Release 13 for DOS

AutoCAD
and its applications
Basics

by

Terence M. Shumaker
Manager
Autodesk Premier Training Center
Clackamas Community College, Oregon City, OR

David A. Madsen
Chairperson
Drafting Technology
Autodesk Premier Training Center
Clackamas Community College, Oregon City, OR
Former Board of Director
American Design Drafting Association

South Holland, Illinois
THE GOODHEART-WILLCOX COMPANY, INC.
Publishers

Library of Congress Catalog Card Number 95-4557
International Standard Book Number 1-56637-177-5

1 2 3 4 5 6 7 8 9 10   96   01 00 99 98 97 96 95

Library of Congress Cataloging-in-Publication Data
Shumaker, Terence M.
    AutoCAD and its applications—basics: release 13 for DOS / by Terence M. Shumaker, David A. Madsen.

    p. cm.
    Includes index.
    ISBN 1-56637-177-5. -- ISBN 1-56637-177-5
    1. Computer graphics. 2. AutoCAD (Computer file)

I. Madsen, David A. II. Title.
T385.S415 1996
620' .0042' 02855369--dc20   95-4557
                                           CIP

Materials used for the cover art courtesy of Arthur Baker, CalComp, Moraine Valley Community College, David Ward, and FLIR Systems Inc.

INTRODUCTION

AutoCAD and its Applications–Basics, Release 13 for DOS is a text and workbook combination that provides complete instruction in mastering the AutoCAD Release 13 for DOS commands and drawing techniques. Typical applications of AutoCAD are presented with basic and design concepts. The topics are covered in an easy-to-understand sequence, and progress in a way that allows you to become comfortable with the commands as your knowledge builds from one chapter to the next. In addition, *AutoCAD and its Applications–Basics, Release 13 for DOS* offers the following features:

* Step-by-step use of AutoCAD commands.
* In-depth explanations of how and why the commands function as they do.
* Examples and discussion of actual industrial practices and standards.
* Professional tips explaining how to use AutoCAD effectively and efficiently.
* Over 200 exercises involving several tasks to reinforce the chapter topics.
* Chapter tests for review of commands and key AutoCAD concepts.
* A large selection of drafting problems supplement each chapter. Problems are presented as, 3-D illustrations, actual plotted industrial drawings, or engineering sketches.

With *AutoCAD and its Applications–Basics, Release 13 for DOS,* you not only learn AutoCAD commands, but you also become acquainted with:

* Professional CAD practices.
* Preliminary planning, sketches, and drawing plan sheets.
* Linetypes and their uses.
* Drawing geometric shapes and constructions.
* Special editing operations that increase productivity.
* Making multiview drawings.
* Dimensioning and tolerancing techniques and practices, as interpreted through accepted standards.
* Drawing sectional views and designing graphic patterns.
* Creating shapes and symbols for multiple use.
* Designing and managing symbol libraries.
* Sketching with AutoCAD.
* Basic 3-D drawing and display.
* Plotting and printing drawings.
* Using DOS commands for system and file manipulations.

The most important factor in learning AutoCAD is to find a reference that:

1. Answers all the questions.
2. Presents the commands in an easy-to-understand, logical sequence.
3. Applies AutoCAD to typical drafting and design tasks.
4. Provides proper drafting standards.
5. Reduces the fear of using AutoCAD.

AutoCAD and its Applications–Basics, Release 13 for DOS does this… and even more!

Checking the AutoCAD reference manuals

No other reference should be needed when using this worktext. However, the authors have referenced the major topic areas to the *AutoCAD User's Guide* and the *AutoCAD Customization Guide*. To the right of most major headings in this text, you will find an abbreviation and a chapter reference number. References are shown in a box similar to the following examples:

| AUG 4 |

| ACG 5 |

The "AUG" in the first example refers to the *AutoCAD User's Guide*. The "4" indicates Chapter 4 of that guide. The reference "ACG" indicates that the topic is referenced to Chapter 5 of the *AutoCAD Customization Guide*.

AutoCAD is also delivered with the *AutoCAD Command Reference.* This is conveniently designed with commands and variables presented in alphabetical order.

Other text references

For additional information, standards from organizations such as ANSI (American National Standards Institute) and ASME (American Society of Mechanical Engineers) are referenced throughout the text. These standards are used to help you work to industrial, national, and international standards.

Also for your convenience, other Goodheart-Willcox textbooks are referenced. Textbooks that are referenced include *AutoCAD and its Applications* (Releases 10, 11, and 12), *AutoLISP Programming–Principles and Techniques, AutoCAD AME–Solid Modeling for Mechanical Design, and Geometric dimensioning and Tolerancing.* All of these textbooks can be ordered directly from Goodheart-Willcox.

Introducing the AutoCAD commands

There are several ways to select AutoCAD drawing and editing commands. Selecting commands from the screen menu, pull-down menus, or the digitizer tablet template menu is slightly different than entering them from the keyboard. All AutoCAD commands and related options in this text are presented using a variety of command entry methods.

Unless otherwise specified, command entries are shown as if they are typed at the keyboard. This allows the text to present the full command name and the prompts that appear on screen. Commands, options, and values you must enter are given in bold text as shown in the following example. Pressing the ENTER (RETURN) key is indicated with the ENTER symbol (↵).

```
Command: LINE ↵
From point: 2,2 ↵
To point: 4,2 ↵
To point: ↵
```

General input such as picking a point or selecting an object is presented in italics.

```
Command: LINE ↵
From point: (pick a point)
To point: (pick another point)
To point: ↵
```

Other command entry methods presented throughout the text are pull-down and screen menus. Pull-down menus are illustrated throughout, and command entries are highlighted. When a pull-down menu is on screen, a command can be entered by picking the desired command name, or by typing the underscored letter in that command.

The AutoCAD digitizer tablet template is presented in Chapter 31. This gives you the opportunity to become familiar with other input formats before using the template menu. Also, not everyone uses a digitizer tablet in their daily CAD projects. Because the commands should be entered in the most convenient manner, experimentation with all command entry methods is encouraged.

Prerequisites

The only prerequisite to using this text is an interest in *AutoCAD. AutoCAD and its Applications–Basics, Release 13 for DOS* takes you through the entire AutoCAD command structure and applies AutoCAD functions to basic drafting concepts.

Flexibility in design

Flexibility is the key word when using *AutoCAD and its Applications–Basics, Release 13 for DOS.* This worktext is an excellent training aid for individual, as well as classroom instruction. *AutoCAD and its Applications–Basics, Release 13 for DOS* teaches you AutoCAD and how it applies to common drafting tasks. It is also an invaluable resource for any professional using AutoCAD.

When working through the text, you will see a variety of notices throughout the text. These notices consist of technical information, hints, and cautions that help you with the development of AutoCAD skills. These notices appear in the text with identifying icons and rules around the text. The professional tips appear as follows:

PROFESSIONAL TIP

Professional Tips. These ideas and suggestions are aimed at increasing your productivity and enhancing your use of AutoCAD commands and techniques.

The notes appear as follows:

NOTE

Notes. A note alerts you to important aspects of the command function, menu, or activity that is being discussed. These aspects should be kept in mind while you are working through the text.

The cautions appear as follows:

CAUTION

Cautions. A caution alerts you to potential problems if instructions or commands are used incorrectly, or if an action could corrupt or alter files, directories, or disks. If you are in doubt after reading a caution, always consult your instructor or supervisor.

The tests and drafting problems are set up to allow an instructor to select individual or group learning goals. Several optional course syllabi are provided in the *Solution Manual* for the instructor to use or revise to suit individual classroom needs.

AutoCAD and its Applications–Basics, Release 13 for DOS provides several ways for you to evaluate your performance. Included are:

- **Exercises.** Each chapter is divided into short sections covering specific aspects of AutoCAD. An exercise composed of several instructions is found at the end of each section. These exercises help you become acquainted with commands at your own pace.
- **Chapter Tests.** Each chapter includes a written test. Questions may require you to provide the proper command, option, or response to perform a certain task.
- **Drawing Problems.** A variety of drafting and design problems are presented at the end of each chapter. These are presented as "real-world" CAD drawings, 3-D illustrations, or engineering sketches, and like some real-world applications, may contain mistakes, improper techniques, or inaccuracies. Always be sure to modify the drawing as needed and apply accurate dimensions to the completed drawings where required. The problems are designed to make you think, solve problems, use design techniques, research and use proper drawing standards, and correct errors in the drawings or engineering sketches.

Each drawing problem deals with one of seven technical disciplines. Although doing all of the problems will enhance your AutoCAD skills, you may have a particular discipline upon which you wish to focus. The discipline that a problem addresses is indicated by an icon at the left of the problem number. Each icon and its description is as follows:

Mechanical Drafting–These problems address mechanical drafting and design applications, such as manufactured part designs.

Architecture–These problems address architecture drafting and design applications, such as floor plans and presentation drawings.

Electronics Drafting–These problems address electronics drafting and designing applications, such as electronic schematics, logic diagrams, and electrical part design.

 Civil Drafting–These problems address civil drafting and design application, such as plot plans, plats, and landscape drawings.

 Graphic Design–These problems address graphic design applications, such as text creation, title blocks, page layout, graphs, and logo design.

 Piping–These problems address piping drafting and design applications, such as piping flow diagrams, pump design, and pipe layout.

 General–These problems address a variety of general drafting and design applications, and should be attempted by everyone learning AutoCAD for the first time.

NOTE   Some problems presented in this text are presented as engineering sketches. These sketches are intended as representations of the kind of materials a drafter would be expected to work from in a real-word situation. As such, engineering sketches often contain errors or slight inaccuracies, may be out of proportion, and are most often not drawn according to proper drafting conventions and applicable standards. Problems presented in this manner are intentional and are meant to encourage the user to apply appropriate techniques and standards in order to solve the problem. As in real-world applications, sketches should be considered to be preliminary layouts. Always question inaccuracies in sketches and designs, and consult the applicable standards or other resources.

ENHANCING THE TEXT

To help you develop your AutoCAD skills, Goodheart-Willcox offers two disk supplement packages. The first package is a student work disk and the second is an instructor's solution disk.

Disk supplements

Two disk supplement packages are available for use with *AutoCAD and its Applications–Basics, Release 13 for DOS. AutoCAD Release 13 for DOS software is required for Goodheart-Willcox software to operate properly.* The *Student Work Disk* package contains specialized pull-down menus. The menus contain a variety of activities that are intended to be used as a supplement to the exercises and activities found in the text. The Work Disk activities correspond to Chapters 8-29 of the text. These activities can be assigned as a group, or individually which allows you to progress at your own pace. Whether used as a group or individually, you will be cultivating your AutoCAD skills with this package!

The *Instructor's Solution Disk* package has been designed as an aid to instructors who evaluate student drawings on disk. This package enables instructors to mark errors or make comments in student drawing files. The Solution Disks contain all the necessary drawing files for use in evaluating drawings, including template drawings for correcting selected activities. A new feature of the software–*AutoCorrect*–allows an instructor to select the student drawing and a drawing template on screen, and then have the computer automatically correct the drawing. Both of these disk supplement packages can be ordered directly from Goodheart-Willcox.

ABOUT THE AUTHORS

Terence M. Shumaker is Manager of the Autodesk Premier Training Center, and a Drafting Technology Instructor at Clackamas Community College. Terence has taught at the community college level since 1977. He has commercial experience in surveying, civil drafting, industrial piping, and technical illustration. He is the author of Goodheart-Willcox's *Process Pipe Drafting,* and is co-author of the *AutoCAD and its Application Release 13* series, *AutoCAD and its Applications (Release 10, 11, and 12 editions),* and *AutoCAD Essentials.*

David A. Madsen is the Chairperson of Drafting Technology and the Autodesk Premier Training Center at Clackamas Community College. David has been an instructor/department chair at Clackamas Community College since 1972. In addition to community college experience, David was a Drafting Technology instructor at Centennial High School in Gresham, Oregon. David also has extensive experience in mechanical drafting, architectural design and drafting, and construction practices. He is the author of several Goodheart-Willcox drafting and design textbooks, including *Geometric Dimensioning and Tolerancing ,* and is co-author of the *AutoCAD and its Applications Release 13* series, *AutoCAD and its Applications (Release 10, 11, and 12 editions),* and *AutoCAD Essentials.*

NOTICE TO THE USER

AutoCAD and its Applications–Basics, Release 13 for DOS, covers the basic AutoCAD DOS applications that are mentioned in this introduction. For a worktext that covers the advanced AutoCAD DOS applications, please refer to *AutoCAD and its Applications–Advanced, Release 13 for DOS.* The Basics and the Advanced worktexts are also available for the AutoCAD Release 13 for Windows format. Copies of any of these worktexts can be ordered directly from Goodheart-Willcox.

These worktexts are designed as complete entry-level AutoCAD teaching tools. The authors present a typical point of view. Users may find alternate and possibly better techniques for using AutoCAD. The authors and publisher accept no responsibility for any loss or damage resulting from the contents of information presented in these worktexts.

ACKNOWLEDGEMENTS

The authors and publisher would like to thank the following individuals and companies for their assistance and contributions:

Technical assistance and contribution of materials

Margo Bilson of Willamette Industries, Inc.
Fitzgerald, Hagan, & Hackathorn
Dr. Stuart Soman of Briarcliffe College
Gil Hoellerich of Springdale, AR

Contribution of materials

Cynthia B. Clark of the American Society of Mechanical Engineers
Marty McConnell of Houston Instrument, A Summagraphics Company
Grace Avila, Neele Johnston, and Wayne Hodgins of Autodesk, Inc.
Dave Hall of the Harris Group, Inc.

Contribution of photographs or other technical information

Amdek Corporation	JDL, Inc.
Applications Development, Inc.	Jerome Hart
Arthur Baker	Jim Armstrong
Autodesk, Inc.	Jim Webster
CADalyst magazine	Kunz Associates
CADENCE magazine	Matt Slay
CalComp	Mark Stennfeld
Chris Lindner	Mitsubishi Electronics America, Inc.
Computer-Aided Design, Inc.	Microsoft Corporation
Digital Equipment Corp.	Moraine Valley Community College
EPCM Services Ltd.	Mouse Systems Corporation
Far Mountain Corporation	Myonetics Inc.
FLIR Systems Inc.	NEC Technologies, Inc.
Gateway 2000	Norwest Engineering
GTCO Corporation	Schuchart & Associates, Inc.
Harris Group, Inc.	Summagraphics Corporation
Hewlett-Packard	The American Society of Mechanical Engineers
Houston Instrument, A Summagraphics Company	The Xerox Engineering Systems Company Weiser, Inc.
IOLINE Corporation	Willamette Industries, Inc.

Technical assistance and reviews

Rod Rawls, Autodesk Premier Training Center, Clackamas Community College; AutoCAD consultant; and co-author of *AutoLISP Programming: Principles and Techniques,* published by Goodheart-Willcox.

Michael Jones, Autodesk Premier Training Center, Clackamas Community College

J.C. Malitzke, Autodesk Premier Training Center, Moraine Valley Community College

Kevin DeVoll, Margaret Burke, Earl Larson, and Paul Masterson

Hardware contributions

CalComp for use of the Inkjet plotter.

Moraine Valley Community College for use of laboratory, computer, monitor, and digitizer.

TRADEMARKS

Autodesk, AutoCAD, and AutoLISP are registered in the U.S. Patent Trademark Office by Autodesk, Inc.

Autodesk Animator Pro, Autodesk 3D Studio, AutoFlix, AME (Advanced Modeling Extension), and DXF are trademarks of Autodesk, Inc.

dBase is a registered trademark of Ashton Tate

IBM is a registered trademark of International Business Machines

MS-DOS is a registered trademark of Microsoft Corporation

Pizazz Plus is a registered trademark of Applications Software Corporation

RenderMan is a registered trademark of Pixar used by Autodesk, Inc. by license

CONTENTS

DIMENSIONING AND TOLERANCING

CHAPTER 20 Basic Dimensioning Practices

CHAPTER 21 Intermediate Dimensioning

CHAPTER 22 Advanced Dimensioning and Tolerancing

APPENDICES

Describes in detail the procedure of installing AutoCAD Release 13
for DOS. Covers the making of backup copies of the installation
disks, which is an essential part of the installation process.

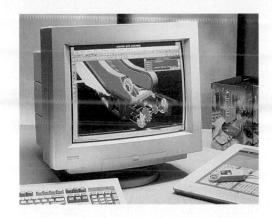

Chapter 1

INTRODUCTION TO COMPUTER-AIDED DRAFTING

Learning objectives

After completing this chapter, you will be able to:

- ○ Identify the tools (equipment) used in computer-aided drafting.
- ○ Describe the methods and procedures used in computer-aided drafting.
- ○ Explain the value of planning and system management.
- ○ Follow the basic rules of hygiene for a computer lab.

THE TOOLS OF CAD

The computer is the principal tool of the drafter's workstation. It is quickly replacing manual drafting tools such as drafting tables, pencils, scales, and templates. The drafter, designer, or engineer can create layouts and designs on a computer screen using the commands of a computer program. Points are chosen with an electronic pointing device such as a digitizer or mouse. Original drawings do not have to be copied with a blueprint machine. Instead, the drawing data is sent to a plotter for an inked original or to a printer for a quick check print. The final drawing is saved on magnetic media such as floppy disks, hard disks, or magnetic tape. The optical CD is becoming a preferred method of data archival. It is much more durable and has greater storage capacity than magnetic media.

The AutoCAD software enables you to create your own drawing commands. This aspect of CAD is often overlooked, and is addressed in this book. You will be learning to use a new set of tools–the computer and AutoCAD. However, you will also be introduced to the methods of customization. Customization is modifying the basic program to meet your specific needs. For example, you may want to create a command to insert a specific symbol at an exact location. It is easy with AutoCAD. This skill allows you to become more productive, and prepares you to move into fields of expertise such as design, engineering, software development, animation and video production, or computer programming.

The nature of AutoCAD allows you to alter the basic program into something that is highly specialized and efficient. Along the way, however, you must pick up many new skills and ways of thinking about the drawing process.

THE NEW METHODS OF CAD

As you begin to use AutoCAD, you will encounter many new drawing methods. These require that you organize your thoughts and plan the project in order to complete the drawing productively. For example, suppose you wish to draw a symmetrical object (an object that is the same on both sides of a centerline). You should not just begin drawing shapes on one side, and then redraw them on the other side. Rather, you should select drawing commands and pick positions on the computer screen using an input device to draw one-half of the object. A special command is then used to reflect or "mirror" the shapes just drawn to complete the object. With CAD, you should never draw the same shape twice.

As you begin your CAD training, plan your drawing sessions thoroughly to organize your thoughts. Sketch the problem or design, noting size and locations of features. List the drawing commands needed in the order they are to be used. Schedule a regular time to use the computer and adhere to that time. Follow the standards set by your school or firm. These might include: specific drawing names, project planning sheets, project logs, drawing layout procedures, special title blocks, and the location where drawings are to be stored. Standards and procedures must be followed by everyone using the computers in your school or company. Confusion may result if your drawings do not have the proper name, are stored in the wrong place, or have the wrong title block.

When using AutoCAD, you will be dealing with a machine that asks questions, follows instructions promptly, and executes every command you give it. Since the computer can destroy your drawing in a fraction of a second, you should develop the habit of saving your work regularly–at least every 10 to 15 minutes. (In Release 13, the SAVETIME system variable can be set to automatically save your drawings at predetermined intervals. SAVETIME is covered in detail in Chapter 5.) Drawings may be lost due to a software error, hardware malfunction, power failure, or your own mistakes. This is not common, but you should still be prepared for such an event.

You should develop methods of managing your work. This is critical to computer drafting and is discussed throughout the text. Keep the following points in mind as you begin your AutoCAD training.
* Plan your work and organize your thoughts.
* Learn and use your classroom or office standards.
* Save your work often.

If you remember to follow these three points, your grasp of the tools and methods of CAD will be easier. In addition, your experiences with the computer will be more enjoyable.

THE APPLICATIONS OF AUTOCAD

You are embarking on a learning process that will take you through a broad range of commands, functions, and applications of the AutoCAD software. Along the way you will learn how to construct, layout, dimension, and annotate two-dimensional drawings. Should you wish to continue your study into 3-D, rendering and customization, *AutoCAD and its Applications–Advanced, R13 for DOS,* provides you with detailed instruction. Your studies will enable you to create a wide variety of drawings, designs and models in any of the drafting, design and engineering disciplines.

The AutoCAD software enables you to create designs and drawings that are more than just two-dimensional constructions. The drawings can have hundreds of colors, and *layers* that contain different kinds of information. See Figures 1-1A and B. In addition, objects in the drawing can be given "intelligence" in the form of *attributes.* These attributes are various kinds of data which turn a drawing into a graphical database. You can then ask questions of your drawing and receive a variety of information.

Figure 1-1.   A–Colors and layers are used to emphasize components in this exploded isometric assembly. (Hewlett-Packard) B–Many different colors and layers were used to create this realistic architectural rendering. (SRG Partnership PC)

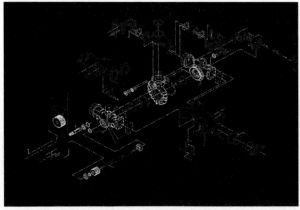

A   B

Using AutoCAD you have the ability to construct 3-D models that appear as wireframes, or have surface colors and textures. The creation of solid models that have mass properties, and can be analyzed is also possible with AutoCAD. The display on the monitor in Figure 1-2 is an example of a solid model created in AutoCAD. 3-D drawings and models can be viewed in several ways. These models can also be colored and shaded, or *rendered,* to appear in a realistic format.

Figure 1-2.   Solid models like this can be created with AutoCAD.
(Digital Equipment Corporation)

A powerful application of CAD software and 3-D models is animation. The simplest form of animation is to dynamically rotate the model in order to view it from any direction. Drawings and models can also be animated so that the model appears to move, rotate, and even explode into its individual components. An extremely useful form of animation is called a *walkthrough.* Using specialized software, you can plot a path through or around a model and replay it just like a movie. The logical next step in viewing the model is to actually be inside it and have the ability to manipulate and change the objects in it. This is called *virtual reality,* and is achieved through the use of 3-D models, and highly specialized software and hardware. Figures 1-3A, B, and C illustrate several kinds of drawings and models that have been created with CAD software.

Figure 1-3.   A–The components of this rendered 3-D piping model retain information in the form of attributes that makes the drawing a graphical database. (Applications Development, Inc.) B–The solid model on this monitor was created with AutoCAD. (Mitsubishi Electronics America, Inc.) C–This model of a F18 jet was created with AutoCAD. (Autodesk, Inc.)

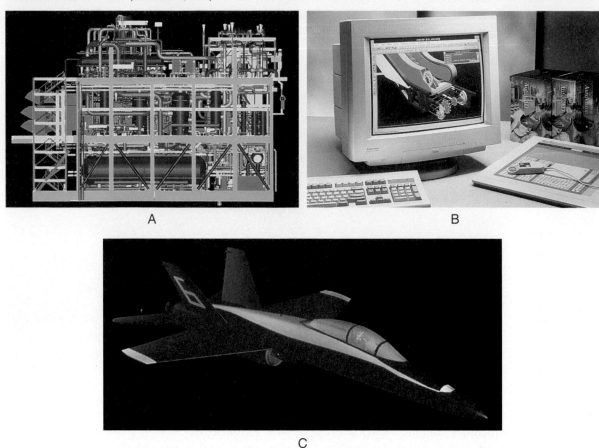

A

B

C

HARDWARE

The physical pieces of equipment used in computer-aided drafting and design are referred to as *hardware*. The microcomputer is the main component. It is accompanied by several other devices called *peripherals*, Figure 1-4. The specific components included in a CAD workstation are presented in the following discussion.

Figure 1-4.   Components of an AutoCAD workstation.

jagged [dʒǽgɪd] : serrado, dentado

Computer

The most commonly used microcomputers for CAD in the education and industrial fields is the IBM, and other microcomputers called "IBM compatibles" or "clones." These clones must be 100% compatible with IBM models for AutoCAD to work properly. The important consideration, regardless of the brand of machine used, is that the computer has the proper components and memory. See Appendix B for the specific hardware requirements of AutoCAD.

A typical microcomputer is a rectangular-shaped metal box containing the central processing unit (CPU), memory, flexible disk drives, and hard disk drive(s).

The heart of the computer–the CPU–is a chip that handles all of the system's calculations. Several printed circuit boards called "cards," occupy the computer. These cards have a variety of integrated circuit chips and electronic components attached. Specific cards or "boards" are required for a video graphics display, the connection for a digitizer or mouse (called *serial ports*), and additional items such as extra memory for the computer.

The computer has a group of blank chips (like empty storage boxes), called *memory*. Memory is also commonly referred to as *random access memory*, or *RAM*. Random access memory refers to the ability of the computer to randomly store and search for data in this area of the memory. When the computer is turned on, the operating system (such as DOS, or the Disk Operating System) is loaded into a small portion of the computer's memory. The operating system remains there because it can be accessed faster than if it was used directly from the hard disk drive.

When AutoCAD is loaded, it is also placed into the computer's RAM. If your computer has a small amount of RAM, for example, 8MB (8 million bytes, or characters), most of the AutoCAD program can be placed in the computer's memory. Then, when you work on a drawing, some (or all) of the drawing may also initially be placed in the computer's memory. If your drawing gets too big, some of it is removed from RAM, and copied, or *paged* to the hard disk. If the "page" of your drawing or AutoCAD is needed again, it is copied back into memory. If you are quick, you may notice when this happens by looking at the flexible and hard disk lights located on the front of your computer. Watch these lights and you will begin to get a good idea of when AutoCAD accesses the flexible disk and hard disk drives.

Most computers are available with a "standard" 640K, or 640,000 bytes of memory. Remember that one byte is roughly equal to one character, such as a letter or number. Memory added to a computer above the basic 640K is called *extended memory*. In order to run AutoCAD Release 13, your computer must have at least 8MB (8 million bytes) of memory, and 16MB is recommended. The more memory a computer has, the faster it can work because it can load programs into memory and not have to work from the hard disk drive, which is much slower.

Monitor

The *monitor* is the output or display device that resembles a small TV, and usually sits atop the computer box, Figure 1-5. Common monitor sizes are 15″, 17″, and 21″ diagonal measurement. Monitors are available in color and monochrome display. *Monochrome* refers to a single text and graphics color, most often white, amber, or green on a black background.

Display *resolution* determines how smooth or jagged text and objects appear on screen. Resolution is measured in *pixels*. The word "pixel" is derived from PIcture ELement. A pixel appears as a dot on the screen, but it is actually a tiny rectangle. The display of a monitor is composed of horizontal rows and vertical columns of pixels. A typical display resolution is 640 × 480, meaning there are 640 dots horizontally and 480 dots vertically. High-resolution monitors may display 1024 × 768 pixels, or more.

The resolution of your monitor is directly related to a component in the computer called a *graphics card*. The graphics card is a "board" that contains a variety of computer chips. This board is inserted in a slot inside the computer that allows the CPU of the computer to communicate with the graphics card and monitor.

Figure 1-5.   The monitor lets
the drafter view the CAD
drawings. (NEC Technologies)

Graphics cards called *accelerator boards* may allow resolution of up to 1600 × 1200, and up to 16.7 million colors. The former VGA standard (Video Graphics Array) has been supplanted by the Super VGA (SVGA), and many industrial applications now demand high-end graphics accelerator boards because of the complexity of the models, renderings, and animations.

Keyboard

If you type well, you will soon discover that the keyboard is the most used input device at your workstation. It resembles a standard typewriter keyboard but has additional keys to the left, right, and top, Figure 1-6. The exact location and number of these keys vary from one model to another. In addition to typing commands, the keyboard can be used for entering precise coordinate values (see Chapter 6), text, and dimensions.

The keys labeled F1-F10, or F1-F12, are called *function keys*. These immediately perform commands that would otherwise have to be typed. AutoCAD uses function keys to control specific operations, many of which are discussed in Chapter 3.

Figure 1-6.   A computer keyboard has many types of keys.

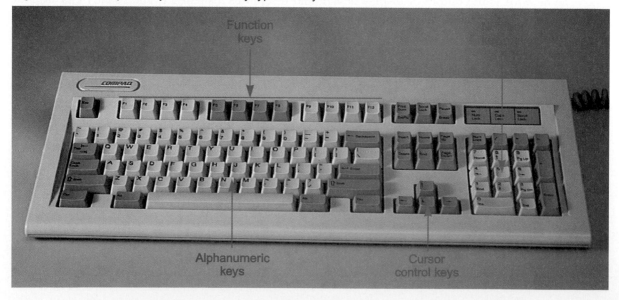

Pointing devices

Another important input device is the pointer, or pointing device. A *pointing device* moves the cursor or crosshairs on the screen. With it, you can select point locations and commands from a screen or digitizer tablet menu. The most commonly used pointing devices are a multibutton *puck* or a pen-shaped *stylus*. See Figure 1-7. Pointing devices are connected to a *digitizer tablet*. Digitizer tablet layout and their use is discussed in Chapter 31 of this text.

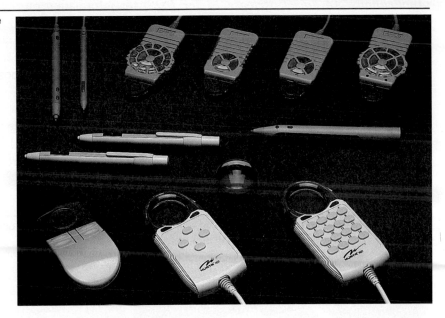

Figure 1-7.   Digitizer pucks are available with different button arrangements. The stylus resembles a pen. (Kurta)

Other commonly used pointing devices include the *mouse* and *trackball*. The mouse or trackball are often suitable choices when cost and table space are concerns (since they do not require a digitizer). Each pointer functions differently, but all put information into the computer.

The digitizer tablet is the drawing board of the CAD workstation. Several examples are shown in Figure 1-8. A plastic or paper *menu overlay* containing AutoCAD commands and/or drawing symbols can also be placed on the digitizer. Items can be selected directly from the menu without looking at the screen. Movement of the puck or stylus is recorded and displayed on the screen as the cursor position. Commands or menus can be picked on the screen by moving the pointing device to the desired item.

Figure 1-8.   Digitizers are available in many different sizes. (CalComp)

Then press the pick button on the puck, or press down on the stylus. Digitizer tablet layout and use is discussed in Chapter 31 of this text.

The multibutton puck, used with a digitizer tablet may have from 1 to 16 buttons. The bottom surface of the puck slides on the digitizer surface. A set of fine crosshairs mounted in the puck serve as the pick point for this device. When the display screen crosshairs move, they are showing the position of the puck's crosshairs on the tablet. One button–the pick button–enters points and selects menu commands. All of the other buttons can be programmed to suit the user. See *AutoCAD and its Applications–Advanced, Release 13 for DOS,* for information on digitizer tablet and button customization.

The stylus, a pen-shaped pointer, attached to the digitizer with a cable, works in a different manner. The point of the stylus is pressed down on the surface of the digitizer. A slight click can be felt and even heard. This indicates that a point or menu item at the cursor's position on the screen has been selected.

The mouse is the most inexpensive pointing device because it does not require a digitizer tablet. A mouse needs only a small flat surface to operate. The mouse is available in two forms: mechanical and optical. See Figure 1-9. An optical mouse uses a special reflective pad with grid lines. A light shines from the mouse to the pad. The location of the mouse is shown as the crosshairs location on the screen. The optical mouse must remain on the special pad in order to work.

Figure 1-9. A–An optical mouse. Note the reflective pad and grid lines in the pad. (Summagraphics) B–A mechanical mouse can be used on almost any surface.

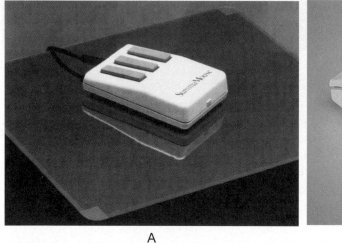
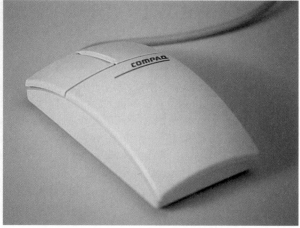

A   B

The mechanical mouse has a roller ball on the bottom. The movement of the roller on any flat surface is sent to the computer and displayed as the screen crosshairs movement. Unlike the stylus and puck, the mouse can be lifted and moved to another position without affecting the location of the screen crosshairs.

If you turn a mouse over, the roller ball is exposed. If this ball was increased in size and enlarged another inch, you would have a trackball. A trackball enables you to move the cursor on the screen by rolling a ball. A trackball requires only the amount of table space needed for it to sit on. The only part you move is the ball. There are a variety of trackballs available, but most have two or three buttons, much like a mouse. See Figure 1-10.

Figure 1-10.   A trackball is a pointing device, which is used by rolling the ball to move the screen cursor or crosshairs.

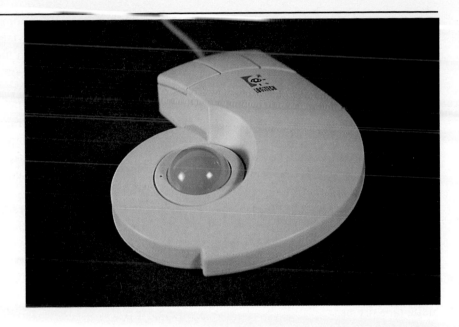

Storage devices and media

Your computer should have an arrangement of floppy and/or hard disk drives. These are the storage areas for AutoCAD and its drawings. A standard 5.25″ floppy disk holds 360,000 (360K) characters of information. A character is referred to as a *byte*. A *high-density* floppy disk holds 1.2 million bytes of information. Million is called *mega*; therefore, a high-density disk's capacity is called 1.2 megabytes, or 1.2MB. Your computer will have one or two of these floppy disk drives, Figure 1-11. Small lights on the fronts of the disk drives indicate when they are being accessed.

Figure 1-11.   A–Floppy disk drives with a hard disk drive to the left. Note the extra compartment that has a CD-ROM drive. B–An external CD-ROM drive. (NEC Technologies)

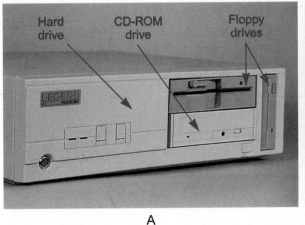

A   B

Many computer users prefer the 3.5″ flexible disk because of its size and the fact that the magnetic media is enclosed in a hard plastic shell, which protects it from damage. The 3.5″ disk was originally designed to fit a shirt pocket, therefore it is convenient to carry around. The 3.5″ disk can be used in either IBM/DOS compatible systems, or Apple Macintosh systems. Most new computers are equipped with a 3.5″ high-density disk drives. The 3.5″ disk drive has now become the standard in new computers. In addition, for persons who may need to use both sizes of diskette, the dual disk drive is available. This drive allows either size diskette to be placed in the same drive slot and used. If you are using an older computer with a low-density disk drive, you will not be able to use the full storage capacity of high-density disks. Chapter 2 provides additional information about preparing disks for use.

Computer users are making increased use of the high-density compact optical digital disk (CD) for data storage. These are much like the compact audio disks. Such devices are now in use for reading CD ROM (Read-Only Memory) disks. The CD ROM drive is found on most CAD workstations now. In fact, the AutoCAD software is less expensive to purchase if ordered on CD ROM. An example of a CD ROM drive is shown in Figure 1-11B.

In addition to flexible disk drives, your computer also has a hard disk drive. AutoCAD requires a hard disk to operate. The hard disk is a sealed unit that contains one or more metal disks, or "platters." These disks have a much greater storage capacity than floppy disks, and are measured in megabytes. Common hard disk sizes are 340MB to 540MB. A small light on the front of the computer indicates when the hard disk drive is being accessed. Before AutoCAD can be used, it must be installed onto the hard disk drive. (See Appendix A for installation information.)

The need for greater storage capacity, and more reliable media has seen the increase in popularity of the re-writable optical drive, or "flopticals." The most popular of these drives accept 3.5″ optical disks that are the same size and style as standard magnetic 3.5″ floppy disks, except the optical disks are a little thicker. They store up to 256MB per disk (512MB compressed), and provide the reliability of optical media without the cost or vulnerability of magnetic media. They can be rewritten with new data as required, just like magnetic floppies. They are faster and more reliable for backups than magnetic tape drives.

Selecting floppy disks

Avoid buying bulk quantities of unpackaged floppy disks that are sold without dust jackets. Often these are sitting out on a store counter exposed to dust, cigarette smoke, and handling. Be safe; purchase packaged unformatted disks, keep them boxed, and store the box in a clean area. Keep disks away from extreme heat or cold and magnetic fields found around stereo speakers and ringing telephones.

A variety of disk drive configurations are now available for most new microcomputers. In some cases, you are able to specify the drive configuration that you desire when purchasing a computer. In many cases you are able to indicate whether you want a drive capable of handling double-density or high-density disks. Since there is such a variety of drive configurations, be careful when purchasing floppy disks to ensure that you have the correct disks for your computer. Check the following:

- 5.25″ vs. 3.5″
- 1.2MB vs. 1.44MB

Be sure that you purchase the proper disks for your computer since you will be saving your AutoCAD drawings on either the hard disk drive or on floppy disks. Even if you store most drawings on the hard disk drive, you will probably use floppy disks for temporary storage of your drawing files, and for data transfer between computers, or to and from a client.

Therefore, you should learn how to prepare a floppy disk to receive drawing files. This preparation process is called *formatting*.

The formatting process is discussed in detail in Chapter 2. You should read that portion of the chapter to gain a better knowledge of the FORMAT command. The section in this chapter provides you with the basics of formatting so you can begin now to save drawings on floppy disks.

CAUTION

Before formatting a floppy disk, check with your instructor or supervisor for information about formatting disks. Some schools and companies have special menu selections that allow you to safely format disks in the floppy disk drives.

Plotter

Paper and film drawings are most often output by a plotter. A plotter uses pencil, felt tip, ballpoint, or wet ink pens to put lines on paper. These devices can plot any size drawing, and are available in a variety of sizes. See Figure 1-12. Plotting is normally done for final documents. Drafters and designers can work for a long time before they ever need to plot their work. For that, and other reasons, most schools and companies have one plotter that is shared by several workstations. The plotting routine is covered in Chapter 12.

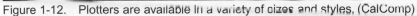

Figure 1-12. Plotters are available in a variety of sizes and styles. (CalComp)

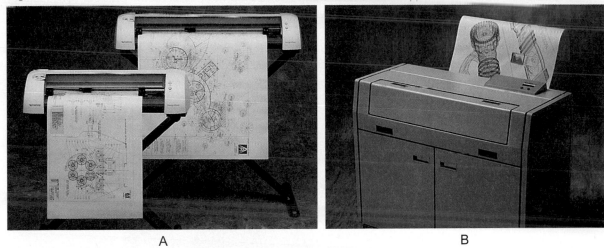

A   B

The *electrophotographic plotter* is increasing in popularity because of its speed and efficiency. Whereas a laser printer "paints" the image onto a sensitized drum with a single beam of light, the electrophotographic plotter uses an array of light-emitting diodes (LED) to draw the image. These tiny LEDs are packed 400 to the inch in the plotter shown in Figure 1-13. This produces a plot resolution of 400 dpi. The electrophotographic technology, when used in a large-format plotter, produces a more accurate image than does a laser beam.

Figure 1-13. The electrophotographic plotter uses an array of LEDs to plot an image at 400 dpi. (CalComp)

A less expensive alternative to the electrostatic plotter is the inkjet plotter. See Figure 1-14. The inkjet technology uses a cartridge that shoots tiny drops of ink at the paper. The cartridge requires no maintenance, and may provide from 200 to 400 prints. Resolutions of 300 to 600 dpi are common. A typical inkjet plotter may be three to eight times faster than a pen plotter, depending on the drawing complexity and printing mode.

Plotters fall into two basic groups–vector and raster. Pen plotters are vector plotters because they draw lines using the XY coordinates of the drawing geometry. Although they are accurate and produce fine quality drawings, they are the slowest of the various plotter technologies. Raster plotters, on the other hand, convert CAD vectors into rows and columns of dots, often called a *bit map*. Raster plotters, such as the inkjet, print an entire row at a time as the paper advances, whereas the pen plotter must constantly move around the paper, drawing each vector.

Figure 1-14.   Inkjet plotters shoot tiny drops of ink at the paper and provide from 300 to 600 dpi resolution. (CalComp/Hewlett-Packard)

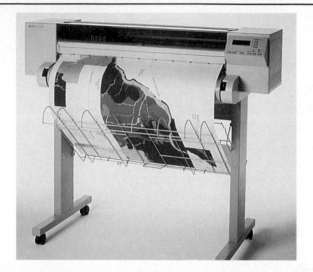

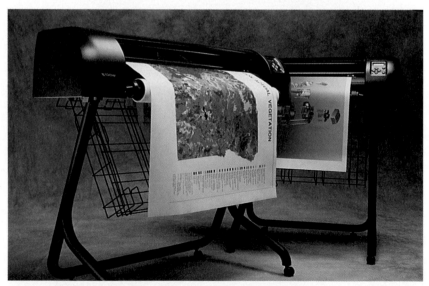

Printer

The raspy sounds of a dot matrix printer are familiar to people who have been to a store or bank. These same printers can render a quick check print of your AutoCAD drawing. Large-format dot matrix printers can produce prints up to C-size (17 × 22). However, other more quiet printing devices–inkjet, laser, and electrophotoghaphic devices–also create high-quality prints. Laser printers can plot up to 600 dpi. An example of a laser printer is shown in Figure 1-15.

Figure 1-15. The laser printer "paints" an image on a sensitized drum and prints up to 600 dpi resolution. (Hewlett-Packard Printers)

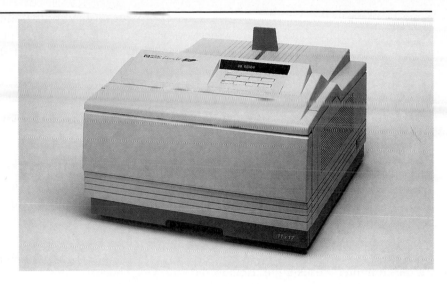

Network systems

There is an increasing need for drawing symbol consistency, accurate project time accounting, instant communications between coworkers, and data security. This has led to the popularity of "network systems." A *network* is nothing more than several computers, connected by a cable, which communicate with each other. Complex networks have hundreds of computers or terminals working off of a central computer or *server*. Each workstation on the network still requires a CPU, input device, and display device. A diagram of a typical network system is shown in Figure 1-16.

The hard disk drives in the server are normally large-capacity drives, in order to store a variety of software, and still have plenty of space for numerous files created by the computer users attached to the network. The network server can also store drawing files that may be needed by computer users in order to complete other new drawings. For example, a base drawing of the walls of a structure can be stored on the server. When a student or employee needs to work on a new drawing of the plumbing or electrical layout of the structure, they simply load the base drawing from the server into their computer and begin working. In most cases, the base drawing is preserved in its original form and a different

Figure 1-16. Layout of a typical computer network system.

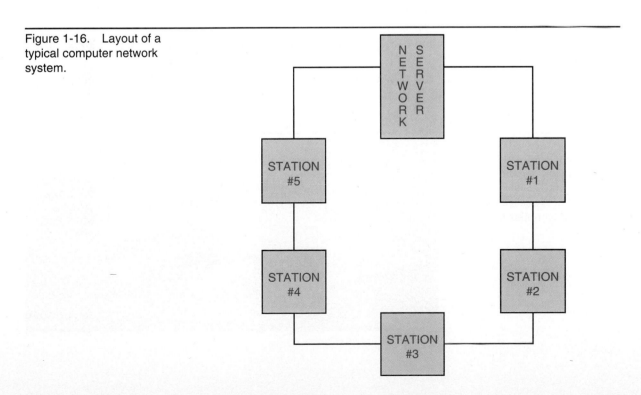

name is given to the new drawing. AutoCAD provides a facility that automatically locks a drawing when a person "checks it out" of the network. This means that only one person can work on a drawing at any given time, thus preventing several people from making different changes to the drawing.

THE ERGONOMIC WORKSTATION

Ergonomics is technically the study of work, but has come to mean the science of adapting the working environment to suit the needs of the worker. Since the advent of computers in the workplace in the early 1980s, an increasing number of work-related injuries and afflictions have been reported. By far, the most common of these are repetitive motion disorders–carpal tunnel syndrome being the most well-known. Most of these injuries and disorders related to computer work are the result of the sedentary nature of the work, and the fast, repetitive motions of the hands and fingers on the keyboard and pointing devices.

Most disorders of this nature can be prevented to some extent by proper workstation configuration, good posture, and frequent exercises. Figure 1-17 illustrates an example of ergonomic equipment for the computer workstation. Review the following checklist, and try to adhere to as many of the items as possible. As is often the case, a small adjustment of equipment, or the investment of a few extra dollars, can prevent unnecessary future injuries and lost productivity.

✓ Obtain a good chair with proper back support, height, and tilt adjustment.

✓ Use adaptive devices such as forearm supports, wrist and palm rests, keyboard drawers, etc., in order to help maintain a level wrist position in relation to the keyboard and pointing device.

✓ Avoid resting your wrists on a table while typing, and use a light stroke on the keys.

✓ Investigate the variety of ergonomic keyboards on the market and test for comfort and efficiency.

✓ Position the equipment and supplies of your workstation for ease of use and access.

✓ The screen should be placed from 18 to 30 inches from the eyes and the top of the display screen should be at eye level.

✓ Lighting should not produce a glare on the screen.

✓ Provide under-desk space so that feet can be placed on a tilted footrest, or at minimum, flat on the floor.

✓ Take short breaks throughout the day.

✓ Practice refocusing your eyes, and engaging in stretching exercises for hands, arms, shoulders, and neck on a regular basis.

✓ Be aware of how your body feels, especially any changes you feel in your shoulders, arms, wrists, and hands.

✓ Consult your doctor if you notice any numbness, aching, or tingling in your hands, wrists, or arms.

Figure 1-17.   The forearm supports provide relief from muscle tension for computer operators, and assist in the prevention of repetitive motion disorders. (Myonetics Inc.)

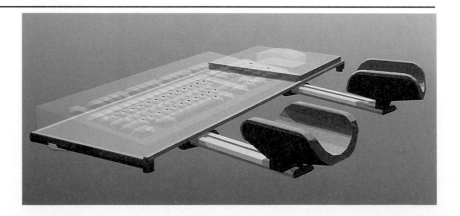

COMPUTER DRAFTING PROCEDURES

The finished product of a CAD drafter is similar to that of a manual drafter. However, some of the thought processes and procedures used to produce the final product are different. A drawing plan must be developed in which all the aspects of the project are considered. This requires careful management of the CAD system and the creation and use of detailed standards for the planning and drawing process.

Drawing planning

Drawing planning involves looking at the entire process or project in which you as a drafter, designer, or engineer, are involved. A plan determines how a project is going to be approached. It includes the drawings to be created, how they will be titled and numbered, the information to be presented, and the types of symbols needed to show the information.

More specifically, drawing planning applies to how you create and manage a drawing or set of drawings. Drafters who begin constructing a drawing from the seat of their pants–creating symbols and naming objects, shapes, and views as they go–do not possess a good drawing plan. Those who plan, use consistent techniques, and adhere to school or company standards are developing good drawing habits.

Throughout this text you will find aids to help you develop good drawing habits. One of the first steps in developing your skills is to learn how to plan your work. The importance of planning cannot be emphasized enough. There is no substitute. Just because you are using a computer does not mean you can be sloppy and take shortcuts. Now, more than ever, there is a need for planning.

Creating and using drawing standards

Standards are guidelines for operating procedures, drawing techniques, and record keeping. Most schools and companies have established standards. It is important that standards exist and are used by all CAD personnel. Drawing standards may include:

- Methods of file storage: location and name.
- Dimensioning techniques.
- File naming conventions.
- Text styles.
- Drawing sheet sizes and title blocks to be used.
- Linetypes.
- Drawing symbols.
- Color schemes for plotting.
- File backup methods and times.

Your standards may vary in content, but the most important aspect of standards is that they are used. The more your standards are used, the more efficiently the classroom or office will run. In addition, it will be easier to manage the system and plan projects. As they are used, standards will change to reflect new methods, techniques, and symbols. All students and employees using the CAD system must be informed of changes immediately. This increases communication and maintains a high level of consistency and productivity.

Planning your work

Study the planning pyramids in Figure 1-18. The horizontal axes of the pyramids represent the amount of time spent on the project. The vertical axes represent the life of the project. The top level is the planning stage and the bottom level is the final execution of the project. The pyramid on the left is pointed at the top and indicates a small amount of planning. As the project progresses, more and more time is devoted to planning and less time is available for other tasks. This is *not* an ideal situation. The inverted pyramid on the right shows a lot of time devoted to initial planning. As the project advances, less planning time is needed, thus freeing more time for other tasks.

Remember the message of the planning pyramids as you begin your study of AutoCAD. When you feel the need to dive blindly into a drawing or project, restrain yourself. Take the time needed for development of the project goals. Then proceed with the confidence of knowing where you are heading.

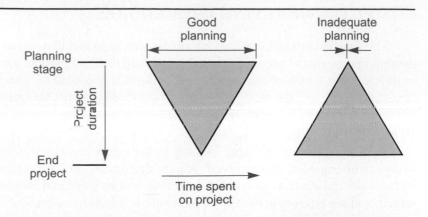

Figure 1-18. Planning pyramids illustrate time required for well-planned and poorly-planned projects.

During your early stages of AutoCAD training, write down all of the instructions needed to construct your drawing. Do this especially for your first few assignments. This means documenting every command and every coordinate point (dimension) needed. Develop a planning sheet for your drawings or use an example shown in Chapter 6. Your time spent at the computer with AutoCAD will be more productive and enjoyable.

System management

The concepts of drawing planning and project planning are parts of system management. (See Appendix C.) System management means that the entire CAD system and related functions are governed by set guidelines. However, simply having guidelines does not mean that the system is being managed. A person or persons must see that procedures and standards are followed throughout the life of a project. If a system is not managed, it soon falls apart. A well-managed system functions smoothly.

Right now, you are probably anxious to begin learning AutoCAD and are wondering why planning, standards, and management are being discussed. It is because you are about to encounter many details, possibilities, methods, and options that you may have never dealt with before. Even if you have never drafted, a basic understanding of AutoCAD will provide you with a solid footing on which to build your experience and knowledge.

You personally may not be the ultimate manager of the CAD system. However, you still need to possess a knowledge of what is meant by system management. Therefore, it is important that you develop an early knowledge of:
- When to store drawings on floppy disks and when to store them on hard disks or other magnetic media.
- How names are assigned to drawings so other employees or your instructor understand their meaning.
- When and how to make backup copies of drawings and store them in a safe place.
- Where to physically store backup floppy disks and magnetic tapes.
- Who should have access to drawings you create.
- Who creates drawing standards and symbols.
- How symbols and standards are distributed to all CAD users.
- Who maintains the hardware and handles software upgrades.

These are just a few aspects of system management affecting your use of AutoCAD in the educational and industrial environments. Before you ever begin a drawing, you should be aware of the items listed above. Know how they relate to your standards and planning procedures because they are a part of system management.

Interactive process

A CAD drafter "interacts" with the drawing much more than a manual drafter. The CAD program asks questions, provides hints, and prompts for information that is needed to complete certain steps. The drawing taped to a drafting board just lies there. It doesn't glow, ask questions, or make demands of the drafter. CAD drafters find themselves involved in an exciting, interactive process. They communicate with the computer to create a drawing.

As you begin learning AutoCAD, you will realize that several skills are required to become a proficient CAD user. The following list provides you with some hints to help you to become comfortable with AutoCAD. They will also allow you to work quickly and efficiently. The following items are discussed in detail in later chapters.

- Plan all work with pencil and paper before using the computer.
- Check the screen menu bar to see if you are in the correct menu and are picking the right command. A command is an instruction that you give to the computer so it can perform a specific task. For example, the LINE command instructs the computer to draw a line between two points you pick.
- Check the status line at the top of the display screen to see which layer(s) and drawing aid(s) are in effect.
- Read the command line at the bottom of the display screen. Constantly check for the correct command, instructions, or proper keyboard entry of data.
- Read the command line after keyboard entry of data before pressing the ENTER or RETURN key. Backspacing to erase incorrect typing is quicker than redoing the command.
- If using a multibutton puck, develop a good hand position that allows easy movement. Your button-pressing finger should move without readjusting your grip of the puck.
- Learn the meanings of all the buttons on your puck or mouse and use them regularly.
- Watch the floppy disk and hard disk drive lights to see when the disks are being accessed. Some disk access may take a few seconds. Knowing what is happening will lessen frustration and impatience.
- Think ahead. Know your next move.
- Learn new commands every day. Don't rely on just a few that seem to work. Find commands that can speed your work and do it more efficiently.
- Save your work every 10 to 15 minutes in case a power failure or system crash deletes the drawing held in computer memory.
- If you're stumped, ask the computer for help. Use the HELP command to display valuable information about each command on the screen.

Computer lab hygiene

Computer equipment is not only costly and complex, it is sensitive. Special cautions should be taken when working with computer equipment and magnetic media.

- It is better to leave computers on all day than to turn them on and off.
- Static electricity can damage computer memory chips. Always ground yourself by stepping on antistatic mats or touching static discharge plates or a metal chair before touching computer hardware.
- Touching the display screen often can build up a static charge in your body. If you must touch the screen, ground yourself often by touching some piece of metal not connected to the computer equipment.
- Keep computers out of dusty areas and away from chalkboards.
- Keep food and drinks away from computer hardware. Coffee and soft drinks spilled in keyboards can ruin your whole day.
- Use a gentle, but firm press on keyboard keys. Avoid sharp strikes.
- Keep magnetic media (floppy disks, magnetic tape) away from magnetic fields such as radio speakers, phones, digitizer tablets, and other computer equipment.
- Store magnetic media in rooms with a moderate, even temperature. Avoid extreme temperature changes.
- Write on disk labels before attaching them to disks.
- Avoid touching the exposed portions of floppy disks and magnetic tapes.

CHAPTER TEST

Write your answers in the spaces provided.

1. How are points chosen on a screen in computer-aided drafting? _____

_____

2. What type of machine produces an inked original drawing? _____

3. What is customization? _____

_____

4. Why is drawing planning important? _____

_____

_____

5. Why should you save your work every 10 to 15 minutes? _____

_____

_____

6. List the seven components of a CAD workstation. _____

_____

_____

_____

7. What is "drawing planning"? _____

_____

_____

_____

8. What are standards? _____

_____

9. Describe system management. _____

_____

_____

_____

10. How do the CAD drafter and the computer "interact"? _____

_____

_____

11. Why should you read the command line at the bottom of the screen? _____

_____

_____

12. What type of storage device can be used for backup storage, hold up to 256MB of data, and be rewritten with new data as required? _____

_____

13. Name three different types of plotter technologies. _____

_____

14. What is the difference between vector and raster plotters? ___

___

___

15 Why is static electricity an important concern in computer rooms? ___

___

PROBLEMS

1. Read through several computer magazines or AutoCAD journals and list three brand names of each piece of hardware required for a computer drafting workstation. Call or visit a local computer equipment dealer and get prices for each piece of equipment.

2. Write a comparative report on using dot matrix printers or pen plotters to satisfy your school or company requirements. Take into account the type of drawings you create and their uses. Determine the minimum quality print you need. Compare this to the final products produced by printers and pen plotters. Based on your needs, recommend a product and include in your recommendation the following:

   A. Price.

   B. Size.

   C. Location (where the equipment will be installed).

   D. Maintenance costs (maintenance contract, if available).

   E. Who will operate the equipment.

   F. Cost of supplies and frequency of purchase.

   G. Savings to school or company over a given period of time.

3. Compare the following types of input devices. List the advantages and disadvantages of each. Provide general price comparisons, ease of use, space, and maintenance requirements.

   A. Mouse.

   B. Digitizer with stylus.

   C. Digitizer with multibutton puck.

   D. Keyboard.

4. Visit an AutoCAD dealer, hardware vendor, or local engineering or manufacturing firm and request a plotter demonstration. Ask questions about paper sizes, speed, pen types, price, and maintenance. Call or visit a local plotting service. Get information on their services and rates. Write a report on the uses and benefits of owning a plotter. Compare this to the benefits of using a plotting service to create final plots.

5. Write a report on the benefits of using a dot matrix printer for generating all check prints. Visit hardware vendors and research the types and sizes of printers available.

6. Interview your drafting instructors or supervisors and try to determine what type of drawing standards exist at your school or company. Write this down and keep it with you as you learn AutoCAD. Make notes as you progress through this text on how you use these standards. Also note how the standards could be changed to match the capabilities of AutoCAD.

7. Research your drafting department standards. If you do not have a copy of the standards, acquire one. If AutoCAD standards have been created, make notes as to how you can use these in your projects.

If no standards exist in your department or company, make notes as to how you can help develop standards. Write a report on why your school or company should create CAD standards and how they would be used. Discuss who should be responsible for specific tasks. Recommend procedures, techniques, and forms if necessary. Develop this report as you progress through your AutoCAD instruction, and as you read through this book.

8. Work up an equipment proposal for the purchase of three different CAD workstation configurations that can run AutoCAD. Visit or call an Authorized AutoCAD Dealer to determine exactly what you need for each item listed below. Record prices for each piece of equipment. Write an introductory statement for each workstation proposal listing the benefits of each. The three proposals should include the following: (You may revise these lists to suit your needs or to reflect changing technologies.)

EQUIPMENT	PROPOSAL #1	PROPOSAL #2	PROPOSAL #3
Computer	CPU: 486/33 ISA 8MB RAM 2 serial ports 1 parallel port MS-DOS	CPU:486/66 VLB 16MB RAM 2 serial ports 1 parallel port MS-DOS MS Windows (optional)	CPU: Pentium 90MHz 32MB RAM 2 serial ports 1 parallel port MS-DOS MS-Windows

Monitor and Graphics Array Card	14″ Multi-scan monitor
	SVGA graphics card
	  w/512K VRAM
		VGA card with 2MB
		  RAM
		17″ color monitor
			VGA card with 4MB
			  RAM
			21″ color monitor

Storage Device	single 3.5″ HD floppy
	  disk drive
	340MB Hard disk drive
		Dual floppy disk drive
		540MB hard disk drive
		256MB tape drive
		Double speed CD-ROM
			Dual floppy disk drive
			1 gigabyte hard disk
			  drive
			256MB re-writable
			  CD drive
			4X speed CD-ROM

Input Device	keyboard and mouse	Keyboard & mouse
		11 × 11 digitizer tablet
		  with 4-button cursor
		Scanner (optional)
			Keyboard & mouse
			11 × 11 digitizer tablet
			  with 4-button cursor
			Color scanner (optional)

Surge Protector	Power center with surge
	  protection
		Light duty UPS
		(Uninterruptible Power
		  Supply)
			Heavy duty UPS

Hardcopy Device	A-size and B-size inkjet
	  printer,
	or Laser printer
	  (2MB memory)
		A-size through E-size
		  pen plotter
		8 1/2 × 11 inkjet printer
			A-size through E-size
			  color inkjet plotter
			A-size and B-size color
			  inkjet printer

Communications	9600 bps modem	14,400 bps FAX/Modem	14,400 bps FAX/Modem

9. Develop a drawing planning sheet for use in your school or company. List items that you think are important for planning a CAD drawing. Make changes to this sheet as you learn more about AutoCAD.

10. Interview your instructors or supervisors to determine how CAD system management is applied in your school or company. Ask questions about the following items:

   A. Drawing storage methods.

   B. Drawing naming standards.

   C. Drawing backup procedures.

   D. Symbol creation and storage.

   E. Hardware and software maintenance and upgrades.

11. List ways in which your computer room can be made cleaner and more secure. Look for problems such as chalkboards, traffic patterns, radios, telephones, garbage cans, heating vents and elements, and locations where people drink and eat.

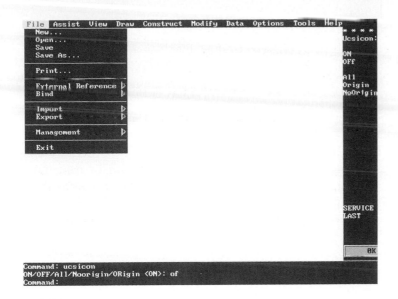

Chapter 2

Learning objectives

After completing this chapter, you will be able to:

- ○ Identify the meaning of DOS disk drive prompts.
- ○ Define the meaning of directories and path names.
- ○ Begin the AutoCAD program from a DOS prompt.
- ○ Describe the AutoCAD screen layouts and menu structure.
- ○ Describe the function of dialog boxes.
- ○ Operate the input device to select commands.
- ○ Use the keyboard keys and input device buttons to select commands, enter text, and pick locations on the screen.
- ○ Use the HELP command for assistance.
- ○ Format a floppy diskette.

AutoCAD, like most computer software, must first be installed on the hard disk drive of your computer. The AutoCAD program is included on several floppy disks, or on a CD-ROM, and contains an installation program called Install.exe. This program transfers files from the release disks or CD to subdirectories on the computer's hard disk. Instructions are given on-screen during the installation process to assist you in proper installation. Refer to Appendix A for installation procedures.

After the AutoCAD files have been installed on the hard disk, AutoCAD must be configured. Configuring tells AutoCAD what brand names of equipment you are using. You can select from a variety of graphics devices, printers, plotters, and pointing devices. You are also able to choose the appearance of the screen display during configuration. Installing and configuring AutoCAD are discussed in detail in Appendix A.

This chapter discusses how to get started once you have configured AutoCAD. It shows how the screen display will look when you begin a drawing. You can choose either of two different screen formats, or switch between them if you wish. You will also learn how to select commonly used commands and special functions given to keyboard keys and digitizer puck buttons.

GETTING STARTED

When you turn on your computer, the DOS software is automatically loaded. As you may recall, DOS stands for *Disk Operating System*, and is the "traffic cop" of your computer system. DOS enables the computer to work with files (including drawings), peripheral equipment, and software such as AutoCAD. DOS commands and functions are covered in several chapters throughout this book. Some schools or companies have a menu displayed on the screen from which you can make selections. The DOS prompt might be located below this menu.

DOS prompts

A *prompt* is a statement or response issued by the computer to show that it awaits your command. The first prompt you see is a letter followed by the greater-than symbol, or *caret* (⟩). These prompts are part of your DOS software and not part of AutoCAD. The prompt on your screen may be A⟩, B⟩, C⟩, or D⟩. The prompt may also display other information.

The letter indicates the DOS name of the current disk drive. If your computer has both a 5.25″ and 3.5″ floppy drives, most newer configurations specify the 3.5″ drive as the A: drive, regardless of its location. If you have a computer with a CD-ROM drive and one floppy drive, the CD-ROM drive is usually named D:. In this configuration the floppy drive is usually a 3.5″ drive and is usually named A:. The first hard disk name is C:. Figure 2-1 illustrates the names of the different drives. If you have an older computer, the top or left floppy drive is named A: and the lower or right floppy drive is B:. The colon (:) is part of the disk drive name, and must be included when you type DOS commands that require the name of the disk drive.

Figure 2-1. This illustration shows a typical disk drive arrangement and the DOS names usually given to the drives.

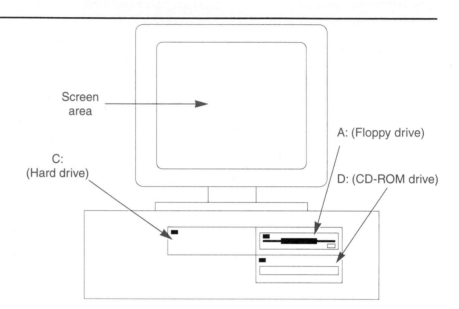

Screen area

A: (Floppy drive)

C: (Hard drive)

D: (CD-ROM drive)

Starting AutoCAD from DOS

To run AutoCAD, the DOS prompt must display the name of the drive that AutoCAD is stored on. This text assumes that AutoCAD is on the C: hard disk drive. The prompt that is on your screen now indicates which disk drive is current, or being looked at by the computer. You need to change drives if the display is anything other than "C⟩" or "C:\⟩". To change drives, type:

C: ↵

Now the display should read:
C⟩ or C:\⟩
If the display on the screen was already "C⟩" or "C:\⟩", you are ready to go.

PROFESSIONAL TIP

AutoCAD can be started automatically using a batch file. A *batch file* is a short program written using DOS commands. It performs a series of DOS commands that otherwise would have to be typed separately. When AutoCAD is installed, it asks if you want a batch file to be automatically created. This batch file is named ACADR13.BAT, and is used to begin an AutoCAD drawing session. You can use this batch file by typing ACADR13 at the C:\) prompt. (You can also modify this file or create your own.) Batch files can be used to load programs and accomplish specific tasks. If your computer does not have a batch file to load AutoCAD, you might want to make one. Appendix C contains information on creating your own batch file that automatically runs AutoCAD from the DOS prompt.

Now you are ready to load AutoCAD from the hard disk into the computer's memory and begin working. First, be certain that the current directory is the one that contains AutoCAD. A directory is like a file drawer. You must be in the right drawer to access the file (AutoCAD). In most cases, the directory name will be ACAD. Make sure ACAD is current by typing the following instructions at the DOS prompt:

C⟩ **CD \ACADR13\DOS** ↲ *(this can be in upper or lower case letters)*
C⟩ **ACADR13** ↲

The DOS command "CD \ACADR13\DOS" changes the current directory to ACADR13\DOS. The command "ACADR13" loads and runs the AutoCAD program. As AutoCAD is loading into the computer's memory, a message is displayed containing copyright and release information, in addition to the Autodesk® logo. This appears briefly, and is replaced by the graphics screen and menus. You are now inside AutoCAD in what is referred to as the *drawing editor*. This is where you construct and edit drawings.

NOTE   If you are working on a network, and are required to "login," a small "Login to AutoCAD" dialog box appears when you enter the drawing editor. Simply type the appropriate login name in the Name: edit box. You can save this login name by picking the "Save as default" check box, and the dialog box will not appear the next time you enter AutoCAD. Check with your instructor or supervisor for proper login names.

AUTOCAD'S MENU STRUCTURE   ARM 2

The graphics screen of AutoCAD is composed of several different menus and elements. The *screen menu* appears on the right side of the screen, whereas the *pull-down menus* are hidden behind the top line of the screen display called the *status line*. Any time you pick an item in the pull-down menus that is followed by ellipses (…), it displays a dialog box. A *dialog box* is a rectangular area that appears on the screen after you type or select certain commands. It contains a variety of options related to a specific command or function. A wide variety of the items you pick and select are found in dialog boxes. In addition, a pick inside a dialog box may display an *icon menu*. Each of these items is discussed in detail in this chapter. Learn the layout, appearance, and proper use of these areas, and your mastery of AutoCAD will come quickly.

Standard screen layout

The standard screen layout provides a large graphics or drawing area. The drawing area is surrounded by a screen menu on the right, status line along the top, and command line at the bottom. The graphics area is either gray or black and is bounded on two sides (right and bottom) by lines. All AutoCAD text surrounding the drawing area is white on a dark blue background in its uncustomized format. Look at your screen now and study the illustration in Figure 2-2.

Figure 2-2. The standard AutoCAD screen layout. The screen menu shown on the right is the "root" menu.

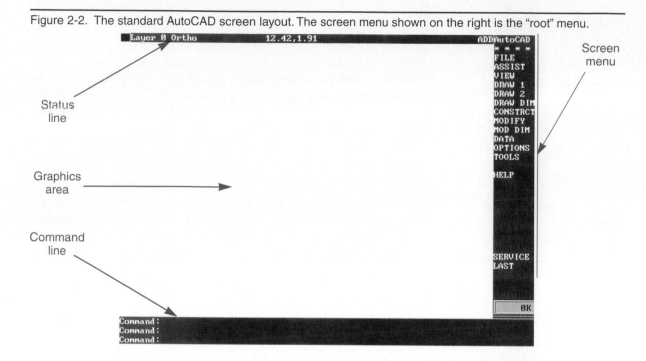

Become familiar with these unique areas of the screen and the information they provide. The list below describes the function of each area.

- **Screen menu.** The screen menu is located along the right side of the screen. Menu names and commands are displayed here. *Menu names* are shown in all capital letters, for example, DRAW 1. Commands and options are selected from menus by moving your cursor to highlight the item you want, and pressing the pick button of your pointing device. A *command name* is followed by a colon and is shown with only the first letter capitalized, for example, Line:. An *option* is one aspect of a command you select. Commands and options are discussed in greater detail later in this chapter. The word "AutoCAD" is shown at the top of each screen menu. Selecting "AutoCAD" returns you to the Root (beginning) screen menu shown in Figure 2-2. Selecting the "* * * *" displays the object snap modes screen menu discussed in Chapter 8.

- **Command line** or **prompt line.** The command line is located along the bottom of the screen. It displays the Command: prompt and reflects any entries you make. It also displays prompts that supply information to you or request values and text. Keep your eye on this line. This is where your communication with AutoCAD is shown.

- **Status line.** The status line is located along the top of the screen. It displays several items, Figure 2-3. The first item on the left of the status line is the name of the current layer. Chapter 17 discusses layers. Next to the layer name, the words "Ortho" and "Snap" are displayed when these two toggle functions are in use. (A *toggle* function is either on or off.) These two toggle functions are discussed in Chapters 4 and 6. Farther to the right are two numbers separated by a comma. This is the X,Y coordinate display, giving the current location of the pointing device on the drawing. The coordinate display is covered in Chapter 6. You will refer to the coordinate display often.

Figure 2-3. The status line shows several different items.

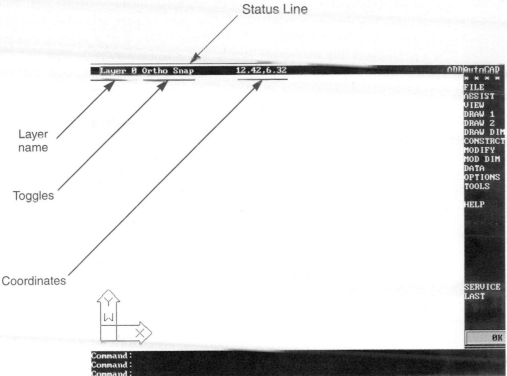

Status Line

Layer name

Toggles

Coordinates

Notice the items located in the screen menu at the right side of the screen. Move your pointing device so that the items in the sidebar menu are highlighted. When an item is highlighted, it can be selected by pressing the *pick button* on your mouse or puck. With a stylus, press it until it clicks.

The first menu that AutoCAD displays is the Root Menu. It is shown in Figure 2-4A, and is composed of menu names only. You must pick one of the menus in order to display a list of commands. For example, if you pick DRAW 1, the list of commands shown in Figure 2-4B is displayed. Commands are shown in lower case letters followed by a colon.

Figure 2-4. The AutoCAD Root menu. Click on an item for the sub menu.

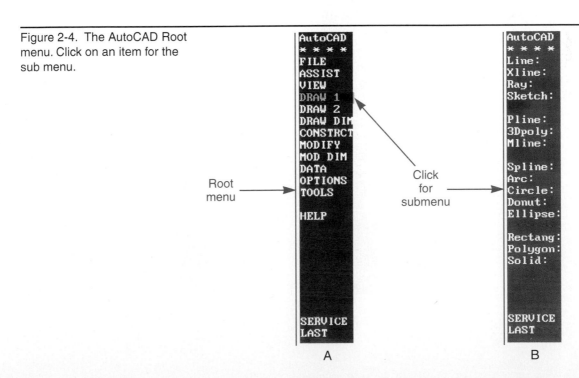

Root menu

Click for submenu

A

B

Some of the commands you select display a dialog box, which provides the options of a command in a graphical format. Commands that begin with the letters "DD" always display a dialog box. The DD stands for Dynamic Dialog. These commands usually have a command line version that does not display a dialog box. For example, if you type GRIPS at the Command: line, a prompt for the grips value is displayed. But if you type DDGRIPS, the "Grips" dialog box is displayed.

The menu, command, and option structure of AutoCAD is a *nested* arrangement. Options nest inside a command, and commands nest inside a menu. Related commands such as drawing commands are grouped together in the DRAW 1 menu. Figure 2-5 shows a schematic of this concept. The actual nesting arrangement of the DRAW 1 menu is shown in Figure 2-6. The entire AutoCAD command structure is shown in Appendix D.

Figure 2-5. This is a schematic representation of nested commands and options.

Figure 2-6. The nesting arrangement of the DRAW menu.

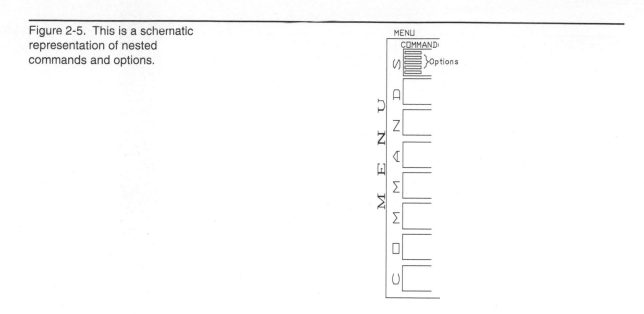

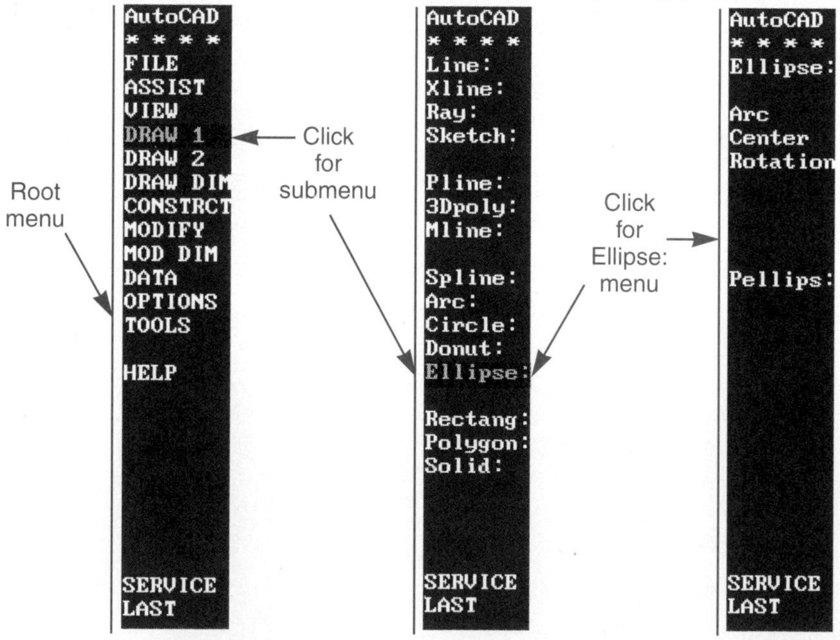

Select the DRAW 1 menu with your pointing device. The menu changes and now consists mostly of commands, Figure 2-7. The commands are grouped according to the similar functions that they perform. Two items are displayed at the bottom of the menu:

SERVICE
LAST

The SERVICE menu provides commands and options that enable you to accurately select items for editing, construct new shapes, and establish a drawing environment in which to work. All of these items are discussed in detail in later chapters. Picking LAST takes you back to the menu that was previously displayed on screen. You can display up to eight previous screen menus using the LAST selection.

Figure 2-7. Commands in a menu are grouped by similar functions.

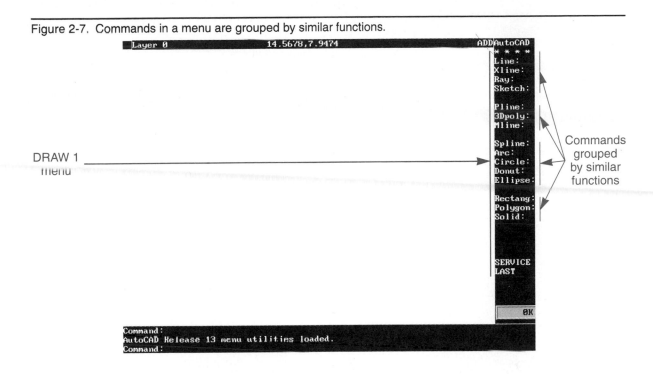

Two additional items are displayed on every menu at the top of the menu bar.

AutoCAD
*   *   *   *

If you select "AutoCAD" from the screen menu, the Root Menu is redisplayed. This is good to remember if you get into the menus and forget how to get back. When in doubt, just pick "AutoCAD" from the top of the menu and you will be put back at the Root Menu. As previously mentioned, when the asterisks (* * * *) are picked, the object snap modes are displayed.

The remainder of the screen between the status line and the command, and to the left of the screen menu is the drawing area. Move your crosshairs around to determine the extents of this area. Note how far you must move your pointing device to locate the crosshairs on the screen.

Pull-down menus

When you move your pointing device so the crosshairs touch the status line at the top, the *menu bar* appears. Your crosshairs also change to an arrow pointer. The menu bar is composed of nine items. They are:

File   Assist   View   Draw   Construct   Modify   Data   Options   Tools   Help

As you move the screen cursor along this row, the items are highlighted when the cursor touches them. These "items" are AutoCAD menus. Their placement enables you to quickly select a variety of commands without moving into nested screen menus. Move the cursor to highlight the "Draw" menu and press the pick button. A pull-down menu appears below Draw, Figure 2-8A. Commands within this menu are selected by moving the cursor to highlight the command. Then press the pick button. Take note of what happens to the screen menu when a pull-down menu selection is made. In many cases, the screen menu displays the options found in the chosen command.

Several of the commands in the Draw pull-down menu have a small arrow to the right. When the arrow pointer is moved over this, a *cascading menu* appears. This menu offers you additional options for that command. See Figure 2-8B. Each of these commands and options are discussed in the appropriate chapters of this text. If you choose an item from a cascading menu, the menu disappears, allowing you to draw and edit as you desire. If you want to select the same item from the cascading menu again, pick the pull-down menu name twice and the same command or option is automatically executed.

Figure 2-8. A–AutoCAD's Draw pull-down menu. B–When the pointer is moved over an arrow in a pull-down menu, a cascading menu appears.

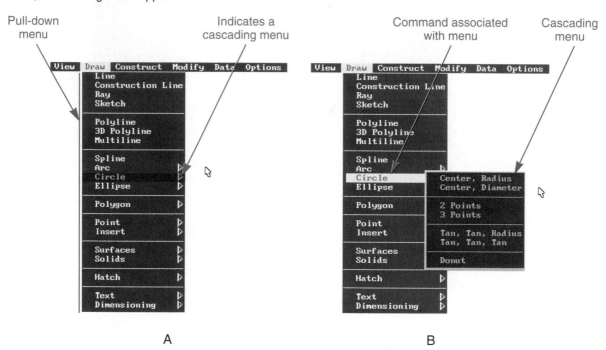

A   B

Some of the menu selections are followed by ellipses (…). If you pick one of these items, a dialog box is displayed. Dialog boxes are discussed in the next section.

If you pick the wrong pull-down menu, simply move the cursor to the one you want and pick it. The first menu is removed and the one you pick is displayed. The pull-down menu disappears after you pick an item in the menu, pick a point in the drawing area, or type on the keyboard.

Dialog boxes

One of the most important aspects of AutoCAD Release 13 is the graphical user interface (GUI). A *graphical user interface* is the manner in which information, options, and choices are displayed for you by the software. The most common aspect of the GUI is the dialog box. The *dialog box* is a box in which a variety of information is presented to you, and in which you can select an item by simply moving your cursor to it and picking. This process eliminates a lot of typing, thus potentially saving time and increasing productivity.

Commands and selections in the pull-down and screen menus that are followed by ellipses (...) or have the prefix of "DD", display a dialog box when they are picked. A good example of a simple dialog box is shown in Figure 2-9. This dialog box is displayed when you pick the New... command from the File pull-down menu. A detailed discussion of this dialog box is included in Chapter 5.

Figure 2-9. A dialog box appears when you pick an item that is followed by ellipses.

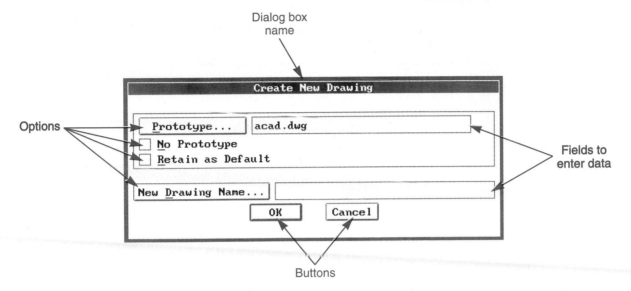

You will encounter a wide variety of dialog boxes in your exploration of AutoCAD. Some of these dialog boxes are very simple, while others are quite detailed. If you pick items followed by ellipses in some dialog boxes, a subdialog box is then displayed. The subdialog box will be displayed on top of the original dialog box much like laying a sheet of paper on top of another. You must make a selection from the subdialog box before returning to the original dialog box.

There are standard parts to all dialog boxes. If you take a few minutes to review them here, you will find it much easier to work with the dialog boxes. A brief description of the dialog box components is given here, and detailed discussions are provided in later chapters.

• **Buttons.** When you pick a button, something happens immediately. The most common buttons are OK and Cancel. Help... is another very common button. See Figure 2-10. If a button has a dark border (such as OK in the given figure), it is the default. Pressing the ENTER key accepts

Figure 2-10. When you select a
button, something immediately
happens. Note the dark border
around the OK button. This
indicates that this button
is the default.

UCS Control

UCS Names

WORLD   Current

Current   Delete   List...

Rename To:

OK   Cancel   Help...

Accepts current
settings

Closes dialog box without
making changes

Accesses the
help files

the default. If a button is "grayed out," then that item is not available for selection. Buttons can also lead to other things:

...   The ellipses lead to another dialog box.
⟨   This symbol requires that you make a selection in the graphics screen then returns you to the dialog box.

- **Radio buttons.** When you press a selector button on your car radio, the station changes. Only one station can play at a time. Likewise, only one item in a group of radio buttons can be highlighted or active at one given time. See Figure 2-11.

Figure 2-11. Radio buttons. Only one button in the group can be highlighted at any one given time.

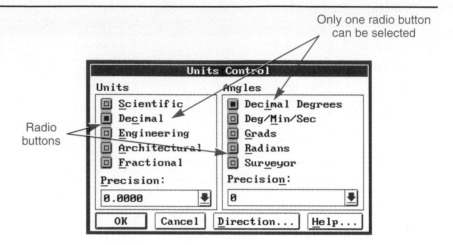

- **Check box.** A check box actually contains an "X" when it is active. The item represented by the "X" is either on or off. See Figure 2-12.

Figure 2-12. Examples of check boxes. An "X" indicates which item is active. More than one can be checked in a group.

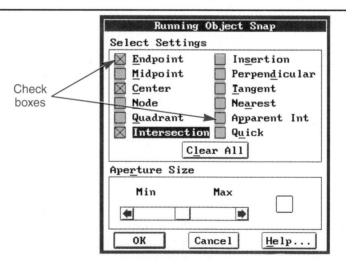

- **List box.** List boxes display a variety of named items such as layer names, text styles, linetype names, etc. The most common list boxes contain lists of directories and files. You can pick from the list, or scan through it using the scroll bar. If you pick the name of a directory, it is highlighted. Press the ENTER key to see the list of files in that directory. You can also *double click* (press the pick button twice quickly) and get the same results. If you pick a file, and it is highlighted, you can pick the OK button, or press the ENTER key to select it. If you double click on the file name, it is selected and loaded automatically. See Figure 2-13.

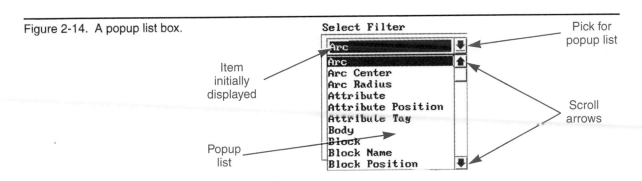

Figure 2-13. List boxes contain a list of directories or files.

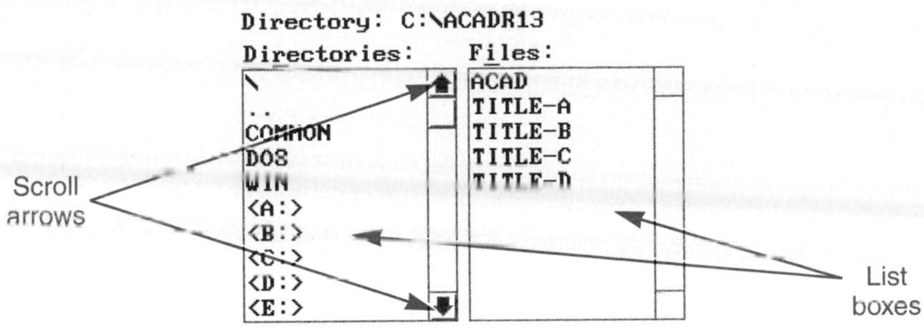

• **Popup list box.** The popup list box is similar to the standard list box, except only one item is initially shown. The remaining items are hidden until you pick the down arrow. When you pick the down arrow, the popup list pops "down" below the initial item. You can then pick from the expanded list, or use the scroll bar to find the item you need. See Figure 2-14.

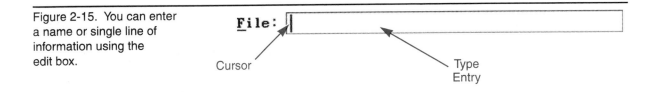

Figure 2-14. A popup list box.

• **Edit box.** You can enter a name or single line of information using the edit box. A blinking cursor is positioned at the left of the box. See Figure 2-15. You can type an entry when it is blinking, or pick a selection from the list box. If there is text in the edit box, it appears highlighted. Any characters you type replace the highlighted text. Pressing either the Backspace key, Space bar, or the Delete key, deletes all of the highlighted text. You can edit text using Home, End, Insert, Delete, and the left and right arrow keys.

Figure 2-15. You can enter a name or single line of information using the edit box.

File: |

Cursor

Type Entry

The home key moves the cursor to the extreme left end of the box. The End key moves the cursor to the end of the line. The Insert key can be used to toggle between the "insert mode" and the "strikeover" mode. When the flashing vertical cursor is thin and positioned between two characters, the insert mode is active. Pressing the Insert key activates strikeover mode and changes the cursor to a solid blinking rectangle that covers a character. Any characters you type will replace the character the cursor rests on. The Delete key removes the character that is directly under the cursor.

• **Scroll bar.** The scroll bar can be compared to an elevator sitting next to a list of files or directories. The top arrow points to the top floor, and the bottom arrow points to the basement. The
box in the middle is the elevator. If you pick the elevator and hold down the pick button, you
can move the box up or down, thus displaying additional files in the upper or lower floors of
your directory. Pick the blank area above the elevator box, and you scroll one page up. Pick
below the elevator box, and the list scrolls down one page. If you want to scroll up or down one
file at a time, simply pick the up or down arrows. See Figure 2-16.

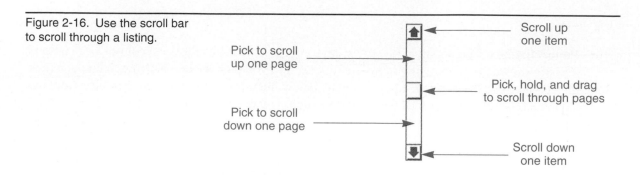

Figure 2-16. Use the scroll bar
to scroll through a listing.

• **Label.** A label displays the value of a setting you made in another area of the dialog box or
drawing. You cannot change the label, but it changes when you alter other items. The plot area
shown in Figure 2-17 is an example of a label.

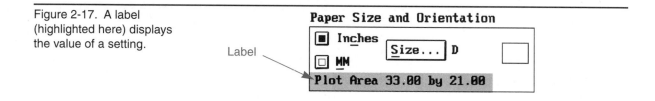

Figure 2-17. A label
(highlighted here) displays
the value of a setting.

• **Image tile.** An image tile is an area of a dialog box that displays a "picture" of the item you
selected, such as a hatch style, linetype, dimension style, or text font. See Figure 2-18A.
• **Image button.** An image button is similar to an image tile, but you can actually pick the image,
or part of it, to make a selection. Note in Figure 2-18B that when an image button is selected,
the defining text to the left is also highlighted.
• **Alerts.** Alerts can be displayed in two forms: a note in the lower-left corner of the original dialog box, or in a separate small dialog box. See Figure 2-19.
You can become efficient in your use of dialog boxes by remembering two things: pick a *button*,
and enter text in an edit box.

Figure 2-18. A—Image tiles change to show the affects of selecting different options. B—Image buttons can be used to select options.

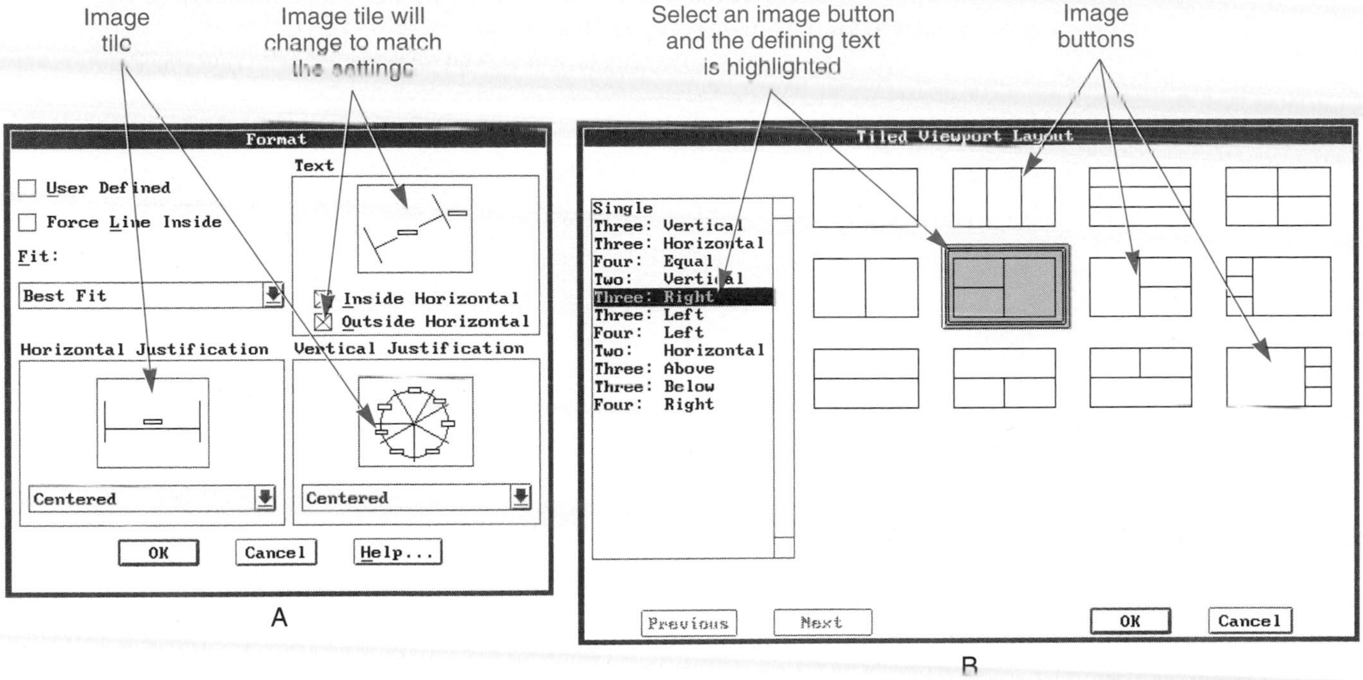

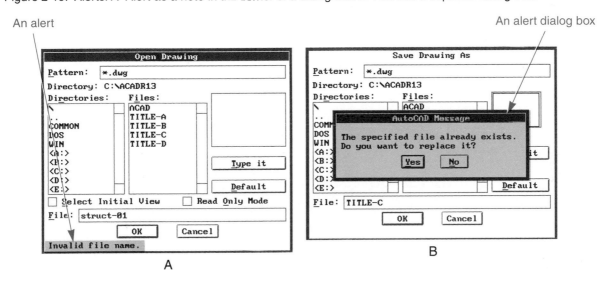

Figure 2-19. Alerts. A—Alert as a note in the corner of a dialog box. B—Alert as a separate dialog box.

AutoCAD tablet menu

The digitizer tablet can accept an overlay or menu that contains most all of AutoCAD's commands. Other specialized programs that operate with AutoCAD may have similar menus.

This text presents commands as if they are typed at the keyboard or selected from menus and dialog boxes. If you wish to use your digitizer tablet to pick commands, the tablet must first be *configured* (arranged) before the menu can be used. See ***AutoCAD and its Applications–Advanced, Release 13 for DOS,*** for information on tablet configuration and customization. After the tablet has been configured, you can select most AutoCAD commands directly from the tablet overlay. All of the AutoCAD commands do not fit on the tablet; some must be picked from the screen. Using the tablet requires that you take your eyes off the screen and look down at the overlay. After picking a tablet command, look at the command line to be sure you picked what you wanted.

The AutoCAD tablet menu is shown in Figure 2-20. If you plan on using a digitizer with tablet menu, take some time and study its arrangement. Become familiar with the command groups. Try to remember where each command is located. The quicker you learn the layout of the menu, the more efficient your drawing sessions will be.

Figure 2-20. AutoCAD tablet menu. (Autodesk, Inc.)

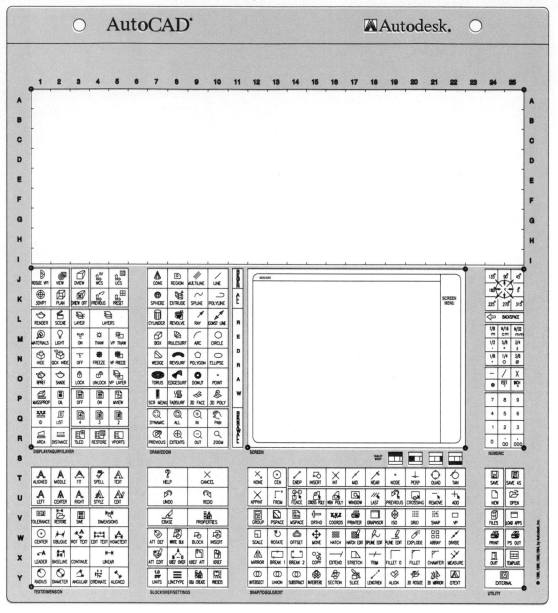

SELECTING AUTOCAD COMMANDS

Commands can be selected in AutoCAD three different ways. They can be:
- Selected from one of the pull-down or screen menus.
- Selected from the digitizer tablet menu overlay.
- Typed at the keyboard.

To use the screen menu, move the pointing device to highlight the desired command and select it by pressing the pick button. You can select a command option in the same manner. An advantage of using the screen menus is that you do not have to remove your eyes from the screen, whereas you must look down to pick tablet menu commands.

The pull-down menus place lists of commands directly over your work area in your line of sight. You do not have to look to the side of the screen to pick a command. In addition, pull-down menus offer immediate access to all dialog boxes.

On the other hand, tablet menus have advantages. They can show almost every command, including small icons that represent the command. The user does not have to page through several screen menus to find the needed command.

Typed commands do not require that you turn your eyes from the screen. There is no need to page through several menus on the screen, because the screen menu changes when a command is typed. You can learn commands quicker by typing them. Try typing commands before other selection methods are used. You will find that work progresses faster. You will also be able to concentrate on the screen for longer periods.

GETTING HELP

If you need some help with a specific command or option, use the HELP command. Whether you type "HELP" at the Command: prompt or pick Help... from the Help pull-down menu, the "Help" dialog box is displayed. See Figure 2-21A.

The Help table of contents is displayed in this first screen. There are three major areas in the table of contents:

- Menu access
- Command line access
- Glossary

Listed under each of these headings are topics inside double brackets. For example, 《《Commands》》 is shown under Command line access. Any item that is enclosed in double brackets is accessible for help. You can either highlight the specific item and pick the OK button, or double-click on the item. Figure 2-21B shows the display that appears after double-clicking on the 《《Commands》》 item.

Figure 2-21. Getting help while drawing. A–The AutoCAD Help dialog box. B–The alphabetical command listing displayed after picking 《《Commands》》 in the "AutoCAD Help" dialog box.

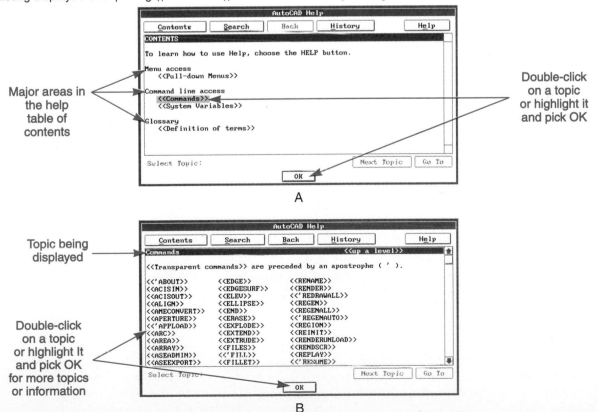

How to use Help

The Help files for AutoCAD Release 13 are extensive, and you can access them in a variety of ways. For that reason there is some assistance available in order to help you learn how to use Help. From the Help pull-down menu pick How to Use Help. The dialog box shown in Figure 2-22 is displayed. Read through these instructions and you will be able to navigate more efficiently through AutoCAD's Help files.

Figure 2-22. The "Help on AutoCAD Help" dialog box provides instructions on the use of the AutoCAD Help functions.

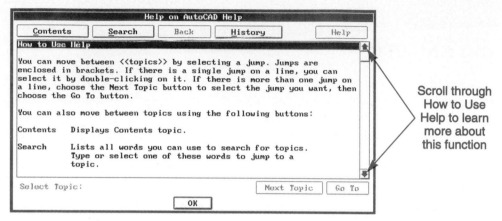

Searching for a specific item

Should you need help for a specific item, command, or technique, the search function may be the most efficient. Pick Search for Help On… in the Help pull-down menu. The "AutoCAD Help Search" dialog box is displayed. See Figure 2-23. To begin a search, place your pointer in the edit box, pick, and type a word you want to search for. Next pick Show Topics, and AutoCAD will display the item in the list box and highlight it. If an exact match is not found, AutoCAD will highlight the closest match. When the item you want information on is highlighted, pick the Go To button and the information is displayed in the "AutoCAD Help" dialog box.

The search function button is also available in all main Help dialog boxes.

Figure 2-23. The "AutoCAD Help Search" dialog box enables you to get Help on a specific item, command, or technique.

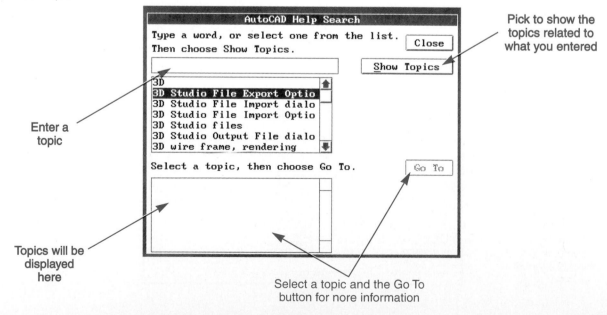

New Features in Release 13

If you are curious about the changes that were made to the Release 13 version of AutoCAD, pick What's New in Release 13... from the Help pull-down menu. There are three selections available in the "What's New in Release 13" dialog box. See Figure 2-24. The Using What's New selection helps you navigate this portion of AutoCAD's help files. New Features gives you a quick tour–with color image tiles–of some of the new features in Release 13. The Command Summary selection provides lists of new, changed, and deleted commands in Release 13.

Figure 2-24. The "What's New in Release 13" dialog box provides a review of Release 13 features and commands.

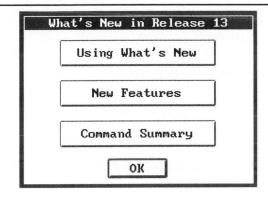

Getting help while working inside a command

You can also ask for help while you are working inside a command. For example, suppose you are using the ARC command and forget what type of information is required by AutoCAD for the specific prompts that are on screen. Pick Help... from the Help pull-down menu. The help you need for that command is then displayed. You can accomplish the same thing by entering either an apostrophe and a question mark ('?), or an apostrophe and the word HELP ('HELP) at the prompt for any command. If the Command: prompt is displayed, you can omit the apostrophe and type a ? or HELP.

KEYS, BUTTONS, FUNCTIONS AND TERMINOLOGY

AutoCAD provides several ways of performing the same task. There are a variety of keys on the keyboard. Some of them you may find handy, but only if you know their meanings. Keyboard keys allow you to perform many functions. In addition, multibutton pointing devices also utilize the extra buttons for AutoCAD commands. Become familiar with the meaning of these keys and buttons.

Control keys

Most computer programs use *control key* functions to perform common tasks. Control key functions are activated by pressing and holding the CTRL key while pressing a second key. Keep the following list close at hand and try them occasionally. (If a command or key is noted as a "toggle," it is either on or off–nothing else.)

CTRL+B–Snap mode (toggle).
CTRL+C–Cancel.
CTRL+D–Coordinate display on status line (toggle).
CTRL+E–Crosshairs in isoplane positions left/top/right (toggle).
CTRL+G–Grid (toggle).
CTRL+H–Same as backspace.
CTRL+O–Ortho mode (toggle).
CTRL+Q–Echo all status listings, prompts, and keyboard inputs to an attached printer.
 AutoCAD DOS versions only. (toggle) *If not, select Preferences in the Options*
Pull-Down Menu, check the log file box and
CTRL+T–Tablet mode (toggle).
CTRL+V–Moves through active viewports, making each one current in succession. *(write down the log file name before).→ enter: LPT1*
CTRL+X–Cancels all characters on command line. *on the edit box next to the check box*
To disable this feature, check again
the box and enter the former log file.

Function keys

Function keys provide instant access to commands and can be programmed to perform a series of commands. The function keys are either to the left or along the top of the keyboard, Figure 2-25. Depending on the brand of keyboard, there will be either 10 or 12 function keys. These are numbered F1-F10 (or F1-F12). AutoCAD uses only seven function keys.

F1—Flip screen from graphics to text (toggle).

F5—Isoplane crosshair mode, left, top, right, bottom (toggle).

F6—Coordinate display (toggle).

F7—Grid (toggle).

F8—Ortho mode (toggle).

F9—Snap mode (toggle).

F10—Tablet mode (toggle).

As you become proficient with AutoCAD, you might program the function keys to do specific tasks using other computer programs.

Figure 2-25. The standard function keys are found along the top or side of a keyboard. In this photo, the function keys are along the top.

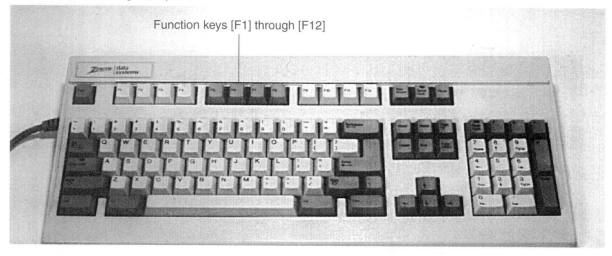

Cursor keys

Cursor keys control the movement of the screen cursor (crosshairs). They are also called *arrow keys,* and are located on the right side of your keyboard, Figure 2-26. Each of the four keys has an arrow pointing in one of the directions of the compass. Cursor keys can be used instead of a pointing device, although this method is slow and tedious.

Press one of the cursor keys one time and watch the screen. Notice the small movements of the crosshairs. The distance of this movement can be increased by pressing the Page Up key located near the cursor keys. Press a cursor key again. You should notice a greater movement of the crosshairs. Press the Page Up key again, and then press a cursor key. The movement is much more dramatic. The amount of cursor movement can be decreased by pressing the Page Down key. Try this a few times to get the feel of it.

The keyboard can also be used to select screen menu items. Press the right arrow key until the crosshairs touch the screen menu. Additional presses of the right arrow key will not move the cursor into the menu bar. Press the Insert key; it is above the arrow keys. One of the screen menu items highlights. Press the up or down arrow key to move around the screen menu. Pressing Insert again or the ENTER key selects the highlighted item.

Figure 2-26. The arrow keys, PAGE UP, PAGE DOWN, and INSERT keys are used to move the screen cursor and select menu items.

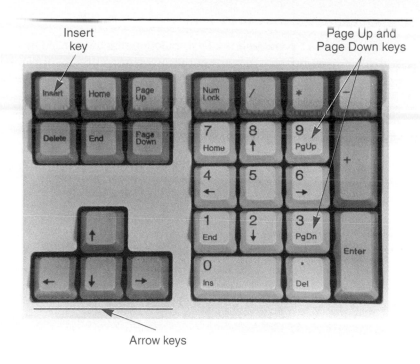

Insert key

Page Up and Page Down keys

Arrow keys

Button functions

If you are using a multibutton pointing device, you can select control key functions by pressing a single button. The meaning of the pointing device's buttons are:

0–Pick.
1–Return.
2–Object snap submenu displayed on screen.
3–Cancel.
4–Snap mode (toggle).
5–Ortho mode (toggle).
6–Grid (toggle).
7–Coordinate display (toggle).
8–Crosshairs isoplane positions top/left/right (toggle).
9–Tablet mode (toggle).

Understanding terminology

Become familiar with the following terms to help you select AutoCAD functions.
- **Default.** A value that is maintained by the computer until you change it.
- **Select.** Choose a command or option from the screen or tablet menu.
- **Pick.** Use the pointing device to select an item on the screen or tablet.
- **Button.** One of the dialog box or pointing device (puck) buttons.
- **Key.** A key on the keyboard.
- **Function key.** One of the keys labeled F1-F12 along the top or side of the keyboard.
- **ENTER (↵).** The ENTER or RETURN key on the keyboard.
- **Command.** An instruction issued to the computer.
- **Option.** An aspect of a command that can be selected. Displayed in lowercase letters.

PREPARING A DISK FOR USE

Before a disk can be used by the computer, it must be formatted. This divides the disk into pie-shaped sectors, checks it for defects, and creates a file location directory on the disk. This is all accomplished with the FORMAT command. The DOS external command that handles this is FORMAT.COM. In order to use this command you must be at the DOS prompt.

A word about the FORMAT command

The FORMAT command is a DOS function that has caused many people grief. It is a helpful command when used properly. However, when used incorrectly, it can be a lethal weapon to floppy and hard disks. The FORMAT command erases a disk before it prepares the disk for use. Respect the FORMAT command and use it carefully.

Floppy disks are the only disks you should ever need to format. Most new floppy disks must be formatted before they can be used. The FORMAT command divides the disk into pie-shaped *sectors* and checks the disk for any bad spots. If bad spots are found, DOS marks them and informs you of their size. The bad spots are then avoided in the future. You can still use a disk with bad spots. Most of the time, the disks are in good shape. The most important thing to remember is that FORMAT's first job is to erase all information on the disk.

CAUTION

 Always run a directory on your floppy disks before formatting them by typing DIR A: or DIR B: and pressing the ENTER key. Be sure the disk does not contain drawings or files that you need. If you must format the disk, be sure the files on it have been copied to another disk.

Using the FORMAT command

In order to use FORMAT, the DOS prompt must be displayed on the screen. It may appear as:

C:\⟩ or C⟩ or C:\ACADR13\DOS⟩

You may see one of these prompts on the screen now. If you are in AutoCAD, exit the program as follows to get the DOS prompt:

Command: **QUIT** ⏎

The DOS prompt returns. Now insert a blank floppy disk into the A: drive and close the lever (if equipped with one). Enter the following DOS command at the prompt. **Do not press ENTER.** Always check your entry at the prompt before continuing.

C:\⟩ **FORMAT A:** ⏎

If you make a typing mistake, simply press the BACKSPACE key until the error is erased and type it over. When the entry looks exactly like the one shown above, press ENTER. The following prompt is displayed:

Insert new diskette for drive A:
and press ENTER when ready...

Press the ENTER key. The following prompt is displayed during the format process:

Checking existing disk format.
Formatting 1.44MB

The following appears when the process is complete:

Format complete.
Volume label (11 characters, ENTER for none)?

The volume label is a name that you can give your disk. It can contain up to 11 characters. If you give your disk a name, write the same name on the adhesive label that you attach to the disk. Should you neglect to name the disk, now you can name it at any time with the LABEL command at the DOS prompt.

If you formatted a 3.5″ 1.44MB floppy disk, the following prompt appears after you supply a disk name, or press ENTER at the volume label prompt:

```
1,457,664 bytes total disk space
1,457,664 bytes available on disk
Format another (Y/N)?
```

If you are using 5.25″ 1.2MB, 3.5″ 720K, or 5.25″ 360K disks, different values than those previously shown will be displayed. Notice that DOS did not report any bad spots on the disk; therefore, the entire disk is good. You are asked if you want to format another. You should format several disks at one sitting. This saves time later when you find you need another disk. If you want to format another, simply type Y and press the ENTER key:

```
Format another (Y/N)? Y ↵
Insert new diskette for drive A:
and press ENTER when ready...
```

The formatting procedure continues to cycle until you answer N or NO to the Format another (Y/N)? prompt.

Once a disk is formatted, it is ready to accept AutoCAD drawing files and files from other programs. Remember, the FORMAT command has the potential to ruin your whole day if you accidentally insert a disk full of drawings to format. Use the FORMAT command carefully.

Refer to Chapter 30 for additional information on formatting disks with different capacities.

UNDERSTANDING DISK DRIVES AND DIRECTORIES

One of the keys to functioning at your job in a productive and efficient manner is to have a good working knowledge of the location and structure of filing systems and resources. Basically, you should become efficient at finding things in a filing cabinet, putting them back where they belong, and filing new documents with the proper name.

As you work with DOS and AutoCAD, you will become more comfortable with the computerized filing system of disk drives. This information is presented now to prepare you for the techniques of storing files in disk drive directories.

Disk drive names

Disk drives have names, as discussed previously in this chapter. When you turn the computer on (before loading AutoCAD), the following DOS prompt appears:

```
C⟩
```

This is the basic DOS prompt, and means that the hard disk drive is current. Your computer may show something different, such as:

```
C:\⟩
```

If it does, do not worry. Your computer has been set to display the current directory as part of the prompt. This is discussed in the next section.

If you want to make the A: drive current, insert a disk in the A: drive and type:

```
C⟩ A: ↵
```

The prompt changes to reflect the new current drive:

```
A⟩
```

If your computer has a second flexible disk drive, access it in the same manner. Be sure a disk is in the B: drive, and type:

```
A⟩ B: ↵
```

Again, the prompt changes.

    B⟩

Remember the difference between a DOS prompt and a disk drive name. A DOS prompt is followed by a caret (⟩), and a disk drive name is followed by a colon (:).

    A⟩ = *prompt*
    A: = *drive name*

When you wish to change drives (at the DOS prompt) be sure to type the colon after the drive letter before pressing ENTER. You can get back to the hard disk drive by entering:

    B⟩ **C:** ↵
    C⟩

The prompt again indicates the hard disk drive is current.

NOTE   If you get the error message:

    Not ready error reading drive A:
    Abort, Retry, Fail?

It means that there is no disk in the drive you are trying to access. Insert a disk in the drive and type "R," but do not press ENTER.

Directories and path names

Before you begin working with files and disks, there is one important concept to learn: directories. Think of your hard disk drive as one big filing cabinet. It would be a mess if you dumped all of your files and records into a filing cabinet without drawers or file folders. Rather, the drawers and folders help you to organize your materials. The same is true with your hard disk. See Figure 2-27. You divide the hard disk (file cabinet) into directories (drawers). Here you might store the AutoCAD main program files. You can then further divide the directories into subdirectories (file folders). These subdirectories–possibly named ELEC (electrical), STRUCT (structural), etc.–hold individual drawing files.

When working with files, you need to specify where a file is located. For example, suppose you want to delete the file TEST1.DWG on drive A:. You would enter:

    C⟩ **DEL A:TEST1.DWG** ↵

Figure 2-27. Organize your hard disk into directories and subdirectories.

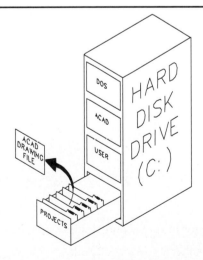

The A: is needed to tell DOS you want to delete the file located on the disk in the A: drive. How then do you delete a file that is located in the ELEC subdirectory of the ACADR13 directory on your hard disk? Here, you need to specify a "path" for the DOS command to follow to find your file. A *path* is the direction, through the directory tree, that DOS must follow. It is composed of the drive letter, the back-slash symbol (\) representing the root directory, and any additional directories and subdirectories (tree branches) that lead to the file. Look at Figure 2-28. Suppose you want to delete the drawing PROJECT1.DWG located in the STRUCT subdirectory of the ACADR13 directory on drive C: (the hard disk). You would enter:

C⟩ **DEL \ACADR13\STRUCT\PROJECT1.DWG** ↵

Figure 2-28. Using a path to find files.

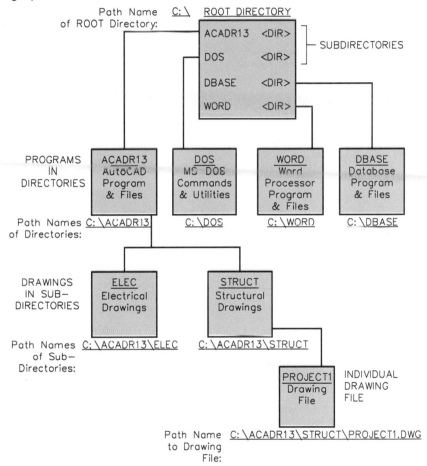

You do not need to include the drive name (C:) because the hard disk drive is already current (C⟩). The first backslash (\) means to begin the path at the root directory. The second backslash means that you are digging deeper by entering a subdirectory. The final backslash separates the subdirectory from the file you wish to delete. You must enter the full file name and its extension, if it has one.

Study Figure 2-28 until you understand the nature of the root directory, and the tree structure of the directories and subdirectories under it. It often helps to think of a subdirectory as the child of the directory in which it resides. For example, in Figure 2-28, the ACADR13 directory is a child of the root directory. Therefore, the root directory must be the parent of ACADR13. Find the STRUCT subdirectory and note that ACADR13 is its parent. When writing a path to a specific file, it may help to remember to list the file last, then the child, then the parent. Each directory and subdirectory name must be separated from the other by a backslash (\).

❑ After each of the following file and directory descriptions, write the correct path notations.
❑ On the D drive the MOUSE directory contains a file named MOUSE.EXE.

_____

❑ The file ACAD.ERR is located in the ACADR13 directory on the C drive.

_____

❑ MACROS is a child of WORD, located on the D drive.

_____

❑ The drawing file 1007-004 is in the PIPING subdirectory, which is a child of PROJECTS. The drawing file is on the C drive, and the parent of the PROJECTS directory is ACADR13.

_____

AVOIDING "DISK FULL" PROBLEMS

When you begin a new drawing, AutoCAD "looks" at the drawing file name to determine where the drawing will be stored. When you enter the drawing name, AutoCAD creates a space for it in the current directory of the active disk drive. AutoCAD does this automatically to the hard disk if you do not put a disk name in front of the file name. Suppose you give the name A:P15-5. AutoCAD creates a space on the floppy disk in the A: drive for drawing P15-5. Note that the "A:" indicates the drive, and "P15-5" is the drawing name.

Creating a drawing on a floppy disk is not the most efficient method of operating AutoCAD. This is because AutoCAD looks at the disk and then creates space for several temporary open files that it uses during a drawing session. There must be room for these open files, in addition to your drawing file, for AutoCAD to function properly. Floppy drives are slow to store and access data. In addition, limited space on the floppy disk can eventually lead to a "disk full" error, or worse a system crash. The disk full error still allows you to save the current drawing. A system crash destroys the current drawing in memory.

Creating a new drawing

It is best to begin new and edit existing drawings on the hard disk during a drawing session. If you are starting a new drawing called P15-5, begin the drawing session with the new drawing name P15-5. AutoCAD then works on the hard disk, which should have plenty of room for the temporary open files. Save the drawing as A:P15-5 by typing the SAVE command to store it on a floppy, then quit without saving. This places the drawing on the floppy disk, but does not put anything on the hard disk drive.

See Chapter 5 for detailed information on saving drawing files.

Editing an existing drawing

If you are in training with AutoCAD, you should save all of your drawings and exercises on floppy disks, not on the hard disk drive. Keep two copies of each floppy disk. One is the original; the other is a backup copy. Each time you save a drawing on a floppy disk, save it a second time on the backup disk. This is discussed again later in the text.

When you need to edit a drawing that is on a floppy disk, select New... from the File pull-down menu. If you want to work on drawing P15-5, enter the following in the New Drawing Name edit box and press ENTER:

P15-5=A:P15-5 ⏎

This technique instructs AutoCAD to retrieve a copy of drawing P15-5 from the floppy disk in the A: drive and begin a new drawing located on the hard disk named P15-5 using that copy. This is called the *prototype drawing method*, and preserves the original drawing.

Another way to use the prototype drawing method is by picking the Prototype edit box of the "Create New Drawing" dialog box. The drawing name–acad–should be the current name in the File edit box. If you double click on the word acad, you can type A:P15-5 and acad is replaced. Now pick the New Drawing Name edit box and type P15-5. When you pick the OK button, AutoCAD gets a copy of the prototype drawing and begins a new one with the same name. This process is explained in greater detail in Chapter 5.

When you are ready to save the drawing, type the SAVE command. Use A:P15-5 as the drawing name. You will then get an alert message that says:

The specified file already exists.
Do you want to replace it?

Pick the YES button. Saving the drawing as A:P15-5 means you want to place the drawing on the floppy drive. (Remember you first loaded the drawing by this name from the floppy disk.) AutoCAD says that a drawing with the same name already exists on the floppy disk in that drive. By entering Y or YES, you replace the old copy with the edited (updated) version.

Use these techniques for working with drawings. You will avoid the problems associated with editing a drawing you want preserved as a prototype.

NOTE   You can instruct AutoCAD to store its temporary files in specified directory by using the CONFIG command. First be sure that you have made a new directory on your hard disk with a name such as C:\ACADTEMP. Then type CONFIG at the Command: prompt, and press ENTER three times until the Configuration menu is displayed. Then type 7, Configure operating parameters. This displays the Configure operating parameters menu. Now select 5, Placement of temporary files. You will be asked to enter a directory name for temporary files. Enter the following:

C:\ACADTEMP

Now AutoCAD will always place its temporary work files in the C:\ACADTEMP directory, and not in the current directory or the one that contains the drawing you are working on. This simplifies the process of purging old, tempory files from the hard disk.

CHAPTER TEST

Write your answers in the spaces provided.

1. What is the difference between installing, configuring, and loading AutoCAD? _____

   _____

   _____

   _____

   _____

   _____

2. What do the following DOS prompts mean? _____

   A⟩ _____

   B⟩ _____

   C⟩ _____

3. What do you type at the DOS prompt to load AutoCAD? _____

   C⟩ _____

4. What four areas comprise the AutoCAD screen layout? _____

   _____

   _____

   _____

5. Which area displays the communications between AutoCAD and the user?_____

   _____

6. What is the difference between a command and a menu, and how is this handled in the screen
   menus? _____

   _____

   _____

   _____

7. What is an option? _____

8. Commands are listed _____ in screen menus.

9. What is the purpose of the SERVICE screen menu? _____

   _____

   _____

   _____

10. How do you return to the Root Menu?_____

   _____

11. List the ten AutoCAD pull-down menus. _____

   _____

   _____

12. What is an image title? _____

   _____

13. What must you do to the tablet menu before it can be used?_____

   _____

14. What are the functions of the following control keys?

   A. CTRL+B–_____

   B. CTRL+C–_____

   C. CTRL+D–_____

   D. CTRL+G–_____

   E. CTRL+O–_____

15. Name the function keys that execute the same task as the following control keys.

   Control Key   Function Key

   A. CTRL+B _____

   B. CTRL+D _____

   C. CTRL+G _____

   D. CTRL+O _____

   E. CTRL+T _____

16. What is the difference between a "button" and a "key?" _____

_____

17. What do you call a value that is maintained by the computer until you change it? _____

_____

18. What type of pull-down menu has an arrow to the right of the item? _____

_____

19. The scroll bar is normally associated with what portion of the dialog box? _____

_____

20. When using AutoCAD's help menus, what is important to know about items that are enclosed in

double brackets, such as ⟨⟨Command⟩⟩?_____

_____

21. How do you get help when working inside of a command? _____

_____

_____

22. What command allows you to prepare a disk for use?_____

_____

23. What is a DOS path? _____

_____

24. What command do you use, and how do you enter it, when you want to save a drawing file on a

floppy disk? _____

_____

PROBLEMS

1. Read the instructions in Appendix A for installing AutoCAD. Make a list of the steps required to perform the task. List the correct order in which the disks should be copied.

2. List the steps required to configure AutoCAD. (Do not list all the hardware options in the configuration routine.)

3. List the steps required to run AutoCAD and begin a new drawing named FIRST.

4. Begin AutoCAD and pick the File pull-down menu. Perform the following tasks using this menu:
   A. Open one of the drawings that are provided with AutoCAD. You may have to pick one or more of the directories to find them. (Hint: Try one of the SAMPLE subdirectories.)
   B. Open another drawing and do not save the previous one.
   C. Save the drawing you just opened as CH2TEST.
   D. Exit AutoCAD and do not save the changes.

5. Draw a freehand sketch of the screen display. Label each of the screen areas. To the side of the sketch, write a short description of each screen area's function.

6. Draw a freehand sketch of your keyboard by blocking each specific group of keys. Label the groups. Label the function keys, arrow keys, and control keys. To the side of your sketch write a short description of the function of each group of keys.

7. Use a C-size sheet of vellum or butcher paper for this problem. Create a freehand sketch of the screen menu layout of AutoCAD. (You will have to refer to the computer for this problem.)

   A. Write the items for the Root Menu as they appear on the screen. Place them at the left or upper portion of the sheet.

   B. Select each menu item to display that menu on the screen.

   C. Write the commands displayed in the menu on your sketch.

   D. Draw connecting lines between menus.

   E. Use this process for all the menus in AutoCAD until you have drawn a "menu tree" or menu flow chart.

8. Draw a freehand sketch of the AutoCAD overlay menu. (Do not draw each individual box.) Block in the four menu areas and the screen area. Label each menu area that is shown in red on the template.

9. Identify the parts of the dialog boxes shown in the following screen displays.

   A. _____   E. _____

   B. _____   F. _____

   C. _____   G. _____

   D. _____

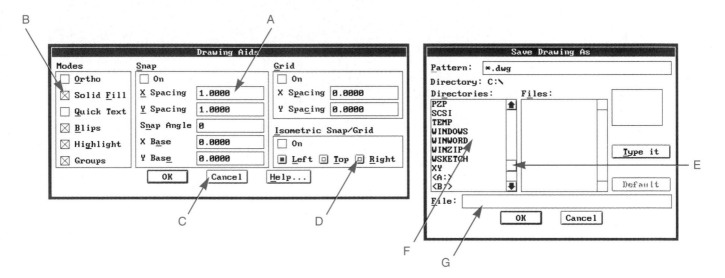

Chapter 3

DRAWING SETUP

Learning objectives

After completing this chapter, you will be able to:

- ❍ Load AutoCAD and enter the drawing editor.
- ❍ Draw and erase lines.
- ❍ Use the UNITS command to establish units of measure.
- ❍ Set drawing limits.

Effective planning can greatly reduce the amount of time it takes to set up and complete a drawing. Drawing setup involves a number of factors that affect the quality and accuracy of your final drawing. Some basic planning decisions include:

- • Sheet size needed to fit the drawing.
- • Units of measure needed to create the drawing.
- • Degree of accuracy required.
- • Name of the drawing.

STARTING A DRAWING

AUG 1

When you turn on the computer and load AutoCAD, the standard AutoCAD screen, which was discussed in Chapter 2, is displayed. This is referred to as the *drawing editor*. See Figure 3-1.

Figure 3-1. The AutoCAD drawing editor.

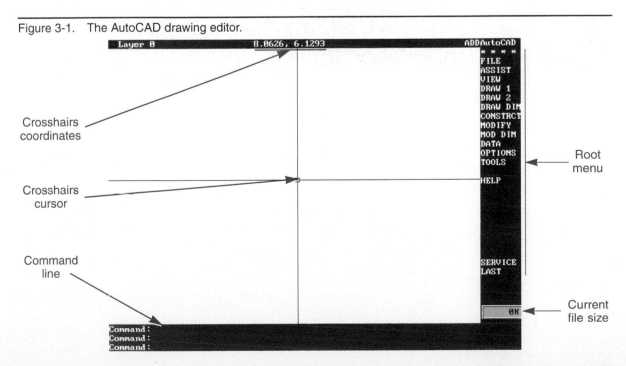

Now that you are in the drawing editor, you are ready to start drawing. Notice the screen crosshairs. Move your pointing device and watch the crosshairs also move. Try doing some drawing by entering the following from the keyboard.

Command: **LINE** ↵
From point: *(move your pointer to any desired place on the screen and pick a point)*
To point: *(move your pointer and pick another point)*
To point: *(move your pointer and pick another point)*
To point: ↵
Command:

You should now have two lines drawn on screen. Now erase the lines as follows:

Command: **ERASE** ↵

Notice that the crosshairs have changed to a small box called the *pick box*.

Select objects: *(move the pick box to one of the lines and pick it by pressing your pick button)*
Select objects: *(move pick box and pick the other line)*
Select objects: ↵

Now you have erased the two lines you just drew. Look at the screen and notice some points still remain. These points are call *blips*. They are located at points that you picked when drawing. If you want to get rid of the blips, enter the following:

Command: **REDRAW** ↵

(You can also pick Redraw View from the View pull-down menu for the same results.) As you can see, you can immediately start drawing as soon as you see the drawing editor. You can continue to practice if you wish.

Even though you can begin work when the drawing editor first appears, there are a few setup tasks that make the drafting job easier and more realistic.

SETTING UP DRAWING UNITS

AUG 1

When drawing with AutoCAD, you do not have to scale a drawing. All lines, circles, and other entities are drawn and measured as full size. For example, if a part is 36 inches long, it is drawn 36 units (inches) long. Therefore, the size of the product determines the size of the drawing. Inches, millimeters, or feet can be used as the unit of measurement. The drawing may have to be scaled to fit on a given sheet size when the drawing is plotted. You can even position and plot different views of the drawing at different scales using AutoCAD's paper space capabilities. The use of paper space is explained in Chapters 10 and 12.

To set the units of measurement, pick UNITS... from the Data pull-down menu, pick Units: from the DATA screen menu, or type UNITS at the Command: prompt as follows:

Command: **UNITS** ↵

The display then changes to the text screen. You are given examples showing how the units are displayed, and are then asked what type of units are desired:

Report formats:	(Examples)
1. Scientific	155E+01
2. Decimal	15.50
3. Engineering	1'-3.50″
4. Architectural	1'-3 1/2″
5. Fractional	15 1/2
Enter choice, 1 to 5	⟨*default*⟩

With the exception of Engineering and Architectural formats, these formats can be used with any basic unit of measurement. For example, Decimal mode is perfect for metric units as well as decimal English units. The examples given show how 15.5 drawing units are displayed in each format. The default (in brackets) shows the units currently in effect. For this example, decimal units are chosen. Enter choice 2 at the prompt and press ENTER:

Enter choice, 1 to 5 ⟨default⟩ **2** ↵

Selecting decimal units

The American National Standard ASME Y14.5M, *Dimensioning and Tolerancing*, specifies that decimal inch or metric units in millimeters are to be used on engineering drawings. Decimal units are used widely in mechanical drafting. Dimensions are in inches, such as 2.5 or 1.875, or in millimeters such as 25 or 30.5. Decimal units are selected by entering 2 at the prompt as previously shown.

Selecting engineering units

Engineering units are used in civil drafting. Civil drafting deals with detailed construction drawings and topographic maps for planning and constructing highways, harbors, drainage, and related projects. Engineering units are measured in feet, inches, and decimal parts of an inch, for example, 5'-6.75". Each engineering unit in AutoCAD is one inch. Respond with a 3 at the prompt for engineering units.

Selecting architectural units

Residential and commercial planning and construction drawings use architectural units. Dimensions are given in feet, inches, and fractional parts of an inch, for example, 8'-10 3/4". Enter choice 4 for architectural units.

Selecting fractional units

Units may also be fractional parts of a unit. The fractional units may take on any desired value such as inches, feet, or miles. Dimensions will be shown giving whole units and parts of a unit as a fraction, for example, 24 3/4. Enter choice 5 for fractional units.

Accuracy of decimal and fractional units

The accuracy of units is based on either the number of decimal places or the smallest fraction. When scientific, decimal, or engineering units are selected, the next prompt is:

Number of digits to right of decimal point (0 to 8) ⟨default⟩

The default value is the number of digits previously selected. Here you make some decisions about the accuracy of the drawing display. For example, two digits is shown as 2.88, three digits 2.875, and four digits 2.8751. For mechanical drawings, three to four digits is normally adequate for inch drawings. For metric drawings, one or two place decimals are commonly used, such as 12.5 or 12.50.

When architectural or fractional units are used, the accuracy is determined by the size of the fraction's denominator. The following prompt is given:

Denominator of smallest fraction to display
(1, 2, 4, 8, 16, 32, 64, 128, or 256) ⟨default⟩:

Press the ENTER key to use the default value or select a new value. Entering 16 shows parts of an inch that are displayed no smaller than 1/16-inch increments. For example, the display might read 4'-8 7/16". If 8 was chosen as the denominator, the same dimension would be rounded off to the nearest 1/8-inch increment, or 4'-8 3/8".

Measuring angles

After the accuracy of decimal or fractional units has been set, the next option determines the method of measuring angles. The screen displays:

```
System of angle measure:        (Examples)
  1.  Decimal degrees           45.0000
  2.  Degrees/minutes/seconds   45d0'0"
  3.  Grads                     50.0000g
  4.  Radians                   0.7854r
  5.  Surveyor's units          N 45d0'0" E
Enter choice, 1 to 5 ⟨default⟩:
```

The given examples show how a 45° angle is displayed in each format. Pressing the ENTER key gives you the default value currently in effect. If the default is not appropriate, make a selection 1 through 5. The angular measurement format recommended by the American National Standards Institute is degrees (°), minutes ('), and seconds (") or decimal degrees, therefore, select 1 or 2. The next prompt requests the accuracy of angular measure:

```
Number of fractional places for display of angles (0 to 8) ⟨default⟩:
```

The degree of accuracy is determined by the drawing requirements. Two-place decimal degrees or degrees and minutes are normally adequate for mechanical drawings. Therefore, select 2. Civil (mapping) drawings often require degrees, minutes, and seconds. In this case, select 2 or 5.

Next you are asked to specify the direction for an angle of 0 degrees. In other words, where is the origin for making angular measurements? The AutoCAD default is an angle starting to the right (East) and heading in a counterclockwise direction, Figure 3-2. If this is appropriate for your drawing, respond with 0 as follows:

```
Direction for angle 0:
  East              3 o'clock = 0
  North            12 o'clock = 90
  West              9 o'clock = 180
  South             6 o'clock = 270
Enter direction for angle 0 ⟨default⟩: 0 ↵
```

Figure 3-2.   Angle, clock, and compass orientation.

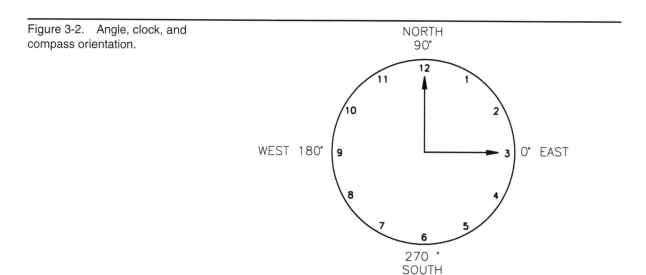

The next prompt is:

```
Do you want angles measured clockwise? ⟨default⟩
```

The AutoCAD default is angles measured in a counterclockwise direction. To maintain this, a NO or N response is needed. If you want angles to be measured clockwise, a YES or Y response is required. Press the F1 function key to get back to the drawing editor.

Setting units using the "Units Control" dialog box

You can also adjust drawing units in the "Units Control" dialog box by picking Units... from the Data pull-down menu. This dialog box allows you to set units quicker and easier than the other two methods previously discussed. The "Units Control" dialog box, Figure 3-3, has the units set to four-place decimals, decimal degrees to zero, East angle direction, and angles measured counterclockwise. Pick Direction... to display the "Direction Control" subdialog box.

Figure 3-3. A–The "Units Control" dialog box. Notice that the selected radio buttons set the Units and Angles settings. The Precision: settings should also be entered. B–The "Direction Control" subdialog box appears when you pick Direction... in the "Unit Control" dialog box. Select the appropriate settings.

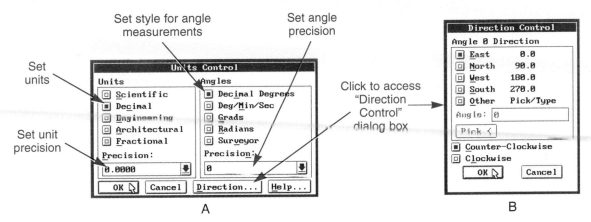

SIZING OF THE DRAWING AREA

AUG 1

ASME/ANSI standard sheet sizes and format are specified in the ANSI Y14.1 *Drawing Sheet Size and Format,* and ASME Y14.1M *Metric Drawing Sheet Size and Format.* See Figure 3-4A and Figure 3-4B. The proper presentation of engineering changes are given in ASME Y14.35M *Revision of Engineering Drawings and Associated Documents.*

ANSI Y14.1 specifies sheet size specifications in inches as follows:

Size Designation	Size in Inches Vertical × Horizontal
A	8 1/2 × 11 (horizontal)
	11 × 8 1/2 (vertical)
B	11 × 17
C	17 × 22
D	22 × 34
E	34 × 44
F	28 × 40

Sizes G, H, J, and K are roll sizes.

ASME Y14.1M provides sheet size specifications in metric (M). Standard metric drawing sheet sizes are designated as follows:

Size Designation	Size in Millimeters Vertical × Horizontal
A0	841 × 1189
A1	594 × 841
A2	420 × 594
A3	297 × 420
A4	210 × 297

Longer lengths are referred to as elongated and extra-elongated drawing sizes. These are available in multiples of the short side of the sheet size.

The size or limits of the AutoCAD drawing area is usually determined by:
✓ The actual size of the drawing.
✓ Space for dimensions and notes.
✓ Free space to avoid crowding and provide for future revisions.
✓ A border and title block area.

Figure 3-4A.   A–Standard drawing sheet sizes. Note: Dimensions are given in inches. (ANSI Y14.1)

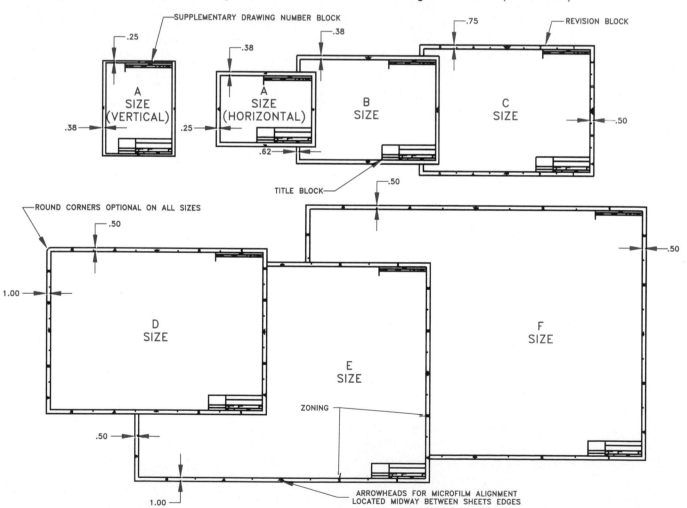

Figure 3-4B. Standard metric drawing sheet sizes. Note: Dimensions are given in millimeters. (ASME Y14.1M)

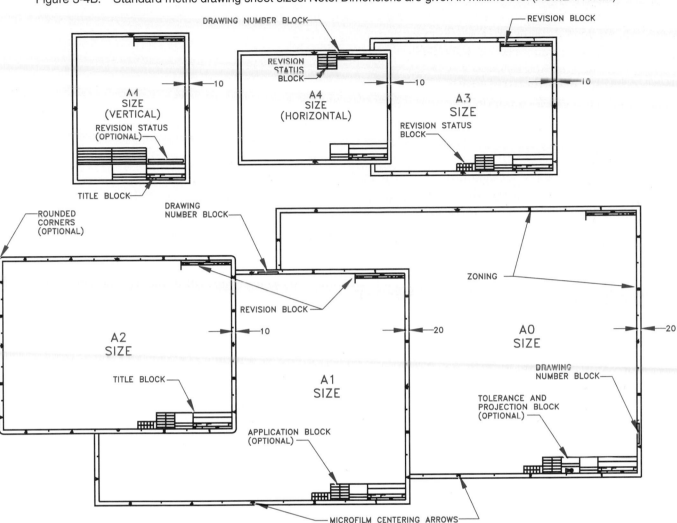

The drawing area is determined by two sets of coordinates. These coordinates are set with the LIMITS command. One set of coordinates marks the lower-left corner of your drawing area. The other set marks the upper-right corner.

It takes some practice to decide how to set the limits relative to the actual size of the object. It is always a good idea to first make a sketch of the drawing to help calculate the area needed. For example, suppose a machine part is 20 inches long and 14 inches high. An additional 4 inches around the part (2 inches on each side) is necessary for dimensions, notes, and free space. In this case, the limits should be set at 24 × 18. Suppose a house floor plan measures 68 feet by 44 feet. An additional 20 feet is needed (10 feet on each side) all around the plan for dimensions, notes, and a border. Then, the limits should be set at 88' × 64'.

Plan your drawing area in relation to sheet sizes during drawing setup or when the drawing is plotted. When plotting, the drawing can be made to fit the sheet or scaled as needed. AutoCAD has standard paper sizes established for plotting, or you can define your own paper size at that time. Chapters 6 and 12 cover plotting an AutoCAD drawing. The preferred method is to consider the standard drawing sheet sizes when setting the required drawing area. The screen format is much like a sheet of paper, with the length measured horizontally and the width measured vertically. This is the same as laying a sheet on a drawing board when manual drafting. Standard sheet sizes are shown in Appendix E.

Setting inch limits

If the limits are based on an A-size sheet, then choose limits of 11 × 8.5 or 12 × 9. A B-size sheet is set up as 17 × 11 or 18 × 12. A C-size drawing is 22 × 17 or 24 × 18; a D-size sheet is 34 × 22 or 36 × 24.

Setting architectural limits

Most architectural floor plans are drawn at 1/4″ = 1′ − 0″ scale. If a C-size (22 × 17) sheet is used, then the drawing limits should be set at 88′ × 68′, where 4′ (4 units/inch) × 22 = 88′ and 4′ × 17 = 68′.

Setting metric limits

The limits are set in millimeters when the drawing is in metric units. If you decide to use A3 metric sheet size, then you will set the limits to 420 × 297 based on the recommended ASME standard shown in Figure 3-4B. If you want to convert a standard inch sheet to metric, then use the multiplication factor 25.4mm = 1 inch. This is referred to as a *hard metric conversion,* because it does not match the recommended metric standard, which is a *soft metric conversion.* For example, suppose you decide to set the limits to 17 inches by 11 inches, then the metric drawing limits are 25.4 × 17 = 431.8 and 25.4 × 11 = 279.4. To provide limits with even units of measure, round off to the next higher whole number. This makes the metric limits 432 × 280.

Using the LIMITS command

The LIMITS command can be accessed by picking Limits: from the DATA screen menu, by picking Drawing Limits from the Data pull-down menu, or by typing LIMITS at the Command: prompt. The following command sequence is used to set the drawing limits:

Command: **LIMITS** ⏎
Reset Model space limits:
ON/OFF/⟨Lower left corner⟩⟨*current value*⟩: **0,0** ⏎

This prompt sets the lower-left corner of the "sheet size" to the lower-left corner of the display screen. A response of 0,0 places the lower-left corner as shown in Figure 3-5. The lower-left corner may be placed at any convenient location other than 0,0, however, 0,0 is common and recommended. The LIMITS command continues with a request for the upper-right corner. The AutoCAD default for upper-right corner is 12,9. This is a standard A-size sheet. The value you enter here determines the upper-right corner of the "sheet size." For example, if a 17 × 11 or B-size sheet is to be used, then the response is:

Upper right corner ⟨*current*⟩: **17,11** ⏎

The horizontal distance is given first, followed by a comma, and then the vertical distance is entered. See the screen display shown in Figure 3-5.

Figure 3-5. Using the LIMITS command. In this example, the lower-left limit is 0,0 and the upper right limit is 17,11.

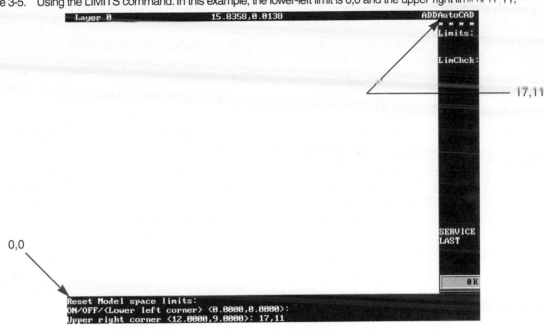

If a D-size (17 × 11) architectural drawing is needed and 4 feet per inch is the scale when plotted, first set Architectural units. Then, set the limits as follows:

Command: **LIMITS** ↵
Reset Model space limits:
ON/OFF/⟨Lower left corner⟩⟨*current value*⟩: **0,0** ↵
Upper right corner ⟨*current*⟩: **68′,44′** ↵

If an A3-size (420 × 297) drawing is set up for millimeters, the limits are set as follows:

Command: **LIMITS** ↵
Reset Model space limits:
ON/OFF/⟨Lower left corner⟩⟨*current value*⟩: **0,0** ↵
Upper right corner ⟨*current*⟩: **420,297** ↵

Limits can be changed at any time by executing the LIMITS command. The ON/OFF portion of the first LIMITS prompt refers to a limits check. The intent of the limits is to set up a work area that confines the drawing. However, it is possible to draw outside of the limits on purpose or accidentally. An ON response to this prompt turns the limits check on. You can still draw outside the limits area; however, if you pick or input a coordinate outside the limits, an "Outside limits" error message is shown. With limits check turned off, the "Outside limits" error is not given. If, for some reason, you draw beyond the limits you can either edit the drawing so it is within limits or increase the limits to include the extended work area.

Setting limits using the Data pull-down menu

The drawing limits can also be changed by moving the screen cursor to the menu bar and picking Data. When the Data pull-down menu appears, move the cursor arrow to the menu and pick Drawing Limits. This activates the LIMITS command at which time you can type the revised limit values, if necessary.

EXERCISE 3-1

❑ Turn on your computer and load AutoCAD.
❑ Using the UNITS command, set the units to decimal with two digits to the right of the decimal point.
❑ Set the angular measure to decimal, one fractional place, 0 direction, and counterclockwise.
❑ Using the LIMITS command, set the limits to the default value of 12,9. (Set the lower-left corner at 0,0 and for the upper-right corner, press ENTER or enter 12,9.)
❑ Type SAVE at the Command: prompt. The "Save drawing as" dialog box then appears. If you want to save the drawing in the current directory, move the cursor to the File box and type EX3-1. Pick the OK box or press the ENTER key.
   If you want to save the drawing on another drive, such as your floppy disk in the A: drive, move the cursor to the File box, and type A:EX3-1. Then, pick OK or press ENTER.
❑ Type QUIT at the Command: prompt and press ENTER if you want to exit AutoCAD.

CHAPTER TEST

Write your answers in the spaces provided.

1. The drafting table and tools of computer-aided drafting is called the _____.

2. How do you get to the standard AutoCAD screen? _____

3. When you type UNITS at the Command: prompt and press ENTER, what happens to the screen? _____

4. What do you do when you are finished with the UNITS command and you want to get to the standard AutoCAD screen? _____

5. The display of a measurement will change when a different number of digits to the right of the decimal point is specified. If a 1.6250 dimension is to be displayed, and the number of digits to the right of the decimal points is as follows, what will actually be displayed?
   A. One digit– _____
   B. Two digits– _____
   C. Three digits– _____
   D. Four digits– _____

6. The AutoCAD default for an angle is in a _____ direction.

7. What are the limits of an architectural drawing using a C-size (22 × 17) sheet and a scale of 4 feet per inch when plotted?
   A. Lower-left corner _____
   B. Upper-right corner _____

8. Name the five systems of units options. _____

9. Name the pull-down menu that contains the LIMITS command. _____

10. How do you access the "Units Control" dialog box? _____ _____

_____

11. Give the entries or commands needed to set the drawing units to three-digit decimal, two-place decimal degrees, East direction for angle 0, and to measure angles counterclockwise:

Command: _____

System of units: _____

Enter choice 1 to 5 ⟨*default*⟩: _____

Number of digits to right of decimal point (0 to 8) ⟨*default*⟩: _____

System of angular measure: _____

Enter choice 1 to 5 ⟨*default*⟩: _____

Number of fractional places for display of angles (0 to 8) ⟨*default*⟩: _____

Enter direction for angle 0 ⟨*current*⟩: _____

Do you want angles measured clockwise? ⟨*current*⟩: _____

12. Give the commands and coordinate entries to set the drawing limits to 22 × 17:

Command: _____

Reset Model space limits: _____

ON/OFF/⟨Lower left corner⟩ ⟨*current value*⟩: _____

Upper right corner ⟨*current*⟩: _____

PROBLEMS

In the following problems, it is suggested that you save the drawings for future use. Saving the drawings as specified will save them to your floppy disk in the A: drive. If you prefer to save your drawings on a floppy disk in the B: drive, insert your floppy disk in the appropriate drive, and type "B:" before the file name. If in doubt, consult your instructor.

1. A. Load AutoCAD.

B. Enter the UNITS command. Select decimal units with four digits behind the decimal. Select decimal degrees with two digits behind the decimal point and 90 (North) for direction of the 0° angle. Angles should be measured counterclockwise.

C. Enter the UNITS command. Select architectural units with 32 as the denominator of the smallest fraction. Angles should be measured by degrees/minutes/seconds with 4 as the number of fractional places. The direction for angle 0° should be East. Angles are to be measured counterclockwise.

D. Set the limits to correspond with a 12 × 9 (A-size) sheet. The scale to be used in calculating the limits is 1/4" = 1'-0". The lower-left corner of your drawing area should be at 0,0.

E. Type SAVE at the Command: prompt and enter A:A12-9 to save your drawing.

F. Type QUIT at the Command: prompt and press ENTER.

2. A. Load AutoCAD.

B. Use the "Units Control" dialog box. Select decimal units with three digits behind the decimal point. Select decimal degrees with two digits behind the decimal point and 90 (North) for direction of the 0° angle. Angles should be measured counterclockwise.

C. Set the limits to correspond with a 17 × 11 (B-size) sheet (0,0; 17,11).

D Save the problem as A:B17-11 and quit.

3. A. Load AutoCAD.

B. Enter the UNITS command. Select decimal units with two digits behind the decimal point. Select decimal degrees with two digits behind the decimal and 0 (East) for direction of the 0° angle. Angles should be measured counterclockwise.

C. Set the limits to correspond with metric (millimeters) and an A3-size sheet.

D. Save as A:MA3 and quit.

Chapter 4

INTRODUCTION TO DRAWING AND DRAWING AIDS

Learning objectives

After completing this chapter, you will be able to:

❍ Set up the drawing aids in a prototype drawing, including limits, units, grid, and snap.

❍ Use the LINE command to draw several different geometric shapes.

❍ Experiment with snap grid turned on and off.

AutoCAD provides aids that help prepare the drawing layout, increase speed and efficiency, and ensure accuracy. These "drawing aids" include GRID, SNAP, and ORTHO. This chapter discusses each of these aids and how they are used to assist you when drawing lines. Drawing aids may be accessed by picking DDrmode: from the OPTIONS screen menu, by picking Drawing Aids from the Options pull-down menu, or by typing the command name at the Command: prompt.

ESTABLISHING A GRID ON THE SCREEN

AUG 1

Some drafting paper used for manual drafting is printed with a grid to assist the drafter in laying out the drawing. A similar type of grid can be used in AutoCAD. The GRID command places a pattern of dots on the screen at any spacing, Figure 4-1. The grid pattern shows only within the drawing limits to help clearly define the working area. Entering the GRID command provides a prompt showing the default grid spacing and several other options. You can press ENTER to accept the default spacing value shown in brackets or enter a new value as follows:

Command: **GRID** ↵
Grid spacing(X) or ON/OFF/Snap/Aspect ⟨0.0000⟩: **.5** ↵

Figure 4-1.   The Grid is a pattern of dots to help locate points.

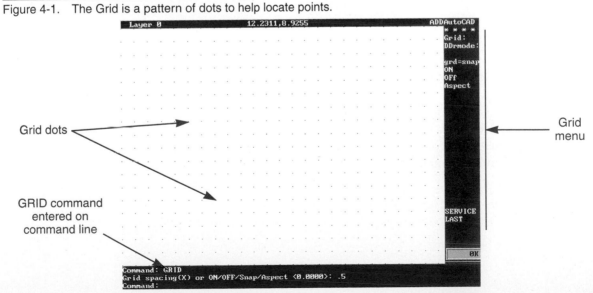

Grid dots

GRID command entered on command line

Grid menu

The dot spacing of the grid may be set by entering a specified unit of measure such as .5. This grid is shown in Figure 4-1. If the grid dot spacing you enter is too close to display on the screen, you will get the "Grid too dense to display" message. A larger grid spacing is required.

The grid spacing may be changed at any time. Also, the grid may be turned on (displayed) or off (not displayed) at any time by typing ON or OFF at the GRID prompt line. Other methods for turning the grid on and off include pressing CTRL+G, the F7 function key, or puck button 6. When the grid is turned on after previously being off, it is set to the previous spacing.

Setting a different horizontal and vertical grid

Type A (for the Aspect option) at the GRID prompt line to set different values for the horizontal and vertical grid dot spacing. For example, suppose you want a horizontal grid spacing of 1 and a vertical spacing of .5. Enter the following:

Command: **GRID** ↵
Grid spacing(X) or ON/OFF/Snap/Aspect ⟨*current*⟩: **A** ↵
Horizontal spacing(X) ⟨*current*⟩: **1** ↵
Vertical spacing(X) ⟨*current*⟩: **.5** ↵

The Aspect option provides the grid dot spacing shown in Figure 4-2.

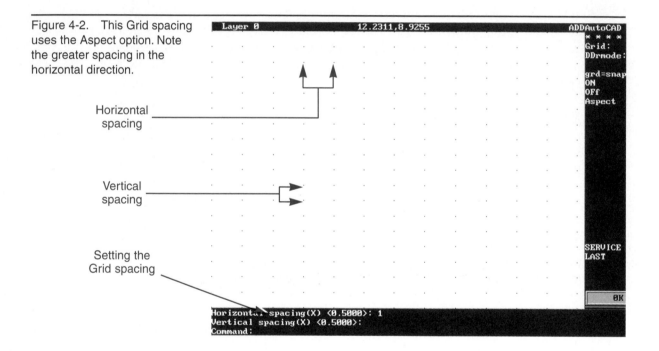

Figure 4-2. This Grid spacing uses the Aspect option. Note the greater spacing in the horizontal direction.

INTRODUCTION TO DRAWING LINES

AUG 2

This section is a brief introduction to drawing lines so you can get started with AutoCAD drawing commands. It will let you see how the different drawing setup options affect the speed and accuracy of drawing lines. There are several ways to use the LINE command, but for now one method is discussed. The LINE command is explained in detail in Chapter 6.

Command: **LINE** ↵
From point: *(move the screen cursor to any position on the screen and pick that point)*
To point: *(move the screen cursor to another location and pick a point)*

Notice that a line has been drawn between the two points. A "rubberband" line is attached to the last point selected and the cursor. The "rubberband" shows the line's location if you picked the current cursor location. The next prompt is:

To point: *(pick the next point)*

You can continue to draw connected lines until you press the ENTER key or space bar to exit the LINE command. The following command sequence is displayed in Figure 4-3.

Command: **LINE** ↵
From point: *(pick point number 1)*
To point: *(pick point number 2)*
To point: *(pick point number 3)*
To point: *(pick point number 4)*
To point: ↵
Command: *(meaning AutoCAD is ready for a new command)*

Figure 4-3. Using the LINE command. Select the points in order from Point 1 to Point 4 to draw this three-segment line.

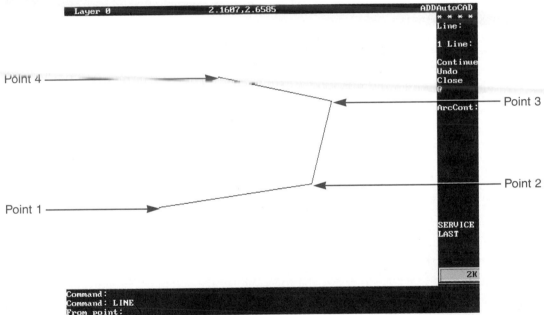

EXERCISE 4-1

❑ Turn on your computer and load AutoCAD to access the drawing editor.
❑ Set the grid spacing at .5.
❑ Use the LINE command to draw two sets of four connected line segments.
❑ Turn off the grid and draw two sets of three connected line segments. Notice how having the grid on provides some guidance for locating points.
❑ Type SAVE at the Command: prompt. When the "Save Drawing As:" dialog box appears, type the file name EX4-1 to save this exercise on your hard disk, or type A:EX4-1 to save it on your floppy disk. Press ENTER or pick the OK button.
❑ Type QUIT at the Command: prompt and press ENTER if you want to exit AutoCAD.

SETTING INCREMENTS FOR CURSOR MOVEMENT
AUG 1, 3

When you move your pointing device, the cursor crosshairs move freely on the screen. Sometimes it is hard to place a point accurately. You can set up an invisible grid that allows the cursor to move only in exact increments. This is called the *snap resolution* or *snap grid*. The snap grid is different than using the GRID command. The snap grid controls the movement of the crosshairs; the grid is only a visual guide. However, the SNAP and GRID commands can be used together.

Properly setting the snap grid can greatly increase your drawing speed and accuracy. The SNAP command is used to set the invisible snap grid. Entering SNAP gives you the following prompt:

Command: **SNAP** ↵
Snap spacing or ON/OFF/Aspect/Rotate/Style ⟨*current*⟩:

Pressing ENTER accepts the value shown in brackets. If a new snap spacing is required, such as .25, enter the amount as shown:

Command: **SNAP** ↵
Snap spacing or ON/OFF/Aspect/Rotate/Style ⟨*current*⟩: **.25** ↵

This sets up the invisible snap spacing at .25 increments both horizontally and vertically.

The OFF selection turns snap off, but the same snap spacing is again in effect when you turn snap back on. The snap spacing may be turned on or off at any time by pressing CTRL+B, function key F9, or puck button 4.

Different horizontal and vertical snap grid units

The normal application of the SNAP command is equal horizontal and vertical snap grid units. However, it is possible to set different horizontal and vertical snap grid units. This is done using the Aspect option as follows:

Command: **SNAP** ↵
Snap spacing or ON/OFF/Aspect/Rotate/Style ⟨*current*⟩: **A** ↵
Horizontal spacing ⟨*current*⟩: **.5** ↵
Vertical spacing ⟨*current*⟩: **.25** ↵

Rotating the snap grid

The normal snap grid pattern is horizontal rows and vertical columns. However, another option is to rotate the snap grid to an angle other than horizontal. This technique is helpful when drawing an auxiliary view that is at an angle to other views of the drawing. (Auxiliary views are discussed in Chapter 17.) When the snap grid is rotated, you are given the option of setting a new base point. The base point is the pivot around which the snap grid is rotated. The base point of a normal snap grid is the lower-left corner. It may be more convenient to set the base point at the location where you will begin the view. You will also be asked to set the rotation angle. The range is 0 to 90 or 0 to –90 degrees:

Command: **SNAP** ↵
Snap spacing or ON/OFF/Aspect/Rotate/Style ⟨*current*⟩: **R** ↵
Base point ⟨0.0000,0.0000⟩: (*press* ENTER *or pick a new base point*)
Rotation angle ⟨0⟩: **25** ↵

The grid automatically rotates about the base point in a counterclockwise direction when a positive rotation angle is given. It rotates clockwise if you enter a negative rotation angle. Figure 4-4 shows the relationship between the regular and rotated snap grids. Remember, the snap grid is invisible and is shown only for illustrative purposes.

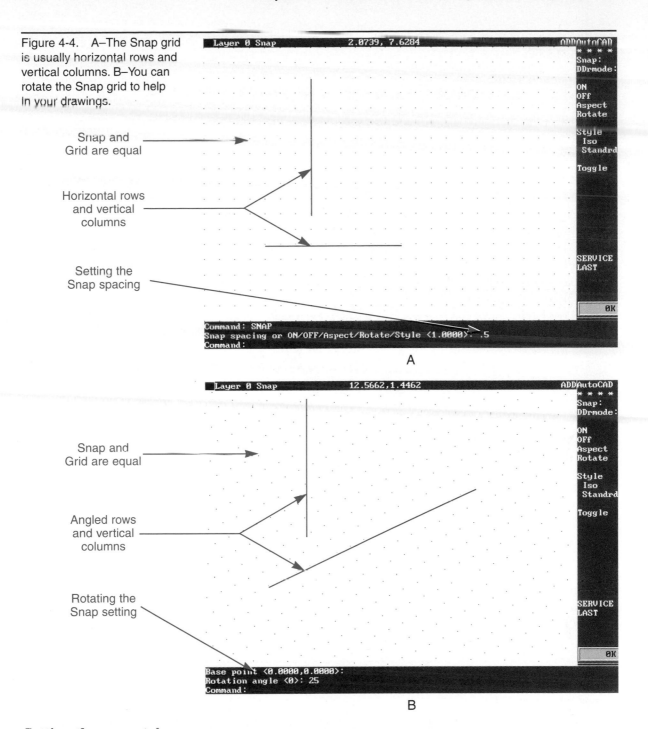

Figure 4-4. A—The Snap grid is usually horizontal rows and vertical columns. B—You can rotate the Snap grid to help in your drawings.

Setting the snap style

The Style option allows you to set the snap grid to either a standard (default) or isometric pattern. The isometric pattern is useful when doing isometric drawings, discussed in Chapter 23. If the snap grid is set to Isometric, use the Style option to return it to the Standard mode:

```
Command: SNAP ⏎
Snap spacing or ON/OFF/Aspect/Rotate/Style ⟨current⟩: S ⏎
Standard/Isometric ⟨current⟩ : S ⏎
Spacing/Aspect ⟨current⟩ : ⏎
```

Setting the grid spacing relative to the snap spacing

The visible grid can be set to coincide with the invisible snap grid by choosing the Snap option after entering the GRID command. You may also set the dot spacing as a multiple of the snap units by entering the number of snap units between grid points. For example, 2X places grid points at every other snap unit.

Command: **GRID** ↵
Grid spacing(X) or ON/OFF/Snap/Aspect ⟨0.0000⟩: **2X** ↵

Therefore, if the snap units are .25 and you specify 2X at the Grid spacing prompt, the grid point spacing will be .5 units.

EXERCISE 4-2

❑ Turn on your computer and load AutoCAD to access the drawing editor.
❑ Set the units to decimal, and two digits to the right of the decimal point.
❑ Set the angular measure to decimal, one fractional place, 0 direction, and counterclockwise.
❑ Set the limits to an A-size (12 x 9) sheet. (Lower-left corner: 0,0; upper-right corner: 12,9.)
❑ Set the grid spacing to .5.
❑ Set the snap spacing to .25.
❑ Use the LINE command to draw two sets of four connected line segments.
❑ Turn snap off and draw two sets of three connected line segments. Notice how snap on allows you to "snap" exactly at .25 intervals.
❑ Type SAVE at the Command: prompt and save the drawing as A:EX4-2, and then quit the drawing editor.

USING THE PULL-DOWN MENU TO SET OR CHANGE THE DRAWING AIDS

AUG 1, 3

The AutoCAD drawing aids may be set or changed using the Options pull-down menu. Pick Options from the menu bar, and then select Drawing Aids… from the pull-down menu. The "Drawing Aids" dialog box then appears on the screen. Typing DDRMODES at the Command: prompt also displays the same dialog box.

Use the dialog box to set or change the grid and snap spacing values. Other controls in the "Drawing Aids" dialog box are discussed later. Turn Snap and Grid on or off by picking the On button. Enter your desired grid and snap spacing in the X/Y Spacing boxes as needed. Look at Figure 4-5 and notice that the Grid and Snap are both on as indicated by the "X" in the On buttons. The grid has an equal horizontal (X) spacing and vertical (Y) spacing of 0.500 units; the snap has an equal X and Y spacing of 0.250.

Figure 4-5.   The "Drawing Aids" dialog box. You can change the Grid and Snap settings. You can also turn Grid and Snap on or off in this dialog box.

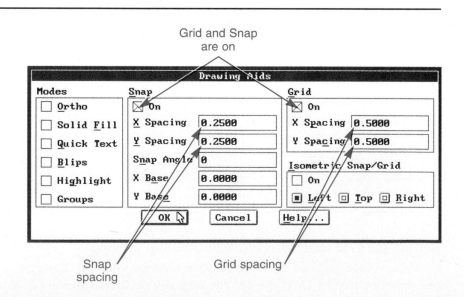

PROFESSIONAL TIP

In actual drafting practice, the SNAP and GRID commands aid in the speed and accuracy of the drawing. Thus, they are referred to as *drawing aids*. The most effective use of snap quite often comes from setting an equal X and Y spacing to the lowest or near lowest increment of the majority of the feature dimensions. For example, in a mechanical drawing this might be .0625 units, or maybe 6" in an architectural application. If it is found that many horizontal features conform to one increment and vertical features to another, then a corresponding snap grid can be set up using different X and Y values. The snap and grid drawing aids may be set at different values to complement each other. For example, snap may be set at .25 and the grid at .5. With this type of format, each plays a separate role in assisting drawing layout and may keep the grid pattern from being too close together. You can quickly change these values to fit your individual needs.

FACTORS TO CONSIDER WHEN SETTING DRAWING AIDS

Factors that influence drawing aid values include:
- Drawing units. If the units are decimal inches, set the grid and snap values to standard decimal increments such as .0625, .125, .25, .5, 1; or .05, .1, .2, .5, 1. If you are using architectural units, use 1, 6, 12 inches, or 1, 2, 4, 5, 10 feet increments.
- Drawing size. A very large drawing might have a 1.00 grid spacing, while a small drawing uses a 0.5 spacing or less.
- Value of the smallest dimension. For example, if the smallest dimension is .125, then an appropriate snap value would be .125 and grid spacing .25.
- Change the values at any time. You can change the snap and grid values at any time without changing the location of points or lines already drawn. This should be done when larger or smaller values would assist you with a certain part of the drawing. For example, suppose a few of the dimensions are in .0625 multiples, but the rest of the dimensions are .250 multiples. Change the snap spacing from .250 to .0625 when laying out smaller dimensions.
- Use the visible grid to help you place views and lay out the entire drawing. Always prepare a sketch before starting a drawing.
- Use whatever method works best and fastest for you when setting or changing the drawing aids.

EXERCISE 4-3

❑ Load AutoCAD to access the drawing editor.
❑ Set decimal units with three digits to the right of the decimal point.
❑ Set the angular measure to degrees/minutes/seconds, one fractional place, and default values for the rest of the options.
❑ Set the limits to 17,11. (Lower-left corner: 0,0; Upper-right corner: 17,11.)
❑ Set the grid spacing at .5.
❑ Set the snap spacing at .25.
❑ Use the LINE command to draw two sets of eight connected line segments.
❑ Change the snap value to .125 and the grid spacing to .25. Draw several more lines and see what happens.
❑ Change the snap value to .5 and the grid spacing to 1. Draw several more lines and observe the results.
❑ Save the drawing as A:EX4-3 and quit.

INTRODUCTION TO PROTOTYPE DRAWING

AUG 1

When doing manual drafting, you normally begin with a sheet of drafting paper. The paper may even have a preprinted border line and title block. The title block might be labeled with the company name and address, and a place for the drawing title, part number, scale, material, and drafter's name. You tape down the sheet and add the views, dimensions, and fill in the title block information. It could be said that you began with a *prototype drawing*–the clean sheet of preprinted paper. The prototype, or drawing format, was then changed when adding the new information. The same type of process occurs when using AutoCAD. A simple prototype drawing is one set up with values for limits, grid, and snap. A complex prototype might have a border and title block, established text styles, layer names, and other drawing variables.

AutoCAD has a standard prototype drawing named ACAD which is available every time you start a new drawing. One big drawback with the ACAD prototype is that it is often too general to be used without some customization. In time you will set up a prototype for each drawing size and type. For example, there may be a border and title block format for A-, B-, and C-size drawings. There may be a different prototype for mechanical, electrical, or architectural drawings. The values for limits, units, drawing aids, and other parameters are different for each.

When you design a prototype drawing in AutoCAD, set the units, limits, snap, and grid values to your own or your company's or school's specifications. When you have all of the desired items set, save the prototype drawing with a name such as PROTODR1. A drawing name is limited to eight characters (with no spaces). To save the prototype drawing as PROTODR1, type SAVE at the Command: prompt or pick Save…from the File pull-down menu. Type the name PROTODR1 at the File box and press ENTER or pick the OK box. The prototype is now saved as PROTODR1. The prototype is ready to use anytime you need it.

When you are ready to use the prototype, turn on your computer, load AutoCAD, and pick Open…from the File pull-down menu. When you get the "Open Drawing" dialog box, select PROTO-DR1 from the list of files. Now, use the prototype as the setup for doing your drawing. When finished with the drawing, pick Save As…from the File pull-down menu. Save your drawing with a new file name such as PROB4-1. By doing this, you now have the new drawing while the prototype remains as PROTODR1, to be used again. Additional prototype information is discussed in the following chapters. Saving a drawing is discussed in Chapter 5.

When you develop prototype drawings, it is a good idea to record the name of the prototype and the setup values. The following are some sample prototypes:

- A prototype for B-size mechanical drawings using inch values might be set up as:
  Name: M-IN-B (M = mechanical; IN = inches; B = B-size)
  Units: Three-place decimal, two-place decimal degrees
  Limits: 17,11
  Grid: .5
  Snap: .25
- A prototype for B-size mechanical drawings using metric values may be set up as:
  Name: M-MM-B (M = mechanical; MM = millimeters; B = B-size)
  Units: Two-place decimal, two-place decimal degrees
  Limits: 432,280
  Grid: 10
  Snap: 5
- A prototype for a C-size architectural floor plan drawing may be set up as:
  Name: ARCHFL-C (ARCH = architectural; FL = floor plan; C = C-size)
  Units: Architectural, 16 fractional denominator, two-place degrees/minutes/seconds
  Limits: 88,68
  Grid: 5
  Snap: 1

EXERCISE 4-4

❑ Load AutoCAD to access the drawing editor.
❑ Set the values for your prototype drawing as follows:
   ❑ UNITS: Three-place decimal, two-place angular decimals.
   ❑ LIMITS: 12,9
   ❑ GRID: .5
   ❑ SNAP: .25
❑ On a piece of notebook paper, record the prototype name and all of the specifications set in this exercise. Keep this record for future reference. This is part of preparing a drawing plan sheet, discussed in detail in Chapter 6.
❑ Save the drawing as PRODR1 and quit. This prototype is used in future exercises and problems. Save it a second time as A:PRODR1.

CHAPTER TEST

Write your answers in the spaces provided.

1. Give the command and value entered to set a grid spacing of .25:

   Command:_____

   Grid spacing(X) or ON/OFF/Snap/Aspect ⟨0⟩:_____

2. Give the command and value entered to set snap at .125:

   Command:_____

   Snap spacing or ON/OFF/Snap/Aspect/Rotate/Style ⟨*current*⟩ : _____

3. Name the command used to place a pattern of dots on the screen. _____

4. Identify the pull-down menu used to select drawing aids. _____

5. How do you activate the snap grid so the screen cursor will automatically move in precise increments?_____

   _____

   _____

6. How do you set different horizontal and vertical snap units? _____

   _____

   _____

7. Name three ways to access the drawing aids. _____

   _____

   _____

8. Name two ways to access the "Drawing Aids" dialog box._____

   _____

   _____

9. Describe a prototype drawing. _____

   _____

   _____

   _____

10. A drawing name is limited to _____ characters.

DRAWING PROBLEMS

P4-1

1. Load AutoCAD and enter the drawing editor. Insert your floppy disk. Set up the following specifications for the new drawing.

   LIMITS: 12,9

   GRID: .5

   SNAP: .25

   UNITS: three-place decimals, two-place decimal angular, East direction for angle 0, angles measured counterclockwise.

   Save the prototype drawing as D12-9. (The D denotes decimal drawing units; the 12-9 specifies the limits.) Save the drawing a second time as A:D12-9.

P4-2

2. Load AutoCAD and enter the drawing editor. Insert your floppy disk. Pick New...from the File pull-down menu. Enter A:D12-9 in the Prototype: box, and enter P4-2 in the New Drawing Name: box. Then pick OK. Turn on the grid and snap features. Draw the following objects using the LINE command so that they fit within the left half of the specified limits.

   A. Right triangle.

   B. Isosceles triangle.

   C. Rectangle.

   D. Square.

   Type SAVE and save the drawing as A:P4-2. Do not quit this drawing session, continue with Problem 3.

P4-3

3. Draw the same object specified in Problem 2 on the right side of the screen. This time, make sure the snap grid is turned off. Observe the difference between having snap on and off. Type SAVE at the Command: prompt, change the drawing name to A:P4-3, and pick OK. Then type QUIT at the Command: prompt and press ENTER twice. This saves the drawing as A:P4-3 while the prototype remains as D12-9.

Chapter 5

SAVING DRAWINGS

Learning objectives

After completing this chapter, you will be able to:

❍ Preview a drawing in current directory and open a drawing that was saved in a previous drawing session.

❍ Change the FILEDIA system variable.

❍ Save a drawing and change the drawing name.

❍ End a drawing session, saving all previous work with the current drawing name.

❍ Quit a drawing.

❍ Identify at least four ways to cancel a command.

❍ Explain the difference between the SAVE, SAVEAS, and QSAVE commands.

❍ Specify how often work should be saved, and use the SAVETIME command to automatically save your work.

❍ List two ways to move between the alphanumeric screen and the drawing editor.

❍ Explain the difference between the END and QUIT commands.

This chapter covers how to get out of a command at any time, and the methods to save or end a drawing. The commands to save or end a drawing include SAVE, SAVEAS, QSAVE, QUIT, and END. Current default values and other drawing characteristics may be displayed using the STATUS command.

CANCELING A COMMAND $\boxed{\text{AUG 1}}$

It is often necessary to get out of a command. You may decide to do something else–perhaps you made an error and want to start over again. Many commands can be discontinued by pressing the ENTER key or the space bar on the keyboard. This normally exits the command and brings back a new Command: prompt. However, there are some situations where this does not work. For example, using the space bar to discontinue a command does not work when adding text. It is simply recognized as a space in the line of text. If you find that one method does not work, do not panic; try another method.

If you are entering a command and misspell it, you can backspace to remove the unwanted letters and retype the command. This can only be done if the mistake is noticed before the ENTER key is pressed. If improper information is entered, you may get an error message. When this happens, press ENTER to get back to a new Command: prompt.

You can get out of any bad command or unwanted entry by using the CONTROL+C option. The "C" stands for cancel. Most computers have a CONTROL or CTRL key on the keyboard. Hold down the CTRL key and press the letter C key at the same time. You can use this method at any time to terminate a command.

Many drafters using a multibutton puck use button number 3 to cancel a command. The symbol "^" stands for CONTROL. If you see the symbol "^C" it also means CONTROL+C or CANCEL. When using this method to cancel a command, the message *Cancel* appears and the Command: prompt returns. You can also delete a line of input by holding down the CTRL key and pressing the let-

ter X key. This is referred to as "CTRL+X" or "^X". A *Delete* message appears and a new Command: prompt is shown. This also must be done prior to pressing the ENTER key.
There is also a Cancel option located in the Assist pull-down menu.

INTRODUCTION TO SAVING AND QUITTING A DRAWING | AUG 1 |

In Chapter 3, you were shown how to begin drawing when you access the AutoCAD drawing editor, and you also saved work or quit the drawing in the exercises and problems. The following discussion provides you with detailed information about saving and quitting a drawing.

When saving drawings files using the SAVE and SAVEAS commands, you can have dialog boxes appear, or you can type everything at the Command: prompt. This is controlled by the FILEDIA system variable. A *system variable* is a command that lets you change the way AutoCAD works. These variables are remembered by AutoCAD and remain in effect until you change them again. There are two FILEDIA system variable options. The default is 1, which displays dialog boxes at the appropriate times. When FILEDIA is set to 0, a dialog box does not appear, and you must type the desired information at the prompt line. You can quickly change the FILEDIA system variable as follows:

    Command: **FILEDIA** ↵
    New value for FILEDIA ⟨1⟩: **0** ↵

In the following discussion, the FILEDIA variable is set to 1, unless otherwise specified.

NAMING DRAWINGS | AUG 1 |

Drawing names may be chosen to identify a product by name and number, for example VICE-101, FLPLN-95, or 6DT1005. Your school or company probably has a drawing numbering system that you can use. These drawing names should be recorded in a part numbering or drawing name log for future reference.

It is important to set up a system where you can determine the content of a drawing by the drawing number. The following rules and restrictions apply to naming a drawing:
- Drawing names contain 8 characters maximum.
- Drawing names include only letters, numbers, dashes (–), dollar signs ($), or underlines (_).
- Spaces, slashes (/ or \), periods, asterisks, or question marks cannot be used in a drawing name.

STARTING A NEW DRAWING | AUG 1 |

Once you have entered the drawing editor, you can name a new drawing, or you can use a prototype drawing that was created earlier. To do this, type NEW at the Command: prompt and press ENTER, or pick New… from the File pull-down menu, Figure 5-1.

Figure 5-1.   The File pull-down menu. To name a new drawing or use a prototype, select New… (shown here highlighted) from the File pull-down menu.

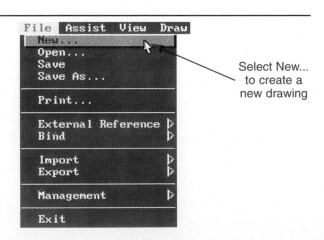

Select New... to create a new drawing

At this time, the "Create New Drawing" dialog box appears. See Figure 5-2.

Figure 5-2.   The "Create New Drawing" dialog box. Notice the prototype is the standard ACAD prototype and the new drawing name is TEST.

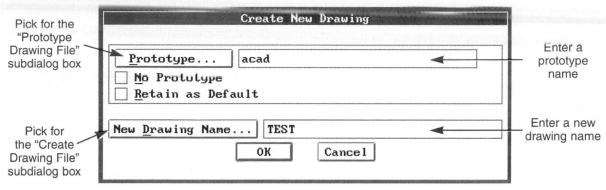

The New Drawing Name... edit box

You enter the new drawing file name in this edit box. When you enter a new drawing named TEST and pick the OK button, AutoCAD creates a new drawing file called TEST.DWG. The drawing file name TEST is entered in Figure 5-2.

The Drawing Name... button

If you want to see a list of existing drawings, pick the New Drawing Name... button. The "Create Drawing File" dialog box is then displayed. You can pick an existing drawing name from this dialog box. See Figure 5-3A.

Figure 5-3.   A–The "Create Drawing File" subdialog box. B–The "Prototype Drawing File" subdialog box. Notice D12-9 has been picked from the Files: list and is shown at the File: edit box.

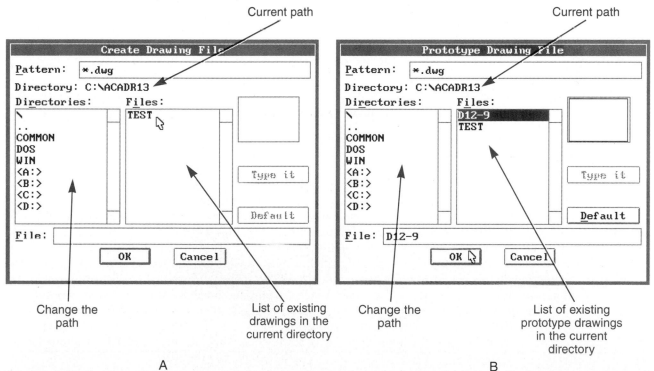

The Prototype edit box

As you may recall, a prototype drawing contains all of the standard elements that you need in the drawing format. These elements might be a border, title block, text style, and AutoCAD system variables set for your application. The Prototype edit box is the place where you enter the name of the prototype drawing that you want to use as the basis for your new drawing. You can also create your own prototype drawing and enter its name in the Prototype edit box. The prototype drawing in Figure 5-2 is ACAD, which is the standard AutoCAD prototype. (All of the values of the ACAD prototype drawing are shown in Appendix Section in the back of this text.)

In Chapter 4, you created a simple prototype drawing named D12-9 (A:D12-9 if the file is on your floppy disk). To use this prototype as the basis for a drawing named EX5-1, enter D12-9 at the Prototype edit box and the drawing name EX5-1 at the New Drawing Name… edit box. Now, any work you do is saved as EX5-1 and the prototype remains unchanged and ready for use again.

The Prototype… button

To see a list of the existing drawings, pick the Prototype… button to get the "Prototype Drawing File" dialog box shown in Figure 5-3B. Notice the D12-9 prototype in the file list (if you saved it to the hard disk drive). You can use D12-9 as your prototype by picking it and pressing ENTER, or pick the OK button. The "Prototype Drawing File" dialog box then disappears and the D12-9 prototype is listed in the Prototype… edit box of the "Create New Drawing" dialog box. Enter a drawing name at the New Drawing Name… edit box and then pick the OK button. You are then ready to start drawing.

When you pick the Prototype… button, you get some optional architectural and mechanical prototypes based on US and international standards. These optional prototypes are in addition to the standard AutoCAD prototype. They have preset values for units, limits, drawing aids, and dimensioning in inches or millimeters depending on the application.

PROFESSIONAL TIP

An entry in a dialog box can be approved by moving the cursor arrow to the OK action button and picking, or by simply pressing the ENTER key.

The No Prototype check box

Pick this check box if you don't want to use a prototype drawing. An X in this box sets all variables to AutoCAD default values. This is essentially how the ACAD.DWG prototype drawing was created.

The Retain as Default check box

If you pick this check box, the current prototype is kept for the next time you set up a new drawing.

PROFESSIONAL TIP

When AutoCAD is operating, it uses what is called *virtual memory*. This means that when it fills up memory, it uses temporary disk files to store program and drawing information. In its default configuration, AutoCAD will create and store these files on the disk drive that was current when the program was started. It is, therefore, very important to be sure that you are not currently on a floppy disk drive when you start AutoCAD. High density disk drives can store just over one megabyte of information, which leaves very little room for temporary files. The problem with this is that AutoCAD can quickly fill this space, and when AutoCAD runs out of temporary file storage space, it can *crash*. When the program crashes, AutoCAD stops working and exits immediately, attempting to save your drawing as it does so. Although it is possible to save your work, this situation can be very inconvenient – and can be easily avoided. Be sure that the current disk drive is not a floppy disk drive when you start the AutoCAD program.

EXERCISE 5-1

❑ Load AutoCAD and enter the drawing editor.
❑ Pick New... from the File pull-down menu and look at the "Create New Drawing" dialog box.
❑ Pick the New Drawing Name... button and see if there are any existing drawings identified in the Files: list. Pick the OK button.
❑ Enter a new drawing name called TEST at the New Drawing Name... edit box and pick the OK button.
❑ Watch the pull-down menu disappear and the drawing editor screen appear. This means that the new drawing named TEST has set up a work space for temporary files. You are ready to begin drawing.
❑ Type QUIT at the Command: prompt.

SAVING YOUR WORK

AUG 1

The SAVE command allows you to protect your work by writing the existing status of your drawing to disk while remaining in the drawing editor. While working in the drawing editor, you should save your drawing every 10 to 15 minutes. This is very important! If there is a power failure, a severe editing error, or other problems, all of the work saved prior to the problem will likely be usable. If you save only once an hour, a power failure results in an hour of lost work. Type SAVE at the Command: prompt, or pick Save... from the File pull-down menu (if the drawing is unnamed) to display the "Save Drawing As" dialog box shown in Figure 5-4. These are the dialog box features.

- **Pattern.** The file type, such as .DWG.
- **Directory.** The current AutoCAD directory. The directory shown in Figure 5-4 is C:\ACADR13.
- **Directories.** This is a list of the current available directories, subdirectories, and drive letters such as A: and B:.
- **File.** This is a list of the current files that are available for the pattern type listed. This list of drawing (.DWG) files listed in Figure 5-4 are D12-9 and TEST.

Figure 5-4.   The "Save Drawing As" dialog box. The pattern is a .DWG (drawing) file, the current directory is ACADR13 on the C: drive, and the drawing to be saved is named FLRPLN in the File: edit box.

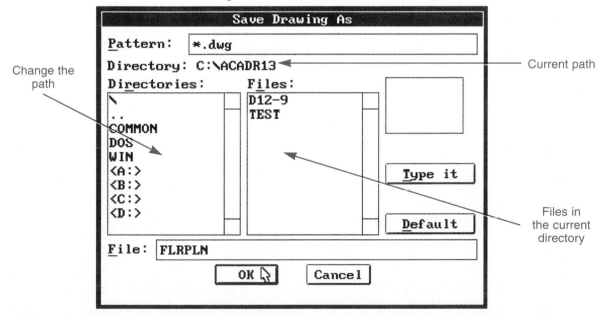

Enter the desired drawing name in the File edit box, pick a drawing name from the list, or pick Type it to enter the drawing name at the prompt line. Remember to change to the drive and directory to where you want the drawing saved. If you are working on a drawing and then try to save it with a name that already exists, AutoCAD displays the alert box shown in Figure 5-5. The question in the box states: "Do you want to replace it?" Pick YES if you want the existing drawing replaced with the current one. If you do not want it replaced, pick NO. Be sure to make the right choice since the existing drawing is replaced if you pick YES. Sometimes it may be appropriate to replace an existing drawing when you are changing it.

Figure 5-5.   The "AutoCAD Message" alert box appears when a drawing with the same name already exists.

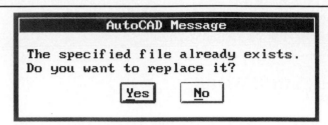

PROFESSIONAL TIP

Never begin a drawing on a floppy disk when in AutoCAD. All work during your drawing session is done on the hard disk.

Save your work in two places. If anything happens to one disk, you have the other one to depend on. If you have two disk drives, backup disks may be placed in the A: and B: drives. When finished with your drawing, save it once with an A: prefix and a second time with the B: prefix. If you have only one floppy disk drive, then save your work on two separate disks in the A: drive.

While saving drawings on floppy disks may be practical at school, it is not recommended for professional applications. The most common practice in industry is to store drawings on its system's hard drive. Saving drawings on the hard drive is much more reliable and convenient than dealing with floppies. Working from the hard drive also offers a noticeable speed increase, and large capacity hard drives are economical.

Another growing practice is the use of rewritable optical disks as archival and drawing storage. Optical disks are safe because they are unaffected by magnetic fields, changes in temperature, and they do not deteriorate over time, which can be a problem with magnetic media. Saving work on floppies is often the last choice, even when sending drawings between users. Sending work through modems is the safest and fastest method of transmission.

SAVING YOUR WORK AUTOMATICALLY   AUG 1

One of the most important things to remember when working with AutoCAD is to save your drawing every 10 to 15 minutes. If something goes wrong, you will lose 10 or 15 minutes of work rather than hours. Unfortunately, most people learn this the hard way! AutoCAD provides you with an automatic work-saving tool in the SAVETIME system variable. All you need to do is decide how often you want your work saved, and enter the amount of time (in minutes) between saves. For example:

Command: **SAVETIME** ↵
New value for SAVETIME ⟨*current*⟩: **15** ↵

The value used for the SAVETIME variable indicates the automatic save interval. The SAVETIME timer starts as soon as a change is made to the drawing, and is reset upon use of the SAVE, QSAVE, or SAVEAS command. If you set SAVETIME to 15, work for 14 minutes, and then let the computer remain idle for 5 minutes, the automatic save will be executed when you access the next command. In this instance, an automatic save is not executed until the 19 minute interval, so be certain to manually save your drawing if you plan to be away from your computer for an extended period of time. The autosaved drawing is always saved with the name of AUTO.SV$. If you need to use the file, it can be renamed to a drawing file using the DOS RENAME command. See Chapters 17 and 32 for DOS commands.

PROFESSIONAL TIP

     While an automatic save is a safeguard, it is an inconvenience to rename the AUTO.SV$ file. Using the SAVE command to continually save work in progress is advised.

WHERE TO SAVE THE DRAWING   AUG 1

When you save a drawing, it is stored in the current directory. If you have one or two floppy disk drives, you can save the drawing on your own floppy disk. To do this, place the floppy disk in the A: drive and enter the drawing name as A:NAME. The "A:" part of the name directs the drawing "NAME" to be saved on the A: drive where your floppy disk is located. Suppose you want the drawing saved on the disk in the B: drive. Place your disk in the B: drive and save the drawing as B:NAME.

It is best to do your work on the hard drive and save to a floppy disk unless otherwise specified by your instructor or CAD system manager. In fact, save your work to two floppy disks so you have a backup in case something happens to one disk. After you save your work to a floppy disk and quit the drawing session, it is best to access the hard disk when you resume your work. However, this requires that you transfer the previous work from the floppy disk to the hard disk if the drawing was not saved on the hard disk. It is easy to do if you follow these steps for an example drawing saved as A:NAME.

1. Load AutoCAD and enter the drawing editor.
2. Put your disk with the drawing NAME in the A: drive.
3. Enter the NEW command to get the "Create New Drawing " dialog box.
4. At the New Drawing Name… edit box, type a drawing name, equal sign, and the name of the drawing on the A: drive as follows:

WORK=A:NAME

This method directs the A:NAME drawing to be copied to the hard drive with the name WORK.

5. Now you are working on the hard drive. You can leave the disk in the A: drive or you can remove it.
6. Save your work every 10 to 15 minutes.
7. When finished for the day, save your work on the disk in the A: drive. Put the floppy disk in the A: drive (if removed) and enter the SAVEAS command.
8. Change the Directory to A: and type NAME in the File: box, or type A:NAME in the File box.
9. The "AutoCAD Message" alert box shown in Figure 5-5 is then displayed. Pick the Yes button. This saves the work you have done on the C: drive as A:NAME.

The SAVEAS command lets you save the current drawing under a new file name. For example, if you are working on an existing drawing and make changes that you want saved with a different name, then use the SAVEAS command. This leaves the current drawing intact with the old name (before changes were made), and saves the modified drawing with the new name. When you pick Save As… from the File pull-down menu, or type SAVEAS at the Command: prompt, the "Save Drawing As" dialog box appears, Figure 5-4, if the FILEDIA system variable is set to 1.

SAVING YOUR DRAWING QUICKLY

AUG 1

The QSAVE (Quick SAVE) command works like the SAVE command except that the drawing you are working on is automatically saved without displaying the "Save Drawing As" dialog box. If you have not used the SAVETIME command to set time intervals between automatic saves, remember to use the QSAVE command every 10 to 15 minutes to ensure your drawing is saved in the event that there is a problem with your computer.

If the drawing is not yet named, the "Save Drawing As" dialog box is displayed. Pick a file name from the Files: list box, or type the drawing name at the File: edit box.

To use the QSAVE command, type QSAVE at the Command: prompt and press the ENTER key. The drawing is then saved without allowing you to change the name, directory, or drive. Picking Save... from the File pull-down menu activates the QSAVE command if a drawing has been named and previously saved.

SAVING A RELEASE 13 DRAWING IN RELEASE 12 FORMAT

AUG 14

Your AutoCAD Release 13 drawings can be saved in a Release 12 format. This allows you to send Release 13 drawings to a business where Release 12 is being used. This capability can also be beneficial if you use Release 13 at work or school and have Release 12 at home.

To save Release 13 drawings in a Release 12 format, type SAVEASR12 at the Command: prompt. The "Save release 12 drawing as" dialog box appears. See Figure 5-6. Type the desired drawing name at the File: edit box. It is best to save the drawing as Release 13 with one file name and again using SAVEASR12 with a different file name. This protects you from accidentally writing over the Release 13 file. Converting from Release 13 back to Release 12 adds handles to the drawing. *Handles* are an alphanumeric representation of the drawing in the AutoCAD data base that can be used for access by other applications. Remove these handles by typing HANDLES at the Command: prompt after entering Release 12. The information that is unique to Release 13 is lost in the Release 12 conversion. However, during the process, a log list changes any lost information for your reference. You can look at the log by pressing the F1 key to get the text screen. When the SAVEASR12 command is used, if the current drawing name is used, the .DWG file is saved as R12 and the original R13 drawing is saved as .BAK.

Figure 5-6.   The "Save release 12 drawing as" dialog box is used to save Release 13 drawings in Release 12 format.

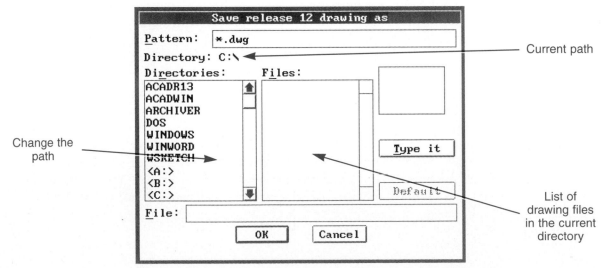

❑ Load AutoCAD and enter the drawing editor.
❑ Insert your floppy disk in the A: drive, and pick Save... from the File pull-down menu. The "Save Drawing As" dialog box then appears.
❑ Pick ⟨A:⟩ from the Directory: list and press ENTER.
❑ Pick the OK button.
❑ Pick Save As... from the File pull-down menu.
❑ Be sure C: is the current directory, then type A:EX5-2A at the File: box and press ENTER. You have now saved EX5-2 and EX5-2A to the floppy disk in the A: drive.
❑ Type QUIT at the Command: prompt and press ENTER.

OPENING AN EXISTING DRAWING

An existing drawing is one that has been previously saved. You can easily access any existing drawing on the hard disk with the OPEN command. Pick Open... from the File pull-down menu, or type OPEN at the Command: prompt. If the drawing is on your floppy disk, use the NEW command and the prototype method discussed earlier. The "Open Drawing" dialog box shown in Figure 5-7 appears when you enter the OPEN command and FILEDIA is set to 1.

The "Open Drawing" dialog box contains Directories and Files lists just as in the "Save Drawing As" dialog box. Pick the desired directory or file from the lists for quick access, or type the file name at the File edit box. If you specify a file name that does not exist, AutoCAD provides the following alert at the bottom of the dialog box:

Cannot find the specified file.

If this happens, be sure you have correctly entered the file name and that you are in the appropriate directory. You cannot open a drawing file that does not exist, or is not in the directory you have specified.

When you pick an existing drawing that was created in AutoCAD Release 13, a picture of the drawing is displayed in the Preview image tile. The Preview image tile is found just to the right of the Files: list. This is an easy way for you to get a quick look at the drawing without going into the AutoCAD drawing editor. You can view each drawing until you find the one you want. Hold the pick button down or use the keyboard arrow keys as you move the cursor arrow up or down the files list to view drawings very fast. The "Open Drawing" dialog box has the Preview image tile that shows you the drawing that is associated to the name. See Figure 5-7. The Preview feature was discussed earlier in this text.

A quick method in becoming familiar with the Preview image tile feature is to look at the sample drawings that come with AutoCAD. The sample drawings must have been loaded during AutoCAD installation to perform this exercise.
❑ Load AutoCAD and enter the drawing editor.
❑ Pick Open... from the File pull-down menu to access the "Open Drawing" dialog box.
❑ Double click on the directory that contains AutoCAD Release 13, such as ACADR13.
❑ Double click on SAMPLE if it is displayed, or double click on COMMON and then SAMPLE. The COMMON directory contains subdirectories that are common to both DOS and Windows.
❑ The Files: list should display all of the sample AutoCAD files.
❑ Pick any sample drawing and watch it display in the Preview image tile. Pick as many as you like to preview, and hold the pick button while you move the cursor arrow across several file names to see them quickly. Use the scroll bar to access additional sample drawings.
❑ Pick the Cancel button.
❑ Type QUIT at the Command: prompt and press ENTER.

Select Initial View

Look at Figure 5-7 and notice the Select Initial View check box. When you pick this box, you are allowed to select a named view that is displayed when you open the drawing. A detailed discussion on views is included in Chapter 10, of this text.

Figure 5-7.   The "Open Drawing" dialog box. Notice the drawing STRUCTUR has been picked from the Files: list, and is displayed at the File: edit box. A preview of this file is shown in the preview area (highlighted here).

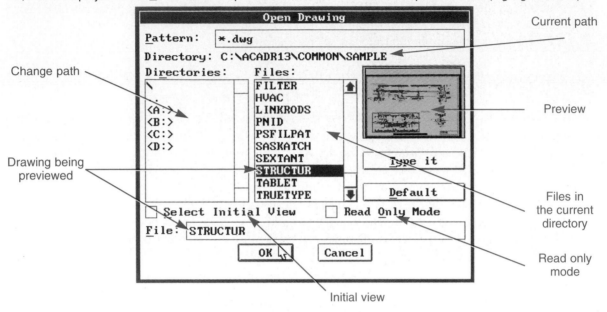

Read Only Mode check box

Refer to Figure 5-7 again and note the Read Only Mode check box. When you pick this box, the drawing you open is available for viewing only, and any changes or modifications made to the drawing cannot be saved. This is one way to protect your drawing file from any changes made by an unauthorized user. You can also use this mode if you want to practice on your drawing without the fear of altering it.

OPENING RELEASE 11 AND 12 DRAWINGS AUG 1

You can open AutoCAD Release 11 and 12 drawings in Release 13 and also continue to open them in Release 11 and 12. When you open a drawing from a previous release and work on it, AutoCAD automatically updates the drawing to Release 13 standards when you save. After the previous release drawing is saved in Release 13, it can be viewed in the Preview image tile during future applications.

MAKING A PREVIEW IMAGE OF OLDER RELEASE DRAWINGS AUG 1

When working with AutoCAD drawings from an older release, the MAKEPREVIEW command can be used to preview files without saving them in AutoCAD Release 13. To do this, enter AutoCAD Release 13 and open a drawing file from a previous release. Now enter the MAKEPREVIEW command.

Command: **MAKEPREVIEW** ↵
Command:

The MAKEPREVIEW command makes a compressed .BMP file of the drawing and places it in the same directory as the drawing file. You do not have to save the drawing in Release 13. Now, when opening this drawing, the "Select Drawing" dialog box displays the image in the Preview image tile just as if the drawing had been saved in Release 13. See Figure 5-3A.

EXERCISE 5-4

❏ Load AutoCAD and enter the drawing editor.
❏ Pick Open… from the File pull-down menu to access the "Open Drawing" dialog box.
❏ PROTO1 and D12-9 should be in the Files list if you did Exercise 4-4 and Drawing Problem 4-1.
❏ Pick D12-9 to insert it at the File: edit box and press ENTER, or pick the OK button to open the prototype drawing D12-9.
❏ Type QUIT at the Command: prompt and press ENTER.

ENDING A DRAWING

AUG 1

When you have completed your drawing session, you can exit the drawing editor, save your work, and return to the operating system prompt all at once using the END command. Simply type END at the Command: prompt as follows:

Command: **END** ↵

When you enter END, the revised drawing is saved with the drawing name and a .DWG file extension. The old version is saved as a backup, with a .BAK file extension. The file extension is provided by AutoCAD. You only enter the drawing name. For example, if you work on the drawing named PROTO1 and type END, it is saved as PROTO1.DWG. The previous version of PROTO1 is saved as PROTO1.BAK. Use the OPEN command when you want to work on PROTO1 again. AutoCAD looks for the .DWG file. If you did not previously name the drawing, AutoCAD prompts you to specify a name before exiting.

If you have done a substantial amount of work on a drawing, some caution should be considered before using the END command. The END command writes the drawing to disk and exits AutoCAD, without purging deleted object data from the drawing file. Use the SAVE, QSAVE, or SAVEAS command to have AutoCAD automatically reduce the file size.

PROFESSIONAL TIP

 The SAVE, QSAVE, and SAVEAS decrease the size of the drawing by varying amounts as compared to the END command. The actual amount of reduction can often be fairly insignificant. However, in larger drawings where a great amount of editing has occurred, the reduction in size can be considerable.

USING THE QUIT COMMAND

AUG 1

The QUIT command lets you exit AutoCAD if any changes you made to the drawing were saved before quitting. You can pick Exit AutoCAD from the File pull-down menu, or type QUIT at the Command: prompt as follows:

Command: **QUIT** ↵

If you enter QUIT before saving your work, then AutoCAD gives you a chance to decide what you want to do with unsaved work by displaying the "Drawing Modification" dialog box shown in Figure 5-8. Press ENTER to activate the highlighted Save Changes… button. This saves the drawing as previously named, or displays the "Save Drawing As" dialog box if the drawing had not been previously saved. You can also pick the Discard Changes button if you plan to discard any changes made to the drawing since the previous SAVE. This is a good way to use AutoCAD for practice. To use AutoCAD for practice without saving, enter the QUIT command when you are done and pick the Discard Changes button. All of the practice work is gone. Pick the Cancel Command button if you decide not to quit.

If you QUIT and pick the Save Changes... button when the drawing is in Read Only Mode, then the QUIT command is automatically canceled. Use the SAVEAS command and give the drawing a new name to save these changes.

Figure 5-8.   While using the QUIT command, the "Drawing Modifications" dialog box appears to indicate that changes to the drawing have been made, but not saved.

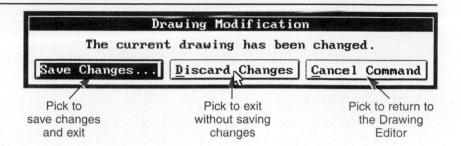

DETERMINING THE DRAWING STATUS

AUG 3

While working on a drawing, you may want to refresh your memory about some of the drawing parameters, such as the limits, grid spacing, or snap value. All of the information about the drawing is displayed by typing STATUS at the Command: prompt. You can also pick STATUS: from the INQUIRY option in the Root Menu. The information displayed looks like this:

```
52 entities in DRAWING
Model space limits are          X:     0.0000      Y:     0.0000      (Off)(World)
                                X:    12.0000      Y:     9.0000
Model space uses                X:     0.9600      Y:     3.5398
                                X:     6.2500      Y:     8.0400
Display shows                   X:     0.0000      Y:    15.4985
                                X:     0.0000      Y:     9.4527
Insertion base is               X:    *0.0000      Y:     0.0000      Z:    0.0000
Snap resolution is              X:     0.5000      Y:     0.5000
Grid spacing is                 X:     0.2500      Y:     0.2500
Current space:              Model space
Current layer:              0
Current color:              BYLAYER–7 (white)
Current linetype:           BYLAYER–CONTINUOUS
Current elevation:          0.0000 thickness:     0.0000
Fill on    Grid on    Ortho off    Qtext off    Snap on    Tablet off
Object snap modes:          None
Free disk:                  14518272 bytes
Virtual memory allocated to program: 2128K
Amount of program in physical memory/Total (virtual) program size: 95%
Total conventional memory: 404K       Total extended memory: 3328K
–Press RETURN for more –
Swap file size: 388KB
Page faults: 136            Swap writes: 0        Swap reclaims: 14
Command:
```

The number of entities in a drawing refers to the total number of entities–both erased and unerased. The (Off) on the "Model space limits are" line refers to the limits check discussed in Chapter 3, and (World) means that the limits are given in World coordinates. If the message "**Over" appears to the right of "Model space uses," this indicates that the drawing extends outside the drawing limits. Free disk represents the space left on the drive containing your drawing file.

PROFESSIONAL TIP

Refer to the drawing STATUS command periodically to see how much "free disk" space is available. If this free disk space becomes dangerously low, you may be unable to complete and save the drawing. This has been known to cause severe problems. AutoCAD automatically saves your work and ends use of the drawing editor if it runs out of disk space.

EXERCISE 5-5

❑ Load AutoCAD and enter the drawing editor.
❑ Pick Open... from the File pull-down to access the "Open Drawing" dialog box.
❑ PRODR1 and D12-9 should be in the Files: list if you did Exercise 4-4 and Drawing Problem 4-1.
❑ Pick D12-9 to insert it at the File: edit box and press ENTER, or pick the OK button to open the prototype drawing D12-9.
❑ Enter the STATUS command and read all of the items displayed. Press the ENTER key to view the information on the second page.
❑ Press the F1 function key to get back to the drawing editor.
❑ Type QUIT at the Command: prompt and press ENTER.

CHAPTER TEST

Write your answers in the spaces provided.

1. Name the command used to start a new drawing. _____

2. What command saves your drawing and returns you to the operating system prompt? _____

_____

3. Identify the command that you use to leave the drawing editor without saving. _____

_____

4. What command would you use to save an existing drawing with a different name? _____

_____

5. Identify at least four ways to cancel a command. _____

_____

_____

6. Explain the difference between the SAVE, END, and QUIT commands. _____

_____

_____

_____

_____

_____

_____

7. How do you change the name of a drawing while in the drawing editor? _____

_____

_____

8. How often should work be saved? _____

9. Name the command that allows you to quickly save your work without displaying the dialog box.

   _____

10. The status of an AutoCAD drawing is currently displayed on screen. List one method to get back to the drawing editor. _____ _____ _____

   _____ _____ _____

11. Name the system variable that allows you to control the dialog box display. _____

   _____

12. List the settings for the system variable described in the previous question that is used to achieve the following results:

   dialog box displayed _____

   dialog box not displayed _____

13. Why is it important to record drawing names in a log? _____

   _____

14. List at least three rules and restrictions for drawing names. _____

   _____

   _____

   _____

   _____

15. Name the pull-down menu where the SAVE, SAVEAS, and OPEN commands are located.

   _____

16. Identify two ways to exit AutoCAD without saving your work. _____

   _____

17. Name the command that allows AutoCAD to automatically save your work at designated intervals.

   _____

18. Explain how you can get a list of existing drawing prototypes._____

   _____

   _____

19. It is recommended that you resume work on the hard drive when you have saved the drawing file on a floppy disk. Name the file entry needed to transfer the drawing file named A:PROJECT to the hard disk in a file called WORK. _____

   _____

20. Why is it a good idea to save your work on two floppy disks, to a hard drive, or to an optical disk?

   _____

   _____

21. Define temporary files._____

   _____

22. Where are temporary files stored if the AutoCAD configuration for the placement of temporary files is set to the default ⟨DRAWING⟩? _____

   _____

23. What is the command to use if you want to change the configuration for the placement of temporary files? _____

24. Give at least two reasons why it is a good idea to direct temporary files to a directory on the hard drive. _____

_____

_____

25. How do you access the Preview image tile and what is its purpose? _____

_____

_____

26. Name the command used to change a drawing created in AutoCAD Release 13 back to Release 12.

_____

DRAWING PROBLEMS

P5-1

1. Enter the drawing editor and open drawing D12-9. This is the prototype that you set up in Problem 4-1. (If you did not set up this prototype, refer back to Problem 4-1 and set up the drawing now.) Draw the same objects that you drew in Problem 4-2. Use the SAVEAS command and change the file name to P5-1. This keeps the prototype unchanged for future use and saves the drawing on the hard drive as P5-1 (P=Problem, 5=Chapter 5, 1=Problem 1). Now, type QUIT at the Command: prompt and press ENTER.

2. Start AutoCAD and open drawing P5-1. Draw the objects in the same manner as required in Problem 4-3. Enter QUIT, press the ENTER key, and discard all changes. This procedure deletes all changes to the drawing and brings you back to the operating system prompt.

3. Start AutoCAD and open drawing P5-1. Observe that the work done in Problem 2 does not exist. This is because you used the QUIT command. Now enter END. This saves P5-1 as is and returns you to the operating system prompt.

P5-4

4. Start AutoCAD and access the "Create New Drawing" dialog box. Enter P5-4=P5-1 at the New Drawing Name... edit box. This procedure does the following:

   - Creates a new drawing titled P5-4.
   - Copies the drawing P5-1 to P5-4.
   - When you SAVE, there is a new drawing titled P5-4. The previous drawing, P5-1, remains unchanged.

   On the right side of the screen draw a right triangle, a square, and a rectangle. Use the SNAP and GRID commands to your best advantage. Enter END to save the drawing when finished.

5. Start AutoCAD and open drawing P5-4. Enter the STATUS command and observe the drawing status. Press the F1 function key to return to the drawing editor. Draw a box around the items previously drawn. Enter the QSAVE command and press ENTER. Then, type QUIT and press ENTER to go back to the operating system prompt.

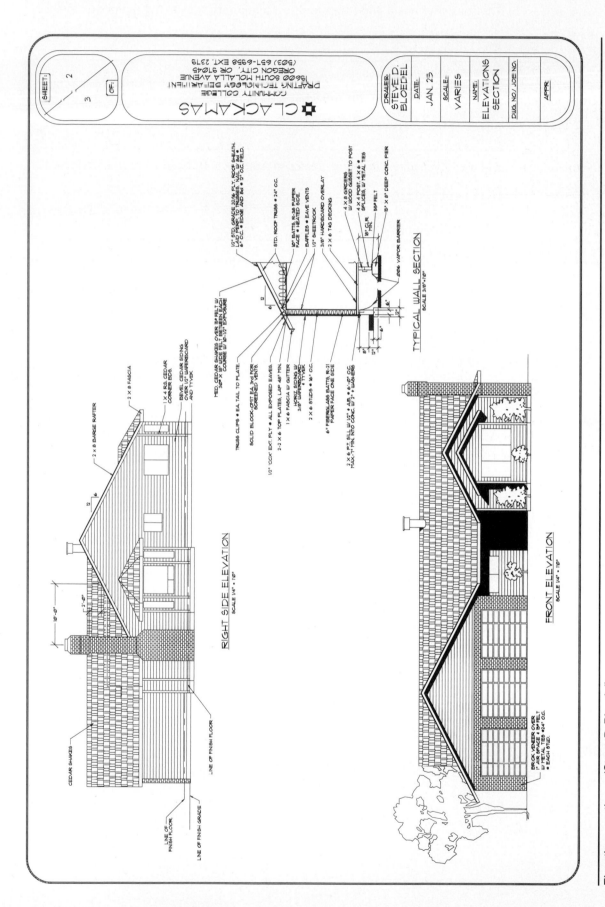

Elevations section. (Steve D. Bloedel)

Chapter 6

DRAWING LINES, ERASING LINES, AND MAKING PRINTS

Learning objectives

After completing this chapter, you will be able to:

- ○ Use the absolute, relative, and polar coordinate point entry systems.
- ○ Use the screen cursor for point entry.
- ○ Use the Ortho mode and coordinate display.
- ○ Select the LINE command to draw given objects.
- ○ Make revisions to objects using the ERASE command and its options.
- ○ Make selection sets using the Multiple, Window, Crossing, WPolygon, CPolygon, and Fence options.
- ○ Use the OOPS command to bring back an entity.
- ○ Remove and add objects to the selection set.
- ○ Use the MULTIPLE command modifier.
- ○ Clean up the screen with the REDRAW command.
- ○ Draw objects with different linetypes.
- ○ Add color to the drawing.
- ○ Use drawing plan sheets.

Drafting is a graphic language that uses lines, symbols, and words to describe products to be manufactured or constructed. Line conventions are standards based on line thickness and type, and are designed to enhance the readability of drawings. This chapter introduces line standards and shows you how to use the AutoCAD drawing editor to perform basic drafting tasks.

LINE CONVENTIONS

The American National Standards Institute (ANSI) recommends two line thicknesses to establish contrasting lines on a drawing. Lines are described as thick and thin. Thick lines are .032 in. (0.6 mm) wide and thin lines are .016 in. (0.3 mm) wide. Figure 6-1 shows recommended line width and type as taken from ANSI Y14.2M, *Line Conventions and Lettering*.

Figure 6-1. Line conventions. (ANSI Y14.2M)

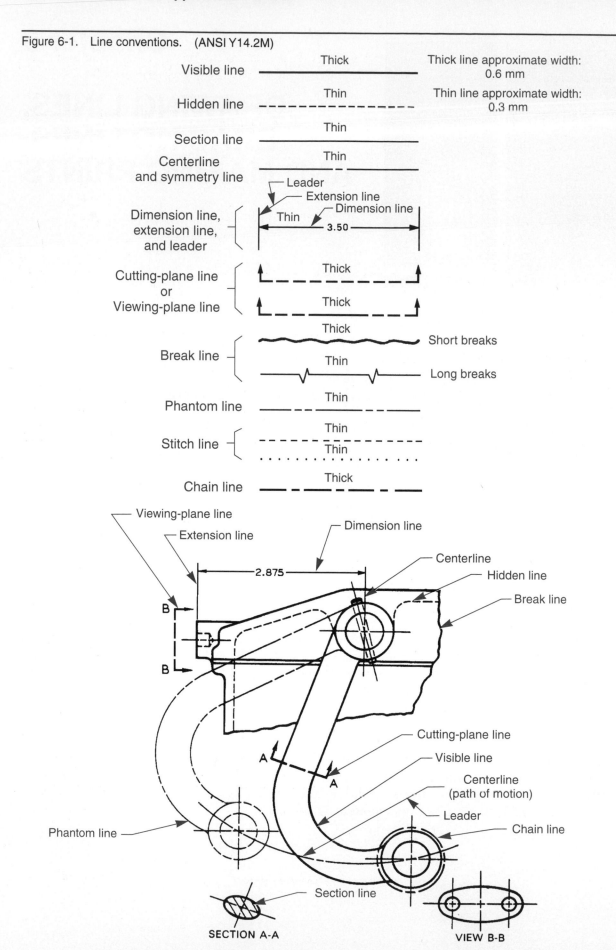

contour [kántʊr]: contorno, perímetro

Object lines

Object lines, also called *visible lines*, are thick lines used to show the outline or contour of an object, Figure 6-2. Object lines are the most common type of lines used on drawings.

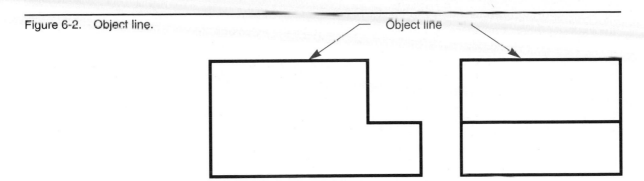

Figure 6-2.   Object line.

Object line

Hidden lines

Hidden lines, often called *dashed lines*, are used to represent invisible edges of an object, Figure 6-3. Hidden lines are drawn thin so they clearly contrast with object lines. Properly drawn, the dashes are .125 in. (3 mm) long and spaced .06 in. (1.5 mm) apart. This is the recommended full size of hidden line dashes. Be careful if the drawing is to be greatly reduced or scaled down during the plotting process. Reduced dashes may appear too small.

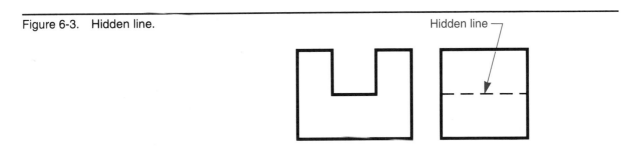

Figure 6-3.   Hidden line.

Hidden line

Centerlines

Centerlines locate the centers of circles and arcs, and show the axis of a cylindrical or symmetrical shape, Figure 6-4. Centerlines are thin lines consisting of alternately spaced long and short dashes. The recommended dash lengths are .125 in. (3 mm) for the short dashes and .75 to 1.5 in. (20 to 38 mm) for the long dashes. These lengths can be altered depending on the size of the drawing. The dashes should be separated by spaces approximately .06 in. (1.5 mm). The small centerline dashes should cross only at the center of a circle.

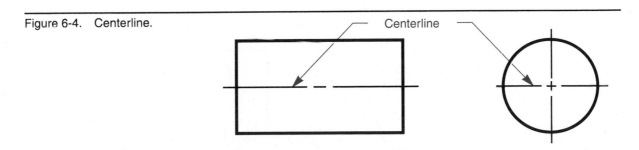

Figure 6-4.   Centerline.

Centerline

Extension lines

Extension lines are thin lines used to show the extent of a dimension, Figure 6-5. Extension lines begin a small distance from the object and extend .125 in. (3 mm) beyond the last dimension line. Extension lines may cross object lines, hidden lines, and centerlines, but they may not cross dimension lines. Centerlines become extension lines when they are used to show the extent of a dimension. When this is done, there is no space where the centerline joins the extension line.

Figure 6-5.　Extension line.

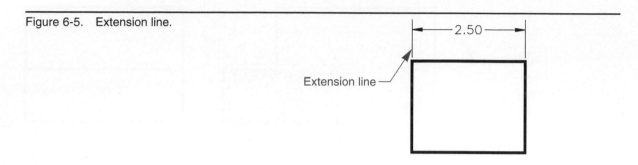

Dimension lines

Dimension lines are thin lines placed between extension lines to indicate a measurement. In mechanical drafting, the dimension line is normally broken near the center for placement of the dimension numeral, Figure 6-6. The dimension line normally remains unbroken in architectural and structural drawings. The dimension numeral is placed on top of an unbroken dimension line. Arrows terminate the ends of dimension lines, except in architectural drafting where slashes or dots are often used.

Figure 6-6.　Dimension line.

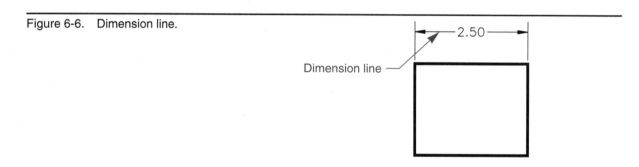

Leader lines

Leader lines are thin lines used to connect a specific note to a feature on a drawing. A leader line terminates with an arrowhead at the feature and has a small shoulder at the note, Figure 6-7. Dimension and leader line usage is discussed in detail in Chapter 18.

Figure 6-7.　Leader line.

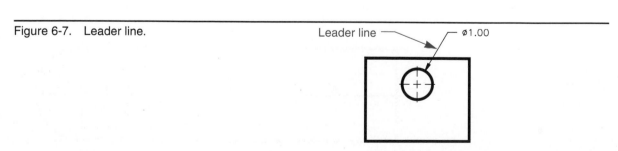

Cutting-plane and viewing-plane lines

Cutting-plane lines are thick lines that identify the location of a section or view. *Viewing-plane lines* are drawn in the same style as cutting-plane lines, but identify the location of a view. Cutting-plane and viewing-plane lines may be drawn one of two ways as shown in Figure 6-1. The use of viewing-plane and cutting-plane lines is discussed in detail in Chapters 19 and 20.

Section lines

Section lines are thin lines drawn in a sectional view to show where material has been cut away, Figure 6-8. Section line types and applications are discussed in Chapter 24.

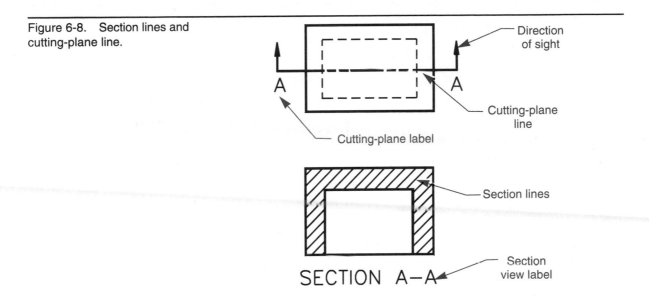

Figure 6-8.   Section lines and cutting-plane line.

Break lines

Break lines show where a portion of an object has been removed for clarity or convenience. For example, the center portion of a very long part may be broken out so the two ends can be moved closer together for more convenient representation. There are several types of break lines shown in Figure 6-9.

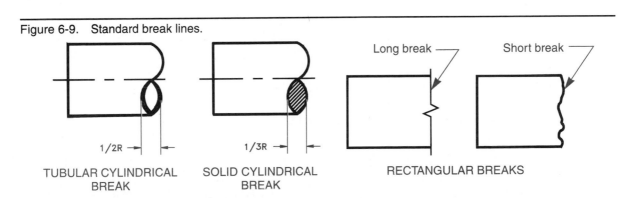

Figure 6-9.   Standard break lines.

Phantom lines

Phantom lines are thin lines with two short dashes alternately spaced with long dashes. The short dashes are .125 in. (3 mm) and the long dashes range from .75 to 1.5 in. (20 to 38 mm) in length depending on the size of the drawing. Spaces between dashes are .06 in. (1.5 mm). Phantom lines identify repetitive details, show alternate positions of moving parts, or locate adjacent positions of related parts, Figure 6-10.

Figure 6-10.   Phantom lines.

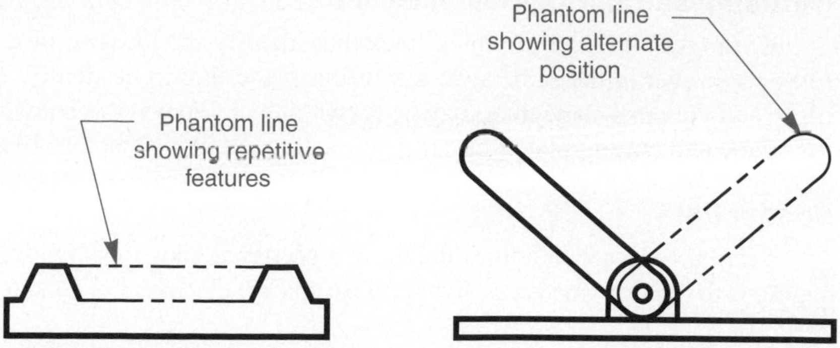

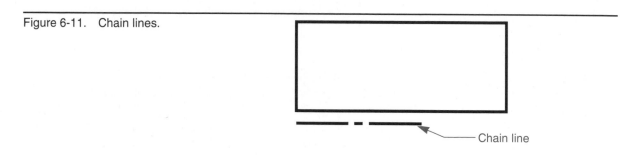

Chain lines

Chain lines are thick lines of alternately spaced long and short dashes. They show that the portion of the surface next to the chain line has special features or receives unique treatment. See Figure 6-11.

Figure 6-11.   Chain lines.

Chain line

DRAWING LINES WITH AUTOCAD

AUG 2

Individual line segments are drawn between two points on the screen. This is referred to as *point entry* and is the simplest form of drafting. Enter endpoints for drawing lines after selecting the LINE command.

The command name LINE may be typed at the Command: prompt. It can also be selected from the DRAW screen menu or the Draw pull-down menu. When you enter the LINE command, AutoCAD asks for the "from point" and "to point" of the line. Enter these points by typing point coordinates using the keyboard or picking points by moving the crosshairs to desired locations. When you select the LINE command, a prompt asks you to select a starting point. When the first point is selected, the next point is requested. When the third To point: prompt is given, you may stop adding lines by pressing the ENTER key or the space bar. If you want to connect a series of lines, continue selecting as many additional points as you like. When finished, press ENTER or press the space bar to get back to the Command: prompt.

The command sequence is for the LINE command:

Command: **LINE** ⌐
From point: *(select the first point)*
To point: *(select the second point)*
To point: *(select the third point or press* ENTER *to get a new Command: prompt)*
Command: *(this appears if you press* ENTER *at the previous prompt)*

Responding to AutoCAD prompts with numbers

Many of the AutoCAD commands require specific types of numeric data. Each situation is explained as you learn new commands in this text. Some of AutoCAD's prompts require you to enter a number as the proper response. For example, later in this book you will learn how to divide an object into a number of equal parts using the DIVIDE command. This command requires that you specify a number of segments as follows:

Command: **DIVIDE** ⏎
Select object to divide: *(pick the object)*
⟨Number of segments⟩/Block: **6** ⏎

The above example illustrates the simplest form of numeric entry where any whole number may be used. Other entries require whole numbers that may be positive or negative. A number is understood to be positive without placing the plus (+) sign before the number. However, a negative number must be preceded by the minus (–) sign.

Much of your data entry is other than whole numbers. In these cases, any real number may be used and can be expressed as decimals, fractions, or scientific notation. They may be positive or negative. Here are some examples:

4.250
–6.375
1/2
1-3/4
2.5E+4 (25,000)
2.5E–4 (0.00025)

When entering fractions, the numerator and denominator must be whole numbers greater than zero such as 1/2, 3/4, or 2/3. Numbers containing fractions that are greater than one must have a dash between the whole number and the fraction, for example, 2-3/4. The dash (-) separator is needed because a space acts just like pressing ENTER, which automatically ends the input. The numerator may be larger than the denominator as in 3/2 only if a whole number is not used with the fraction.

When you enter coordinates or measurements, the value used depends on the units of measure such as feet, inches, or millimeters. Values on inch drawings are understood to be in inches without placing the inch (″) marks after the numeral. For example, 2.500 is automatically 2.500 inches. When your drawing is set up for metric values, then any entry is automatically expressed as millimeters. If you are working in an engineering or architectural environment, any value greater than one foot is expressed in inches, feet, or feet and inches. The values can be whole numbers, decimals, or fractions. For measurements in feet, the foot (′) symbol must follow the number, as in 24′. If the value is in feet and inches, there is no space between the feet and inch value. For example, 24′6 is the proper input for the value 24′-6″. If the inch part of the value contains a fraction, the inch and fractional part of an inch are separated by a dash as previously explained. For example, 24′6-1/2. Never mix feet with inches greater than one foot, for example, 24′18″ is an invalid entry. In this case, you should enter 25′6.

PROFESSIONAL TIP

Placing the inch (″) marks after an inch value at the prompt line is acceptable, but not necessary. It takes more time and reduces productivity.

POINT ENTRY METHODS

AUG 2

There are several point entry techniques for drawing lines. Being familiar and skillful with these methods is very important. It is not necessary to use only one point entry system when drawing. A combination of techniques may be used to help reduce drawing time. Each of the point entry methods uses the Cartesian, or rectangular coordinate system. The *Cartesian coordinate system* is based on selecting distances that locate a point from two intersecting axes. Each point distance is measured along a horizontal "X" axis and a vertical "Y" axis. The intersection of the axes, called the *origin*, divides the coordinate system into four quadrants. Points are located in relation to the origin where X = 0 and Y = 0, or (0,0). Figure 6-12 shows the X,Y values of points located in the Cartesian coordinate system.

Figure 6-12.   The Cartesian coordinate system.

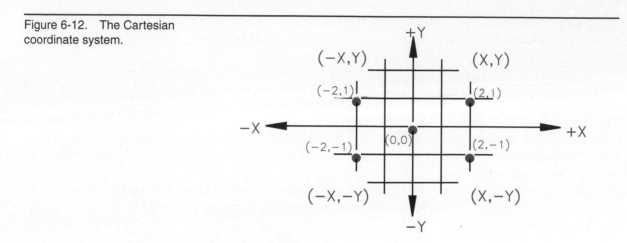

When using AutoCAD, the 0,0 point (origin) is usually at the lower-left corner of the drawing. This point also coincides with the lower-left corner of the drawing limits. This setup places all points in the upper-right quadrant where both X and Y coordinate values are positive, Figure 6-13.

Methods of establishing points in the Cartesian coordinate system include absolute coordinates, relative coordinates, and polar coordinates.

Figure 6-13.   X,Y coordinate axes on the screen.

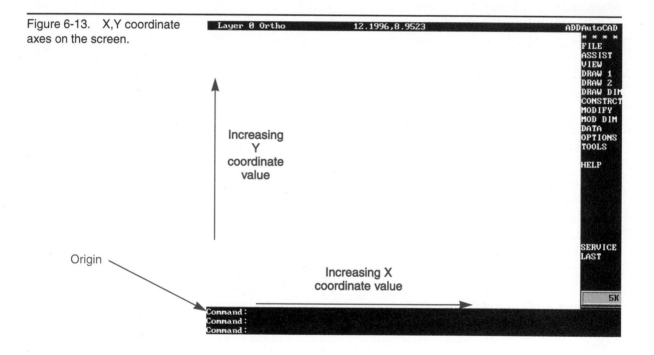

Absolute coordinates

Points located using the absolute coordinate system are measured from the origin (0,0). For example, a point with X = 4 and Y = 2 (4,2) is measured 4 units horizontally (X) and 2 units vertically (Y) from the origin, Figure 6-14. Notice the status line at the top right of the screen registers the location of the selected point in X and Y coordinates. This is referred to as the *coordinate display*. The coordinate display may be turned on or off by pressing CTRL+D on the keyboard or puck button 7.

Remember, when the absolute coordinate system is used, each point is located from 0,0. Follow through these commands and point placements at your computer as you refer to Figure 6-15.

Figure 6-14. Locating points with absolute coordinates.

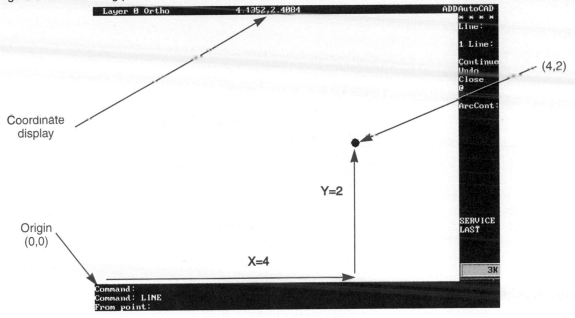

Command: **LINE** ↵
From point: **4,2** ↵
To point: **7,2** ↵
To point: **7,6** ↵
To point: **4,6** ↵
To point: **4,2** ↵
To point: ↵
Command: **LINE** ↵
From point: **9,1.5** ↵
To point: **11,1.5** ↵
To point: **10,5.25** ↵
To point: **9,1.5** ↵
To point: ↵
Command:

Figure 6-15. Drawing simple shapes using the LINE command and absolute coordinates.

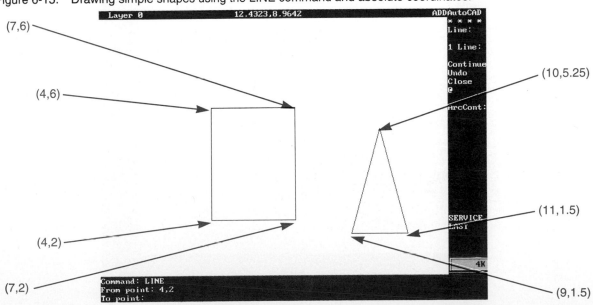

EXERCISE 6-1

❑ Load AutoCAD, enter the drawing editor, and open PRODR1 from Exercise 4-4, or start a new drawing and set up your own variables.

❑ Given the following absolute coordinates, use the LINE command to draw the object:

Point	Coordinates	Point	Coordinates
1	0,0	5	0,2
2	9,0	6	0,1.5
3	9.5,.5	7	.25,.5
4	9.5,2	8	0,0

❑ Save the drawing as A:EX6-1 and quit the drawing editor.

Relative coordinates

Relative coordinates are located from the previous position, rather than from the origin. The relationship of points in the Cartesian coordinate system shown in Figure 6-12 must be clearly understood before beginning with this method. For relative coordinates, the @ symbol must precede your entry. (This symbol is selected by holding the SHIFT key and pressing the "2" key at the top of the keyboard.) Follow through these commands and relative coordinate point placements as you refer to Figure 6-16.

```
Command: LINE ↵
From point: 2,2 ↵
To point: @6,0 ↵
To point: @2,2 ↵
To point: @0,3 ↵
To point: @–2,2 ↵
To point: @–6,0 ↵
To point: @0,–7 ↵
To point: ↵
Command:
```

Figure 6-16.   Drawing a simple shape using the LINE command and relative coordinates. Notice that the coordinates are entered counterclockwise from the first point (2,2).

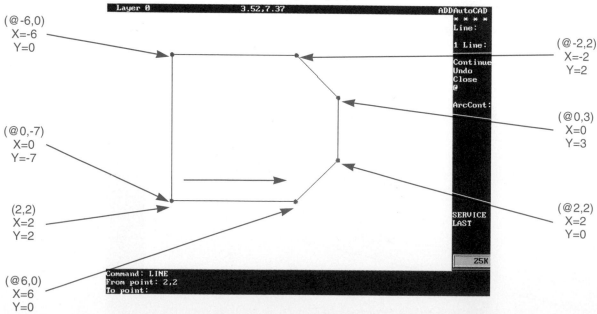

EXERCISE 6-2

❑ Load AutoCAD, enter the drawing editor, and open PRODR1 from Exercise 4-4, or start a new drawing and set up your own variables.
❑ Use the LINE command to draw the object with the following relative coordinates:

Point	Coordinates	Point	Coordinates
1	1,1	5	@–9.5,0
2	@9,0	6	@0,–.5
3	@.5,.5	7	@.25,–.5
4	@0,1.5	8	@–.25,–.5

❑ Save the drawing as A:EX6-2 and quit.

Polar coordinates

A point located using *polar coordinates* is based on the distance from a fixed point at a given angle. When using AutoCAD, a polar coordinate point is determined by distance and angle measured from the previous point. It is important to remember that points located using polar coordinates are always positioned relative to the *previous* point, not the origin (0,0). The angular values used for the polar coordinate format are shown in Figure 6-17.

Figure 6-17.   Angles used in the polar coordinate system.

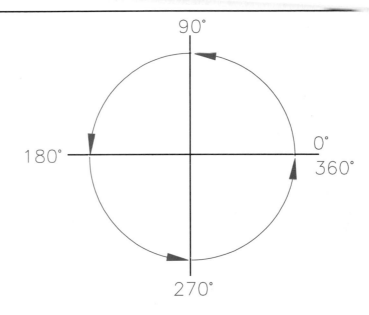

When establishing points using the polar coordinate system, AutoCAD needs a specific symbol entered. For example, if you want to locate a point 4 units from point 0,0 at a 45° angle, the following information must be typed:

```
Command: LINE ↵
From point: 0,0 ↵
To point: @4⟨45 ↵
To point: ↵
```

Figure 6-18 shows the result of this command. The entry @4⟨45 means the following:

@–Tells AutoCAD to measure from the previous point. This symbol must precede all polar
coordinate prompts.

4–Denotes the distance from the previous point.

⟨–Establishes a polar or angular increment to follow.

45–Determines the angle as 45° from 0°.

Figure 6-18.   Using polar coordinates for the LINE command.

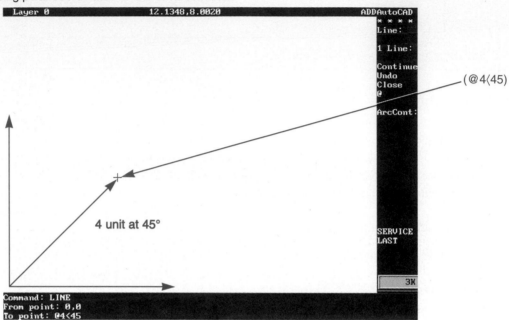

Now, follow through these commands and polar coordinate points on your computer as you refer to
Figure 6-19.

Command: **LINE** ↵
From point: **1,1** ↵
To point: **@4⟨0** ↵
To point: **@2⟨90** ↵
To point: **@4⟨180** ↵
To point: **@2⟨270** ↵
To point: ↵
Command: **LINE** ↵
From point: **2,6** ↵
To point: **@2.5⟨0** ↵
To point: **@3⟨135** ↵
To point: **2,6** ↵
To point: ↵
Command:

Figure 6-19.   Drawing simple shapes using polar coordinates.

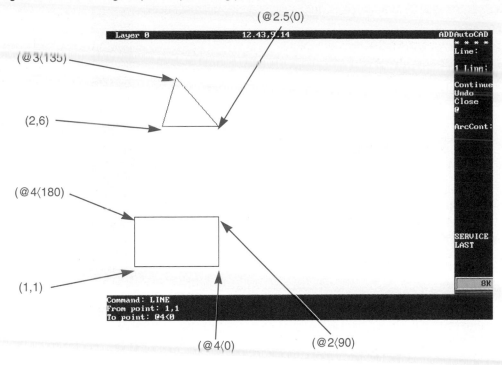

EXERCISE 6-3

❑ Load AutoCAD, enter the drawing editor, and open PRODR1 from Exercise 4-4, or start a new drawing and set up your own variables.
❑ Use the LINE command to draw an object using the following polar coordinates:

Point	Coordinates
1	1,1
2	@9⟨0
3	@.7⟨45
4	@1.5⟨90
5	@9.5⟨180
6	@2⟨270

❑ Save the drawing as A:EX6-3 and quit.

Picking points using the screen cursor

The cursor crosshairs may be moved to any location. Pick points at the cursor using the stylus, mouse, or puck. The GRID and SNAP modes normally should be on for precise point location. This assists in drafting presentation and maintains accuracy when using a pointing device. With snap grid on, the crosshairs move in designated increments without any guesswork.

When using a pointing device, the command sequence is the same as using coordinates except that points are picked when the crosshairs are at the desired location on the screen. After the first point is picked, the distance to the second point and the point's coordinates are displayed on the status line for reference. Also, use a visible grid and invisible snap grid for reference. For example, if the distance is 2.75, then .25 snap units and .5 grid units allow you to quickly locate the point. When picking points in this manner, there is a "rubberband" line connecting the "from point" and the crosshairs. The rubberband line moves as the crosshairs are moved. It provides a clue to where the new line will be placed. The rubberband line remains attached to the crosshairs until you complete the LINE command. See Figure 6-20.

Figure 6-20. The rubberband line is visible when using a pointing device to input points for lines.

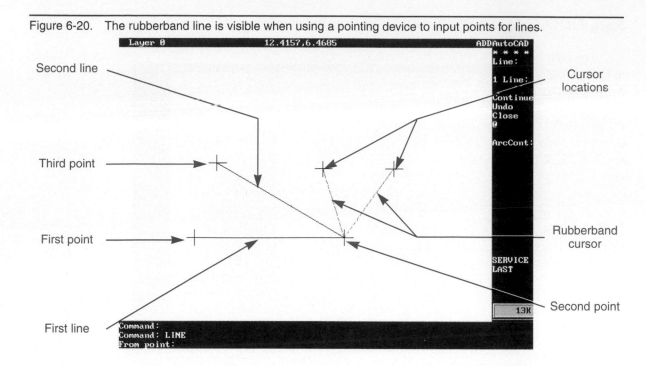

DRAWING MULTIPLE LINES

ARM 4

The MULTIPLE command modifier is a method used to automatically repeat commands issued at the keyboard. It is available if your computer supports the AutoCAD pull-down menus. This technique may be used to draw repetitive lines, polylines, circles, arcs, ellipses, or polygons. For example, if you plan to draw several sets of line segments, type the word MULTIPLE before LINE at the Command: prompt. AutoCAD automatically repeats the LINE command until you have finished drawing all of the desired lines. You must then cancel to get back to the Command: prompt. The MULTIPLE option is used as follows:

Command: **MULTIPLE LINE** ↵
From point: *(pick the first point)*
To point: *(pick the second point)*
To point: *(pick the third point or press* ENTER)
To point: ↵
LINE From point: *(pick the first point of the next line)*
To point: *(pick the second point of the next line)*
To point: *(pick the third point or press* ENTER)
To point: ↵
LINE From point: *(pick first point of third line)*
To point: *(pick the second point of third line)*
To point: ↵
LINE From point: *(press* CTRL+C) *Cancel*
Command:

AutoCAD automatically reissues the LINE command so you can draw another line or lines, or press CTRL C to cancel the repeating command.

THE COORDINATE DISPLAY

AUG 1

The coordinate display is found just to the right of center on the status line. The number of places to the right of the decimal point is determined by the units setting. When you begin a new drawing and before any point entry is made, the coordinate display shows the X and Y coordinates as 0.0000,0.0000. When point entries are made, the coordinate display changes to represent the location of the point relative to the origin. For example, if the first point picked is X = 4.2500, Y = 3.6250, the coordinate display reads 4.2500,3.6250. If the units are set at two places to the right of the decimal, then the reading is 4.25,3.63. Each time a new point is picked, the coordinates are updated. The coordinate display may be changed from recording the location of each point picked to a constant update as you move the cursor. By turning the coordinates on, the display then shows point location or the length and angle of a line being drawn. The coordinate display is turned on and off by pressing CTRL+D, F6, puck button 7, or pick Coordinate Display in the Options pull-down menu. With coordinates on, the coordinates constantly change as the crosshairs move. There are two modes. One shows absolute coordinates and the other provides polar coordinates. A typical absolute coordinate display gives X and Y coordinates like 6.2000,5.9000. A polar coordinate display shows the distance and angle from the last point, such as 3.4000⟨180.

EXERCISE 6-4

❑ Load AutoCAD, enter the drawing editor, and open PRODR1 from Exercise 4-4.
❑ Draw rectangles 3 in. (76 mm) wide by 2 in. (50 mm) high using each point entry method from the following list. Experiment with the coordinate display options as you draw the rectangles.
  ❑ Absolute coordinates.
  ❑ Relative coordinates.
  ❑ Polar coordinates.
  ❑ Using the screen cursor.
❑ Use the MULTIPLE LINE command to draw several different lines or shapes. Notice the advantage of remaining in the LINE command when several different line segments or shapes must be drawn.
❑ Save the drawing as A:EX6-4 and quit.

DRAWING AT RIGHT ANGLES USING
THE ORTHO COMMAND

AUG 3

The ORTHO command puts AutoCAD in the Ortho mode. Ortho allows lines drawn by the crosshairs movement to be only horizontal or vertical, in alignment with the current snap grid. The term *ortho* comes from "orthogonal" which means "at right angles." The Ortho mode has a special advantage when drawing rectangular shapes because all corners are guaranteed to be square. It is impossible to draw a line at an angle to the snap grid with a pointing device while Ortho is On. See Figure 6-21. Ortho may be turned On or Off by typing ORTHO at the Command: prompt, or while in another command by using function key F8, puck button 5, or CTRL+O.

Command: **ORTHO** ⏎
ON/OFF: (**ON** *or* **OFF** *as desired*) ⏎

Figure 6-21.   A—Angled lines cannot be drawn with Ortho mode on. B—With the Ortho mode off, angled lines can be drawn.

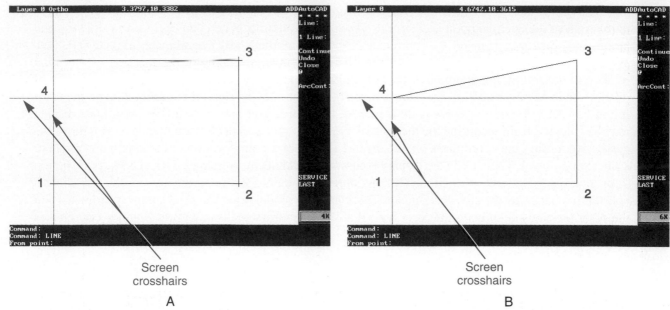

Screen
crosshairs

A

Screen
crosshairs

B

Remember, the Ortho mode is easy to turn on or off using function key F8, puck button 5, or pressing CTRL+O.

EXERCISE 6-5

❑ Load AutoCAD, enter the drawing editor, and open PRODR1 from Exercise 4-4.
❑ Draw an equilateral triangle (three equal sides and angles). Ortho must be off to do this.
❑ Draw a 3 in. (76 mm) by 2 in. (50 mm) rectangle using the screen cursor for point entry with Ortho off. Draw a second rectangle with Ortho on. Compare the difference.
❑ Save the drawing as A:EX6-5 and quit.

PROFESSIONAL TIP

 Practice using the different point entry techniques and decide which method works best for certain situations. Keep in mind that you may mix methods to help enhance your drawing speed. For example, absolute coordinates may work best to locate an initial point or to draw a simple shape. These calculations are easy. Polar coordinates may work better to locate features in a circular pattern, or at an angular relationship. Practice with Ortho and snap settings to see the advantages and disadvantages of each. Change the snap setting at any time to assist in drawing layout accuracy. Remember, the snap grid is a drawing aid, so set the snap increment to assist in drawing accuracy.

USING THE CLOSE POLYGON OPTION

ARM 5

A *polygon* is a closed plane figure with at least three sides. A triangle or rectangle are examples of polygons. When you are drawing a polygon, the last point may automatically be connected to the first point using the Close option. This option may be picked from the LINE screen menu or by typing CLOSE or C at the prompt line. In Figure 6-22, the last line is drawn using the Close option as follows:

Command: **LINE** ↵
From point: *(pick point 1)*
To point: *(pick point 2)*
To point: *(pick point 3)*
To point: *(pick point 4)*
To point: **C** ↵
Command:

Figure 6-22.   Using the Close option to complete a box.

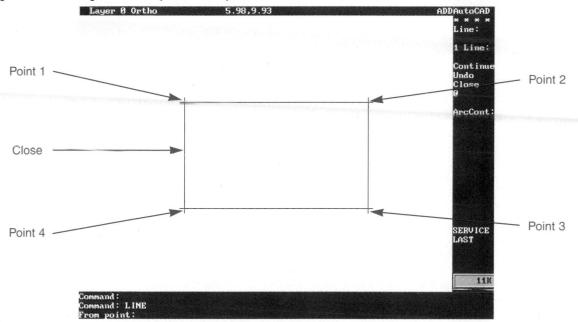

USING THE LINE CONTINUATION OPTION

AUG 2

Suppose you draw a line, then exit the LINE command, but decide to go back and connect a new line to the end of the previous one. Go to the LINE screen menu and pick "continue." This automatically connects the next line to the last endpoint of the previous one as shown in Figure 6-23. (The line continuation option may also be used to continue drawing arcs, as discussed in Chapter 8.) The command sequence for continuing a line looks like this:

First line:
    Command: **LINE** ↵
    From point: *(pick point 1)*
    To point: *(pick point 2)*
    To point: ↵

Next line:
    Command: *(pick "continue" from the LINE screen menu)*
    Command: _LINE
    From point: *(AutoCAD automatically picks the last endpoint of the previous line)*
    To point: *(pick point 3)*
    To point: ↵
    Command:

Figure 6-23.   Using the Continue option.

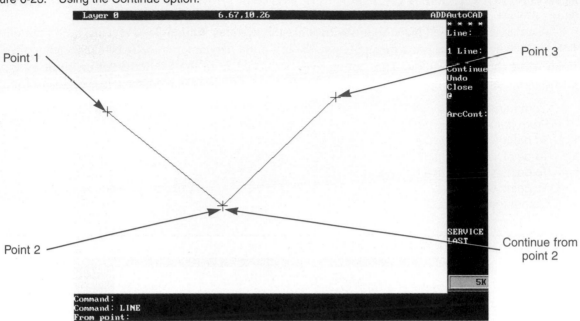

Point 1

Point 3

Point 2

Continue from
point 2

A quicker way to select the "continue" option is to press the space bar after entering the LINE command.

Command: **LINE** ↵
From point: *(press space bar; AutoCAD automatically picks the last endpoint of the previous line)*
To point: *(pick the next point)*
To point: ↵
Command:

UNDOING THE PREVIOUSLY DRAWN LINE

AUG 1

When drawing a series of lines, you may find that you made an error. To delete the mistake, type U at the prompt line and press ENTER. You can also pick "undo" from the LINE screen menu while still in the LINE command. Doing this erases the previously drawn line and allows you to continue from the previous endpoint. A series of U's followed by ENTERs may be typed to erase line segments as far back as needed. The endpoints of the removed lines remain as blips, for reference, until you enter the REDRAW or REGENERATE command, or change the drawing display area. See Figure 6-24.

Command: **LINE** ↵
From point: *(pick point 1)*
To point: *(pick point 2)*
To point: *(pick point 3)*
To point: *(pick point 4)*
To point: *(pick point 5)*
To point: **U** ↵
To point: **U** ↵
To point: *(pick revised point 4)*
To point: ↵
Command:

Figure 6-24.   Using the Undo option while in the LINE command. Notice that the original points 4 and 5 remain as blips until the screen is redrawn.

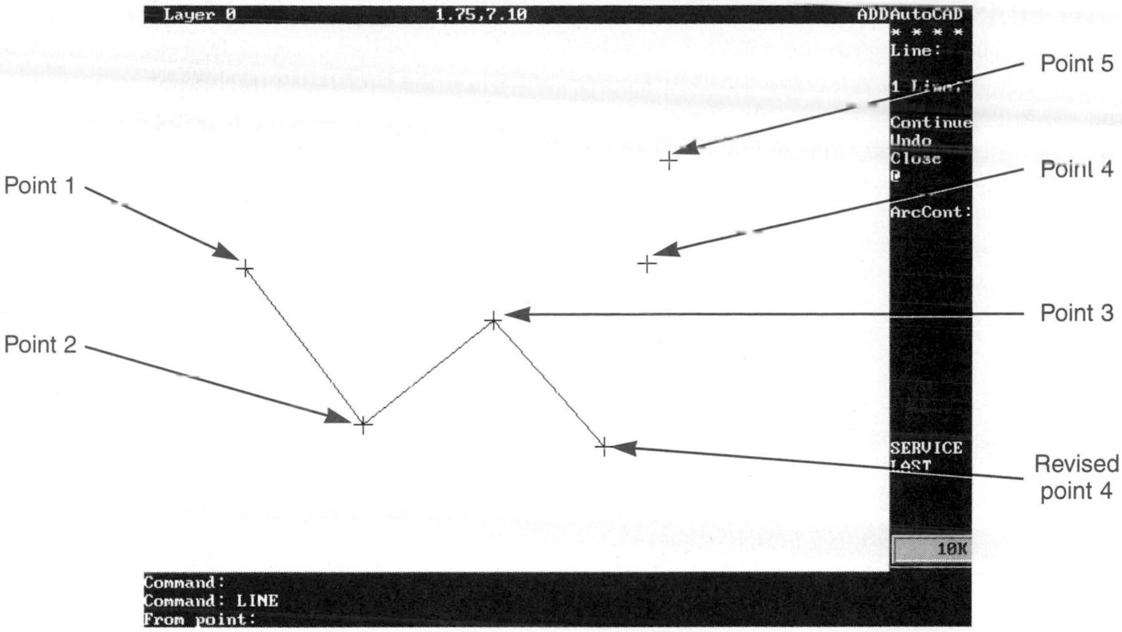

EXERCISE 6-6

❑ Load AutoCAD, enter the drawing editor, and open PRODR1, or begin a new drawing using your own variables.
❑ Experiment drawing lines using the following guidelines and options:
  ❑ Draw two polygons using the Close option.
  ❑ Draw two connected lines, end the LINE command, and then select "continue" to draw additional lines.
  ❑ Draw eight connected lines. Then use the "undo" option to remove the last four lines while remaining in the LINE command. Finally, draw four new connected lines.
❑ Save the drawing as A:EX6-6 and quit.

INTRODUCTION TO EDITING   AUG 5

The procedure used to correct mistakes or revise an existing drawing is referred to as *editing*. There are many editing functions that help increase productivity. This discussion introduces the basic editing operations ERASE and OOPS.

When you edit a drawing, you will be selecting items when you see this prompt:

Select objects:

The items that you select are called a *selection set*. You can select one or more objects using a variety of selection set options, including Window, Crossing, WPolygon, CPolygon, and Fence. When you become familiar with the selection options, you will find that they increase your flexibility and performance. The following discussion introduces several of the selection set methods used with the ERASE command. Keep in mind, however, that these techniques may be used with any of the editing commands where the Select objects: prompt appears.

USING THE ERASE COMMAND

The ERASE command acts the same as using an eraser in manual drafting to remove unwanted information. However, with the ERASE command you have a second chance. If you erase the wrong item, it can be brought back using the OOPS command. Enter the ERASE command by typing ERASE at the Command: prompt, selecting Erase: from the EDIT screen menu, or picking Erase from the Modify pull-down menu. The next screen menu you see after selecting Erase from the screen menu lists four choices: Erase:, Oops:, SERVICE, and LAST. Picking SERVICE from the screen menu accesses several options that may be used for erasing applications. These options include:

Last	Fence
Previous	Group
All	Add
Cpolygon	Remove
Wpolygon	Undo

When you enter the ERASE command, a prompt is given to select an object to be erased:

Command: **ERASE** ↵
Select objects: *(select an object)*
Select objects: ↵
Command:

When you see the Select objects: prompt, a small box replaces the screen crosshairs. This box is referred to as the *pick box*. Move the pick box over the item to be erased and pick it. For example, suppose you draw a square and want to erase it. You must erase one line at a time because each line of the square is a single "*entity or object*." Thus, using ERASE in this manner only erases single entities. The terms *entity* and *object* are interchangeable in AutoCAD. An entity or object is a predefined element that you place in a drawing by means of a single command. For example, a line, circle, arc, or single line of text is an entity or object.

When you pick a line to erase, the line is highlighted to acknowledge that you have chosen that entity. When this happens, the Select objects: prompt returns and you can select another entity to erase, Figure 6-25. Press ENTER to complete the ERASE command and return to the Command: prompt. You can get back into the ERASE command immediately by pressing the space bar or ENTER key. This procedure, as shown in the following sequence, is an easy way to re-execute any AutoCAD command:

Command: **ERASE** ↵
Select objects: *(select an object)*
Select objects: ↵
Command: *(press* ENTER *or space bar)*
ERASE
Select objects: *(select another object to erase)*
Select objects: ↵
Command:

Figure 6-25.   Using the ERASE command to erase a single entity.

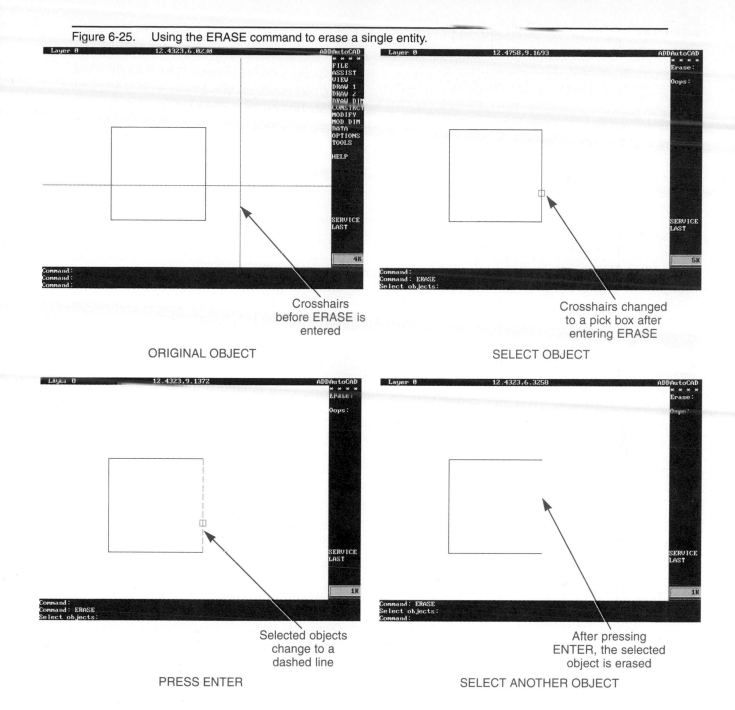

Crosshairs
before ERASE is
entered

ORIGINAL OBJECT

Crosshairs changed
to a pick box after
entering ERASE

SELECT OBJECT

Selected objects
change to a
dashed line

PRESS ENTER

After pressing
ENTER, the selected
object is erased

SELECT ANOTHER OBJECT

Making a single selection automatically

Normally, AutoCAD lets you pick as many items as you want for a selection set, and selected items are highlighted to let you know what has been picked. You also have the option of selecting an item or items and have them automatically edited without first being highlighted. To do this, enter SI for SIngle at the Select objects: prompt. The command sequence is as follows:

Command: **ERASE** ↵
Select objects: **SI** ↵
Select objects: *(pick an individual item, or use one of the Window or Crossing options to
pick several items)*

Note that the Select objects: prompt did not return after the items were picked. You can pick a group of entities using any of the Window or Crossing selection options. The entire group is automatically erased when you press ENTER or pick the second corner of a window or crossing box.

Using the Last selection option

The ERASE command's Last option is a handy option that saves time if you need to erase the last entity drawn. For example, suppose you draw a box using the LINE command. The ERASE command's Last option erases the last line drawn. The Last option erases entities in the reverse order in which they were drawn. The Last option may be selected by first picking SERVICE from the screen menu and then pick Last, or by typing L at the prompt line as follows:

```
Command: ERASE ↵
Select objects: L ↵
1 found
Select objects: ↵
Command: (press space bar or ENTER)
Select objects: L ↵
1 found
Select objects: ↵
Command:
```

Keep in mind that using the Last option highlights the last item drawn. You must press ENTER for the object to be erased.

EXERCISE 6-7

❑ Load AutoCAD, enter the drawing editor, and open PRODR1, or begin a new drawing using your own variables.
❑ Use the LINE command to draw a square similar to the "ORIGINAL OBJECT" in Figure 6-25.
❑ Type ERASE at the Command: prompt and erase two of the lines.
❑ Observe the difference between erasing the first two and the last two lines.
❑ Draw another square, similar to the previous one.
❑ Type ERASE at the Command: prompt and enter L at the Select objects: prompt.
❑ Pick Last from the SERVICE screen menu twice to erase the last two lines.
❑ Observe the difference between erasing the first two and the last two lines.
❑ Type QUIT and exit the drawing editor without saving.

The Window selection option

The Window or W option can be used with several commands. This option allows you to draw a box or "window" around an object or group of objects. Everything *entirely within* the window can be erased at the same time. If portions of entities project outside the window, they are not erased. Use the automatic Window selection process, as follows:

1. Enter the ERASE command.
2. Pick a point outside and to the upper- or lower-left of the object to be erased. This is shown as the first window point in Figure 6-26.
3. Move the pointing device so the window completely encloses the object. Pick the second window point shown in Figure 6-26.

The command sequence looks like this:

```
Command: ERASE ↵
Select objects: (pick a point outside and to the upper- or lower-left of the object)
Other corner: (move the cursor so the window completely encloses the object and pick)
Select objects: ↵
Command:
```

Figure 6-26.   Using the ERASE Window option.

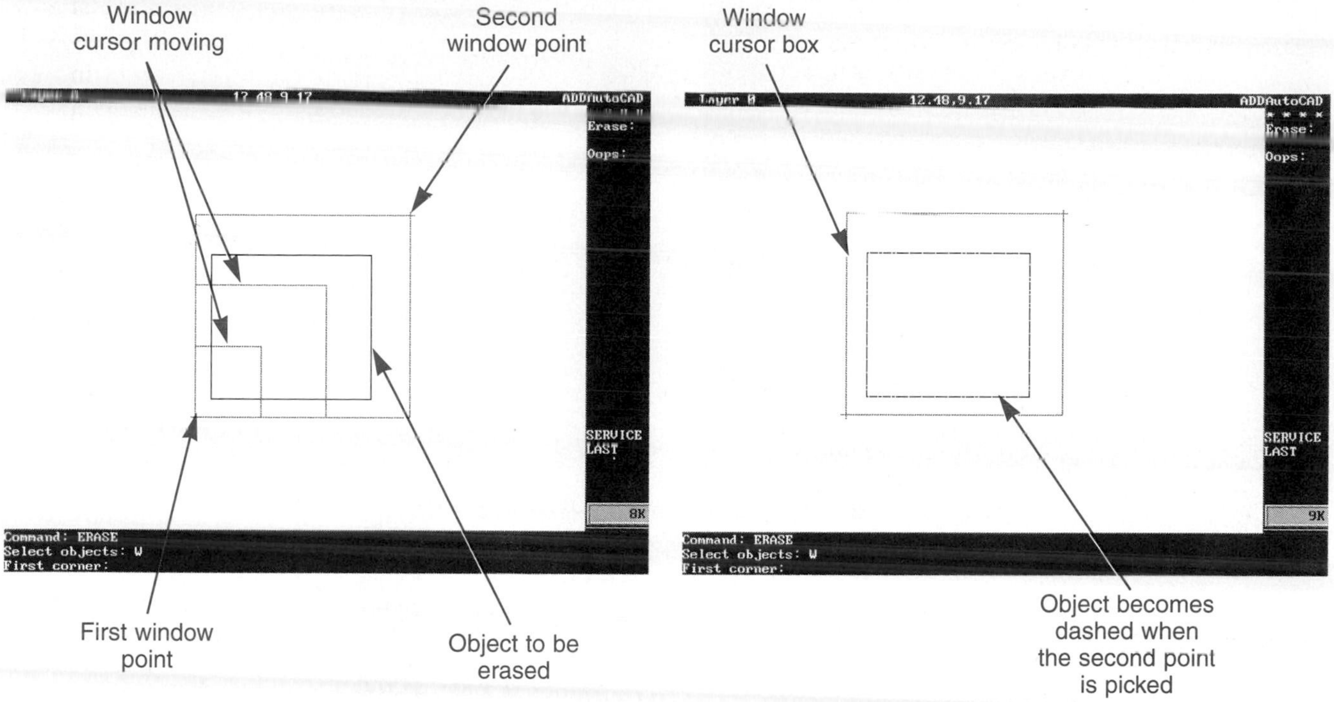

Window
cursor moving

Second
window point

Window
cursor box

First window
point

Object to be
erased

Object becomes
dashed when
the second point
is picked

The Crossing selection option

Another selection option called "Crossing," is similar to the Window option. Entities *entirely within and those crossing* the box are selected. Pick a location to the right of the object(s) to be erased. This automatically activates the first corner of the crossing box. Then move the pointing device to the left. This forms a box around the object(s) to be erased. The crossing box outline is dashed to distinguish it from the solid outline of the window box. The command sequence for the Crossing selection is:

Command: **ERASE** ↵
Select objects: *(pick a point outside and to the upper- or lower-right side of the object)*
Other corner: *(move the crossing box to enclose or cross the object(s) and pick)*
Select objects: ↵
Command:

Remember, the crossing box does not have to enclose the entire object to erase it. The window box does. The crossing box must only "cross" part of the object to be erased or edited. Figure 6-27 shows how to erase three of four lines of a rectangle using the Crossing option.

PROFESSIONAL TIP

 Remember, you can pick any left point outside the object and then move the cursor to the right for a Window selection; the window is a solid image. Pick any right point outside the object and move the cursor to the left for a Crossing selection; the crossing box is a dashed image.

Figure 6-27.   Using the Crossing box to erase objects.

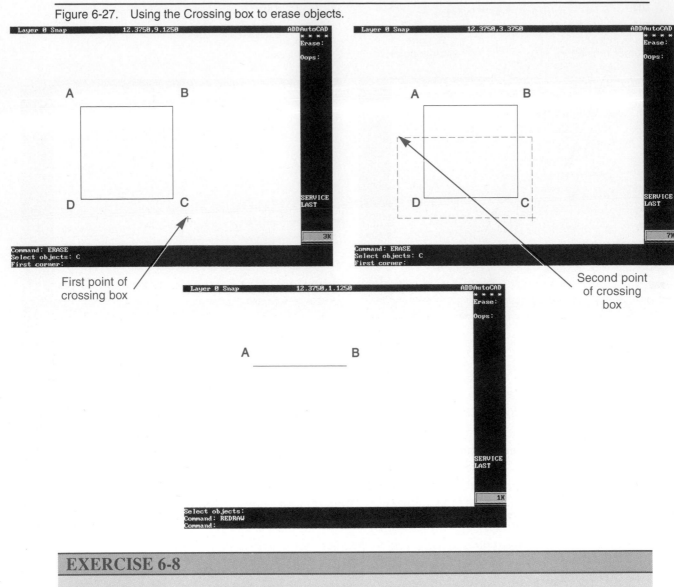

First point of
crossing box

Second point
of crossing
box

EXERCISE 6-8

❑ Load AutoCAD, enter the drawing editor, and open PRODR1, or begin a new drawing using your own variables.
❑ Use the LINE command to draw a square similar to the "ORIGINAL OBJECT" shown in Figure 6-25.
❑ Type ERASE at the Command: prompt and use the Window selection option. Place the window around the entire square to erase it.
❑ Draw another square.
❑ Now, erase three of the four lines by using the Crossing selection.
❑ Type QUIT and exit the drawing editor without saving.

Using the WPolygon selection option   AUG 5

The Window selection option requires that you place a rectangle completely around the entities to be erased. Sometimes it is awkward to place a rectangle around the items to erase. When this situation occurs, you can place a polygon (closed figure with three or more sides) of your own design around the objects. To use the WPolygon options, enter WP at the Select objects: prompt, or pick WPolygon from the SERVICE screen menu, and proceed to draw a polygon. As you pick corners, the polygon drags into place. The command sequence for erasing the four squares in the middle of Figure 6-28 is as follows:

Command: **ERASE** ↵
Select objects: **WP** ↵
First polygon point: *(pick point 1)*
Undo/⟨Endpoint of line⟩: *(pick point 2)*
Undo/⟨Endpoint of line⟩: *(pick point 3)*
Undo/⟨Endpoint of line⟩: *(pick point 4)*
Undo/⟨Endpoint of line⟩: ↵
Select objects: ↵
Command:

Figure 6-28.   Using the WPolygon selection option to erase objects.

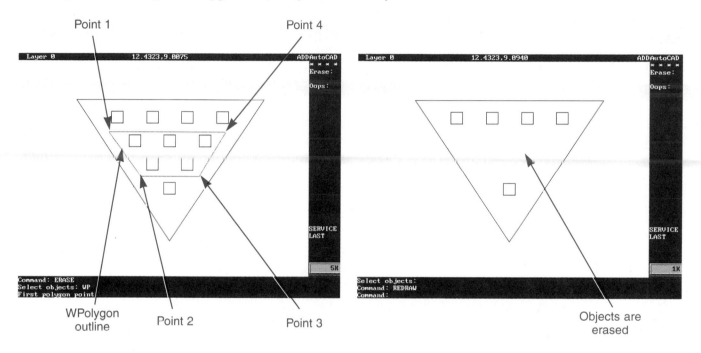

Use the Undo option by entering U at the Undo/⟨Endpoint of line⟩: prompt if you do not like the last polygon point you picked.

EXERCISE 6-9

❏ Load AutoCAD and open PRODR1, or start a new drawing using your own variables.
❏ Draw an object similar to the one shown in Figure 6-28.
❏ Use the WPolygon selection option to erase the same items as shown in the figure.
❏ Save the drawing as A:EX6-9 and quit the drawing session.

Using the CPolygon selection option   AUG 5

The Crossing selection option lets you place a rectangle around or through the objects to be erased. Sometimes it is difficult to place a rectangle around or through the items to be erased without coming into contact with other entities. When you want to use the features of the Crossing selection option, but prefer to use a polygon instead of a rectangle, enter CP at the Select objects: prompt, or pick CPolygon from the SERVICE screen menu. Then, proceed to erase everything enclosed within or crossed by the polygon. As you pick the points, the polygon drags into place. Note that the CPolygon is a dashed rubberband cursor, while the WPolygon is a solid rubberband cursor.

Suppose you want to erase everything inside the large triangle in Figure 6-29A except for the top and bottom horizontal lines. The command sequence to erase these lines is as follows:

Command: **ERASE** ↵
Select object: **CP** ↵
First polygon point: *(pick point 1)*
Undo/⟨Endpoint of line⟩: *(pick point 2)*
Undo/⟨Endpoint of line⟩: *(pick point 3)*
Undo/⟨Endpoint of line⟩: *(pick point 4)*
Undo/⟨Endpoint of line⟩: ↵
Select objects:
Command:

Figure 6-29.   Using the CPolygon selection option. Everything enclosed within or crossing the polygon is selected.

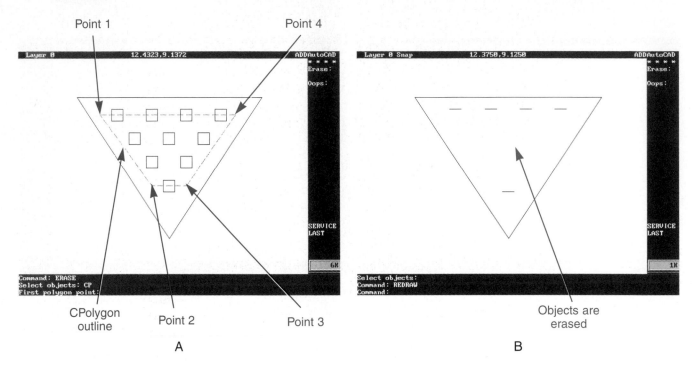

If you want to change the last CPolygon point you picked, enter U at the Undo/⟨Endpoint of line⟩: prompt.

EXERCISE 6-10

❑ Load AutoCAD and open PRODR1, or start a new drawing using your own variables.
❑ Draw an object similar to the one shown in Figure 6-29A.
❑ Use the CPolygon selection option to erase the same items as shown in the figure.
❑ Save the drawing as A:EX6-10 and quit.

Using the Fence selection option   ARM 2

Fence is another selection option used to select several objects at the same time when performing editing functions. When using the Fence option, you simply need to place a fence through the objects you want to select. Anything that the fence passes through is included in the selection set. The fence

stagger:

can be straight or it can stagger to pass through items as shown in Figure 6-30. Select Fence in the SERVICE screen menu, or enter F at the Select objects: prompt as follows:

Command: **ERASE** ↵
Select objects: **F** ↵
First fence point: *(pick the starting point of the first fence)*
Undo/⟨Endpoint of line⟩: *(pick point 2)*
Undo/⟨Endpoint of line⟩: ↵
6 found
Select objects: **F** ↵
First fence point: *(pick point 3)*
Undo/⟨Endpoint of line⟩: *(pick point 4)*
Undo/⟨Endpoint of line⟩: *(pick point 5)*
Undo/⟨Endpoint of line⟩: *(pick point 6)*
Undo/⟨Endpoint of line⟩: *(pick point 7)*
Undo/⟨Endpoint of line⟩: *(pick point 8)*
Undo/⟨Endpoint of line⟩: ↵
6 found
Select objects: ↵
Command:

Figure 6-30.   Using the Fence selection option to erase entities. Notice that the fence can be either straight or staggered.

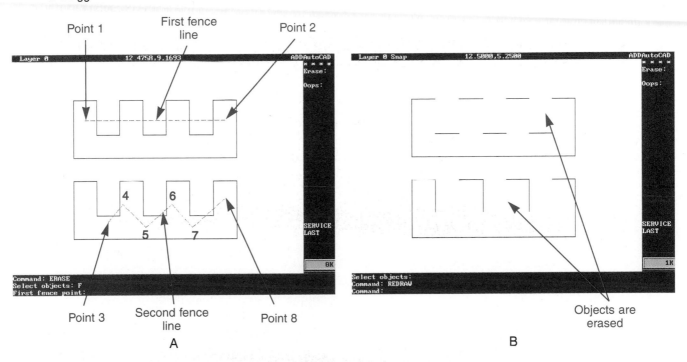

EXERCISE 6-11

❑ Load AutoCAD and open PRODR1, or start a new drawing using your own variables.
❑ Draw an object similar to the one shown in Figure 6-30A.
❑ Use the Fence selection option to erase the items shown in the figure.
❑ Use the REDRAW command to clean up the drawing.
❑ Save the drawing as A:EX6-11 and quit.

Removing and adding entities to the selection set

When editing a drawing, a common mistake is to accidentally select an entity that you did not want, or not to select an entity that you want included. Do not worry; you can remove or add the entity to the selection set anytime you are at the Select objects: prompt. For example, suppose you are using the ERASE command and you selected several items to be erased. Then you decide that two of the items should not be erased. When this happens, pick Remove from the SERVICE screen menu, or enter R for Remove like this:

> Command: **ERASE** ⏎
> Select objects: *(pick several items using any of the selection techniques)*
> Select objects: **R** ⏎
> Remove objects: *(pick the items you want removed from the selection set)*

Now if you decide that you want to add more items to the selection set, pick Add from the SERVICE screen menu, or enter A for Add and pick the additional objects to be erased:

> Remove objects: **A** ⏎
> Select objects: *(pick additional items to be erased)*
> Select objects: ⏎
> Command:

Selecting all entities on a drawing

Sometimes you may want to select every item on the drawing to erase or use with other editing functions. To do this, pick All in the SERVICE screen menu, or enter ALL at the Select objects: prompt as follows:

> Command: **ERASE** ⏎
> Select objects: **ALL** ⏎
> Select objects: ⏎
> Command:

This procedure erases everything on the drawing, but you can use the Remove option at the Select objects: prompt and enter ALL again to remove everything from the selection set before you leave the command. If you do not leave the command, you can immediately get everything back by picking Undo in the SERVICE screen menu, or enter U for Undo at the Command: prompt.

EXERCISE 6-12

❑ Load AutoCAD and open PRODR1, or start a new drawing using your own variables.
❑ Draw an object similar to the one shown in Figure 6-30A.
❑ Use the Fence option to erase lines similar to those erased in Figure 6-30B.
❑ Experiment using the Remove and Add selection options by selecting six items to erase, remove two of the items from the selection set, and then add three different entities to the selection set.
❑ Use the ALL selection option to erase everything from the drawing.
❑ Enter U at the Command: prompt to get everything back that you erased.
❑ Save the drawing as A:EX6-12 and quit.

Using the Box selection option

Another way to begin the window or crossing selection option is to type BOX at the Select objects: prompt. You are then prompted to pick the left corner of a window or right corner of a crossing box, depending on your needs. The command sequence is as follows:

> Command: **ERASE** ⏎
> Select objects: **BOX** ⏎
> First corner: *(pick the left corner of the window box or the right corner of the crossing box)*
> Select objects: ⏎
> Command:

Using the Multiple selection option

The MULTIPLE option of the select mode provides easy access to stacked objects. *Stacked objects* are when one feature such as a line overlays another in a 2-D drawing. These lines have the same Z values, so one is no higher or lower than the other. Although, the last one drawn appears to be on top. When a point on an object is picked in select mode, the data base is scanned and the first object found to pass through the pick box area, at the point picked, is the object selected. Additional picks will only duplicate the original results. This means that unless a window, crossing, fence, or multiple is used, the underlying objects are inaccessible. Using the MULTIPLE option allows multiple picks at the same point to find more than one entity. The first pick finds the first object. A second pick in the same place ignores the already selected object and finds the next object. This process continues for each pick made in multiple mode. The command sequence used to erase two stacked lines with the multiple mode is as follows:

but it is still kept selected

Command: **ERASE** ↵
Select objects: **M** ↵
Select objects: *(pick the stacked objects twice)*
 2 selected, 2 found
Select objects: ↵
Command:

PROFESSIONAL TIP

When objects are selected using the Multiple option, the selected objects are not high-lighted until the ENTER key is pressed. This can speed up the selection process for text and other complex objects on workstations with slower display systems. Often times you may want to modify an object underlying another, without affecting the "top" object. To do this, enter the multiple mode as previously discussed. Pick a point on the object twice and press ENTER to end the multiple mode and find both objects are selected. Now, use the REMOVE option and select the same point again. The "top" object is now removed from the selection set. The Command sequence is as follows:

Command: **ERASE** ↵
Select objects: **M** ↵
Select objects: *(pick the object twice)*
 1 selected, 2 found
Select objects: **R** ↵
Select objects: *(pick the point again)*
 1 selected, 1 found
Remove objects: ↵
Command:

NOTE   When selecting objects to be erased, AutoCAD only accepts qualifying objects. A *qualifying object* refers to an object that is not on a locked layer and that passes through the pickbox area at the point selected. Layers are discussed in Chapter 19 of this text.

Cycling through stacked objects

Another way to deal with stacked objects is to let AutoCAD cycle through the objects. *Cycling* means that you can go through a series of stacked objects until the desired object is highlighted. This works best when several objects cross at the same place or are very close together. See Figure 6-31. To do this, hold down the CTRL key and pick the object as you normally pick a single object. With objects as in Figure 6-31, pick where the four circles intersect. If there are two or more objects that are found crossing through the pickbox area, the top object is highlighted.

Now you can release the CTRL key. When you pick again, the top object returns and the next one is highlighted. Every time you pick in the same place another object becomes highlighted, until you have cycled through all of the objects. When you have the desired object highlighted, press ENTER to end the cycling process and return to the Command: prompt. The following command sequence is used to erase one of the circles in Figure 6-31, but you can use this for any editing function:

Command: **ERASE** ⏎
Select objects: *(hold down the* CTRL *key and pick)* ⟨Cycle on⟩
 (pick until you have highlighted the desired object and press ENTER*)*
⟨Cycle off⟩1 found
Select objects: *(select additional objects or press* ENTER*)*
Command:

Figure 6-31. Cycling through a series of stacked circles until the desired object is highlighted.

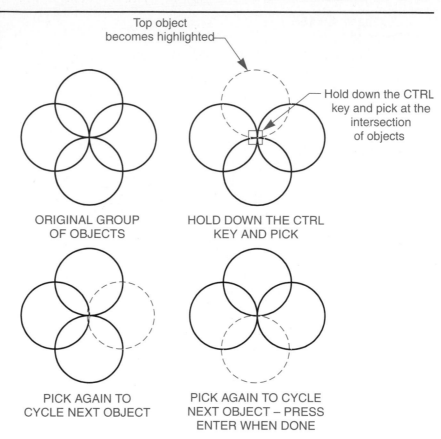

Top object becomes highlighted

Hold down the CTRL key and pick at the intersection of objects

ORIGINAL GROUP OF OBJECTS

HOLD DOWN THE CTRL KEY AND PICK

PICK AGAIN TO CYCLE NEXT OBJECT

PICK AGAIN TO CYCLE NEXT OBJECT – PRESS ENTER WHEN DONE

OOPS, I MADE A MISTAKE

AUG 5

The OOPS command is handy to bring back the last object you erased. If you erased several objects in the same command sequence, all are brought back to the screen. The OOPS command must be given *immediately* after making the error and prior to issuing another command. OOPS can only be used with the ERASE command. If you erased entities within a window, they could be brought back as follows:

Command: **ERASE** ⏎
Select objects: **W** ⏎
First corner: *(select a point)*
Other corner: *(select a point)*
Select objects: ⏎
Command: **OOPS** ⏎

CLEANING UP THE SCREEN

When you draw or erase a number of objects on a drawing, the screen is cluttered with small crosses or markers called *blips*. In addition, many of the grid dots may be removed. There is no problem caused by this, but it can be distracting. It is easy to clean up the screen, and restore the drawing by choosing the REDRAW command. The REDRAW command cleans the screen in the current viewport. (Viewports and the REDRAWALL command are discussed in detail in Chapter 12.) The REDRAW command can be typed at the keyboard, or selected from the VIEW screen menu, or pick Redraw View in the View pull-down menu.

Command: **REDRAW** ↵

The screen goes blank for an instant, and the cleaned drawing and screen return.

DISABLING THE AUTOMATIC WINDOWING

The PICKAUTO system variable controls automatic windowing when the Select object prompt appears. The PICKAUTO settings are ON=1, which is the default, and OFF=0. You can change the PICKAUTO setting like this:

Command: **PICKAUTO** ↵
New value for PICKAUTO ⟨1⟩: **0** ↵

With PICKAUTO set at 0 you are forced to enter W for window or C for crossing at the Select objects: prompt.

You can use the automatic Window or Crossing selection options if PICKAUTO is 0 (off). To do this, enter AU for AUto at the Select objects: prompt, and then proceed as previously discussed. The command sequence looks like this:

Command: **ERASE** ↵
Select objects: **AU** ↵
Select objects: *(pick a point outside and to the upper- or lower-left side of the object for a window, or pick a point outside and to the upper- or lower-right side of the object for a crossing box)*
Other corner: *(move the cursor so the window entirely encloses the object, or move the cursor to enclose or cross the object for a crossing box)*
Select object: ↵
Command:

Exercise 6-13

❏ Load AutoCAD and open PRODR1, or start a new drawing using your own variables.
❏ Use the LINE command to draw a rectangle that fills much of the screen, and then draw another rectangle directly over the first. Use snap and grid to help you.
❏ Use the Multiple option to select and erase both lines on the left side of the rectangle.
❏ Use the Multiple and Remove options to erase only the underlying line on the right side of the rectangle.
❏ Use the Box option to erase the top and bottom lines of the rectangle with the crossing box.
❏ Type OOPS at the Command: prompt to bring back the lines that were previously erased.
❏ Use the REDRAW command to clean up the screen.
❏ Save the drawing as A:EX6-13 and quit.

INTRODUCTION TO LINETYPE   AUG 6

Earlier in this chapter you were introduced to line standards. AutoCAD has standard linetypes supplied with the program that may be used at any time. Standard AutoCAD linetypes are a single thickness. In order to achieve different line thicknesses, it is necessary to use the PLINE or TRACE commands introduced in Chapter 7. Line thickness may also be varied using different plotter pen tip widths. Draw different width lines on separate layers. Then plot with the appropriate width of pen or line thickness settings when plotting. This is further discussed in this chapter and Chapter 12.

AutoCAD linetypes   AUG 6

AutoCAD has a standard library of linetypes as shown in Figure 6-32. The AutoCAD standard linetype library does not show a solid object line. AutoCAD refers to this line as CONTINUOUS. The LINETYPE command allows you to change the current linetype. Individual lines or entities may be drawn with a specified linetype at any time. (Linetypes may also be set by layers. This is discussed in Chapter 19.) The LINETYPE command is typed at the Command: prompt. If you want to look at the AutoCAD linetypes, enter ? as follows:

    Command: **LINETYPE** ⏎
    ?/Create/Load/Set: **?** ⏎

Figure 6-32. Standard AutoCAD linetype library.

Border	
Border2	
BorderX2	
Center	
Center2	
CenterX2	
Dashdot	
Dashdot2	
DashdotX2	
Dashed	
Dashed2	
DashedX2	
Divide	
Divide2	
DivideX2	
Dot	
Dot2	
DotX2	
Hidden	
Hidden2	
HiddenX2	
Phantom	
Phantom2	
PhantomX2	

This displays the "Select Linetype File" dialog box shown in Figure 6-33. Notice ACAD is highlighted in the Files list and at the File edit box. Press ENTER or pick OK. An alphanumeric screen is displayed with the linetypes shown in Figure 6-32. Look at the linetypes and press function key F1 to return to the drawing editor. Also found in the "Select Linetype File" dialog box is LTYPESHP. Pick this to see standard linetypes symbols for maps.

Figure 6-33.   The "Select Linetype File" dialog box.

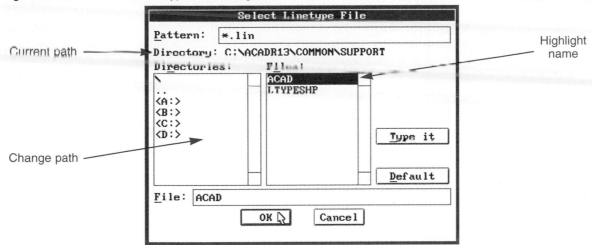

When you want to change the linetype for the next line or series of lines, use the Set option in the LINETYPE command as follows:

Command: **LINETYPE** ↵
?/Create/Load/Set: **S** ↵
New entity linetype (or ?) ⟨*current*⟩:

The current linetype is shown in brackets. The default is the solid linetype named "continuous." If you have just started using the drawing editor and have not changed the linetype, "BYLAYER" is shown in brackets. If you want to see a sample of the current linetype, type a ?. The sequence then looks like this:

New entity linetype (or ?) ⟨CONTINUOUS⟩: **?** ↵
Linetype(s) to list ⟨*⟩: ↵

If you want to set a new linetype, such as "dashed," for drawing the next entity or series of entities, type the linetype name:

New entity linetype (or ?) ⟨CONTINUOUS⟩: **DASHED** ↵
?/Create/Load/Set: ↵
Command:

The next lines are drawn as a dashed linetype until the linetype is set again.

LINETYPE can also be used as *transparent command*. This means it can be used while you are working inside another command. When the transparent command is completed, the command you were using returns. Use the transparent command by entering an apostrophe (') before the command name, for example 'LINETYPE.

The Create and Load options of the ?/Create/Load/Set: prompt are discussed in Chapter 19 along with accessing the Ddltype command in the screen and pull-down menus.

EXERCISE 6-14

❏ Load AutoCAD, enter the drawing editor, and open PRODR1, or begin a new drawing using your own variables.
❏ Use the LINETYPE command to do the following:
  ❏ Look at the standard AutoCAD linetypes.
  ❏ Draw objects of your own choosing using at least six of the standard AutoCAD linetypes.
❏ Save the drawing as A:EX6-14 and quit.

ADDING COLOR TO THE DRAWING

You may change the color of any part of the drawing. Whether you are drawing using a single layer or multiple layers, the color may be changed by typing COLOR at the Command: prompt, and entering the color name or number at the next prompt. The seven standard colors are:

- 1–Red
- 5–Blue
- 2–Yellow
- 6–Magenta
- 3–Green
- 7–White
- 4–Cyan

After entering COLOR, you are asked for the new color. Type either the color number or name as follows:

Command: **COLOR** ↵
New object color ⟨*current*⟩: *(type the desired color number or name,* **5** *or* **BLUE***, for example)* ↵

COLOR is a transparent command. Enter 'COLOR to change entity color while inside another command. Additional information on color is found in Chapter 19.

EXERCISE 6-15

❑ Load AutoCAD and open PRODR1, or begin a new drawing using your own variables.
❑ Change the color to yellow. Use the LINE command to draw a 2 unit by 4 unit rectangle.
❑ Change the color to blue. Use the LINE command to draw a rectangle 2 units by 4 units.
❑ Save the drawing as A:EX6-15 and quit.

INTRODUCTION TO PRINTING AND PLOTTING

There are two types of drawing in CAD: hard copy and soft copy. A *hard copy* is the paper drawing produced by a printer or plotter. It is called hard copy because it has substance and can be held and felt. A *soft copy* is a screen display. It is called soft because it has no substance. If the power to the screen is turned off, then the soft copy drawing is gone.

AutoCAD supports two types of hard copy devices, which are printers and plotters. Printers and plotters take the soft copy images that you draw in AutoCAD and transfer them on paper to make the hard copy.

There are several types of printers including dot matrix, ink-jet, laser, and thermal transfer. Dot matrix printers are normally used to make low-quality check prints. The other printers produce higher quality prints and are used to make quick check prints of formal drawings. Print size for most of these printers is 8.5 x 11 in. or 8.5 x 14 in.

Large format hard copy devices are commonly referred to as plotters. Plotters include ink-jet, thermal electrostatic, electrophotographic, pen, and pencil types. These plotters are capable of producing hard copies with varying line widths and with color output. These specific features of a plotter should be verified. Pen plotters have been the industry standard for preparing large format hard copies. They are called pen plotters because they use liquid ink, fiber tip pens, or pens with pencil lead to reproduce computer drawings. Multi-pen plotters can provide different line thicknesses and colors. During plotting, the pens move quite fast, but it still can take some time to plot a large and complex drawing.

Because plotting with pen plotters can be time consuming, they are rapidly being replaced in industry by laser plotters, thermal transfer, and ink-jet. Laser plotters draw lines on a revolving plate that is charged with high voltage. The laser light causes the plate to discharge while an ink toner adheres to the laser-drawn image. The ink is then bonded to the paper by pressure or heat. The quality of the laser printer depends mostly on the number of dots per inch (dpi). Laser printers are commonly 300 to 600 dpi. Thermal transfer printers use tiny heat elements to burn dots into treated paper. The electrostatic process uses a line of closely spaced electrically charged wire nibs to produce dots on coated paper. The ink-jet sprays droplets of ink on the paper to produce dot-matrix images.

PROFESSIONAL TIP

The stereo lithography process involves using a movable table immersed in a bath of liquid polymer. A laser beam is used to plot one very thin slice of a 3-D CAD model on the table top, which has the effect of hardening the polymer wherever the beam passes. Then the table moves down slightly and the process continues until the entire object has been plotted into an accurate 3-D model. Thus, an engineer can hold a prototype of the design in just minutes after completing the design. While AutoCAD does not yet talk directly to stereo lithography machines, it does output Stereo Lithography file formats (.STL).

This chapter gives you an introduction to making prints and plots, while Chapter 12 explores the detailed aspects of printing and plotting. Prints and plots are made using the PLOT command, which can be typed at the Command: prompt, accessed by picking Print... in the File pull-down menu, or accessed by picking Print: in the FILE screen menu. Doing one of these things displays the "Plot Configuration" dialog box shown in Figure 6-34. Some of the features in the "Plot Configuration" dialog box are discussed in more detail in Chapter 12 of this text.

Figure 6-34.   The "Plot Configuration" dialog box.

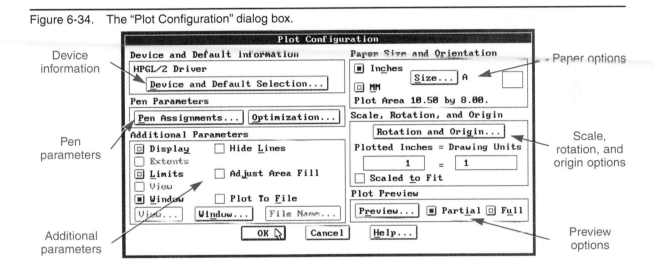

Device and default selection

As you look at the "Plot Configuration" dialog box, notice the Device and Default Information area in the upper-left corner. This is where AutoCAD displays information about the current configured printers and plotters. For now, the assumption is made that your instructor or CAD systems manager has taken care of the device and default selection.

Pen parameters

The "Plot Configuration" dialog box allows you to set pen parameters based on your drawing standards, such as line thickness or text style. You should be able to make a print at this time without changing any pen parameters. This should be set by your instructor or CAD systems manager. Making changes to the pen parameter settings is covered in Chapter 12 of this text.

Additional parameters

Look at the Additional Parameters area in the "Plot Configuration" dialog box, and you can see the options for the part of the drawing to be plotted, and how it is plotted. These are Display, Extents,

Limits, Views, and Window, and are shown with radio buttons. Therefore, they are either On or Off. the following describes the function of each option:
  • **Display.** This request prints or plots the current screen display.
  • **Extents.** The Extents option prints or plots only that area of the drawing in which objects are drawn. Before using this option, zoom the extents to include all recently edited objects to check exactly what will be plotted. The Zoom command is discussed in Chapter 9.

NOTE   Border lines around your drawing may be clipped off if they are at the extreme edges of the screen. This often happens because you are requesting the plotter to plot at the extreme edge of its active area.

  • **Limits.** This option plots everything inside your drawing limits.
  • **Views.** This option plots views saved with the VIEW command. AutoCAD prompts you for the name. The view you enter does not have to be displayed on the screen. The View radio button is inactive unless a view has been previously saved using the View command discussed in Chapter 10 of this text.
  • **Window.** This option allows you to pick two opposite corners of a window around the portion of the drawing to be plotted. These can be chosen with the pointing device or entered as coordinates at the keyboard. If the window is defined close to an object, some lines may be clipped off in your plot. If this happens, adjust the window the next time you plot. The Window radio button is inactive unless you pick the Window… button.

     Picking the Window… button displays the "Window Selection" subdialog box shown in Figure 6-35. Enter the first corner and second corner Coordinates of the desired window in the X: and Y: edit boxes. Pick the OK button to accept the coordinates. The Window radio button is then active. You can also use the Pick ⟨ button in the "Window Selection" subdialog box. This clears the dialog boxes and displays the screen. The prompt asks you to pick the window corners that surround the part of the drawing you want printed or plotted:

     Command:_plot
     First corner: *(pick the first window corner)*
     First corner: *(pick the second window corner)*

The "Plot Configuration" dialog box reappears after you pick OK in the "Window Selection" subdialog box.

Figure 6-35.   Specify a plot window using the "Window Selection" dialog box.

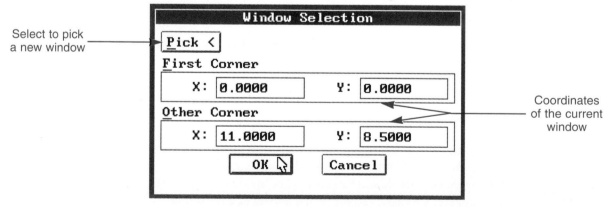

The Hide Lines check box is picked if you want to plot a 3-D drawing with hidden lines removed. Note that plotting takes a little longer when removing hidden lines since AutoCAD must calculate the lines to be removed. The Adjust Area Fill check box is activated if you want areas such as polylines and solids filled completely. If you want to send the plot to a file, pick the Plot to File check box. This activates the File Name… button. Pick this button to get the "Create Plot File" subdialog box.

Paper size and orientation

The upper-right area of the "Plot Configuration" dialog box shown in Figure 6-34 controls the paper size and orientation. Pick either the Inches or the MM radio button to make inches or millimeters the units for all plot specifications. Pick the Size... button to access the "Paper Size" subdialog box. This should be set by your instructor or CAD systems manager. You can make your own settings after studying Chapter 12 of this text. Also indicated is the orientation, either landscape or portrait. The paper orientation icon is a rectangle on the right side of the "Paper Size" subdialog box, and is shown in Figure 6-36. Figure 6-36A shows the icon in the landscape position, while Figure 6-36B displays the portrait orientation. The term *landscape* position comes from the idea that landscape artwork is normally placed horizontally, while *portrait* artwork is usually prepared vertically. This icon changes depending on the natural orientation of the paper in the current plotting device.

Figure 6-36.   A–The landscape sheet size icon. B–The portrait sheet size icon.

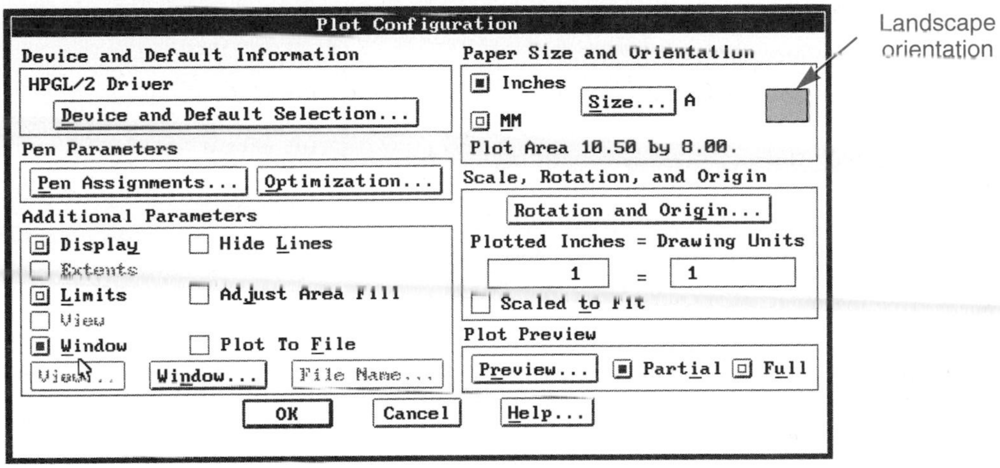

A

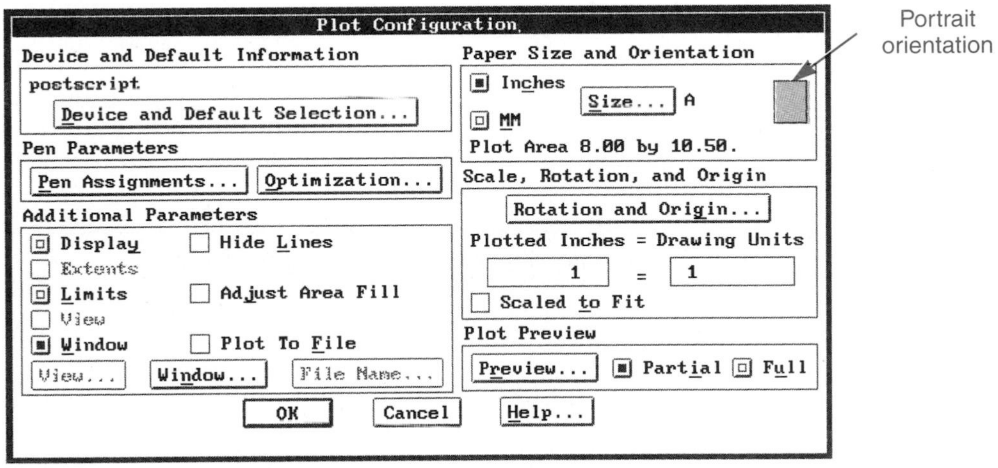

B

Scale, rotation, and origin

The items Scale, Rotation, and Origin are found on the right side of the "Plot Configuration" dialog box. See Figure 6-37A. Pick the Rotation and Origin... button to access the "Plot Rotation and Origin" subdialog box shown in Figure 6-37B. Figure 6-38 shows the same drawing plotted at the different rotation angles. The Plot Rotation area of the "Plot Rotation and Origin" subdialog box has radio buttons for 0, 90, 180, and 270 degree rotation settings. The Plot Origin section has edit boxes for you to specify desired X and Y plot origin settings. Pick OK when done.

Figure 6-37.   A–The "Plot Rotation and Origin" dialog box. The plotting scale is shown in the Plotting Inches = Drawing Units edit boxes. B–Select a rotation and change the origin if necessary.

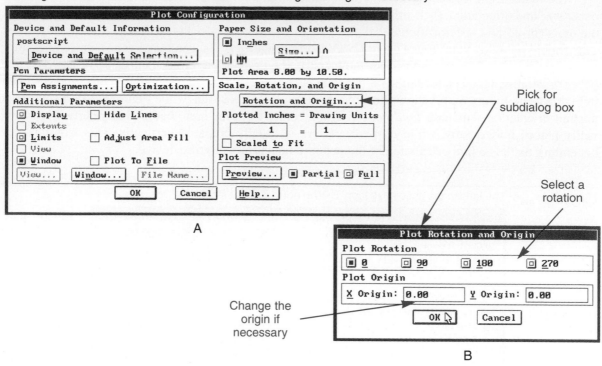

A

Pick for
subdialog box

Select a
rotation

Change the
origin if
necessary

B

Figure 6-38.   An example of a drawing plotted at different rotation angles.

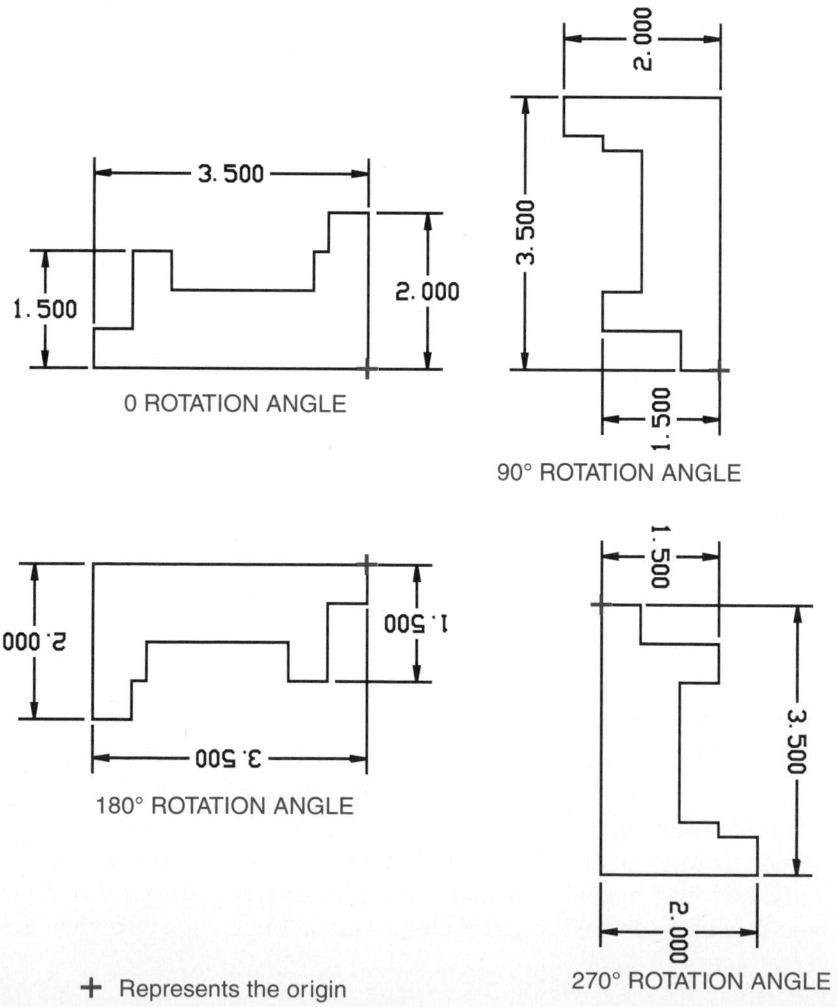

0 ROTATION ANGLE

90° ROTATION ANGLE

180° ROTATION ANGLE

270° ROTATION ANGLE

+ Represents the origin

The Plotted Inches = Drawing Units edit boxes (or Plotted MM = Drawing Units edit boxes if using metric units) let you set the plot scale. Plotting scale factors are discussed in Chapter 12 of this text.

Pick the Scaled to Fit check box if you want AutoCAD to automatically adjust your drawing to fit on the paper. Pick this box until you study other options in Chapter 12 of this text.

Preview plot

The plot preview feature allows you to check the layout of your drawing on the paper before plotting or printing. The Plot Preview is located in the lower-right corner of the "Plot Configuration" dialog box. It often takes a long time to plot a drawing. The Plot Preview option lets you save material and valuable time. The Partial and Full preview options are each controlled by a radio button.

When the Partial radio button is active and you pick the Preview… button, AutoCAD quickly displays the "Preview Effective Plotting Area" subdialog box shown in Figure 6-39. The red outline is the paper size, and the paper dimensions are given below for reference. The area the image occupies is called the *effective area*. The effective area dimensions are noted and the blue outline of this area is provided within the paper size. AutoCAD displays a red and blue dashed line when the effective area and the paper size are the same. While this shows you how the drawing compares to the paper size, the final plot depends on how the printer or plotter is set up.

Figure 6-39.   Selecting Preview… when Partial is checked displays the "Preview Effective Plotting Area" subdialog box. The effective area is shown here highlighted.

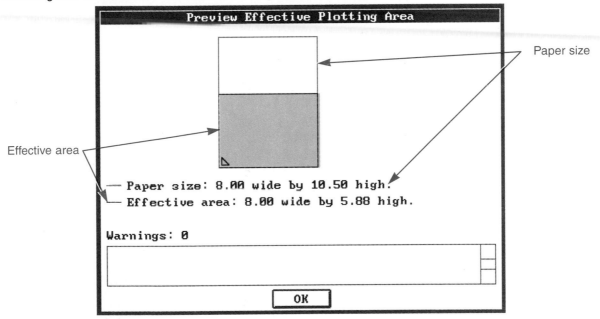

AutoCAD gives you messages in the Warnings: box if there is something wrong with the relationship of the display and the paper. The warnings give you an opportunity to make corrections and then preview the plot again. These are the types of warnings you might expect:
- Effective area too small to display.
- Origin forced effective area off display.
- Plotting area exceeds paper maximum.

Notice the small symbol in the lower-left corner of the effective area in Figure 6-39. This is called the *rotation icon*. The rotation icon in the lower-left corner represents the 0 default rotation angle. The icon is in the upper-left corner when the rotation is 90°, the right corner for 180° rotation, and in the lower-right corner for a 270° rotation. Figure 6-40 clearly shows the rotation icon placement.

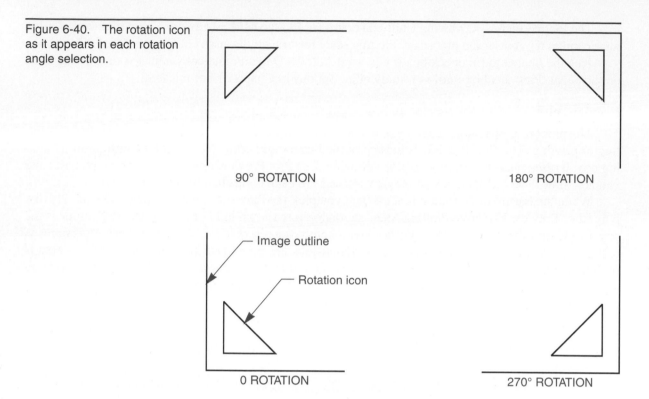

Figure 6-40.   The rotation icon as it appears in each rotation angle selection.

90° ROTATION

180° ROTATION

Image outline

Rotation icon

0 ROTATION

270° ROTATION

Pick the Full radio button followed by picking the Preview… button if you want a full preview. The full preview takes more time, but it displays the drawing on the screen as it will actually appear on paper. This takes the same amount of time as a drawing regeneration, which means that the drawing size determines how fast this happens. AutoCAD displays a 0-100% meter in the lower-right corner of the "Plot Configuration" dialog box as the full plot preview is generated. The graphics screen then returns with the drawing displayed inside the paper outline. At the same time, there is a "Plot Preview" dialog box positioned near the center of the screen. See Figure 6-41. If this dialog obscures the drawing, just move the cursor arrow to the black title bar at the top of the dialog box, and pick and hold to move the dialog box to a desired location. Pick the End Preview button to return to the "Plot Configuration" dialog box.

Figure 6-41.   The "Plot Preview" subdialog box is displayed when a full preview is selected.

Pick and hold to drag to a new location

Pick to pan or zoom

Pick to end the preview

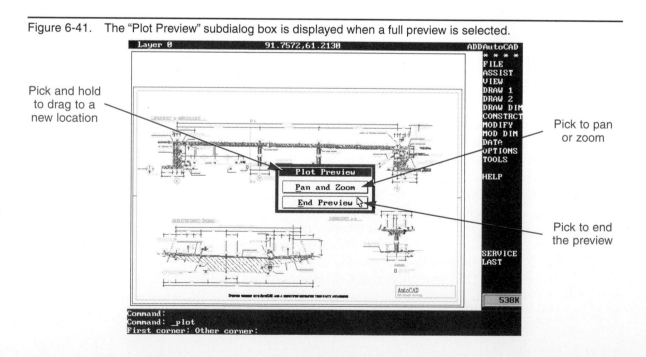

The full preview also allows you to examine details on the drawing or evaluate how a multiview arrangement fits together by picking the Pan and Zoom button. This is discussed in Chapter 10.

Completing the print process

Setting up the "Plot Configuration" dialog box is easy when you become familiar with it. Before you pick the OK button, there are several items you should check:
- Printer or plotter is plugged in.
- Cable from your computer to printer or plotter is secure.
- Printer has paper.
- Paper is properly loaded in the plotter and grips or clamps are in place.
- Plotter pens are inserted in holder and proper color or thickness are in correct places.
- Plotter area is clear for unblocked paper movement.

Pick the OK button when you are ready to send the print or plot to paper. You can also cancel or get help at any time by picking the Cancel or Help buttons. After you pick the OK button, you get one of these messages:

Plot Complete, or
Position paper in plotter.
Press RETURN to continue or S to Stop for hardware setup.

Press ENTER to send the drawing to the plotter if you get the second message.

PROFESSIONAL TIP

 You can stop a plot in progress at any time by canceling with CTRL+C. Keep in mind that it may take a while for some printers or plotters to terminate the plot, depending on the amount of the drawing file that has already been sent to the printer or plotter.

EXERCISE 6-16

❏ Load AutoCAD and open any of your previous drawings.
❏ Access the "Plot Configuration" dialog box.
❏ There should be an "X" in the Scale to Fit button, and the Partial preview and Display buttons should be highlighted.
❏ Pick the Preview... button and observe what happens. Pick OK.
❏ Pick the Full preview button and then pick the Preview... to see the results. A full representation of your drawing should be displayed as it will appear when printed on the paper. Pick End Preview.
❏ Experiment by changing the rotation angle followed by doing a full preview each time.
❏ Pick the Window... button and then pick the Pick ⟨ button in the "Window Selection" dialog box. Window a small portion of the drawing and then pick OK.
❏ Do another full preview to see the results. End the preview.
❏ Pick the Display radio button, preview the drawing to see if it is what you want, and make a print if a printer is available.
❏ Quit AutoCAD.

USING DRAWING PLAN SHEETS

A good work plan almost always saves drafting time in the long run. Planning should include sketches and drawing plan sheets. A rough preliminary sketch and completed drawing plan sheet help in the following ways:
- Determines the drawing layout.
- Sets the overall size or limits of the drawing by laying out the views and required free space.

- Confirms the drawing units based on the dimensions provided.
- Predetermines the point entry system and locates the points.
- Establishes the grid and snap settings.
- Presets some of the drawing variables, such as LINETYPE, FILL, and polyline width.
- Establishes how and when various activities are to be performed.
- Determines the best use of AutoCAD.
- Results in an even work load.
- Maintains maximum use of equipment.

Drawing plan sheets may range in content depending on the nature of the drafting project. One basic drawing plan sheet is shown in Figure 6-42. Copies of plan sheets are available for duplication in the Solution Manual.

Figure 6-42. A drawing plan sheet and project log combination. They are generally printed on the front and back of one piece of paper. (Courtesy of Harlton Terrie Gaines; Palmer, Alaska)

DRAWING PLANNING SHEET   Page 1 of 2

The following information is to be furnished by the Assigned Project Engineer requesting design support:

PROJECT TITLE: _____
DISCIPLINE: _____
PROJECT NO. : _____   A.F.E. NO. : _____
PROJECT ENGINEER: _____   PHONE NO. : _____
CLIENT: _____
DRAWING SCOPE OF WORK: _____
_____
_____
_____

The following information will be furnished by the assigned Lead Designer:

LEAD DESIGNER: _____   PHONE NO. : _____
DISK NAME: _____
FILE NAME: _____   DRAWING NO.: _____
DWG. GHOST (SIZE & FORMAT): _____

DRAFTER: _____   PHONE NO. : _____
DATE ASSIGNED: _____   DATE REQUIRED: _____
DATE I.F.A. : _____   DATE I.F.C. : _____
ESTIMATED M.H. : _____   ACTUAL M.H. : _____
DRAWING STANDARD: _____   MAT'L SPEC.: _____
AFFECTED TAG NO'S: REFERENCE SHEETS

_____ _____ _____   _____ _____ _____
_____ _____ _____   _____ _____ _____

Freehand sketch by drafter:

Approved by: _____   Date: _____

Figure 6-42.   (Continued)

DRAWING PLANNING SHEET

Drafters notes: _____
_____
_____
_____
_____
_____
_____
_____
_____

Commands used by the drafter:

Commands	Values	Commands	Values
1.		34.	
2.		35.	
3.		36.	
4.		37.	
5.		38.	
6.		39.	
7.		40.	
8.		41.	
9.		42.	
10.		43.	
11.		44.	
12.		45.	
13.		46.	
14.		47.	
15.		48.	
16.		49.	
17.		50.	
18.		51.	
19.		52.	
20.		53.	
21.		54.	
22.		55.	
23.		56.	
24.		57.	
25.		58.	
26.		59.	
27.		60.	
28.		61.	
29.		62.	
30.		63.	
31.		64.	
32.		65.	
33.		66.	

CHAPTER TEST

Write your answers in the spaces provided.

1. Give the commands and entries you must make to draw a line from point A to point B, to point C, back to point A. Finally, be ready to give a new command:

   Command: _____

   From point: _____

   To point: _____

   To point: _____

   To point: _____

   To point: _____

   Command: _____

2. Give the commands needed to turn on the Ortho mode:

   Command: _____

   ON/OFF: _____

3. Give the command and actions needed to quickly connect a line to an existing line and then undo it because it was wrong:

   Command: _____

   From point: _____

   To point: _____

   To point: _____

   To point: _____

4. Give the command and related responses used to erase a group of objects at the same time and then bring them all back:

   Command: _____

   Select objects: _____

   First corner: _____

   Other corner:_____

   Select objects: _____

   Command: _____

5. Give the command necessary to clean the screen:

   Command: _____

6. Give the commands to change the linetype from a solid line to a centerline:

   Command: _____

   ?/Create/Load/Set: _____

   New entity linetype (or ?): ⟨continuous⟩: _____

7. Identify the following linetypes.

A. _____

B. _____

C. _____

D. _____

E. _____

F. _____

G. _____

H. _____

I. _____

J. _____

K. _____

A ————————————

B – – – – – – – – – –

C ———————— F

D   E

G ————————————

H ← – – – – – – – →

I ———⌄———⌄———

J —— – – —— – – ——

K ····························

8. List two ways to discontinue drawing a line. _____

_____

_____

9. Name four point entry systems. _____

_____

_____

10. Identify three ways to turn on the coordinate display. _____

_____

_____

11. What does a coordinate display of 2.750<90 mean? _____

_____

_____

12. What does the coordinate display of 5.250,7.875 mean? _____

_____

_____

13. List four ways to turn on the Ortho mode. _____

_____

_____

_____

14. What do you enter at the Command: prompt if you want to have AutoCAD automatically repeat the LINE command?_____

_____

15. Identify two ways to continue drawing another line from a previously drawn line. _____

_____

_____

16. Name the screen menu where you can access several options that may be used for erasing applications. _____

_____

17. Define stacked objects. _____

_____

_____

18. Name the command that you use if you want to draw new entities in red. _____

_____

19. How do you automatically use the Window selection method when you want to erase a group of objects? _____

_____

_____

_____

_____

20. How do you automatically use the Crossing selection option when you want to erase three out of four lines of a square? _____

_____

_____

_____

_____

21. How does the appearance of a window and crossing box differ? _____

_____

_____

22. Name the command that is used to bring back the last object you erased and before you issue another command. _____

23. What command and option do you use if you are drawing object lines and you want to change to draw hidden lines? _____

24. How do you get an alphanumeric screen showing the AutoCAD standard linetypes? _____

_____

25. List at least five ways to select an object to erase. _____

_____

_____

26. Define hard copy and soft copy. _____

_____

_____

27. Identify three ways to access the "Plot Configuration" dialog box. _____

_____

_____

28. Describe the difference between the Display and the Window Plot Parameter options.

_____

_____

_____

_____

29. What is a major advantage of doing a plot preview? _____

_____

_____

_____

30. Identify at least four reasons for using a drawing plan sheet. _____

_____

_____

DRAWING PROBLEMS

1. Draw an object by connecting the following point coordinates. Save your drawing as A:P6-1. Make a print of your drawing if a printer is available.

P6-1

Points	Coordinates	Points	Coordinates
1	2,2	8	@-1.5,0
2	@1.5,0	9	@0,1.25
3	@.75<90	10	@-1.25,1.25
4	@1.5<0	11	@2<180
5	@0,-.75	12	@-1.25,-1.25
6	@3,0	13	@2.25<270
7	@1<90		

2. With the absolute, relative, and polar coordinate entry methods, use the digitizer, keyboard, and cursor keys to draw the following shapes. Be sure to use a drawing plan sheet. Set the limits to 22,17, units to decimal, grid to .5, and snap to .0625. Draw rectangle A three times using a different point entry system each time. Draw object B once, using at least two methods of coordinate entry. Do not draw dimensions. Save your drawing as A:P6-2. Make a print of your drawing if a printer is available.

P6-2

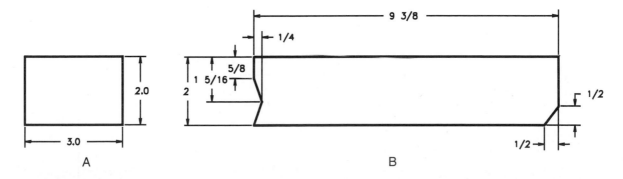

P6-3

3. With the absolute, relative, and polar coordinate entry methods use the digitizer, keyboard, and cursor key to draw the following object. Use a drawing plan sheet. Set the limits to 22,17, units to decimal, grid to .25, and snap to .0625. Use the LINE command. Do not draw dimensions. Save your drawing as A:P6-3. Make a print of your drawing if a printer is available.

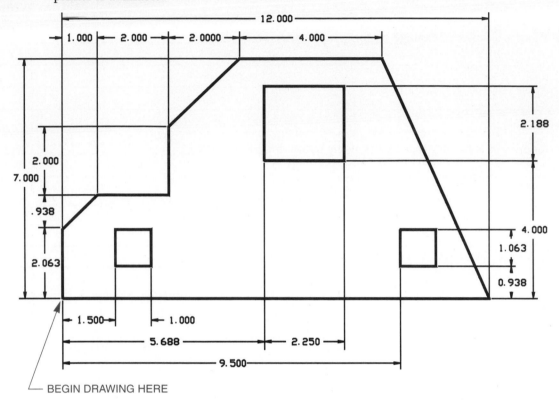

BEGIN DRAWING HERE

P6-4

4. Edit problem P6-3 so that it takes on the following changes. The dimensions shown are revisions and are not to be added. Save your drawing as A:P6-4. Make a print of your drawing if a printer is available.

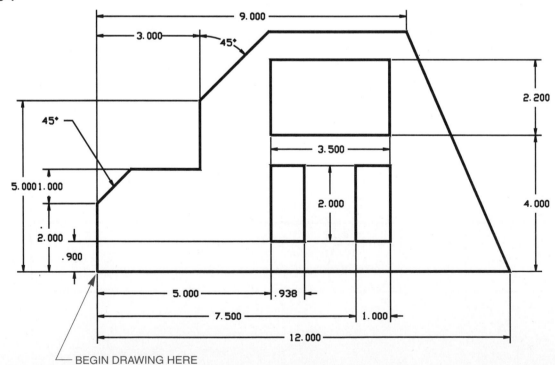

BEGIN DRAWING HERE

P6-5

3. Draw the objects shown at A and B below using the following instructions:

   A. Use a drawing plan sheet.

   B. Draw each object using the LINE command.

   C. Start each object at the point shown and then discontinue the LINE command where shown

   D. Complete each object using the Continue option.

   E. Do not draw dimensions.

   F. Save the drawings as A:P6-5.

   G. Make a print of your drawing if a printer is available.

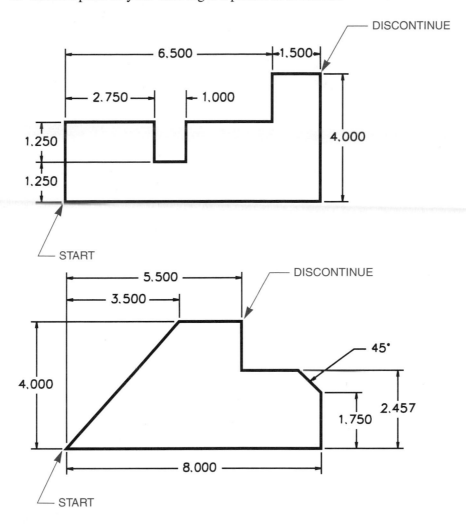

P6-6

6. Draw the plot plan shown below. Use the linetypes shown, which include:
   A. ACAD-Continuous, hidden, phantom, and centerline.
   B. LTYPESHP-Fenceline1 and Gas-line.
   C. Make your drawing proportional to the given example.
   D. Save the drawings as A:P6-6.

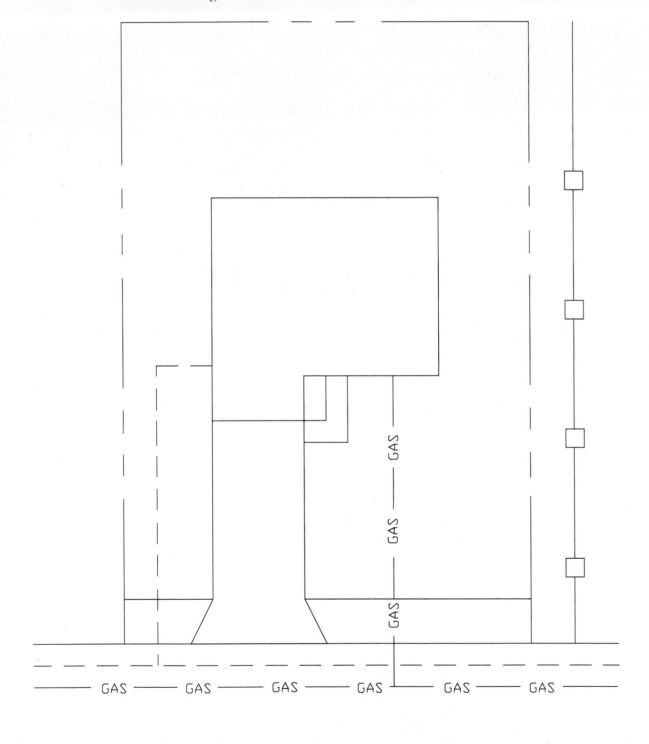

7. Draw the line chart shown below. Use the linetypes shown, which include:

   A. ACAD-Continuous, hidden, phantom, and centerline.

P6-7   B. LTYPESHP-Fenceline1 and Fenceline2.

   C. Make your drawing proportional to the given example.

   D. Save the drawings as A:P6-7.

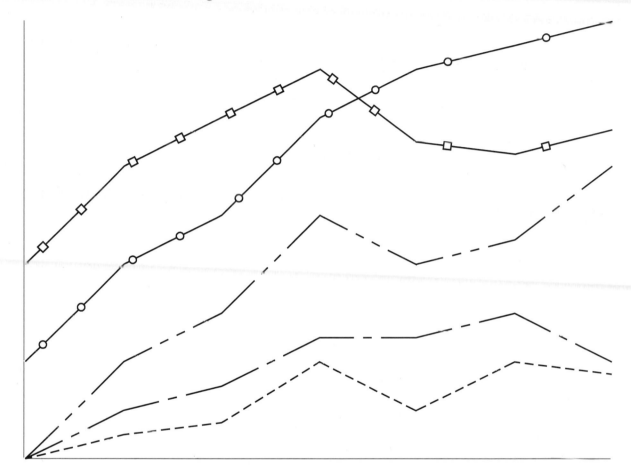

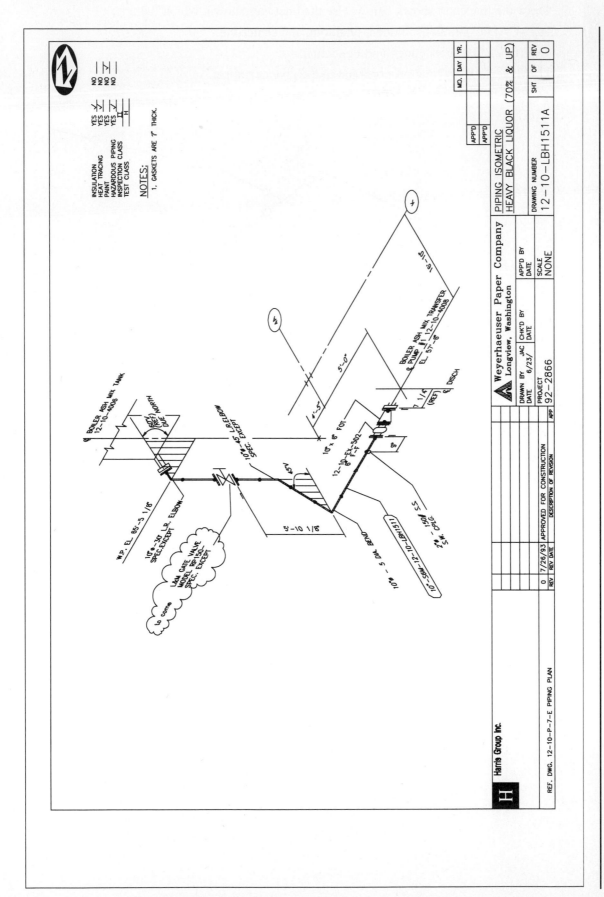

Piping isometric drawing. (Harris Group Inc.)

Chapter 7

INTRODUCTION TO POLYLINES AND MULTILINES

Learning objectives

After completing this chapter, you will be able to:

- ○ Use the PLINE command to draw given objects.
- ○ Observe the results of using FILL On and Off, and REDRAW.
- ○ Draw given objects using the TRACE command.
- ○ Use the MLINE command to draw given features.
- ○ Create your own multiline styles with the MISTYLE command.
- ○ Sketch with AutoCAD.

AutoCAD has two features that provide you with endless possibilities for design and drafting applications. These are polylines and multilines. The term *polyline* is composed of the words "poly" and "line". *Poly* means many and a polyline is a single object that can be made up of many different or multiple line segments. Polylines are drawn with the PLINE command and its options. While the PLINE command is popular for drawing thick lines, AutoCAD also provides the TRACE command.

Multilines are combinations of parallel lines consisting of between 1 and 16 features called elements. You can offset the elements to create any desired pattern for any field of drafting, including architectural, schematic, or mechanical as needed. Multilines are drawn using the MLINE command and related commands.

This chapter introduces you to the use of polylines and fully explains how to create drawings with multilines. You will also see how to sketch with AutoCAD. A complete discussion of polyline use is provided in Chapter 18.

INTRODUCTION TO DRAWING POLYLINES

AUG 2

PLINE is the AutoCAD command used for drawing polylines (PolyLINEs). Polylines have advantages over normal lines because there are an unlimited number of possibilities, including:

- • Much more flexibility than lines drawn with the TRACE command (discussed later in the chapter).
- • Making thick or tapered lines.
- • May be used with any linetype.
- • May be used to draw a filled circle or donut shape.
- • Can be edited using advanced editing features.
- • Closed polygons may be drawn.
- • The area or perimeter of a polyline feature may be determined without extra effort.
- • Arcs and straight lines of varying thicknesses may be joined as a single entity.

The PLINE command basically functions like the LINE command except that additional options are offered, and all segments of a polyline are a single entity. PLINE can be typed at the Command: prompt, picked from the DRAW screen menu, or picked as polyline from the Draw pull-down menu:

```
Command: PLINE ↵
From point: (select a point)
Current line-width 0.0
```

The current linewidth is shown as 0.0, which produces a line of minimum width. If this linewidth is acceptable, you may begin by selecting the endpoint of a line when the following prompt appears:

```
Arc/Close/Halfwidth/Length/Undo/Width/⟨Endpoint of line⟩: (select a point)
```

If additional line segments are added to the first line, the endpoint of the first line automatically becomes the starting point of the next line.

Setting the polyline width

If it is necessary to change the linewidth, this may be done by entering W for Width as follows:

```
Arc/Close/Halfwidth/Length/Undo/Width/⟨Endpoint of line⟩: W ↵
```

When the Width option is selected, you are asked for the starting and ending widths. If a tapered line is desired follow this procedure:

```
Starting width ⟨0.0000⟩: (type a width value and press ENTER)
Ending width ⟨starting width⟩: (type a width value and press ENTER)
```

The starting width that you select becomes the default for the ending width. Therefore, to keep the line the same width, press ENTER at the Ending width ⟨starting width⟩: prompt. The following command sequence draws the line shown in Figure 7-1. Notice that the start and endpoints of the line are located at the center of the line.

```
Command: PLINE ↵
From point: 4,4 ↵
Current line-width 0.0
Arc/Close/Halfwidth/Length/Undo/Width/⟨Endpoint of line⟩: W ↵
Starting width ⟨0.0000⟩: .25 ↵
Ending width ⟨.25⟩: ↵
Arc/Close/Halfwidth/Length/Undo/Width/⟨Endpoint of line⟩: 8,4 ↵
```

Figure 7-1.   A thick polyline drawn with the PLINE Width option.

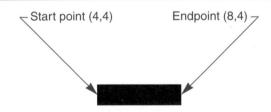

Start point (4,4)   Endpoint (8,4)

Drawing a tapered polyline

Enter different starting and ending widths if you want to draw a tapered polyline. See Figure 7-2.

```
Command: PLINE ↵
From point: 4,4 ↵
Current line-width 0.0
Arc/Close/Halfwidth/Length/Undo/Width/⟨Endpoint of line⟩: W ↵
Starting width ⟨0.0000⟩: .25 ↵
Ending width ⟨.25⟩: .5 ↵
Arc/Close/Halfwidth/Length/Undo/Width/⟨Endpoint of line⟩: 8,4 ↵
```

Figure 7-2.   Using PLINE to
draw a wide tapered line.

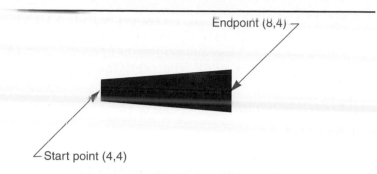

If you want to draw an arrow, give 0 as the starting width and then use any desired ending width.

Using the Halfwidth option

The Halfwidth option allows you to specify the width from the center to one side. This is done by selecting the H option and then specifying the widths. See Figure 7-3.

Arc/Close/Halfwidth/Length/Undo/Width/⟨Endpoint of line⟩: **H** ↵
Starting half-width ⟨0.0000⟩: **.25** ↵
Ending half-width ⟨.25⟩: **.5** ↵

Figure 7-3.   Using the PLINE
Halfwidth option.

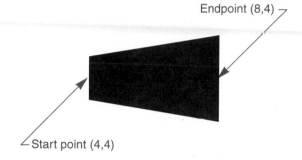

Using the Length option

The Length option allows you to draw another polyline at the same angle as the previous polyline. This is done by selecting the L option and then specifying the desired length. For example:

Command: **PLINE** ↵
From point: *(pick a starting point for polyline number 1)*
Current line-width is 0.0000
Arc/Close/Halfwidth/Length/Undo/Width/⟨Endpoint of line⟩: *(pick the ending point for poly-line number 1)*
Arc/Close/Halfwidth/Length/Undo/Width/⟨Endpoint of line⟩: ↵
Command: ↵
PLINE
From point: *(pick a starting point for polyline number 2)*
Current line-width is 0.0000
Arc/Close/Halfwidth/Length/Undo/Width/⟨Endpoint of line⟩: **L** ↵
Length of line: *(enter any desired length for polyline number 2)*
Arc/Close/Halfwidth/Length/Undo/Width/⟨Endpoint of line⟩: ↵
Command:

The second polyline is drawn at the same angle as the previous polyline and at the length you specify.

UNDOING PREVIOUSLY DRAWN POLYLINES

AUG 2

While in the PLINE command you may pick the Undo option in the screen menu or type U at the prompt line and press ENTER. This erases the last polyline segment drawn. Each time you use Undo, another polyline segment is erased. A quick way to go back and correct the polyline while you remain in the PLINE command is as follows:

> Command: **PLINE** ↵
> From point: (pick a starting point)
> Current line-width is 0.0000
> Arc/Close/Halfwidth/Length/Undo/Width/⟨Endpoint of line⟩: (pick the endpoint)
> Arc/Close/Halfwidth/Length/Undo/Width/⟨Endpoint of line⟩: (pick another endpoint)
> Arc/Close/Halfwidth/Length/Undo/Width/⟨Endpoint of line⟩: (pick another endpoint)
> Arc/Close/Halfwidth/Length/Undo/Width/⟨Endpoint of line⟩: **U** ↵
> Arc/Close/Halfwidth/Length/Undo/Width/⟨Endpoint of line⟩: (pick another endpoint or
>   enter **U** again to remove an additional segment)

After you type U followed by pressing ENTER, the last polyline segment you drew is automatically removed, but the rubberband cursor remains attached to the end of the previous polyline segment. You may now continue drawing additional polyline segments, or enter U again to undo more polyline segments. You can keep using Undo to remove all of the polyline segments up to the first point of the polyline. The polyline segments are removed in reverse order from which they were drawn.

The U command works in much the same way. However, the U command may be used at any time to undo any previous command. This is done by typing U at the Command: prompt or picking Undo from the Assist pull-down menu. AutoCAD gives you a message telling you which command was undone:

> Command: **U** ↵
> LINE
> Command:

In this example, the LINE command was the last command to undo. The U command is different from the UNDO command, which is discussed later in the chapter.

EXERCISE 7-1

❑ Load AutoCAD, enter the drawing editor, and open PRODR1, or begin a new drawing using your own variables.

❑ Use the PLINE command to draw several objects of your own design. Vary the width for each object.

❑ Draw three different types of arrows by specifying different starting and ending widths.

❑ Set the polyline width to .125. Draw a single polyline. Using the Length option, draw two more .125 wide polylines with a 4 unit length.

❑ Save the drawing as A:EX7-1 and quit.

mitered:

DRAWING THICK LINES USING THE TRACE COMMAND

When it is necessary to draw thick lines, the TRACE command may be used instead of the PLINE command. The TRACE command is located in the DRAW 2 screen menu or TRACE can be typed at the Command: prompt. All of the LINE command procedures apply to TRACE except that the linewidth is set first, and it cannot be closed.

The current trace width is specified in brackets. Type .032 if you want to specify a trace width equal to the ANSI standard width for object lines. The following command and prompts produce a six-sided object. Try using the TRACE command while responding as follows to the prompts:

Command: **TRACE** ↵
Trace width ⟨*current*⟩: **.032** ↵
From point: **2,2** ↵
To point: **@6,0** ↵
To point: **@2,2** ↵
To point: **@0,3** ↵
To point: **@–2,2** ↵
To point: **@–6,0** ↵
To point: **@0,–7** ↵
To point: **2,2** ↵
To point: ↵
Command:

When you use the TRACE command, the lines are made up of *trace segments*. The previous trace segment is not drawn until the next endpoint is specified. This is because trace segment ends are mitered to fit the next segment.

EXERCISE 7-2

❏ Load AutoCAD, enter the drawing editor, and open PRODR1, or begin a new drawing using your own variables.
❏ Use the TRACE command to draw several objects of your own design. Vary the trace width for each object.
❏ Save the drawing as A:EX7-2 and quit.

USING THE UNDO AND U COMMANDS   AUG 1

After you leave the PLINE or LINE commands, picking Undo from the Pline: or Line: screen menu and typing UNDO at the Command: prompt works in a different manner. The UNDO command can be used to undo any previous command. When you select the UNDO command, the following sub-options appear:

Command: **UNDO** ↵
Auto/Control/BEgin/End/Mark/Back/⟨Number⟩:

The default is "Number." If you enter a number such as 1, the entire previous command sequence is removed. If you enter 2, the previous two command sequences are removed. You designate the number of previous command sequences you want removed. When using this command, AutoCAD tells you which previous commands were undone with a message after you press ENTER:

Command: **UNDO** ↵
Auto/Control/BEgin/End/Mark/Back/⟨Number⟩: **2** ↵
PLINE LINE
Command:

Other options of the UNDO command are defined as follows:
- **Auto (A).** Entering A gives you this prompt:

> ON/OFF ⟨*current*⟩: *(select* **ON** *or* **OFF***)*

With UNDO Auto turned On, any group of commands that are used to insert an item are removed together. For example, when a command contains other commands, all of the commands in that group are removed as one single command with UNDO Auto turned On. If UNDO Auto is Off, each individual command in a group of commands is treated individually.
- **Control (C).** Allows you to decide how many of the UNDO suboptions you want active. You can even disable the UNDO command altogether. When you enter C, you get this prompt:

> All/None/One ⟨All⟩:

The control options do the following:
- **All (A)**–Keeps the full range of UNDO options active.
- **None (N)**–This suboption disables both the U and UNDO commands.

> Auto/Control/BEgin/End/Mark/Back/⟨Number⟩: **C** ↵
> All/None/One ⟨All⟩: **N** ↵

You are now unable to use either the U or UNDO commands. If you try to use UNDO, all you get is the Control options:

> Command: **UNDO** ↵
> All/None/One⟨All⟩:

You must activate the UNDO options by pressing ENTER for All or entering O for the One mode. If you have U and UNDO disabled and try to use the U command, AutoCAD gives you this message:

> Command: **U** ↵
> U command disabled: Use UNDO command to turn it on

- **One (O)**–This suboption limits UNDO to one operation only:

> Auto/Control/BEgin/End/Mark/Back/⟨Number⟩: **C** ↵
> All/None/One ⟨All⟩: **O** ↵

Now, when you enter the UNDO command, you get the following prompt:

> Command: **UNDO** ↵
> Control/⟨1⟩:

You may press ENTER to undo only the previous command, or enter C to return to the Control options. With One active, you can remove only those items drawn with the previous command. AutoCAD acknowledges this with the message:

> Command: **UNDO** ↵
> Control/⟨1⟩: ↵
> LINE
>   Everything has been undone
> Command:

PROFESSIONAL TIP

When you use the UNDO command, AutoCAD maintains an UNDO file which saves previously used UNDO commands. All UNDO entries saved before disabling UNDO with the Control None option are discarded. This frees up some disk space, and may be valuable information for you to keep in mind if you ever get close to a full disk situation. If you want to continue using U or UNDO to some extent, then you might consider using the UNDO Control One suboption. This allows you to keep using U and UNDO to a limited extent while freeing disk space holding current UNDO information.

- **BEgin (BE) and End (E).** These UNDO options work together to cause a group of commands to be treated as a single command. Entering the U command removes commands that follow the BEgin suboption but precede the End suboption. These options can be used if you can anticipate the possible removal of a consecutive group of commands. For example, if you think you may want to undo the next three commands all together, then do the following:

> Command: **UNDO** ↵
> Auto/Control/BEgin/End/Mark/Back/⟨Number⟩: **BE** ↵
> Command: **LINE** ↵
> From point: *(pick a point)*
> To point: *(pick other endpoint)*
> To point: ↵
> Command: **PLINE** ↵
> From point: *(pick one endpoint)*
> Current line-width is 0.0000
> Arc/Close/Halfwidth/Length/Undo/Width/⟨Endpoint of line⟩: *(pick the other endpoint of the polyline)*
> Arc/Close/Halfwidth/Length/Undo/Width/⟨Endpoint of line⟩: ↵
> Command: **LINE** ↵
> From point: *(pick a point)*
> To point: *(pick other endpoint)*
> To point: ↵
> Command: **UNDO** ↵
> Auto/Control/BEgin/End/Mark/Back/⟨Number⟩ **E** ↵
> Command: **U** ↵

This U undoes the three commands that you executed between entering UNDO Group and UNDO End.

- **Mark (M).** The UNDO Mark option inserts a marker in the UNDO file. The Back option allows you to delete commands "back" to the marker. For example, if you do not want any work to be undone by the UNDO Back option, then enter the Mark option following this work:

> Auto/Control/BEgin/End/Mark/Back/⟨Number⟩:**M** ↵
> Command:

Then, use the UNDO Back option to undo everything back to the marker.

> Command: **UNDO** ↵
> Auto/Control/BEgin/End/Mark/Back/⟨Number⟩:**B** ↵

- **Back (B).** This option undoes everything in the entire drawing. AutoCAD questions your choice with the following message:

> This will undo everything: OK? ⟨Y⟩:

If you want everything that you have drawn to be removed, press ENTER. If not, type N or NO followed by an ENTER, or use CTRL+C.

PROFESSIONAL TIP

The UNDO Mark option can be used to assist in the design process. For example, if you are working on a project and have completed the design on a portion of the structure you can mark the spot with the Mark option and then begin work on the next design phase. If anything goes wrong with this part of the design, you can simply use UNDO Back to remove everything back to the Mark.

REDOING THE UNDONE

AUG 1

Type REDO or pick Redo from the Assist pull-down menu to bring back objects that were previously removed using the UNDO or U command:

Command: **REDO** ↵

REDO does not bring back polyline segments that were removed using the Undo option within the PLINE command. Remember, REDO only works immediately after undoing something.

EXERCISE 7-3

❑ Load AutoCAD, enter the drawing editor, and open PRODR1, or begin a new drawing using your own variables.
❑ Use the PLINE command to draw the following:
  ❑ A rectangle 2 units by 4 units, 0 width.
  ❑ A rectangle 2 units by 4 units, .125 width.
  ❑ A line 6 units long with a .125 starting width and .250 ending width.
  ❑ A line 6 units long using the Halfwidth option. Starting width is .125 and ending width is .250.
❑ Use the UNDO command to remove the last three polylines.
❑ Use REDO to bring back the last removed polyline.
❑ Save the drawing as A:EX7-3 and quit.

FILLING THE PLINE AND TRACE

AUG 4

In the discussion on the PLINE and TRACE commands, the results were shown as if they were solid, or filled in. You may decide to leave traces and polylines filled in, or show an outline. This is controlled by the FILL command, Figure 7-4. The FILL command only has ON and OFF options.

Command: **FILL** ↵
ON/OFF ⟨*current*⟩:

The value specified in brackets is the default, or previous setting. FILL may be turned On or Off in the prototype drawing. When FILL is Off, traces and polylines appear as outlines and the corners are mitered. After turning FILL Off, enter REGEN at the Command: prompt to have the fill removed.

Figure 7-4.   Examples of FILL when it is turned On and Off.

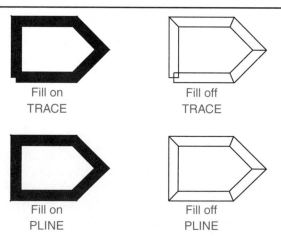

Fill on
TRACE

Fill off
TRACE

Fill on
PLINE

Fill off
PLINE

PROFESSIONAL TIP

When there are many wide polylines or traces on a drawing, it is best to have the FILL mode turned Off. This saves time when redrawing, regenerating, or plotting a check copy. Turn the FILL mode On for the final drawing.

EXERCISE 7-4

❏ Load AutoCAD and open PRODR1, or begin a new drawing using your own variables.
❏ Use the TRACE command to draw a 2 unit by 4 unit rectangle with a .125 linewidth. Draw another with .25 linewidth.
❏ Use the PLINE command to draw a rectangle 2 units by 4 units with .125 linewidth. Draw another with .25 linewidth.
❏ Turn FILL Off and On, and notice the regeneration speed in each situation. There may not be much difference with a fast computer unless the file begins to get large.
❏ Save the drawing as A:EX7-4 and quit.

DRAWING MULTILINES

AUG 2

The Multiline function has two related commands: MLINE and MLSTYLE. The MLINE command actually draws the multiline, whereas the MLSTYLE command allows configuration of the multiline to be drawn by future uses of the MLINE command. The multiline consists of between 1 and 16 parallel lines. The lines in a set of multilines are called *elements*. The style of the multiline is defined using the MLSTYLE command. The AutoCAD default style has two elements and is called STANDARD.

The MLINE command is accessed by picking Mline: from the DRAW 1 screen menu, by picking Multiline from the Draw pull-down menu or by typing MLINE at the Command: prompt as follows:

```
Command: MLINE ↵
Justification = Top, Scale = 1.00, Style = STANDARD
Justification/Scale/STyle/⟨From point⟩: 2,2 ↵
⟨To point⟩: 6,2 ↵
Undo/⟨To point⟩: 6,6 ↵
Close/Undo/⟨To point⟩: 2,6 ↵
Close/Undo/⟨To point⟩: C ↵
Command:
```

Notice the familiar ⟨From point⟩: and ⟨To point⟩: prompts, plus some other options, that are found in the MLINE command. These prompts work just as they did in the LINE command. The other options are Close and Undo. Use the Close option by typing C at the last prompt to close a polygon. Enter U during the command sequence to undo the previously drawn multiline segment. The object created in the previous command sequence is shown in Figure 7-5. Two lines are drawn because this is the STANDARD AutoCAD multiline style.

Figure 7-5.   This multiline object was created with the command sequence given in the text.

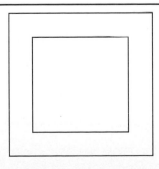

Multiline justification

Multiline justification determines how the resulting lines are offset based on the definition points provided. The *definition points* are the points you enter when drawing the multilines. Justification can be specified only once during a single MLINE command sequence for a given multiline object. Justification is based on a counter-clockwise rotation direction. The justification value is stored in the AutoCAD system variable CMLJUST. The justification options are Top, Zero, and Bottom. Top justification is the AutoCAD default, but the current value remains in effect until changed. To change the justification, pick Justify in the Mline: screen menu, or enter J at the first prompt followed by the first letter of the desired justification format (T, Z, or B) as follows:

```
Command: MLINE ↵
Justification = Top, Scale = 1.00, Style = STANDARD
Justification/Scale/STyle/⟨From point⟩: J ↵
Top/Zero/Bottom ⟨top⟩: (type T, Z, or B and press ENTER)
Justification = as specified, Scale = 1.00, Style = STANDARD
Justification/Scale/STyle/⟨From point⟩: 2,2 ↵
⟨To point⟩: 6,2 ↵
Undo/⟨To point⟩: 6,6 ↵
Close/Undo/⟨To point⟩: 2,6 ↵
Close/Undo/⟨To point⟩: C ↵
Command:
```

Figure 7-6 shows the results of the three different justification options using the same point entries from the previous command sequence.

Figure 7-6.   Multiline justification options.

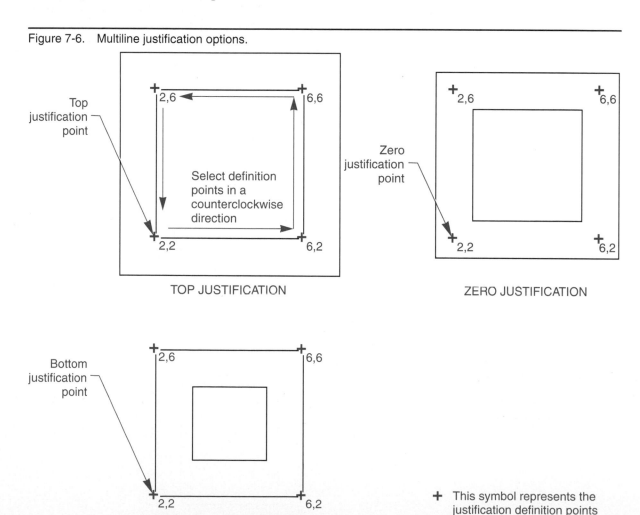

PROFESSIONAL TIP

As demonstrated in Figure 7-6, the justification option controls the direction of the offsets for multiline elements for the current style. These examples draw the multiline segments in a counterclockwise direction. Unexpected results often occur when drawing multiline segments in a clockwise direction.

EXERCISE 7-5

❏ Load AutoCAD and open PRODR1, or begin a new drawing using your own variables.
❏ Use the MLINE command and justification options to draw three objects similar to the ones shown in Figure 7-6.
❏ Use your own point input that results in a layout that is similar to the illustration in Figure 7-6.
❏ Observe the difference between the justification options.
❏ Save the drawing as A:EX7-5 and quit.

Adjusting the Multiline Scale

The Scale option controls the multiplier for the offset values specified in the MLSTYLE command and is stored in the CMLSCALE system variable. In the previous command sequence the Scale is 1.00. This means that the distance between multiline elements is 1 unit. In the case of Zero justification, the lines are offset 0.5 units on either side of the definition points picked. AutoCAD calculates a distance of 0.5 on one side and -0.5 on the other side. If the Scale value is 2, the offset values use this as the multiplier and result in the 2 units offset for the Top and Bottom justification and Zero offset of 1 and -1 each side of the definition points. Change the offset Scale to 2 by picking Scale in the Mline: screen menu, or type S and 2 at the appropriate prompts like this:

```
Command: MLINE ↵
Justification = Top, Scale = 1.00, Style = STANDARD
Justification/Scale/STyle/〈From point〉: S ↵
Set Mlinescale 〈1.00〉: 2 ↵
```

Figure 7-7 shows a comparison between multilines drawn at several different offset Scale values.

Figure 7-7. Multiline scales.

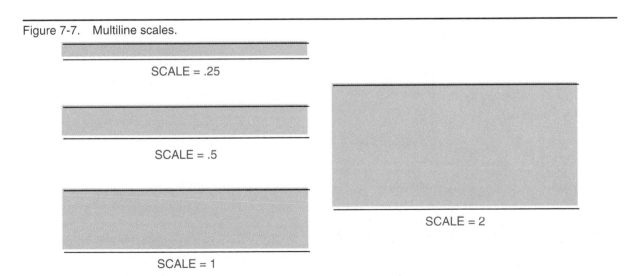

Setting Your Own Multiline Style

The STyle option in the MLINE command allows you to define multiline styles to be set as the current style. However, the multiline style has to be saved using the MLSTYLE command before it can be accessed. To use multiline styles that have been saved in the MLSTYLE command, access the STyle option in the Mline: screen menu or type ST as follows:

```
Command: MLINE ↵
Justification = Top, Scale = 1.00, Style = STANDARD
Justification/Scale/STyle/⟨From point⟩: ST ↵
Mstyle name (or?): ROAD 1 ↵
Justification = Zero, Scale = 1.00, Style = ROAD1
```

If you forget the name of the desired multiline style, you can type a ? as follows to get the Loaded multiline styles: text screen shown in Figure 7-8:

```
Justification/Scale/STyle/⟨From point⟩: ST ↵
Mstyle name (or ?): ? ↵
```

Figure 7-8.   Loaded multiline styles: text screen.

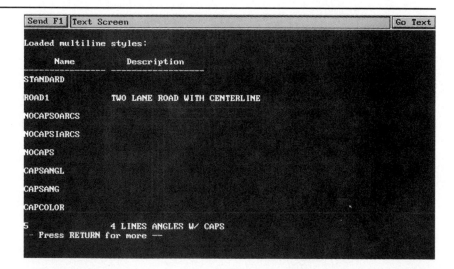

Styles are defined in the MLSTYLE command and stored in the CMLSTYLE system variable. The MLSTYLE command is found under the Data pull-down menu as Multiline Style… in the Data screen menu as MLstyle:, by picking MLstyle after picking Mline: in the DRAW 1 screen menu, or by typing at the Command: prompt. The MLSTYLE command displays the "Multiline Styles" dialog box where multiline styles can be defined, edited, and saved. See Figure 7-9. Styles can be saved either to the drawing's symbol table, or externally in a file so they can be used in other drawings.

Figure 7-9.   "Multiline Styles" dialog box.

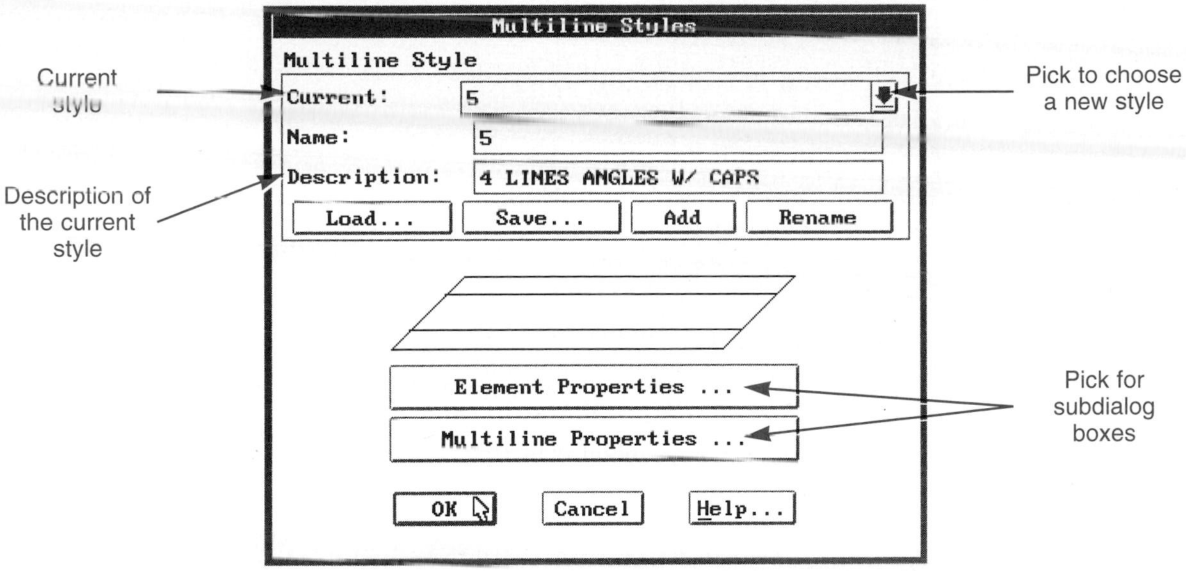

Introduction to the Multiline Styles

Look at Figure 7-9. The options found in the Multiline Styles part of the dialog box are described as followes:

- **Current:.** The Current: text box makes the identified multiline style current. This adjusts the value of the AutoCAD system variable CMLSTYLE. The use of this option provides a list box showing currently defined multiline styles. Use the down arrow to show the list and to pick the style that you want to make current. The only style listed is for the STANDARD AutoCAD multiline until you create others.
- **Name:.** This is where you enter a new style name, but this is done after you have created a new style. This is discussed again after you create a style. See page 172.
- **Description:.** An optional description of your multiline style may be entered here. This is discussed again after you create a style. See page 172.
- **Load....** The Load... button allows you to load a multiline style contained in an external multiline definition file or from the symbol table of the current drawing. You can only load a style that has been created, so this is discussed again after you create a style. See page 172.
- **Save....** The Save... button lets you save a style to an external file. The style is saved to an MLN file. This is covered again after you create a style. See page 172.
- **Add.** Pick the Add button after entering a multiline style name in the Name: text box. This adds the multiline style name to the Current: list.
- **Rename.** Pick this button to rename a multiline style. The image tile in the center of the "Multiline Style" dialog box displays a representation of the current multiline elements.

Using the "Element Properties" Subdialog Box

The previous information introduced you to the Multiline Style parts of the "Multiline Styles" dialog box. Picking the Element Properties... button is where you do the work to create a new multiline style. This button accesses the "Element Properties" subdialog box shown in Figure 7-10.

Figure 7-10.   "Element Properties" subdialog box.

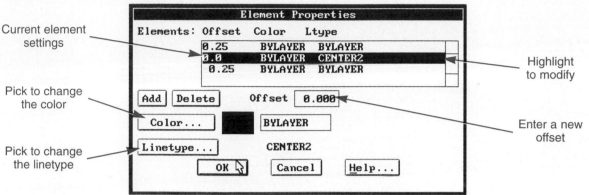

The following items describe how to use this subdialog box:
- **Elements:.** This part of the dialog box displays the current Offset values, Color, and Linetype. Picking a set of elements highlights the items for further definition in this dialog box.
- **Add.** Pick this button to add a new element to the multiline definition. Doing this adds an element with these settings:
  Offset = 0.0, Color = BYLAYER, and Ltype = BYLAYER. This allows you to draw a multiline element between the two existing elements shown in Figure 7-10.
- **Delete.** Pick this button to delete the highlighted items in the Elements: list.
- **Offset.** Type either a positive or negative offset value for the highlighted offset in the Elements: list. Press ENTER to accept what you type.
- **Color….** The Color… button accesses the "Select Color" subdialog box. Pick the desired color to change the color of the highlighted item in the Elements: list. Now the color is displayed in an image tile next to the Color… button.
- **Linetype….** Pick this button to get the "Select Linetype" subdialog box. Pick the desired linetype from the Loaded Linetypes list. Linetypes must be loaded before they can be used. Load the needed linetype by picking Load… in the "Select Linetype" subdialog box followed by picking the linetypes from the "Load or Reload Linetypes" subdialog box, and then pick OK. The selected linetype is now displayed at the highlighted items in the Elements: list.

If you add a new set of elements to the Elements: list, leave the color BYLAYER, and change the linetype to CENTER2, you get the display shown in Figure 7-10. Pick OK to leave the "Element Properties" subdialog box. The current status of the multiline is displayed in the Multiline Style image tile. You can continue in this manner to add up to 16 different color and linetype elements to the custom multiline style.

Using the "Multiline Properties" subdialog box

You can continue to customize the multiline style by adding various end caps, segment joints, and background color by picking the Multiline Properties… button in the "Multiline Styles" dialog box. Doing this displays the "Multiline Properties" subdialog box shown in Figure 7-11. The following explains the options for you to use in the "Multiline Properties" subdialog box:

Figure 7-11. "Multiline Properties" subdialog box.

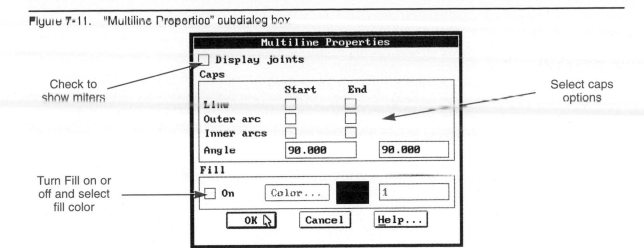

Check to
show miters

Turn Fill on or
off and select
fill color

Select caps
options

- **Display joints.** This is an On/Off toggle for the display of joints. Joints are lines that connect the vertices between adjacent multiline elements. Joints are also referred to as *miters*. Figure 7-12 displays a multiline drawn with joints On and with joints Off.

Figure 7-12.   How an object
appears with multiline joints On
and Off.

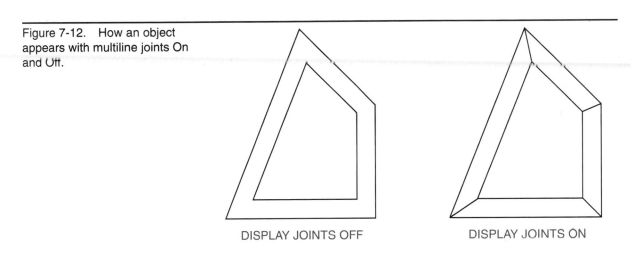

DISPLAY JOINTS OFF   DISPLAY JOINTS ON

- **Caps.** There are several selections in the category of Caps that control the placement of end-caps on the multilines. *End caps* are lines drawn between the corresponding vertices of the beginning or ending points of the elements of the multiline. Caps can be set on either the start point, end point, or both points of the multiline. Arcs may also be specified. Arcs can be set to connect the ends of the outermost lines only, between pairs of interior elements, or both the outer and interior lines. These arcs are drawn tangent to the elements they connect. Drawing outermost arcs requires at least two multiline elements.

You can also change the angle of the cap relative to the direction of the last drawn line segment. All you have to do to customize the end lines is to turn On or Off the Start and End toggles in the Caps area as needed. An "X" in a box means that the end option is On. To change the ending angle, enter a new value in the Angle text boxes as desired. Figure 7-13 shows examples of several different end cap options.

Figure 7-13.   Several different
multiline end cap options.

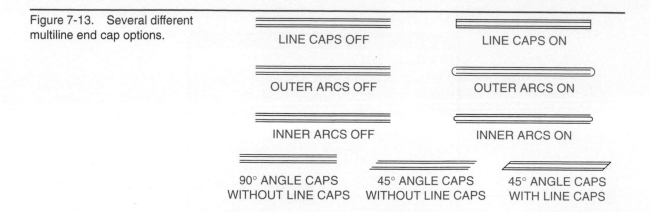

LINE CAPS OFF

LINE CAPS ON

OUTER ARCS OFF

OUTER ARCS ON

INNER ARCS OFF

INNER ARCS ON

90° ANGLE CAPS
WITHOUT LINE CAPS

45° ANGLE CAPS
WITHOUT LINE CAPS

45° ANGLE CAPS
WITH LINE CAPS

- **Fill.** If turned On, the multiline is filled with a solid fill pattern in the color specified using the fill color option. Pick the On switch to activate the Color... button. You can leave the color set BYLAYER or change it by picking the Color... button which displays the "Select Color" sub-dialog box. Figure 7-14 shows multilines drawn with Fill turned On and Off.

Figure 7-14.   Multiline Fill On
and Off.

MULTILINE WITH FILL OFF

MULTILINE WITH FILL ON

Steps in creating and drawing a multiline

Now that you have seen how the MLINE and MLSTYLE commands work, you can put it all together by creating and drawing your own multiline style. You need to draw a multiline for a two lane road to be used on a mapping project. The following is the procedure for drawing the multiline:

1. Access the "Multiline Styles" dialog box, pick Element Properties... and set the following Elements:

Elements: Offset	Color	Ltype
0.25	BYLAYER	BYLAYER
0.0	BYLAYER	CENTER2
-0.25	BYLAYER	BYLAYER

2. Pick OK.
3. Pick the Multiline Properties... button in the "Multiline Styles" dialog box. Be sure the Display joints, Caps, and Fill toggles are turned Off, and the Caps Angle is 90°.
4. Pick OK.
5. Type ROAD1 in the Name: text box in the Multiline Style area of the "Multiline Styles" dialog box.
6. In the Description: text box type: TWO LANE ROAD WITH CENTER LINE.
7. Pick the Save... button in the "Multiline Styles" dialog box to get the "Save Multiline Style" sub-dialog box.
8. Double click on the ACAD file, or pick ACAD and then OK.
9. Pick the Load... button in the "Multiline Styles" dialog box to access the "Load Multiline Styles" subdialog box.
10. Find the ROAD1 style and pick to highlight it. Pick OK.
11. Pick OK to exit the "Multiline Style" dialog box.
12. Enter the MLINE command to draw the ROAD1 multiline and set Zero justification like this:

```
Command: MLINE ↵
Justification = Top, Scale = 1.00, Style = ROAD1
Justification/Scale/STyle/⟨From point⟩: J ↵
Top/Zero/Bottom ⟨top⟩: Z ↵
Justification = Zero, Scale = 1.00, Style = ROAD1
```

If the ROAD1 multiline style was not loaded in the "Multiline Style" dialog box but does exist then use the STyle option to access it and draw the multiline shown in Figure 7-15:

```
Justification/Scale/STyle/<From point>: ST ↵
Mstyle name (or?): ROAD1 ↵
Justification = Zero, Scale = 1.00, Style = ROAD1
Justification/Scale/STyle/<From point>: 2,2 ↵
<To point>: 6,2 ↵
Undo/<To point>: ↵
Command:
```

Figure 7-15.   Drawing the ROAD1 multiline style.

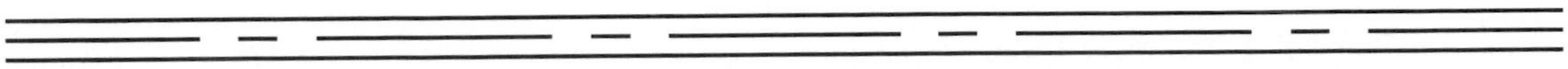

EXERCISE 7-7

❏ Load AutoCAD and open PRODR1, or begin a new drawing using your own variables.
❏ Use the MISTYLE and the MLINE commands to create and draw the following:
  ❏ A multiline with joints similar to Figure 7-12.
  ❏ Multilines with several end cap options similar to Figure 7-13.
  ❏ A multiline with Fill On.
  ❏ A multiline with a different linetype similar to Figure 7-15.
❏ Save the drawing as A:EX7-7 and quit.

EDITING MULTILINES

[AUG 5]

The MLEDIT allows limited editing of multiline objects. The MLEDIT command may be accessed by picking Mledit: from the MODIFY screen menu, pick Edit Multiline... in the Modify pull-down menu or by typing at the Command: prompt. Selecting the MLEDIT command displays the "Multiline Edit Tools" dialog box shown in Figure 7-16. This dialog box displays image buttons that show you an example of what to expect when using each option.

Figure 7-16.   "Multiline Edit Tools" dialog box.

Select the option you want

Name of the selected option

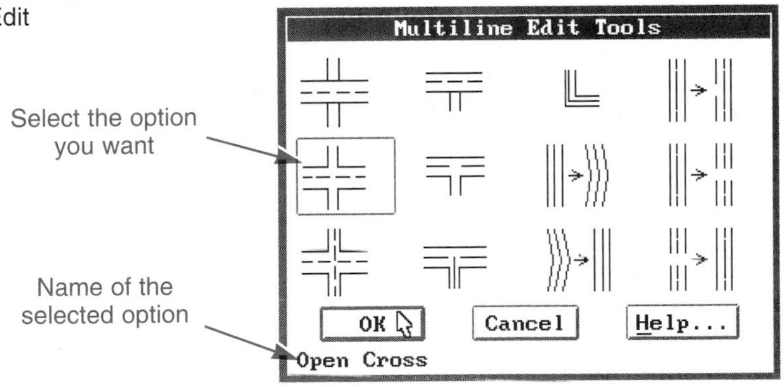

Editing the crossing

The "Multiline Edit Tools" dialog box gives twelve options presented in four columns. The first column has three image buttons, each displaying a different type of intersection. Picking one of these buttons allows you to create the type of intersection shown in the image buttons. The name of the MLEDIT option is displayed in the lower left corner of the dialog box when you pick an image button. The following describes these first three options:

- **Closed Cross.** This option lets you create what is referred to as a Closed Cross. This is where the first multiline, which is called the foreground, remains unchanged while the intersecting multiline is trimmed to intersect with the foreground multiline as shown in Figure 7-17. Note that the trimming is apparent, not actual. The line visibility is changed, but it is still one multiline element. The command sequence is like this:

   Command: **MLEDIT** ⏎ *(pick the Closed Cross image button and pick OK)*
   Select first mline: *(pick the foreground multiline)*
   Select second mline: *(pick the intersecting multiline)*

   The Closed Cross intersection is automatically made, and AutoCAD issues a prompt to let you pick additional multilines for intersection or type U to Undo the intersection you just made. If you Undo, AutoCAD gives the Select first mline: prompt again.

   Select first mline (or Undo): **U** ⏎
   Select first mline: *(pick the foreground multiline)*
   Select second mline: *(pick the intersecting multiline)*
   Select first mline (or Undo): ⏎
   Command:

Figure 7-17.   MLEDIT Closed Cross option.

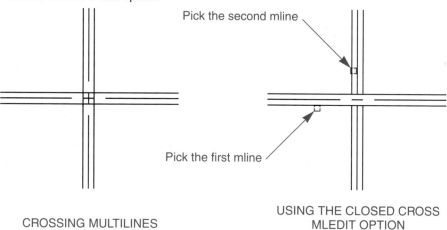

Pick the second mline

Pick the first mline

CROSSING MULTILINES

USING THE CLOSED CROSS
MLEDIT OPTION

- **Open Cross.** Select the Open Cross image button to trim all of the elements of the first picked multiline and only the outer elements of the second multiline are trimmed as shown in Figure 7-18. The command sequence is the same as previously discussed.

Figure 7-18. MLEDIT Open Cross option.

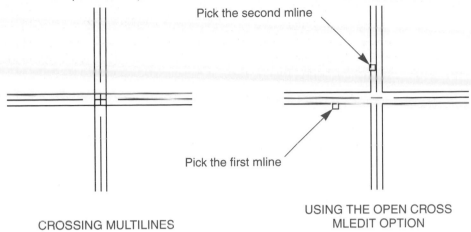

Merged Cross. The Merged Cross image button allows you to trim all outer elements while all interior elements remain the same as shown in Figure 7-19.

Figure 7-19. MLEDIT Merged Cross option

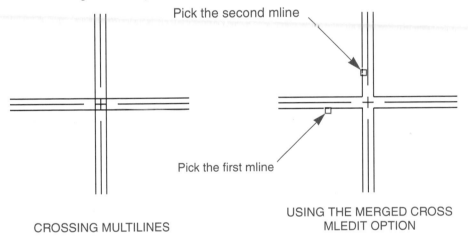

Editing the tees

The second column of the "Multiline Edit Tools" dialog box is for editing tees. The MEDIT tee options are illustrated in Figure 7-20. The options are described as follows:
- **Closed Tee.** Pick the Closed Tee option to have AutoCAD trim or extend the first selected multiline to its intersection with the second multiline.

Figure 7-20.   MLEDIT Tee options.

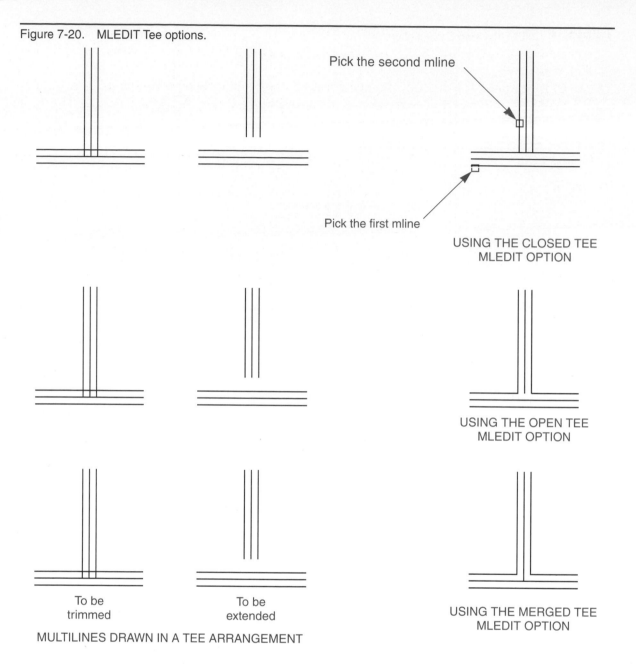

- **Open Tee.** The first pick of the Open Tee option is the multiline to trim or extend and the second is the intersecting multiline. The intersecting multiline is trimmed and left open where the first multiline joins. See Figure 7-20.
- **Merged Tee.** The Merged Tee option trims or extends the intersecting multiline by creating an open appearance with the outer elements and joining the interior elements. See Figure 7-20.

EXERCISE 7-9

❏ Load AutoCAD and open PRODR1, or begin a new drawing using your own variables.
❏ Use the MLINE and MEDIT commands to do the following:
   ❏ Draw three sets of multilines that meet or nearly meet at a tee and then use the Closed Tee option to edit the first, Open Tee for the second, and Merged Tee to edit the third. Use Figure 7-20 as an example.
❏ Save the drawing as A:EX7-9 and quit.

Editing the corner joint and multiline vertices

The third column of the "Multiline Edit Tools" dialog box has a corner joint option and vertex control options. The options are described in the following:

- **Corner Joint.** This MLEDIT option creates a corner joint between two multilines. The first multiline is trimmed or extended to its intersection with the second multiline as shown in Figure 7-21.

Figure 7-21.   MLEDIT Corner Joint option

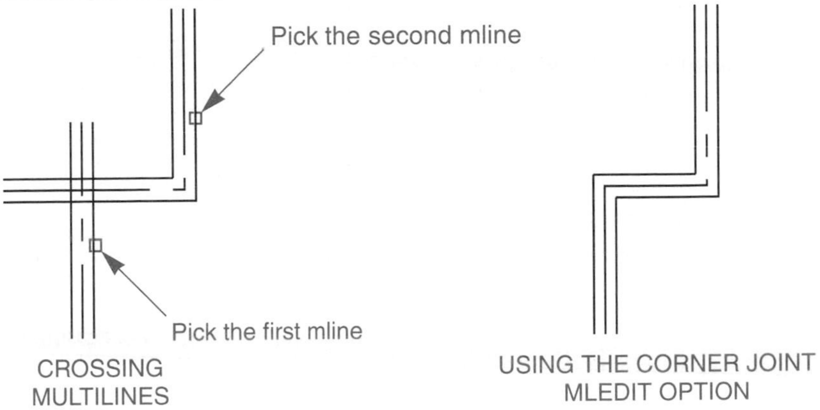

Pick the second mline

Pick the first mline

CROSSING MULTILINES

USING THE CORNER JOINT MLEDIT OPTION

- **Add Vertex.** This MLEDIT option adds a vertex to an existing multiline at the location where you pick as shown in Figure 7-22. The command sequence is a little different than before and looks like this:

Command: **MLEDIT** ↵ *(pick the Add Vertex image button and pick OK)*
Select mline: *(pick the place on the mline for the new vertex)*
Select mline (or Undo): ↵
Command:

Figure 7-22.   MLEDIT add and delete vertices option.

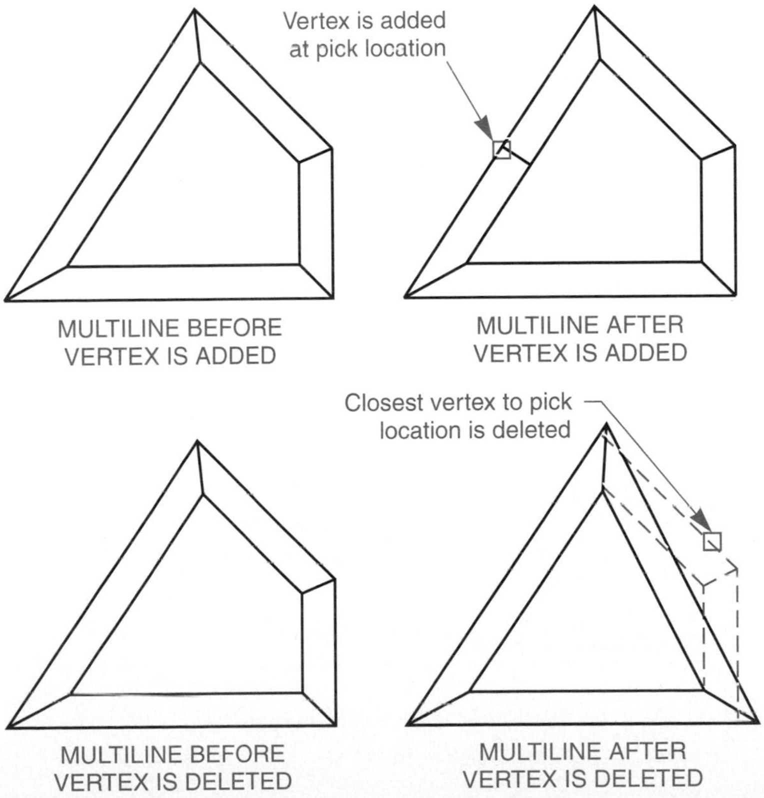

Vertex is added at pick location

MULTILINE BEFORE VERTEX IS ADDED

MULTILINE AFTER VERTEX IS ADDED

Closest vertex to pick location is deleted

MULTILINE BEFORE VERTEX IS DELETED

MULTILINE AFTER VERTEX IS DELETED

- **Delete Vertex.** The Delete Vertex option removes a vertex from an existing multiline nearest to the location where you pick as shown in Figure 7-22.

EXERCISE 7-10

❑ Load AutoCAD and open PRODR1, or begin a new drawing using your own variables.
❑ Use the MLINE and MEDIT commands to do the following:
  ❑ Draw multilines similar to the before example in Figure 7-21 and then use the Corner Joint option to edit similar to Figure 7-21.
  ❑ Draw multilines similar to the before example in Figure 7-22 and then use the Add and Delete Vertex options to edit similar to Figure 7-22.
❑ Save the drawing as A:EX7-10 and quit.

Cutting and welding multilines

The fourth column of image buttons in the "Multiline Edit Tools" dialog box is for cutting a portion out of a single multiline element or the entire multiline, or connecting a space between multiline ends. AutoCAD refers to the connecting operation as *welding*. The options are illustrated in Figure 7-23.

Figure 7-23.   MLEDIT cut single, cut all, and weld options.

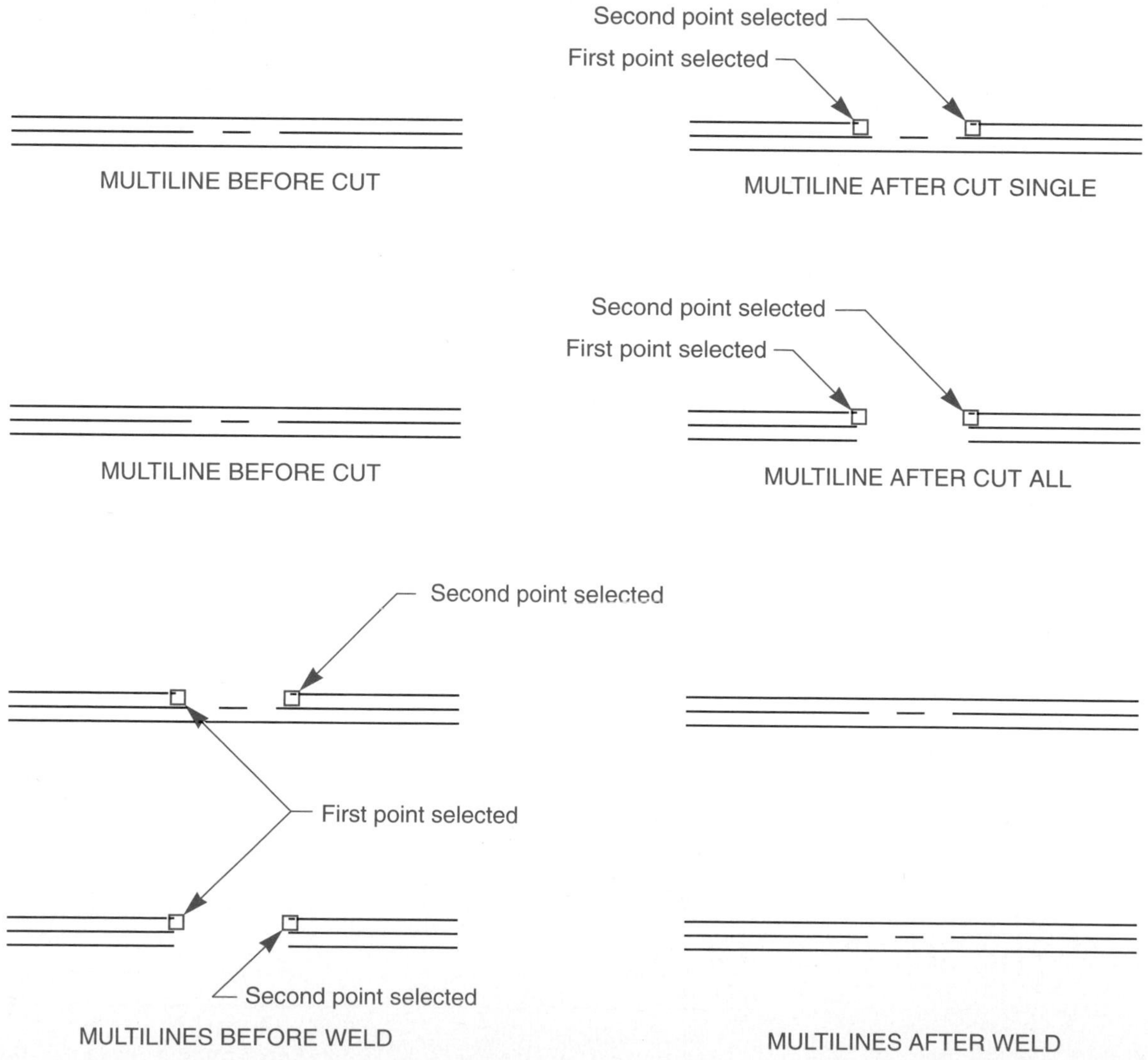

- **Cut Single.** This option allows you to *cut* a single element between two specified points. Cutting only affects visibility of elements, and does not separate a multiline object. The multiline is still a single object. AutoCAD uses the points you pick on the multiline as the cut points. Be sure you pick the points where you want the cut to occur, or enter U to Undo the operation and try again. The command is performed as follows:

> Command: **MLEDIT** ↵ *(pick the Cut Single image button and pick OK)*
> Select mline: *(pick the place for the first cutpoint on the mline)*
> Select second point: *(pick the place for the second cut point)*
> Select mline (or Undo): ↵
> Command:

- **Cut All.** This MLEDIT option cuts all of the elements of a multiline between specified points. The multiline is still a single object even though it appears to be separated.
- **Weld All.** This option repairs all cuts in a multiline between two selected points.

EXERCISE 7-11

❑ Load AutoCAD and open PRODR1, or begin a new drawing using your own variables.
❑ Use the MLINE and MEDIT commands to do the following:
   ❑ Draw multilines similar to those in Figure 7-23 and then use the Cut Single, Cut All, and Weld options to edit the multilines similar to those edited in that figure.
❑ Save the drawing as A:EX7-11 and quit.

PROFESSIONAL TIP

    Multiline objects are complex objects similar to blocks, and can be exploded. Multiline objects become individual line segments after being exploded. A block is a symbol that is created for future use. Blocks are discussed in detail in Chapter 25. The EXPLODE command is completely explained in Chapters 18, 22, and 25. The following is a brief look at the EXPLODE command sequence:

> Command: **EXPLODE** ↵
> Select objects: *(pick the object to explode)*
> Select objects: ↵
> Command:

SKETCHING WITH AUTOCAD   AUG 2

    While the SKETCH command is not commonly used, it does have value for certain applications. Sketching with AutoCAD allows you to draw as if you are sketching with pencil on paper. The SKETCH command is used when it is necessary to draw a contour that is not defined by geometric shapes or straight lines. Examples of freehand sketching with AutoCAD include:
- Contour lines on topographic maps.
- Maps of countries and states.
- Architectural landscape symbols, such as trees, bushes, and plants.
- Graphs and charts.
- Graphic design, such as found on a greeting card.
- Short breaks, such as those used in mechanical drafting.

USING THE SKETCH COMMAND   AUG 2

    The SKETCH command requires the use of a pointing device. Sketching may not be done using the keyboard cursor movement keys. Before using the SKETCH command, it is best to turn SNAP and

ORTHO modes off since they limit the cursor's movement to horizontal and vertical increments of the snap grid. Normally, you want total control over the cursor when sketching. The SKETCH command can be entered at the keyboard, DRAW 1 screen menu, or Draw pull-down menu. When you enter SKETCH, AutoCAD responds with the following:

    Command: **SKETCH** ⏎
    Record increment ⟨0.1000⟩:

The "Record increment" is the length of each sketch line element generated as you move the cursor. For example, if the record increment is 0.1 (default value), sketched images consist of 0.1 long lines. An increment setting of 1 creates sketched line segments 1 unit long. Reducing the record increment increases the accuracy of your sketched image. However, record increments less than .1 consume great amounts of computer storage. To view the chosen record increment, turn the ORTHO mode on and draw stair steps. Each horizontal and vertical element is the length of the record increment. If the SNAP mode is also on, the record increment automatically equals the snap increment. Figure 7-24 shows a comparison of .1 and 1 record increments.

Figure 7-24.   Sketching record increments.

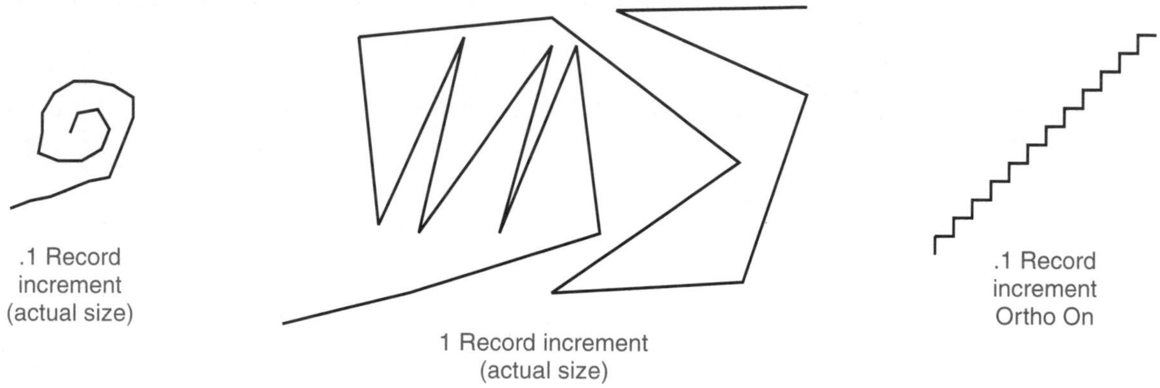

.1 Record
increment
(actual size)

1 Record increment
(actual size)

.1 Record
increment
Ortho On

To set a .1 record increment, type .1 or press ENTER to accept the default value.

    Record increment ⟨0.1000⟩: ⏎

AutoCAD then issues the following prompt:

    Sketch. Pen eXit Quit Record Erase Connect .

Once you see the Sketch. prompt, the buttons on your puck activate the SKETCH subcommands. If you do not use a puck, the subcommands may be entered at the keyboard. Simply type the capitalized letter in each. The following list shows the puck button and keyboard letters used to access each subcommand.

Keyboard Entry	Puck Button	Subcommand Function
Pen (P)	0	Pen up, Pen down.
"." (period)	1	To draw a line from endpoint of sketched line.
Record (R)	2	Records skatched lines as permanent.
eXit (X, space, or Return)	3	Records sketched lines and exists SKETCH command.
Quit (Q, CTRL+C)	4	Removes all entities created before R or X.
Erase (E)	5	Erases all entities created before R or X.
Connect (C)	6	Connects to endpoint of sketched line after a pen up has been issued.

The normal puck buttons for SNAP (4) and ORTHO (5) modes remain disabled as long as the SKETCH command is active. However, you can access ORTHO and SNAP with their function keys, F8 and F9.

Drawing sketched lines

Sketching is done with the Pen subcommand. It is similar to sketching with paper and pencil. When the pencil is "down," you are ready to draw. When the pencil is "up," you are thinking about what to draw next or moving to the next location. Type P to select "pen down," and sketch. Move your cursor around to create a line. Type P again to select pen up to stop sketching. When you type "P" or use the pick button 0, the prompt line reads:

Sketch. Pen eXit Quit Record Erase Connect . ⟨Pen down⟩ ⟨Pen up⟩

PROFESSIONAL TIP

 If you do not consider yourself an artist, trace an existing design. Tape it to the digitizer and move the cursor along the outline of the shape with the pen down. Do not forget to select "pen up" when moving to a new sketching location.

Using the . subcommand

To draw a straight line from the endpoint of the last sketched line to a selected point, do the following:
1. Make sure the "pen" is up.
2. Move the screen cursor to the desired point.
3. Type . or press puck button 1.
A straight line is automatically drawn.

Using the Erase subcommand

You can erase while sketching. If you make a mistake, type E or press puck button 5. The pen may be up or down. If the pen is down, it is automatically raised. AutoCAD responds with the message:

Erase: Select end of delete. ⟨Pen up⟩

Move the cursor to erase any portion of the sketch, beginning from the last point. When finished, type P or press the pick button 0. If you decide not to erase, type E or press button 5. AutoCAD returns to the SKETCH command after issuing the "Erase aborted" message.

Recording sketched lines

As you sketch, the lines are displayed in color and are referred to as *temporary lines*. Temporary lines become *permanent lines* and are displayed in their final color after they are recorded. You can record the lines and remain in the SKETCH command by typing R or pressing puck button 2. You may also record and exit the SKETCH command by typing X, pressing the space bar, pressing ENTER, or using puck button 3. AutoCAD responds with a message indicating the number of lines recorded. For example, suppose you created 32 lines, the message reads: "32 lines recorded."

Quitting the SKETCH command

To get out of the SKETCH command without recording temporary lines, type Q, press CTRL+C, or press puck button 4. This removes all temporary lines and returns the Command: prompt.

Connecting the endpoint of the line

It is customary to select "pen up" to pause or to make a menu selection. When the pen is up, return to the last sketched point and resume sketching by typing C, or pressing puck button 6. AutoCAD responds with this message:

Connect: Move to the endpoint of line.

Move the cursor to the end of the previously sketched temporary line. As soon as the crosshairs touch the previously drawn line, the pen automatically goes down and you can resume sketching.

Consuming storage space with the SKETCH command

Sketching consumes computer storage rapidly. A drawing with fine detail will quickly fill your floppy disk. Therefore, the SKETCH command should be used only when necessary. The record increment should be set as large as possible, yet still appear pleasing. In commercial applications, such as topographical maps, the storage capacity is designed to accept the required input. Figure 7-25 shows a sketch of a rose. This drawing nearly filled one high-density disk (1,440,000 bytes).

Figure 7-25.   A rose drawn using the SKETCH command. (Susan Waterman)

EXERCISE 7-12

❑ Load AutoCAD and enter the drawing editor.
❑ Use the SKETCH command to sketch a bush, tree, or houseplant in plan (top) view.
❑ Save the drawing as A:EX7-12 and quit.

CHAPTER TEST

Write your answers in the spaces provided.

1. Give the commands to draw a polyline from point A to point B with a beginning width of .500 and an ending width of 0. Then undo the polyline because you think you made a mistake. Finally, bring it back because you realized you did not make a mistake:

   Command:_____

   From point: _____

   Current line-width 0.0 _____

   Arc/Close/Halfwidth/Length/Undo/Width/⟨End point of line⟩:_____

   Starting width ⟨0.0000⟩: _____

   Ending width ⟨.5000⟩: _____

   Arc/Close/Halfwidth/Length/Undo/Width/⟨End point of line⟩:_____

   Arc/Close/Halfwidth/Length/Undo/Width/⟨End point of line⟩:_____

   Command:_____

   Auto/Back/Control/End/Group/Mark/⟨Number⟩:_____

   Command:_____

2. Give the command and entries needed to draw two parallel lines, with a center line between, with center justification, and end line caps, and the style is already saved as ROAD1:

   Command:_____

   Justification = Top, Scale = 1.00, Style = STANDARD _____

   Justification/Scale/STyle/⟨From point⟩: _____

   Mstyle name (or?): _____

   Justification = Top, Scale = 1.00, Style = ROAD1 _____

   Justification/Scale/STyle/⟨From point⟩: _____

   Top/Zero/Bottom ⟨top⟩: _____

   Justification = Zero, Scale = 1.00, Style = ROAD1 _____

   Justification/Scale/STyle/⟨From point⟩: _____

   ⟨To point⟩: _____

   Undo/⟨To point⟩:_____

3. How do you draw a filled arrow using the PLINE command? _____

   _____

4. Name two commands that may be used to draw wide lines. _____

   _____

5. Which PLINE option allows you to specify the width from the center to one side?_____

   _____

6. What is an advantage of leaving the FILL mode turned Off? _____

   _____

7. What is the difference between picking Undo from the Pline: screen menu as compared with entering the UNDO command? _____

_____

8. Name the command that is used to bring back an object that was previously removed using UNDO. _____

9. Name the MLINE command option that establishes how the resulting lines are offset based on the definition points provided. _____

_____

10. Name the option that controls the multiplier for the offset values specified in the MLINE command. _____

_____

11. How do you access the "Multiline Style" dialog box? _____

_____

12. Describe the function of the Add button in the "Element Properties" subdialog box._____

_____

13. Describe the function of the Linetype… button in the "Element Properties" subdialog box. _____

_____

14. Define end caps. _____

_____

_____

15. Name the Multiline Properties Caps options. _____

_____

16. Define joints. _____

_____

_____

17. What do you get when you enter the MLEDIT command?_____

_____

18. How do you access one of the MLEDIT options?_____

_____

19. List the three options that are used for editing crossings in the MLEDIT command. _____

_____

20. Name the MLEDIT option where the intersecting multiline is trimmed or extended and left open where the first multiline joins. _____

_____

21. Name the MLEDIT option that allows you to remove a vertex from a multiline._____

_____

22. Name the MLEDIT option that lets you remove a portion from an individual multiline element.

_____

23. Name the MLEDIT option that removes all of the elements of a multiline between two specified points. _____

_____

24. Name the MLEDIT option that repairs all cuts in a multiline. _____

_____

25. Explain why the SNAP and ORTHO modes should be turned off for most sketching applications.

_____

DRAWING PROBLEMS

1. Use the PLINE command to draw the following object with a .032 line width. Do not draw dimensions. Save the drawing as A:P7-1.

P7-1

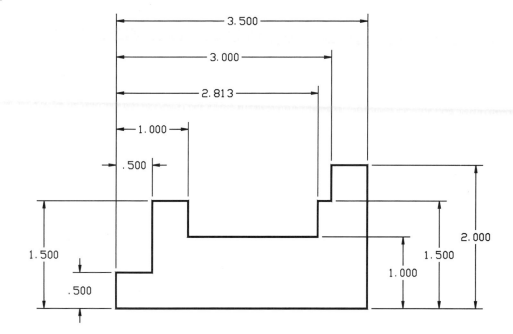

P7-2

2. Use the PLINE command to draw the following object with a .032 line width. Do not draw dimensions. Save the drawing as A:P7-2.

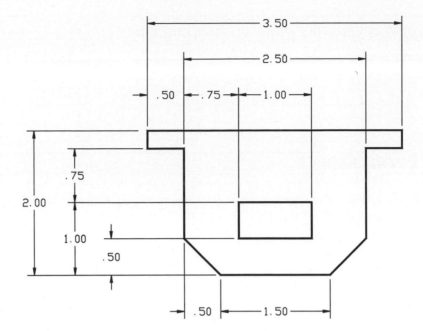

P7-3

3. Use the TRACE command to draw the following object with a .032 line width. Do not draw dimensions.

A. Turn off the FILL mode and use the REGEN command. Then, turn on FILL and do REGEN again.

B. Observe the difference with FILL on and off.

C. Save the drawing as A:P7-3.

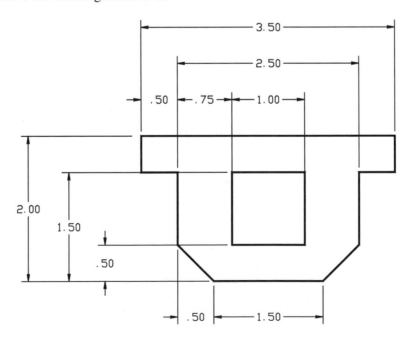

4. Use the PLINE command to draw the filled rectangle shown below. Do not draw dimensions. Save the drawing as A:P7-4.

P7-4

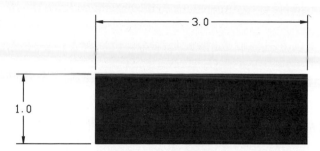

5. Draw the objects shown at A and B below. Then, use the Undo option to remove object B. Use the REDO command to get object B back. Save this drawing as A:P7-5.

P7-5

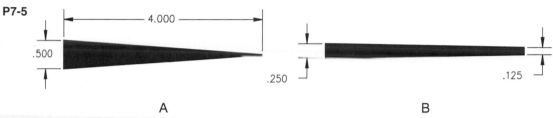

A   B

6. Draw the object shown below. Set limits at 11,8.5, decimal units, .25 grid, and .0625 snap. Save your drawing as A:P7-6.

P7-6

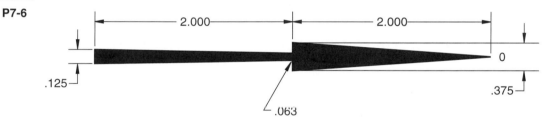

P7-7

7. Draw the following objects using the multiline commands. Use the options indicated with each illustration. Set limits to 11,8.5, grid at .50, and snap at .25. Set the line offset to .25. Do not add text or dimensions to the drawings. Save the drawings as A:P7-7.

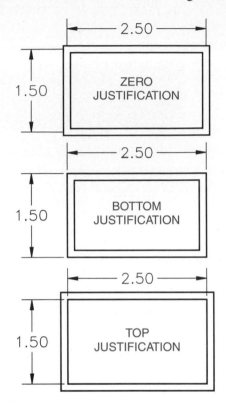

P7-8

8. Draw the following objects using the multiline commands. Establish a line offset proportional to the given objects. Do not draw the dimensions or text. Save the drawing as A:P7-8.

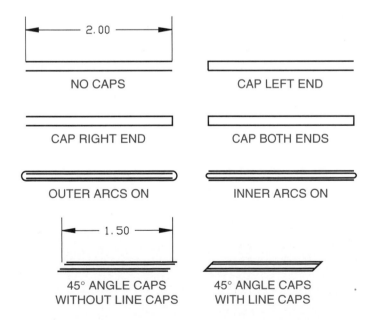

P7-9

9. Draw the partial floor plan using the MLINE command. Carefully observe how the dimensions correlate with the walls to determine your offset settings. Also, use the end cap and MLEDIT Break options appropriately. Set limits to 88",68", grid to 24, snap to 12, and use architectural units. Make all walls 6 in. thick. Do not add text or dimensions to the drawing. Save the drawing as A:P7-9.

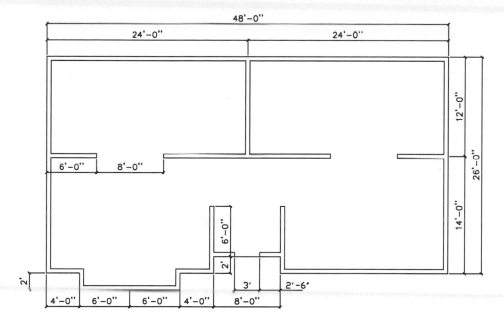

P7-10

10. Draw the following proposed subdivision map using the multiline commands. Establish a line offset proportional to the given map. Use a centerline for the linetype at the center of the roads. The absolute coordinates are given at the road end and intersection centerlines. Do not draw the text. Save the drawing as A:P7-10.

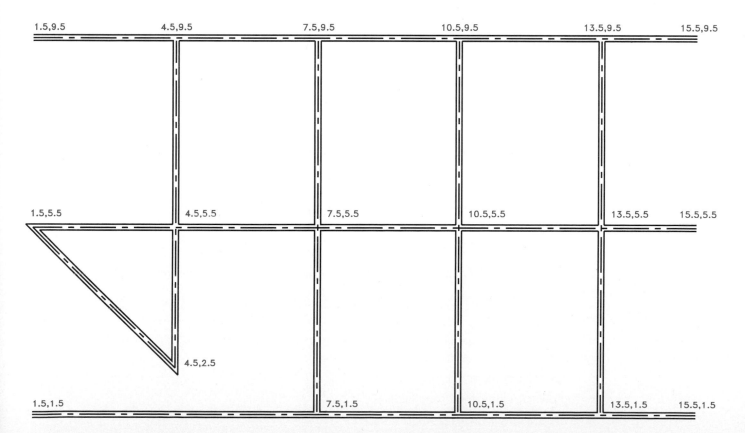

P7-11

11. Draw the following proposed electrical circuit using the multiline commands. Establish a line offset proportional to the given layout. Use a phantom line for the linetype at the center of the runs. The absolute coordinates are given at the connections. Do not draw the text. You establish any drawing features that are not defined by coordinates. Save the drawing as A:P7-11.

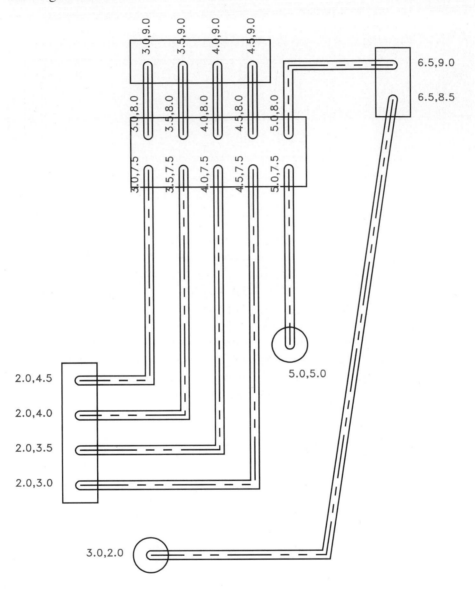

P7-12

12. Use the SKETCH command to sign your name. Save the drawing as A:P7-12.

P7-13

13. Use the SKETCH command to design the cover of a greeting card. Save the design as A:P7-13.

P7-14

14. Find a map of your state and make a photocopy. Tape the copy to your digitizer tablet. Using the SKETCH command, do the following:

A. Trace the outline of the map.

B. Include all major rivers and lakes.

Save the drawing as A:P7-14.

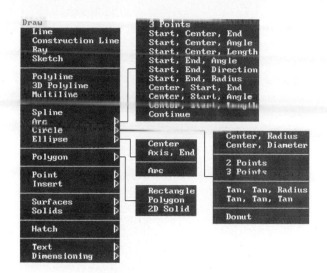

Learning objectives

After completing this chapter, you will be able to:

- ○ Use DRAGMODE to observe an object drag into place.
- ○ Draw circles using the CIRCLE command options.
- ○ Identify and use the @ symbol function.
- ○ Draw arcs using the ARC command options.
- ○ Draw an arc extending from a previously drawn arc.
- ○ Draw an arc extending from a previously drawn line.
- ○ Use the pull-down menu to draw multiple shapes.
- ○ Use the ELLIPSE command to draw ellipses and elliptical arcs by various methods.
- ○ Draw polygons from given information.
- ○ Explain and use the MULTIPLE command modifier.
- ○ Draw doughnuts.
- ○ Preset polygon and doughnut specifications.

The decisions made when drawing circles and arcs with AutoCAD are similar to those required when drawing the items manually. You have options to consider. These include the center location and radius or diameter, or where the outline of the circle or arc should be located. AutoCAD provides many ways to create circles and arcs using the CIRCLE and ARC commands. AutoCAD also provides the ELLIPSE and POLYGON commands, which draw a wide variety of shapes.

WATCHING OBJECTS DRAG INTO PLACE $\boxed{\text{AUG 4}}$

Chapter 6 showed how the LINE command displays a dashed image that is "dragged" across the screen before the second endpoint is picked. This same dashed image, called a *rubberband*, drags across the screen when drawing other entities, too. The CIRCLE, ARC, ELLIPSE, and POLYGON commands display a rubberband image to help you decide where to place the entity.

When a circle is drawn using the Center and Radius options, a dashed circle image appears on the screen. This image gets larger or smaller as you move the pointer. When the desired circle size is picked, the dragged image is replaced by a solid-line circle as shown in Figure 8-1.

Figure 8-1.   Dragging a circle to its desired size.

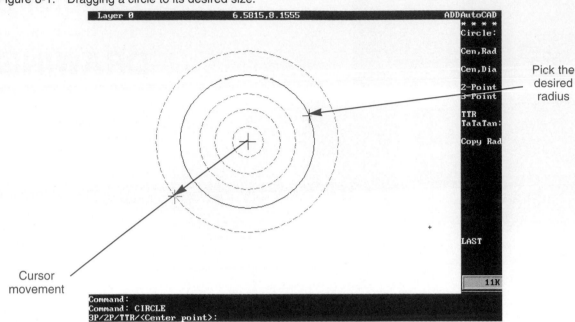

The DRAGMODE may be set to be ON, OFF, or Automatic by typing DRAGMODE at the Command: prompt and pressing ENTER as follows:

Command: **DRAGMODE** ↵
OFF/ON/Auto ⟨current⟩: *(type* **OFF, ON,** *or* **A** *and press* ENTER*)*

The current (default) mode is shown in brackets. Pressing the ENTER key keeps the existing status. An ON response turns DRAGMODE on. When DRAGMODE is on, dragging is permitted by entering DRAG at the appropriate time in the command sequence or by menu selection. When the DRAGMODE is on, you decide when to use DRAG. Selecting OFF disables the DRAGMODE, and all DRAG requests are ignored by AutoCAD. When you set DRAGMODE to AUTO by typing an A, the drag capabilities are automatically used by AutoCAD for all commands that support dragging. Many users prefer to have the DRAGMODE set to Auto. However, some computer configurations slow down the drag process. When this occurs, you may prefer to turn DRAGMODE On and Off by choice. The following command sequence shows you how to activate the DRAGMODE when in another command.

Command: **CIRCLE** ↵
3P/2P/TTR/⟨Center point⟩: *(pick a center point)*
Diameter/⟨Radius⟩: **DRAG** ↵ *(pick the desired radius)*

DRAWING CIRCLES   AUG 2

The CIRCLE command is located in the DRAW 1 screen menu and the Draw pull-down menu, or access it by typing CIRCLE or C at the Command: prompt. The CIRCLE command has these options: Center, Radius; Center Diameter; 2 Points; 3 Points; Tan, Tan, Radius; and Tan, Tan, Tan. *Tan* is the AutoCAD abbreviation for tangent. The CIRCLE command options are explained in the following section.

Drawing a circle by radius

When you select CEN,RAD: (CENter,RADius), AutoCAD asks you to first pick a center point. Then either pick the radius on the screen or type the radius value, Figure 8-2. If the radius is picked on the screen, watch the coordinate display to locate the exact radius. CEN,RAD is also the circle command's default option. The CIRCLE command gives the following as you use the CEN,RAD option:

Command: **CIRCLE** ↵
3P/2P/TTR/⟨Center point⟩: *(select a center point)*
Diameter/⟨Radius⟩: *(drag the circle to the desired radius and pick, or type the radius size and press* ENTER*)*

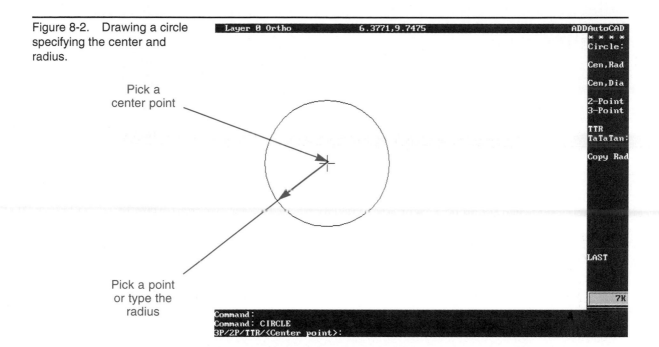

Figure 8-2.   Drawing a circle specifying the center and radius.

Pick a center point

Pick a point or type the radius

The radius value you enter becomes the default setting for the next time you use the CIRCLE command. Use the CIRCLERAD system variable if you want to set a radius default. This provides you with the same circle radius default value each time you use the CIRCLE command until you use a different value. The CIRCLERAD system variable works like this:

Command: **CIRCLERAD** ↵
New value for CIRCLERAD ⟨0⟩: *(set the desired default,* **.50** *for example)*

The CIRCLE command sequence then looks like this:

Command: **CIRCLE** ↵
3P/2P/TTR/⟨Center point⟩: *(pick the center point)*
Diameter/⟨Radius⟩ ⟨.50⟩: ↵
Command:

When the CIRCLERAD system variable is set to a non-zero value, all you have to do is pick the center point of the circle and press ENTER to accept the default value. You can always enter a different radius or pick a desired radius point if you want to ignore the default value. Set CIRCLERAD to 0 if you do not want a constant radius default.

Drawing a circle by diameter

You can select the center point and the diameter of a circle by picking CEN,DIA: from the screen menu. If the CIRCLE command is typed, the Diameter option is required at the prompt line because "Radius" is the default:

> Command. **CIRCLE** ⏎
> 3P/2P/TTR/⟨Center point⟩: *(select a center point)*
> Diameter/⟨Radius⟩: **D** ⏎
> Diameter: *(drag the circle to the desired diameter and pick, or type the diameter size and press* ENTER*)*

Figure 8-3. Drawing a circle using the CEN,DIA: option. Notice that AutoCAD calculates the circle's position as you move the cursor.

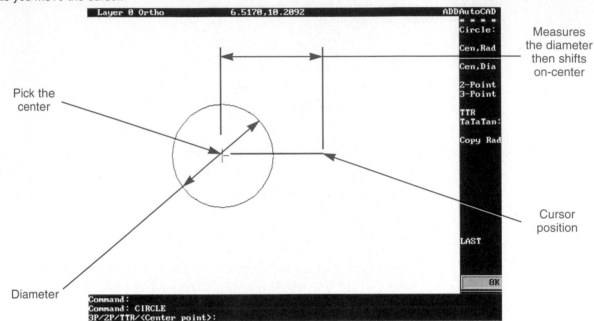

Watch the screen carefully when using the CEN,DIA: option; something a little strange happens. The pointer measures the diameter, but the circle passes midway between the center and the cursor as shown in Figure 8-3. The CEN,DIA: option is convenient because most circle dimensions are given as diameters.

After you draw a circle, the radius you selected becomes the default for the next circle if CIRCLERAD is set to 0. If you use the Diameter option, the previous default setting is converted to a diameter. If you use the Radius option to draw a circle after using the Diameter option, AutoCAD changes the default to a radius measurement based on the previous diameter. If you set CIRCLERAD to a value such as .50, then the default for a circle drawing with the Diameter option is automatically 1.00 (twice the radius).

Drawing a two-point circle

A two-point circle is drawn by picking two points on opposite sides of the circle, Figure 8-4. This option is useful if the diameter of the circle is known, but the center is difficult to find. One example is locating a circle between two lines. The command sequence for a two-point circle is as follows:

> Command: **CIRCLE** ⏎
> 3P/2P/TTR/⟨Center point⟩: **2P** ⏎
> First point on diameter: *(select a point)*
> Second point on diameter: *(select a point)*

Figure 8-4. Drawing a circle by selecting two points on the circle.

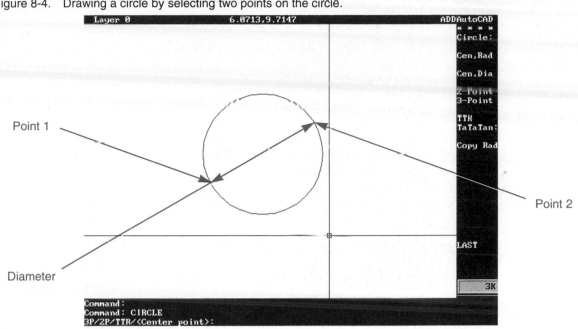

If the CIRCLERAD variable is set to 0, AutoCAD uses this radius as the default for the next circle.

Drawing a three-point circle

If three points on the circumference of a circle are known, the three-point option is the best method to select, Figure 8-5. The three points may be selected in any order. The three-point option gives the following prompts:

Command: **CIRCLE** ↵
3P/2P/TTR/⟨Center point⟩: **3P** ↵
First point: *(select a point)*
Second point: *(select a point)*
Third point: *(select a point)*

Figure 8-5. Drawing a circle given three points on the circle.

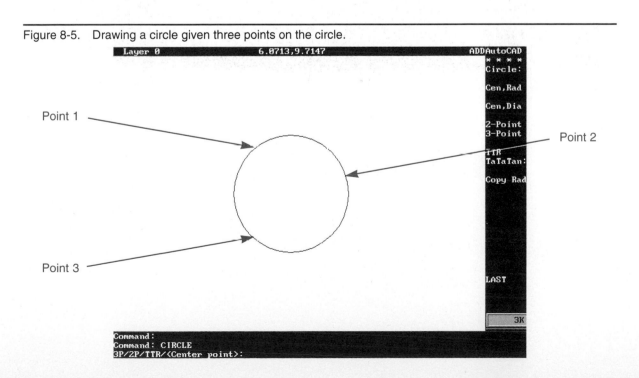

If CIRCLERAD is set to 0, AutoCAD automatically calculates the radius of the circle and uses this value as the default for the next circle.

Drawing a circle tangent to two objects with a known radius

The term *tangent* refers to a line, circle, or arc that comes into contact with an arc or circle at only one point. That point is called the *point of tangency.* A line drawn from the circle's or arc's center to the point of tangency is perpendicular to the tangent line. Circles are tangent when they touch at only one point. A line drawn between the centers passes through the point of tangency. When it is necessary to draw a circle tangent to given lines, circles, or arcs, select the TTR: option. Then select the lines or line and arc to which the new circle will be tangent. The radius of the circle is also required. To assist you in picking the three objects, the screen cursor takes on the shape of a box and crosshairs. This is called an *aperture* and is discussed in detail in Chapter 9. When you see the aperture, move it to the objects that you want to pick. The command sequence is as follows:

> Command: **CIRCLE** ⏎
> 3P/2P/TTR/ ⟨Center point⟩: **TTR** ⏎
> Enter Tangent spec: *(pick the first line, circle, or arc)*
> Enter second Tangent spec: *(pick the second line, circle, or arc)*
> Radius: *(type a radius value and press* ENTER*)*

If the radius entered is too small, AutoCAD gives you the message: Circle does not exist. If the CIR-CLERAD system variable is set to 0, the radius you use for the TTR: option becomes the default for the next circle. Two examples of the TTR option are shown in Figure 8-6.

Figure 8-6.   Two examples of drawing circles tangent to two given objects using the TTR: option.

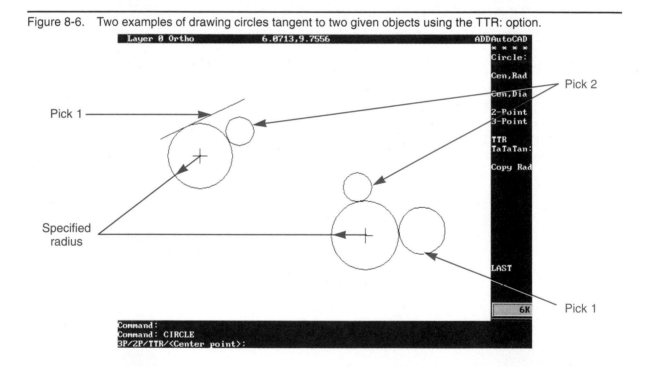

Drawing a circle tangent to three objects

You can draw a circle tangent to three existing objects by using the Tan, Tan, Tan option. This option is found in the Draw pull-down menu as Tan, Tan, Tan in the Circle cascading menu, and in the Circle: screen menu as TaTaTan: You need to pick one of these to access this option. This works like the 3 point option by automatically drawing a circle tangent to three objects that you pick. The Command sequence looks like this and is illustrated in Fig. 8-7.

Command: circle 3P/2P/TTR/⟨Center point⟩: _3p First point: _tan to *(pick the first object)*
Second point:_tan to *(pick the second object)*
Third point:_tan to *(pick the third object)*
Command:

Figure 8-7. Two examples of drawing circles tangent to three given objects.

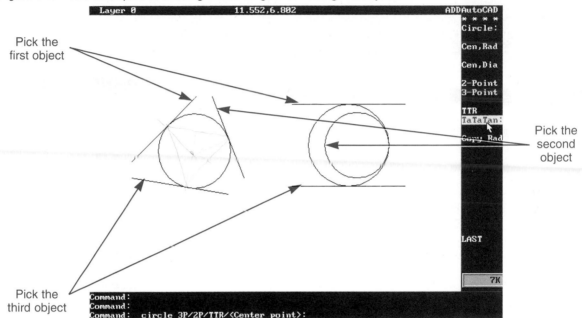

NOTE If a point prompt is answered with a pick where no tangent exists, the TAN mode must be manually reactivated for the second attempt at that pick. TAN is one of the object snap modes that is discussed in Chapter 9. For now, type TAN and press ENTER if you miss an object when trying to pick it. This returns the aperture box so you can pick again as follows:

Command: circle 3P/2P/TTR/⟨Center point⟩: _3p First point: _tan to *(pick the first object)*
Second point:_tan to *(pick the second object)*
Third point:_tan to *(you try but fail to pick the third object)*
No Tangent found for specified point.
Invalid 2D point.
Third point: **TAN** ⏎
to_*(pick the third object)*
Command:

PROFESSIONAL TIP

Using the CIRCLERAD system variable to set a fixed default is helpful and saves drafting time when you plan to draw several circles with the same radius.

The Copy Rad option

The Circle: screen menu also contains the Copy Rad option. Picking this activates the AutoCAD geometry calculator, which is discussed in detail in Chapter 9. While this is not a complete explanation of the geometry calculator, you can use the Copy Rad option to draw a circle with exactly the same radius as an existing circle or arc, or length of a polyline arc segment. To make this work, draw a circle, arc, or polyline arc segment. A circle is shown in Figure 8-8. Next, pick Copy Rad from the Circle: screen menu to get this prompt:

New value for CIRCLERAD: '_cal Expression: rad
〉〉Select circle, arc or polyline segment for RAD function *(pick the existing circle)*
Command: **CIRCLE** ↵
3P/2P/TTR/〈Center point〉: Diameter/〈Radius〉〈1.5000〉: ↵
Command:

Figure 8-8.   Drawing a circle with the same radius as an existing arc or circle, or length of polyline, using the Copy Rad option. Pressing Enter at the Radius: prompt draws the new circle.

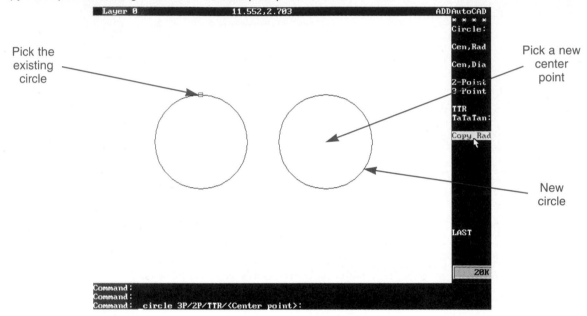

USING THE @ SYMBOL TO SPECIFY THE LAST COORDINATES

| AUG 2 |

The @ symbol may be used alone to input the same coordinates as previously selected. For example, suppose you want to draw a circle with its center at the end of a previously drawn line. Enter the @ symbol at the 〈Center point〉: prompt as follows:

Command: **LINE** ↵
From point: **4,4** ↵
To point: **8,4** ↵
To point: ↵
Command: **CIRCLE** ↵
3P/2P/TTR/〈Center point〉: **@** ↵

The @ symbol automatically issues the coordinate 8,4 (end of the last line) as the center of the circle. The 8,4 value is saved in the LASTPOINT system variable. The @ retrieves the LASTPOINT value.

Another application is drawing concentric circles (circles which have the same center). To do this, draw a circle using the CEN,RAD: or CEN,DIA: options. Then enter the CIRCLE command again and type @ at the 〈Center point〉: prompt. This automatically places the center of the new circle at the center of the previous circle.

EXERCISE 8-1

❑ Load AutoCAD and open PRODR1, or start a new drawing and set up your own variables.
❑ Set the CIRCLERAD system variable to 0.
❑ Use the CIRCLE command's CEN,RAD: option to draw a circle similar to the one shown in Figure 8-2.
❑ Use the CIRCLE command's CEN,DIA: option to draw the circle shown in Figure 8-3.
❑ Draw two vertical parallel lines two units apart. Then use the CIRCLE command's 2P option to draw the circle tangent to the two lines.
❑ Use the CIRCLE command's 3P option to draw the circle shown in Figure 8-5.
❑ Use the CIRCLE command's TTR option to draw the circles shown in Figure 8-6.
❑ Draw existing objects similar to those in Figure 8-7 and then pick Tan, Tan, Tan from the Circle cascading menu in the Draw pull-down menu or TaTaTan in the Circle: screen menu to draw circles tangent to the existing objects as in Figure 8-7.
❑ Draw a line. Enter the CIRCLE command's CEN,RAD: option and the @ symbol to place the circle's center at the endpoint of the line.
❑ Draw three concentric circles using the @ symbol to automatically place the circles on the same center.
❑ Set CIRCLERAD to .5 and draw circles using each CIRCLE option to observe the difference in the prompts for the previously drawn circles.
❑ Draw a circle with any desired radius and then use the Copy Rad option in the Circle: screen menu to draw another circle with the same radius as the first, similar to Figure 8-8.
❑ Save the drawing as A:EX8-1 and quit the drawing editor.

DRAWING ARCS

AUG 2

An *arc* is defined as any part of a circle or curve. Arcs are commonly dimensioned with a radius, but may be drawn by a number of different methods. The ARC command is located in the DRAW 1 screen menu and the Draw pull-down menu. AutoCAD provides eleven methods for drawing arcs.

The three-point option is the default if ARC is typed at the Command: prompt. The other options arc given with letters that designate the option prompt sequence. The following list gives the meanings of the ARC option letters. These are illustrated in Figure 8-9.

C *or* Ce   Center of the arc as part of a circle.
S *or* St   Start point. First point on the arc.
E *or* End   Endpoint. Last point on the arc.
Ang   Angle. Refers to the included angle.
Rad   Radius of the arc.
Dir   Direction arc is drawn.
Len   Length of chord. A *chord* is a line connecting the arc end points.

Figure 8-9.   The meaning of the ARC command option abbreviations.

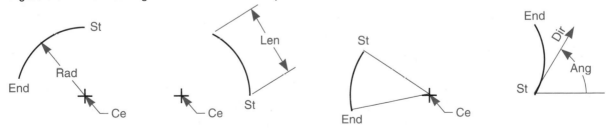

The last element of any arc construction option is automatically dragged into place if DRAGMODE is set to Auto.

Drawing a 3-point arc

The 3-point option asks for the start point, point along the arc, and then the endpoint, Figure 8-10. The arc may be drawn clockwise or counterclockwise, and is dragged into position as the endpoint is located. The following shows the prompts of the three-point option:

Command: **ARC** ↵
Center/⟨Start point⟩: *(select the first point on the arc)*
Center/End/⟨Second point⟩: *(select the second point on the arc)*
End point: *(select the arc's endpoint)*

Figure 8-10.   Drawing an arc by picking three points.

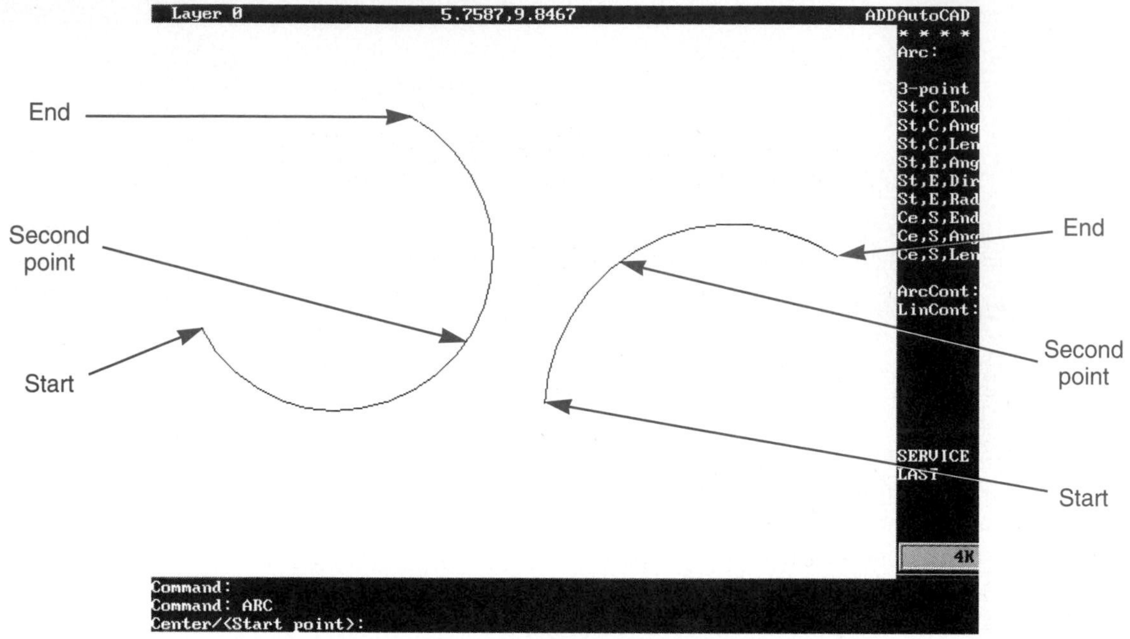

Drawing an arc with the Start, Center, End (St,C,End) option

The St,C,End option is chosen when the start, center, and endpoints are known. Picking the start and center points establishes the arc's radius. The endpoint provides the arc length. For this reason, the arc does not pass through the endpoint, unless this point is also on the radius, Figure 8-11. The following command sequence is used and the arc is drawn counterclockwise:

Command: **ARC** ↵
Center/⟨Start point⟩: *(select the first point on the arc)*
Center/End/⟨Second point⟩: **C** ↵
Center: *(select the arc's center point)*
Angle/Length of chord/⟨End point⟩: *(select the arc endpoint)*

Figure 8-11.   Using the St,C,End option. Notice that the endpoint may not be on the arc's surface.

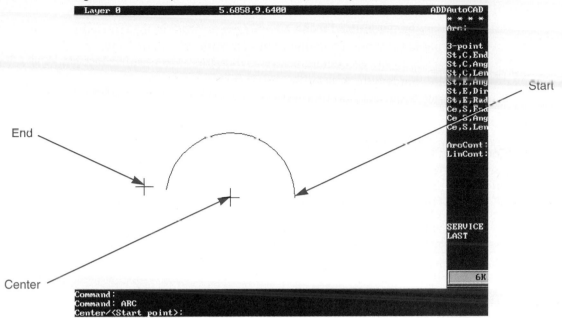

Drawing an arc with the Start, Center, Angle (St,C,Ang) option

When the arc's included angle is known, the St,C,Ang option may be the best choice. The *included angle* is an angle formed between the center, and start and endpoints of the arc. The arc is drawn counterclockwise, from start to end, unless a negative angle is specified. See Figure 8-12. The following command sequence uses the Angle option and specifies a 45° included angle:

Command: **ARC** ↵
Center/⟨Start point⟩: *(select the first point on the arc)*
Center/End/⟨Second point⟩: **C** ↵
Center: *(select the arc center point)*
Angle/Length of chord/⟨End point⟩: **A** ↵
Included angle: **45** ↵

Figure 8-12.   How positive and negative angles work with the Start, Center, Angle option.

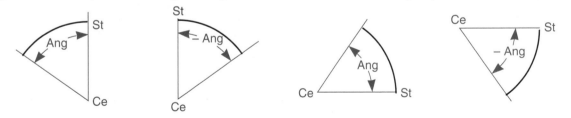

Notice that "DRAG" automatically appears after the Included angle: prompt if the St,C,Ang option is picked from the Arc submenu and the DRAGMODE is set to Auto. This acknowledges that drag is working.

Drawing arcs with the Start, Center, and Length of chord (St,C,Len) option

The chord length may be determined using *Chord Length Table* in the Appendix Section in the back of this text. Referring to the table, a one-unit radius arc with an included angle of 45° has a chord length of .765 units. Arcs are drawn counterclockwise; therefore, a positive chord length gives the smallest possible arc with that length. A negative chord length results in the largest possible arc. See Figure 8-13. The command sequence is as follows:

Command: **ARC** ↵
Center/〈Start point〉: *(select the first point on the arc)*
Center/End/〈Second point〉: **C** ↵
Center: *(select the arc center point)*
Angle/Length of chord/〈End point〉: **L** ↵
Length of chord: DRAG *(type* **.765** *for the smallest arc, or* **–.765** *for the largest arc and press* ENTER*)*

Figure 8-13. How positive and negative chord lengths work with the Start, Center, Length option.

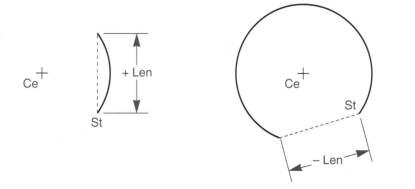

Drawing arcs using the Start, End, and Included Angle (St,E,Ang) option

An arc may also be drawn by picking the start point, endpoint, and entering the included angle. A positive included angle draws the arc counterclockwise, while a negative angle produces a clockwise arc, Figure 8-14. The command sequence is as follows:

Command: **ARC** ↵
Center/〈Start point〉: *(select the first point on the arc)*
Center/End/〈Second point〉: **E** ↵
End point: *(select the arc endpoint)*
Angle/Direction/Radius/〈Center point〉: **A** ↵
Included angle: *(type or pick a positive or negative angle and press* ENTER*)*

Figure 8-14.   How positive and
negative angles work with the
Start, End, Angle option.

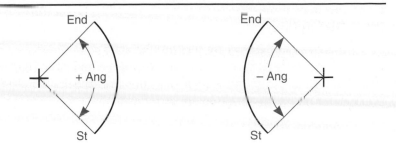

Drawing arcs using the Start, End, Radius (St,E,Rad) option

The start, end, radius method allows an arc to be drawn only counterclockwise, as are most arcs. A positive radius value results in the smallest possible arc between the two endpoints. A negative radius gives the largest arc possible, Figure 8-15. The command sequence is as follows:

Command: **ARC** ↵
Center/⟨Start point⟩: *(select the first point on the arc)*
Center/End/⟨Second point⟩: **E** ↵
End point: *(select the arc endpoint)*
Angle/Direction/Radius/⟨Center point⟩: **R** ↵
Radius: *(pick, or type a positive radius or negative radius and press ENTER)*

Figure 8-15.   Using the Start, End, Radius option with a positive or a negative radius.

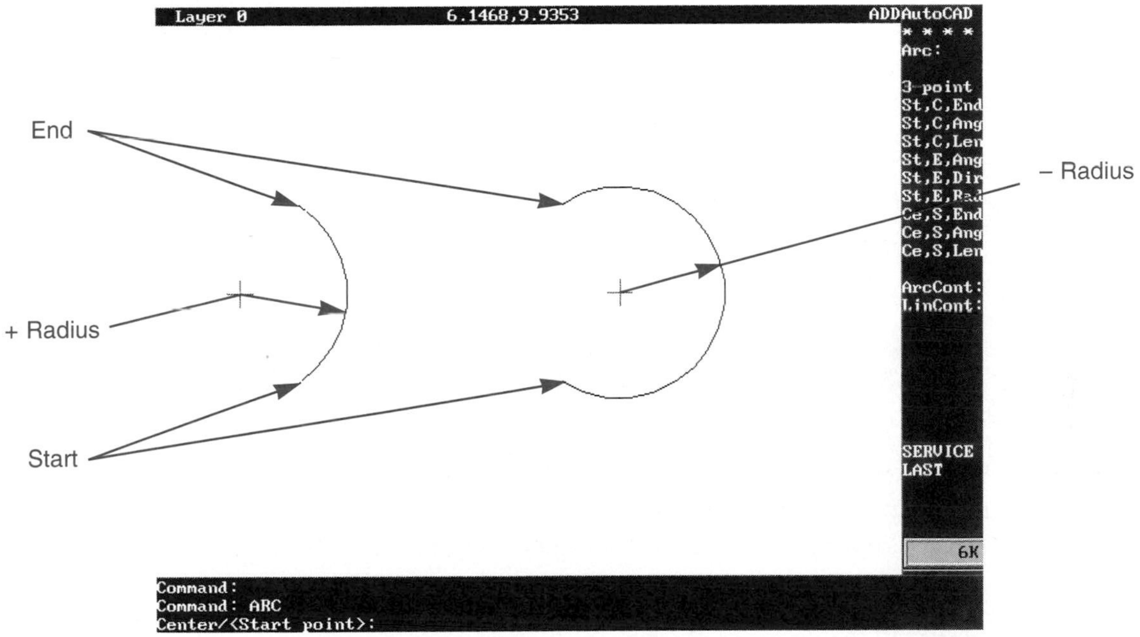

Drawing arcs using the Start, End, starting Direction (St,E,Dir) option

An arc may be drawn by picking the start point, endpoint, and entering direction of rotation in degrees. The distance between the points and the number of degrees determines the arc's location and size. The arc is started tangent to the direction specified as shown in Figure 8-16. The command prompts for the St,E,Dir option are as follows:

Command: **ARC** ↵
Center/〈Start point〉: *(select the first point on the arc)*
Center/End/〈Second point〉: **E** ↵
End point: *(select the arc endpoint)*
Angle/Direction/Radius/〈Center point〉: **D** ↵
Direction from start point: *(pick the direction from the start point, or type the direction in
    degrees and press* ENTER*)*

Figure 8-16.   Using the Start, End, Direction option.

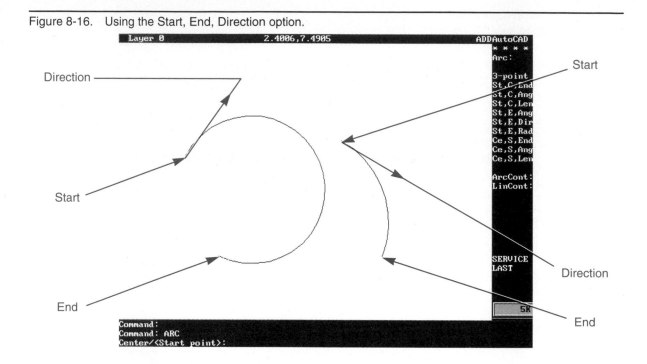

Drawing arcs using the Center, Start, End (Ce,S,End) option

The center, start, end option is a variation of the St,C,End option. Use the Ce,S,End option when it is easier to begin by locating the center. The command sequence is as follows:

Command: **ARC** ↵
Center/〈Start point〉: **C** ↵
Center: *(pick the center point)*
Start point: *(pick the start point)*
Angle/Length of chord/〈End point〉: *(pick the arc's endpoint)*

A drawing showing the use of the Ce,S,End option is displayed in Figure 8-17.

Figure 8-17. Using the Center, Start, End option. Note that the endpoint may not be on the arc's surface.

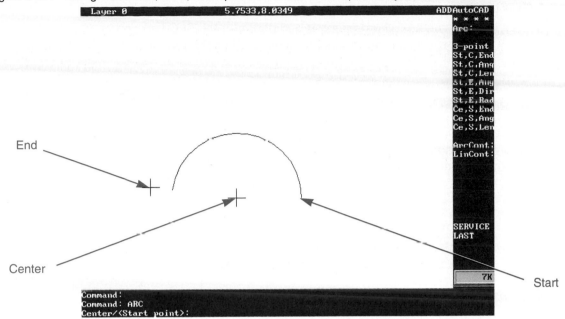

❑ Load AutoCAD and open PRODR1, or start a new drawing and set up your own variables.
❑ Use the ARC command's St,E,Ang option to draw an arc similar to that shown in Figure 8-14.
❑ Use the ARC command's St,E,Rad option to draw the arc shown in Figure 8-15.
❑ Use the ARC command's St,E,Dir option to draw the arcs shown in Figure 8-16.
❑ Use the ARC command's Ce,S,End option to draw the arcs shown in Figure 8-17.
❑ Save the drawing as A:EX8-3 and quit.

Drawing arcs using the Center, Start, Angle (Ce,S,Ang) option

The center, start, angle option is a variation of the St,C,Ang option. Use the Ce,S,Ang option when it is easier to begin by locating the center, Figure 8-18. The command sequence is as follows:

Command: **ARC** ↵
Center/⟨Start point⟩: **C** ↵
Center: *(pick the center point)*
Start point: *(pick the start point)*
Angle/Length of chord/⟨End point⟩: **A** ↵
Included angle: *(pick the included angle or type a positive angle or negative angle and press ENTER)*

Figure 8-18. How positive and negative angles work with the Center, Start, Angle option.

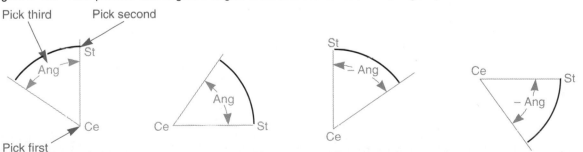

Drawing arcs with the Center, Start, Length of chord (Ce,S,Len) option

The center, start, length of chord option is a variation of the St,C,Len option. Use the Ce,S,Len option when it is easier to begin by locating the center, Figure 8-19. The command sequence is as follows:

Command: **ARC** ↵
Center/⟨Start point⟩: **C** ↵
Center: (*pick the center point*)
Start point: (*pick the start point*)
Angle/Length of chord/⟨End point⟩: **L** ↵
Length of chord: (*pick, or type the chord length and press* ENTER)

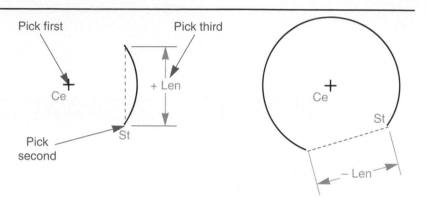

Figure 8-19.   How positive and negative chord lengths work with the Center, Start, Length option.

Continuing an arc from a previously drawn arc or line

An arc may be continued from the previous arc. Press the ENTER key or space bar at the ⟨Start point⟩: prompt, or using the Arc: screen menu, pick ArcCont: to continue an arc or LinCont: to continue a line from the last point of a previously drawn arc. When arcs are drawn in this manner, each consecutive arc is tangent. The start points and direction are taken from the endpoint and direction of the previous arc. Figure 8-20 shows the arc continuation described below.

Command: **ARC** ↵
Center/⟨Start point⟩: (*select the first point on the arc*)
Center/End/⟨Second point⟩: **E** ↵
End point: (*select the arc's endpoint*)
Angle/Direction/Radius/⟨Center point⟩: **D** ↵
Direction from start point: (*pick, or specify the direction from the start point in degrees and press* ENTER)
Command: ↵
ARC Center/⟨Start point⟩: (*press space bar or* ENTER)
End point: (*select the endpoint of the second arc*)
Command: ↵
ARC Center/⟨Start point⟩: (*press space bar or* ENTER)
End point: (*select the endpoint of the third arc*)

Figure 8-20.   Using the CONTIN option to draw three arcs.

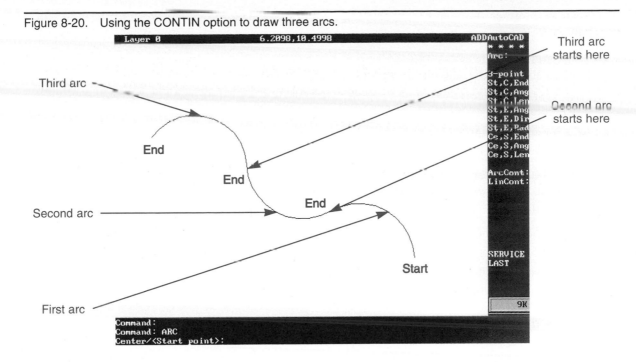

You can quickly draw an arc tangent to the endpoint of a previously drawn line or arc, as shown in Figure 8-21. The command sequence is as follows:

Command: **LINE** ↵
From point: *(select a point)*
To point: *(select the second point)*
To point: ↵
Command: **ARC** ↵
Center/⟨Start point⟩: *(press space bar or ENTER to place start point of arc at end of previous line)*
End point: *(select the endpoint of the arc)*

Figure 8-21.   An arc continuing from the previous line. Point 2 is the start of the arc. Point 3 is the end of the arc.

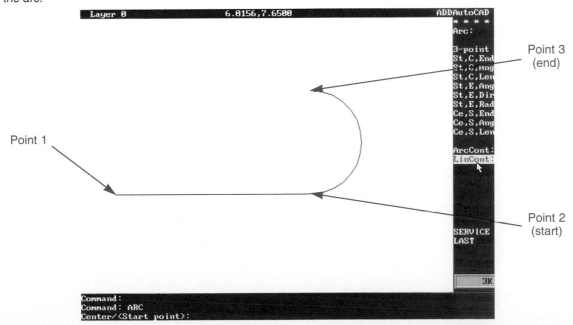

You can continue drawing an arc or a line from a previously drawn arc faster by picking either ArcCont: or LinCont: from the Arc: screen menu at the Command: prompt like this:

Command: **ARC** ↵
Center/⟨Start point⟩: *(pick the start point)*
Center/End/⟨Second point⟩: *(pick the second point)*
End point: *(pick the endpoint)*

Pick ArcCont: or LinCont: from the Arc: screen menu to automatically activate the ARC or LINE command. If you pick ArcCont:, the AutoCAD prompt looks like this:

Command: _arc Center/⟨Start point⟩:
End point: *(pick the arc endpoint)*
Command:

If you pick LinCont:, the AutoCAD prompt looks like this:

Command:_line From point:
Length of line: *(pick the endpoint of the desired line)*
To point: *(pick another line endpoint or press ENTER)*
To point: ↵
Command:

EXERCISE 8-4

❑ Load AutoCAD and open PRODR1, or start a new drawing and set up your own variables.
❑ Use the ARC command's Ce,S,Ang option to draw arcs similar to those shown in Figure 8-18.
❑ Use the ARC command's Ce,S,Len option to draw the arc shown in Figure 8-19.
❑ Use the ARC command's CONTIN option and draw the arcs shown in Figure 8-20.
❑ Use the ARC command's CONTIN option to draw an arc connected to a previously drawn line as shown in Figure 8-21.
❑ Save the drawing as A:EX8-4 and quit.

USING THE PULL-DOWN MENU TO DRAW CIRCLES AND ARCS

AUG 2

The Draw pull-down menu displays Arc and Circle as two of the selections. Picking either of these selections displays the cascading menus shown in Figure 8-22.

When you select Circle from the Draw pull-down menu, the Circle cascading submenu appears with the CIRCLE options listed, Figure 8-22A. Pick the desired option and the command sequence continues as discussed earlier in this chapter.

When you pick Arc from the pull-down menu, the Arc cascading submenu with the Arc options is displayed, Figure 8-22B.

Figure 8-22. A—The Circle cascading submenu (shown here highlighted). B The Arc cascading submenu (shown here highlighted).

A

B

DRAWING ELLIPSES

AUG 2

When a circle is viewed at an angle, an elliptical shape is seen. For example, a 30° ellipse is created if a circle is rotated 60° from the line of sight. The parts of an ellipse are shown in Figure 8-23.

Figure 8-23. Parts of an ellipse.

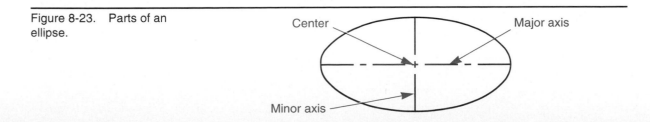

An ellipse may be drawn using different options of the ELLIPSE command. The ELLIPSE command is found in the DRAW 1 screen menu or the Draw pull-down menu, or can be typed at the Command: prompt:

> Command: **ELLIPSE** ⏎
> Arc/Center/⟨Axis endpoint 1⟩: *(select an axis endpoint)*
> Axis endpoint 2: *(select the other endpoint of the axis)*

The Axis endpoints option establishes either the major or minor axis. The next prompt determines which axis is entered first, as shown in Figure 8-24.

> ⟨Other axis distance⟩/Rotation: *(select a distance from the midpoint of the first axis to the end of the second axis and press* ENTER*)*

The ellipse is dragged by the cursor until the point is picked.

Figure 8-24. Constructing the same ellipse twice by choosing different axis endpoints.

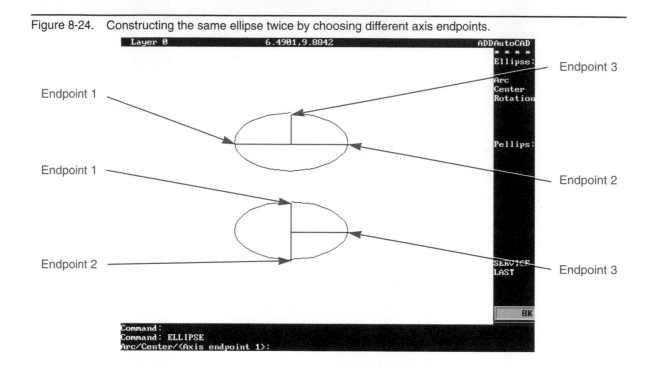

If you respond to the ⟨Other axis distance⟩/Rotation: prompt with R for Rotation, AutoCAD assumes you have selected the major axis with the first two points. The next prompt requests the angle that the ellipse is rotated from the line of sight. The command sequence is as follows:

> Command: **ELLIPSE** ⏎
> Arc/Center/⟨Axis endpoint 1⟩: *(select an axis endpoint)*
> Axis endpoint 2: *(select the other endpoint of the axis)*
> ⟨Other axis distance⟩/Rotation: **R** ⏎
> Rotation around major axis: *(type a rotation angle, such as* **30**, *and press* ENTER*)*

The 30 response draws an ellipse that is 30° from the line of sight. A 0 response draws a circle with both major and minor axes equal to the circle's diameter. Any angle greater than 89.4° is rejected by AutoCAD because the ellipse appears as a line. Figure 8-25 shows the relationship between several ellipses having the same major axis length, but different rotation angles.

Figure 8-25. Ellipse rotation angles.

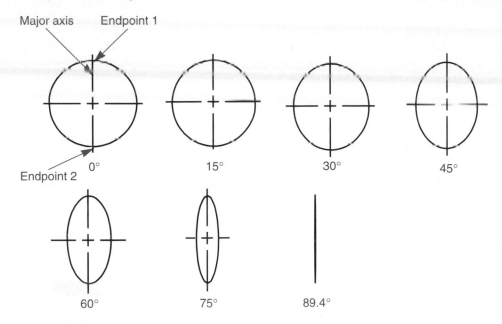

An ellipse may also be constructed by specifying the center point and endpoints of the two axes, Figure 8-26. Use the following command sequence:

Command: **ELLIPSE** ↵
Arc/Center/⟨Axis endpoint 1⟩: **C** ↵
Center of ellipse: *(select the ellipse center point)*
Axis endpoint: *(select the endpoint of one axis)*
⟨Other axis distance⟩/Rotation: *(select the endpoint of the other axis)*

Figure 8-26. Drawing an ellipse by picking the center and endpoints of two axes.

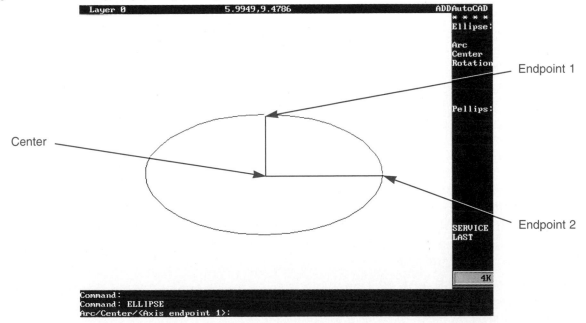

The rotation option may be used instead of selecting the second axis endpoint. See Figure 8-27. The command sequence is as follows:

Command: **ELLIPSE** ↵
Arc/Center/⟨Axis endpoint 1⟩: **C** ↵
Center of ellipse: *(select the ellipse center point)*
Axis endpoint: *(select the endpoint of one axis)*
⟨Other axis distance⟩/Rotation: **R** ↵
Rotation around major axis: **30** ↵

Figure 8-27.   Drawing an ellipse using the center option and the rotation angle. This ellipse was drawn using a 30° rotation angle.

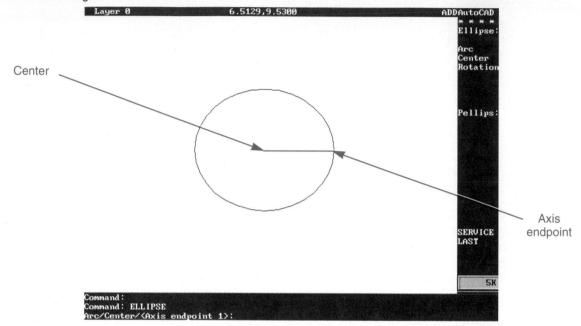

EXERCISE 8-5

❑ Load AutoCAD and open PRODR1, or start a new drawing and set up your own variables.
❑ Use the ELLIPSE command's Axis endpoints option to draw the ellipse shown in Figure 8-24.
❑ Use the ELLIPSE command's center and axis endpoints option to draw the ellipse shown in Figure 8-26.
❑ Use the ELLIPSE command's center and rotation angle option to draw the ellipse shown in Figure 8-27.
❑ Save the drawing as A:EX8-5 and quit.

Drawing elliptical arcs

The ELLIPSE command may also be used to draw elliptical arcs with the Arc option. Pick Arc from the Ellipse screen menu, Arc from the cascading Ellipse pull-down menu, or type the ELLIPSE command and enter the Arc option:

Command: **ELLIPSE** ↵
Arc/Center/⟨Axis end point 1⟩: **A** ↵
⟨Axis endpoint 1⟩/Center: *(pick the first axis endpoint)*
Axis endpoint 2: *(pick the second axis endpoint)*

You can now drag the shape of a full ellipse on the screen to help you visually select the other axis distance if needed. The other axis distance is from the ellipse center to the point picked:

⟨Other Axis distance⟩/Rotation: *(pick the other axis distance)*

Next, enter a start angle. The start and end angles are the angular relation between the ellipse center and where arc begins. The angle of the elliptical arc is established from the angle of the first axis. A 0 start angle is the same as the Axis end point 1 while a 45° start angle is 45° counterclockwise from the start angle. End angles are also established counterclockwise from the start point:

Parameter/⟨start angle⟩: **0** ↵
Parameter/Included/⟨end angle⟩: **90** ↵
Command:

Figure 8-28 shows the elliptical arc drawn with the previous command sequence, and displays samples of different start and end angle arcs.

Figure 8-28.   Drawing elliptical arcs with the Arc option. Note the three examples at the bottom using three different angle settings.

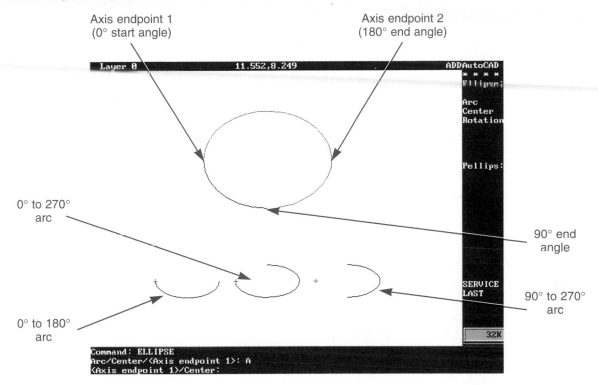

Using the Parameter option

The Parameter option requires the same input as the start angle. The difference is that AutoCAD creates the elliptical arc using a different means of vector calculation. The results are similar but the command sequence looks like this:

Parameter/⟨start angle⟩: **P** ↵
Angle/⟨start parameter⟩: *(pick the start point)*
Angle/Included/⟨end parameter⟩: *(pick the endpoint)*
Command:

Using the Included Angle option

The Included option establishes an included angle beginning at the start angle. An included angle is an angle that is formed by two sides or in this case an angle that is formed as a number of degrees from the start angle. The command sequence looks like this:

Command: **ELLIPSE** ↵
Arc/Center/⟨Axis endpoint 1⟩: **A** ↵
⟨Axis endpoint 1⟩/Center: *(pick the first axis endpoint)*
Axis endpoint 2: *(pick the second axis endpoint)*
⟨Other axis distance⟩/Rotation: *(pick the other axis distance)*
Parameter/⟨start angle⟩: **0** ↵
Parameter/Included/⟨end angle⟩: **I** ↵
Included angle ⟨*current*⟩: **180** ↵
Command:

Rotating an elliptical arc around its axis

The Rotation option for drawing an elliptical arc is similar to the Rotation option when drawing a full ellipse as discussed earlier. Refer back to Figure 8-25 for an example of various rotation angles. This option allows you to rotate the elliptical arc about the first axis by specifying a rotation angle as follows:

Command: **ELLIPSE** ↵
Arc/Center/⟨Axis endpoint 1⟩: **A** ↵
⟨Axis endpoint 1⟩/Center: *(pick the first as endpoint)*
Axis endpoint 2: *(pick the second axis endpoint)*
⟨Other axis distance⟩/Rotation: **R** ↵
Rotation around major axis: **45** ↵
Parameter/⟨start angle⟩: **90** ↵
Parameter/Included/⟨end angle⟩: **180** ↵
Command:

Drawing an elliptical arc using the Center option

The Center option for drawing an elliptical arc lets you establish the center of the ellipse using this command sequence, as shown in Figure 8-29:

Command: **ELLIPSE** ↵
Arc/Center/⟨Axis endpoint 1⟩: **A** ↵
⟨Axis endpoint 1⟩/Center: **C** ↵
Axis endpoint: *(pick the first axis endpoint)*
⟨Other axis distance⟩/Rotation: *(pick the other axis distance)*
Parameter/⟨start angle⟩: **0** ↵
Parameter/Included/⟨end angle⟩: **180** ↵
Command:

Figure 8-29.   Drawing elliptical arcs with the Center option.

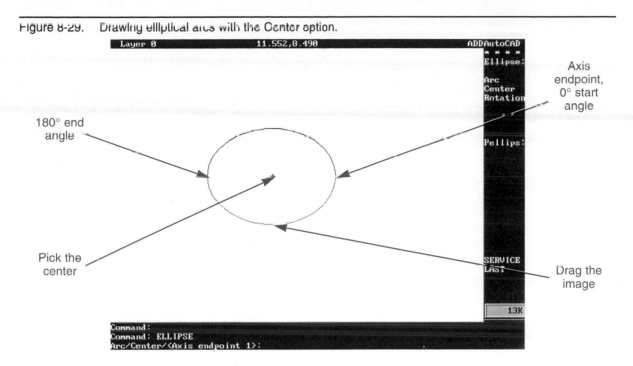

The PELLIPSE system variable

PELLIPSE is an AutoCAD system variable having a value of either 0 or 1. When the value is 0, the object created using the ELLIPSE command is a true elliptical object. A true elliptical object can be grip edited while keeping the object elliptical. Grip editing is discussed in Chapter 14. If the PELLIPSE value is 1, the object created is a polyline ellipse. An elliptical polyline can be grip edited or PEDITed with each vertex able to move without maintaining the elliptical shape. The ELLIPSE command's Arc option is not available when PELLIPSE is set to 1. The AutoCAD default is 0, but you can change it like this:

Command: **PELLIPSE** ↵
New value for PELLIPSE ⟨0⟩: **1** ↵
Command:

EXERCISE 8-6

❑ Load AutoCAD and open PRODR1, or start a new drawing and set up your own variables.
❑ Use the ELLIPSE command's Arc option to draw the following elliptical arcs:
  ❑ Use axis endpoints, axis distance, start angle = 0, and end angle = 90; similar to Figure 8-28.
  ❑ Use the same options as in the previous instructions to draw a 0° to 180° arc, 0° to 270° arc, and a 90° to 270° arc similar to the samples in Figure 8-28.
  ❑ Use the Parameter option to draw an elliptical arc of your own design.
  ❑ Use the Rotation option to rotate an elliptical arc 45° about its axis.
  ❑ Use the included option to draw an elliptical arc with a 180° included angle and another with a 90° included angle.
  ❑ Use the Center option to draw an elliptical arc of your own design.
❑ Save the drawing as A:EX8-6 and quit.

DRAWING REGULAR POLYGONS   AUG 2

A *regular polygon* is any closed plane geometric figure with three or more equal sides and equal angles. A hexagon, for example, is a six-sided regular polygon. After drawing regular polygons using manual drafting techniques, you will be impressed with AutoCAD's POLYGON command. The command is used to draw any regular polygon with 3 to 1024 sides. A large number of sides is usually impractical; too many sides make the polygon look like a circle.

The POLYGON command is located in the DRAW 1 screen menu and the Draw pull-down menu, and can also be typed in at the Command: prompt. It prompts for the number of sides. If you want an octagon (polygon with eight sides), enter 8 as follows:

Command: **POLYGON** ↵
Number of sides ⟨*current*⟩: **8** ↵

The number of sides you enter becomes the default for the next time you use the POLYGON command. Next, AutoCAD prompts for the edge or center of the polygon. If you reply by picking a point on the screen, this point becomes the center of the polygon. You are then asked if you want to have the polygon inscribed within, or circumscribed outside, an imaginary circle, Figure 8-30. A polygon is *inscribed* when it is drawn inside a circle and its corners touch the circle. *Circumscribed* polygons are drawn outside of a circle where the sides of the polygon are tangent to the circle. You must specify the radius of the circle. The command continues as follows:

Edge/⟨Center of polygon⟩: (*pick center of polygon*)
Inscribed in circle/Circumscribed about circle (I/C): (*respond with* **I** *or* **C** *and press* ENTER)
Radius of circle: (*type the radius, such as* **2** *and press* ENTER, *or pick a point on the screen at the desired distance from the center*)

The I or C option you select becomes the default for the next polygon.

Figure 8-30.   Drawing an inscribed and a circumscribed polygon.

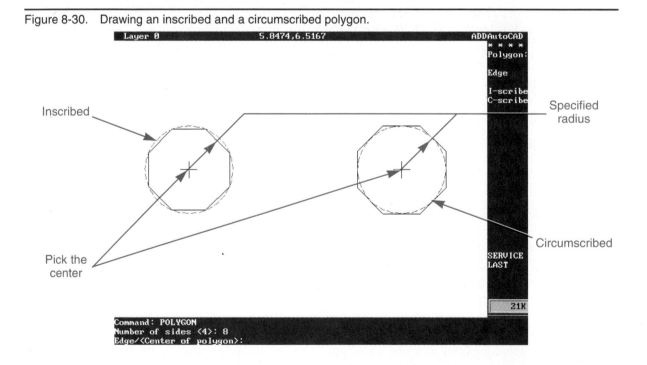

The Edge/⟨Center of polygon⟩: prompt allows you to pick the center or specify the edge. Notice that "Center of polygon" is the default. If you want to draw the polygon on an existing edge, specify the Edge option and pick edge endpoints as follows:

Command: **POLYGON** ↵
Number of sides/⟨4⟩: **8** ↵
Edge/⟨Center of polygon⟩: **E** ↵
First endpoint of edge: (*pick a point*)
Second endpoint of edge: (*pick second point*)

After you pick the endpoints of one side, the rest of the polygon sides are drawn counterclockwise, Figure 8-31.

Figure 8-31.   Drawing a polygon by giving the number of sides and the length of the first side. Note that the sides are drawn counterclockwise.

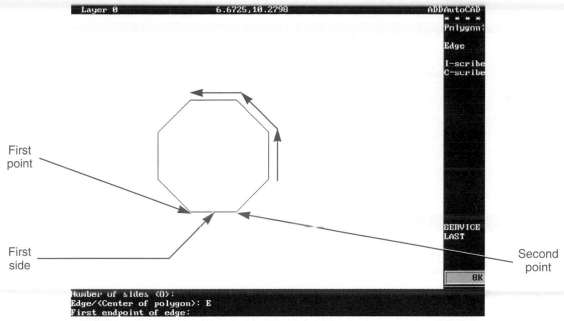

Ellipses and polygons are polylines, and may easily be edited using the PEDIT (Polyline EDIT) command. For example, a polygon may be given width using the Width option of the PEDIT command discussed in Chapter 18.

Hexagons (six-sided polygons) are commonly drawn as bolt heads and nuts on mechanical drawings. Keep in mind that these features are normally dimensioned across the flats. To draw a hexagon, or any polygon, dimensioned across the flats, circumscribe it. The radius you enter is equal to one-half the distance across the flats. The distance across the corners (inscribed polygon) is specified when the polygon must be confined within a circular area. One example is the boundary of a swimming pool in architectural drafting. Notice the distance across the flats and the distance across the corners in Figure 8-32.

Figure 8-32.   Specifying the distance across the flats and between corners of a polygon.

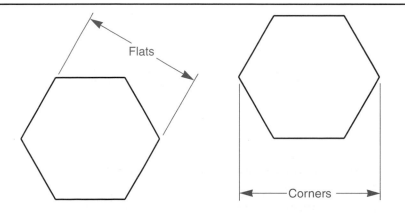

Setting the Polygon SIDES default

AutoCAD allows you to set the number of polygon sides default using the POLYSIDES system variable. Set POLYSIDES like this:

Command: **POLYSIDES** ⏎
New value for POLYSIDES ⟨4⟩: **6** ⏎
Command:

The value you specify for the default is used until you change the value again.

DRAWING RECTANGLES

AutoCAD's RECTANGLE command allows you to easily draw rectangles; simply pick one corner, and then the opposite corner. See Figure 8-33. RECTANGLE can be accessed by picking Rectang: in the DRAW 1 screen menu, by accessing the Polygon cascading menu in the Draw pull-down menu, or by typing RECTANG at the Command: prompt as follows:

Command: **RECTANG** ⏎
First corner: *(pick first corner)*
Other corner: *(pick the opposite corner)*
Command:

Figure 8-33. Using the RECTANGLE command. Simply pick opposite corners of the rectangle.

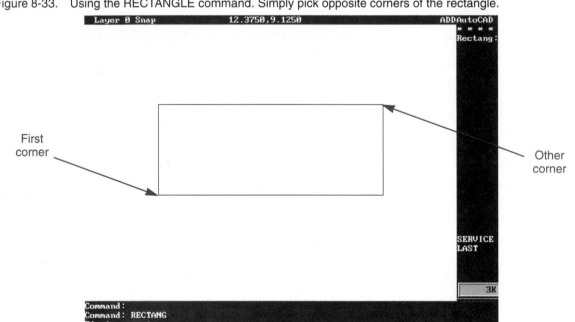

After the rectangle has been placed in the drawing, it is treated as one entity until it is exploded. Then the individual sides can be edited as desired. (The EXPLODE command is discussed in Chapter 18.)

Using the pull-down menu to draw polygons

When you select Polygon from the Draw pull-down menu, the cascading submenu shown in Figure 8-34 is displayed. The commands in the cascading submenu are Rectangle, Polygon, and 2D Solid. The Rectangle and Polygon commands work as previously described. Picking 2D Solid activates the SOLID command. This command is explained in detail in Chapter 24 with regard to creating graphic patterns.

Figure 8-34   The Polygon cascading menu (shown here highlighted) is found in the Draw pull-down menu.

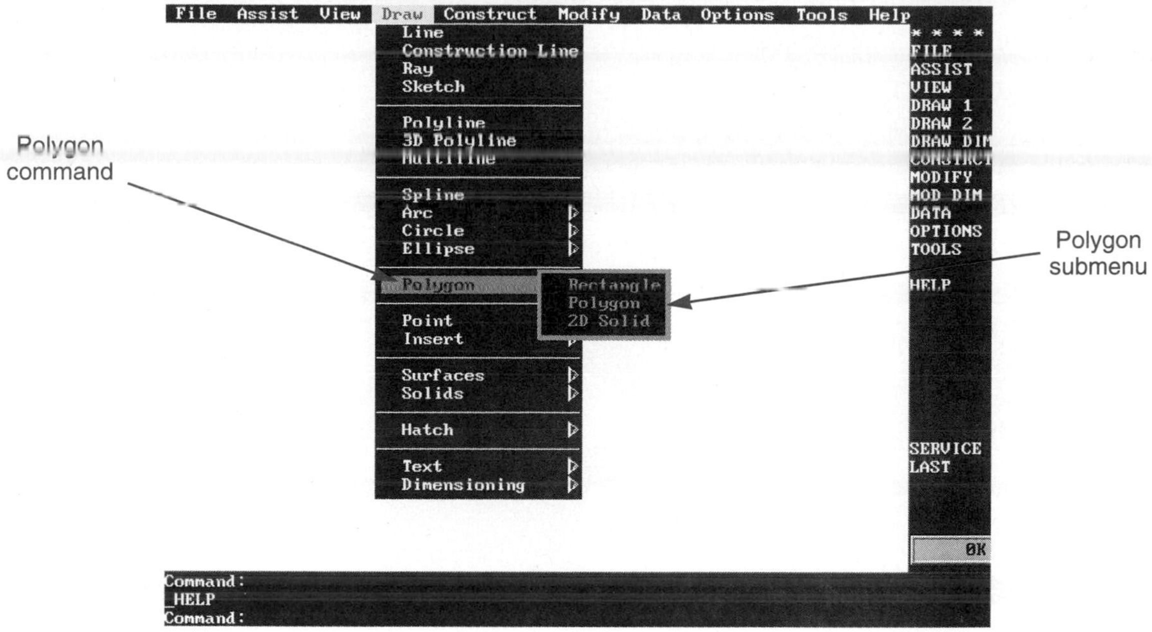

Polygon
command

Polygon
submenu

PROFESSIONAL TIP

The MULTIPLE command modifier, introduced in Chapter 6, automatically repeats commands issued at the keyboard. It may be used to draw repetitive circles, arcs, ellipses, or polygons. For example, if you plan to draw multiple circles, do the following:

> Command: **MULTIPLE CIRCLE** ↵
> 3P/2P/TTR/⟨Center point⟩: *(pick the center point)*
> Diameter/⟨Radius⟩: *(pick, or type the radius and press* ENTER*)*
> CIRCLE 3P/2P/TTR/⟨Center point⟩: *(pick the center point)*
> Diameter/⟨Radius⟩: *(pick, or type the radius and press* ENTER*)*
> CIRCLE 3P/2P/TTR/⟨Center point⟩: *(continue drawing additional circles or cancel*
> *to get back to the Command: prompt)*

AutoCAD automatically reissues the CIRCLE command. Enter CTRL+C to cancel the repeating action.

EXERCISE 8-7

❑ Load AutoCAD and open PRODR1, or start a new drawing and set up your own variables.
❑ Draw a hexagon with a distance of three units across the flats. Then draw another hexagon measuring three units across the corners.
❑ Draw an octagon with a horizontal edge that is 1.75 units long.
❑ Draw a pentagon circumscribed about a circle having a 2.25 inch diameter.
❑ Draw a rectangle measuring 3 x 5 units.
❑ Save the drawing as A:EX8-7 and quit.

DRAWING DOUGHNUTS AND SOLID CIRCLES   AUG 2

AutoCAD's doughnuts are actually circular polylines. Drawing polylines was introduced in Chapter 6 and is covered in detail in Chapter 18. The DONUT command allows you to draw a thick circle. It can have any inside and outside diameter or be completely filled in, Figure 8-35. When the FILL mode is turned off, doughnuts appear as segmented circles or concentric circles as shown on the bottom in Figure 8-35. FILL may be used transparently by entering 'FILL while inside the command. Then, simply enter ON or OFF as needed. The fill in previously drawn donuts remains on until the drawing is regenerated. The command may be issued as DOUGHNUT, or DONUT to save time:

Command: **DONUT** ⏎
Inside diameter ⟨*current*⟩: *(specify a new inside diameter and press* ENTER, *or press* ENTER *to accept the current value)*
Outside diameter ⟨*current*⟩: *(specify a new outside diameter and press* ENTER, *or press* ENTER *to accept the current value)*

Figure 8-35.   Examples of doughnuts. A–With FILL mode On. B–With FILL mode Off.

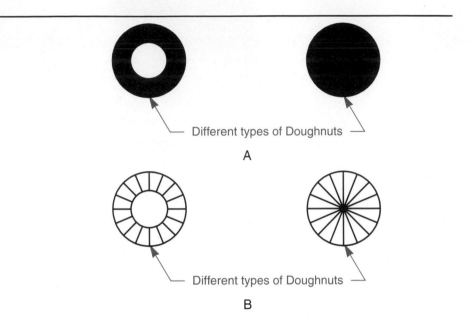

The previously set inside diameter is shown in brackets. A new inside diameter may be entered at this time, or press the ENTER key to keep the existing value. A 0 response to the Inside diameter ⟨current⟩: prompt gives you a solid circle, Figure 8-36. The next request is for a new outside diameter. Press ENTER to keep the current value. AutoCAD then asks:

Center of doughnut: *(select the doughnut center point)*

Figure 8-36.   Doughnuts can be drawn with a 0 inside diameter to create solid circles.

When a center point is picked, the doughnut is drawn with its center at that point. Next, a new Center of doughnut: prompt is issued. You may pick another center point to draw the same size doughnut in a new location. Press ENTER if you wish to get back to the Command: prompt. The DONUT command remains active until you press ENTER or CTRL+C to end it.

If you want to draw a doughnut with a .5 inside diameter and a 1.25 outside diameter, respond as follows:

Command: **DONUT** ↵
Inside diameter ⟨*current*⟩: **.5** ↵
Outside diameter ⟨*current*⟩: **1.25** ↵
Center of doughnut: *(select the doughnut center point)*
Center of doughnut: *(select a center point or* ENTER*)*

This doughnut is shown in Figure 8-37.

Figure 8-37. The doughnut that results from the command sequence given in the text.

Doughnut with ø.5 inside
and ø1.25 outside

Presetting the DONUT options

AutoCAD allows you to preset the DONUT options so the inside and outside diameters have defaults. This saves time when you plan to draw only doughnuts with a given inside and outside diameter. To set DONUTS to automatically issue a default inside and outside diameter, use the DONUTID and DONUTOD system variables to set the inside and outside diameters respectively. The DONUTID variable can be 0 or any other value. The DONUTOD variable must be a nonzero value. If DONUTID is larger than DONUTOD, the two values are interchanged by the next command. The command sequences for DONUTID and DONUTOD variables is as follows:

Command: **DONUTID** ↵
New value for DONUTID ⟨0.5000⟩: **.25** ↵
Command: **DONUTOD** ↵
New value for DONUTOD ⟨1.000⟩: **.75** ↵
Command:

Now, when you type or pick the DONUT command from the screen menu or Draw pull-down menu the previously set values are the defaults.

EXERCISE 8-8

❑ Load AutoCAD and open PRODR1, or start a new drawing and set up your own variables.
❑ Draw a doughnut with a .5 inside diameter and a 1.5 outside diameter.
❑ Draw a doughnut with a 0 inside diameter and a 1.5 outside diameter.
❑ Turn the FILL mode off and type REGEN to see what happens to the doughnuts.
❑ Set DONUTID to .25 and DONUTOD to .75.
❑ Type DONUT at the Command: prompt and draw a doughnut using the defaults.
❑ Use a transparent FILL command ('FILL) to turn FILL on while in the DONUT command. Now, draw two more doughnuts. Regenerate the drawing.
❑ Select Donut from the Circle options of the Draw pull-down menu and draw three more doughnuts. Notice the inside and outside presets you set earlier are automatically used.
❑ Save the drawing as A:EX8-8 and quit.

CHAPTER TEST

Write your answers in the spaces provided.

1. Give the command, entries, and actions required to draw a circle with a 2.5 unit diameter:

   Command:_____

   3P/2P/TTR/⟨Center point⟩: _____

   Diameter/⟨Radius⟩: _____

   Diameter:_____

2. Give the command, entries, and actions to draw a 1.75 unit radius circle tangent to an existing line and circle:

   Command:_____

   3P/2P/TTR/⟨Center point⟩: _____

   Enter Tangent spec: _____

   Enter second Tangent spec: _____

   Radius: _____

3. Give the command, entries, and actions needed to draw a three-point arc:

   Command:

   Center/⟨Start point⟩:_____

   Center/End/⟨Second point⟩:_____

   End point: _____

4. Give the command, entries, and actions needed to draw an arc, beginning with the center point and having a 60° included angle:

   Command:_____

   Center/⟨Start point⟩:_____

   Center: _____

   Start point:_____

   Angle/Length of chord/⟨End point⟩: _____

   Included angle: DRAG _____

5. Give the command, entries, and actions required to draw an arc tangent to the endpoint of a previously drawn line:

   Command:_____

   Center/⟨Start point⟩:_____

   End point: _____

6. Give the command, entries, and actions needed to draw an ellipse with the Axis endpoint option:

   Command:_____

   Arc/Center/⟨Axis endpoint 1⟩: _____

   Axis endpoint 2:_____

   ⟨Other axis distance⟩/Rotation: _____

7. Give the command, entries, and actions necessary to draw a hexagon measuring 4 inches (101.6 mm) across the flats:

   Command:_____

   Number of sides:_____

   Edge/⟨Center of polygon⟩:_____

   Inscribed in circle/Circumscribed about circle (I/C): _____

   Radius of circle:_____

8. Give the responses required to draw two doughnuts with a .25 inside diameter and a .75 outside diameter:

   Command:_____

   Inside diameter ⟨*current*⟩: _____

   Outside diameter ⟨*current*⟩: _____

   Center of doughnut: _____

   Center of doughnut: _____

   Center of doughnut: _____

9. Describe why the @ symbol may be used by itself for point selection. _____

10. Define the term "included angle." _____

    _____

11. List the three input options that may be used to draw an arc tangent to the endpoint of a previously drawn arc._____

12. Given the distance across the flats of a hexagon, would you use the I or C option to draw the hexagon? _____

13. Describe how a solid circle may be drawn. _____

    _____

14. To use the MULTIPLE command modifier to draw a series of arcs, what command do you type?

    _____

15. Explain how you turn the FILL mode off while inside the DONUT command. _____

    _____

    _____

16. Name the system variable used to set the radius default value when drawing circles. _____

    _____

17. Name the system variables used to preset the inside and outside doughnut diameters. _____

    _____

18. Identify two ways to access the option that allows you to draw a circle tangent to three objects.

    _____

    _____

19. Describe the purpose of the Copy Rad option. _____

    _____

    _____

    _____

    _____

20. Name the two picks that are found in the Arc: screen menu for continuing an arc or a line from a previously drawn arc or line. _____

21. Identify three ways to access the Arc option for drawing elliptical arcs. _____

_____   _____

_____   _____

22. Name the AutoCAD system variable that lets you draw a true ellipse or a polyline ellipse with the ELLIPSE command._____

23. Where is the RECTANGLE command found in a pull-down menu? _____

_____

24. What is the AutoCAD default if the ARC command is typed at the Command: prompt?_____

_____

25. Name the AutoCAD system variable and its setting that allows AutoCAD to automatically calculate the radius of the current circle and use this value as the default for the next circle._____

_____

DRAWING PROBLEMS

Load AutoCAD for each of the following problems and use the prototype PRODR1, or start a new drawing with your own variables.

P8-1

1. You have just been given the sketch of a new sports car design (shown below). You are asked to create a drawing from the sketch. Use the LINE command and selected shape commands to draw the car. Do not be concerned with size and scale. Consider the commands and techniques used to draw the car, and try to minimize the number used. Save your drawing as A:P8-1 and quit.

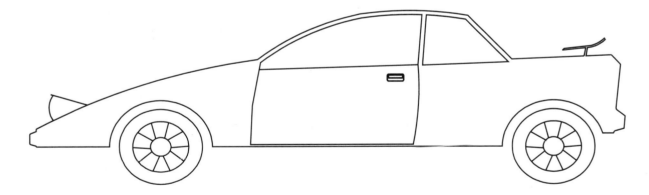

2. You have just been given the sketch of an innovative new truck design (shown below). You are asked to create a drawing from the sketch. Use the LINE and selected shape commands to draw the truck resembling the sketch. Do not be concerned with size and scale. Save your drawing as A:P8-2.

P8-2

3. Use the LINE command and CIRCLE command options to draw the objects below. Do not include dimensions. Save the drawing as A:P8-3.

P8-3

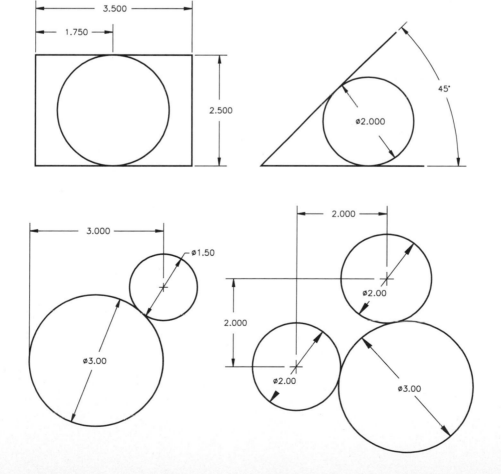

4. Use CIRCLE and ARC command options to draw the object below. Do not include dimensions. Save the drawing as A:P8-4.

P8-4

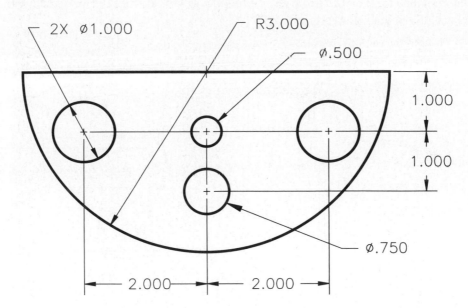

5. Select the ELLIPSE command to draw four ellipses using the following options. Then, save the drawing as A:P8-5.

P8-5

Ellipse 1: Axis endpoint 1/axis endpoint 2/other axis distance.
Ellipse 2: Center/axis endpoint/other axis distance.
Ellipse 3: Center/axis endpoint/rotation (use cursor and read coordinate angle display).
Ellipse 4: Center/axis endpoint/rotation (type angle value).

6. Draw the pressure cylinder shown below. Use the ELLIPSE command's Arc option to draw the cylinder ends. Do not draw the dimensions. Save the drawing as A:P8-6.

P8-6

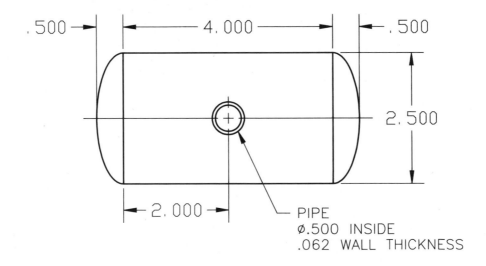

7. Use the ELLIPSE command's Arc option to draw samples of elliptical arcs with different start and end angle arcs all with the same major axis length and a 45° rotation angle based on the following information: (see the samples at the bottom of Figure 8-28)

Arc 1 = 0° to 90°
Arc 4 = 90° to 180°
Arc 2 = 0° to 180°
Arc 5 = 90° to 270°
Arc 3 = 0° to 2700°
Arc 6 = 180° to 0°

8. Draw the hex head bolt pattern shown below. Do not draw dimensions. Save the drawing as A:P8-8.

P8-8

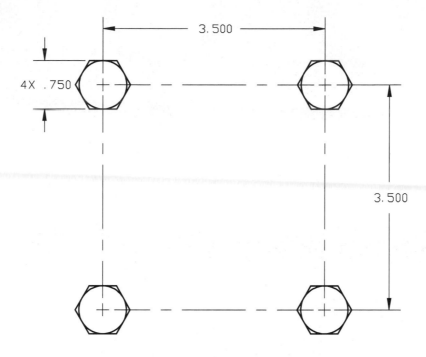

9. Use the POLYGON command to draw the three polygons shown below. Save the drawing as A:P8-9.

P8-9

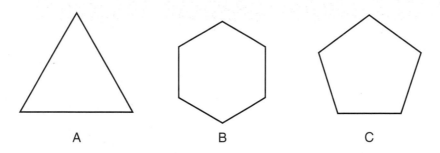

A   B   C

10. Use the DONUT command to draw the objects shown below using the following values. Save the drawing as A:P8-10.

P8-10

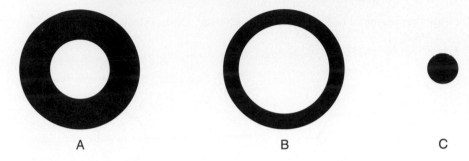

	Inner Diameter	Outer Diameter
A	.5	1.0
B	1.0	1.2
C	0	.2

A   B   C

 11. Use the MULTIPLE command modifier to draw four hexagons similar to the one shown in Problem 9, Example B. Save the drawing as A:P8-11.

P8-11

 12. Preset the doughnut inside diameter to .25 and the outside diameter to 1.25. Turn FILL on. Use the pull-down menu selection to draw four doughnuts with these settings. Place the doughnuts 1.5 units apart in a straight horizontal line. Save the drawing as A:P8-12.

P8-12

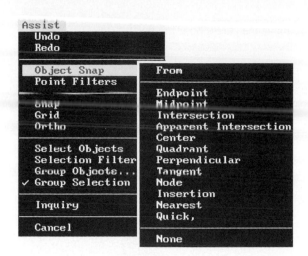

Chapter 9

GEOMETRIC CONSTRUCTIONS AND OBJECT SNAP

Learning objectives

After completing this chapter, you will be able to:

- ○ Select the OSNAP command to set running object snaps.
- ○ Use the OSNAP override.
- ○ Identify three ways to discontinue a running OSNAP.
- ○ List four ways to access the object snap modes.
- ○ Describe the QUICK mode.
- ○ Use the object snap interrupt and running modes to make several geometric constructions.
- ○ Adjust aperture size.
- ○ Use the OFFSET command to draw parallel lines and curves.
- ○ Divide existing objects into equal parts using the DIVIDE command.
- ○ Use the MEASURE command to set designated increments on an existing object.
- ○ Set point sizes and options to draw points.
- ○ Use the geometry calculator to draw and edit geometric constructions.

This chapter explains how the powerful OSNAP command and its snap modes are used to perform geometric constructions. OSNAP is the command name for object snap. Object snap allows you to precisely place points on existing objects. This chapter also explains how to draw parallel lines, divide objects, and place point symbols.

SNAPPING TO SPECIFIC OBJECTS OR FEATURES

AUG 3

Object snap is one of the most useful tools found in AutoCAD. It increases your drafting ability, performance, and productivity. The term *object snap* refers to the cursor's ability to "snap" exactly to a specific point or place on an object. The advantage of object snap is that you do not have to pick an exact point. For example, suppose you want to place a point on the end of a line. Normally you would try to pick the endpoint, but probably miss. Using object snap, all you do is pick somewhere near the end of the line. AutoCAD automatically snaps to the exact end. There are many object snap modes to help simplify drawing and design.

When a point is to be picked using object snap, the screen cursor takes the shape of a box and crosshairs. This cursor box, called an *aperture,* is then used to pick the desired object. For example, suppose you want to connect a line to the end of another line. Move the aperture near the end of the line and pick. You do not have to place the aperture exactly at the endpoint. If you are drawing a line to the point of tangency on a circle, pick the "tangent" option. Then pick a point on the circle near the estimated point of tangency. See Figure 9-1.

Figure 9-1. The object snap cursor box, or aperture. Simply move the cursor near the point to select and pick.

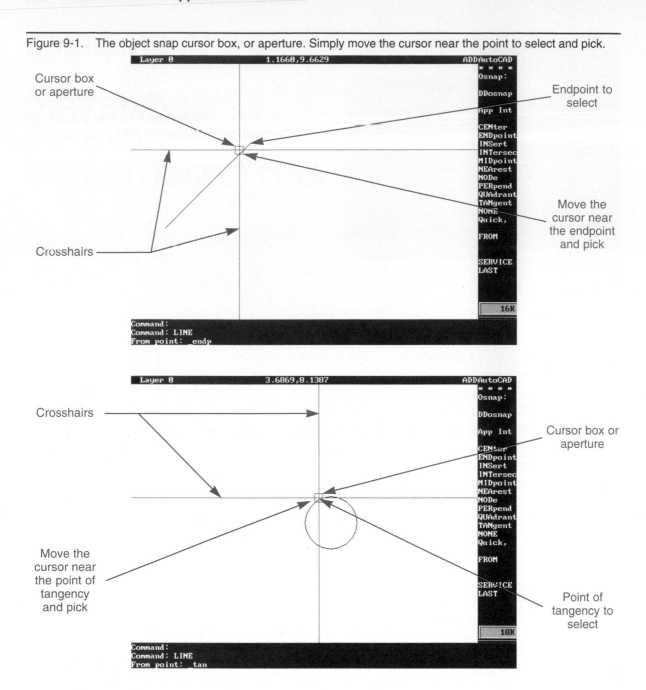

THE OBJECT SNAP MODES

$\boxed{\text{AUG 3}}$

The object snap modes determine what the aperture snaps to. Object snap modes may be typed at the prompt line, displayed by picking "* * * *" from the top of the screen menu, or picking Object snap from the Assist pull-down menu. The Osnap: submenu is shown in Figure 9-1. Button number 2 of a multibutton puck or holding down the Shift key while pressing the right button on a mouse also activates the object snap options in a cursor menu.

Object snap modes defined

Each object snap mode has a specific application. When typed at the prompt line, only the first three letters are required. The object snaps are defined as follows:
- **APPint.** Finds the apparent intersection point where two objects would intersect if they were extended.
- **CENter.** Locates the center point of any radial object. This includes circles, arcs, ellipses, elliptical arcs, and radial solids.

Figure 9-2.   Object snap to the endpoint of a line.

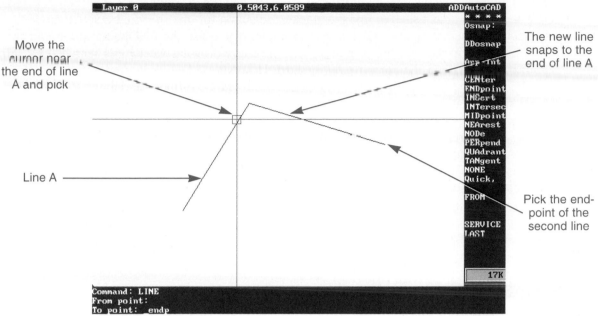

Figure 9-3.   Object snap to the endpoint of an arc.

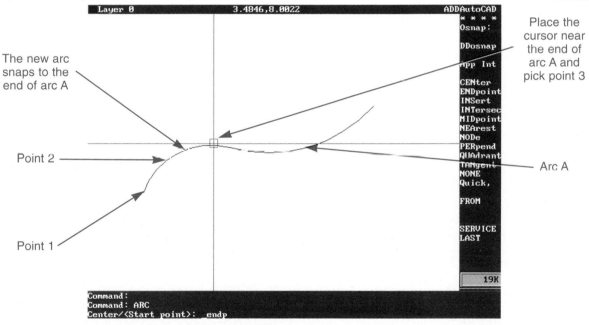

- **ENDpoint.** Finds the nearest applicable endpoints of a line, arc, elliptical arc, spline, ellipse, ray, solid, xline, or mline.
- **INSert.** Snaps to the insertion point of text, objects, and blocks.
- **INTersection.** Picks the closest intersection of two features.
- **MIDpoint.** Finds the midpoint of any object having two endpoints, such as a line, arc, elliptical arc, spline, ellipse, ray, solid, xline, or mline.
- **NEArest.** Locates a point on an object closest to the crosshairs.
- **NODe.** Snaps to a point drawn with the POINT command.
- **PERpendicular.** Finds a point on an object that is perpendicular to the object from the last point picked. Perpendicularity can be found on a line, polyline, arc, elliptical arc, ellipse, spline, ray, xline, mline, solid, trace, or circle.

- **QUAdrant.** Picks one of four quadrants on a circle closest to the crosshairs. Also finds applicable quadrant points on arcs, elliptical arcs, ellipses, and radial solids.
- **QUIck.** Allows object snap to find the quickest selection for the specified OSNAP mode that is selected immediately after QUIck. For example, if you use the ENDpoint option and two lines are found in the aperture pick area, then the entire drawing database is searched for all applicable points and the closest point is used. However, if QUIck is used, the data base is searched and the first applicable point found is used with no further searching. Thus the term quick, since it can be much faster in a large drawing file.
- **TANgent.** Forms a line, circles, and arcs tangent to lines, arcs, or circles as needed.
- **NONe.** Turns running object snap off, and can also be used as an override that causes AutoCAD to ignore any currently running object snap modes.

Using the object snap modes

Practice with the different object snap options to find which works best in various situations. Object snap may be invoked during many commands, such as LINE, CIRCLE, ARC, MOVE, COPY, and INSERT. The most common object snap uses are discussed in detail in the following sections.

Find the endpoint

Often, you need to connect a line, arc, or center point of a circle to the endpoint of an existing line or arc. Select the ENDpoint and move the aperture past the midpoint of the line or arc toward the end to be picked. To connect a line to the endpoint of existing line A in Figure 9-2, the following command sequence is used:

```
Command: LINE ↵
From point: (pick a point)
To point: END ↵
of (move the aperture near the end of line A and pick)
To point: ↵
Command:
```

Another application is to snap an arc or line to the endpoint of an existing arc. To connect a new arc to the endpoint of existing arc A in Figure 9-3, use the following command sequence:

```
Command: ARC ↵
Center/⟨Start point⟩: (pick a point)
Center/End/⟨Second point⟩: (pick the second point)
End point: END ↵
of (move the aperture to somewhere near the end of arc A and pick)
```

PROFESSIONAL TIP

Be careful about using the ENDpoint mode when entering object snap modes from the keyboard. If you accidentally type END at the Command: prompt, your drawing will be saved to disk and you will be dumped out of AutoCAD. It is safer to type ENDP if you are using the keyboard. You may have noticed that when ENDpoint is picked from a menu, the command line entry is automatically _endp.

Find the midpoint

The MIDpoint object snap mode finds and picks the midpoint of a line or arc. For example, to connect a line from any point to the midpoint of line A, shown in Figure 9-4, use the following command sequence:

```
Command: LINE ↵
From point: (pick a point)
To point: MID ↵
of (move aperture to anywhere on line A and pick)
```

Figure 9-4.   Using object snap to locate the midpoint of a line.

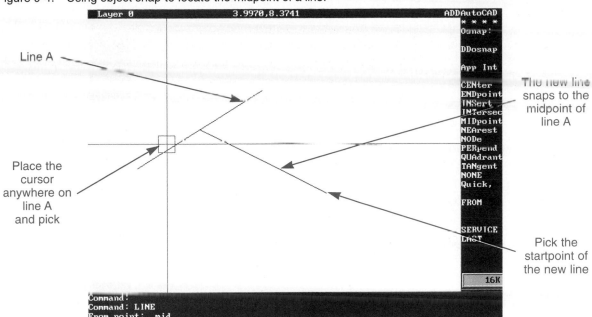

EXERCISE 9-1

❑ Load AutoCAD and open PRODR1, or start a new drawing and set up your own variables.
❑ Use the ENDpoint or MIDpoint snap options to draw the object shown below. Draw line 1, then line 2 connecting to the endpoint of line 1. Draw line 3 from the endpoint of line 2 to the midpoint of line 1. Draw arc A with one end connected to the endpoint of line 1.

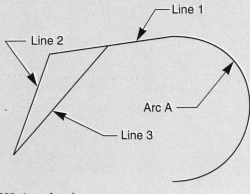

❑ Save the drawing as A:EX9-1 and quit.

Find the center of a circle or arc

The CENter option allows you to snap to the center point of a circle or arc. The following command sequence, as shown in Figure 9-5, draws a line from the center of circle A to the center of circle B.

Command: **LINE** ↵
From point: **CEN** ↵
of *(move aperture to anywhere on circle A and pick)*
To point: **CEN** ↵
of *(move aperture to anywhere on circle B and pick)*

Figure 9-5.   Using object snap to find the center of a circle. Note that the cursor is placed on the circle, not near the center.

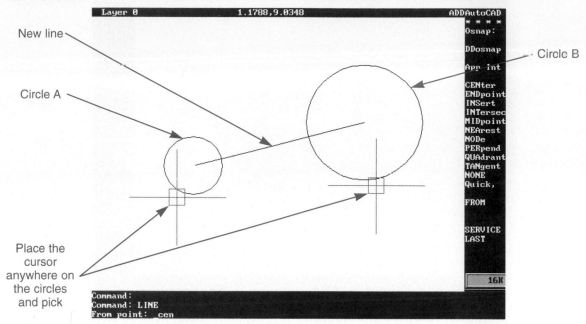

Find the quadrant of a circle or arc

A *quadrant* is a quarter section of a circle or arc. The object snap QUAdrant option finds the 0, 90, 180, and 270 degree positions on a circle or arc, Figure 9-6.

Figure 9-6.   The quadrants of a circle.

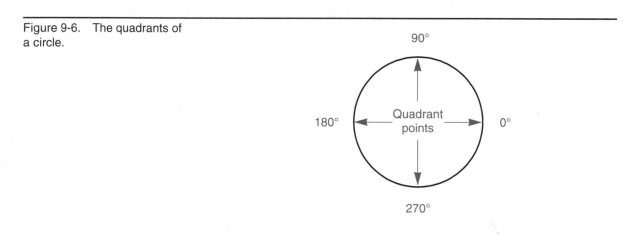

NOTE   Quadrant points are unaffected by the angle zero direction, but always coincide with the current UCS (User Coordinate System). The UCS is discussed in more detail in Chapters 19 and 21. The quadrant points of a circle or arc are at the top, bottom, left, and right regardless of the rotation of the object. However, the quadrant points of an ellipse or elliptical arc do rotate with the object.

When picking quadrants, locate the aperture on the circle closest to the intended quadrant. For example, circle B in Figure 9-7 may be drawn with its center located at one of the quadrants of circle A. The command sequence using the QUAdrant option is as follows:

Command: **CIRCLE** ↵
3P/2P/TTR/⟨Center point⟩: **QUA** ↵
of *(move the aperture to anywhere near the desired quadrant on circle A and pick)*
Diameter/⟨Radius⟩: *(pick a radius)*

Figure 9-7.   Using object snap to locate the quadrant of a circle.

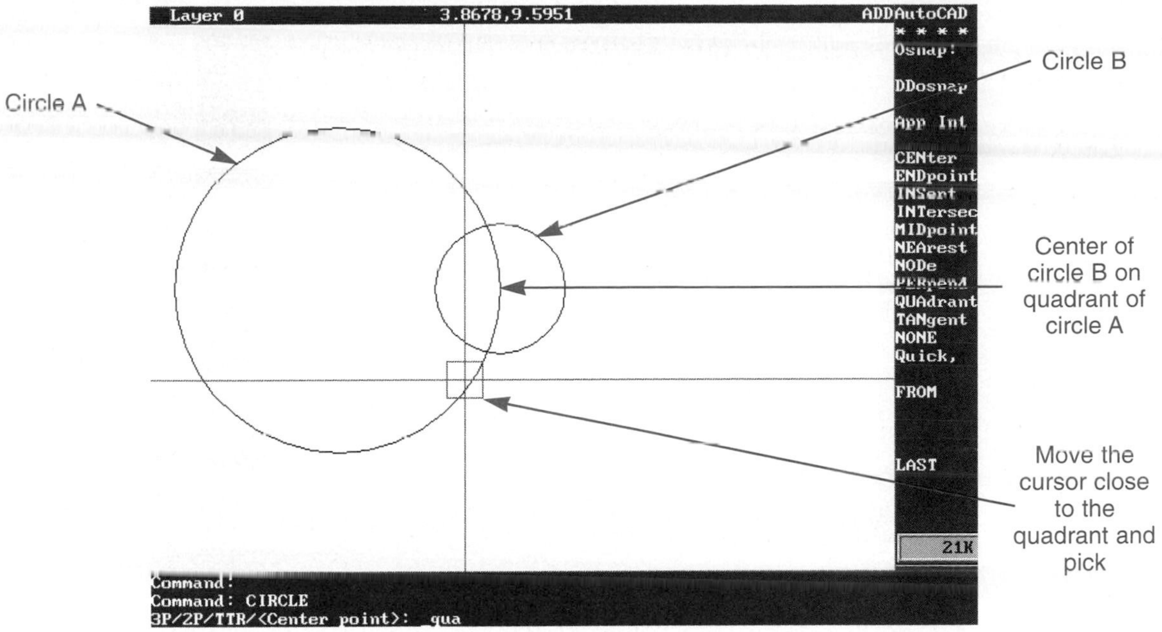

EXERCISE 9-2

❑ Load AutoCAD and open PRODR1, or start a new drawing and set up your own variables.
❑ Use the object snap center or quadrant options for the following situations:
　❑ Draw two separate circles and refer to the one on the left as circle A and the other as circle B.
　❑ Draw a line from the center of circle A to the 180° quadrant of circle B.
　❑ Draw a line from the center of circle B to the 270° quadrant of circle B to the 270° of circle A, and finally to the center of circle A.
❑ Save the drawing as A:EX9-2 and quit.

Finding the intersection of lines

If it is necessary to snap to the intersection of two entities, use the INTersect option. Given line A intersecting arc A in Figure 9-8, the method to draw another line to the point of intersection is as follows:

Command: **LINE** ↵
From point: *(pick a point)*
To point: **INT** ↵
of *(move the cursor so the intersection is somewhere inside the aperture and pick)*

While picking with the aperture box over the intersection is the fastest way to select an intersection, the INTersection mode gives you a second chance if you miss the intersection. When this happens, you are prompted with an "and," which allows you to pick the second object. The intersection point is found if these objects intersect:

Command: **LINE** ↵
From point: *(pick a point)*
To point: **INT** ↵
of *(pick line A in Figure 9-8 and not the intersection)*
and *(pick Arc A)*
To point: ↵
Command:

Figure 9-8.   Using the object snap intersect mode.

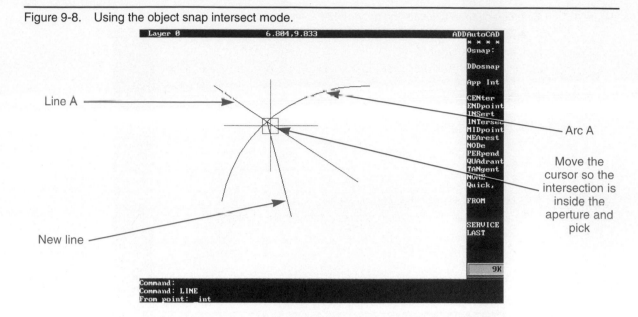

Find the apparent intersection of lines

The object snap mode AppInt means Apparent Intersection and is used to find the point where two objects would intersect if they were extended far enough as shown in Figure 9-9. For example, if you want to draw a line from the endpoint of an existing line to where it would intersect another line if it were extended, do this:

Command: **LINE** ↵
From point: **END** ↵
of *(pick the endpoint of Line 1)*
To point: **APP** ↵
of *(pick Line 2)*
and *(pick Line 1 again)*
To point: ↵
Command:

This object snap mode works even if the objects do actually intersect.

Figure 9-9.   Using object snap to find the apparent intersection of two objects.

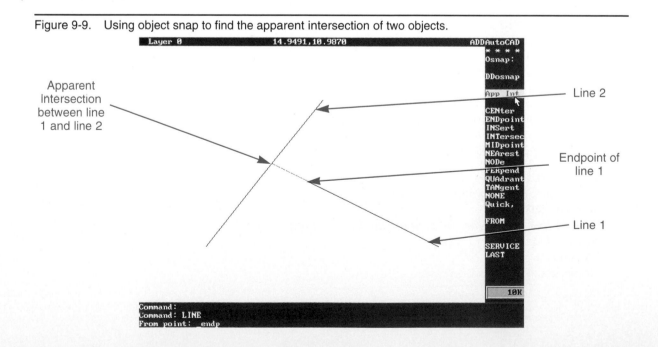

Drawing a perpendicular line

A typical geometric construction is to draw one line perpendicular to another. This is easily done using the object snap PERpendicular mode. For example, note line A and circle A in Figure 9-10. A line perpendicular to line A from the center point of circle A is drawn as follows:

Command: **LINE** ↵
From point: **CEN** ↵
of *(move the aperture to any location on the circumference of the circle and pick)*
To point: **PER** ↵
to *(move the aperture to any place on line A and pick)*

Figure 9-10. Using the object snap perpendicular option.

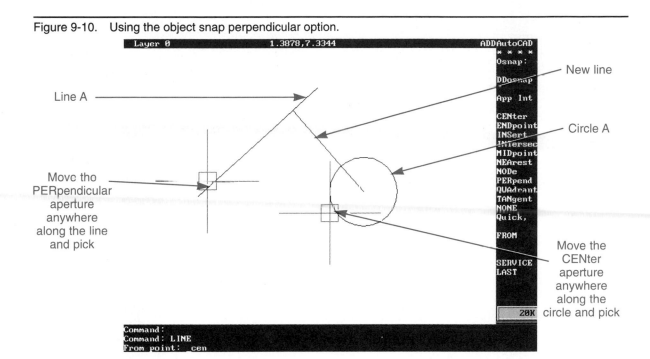

Drawing a line tangent to a circle or arc

A common geometric construction is a line tangent to a circle or arc. In Chapter 9 you were shown how to draw circles tangent to lines, circles, and arcs. Now, you will use the object snap TANgent option to draw lines tangent to an existing circle or arc. Given two circles as shown in Figure 9-11, two lines are drawn tangent to the circles. The command sequence is:

Command: **LINE** ⏎
From point: **TAN** ⏎
to *(pick a point on circle A near the intended point of tangency)*
To point: **TAN** ⏎
to *(pick a point on circle B near the intended point of tangency)*
To point: ⏎
Command: ⏎
LINE From point: **TAN** ⏎
to *(pick a point on circle A near the intended point of tangency)*
To point: **TAN** ⏎
to *(pick a point on circle B near the intended point of tangency)*
To point: ⏎
Command:

Figure 9-11. Using object snap to draw lines tangent to circles.

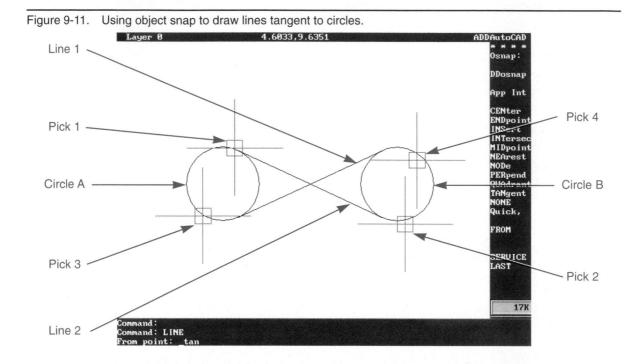

EXERCISE 9-4

❑ Load AutoCAD and open PRODR1, or start a new drawing and set up your own variables.
❑ Use the object snap TANgent option to draw two circles with tangent lines similar to those shown in Figure 9-11.
❑ Draw two lines that do not cross tangent to the same circles.
❑ Save the drawing as A:EX9-4 and quit.

Using fast object snaps

When AutoCAD draws using object snap modes, it searches for the best solution to your request. In a simple drawing, this process happens very fast. However, as your drawing becomes complex, it may take some time for the snap object to be found. You can speed up the process by selecting the object snap QUICK mode. Enter QUI, followed by a comma, and then the desired object snap option. (The QUICK mode is not effective on the object snap INTersection option.) The QUICK mode directs

AutoCAD to look only for the first solution to your request, and then end the search. The only problem you may find is that the first AutoCAD selection may not be the best choice. However, in most cases the QUICK mode works to your advantage and helps increase productivity. The following command sequence shows the QUICK mode used on the example illustrated in Figure 9-11.

Command: **LINE** ⏎
From point: **QUI,TAN** ⏎
to *(pick a point on circle A near the intended point of tangency)*
To point: **QUI,TAN** ⏎
to *(pick a point on circle B near the intended point of tangency)*
To point: ⏎
Command: ⏎
LINE From point: **QUI,TAN** to *(pick a point on circle A near the intended point of tangency)*
To point: **QUI,TAN** to *(pick a point on circle B near the intended point of tangency)*

Using the cursor menu for object snaps

Button number 2 of a multibutton puck, or holding down the Shift key and pressing the right button on a mouse activates the object snap options in a cursor menu, which is displayed at the screen crosshairs. This feature is convenient and saves drafting time. When you need to use an object snap, use one of the two accessing methods just discussed, and the cursor menu shown in Figure 9-12 is displayed on screen. Move the cursor arrow to the desired object snap and pick. The cursor menu disappears and the aperture is ready for you to use as you had planned.

Figure 9-12.   The object snap cursor menu.

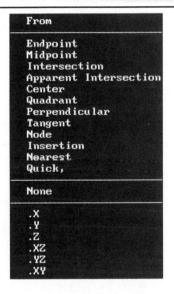

Using the FROM point selection mode

The FROM point selection mode allows you to establish a relative or polar coordinate point as a distance from a reference base point. Access the FROM option by selecting Osnap: from the ASSIST screen menu. It can also be accessed from the Object Snap cascading submenu in the Assist pull-down menu, or by typing FROM at the point selection prompt of the Circle command sequence. For example, use FROM if you want to draw a circle a specific distance from the midpoint of an existing line as shown in Figure 9-13 and with this command sequence:

Command: **CIRCLE** ⏎
3P/2P/TTR/〈Center point〉: **FROM** ⏎
Base point: **MID** ⏎
of (pick the line) 〈Offset〉: **@2〈45** ⏎
Diameter/〈Radius〉: **.75** ⏎
Command:

Figure 9-13. Using the FROM point selection mode following the command sequence given in the text.

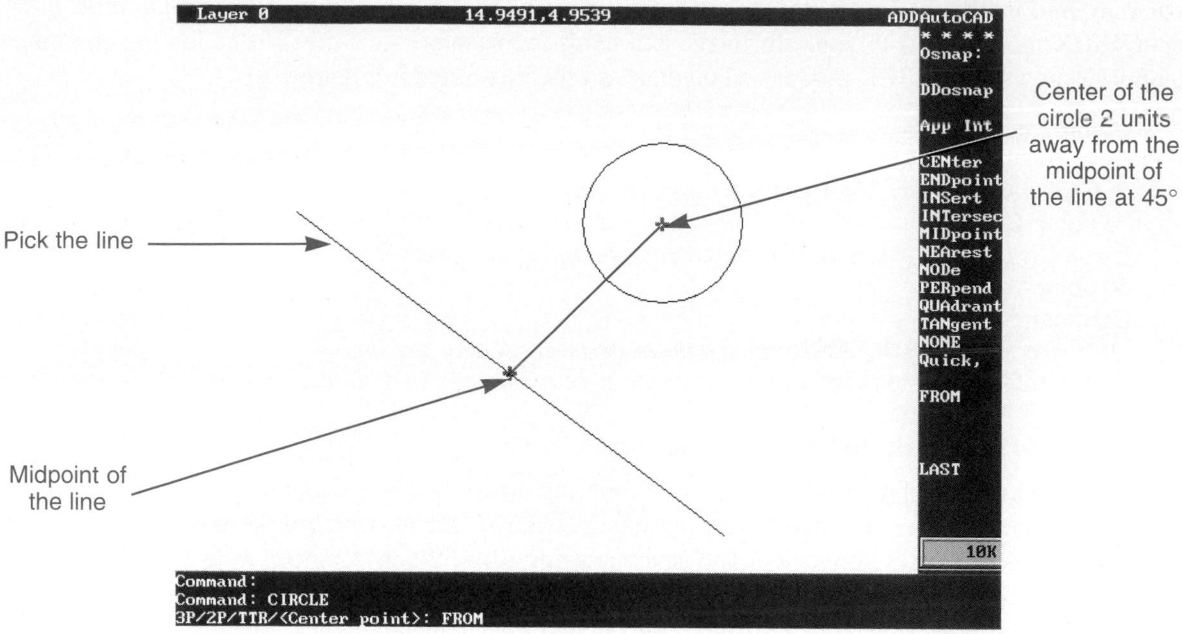

SETTING A RUNNING OBJECT SNAP

AUG 3

The previous discussion explained how to use object snap options by typing the first three letters, or selecting the desired mode from the screen, pull-down, or cursor menus. These are called the OSNAP *interrupt modes*. The interrupt mode works well in many situations. However, if you plan to use one object snap frequently, you can set a *running object snap*. AutoCAD automatically uses only the running object snap mode that you have selected. Set running object snaps by typing OSNAP at the Command: prompt or selecting DDosnap: from the OPTIONS screen menu. You can also pick Running Object Snap... from the Options pull-down menu to access the "Running Object Snap" dialog box. When the OSNAP command is typed, the Object snap modes: prompt is given. For example, if you want to set ENDpoint as the running OSNAP, type END as follows:

Command: **OSNAP** ↵
Object snap modes: **END** ↵

If you plan to use several object snaps frequently, then set all by typing the first three letters of each, separated by commas. For example:

Command: **OSNAP** ↵
Object snap modes: **END,PER,TAN** ↵

Now the running object snap is set to perform endpoint, perpendicular, and tangency operations. All other object snaps are ignored unless picked from the screen menu or typed during a command.

Using the dialog box to set running object snaps

You can also set running object snaps using the "Running Object Snap" dialog box. Pick Running Object Snap... from the Options pull-down menu, pick DDosnap: from the OPTIONS screen menu, or type DDOSNAP to access this dialog box. Notice in Figure 9-14 that the Endpoint, Perpendicular, and Tangent running object snaps are active. You can use this dialog box at any time to discontinue the running object snaps or to set other object snaps. Pick the Clear All button to discontinue all running object snaps.

Figure 9-14.   Setting running object snap modes using the "Running Object Snap" dialog box.

Select the needed settings

Select to clear all of the settings

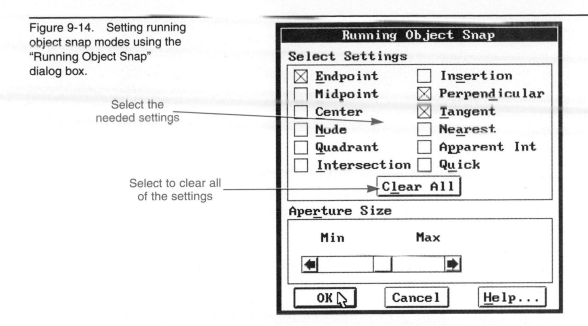

Overriding or getting out of the running OSNAP

You can temporarily override the running OSNAP by typing a different object snap request at the prompt. This is referred to as an *OSNAP override*. After the new object snap operation has been performed, the running snaps remain in effect.

The current running OSNAP may also be discontinued. Type NONE, OFF, or press the ENTER key as follows:

Command: **OSNAP** ↲
Object snap modes: *(type **NONE** or **OFF** and press* ENTER, *or press* ENTER)

You may also remove the active checks in the "Running Object Snap" dialog box.

PROFESSIONAL TIP

Use the object snap modes not only when drawing, but also when editing. With practice, using object snaps becomes second nature. In time, your drawing productivity will increase.

CHANGING THE APERTURE SIZE

Earlier in this chapter, you were introduced to the aperture. It appears on the screen when you enter object snap modes or use the OSNAP command. The size of the aperture may be enlarged to provide a bigger pick area. It may also be reduced in size to provide more accurate picking of a complex detail. The size of the aperture is measured in *pixels*, short for picture elements. Pixels or picture elements are the dots that make up a display screen. The AutoCAD prototype drawing sets the aperture size at 10 pixels. If you want to change the size of the aperture, type APERTURE at the Command: prompt. You are then asked to enter the desired aperture box size in pixels. This is limited to a number between 1 and 50 pixels. To change the aperture size to 5 pixels, do the following:

Command: **APERTURE** ⏎
Object snap target height (1-50 pixels) ⟨*current*⟩: **5** ⏎
Command:

Examples of different aperture box sizes measured in pixels are shown in Figure 9-15.

Keep in mind that the "aperture" and the "pick box" are different. The aperture, as previously discussed, is displayed on the screen when object snap modes are used. The pick box appears on the screen for any command that activates the Select objects: prompt. For example, the ERASE command issues the Select objects: prompt.

Figure 9-15.   Aperture box
sizes measured in pixels.

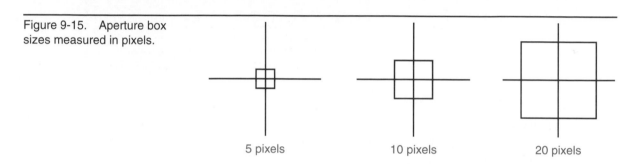

5 pixels   10 pixels   20 pixels

Another easy way to change the aperture size is found in the "Running Object Snap" dialog box. Look at Figure 9-14 and notice the Aperture Size area. Move the scroll bar between Min and Max and watch the sample aperture in the image tile change size accordingly. Pick OK when the aperture is the size you want.

DRAWING PARALLEL LINES AND CURVES

AUG 5

If you want to draw parallel lines, or concentric circles, arcs, curves, or polylines, use the OFFSET command. OFFSET is located in the CONSTRCT screen menu and the Construct pull-down menu. The command sequence is as follows:

Command: **OFFSET** ⏎
Offset distance or Through ⟨*current*⟩:

In response to this prompt you may type a desired distance, or pick a point for the parallel entity to be drawn through. The last offset distance used is shown in brackets. If you want to draw two parallel circles a distance of .1 unit apart, Figure 9-16, use the following command sequence:

Command: **OFFSET** ↵
Offset distance or Through ⟨*current*⟩: **.1** ↵
Select object to offset: *(pick the object)*
Side to offset? *(pick the side of the object for the offset to be drawn)*
Select object to offset: *(select another object or press* ENTER*)*

Figure 9-16.   Drawing an offset by a designated distance.

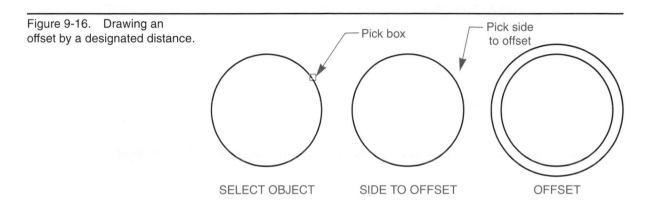

SELECT OBJECT   SIDE TO OFFSET   OFFSET

When the Select object to offset: prompt first appears, the screen cursor turns into a pick box. After the object is picked, the screen cursor resumes the appearance of crosshairs. The Window, Crossing, and Fence options do not work with the OFFSET command.

The other option is to pick a point through which the offset is drawn. Type T as follows to produce the results shown in Figure 9-17:

Command: **OFFSET** ↵
Offset distance or Through ⟨*current*⟩: **T** ↵
Select object to offset: *(pick the object)*
Through point: *(pick the point that the offset will be drawn through)*
Select object to offset: ↵

Figure 9-17.   Drawing an offset through a given point.

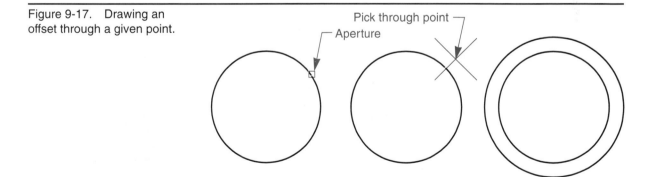

SELECT OBJECT   THROUGH POINT   OFFSET

PROFESSIONAL TIP

Object snap modes may be used to assist in drawing an offset. For example, suppose you have a circle apart from a line, as shown in Figure 9-18A. You want to draw another concentric circle tangent to the line as shown in Figure 9-18B. Enter the following:

Command: **OFFSET** ↵
Offset distance or Through ⟨*current*⟩: **QUA** ↵
of *(pick the existing circle)*
Second point: **PER** ↵
to *(pick existing line)*
Select object to offset: *(pick existing circle)*
Side to offset? *(pick between circle and line)*
Select object to offset: ↵

Figure 9-18.   Using object snap modes to draw an offset.

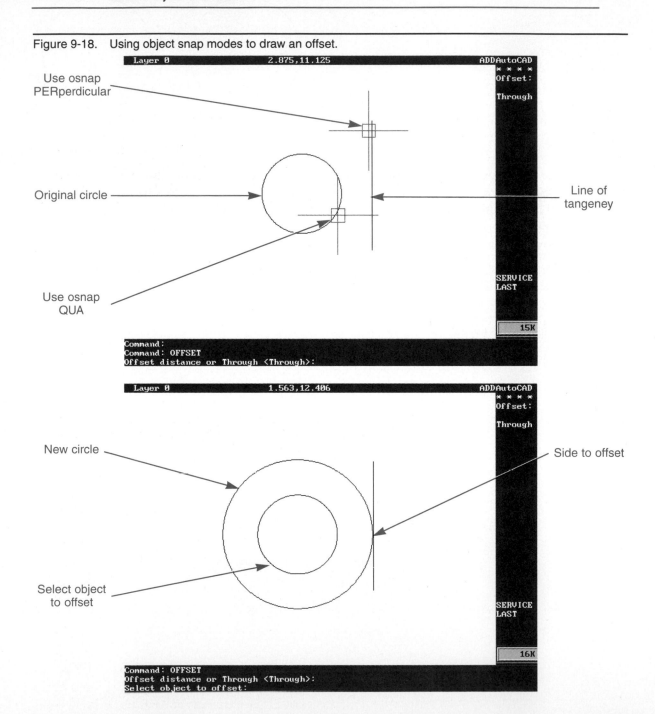

Setting the offset distance

The OFFSETDIST system variable lets you set an offset distance default. The next time you offset an entity, the preset default will appear. To enter a .2 unit offset for the default value, respond to the prompts as follows:

> Command: **OFFSETDIST** ↵
> New value for OFFSETDIST ⟨–1 ⟩: **.2** ↵
> Command:

A setting of –1 makes the Through option the default.

EXERCISE 9-7

❏ Load AutoCAD and open PRODR1, or start a new drawing and set up your own variables.
❏ Draw two circles and two polylines made up of line and arc segments.
❏ Use the OFFSET command to draw parallels a distance of .2 unit on the inside of one circle and one polyline.
❏ Use the OFFSET command again, this time specifying Through point on the outside of the other circle and polyline.
❏ Use the command sequence shown with Figure 9-18 to draw a similar object.
❏ Save the drawing as A:EX9-7 and quit.

DIVIDING AN OBJECT INTO AN EQUAL NUMBER OF PARTS | AUG 3 |

A line, circle, arc, or polyline may be divided into an equal number of segments using the DIVIDE command. The Divide: command is located in the DRAW 2 screen menu and the Point selection of the Draw pull-down menu. Suppose you have drawn a line and want to divide it into eight equal parts. Enter the DIVIDE command and select the object to divide. Then enter the number of divisions or segments. The procedure is as follows:

> Command: **DIVIDE** ↵
> Select object to divide: *(pick the object)*
> ⟨Number of segments⟩/Block: *(enter the number of parts and press* ENTER*)*

After the number of segments is given, the object is divided with dots. However, the dots do not show very well. To see the divisions, the appearance of the points must be changed as shown in Figure 9-19.

Figure 9-19.   Using the DIVIDE command.

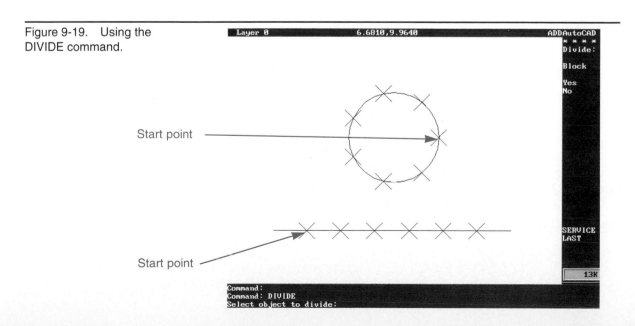

The marks placed by the DIVIDE command are controlled by the PDMODE system variable. Pdmode: is also an option of the Point: submenu found in the DRAW 2 screen menu. The PDMODE can be used to establish a mark that shows on the screen. PDMODE values range from 0 to 4. The points drawn using each PDMODE value are shown in Figure 9-20. The PDMODE default value is 0, which draws dots.

Figure 9-20. PDMODE values and symbols.

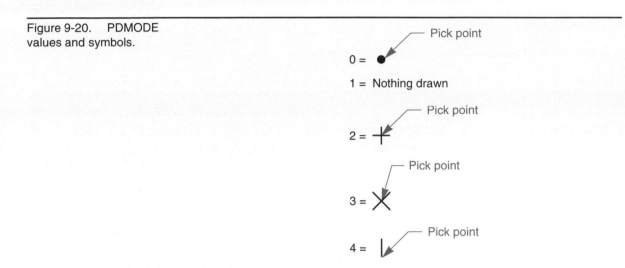

As previously mentioned, a problem with dots when using the DIVIDE command is that they may not show up. Therefore, a different PDMODE value must be set. Use the following sequence to set one of the PDMODE values.

Command: **PDMODE** ↵
New value for PDMODE ⟨0⟩: **3** ↵

After setting a different PDMODE value, type REGEN at the Command: prompt. The DIVIDE points change to the current PDMODE and can be seen.

The Block option of the DIVIDE command allows you to place a block at each division point. A *block* is a previously drawn symbol or shape. To initiate the Block option, type B or BLOCK at the prompt. You are then asked if the block is to be aligned with the object. Answer YES or NO. Blocks are discussed in Chapter 25.

MEASURE AN OBJECT INTO SPECIFIED DISTANCES $\boxed{\text{AUG 3}}$

Unlike the DIVIDE command in which a given entity is divided into a predetermined number of parts, the MEASURE command places marks a designated distance apart. The line shown in Figure 9-21 is measured with .75 unit segments as follows:

Command: **MEASURE** ↵
Select object to measure: *(pick an object)*
⟨Segment length⟩/Block: **.75** ↵

Measuring begins at the end closest to where the object is picked. All increments are equal to the entered segment length except the last segment. It may be shorter depending on the entity's length, Figure 9-21. The PDMODE affects the marks placed on the object in the same manner that the DIVIDE command does. Blocks may be inserted at the given distances using the Block option of the MEASURE command.

Figure 9-21.   Using the MEASURE command.

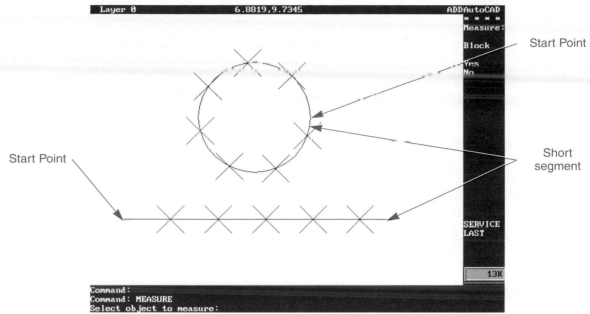

EXERCISE 9-8

❑ Load AutoCAD and open PRODR1, or start a new drawing and set up your own variables.
❑ Set the PDMODE to 3 before marks are drawn in this exercise.
❑ Draw two circles of any diameter, and two lines of any length.
❑ Use the DIVIDE command to divide one circle into 10 equal parts and one line into 5 equal parts.
❑ Use the MEASURE command to divide the other circle into .5 unit parts and the other line into .75 unit parts.
❑ Draw two parallel vertical lines. Make each line 3 in. (76.2 mm) long and space them 4 in. (101.6 mm) apart. Use the DIVIDE command to divide the line on the left into 10 equal increments. Draw horizontal parallel lines from each division on the left line over to the right line. Use the OSNAP NODe and PERpendicular options to assist you.
❑ Save the drawing as A:EX9-8 and quit.

DRAWING POINTS

AUG 2

You can draw points anywhere on the screen using the POINT command. The Point: submenu is found in the DRAW 2 screen menu and in the Draw pull-down menu, or POINT can be typed in at the Command: prompt. The specific type of point drawn is controlled by PDMODE discussed earlier. If you want to draw a dot (.), set the PDMODE to the default value of 0. Then proceed as follows:

Command: **POINT** ↵
Point: *(type point coordinates or pick with pointing device)*

Notice when you pick the point, it shows on the screen as a blip. The blip changes to a dot after using the REDRAW command, as shown in Figure 9-22. If you want to change the point style to a +, ×, or ¦, use the PDMODE command, or choose the POINT submenu to set the PDMODE value as discussed earlier.

Figure 9-22.　Using the POINT command.

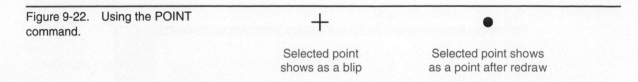

Selected point
shows as a blip

Selected point shows
as a point after redraw

Adding additional symbols to the point

So far you have changed the PDMODE to draw four different point types. You can draw either a circle, square, or circle and square around the selected PDMODE symbol. Do this by adding another value, Figure 9-23. Draw a circle by adding 32 to the original PDMODE value. Add 64 to draw a square. Add 96 to draw a circle and square. For example, a point display of an X inside a circle has a PDMODE value of 35. That is the sum of the X value of 3 and the circle value of 32. If you want to draw a point with an X inside of a circle and square, enter the PDMODE value 99. Then use the POINT command as follows:

Command: **PDMODE** ↵
New value for PDMODE ⟨*current*⟩: **99** ↵
Command: **POINT** ↵
Point: *(pick the point)*
Command:

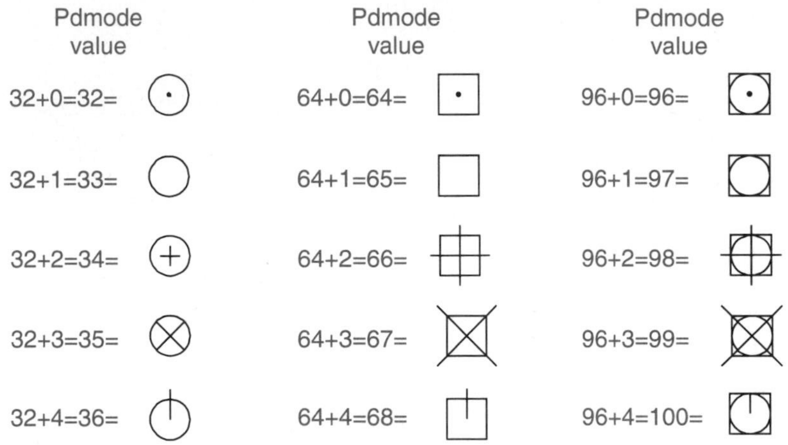

Figure 9-23.　PDMODE values for expanded symbols.

Pdmode value		Pdmode value		Pdmode value	
32+0=32=	⊙	64+0=64=	▫	96+0=96=	(⊙)
32+1=33=	○	64+1=65=	□	96+1=97=	(○)
32+2=34=	⊕	64+2=66=	⊞	96+2=98=	⌖
32+3=35=	⊗	64+3=67=	⊠	96+3=99=	⊗̸
32+4=36=	○̍	64+4=68=	⊓	96+4=100=	⊙̍

When the PDMODE value is changed, all previously drawn points stay the same until the drawing is regenerated. After REGEN, all points take on the shape of the current value.

Changing the point size

The point size can be modified using the PDSIZE variable. You can also use the Pdsize option in the Point: submenu found in the DRAW 2 screen menu. The default PDSIZE value of 0 displays points at the size shown in Figures 9-20 and 9-23. If you want to draw a point with a PDSIZE of 1, use the following command sequence:

Command: **PDSIZE** ↵
New value for PDSIZE ⟨0.0000⟩: **1** ↵
Command: **POINT** ↵
Point: *(pick the point)*
Command:

The point retains the set PDMODE value, but the size changes. Figure 9-24 shows the point sizes of different PDSIZE values. Positive PDSIZE values change points in relation to different display options. For example, if the view is enlarged with the ZOOM command, the point size also increases. (Zoom is discussed in Chapter 10.) A negative PDSIZE value makes the points appear the same size no matter how much you ZOOM the drawing. Points drawn with negative PDSIZE values are shown in Figure 9-25.

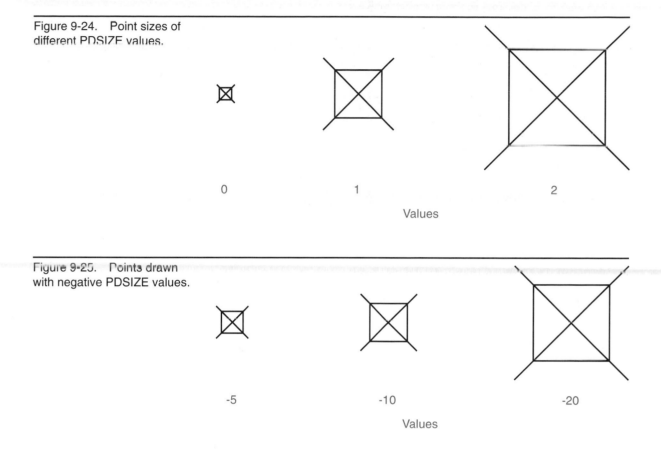

Figure 9-24.   Point sizes of different PDSIZE values.

0   1   2

Values

Figure 9-25.   Points drawn with negative PDSIZE values.

-5   -10   -20

Values

Using the Point Style icon menu

The "Point Style" icon menu, shown in Figure 9-26, is accessed by selecting the Display option of the Options pull-down menu and then selecting the Point Style… option. This is convenient since it lets you see and pick the point symbols displayed as graphic images. Pick the desired style to be used next time you draw a point. Set the point size by entering a value in the Point Size: box. Pick the Set Size Relative to Screen radio button if you want the point size to change in relation to different display options. Picking the Set Size in Absolute Units radio button makes the points appear the same size no matter what display option is used.

Figure 9-26.   The "Point Style" icon menu.

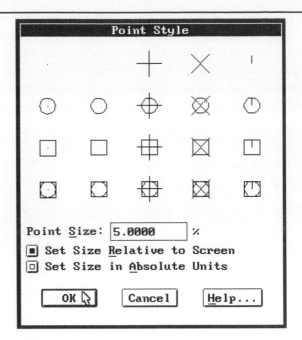

USING THE CALCULATOR FOR MATH AND GEOMETRIC CONSTRUCTION   AUG 3

AutoCAD's geometry calculator is a convenient tool to use when drawing and editing geometric constructions, and performing basic mathematical calculations. The geometry calculator is accessed by typing CAL at the Command: prompt, or by picking Calculator from the Tools pull-down menu. 'CAL can also be entered transparently when needed during any AutoCAD command. The calculator is especially helpful when entering points that are not easily located by other means, and for editing objects using mathematical calculations. You can also enter a math equation when you see the ⟩⟩Expression: prompt, such as shown in the following command sequence:

    Command: **CAL** ↵
    ⟩⟩ Expression: 2+2 ↵
    4
    Command:

The following discussion introduces the techniques and applications for using the geometry calculator. Additional information regarding the CAL command is found in the *AutoCAD Command Reference*.

Making entries

Numbers are entered in the calculator in the same manner they are entered when locating coordinates on screen. (Refer to Chapter 6 for details about entering numbers.) The standard format is inches. You can use decimal inches or scientific notation. Two formats are used for entering feet and inches:

feet'-inches" or feet'inches". In the following example, 5'6" is converted to 66". The value 5'6" is converted as follows:

> Command: **CAL** ⏎
> ⟩⟩ Expression: **5'6"** ⏎
> 66.0
> Command:

Angles are entered in decimal degrees, for example, 30d. Minutes and seconds can be omitted if their values are 0. When minutes (') and seconds (") are also included, they can be entered as 30d45'15". When *only* minutes and seconds are used, degrees are entered as 0d, for example, 0d30'10". You can also enter angles in radians by adding an r (3.5r), or in grads with a g (12.25g).

When entering coordinate values in the calculator, enclose them in square brackets ([]). Use the standard absolute, relative, and polar coordinate notation (discussed in Chapter 6). Absolute values are entered as [X,Y,Z], for example, [4,6,0]. Relative values are entered as [@X,Y,Z], such as [@2,4,0]. Polar values require a distance and angle value [distance⟨angle,Z], for example, [6⟨45d,0]. The Z value is used for 3-D applications, and may be entered as 0 or omitted for 2-D applications. Coordinate values can be added in the calculator like this:

> Command: **CAL** ⏎
> ⟩⟩ Expression: **[4,2,0]+[2,6,0]** ⏎
> (6.0 8.0 0.0)
> Command:

Other mathematical functions can also be performed using the calculator. The following symbols are used in mathematical expressions:

+ Add
− Subtract
× Multiply
/ Divide
^ Exponents
( ) Grouped expressions

Parentheses are used to group the symbols and values into sets. Complex mathematical expressions in which more than one set is involved are calculated beginning with the innermost grouped set. In any given set, exponents are calculated first, followed by multiplication and division, and then addition and subtraction. Calculations are then made from left to right.

EXERCISE 9-10

❏ Load AutoCAD.
❏ Use the CAL command to make the following calculations:
   A. 28.125 + 37.625
   B. 16.875 − 7.375
   C. 6.25 × 3.5
   D. (25.75 ÷ 4) + (5.625 × 3)
❏ Do not save this exercise.

Additional geometric calculations

In addition to the basic math functions previously discussed, AutoCAD's CAL command also allows you to obtain information about objects or make the following calculations:
- **RXOF(P).** Provides the X coordinate of a point.
- **RYOF(P).** Provides the Y coordinate of a point.
- **SIN(angle).** Sine of angle.

- **COS(angle).** Cosine of angle.
- **TANG(angle).** Tangent of angle.
- **ASIN(number).** Arcsine of number between –1 and 1.
- **ACOS(number).** Arccosine of number between –1 and 1.
- **ATAN(number).** Arctangent of number.
- **IN(number).** Natural log of number.
- **LOG(number).** Base-10 logarithm of number.
- **EXP(number).** Natural exponent of number.
- **EXP10(number).** Base-10 exponent of number.
- **SQR(number).** Square of number.
- **SQRT(number).** Square root of positive number.
- **ABS(number).** Absolute value of number.
- **ROUND(number).** Rounds number to nearest integer.
- **TRUNC(number).** Provides integer part of number (portion preceding the decimal point).
- **R2D(angle).** Converts angle in radians to degrees.
- **D2R(angle).** Converts angle in degrees to radians.
- **CVUNIT(value,from,to).** Converts a value from one unit of measurement to another, such as inches to millimeters, like this: CVUNIT(6,IN,MM).
- **PI.** Constant value π (3.1415926).

The CVUNIT expression can be used to convert 6 in. to millimeters as shown in the following example:

Command: **CAL** ↵
⟩⟩ Expression: **CVUNIT(6,IN,MM)** ↵
152.4
Command:

To calculate the square root of 25, use the following procedure:

Command: **CAL** ↵
⟩⟩ Expression: **SQRT(25)** ↵
5.0
Command:

EXERCISE 9-11

❏ Load AutoCAD.
❏ Use the CAL command to perform the following calculations:
  A. Sine of 30°
  B. Cosine of 18°
  C. Circumference of a 4 in. diameter circle. Use the formula: $C = \pi \times D$
  D. Round off 9.875 to nearest integer
  E. Convert 18 inches to millimeters
  F. 23^2
  G. Square root of 79
❏ Do not save this drawing.

2-D entity calculations

Some functions of the geometry calculator can be used to help create or edit a drawing. The following functions involve calculations in a 2-D or XY plane environment. Additional functions are used for 3-D (XYZ) vector calculations for descriptive geometry. The *AutoCAD Command Reference* details the use of 3-D functions.

- **CUR.** Allows you to pick a point using the cursor.

- **DEE.** Distance between two endpoints of entities. Same as DIST(END,END).
- **DIST(P1,P2).** Distance between points 1 and 2.
- **DPL(P,P1,P2).** Distance between point P and line with endpoints P1 and P2.
- **ILL(P1,P2,P3,P4).** Gives the intersection between two lines, one with endpoints P1,P2 and the other with endpoints P3,P4.
- **ILLE.** This is a short-cut function that is the same as ILL(P1,P2, P3, P4) previously discussed.
- **MEE.** Gives the midpoint between two endpoints. Abbreviated version of (END+END)/2.
- **PLD(P1,P2,DIST).** Point of line P1,P2, which is DISTance from P1.
- **PLT(P1,P2,T).** Point on line P1,P2, defined by parameter T.
- **RAD.** Gives the radius of the circle or arc selected.
- **ROT(P,ORIGIN,ANGLE).** Rotates point P through an angle about the origin.
- **ROT(P,P1AX,P2AX).** Rotates point P through an angle using line with endpoints P1,P2 as the rotation axis.

To determine the length of a line, use the following command sequence:

Command: **CAL** ↵
⟩⟩ Expression: **DEE** ↵
⟩⟩ Select one endpoint of DEE: *(pick one end of the line)*
⟩⟩ Select another endpoint for DEE: *(pick the other end)*
6.30064

The radius of a circle, arc, or polyline is determined using the following procedure:

Command: **CAL** ↵
⟩⟩ Expression: **RAD** ↵
Select circle, arc, or polyline segment for RAD function: *(pick one of specified entities)*
1.06682
Command:

Using the object snap modes

The object snap modes can be used in place of point coordinates in 2-D entity calculations. This instructs AutoCAD to automatically issue the OSNAP mode you need to easily pick an exact point, thus eliminating the need for you to enter the point coordinates at the keyboard. All you need to enter are the first three letters of the object snap mode, as with any OSNAP operation. The CAL command supports the following OSNAP modes:

- ENDpoint
- INSert
- INTersection
- MIDpoint
- CENter
- NEArest
- NODe
- QUAdrant
- PERpendicular
- TANgent

Calculating the angle between lines

Some calculator functions allow you to find the angle from the X axis or between given lines. The angle is measured counterclockwise. The formulas for these functions are:

- **ANG(P1,P2).** Provides the angle between the X axis and a line where P1 and P2 are the endpoints on the line. Use the ENDpoint object snap mode to pick the endpoints.
- **ANG(APEX,P1,P2).** Returns the angle between lines in an XY plane. For example, if you want to find the angle between the two lines in Figure 9-27, use the following command sequence:

Command: **CAL** ↵
⟩⟩ Expression: **ANG(END,END,END)** ↵
⟩⟩ Select entity for END snap: *(pick the vertex)*
⟩⟩ Select entity for END snap: *(pick P1)*
⟩⟩ Select entity for END snap: *(pick P2)*
60.5
Command:

Figure 9-27.   Using the
geometry calculator to
determine the angle between
lines in the XY plane.

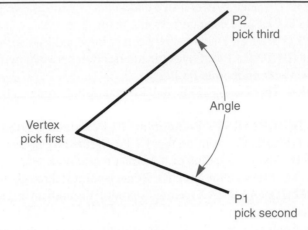

The (END,END,END) notation instructs AutoCAD to issue the ENDpoint object snap mode to assist you in picking the desired points.

EXERCISE 9-12

❑ Load AutoCAD and open TITLEA.
❑ Use the LINE command to draw an angle similar to Figure 9-27.
❑ Determine the angle formed using the CAL command.
❑ Save the drawing as A:EX9-12 and quit.

Making point calculations

You can easily calculate the distance between two points using the following command sequence:

Command: **CAL** ↵
⟩⟩ Expression: **DIST(NOD,NOD)** ↵
⟩⟩ Select entity for NOD snap: *(pick the first point)*
⟩⟩ Select entity for NOD snap: *(pick the second point)*

If you want to calculate one-half the distance between any two entities, such as the endpoints of a line, follow this procedure:

Command: **CAL** ↵
⟩⟩ Expression: **DIST(END,END)/2** ↵
⟩⟩ Select entity for END snap: *(pick the first point)*
⟩⟩ Select entity for END snap: *(pick the second point)*

Determining the radius of an arc or circle

Use the RAD function to determine the radius of a circle, arc, or 2-D polyline in this manner:

Command: **CAL** ↵
⟩⟩ Expression: **RAD** ↵
⟩⟩ Select circle, arc, or polyline segment for RAD function: *(pick the circle or arc to automatically obtain the radius value)*

EXERCISE 9-13

❑ Load AutoCAD and start a new drawing.
❑ Without the assistance of either snap or grid, use the LINE command to draw a single line anywhere on the screen.
❑ Use the CAL command to determine the distance between the endpoints.
❑ Use the CAL command to determine one-half the distance between the endpoints.
❑ Draw a circle without a specified radius or diameter.
❑ Use the CAL command's RAD function to determine the radius of the circle.
❑ Save the drawing as A:EX9-13 and quit.

CALCULATOR APPLICATIONS

In some instances, using the geometry calculator to perform simple tasks that may otherwise be performed on a hand-held calculator may seem to be a poor use of time. However, the real power of AutoCAD's geometry calculator is apparent when using the calculator as part of your drawing and editing process. The following applications provide you with a few of the many tasks that can be performed using the geometry calculator.

Circular applications

You can place a circle or other entity centered inside an object such as a rectangle, Figure 9-28, using the following calculation:

Command: **CIRCLE** ↵
3P/2P/TTR/⟨Center point⟩: **'CAL** ↵
⟩⟩ Expression: **MEE** ↵

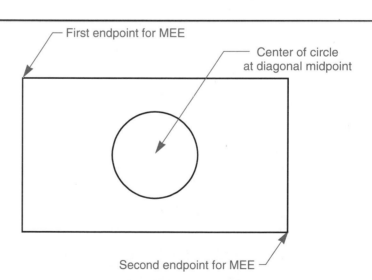

Figure 9-28.   Centering a circle within a rectangle using the CAL command.

First endpoint for MEE

Center of circle at diagonal midpoint

Second endpoint for MEE

MEE is the midpoint between two endpoints. This expression allows you to pick the opposite corners of the rectangle to get the midpoint of the diagonal, which is the center of the rectangle.

⟩⟩ Select one endpoint for MEE: *(pick one corner of the rectangle)*
⟩⟩ Select another endpoint for MEE: *(pick the opposite corner)*
Diameter/⟨Radius⟩ ⟨*current*⟩: *(type a radius and press ENTER, or pick a radius)*

If you have an existing circle on a drawing, you can create another circle of equal radius using the RAD expression. The command sequence is as follows, and is shown in Figure 9-29:

    Command: **CIRCLE** ⏎
    3P/2P/TTR/⟨Center point⟩: *(pick a center point for the new circle)*
    Diameter/⟨Radius⟩ ⟨*current*⟩: **'CAL** ⏎
    ⟩⟩ Expression: **RAD** ⏎
    ⟩⟩ Select circle, arc, or polyline segment for RAD function: *(pick the original circle)*

After you pick the original circle, a circle equal in radius to the original is automatically drawn at the new center point. This technique is helpful if you do not know the size of the original circle.

Figure 9-29.   Using the RAD function to create a circle equal in size to an existing circle.

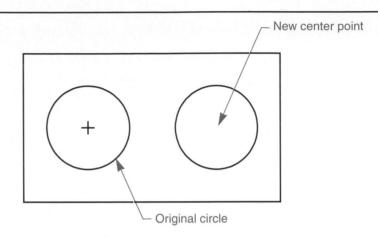

Picking Copy Rad option from the Circle: submenu of the DRAW 1 screen menu also activates the AutoCAD geometry calculator. You can use the Copy Rad option to draw a circle with exactly the same radius as an existing circle or arc, or length of a polyline segment just as in the previous example. To make this work, draw a circle as shown in Figure 9-29. Next, pick Copy Rad from the Circle: submenu to get this prompt:

    New value for CIRCLERAD ⟨*current*⟩: '_cal Expression: rad
    ⟩⟩Select circle, arc or polyline segment for RAD function: *(pick the existing circle)*
    Command: **CIRCLE** ⏎
    3P/2P/TTR/⟨Center point⟩: *(pick a center point)*
    Diameter/⟨Radius⟩ ⟨1.5000⟩: ⏎
    Command:

EXERCISE 9-14

❏ Load AutoCAD and open TITLEA.
❏ Use the CAL command's MEE function to assist you in making a drawing similar to Figure 9-28.
❏ Use the CAL command to assist you in making a drawing similar to Figure 9-29.
❏ Save the drawing as A:EX9-14 and quit.

Calculator functions can also be combined and used productively. For example, suppose you want to draw a new circle that is 25 percent the size of the original circle, which is to be placed in a new position that also needs to be calculated. Refer to Figure 9-30 as you follow this command sequence:

    Command: **CIRCLE** ⏎
    3P/2P/TTR/⟨Center point⟩: **'CAL** ⏎
    ⟩⟩ Expression: **(MID+MID)/2** ⏎
    ⟩⟩ Select entity for MID snap: *(pick line 1)*
    ⟩⟩Select entity for MID snap: *(pick line 2)*

Now, instruct AutoCAD to calculate a new radius that is 25 percent (.25) of the size of the original circle:

> Diameter/⟨Radius⟩ ⟨*current*⟩: **'CAL** ↵
> ⟩⟩ Expression: **.25*RAD** ↵
> ⟩⟩ Select circle, arc, or polyline segment for RAD function: *(pick one of the original circles)*

The new circle is automatically placed at the point specified, and at 25 percent of the size of the original circle.

Figure 9-30.   Combining calculator functions to resize a circle and place it in a new position.

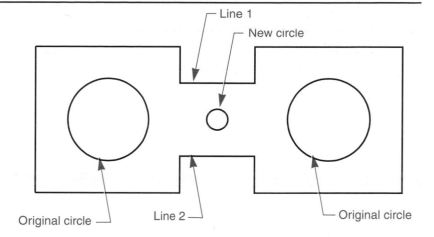

Another application of the CAL command is demonstrated in Figure 9-31, where a new circle is 3.00 in. from an existing circle along a centerline. The new circle is 1 1/2 times (1.5X) larger than the original circle. The following command sequence can be used:

> Command: **CIRCLE** ↵
> 3P/2P/TTR/⟨Center point⟩: **'CAL** ↵
> ⟩⟩ Expression: **PLD(CEN,END,3.00)** ↵
> ⟩⟩ Select entity for CEN snap: *(pick the original circle)*
> ⟩⟩ Select entity for END snap: *(pick near the right end of the centerline)*
> Diameter/⟨Radius⟩ ⟨*current*⟩: **'CAL** ↵
> ⟩⟩ Expression: **1.5*RAD** ↵
> ⟩⟩ Select circle, arc, or polyline segment for RAD function: *(pick the original circle)*

Figure 9-31.   Moving a circle along a centerline and resizing it.

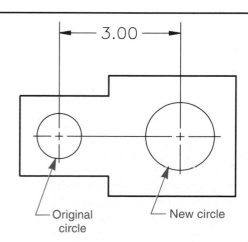

EXERCISE 9-15

❑ Load AutoCAD and open TITLEA.
❑ Use the CAL command to assist you in creating a drawing similar to Figure 9-30.
❑ Use the CAL command to assist you in making a drawing similar to Figure 9-31.
❑ Save the drawing as A:EX9-15 and quit.

Still another situation might exist where you want to draw a new circle that is .5 in. higher than one-half the distance between the center of an existing circle and the side (line) of an object. The command sequence is as follows, and is shown in Figure 9-32:

    Command: **CIRCLE** ⏎
    3P/2P/TTR/⟨Center point⟩: **'CAL** ⏎
    ⟩⟩ Expression: **(CEN+MID)/2+[0,.5]** ⏎

The (CEN+MID)/2 expression places the center point of the new circle one-half the distance between the center of the original circle and the midpoint of the line. Adding the [0,.5] locates the center point 0 units in the X direction and .5 units above (Y direction) the center point located with the (CEN+MID)/2 expression.

    ⟩⟩ Select entity for CEN snap: *(pick the original circle)*
    ⟩⟩ Select entity for MID snap: *(pick the right line)*
    Diameter/⟨Radius⟩ ⟨*current*⟩: **'CAL** ⏎
    ⟩⟩ Expression: **RAD** ⏎
    ⟩⟩ Select circle, arc, or polyline segment for RAD function: *(pick the original circle)*

Figure 9-32.   Combining calculator functions to create a new circle not on the same centerline as the original.

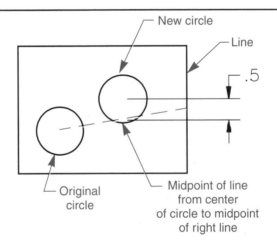

EXERCISE 9-16

❑ Load AutoCAD and open TITLEA.
❑ Use the CAL command to assist you in making a drawing similar to Figure 9-32.
❑ Save the drawing as A:EX9-16 and quit.

These are only a few of the possibilities for using the CAL command. Although the examples shown here involve the CIRCLE command, similar tasks involving other commands can also be performed. More examples, related to editing drawings, are given in Chapter 14.

DRAWING WITH X AND Y FILTERS   AUG 5

Filters allow you to select any aspect of an entity on the screen while "filtering out" other items or features. There are many uses for filters. While a variety of applications for filters are discussed throughout this text, this discussion centers on X and Y filters–filters that let you control X and Y coordinates, respectively. (In actuality, there are X, Y, and Z coordinates, but the Z coordinate is used for 3-D applications. Only X and Y filters are used in the following examples.) This discussion centers around working with the LINE command to create geometric constructions with X and Y filters. When you are prompted for a point, you can respond with any combination of .X, .Y, or .XY, as needed. If AutoCAD asks you for a Z value, simply answer with a 0.

Suppose you want to construct an isosceles triangle with a given height of 4 in. on a baseline that already exists. The drawing is shown in Figure 9-33. First, follow this command sequence to establish the base of your triangle:

> Command: **LINE** ⏎
> From point: **2,2** ⏎
> To point: **@3⟨90** ⏎

Now, place the vertex (Y) 4 in. from the midpoint of the baseline:

> To point: **.Y** ⏎
> of **MID** ⏎
> of *(pick the baseline)*
> of (need XZ): **4,0** ⏎

Finally, complete the triangle:

> To point: **END** ⏎
> of *(pick the endpoint of the baseline)*
> To point: ⏎
> Command:

Filters can also be picked from the bottom part of the cursor object snap menu. See Figure 9-12.

Figure 9-33.   Constructing an isosceles triangle using the geometry calculator.

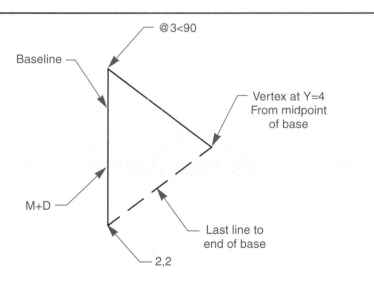

EXERCISE 9-17

❑ Load AutoCAD and open TITLEA.
❑ Use the X and Y filters as previously discussed to assist you in making a drawing similar to Figure 9-33.
❑ Save the drawing as A:EX9-17 and quit.

CHAPTER TEST

Write your answers in the spaces provided.

1. Give the command and entries needed to draw a line to the midpoint of an existing line:
   Command:_____
   From point: _____
   To point: _____ of _____

2. Give the command and entries necessary to draw a line tangent to an existing circle and perpendicular to an existing line:
   Command:_____
   From point: _____ to _____
   To point: _____ to _____

3. Give the command and entries needed to set ENDpoint, CENter, and MIDpoint as the running object snaps: _____
   Command:_____
   Object snap modes: _____

4. Give the command sequence required to draw a concentric circle inside an existing circle at a distance of .25:
   Command:_____
   Offset distance or Through ⟨*current*⟩: _____
   Select object to offset:_____
   Side of offset?: _____
   Select object to offset:_____

5. Give the command and entries needed to divide a line into 24 equal parts:
   Command:_____
   Select the object to divide: _____
   ⟨Number of segments⟩/Block: _____

6. Give the command and entries used to draw a point symbol that is made up of a circle over "X":
   Command:_____
   New value for _____ ⟨0⟩: _____
   Command:_____
   Point: _____

7. Suppose after drawing the point in Question 6, you find that it is too small. Give the command and prompts needed to draw the point larger:
   Command:_____
   New value for _____ ⟨0.0000⟩: _____

8. Define object snap._____
   _____

9. What do you call the cursor box that appears on the screen when an object snap mode is selected?
   _____

10. List four methods to access the object snap modes _____ _____

11. When typed at the prompt line, which three letters are required to activate any desired object snap?_____ _____ _____

12. Define quadrant._____ _____

13. Describe the "quick mode." _____ _____ ____

14. Describe the OSNAP interrupt mode. _____ _____

15. Define running object snap. _____ _____ _____

16. Identify two ways to set a running object snap._____ _____

17. How do you access the "Running Object Snap" dialog box? _____

18. Describe the OSNAP override. _____ _____ _____

19. What command is used to change the aperture size?_____ _____

20. In addition to the command identified in Question 19, what is another way to change the aperture size?_____ _____

21. What value would you specify to make the aperture half the default value? _____

22. How is the running OSNAP discontinued? _____ _____ _____ _____

23. List two ways to establish an offset distance using the OFFSET command._____ _____

24. Name the system variable used to set the offset distance default. _____

25. The DIVIDE command is located in which screen menu? _____

26. What is the difference between the DIVIDE and MEASURE commands? _____ _____ _____

27. The object snap quick mode is not effective on which object snap option? _____

28. If you use the DIVIDE command and nothing appears to happen, what should you do? _____ _____ _____

29. Name the system variable used to set a point style. ____ _____

30. Name the system variable used to set a point size. _____

31. How do you access the "Point Style" icon menu? _____

    _____

32. How do you change the point size in the "Point Style" icon menu? _____

33. List the command that is used to make geometric calculations with AutoCAD._____

34. Identify three ways the value "four feet and eight inches" can be entered in the calculator._____

    _____

    _____

35. How is "45 degrees, 15 minutes, 30 seconds" entered in the calculator? _____

36. How are point coordinates entered in the AutoCAD calculator?_____

37. Cite the proper input for the following calculations: _____

    A. Sine of a 35° angle:_____

    B. Tangent of a 50° angle: _____

    C. Square root of 49: _____

    D. Convert 86 millimeters to inches:_____

    E. Area of a 6 in. diameter circle, where A=πx∅: _____

38. Give the calculator functions used to achieve the following results:

    A. Distance between two points: _____

    B. Intersection of two lines: _____

    C. Midpoint between two endpoints: _____

    D. Radius of a circle or arc:_____

39. Define "filters." _____

    _____

40. What value do you enter for Z when working with X and Y filters in a 2-D drawing?_____

    _____

    _____

DRAWING PROBLEMS

Load AutoCAD for each of the following problems and use the PRODR1 prototype drawing, or start a new drawing with your own variables.

1. Draw the object below using the object snap modes. Save the drawing as A:P9-1 (omit dimensions).

P9-1

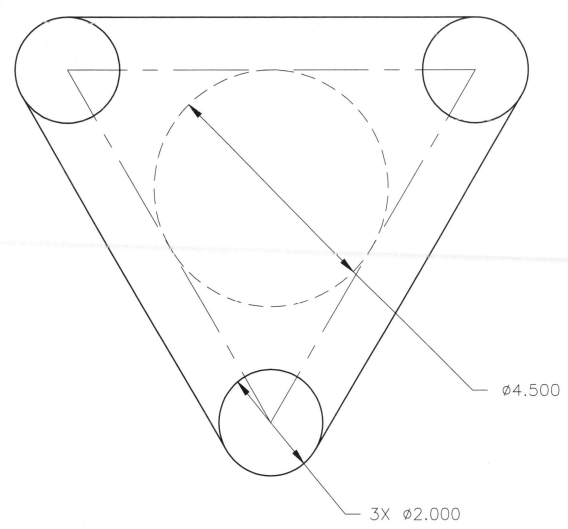

Ø4.500

3X Ø2.000

2. Draw the object below using the object snap modes indicated. Save the drawing as A:P9-2.

P9-2

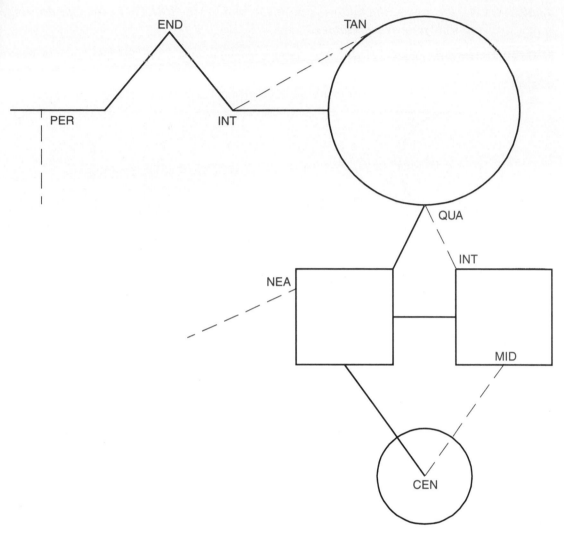

3. Draw the object below using ENDpoint, TANgent, CENter, PERpendicular, and QUAdrant running object snap modes. Save the drawing as A:P9-3.

P9-3

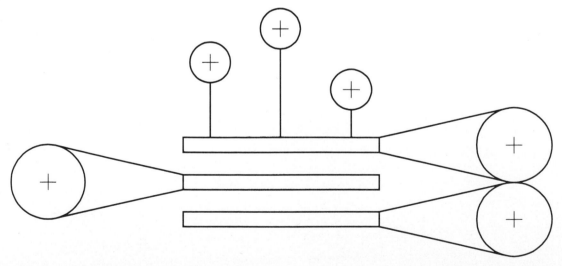

P9-4

1. Draw the following object using the information provided in the layout, and the FROM option with these instructions: (Dimensions are in inches. Do not draw dimensions.)

A. Hole A is .523 from the midpoint of Line 1.

B. Hole B is .523 from the midpoint of Line 2.

C. Hole C is .833 from the midpoint of Line 3.

D. Hole D is .399 from the midpoint of Line 4.

E. Hole E is .738 from the midpoint of Line 5.

F. Hole F is 1.295 from the midpoint of Line 6.

G. Hole G is .574 from Corner 1.

H. Hole H is .574 from Corner 2.

I. Save the drawing as A:P9-4.

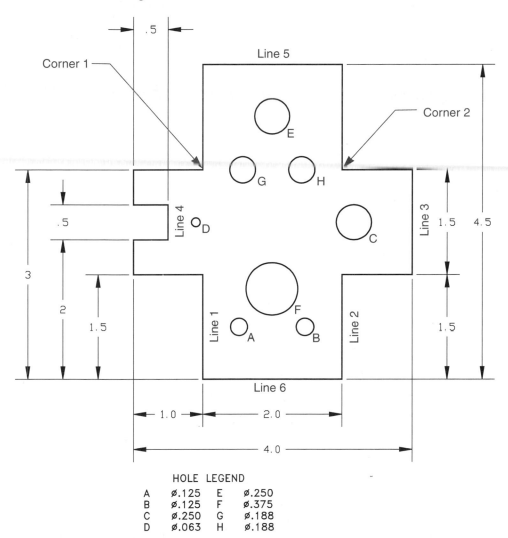

HOLE LEGEND

A	Ø.125	E	Ø.250
B	Ø.125	F	Ø.375
C	Ø.250	G	Ø.188
D	Ø.063	H	Ø.188

P9-5

5. Draw the floor plan layout about three times the size of that shown. Use the following AutoCAD functions:

A. Set architectural units; 48′,36′ limits; 2 ft. grid; and 6 in. snap.

B. Use the PLINE command to draw plan A. (The LINE command may be used, but it will take longer to complete the problem.)

C. Use the OFFSET command to draw a parallel line 6 in. on the inside of plan A. Your final drawing should look like that shown in plan B.

D. Save the drawing as A:P9-5.

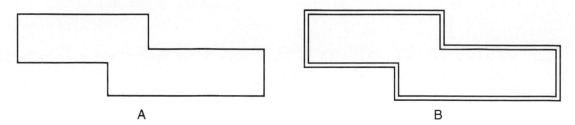

A   B

P9-6

6. Create a drawing proportional, but about three times the size of the object shown below. Proceed as follows:

A. Draw the outer circle first.

B. Use the OFFSET command to create other concentric circles. (Try to draw the object without leaving the OFFSET command.) Select the Through option and point to the spot where you want the offset circles to be placed.

C. Save the drawing as A:P9-6.

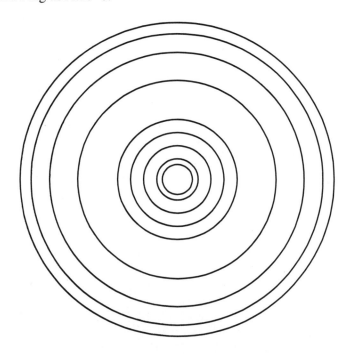

7. Draw two horizontal lines, each 8 in. (203 mm) long. Use the DIVIDE command to divide one of the lines into 10 equal parts. Use the MEASURE command to set off .8 in. (20 mm) increments on the second line. Save the drawing as A:P9-7.

P9-7

8. Draw two circles, each having a 4 in. (102 mm) diameter. Then use the DIVIDE command to divide one of the circles into 12 equal parts. Use the MEASURE command to set off .75 in. (19 mm) increments on the second circle. Save the drawing as A:P9-8.

P9-8

9. Draw two closed polylines each made up of line and arc segments. Then, use the DIVIDE command to divide one of the polylines into 24 equal parts. Use the MEASURE command to set off 1.5 increments on the second polyline. Save the drawing as A:P9-9.

P9-9

10-13. If several PDMODE symbols are displayed on the screen, they will all be updated to the current PDMODE value when a regeneration occurs.

10. Set the PDSIZE to 1 and draw points with each of the following PDMODEs: 0, 2, 3, and 4. Save the drawing as A:P9-10.

P9-10

11. Set the PDSIZE to 2 and draw a point with each of the following PDMODEs: 32, 34, 35, 64, 65, 66, 96, 97, 98, 99, and 100. Save the drawing as A:P9-11.

P9-11

12. Use the "Point Style" icon menu to draw five different point symbols. Save the drawing as A:P9-12.

P9-12

13. Use the "Point Style" icon menu to change the size of each of five different point symbols. Save the drawing as A:P9-13.

P9-13

14. Use the LINE command to draw the angle shown in the following illustration using the given coordinates. Use the CAL command to determine the angle, in degrees, between the lines. Save the drawing as A:P9-14.

P9-14

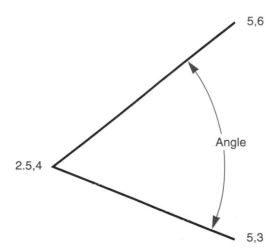

15. Draw a rectangle measuring 3.125 × 5.625. Use the CAL command to center a circle with a .75 diameter inside the rectangle. Save the drawing as A:P9-15.

P9-15

16. Draw the following object. Then use the CAL command to place another circle to the left of the existing circle so the completed object is symmetrical. Do not include the dimensions. Save the drawing as A:P9-16.

P9-16

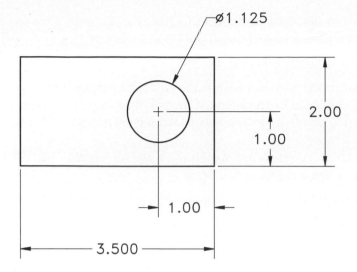

17. Draw the following object. Then use the CAL command to add another circle with a diameter which is 30 percent of the size of the existing circle. Center the new circle between the midpoints of line 1 and 2. Do not include dimensions. Save the drawing as A:P9-17.

P9-17

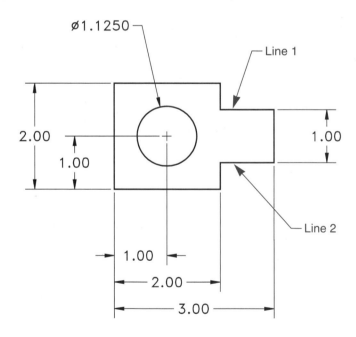

P9-18

18. Draw the object shown below. Then use the CAL command to create another circle with a diameter which is 150 percent (1.5X) of the existing circle. Center the new circle 3 in. horizontally to the right of the existing circle. Do not dimension the drawing. Save the drawing as A:P9-18.

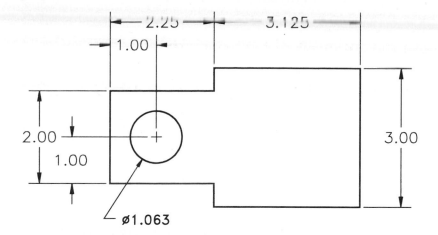

P9-19

19. Draw the following object. Then use the CAL command to create another circle with the same diameter as the existing circle. Place the center of the new circle .5 in. above a point that is midway between the center of the existing circle and the midpoint of the right line of the object. Do not include dimensions. Save the drawing as A:P9-19.

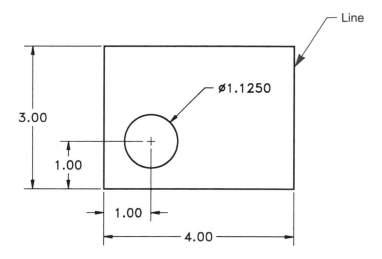

P9-20

20. Use the X and Y filters to draw an isosceles triangle with a vertical baseline measuring 4.5 in. long, and a height of 5.75 in. Save the drawing as A:P9-20.

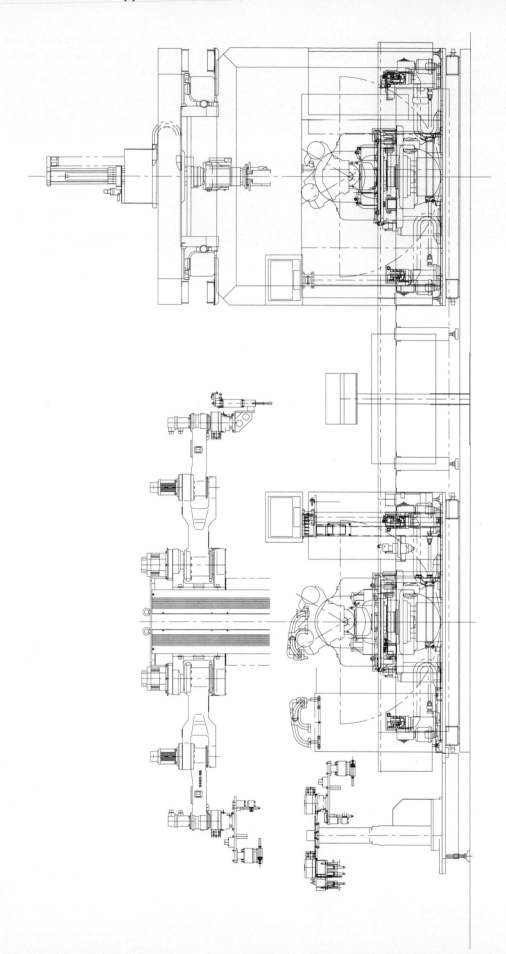

Flexible Assembly cell system. (Hirata Corporation)

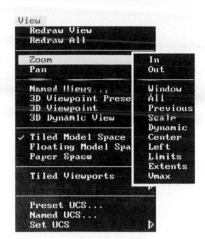

Chapter 10

DRAWING DISPLAY OPTIONS

Learning objectives

After completing this chapter, you will be able to:

○   Magnify a small part of a drawing to work on details.

○   Move the drawing around the screen to display portions outside the boundaries of the monitor.

○   Create named views that can be recalled instantly.

○   Create multiple viewports on the screen.

○   Define and use model space and paper space.

You can view the exact portion of the drawing you need using AutoCAD's Display commands. The ZOOM command enables you to enlarge or reduce the amount of the drawing displayed. The portion displayed can also be moved back and forth or up and down using the PAN command. PAN can be compared to looking through a camera lens and moving the camera across the drawing. The Aerial View Command in the Tools pull-down menu enables the Aerial View window. The Aerial View functions allow you to see the entire drawing in a separate display window, locate the particular area you want to view, and move to it using both zoom and pan functions. The VIEW command allows you to create and name specific views of the drawing. When additional drawing or editing is required in a saved view, the view can be quickly recalled.

Specialized display functions allow you to work in "space." They are called model space and paper space, and are found by picking Mview: in the VIEW screen menu. The MVIEW command can also be executed by selecting Floating Model Space from the View pull-down menu. These two functions allow you to switch between the drawing and design world called *model space,* and the plotting world called *paper space.* Detailed information regarding the use of model space and paper space as related to plotting multiview drawings is provided in Chapter 12.

This chapter also discusses the differences between REDRAW and REGEN. It also describes how to set the REGENAUTO and VIEWRES commands to achieve optimum display speeds and quality.

REDRAW THE SCREEN

ARM 7

The REDRAW command cleans the screen of blips that appear when a point is picked. It also fills gaps left behind when entities are erased. Redraw the screen by picking Redraw View from the View pull-down menu, by selecting Redraw: from the VIEW screen menu, or by entering REDRAW at the Command: prompt. You may also redraw the screen while working inside another command.

Working inside another command

REDRAW is one of AutoCAD's transparent commands. *Transparent commands* can be used while you are working inside another command. Transparent commands include SETVAR, HELP, ZOOM, PAN, VIEW, AV (Aerial View), and REDRAW. When the transparent command is completed, the command with which you were working returns. REDRAW does not prompt you; it just does its job. Select REDRAW from the screen, pull-down, or tablet menu and notice the command line display.

    Command: '_redraw

The apostrophe in front of the command tells AutoCAD that this is a transparent command. All of the commands discussed in this chapter, with the exception of REGEN, VIEWRES, and VPORTS are transparent. A detailed discussion of transparent commands and how they are used is given later in the chapter.

Cleaning the screen display

REDRAW is commonly used to clean away the clutter of drawing and editing work. Most of the clutter is that of blips. A *blip* is a small cross displayed when a point is picked on the screen, Figure 10-1. These blips are indicators of selected points and are not part of your drawing. They simply stay on the screen until it is redrawn. Using REDRAW for removing blips is fine, but it may begin to slow your drawing sessions. When you begin working on complex drawings, REDRAW takes much longer.

Figure 10-1. Tiny crosshairs, or blips, show on the screen when a point is selected.

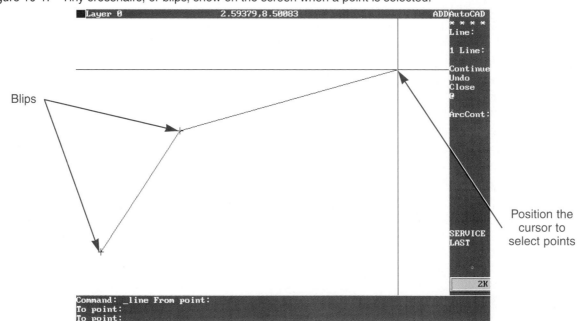

Blips remind you where points were selected, but they may be omitted. This eliminates the need to redraw as often. If you turn blips off, it may be more difficult to identify points on the screen using XYZ filters or the ID command. Therefore, if you decide you do not want blips, you may turn them off with the BLIPMODE command, by typing the following:

    Command: **BLIPMODE** ↵
    ON/OFF ⟨*current*⟩: **OFF** ↵

Blips may also be turned off from the "Drawing Aids" dialog box. Select Drawing Aids from the Options pull-down menu or pick DDrmode: from the OPTIONS screen menu, and then click the X in the Blips check box (or type B and press the spacebar), to turn off blips. The blips will not show on the screen for the current drawing until BLIPMODE is turned back on. The blips will not show on the screen unless you access BLIPMODE again and enter ON.

PROFESSIONAL TIP

Turning BLIPMODE off affects the current drawing only. If you want blips to be off in any new drawings yet to be created, turn off BLIPMODE in acad.dwg and any other prototype drawings that you use. Be sure to save this drawing if you want the setting to remain in effect the next time you open it.

GETTING CLOSE TO YOUR WORK ARM 7

It is doubtful whether many drafters would create drawings on a computer screen if they could not move in close to their work. This ability to "zoom in" (magnify) a drawing was an advancement that enabled designers to create the tiny circuits found in computers. The ZOOM command is a tool that you will use often because it is so helpful. It also is a transparent command and can be used while inside other commands. Twelve different menu pull-down options allow you to use ZOOM in a variety of ways.

The ZOOM options

To use the ZOOM command, pick Zoom: from the VIEW screen menu or enter ZOOM at the Command: prompt. This lists the options as follows:

Command: **ZOOM** ↵
All/Center/Dynamic/Extents/Left/Previous/Vmax/Window/⟨Scale(X/XP)⟩:

Brief explanations of the ZOOM options are as follows:
- **In.** This option is available only if Zoom is picked from the View pull-down menu. It automatically executes a 2X zoom scale factor.
- **Out.** This option is available only if Zoom is picked from the View pull down menu. It automatically executes a .5X zoom scale factor.
- **All.** Zooms to display drawing limits. If objects are beyond limits, they are included in the display. Always use the All option after you change limits.
- **Center.** Pick the center and height of the next screen display. A magnification factor instead of a height can be entered by typing a number followed by "X," such as "4X." The current value represents the height of the screen in drawing units. Entering a smaller number enlarges the image size, while a larger number reduces it. The command sequence is as follows:

  All/Center/Dynamic/Extents/Left/Previous/Vmax/Window/⟨Scale(X/XP)⟩: **C** ↵
  Center point: *(pick a center point)*
  Magnification or Height ⟨*current*⟩: **4X** ↵

- **Dynamic.** Allows for a graphic pan and zoom with the use of a view box that represents the screen. This option is discussed in detail later in the chapter.
- **Extents.** Zooms to extents of the drawing. This is the portion of the drawing area that has entities drawn in it.
- **Left.** Pick the lower-left corner and height of next screen display. A magnification factor instead of a height can be entered as follows:

  All/Center/Dynamic/Extents/Left/Previous/Vmax/Window/⟨Scale(X/XP)⟩: **L** ↵
  Lower left corner point: *(pick a point)*
  Magnification or Height ⟨*current*⟩: **3X** ↵

- **Previous.** Returns to the previous display. You can go back 10 displays in Release 13.
- **Vmax.** AutoCAD maintains a "virtual screen" composed of 4 billion pixels in each axis (X and Y). This means that each time a regeneration is required, the virtual screen is recalculated. Then, you can view any detail of your drawing that you want, within the virtual screen, and AutoCAD displays it at redraw speed. The image is redrawn (not regenerated) if the next display you request is inside the limits of the virtual screen. However, if the requested display (a small zoom window, for example) will not provide an accurate representation of the drawing entities, AutoCAD performs a regeneration. You can test Vmax by zooming in on a small detail on your drawing. You may want to do this a couple of times until AutoCAD regenerates. Then use ZOOM Vmax. The resulting display is the virtual screen.
- **Window.** Pick opposite corners of a box. Objects in the box enlarge to fill the display. The Window option is the default if you pick a point on the screen.
- **Scale(X).** A positive number is required here to indicate the magnification factor of the original display. You can enlarge or reduce relative to the current display by typing an X after the scale. Type 2X if you want the image enlarged two times. Type .5X if you want the image reduced by half. Typing just a number without the X zooms the *original* drawing. On the other hand, typing a number followed by an X zooms the *current view* by that scale value.
- **Scale(XP).** This option is used in conjunction with model space and paper space, both discussed later in this chapter. Its purpose is to scale a drawing in model space relative to paper space, and is used primarily in the layout of scaled multiview drawings for plotting purposes. A detailed discussion of this option is given in Chapter 26–*External References and Multiview Layouts.*

Enlarging with a window

The most-used ZOOM option is Window. Two opposite corners of a rectangular window enclosing the feature to be zoomed are picked. The command sequence is as follows:

Command: **ZOOM** ↵
All/Center/Dynamic/Extents/Left/Previous/Vmax/Window/⟨Scale(X/XP)⟩: *(pick a corner)*
Other corner: *(pick the opposite corner)*

The first point you pick is automatically accepted as the first corner of the zoom window. After this corner is picked, a box appears attached to the crosshairs. It grows and shrinks as you move the pointing device. When the second corner is picked, the center of the window becomes the center of the new screen display. If you wish to return to the previous display, select ZOOM and use the P (Previous) option. If you want to see the entire drawing, use the A (All) option. Figure 10-2 shows the difference between ZOOM Window and ZOOM All.

The Window option can also be selected by entering a W at the options prompt. This method is useful for customized applications that are designed to operate on earlier releases of AutoCAD. See **AutoCAD and its Applications–Advanced, R13 for DOS**, for information on customizing AutoCAD menus.

Figure 10-2. A–When using the ZOOM Window command, select two corners of a window (shown highlighted here). B–The selected window will fill the drawing screen. C–To view all of the objects in your drawing, use the ZOOM All options.

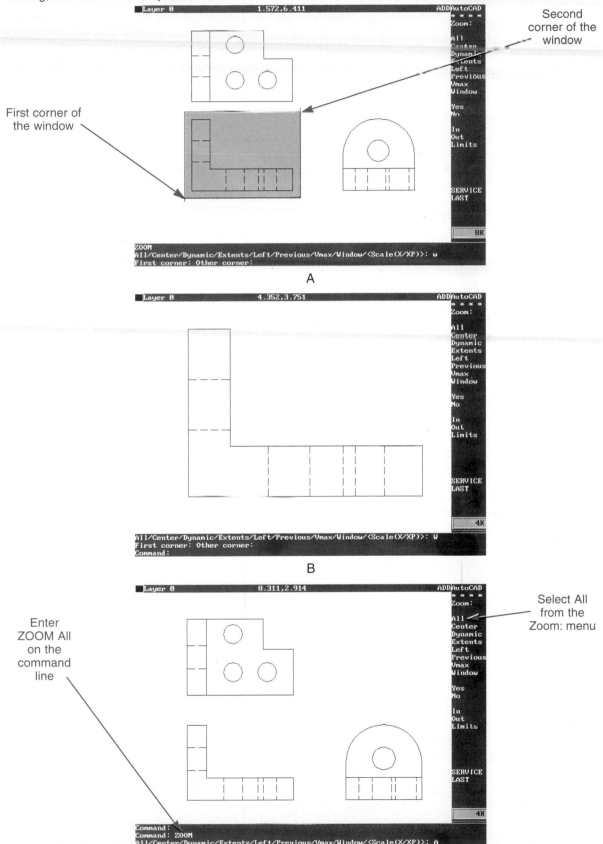

Accurate displays with dynamic zoom

The ZOOM Dynamic option allows you to accurately specify the portion of the drawing you want displayed. This is done by constructing a *view box*. This view box is proportional to the size of the display area. If you have zoomed in already when ZOOM Dynamic is selected, the entire drawing is displayed on the screen. To practice with this command, load any drawing into AutoCAD. Then select the ZOOM command's Dynamic option as follows:

Command: **ZOOM** ⏎
All/Center/Dynamic/Extents/Left/Previous/Vmax/Window/⟨Scale(X/XP)⟩: **D** ⏎

Figure 10-3.   Features of the ZOOM Dynamic command. A–Drawing extents. B–Current view. C–Generated area. D and E–Panning view box/Zooming view box. F–Hourglass.

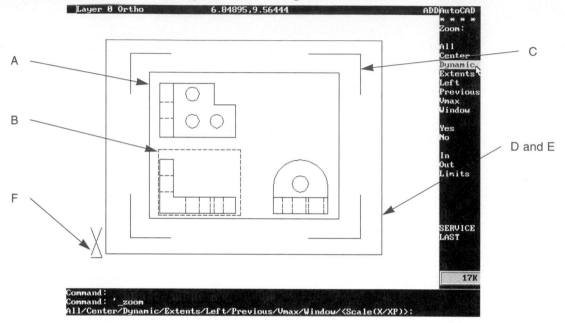

The screen is now occupied by four boxes, Figure 10-3. A fifth box is displayed later. Each one has a specific function. The boxes and their functions are:

- **Drawing extents (white line).** This box shows the area of the drawing that is occupied by drawing features (entities). It is the same area that would be displayed with ZOOM Extents.
- **Current view (green dotted line).** This is the view that was displayed before you selected ZOOM Dynamic. It may be considerably smaller than the red corners of the generated area.
- **Generated area (red corners).** This is the most obvious box because its corners are red lines. It represents the generated area of the drawing. AutoCAD keeps a *virtual screen* of over 4 billion pixels in both the X and Y coordinate directions. (Pixels were discussed in Chapter 8.) The virtual screen is the area AutoCAD calculates with the REGEN command. Many users have screens with 640×480 pixels; thus, the virtual screen is much larger than the display area. This is why the generated area extends beyond the actual drawing. Note that all, some, or even none of the red corners may be visible. This depends on the current size of the virtual screen.

  The generated area is important because it displays the portion of the drawing that can be zoomed without causing a regeneration. This means the next display is calculated at the faster redraw speed. If you select a zoom box that lies outside the generated area, a REGEN is performed, thus slowing the next display. Try to size your view and pan boxes inside the generated area.
- **Panning view box (X in the center).** The box with an X in the center is the panning view box. Move the pointing device to find the center point of the desired zoomed display. When you press the pick button, the fifth and final box appears.

- **Zooming view box (arrow on right side).** This box allows you to decrease or increase the area that you wish to zoom. Move the pointer to the right and the box increases in size. Move the pointer to the left and the box shrinks. You can also pan up or down with the zooming view box. The only restriction is that you cannot move the box to the left.

The ZOOM Dynamic command is not complete until you press ENTER. If you press the pick button to select the zooming view box, the panning view box reappears. Then you can reposition it if necessary. Press the pick button again and the zooming view box is displayed. In this manner, you can fine-tune the exact display needed. This is also helpful in defining permanent views, which is discussed later in this chapter.

One final aspect of ZOOM Dynamic is the "hourglass" displayed in the lower-left corner of the screen. See F in Figure 10-3. The hourglass informs you that the zooming view box is outside the generated area (red corners). AutoCAD is then forced to regenerate the drawing. The hourglass is a reminder to help you save time by avoiding unnecessary regenerations. As you adjust the view box, the hourglass may disappear. When it does, notice where the view box is located. All lines of the view box are inside the generated area. Move the view box so that one side is touching the generated area box. The hourglass then reappears. If you pick that view box location, a regeneration takes place.

EXERCISE 10-1

❏ Load a drawing from a previous exercise or drawing problem.
❏ Select ZOOM Window and enlarge a portion of the drawing.
❏ Select ZOOM Window again to move in closer to a detail.
❏ Select ZOOM Vmax to show the virtual screen.
❏ Use ZOOM Previous to return to the last display.
❏ Select ZOOM Extents to show only the drawing entities.
❏ Select ZOOM All to display the entire drawing limits.
❏ Select ZOOM Dynamic. Maneuver the view box to select a portion of the drawing.
❏ Use ZOOM Dynamic to enlarge the display. Force a regeneration of the drawing by placing the view box partially outside the generated area.
❏ Save the drawing as A:EX10-1, then quit the drawing session.

CREATE YOUR OWN WORKING VIEWS

ARM 7

On a large drawing that involves a number of separate details, using the ZOOM command can become time-consuming. Being able to specify a certain view would make better use of your time. This is possible with the VIEW command. It allows you to create named views. A view can be a portion of the drawing, such as the upper-left quadrant, or it can denote an enlarged portion. After the view is created, you can instruct AutoCAD to display it at any time.

Creating views

The VIEW command is listed in the VIEW screen menu as DDview:, and as Named Views... in the View pull-down menu. When VIEW is entered at the Command: prompt, you are presented five options. Two of the options, Save and Window, allow you to create views. The Save option saves the current screen display under a name you enter. To name the view FRONT, you would follow this procedure:

```
Command: VIEW ↵
?/Delete/Restore/Save/Window: S ↵
   View name to save: FRONT ↵
```

The second method of choosing a view to save is by windowing. This is much like zooming in on an area with the ZOOM Window option.

Command: **VIEW** ↵
?/Delete/Restore/Save/Window: **W** ↵
View name to save: *(enter the view name and press* ENTER*)*
First cornor: *(pick one window corner)*
Other corner: *(pick the second corner)*

Getting information on existing views

Part of your drawing sessions should involve planning and bookkeeping activities. Keep a sheet or form containing all of the drawing variables. These might include symbols, text styles, dimensioning variables (see Chapters 20-22), and view names. If you do not remember the view names, list them by selecting the inquiry option (?) of the VIEW command.

Command: **VIEW** ↵
?/Delete/Restore/Save/Window: **?** ↵
   View(s) to list⟨*⟩: ↵

The alphanumeric screen appears with the display shown in Figure 10-4. Write down these view names and keep them with the other drawing information.

When you press ENTER at the View(s) to list(*): prompt, AutoCAD switches to the Text Screen window as shown in Figure 10-4. Notice in the upper-right corner of Figure 10-4 that the cursor has four arrows on it. You can physically move this text "window" around on your screen by clicking once on your pointer, moving it, then clicking a second time to place the screen. The text screen cannot be resized, just repositioned. You can pick the Go Text button in the upper right to switch to a full text screen, or pick the Send F1 button in the upper left to return to the graphics screen. The Send F1 button is the same as pressing the F1 key on the keyboard. You can get a printout of the list of views shown on the text screen if you have a printer attached to your computer. First be sure that your screen displays a full text screen, and not the Text Screen window. Next press the Print Screen key. You may have to press the Form Feed button on your printer to receive the print.

Figure 10-4.   The alphanumeric screen showing view names. You can use the cursor to reposition the window.

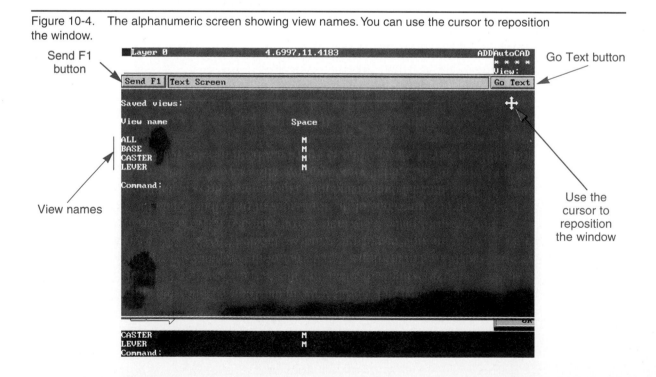

Send F1 button

Go Text button

View names

Use the cursor to reposition the window

Recalling a saved view

A saved view can be restored to the screen at any time by selecting the Restore option of the VIEW command. Then enter the name of the view you want to display.

    Command: VIEW ↵
    ?/Delete/Restore/Save/Window: R ↵
        View name to restore: (type the view name and press ENTER)

The view you enter is immediately displayed.

THE VIEW DIALOG BOXES   ARM 7

You can also work with views by selecting the Name Views… in the View pull-down menu, or by selecting DDview: from the VIEW screen menu. This displays the "View Control" dialog box. See Figure 10-5.

Figure 10-5.   Select a different view in the "View Control" dialog box. Create a new view by selecting the New… button.

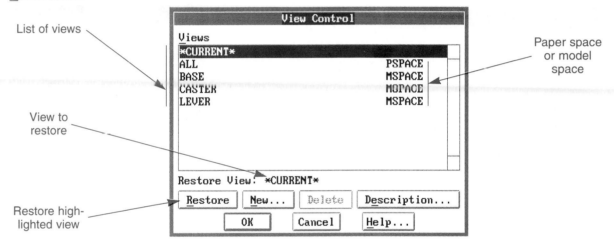

Defining views

A list of views is shown in the Views list box. If you wish to window a new view, pick the "New…" button and the "Define New View" dialog box is displayed. See Figure 10-6. Then pick the "Define Window" radio button. Type the name in the New Name: edit box. Pick the Window ⟨ button, and you are prompted for the first corner. Select the view window in the normal fashion. After you pick the second corner, the "Define New View" dialog box reappears. Pick the Save View button and the "View Control" dialog box is updated to reflect the new view.

Figure 10-6.   In the "Define New View" dialog box, name the new view and define the window.

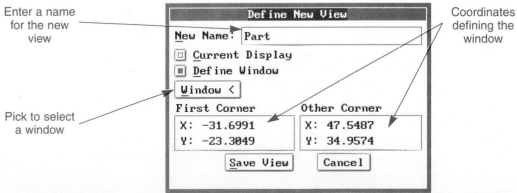

NOTE   The crosshairs in a 3-D view remain on the 3-D axis until you pick the first window point, then the window is displayed. After entering a name in the New Name edit box, you must pick the Save View button, rather than pressing ENTER.

Restoring a saved view

If you wish to display any of the listed views, simply pick its name from the file list, then pick the Restore button. The name of the view to be restored appears in the Restore View: label. Now, pick the OK button and the screen displays the selected view.

Saving the current display

If you want to save the current display as a view, pick the New button in the "View Control" dialog box, then type the new name. The Current Display radio button is the default, so just pick Save View, and the view name is added to the list.

Deleting a view

If you wish to delete a view displayed in the dialog box, first pick the view name in the list, then pick Delete. Notice that the view name is immediately removed from the list. If no view name is highlighted, the Delete button is grayed out, and thus not a valid option.

View description

You can get a detailed description of the selected view by picking the Description... button. This opens another dialog box that provides a variety of information about the view. See Figure 10-7. A discussion of these values related to 3-D drawings is given in *AutoCAD and its Applications–Advanced, R13 for DOS*.

Figure 10-7.   Picking the Description... button in the "View Control" dialog box accesses this informative dialog box.

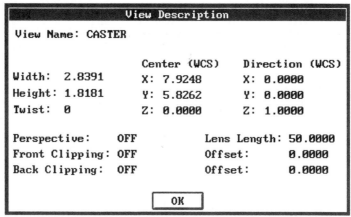

PROFESSIONAL TIP

Part of your project planning should be view names. A consistent naming system ensures that all users will know the view names without having to list them. The views can be set as part of the prototype drawings. Then, view names might be placed in a custom screen menu as discussed in *AutoCAD and its Applications–Advanced, R13 for DOS*.

MOVING AROUND THE DISPLAY SCREEN ARM 7

Imagine that you could put a hook in one side of the drawing and drag it across the screen. This is what the PAN command does. PAN allows you to move around the drawing without changing the magnification factor. You can then view objects which lie just outside the edges of the display screen.

Picking the pan displacement

Type PAN at the Command: prompt, or select Pan: from the VIEW screen menu. You can also select Pan and then Point from the View pull-down menu. AutoCAD then prompts for a point you want to drag. Pick that point. Next, you must pick where you want that point in the next display. The drawing is moved the distance between your two points, Figure 10-8.

Command: **PAN** ↵
Displacement: *(pick the point to drag)*
    Second point: *(pick the final location of the first point)*

Figure 10-8.   PAN moves the drawing around the screen. A–Panning to the left. B–Panning up. C–Completed pan.

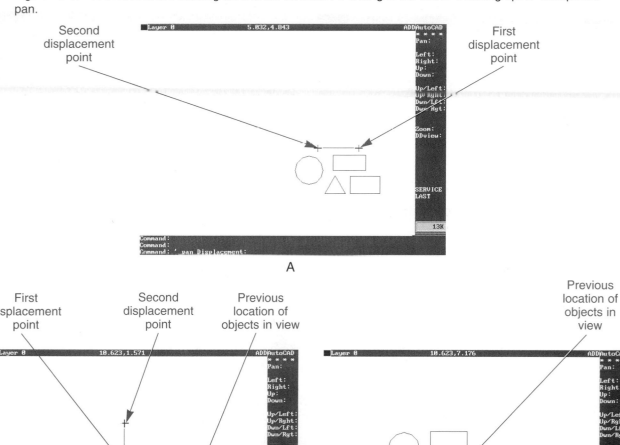

A

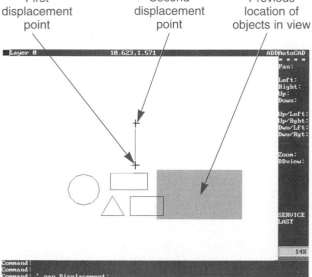

B

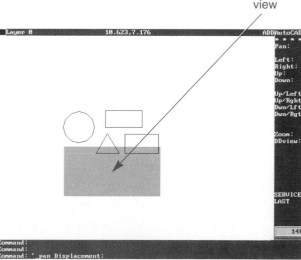

C

You can also enter the displacement, or the distance the drawing is to be moved by giving coordinates. See Figure 10-9. The coordinates can be either relative or absolute. A relative displacement to move the drawing 8 units to the right and 3 units up is:

Command: **PAN** ↵
Displacement: **8,3** ↵
   Second point: ↵

Figure 10-9.   Relative coordinates can be used to pan across a drawing.

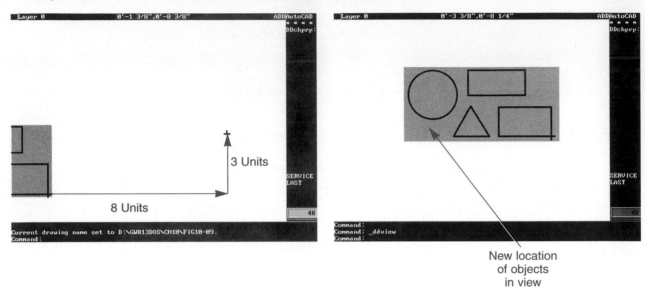

New location
of objects
in view

Suppose the absolute coordinate location of the point you wanted to move was 4,5. Then, the absolute displacement for the above movement is calculated as 8,3 + 4,5 = 12,8 for the second point. Enter this as follows:

Command: **PAN** ↵
Displacement: **4,5** ↵
   Second point: **12,8** ↵

Using pan presets

You can automatically pan from the center of your drawing to one of the four edges or corners by using one of the presets provided in the screen and pull-down menus. These eight options of the PAN command are shown in Figure 10-10 as they appear in the View pull-down menu. These options must be picked from a menu. They cannot be typed at the Displacement: prompt.

Figure 10-10. The View pull-down menu and the eight options of the PAN command.

Select the view pull-down menu

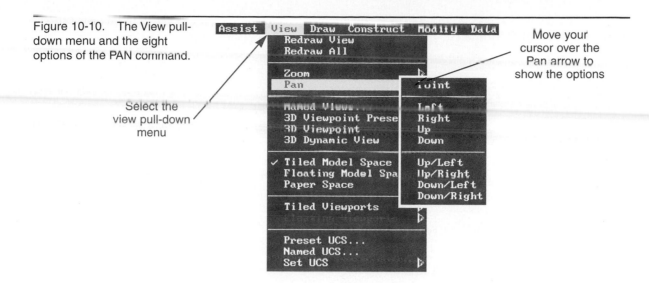

Move your cursor over the Pan arrow to show the options

SETTING VIEW RESOLUTION FOR QUICK DISPLAYS   ARM 7

AutoCAD allows you to save time on zooms and pans at the expense of display accuracy. On the other hand, AutoCAD provides a perfect display at the expense of zoom and pan speed. The main factor in this decision is called the view resolution. The *view resolution* refers to the number of lines used to draw circles and arcs. High resolution values display smooth circles and arcs. You can control the view resolution of circles and arcs with the VIEWRES command. It asks if you want zooms to be fast and what zoom percentage you want for circles:

Command: **VIEWRES** ↵
Do you want fast zooms? ⟨Y⟩ ↵
Enter circle zoom percent (1-20000) ⟨100⟩:

If your response to the first prompt is Yes, AutoCAD "repaints" the screen using REDRAW speed for ZOOM, PAN, or VIEW Restore. (The REDRAW speed can only be used if you do not reduce or enlarge outside of the generated areas.) After zooming in on a circle, the circle will appear less smooth.

If speed is not a concern, then answer "No" to the first prompt. This causes AutoCAD to use REGEN when any display command is issued. Circles and arcs will always appear to have the same smoothness.

The actual smoothness of circles and arcs is controlled by the circle zoom percent. It can vary between 1 and 20000. The default is 100. This produces a relatively smooth circle. A number smaller than 100 causes circles and arcs to be drawn with fewer vectors (straight lines). A number larger than 100 places more vectors in the circles, as shown in Figure 10-11. The circle zoom percent is only used when AutoCAD is forced to do a regeneration. That is why a circle may appear to be composed of several straight sides after you zoom in on it. If you want a smooth circle, just use the REGEN command.

Figure 10-11. The higher the VIEWRES value, the smoother a circle will appear.

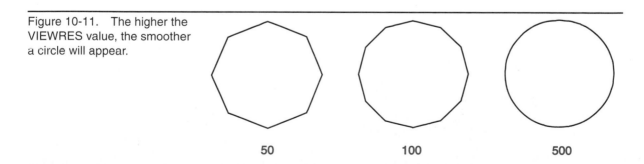

50   100   500

The VIEWRES command is a display function only and has no effect on the plotted or printed drawing. A drawing is printed or plotted using an optimum number of vectors for the size of circles and arcs. See Chapter 12 for detailed information on plotting.

PROFESSIONAL TIP

If you are concerned with speed, set VIEWRES for fast zooms and set the circle zoom percent to 100 or less. Circles may look like they have straight line sides, but drawing regenerations take less time.

EXERCISE 10-2

❑ Load AutoCAD and begin a new drawing named EX10-2.
❑ Draw three circles and three arcs of different sizes.
❑ Zoom in on the smallest circle using the Dynamic option. Notice the straight line segments that make up the circle.
❑ Keep zooming in on the circle edge (with ZOOM Window) until you force a regeneration. At that time, you have gone beyond the virtual screen.
❑ Set the VIEWRES command for fast zooms and a 10 percent circle zoom. ZOOM All and notice the shape of the circles and arcs after a regeneration.
❑ Select the VIEWRES command and answer "No" for fast zooms. Set circle zoom to 20 percent. Zoom in on a circle three times. Notice when regenerations are performed.
❑ Save the drawing as A:EX10-2 and quit the drawing session.

THE VIEW PULL-DOWN MENU   ARM A

Often-used display commands can be accessed by selecting View from the menu bar. The View pull-down menu with two display cascading submenus are shown in Figure 10-12.

The View pull-down menu provides access to all of AutoCAD's display and viewing commands. Seven of the selections are followed by arrows, which lead to cascading submenus that provide additional options or other commands.

A brief description of each of the picks in the View pull-down menu is provided here.

- **Redraw View.** Redraws the current viewport.
- **Redraw All.** Redraws all viewports in model or paper space.
- **Zoom.** Provides access to all ZOOM command options. See Figure 10-12B.
- **Pan.** Provides access to all PAN command options. See Figure 10-10.
- **Named Views....** Displays the View Control dialog box which enables you to work with views. Allows access to related view control dialog boxes (previously discussed). See Figure 10-12C.
- **3D Viewpoint Presets.** Provides access to eleven different preset 3-D views. The current viewport is affected by the preset that is selected.
- **3D Viewpoint.** Provides access to three different methods of selecting a 3-D viewpoint.
- **3D Dynamic View.** Activates the DVIEW command, which provides total control over the creation of a 3-D viewpoint and display.
- **Tiled Model Space.** This is the default display setting, and indicates that the TILEMODE system variable is set to a value of 1, and the VPORTS command must be used to construct "tiled" viewports. This is the model space mode in which you draw.
- **Floating Model Space.** Switches the TILEMODE variable to 0, and activates the current model space "floating" viewport. If no floating viewports have been cut into the paper space drawing with the MVIEW command, AutoCAD executes MVIEW and allows you to create a viewport.
- **Paper Space.** Switches the TILEMODE variable to 0, and activates paper space. If floating viewports have been created, the crosshairs appear to be laying over the top of them. Paper

Figure 10-12. The View pull-down menu with the "Zoom" and "Set View" cascading menus.

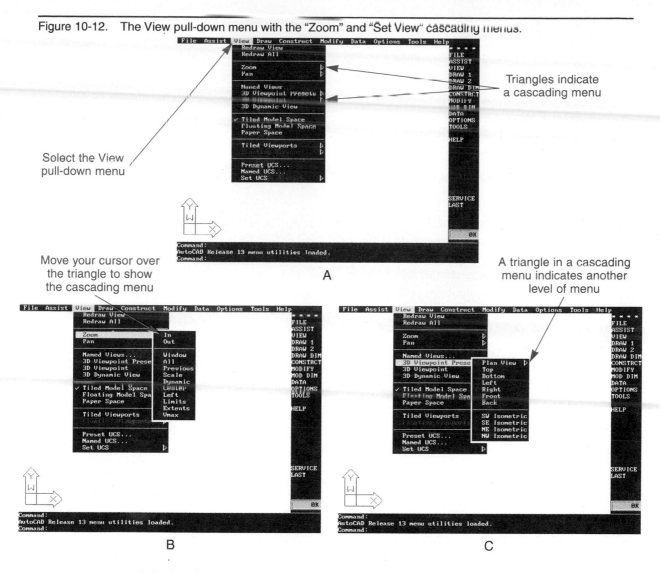

Select the View pull-down menu

Triangles indicate a cascading menu

Move your cursor over the triangle to show the cascading menu

A triangle in a cascading menu indicates another level of menu

A

B

C

space is a 2-D drawing space. Therefore, when this item has a check mark by it, the three 3-D selections in the View pull-down menu are grayed out and unselectable.

- **Tiled Viewports.** Enables you to create tiled viewports with the VPORTS command. This selection is only available if there is a check mark by **Tiled Model Space**, because the VPORTS command is only active when TILEMODE is set to 1.
- **Floating Viewports.** Enables you to create floating viewports with the MVIEW command. This selection is only available if there is a check mark by **Floating Model Space**, or **Paper Space**, because the MVIEW command is only active when TILEMODE is set to 0.
- **Preset UCS....** Activates the UCS Orientation dialog box in which you can graphically change the orientation of the User Coordinate System to a specific face of a cube. User coordinate systems are discussed in greater detail in Chapter 19.
- **Named UCS....** Activates the UCS Control dialog box in which you can display, delete, list, or rename user coordinate systems that have been previously named and saved with the UCS command.
- **Set UCS.** Provides access to all of the options of the UCS command in a cascading menu.

USING TRANSPARENT DISPLAY COMMANDS

ARM 7

As mentioned earlier, certain commands can be used while you are inside another command. These commands are said to be "transparent" to the computer user. The display commands ZOOM, PAN, and VIEW are transparent. Suppose that while drawing a line, you need to place a point somewhere off the screen. One option is to cancel the LINE command. Then zoom out to see more of the drawing and select LINE again. A more efficient method is to use PAN or ZOOM while still in the LINE command. An example of drawing a line to a point off the screen is as follows:

> Command: **LINE** ⏎
> From point: *(pick a point)*
> To point: **'PAN** ⏎
> 〉〉Displacement: *(pick a point to drag at edge of screen)*
> 〉〉Second point: *(pick a second point of displacement)*
> Resuming LINE command.
> To point: *(pick a point)*
> To point: ⏎

The double prompt (〉〉) indicates that a command has been put on "hold" while you use a transparent command. The transparent command must be completed before the original command is returned. At that time, the double prompt disappears.

The above procedure is similar when using the ZOOM and VIEW commands. An apostrophe (') is entered before the command. To connect a line to a small feature, enter 'ZOOM at the "To point:" prompt. To perform a drawing or editing function across views, enter 'VIEW. If the current display you see is not a saved view, create a view. Then you can do a transparent PAN or ZOOM to continue drawing. Finally, do a transparent 'VIEW Restore.

When trying to perform a transparent display, you may receive the following message:

> **Requires a regen, cannot be transparent.
> Resuming *(current)* command.

In this situation, you might try a less dramatic ZOOM, PAN, or VIEW that does not require AutoCAD to regenerate the display, or you can try ZOOM Vmax.

AutoCAD system variables can also be used in the transparent mode. Remember, when typing any transparent command, first type an apostrophe before the command name.

EXERCISE 10-3

❏ Load AutoCAD and begin a new drawing named EX10-3.
❏ Set the drawing limits at 12,9, grid spacing at .5, and snap spacing at .25.
❏ Construct the two arcs shown below.

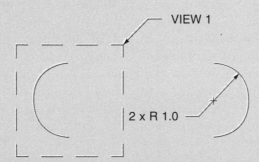

❏ Window a view of the left arc and name it 1. Restore view 1.
❏ Select the LINE command and snap to the top of the arc.
❏ Select 'ZOOM Dynamic. Increase the zooming view box to include both arcs, but do not cause a regeneration.
❏ Extend the line to the top of the other arc. Begin a second line at the bottom of the right arc.
❏ Select 'VIEW and restore view 1. Attach the line to the bottom of the left arc.
❏ ZOOM Dynamic to show the completed object.
❏ Save the drawing as A:EX10-3 and quit the drawing session.

endeavor:

USING THE AERIAL VIEW

The use of display commands to view different aspects of your drawing can become a time-consuming endeavor, especially if you are working with a large drawing. Therefore, it is worth the effort for you to become familiar with a powerful display feature called the Aerial View. The Aerial View enables you to see your entire drawing in a small window, then move to any feature quickly. You can zoom in to any area on the drawing in the Aerial View, and the graphics screen is updated automatically to reflect your selection. In addition, you can use the dynamic zoom function that allows you to move the zoom box around in the Aerial View and the graphics screen is continuously updated to reflect the location of the zoom box.

To open the Aerial View window, pick Aerial View in the Tools pull-down menu, or type AV at the Command: prompt. The entire drawing is displayed in the Aerial View. See Figure 10-13. The Aerial View window is initially displayed in the upper-left corner of the graphics screen, but can be moved to any location. To do so, pick the title bar of the window, labeled "AV-2." Move your pointer to the desired location and pick again to place the window. You can also resize the Aerial View to make it larger or smaller. Move your pointer to one of the four sides of the window, and the cursor changes to a double-pointed arrow. Press the pick button and move the pointer. Press again to complete the resizing action. Picking a corner of the Aerial View window allows you to scale the entire window by stretching it diagonally. The Aerial View in Figure 10-14 has been resized. Note how the title bar and buttons have changed.

Figure 10-13. Aerial View window is initially in the upper-left corner of the graphics screen (shown highlighted here).

Aerial view window

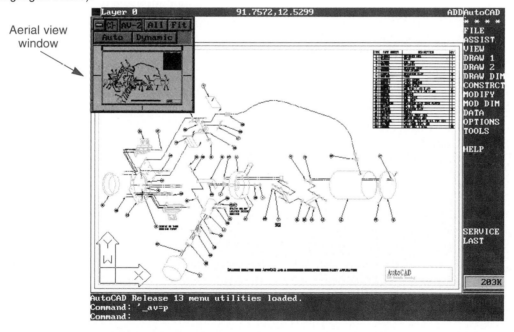

Aerial View window description

The Aerial View contains a title bar, four buttons labeled All, Fit, Auto, and Dynamic, and a button that resembles a push-pin. The button in the extreme upper-left corner is the control button, and closes the window when it is pressed. The buttons in the Aerial View window are described here. Refer to Figure 10-14 as you read.

- **All.** Redisplays the entire drawing in the center of the Aerial View.
- **Fit.** Redisplays the entire drawing in the Aerial View similar to Zoom extents.
- **Auto+Dynamic/Static.** Functions as both a zoom and pan tool. Pick a point in the Aerial View, then pick a second window corner. The graphics screen automatically displays the contents of

Figure 10-14.   The Aerial View window can be resized and moved to any location.

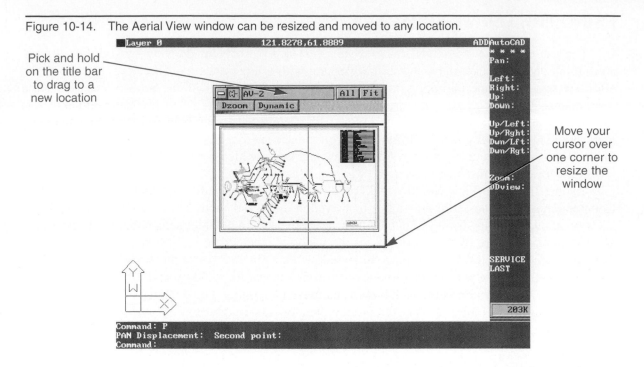

Pick and hold
on the title bar
to drag to a
new location

Move your
cursor over
one corner to
resize the
window

the window. Now, pick any point inside the zoom box in the Aerial View and move the pointer. Notice that the graphics display is continuously updated to show the area inside the zoom box. That is because the Dynamic button is active. Pick the Dynamic button and it changes to Static. Now, pick inside the Aerial View zoom box and move the pointer. The graphics display does not change until you pick a second point.

You can quickly zoom in on any point and double the current magnification. First, move your pointer to where you want the center of the next screen display. Now, press the right mouse button. The graphics display changes and the zoom box in the Aerial View moves to the pick point and is reduced in size by half.

- **Dzoom+Dynamic/Static.** This is the dynamic zoom mode. When you press the Auto button it changes to Dzoom. Pick inside the Aerial View window and an arrow appears on the right side of the zoom box. It functions exactly the same as the dynamic zoom command. Pick again and the entire box moves, or pans. This is the pan box. When you are satisfied with the zoom box size and location, press ENTER. If the Dynamic button is displayed, you can see the results of your zooming and panning in the graphics screen. If the Static button is displayed, the graphics screen is not redrawn to reflect your changes until you press ENTER.
- **Zoom.** Functions exactly like the ZOOM command. Pick two points in the Aerial View and the graphics display reflects the zoom. You can use the same automatic zoom and double magnification procedure as discussed previously when the Zoom button is active. The Dynamic and Static functions are not available with Zoom or Pan.
- **Pan.** Allows you to pan the current zoom box to a new location. The automatic zoom and double magnification procedure is also available when the Pan button is active.
- **Pushpin icon.** This button in the upper-left corner of the Aerial View, appears depressed. This means that the Aerial View is "pinned" to your display screen, even as you continue to work on your drawing. If you do not want the Aerial View to remain displayed as you work, you can dismiss it the next time you pick any point on the graphics screen. To activate this "unpinned" option, click on the pushpin button to release it. You have now removed the pin from the screen. When you move the pointer outside the Aerial View, it changes to a large X to indicate that the pin is removed. As soon as you pick any point outside the Aerial View, it is removed from the display.

PROFESSIONAL TIP

You should try to avoid regenerations. They slow your work and thought processes. Try the following tips for all your new drawings:
* Set your drawing limits to include a little extra for a border.
* ZOOM All.
* Create a view named ALL (or a name of your choice) of the entire drawing area.
* Avoid using ZOOM Window, ZOOM Extents, PAN, or REGEN again.
* Create additional smaller views as you need them.
* Use ZOOM Dynamic in place of all other display commands. The hourglass in the display will appear if AutoCAD plans to regenerate the drawing.
* Use ZOOM Vmax to check the contents of the virtual screen.
* Use the Aerial View for all zooming and panning.

EXERCISE 10-4

❑ Load AutoCAD and open the ASESMP drawing in the acadr13\sample directory.
❑ Activate the Aerial View and zoom in on office #109 in the upper-right corner of the drawing. Use the default Auto+Dynamic buttons.
❑ Pick inside the zoom box in the Aerial View and slowly move your pointer around the drawing to see the contents of each room in the building.
❑ Pick the Dynamic button to activate Static. Move the zoom box in the Aerial View to the upper-left corner of the building and click so that office #101 is displayed.
❑ Place your pointer over one of the green desks inside the zoom box in the Aerial View and press the ENTER button of your pointer to zoom in. Keep zooming in like this until you can clearly see the green phone on the desk.
❑ Zoom out to view the entire building.
❑ Pick Auto to display Dzoom, then be sure the Dynamic button is active. Resize your zoom box so you can see three offices at one time and take another tour of the building.
❑ Pick Dzoom to activate the Zoom button and create a zoom box in the Aerial View just large enough to view one office.
❑ Pick the Zoom button to activate Pan and move the zoom box around the Aerial View, picking different locations to look at as you go.
❑ When you are finished experimenting with the Aerial View, quit the session without saving.

MODEL SPACE AND PAPER SPACE   ARM 7

Model space can be thought of as the method and place in which you draw and design in AutoCAD. It is the "space" in which you create your drawing or model. The term "model" has more meaning when working in 3-D, but you can consider any drawing or design a model, even if it is two-dimensional. The best way to tell if you are in model space is to look at the UCS (User Coordinate System) icon. It is the symbol located in the lower-left corner of the screen, and represents the current directions of the X and Y coordinates. See Figure 10-15. A detailed discussion of User Coordinate Systems and the UCS icon is given in Chapter 29.

Figure 10-15.   The UCS icons for model space and paper space.

Model space UCS

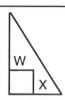

Paper space USC

Paper space, on the other hand, is a "space" you create when you are ready to lay out a drawing or model to be plotted. Basically, you place a sheet of paper on the screen, then insert, or "reference," one or more drawings to the paper. In order to create this plotting layout, you must first enter paper space by typing PSPACE or PS at the Command: prompt.

Command: **PS** ↵
Command not allowed unless TILEMODE is set to 0

As you can see, AutoCAD does not allow you to enter paper space until you have changed the manner in which viewports are handled. This system variable is called TILEMODE. The function of tiled viewports is discussed later in this chapter, but for now, in order to enter paper space you must reset the TILEMODE value.

Command: **TILEMODE** ↵
New value for TILEMODE ⟨1⟩: **0** ↵

After entering the TILEMODE variable of 0 you are automatically placed in paper space. Notice the "P" that appears in the status line after the layer name and the paper space icon displayed in the lower-left corner of the screen.

Remember that you should create all your drawings and designs in model space, not in paper space. Only paper layouts for plotting purposes should be created in paper space. Therefore, you should return to model space by entering either MSPACE or MS at the Command: prompt.

Command: **MS** ↵
MSPACE
There are no active Model space viewports.

Notice that you are *not* returned to model space. You must first reset the TILEMODE system variable to 1 to return to model space.

Command: **TILEMODE** ↵
New value for TILEMODE ⟨0⟩: **1** ↵

As previously mentioned, the View pull-down menu allows you to quickly switch back and forth from model space to paper space. Pick View and notice that a check mark is by Tiled Model Space. This informs you that TILEMODE is set to one and model space is current. If you wish to display paper space just pick Paper Space in the View menu.

Press the F1 key to display the text screen and you will see that when you pick Paper Space, AutoCAD automatically resets the value of the TILEMODE variable. You will find that using the View pull-down menu to switch between paper and model space is quick and easy.

Do not be confused by TILEMODE, model space, and paper space. The detailed discussion in Chapter 26 will give you greater confidence. Right now, think of these terms in the following manner:

ACTIVITY	SPACE	TILEMODE
Drawing and design	Model	1
Plotting and printing layout	Paper	0

CREATING MULTIPLE VIEWPORTS   ARM 7

Viewports are created with the VPORTS command. The screen of a DOS computer can be divided into sixteen "tiled" viewports. The edges of tiled viewports butt against one another like floor tile. The TILEMODE variable must be set to 1 or "ON" to display tiled viewports. The arrangement of the viewports can vary, as indicated by the options of the VPORTS command. The default arrangement of viewports–the 3 option–is shown in Figure 10-16.

Command: **VPORTS** ↵
Save/Restore/Delete/Join/SIngle/?/2/⟨3⟩/4: ↵
Horizontal/Vertical/Above/Below/Left/⟨Right⟩: ↵
Regenerating drawing.

Figure 10-16. The default arrangement of viewports.

By default, all three viewports are the same

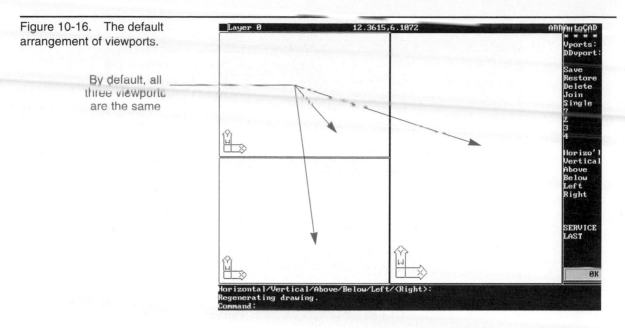

When you accept the defaults, AutoCAD displays an arrangement of two viewports on the left side of the screen, and a large viewport on the right. The possible combinations of three viewports are shown in Figure 10-17.

Figure 10-17. A variety of viewport arrangements are possible with the VPORTS command and the 3 option.

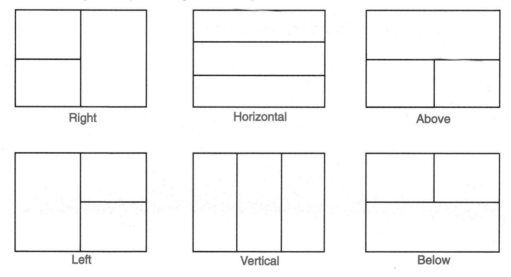

| Right | Horizontal | Above |
| Left | Vertical | Below |

Move the pointing device around and notice that only one viewport contains crosshairs. This is called the *active viewport*. The pointer is represented by an arrow in the others. To make a different viewport active, move the pointer into it and press the pick button. As you draw in one viewport, the image is displayed in all of them. Try drawing lines and other shapes and notice how the viewports are affected. Then use a Display command, such as ZOOM, in the current viewport and notice the results. Only the current viewport reflects the use of the ZOOM command.

Preset tiled viewport layouts can be selected from a dialog box. Pick the View pull-down menu, Tiled Viewports, then pick select "Layout..." to display the "Tiled Viewport Layout" icon menu. You can select a pre-arranged layout by either picking the icon on the right, or by picking the written description from the list on the left. See Figure 10-18. After you pick a layout, the icon is highlighted (as is the description). If this is the desired layout, pick OK and the screen automatically reflects your selection.

Figure 10-18.   The Tiled Viewport Layout icon menu.

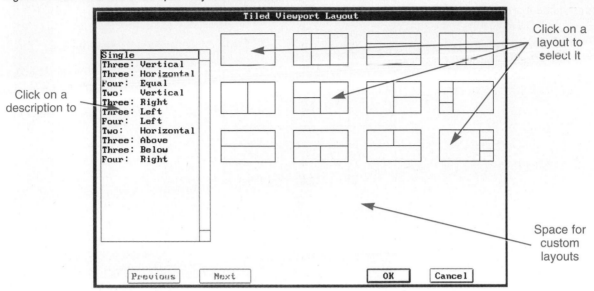

Notice in Figure 10-18 that there are several additional spaces in the icon menu. You can create custom viewport layouts and add them to this icon menu. See *AutoCAD and its Applications–Advanced, R13 for DOS*, for menu customization techniques.

Uses of viewports

Viewports in model space can be used for both 2-D and 3-D drawings. They are limited only by your imagination and need. See Chapter 29 for examples of the VPORTS command in 3-D. The nature of 2-D drawings, whether they are mechanical multiview, architectural construction details, or unscaled schematic drawings, lend themselves well to viewports.

PROFESSIONAL TIP

When dialog boxes appear on screen, many times they obstruct your view of the drawing. Pick the title bar that contains the dialog box name and hold down the pick button. You can then move the dialog box to a new location on screen.

PROFESSIONAL TIP

Several sample drawings are included with the AutoCAD software. These files have been compressed and can only be viewed if you used the INSTALL program to copy the AutoCAD files to your hard disk. If AutoCAD was installed properly, the sample drawings should be located in the \ACADR13\COMMON\SAMPLE subdirectory. The name of the directory and subdirectories may vary depending on how the software was installed, and what the directories were named during installation. Check with your instructor or supervisor to locate these drawings, or browse through the directories and subdirectories to determine their locations. The sample drawings include a variety of drawing and design disciplines and are excellent for testing and practice. It is suggested that you use these drawings, especially when learning the Display commands.

EXERCISE 10-5

❏ Load AutoCAD and open the SASKATCH drawing from your \ACADR13\SAMPLE subdirectory. (SASKATCH will reside here if AutoCAD was installed according to suggestions in the "Installation and Performance Guide.")
❏ When the drawing is displayed on the screen, you should see a map of the Canadian province of Saskatchewan. Zoom into various locations to get familiar with the drawing.
❏ Use the VPORTS command to create the default arrangement of three viewports. (Make sure TILEMODE is set to 1.) The large viewport should be on the right.
❏ Use PAN to move the drawing up in the large viewport.
❏ In the upper-left viewport, use ZOOM Window to find the lower-left corner of the legend.
❏ Pick the lower-left viewport and zoom in on the center of the map. Locate the towns of McMahon and Neville.
❏ While in this same viewport, use ZOOM Vmax. This displays the virtual screen for the current viewport.
❏ Quit and do not save the drawing.

INTRODUCTION TO 3-D DISPLAY COMMANDS   ARM 7

An introduction to the basics of 3-D drawing is provided in Chapter 29. However, a short introduction to two additional display commands will conclude the discussion of viewing drawings. The two commands are DVIEW (Dynamic VIEW), and VPOINT (ViewPOINT).

Establishing a dynamic view

When using the DVIEW command to view a 3-D drawing, you can see the object move as you perform the viewing manipulations such as rotate, turn, twist, and pan. You can rotate the "camera" (your eyes), and the "target" (focus point). Follow the given example for a brief overview of this command. Use the OPEN command and recall the LINKRODS drawing. Again, this drawing may be in a separate subdirectory such as \ACADR13\COMMON\SAMPLE.

The "Open Drawing" dialog box appears. Find SAMPLE in the Directories box and double click on it. A list of files should appear in the Files box. Pick LINKRODS, then pick OK. The drawing that appears is a 3-D wireframe model of a linkrod, and is displayed at an odd angle. Use the PLAN command to obtain the plan, or top view of the model:

    Command: **PLAN** ↵
    ⟨Current UCS⟩/Ucs/World: ↵
    Regenerating drawing.

Your display should look like Figure 10-19. Use the following commands to create viewports and a dynamic view in the large viewport.

    Command: **VPORTS** ↵
    Save/Restore/Delete/Join/SIngle/?/2/⟨3⟩/4: ↵
    Horizontal/Vertical/Above/Below/Left/⟨Right⟩: ↵

Your screen should now look like the one in Figure 10-20.

Figure 10-19.   The LINKRODS drawing displayed in a single viewport.

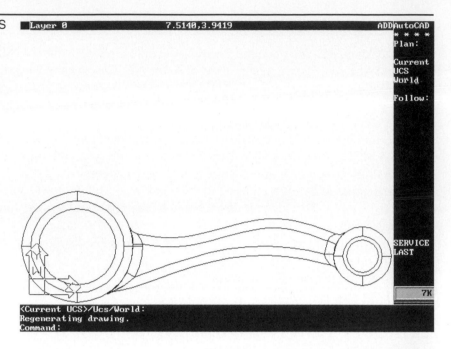

Figure 10-20.   The VPORTS command is used to display three viewports.

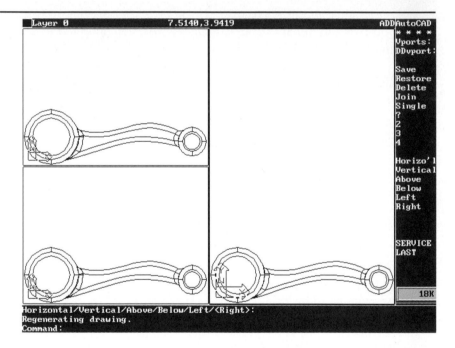

The DVIEW command is used next to create the 3-D view of the linkrod in the large viewport. Make the large viewport active. Instead of picking the viewport to make it active, you can press CTRL+V (hold down the CTRL key while pressing the V key) to change the active viewport. In order to speed up the DVIEW process, press ENTER at the Select objects: prompt. This displays a small house that requires less regeneration time. Your drawing returns to the screen at the completion of the DVIEW command, and is displayed in the same viewpoint as the house. If you want to work with your drawing on the screen using the DVIEW options, you must select it using any of the selection methods.

NOTE It is best to use the house for DVIEW purposes. If your drawing is complex, the comput er slows down because it is constantly regenerating the highlighted display as the drawing is dynamically moved on the screen.

Command: **DVIEW** ↵
Select objects: ↵
CAmera/TArget/Distance/POints/PAn/Zoom/TWist/CLip/Hide/Off/Undo/⟨eXit⟩: **TA** ↵
Toggle angle in/Enter angle from XY plane ⟨–90.0000⟩: **–15** ↵
Toggle angle from/Enter angle in XY plane from X axis ⟨90.0000⟩: **–40** ↵
CAmera/TArget/Distance/POints/PAn/Zoom/TWist/CLip/Hide/Off/Undo/⟨eXit⟩: ↵
Command: **ZOOM** ↵
All/Center/Dynamic/Extents/Left/Previous/Vmax/Window/⟨Scale(X/XP)⟩: **E** ↵
Regenerating drawing.

Try to determine the direction in which you are viewing the linkrod. Notice in the small viewports that the large end of the linkrod is toward the left of the screen, and the small end is oriented in the positive Y direction. Now look at the UCS in the large view. If it now appears that the large end of the linkrod is closest to you, then it is correct. If you have trouble visualizing this, make the large viewport active, and then type HIDE at the Command: prompt. The hide operation may take from 45 seconds to two minutes depending on the model and speed of your computer. That is because this drawing is a 3-D solid model and AutoCAD must first construct a "skin" to wrap around the model, and then calculate which parts of the model will be hidden from view. After using the DVIEW command in the large viewport, the screen display should look similar to Figure 10-21.

Figure 10-21. The DVIEW command is used in the large viewport.

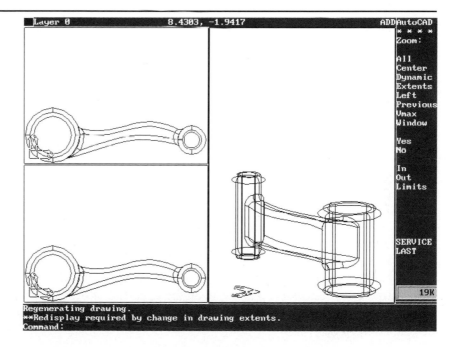

There are several other options and possibilities with the DVIEW command. You can create a true perspective view by specifying the distance from camera to target. In addition, you can zoom in or away from the object, or "clip" the front or rear of the screen image. Additional information regarding these options is found in *AutoCAD and its Applications–Advanced, R13 for DOS*.

Creating a 3-D viewpoint

The VPOINT command enables you to specify the direction from which you will view the object. You can enter XYZ coordinates, or you can visually determine your viewpoint using an XYZ "tripod."

This introductory example uses coordinate entry to determine both viewpoints. See Chapter 29 for a discussion of the tripod method. Make the upper-left viewport active and enter the following commands:

> Command: **VPOINT** ↵
> Rotate/⟨View point⟩ ⟨0.0000,0.0000,0.0000⟩: **−1,−1,1** ↵
> Regenerating drawing.

Activate the lower-left viewport and enter the following:

> Command: **VPOINT** ↵
> Rotate/⟨View point⟩ ⟨0.0000,0.0000,0.0000⟩: **1,−1,1** ↵
> Regenerating drawing.

The two new displays created with VPOINT should resemble those in Figure 10-22.

Figure 10-22.   The VPOINT command creates two different views in the small viewports.

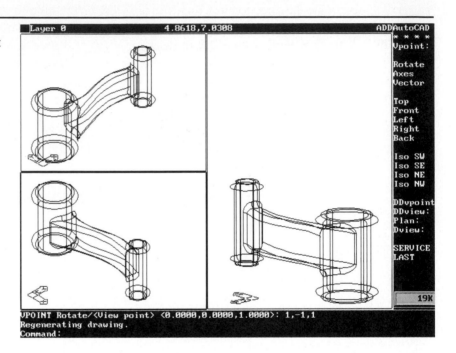

One advantage of multiple viewports is that each viewport is a separate screen. Therefore, you can display any view of the drawing you wish in each screen. In addition, 3-D drawings can appear as either wireframe or solid. The views currently on your screen are in wireframe. The final aspect of this example illustrates these additional possibilities.

Make the lower-left viewport active and zoom in on the small end of the linkrod. Next, make the upper-left viewport active and zoom in on the large end of the linkrod. Now, use the HIDE command in all viewports to remove hidden lines. This process may take a few minutes depending on the speed of your computer.

> Command: **HIDE** ↵
> Regenerating drawing.
> Hiding lines 100% done.

Your screen now shows three separate 3-D views, with hidden lines removed to represent a solid. See Figure 10-23.

Figure 10-23.   Three separate views of the linkrod with hidden lines removed.

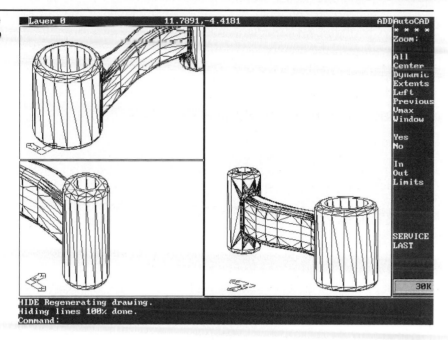

REDRAWING AND REGENERATING VIEWPORTS

ARM 7

Since each viewport is a separate screen, you can redraw or regenerate a single viewport at a time without affecting the others. The REGEN (REGENerate) command instructs AutoCAD to recalculate all of the entities in the drawing. This takes considerably longer than a REDRAW, especially if the drawing is large. However, a REGEN can clarify a drawing by smoothing out circles, arcs, ellipses, and splines.

In order to redraw all of the viewports, use the REDRAWALL command. If you need to regenerate all of the viewports, use the REGENALL command.

EXERCISE 10-6

❑ Use the display of the LINKRODS drawing that is currently on your screen. If the display is not on your screen, refer to the previous section of this text entitled "Establishing a dynamic view," and follow the example to this point.
❑ Make the upper-left viewport active and draw some lines near the top of the linkrod. The lines should be displayed in all viewports.
❑ Make the lower-left viewport active and draw some lines.
❑ Use the REDRAW command while the lower-left viewport is active. Notice that it is the only viewport that is redrawn.
❑ Use the REDRAWALL command.
❑ Pick the large viewport and enter the REGEN command.
❑ Use the REGENALL command. Notice how much longer it takes to perform this command than the REDRAWALL command.
❑ Save your drawing as A:EX10-6, then quit the drawing session.

Controlling automatic regeneration

When developing a drawing, you may issue a command that changes certain aspects of the entities in it. When this occurs, AutoCAD does an automatic regeneration to update the entities. This may not be of concern to you when working on small drawings, but this regeneration may take a considerable amount of time on larger and more complex drawings. In addition, it may not be necessary to have a regeneration of the drawing at all times. If this is the case, set the REGENAUTO command to off.

Command: **REGENAUTO** ↵
ON/OFF ⟨*current*⟩: **OFF** ↵

When REGENAUTO is off, you are given a warning if a regeneration is required:

About to regen – proceed? ⟨Y⟩

If you answer "No" to this prompt, the command you issued is not executed. The following commands may automatically cause a regeneration: ZOOM, PAN, and VIEW Restore.

MULTIPLE VIEWPORTS IN PAPER SPACE   ARM 7

The viewports created with the VPORTS command in model space are called *tiled viewports* because they butt against one another. However, the viewports created in paper space are constructed with the MVIEW command, and are separate entities. You may create as many viewport entities as needed, and they can overlap. AutoCAD can only display a certain number of active viewports. A model space drawing is displayed in an active viewport. The type of operating system used by your computer and the display device determine the number of active viewports. You can check this number by entering the MAXACTVP (MAXimum ACTive ViewPorts) system variable:

Command: **MAXACTVP** ↵
New value for MAXACTVP ⟨16⟩:

The viewports created by the MVIEW command are used when laying out a multiview drawing for plotting or printing. Since these viewports are created in paper space, and they can overlap, the TILEMODE system variable must be set to 0. This places you in paper space so you can make "cutouts" or viewports in your sheet of paper with the MVIEW command. Think of the relationship of TILEMODE and viewports as follows:

ACTIVITY	SPACE	TILEMODE	COMMAND
Drawing and design	Model	1	VPORTS (tiled)
Plotting and printing layout	Paper	0	MVIEW (entities)

This procedure, and all of the options of the MVIEW command, are discussed in detail in Chapter 26.

CHAPTER TEST

Write your answers in the spaces provided.

1. What is the difference between the REDRAW and 'REDRAW commands?_____

   _____

2. What are "blips" and how does REDRAW deal with them? _____

   _____

   _____

3. Which command allows you to change the display of blips? _____

4. Give the proper command option and value to zoom in on the center of a drawing with a magnification factor of 3. _____

5. What is the difference between ZOOM Extents and ZOOM All? _____ _____

_____

_____

6. During the drawing process, when should you use ZOOM? _____ _____

_____

_____

7. How many different boxes are displayed during the ZOOM Dynamic command?_____

8. What is a "virtual screen?"_____

_____

_____

_____

9. When using the ZOOM Dynamic option, what symbol informs you that a regeneration is about to take place? _____

10. Which command and option allows you to create a view, named FULL, of the current screen display_____

11. What option would you choose to display an existing view? _____

12. How would you obtain a listing of existing views? _____

_____

13. What is the purpose of the PAN command?_____

_____

14. How does PAN work? _____

_____

15. How do you access the PAN command presets? _____

_____

16. What is "view resolution?"_____

_____

17. What is the purpose of the VIEWRES command?_____

_____

_____

18. If you answer No to the Do you want fast zooms prompt, what does AutoCAD do when you issue any display command? _____

19. What does the VIEWRES zoom percentage refer to? _____

_____

20. What is the difference between Tiled Model Space and Floating Model Space? _____

_____

_____

_____

21. How does the Dynamic button in the Aerial View window affect the main display screen?_____

_____

_____

_____

22. The Dzoom button in the Aerial View window is similar to which command/option combination?
_____

23. How is a transparent display command entered at the keyboard? _____

24. When will AutoCAD refuse to execute a transparent display command? _____

25. Explain the difference between model space and paper space. _____
_____
_____

26. What is the purpose of the TILEMODE system variable? _____
_____
_____

27. Describe the default viewport layout for the VPORTS command. _____
_____

28. What type of object does the DVIEW command use to initially establish a 3-D view? _____
_____

29. How do the DVIEW and VPOINT commands differ? _____
_____
_____

30. Which command regenerates all of the viewports? _____

31. What is the function of REGENAUTO? _____
_____

DRAWING PROBLEMS

1. Load a drawing from an earlier chapter. Use the following display commands and options on the drawing:
   A. ZOOM All.
   B. ZOOM Window on one detail three times.
   C. ZOOM Previous.
   D. ZOOM Extents.
   E. ZOOM Center.
   F. ZOOM Vmax.
   G. PAN in four directions.
   H. PAN diagonally.

2. Load a previous drawing that contains a large amount of detail. Use the VIEW command to create views of two areas containing detail. Also create a view that shows the entire drawing. Use the VIEW command to restore each of the views.

P10-3

3. The purpose of this problem is to add six views to an existing prototype drawing that is C-size or larger. If you do not have a C-size prototype drawing, set up one for this problem. Use the following display aspects in your drawing:

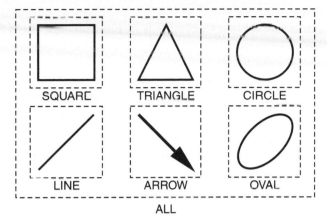

A. Create one view of the entire drawing limits and name it ALL or FULL.

B. Window four additional views of the drawing area. Create one view for each quadrant of the drawing.

C. Create a view of the title block.

D. Set VIEWRES for fast zooms and a circle zoom percent of 50.

E. Save the drawing as A:PRODRCV.

4. Load one of your B-size prototype drawings into the drawing editor. Create two views of the drawing area and one view of the title block. Set the VIEWRES for fast zooms and a circle zoom percent of 500. Save the drawing as A:PRODRBV.

P10-5

5. Open the drawing named HVAC. (If AutoCAD was installed properly, this drawing should be in the ACADR13\COMMON\SAMPLE subdirectory.) When the drawing is displayed, perform the following:

A. Make sure you are in paper space. Use the View command to create views of the following parts of the drawing. Name the views using the names provided in parentheses.

- Stairwell (STAIRS)
- Lower-right quadrant of building (LR)
- Lower-left quadrant of building (LL)
- Upper-left quadrant of building (UL)
- Upper-right quadrant of building (UR)
- Entire drawing (ALL)

B. Use the VIEW command's Restore option to check all the views you just made.

C. Restore the enter drawing with the proper view.

D. Set the TILEMODE system variable to 0. You are now in paper space. Try to restore one of your views. What happens?

E. Use the MVIEW command, or pick Floating Viewports in the View pull-down menu to create an arrangement of four viewports in paper space. Enter model space by typing MS, or picking Floating Model Space from the View pull-down menu.

F. Pick the lower-right viewport to make it active, then restore the lower-right view. Pick the upper-right viewport to make it active, then restore the upper-right view. Continue until the four quadrant views are displayed in their respective viewports.

G. Return to tiled model space. Pick Tiled Viewports from View and select 4 Viewports. Restore the stair view in the upper-right viewport, the full drawing in the upper-left, and the LL and LR views in the bottom two viewports. Use the Tiled Viewports command again to save this viewport configuration with the name "four".

H. Use the VPORTS command and the Single option, return the screen to a single viewport.

I. Pick Floating Model Space from the View menu. Use the Aerial View to change the zoom area and magnification in the upper-right viewport.

J. Set the value of TILEMODE to 1. Use the VPORTS command to restore the viewport configuration named four. Activate the Aerial View and use it to change the zoom magnification of the lower-right viewport. Pick the upper-right viewport and return to the Aerial View. Notice as you try to change the magnification, the lower-right viewport is affected. Remember to dismiss the Aerial View and reactivate it if you wish to change the view in another viewport.

K. Save the drawing as AP10-5 only if required by your instructor.

P10-6

6. Open the drawing named SEXTANT. It should be located in the \ACADR13\COMMON\SAMPLE subdirectory. The object is a 3-D drawing that is displayed in a perspective view. In order to use the Display commands such as ZOOM, you must first remove the perspective view.

A. Set the TILEMODE system variable to 1.

B. Type DVIEW, then press ENTER at the Select objects: prompts. Now type OFF and press ENTER twice to remove the perspective view and return to your drawing.

C. Then perform the following display functions on the SEXTANT drawing:
- Use ZOOM Dynamic to display the entire sextant on the screen.
- Create an arrangement of three viewports using the VPORTS command. Place the large viewport on the right.
- Use the PAN command to center the sextant in the large viewport.
- Pick the upper-left viewport and type PLAN. This creates a top view. The PLAN command is discussed in Chapter 29.
- Pick the lower-left viewport and use the Aerial View's Dzoom/Dynamic function to zoom in on the angled green box at the top of the sextant. Your display should look similar to the one shown below.
- Pick the large viewport and type HIDE. This removes the hidden lines. Now type SHADE. This colors in the solid faces of the object using the colors of the object. The HIDE and SHADE commands are discussed in Chapter 29.
- Use the VPORTS command to save the present configuration as THREE.
- Return the TILEMODE variable to 0.

D. Save your drawing as A:P10-6 and quit the drawing session.

E. Load AutoCAD and open P10-6 from your floppy disk using the prototype method.

F. Set TILEMODE to 1. Notice the configuration that is displayed.

G. Continue experimenting with naming views and creating other viewport configurations.

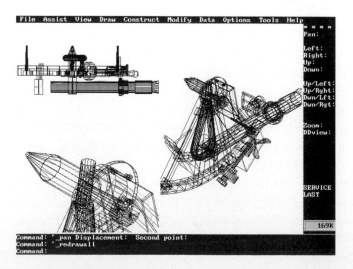

Chapter 11

PLACING TEXT ON A DRAWING

Learning objectives

After completing this chapter, you will be able to:

- ❍ Use the TEXT command to add words to a drawing.
- ❍ Make multiple lines of text with the MTEXT command.
- ❍ Change text styles using the STYLE command.
- ❍ Use the DTEXT command to display text on the screen while typing.
- ❍ Draw special symbols using control characters.
- ❍ Underscore and overscore text.
- ❍ Explain the purpose of the Quick Text mode and use the QTEXT command.
- ❍ Identify and use the pull-down menus for creating and drawing text.
- ❍ Design prototype drawings with title blocks for A-, B-, and C-size drawings.
- ❍ Draw objects with associated text.
- ❍ Edit existing text.
- ❍ Check your spelling.

Words and notes on drawings have traditionally been added by hand lettering. Lettering is a slow, time-consuming task when done by hand using a pencil, pen, or a lettering device. Computer-aided drafting programs have reduced the tedious nature of adding notes to a drawing. In computer-aided drafting, lettering is referred to as *text*. There are some advantages of computer-generated text over hand-lettering techniques. Now, lettering is fast, easier to read, and follows the same consistent style. This chapter shows how text can be added by different methods. It also explains proper text presentation as recommended by ANSI Y14.2M, *Line Conventions and Lettering*.

TEXT STANDARDS

Company standards often dictate how text should appear on a drawing. The minimum recommended text height on engineering drawings is .125 inch (3 mm). All dimension numerals, notes, and other text information should be the same height. Titles, subtitles, captions, revision information, and drawing numbers may be .188 to .25 in. (5 to 6.5 mm) high. Many companies specify a .188 or 5/32 in. (5 mm) lettering height for standard text. This text size is easy to read even after the drawing is reduced.

Vertical or inclined text may be used on a drawing depending on company preference, Figure 11-1. One or the other is recommended; do not use both. The recommended slant for inclined text is 68° from horizontal. Computer-generated text offers a variety of styles for specific purposes, such as titles or captions.

Text on a drawing may be uppercase or lowercase letters. Most companies use uppercase letters.

Figure 11-1.   Vertical and
inclined text.

ABC.. abc.. 123..
ABC.. abc.. 123..

Numerals in dimensions or notes are the same height as standard text, excluding titles. Most numeral dimensions on an engineering drawing are in decimal inches or millimeters. On architectural drawings, enter dimensions as feet and inches. Fractional dimensions are not commonly used in mechanical drafting because they express a tolerance larger than the decimal equivalent. When fractions *are* used, each numeral should be the same height as the other drawing numerals. The ANSI standard recommends that the fraction bar be placed horizontally between the numerator and denominator, with full-size numerators and denominators. However, this is difficult with computer-generated text. Therefore, the fraction bar is placed diagonally. A dash or space is placed between the whole number and the fraction, Figure 11-2. Dimensioning is discussed in detail in Chapters 20 through 23 of this text.

Figure 11-2.   Examples of numbers for different unit of measure.

UNITS	EXAMPLES	
Decimal-Inches	2.750	
Millimeters	3	0.5
Fractional Inches	2 3/4 2–3/4	

DETERMINING DRAWING SCALE FACTORS FOR TEXT HEIGHT

AUG 1

Before plotting a drawing, you should determine the scale factor. You can do this at the time of plotting, but more work is required to update text heights. Scale factors are important numbers because this value is used to ensure that the text is plotted at the proper height. The scale factor is multiplied by the desired plotted text height to get the AutoCAD text height.

The scale factor is always a reciprocal of the drawing scale. For example, if you wish to plot a drawing at a scale of 1/2″ = 1″, calculate the scale factor as follows:

1/2″ = 1″
.5″ = 1″
1/.5 = 2   The scale factor is 2.

An architectural drawing that is to be plotted at a scale of 1/4″ = 1′-0″ has a scale factor calculated as follows:

1/4″ = 1′-0″
.25 = 12″
12/.25 = 48   The scale factor is 48.

The scale factor of a civil engineering drawing that has a scale of 1″ = 60′ is calculated as follows:

1″ = 60′
1″ = (60 × 12)
720/1 = 720   The scale factor is 720.

If your drawing is in millimeters where the scale is 1.1, the drawing scale factor may be converted to inches with the formula 1″ = 25.4 mm. Therefore, the scale factor is 25.4. When the metric drawing scale is 1:2, then the scale factor is 1″ = 50.8 (25.4 × 2). The scale factor is 50.8.

After the scale factor has been determined, you should then calculate the height of the AutoCAD text. If the text is to be plotted at 1/8″ (.125″) high, it should be drawn at that height. If the drawing scale is FULL or 1″ = 1″, then the text height is 1/8″ or .125″. However, if you are working on a civil engineering drawing with a scale of 1″ = 60′, text drawn at 1/8″ high appears as a dot. Remember that the drawing you are working on is 720 times larger than it is when plotted at the proper scale. Therefore, you must multiply the text height by the 720 scale factor to get text that appears in correct proportion on the screen. If you want 1/8″ (.125″) high text to appear correctly on a drawing with a 1″ = 60′ scale, calculate the AutoCAD height as follows:

1″ = 60′
1″ = (60 × 12)
720/1 = 720   The scale factor is 720.
text height × scale factor = scaled text height
.125″ × 720 = 90   The proper text height is 90″.

An architectural drawing with a scale of 1/4″ = 1′-0″ has a scale factor of 48. Text that is to be 1/8″ high should be drawn 6″ high.

1/4″ = 1′-0″
.25″   12″
12/.25 = 48   The scale factor is 48.
.125 × 48 = 6   The proper text height is 6″.

Scale factors and text heights should be determined before beginning a drawing, and are best incorporated as values within your prototype drawing files.

TEXT COMPOSITION

Composition refers to the spacing, layout, and appearance of the text. With manual lettering, it is necessary to space letters freehand. This task is performed automatically with computer-generated text.

Notes should be placed horizontally on the drawing. AutoCAD automatically sets lines of text apart a distance equal to one-half the text height. This helps maintain the identity of individual notes.

Most lines of text are "left-justified." The term *justify* means to align the text to fit a given location. Left-justified text, for example, is text that is aligned along an imaginary left border. Figure 11-3 shows default spacing between lines of left-justified text.

Figure 11-3.   Default spacing between lines of left-justified text.

USING AUTOCAD TO DRAW TEXT

The TEXT command places notes and other written information on a drawing. TEXT may be typed at the Command: prompt, or pick Text in the Draw pull-down menu followed by selecting Single-Line Text from the cascading submenu. When you select or type the TEXT command, the prompt reads:

Command: **TEXT** ↵
Justify/Style/⟨Start point⟩:

The default option is Start point. If you want another option, type the option's first letter, such as J for Justify or S for Style, or select the option from the screen menu. The TEXT command allows you to compose the words in a variety of formats.

Selecting the Start point option

The default mode, Start point, allows you to select a point on the screen where you want the text to begin. This point becomes the lower-left corner of the text. After you pick the point, the prompt reads:

Height ⟨0.2000⟩:

This allows you to select the text height. The default value is 0.2000. A previously selected letter height may be displayed as the current value. If you want letters that are .5 unit high, then type .5. The next prompt is:

Rotation angle ⟨0⟩:

The default value of the rotation angle is 0. This places the text horizontally at the specified start point. Rotation angle values rotate text in a counterclockwise direction. The text pivots about the starting point, Figure 11-4. Press ENTER for 0° rotation to place horizontal text.

Figure 11-4. Different rotation angles for text.

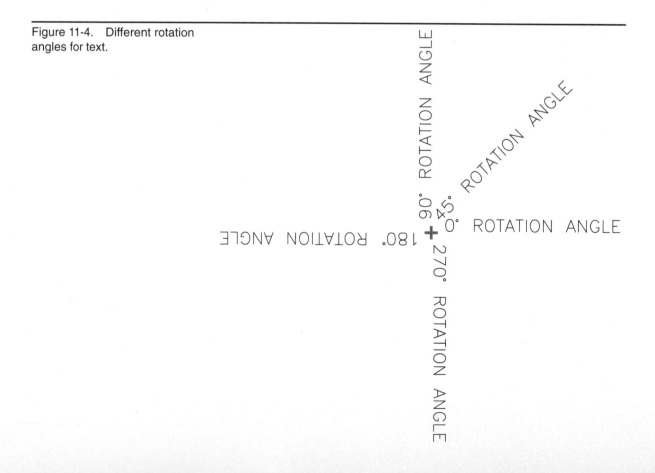

The last prompt is:

Text:

Type the desired text and press ENTER. Text added with the Start point option is left-justified. For example:

Text: **AUTOCAD LEFT JUSTIFIED TEXT** ⌐

After you type the note, press ENTER to insert the text. The information typed using the Start point option generates text as shown in Figure 11-5. The "+" in Figure 11-5 and future examples shows the pick point. The pick point is the point you select to locate the text.

Figure 11-5.   Left-justified text using the Start point option.

AUTOCAD LEFT JUSTIFIED TEXT

Justifying your text

When you select the Justify option, you can use one of several text alignment options.

Command: **TEXT** ⌐
Justify/Style/⟨Start point⟩: **J** ⌐
Align/Fit/Center/Middle/Right/TL/TC/TR/ML/MC/MR/BL/BC/BR:

Using the Align text option

The Align option allows you to pick two points between which the text string is confined. The beginning and endpoints may be placed horizontally or at an angle. The computer automatically adjusts the text width to fit between the points selected. One caution with this option is that the text height is also changed. This varies according to the distance between points and the number of characters. To use this option, enter J for Justify, and then A for Align as follows:

Command: **TEXT** ⌐
Justify/Style/⟨Start point⟩: **J** ⌐
Align/Fit/Center/Middle/Right/TL/TC/TR/ML/MC/MR/BL/BC/BR: **A** ⌐
First text line point: *(pick a point)*
Second text line point: *(pick a point)*
Text: **AUTOCAD ALIGNED TEXT** ⌐

Figure 11-6 shows how information is aligned between the first and second points. Notice that the text is confined. The letter height and width changes in relation to the distance between points.

Figure 11-6.   Examples of Aligned text.

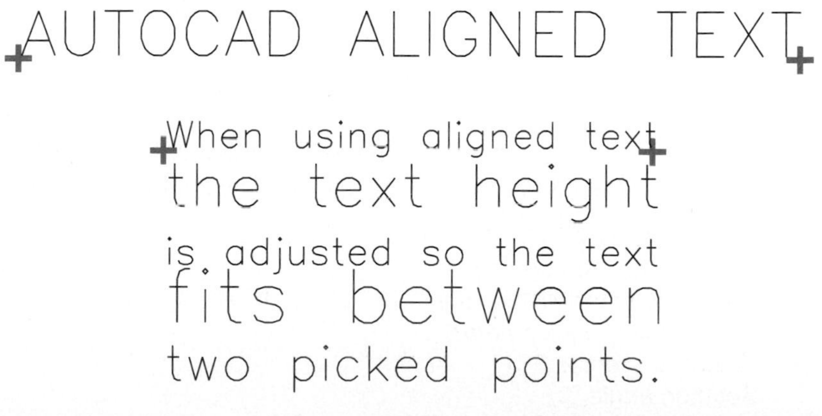

AUTOCAD ALIGNED TEXT

When using aligned text
the text height
is adjusted so the text
fits between
two picked points.

Using the Fit text option

The Fit option is similar to the Align option, except that you may select the text height. AutoCAD adjusts the letter width to fit between two given points. The height default value is .20, but you may change this.

Command: **TEXT** ↵
Justify/Style/⟨Start point⟩: **J** ↵
Align/Fit/Center/Middle/Right/TL/TC/TR/ML/MC/MR/BL/BC/BR: **F** ↵
First text line point: *(pick a point)*
Second text line point: *(pick a point)*
Height ⟨*current*⟩: **.5** ↵
Text: **AUTOCAD FIT TEXT** ↵

Figure 11-7 shows the note above as it appears on the screen in two different locations. Notice that the letter height remains the same, but the letter width is adjusted. In both cases, the line of text fits between the chosen points.

Figure 11-7. Using the Fit text option.

The Center text option

The Center option allows you to select the center point for the baseline of the text. Enter the letter height and rotation angle after picking the center point. This example uses a .5 unit height and a 0° rotation angle. The prompts appear as follows:

Command: **TEXT** ↵
Justify/Style/⟨Start point⟩: **J** ↵
Align/Fit/Center/Middle/Right/TL/TC/TR/ML/MC/MR/BL/BC/BR: **C** ↵
Center point: *(pick a point)*
Height ⟨*current*⟩: **.5** ↵
Rotation angle ⟨0⟩: ↵
Text: **AUTOCAD CENTERED TEXT** ↵

Figure 11-8 shows how the AUTOCAD CENTERED TEXT note appears.

Figure 11-8. Using the Center text option.

Using the Middle text option

The Middle text option allows you to center text both horizontally and vertically at a given point. The letter height and rotation may be changed. The command sequence is as follows:

Command: **TEXT** ↵
Justify/Style/⟨Start point⟩: **J** ↵
Align/Fit/Center/Middle/Right/TL/TC/TR/ML/MC/MR/BL/BC/BR: **M** ↵
Middle point: *(pick a point)*
Height ⟨*current*⟩: **.5** ↵
Rotation angle ⟨0⟩: ↵
Text: **AUTOCAD MIDDLE TEXT** ↵

Figure 11-9 shows the above note as it appears on the screen.

Figure 11-9.   Using the Middle
text option.

AUTOCAD MIDDLE TEXT

The Right text option

The Right option is similar to Start point, except text is aligned with the lower-right corner. The text is right-justified. This option also allows you to enter letter height and rotation angle. The command sequence appears as follows:

Command: **TEXT** ↵
Justify/Style/⟨Start point⟩: **J** ↵
Align/Fit/Center/Middle/Right/TL/TC/TR/ML/MC/MR/BL/BC/BR: **R** ↵
End point: *(pick a point)*
Height ⟨*current*⟩: **.5** ↵
Rotation angle ⟨0⟩: ↵
Text: **AUTOCAD RIGHT - JUSTIFIED TEXT** ↵

Figure 11-10 shows right-justified text.

Figure 11-10.   Using the Right text option.

AUTOCAD RIGHT — JUSTIFIED TEXT

EXERCISE 11-1

❑ Load AutoCAD.
❑ Use the TEXT command to type the following information. Each time, change the text option to obtain the format given. Use .5 letter height and 0° rotation angle.
 AUTOCAD TEXT LEFT-JUSTIFIED USING THE START POINT OPTION.
 AUTOCAD TEXT RIGHT-JUSTIFIED USING THE RIGHT OPTION.
 AUTOCAD TEXT ALIGNED USING THE ALIGN OPTION.
 AUTOCAD TEXT CENTERED USING THE CENTER OPTION.
 AUTOCAD FIT TEXT USING THE FIT OPTION.
 AUTOCAD TEXT USING THE MIDDLE OPTION.
❑ Save the drawing as A:EX11-1 and quit.

PROFESSIONAL TIP

If you already know which text alignment option you want to use in your drawing, you can enter it at the Justify/Style/⟨Start point⟩: prompt without entering J for Justify.

Using the other text alignment options

There are a number of text alignment options that allow you to place text on a drawing in relationship to the top, bottom, middle, left, or right side of the text. These alignment options are displayed in Figure 11-11.

Figure 11-11. Using the TL, TC, TR, ML, MC, MR, BL, BC, and BR text alignment options.

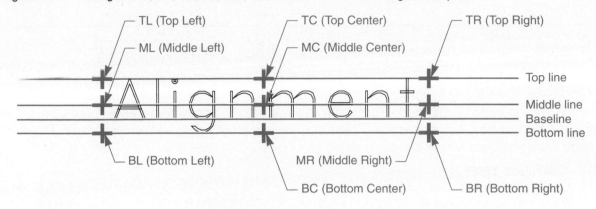

The alignment options displayed in Figure 11-11 are also shown as abbreviations. Note the abbreviations shown in the illustration and those found in the TEXT prompt line.

When you select the Justify option using the prompt line or screen menu, one of several text alignment options is available to use. The command sequence for these options is similar to what was previously discussed:

Command: **TEXT** ↵
Justify/Style/⟨Start point⟩: **J** ↵
Align/Fit/Center/Middle/Right/TL/TC/TR/ML/MC/MR/BL/BC/BR:

Left-justified text

The TL option allows you to justify the text at the top left, as shown in Figure 11-12.

Command: **TEXT** ↵
Justify/Style/⟨Start point⟩: **J** ↵
Align/Fit/Center/Middle/Right/TL/TC/TR/ML/MC/MR/BL/BC/BR: **TL** ↵
Top/left point: *(pick a point)*
Height ⟨*current*⟩: **.5** ↵
Rotation angle ⟨0⟩: ↵
Text: **AUTOCAD TOP/LEFT TEXT** ↵

Figure 11-12. Using the TL
text alignment option.

⁺AUTOCAD TOP/LEFT TEXT

Center-justified text

The TC option allows you to justify the text at the top center, as shown in Figure 11-13.

Command: **TEXT** ↵
Justify/Style/⟨Start point⟩: **J** ↵
Align/Fit/Center/Middle/Right/TL/TC/TR/ML/MC/MR/BL/BC/BR: **TC** ↵
Top/center point: *(pick a point)*
Height ⟨*current*⟩: **.5** ↵
Rotation angle ⟨0⟩: ↵
Text: **AUTOCAD TOP/CENTER TEXT** ↵

Figure 11-13. Using the TC
text alignment option.

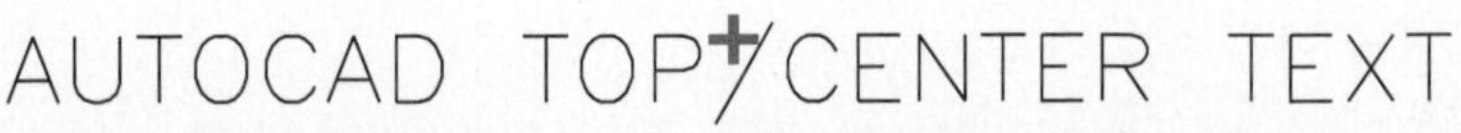

AUTOCAD TOP⁺CENTER TEXT

Right-justified text

The TR option allows you to justify the text at the top right, as shown in Figure 11-14.

Command: **TEXT** ↵
Justify/Style/⟨Start point⟩: **J** ↵
Align/Fit/Center/Middle/Right/TL/TC/TR/ML/MC/MR/BL/BC/**BR**: **TR** ↵
Top/right point: (*pick a point*)
Height ⟨*current*⟩: **.5** ↵
Rotation angle ⟨0⟩: ↵
Text: **AUTOCAD TOP/RIGHT TEXT** ↵

Figure 11-14.   Using the TR
text alignment option.

AUTOCAD TOP/RIGHT TEXT⁺

In the previous discussion you have seen how the TL, TC, and TR options work. The remaining text alignment options function in the same manner. If you forget what the different abbreviations refer to, look back at Figure 11-11 for reference.

EXERCISE 11-2

❑ Load AutoCAD.
❑ Use the TEXT command to type the following information. Each time, change the text option to obtain the format given in each statement. Use .5 letter height and 0° rotation angle.
  AUTOCAD TOP/LEFT OPTION.
  AUTOCAD TOP/CENTER OPTION.
  AUTOCAD TOP/RIGHT OPTION.
  AUTOCAD MIDDLE/LEFT OPTION.
  AUTOCAD MIDDLE/CENTER OPTION.
  AUTOCAD MIDDLE/RIGHT OPTION.
  AUTOCAD BOTTOM/LEFT OPTION.
  AUTOCAD BOTTOM/CENTER OPTION.
  AUTOCAD BOTTOM/RIGHT OPTION.
❑ Save the drawing as A:EX11-2 and quit.

MAKING MULTIPLE LINES OF TEXT

AUG 8

Lines of text may be automatically spaced, each string having the same angle, height, and alignment. Press ENTER after the first line has been entered. This brings back the Command: prompt. A second ENTER repeats the previous TEXT command. The Start point: prompt is displayed again and the previous line of text is highlighted. Press the ENTER key again to automatically justify the next line of text below the previous. The same procedure is used to continue drawing additional lines of text, Figure 11-15. Each line of text is an individual text object. The command sequence is as follows:

Command: **TEXT** ↵
Justify/Style/⟨Start point⟩: (*pick the start point*)
Height ⟨*current*⟩: **.5** ↵
Rotation angle ⟨0⟩: ↵
Text: **THIS IS THE FIRST LINE OF TEXT** ↵
Command: ↵
TEXT Justify/Style/⟨Start point⟩: ↵
Text: **THIS IS THE SECOND LINE OF TEXT** ↵

The MTEXT command is discussed in the next section. This command makes multiline text objects.

Figure 11-15.   Drawing multiple lines of text with the TEXT command.

Words on a drawing have traditionally
been referred to as lettering. Lettering
has typically been a slow, time—consuming,
task. Computer—aided drafting has
reduced the tedious nature of preparing
lettering on a drawing.

EXERCISE 11-3

❏ Load AutoCAD.
❏ Use the TEXT command to type the following multiple lines of text exactly as shown. Use .25
   letter height and 0° rotation angle.
   LETTERING HAS TYPICALLY BEEN A SLOW, TIME-CONSUMING TASK.
   COMPUTER-AIDED DRAFTING HAS REDUCED THE TEDIOUS NATURE OF
   PREPARING LETTERING ON A DRAWING. IN CAD, LETTERING IS NOW
   REFERRED TO AS TEXT. COMPUTER-GENERATED TEXT IS FAST,
   CONSISTENT, AND EASIER TO READ.
❏ Save the drawing as A:EX11-3 and quit.

PROFESSIONAL TIP

Multiple lines of text may be placed in a box format with the Fit option. This justifies the
text on the left and right. The letter height is the same for each line of text. However, the letter
width is different, Figure 11-16.

Figure 11-16.   Boxing text
using the Fit option.

When using FIT text,
text height remains the
same. The text
width is adjusted to fit
between the picked points.

MAKING MULTIPLE LINES OF TEXT WITH
THE MTEXT COMMAND

AUG 8

The MTEXT command allows the creating of multiline text objects. Instead of each line being an
individual object as previously discussed, all of the lines are part of the same object. Single line text
objects are handled as previously explained, but multiple text objects have a different set of rules. The
command for multiple text objects is MTEXT, but the pull-down menu is found by picking Text in the

draw pull down and then Text in the cascading menu. You can also find Mtext: in the DRAW 2 screen menu. The use of the MTEXT command is as follows:

Command: **MTEXT** ↵
Attach/Rotation/Style/Height/Direction/⟨Insertion point⟩:

The following gives a brief description of each MTEXT option:

- **Attach.** Sets the text justification method. This sets the same type of text justification that you learned with single text lines except that the alignment of the entire text boundary is set relative to the justification point. For example, all left justification controls align the paragraph with the left margin, center justification centers each line of the paragraph, and all right justification controls align the paragraph with the right margin as shown in Figure 11-17.
- **Rotation.** Controls the rotation angle of the paragraph.
- **Style.** Sets the text style to be used.
- **Height.** Sets the text height.
- **Direction.** This sets the reading direction. For example, English is read horizontally, but Japanese is read vertically.
- **Insertion point.** This is the MTEXT default that lets you pick the first corner of a boundary used to enclose the paragraph. When selecting an insertion point, the following are additional options:
  - **Width–**Numerically sets the paragraph width.
  - **2Points–**Allows you to select 2 points to define the paragraph width rather than a boundary box.
  - **Other corner–**This prompt asks you to pick the other corner of a text boundary box after you have picked the Insertion point previously defined.

Figure 11-17.   The effects of the different MText justification options.

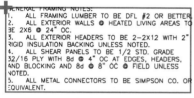

TOP LEFT
LEFT JUSTIFIED

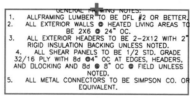

TOP CENTER
CENTER JUSTIFIED

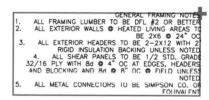

TOP RIGHT
RIGHT JUSTIFIED

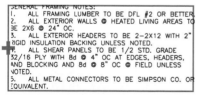

MIDDLE LEFT
LEFT JUSTIFIED

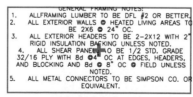

MIDDLE CENTER
CENTER JUSTIFIED

MIDDLE RIGHT
RIGHT JUSTIFIED

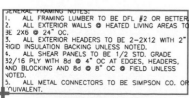

BOTTOM LEFT
LEFT JUSTIFIED

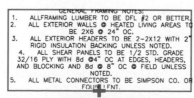

BOTTOM CENTER
CENTER JUSTIFIED

BOTTOM RIGHT
RIGHT JUSTIFIED

✚ This symbol represents the insertion point

The MTEXT options act the same as the TEXT command options that you learned earlier. You can use the MTEXT options to create desired text by setting each before you begin typing text. It is best to have a plan about how you want the paragraph to look before you begin. The following shows the prompts and inputs you might use to set up the MTEXT command:

Command: **MTEXT** ⏎
Attach/Rotation/Style/Height/Direction/⟨Insertion point⟩: **A** ⏎
TL/TC/TR/ML/MC/MR/BL/BC/BR: **BL** ⏎
Attach/Rotation/Style/Height/Direction/⟨Insertion point⟩: **R** ⏎
Rotation angle ⟨0⟩: ⏎
Attach/Rotation/Style/Height/Direction/⟨Insertion point⟩: **S** ⏎
Style name (or ?) ⟨STANDARD⟩: **ROMANS** ⏎ *(Note: Text styles are explained fully later in this chapter)*
Attach/Rotation/Style/Height/Direction/⟨Insertion point⟩: **H** ⏎
Height ⟨0.0800⟩: **.125** ⏎
Attach/Rotation/Style/Height/Direction/⟨Insertion point⟩: **D** ⏎
Horizontal/Vertical: **H** ⏎
Attach/Rotation/Style/Height/Direction/⟨Insertion point⟩: *(pick the insertion point)*

Inserting multiline text

After you have set up the text the way you want it, the MTEXT default asks for an ⟨Insertion point⟩. Pick an insertion point or type the coordinates to start a corner of the text boundary. Now, the screen cursor forms a box, and you get the ⟨Other corner⟩ prompt. Pick the other corner of the box to establish the boundary for your paragraph of text. These are the prompts as continued from above:

Attach/Rotation/Style/Height/Direction/⟨Insertion point⟩: *(pick the insertion point)*
Attach/Rotation/Style/Height/Direction/Width/2Points/⟨Other corner⟩: *(pick the other corner of the text boundary)*

The ⟨Other corner⟩ selection sets the second corner of the text boundary. The boundary width is important because AutoCAD automatically starts the next line when your text gets to the boundary edge. The length is not as important, because if the text supplied spills over the defined boundary, the boundary is automatically resized to fit as related to the current attach setting. If the text is not enough to fill the boundary, the boundary size is contracted accordingly. Once all options have been set and you are ready to enter the actual text content for the paragraph, AutoCAD leaves the drawing editor and enters the MS-DOS EDIT program shown in Figure 11-18. This is a basic text editor that allows simple text editing functions such as cutting and pasting.

Figure 11-18.   The MS-DOS EDIT program is a basic text editor.

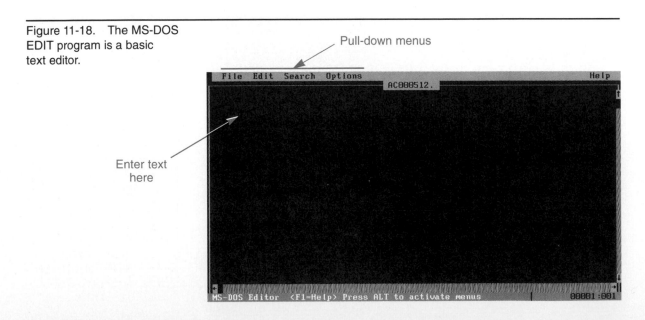

Using the MS-DOS Text Editor

In the text editor, the cursor appears as a flashing underscore or rectangle that initially shows up in the upper left corner of the editor screen. Pull-down menus appear across the top of the screen where text editor functions can be accessed. The pull-down menus, File, Edit, Search, and Options, each have several options. Bold letters are highlighted letters in the pull-down menus used to access the options by key strokes. Combination key strokes may be used to access the options where appropriate. The following is a list of the pull-down menus, their options, bold letters, and combination keys:

File	Edit	Search	Options
New	**Cut Shift+Del**	**F**ind...	**D**isplay...
Open...	**Copy Ctrl+Ins**	**R**epeat Last Find F3	Help **P**ath...
Save	**Paste Shift+Ins**	**C**hange...	
Save **A**s...	**Clear Del**		
Print...			
E**x**it			

The MS-DOS EDIT program has mouse support, and provides a cursor for mouse activity. The pull-down menus are accessed either by selecting the menu name with the mouse cursor or by using an alternate key stroke. When the ALT key is pressed and held, one character in each of the menu names is highlighted. Continuing to hold the ALT key, press the key of the highlighted character and the menu will pop down. Now, either use the cursor keys or mouse to pick the highlighted character in the menu selection. For example, to use the Find function in the Search pull-down menu, you should first press ALT+S to access the Search menu. Next, press the F key to begin the find function. For additional information, the Help menu can be accessed by pressing the F1 key. Help contains listings for each of the editor functions and how to use them.

The keyboard keys have functions within the text editor to assist you in the preparation of your paragraph. The following is a description of the basic keyboard functions:

- **Caps Lock.** When ON, all alphabetical characters appear as uppercase. When OFF, characters appear as lower-case.
- **Shift.** Pressing this key reverses the upper-case or lower-case state of the Caps Lock alphabetical characters.
- **Arrow Keys.** Moves the text cursor one character or column in the direction of the arrows.
- **Ctrl+Arrow.** Moves the text cursor one word right or left.
- **Insert.** This toggles the INSERT state. When Insert is OFF, new text entry overwrites existing text. When Insert is ON, new text entry pushes existing text to the right or the next line, saving it from being overwritten.
- **Backspace.** Moves the cursor one column left, removing any existing characters as it moves.
- **Delete.** Deletes the character directly to the right of the cursor.
- **Home.** Moves the text cursor to the first column of the current line.
- **End.** Moves the text cursor to the right of the last character in the current line.
- **Page Up.** Moves the cursor location one page up.
- **Page Down.** Moves the cursor location one page down.

Typing the text

The formatting of the text within the editor is not important. AutoCAD automatically reformats the text to fit within the boundary defined in the drawing, as described earlier. To create a new paragraph, type \P or press ENTER and a new paragraph will begin on the next line. This may seem a little strange at first, because you just keep typing a string of text in the editor and then when you return to AutoCAD, the text is placed within the boundary that you established. See Figure 11-19.

Figure 11-19. The multiline
text boundary

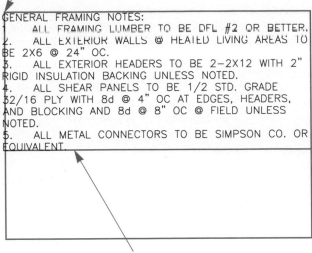

Insertion point–first corner
of the text boundary

The text boundary is automatically resized
to fit the actual text that you type

Saving the text

To save the text and return to the AutoCAD drawing editor, select the File pull-down menu and the Exit option. As the editor is exiting, it asks you if you wish to save the file by giving this message:

Loaded file is not saved. Save it now?
⟨Yes⟩   ⟨No⟩   ⟨Cancel⟩   ⟨Help⟩

Be sure to pick Yes or press ENTER, because Yes is the default. The name of the file is assigned by AutoCAD as "AC000512." and should not be changed. Entering Yes as recommended, saves the file using this AutoCAD default name. This file is stored where your AutoCAD temporary files are stored. If the file name "AC000512.11" is changed, any changes to the text will not be updated. Now, the AutoCAD drawing editor returns and the text that you typed in the editor is displayed within the boundary you established earlier. Finally, just save the text along with the rest of your drawing as you normally do.

Entering Multiline text at the prompt line

If you prefer to enter multiple lines of text at the prompt line without access to the text editor, use the -MTEXT command. You still get the MTEXT prompts that were previously described, but you enter the text at the prompt line after establishing the text boundary. Everything else works the same as before except these are the prompts:

Command: **-MTEXT** ↵
Attach/Rotation/Style/Height/Direction/⟨Insertion point⟩: *(pick the insertion point)*
Attach/Rotation/Style/Height/Direction/Width/2Points/⟨Other corner⟩: *(pick the other corner*
  of the text boundary)
MText: **TYPE THE MULTIPLE LINES OF TEXT DIRECTLY AT THE PROMPT LINE.**
  AUTOCAD AUTOMATICALLY PLACES THE TEXT WITHIN THE BOUNDARY THAT
  YOU HAVE ESTABLISHED. ↵
Command:

Setting a zero width causes lines of text to proceed in a continuous line until you press ENTER. When you do this, AutoCAD only asks for the Insertion point. You control the length of each line, so do not forget to press ENTER when you want a new line to begin. This is the command sequence:

Command: **-MTEXT** ↵
Attach/Rotation/Style/Height/Direction/⟨Insertion point⟩: *(pick the insertion point)*
Attach/Rotation/Style/Height/Direction/Width/2Points/⟨Other corner⟩: **W** ↵
Object Width: **0** ↵
MText: **ENTER THE DESIRED MULTIPLE LINES OF TEXT** ↵
MText: **AT THE PROMPT LINE, BUT DO NOT FORGET TO** ↵
MText: **PRESS ENTER TO HAVE YOUR TEXT GO TO THE** ↵
MText: **NEXT LINE. PRESS ENTER TWICE TO GET BACK** ↵
MText: **TO THE COMMAND: PROMPT.** ↵
MText: ↵
Command:

PROFESSIONAL TIP

The AutoCAD default text editor program for multiple lines of text is the MS-DOS EDIT program. This can be changed by setting the MTEXTED system variable to the path and file name of your preferred text editor. For example, you can try another text editor program such as Q-EDIT. To use it, you must execute the file Q.EXE in the C:\Q directory. Setting this as the default editor looks like this:

Command: **MTEXTED** ↵
New value for MTEXTED, or . for none ⟨""⟩: **C:\Q\QEXE** ↵
Command: .

EXERCISE 11-4

❑ Load AutoCAD and set your own variables as you feel are needed for this exercise.
❑ Type multiple lines of text based on the following requirements:
Justification = TL, Rotation angle = 0, Style = STANDARD (AutoCAD's default), Text height = .125, Text direction = horizontal. Establish a text boundary beginning with the upper left corner to the lower right corner that is 4 in. wide × 5 in. long.
❑ Type the following:
The MTEXT command allows the creating of multiline text objects. Instead of each line being an individual object, all of the lines are part of the same object. The command for multiple text objects is MTEXT. It is accessed in the pull-down menu by picking Text in the draw pull-down and then Text in the cascading menu. You can also find MText: in the DRAW 2 screen menu. After you have set up the text the way you want it, the MTEXT default asks for an ⟨Insertion point⟩. Pick an insertion point or type the coordinates to start a corner of the text boundary. Now, the screen cursor forms a box, and you get the ⟨Other corner⟩ prompt. Pick the other corner of the box to establish the boundary for your paragraph of text. Once all options have been set and you are ready to enter the actual text content for the paragraph, AutoCAD leaves the drawing editor and enters the MS-DOS EDIT program.
❑ Save the drawing as A:EX 11-4 and quit.

AUTOCAD TEXT FONTS   AUG 8, C

A *font* is all of the uppercase and lowercase letters and numerals of a particular letter face design. The standard AutoCAD text fonts are shown in Figure 11-20. The TXT font is the AutoCAD default when you begin a new drawing. The TXT font is rather rough in appearance and may not be the best choice for your application. On the other hand, TXT requires less time to regenerate than other fonts. The ROMANS (ROMAN Simplex) font is smoother than TXT. It closely duplicates the single-stroke Gothic lettering that has long been the standard for drafting. The COMPLEX and TRIPLEX fonts are multistroke fonts for drawing titles and subtitles. The GOTHIC and ITALIC fonts are ornamental styles. In addition, AutoCAD provides several standard symbol fonts as shown in Figure 11-21.

Figure 11-20. Standard AutoCAD text fonts. (Autodesk, Inc.)

FAST FONTS

Txt	The quick brown fox jumps over the lazy dog. ABC123
Monotxt	The quick brown fox jumps over the lazy dog. ABC123

SIMPLEX FONTS

Romans	The quick brown fox jumps over the lazy dog. ABC123
Scripts	*The quick brown fox jumps over the lazy dog. ABC123*
Greeks	Τηε ϑυιχκ βροων φοξ ϑυμπσ οϵερ τηε λαζψ δογ. ΑΒΧ123

DUPLEX FONTS

Romand	The quick brown fox jumps over the lazy dog. ABC123

COMPLEX FONTS

Romanc	The quick brown fox jumps over the lazy dog. ABC123
Italicc	*The quick brown fox jumps over the lazy dog. ABC123*
Scriptc	*The quick brown fox jumps over the lazy dog. ABC123*
Greekc	Τηε ϑυιχκ βροων φοξ ϑυμπσ οϵερ τηε λαζψ δογ. ΑΒΧ123
Cyrillic	Узд рфивк бсоцн еоч йфмпт охдс узд лащш гож. АБВ123
Cyriltlc	Тхе цуичк брошн фож щумпс овер тхе лазй дог. АБЧ123

TRIPLEX FONTS

Romant	**The quick brown fox jumps over the lazy dog. ABC123**
Italict	***The quick brown fox jumps over the lazy dog. ABC123***

GOTHIC FONTS

Gothice	The quick brown fox jumps over the lazy dog. ABC123
Gothicg	The quick brown fox jumps over the lazy dog. ABC123
Gothici	The quick brown fox jumps over the lazy dog. ABC123

Figure 11-21. Standard AutoCAD symbol fonts. (Autodesk, Inc.)

SYMBOL FONTS

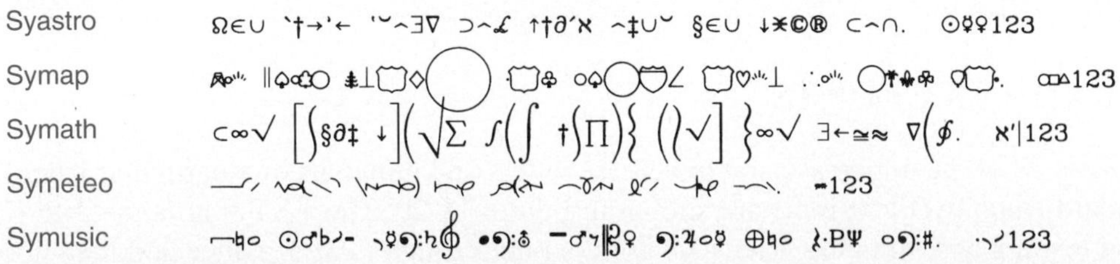

Several additional AutoCAD fonts provide special alphabets or symbols that you must access by typing specific keys. This method is referred to as *character mapping* for non-Roman and symbol fonts as displayed in Figure 11-22.

AutoCAD Release 13 also provides PostScript fonts for use in drawings. See Figure 11-23. PostScript fonts are available by using the STYLE command and techniques previously discussed for

Figure 11-22.   Character mapping for non-Roman and symbol fonts.   (Autodesk, Inc.)

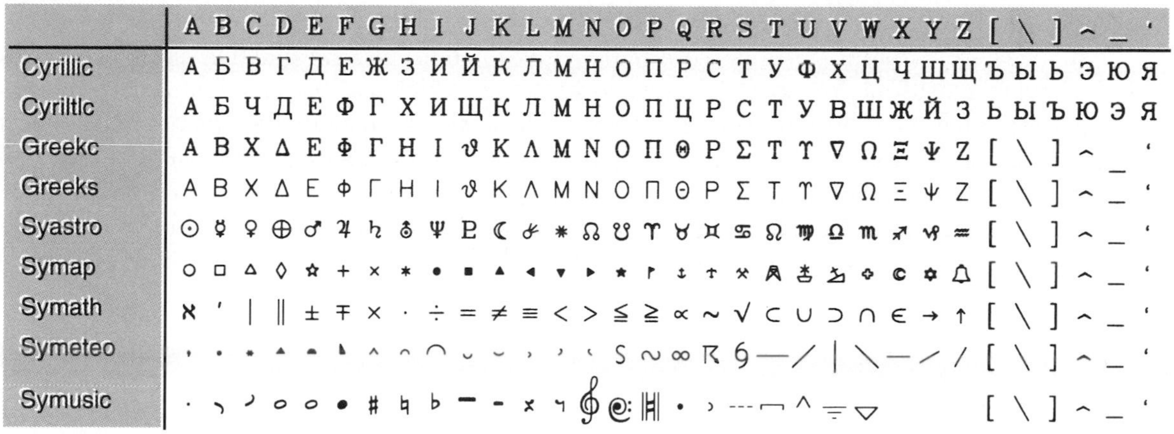

Figure 11-23.   AutoCAD PostScript fonts.   (Autodesk, Inc.)

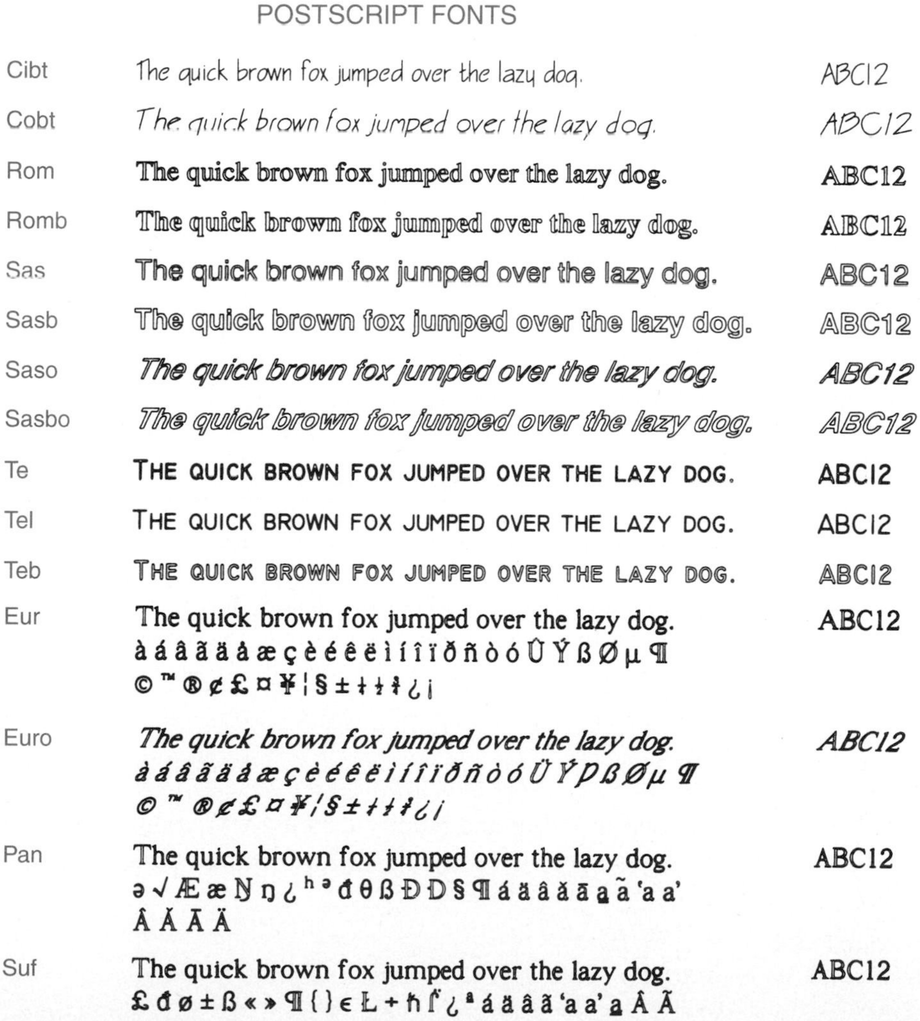

POSTSCRIPT FONTS

Cibt	The quick brown fox jumped over the lazy dog.	ABC12
Cobt	The quick brown fox jumped over the lazy dog.	ABC12
Rom	The quick brown fox jumped over the lazy dog.	ABC12
Romb	The quick brown fox jumped over the lazy dog.	ABC12
Sas	The quick brown fox jumped over the lazy dog.	ABC12
Sasb	The quick brown fox jumped over the lazy dog.	ABC12
Saso	The quick brown fox jumped over the lazy dog.	ABC12
Sasbo	The quick brown fox jumped over the lazy dog.	ABC12
Te	THE QUICK BROWN FOX JUMPED OVER THE LAZY DOG.	ABC12
Tel	THE QUICK BROWN FOX JUMPED OVER THE LAZY DOG.	ABC12
Teb	THE QUICK BROWN FOX JUMPED OVER THE LAZY DOG.	ABC12
Eur	The quick brown fox jumped over the lazy dog.	ABC12
Euro	The quick brown fox jumped over the lazy dog.	ABC12
Pan	The quick brown fox jumped over the lazy dog.	ABC12
Suf	The quick brown fox jumped over the lazy dog.	ABC12

the standard AutoCAD fonts. You can set a width factor or obliquing angle, but you cannot apply both options to these fonts. Two of the PostScript fonts that might work well for architectural applications are the Cibt (city blueprint) and the Cobt (country blueprint). Additional information regarding PostScript fonts is included in ***AutoCAD and its Applications—Advanced, R13 for DOS.*** AutoCAD Release 13 also provides TrueType® fonts with a .TTF file extension. Refer to the *AutoCAD User's Guide* for a listing of these fonts, or open the TRUETYPE.DWG drawing to view them.

SELECTING AUTOCAD TEXT STYLES

AUG 8

Text styles are variations of fonts. A *text style* gives height, width, obliquing angle (slant), and other features to a text font. You may have several text styles which use the same font. Text styles may be created using the STYLE command, to be discussed later. The default style name used with the TEXT command is STANDARD. If the Style option is selected, you can select another text style. The Style option is entered at the TEXT prompt line by typing S. You can also select Style from the TEXT screen menu. The following sequence shows the TEXT command's Style option prompts:

```
Command: TEXT ↵
Justify/Style/⟨Start point⟩: S ↵
Style name (or ?) ⟨current⟩:
```

You may respond in one of the following ways:
- Press the ENTER key to activate the current style.
- Type the name of a style that was previously created using the STYLE command. If you enter a text style that was not previously created using the STYLE command, AutoCAD gives this message:

```
Unknown or invalid text style name.
Style name (or ?) ⟨current⟩:
```

- Type ? to get a list of the available text styles. Entering ? gives you this prompt:

```
Style name (or ?)⟨current⟩: ? ↵
Text style(s) to list ⟨*⟩:
```

You may type the specific text styles to list, or press ENTER to display all of the available text styles. The available text styles are shown on the alphanumeric screen. The style name, font file, height, width factor, obliquing angle, and generation of each are listed. Press the F1 key to return to the graphics screen.

After your response, AutoCAD displays the Start point: prompt for you to continue the TEXT command.

PROFESSIONAL TIP

The TEXT command's Style option allows you to select text styles that have already been created. The STYLE command allows you to custom design one of the standard fonts to make a new style. The Style option then allows you to select that new style to use for text added to the drawing.

MAKING FONT STYLES

AUG 8

The STYLE command is used to create and modify existing text styles or list existing styles. Access Style: from the DRAW 2 screen menu, or type STYLE at the Command: prompt. The prompts associated with the STYLE command are as follows:

```
Command: STYLE ↵
Text style name (or ?) ⟨current⟩: (enter text style name and press ENTER)
```

After entering the desired text style name, AutoCAD displays the "Select Font File" dialog box shown in Figure 11-24. If the chosen style exists, you get an "Existing style" message on the command line, and the existing font is displayed in the File: edit box. You can press ENTER to keep the existing style. If the entered style is new, AutoCAD gives you a "New style" message and the default font for that style is shown in the File: edit box.

In order to create or change a style, enter the style name at the Text style name: prompt, then select a font to use in one of four ways:

- Page through the list of available text fonts, move the cursor arrow to the desired font, and pick. In Figure 11-24, the ROMANS font is picked and is shown in the File: edit box to acknowledge its selection. Now press ENTER or pick the OK button.
- Type the font name in the File: edit box. When ready, pick OK or press ENTER.
- Move the cursor arrow to the Type it button and pick. This removes the "Select Font File" dialog box and allows you to type the desired font name:

   Font file ⟨*current*⟩: **ROMANS** ↵

- Pick the Default button to accept the default font style.

Figure 11-24.   The "Select Font File" dialog box displays the names of fonts available to use.

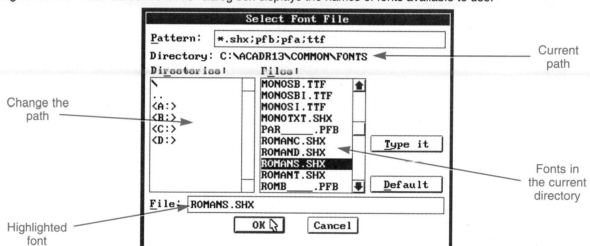

No matter which entry method you use, the rest of the prompts let you establish the style characteristics.

   Height ⟨*default*⟩: *(enter the height value,* **.25,** *for example, and press* ENTER*)*
   Width factor ⟨*default*⟩: *(enter the width factor,* **1,** *for example and press* ENTER*)*
   Obliquing angle ⟨*default*⟩: *(enter the obliquing angle,* **0,** *for example and press* ENTER*)*
   Backwards? ⟨N⟩: *(type* **Y** *or* **N** *and press* ENTER*)*
   Upside-down? ⟨N⟩: *(type* **Y** *or* **N** *and press* ENTER*)*
   Vertical? ⟨N⟩: *(type* **Y** *or* **N** *and press* ENTER*)*
   ROMANS is now the current text style.

STYLE command prompts

The following discussion explains each of the STYLE command prompts.

   Text style name (or ?) ⟨*current*⟩:

The first prompt in the STYLE command allows you to create a new style or modify an existing style. A ? response produces a list of existing styles. Pressing the space bar or ENTER key selects the current style shown in brackets (⟨⟩). To create or modify an existing style, use one of the methods previously discussed. For example, suppose you want to create a ROMANS style with a height of .125. Enter the style name as ROMANS-125. The style name may contain up to 31 characters.

Font file ⟨*default*⟩:

This prompt appears if the FILEDIA system variable is set to 0. Type the name of the font to be used. In this example, the font you are using is ROMANS. If you respond by pressing the ENTER key, the default font shown in brackets is made current. If FILEDIA is 1, the "Select Font File" dialog box appears. Select the desired font from the list, or enter the font file name using the procedure discussed earlier.

Height ⟨*default*⟩:

The Height: prompt allows you to enter a fixed character height. For example, typing .125 draws text .125 in. high for the text style. A 0 response here gives you the opportunity to specify the text height each time you use this style. You may also press ENTER to choose the default height shown in brackets.

Width factor ⟨*default*⟩:

The *width factor* is a numerical value that defines the character width relative to the height. A width factor of 1 is the default. A width factor greater than 1 expands the letters. A factor less than 1 compresses the letters, Figure 11-25.

Obliquing angle ⟨*default*⟩:

Figure 11-25. AutoCAD text width factors.

Width factor	Text
1	ABCDEFGHIJKLM
.5	ABCDEFGHIJKLMNOPQRSTUVWXY
1.5	ABCDEFGHI
2	ABCDEFG

The obliquing angle allows you to slant the letters to the right or left. A 0 response draws vertical text. A value greater than 0 slants the letters to the right. A negative angle slants the characters to the left. See Figure 11-26.

Backwards ⟨N⟩:

Figure 11-26. AutoCAD obliquing angles.

Obliquing angle	Text
0	ABCDEFGHIJKLM
15	ABCDEFGHIJKLM
−15	ABCDEFGHIJKLM

If you want the text to appear backwards, respond Y to this prompt. For text that appears normal, respond with N. Backward characters may be used when the text is to be printed on the back of poly-ester film. When the film is turned around, the image will be legible. An example of backward text is shown in Figure 11-27.

Upside-down? ⟨N⟩:

Figure 11-27. Backward text.

If you want the text to appear upside-down, respond with Y to this prompt. See Figure 11-28. For text that appears normal, respond with N.

Vertical? ⟨N⟩:

Figure 11-28. Upside-down text.

Text is normally placed horizontally on a drawing. However, it is possible to add text in a vertical format. This application may be used for graphic designs or custom layouts. Vertical text is shown in Figure 11-29.

Figure 11-29. Vertical text orientation.

Vertical text works best when the rotation angle is set at 270°. For prompts that require two points, the second point should be directly below the first. Obliquing, underscoring, or overscoring are not intended for use with the vertical format. If vertical text is desired, then a Y response is required. Enter an N for standard horizontal text.

CREATING A NEW TEXT STYLE

AUG 8

Assume that you have entered the drawing editor to begin a new drawing. Remember, the only text style available is TXT. Text style names can be up to 31 characters in length. The following command and prompts sets a new style called ROMANS-125:

Command: **STYLE** ↵
Text style name (or ?) ⟨STANDARD⟩: **ROMANS-125** ↵

The "Select Font File" dialog box then appears (if FILEDIA is 1). Type ROMANS in the File: edit box and pick the extended OK box, or pick ROMANS.SHX from the list of font files. Pick OK to close the dialog box, and then enter the following values:

Height ⟨*current*⟩: **.125** ↵
Width factor ⟨*current*⟩: **1** ↵
Obliquing angle ⟨*current*⟩: **0** ↵
Backwards? ⟨N⟩: ↵
Upside-down? ⟨N⟩: ↵
Vertical? ⟨N⟩: ↵
ROMANS-125 is now the current text style.

Keep reference notes stating the name and features of text styles that you design. However, if you forget, enter ? at the Text style name: prompt. A listing of created styles appears.

Using the new text style

The new text style may now be used by entering the TEXT command. Select the Start point or any of the other options. In this example, the ROMANS-125 style is now the default until you change it using the Style option. Remember, that you may use the TEXT command's Style option to select those text styles already created with the STYLE command.

PROFESSIONAL TIP

It is recommended that you use fancy text styles, such as COMPLEX and ITALIC, only on rare occasions. They require much more computer regeneration time. They also take longer to plot than TXT or SIMPLEX fonts, and make drawing files larger.

EXERCISE 11-5

❑ Load AutoCAD.
❑ Use the TEXT command to type the following information. Change the text style to represent each of the four standard AutoCAD fonts named. Use .5 unit letter height and 0° rotation angle.
   TXT–AUTOCAD'S DEFAULT TEXT FONT.
   ROMANS–A SMOOTH FONT OF CONVENTIONAL LETTERING STYLE.
   COMPLEX–A MULTISTROKE FONT THAT IS GOOD FOR TITLES.
   ITALIC–AN ORNAMENTAL FONT SLANTED TO THE RIGHT.
❑ Save the drawing as A:EX11-5 and quit.

Changing the format or name of existing styles

You can change text style without affecting existing text entities. The changes are applied only to newly added text using that style. However, you may not alter the text font or the orientation from horizontal or vertical. You can change the name of an existing text style using the RENAME command.

The RENAME command may be used to rename existing files such as blocks, dimension styles, layers, linetypes and text styles. The options are discussed throughout this text where appropriate. The option relating to text styles is Style. Type the RENAME command and the Style option as follows:

```
Command: RENAME ↵
Block/Dimstyle/LAyer/LType/Style/Ucs/VIew/VPort: S ↵
Old text style name: ROMANS-125 ↵
New text style name: 125-ROMANS ↵
Command:
```

The RENAME command can also be accessed by picking Rename... in the Data pull-down menu, or selecting Rename: from the DATA screen menu. These selections open the "Rename" dialog box. Using this dialog box, pick Style from the Named Objects list. This gives you an Items list where all of the current text styles are listed. A text style must have been loaded using the STYLE command for it to be listed here. Pick the current style that you want to rename from the Items list, or type the name of the current text style in the Old Name: edit box. Next, type the new name in the Rename To: edit box and finally pick the Rename To: button. The old name is changed and you can see the new name listed in the Items list.

Suppose you change the values of an existing text style, including the font and orientation. *All* text items with that style are redrawn with the new values. They are displayed when the drawing is regenerated. This type of a change causes automatic regeneration if the REGENAUTO mode is on.

Check or change the current text style name

You can check the current text style name or change the text style to a previously set style with the TEXTSTYLE system variable like this:

Command: **TEXTSTYLE** ↵
New value for TEXTSTYLE ⟨"STANDARD"⟩: **ROMANS** ↵

Press ENTER to accept the current text style shown in brackets, or enter a new text style that was previously set using the STYLE command. If you make a mistake when typing, AutoCAD gives you an *Invalid* error message and returns you to the Command: prompt.

SPECIAL CHARACTERS FOR SINGLE-LINE TEXT | AUG 8 |

Many drafting applications require special symbols for text and dimensions. These are different methods for entering special characters depending on if you are using single-line text with the TEXT or DTEXT commands or multiline text with the MTEXT command. In order to draw symbols, AutoCAD requires a sequence of *control characters*. The *control sequence* for a symbol begins with a double percent sign (%%). The next character you enter represents the symbol. These control characters are used for single line text objects that are generated with the TEXT or DTEXT commands. The following list gives the most used control sequences:

%%D = Draw degrees symbol (°).
%%P = Draw plus/minus tolerance symbol (±).
%%C = Draw diameter symbol (∅).
%%% = Draw a single percent symbol (%).

In order to draw the note, ∅2.75, you would use the control sequence %%C2.75. The results are shown in Figure 11-30.

Figure 11-30.   The control sequence %%C creates the ∅ (diameter) symbol.

$$\varnothing 2.75$$

A single percent sign may be also drawn without using the %%% control sequence; simply use the percent (%) key. However, when a percent sign must precede another control sequence, the %%% characters force a single percent sign. For example, suppose you want the note 25% ±2. You must type the following sequence: 25 %%%%P2.

Special symbols may also be drawn by entering a three-digit code between 1 and 126. For example, the ampersand (&) symbol is drawn by the sequence %%038. The control sequence for symbols that are often found on drawings include:

%%035 = #   %%047 = /
%%037 = %   %%060 = ⟨
%%038 = &   %%061 = =
%%040 = (%%062 = ⟩
%%041 =)   %%064 = @
%%044 = ,

Drawing underscored or overscored text

Text may be underscored (underlined) or overscored by typing a control sequence in front of the line of text. The control sequences are:

%%O = overscore
%%U = underscore

For example, to underline the note: UNDERSCORING TEXT, type the note as %%UUNDERSCORING TEXT. The resulting text is shown in Figure 11-31. If a line of text requires both underscoring and overscoring, the control sequence is typed as %%O%%ULINE OF TEXT.

The %%O and %%U control codes are toggles that turn overscoring and underscoring On and Off. Type %%U preceding a word or phrase to turn underscoring On, followed by typing %%U after the desired word or phrase to turn underscoring Off. Any text following the second %%U appears without underscoring.

Figure 11-31. The %% U
control sequence underscores
text.

UNDERSCORING TEXT

SPECIAL CHARACTERS FOR MULTILINE TEXT

AUG 8

The previous discussion explained the use of special characters in single-line text objects that are created with the TEXT and DTEXT commands. Special characters are also available in multiline text objects that are created with the MTEXT command (and LEADER command discussed in Chapter 20. These multiline special characters are created in the text editor by using format codes for paragraphs and Unicode characters. Available format codes for paragraphs and their results are shown in the following chart.

PARAGRAPH FORMAT CODES	
Format Code	**Result**
\O	Overscore toggle on.
\o	Overscore toggle off.
\L	Underscore toggle on.
\l	Underscore toggle off.
\~	Non-breaking space.
\\	Backlash (\).
\{ and \}	Inserts opening and closing braces ({}).
\Cvalue;	Changes to 'value' color. For example, \Cred changes the color to red.
\Hvalue;	Changes to 'value' text height. For example, \H.250 changes the text height from its current value to .250.
\Ffilnam;	Changes font to 'filnam'. For example, if the current font is ROMANS and you want a bolder ROMAND, then enter \Fromand;.
\S ... /...; or \S...^...;	Stacks text at the / or ^ symbol. This is used for stacking fraction numerals, for example.
\Tvalue;	Changes character spacing between .75 X and 4X normal. Normal text spacing is 1X. Enter \T2; if you want double character spacing.
\Qangle;	Changes the obliquing angle of the text to 'angle'. Standard obliquing angle is 0°. Change to a 15° slant on the characters with \Q15;.
\A0;	Changes the alignment for dimensions: \A0; = Baseline.
\A1;	Changes the alignment for dimensions: \A1; = Centerline.
\A2;	Changes the alignment for dimensions: \A2; = Topline.
\Wvalue;	Changes the character width factor to 'value'. For example, if you want to double the character width, enter \W2;.
\P	This entry begins a new paragraph on the next line.

Using the curly braces { } applies the formatting changes only to the code and text within the braces. The braces are not needed for underscoring or overscoring. A \L typed before the text starts the underscoring and \l after the text ends the underscoring. \O and \o is used for overscoring. The following sections cover some special character entries and their results.

Underscoring

If you enter the following:

INTERPRET DIMENSIONS AND TOLERANCES PER \LASME Y14.5M-1994\l FOR ALL DRAWING FEATURES.

The text result is:

INTERPRET DIMENSIONS AND TOLERANCES PER <u>ASME Y14.5M-1994</u> FOR ALL DRAWING FEATURES.

Changing the font filename

If you enter the following:

INTERPRET DIMENSIONS AND TOLERANCES PER {\Fromand;ASME Y14.5M-1994} FOR ALL DRAWING FEATURES.

The text result is:

INTERPRET DIMENSIONS AND TOLERANCES PER **ASME Y14. 5M-1994** FOR ALL DRAWING FEATURES.

Changing the character spacing

If you enter the following:

All drawing titles are required to be entered with {\T2;DOUBLE SPACE TEXT} unless otherwise specified

The text result is:

All drawing titles are required to be entered with D O U B L E   S P A C E   T E X T unless otherwise specified.

Entering special characters using the Unicode system

AutoCAD now supports what is known as the *Unicode* character encoding standard. This standard replaces the old SHP and SHX file formats which will no longer be supported after Release 13. This new font standard is no longer limited to 256 characters as is the SHP and SHX font files. A Unicode font can have up to 65,535 separate characters in a font file, with figures for many different languages. This standard provides support for these languages by allowing typing of characters not on the keyboard. The Unicode standard is used for multiline text objects created with the MTEXT command (or the LEADER command discussed in Chapter 20). The prefix for a Unicode special character is \U+, and is followed by a four digit hexadecimal number indicating the value of the character in the font file. A *hexadecimal* number is a base 16 number as opposed to a base 10 number which was previously used. The Unicode special characters are accessed by typing an escape sequence. For example, \U+2205 is the escape sequence for entering a diameter symbol. It is referred to as an *escape sequence,* probably because it allows you to escape the confines of the limited keyboard or it escapes from the standard text processing. The Unicode entry for special characters is in the format \U+*nnnn* where *nnnn* is the hexadecimal value of the character. The following are some examples that may commonly be used in drafting technology:

- **\U+2205.** Enters the diameter symbol.
  For example: \U+2205.750 = ∅.750
- **\U+00B0.** Places the degree symbol.
  For example: 45\U+00B0 = 45°
- **\U+00B1.** Inserts the Plus/Minus symbol.
  For example: 2.625\U+OOB1.005 = 2.626±.005

EXERCISE 11-6

❏ Load AutoCAD and set up your own variables.
❏ Use the TEXT command and control characters to type the following:
    45°
    1.375±.005
    ∅3.875
    79%
    <u>UNDERSCORING TEXT</u>
❏ Use the MTEXT command and appropriate control characters to type the following:
    N O T E 1:
    EACH BEDROOM TO HAVE A <u>MINIMUM</u> WINDOW OPENING OF **5.7 SQ.**
    FT. WITH A <u>MINIMUM</u> WIDTH OF **20″** AND A SILL LESS THAN **44″**
    OFF THE FLOOR.
    N O T E 2:
    BATHROOMS AND UTILITY ROOMS ARE TO BE VENTED TO THE
    OUTSIDE WITH A <u>MINIMUM</u> OF A 90CFM FAN WITH A <u>**MINIMUM**</u>
    ∅4″ SCREENED DUCT.
❏ Save the drawing as A:EX11-6 and quit.

DYNAMIC TEXT–SEE THE TEXT AS YOU TYPE   AUG 8

The DTEXT (Dynamic TEXT) command allows you to see the text on the screen as you type. All of the options are the same as the TEXT command. DTEXT also allows you to use the backspace key to edit what has been typed on the screen. The TEXT command only lets you backspace to edit at the prompt line. Enter multiple lines of text simply by pressing ENTER at the end of each line. Press ENTER twice to exit the DTEXT command. The sequence of prompts is the same as the TEXT command, except that the Text: prompt is repeated. When the Text: prompt appears, a cursor box equal in size to the text height also appears on the screen at the text start point.

The Draw pull-down menu offers the DTEXT command. Pick Text from the Draw pull-down menu, and then pick Dynamic text in the cascading submenu. This works the same as picking Dtext: from the DRAW 2 screen menu. You can also type DTEXT at the Command: prompt. Use the method that works best and fastest for you.

You can cancel the DTEXT command at any time by entering CTRL C. This action erases all of the text entered during the command.

A great advantage of DTEXT over TEXT is that additional lines of text can be entered. Simply press ENTER at the end of each line. The cursor box automatically moves to the start point one line below the preceding line. While in the DTEXT command, the screen crosshairs can be moved independently of the text cursor box. Selecting a new start point completes the line of text being entered and begins a new line at the selected point. Using DTEXT, multiple lines of text may be entered anywhere on the drawing without exiting the command. This saves a lot of drafting time.

A few aspects of the DTEXT command may cause you some concern at first. They are:
- When you end the DTEXT command, the entered text is erased from the screen, then regenerated.
- If you select C, M, R, TL, TC, TR, ML, MC, MR, BL, BC, or BR justification, the cursor box appears as if the text is left-justified. However, when you end the DTEXT command, the text disappears and is then regenerated with the alignment you requested.
- When you use a control code sequence for a symbol, the control code, not the symbol, is displayed. When you end the command, the text disappears and is then regenerated showing the proper symbol. For example, if the desired text is 98.6°F it first appears as typed, 98.6%%DF. However, when you end the DTEXT command, the note is redisplayed as 98.6°F.
- If you cancel the DTEXT command, all text entered while in the command is discarded. All DTEXT entries must be from the keyboard. Tablet menu picks are ignored.

PROFESSIONAL TIP

DTEXT is not recommended for aligned text because the text height for each line is adjusted according to the width. Other justification options work well with the DTEXT command.

EXERCISE 11-7

❏ Load AutoCAD and set your own variables.
❏ Use the STYLE command to create the text styles described below. Change the options as specified. Then use the DTEXT command to type the text, changing the style for each of the four standard AutoCAD fonts. Enter a .5 letter height.
  TXT–EXPAND THE WIDTH.
  ROMANS–SLANT TO THE LEFT.
  ROMANC–SLANT TO THE RIGHT.
  ITALICC–BACKWARDS.
❏ Select any four fonts from the "Select Font File" dialog box. Customize the text fonts to your own specifications such as height, width, or slant. Type the alphabet and numerals 1-10 for each of the four styles you developed.
❏ Save the drawing as A:EX11-7 and quit.

PRESETTING TEXT HEIGHT

If you set a text height in the STYLE command, then this value is automatically used when you use the TEXT or DTEXT commands. A default value for text height can be preset if the text height in the STYLE command is set to 0. When the text height is set to 0 in the STYLE command, then the TEXTSIZE system variable can be used to establish the text height default. The command sequence is as follows:

Command: **TEXTSIZE** ↵
New value for TEXTSIZE ⟨*current*⟩: **.125** ↵

QUICKLY REDRAWING TEXT   AUG 4

Text requires a great deal of time to regenerate, redraw, and plot. This is because each character is made up of many individual entities. The Quick Text mode makes text appear as rectangles equal to the height of each text string. This speeds regeneration and plotting time. The Quick Text mode is turned on and off with the QTEXT (Quick TEXT) command. Figure 11-32 shows a comparison between displays when QTEXT is on and off.

Figure 11-32.   Comparison of QTEXT turned on and off.

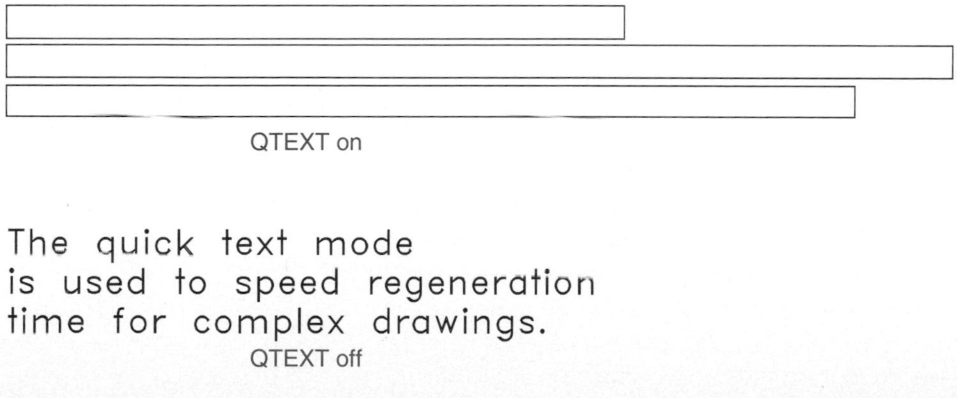

QTEXT on

The quick text mode
is used to speed regeneration
time for complex drawings.
QTEXT off

The QTEXT command is entered at the Command: prompt or picked from the SETTINGS screen menu. The options ON/OFF are shown along with the current QTEXT setting. If the last setting was off, the command line appears as follows:

Command: **QTEXT** ↵
ON/OFF ⟨Off⟩:

Type ON to quicken the redraw time. When quick text is on, new text entities first appear as text so you can check them. The text converts to the QTEXT appearance when the drawing is regenerated. If you want to review the text after QTEXT has been turned on, you need to turn QTEXT off. Follow this by the REGEN command to display the text in the normal format.

PROFESSIONAL TIP

 Consider setting up QTEXT in your prototype drawing. Use QTEXT when a large amount of text or complex text begins to slow down regeneration. This helps you save valuable drafting time.

CHANGING THE LOCATION OF EXISTING TEXT

Existing text can be modified or moved to a new location using the CHANGE command. Enter the CHANGE command, and follow this command sequence:

Command: **CHANGE** ↵
Select objects: *(pick text to be changed)*
Select objects: ↵
Properties/⟨Change point⟩: ↵
Enter text insertion point: *(pick a new text location)*
Text style: ROMANS
New style or RETURN for no change: ↵
New height ⟨0.2000⟩: ↵
New rotation angle ⟨0⟩: ↵
New text ⟨selected text string⟩: *(type new text or press* ENTER *to keep the same text)*
Command:

Figure 11-33 shows how text can be moved.

Figure 11-33.   Using the CHANGE command to move text.

If the text location is acceptable, but you want to change other characteristics of your text, simply press ENTER at the Enter text insertion point: prompt.

If you want to change the text style and already have defined an ITALICC text style, do the following:

    Properties/⟨Change point⟩: ↵
    Enter text insertion point: *(pick a new text location)*
    Text style: ROMANS
    New style or RETURN for no change: **ITALICC** ↵
    New height ⟨0.2000⟩: **.25** ↵
    New rotation angle ⟨0⟩: ↵
    New text ⟨selected text string⟩: *(type new text or press* ENTER *to keep the same text)*
    Command:

Figure 11-34 shows the new text location and style.

Figure 11-34.   Using the CHANGE command to relocate and change text style.

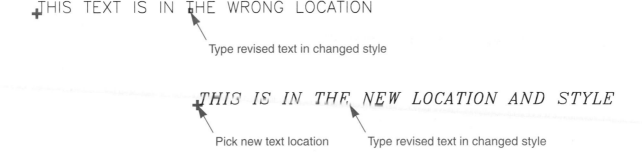

THIS TEXT IS IN THE WRONG LOCATION

Type revised text in changed style

THIS IS IN THE NEW LOCATION AND STYLE

Pick new text location   Type revised text in changed style

EXERCISE 11-8

❑ Load AutoCAD and set up your own variables.
❑ Place the following text on your drawing using .25 high letters: THIS IS THE ORIGINAL TEXT.
❑ Use the CHANGE command to move and change the above text to read: THIS IS THE REVISED TEXT IN A NEW LOCATION.
❑ Use the CHANGE command to move the previous text, change its style, and reword it as follows: THIS IS THE NEW TEXT WITH CHANGED STYLE AND LOCATION.
❑ Turn QTEXT on, then off. Observe the results. Do not forget to use REGEN to change the display.
❑ Save the drawing as A:EX11-8 and quit.

ADDITIONAL TEXT TIPS

Text presentation is important on any drawing. It is a good idea to plan your drawing using rough sketches to allow room for text and notes. Some things to consider when designing the drawing layout include:

- Placement of the views.
- Arrange text to avoid crowding.
- Place related notes in groups to make the drawing easy to read.
- Place all general notes in a common location. Locate notes in the lower-left corner or above the title block when using ANSI standards. Place notes in the upper-left corner when using military standards.
- Place numbered notes away from the border so that additional notes can be added later.
- Provide extra clear space to avoid crowding and allow for future revisions.

REVISING TEXT ON THE DRAWING

AUG 8

AutoCAD provides the means to revise existing text. This is referred to as *text editing*. Text editing is accomplished in a dialog box that is accessed using the DDEDIT command. Pick Edit Text… from the Modify pull-down menu, or Ddedit: from the MODIFY screen menu, or DDEDIT may be typed at the Command. prompt as follows:

Command: **DDEDIT** ↵
⟨Select a TEXT or ATTDEF object⟩/Undo: *(pick the line of text to edit)*

The default asks you to "Select a TEXT" and the screen cursor takes the shape of a pick box. Move the pick box to the desired text and pick. When you pick a single-line text object, the "Edit Text" dialog box is then displayed with the line of text that you picked ready for editing. Figure 11-35 shows a line of text and the "Edit Text" dialog box with the first line of text displayed. Notice that if you pick a multiline text object, the text editor is opened. This is explained later in this chapter.

Figure 11-35.   The "Edit Text" dialog box is shown here highlighted. The selected text is displayed in the text box.

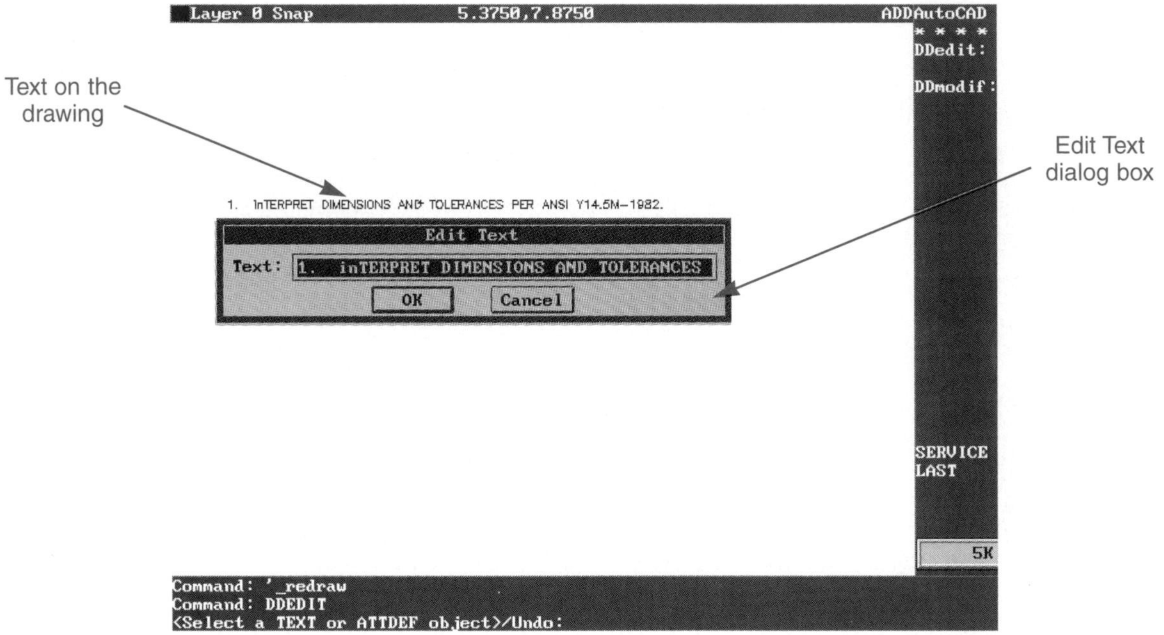

Notice the line of text to be edited is highlighted in the Text: box. Also notice the text cursor is flashing at the end of the Text: box. If you press the space bar or Backspace key, the highlighted text disappears and you can enter new text. If you make a mistake, pick Cancel and pick the desired text again. Move the cursor arrow inside the Text: box and pick to remove the highlight around the text. Use the left and right arrow keys to move through the entire line of text, and access the portion of the text that is hidden beyond the limits of the box. When you are ready to edit the text, move the cursor arrow just to the right of the letters to be changed and pick. This places the text cursor in that location. Edit the line of text shown in Figure 11-36 following this procedure:

• Notice the word "inTERPRET" should read "INTERPRET." Move the cursor arrow so it is located directly after the "n" and pick, as shown in Figure 11-36.

Figure 11-36. Editing an incorrect line of text. Note the position of the text cursor.

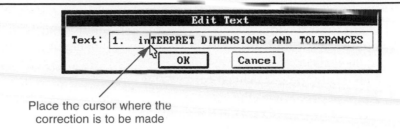

Place the cursor where the correction is to be made

- Backspace through the "in", removing them. Type the new "IN," as shown in Figure 11-37.

Figure 11-37. The error corrected in the line of text.

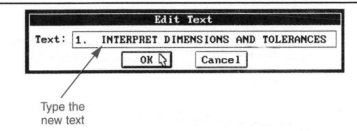

Type the new text

- To see the text at the end of the line, use the right arrow to move the text cursor until the text "ANSI Y14.5M-1982." is displayed in the text edit box.
- Move the cursor arrow and highlight "NSI" then press the BACKSPACE key The "NSI" text is removed.
- Type SME.
- Change 1982 to 1994.
- Pick OK and press ENTER to accept the text changes. The revised text is then displayed on your drawing as shown in Figure 11-38.

Figure 11-38. After picking OK, the revised text is placed on the drawing.

1. INTERPRET DIMENSIONS AND TOLERANCES PER ASME Y14.5M−1994.

- Cancel to exit the DDEDIT command, or enter U to undo the editing if you made a mistake.

Editing techniques

Although it is recommended that you enter text as carefully as possible initially, there will likely be times when you must revise text using the DDEDIT command. The following techniques can be used to help edit text.
- **Highlighting text in the Text: box.** Text can be highlighted by moving the cursor arrow to the desired text and picking. Hold the pick button down while you move the cursor across the text to be highlighted. Release the pick button when you have highlighted all of the intended text.
- **Removing highlighting from text in the Text: box.** When the Text: box, or a portion of the text in the Text: box is highlighted, pressing the space bar, the Delete key, or the Backspace key removes the highlighted text.
- **Moving around inside the Text: box.** Move the cursor arrow inside the Text: box and pick. Then use the left arrow key to move the text to the right or the right arrow key to move the text to the left. You may also pick inside the Text: box, and while holding the pick button down, move the cursor arrow either to the right or left to move around.
- **Inserting text.** Type any desired text at the text cursor location. This inserts new text and shifts all existing text to the right.

- **Backspace key.** Pressing the Backspace key when text is not highlighted removes text to the left of the text cursor and moves the text to the right along with the text cursor.
- **Space bar.** Pressing the space bar when text is not highlighted moves all of the text to the right of the text cursor.
- **Left arrow.** Moves the text cursor to the left.
- **Right arrow.** Moves the text cursor to the right.
- **Control+X (Ctrl+X).** Highlights the entire string of text in the Text: box.

The previous discussion explained how to edit single-line text objects by using the DDEDIT command to access the "Edit Text" dialog box. The DDEDIT command is also used when you want to edit multiline text, except the default text editor is opened with the selected text:

Command: **DDEDIT** ⏎
⟨Select a TEXT or ATTDEF object⟩/Undo: *(pick the multiline text)*

Use the text editor to edit the text as you wish and then pick Exit from the File pull-down menu to return to the drawing editor as discussed previously with the MTEXT command.

PROFESSIONAL TIP

    If you try to create or edit a MTEXT object and get a DOS error message: Bad command or file name, and are returned immediately to AutoCAD, then DOS cannot find the editor's program file called EDIT.COM. First, check that the file exists in your DOS directory. If it does exist, but you still get the error message, it is probably not on your DOS directory search path. This is an environmental variable that tells DOS where to look for program files. You can check your current directory search path by typing PATH at the DOS prompt. Consult your DOS manual to fix either of these problems.

You can also edit multiline text using the DDMODIFY command:

Command: **DDMODIFY** ⏎
Select object to modify: *(pick the line of text you want to edit)*

After you pick the specific line of text that you want to edit, the "Modify MText" dialog box, is displayed see Figure 11-39. The following describes the elements of the "Modify MText" dialog box:

- The Properties area of the "Modify MText" dialog box lets you change color by picking the <u>C</u>olor... button. This opens the "Select Color" subdialog box where you can select a desired color. The <u>L</u>ayer... button accesses the "Select Layer" subdialog box which is explained in detail in Chapter 19 of this text.

Figure 11-39.   The "Modify MText" dialog box.

Modify MText

Properties

Color...   ■ BYLAYER   Handle: 30A

Layer...   0   Thickness: 0.0000

Linetype... CONTINUOUS   Linetype Scale: 1.0000

Insertion Point

Pick Point <

X: 1.5000
Y: 8.5000
Z: 0.0000

Contents

O BE 1/2 STD. GRADE 32/16 PLY WITH 8d @ 4

Edit Contents...   Edit Properties...

OK   Cancel   Help...

Pick to change the color or layer of the text

Change the insertion point if needed

Pick to edit the contents of the text

Pick to open the "MText Properties" subdialog box

- The Insertion Point section of the "Modify MText" dialog box lets you change the X and Y coordinates of the text insertion point by changing the values in the X: or Y: edit boxes. You can also choose the Pick Point ⟨ button to change the pick point with the screen cursor.
- Pick the Edit Contents... button to edit the text found in the Contents edit box.
- The Edit Properties... button accesses the "MText Properties" subdialog box shown in Figure 11-40. Use this dialog box to change the text style, text height, direction, attachment justification, width, or rotation.

Figure 11-40.   The "MText Properties" dialog box.

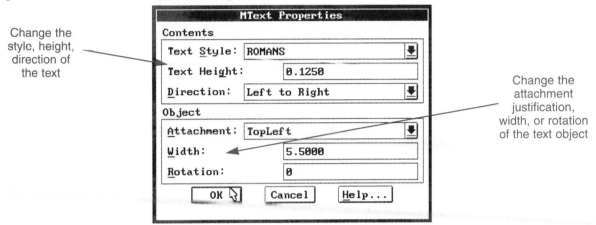

Change the style, height, direction of the text

Change the attachment justification, width, or rotation of the text object

You can also use the DDMODIFY command to access the Modify Text dialog box for editing single-line text objects in a similar manner. This allows you to change the insertion point origin, justification, height, rotation, width factor, obliquing angle, style, properties, and edit the text.

EXERCISE 11-9

❏ Load AutoCAD and set up your own variables.
❏ Use the DTEXT to place the following text on your drawing (incorrectly as shown) using ROMANS style and .125 text height.
    1. iNTERPRET DEMINSIONIN AND TOLERENCING PER ANSI Y14.5M-1982.
    2. REMOVE ALL BURRS AND EDGES.
    3. ALL FILLETS AND ROUNDS ARE .125 R.
    4. FINISH ALL OVER.
❏ Use the DDEDIT command to revise the above text as follows:
    1. INTERPRET DIMENSIONING AND TOLERANCING PER ASME Y14.5M-1994.
    2. REMOVE ALL BURRS AND SHARP EDGES.
    3. ALL FILLETS AND ROUNDS R.125.
    4. FINISH ALL OVER 62 MICROINCHES.
❏ Do the previous steps again, but this time enter the text with the MTEXT command and edit the text using DDEDIT and DDMODIFY commands.
❏ Save the drawing as A:EX11-9 and quit.

USING THE AUTOCAD SPELL CHECKER   AUG 8

You have been introduced to editing text on the drawing with the DDEDIT and DDMODIFY commands. You can use these commands to change lines of text and even correct spelling errors. However, AutoCAD has a powerful and convenient tool for checking the spelling on your drawing. To check the spelling type SPELL at the Command: prompt, pick Spelling… from the Tools pull-down menu, or select Spell: from the TOOLS screen menu. After entering the command, you are asked to select the text to be checked. You need to pick each line of single-line text or one pick on multiline text selects the entire paragraph. Enter the command and pick the text like this:

    Command: **SPELL** ⏎
    Select objects: *(pick the text)*
    Select objects: ⏎

The "Check Spelling" dialog box, shown in Figure 11-41, is displayed after picking the text that needs spell checking.

Figure 11-41.   The "Check Spelling" dialog box.

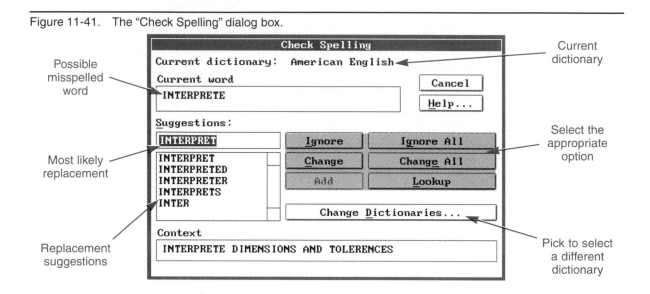

The following describes the features found in the Check Spelling dialog box:
- **Current dictionary:.** The current dictionary (American English) that is being used to check the spelling of the text you picked is identified at the top of the dialog box. You can change to a different dictionary by picking the Change Dictionaries… button discussed later.
- **Current word.** The Current word box displays a word that AutoCAD thinks may be spelled incorrectly.
- **Context.** At the bottom of the dialog box, AutoCAD displays the line of text where the current word was found.
- **Suggestions:.** This gives you a list of possible correct spellings for the current word. The first box is called the Suggestion: box and is AutoCAD's best guess. The word in the Suggestion: box is highlighted. Following the highlighted word is a list of other possible choices. If there are many choices, the scroll bar is available for you to use. If you do not like the word that AutoCAD has highlighted, move the cursor arrow to another word and pick it. The word you pick then becomes highlighted in the list and is shown in the Suggestion: box. When you think the highlighted word is correct, you have these options:
  - **Ignore–**Pick the Ignore button to skip the current word. For example, AutoCAD considers ASME in the Figure 11-41 note to be a misspelling, but ASME stands for American Society of Mechanical Engineers. So, you may chose to ignore this entry.

- **Ignore All**–Pick this button if you want AutoCAD to ignore all of the words that match the current word.
- **Change**–Pick the Change button to replace the Current word with the word in the Suggestion: box.
- **Change All**–Pick this button if you want to replace the Current word with the word in the Suggestion: box throughout the entire text object.
- **Add**–Pick this button to add the current word to the custom dictionary. You can add a word with up to 63 characters in length.
- **Lookup**–The Lookup button asks AutoCAD to check the spelling of the word in the Suggestion: box. For example, if you want to verify the spelling of a word that you type in the Suggestion: box and pick Lookup, a new suggestion and list of possible words follows.

Changing Dictionaries

AutoCAD provides you with spelling dictionaries for 24 different languages. A full list of the available language dictionaries is in Appendix A of the AutoCAD Command Reference. Pick the Change Dictionaries… button in the "Check Spelling" dialog box to access the "Change Dictionary" subdialog box shown in Figure 11-42. The first item in this dialog box is Main dictionary. This is where you can select one of the many language dictionaries to use as the current Main dictionary. To change the main dictionary, pick the down arrow to access the pop-up list. Next, pick the desired language dictionary from the pop-up list. The main dictionary is protected and cannot be added on to. The additional features found in the "Change Dictionaries" subdialog box are as follows:

- **Custom dictionary.** This displays the name of the current custom dictionary, or you can type the name of another custom dictionary in the text box. The name can take two forms:

  A. The name can be a textual description using up to 63 characters in sentence form. You can use spaces and characters such as #, or &. When named in this manner, it is referred to as *volatile*. This means that if an alternate custom dictionary is specified, the previous one is lost forever.

  B. If you wish to save a custom dictionary file for later access, name it in a standard DOS fashion using up to 8 characters and place a .CUS file extension after the name, like this: ARCH.CUS.

Figure 11-42.   The "Change Dictionaries" subdialog box.

Select the language dictionary

Select a custom dictionary

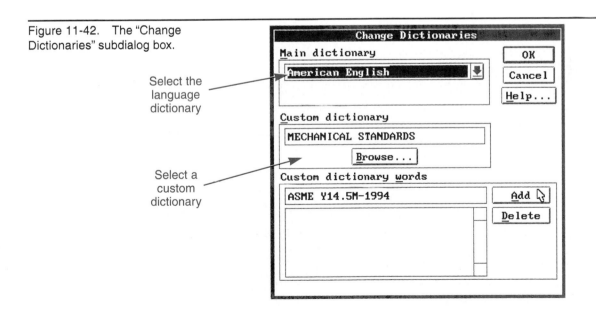

PROFESSIONAL TIP

Creating a .CUS file allows that name to be specified later for loading as the custom dictionary. A reason for this might be for a drafter who practices multiple disciplines. For example, when in a mechanical drawing, certain nonwords such as abbreviations or brand names that are commonly encountered might be added to a MECH.CUS file. In the same manner, a separate file named ARCH.CUS might contain common architectural abbreviations and frequently used brand names. These CUS files are standard American National Standard Code for Information Interchange (ASCII) text files and can be edited in any standard text editor. This is where words can be added, deleted, or dictionaries can be combined. These should not be edited using a word processor such as MS Word or Word Perfect unless the output is saved as "text only" with no special text formatting or printer codes.

*   **Browse…**–Pick the <u>B</u>rowse… button to get the "Select Custom Dictionary" subdialog box shown in Figure 11-43.

Figure 11-43.   The "Select Custom Dictionary" dialog box.

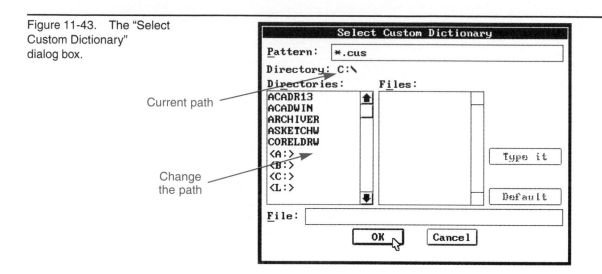

Current path

Change the path

*   **Custom dictionary <u>w</u>ords.** Type a word in the text box that you either want to add or delete from the custom dictionary. For example, look at Figure 11-42 and see ASME Y14.5M-1994 entered in the text box. This is an example of custom text used in engineering drafting. Pick the <u>A</u>dd button to accept the custom word in the text box, or pick the <u>D</u>elete button to remove the word from the <u>C</u>ustom dictionary. <u>C</u>ustom dictionary entries may be up to 32 characters in length. Pick OK when you are done, or pick Cancel or Help as needed.

When the spelling check is complete, you get the "AutoCAD Alert" box shown in Figure 11-44. Pick the OK button or press ENTER to return the drawing editor.

Figure 11-44.   When AutoCAD is finished spell-checking the selected text, this alert box is displayed.

The current custom dictionary may be displayed at the prompt line by using the DCTCUST system variable like this:

Command: **DCTCUST** ↵
New value for DCTCUST, or for none ⟨"MECHANICAL STANDARDS"⟩:

Typing the DCTMAIN system variable at the Command: prompt displays the current Main dictionary:

Command: **DCTMAIN** ↵
New value for DCTMAIN, or. for none ⟨"enu"⟩:

The "enu" is the abbreviation for the American English main dictionary. The abbreviations for all available AutoCAD language dictionaries is found in Appendix A of the *AutoCAD Command Reference.*

EXERCISE 11-10

❏ Load AutoCAD and set up your own variables.
❏ Use the MTEXT command to type a short paragraph of your own choice with purposely made spelling errors.
❏ Check the spelling and correct the misspelled words.
❏ Save as A:EX 11-10 and quit.

CHAPTER TEST

Write your answers in the spaces provided.

1. Give the command and entities required to display "IT IS FAST AND EASY TO DRAW TEXT USING AUTOCAD." The text must be .375 unit high, have the default TXT font, and fit between two points:

   Command:_____

   Justify/Style/⟨Start point⟩: _____

   Align/Fit/Center/Middle/Right/TL/TC/TR/ML/MC/MR/BL/BC/BR: _____

   First text line point: _____

   Second text line point:_____

   Height ⟨.2000⟩: _____

   Text:_____

2. Give the command and entries required to create a new text style. The style should have the following specifications. Assume FILEDIA equals 0.
    - Style name: 25-TITLES.
    - Used for titles .25 inch height.
    - Double width.
    - ROMANC font.

    Command:_____

    Text style name (or ?) ⟨TXT⟩:_____

    Font file ⟨*default*⟩: _____

    Height ⟨*current*⟩: _____

    Width factor ⟨1⟩:_____

    Obliquing angle ⟨0⟩:_____

    Backwards? ⟨N⟩: _____

    Upside-down? ⟨N⟩: _____

    Vertical? ⟨N⟩: _____

    _____ is now the current text style.

3. Give the command and entries to underscore the following text and place it at a selected start point: "VERIFY ALL DIMENSIONS DURING CONSTRUCTION."

    Command:_____

    Justify/Style/⟨Start point⟩: _____

    Height ⟨*current*⟩: _____

    Rotation angle ⟨0⟩:_____

    Text:_____

4. How would you turn On the Quick Text mode if it is currently Off?

    Command:_____

    ON/OFF ⟨Off⟩: _____

5. Give the letter you must enter at the TEXT prompt to place text as follows:

    A. Left-justified text: _____

    B. Right-justified text:_____

    C. Text between two points without regard for text height: _____

    D. Center the text horizontally and vertically: _____

    E. Text between two points with a fixed height:_____

    F. Center text along a baseline:_____

    G. Top and Left horizontal: _____

    H. Middle and Right horizontal: _____

    I. Bottom and Center horizontal: _____

6. List the Justify options. _____

7. How would you specify a text style with a double width factor? _____

8. How would you specify a text style with a 15° angle? _____

   _____

9. How would you specify vertical text? _____

   _____

10. How is the "Select Font File" dialog box accessed? _____

11. Give the control sequence required to draw the following symbols and associated text for the two formats specified:

	Select Line Text	**Paragraph or Unicode for Multiline Text**
A. 30°	_____	_____
B. 1.375 ± .005	_____	_____
C. ∅24	_____	_____
D. <u>NOT FOR CONSTRUCTION</u>	_____	_____

12. What command is used so you can see the text on the screen as it is typed? _____

13. Why use the Quick Text mode rather than have the actual text displayed on the screen?_____

    _____

    _____

14. Name three ways to access the DTEXT command. _____

    _____

15. When setting text height in the STYLE command, what value do you enter at the Height: prompt so text height can be altered each time the TEXT or DTEXT commands are used?_____

    _____

16. Give the command that lets you alter the location, style, height, and wording of existing text. ___

    _____

17. Identify the command used to revise existing text on the drawing by using the "Edit Text" dialog box._____

18. List the sequence of activities required to access the "Edit Text" dialog box._____

    _____

    _____

19. When editing single-line text, how do you remove the character located in front of the text cursor? _____

    _____

    _____

20. When using the "Edit Text" dialog box, how do you move the text cursor to the left without removing text characters? _____

21. How do you remove all of the text to the right of the text cursor when editing text in the "Edit Text" dialog box?_____

    _____

    _____

22. When editing text in the Text: box, the flashing vertical bar is called the _____.

23. Determine the AutoCAD text height for text to be plotted .188″ high using a HALF (1:2) scale. (Show your calculations.)_____

_____

24. Determine the AutoCAD text height for text to be plotted .188″ high using a scale of 1/4″ = 1′- 0″. (Show your calculations.)_____

_____

25. What would you do if you just completed editing a line of text and discovered you made a mistake? Assume you are still in the "Edit Text" dialog box. _____

_____

26. Identify two ways to move around inside the Text: box of the "Edit Text" dialog box. _____

_____

_____

_____

_____

27. What happens when you press the space bar or the Backspace key when the text inside the Text: box is highlighted? _____

28. What happens when you press CTRL+X when using the "Edit Text" dialog box?_____

_____

_____

29. Name the command that lets you make multiple line text objects. _____

_____

30. What do you get when you pick Text from the Draw pull-down menu followed by selecting Text from the cascading submenu? _____

_____

31. Describe the purpose of the Attach option when setting up multiline text. _____

_____

_____

_____

32. How does the width of the multiline text boundary affect what you type? _____

_____

_____

33. What happens if the multiline text that you are entering exceeds or is not as long as the boundary length that you initially establish? _____

_____

_____

34. What happens when you pick the Insertion point followed by the Other corner of the multiline text boundary? _____

35. Describe two ways to access the pull-down menus in the MS DOS EDIT program.

_____

_____

36. Why is it not important to do formatting while you are typing in the text editor?

_____

_____

37. Describe how you save multiline text that you have created in the text editor and return to
AutoCAD. _____

_____

_____

38. Name the command that you enter if you want to enter multiple lines of text at the prompt line
rather than in a text editor. _____

_____

39. What command do you use if you want to change the name of a text style? _____

_____

40. Name two commands that allow you to edit multiline text. _____

_____

41. Identify three ways to access the AutoCAD Spell Checker. _____

_____

_____

42. What is the purpose of the word found in the Current word box of the "Check Spelling" dialog
box? _____

43. How do you change the Current word if you do not think the word that is displayed in the
Suggestion: box of the "Check Spelling" dialog box is the correct word, but one of the words in
the list of suggestions is the correct word? _____

_____

_____

_____

44. What is the purpose of the Add button in the "Check Spelling" dialog box? _____

_____

_____

_____

45. How do you change the main dictionary for use in the "Check Spelling" dialog box? _____

_____

_____

_____

DRAWING PROBLEMS

1. Make three prototype drawings with borders and title blocks for your future drawings. Use the following guidelines:

   A. Prototype 1 for A-size, 8 1/2 × 11 drawings, named TITLEA.

   B. Prototype 2 for B-size, 11 × 17 drawings, named TITLEB.

   C. Prototype 3 for C-size, 17 × 22 drawings, named TITLEC.

   D. Set the following values for the drawing aids:

   Units = three-place decimal.

   Grid = .500.

   Snap = .250.

   E. Draw a polyline border, .032 wide, 1/2 in. from the drawing limits.

   F. Design a title block using created text styles. Place it in the lower-right corner of each drawing. The title block should contain the following information: company or school name, address, date, drawn by, approved by, scale, title, drawing number, material, revision number. See the following example.

   G. Set a standard text style titled ROMANS-125. This style was discussed in this chapter.

SPECIFICATIONS			R -	CHANGE			DATE	ECN
			HYSTER COMPANY					
			THIS PRINT CONTAINS CONFIDENTIAL INFORMATION WHICH IS THE PROPERTY OF HYSTER COMPANY. BY ACCEPTING THIS INFORMATION THE BORROWER AGREES THAT IT WILL NOT BE USED FOR ANY PURPOSE OTHER THAN THAT FOR WHICH IT IS LOANED.					
UNLESS OTHERWISE SPECIFIED DIMENSIONS ARE IN ~~INCHES~~ MILLIMETERS AND TOLERANCES FOR: ____ PLACE DIMS± _____:____ PLACE DIMS± _____ ANGLES ± _____ : WHOLE DIMS± _____			DR.		SCALE		DATE	
			CK. MAT'L.		CK. DESIGN		REL. ON ECN	
			NAME					
MODEL	DWG. FIRST USED	SIMILAR TO						
DEPT.	PROJECT	LIST DIVISION	H	PART NO.				R

P11-2

2. Recall your TITLEA prototype drawing. Use the TEXT or DTEXT command to type the following information. Change the text style to represent each of the four standard AutoCAD fonts named. Use a .5 unit text height and 0° rotation angle.

TXT–AUTOCAD'S DEFAULT TEXT FONT WHICH IS AVAILABLE FOR USE WHEN YOU BEGIN A DRAWING.

ROMANS–SMOOTHER THAN TXT FONT AND CLOSELY DUPLICATES THE SINGLE-STROKE LETTERING THAT HAS BEEN THE STANDARD FOR DRAFTING.

ROMANC–A MULTI-STROKE DECORATIVE FONT THAT IS GOOD FOR USE IN DRAWING TITLES.

ITALICC–AN ORNAMENTAL FONT SLANTED TO THE RIGHT AND HAS THE SAME LETTER DESIGN AS THE COMPLEX FONT.

Save the drawing as A:P11-2 and quit.

P11-3

3. Recall your TITLEA prototype drawing. Use the STYLE command to create the following text styles. Change the options as noted in each line of text. Then use the DTEXT command to type the text, changing the text style to represent each of the four standard AutoCAD fonts named. Use a .25 unit text height.

TXT–EXPAND THE WIDTH BY THREE.
MONOTXT–SLANT TO THE LEFT –30°.
ROMANS–SLANT TO THE RIGHT 30°.
ROMAND–BACKWARDS.
ROMANC–VERTICAL.
ITALICC–UNDERSCORED AND OVERSCORED.
ROMANS–USE 16d NAILS @ 10″ OC.
ROMANT–3⌀32 (812.8).

Save the drawing as A:P11-3 and quit.

P11-4

4. Open drawing P11-3. Select the following fonts from the text font icon menu: SCRIPTC, ROMANT, GOTHICE, SYMAP, and SYMUSIC.

   A. Type a complete alphabet and numbers 1-10 for the text fonts, and all available symbols for the symbol fonts.

   B. Use .375 unit height with all other variables at default values.

   C. Save the drawing as A:P11-4 and quit.

P11-5

5. Draw a Parts List (similar to the one shown below) connected to your A-size prototype title block.

   A. Enter "PARTS LIST" with a COMPLEX style.

   B. Enter the other information using ROMANS text and the DTEXT command. Do not exit the DTEXT command to start a new line of text.

   C. Save the drawing as A:P11-5 and quit.

3	HOLDING PINS	12
2	SIDE COVERS	3
1	MAIN HOUSING	1
KEY	DESCRIPTION	QTY

PARTS LIST

UNLESS OTHERWISE SPECIFIED
ALL DIMENSIONS IN

INCHES

AND TOLERANCES FOR:

1 PLACE DIMS: ±.1
2 PLACE DIMS: ±.01
3 PLACE DIMS: ±.005
ANGULAR: ±30'
FRACTIONAL: ±.1/32
FINISH: 125? in.

JANE'S
DESIGN

| DR: JANE | SCALE: FULL | DATE: XX–XX–XX | APPD: |

MATERIAL:
MILD STEEL

NAME:
XXX–XXXX

FIRST USED ON: SIMILAR TO:

B   PART NO: 123–321   REV: 0

P11-6

6. Draw an architectural prototype drawing for a 17″ × 22″ or 22″ × 44″ sheet size with a title block along the right side similar to the one shown below. Save the drawing as A:P11-6.

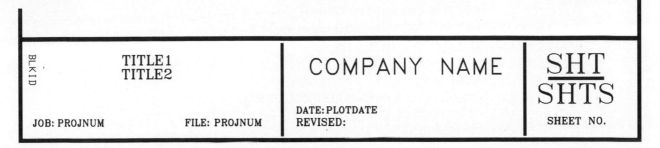

P11-7

7. Complete the following drawing.

   A. Make the symbols proportional to the ones shown. They will not necessarily be the same size.

   B. Use the DTEXT command and the variables studied in this chapter.

   C. Save the drawing as A:P11-7 and quit.

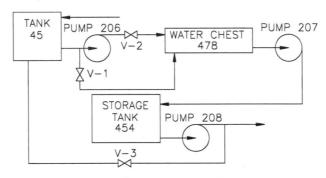

4. ALL PUMPS ON 6″ THICK CONCRETE PADS.
3. ALL TANKS AND CHESTS BUILT TO CUSTOMERS SPECIFICATIONS.
2. ALL VALVES FABRIVALVE FIG. 71.
1. TEST ALL TANKS TO 175 PSI.

NOTES:

P11-8

8. Complete the drawing shown on the following page.

   A. Make the symbols proportional to the ones shown, but not necessarily the same size.

   B. Use the DTEXT command and the variables studied in this chapter.

   C. Save the drawing as A:P11-8 and quit.

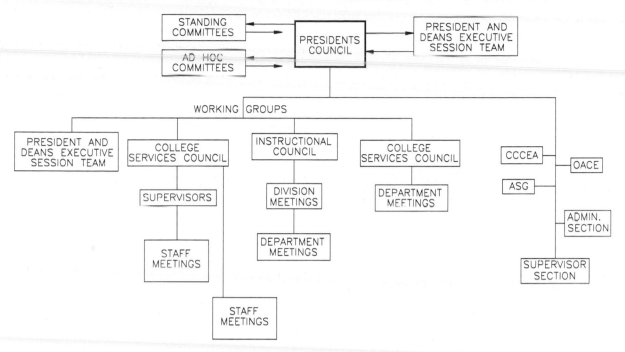

GROUP DECISION MAKING PROCESS

*NOTE: STANDING OR AD HOC COMMITTEES MAY BE FORMED AT ANY LEVEL.

P11-9

9. Use the MTEXT command to type the following text using the font settings of ROMANS and .125 text height with .25 heading text height.

NOTES:
1.   INTERPRET DIMENSIONS AND TOLERANCES PER ASME Y14.5M—1994.
2.   REMOVE ALL BURRS AND SHARP EDGES.

CASTING NOTES UNLESS OTHERWISE SPECIFIED:
1.   .31 WALL THICKNESS.
2.   R.12 FILLETS.
3.   R.06 ROUNDS.
4.   1.5°—3.0° DRAFT.
5.   TOLERANCES:
      ± 1° ANGULAR
      ±.03 TWO PLACE DIMENSIONS.
6.   PROVIDE .12 THK MACHINING STOCK ON ALL MACHINE SURFACES.

P11-10

10. Use the MTEXT command to type the following text using the font settings of City Blueprint (cibt) and .125 text height with .188 heading text height. After typing the text exactly as shown, edit the text with the following changes:

A. Change the \ in item 7 to 1/2.

B. Change the [in item 8 to 1.

C. Change the 1/2 in item 8 to 3/4.

D. Change the ^ in item 10 to a degree symbol.

Save as drawing A:P11-10

COMMON FRAMING NOTES:
1.　ALL FRAMING LUMBER TO BE DFL #2 OR BETTER.
2.　ALL HEATED WALLS @ HEATED LIVING AREAS TO BE
　　2 X 6 @ 24" OC.
3.　ALL EXTERIOR HEADERS TO BE 2-2 X 12 UNLESS
　　NOTED, W/ 2" RIGID INSULATION BACKING UNLESS
　　NOTED.
4.　ALL SHEAR PANELS TO BE 1/2" CDX PLY W/ 8d
　　@ 4" OC @ EDGE, HDRS, & BLOCKING AND 8d @
　　8" OC @ FIELD UNLESS NOTED.
5.　ALL METAL CONNECTORS TO BE SIMPSON CO. OR
　　EQUAL.
6.　ALL TRUSSES TO BE 24" OC.　SUBMIT TRUSS
　　CALCS TO BUILDING DEPT. PRIOR TO ERECTION.
7.　PLYWOOD ROOF SHEATHING TO BE \ STD GRADE
　　32/16 PLY LAID PERP TO RAFTERS.　NAIL W/ 8d
　　@ 6" OC @ EDGES AND 12" OC @ FIELD.
8.　PROVIDE [1/2" STD GRADE T&G PLY FLOOR
　　SHEATHING LAID PERP TO FLOOR JOISTS.　NAIL W/
　　10d @ 6" OC @ EDGES & BLOCKING AND 12" OC
　　@ FIELD.
9.　BLOCK ALL WALLS OVER 10'-0" HIGH AT MID.
10. LET-IN BRACES TO BE 1 X 4 DIAG BRACES @ 45^
　　FOR ALL INTERIOR LOAD BEARING WALLS.

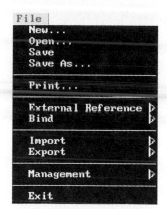

Chapter 12

PLOTTING AND PRINTING

Learning objectives

After completing this chapter, you will be able to:
- ○ Identify options and variables found in the PLOT command.
- ○ Determine the scale factor of a drawing.
- ○ Use the "Plot Configuration" dialog box to prepare a drawing for plotting.
- ○ Print and plot a drawing.
- ○ Configure a new plotting device.

The *Introduction to Printing and Plotting* section in Chapter 6, provided you with a brief overview of the steps involved in generating a printed paper copy of your drawing or design. This chapter introduces you to all of the options of the PLOT command as it appears at the Command: prompt, and then discusses the "Plot Configuration" dialog box in detail. In addition, you will step through the procedure to configure AutoCAD for additional hardcopy devices.

USING THE PLOT COMMAND

AUG 10

The PLOT command can be typed at the Command: prompt. In order to generate a plot or print from the screen menus you must pick Print... from the File pull-down or Print: from the File screen menu. If the CMDDIA system variable is set to 1, the "Plot Configuration" dialog box is displayed. This is the AutoCAD default. Plotting prompts are issued at the command line when CMDDIA is 0. To issue plot prompts at the command line, set the CMDDIA system variable to 0 like this:

> Command: **CMDDIA** ↵
> New value for CMDDIA ⟨1⟩: **0** ↵

The PLOT command asks for the part of the current drawing you want to plot, then allows you to change a variety of plotting specifications. You can choose to change the specifications or leave them as they are. When the plot is finished, AutoCAD returns you to the drawing editor.

Most AutoCAD users will generate prints and plots by using the "Plot Configuration" dialog box. It is convenient because all of the plotting options are displayed and can be accessed quickly. But it is also a good idea to become familiar with the various options that are part of the PLOT command. It is good information to know if you plan to learn how to customize AutoCAD with command macros, screen menus, and script files. If you want to skip PLOT's Command: line entry discussion, move ahead to the *Using the Plot Configuration dialog Box* section in this chapter. But be sure to review the *Scaling the plot* section in this chapter, for an in-depth look at drawing and plot scales.

Choose what to plot

After entering the PLOT command, decide the part of the drawing you want to plot.

> Command: **PLOT** ↵
> What to plot – Display, Extents, Limits, View or Window ⟨D⟩:

Press ENTER to plot the screen display. Type the first letter of any other option to change the selection. The following describes the function of each option.

- **Display (D).** This request prints or plots the current screen display.
- **Extents (E).** The Extents option prints or plots only that area of the drawing in which objects (entities) are drawn. Before using this option, zoom the extents to include all recently edited entities to check exactly what will be plotted.

  Border lines around your drawing may be clipped off if they are at the extreme edges of the screen. This often happens because you are requesting the plotter to plot at the extreme edge of its active area.
- **Limits (L).** This option plots everything inside your drawing limits.
- **View (V).** This option plots views saved with the VIEW command. AutoCAD prompts you for the name. The view you enter does not have to be displayed on the screen.
- **Window (W).** This option allows you to pick two opposite corners of a window around the portion of the drawing to be plotted. These can be chosen with the pointing device or entered as coordinates at the keyboard. If the window is defined close to an entity, some lines may be clipped off in your plot. If this happens, adjust the window next time you plot.

NOTE   The FILEDIA system variable controls the display of any file name dialog box regardless
    of the CMDDIA setting.

SETTING THE PLOT SPECIFICATIONS   AUG 10

After choosing the portion of the drawing to plot, you are presented with a list of default settings for the plot specifications. These specifications might read like this for a PostScript printer:

```
A ^Z will not be appended to the end of the file
A ^D will not be appended to the end of the file
Plot device is PostScript device ADI 4.2 - by Autodesk, Inc
Description:  HP Laserjet IV Adesk ADI
Plot optimization level = 1
Plot will NOT be written to a selected file
Sizes are in Inches and the style is portrait
Plot origin is at (0.00,0.00)
Plotting area is 8.00 wide by 10.50 high (A size)
Plot is NOT rotated
Area fill will NOT be adjusted for pen width
Hidden lines will NOT be removed
Plot will be scaled to fit available area
Do you want to change anything? (No/Yes/File/Save) ⟨N⟩: ↵
```

These specifications may be suitable for some of your drawings. If so, press ENTER to accept the default "NO" response. AutoCAD sends the drawing to the printer and displays a message similar to this:

```
Effective plotting area: 8.00 wide by 5.77 high
Regeneration done 100%
Plot complete.
Command:
```

Answer Y to the Do you want to change anything? prompt if you want to change any of the values. First you get some questions asking for changes to your printer or plotter configuration. You can respond with changes or press ENTER to keep defaults. This example shows how you would change the scale to make any size drawing fit on the paper.

Do you want to change plotters? ⟨N⟩ ⏎
Do you wish to append a ^Z ⟨N⟩ ⏎
Do you wish to append a ^D ⟨N⟩ ⏎
Pen widths are in Inches.

Object Color	Pen No.	Line Type	Pen Width	Object Color	Pen No.	Line Type	Pen Width
1 (red)	1	0	0.010	9	1	0	0.010
2 (yellow)	1	0	0.010	10	1	0	0.010
3 (green)	1	0	0.010	11	1	0	0.010
4 (cyan)	1	0	0.010	12	1	0	0.010
5 (blue)	1	0	0.010	13	1	0	0.010
6 (magenta)	1	0	0.010	14	1	0	0.010
7 (white)	1	0	0.010	15	1	0	0.010
8	1	0	0.010	16	1	0	0.010

Do you want to change any of the above parameters? ⟨N⟩ ⏎

Write the plot to a file? ⟨N⟩ ⏎
Size units (Inches or Millimeters) ⟨I⟩: ⏎
Plot origin in Inches ⟨0.00,0.00⟩: ⏎

Standard values for plotting size

Size	Width	Height
A	8.00	10.50
B	10.00	16.00
C	16.00	21.00
D	21.00	33.00
E	33.00	43.00
F	28.00	40.00
G	11.00	90.00
H	28.00	143.00
J	34.00	176.00
K	40.00	143.00
A4	7.80	11.20
A3	10.70	15.60
A2	15.60	22.40
A1	22.40	32.20
A0	32.20	45.90
MAX	218.40	218.40

Enter the Size or Width,Height (in Inches) ⟨A⟩: ⏎

Rotate plot clockwise 0/90/180/270 degrees ⟨0⟩: ⏎
Adjust area fill boundaries for pen width? ⟨N⟩ ⏎
Remove hidden lines? ⟨N⟩ ⏎
Specify scale by entering:
Plotted Inches=Drawing Units or Fit or ? ⟨F⟩: ⏎
Effective plotting area: 7.72 wide by 10.50 high
Regeneration done 100%
Plot complete.

NOTE   For some models of plotters, you will be prompted for a Plotter Port to Time-Out value.
Accept the default value by pressing ENTER.

Additional setup Options for a pen plotter

After responding Y to change plot specifications for a pen plotter, the screen shown in Figure 12-1 appears. Here, you can change pen numbers, linetypes, and pen speeds.

Figure 12-1.   Plot specifications, such as pen number, linetype, and pen speed, can be modified when adding a plotter.

```
Pen widths are in Inches.
Object   Pen  Line  Pen     Pen    Object   Pen  Line  Pen     Pen
Color    No.  Type  Speed   Width  Color    No.  Type  Speed   Width
1 (red)   1    0    36      0.010   9        3    0    36      0.010
2 (yellow) 2   0    36      0.010  10        4    0    36      0.010
3 (green)  3   0    36      0.010  11        5    0    36      0.010
4 (cyan)   4   0    36      0.010  12        6    0    36      0.010
5 (blue)   5   0    36      0.010  13        1    0    36      0.010
6 (magenta) 6  0    36      0.010  14        2    0    36      0.010
7 (white)  1   0    36      0.010  15        3    0    36      0.010
8          2   0    36      0.010  16        4    0    36      0.010

Linetypes
         0 = continuous line
         1 = ...............................
         2 = ----    ----    ----    ----
         3 = -----   -----   -----   -----
         4 = ------. ------. ------. ------.
         5 = ---- -  ---- -  ---- -  ---- -
         6 = --- - - --- - - --- - - --- - -

Note:  Linetypes 7 thru 12 are valid, adaptive linetypes.
Please see your HP plotter manual
Do you want to change any of the above parameters? <N>
```

The possible responses, shown above in the Enter values: prompt, are defined as follows:
- **Blank (ENTER or space bar).** Uses the current value displayed in brackets and moves to the next one. AutoCAD stays in this routine until you move to the next specification by exiting.
- **Cn (color number).** You can proceed to a specific color and set that pen number by typing Cn. The "n" represents the number of the specific color you wish to change. To assign pen number 4 to the green color, first type C3. The screen displays the Pen number: prompt for color 3 (green). Now enter the plotter carousel or pen rack number of the green pen.
- **S (Show values).** Allows you to check the values just entered. Typing S displays an updated list of pen numbers, linetypes, and pen speeds.
- **X (Exit).** This completes the pen and linetype routine and moves to the next plot specification.

The display of linetypes in this prompt depends on the type of plotter you have configured. Normally, do not specify anything but a continuous linetype. Your AutoCAD drawing will already have linetypes set by the software.

Create a plot file

Some computers allow you to continue working on a drawing while another routine is being handled by the computer. This feature of some powerful computers, called *multitasking*, runs more than one program without a noticeable decline in efficiency. The PLOT command allows you to create a file that can be used in this manner. Some computer programs plot a list of files without any additional plotting information input by the user.

Write the plot to a file? ⟨N⟩: **Y** ↵

When the scaling routine is completed (discussed in one of the following sections), you are asked to name the plot file if FILEDIA is 0. If FILEDIA is 1, the "Create Plot File" dialog box is displayed. Here you can enter the plot file name.

Enter file name for plot ⟨current⟩:

You either assign a different name to the plot file or accept the current name by pressing ENTER. AutoCAD assigns the plot file a .PLT extension. The file is now ready to be used by other programs. With some plotters, PLT files can be plotted directly from the DOS prompt.

Computer network systems operating off a central server also use PLT files in a plot queue. A *plot queue* is a lineup or list of files waiting to be plotted. The PLT files can be loaded in the queue and started while users on the network continue other work.

Size of the drawing units

This prompt allows you to specify inches or millimeters.

Size units (Inches or Millimeters) ⟨current⟩:

The "current" size is accepted by pressing ENTER. If needed, select the other by typing I or M.

Origin of the plot

The origin of a pen plotter is the lower-left corner of the paper. To begin the drawing at that point, press ENTER. The default values of the prompt should appear as shown here.

Plot origin in units ⟨0.00,0.00⟩:

To position your drawing away from the origin, enter the coordinate values at the prompt. Put a comma between the X and Y values. For example, to move the drawing four units to the right and three units above the plotter origin, enter:

Plot origin in units ⟨0.00,0.00⟩: **4,3** ↵

The origin of a printer is the upper-left corner of the paper. The coordinates above move the drawing four units to the right and three units down. The "units" in this prompt refers to the units specified in the Size units: prompt.

Size of the plot

The next prompt displays the plot sizes available from the configured plotter. You can choose one of these or enter a size of your own, as long as it is smaller than the maximum (MAX) size indicated in the list. The sizes listed will vary according to the brand and size of plotter you have.

Standard values for plotting size

Size	Width	Height
A	10.50	8.00
B	16.00	10.00
C	21.00	16.00
D	33.00	21.00
E	43.00	33.00
MAX	64.50	36.00
USER	17.00	22.00

Enter the Size or Width, Height (in units) ⟨current⟩:

Remember that all plotters require margins around the edges of the paper. This space allows for the plotter's grit wheels, clamps, or other holding devices. Therefore, the available size may be smaller than the standard ANSI sizes. Figure 12-2 shows standard paper sizes and the approximate available plotting area.

Figure 12-2.   Standard paper sizes and approximate plotting areas.

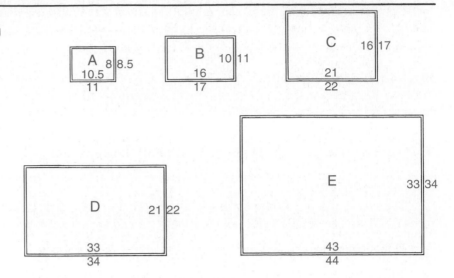

The MAX size is the largest size paper your plotter can handle. The USER values indicate the last size entered. To select a size shown on the list, type the letter. Simply press ENTER to accept the default size. For example, to use an 11 × 17 sheet of paper, the response would be:

Enter the Size or Width, Height (in units)⟨current⟩: **17,11** ↵

Be sure to enter the width (X dimension) of the paper first.

Rotate the plot

In AutoCAD, the horizontal screen measurement relates to the long side of the paper. This orientation is known as *landscape* format. However, you might create a drawing, form, or chart that must be placed in *portrait* format. The long side is positioned vertically. Most A size printers are set to portrait by default. The next prompt allows you to make the change from landscape to portrait.

Rotate plot clockwise 0/90/180/270 degrees ⟨0⟩:

Plots can be rotated in 90 degree increments. If you type 90 the lower-left corner of your drawing is placed at the upper-left corner of the paper. Figure 12-3 shows the effects of a 90 degree clockwise direction.

Figure 12-3.   A–Standard plot with no rotation. B–Effects of a 90 degree clockwise rotation.

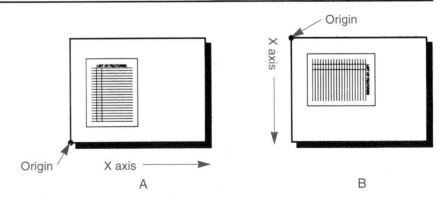

Pen width

You can increase the efficiency of AutoCAD and your plotter by knowing the widths of the pens. This value governs how many passes the pen must make when filling in polylines, trace lines, and solids. The response entered at the Pen width: prompt is measured by the units entered at the Size units: prompt.

Adjust for pen width in area fills

The Adjust area fill boundaries for pen width?: specification is one that most users seldom change. A Y response directs AutoCAD to move the pen inside the boundaries of filled areas one-half the pen width. Do this only if the nature of the plotted material requires extreme accuracy. Pressing ENTER instructs the plotter to place the center of the pen on the exact coordinates given.

A situation in which the pen width is adjusted for area fills is for plotting accurate artwork for printed circuit boards (PCBs). The line on a PCB must be an exact width. When the adjustment is set to Off (Y), the outer edges, or defined area of the line width, are drawn with the center line of the pen on the edge. When the adjustment is set to On (N), the pen is moved inward so the edge of the pen doesn't go beyond the outside of the fill area.

Remove hidden lines

The hidden line removal function works the same as the HIDE command. If used with a detailed drawing, it may require a long wait on your part.

> Remove hidden lines? ⟨N⟩

Answer Y to this prompt *only* if you must have hidden lines removed.

Determining drawing scale factors

You should have already established the scale factor of the drawing by the time you are ready to plot. However, if you haven't, it isn't too late to do so; you will have to spend some time updating dimensions and changing text styles. Scale factors are important because the number is used to ensure that text, dimension text and arrows, and tick marks are plotted or printed at the proper height. The scale factor is multiplied by the desired plotted text height to obtain the AutoCAD text height. The scale factor is also used in the DIMSCALE dimension variable.

The scale factor is always the reciprocal of the drawing scale. For example, if you wish to plot a drawing at a scale of 1/2″ = 1″, calculate the scale factor as follows:

> 1/2″ = 1″
> .5″ = 1″
> 1/.5 = **2** *(The scale factor is 2.)*

An architectural drawing that is to be plotted at a scale of 1/4″ = 1′-0″ would have a scale factor calculated as follows:

> 1/4″ = 1′-0″
> .25″ = 12″
> 12/.25 = **48** *(The scale factor is 48.)*

The scale factor of a civil engineering drawing that has a scale of 1″ = 60′ is calculated as:

> 1″ = 60′
> 1″ = (60 x 12) = **720** *(The scale factor is 720.)*

When the scale factor of any drawing has been determined, you should then calculate the height of the text in AutoCAD. If text height is to be plotted at 1/8″, it should *not* be drawn at that height. For example, if you are working on a civil drawing with a scale of 1″ = 60′ (scale factor = 720), text drawn 1/8″ high appears as a dot. Remember, the drawing you are working on in AutoCAD is 720 times larger than it will be when you plot it at the proper scale. Therefore, you must multiply the text height by

720 in order to get text that appears in correct proportion on the screen. In this case, if you want 1/8″ high text to appear correctly on your screen, calculate the AutoCAD height as follows:

> 1/8″ x 720
> .125″ x 720 = **90** (The proper height of the text is 90.)

Scale factors, text heights, and DIMSCALE values should be determined *before* beginning a drawing, and are best incorporated as values within your prototype drawing files.

Scaling the plot

The final specification to set is the plot scale. Here you decide how big the drawing will be plotted.

> Specify scale by entering:
> Plotted units=Drawing units or Fit or ? ⟨*default*⟩:

Either enter a scale or instruct AutoCAD to fit the entire drawing on the paper. The Fit option can be selected by typing F at the prompt and pressing ENTER. No other values are needed. AutoCAD automatically adjusts your drawing to fit on the paper. You may have considerable blank space left on the paper depending on the size and proportions of your drawing.

To specify a scale you must enter a ratio of plotted units to drawing units. A mechanical drawing to be plotted at a scale of 1/2″ = 1″ is entered as follows:

> Specify scale by entering:
> Plotted units=Drawing units or Fit or ? ⟨*default*⟩: **1/2″=1″** *or* **.5=1** *or* **1=2** ↵

An architectural drawing to be plotted at 1/4″ = 1′-0″ is entered as follows:

> Specify scale by entering:
> Plotted units=Drawing units or Fit or ? ⟨*default*⟩: **1/4″=1′** *or* **.25=12**

To calculate the available area on a sheet of paper at a specific scale, use this formula:

$$\frac{\text{Unit}}{\text{Scale}} \times \text{Paper size} = \text{Limits}$$

To find the limits of a B-size (17 x 11 in.) sheet of paper at 1/2″ = 1″ scale:

$$\frac{1}{.50} \times 17 = 17 \div .5 = 34$$

$$\frac{1}{.50} \times 11 = 11 \div .5 = 22$$

Thus the limits of a B-size sheet at the scale of 1/2″ = 1″ are 34,22. The same formula applies to architectural scales. The limits of a C-size architectural sheet (24 x 18 in.) at a scale of 1/4″ = 1′-0″ can be determined like this:

$$\frac{1'-0''}{1/4''} \times 24 = \frac{12''}{.25''} \times 24 = 48 \times 24 = 1152 \div 12 = 96 \text{ feet (X distance)}$$

Use the same formula to calculate the Y distance of the 18 in. side of the paper. The chart in Figure 12-4 provides limits for common scales on various paper sizes for each drafting field. It also lists text height, scale factors, and linetype scales for the best linetype display.

Each row of the chart lists a different size of paper. Notice in the third column titled Scale, that the same four scales are listed for each sheet size. Therefore, only the top row shows the plotted text height, scale factor, and linetype scales for each scale. For example, the plotted text height of 1/8″ is drawn at the same height (.25″) in AutoCAD on a 1/2″ = 1″ scale drawing, regardless of the sheet size.

Figure 12-4.   Common scales and their drawing limits, text height, scale factors, and linetype scales.

	Paper size	Approx. drawing area	Scale	Limits	Plotted text height (inches)		Scale factor	Ltscale
					1/8	1/4		
Mechanical	11 × 8.5	9 × 7	2″ = 1″ 3/4″ = 1″ 1/2″ = 1″ 1/4″ = 1″	4.5″ × 3.5″ 12″ × 9.33″ 18″ × 14″ 36″ × 28″	.0625 .167 .25 .5	.125 .33 .5 1.0	.5 1.33 2 4	.25 .67 1 2
	17 × 11	15 × 10	2″ = 1″ 3/4″ = 1″ 1/2″ = 1″ 1/4″ = 1″	7.5″ × 5″ 20″ × 13.33″ 30″ × 20″ 60″ × 40″				
	22 × 17	20 × 15	2″ = 1″ 3/4″ = 1″ 1/2″ = 1″ 1/4″ = 1″	10″ × 7.5″ 26.67″ × 20″ 40″ × 30″ 80″ × 60″				
	34 × 22	32 × 30	2″ = 1″ 3/4″ = 1″ 1/2″ = 1″ 1/4″ = 1″	16″ × 10″ 42.67″ × 26.67″ 64″ × 40″ 128″ × 80″				
	44 × 34	42 × 32	2″ = 1″ 3/4″ = 1″ 1/2″ = 1″ 1/4″ = 1″	21″ × 16″ 56″ × 42.67″ 84″ × 64″ 168″ × 128″				

	Paper size	Approx. drawing area	Scale	Limits	Plotted text height (inches)		Scale factor	Ltscale
					1/8	1/4		
Architectural	11 × 8.5	9 × 7	1″ = 1′-0″ 1/2″ = 1′-0″ 1/4″ = 1′-0″ 1/8″ = 1′-0″	9′ × 7′ 18′ × 14′ 36′ × 28′ 72′ × 56′	1.5 3.0 6.0 12.0	3.0 6.0 12.0 24.0	12 24 48 96	6 12 24 48
	17 × 11	15 × 10	1″ = 1′-0″ 1/2″ = 1′-0″ 1/4″ = 1′-0″ 1/8″ = 1′-0″	15′ × 10′ 30′ × 20′ 60′ × 40′ 120′ × 80′				
	22 × 17	20 × 15	1″ = 1′-0″ 1/2″ = 1′-0″ 1/4″ = 1′-0″ 1/8″ = 1′-0″	20′ × 15′ 40′ × 30′ 80′ × 60′ 160′ × 120′				
	34 × 22	32 × 20	1″ = 1′-0″ 1/2″ = 1′-0″ 1/4″ = 1′-0″ 1/8″ = 1′-0″	32′ × 20′ 64′ × 40′ 128′ × 80′ 256′ × 160′				
	44 × 34	42 × 32	1″ = 1′-0″ 1/2″ = 1′-0″ 1/4″ = 1′-0″ 1/8″ = 1′-0″	42′ × 32′ 84′ × 64′ 168′ × 128′ 336′ × 256′				

Figure 12-4.   Continued.

	Paper size	Approx. drawing area	Scale	Limits	Plotted text height (inches)		Scale factor	Ltscale
					1/8	1/4		
Civil Engineering	11 × 8.5	9 × 7	1″ = 10′	90′ × 70′	15	30	120	60
			1″ = 20′	180′ × 140′	30	60	240	120
			1″ = 30′	270′ × 210′	45	90	360	180
			1″ = 50′	450′ × 350′	75	150	600	300
	17 × 11	15 × 10	1″ = 10′	150′ × 100′				
			1″ = 20′	300′ × 200′				
			1″ = 30′	450′ × 300′				
			1″ = 50′	750′ × 500′				
	22 × 17	20 × 15	1″ = 10′	200′ × 150′				
			1″ = 20′	400′ × 300′				
			1″ = 30′	600′ × 450′				
			1″ = 50′	1000′ × 750′				
	34 × 22	32 × 20	1″ = 10′	320′ × 200′				
			1″ = 20′	640′ × 400′				
			1″ = 30′	960′ × 600′				
			1″ = 50′	1600′ × 1000′				
	44 × 34	42 × 32	1″ = 10′	420′ × 320′				
			1″ = 20′	840′ × 640′				
			1″ = 30′	1260′ × 960′				
			1″ = 50′	2100′ × 1600′				

Prepare the plotter

The last step you must take before plotting is to prepare the plotter. The exact procedure varies from one plotter model to the next, but the basic procedure is the same. After setting the plotter specifications, AutoCAD displays the space available for plotting and begins the plot:

Effective plotting area: (xx) wide by (yy) high

These are actual dimensions of the current plotting area. Before you press ENTER at the scale prompt, there are several items you should check.
- Plotter is plugged in.
- Plotter cable to computer is secure.
- Pen carousel is loaded and secure or pen is in plotter arm.
- Pens of proper color and thickness are in correct locations in pen carousel or rack.
- Paper is properly loaded in plotter and paper grips or clamps are in place.
- Plotter area is clear for unblocked paper movement.

PROFESSIONAL TIP

    You can stop a plot in progress at any time by canceling with CTRL+C. Keep in mind that it may take awhile for some plotters to terminate the plot, depending on the amount of the drawing file that has already been sent to the plotter.

USING THE PLOT CONFIGURATION DIALOG BOX   AUG 10

The previous discussion had the CMDDIA variable set to 0 so the PLOT command settings could be issued at the keyboard. When CMDDIA is set to 1, the "Plot Configuration" dialog box can be used. It is displayed when you pick Print… from the File pull-down menu, Print in the File Screen menu, or type PLOT at the Command: prompt. See Figure 12-5.

Figure 12-5.   Plot parameters can be specified in the "Plot Configuration" dialog box.

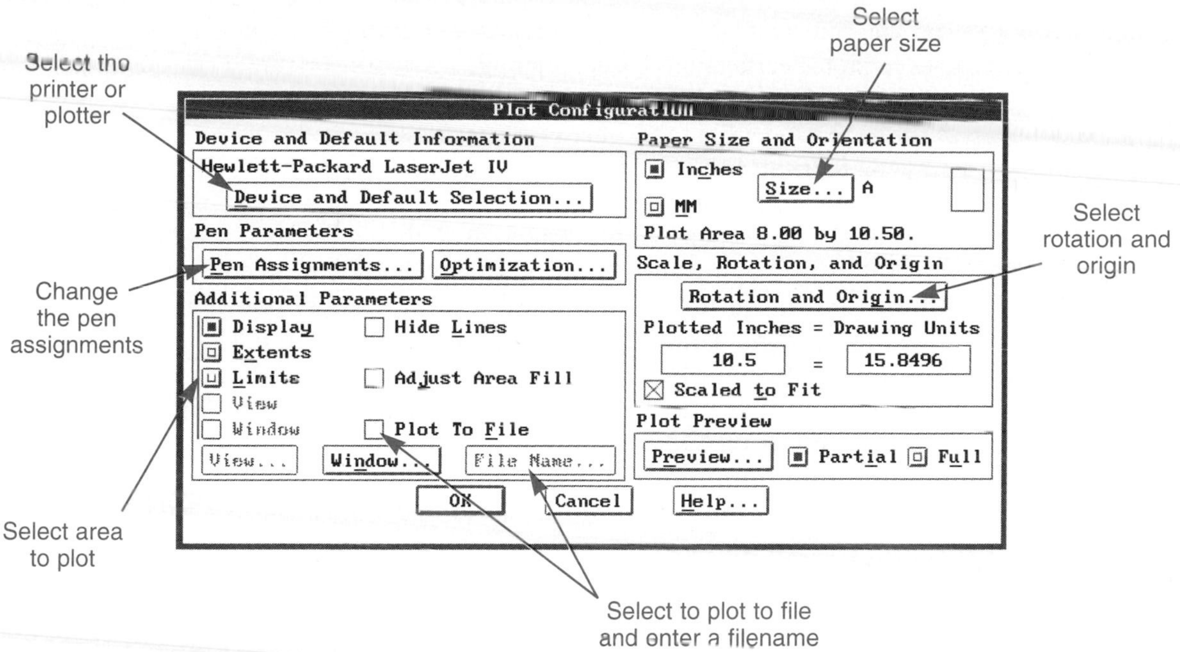

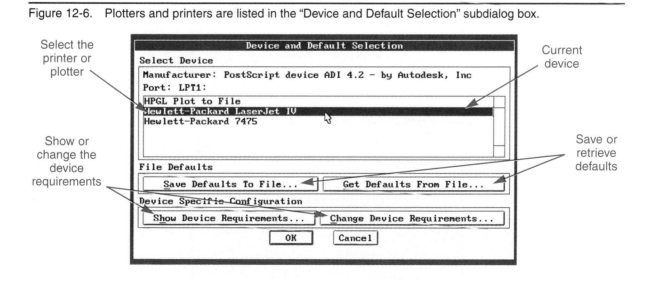

Device and default selection

Pick the Device and Default Selection... button in the upper-left to access the "Device and Default Selection" subdialog box shown in Figure 12-6. You can use this dialog box to review or change any of the printer or plotter specifications. The current device is highlighted in the Select Device area. When additional devices are displayed, you can make a different one current by picking it from the list. The Hewlett-Packard Laserjet IV is being selected in the example shown in Figure 12-6. Add printers and plotters to the list with the CONFIG command's Configure plotter option and choose the Add a plotter configuration selection.

Figure 12-6.   Plotters and printers are listed in the "Device and Default Selection" subdialog box.

The File Defaults area of the "Device and Default Selection" subdialog box provides you with the Save Defaults to File… and Get Defaults from File… buttons. These are called Plot Configuration Parameters (PCP) files. You can create a PCP file for a number of purposes including:
- Making changes to plot specifications before plotting.
- Making plot files for different drawing types.
- Making a plot file for each configured plotter or printer.
- Setting up a drawing to be plotted in a variety of formats.
- Giving a plot file to another person or company.

Each of the values that you set in the "Plot Configuration" dialog box is saved in the PCP file. This means that you can set values for individual prototype drawings. Then, when a prototype is used to construct a new drawing, you only have to retrieve a PCP file, then plot the drawing without making any additional changes to the plotting parameters. Pick the Save Defaults to File… button to save a PCP file. Select the directory or drive in which to save the file and enter the file name as shown in the "Save to File" subdialog box in Figure 12-7A. To get a previously saved PCP file, pick the Get Defaults from File… button. This displays the "Obtain from File" subdialog box shown in Figure 12-7B. If everything is fine with the PCP file you pick, then AutoCAD gives the message "Plot configuration updated without error" in the lower-left corner of the "Device and Default Selection" subdialog box. If there is an error in the PCP file you select, AutoCAD issues an "Error Information on File Defaults" dialog box. Pick the Create Error File button to make an error file (.ERR extension) that can be used to correct the PCP file.

Figure 12-7.   A–The PCP (Plot Configuration Parameters) "Save to File" subdialog box. B–Load a PCP file using the "Obtain from File" subdialog box.

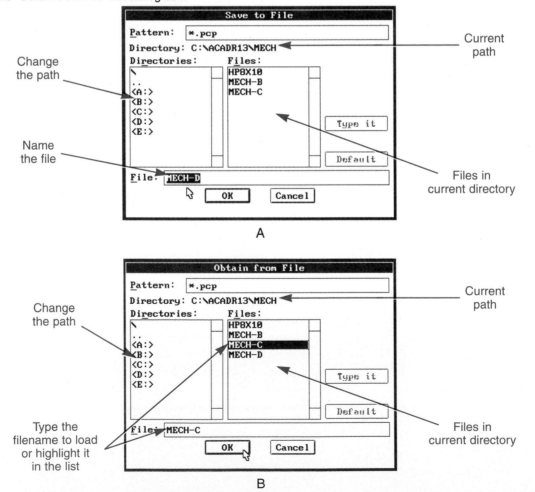

Use the Device Specific Configuration buttons to review or change your printer or plotter settings. The Show Device Requirements… button accesses a dialog box of the same name. Check the current device settings and pick OK when you are satisfied. See Figure 12-8A. Make changes by picking the Change Device Requirements… button. This displays the consecutive subdialog boxes shown in Figure 12-8B through D. Change the current setting in the edit box and pick OK to continue. The content and the number of dialog boxes displayed is a function of the currently configured plotter or printer.

Figure 12-8.   A–The "Show Device Requirements" subdialog box. Device settings can be changed with the "Change Device Requirements" subdialog boxes. B–Changing the paper tray. C–Changing the printer resolution. D–Changing the number of copies plotted.

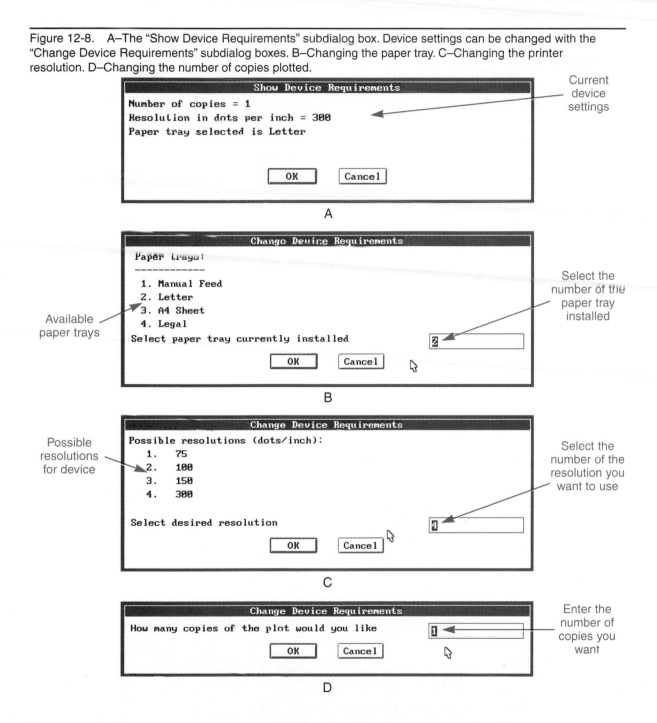

Pen parameters

Using the "Plot Configuration" dialog box you can set pen parameters based on your drawing standards and the type of printer/plotter you are using. To do this, pick the Pen Assignments… button to get the "Pen Assignments" subdialog box. When you highlight a pen assignment by picking it, the values are displayed in the Modify Values edit boxes.

AutoCAD plots drawings based on the color of the entity and the pen number assigned to that color. The default settings for colors and pen numbers are shown in Figure 12-9A. If you were to leave these values unchanged, AutoCAD would plot all of the colors of your drawing with different pens. The first seven colors listed in the "Pen Assignments" dialog box are:

1 red
2 yellow
3 green
4 cyan
5 blue
6 magenta
7 white (or black)

You can see from the settings in the dialog box that color 4 will be plotted with the number 4 pen.

It is more efficient to plot your drawings using a minimum number of pens, unless it is important that you plot in color. Make changes in the edit boxes as needed. Pick a selection to highlight it, and its values are listed in the Modify Values area. Pick the value you need to change and type a new one. The pen assignments shown in Figure 12-9B have been changed, and represent an efficient use of resources. All of the colors 1 through 6 are used for lines such as hidden, center, dimension, text, and hatching, and are plotted with pen number 1 which is thin. Color number 7 is used for object lines and must be set to the proper ANSI thickness of .032 inches. Therefore pen number 2 is used. Now only two pens are used to plot the drawing.

Figure 12-9.   The "Pen Assignments" subdialog box enables you to fine-tune the plotter pen specifications. A–These are the default pen settings. B–These settings have been modified so that all colors except white will be plotted with pen 1.

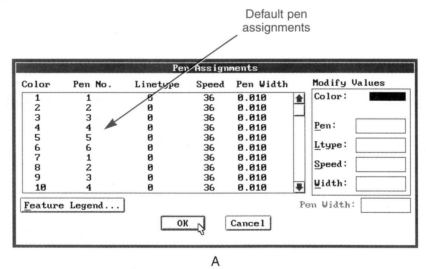

A

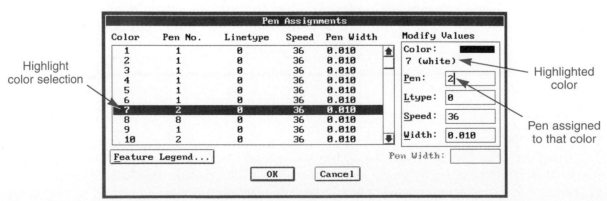

B

A variety of pen styles and widths are available for pen plotters. Some are similar to technical ink pens, and others have fiber or ceramic tips. If your pen plotter is capable of handling a variety of pen widths, you will not need to change the pen width in the "Pen Assignments" subdialog box. Just insert the correct pen in the appropriate numbered pen position of your plotter.

Output devices such as laser and inkjet printers do not use pens. But you can assign pen widths to the color numbers used in your drawing. The colors are then printed with the appropriate line widths even though your printer does not use pens.

Linetypes and Speed can be changed in the "Pen Assignments" subdialog box. You will seldom have to change these settings because most often they are controlled by the plotter. Note also the Feature Legend... button in the lower-left corner of the "Pen Assignments" subdialog box. This displays the Feature Legend subdialog box shown in Figure 12-10. This shows a list of linetypes that are generated by the plotter, and are different from linetypes created in your drawing. Entities drawn with linetypes other than continuous in AutoCAD will plot correctly and should not have to be changed in the "Pen Assignments" subdialog box.

Figure 12-10. The "Feature Legend" subdialog box displays the linetypes generated by the plotter, not AutoCAD.

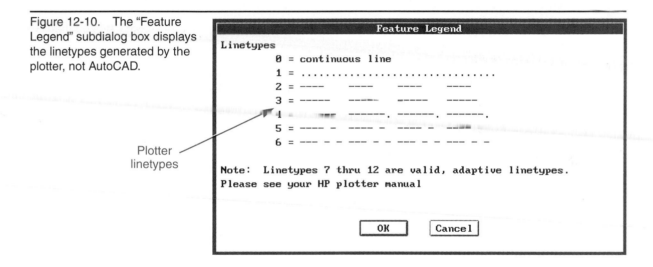

Plotter linetypes

PROFESSIONAL TIP

In the unlikely event that you do need to adjust pen speeds, they should be set according to the type of paper or film you are using. In addition, you should consider the type of pen such as liquid ink or felt tip, and the lines or text to be plotted. A fast pen speed may not draw quality lines and text. Set a slower pen speed to improve the plot quality.

Most plotters generate the required linetypes for AutoCAD drawings. Therefore, the plotter-generated linetypes should remain set as continuous (0) in the "Pen Assignments" subdialog box. This ensures that the lines in your drawing are properly plotted.

The Optimization... button displays the "Optimizing Pen Motion" subdialog box. This subdialog box contains check boxes that let you control the efficiency of pen movement. By default, AutoCAD minimizes wasted pen motion with the check boxes picked in Figure 12-11. With the exception of the No optimization check box, each consecutive check box increases optimization. Picking a higher level option automatically checks all previous options. These options may not be available if you are using a non-pen plotter such as a dot-matrix printer, since they have no affect on these output devices.

Figure 12-11.   The "Optimizing Pen Motion" subdialog box. Each box checked will increase the optimization. Select No optimization if you don't want AutoCAD to optimize the plot.

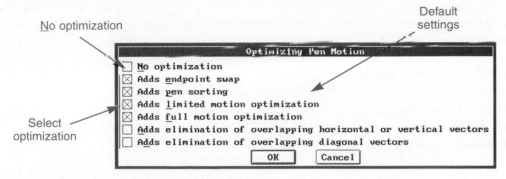

PROFESSIONAL TIP

You need to experiment with your plotter to be sure that optimization is an asset. In most cases, it reduces plotting time, but it may cause problems such as unnecessary pen changes.

Check plots are often created using roller-ball (ball-point) pens, which do not produce the uniform line thickness of a technical pen, but can be reliable at speeds approaching 36 inches per second (in./sec). Standard technical style plotter pens produce the best quality, but can become unreliable beyond 16 to 20 in./sec. Felt-tip plotter pens are usually used for film of transparencies, and work best at speeds below 12 in./sec for this type of media.

Choosing what to plot

Look at the Additional Parameters area in the "Plot Configuration" dialog box, Figure 12-12. After selecting the appropriate plotting device and setting pen assignments, you must select the portion of the drawing you want to plot. Each of the options are discussed on the second page of this chapter, but let's review them here briefly.

Figure 12-12.   The Additional Parameters area of the "Plot Configuration" dialog box is shown here highlighted.

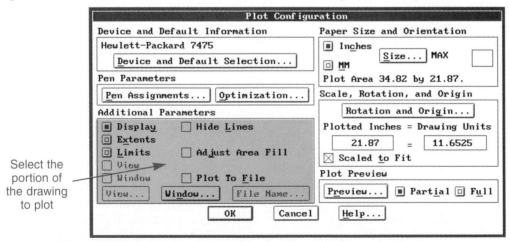

- **Display.** Plots the current screen display.
- **Extents.** Plots only that area of the drawing in which objects (entities) are drawn.
- **Limits.** Plots everything inside the drawing limits.
- **View.** Plots views saved with the VIEW command. To specify a view name pick the View… button. This displays the "View Name" subdialog box. Select the view name to be plotted and pick OK. You can plot any named view regardless of the current screen display.

- **Window.** This item is greyed-out until you pick the Window... button that displays the "Window Selection" subdialog box as shown in Figure 12-13. You must define two diagonal corners around the area to be plotted. You can enter the two diagonal corners of the window box by typing the X, Y coordinates in the First Corner and Other Corner edit boxes. If you want to define the window box with your pointing device, select the Pick ⟨ button at the upper-left of the dialog box. The graphics screen is displayed and you can pick the two window corners. After picking the second corner, the "Window Selection" subdialog box returns. Pick OK to return to the "Plot Configuration" dialog box.

Pick the Hide Lines check box if you want to plot a 3-D drawing with hidden lines removed. This function works the same as the HIDE command. Note that plotting takes a little longer when removing hidden lines since AutoCAD must calculate the lines to be removed.

Figure 12-13. Specify a plot window using the "Window Selection" subdialog box. Enter coordinates or pick a new window.

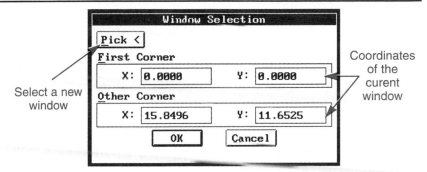

Select a new window

Coordinates of the current window

Pick the Adjust Area Fill check box if you want areas such as polylines and solids filled completely. These precise plots are a result of the pen being adjusted inside the boundary by one-half the pen width. When this is inactive, the pen plots at the center of the boundary, which is fine for most applications, but may be poor in printed circuit board artwork.

Creating a plot file

If you want to send the plot setup to a file, pick the Plot to File check box. This activates the File Name... button that is normally grayed-out. Picking this button displays the "Create Plot File" subdialog box shown in Figure 12-14. A plot file is automatically given a .PLT file extension, and assumes the name of the current drawing unless you supply a different one. If the current drawing is not named, and you neglect to name the plot file, it is saved with the name of unnamed.plt. Enter the appropriate name in the File: text box and pick OK to return to the "Plot Configuration" dialog box. Pick OK again to close the dialog and create the plot file. You are prompted on the Command: line when the file is complete.

Figure 12-14. The "Create Plot File" subdialog box. Select a destination and name the file.

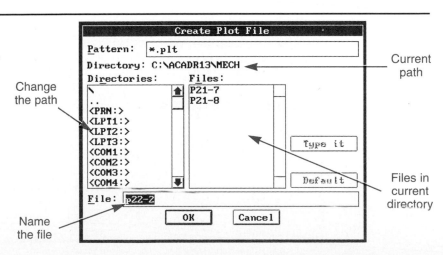

Change the path

Name the file

Current path

Files in current directory

Using PLT files is good practice if you have only one office or class computer connected to a plotter, or if your office or school uses a plot spooler. The plot spooler is cabled to a plotter and is basically a "smart" disk drive with memory. It reads the PLT file from disk and sends the drawing data to the plotter. A plot spooler removes the need of having a computer cabled to the plotter. Plot files (.PLT extension) can also be used by plot spooling software in network systems. Plot spooling software accepts the output of the PLOT command from all workstations that are attached to the network. Each plot file is printed or plotted by the specified hardcopy device in the order in which it is received. When multiple plots are sent to the spooling software, a lineup, or *queue,* is created, and each plot file is handled by its order in the queue.

Paper size and orientation

The upper-right area of the "Plot Configuration" dialog box shown in Figure 12-15 controls the paper size and orientation. This has the same application as input at the prompt line discussed earlier in this chapter. Pick either the Inches or the MM radio button to make inches or millimeters the units for all plot specifications.

Figure 12-15.   The Paper Size and Orientation area of the "Plot Configuration" dialog box is shown here highlighted.

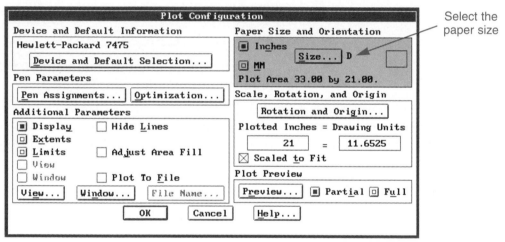

Pick the Size... button to access the "Paper Size" subdialog box. Pick the desired standard size such as D-size as shown in Figure 12-16, or enter your own size specifications in one of the USER Width and Height edit boxes. If you enter a user size, be sure not to exceed the maximum (MAX) size

Figure 12-16.   All available sheet sizes are listed in the "Paper Size" subdialog box. Select the sheet size you want to use.

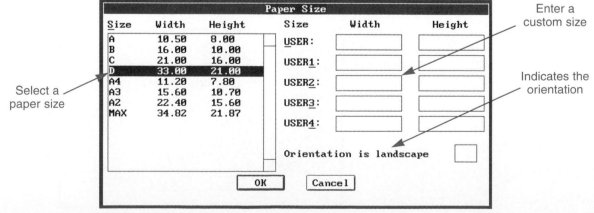

shown in the list. This is the largest size that your plotter can handle, and these sizes will vary between printer and plotter manufacturers. Also indicated is the orientation, either landscape or portrait.

The paper orientation icon is a rectangle on the right side of the "Paper Size" subdialog box and also appears in the "Plot Configuration" dialog box, as shown in Figure 12-17. This icon changes depending on the natural orientation of the paper in the current plotting device.

Figure 12-17. The orientation of the paper you selected is shown as an icon (highlighted here). The portrait icon (shown here) is taller than it is wide. The landscape icon is wider than it is tall.

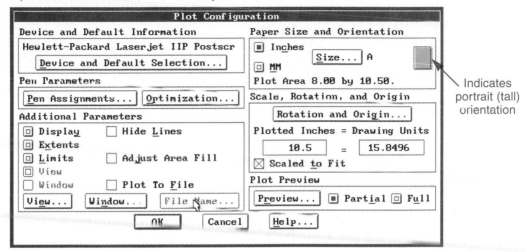

Scale, rotation, and origin

The familiar items Scale, Rotation, and Origin are found on the right side of the "Plot Configuration" dialog box. Pick the Rotation and Origin... button to access the "Plot Rotation and Origin" subdialog box shown in Figure 12-18. The Plot Rotation area has radio buttons for 0, 90, 180, and 270 degree rotation settings. The Plot Origin section has edit boxes for you to specify desired X and Y plot origin settings. Pick OK when done.

Figure 12-18. The "Plot Rotation and Origin" subdialog box can be used to change the origin or the rotation of the plot.

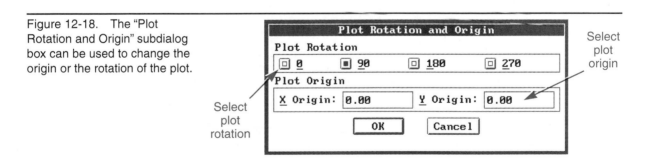

The Plotted Inches = Drawing Units edit boxes (or Plotted MM = Drawing Units edit boxes if using metric units) let you set the plot scale as outlined earlier in this chapter. For example, if you are making an architectural drawing that scales 1/4″ = 1′-0″, then the scale factor is 48. For this scale factor, set the Plotted Inches to 1 and Drawing Units to 48 as shown in Figure 12-19.

Pick the Scaled to Fit check box if you want AutoCAD to automatically adjust your drawing to fit on the paper.

Figure 12-19.   The plotting scale is shown in the Plotted Inches = Drawing Units edit boxes. Select Scale to Fit if you want AutoCAD to automatically fit the drawing onto your paper.

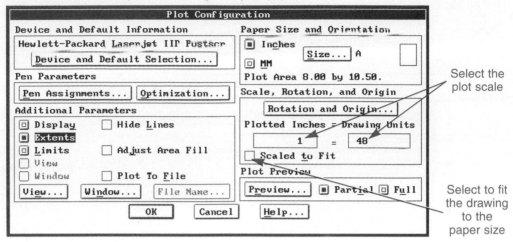

Preview plot

The plot preview feature allows you to check the layout of your drawing on the paper before plotting or printing. The Plot Preview area is located in the lower-right corner of the "Plot Configuration" dialog box, Figure 12-20. It often takes a long time to plot a drawing. The Plot Preview option lets you save material and valuable plot time. The Partial and Full preview options are each controlled by a radio button.

Figure 12-20.   The Plot Preview area of the "Plot Configuration" dialog box is shown highlighted here. Select the type of preview and the Preview… button to preview the plot.

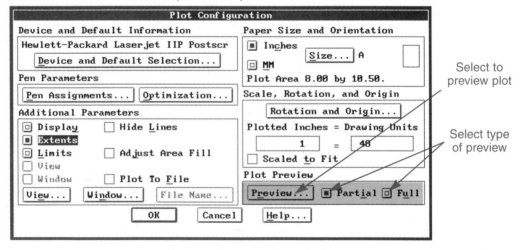

When the Partial radio button is active and you pick the Preview… button, AutoCAD quickly displays the "Preview Effective Plotting Area" subdialog box shown in Figure 12-21. The red outline is the paper size, and the paper dimensions are given below for reference. The area the image occupies is called the *effective area*. The effective area dimensions are noted and the blue outline of this area is provided within the paper size. AutoCAD displays a red and blue dashed line when the effective area and the paper size are the same. While this shows you how the drawing compares to the paper size, the final plot depends on how the printer or plotter is set up.

Figure 12-21.   Selecting the P<u>r</u>eview... button when Part<u>i</u>al is checked displays the "Preview Effective Plotting Area" subdialog box. The red line indicates the paper size. The blue line indicates the plotting area.

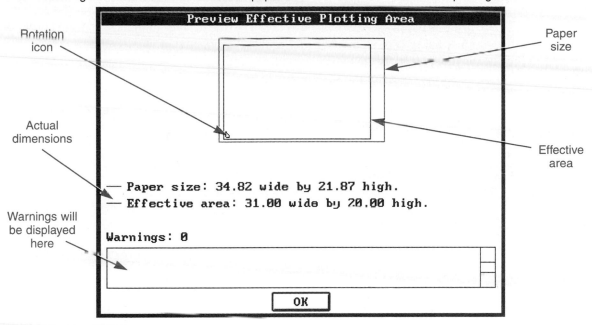

AutoCAD gives you messages in the Warnings: box if there is something wrong with the relationship of the display and the paper. The warnings give you an opportunity to make corrections and then preview the plot again. These are the types of warnings you might expect:

- Effective area too small to display.
- Origin forced effective area off display.
- Plotting area exceeds paper maximum.

Notice the small symbol in the lower-left corner of the effective area in Figure 12-21. This is called the *rotation icon*. The rotation icon in the lower-left corner represents the 0 default rotation angle. The icon is in the upper-left corner when the rotation is 90°, the right corner for 180° rotation, and in the lower-right corner for a 270° rotation. Figure 12-22 clearly shows the rotation icon placement.

Figure 12-22.   The rotation icon as it appears in each rotation angle selection.

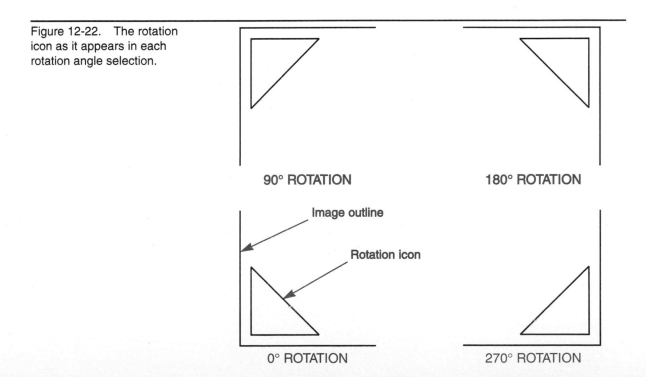

Pick the Full radio button followed by picking the Preview… button if you want a full preview. The full preview takes more time, but it displays the drawing on the screen as it will actually appear on paper. This takes the same amount of time as a drawing regeneration, which means that the drawing size determines how fast this happens. AutoCAD displays a 0-100% meter in the lower-right corner of the "Plot Configuration" dialog box as the full plot preview is generated. The graphics screen then returns with the drawing displayed inside the paper outline. At the same time, there is a "Plot Preview" dialog box positioned near the center of the screen. See Figure 12-23. If this dialog obscures the drawing, just move the cursor arrow to the title bar at the top of the dialog box, and pick and hold to move the dialog box to a desired location. Pick the End Preview button to return to the "Plot Configuration" dialog box.

Figure 12-23.   The "Plot Preview" subdialog box is displayed when a full preview is selected.

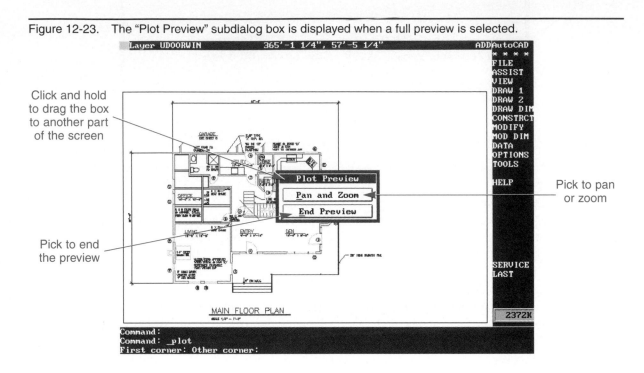

The full preview also allows you to examine details on the drawing or evaluate how a multiview arrangement fits together by picking the Pan and Zoom button. When you first pick the Pan and Zoom button, you get a small view box with an X inside for panning, as shown in Figure 12-24A. This is similar to the ZOOM command's Dynamic option discussed in Chapter 10. Move the pan view box anywhere you want. Pressing the pick button changes the image to a zoom view box. The zoom box image has an arrow on the right side as shown in Figure 12-24B.

Figure 12-24.   The pan and zoom boxes enable you to accurately view areas of the drawing during full preview.

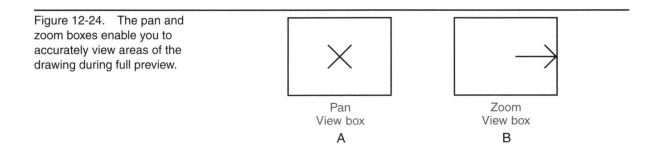

Now you can make the zoom box bigger by moving the arrow to the right, or smaller by moving to the left. The box can be moved vertically without changing its size. Press ENTER when you have the size and position of the pan/zoom box where you want it. This re-displays the drawing at the pan location and zoom scale that you selected. Figure 12-25 shows the result of a selective pan and zoom on the drawing shown in Figure 12-23 to review some specific information on the drawing. Also notice the "Plot Preview" subdialog box has changed and now has a Zoom Previous button. Pick this button to return to the original full preview representation, or pick End Preview to return to the "Plot Configuration" dialog box.

Figure 12-25.   The Zoom Previous button appears after picking a pan and zoom. Note the position of the "Plot Preview" subdialog box on the screen.

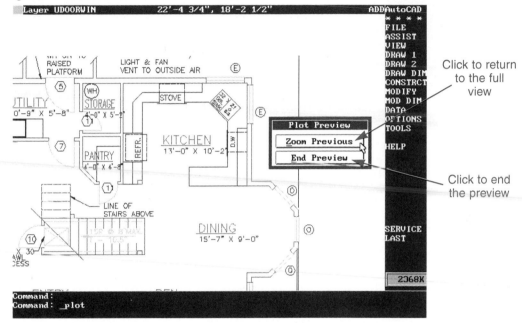

PLOTTING HINTS

Plotting can slow down productivity in an office or a classroom if not done efficiently. Establish and adhere to a system for using the plotter. For a company, this might involve adding a special night shift that plots drawings when computer operators are not working. In a school, a student may be assigned to plot drawings, or specific times can be set aside for the task. In any situation, instruct all drafters, engineers, and other plotter users of the proper operating procedures. Post these in strategic locations.

Planning your plots

Planning is again the key word when dealing with plots. In the same way you planned the drawing, you must plan the plot. A few items to consider when planning are:

✓ Size and type of plotting media, such as bond paper, vellum, or polyester film.
✓ Type of title block.
✓ Location and scale of multiple views.
✓ Origin location.
✓ Scale of the drawing.
✓ Color, thickness, and types of pens to be used.
✓ Speed of pens.
✓ Orientation of 3-D views.
✓ Portion to be plotted: view, window, display, limits, or extents.

This is only a sample of decisions that should be made before you even walk up to the plotter. Remember, the plotter is the funnel through which all the drawings must go before they are evaluated, approved, and sent to production or the client. When a bottleneck develops at the plotter, production can suffer. The time savings of a CAD system can be drastically reduced.

Whether a school or business, your organization may benefit from the creation of a plotting request form. An example is shown in Figure 12-26. This sample is used in one school's CAD lab. Its purpose is to require AutoCAD users to prepare as much as possible before thinking about a plot. Use this form or develop one of your own to increase your plotting efficiency.

Figure 12-26.   An example of a plotting request form.

PLOT REQUEST

REQUESTED BY:			DATE:	

DATE REQUIRED:

CAD STATION NUMBER:	1.	3.	5.	7	9.
	2.	4.	6.	8.	10.

SCALE: ☐1=1   ☐1=12   ☐1=24   ☐1=32   ☐1=48
☐1=96   ☐FIT   ☐OTHER (   )

AREA OF DWG. TO PLOT:
☐DISPLAY   ☐EXTENTS   ☐LIMITS
☐VIEW   ☐WINDOW

TYPE OF PLOT & PAPER SIZE:

CALCOMP:	☐D–SIZE ☐OTHER ( )
JDL:	☐D REDUCED TO C–SIZE ☐B–SIZE ☐OTHER ( )
H–P:	☐D REDUCED TO B–SIZE ☐B–SIZE ☐OTHER ( )
LASER:	☐LANDSCAPE ☐PORTRAIT

PLOT WRITTEN TO FILE:	☐NO ☐YES

PLOTTED BY:	DATE:

PROFESSIONAL TIP

Use preprinted borders and title blocks whenever possible. Use attributes in a block for the information in the title block that will change with each drawing. This block can be inserted into any drawing or plotted separately before or after the drawing. This eliminates drawing borders and title blocks each time.

The creation and use of blocks and attributes is discussed in detail in Chapters 25 and 27 respectively. If you develop title blocks using text entities now, you can always update them later to take advantage of the more efficient use of blocks and attributes.

Establish a plotting center

Many companies and schools have discovered the problems associated with the plotting process. One solution is the creation of a plotting center. A person or department is responsible for plotting drawings and supervising plotter use. The type of center or procedure established depends on the number of plotters available. Other factors include the number of computers serving the plotters, the numbers of computer users, network usage, office space available, and nature of the business.

The plotting center may be a special room with a dedicated computer, a terminal attached to the plotter, or a plot spooler cabled to a plotter. Disks are sent here at prearranged times or left in a "plot request" box with a plot form attached. Large companies that produce many drawings usually have a reproduction department. One or more people are responsible for making prints, copies, or photos. It is unproductive in a large office or classroom to allow all computer users to run their own plots.

Network users can operate a plotting center even more efficiently. Here plot files are created and used by a plot spooler. A plot spooler is a program that creates a plot queue (list). Plots are made as fast as paper can be loaded in the plotter. The network or spooler may also have a method for leaving instructions for the person doing the actual plotting. These instructions might replace the items that would normally be listed on a plot request form.

Establish plotting times in a classroom

In an educational environment, set a schedule for plot times. Set aside a time for plotting and have an instructor or lab assistant available to answer questions and solve problems. Options include:
- ✓ Plot at the end of the class or day.
- ✓ Plot once a week.
- ✓ Have a lab assistant make plots during the evening.
- ✓ Plot only those drawings absolutely necessary during work or class hours. This might occur during final evaluation at the end of the term. Instructors should evaluate drawings on disk whenever possible.

Eliminate unnecessary plots

A potential element in using computers for design and manufacturing is the elimination of paper drawings. This is a difficult concept for many people to grasp, mainly because there is "nothing" to grasp. When design data proceeds directly to manufacturing, there is no paper drawing to approve, touch, mark on, or keep lying around.

When you create plots, a bottleneck is introduced into the classroom or production environment, decreasing productivity. The easiest way to eliminate the problems associated with plotting is to eliminate plotting. Simply don't plot. Make plots *only* when absolutely necessary. This results in time and money savings. A few additional suggestions include:
- ✓ Obtain approvals of designs while the drawings are on the screen. This procedure is good in theory, but for most people it is easier to check a paper print of a drawing for errors.
- ✓ Transfer files or disks for the checker's comments or supervisor's input on layout or designs.
- ✓ Create a special layer with a unique color for markups. Freeze or erase this layer when finally making a plot.
- ✓ Use a "redlining" software package that enables the checker to review the drawing and apply markups to it without using AutoCAD.
- ✓ Classroom instructors should check drawings on disk at the computer screen. Use special layer for instructor comments.
- ✓ Make quick prints with a printer whenever check prints are sufficient.
- ✓ Avoid making plots for backups. Rather, save your drawing files in three different locations such as: hard disk, flexible disk at workstation, and flexible disk at another location. These may also be supplemented with a backup on tape cartridges or optical disks.

If you must plot...

Industry still exists on a paper-based system. Therefore, it is important that plotters are used efficiently–that means using the plotter only for what is required. Here are a few hints for doing just that.
- ✓ Ask yourself, "Do I *really* need a plot?" If the answer is an unqualified YES, then proceed.
- ✓ Plan your plot!
- ✓ Pick the least busy time to make the plot.
- ✓ If more than one plotter is available, use the smallest, least complex model.
- ✓ Select the smallest piece of paper possible.
- ✓ Use the lowest quality paper possible. Select bond for check plots or vellum or polyester film for final plots.

✓ Decide on only one color and thickness of pen to make the plot.

✓ Use the most inexpensive pen possible. Obtain a fiber tip or disposable pen for check plots. Choose a wet ink, steel, jewel, or ceramic tip pen only for final plots on vellum or polyester film.

✓ Enter the fastest pen speed that will still achieve quality without the pen skipping.

✓ Use a continuous linetype when possible. Hidden and center linetypes increase plot time significantly, and cause pen wear. This will not be as much of a factor with penless plotters such as laser and inkjet.

Producing quality plots

The time comes when you must plot the highest quality drawing for reproduction, evaluation, or client use. Then, use your plotter in a manner that does the job right the first time. Keep in mind these points before making that final plot.

✓ If you have several plotters, choose the one that will produce the quality of print you need. Select the right tool for the job.

✓ Choose the paper size appropriate for the drawing.

✓ Select the type of plotting media best suited for the application (drafting film for good reproduction; bond for check prints).

✓ Select the type of pen to achieve the results you need (wet ink for good reproduction; fiber or plastic tip for check prints).

✓ Set pen speeds slow enough to produce good lines without skipping.

✓ Use the proper ink for your climate.

Plotter hygiene

Computer lab hygiene, discussed in Chapter 1, extends to plotters as well. It is true that when properly maintained and cleaned, mechanical equipment works longer, more efficiently, and develops fewer problems. Here are a few suggestions for dealing with plotters and plotter supplies.

✓ Keep the plotter clean. Purchase a plastic or cloth dustcover if possible. Dust or vacuum it regularly. Clean the grit wheels with a stiff bristle brush (usually provided by manufacturer). Use pressurized air to clean internal parts.

✓ Service as soon as problems develop.

✓ Lock wheels on plotters that roll.

✓ Locate plotters out of high traffic areas. A separate room is best.

✓ Properly instruct all plotter users on machine operation.

✓ Have regular plotter operation update sessions.

✓ Assign people on rotating basis to regularly clean the plotter and plotting center, if a specific person is not in charge of plotting duties.

✓ Keep plotter supplies, paper, pens, attachments, in a storage area near the plotter.

✓ Adjust the humidity of the plotter room to suit the media used, or purchase plotter media that works best in the temperature and humidity of the plotter room.

✓ Avoid using wrinkled or creased paper or film in the plotter.

CHAPTER TEST

Write your answers in the spaces provided.

1. What command is used to generate paper copies of your drawings? _____

2. What system variable switches use of the PLOT command from dialog box to Command: line prompts? _____
   _____

3. To what value should you set the system variable in Question 2 to activate Command: line prompts for the PLOT command? _____
   _____

4. List the different displays of a drawing you can select to plot in response to the What to plot: prompt. _____
   _____

5. To change the plotter defaults that are displayed by the PLOT command, you must _____
   _____.

6. Define a "plot file" and explain how it is used. _____
   _____
   _____

7. Define a "plot queue." _____
   _____

8. Explain when you would rotate a plot 90° clockwise. _____
   _____

9. What would you enter at the Plot scale: prompt to make the plotted drawing twice the size of the softcopy drawing? _____

10. What would you enter at the Plot scale: prompt to enter a scale of 1/4″ = 1′-0″? _____
    _____

11. Name the system variable that controls the display of any dialog box. _____
    _____

12. How do you stop a plot in progress? _____

13. Name the pull-down menu where the PLOT command is found. _____

14. How do you add several printers or plotters to the Select Device area of the "Device and Default Selection" dialog box? _____
    _____

15. What is a PCP file? _____

16. How do you save a plot file named PLOT1 to your floppy disk? _____
    _____
    _____

17. How do you set pen assignments in a dialog box? _____
    _____
    _____

18. Identify the two types of paper orientation. _____

19. Specify the radio button that is picked to make millimeters the units for all plot specifications.

    _____

20. List an advantage of the Partial plot preview format._____

21. Enter the rotation indicated by the following rotation icon representations as presented in the Partial plot preview format.

Image outline

Rotation icon

A. _____   B. _____   C. _____   D. _____

22. Cite at least two advantages of the Full plot preview format. _____

    _____

    _____

23. Identify at least one disadvantage of the Full plot preview format. _____

    _____

24. Enter the name of symbols below that are used in the Pan and Zoom application of the Full plot preview format.

A. _____   B. _____

25. Explain the function of the Pan and Zoom boxes in the Full plot preview format. _____

    _____

    _____

    _____

    _____

DRAWING PROBLEMS

1. Open one of your drawings from an earlier chapter. Obtain a print of the drawing on your printer.

2. Use the same drawing from Problem 1 and generate two plots on your printer. The first should be rotated 90° and the second plot should not be rotated.

3. Open one of your detailed drawings from a previous chapter. Use the PLOT command to generate a B-size half-scale drawing of the limits. Use MVIEW to create viewports. Set zoom magnification appropriately.

4. Plot the same drawing used in Problem 3 on the appropriate size paper to give you a full-scale plot.

5. Plot the same drawing used in Problem 3 on B-size paper, but with a scale that will fit the entire drawing on the paper. Add a title block and border to the drawing before making the plots.

6. Open one of your drawings from Chapter 11. Plot the drawing on B-size paper using the Limits option. Use different color pens for each color in the drawing.

7. Zoom in on a portion of the drawing in Problem 6 and select the Display option. Rotate the plot 90° and fit it on the paper.

8. Using the same drawing from Problem 6, first be sure the entire drawing is displayed on the screen. Select PLOT and use the Window option. Window a detailed area of the drawing. Plot the drawing to fit the paper size chosen.

9. Plot a title block and border on a C-size sheet of paper. Put the name PLOT TEST next to Drawing Name: in the title block. Next, plot six different named views of problems from any previous chapters on a separate area of the paper.
   A. Determine the overall dimensions of the object before you plot.
   B. Determine the amount of paper space available for each object.
   C. Set the appropriate scale for each object so that it does not extend beyond the amount of space allotted to it.
   D. Use the appropriate plot format, such as Display, View, or Window.
   E. Use the Remove hidden lines option for one of the plots.
   F. Be sure to change the plot origin before plotting each object.

10. Open your most detailed dimensioned drawing. Generate a final plot with wet ink pens.
   A. Display the entire drawing on the screen.
   B. Load vellum or polyester film into the plotter.
   C. Insert wet ink pens into the pen holder or carousel. Use different pen widths if available.
   D. If you constructed the drawing on different layers, choose different color pens.
   E. Set pen speeds to achieve good quality lines. See the manufacturer's specifications for your particular brand of pen.
   F. Plot the drawing using the Limits or Extents option.

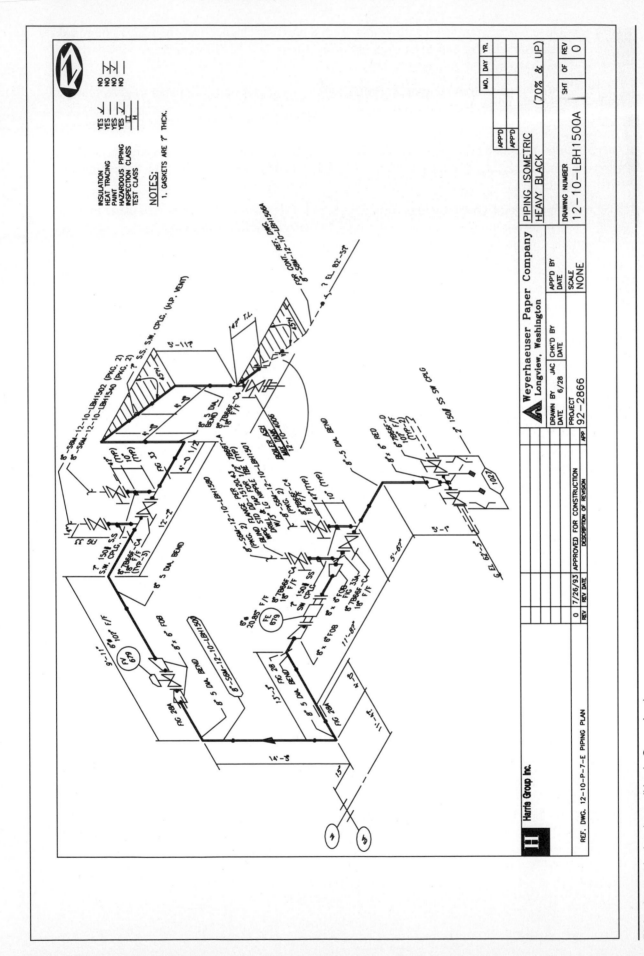

Piping isometric drawing.   (Harris Group Inc.)

Learning objectives

After completing this chapter, you will be able to:

- ❍ Draw chamfers and angled corners with the CHAMFER command.
- ❍ Use the FILLET command to draw fillets, rounds, and other rounded corners.
- ❍ Preset chamfer and fillet specifications.
- ❍ Remove a portion of a line, circle, or arc using the BREAK command.
- ❍ Relocate an object using the MOVE command.
- ❍ Use the TRIM, EXTEND, and LENGTHEN commands to edit an object.
- ❍ Use the CHANGE command to revise an existing object.
- ❍ Make single and multiple copies of existing objects using the COPY command.
- ❍ Draw a mirror image of an object.
- ❍ Change the angular position of an object using the ROTATE command.
- ❍ Use the ALIGN command to move and rotate an object simultaneously.
- ❍ Enlarge and reduce the size of an object using the SCALE command.
- ❍ Change the length and height of an object using the STRETCH command.
- ❍ Set the PICKAUTO, PICKFIRST, and GRIPS system variables to vary your selection techniques.
- ❍ Use the geometry calculator to edit drawings.
- ❍ Create selection sets and object groups.

This chapter explains commands and methods for changing a drawing. Editing and modifying a drawing used to take hours or sometimes days using manual drafting techniques. AutoCAD, however, makes the same editing tasks simpler and quicker. In Chapter 6 you learned how to draw and erase lines. The ERASE command is one of the most commonly used editing commands. You also learned how to select objects to erase by picking, or by using one of the other selection techniques such as a window, crossing box, or fence. The items you selected were referred to as a *selection set*.

The same selection methods and techniques may be used for the editing commands presented in this chapter. You will learn how to easily draw angled and rounded corners. You will also learn how to copy, move, rotate, or change the scale of an existing object. These commands are found in the CON-STRCT and MODIFY screen menus. You can also pick editing commands from the Modify or Construct pull-down menus. The editing commands discussed in this chapter are basically divided into two general groups–editing individual features of a drawing and editing major portions of a drawing. Commands typically used to edit individual features of a drawing are:

- • CHAMFER
- • FILLET
- • BREAK
- • TRIM
- • EXTEND
- • LENGTHEN

Even though you can edit individual features with the following commands, they are often used to edit entire drawings or major portions of a drawing. The commands discussed in the second section of this chapter are:

- MOVE
- COPY
- ROTATE
- MIRROR
- SCALE

- STRETCH
- CHANGE
- SELECT
- GROUP

DRAWING CHAMFERS

AUG 5

A *chamfer* in mechanical drafting is a small angled surface used to relieve a sharp corner. AutoCAD defines a "chamfer" as any angled corner on the drawing. The size of a chamfer is determined by its distance from the corner. A 45° chamfer is equidistant from the corner in each direction, Figure 13-1.

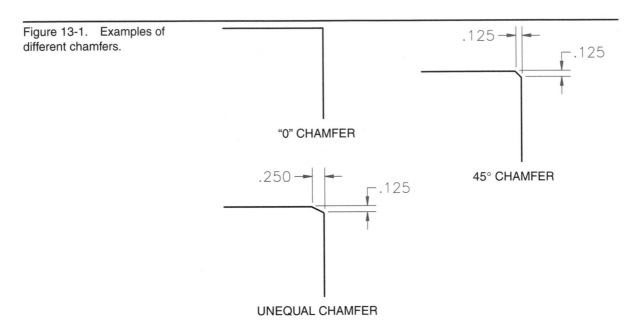

Figure 13-1.   Examples of different chamfers.

"0" CHAMFER

.125   .125

45° CHAMFER

.250   .125

UNEQUAL CHAMFER

Chamfers may be drawn between two lines which may or may not intersect. They are also used on polylines, xlines, and rays. Chamfers are drawn by typing CHAMFER at the Command: prompt, by picking Chamfer from the Construct pull-down menu, or by selecting Chamfer: from the CONSTRCT screen menu. The following shows the default values and the options that are available when you enter the CHAMFER command:

Command: **CHAMFER** ↵
(TRIM mode) Current chamfer Dist1 = 0.0, Dist2 = 0.0
Polyline/Distance/Angle/Trim/Method/⟨Select first line⟩:

The current settings are displayed for your reference. Chamfers are established with distances or a distance and angle. The default distances are 0 which is a corner without a chamfer. The following is a brief description of each CHAMFER option:

- **Polyline.** Use this option if you want to chamfer all of the eligible corners on a polyline. The term eligible means that if a chamfer distance is too large, the corner will not be chamfered and AutoCAD gives you a message such as "4 were too short."
- **Distances.** This option lets you set the chamfer distance for each line from the corner.
- **Angle.** This option uses a chamfer distance on the first selected line and applies a chamfer angle to determine the second line chamfer.

- **Trim.** Enter this to set the Trim mode. This means that if Trim is on, the selected lines are trimmed or extended as required from the corner before creating the chamfer line. If No trim is active, this means that the Trim mode is off. In this case, the selected lines are not trimmed or extended and only the chamfer line is added.
- **Method.** This sets the chamfer method to either Distances or Angle. This is a toggle and just sets the currently active chamfering method. Distance and Angle values can be set without affecting each other.

Setting the chamfer distance

The chamfer distance must be set before you can draw chamfers. The distances that you set remain in effect until changed. Most drafters set the chamfer distance as exact values, but you can also pick to points to set the distance. The chamfer distance is set like this:

Command: **CHAMFER** ↵
(TRIM mode) Current chamfer Dist1 = 0.0, Dist2 = 0.0
Polyline/Distance/Angle/Trim/Method/⟨Select first line⟩: **D** ↵
Enter first chamfer distance ⟨0⟩: *(specify a distance, **.25** for example, and press* ENTER*)*
Enter second chamfer distance ⟨0.25⟩: *(press* ENTER *for the current distance, or type a new value and press* ENTER*)*
Command:

Now you are ready to draw chamfers. Enter the CHAMFER command and select the first and second lines:

Command: **CHAMFER** ↵
(TRIM mode) Current chamfer Dist1 = 0.25, Dist2 = 0.25
Polyline/Distance/Angle/Trim/Method/⟨Select first line⟩: *(pick the first line)*
Select second line: *(pick the second line)*

After the lines are picked, AutoCAD automatically chamfers the corner. Even if the corners do not meet, AutoCAD extends the lines and chamfers the corners unless the TRIM mode is Off. This is discussed later in this chapter. If the lines you want to chamfer are too short for the specified distances, AutoCAD gives you a message such as "2 were too short." If you want to chamfer additional corners, press ENTER to repeat the CHAMFER command. The results of several chamfering operations are shown in Figure 13-2.

Figure 13-2.   Using the CHAMFER command.

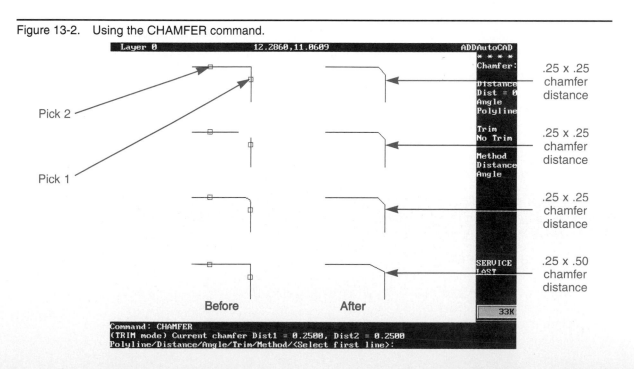

Chamfering the corners of a polyline

All corners of a closed or open polyline may be chamfered in one task. Enter the CHAMFER command, select the Polyline option, and then select the polyline. The corners of the polyline are chamfered to the set distance values. If the polyline appears closed, but the Close option was not used, the beginning corner is not chamfered, Figure 13-3.

Command: **CHAMFER** ↵
Polyline/Distances/Angle/Trim/Method/⟨Select first line⟩: **P** ↵
Select 2D polyline: *(pick the polyline)*
Command:

Figure 13-3.   Using the Polyline option of the CHAMFER command.

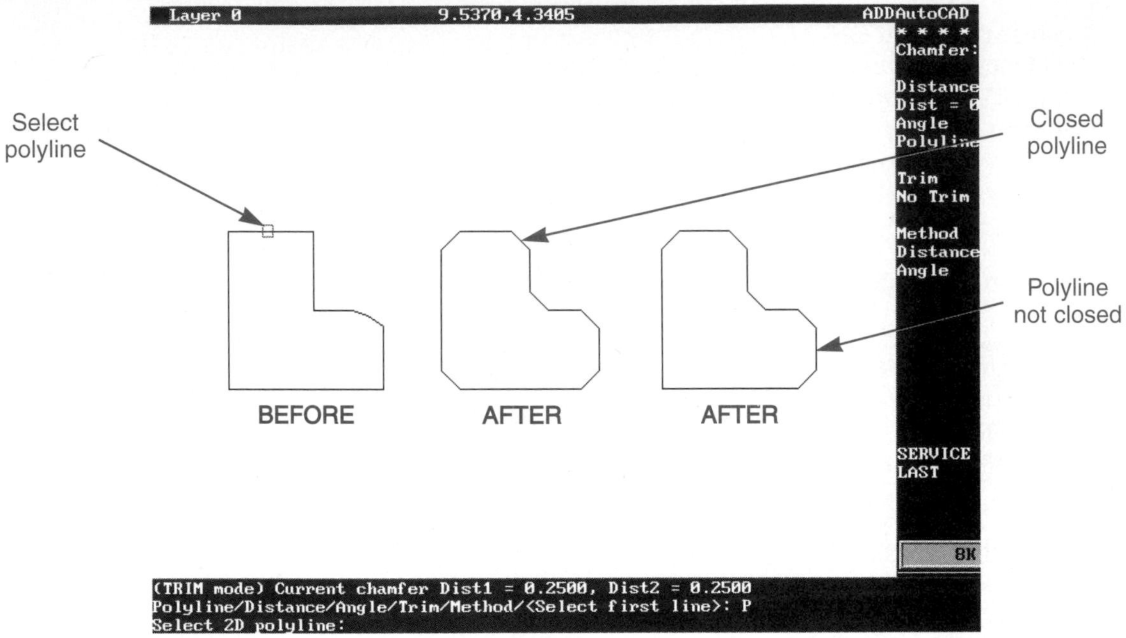

Setting the chamfer angle

You can either set the chamfer distance for two lines or you can set the chamfer distance for one line and an angle to determine the chamfer to the second line. To do this, use the Angle option:

Command: **CHAMFER** ↵
Polyline/Distance/Angle/Trim/Method/⟨Select first line⟩: **A** ↵
Enter chamfer length on the first line ⟨0⟩: *(enter a chamfer distance, .5 for example, and press ENTER)*
Enter chamfer angle from the first line ⟨0⟩: *(enter a chamfer angle, 45 for example, and press ENTER)*
Command:

Now, you are ready to enter the CHAMFER command again and draw a chamfer with the Angle option, as shown in Figure 13-4. You can see in the following command sequence that distance and angle are now the defaults:

Command: **CHAMFER** ↵
(TRIM mode) Current chamfer Length = 0.5, Angle = 45.0
Polyline/Distance/Angle/Trim/Method/⟨Select first line⟩: *(pick line 1)*
Select second line: *(pick line 2)*
Command:

Figure 13-4.   Using the CHAMFER command Angle option.

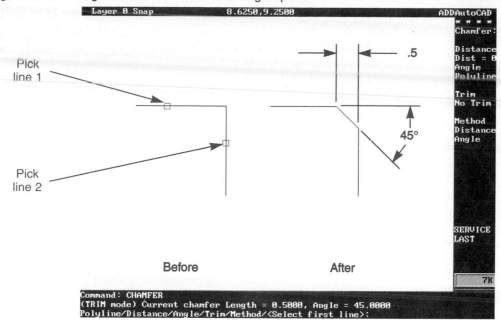

Setting the chamfer method

When you set the chamfer distances using the Distance option or set the distance and angle using the Angle option, AutoCAD keeps the setting until you change it. You can have distance and angle values set without affecting each other. All you have to do is use the Method option if you want to switch between drawing chamfers by Distance or by Angle. The default for this is the Distance and Angle option previously entered. The default option contains the values that you previously set:

Command: **CHAMFER** ↵
(TRIM mode) Current chamfer Length = 0.5, Angle = 45.0
Polyline/Distance/Angle/Trim/Method/〈Select first line〉: **M** ↵
Distance/Angle 〈Angle〉: **D**↵
Polyline/Distance/Angle/Trim/Method/〈Select first line〉: *(pick line 1)*
Select second line: *(pick line 2)*
Command:

Setting the chamfer Trim mode

You can have the selected lines automatically trimmed before chamfering, or you can have the selected lines remain in the drawing when the chamfering happens, as shown in Figure 13-5. To use this, you enter the Trim option and then select either T for Trim or N for No trim as follows:

Command: **CHAMFER** ↵
Polyline/Distance/Angle/Trim/Method/〈Select first line〉: **T** ↵
Trim/No trim 〈Trim〉: **N** ↵
Polyline/Distance/Angle/Trim/Method/〈Select first line〉: *(pick line 1)*
Select second line: *(pick line 2)*
Command:

Figure 13-5.   Using the CHAMFER command Trim option. C–The result when the lines do not extend to the corners.

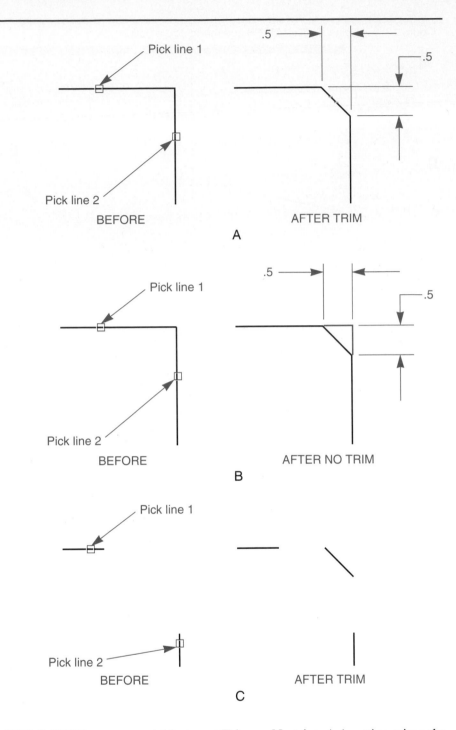

You can also use the TRIMMODE system variable to set Trim or No trim. A 1 setting trims the lines before chamfering, while a 0 setting does not trim the lines:

Command: **TRIMMODE** ↵
New value for TRIMMODE 〈1〉: **0** ↵
Command:

NOTE   The TRIMMODE system variable affects the FILLET command in the same manner as the CHAMFER command. The FILLET command is discussed next. If the Polyline option is used with the No trim mode active, any chamfer lines created are not part of the polyline.

PROFESSIONAL TIP

When the CHAMFER or FILLET command is set to Trim, lines that do not connect at a corner are automatically extended and the chamfer or fillet is applied. However, when the No trim option is used, these lines are not extended, but the chamfer or fillet is drawn anyway. If you have lines that are drawn short of a corner and want them to connect to the chamfer or fillet, you need to extend them before or after you draw in the No trim mode.

DRAWING ROUNDED CORNERS

AUG 6

In mechanical drafting, an inside rounded corner is called a *fillet*. An outside rounded corner is called a *round*. AutoCAD refers to all rounded corners as fillets. The FILLET command draws a rounded corner between intersecting or nonintersecting lines, circles, arcs, polyline, ellipse, rays, xlines, and splines. Fillets are sized by radius. A radius must be entered before a fillet can be drawn. The radius is specified first by selecting the Radius option in the FILLET command as follows:

Command: **FILLET** ↵
(TRIM mode) Current fillet radius = 0
Polyline/Radius/Trim/⟨Select first object⟩: **R** ↵
Enter fillet radius ⟨current⟩: *(type the fillet radius, **.25** for example, and press* ENTER, *or press* ENTER *to accept the current value)*

Once the fillet radius has been given, repeat the FILLET command to fillet the objects. Refer to Figure 13-6 as you follow this command sequence:

Command: **FILLET** ↵
Polyline/Radius/Trim/⟨Select first object⟩: *(pick the first object to be filleted)*
Select second object: *(pick the other object to be filleted)*
Command:

Figure 13-6.   Using the FILLET command.

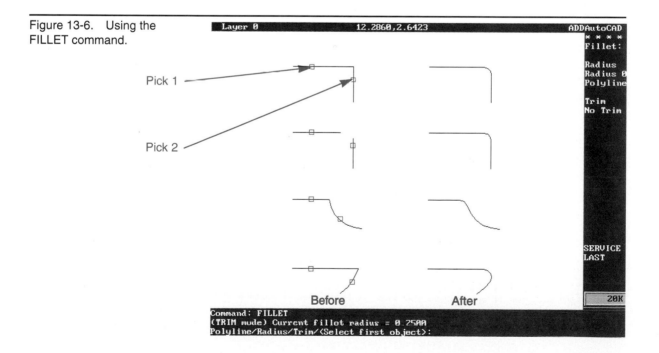

Rounding the corners of a polyline

Fillets may be drawn at all corners of a polyline by selecting the Polyline option. The current fillet radius is used. The command sequence shown in Figure 13-7 is as follows:

Command: **FILLET** ↵
Polyline/Radius/Trim/⟨Select first object⟩: **P** ↵
Select 2D polyline: *(pick the polyline)*

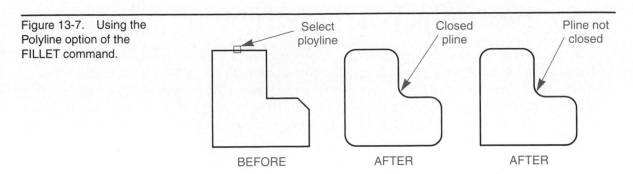

Figure 13-7. Using the Polyline option of the FILLET command.

BEFORE   AFTER   AFTER

AutoCAD tells you how many lines were filleted. Then the Command: prompt returns. If the polyline appears closed, but the Close option was not used, the beginning corner is not filleted.

Setting the fillet Trim mode

The TRIMMODE system variable and the Trim option controls whether or not the FILLET command trims off object segments which extend beyond the fillet radius point. When the Trim mode is active, objects are trimmed. When the Trim mode is inactive, the filleted objects are not changed after the fillet is inserted, as shown in Figure 13-8. Use the Trim option like this:

Command: **FILLET** ↵
(TRIM mode) Current fillet radius = 0.25
Polyline/Radius/Trim/⟨Select first object⟩: **T** ↵
Trim/No trim/⟨Trim⟩: **N** ↵
Polyline/Radius/Trim/⟨Select first object⟩: *(pick the first object)*
Select second object: *(pick the second object)*
Command:

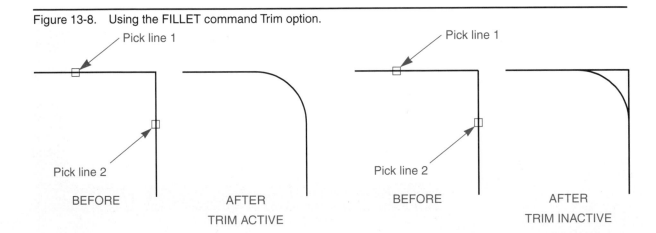

Figure 13-8. Using the FILLET command Trim option.

Pick line 1   Pick line 1

Pick line 2   Pick line 2

BEFORE   AFTER   BEFORE   AFTER
TRIM ACTIVE   TRIM INACTIVE

If the lines to be filleted do not connect at the corner, they are automatically extended when the Trim mode is On. However, they are not extended when using No trim. The results are similar to the bottom example in Figure 13-5. If you do not want these results, then extend the lines to the corner before filleting.

Filleting parallel lines

You can also draw a fillet between parallel lines. When parallel lines are selected, a radius is placed between the two lines. If one of the parallel lines is longer than the other, the longer line is trimmed to match the length of the shorter line if Trim mode is On. The radius of a fillet between parallel lines is always half of the distance between the two lines, regardless of the FILLETRAD settings and this does not change the FILLETRAD.

PROFESSIONAL TIP

You are encouraged to just press the ENTER key or the SPACE bar to automatically return the FILLET or CHAMFER command after the settings are made. This saves you time, because retyping or repicking the command is too much work.

Chamfering and Filleting line and polyline objects together

In Figures 13-2 and 13-6 you observed that line objects, such as lines and arcs, are chamfered or filleted at the corner where they meet. These line objects are automatically extended and chamfered if they do not meet. This also happens when a combination of line objects and polyline objects are chamfered or filleted. For example, if you have a line and a polyline that either meet or do not meet, you can draw a chamfer or fillet between them with the CHAMFER or FILLET command as desired. When you do this, the line is automatically joined with the polyline, resulting in a single polyline. This is only true when TRIMMODE is 1. When TRIMMODE is 0, neither object is affected.

Presetting the chamfer distance and the fillet radius

AutoCAD lets you set the chamfer distance and fillet radius to a designated value. This saves time when the chamfer distance and fillet radius remains constant on your drawing. To do this, use the CHAMFERA, CHAMFERB, and FILLETRAD system variables. You can preset the chamfer distances to different or equal values. For example, if you want .125 for both chamfer distances, type the following:

> Command: **CHAMFERA** ⏎
> New value for CHAMFERA ⟨*current*⟩: **.125** ⏎
> Command: **CHAMFERB** ⏎
> New value for CHAMFERB ⟨*current*⟩: **.125** ⏎
> Command:

Now, enter CHAMFER at the Command: prompt and the preset values are automatically issued. The command sequence looks like this:

> Command: **CHAMFER** ⏎
> (TRIM mode) Current chamfer Dist1= 0.125, Dist2 = 0.125
> Polyline/Distances/⟨Select first line⟩: *(pick the first line)*
> Select second line: *(pick the second line)*

When presetting the fillet radius, first enter FILLETRAD at the Command: prompt. You are then asked to enter a new value. For example, if you want .25 radius, type the following:

> Command: **FILLETRAD** ⏎
> New value for FILLETRAD ⟨*current*⟩: **.25** ⏎
> Command:

To work with the preset specifications, enter the FILLET command and the preset radius for the fillet is automatically issued. The command sequence looks like this:

> Command: **FILLET** ⏎
> (TRIM mode) Current fillet radius = 0.25
> Polyline/Radius/⟨Select first object⟩: *(pick the first object)*
> Select second object: *(pick the second object)*
> Command:

PROFESSIONAL TIP

Using the FILLET or CHAMFER command with a 0 fillet radius or 0 chamfer distances is a quick and convenient way to create square corners.

EXERCISE 13-1

❑ Load AutoCAD and open TITLEB.
❑ Draw two 4 × 2 rectangles using the LINE command. Use the CHAMFER command on the first rectangle to chamfer two corners a distance of .125 with the Trim mode ON. Chamfer the other corners a distance of .25 with no Trim. Use the FILLET command on the second rectangle to round two corners at a .125 radius with the Trim mode ON. Round the other corners at a .25 radius with no trim.
❑ Draw two more 4 × 2 rectangles using the PLINE command. Use the Close option on one but not on the other. Use the CHAMFER command on the first rectangle to chamfer all corners a distance of .25. Use the FILLET command on the second rectangle to round all corners at .25 radius. Have the Trim mode ON for both drawings. Observe what happens on the polyline rectangle that was drawn without using the Close option.
❑ Save the drawing as A:EX13-1 and quit.

PROFESSIONAL TIP

While the previous chamfer and fillet examples had mechanical applications, the CHAMFER and FILLET commands may be used in any drafting field; for example, angled or rounded corners in architectural drafting. If you are working in architectural drafting at a scale of 1/4″ = 1′-0″, be sure to set the chamfer or fillet distances in feet and/or inches accordingly.

REMOVING A SECTION FROM AN OBJECT   AUG 5

The BREAK command is used to remove a portion of a line, circle, arc, trace, or polyline. AutoCAD asks you to first select the object, then pick break points as follows:

Command: **BREAK** ↵
Select object: *(Pick the line, circle, or arc to be broken. If a pick point is used rather than a window, that point becomes the first break point.)*

If the object you pick is a line, the pick point is your first break point. You are then asked for the second break point:

Enter second point (or F for first point): *(pick the second point, or type **F** and press ENTER for another first point option)*

If you pick a second break point, the line is broken between the two points, Figure 13-9. You can also enter F to specify a new first point:

Enter second point (or F for first point): **F** ↵
Enter first point: *(pick a new first point)*
Enter second point: *(pick the second point)*

Figure 13-9. Using the BREAK command.

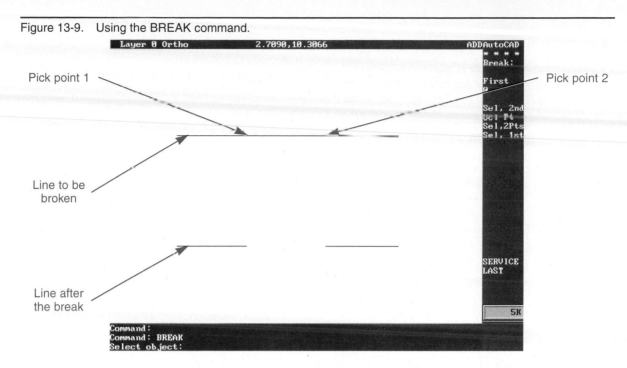

When breaking arcs or circles, always work in a counterclockwise direction. Otherwise, you may break the portion of the arc or circle that you want to keep. If you want to break the end off of a line or arc, pick the first point on the line or arc. Then pick the second point slightly beyond the end to be cut off, Figure 13-10. If you pick a second point that is not on the object, AutoCAD selects the nearest point on the object.

Figure 13-10. Using the BREAK command on circles and arcs.

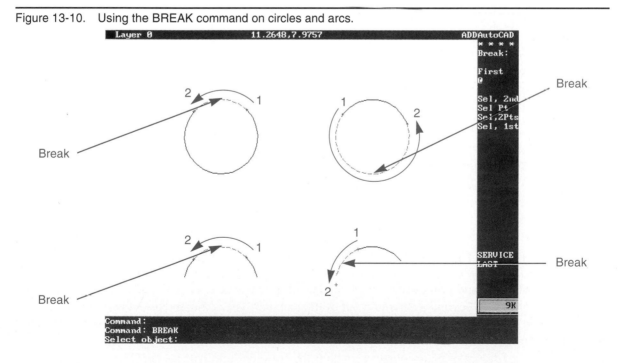

If you want to break a line from the point of intersection with another line, use the object snap INTersect mode as follows:

Command: **BREAK** ↵
Select object: *(pick the line)*
Enter second point (or F for first point): **INT** ↵
of *(move the aperture to the intersection and pick)*

The line is now broken between the first point and the point of intersection.

Using the BREAK cascading menu

The BREAK command can also be accessed from the Modify pull-down menu. When you pick Break (or slide the cursor over its arrow), a cascading submenu appears, displaying four options. The options are 1 Point, 1 Point Select, 2 Points, and 2 Points Select, and are explained as follows:

- **1 Point.** This is used to split an object in two without removing a portion. For example, if you pick a line with this option, the line becomes two lines that are split at the break point. The prompt line looks like this:

      Command: _break Select object: *(pick the desired point on the object)*
      Enter second point (or F for first point): **@**
      Command:

Notice the @ symbol is automatically entered at the end of the second prompt. This means that the second break point is exactly where you picked the first break point. You can also do this manually by entering an @ symbol at the second prompt when typing the command.

- **1 Point Select.** This option asks you for a new first point after you select the object to break and then automatically picks the second point at the same location as your first point:

      Command: _break Select object: *(pick the object)*
      Enter second point (or F for first point): _f
      Enter first point: *(pick the first break point)*
      Enter second point: **@** ↵
      Command:

- **2 Points.** This gives you the prompts that are issued as if you typed the command. Refer to the first part of the discussion on the BREAK command.

- **2 Point Select.** This option automatically asks you for a first point after you select the object. You are then asked for a second point after you pick a first point:

      Command: _break Select object: *(pick the object)*
      Enter second point (or F for first point): _f
      Enter first point: *(pick the first break point)*
      Enter second point: *(pick the second break point)*
      Command:

TRIMMING SECTIONS OF A LINE, CIRCLE, OR ARC   `AUG 5`

The TRIM command prunes lines, arcs, circles, elliptical arcs, open 2-D and 3-D polylines, rays, and splines that extend beyond a desired point of intersection. The command asks that you pick a "cutting edge" and the object(s) to trim. Cutting edges are objects such as lines, arcs, or text that the chosen objects trim to.

The *cutting edge* may be an object to which the trimmed line will be cut. If two corners of an object overrun, select two cutting edges and two objects as follows: (Refer to Figure 13-11.)

Command: **TRIM** ↵
Select cutting edges: (Projmode = UCS, Edgemode = No extend)
Select objects: *(pick the first cutting edge)*
Select objects: *(pick the second cutting edge)*
Select objects: ↵
⟨Select object to trim⟩/Project/Edge/Undo: *(pick the first object to trim)*
⟨Select object to trim⟩/Project/Edge/Undo: *(pick the second object to trim)*
⟨Select object to trim⟩/Project/Edge/Undo: ↵
Command:

Figure 13-11.   Using the TRIM command. Note the cutting edges.

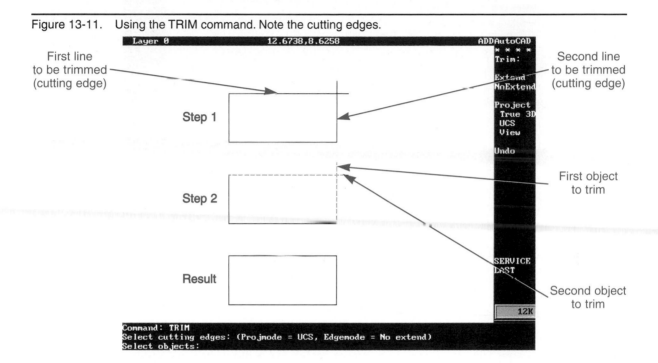

Trimming to an implied intersection

Trimming to an implied intersection is possible using the Edge option in the TRIM command. When you enter the Edge option, the choices are Extend and No extend. When Extend is active, the cutting edge object is checked to see if, when extended, it would intersect. If it would intersect, the implied intersection point can be used to trim the object to be trimmed. This does not change the cutting edge object at all. This is the command sequence for the TRIM operation shown in Figure 13-12:

Command: **TRIM** ↵
Select cutting edges: (Projmode = UCS, Edgemode = No extend)
Select objects: *(pick the first cutting edge)*
Select objects: *(pick the second cutting edge)*
Select objects: ↵
⟨Select object to trim⟩/Project/Edge/Undo: **E** ↵
Extend/No extend/⟨No extend⟩: **E** ↵
⟨Select object to trim⟩/Project/Edge/Undo: *(pick the object to trim)*
⟨Select object to trim⟩/Project/Edge/Undo: ↵
Command:

Figure 13-12. Trimming to an implied intersection.

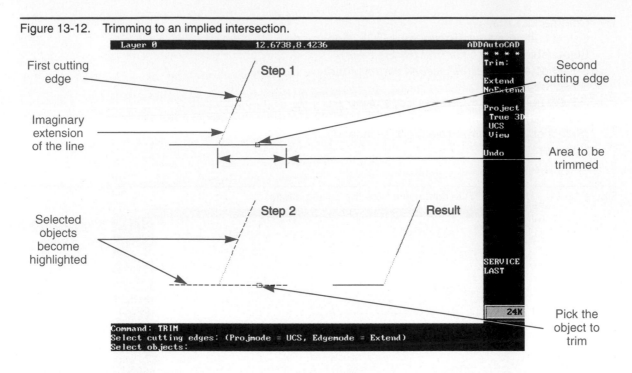

The Edge option may also be set using the EDGEMODE system variable. Extend is active when the EDGEMODE is 1. The cutting edge object is checked to see if, when extended, it would intersect.

Command:**EDGEMODE** ↵
New value for EDGEMODE ⟨0⟩: **1** ↵

Using the Undo option

The TRIM command has an Undo option that allows you to reverse the previous TRIM without leaving the command. This is handy in case what you observe is not what you expected, so you can try another trim:

Command: **TRIM** ↵
Select cutting edges: (Projmode = UCS, Edgemode = No extend)
Select objects: (*pick the first cutting edge*)
Select objects: (*pick the second cutting edge*)
⟨Select object to trim⟩/Project/Edge/Undo: (*pick the object to trim*)
⟨Select object to trim⟩/Project/Edge/Undo: **U** ↵
Command has been completely undone.
⟨Select object to trim⟩/Project/Edge/Undo: (*pick the object to trim*)
⟨Select object to trim⟩/Project/Edge/Undo: ↵
Command:

An introduction to the Project mode

In a 3-D drawing environment, some lines may appear to intersect in a given view, but may not actually intersect. In such a case, using the Project option of the TRIM command can allow trimming operations. This option is also controlled by the PROJMODE system variable. Using AutoCAD for 3-D drawing is explained in *AutoCAD and its Applications–DOS, Advanced.*

EXTENDING LINES

AUG 5

The EXTEND command can be considered the opposite of TRIM. The EXTEND command is used to lengthen lines, arcs, elliptical arcs, open 2-D and 3-D polylines, and rays. EXTEND will not work on closed lines or closed polylines since an opening does not exist. The command format is similar to TRIM. You are asked to select "boundary edges" (rather than cutting edges). *Boundary edges* are those objects such as lines, arcs, or text that the chosen objects extend to meet. The command sequence is shown below and illustrated in Figure 13-13:

Command: **EXTEND** ↵
Select boundary edges: (Projmode = UCS, Edgemode = No extend)
Select objects: *(pick the boundary edge)*
Select objects: ↵
⟨Select object to extend⟩/Project/Edge/Undo: *(pick the object to extend)*
⟨Select object to extend⟩/Project/Edge/Undo: ↵
Command:

Figure 13-13.   Using the EXTEND command. Note the boundary edge.

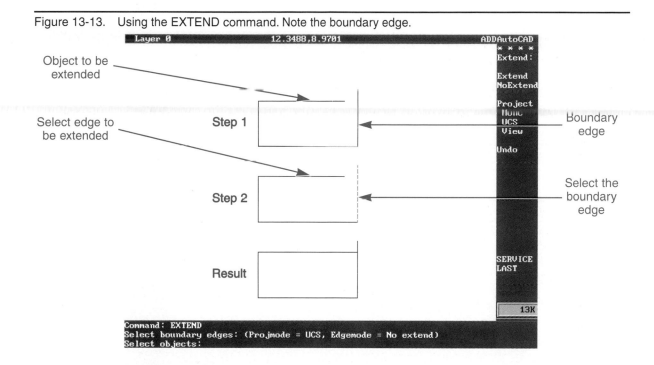

If there is nothing for the selected line to meet, AutoCAD gives the message: "No edge in that direction" or "Entity does not intersect an edge."

Extending to an implied intersection

You can extend an object to an implied intersection using the Edge option in the EXTEND command. When you enter the Edge option, the choices are Extend and No extend just as in the TRIM command. When Extend is active, the boundary edge object is checked to see if it would intersect when extended. If it would intersect, the implied intersection point can be used as the boundary for the object to be extended, as shown in Figure 13-14. This does not change the boundary edge object at all:

Command: **EXTEND** ↵
Select boundary edges: (Projmode = UCS, Edgemode = No extend)
Select objects: *(pick the boundary edge)*
Select objects: ↵
⟨Select object to extend⟩/Project/Edge/Undo: **E** ↵
Extend/No extend/⟨No extend⟩: **E** ↵
⟨Select object to extend⟩/Project/Edge/Undo: *(pick the object to extend)*
⟨Select object to extend⟩/Project/Edge/Undo: ↵
Command:

The Edge option may also be set using the EDGEMODE as previously discussed with the TRIM command.

Figure 13-14.   Extending to an implied intersection

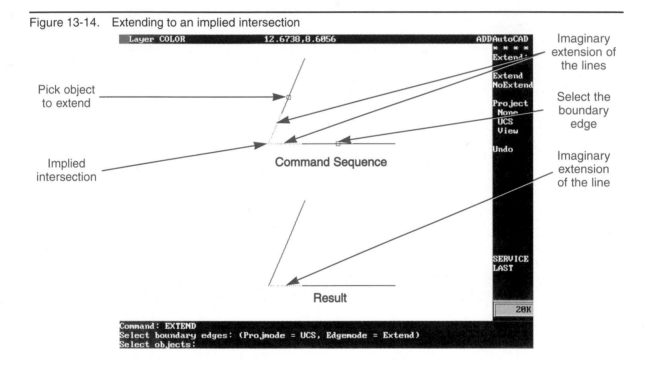

Using the Undo option

The Undo option in the Extend command may be used to reverse the previous Extend operation without leaving the EXTEND command. The command sequence is the same as discussed in the TRIM command.

The EXTEND command's Project mode

In a 3-D drawing, some lines may appear to intersect in a given view, but may not actually be able to intersect. In such a case, you can use the Project option or the PROJMODE as explained with the TRIM command.

PROFESSIONAL TIP

The TRIM and EXTEND commands have a convenient "Smart" mode. To use the Smart mode, press ENTER rather than selecting a cutting or boundary edge. Then, when an object to trim or extend is picked, AutoCAD searches for the nearest intersecting object or implied intersection (depending on the EDGEMODE setting) in the direction of your pick. AutoCAD then uses this object as the cutting or boundary edge. If an actual intersection is found, it is used rather than the implied intersection, even if the implied intersection is closer. The object must be visible on the screen, and cannot be a block or xref object.

Also, trimming can be done between two actual or implied intersections, but not between a combination of one actual and one implied intersection.

CHANGING LINES AND CIRCLES

The endpoint location of a line or the radius of a circle may be altered using the CHANGE command. The endpoint of one or more lines may be moved by picking a new point. This new point is called the *change point*. For example, suppose a corner where two lines meet is not correct. Type CHANGE at the Command: prompt, or pick Change from the MODIFY screen menu. Use the CHANGE command to reposition a corner. At the ⟨Change point⟩: prompt, pick the new point. AutoCAD automatically relocates the endpoints, as shown in Figure 13-15. The command sequence is as follows:

Command: **CHANGE** ↵
Select objects: *(pick the lines individually or with a crossing box)*
Select objects: ↵
Properties/⟨Change point⟩: *(pick the new point)*

Figure 13-15. Using the CHANGE command to relocate a corner.

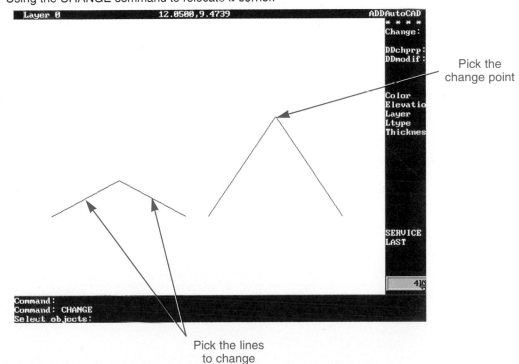

NOTE If ORTHO had been on during the Change point operation shown in Figure 13-15, the lines would have been disconnected and extended parallel to each other up to the new point.

The CHANGE command can also be used to revise the radius of a circle. Do this by picking a change point through which the new circle is to be drawn. See Figure 13-16.

Figure 13-16. Using the CHANGE command to revise the radius of a circle.

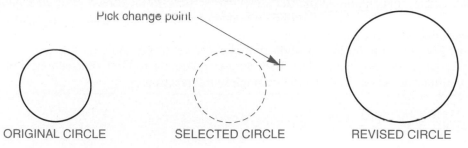

ORIGINAL CIRCLE   SELECTED CIRCLE   REVISED CIRCLE

Using the CHANGE command to move text is discussed in Chapter 11. Changing common properties such as layer, linetype, and color is explained in Chapter 19. Three-dimensional applications are discussed in *AutoCAD and its Applications–Advanced, R13 for DOS*.

EXERCISE 13-2

❑ Make a drawing similar to that shown below and perform the BREAK, TRIM, and EXTEND operations noted.

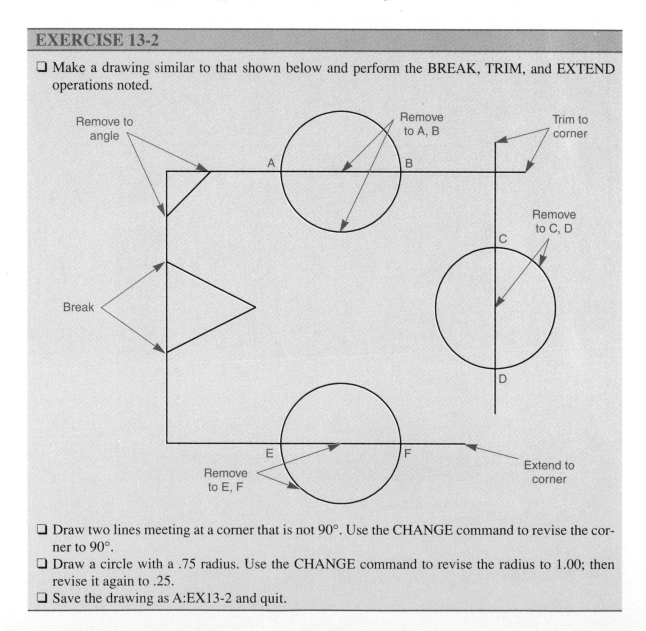

❑ Draw two lines meeting at a corner that is not 90°. Use the CHANGE command to revise the corner to 90°.
❑ Draw a circle with a .75 radius. Use the CHANGE command to revise the radius to 1.00; then revise it again to .25.
❑ Save the drawing as A:EX13-2 and quit.

MOVING AN OBJECT

AUG 5

In many situations, you may find that the location of a view or feature is not quite where you want it. This problem is easily resolved using the MOVE command. After you enter MOVE, AutoCAD requests that you select those objects to be moved. Use any of the selection techniques: fence, window, window polygon, last, crossing, crossing polygon, or pick single items.

The next prompt requests the base point. The *base point* is any point on or adjacent to the feature. It provides a reference point. Most drafters select a point on an object, corner of a view, or center of a circle. The next prompt asks for the second point of displacement. This is the new position. All selected entities are moved the distance from the base point to the displacement point. The following MOVE command relates to the object shown in Figure 13-17. After the base point is picked, the object is automatically dragged into position if the DRAGMODE is set to Auto.

Command: **MOVE** ↵
Select objects: *(pick individual entities or window the object to be moved)*
Select objects: ↵
Base point or displacement: *(enter coordinates or pick a point on screen)*
Second point of displacement: *(establish the new position by typing coordinates or picking a second point on screen)*

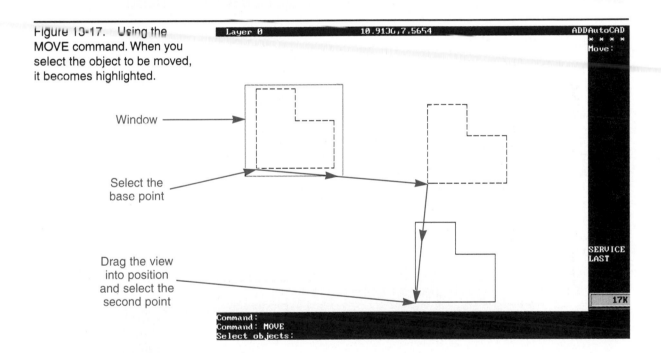

Figure 13-17.   Using the MOVE command. When you select the object to be moved, it becomes highlighted.

COPYING OBJECTS

AUG 5

The COPY command is used to make a copy of an existing view or object. The command prompts are the same as the MOVE command. However, when a second point of displacement is picked, the original object remains and the copy is drawn. The following command sequence is shown in Figure 13-18.

Command: **COPY** ↵
Select objects: *(pick individual entities or window the object to be moved)*
Select objects: ↵
⟨Base point or displacement⟩/Multiple: *(enter coordinates and press* ENTER, *or pick with the pointing device)*
Second point of displacement: *(establish the new position by typing coordinates and pressing* ENTER, *or pick a point on the screen)*

Figure 13-18.   Using the COPY command.

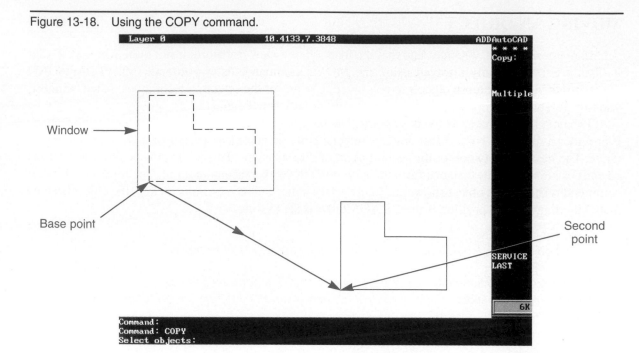

Making multiple copies

To make several copies of the same object, select the Multiple option of the COPY command. Type M or pick Multiple from the COPY screen menu. The prompt for a second point repeats. When you have made all the copies needed, press ENTER. The command sequence after you select objects continues as follows. The results are shown in Figure 13-19.

⟨Base point or displacement⟩/Multiple: **M** ↵
Base point: *(enter coordinates and press* ENTER, *or pick a location with the pointing device)*
Second point of displacement: *(establish the new position by typing coordinates and pressing* ENTER, *or pick a location on screen)*
Second point of displacement: *(pick the second position)*
Second point of displacement: *(pick the third position)*
Second point of displacement: ↵
Command:

Figure 13-19.   Using the Multiple option of the COPY command.

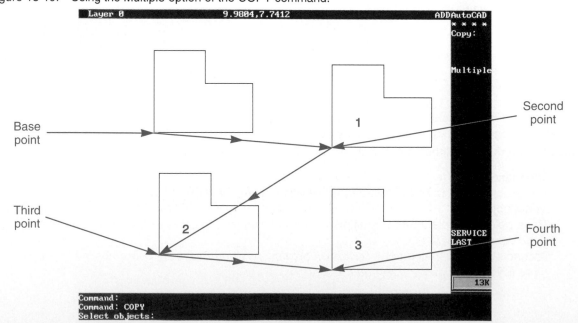

EXERCISE 13-3

❑ Load AutoCAD and open TITLEA.
❑ Draw a square and an equilateral triangle (equal sides and angles). Use the POLYGON command.
❑ Move the square to a new location.
❑ Copy the triangle next to the new square position. Leave a small space between the two objects.
❑ Move all features to a new position in the upper-left corner of the screen.
❑ Make four copies of the square anywhere on the screen. The new copies should not touch other objects.
❑ Save the drawing as A:EX13-3 and quit.

DRAWING A MIRROR IMAGE OF AN EXISTING OBJECT   AUG 5

It is often necessary to draw an object, symbol, or view in a reflected, or mirrored position. The MIRROR command performs this task. Mirroring an entire drawing is common in architectural drafting when a client wants a plan drawn in reverse.

The normal mirroring operation reverses everything, including words and dimensions. However, by using the system variable MIRRTEXT, text retains its normal position. This option is discussed later in the chapter.

Selecting the mirror line

The *mirror line* is the hinge about which objects are reflected. Once you select objects to mirror, you must pick the endpoints of the mirror line. The objects, plus any space between the objects and the mirror line, are reflected, Figure 13-20.

Figure 13-20.   When an object is reflected about a mirror line, the space between the object and the mirror line will also be mirrored.

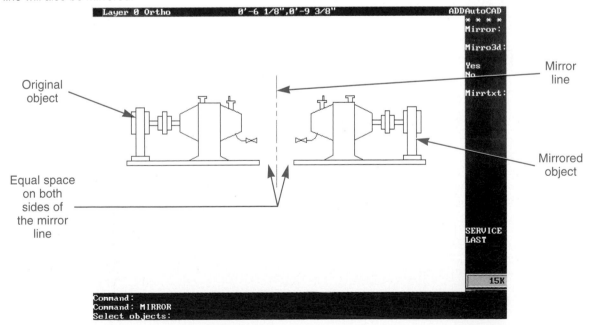

The mirror line can be placed at any angle. Once you select the first endpoint, the chosen objects are displayed as they would be mirrored. Once you select the second mirror line endpoint, you can delete the original objects or make a copy. The command sequence shown in Figure 13-21 is as follows:

Command: **MIRROR** ⏎
Select objects: *(use any selection method; a window is common)*
First point of mirror line: *(pick the first endpoint on or away from the object)*
Second point of mirror line: *(pick the second endpoint)*
Delete old objects? ⟨N⟩: *(type **Y** or press ENTER)*

Figure 13-21.   Using the MIRROR command. You will have the option to keep or delete the old objects.

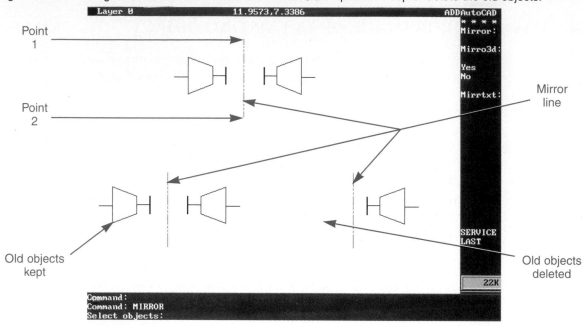

PROFESSIONAL TIP

Always use object snap to your best advantage when using editing commands. For example, suppose you want to move an object to the center point of a circle. Initiate the OSNAP CENter option as follows:

Command: **MOVE** ⏎
Select objects: *(select the object to be moved)*
Base point or displacement: *(pick the base point on the object)*
Second point of displacement: **CEN** ⏎
of *(snap to the center of an existing circle)*

EXERCISE 13-4

❑ Load AutoCAD and open TITLEA.
❑ Draw the half object shown below. Then complete the entire object using the MIRROR command. Do not dimension.

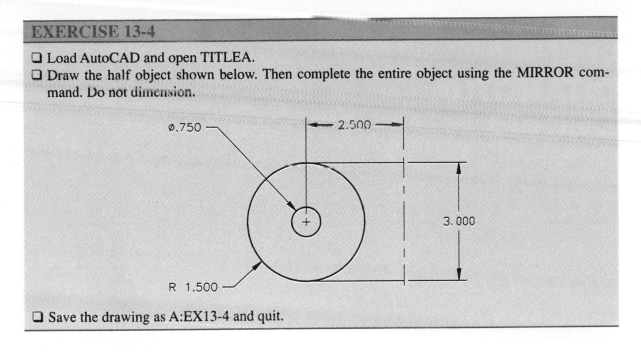

❑ Save the drawing as A:EX13-4 and quit.

MIRRORING TEXT

Normally, the MIRROR command reverses any text associated with the selected object. Backwards text is generally not acceptable. To keep the text readable, the MIRRTEXT system variable must be zero. There are two values for MIRRTEXT, Figure 13-22.
- 1 = Default value. Text is mirrored in relation to the original object.
- 0 = Prevents text from being reversed.

Figure 13-22.   The MIRRTEXT system variable options.

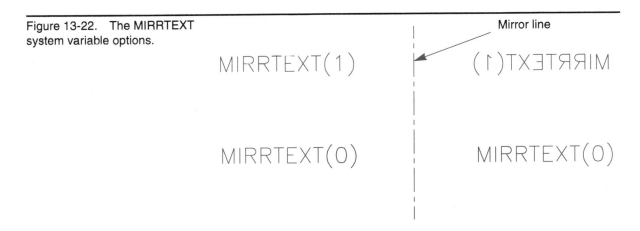

To draw a mirror image of an existing object, but leave the text readable, set the MIRRTEXT variable to 0. Then proceed to the MIRROR command. The entire command sequence is as follows:

Command: **MIRRTEXT** ⏎
New value for MIRRTEXT ⟨1⟩: **0** ⏎
Command: **MIRROR** ⏎
Select objects: *(select objects to mirror)*
Select objects: ⏎
First point of mirror line: *(pick the first mirror line point)*
Second point: *(pick the second mirror line point)*
Delete old objects? ⟨N⟩: *(type **Y** or press ENTER)*
Command:

EXERCISE 13-5

❑ Load AutoCAD and open TITLEA.
❑ Make a drawing similar to the "original" object shown. With the MIRRTEXT variable set to 0, mirror the object as shown in the center example.
❑ With MIRRTEXT set to 1, mirror the object as shown in the right example.

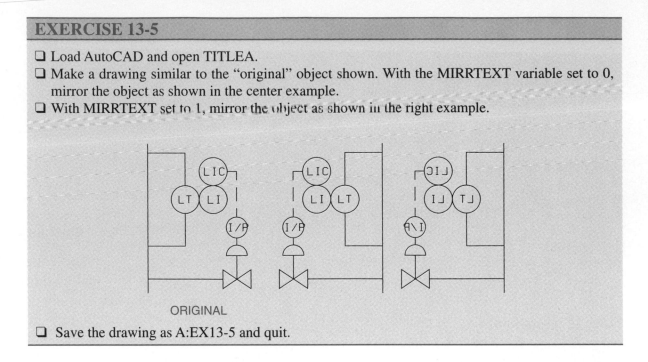

ORIGINAL

❑ Save the drawing as A:EX13-5 and quit.

ROTATING EXISTING OBJECTS

AUG 5

Design changes often require that an object, feature, or view be rotated. For example, in an interior design the office furniture layout may have to be moved, copied, or rotated. AutoCAD allows you to easily revise the layout to obtain the final design.

Objects you select are rotated about a base point. You must pick a base point and enter the rotation angle. A negative rotation angle revolves the object clockwise, Figure 13-23. A positive rotation angle revolves the object counterclockwise. The ROTATE command sequence appears as follows:

Command: **ROTATE** ↵
Select objects: *(use one of the selection methods, such as window)*
Select objects: ↵
Base point: *(pick the base point on or near the object, or enter coordinates and press ENTER)*
⟨Rotation angle⟩/Reference: *(type a positive or negative rotation angle and press ENTER, or pick a point on screen)*

Figure 13-23.   Different rotation angles.

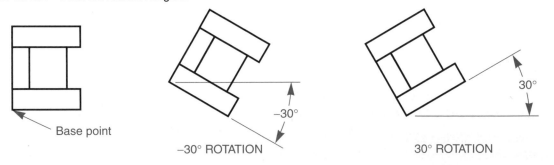

If an object is already rotated and you want a different angle, you can do this two ways using the Reference option after selecting the object for rotation. The first method, shown in Figure 13-24A, is to specify the existing angle followed by the proposed angle:

⟨Rotation angle⟩/Reference: **R** ↵
Reference angle ⟨0⟩: **135** ↵
New angle: **180** ↵

The other method is to pick a reference line on the object and rotate the object in relationship to the reference line, as shown in Figure 13-24B. The prompts are as follows:

⟨Rotation angle⟩/Reference: **R** ↵
Reference angle ⟨0⟩: *(pick the endpoints of a reference line that forms the existing angle)*
New angle: *(specify a new angle, such as **180**, and press ENTER)*

Figure 13-24. Using the ROTATE command's Reference option.

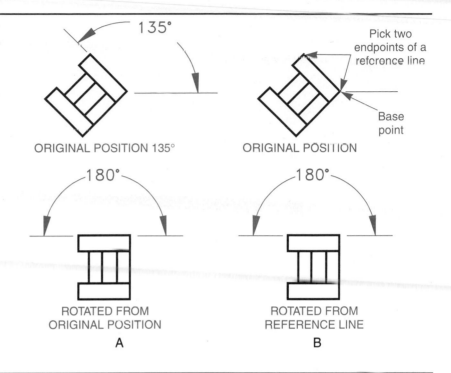

EXERCISE 13-6

❑ Load AutoCAD and open TITLEA.
❑ Draw a 2.25 unit square with one horizontal side.
❑ Rotate the square to 75°. Then, using the Reference option, rotate the square another 45°. Finally rotate the square back to 0°.
❑ Save the drawing as A:EX13-6 and quit.

MOVING AND ROTATING AN OBJECT SIMULTANEOUSLY

The ALIGN command is primarily used for 3-D applications, but it has 2-D applications when you want to move and rotate an object at the same time. The command sequence asks you to select objects, and then asks for three source points and three destination points. For 2-D applications, you only need two source and two destination points. The *source points* are points on the object in its original position. The *destination points* correspond to the location where the object is to be placed. Refer to Figure 13-25A. Press ENTER when the prompt requests the third source and destination points.

Command: **ALIGN** ↵
Select objects: *(select the desired objects)*
Select objects: ↵
1st source point: *(pick the first source point)*
1st destination point: *(pick the first destination point)*
2nd source point: *(pick the second source point)*
2nd destination point: *(pick the second destination point)*
3rd source point: ↵
⟨2d⟩ or 3d transformation: *(press ENTER to accept the default of 2d)*

Figure 13-25B shows the kitchen cabinet layout moved and rotated into the desired wall location.

Figure 13-25.   The ALIGN command rotates and moves an object simultaneously.

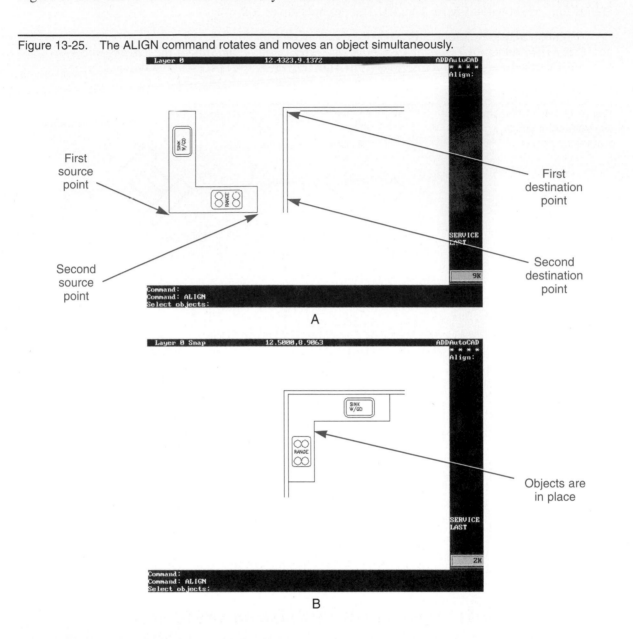

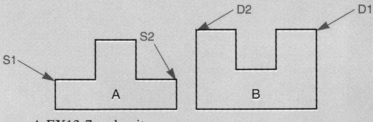

CHANGING THE SIZE OF AN EXISTING OBJECT

A convenient editing command that saves hours of drafting time is the SCALE command. This command lets you change the size of an existing object or complete drawing. The SCALE command enlarges or reduces the entire object proportionately. One advantage of AutoCAD is that if the object is dimensioned, the dimensions also change to reflect the new size.

Command: **SCALE** ↵
Select objects: *(use any selection technique to select objects)*
Select objects: ↵
Base point: *(select the base point)*
⟨Scale factor⟩/Reference:

Scale factors

The scale factor is the default prompt. Specify the amount of enlargement or reduction in size. If you want to double the scale, type 2 at the "⟨Scale factor⟩/Reference:" prompt, Figure 13-26. The chart in Figure 13-27 shows sample scale factors.

Figure 13-26.   Using the SCALE command. A–The original object. B–The object after being scaled.

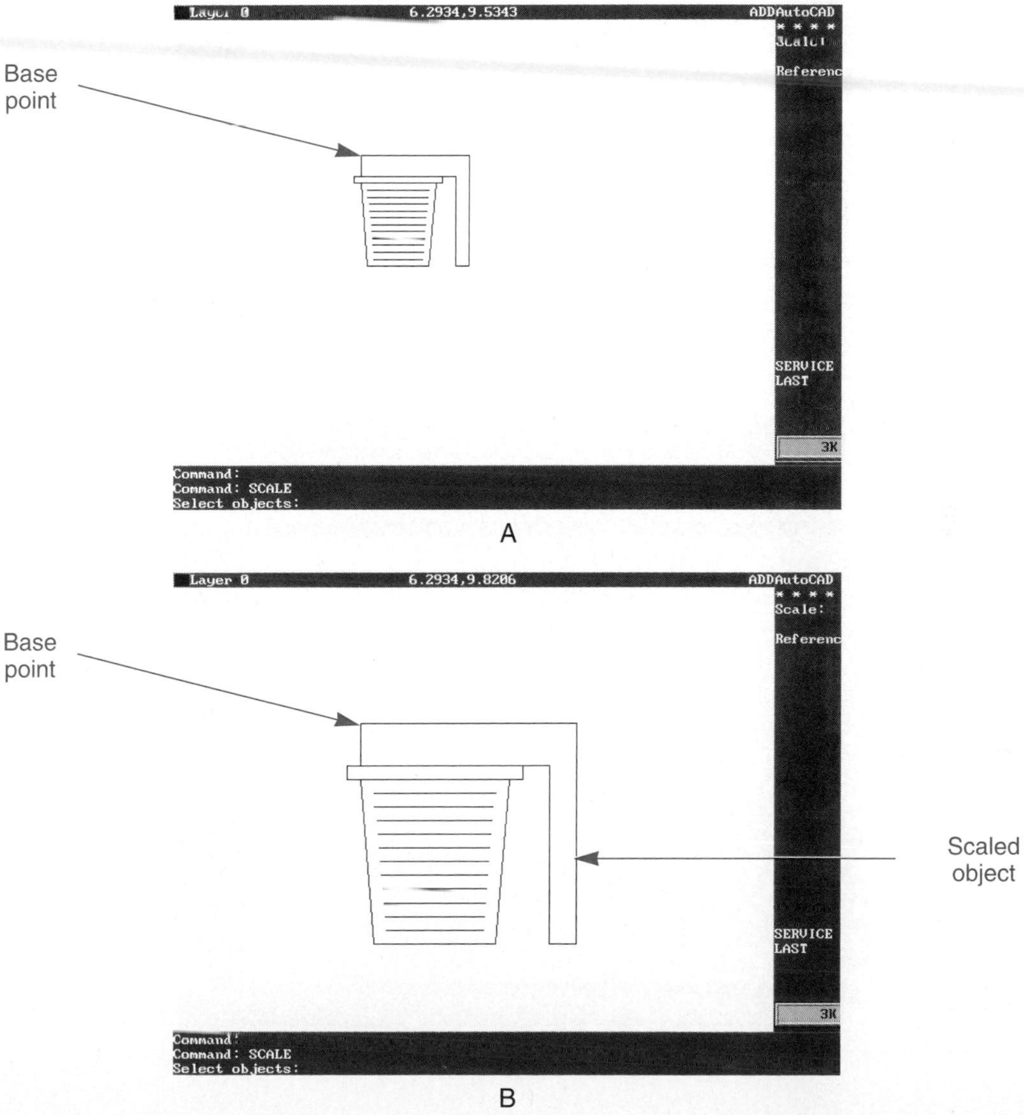

A

B

Figure 13-27. Different scale factors and the resulting sizes.

Scale Factor	Resulting Size
10	10 x bigger
5	5 x bigger
2	2 x bigger
1	Equal to existing size
.75	3/4 of original size
.50	1/2 of original size
.25	1/4 of original size

An object may also be scaled by specifying a new size in relation to an existing dimension. For example, suppose you have a shaft that is 2.50 in. long and you want to make it 3.00 in. long. Use the Reference option, shown in Figure 13-28, as follows:

⟨Scale factor⟩/Reference: **R** ↵
Reference length ⟨1⟩: **2.50** ↵
New length: **3.00** ↵

Figure 13-28. Using the SCALE command's Reference option.

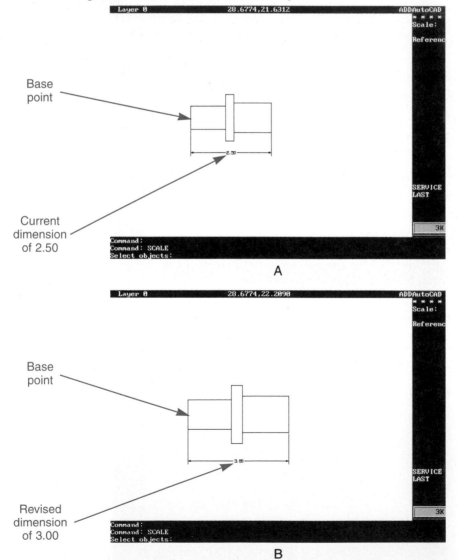

EXERCISE 13-8

- ❑ Load AutoCAD and open TITLEA.
- ❑ Draw two 2.25 in. squares each with one horizontal side.
- ❑ Double the size of one square.
- ❑ Use the Reference option to make the other square 3.25 in. along one side.
- ❑ Save the drawing as A:EX13-8 and quit.

PROFESSIONAL TIP

Always use the running and interrupt OSNAP modes to your best advantage when editing. For example, suppose you want to rotate an object. It may be difficult to find an exact corner without using OSNAP modes. To select the base point, use the ENDpoint or INTersect option.

STRETCHING AN OBJECT

AUG 5

The SCALE command changes the length and width of an object proportionately. The STRETCH command, on the other hand, changes only one dimension of an object or view. In mechanical drafting, it is common to increase the length of a part while leaving the diameter or width the same. In architectural design, room sizes may be stretched to increase the square footage.

When using the STRETCH command, you can select objects individually, or with the crossing, window, or polygon options. For example, at the Select objects: prompt, pick the opposite two corners of a crossing box around the objects you want to stretch.

Stretch may be picked from the Modify pull-down or MODIFY screen menu. It automatically uses the Crossing option at the Select objects: prompt. If you type the STRETCH command, the sequence looks like this:

Command: **STRETCH** ⏎
Select objects to stretch by crossing-window or -polygon...
Select objects: *(use a crossing, window, or one of the polygon options to select the first corner of a crossing box)*
Select objects: *(pick the second corner)*
Select objects: *(pick additional objects or press ENTER)*

Select only that portion of the object to be stretched as in Figure 13-29. If you select the entire object, the STRETCH command works like the MOVE command.

Next, you are asked to pick the base point. This is the point from which the object will be stretched. Then pick a new position for the base point. As you move the screen cursor, the object or objects are stretched or compressed. When the displayed object is stretched to the desired position, pick the new point. The command sequence after selecting objects is as follows:

Base point or displacement: *(pick the base point for the stretch to begin)*
Second point of displacement: *(pick the final location of the base point)*
Command:

The example in Figure 13-29 shows the object being stretched. This is a common use of the STRETCH command. You may also use the STRETCH command to reduce the size of an object.

Figure 13-29. Using the STRETCH command.

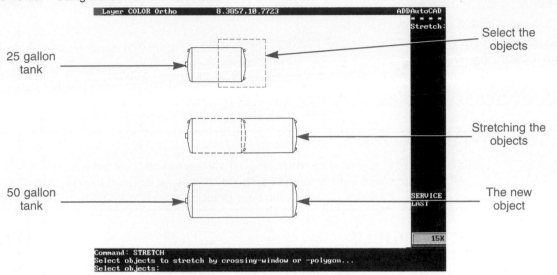

- 25 gallon tank → Select the objects
- Stretching the objects
- 50 gallon tank → The new object

Using the Displacement option

The Displacement option works the same with the STRETCH command as with the MOVE and COPY commands.

Command: **STRETCH** ⏎
Select objects to stretch by crossing-window or -polygon…
Select objects: *(pick the first corner of a crossing, window, or one of the polygon options)*
Other corner: *(pick the second corner)*
Select objects: ⏎
Base point or displacement: *(enter an X and Y displacement value such as 2,3)*
Second point of displacement: ⏎
Command:

When you press ENTER at the Second point of displacement: prompt, the object is automatically stretched as you specified with the X and Y coordinates at the Base point or displacement: prompt. In this case, the object was stretched 2 units in the X direction and 3 units in the Y direction.

PROFESSIONAL TIP

It may not be common to have objects lined up in a convenient manner for using the Crossing selection option with the STRETCH command. You should consider using the Window-polygon or Crossing-polygon selection options to make selecting the objects easier.

Also, make sure the DRAGMODE is turned on when stretching an object; you can watch the object stretch to its new size. If the stretched object is not what you expected, cancel the command with CTRL+C or puck button 3. The STRETCH command and other editing commands discussed in this chapter work well with ORTHO on. This lets you work in only horizontal and vertical directions.

EXERCISE 13-9

❑ Load AutoCAD and open TITLEB.
❑ Design and draw a cylindrical-shaped object similar to the tank in Figure 13-29.
❑ Stretch the object to approximately twice its original length.
❑ Stretch the object to about twice its original height.
❑ Save the drawing as A:EX13-9 and quit.

LENGTHENING OR SHORTENING AN OBJECT

[AUG 5]

The LENGTHEN command may be used to change the length of objects and the included angle of an arc. Objects can only be lengthened one at a time. The LENGTHEN command does not affect closed objects. For example, you can lengthen a line, polyline, arc, elliptical arc, or spline but you cannot lengthen a closed polygon. Pick Lengthen: from the MODIFY screen menu, the Modify pull-down menu, or type LENGTHEN at the Command: prompt. When you select an object, AutoCAD gives you the current length if the object is linear or the included angle if the object is an arc:

Command: **LENGTHEN** ⏎
DElta/Percent/Total/DYnamic/⟨Select object⟩: *(pick an object)*
Current length: 1.500, included angle: 75.000
DElta/Percent/Total/DYnamic/⟨Select object⟩:

The following describes the function of each option:

- **DElta.** The DElta option allows specification of a positive or negative change in length measured from the endpoint of the selected object. The lengthening or shortening happens closest to the selection point and changes the length by the amount you specify. See Figure 13-30.

    Command: **LENGTHEN** ⏎
    DElta/Percent/Total/DYnamic/⟨Select object⟩: *(pick an object)*
    Current length: 3.000
    DElta/Percent/Total/DYnamic/⟨Select object⟩: **DE** ⏎
    Angle/⟨Enter delta length (0.000)⟩: *(enter the desired length, .75 for example)*
    ⟨*Select object to change*⟩/Undo: *(pick the object again)*
    ⟨Select object to change⟩/Undo: *(press ENTER to make the change or type **U** to Undo the change)*
    Command:

Figure 13-30   Using the LENGTHEN command DElta option.

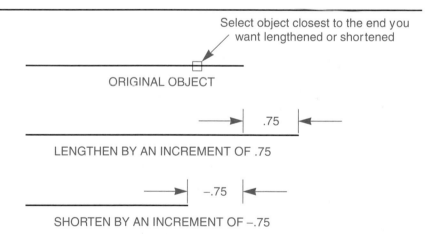

Select object closest to the end you want lengthened or shortened

ORIGINAL OBJECT

.75

LENGTHEN BY AN INCREMENT OF .75

−.75

SHORTEN BY AN INCREMENT OF −.75

You can also change the length of an arc as previously demonstrated on a line, but you can also change the included angle of an arc. The DElta option has an Angle sub option that lets you change the included angle of an arc by a specified angle. The command sequence is as follows and shown in Figure 13-31:

Command: **LENGTHEN** ⏎
DElta/Percent/Total/DYnamic/⟨Select object⟩: **DE** ⏎
Angle/⟨Enter delta length (0.0000)⟩: **A** ⏎
Enter delta angle ⟨0.0000⟩: *(enter an angle such as **45**)*
⟨Select object to change⟩/Undo: *(pick the arc)*
⟨Select object to change⟩/Undo: ⏎
Command:

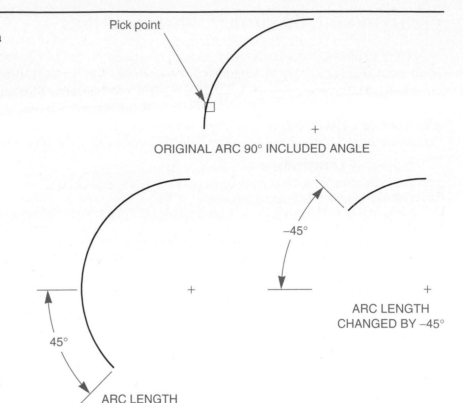

Figure 13-31. Using the LENGTHEN command DElta option's Angle suboption.

Pick point

ORIGINAL ARC 90° INCLUDED ANGLE

−45°

ARC LENGTH CHANGED BY −45°

45°

ARC LENGTH CHANGED BY 45°

- **Percent.** The Percent option allows you to change the length of an object or the angle of an arc by a specified percentage of its total length or angle. If you consider the original length 100% then you can make the object shorter by specifying less than 100% or longer by specifying more than 100%. Look at Figure 13-32 and follow this command sequence:

Command: **LENGTHEN** ↵
DElta/Percent/Total/DYnamic/〈Select object〉: **P** ↵
Enter percent length 〈100.0〉: **125** ↵
〈Select object to change〉/Undo: *(pick the object)*
〈Select object to change〉/Undo: ↵
Command:

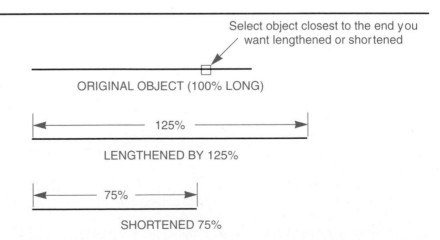

Figure 13-32. Using the LENGTHEN command Percent option.

Select object closest to the end you want lengthened or shortened

ORIGINAL OBJECT (100% LONG)

125%

LENGTHENED BY 125%

75%

SHORTENED 75%

- **Total.** The Total option allows you to set the total length or angle by the value that you specify. See Figure 13-33. You do not have to select the object before entering one of the options, but doing so lets you know the current length and angle of the object (if it is an arc):

Command: **LENGTHEN** ↵
DElta/Percent/Total/DYnamic/⟨Select object⟩: *(pick an object)*
Current length: 3.000
DElta/Percent/Total/DYnamic/⟨Select object⟩: **T** ↵
Angle/⟨Enter delta length (1.000)⟩: *(enter a new length such as* **3.75** *or* **A** *if it is
    an angle)*
⟨Select object to change⟩/Undo: *(pick the object)*
⟨Select object to change⟩/Undo: ↵
Command:

Figure 13-33.   Using the
LENGTHEN command
Total option.

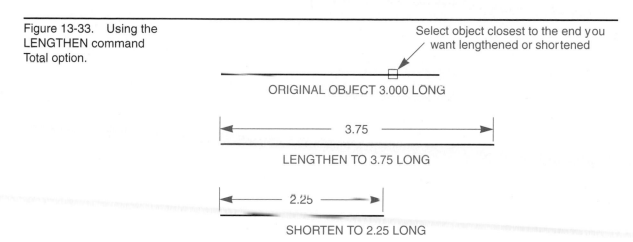

Select object closest to the end you
want lengthened or shortened

ORIGINAL OBJECT 3.000 LONG

◄——————— 3.75 ———————►

LENGTHEN TO 3.75 LONG

◄——— 2.25 ———►

SHORTEN TO 2.25 LONG

• **DYnamic.** This option lets you drag the endpoint of the object to the desired length or angle
with the screen cursor. This allows you to visually change the length or angle by moving the
screen cursor, so it is helpful to have the grid and snap set to usable increments. See Figure 13-
34. This is the command sequence:

Command: **LENGTHEN** ↵
DElta/Percent/Total/DYnamic/⟨Select object⟩: **DY** ↵
Specify new end point.
⟨Select object to change⟩/Undo: *(pick the object and move the cursor to the desired
    length)*
⟨Select object to change⟩/Undo: ↵
Command:

Figure 13-34.   Using the
LENGTHEN command
DYnamic option.

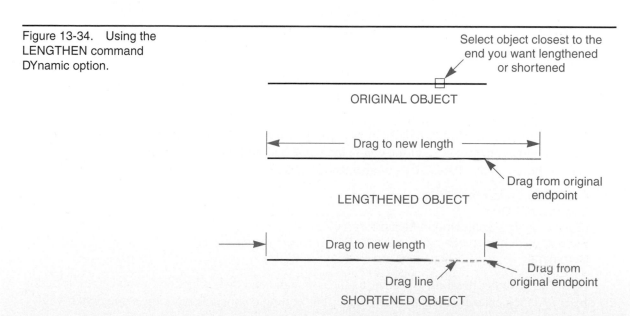

Select object closest to the
end you want lengthened
or shortened

ORIGINAL OBJECT

◄——————— Drag to new length ———————►

Drag from original
endpoint

LENGTHENED OBJECT

Drag to new length

Drag line

Drag from
original endpoint

SHORTENED OBJECT

Identifying the length of an object

The LENGTHEN command may also be used to identify the length of an object such as a line, or length and included angle of an arc. To do this, enter LENGTHEN at the Command: prompt and pick the desired object in response to the ⟨Select object⟩: prompt as follows:

Command: **LENGTHEN** ↵
DElta/Percent/Total/DYnamic/⟨Select object⟩: *(pick a line)*
Current length: 1.25
DElta/Percent/Total/DYnamic/⟨Select object⟩: *(pick an arc)*
Current length: 1.25, included angle: 152.00
DElta/Percent/Total/DYnamic/⟨Select object⟩: ↵
Command:

EXERCISE 13-10

❑ Load AutoCAD and set up your own variables or use a prototype.
❑ Use the LENGTHEN command and the following options to draw objects similar to the ones specified in the given figure numbers: (Note: use the COPY command to make two copies of each original object for the lengthening or shortening)
DElta–Figure 13-30 and Figure 13-31.
Percent–Figure 13-32.
Total–Figure 13-33.
DYnamic–Figure 13-34.
❑ Use the LENGTHEN command to identify the length of a line and an arc.
❑ Save the drawing as A:EX13-10 and quit.

SELECTING OBJECTS BEFORE EDITING   AUG 5

Throughout this chapter, you have worked with the basic editing commands by entering the command name and then selecting the object to be edited. You can also set up AutoCAD to let you select the object first and then enter the desired editing command. The system variables that affect this procedure are PICKAUTO, PICKFIRST, and GRIPS. They should be set as follows:

- **PICKAUTO = 1 (on).** This allows you to automatically pick objects by the method used to pick and move the cursor.
- **PICKFIRST = 1 (on).** This system variable lets you pick the object before entering the editing command. When PICKFIRST is set to 0 (off), you must enter the command name before selecting the object. Notice the difference in the appearance of the crosshairs when PICKFIRST is on and off.
- **GRIPS = 0 (off).** Grips are used for automatic editing, and are discussed in detail in Chapter 14. For PICKFIRST to have its best performance, turn GRIPS off. If you are following along with this text while working at your computer, be sure to turn the GRIPS system variable back on when working in Chapter 14.

You can select objects individually or as a group at the Command: prompt. The selected entities become highlighted; then you enter the command name and proceed with the prompts as discussed in this chapter. For example, the COPY command works like this:

Command: *(select the entities to copy)*
Command: **COPY** ↵
⟨Base point or displacement⟩/Multiple: *(pick a base point)*
Second point of displacement: *(pick the final location for the copy)*
Command:

Now you have the flexibility of entering the command and then selecting the object, or selecting the object and then entering the command name. The editing commands work the same either way.

EXERCISE 13-11

❑ Load AutoCAD and open EX13-3, or start a new drawing and draw a square and triangle of any size.
❑ Set the following system variables as shown:
   PICKAUTO = 1
   PICKFIRST = 1
   GRIPS = 0
❑ Select the square; then enter the MOVE command to move it to a new position.
❑ Select the triangle; then enter the COPY command to make a copy of it.
❑ Experiment by selecting objects followed by using some of the other editing commands such as ROTATE and SCALE.
❑ Erase an object by selecting the object before entering the ERASE command.
❑ Save the drawing as A:EX13-11 and quit.

EDITING WITH THE GEOMETRY CALCULATOR　　　　AUG 3

In Chapter 9, you were introduced to the geometry calculator using the CAL command. This discussion shows you how to use the calculator to perform editing tasks. Review Chapter 9 before proceeding, paying special attention to the symbols, equations, and format detailed there.

Sometimes it is difficult to determine the exact position of an object you are trying to edit since the geometry does not fit into your grid and snap setup. When this occurs, it may be helpful to use the CAL command. There are an endless number of possibilities; this discussion provides you with a few of the many options.

Assume you have a drawing similar to the one shown in Figure 13-35. You can easily locate points 1 and 2 using object snap modes; however, you cannot find the exact center between the points for the final destination of the circular object. Use the MOVE and CAL commands as follows:

    Command: **MOVE** ↵
    Select objects: *(select the circular object on the right)*
    Select objects: ↵
    Base point or displacement: *(use the OSNAP CENter option to locate the center of the circular object)*

Now use the CAL command to locate the center point exactly halfway between points 1 and 2:

    Second point of displacement: **'CAL** ↵
    ⟩⟩ Expression: **(END + END)/2** ↵
    ⟩⟩ Select entity for END snap: *(pick point 1)*
    ⟩⟩ Select entity for END snap: *(pick point 2)*

The circular object automatically moves to the exact center point between points 1 and 2.

Figure 13-35. Centering an object between two endpoints using the CAL command.

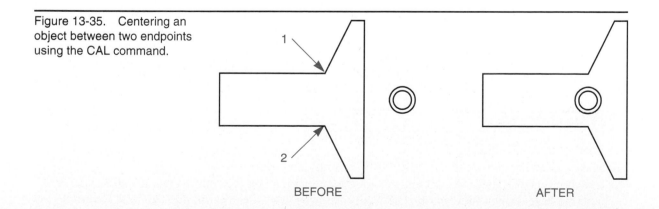

BEFORE   AFTER

EXERCISE 13-12

❑ Load AutoCAD and open TITLEA.
❑ Create a drawing similar to the "BEFORE" example in Figure 13-35.
❑ Use the MOVE and CAL commands to move the circular object exactly halfway between points 1 and 2. Your results should be similar to the "AFTER" example.
❑ Save the drawing as A:EX13-12 and quit.

The object at the left in Figure 13-36 is rotated at an unknown angle. This makes it difficult to rotate the object on the right to the same angle. The objective is to rotate the object on the right so that its base is parallel with the base of the object on the left. The following command sequence accomplishes this task:

Command: **ROTATE** ↵
Select objects: *(select the horizontal object on the right)*
Select objects: ↵
Base point: *(pick point 1)*
⟨Rotation angle⟩/Reference: **'CAL** ↵
⟩⟩ Expression: **ANG(END,END)** ↵
⟩⟩ Select entity for END snap: *(pick point 2)*
⟩⟩ Select entity for END snap: *(pick point 3)*
Command:

Figure 13-36.   Rotating an object so its base is parallel with an existing object.

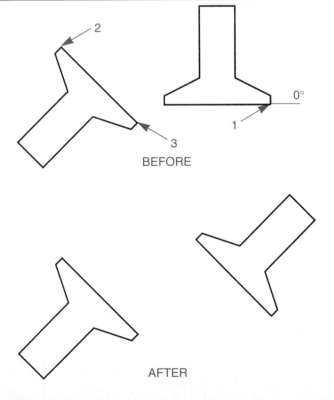

BEFORE

AFTER

EXERCISE 13-13

❑ Load AutoCAD and open TITLEA.
❑ Make a drawing similar to the "BEFORE" example in Figure 13-36.
❑ Use the ROTATE and CAL commands to rotate the object on the right so that its base is parallel with the base of the object on the left. Your results should be similar to the "AFTER" example.
❑ Save the drawing as A:EX13-13 and quit.

SELECTING OBJECTS FOR FUTURE EDITING

AUG 2

The SELECT command is used to preselect an object or group of objects for future editing. It is designed to increase your productivity. Often you are working with the same set of objects, moving, copying, or scaling them. Set these aside as a selection set with the SELECT command. Then continue to perform another drawing or editing task. To return to those objects set aside, enter P at the Select objects: prompt. The command sequences for creating a selection set and then moving it are as follows:

> Command: **SELECT** ↵
> Select objects: *(use any method to select an individual object or group of objects)*
> Select objects: *(select additional objects or press ENTER)*

This sets up a selection set. Later, when you want to move these objects, use the Previous option as follows:

> Command: **MOVE** ↵
> Select objects: **P** ↵ *(this selects the object or group of objects previously selected using the SELECT command)*
> Select objects: ↵
> Base point or displacement: *(pick the base point)*
> Second point of displacement: *(pick the new location of the base point)*

EXERCISE 13-14

❑ Load AutoCAD and open TITLEA.
❑ Draw two circles with 1.5 in. (38.1 mm) radii spaced .25 in. (6.35 mm) apart.
❑ Use the SELECT command to select both circles for future editing.
❑ Draw at least three other small objects.
❑ Use the COPY command and the Previous option to copy the original two circles to a new location.
❑ Save the drawing as A:EX13-14 and quit.

CREATING OBJECT GROUPS

AUG 5

A *group* is a named selection set of objects. These selection sets are saved with the drawing and therefore exist between multiple drawing sessions. Objects can be members of more than one group and groups can be nested. *Nesting* means that one group can be inside of another group. An object existing in multiple groups creates an interesting situation. For example, if a LINE and an ARC are grouped and then the ARC is grouped with a CIRCLE, moving the first group moves the LINE and ARC, and moving the second group moves the ARC and CIRCLE. Nesting can be used to group smaller groups into larger groups for easier editing.

The PICKSTYLE system variable is used to determine whether selecting a grouped object selects the individual object or the entire group. PICKSTYLE has the following settings:

> 0 = No group selection or associative hatch selection. Hatch is used in sectioning and is discussed in Chapter 24. Associative hatch means that the hatch pattern is associated with the object. So, when the object is changed, the hatch pattern changes with it.
> 1 = Group selection is the default.
> 2 = Associative hatch selection.
> 3 = Group selection and associative hatch selection.

Enter PICKSTYLE like this:

> Command: **PICKSTYLE** ↵
> New value for PICKSTYLE ⟨1⟩:

The GROUP command may be typed, or accessed by picking Group objects... from the Assist pull-down menu, or Group: in the ASSIST screen menu. Entering GROUP displays the "Object Grouping" dialog box shown in Figure 13-37.

Figure 13-37. The "Object Grouping" dialog box. The different elements are shown here highlighted.

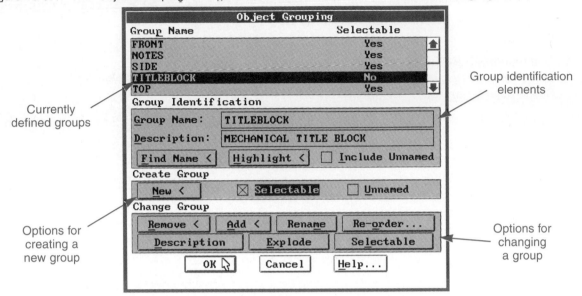

The elements found in the "Object Grouping" dialog box are described in the following:
- **Group Name.** This shows currently defined groups.
- **Selectable.** If a group is selectable, picking any object in it selects the entire group. Making a group nonselectable allows individual objects to be edited while still in the group.
- **Group Identification elements.** This section of the "Object Grouping" dialog box shows the name of the selected group and its description. The elements found in this section are described as follows:
  - **Group Name:**–Displays the name of the currently selected group. Also, this is where a name for a new group is entered. Group names can be a maximum of 31 characters long and include letters, numbers, and the special characters $, _, and -. The group name may not have a space between words, but if you want to use two words, separate them with an underline or dash, such as CHART-EARNINGS.
  - **Description:**–This field allows a text description of the group shown in Group Name:. A maximum of 64 characters may be used, including spaces.
  - **Find Name ⟨**–The Find Name ⟨ button allows selection of an object, then displays a dialog list of all groups the object is associated with. When you pick this button, you get the following prompt:

    Pick a member of a group.

    The drawing editor returns and you can pick an item for identification. This displays the "Group Member List" subdialog box which just lists the group.
  - **Highlight ⟨**–This allows a group name to be specified, then highlights all the members of the specified group in the drawing editor. This allows you to see the parts of the drawing that are identified as the members of that group. There is a Continue button that you can pick or press ENTER to get back to the "Object Grouping" dialog box.
  - **Include Unnamed**–This is a toggle that causes unnamed groups to be listed with named groups. Unnamed groups are given a default name by AutoCAD in the format: *Ax, where x is an integer value that increases with each new group, for example, *A6. Unnamed groups can be named later by using the Rename option.

- **Create Group.** This section of the "Object Grouping" dialog box shows the options for creating a new group. The elements found in this section are described as follows:
  - **New ⟨** –This creates a new group from the selected objects using the name that is entered in the Group Name: text box. AutoCAD issues these prompts after you enter a new name in the Group Name: text box.

    ```
    Select objects for grouping:
    Select objects: (select the objects to group)
    Select objects: ⏎
    ```

    The "Object Grouping" dialog box returns and the newly named group is shown in the Group Name list.
  - **Selectable** –A check in this box sets the initial status of the Selectable value as "Yes" for the new group that is identified under the Selectable list described earlier. No check here specifies "No" under the Selectable list. This can be changed later.
  - **Unnamed** –This indicates whether the new group will be named. If this box is checked, AutoCAD assigns its own default name as detailed previously.
- **Change Group.** This section of the "Object Grouping" dialog box shows the options for changing a group. The elements found in this section are described as follows:
  - **Remove ⟨** –Pick this button to remove objects from a group definition.
  - **Add ⟨** –Allows objects to be added to a group definition.
  - **Rename** –Pick this button to change the name of a existing group. Unnamed groups having AutoCAD's default name can be renamed to a user defined name.
  - **Re-order...** –Objects are numbered in the order in which they are selected in the group definition process. The first object is numbered 0, not 1. This option allows objects to be re-ordered within the group. For example, if a group contains a set of instructions, you can re-order the instructions to suit the typical steps that are used to follow the instructions. The "Order Group" subdialog box is displayed when you pick this button. The elements of this dialog box are briefly described as follows:
    - **Group Name.** Displays the name of the selected group.
    - **Description.** Displays the description that you entered for the selected group.
    - **Remove from position (0-n):.** Position number of the object to re-order, where "n" is the total number of objects found in the group. You place the desired order in the text box to the right of this and the next two features.
    - **Replace at position (0-n):.** Position number to place the object at.
    - **Number of objects (1-n):.** Displays the number of objects or the range to re-order.
    - **Reverse Order.** Pick this button to have the order of all members in the group reversed.
  - **Description** –Updates the group with the new description entered in the Description: text box described earlier.
  - **Explode** –Pick this button to delete the selected group definition, but not the group's objects. The group name is removed and the original group is exploded, but copies of the group are not affected. Explode is an operation that breaks down a complex object into simpler objects. The reason this happens is because copies of a group become unnamed groups. By toggling on the Include Unnamed switch, these unnamed groups are displayed and can then be exploded, if needed.
  - **Selectable** –Toggles the selectable value of a group. This is where, as suggested earlier, you can change the value in the Selectable list from Yes to No or back again.

EXERCISE 13-15

❑ Load AutoCAD and open one of your previous more complex drawings.
❑ Use the GROUP command to name and describe several different elements of the drawing as groups. For example, Views: FRONT, TOP, SIDE, TITLEBLOCK, or NOTES.
❑ Use each element of the "Object Grouping" dialog box to see the effect on the groups that you have named.
❑ Save as A:EX13-15 or quit without saving.

CHAPTER TEST

Write your answers in the spaces provided.

1. Give the command and entries used to draw a 45° x .125 chamfer:

   Command:_____

   Polyline/Distances/Angle/Trim/Method/⟨Select first line⟩: _____

   Enter first chamfer distance ⟨*current*⟩: _____

   Enter second chamfer distance ⟨previous⟩:_____

   Command:_____

   Polyline/Distances/⟨Select first line⟩: _____

   Select second line: _____

2. Give the command and entries required to produce .50 radius fillets on all corners of a closed polyline:

   Command:_____

   Polyline/Radius/Trim/⟨Select first object⟩: _____

   Enter fillet radius ⟨*current*⟩:_____

   Command:_____

   Polyline/Radius/Trim/⟨Select first object⟩: _____

   Select 2D polyline: _____

3. Give the command, entries, and actions required to move an object from position A to position B:

   Command:_____

   Select objects:_____

   Select objects:_____

   Base point or displacement: _____

   Second point of displacement: _____

4. Give the command and entries needed to make two copies of the same object:

Command:_____

Select objects:_____

Select objects:_____

⟨Base point or displacement⟩/Multiple: _____

Base point: _____

Second point of displacement: _____

Second point of displacement: _____

Second point of displacement: _____

5. Give the command and entries necessary to draw a reverse image and then remove an existing object:

Command:_____

Select objects:_____

Select objects:_____

First point of mirror line: _____

Second point of mirror line: _____

Delete old objects? ⟨N⟩:_____

6. Give the command and entries needed to rotate an object 45° clockwise:

Command:_____

Select objects:_____

Select objects:_____

Base point: _____

⟨Rotation angle⟩/Reference: _____

7. Give the command and entries required to reduce the size of an entire drawing by one-half:

Command:_____

Select objects:_____

Select objects:_____

Base point: _____

⟨Scale factor⟩/Reference: _____

8. Give the command and entries needed to change the first break point picked to the intersection of two other lines:

Command:_____

Select object:_____

Enter second point (or F for first point):_____

Enter first point: _____

of _____

Enter second point: _____

9. Give the command sequence which revises the radius of a circle:

   Command:_____

   Select objects:_____

   Select objects:_____

   Properties/(Change point): _____

10. Define the term "displacement" as it relates to the MOVE and COPY commands. _____

    _____

    _____

11. Explain the difference between the MOVE and COPY commands. _____

    _____

    _____

12. List two locations you normally choose as the base point when using the MOVE or COPY
    commands. _____

    _____

13. Describe the purpose of the SELECT command. _____

    _____

14. What is a selection set? _____

    _____

15. How do you select objects for editing that have previously been picked using the SELECT
    command? _____

    _____

16. How is the size of a fillet specified? _____

17. Identify the default selection method issued by AutoCAD for the STRETCH command. _____

    _____

18. List two ways to cancel the STRETCH command. _____

    _____

19. The EXTEND command can be considered the opposite of the _____ command.

20. Name the system variable used to preset the fillet radius. _____

21. In what direction should you pick points to break a portion out of a circle or arc?_____

    _____

22. Name the command which trims an object to a cutting edge. _____

23. Name the command associated with boundary edges._____

24. The MOVE, COPY, TRIM, EXTEND, and STRETCH commands are located in the
    _____ screen menu and the _____ or _____ pull-down menus.

25. Name the command that can be used to move and rotate an object simultaneously._____

    _____

26. Describe the purpose of the PICKFIRST system variable. _____

    _____

27. Describe the difference between Trim and No trim when using the CHAMFER and FILLET commands. _____

_____

_____

_____

28. What is the purpose of the Method option in the CHAMFER command? _____

_____

29. How can you split an object in two without removing a portion? _____

_____

_____

_____

30. Name the option in the TRIM and EXTEND commands that allows you to trim or extend to an implied intersection. _____

_____

31. How do you use the Smart mode? _____

_____

_____

_____

_____

32. Identify the LENGTHEN command option with its descriptions by placing the letter of the command option in the blank in front of its description.

_____ Change a length or arc angle by a percentage of the total.   A. DElta

_____ Drag the end point of the object to the desired length or angle.   B. Percent

_____ Allows a positive or negative change in length from the end point.   C. Total

_____ Set the total length or angle to the value specified.   D. DYnamic

33. Define a group. _____

_____

34. How do you access the "Object Grouping" dialog box?

_____

_____

_____

_____

35. Describe how you create a new group.

_____

_____

_____

_____

DRAWING PROBLEMS

Use the TITLEA or TITLEB prototypes as appropriate for each of the following problems.

P13-1

1. Draw the object shown as view A. Change the angle of the object to 45° as shown in view B. Then rotate it to a 90° rotation angle as shown in view C. Save the drawing as A:P13-1 and quit.

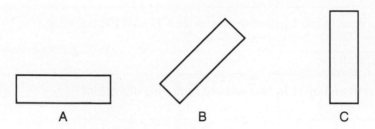

A   B   C

P13-2

2. Draw the object shown as view A. Scale it down to 1/4 size as shown in view B. Then scale the object 10 times as shown in view C. Save the drawing as A:P13-2 and quit.

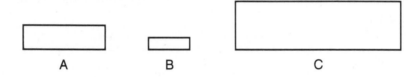

A   B   C

P13-3

3. Draw object A using the LINE command, making sure that the corners overrun. Then trim the lines all at the same time. Select all four lines when asked to select cutting edges. Pick all overruns when asked to select object to trim. The object should appear as shown in view B. Save the drawing as A:P13-3 and quit.

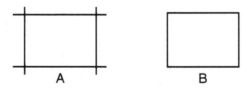

A   B

P13-4

4. Draw object A using the LINE and ARC commands. Make sure that the corners overrun and the arc is centered, but does not touch the lines. Then use the TRIM, EXTEND, and MOVE commands to make the object look like the example shown in view B. Save the drawing as A:P13-4 and quit.

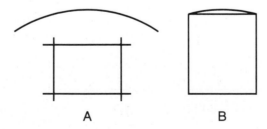

A   B

P13-5

5. Open drawing P13-4 for further editing. Using the STRETCH command, change the shape to that shown in view B. Make a copy of the new revision. Change the copy to represent the example shown in view C. Save the drawing as A:P13-5 and quit.

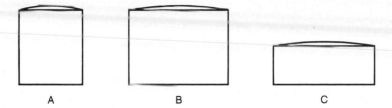

A   B   C

P13-6

6. Refer to Figure 13-29 in this chapter for this problem. Draw and make three copies of the object shown in Option 1. Stretch the first copy to twice its length as shown as Option 2. Stretch the second copy to twice its height. Double the size of the third copy using the SCALE command. Save the drawing as A:P13-6 and quit.

P13-7

7. Draw objects A, B, and C shown below without dimensions. Then, move objects A, B, and C to new positions. Select a corner of object A and the center of objects B and C as the base points. Save the drawing as A:P13-7 and quit.

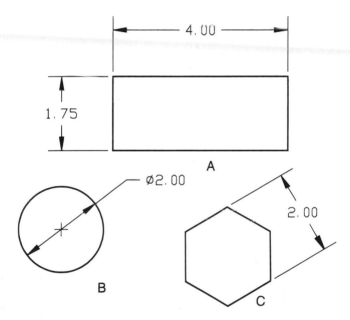

P13-8

8. Draw objects A, B, and C shown in Problem 13-7 at the left side of the screen. Make a copy of object A two units to the right. Make four copies of object B three units, center-to-center, to the right using the Multiple option. Make three copies of object C three units, center-to-center, to the right. Save the drawing as A:P13-8 and quit.

P13-9

9. Draw the object shown using the ELLIPSE, COPY, and LINE commands. The rotation angle of the ellipses is 60°. Use the BREAK command when drawing and editing the lower ellipse. Save the drawing as A:P13-9 and quit.

10. Call up drawing P13-9 for further editing. Shorten the height of the object using the STRETCH command as shown below. Next, add to the object as indicated. Save the drawing as A:P13-10 and quit.

P13-10

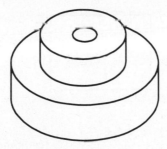

11. Draw the object shown as view A. Use the BREAK command to help change the object to the example shown as view B. Save the drawing as A:P13-11 and quit.

P13-11

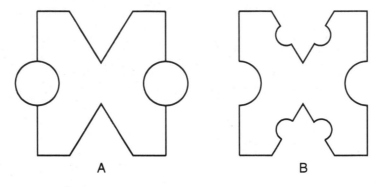

A   B

12. Draw view A, without dimensions. Use the CHAMFER and FILLET commands to your best advantage. Then draw a mirror image of it as shown in view B. Now, remove the original view and move the new view so that point 2 is at the original point 1 location. Save the drawing as A:P13-12 and quit.

P13-12

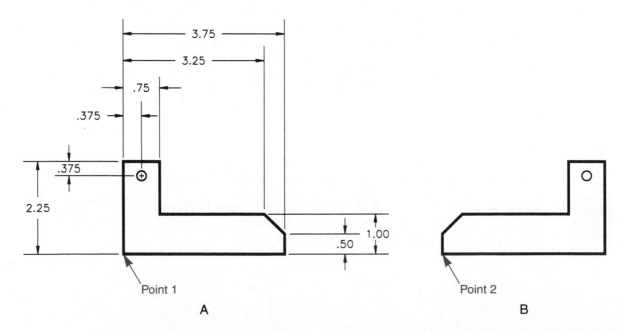

A   B

13. Draw the object shown below, without dimensions. The object is symmetrical; therefore, draw only the right half. Then mirror the left half into place. Use the CHAMFER and FILLET commands to your best advantage. Save the drawing as A:P13-13 and quit.

P13-13

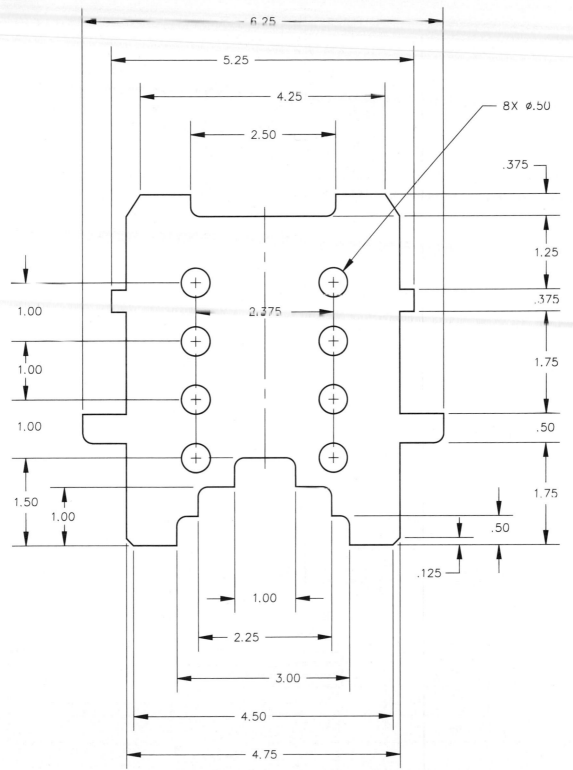

NOTE: ALL FILLETS AND ROUNDS R.125.

P13-14

14. Refer to the view shown below for this problem. Plan to use the TRIM, OSNAP, and OFFSET commands to assist you in drawing the view. Do not draw centerlines or dimensions. Save the completed drawing as A:P13-14 and quit.

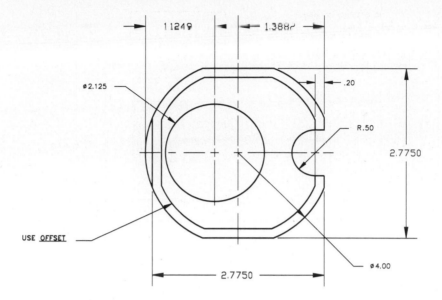

P13-15

15. Draw the object shown below, without dimensions. Then mirror the right half into place. Use the CHAMFER and FILLET commands to your best advantage. Save the drawing as A:P13-15 and quit.

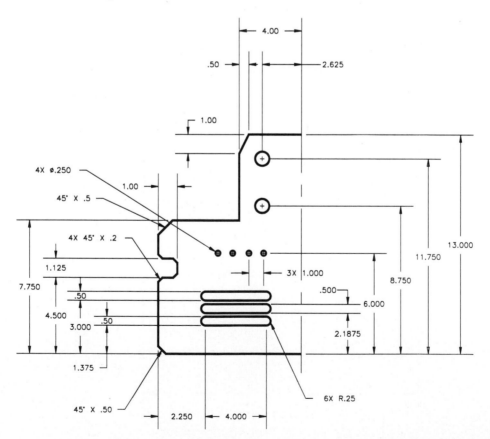

16. Redraw the objects shown below. Then mirror the drawing, but have the text remain readable. Delete the original image during the mirroring process. Save the drawing as A:P13-16 and quit.

P13-16

2b1

TRANSFER

5n2 4a1 8a1

LTS. HTRS. FANS

2b1

1b1

RESET

11b1

BYPASS

17. Draw the kitchen cabinet layout shown in view A and the partial floor plan shown at B. Make the cabinet 24 in. (600 mm) deep and the walls 6 in. (150 mm) wide. Make the sink and range proportional in size to the given illustration. Use the ALIGN command to move and rotate the cabinet layout into the wall location as shown in view C. Save the drawing as A:P13-17.

P13-17

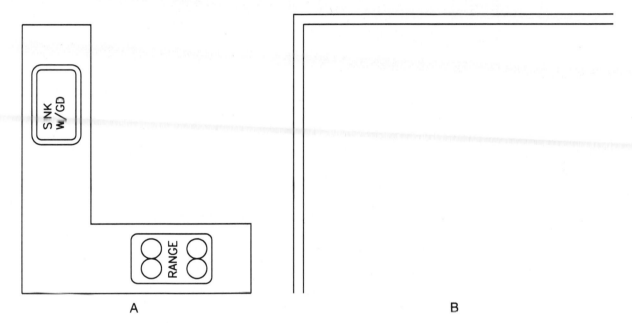

A   B

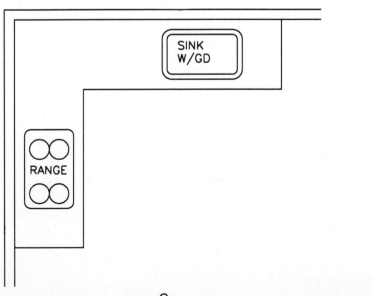

C

18. Draw the following objects. All rounds on the drawing are .250 unit radius. Use the CAL command to assist you in moving the circular object at the right to be centered exactly between points 1 and 2 on the object on the left. Do not dimension the drawing. Save the drawing as A:P13-18.

P13-18

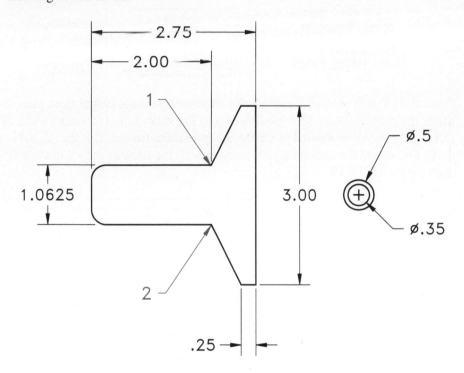

19. Open drawing P13-18. Make a copy of the object and rotate the copy to a horizontal position similar to the object shown at A below. Exact position is not critical. Rotate the original object to 225° as shown at B. Use the ROTATE, MOVE, or ALIGN commands as needed. Your objects should now look like A and B below. Use the ROTATE and CAL commands to rotate the object on the right so that the base is parallel to the base of the object on the left. Save the drawing as A:P13-19.

P13-19

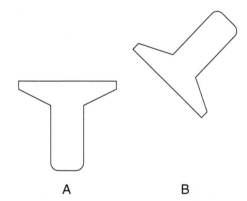

A   B

20. Draw the objects shown using the dimensions given, but do not draw the dimensions. Copy all of the objects and perform the specified TRIM and EXTEND operations to demonstrate a before and after representation. Save the drawing as A:P13-20.

P13-20

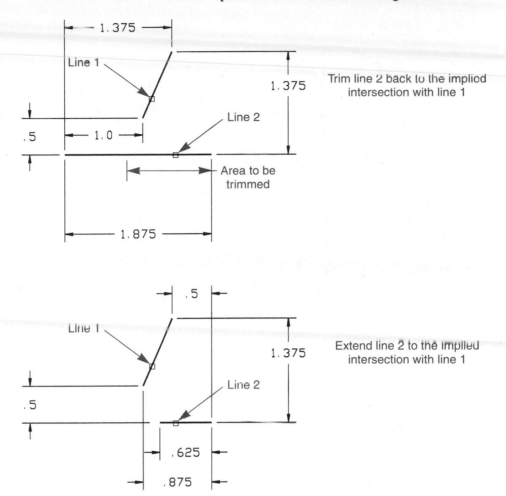

Trim line 2 back to the implied intersection with line 1

Extend line 2 to the implied intersection with line 1

21. Draw the objects shown using the dimensions given, but do not draw the dimensions. Copy all of the objects and perform the specified LENGTHEN operations to demonstrate a before and after representation. Perform all operations from the right end of the copied lines. Save the drawing as A:P13-21.

P13-21

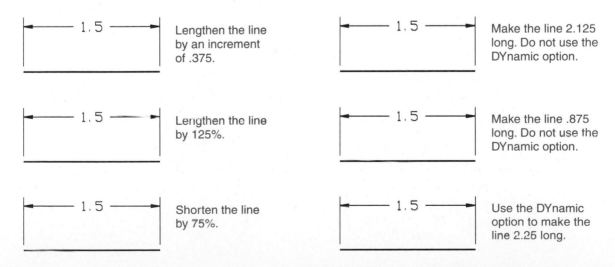

Lengthen the line by an increment of .375.

Make the line 2.125 long. Do not use the DYnamic option.

Lengthen the line by 125%.

Make the line .875 long. Do not use the DYnamic option.

Shorten the line by 75%.

Use the DYnamic option to make the line 2.25 long.

22. Draw the objects shown at the left using the dimensions given, but do not draw the dimensions. Copy all of the objects to a position to the right and perform the specified LENGTHEN operations to demonstrate a before and after representation. Perform all operations from the bottom left end of the copied arcs. Save the drawing as A:P13-22.

P13-22

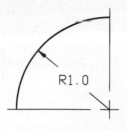

Increase the included angle by 90°.

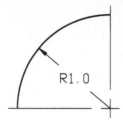

Decrease the included angle by 45°.

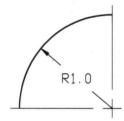

Lengthen the arc by 50%.

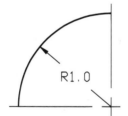

Drag the length of the arc to 270°.

23. Draw the following object without dimensions. Note: Use the TRIMMODE to your advantage. Save the drawing as A:P13-23.

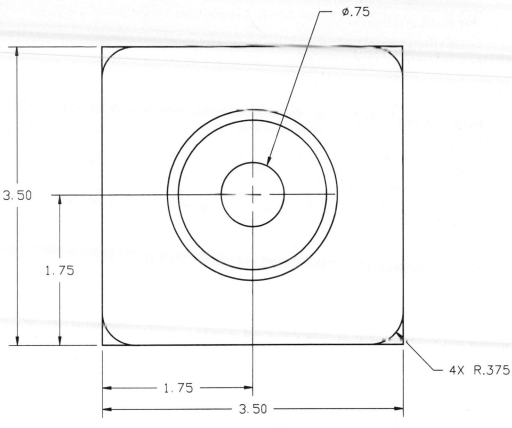

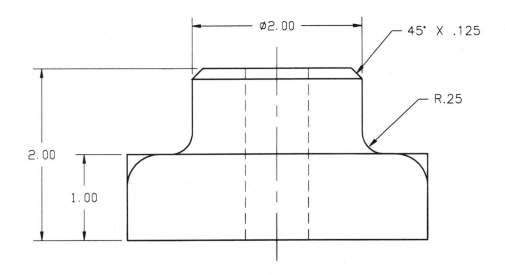

P13-24

24. Draw the objects shown at A, B, C, D, and E below. Use the GROUP command to name each of the drawings as follows:

A=SWITCH

B=REGULATOR

C=GROUND-SWITCH

D=GROUND-OVERCURRENT

E=FUSE

Use the object groups to draw the one-line electrical diagram shown below. Use the Explode option to edit the symbols at 1 and 2 in the diagram as shown. Save the drawing as A:P13-24.

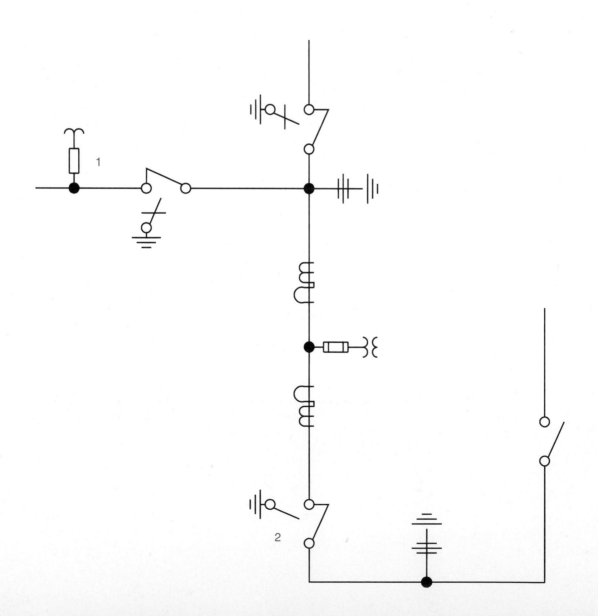

Learning objectives

After completing this chapter, you will be able to:

- ○ Use grips to do automatic editing with the STRETCH, COPY, MOVE, ROTATE, SCALE, and MIRROR commands.
- ○ Identify the system variables used to do automatic editing.
- ○ Perform automatic editing through the "Modify" dialog box.
- ○ Change the properties of an object.
- ○ Use the FILTER command to create a selection set.

In Chapter 13 you learned how to use commands that let you do a variety of drawing and editing activities with AutoCAD. These editing commands are used to give you maximum flexibility and increase productivity. The command format allowed you to enter commands such as COPY, MOVE, and SCALE before selecting objects, or to set system variables that let you select the object before entering the command name. This chapter takes editing a step further by allowing you to select an object and automatically perform editing operations.

AUTOMATIC EDITING WITH GRIPS ⬚ AUG 5

"Hold," "grab," or "grasp" are all words that are synonymous with grip. In AutoCAD, *grips* are features on an object that are highlighted with a small box. For example, the grips on a line are the ends and midpoint. When grips are used for editing, you can select an object to automatically activate the grips, and then pick any of the small boxes to perform stretch, move, rotate, scale, and mirror operations. In order for grips to work, the GRIPS system variable must be On (1). GRIPS is on by default, but if GRIPS is Off (0), turn it on like this:

Command: **GRIPS** ↵
New value for GRIPS ⟨0⟩: **1**↵
Command:

When GRIPS is On there is a pickbox located at the intersection of the screen crosshairs. You can pick any entity to activate the grips. Figure 14-1 shows what grips look like on several different entities. You can even pick text and the grip box is located at the insertion point.

Figure 14-1.   Grips are placed
at strategic locations on
objects.

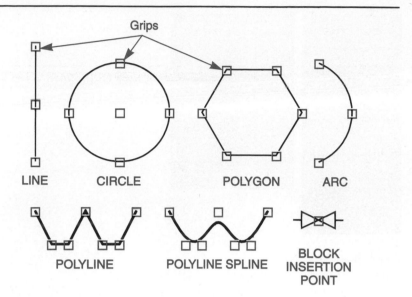

You can also control grips by picking Grips... in the Options pull-down menu, by picking DDgrips: in the OPTIONS screen menu, or by typing DDGRIPS. The "Grips" dialog box shown in Figure 14-2 is then displayed.

Figure 14-2.   The "Grips"
dialog box.

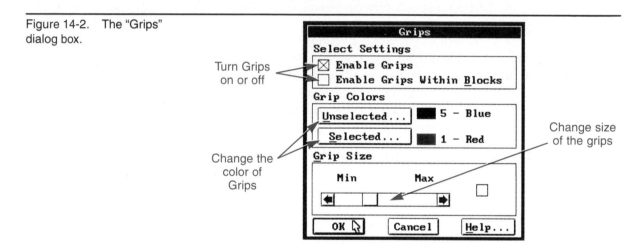

Look at the "Grips" dialog box and notice the Select Settings check boxes. Pick the Enable Grips check box to turn grips On or Off. Pick the Enable Grips Within Blocks check box to have grips displayed on every entity of a block. A *block* is a special symbol designed for multiple use. (Blocks are discussed in detail in Chapter 25.) When this check box is off, the grip location for a block is at the insertion point as shown in Figure 14-1. Grips in blocks may also be controlled with the GRIPBLOCK system variable. The default for GRIPBLOCK is 0. Type 1 and press ENTER to turn on grips within blocks.

The Grip Colors buttons allow you to change the color of grips. The grips are displayed when you first pick an entity. These are referred to as *unselected grips* because you have not yet picked a grip to perform an operation. An unselected grip is a colored square outline. Unselected grips are set to blue as default, and are considered "warm." After you pick a grip it is called a *selected grip,* and is displayed as a filled-in square as shown in Figure 14-3. Selected grips are red by default, and are referred to as "hot." If more than one entity is selected, and they have warm grips, then they are all affected by what you do with the hot grips. Entities that have warm and hot grips are highlighted and are part of the selection set. You can remove highlighted entities from the selection set by holding down the SHIFT key and picking the entity to be removed. The highlighting goes away, but the grips remain. These are called "cold" grips. Entities with cold grips are not affected by what you do to entities with warm grips. Return the entity with cold grips to the selection set by picking it again.

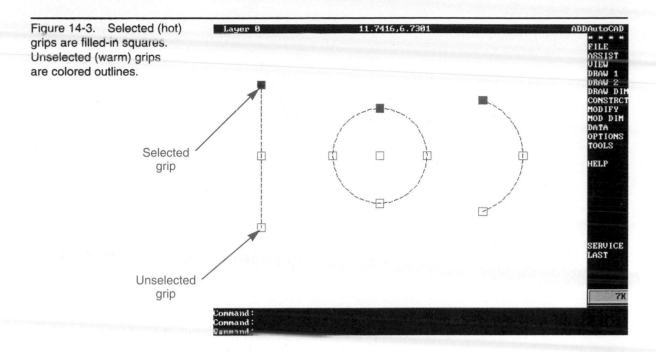

Figure 14-3. Selected (hot) grips are filled-in squares. Unselected (warm) grips are colored outlines.

You can also control grip color with the GRIPCOLOR and GRIPHOT system variables. GRIP-COLOR controls the color of unselected (warm) grips, while GRIPHOT regulates the color of selected (hot) grips. When you enter one of these variables, simply set the color number as desired.

The Grip Size scroll bar in the "Grips" dialog box lets you graphically change the size of the grip box. Change the grip size to whatever works best for your drawing. Very small grip boxes may be difficult to pick. However, the grips may overlap if they are too large.

Grip size can be given a numerical value from the Command: prompt using the GRIPSIZE system variable. To change the default of 3, enter GRIPSIZE at the Command: prompt and then type a desired size in pixels.

Using grips

To activate grips move the pick box to the desired entity and pick. The object is highlighted and the unselected grips are displayed. To select a grip move the pick box to the desired grip and pick it. Notice that the crosshairs "snap" to a grip. A grip becomes solid when selected. See Figure 14-3. When you pick a grip the command line changes to this:

** STRETCH **
⟨Stretch to point⟩/Base point/Copy/Undo/eXit:

This activates the STRETCH command. All you have to do is move the cursor to make the selected object stretch as shown in Figure 14-4. If you pick the middle grip of a line or arc, or the center grip of a circle, the object moves. These are the other options:
- **Base point.** Type B and press ENTER to select a new base point for this editing command.
- **Copy.** Type C and press ENTER if you want to make one or more copies of the selected object.
- **Undo.** Type U and press ENTER to undo the previous operation.
- **eXit.** Type X and press ENTER to exit the command. The selected grip is gone, but the unselected grips remain. You can also use CTRL+C to cancel the command. Canceling twice removes the selected and the unselected grips and returns the Command: prompt.

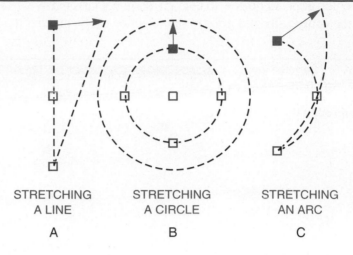

Figure 14-4.   Using the automatic STRETCH command. Note the selected grip. A—Stretching a line. B—Stretching a circle. C—Stretching an arc.

STRETCHING A LINE

A

STRETCHING A CIRCLE

B

STRETCHING AN ARC

C

PROFESSIONAL TIP

More than one grip can be hot at any one time. Simply hold down the Shift key and pick the desired grips.

You can pick objects individually or you can use any of the selection techniques that were discussed in Chapter 6. Figure 14-5 shows how you can stretch features of an object after selecting all of the objects. Step 1 in Figure 14-5A illustrates stretching the first corner and Step 2 stretches the second corner. You could also make more than one grip hot at the same time by holding down the SHIFT key as you pick the grips as shown in Figure 14-5B.

Figure 14-5.   Stretching an object. A—Select corners to stretch individually. B—Select several hot grips by holding down the SHIFT key.

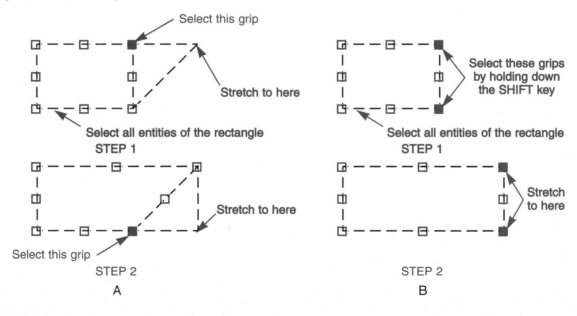

Select this grip

Stretch to here

Select all entities of the rectangle
STEP 1

Stretch to here

Select this grip

STEP 2

A

Select these grips by holding down the SHIFT key

Select all entities of the rectangle
STEP 1

Stretch to here

STEP 2

B

Here are some general rules and guidelines that can help make grips work for you:
✓ Be sure the GRIPS system variable is On.
✓ Pick an object or group of entities to activate grips.
✓ Entities in the selection set are highlighted.
✓ Pick a warm grip to make it hot.
✓ Make more than one grip hot by holding down the SHIFT key while picking warm grips.

✓ If more than one object is selected and they have warm grips, then they are all affected by the editing commands.

✓ Remove objects from the selection set by holding down the SHIFT key and picking them, thus making the grips cold.

✓ Return objects to the selection set by picking them again.

✓ Remove hot grips from the selection set by pressing CTRL+C. Press CTRL+C again to remove all grips from the selection set. If you have not yet picked a hot grip, all you have to do is press CTRL+C once to remove the grips.

PROFESSIONAL TIP

    When editing with grip you can enter coordinates to help improve your accuracy. Remember that any of the coordinate entry methods discussed in Chapter 6 will work.

EXERCISE 14-1

❑ Load AutoCAD and open TITLEA.

❑ Draw a line with coordinates X=2,Y=4 and X=2,Y=7. Draw a circle with the center at X=5.5,Y=5.5, with a radius of 1.5. Finally, draw an arc with its center at X=8.5,Y=5.5, a start point of X=9.5,Y=4, and an endpoint of X=9.5,Y=7.

❑ In the space at the bottom of the screen, draw a polyline on the left similar to the one in Figure 14-1. Copy the polyline to a location approximately one unit to the right of the original. Use the PEDIT command to spline the second polyline. The polylines should be similar to the bottom of Figure 14-1.

❑ Make sure GRIPS are On.

❑ Experiment with the STRETCH command using grips by picking the points as follows:
  ❑ Line–Pick the ends first and then the middle to see what happens.
  ❑ Circle–Pick one of the quadrants, and the center.
  ❑ Arc–Pick the ends and the middle.
  ❑ Polyline–Pick various grips.
  ❑ Spline–Pick various grips. Editing polylines in this manner allows you to create some interesting shapes.

❑ Save the drawing as A:EX14-1 and quit.

You can also use the MOVE, ROTATE, SCALE, and MIRROR commands to automatically edit entities. All you have to do is pick the object and then select one of the grips. When you see the ** STRETCH ** command, press ENTER to get the next command option:

```
** STRETCH **
⟨Stretch to point⟩/Base point/Copy/Undo/eXit: ↵
** MOVE **
⟨Move to point⟩/Base point/Copy/Undo/eXit: ↵
** ROTATE **
⟨Rotation angle⟩/Base point/Copy/Undo/Reference/eXit: ↵
** SCALE **
⟨Scale factor⟩/Base point/Copy/Undo/Reference/eXit: ↵
** MIRROR **
⟨Second point⟩/Base point/Copy/Undo/eXit:
```

Pressing ENTER cycles through each editing command, or you can pick the desired command from the screen menu.

PROFESSIONAL TIP

When warm grips are displayed on the screen, you can also use some of the editing commands from the pull-down and screen menus, or type the editing command name at the Command: prompt. For example, the ERASE command can be used to clear the screen of all entities displayed with warm grips by first picking the entities and then selecting the ERASE command.

Moving an object automatically

If you want to move an object with grips, select the object, pick a grip to use as the base point, and press ENTER to get this prompt:

```
** MOVE **
⟨Move to point⟩/Base point/Copy/Undo/eXit:
```

The selected grip becomes the base point. Then move the object to a new point and the MOVE operation is complete as shown in Figure 14-6. If you accidentally pick the wrong grip or decide to change the grip base point, type B and press ENTER for the Base point option and pick a new one.

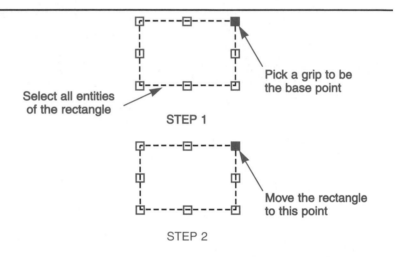

Figure 14-6.   The automatic MOVE command. The selected grip becomes the base point for the move.

Select all entities of the rectangle

Pick a grip to be the base point

STEP 1

Move the rectangle to this point

STEP 2

EXERCISE 14-2

☐ Load AutoCAD and open TITLEA.
☐ Draw a 1.5 in. (38.1 mm) diameter circle with its center at X=2,Y=3.
☐ Use grips to move the circle 2 in. (50.8 mm) to the right.
☐ Save the drawing as A:EX14-2 and quit.

Copying an object automatically

The Copy option is found in each of the editing commands. When using the STRETCH command, the Copy option allows you to make multiple copies of the object you are stretching. Holding down the SHIFT key while performing the first STRETCH operation accesses the Multiple mode. The prompt looks like this:

```
** STRETCH (multiple) **
⟨Stretch to point⟩/Base point/Copy/Undo/eXit: ↵
```

The Copy option in the MOVE command is the true form of the COPY command. You can activate the Copy option by entering C for copy as follows:

** MOVE **
⟨Move to point⟩/Base point/Copy/Undo/eXit: **C** ↵
** MOVE (multiple) **
⟨Move to point⟩/Base point/Copy/Undo/eXit: *(make as many copies as desired and enter* **X** *to exit, or press* CTRL+C)

Holding down the SHIFT key while performing the first MOVE operation also puts you in the Copy mode.

The Copy option works similarly in each of the editing commands. Try it with each to see what happens.

PROFESSIONAL TIP

When in the MOVE command's Copy option, if you make the first copy followed by holding the SHIFT key, the distance of the first copy automatically becomes the snap spacing for additional copies.

EXERCISE 14-3

❑ Load AutoCAD and open TITLEA.
❑ Use the PLINE command to draw the objects shown at A, B, C, and D below. Do not draw dimensions.

❑ Use the STRETCH command's Copy option to make object A look similar to the example at the right.
❑ Use the STRETCH command's Copy option to make object B look similar to the example at the right. Make two grips hot for this to work.
❑ Use the MOVE command's Copy option to make multiple copies to the right of object C.
❑ Use the MOVE command to make multiple copies to the right of object D while holding down the SHIFT key.
❑ Save the drawing as A:EX14-3 and quit.

Rotating an object automatically

To automatically rotate an object, select the object to be rotated, pick a grip to use as the base point, and press ENTER until you see this prompt:

```
** ROTATE **
⟨Rotation angle⟩/Base point/Copy/Undo/Reference/eXit:
```

Now, move your pointing device and watch the object rotate. Pick the desired rotation point, or enter a rotation angle like this:

```
⟨Rotation angle⟩/Base point/Copy/Undo/Reference/eXit: 45 ↵
```

Type R and press ENTER if you want to use the Reference option:

```
⟨Rotation angle⟩/Base point/Copy/Undo/Reference/eXit: R ↵
```

The Reference option may be used when the object is already rotated at a known angle and you want to rotate it to a new angle. The reference angle is the current angle and the new angle is the desired angle:

```
Reference angle ⟨0⟩: 45 ↵
** ROTATE **
⟨New angle⟩/Base point/Copy/Undo/Reference/eXit: 10 ↵
```

Figure 14-7 shows the Rotation options.

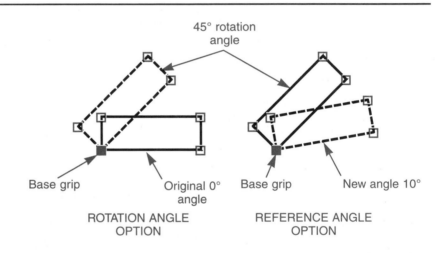

Figure 14-7.   The MOVE command's Rotation angle option and Reference option.

45° rotation angle

Base grip   Original 0° angle   Base grip   New angle 10°

ROTATION ANGLE OPTION   REFERENCE ANGLE OPTION

EXERCISE 14-4

❏ Load AutoCAD and open TITLEA.
❏ Draw a rectangle using the PLINE command similar to the one shown at the left of Figure 14-7. Orient the long sides so they are at 0°.
❏ Use grips to rotate the object 45°.
❏ Rotate the object again to 20° using the Reference option.
❏ Save the drawing as A:EX14-4 and quit.

Scaling an object automatically

If you want to scale an object with grips, cycle through the editing options until you get this prompt:

```
** SCALE **
⟨Scale factor⟩/Base point/Copy/Undo/Reference/eXit:
```

You can move the screen cursor and pick when the object is dragged to the desired size, or enter a scale factor to automatically increase or decrease the scale of the original object. Scale factors are given in Chapter 13 of this text. You can also use the Reference option if you know a current length and a desired length. Enter R for the Reference option:

⟨Scale factor⟩/Base point/Copy/Undo/Reference/eXit: **R** ↵
Reference length⟨⟩: **3.0** ↵
** SCALE **
⟨New length⟩/Base point/Copy/Undo/Reference/eXit: **5.25** ↵

Note that the selected base point remains in the same place when the object is scaled. Figure 14-8 shows the two Scale options.

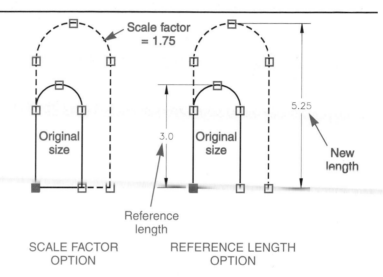

Figure 14-8.   The options for the automatic SCALE command include the Scale factor option and the Reference length option.

EXERCISE 14-5

❏ Load AutoCAD and open TITLEA.
❏ Draw an object similar to the original object at the left in Figure 14-8.
❏ Activate grips to make a copy of the object to the right of the original.
❏ Scale the first object using a scale factor of 1.5.
❏ Use the Reference option to scale the second object to any desired height.
❏ Save the drawing as A:EX14-5 and quit.

Mirroring an object automatically

If you want to mirror an object, the selected grip becomes the first point of the mirror line. Then press ENTER to cycle through the editing commands until you get this prompt:

** MIRROR **
⟨Second point⟩/Base point/Copy/Undo/eXit:

Pick another grip or any point on the screen to be the second point of the mirror line as shown in Figure 14-9. Unlike the MIRROR command accessed through the pull-down, screen menus, and keyboard, the automatic MIRROR command does not give you the option to delete the old objects; it does so automatically. If you want to keep the original object while mirroring, use the Copy option in the MIRROR command.

Figure 14-9.   When using the automatic MIRROR command, the selected grip becomes the first point of the mirror line.

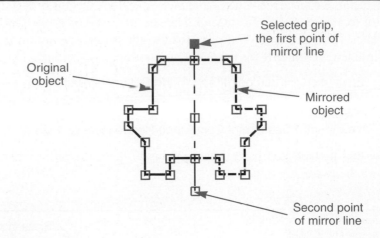

EXERCISE 14-6

❑ Load AutoCAD and open TITLEA.
❑ Draw a shape similar to the original object in Figure 14-9.
❑ Use grips to mirror the object along the centerline.
❑ Save the drawing as A:EX14-6 and quit.

BASIC EDITING VS. AUTOMATIC EDITING   AUG 5

In Chapter 13 you learned what is referred to in this text as *basic editing*. Basic editing allows you to first enter a command and then select the desired object to be edited. You could also set system variables to first select the desired objects and then enter the desired command. The automatic editing features discussed in this chapter use grips and related editing commands to edit an object automatically by picking the object first. The method you use is completely up to you. AutoCAD has given you maximum flexibility to use a variety of techniques that help you increase drafting and design productivity. You will find that certain command formats work best for you in different situations as you become an experienced AutoCAD user.

The "Object Selection Settings" dialog box allows you to control the manner in which you use editing commands. This dialog box is displayed by typing DDSELECT at the Command: prompt, by picking Selection... from the Options pull-down menu, or by picking DDselec: from the OPTIONS screen menu. See Figure 14-10. These are the items found in the "Object Selection Settings" dialog box:

• **Noun/Verb Selection.** AutoCAD refers to Noun/Verb as the format used when you select objects and then enter the desired command. This is the technique discussed in this chapter. The pick box is displayed at the screen crosshairs. An "X" in this check box means that the Noun/Verb method is active. The PICKFIRST system variable may also be used to set the Noun/Verb selection. The opposite of the Noun/Verb selection–Verb/Noun–is the method in which you enter the command before selecting the object. The Verb/Noun method is used primarily in Chapter 13. Remove the "X" from the Noun/Verb check box to enter the command before making a selection. Some editing commands such as FILLET, CHAMFER, DIVIDE, MEASURE, OFFSET, EXTEND, TRIM, and BREAK require that you enter the command before you select the object.

• **Use Shift to Add.** When this check box is not checked (Off), every entity or group of entities you select is highlighted and added to the selection set. If you pick this check box, it changes the way AutoCAD accepts objects you pick. For example, if you pick an object, it is highlighted and added to the selection set. However, if you pick another object, it is highlighted and the first is removed from the selection set. This means that you can only include one object by

Figure 14-10. The "Object
Selection Settings" dialog box.

Default
selection
modes on

Default
pickbox
size

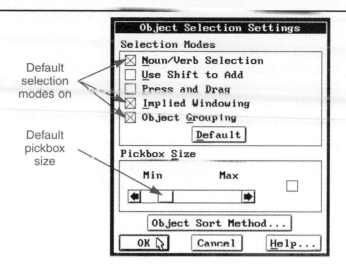

picking, or one group of objects with a selection window, to the selection set. If you want to add more items to the selection set, you must hold down the SHIFT key as you pick them, hence the name Use Shift to Add. Turning on the PICKADD system variable does the same thing as turning on this feature.

- **Press and Drag.** This is the same as turning on the PICKDRAG system variable. With Press and Drag on, you create a selection window by picking the first corner, and then move the puck while holding down the pick button. Release the pick button when you have the desired selection window. The default is to have Press and Drag turned off, which means that you have to pick both the first and second corner of the desired selection window.
- **Implied Windowing.** This option defaults to on. This means that you can automatically create a window by picking the first point, and moving the cursor to the right to pick the second point, or make a crossing box by picking the first point and moving the cursor to the left to pick the second point. This is the same as turning on the PICKAUTO system variable. This only affects selecting objects when the Select objects: prompt appears, and it does not work if PICKDRAG is on.
- **Object Grouping.** Object grouping controls whether or not AutoCAD recognizes grouped objects as singular entities. When off, the individual elements of a group can be selected for separate editing without having to first explode the group.
- **Default.** Picking this button sets the selection methods to the AutoCAD defaults as shown in Figure 14-10.
- **Pickbox Size.** This scroll bar lets you adjust the size of the pick box. Watch the sample in the image tile get smaller or larger as you move the scroll bar. Stop when you have a desired size. The pick box size is also controlled by the PICKBOX system variable.
- **Object Sort Method....** The "Object Sort Method" subdialog box shown in Figure 14-11 appears when you pick this button. The check boxes in the "Object Sort Method" subdialog box allows you to control the order in which objects are displayed or plotted. The check boxes control these features:
  - **Object Selection**–Ensures that objects using a windowing method are placed in the selection set in the order that they occur in the drawing database. A *database* is a collection of information stored in computerized form.
  - **Object Snap**–Ensures that object snap modes find objects in the order that they occur in the drawing database.
  - **Redraws**–Ensures that objects are displayed by a REDRAW command in the order that they occur in the drawing database.
  - **Slide Creation**–Writes the slide file so that when viewing the slide, objects are displayed in the order they occur in the drawing database.

- **Regens**–Ensures that objects are displayed by a drawing regeneration in the order that they occur in the drawing database.
- **Plotting**–Ensures that objects are plotted in the order that they occur in the database.
- **PostScript Output**–Ensures that PSOUT processes objects in the order that they occur in the database. *PostScript* is a copyrighted page description language that is used in the desktop publishing industry. This topic is discussed in **AutoCAD and its Applications–Advanced, R13 for DOS**. The PSOUT command coverts any AutoCAD drawing to a PostScript file.

Figure 14-11. This dialog can be accessed by picking Object Sort Method... from the "Object Selection Settings" subdialog box.

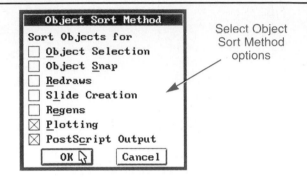

Object sorting is also controlled by the SORTENTS system variable where the following values duplicate the check boxes in the dialog box:

0 = Sorting is turned off.
1 = Object selection sorting.
2 = Object snap sorting.
4 = Sorts entities in a redraw.
8 = Slide creation sorting.
16 = Regeneration sorting.
32 = Plot sorting.
64 = Sort for PostScript output.

The default, 96, specifies sorting for plotting and PostScript output.

PROFESSIONAL TIP

Notice in Figure 14-11 that only a couple of the check boxes are checked by default. Entity sorting takes time and should only be used if the drawing or application software you are using requires entity sorting. Turn the Object Selection sorting on if you want AutoCAD to find the last object drawn when selecting overlapping entities.

EXERCISE 14-7

❏ Load AutoCAD.
❏ Enter the DDSELECT command and look at the "Object Selection Settings" dialog box.
❏ Adjust the pick box size while watching the image tile.
❏ Pick Object Sort Method... and see the "Object Sort Method" subdialog box.
❏ Cancel both dialog boxes.
❏ Quit without saving this drawing session.

AUTOMATIC EDITING IN A DIALOG BOX

AUG 5

You can use the DDMODIFY command or pick Properties... from the Modify pull-down menu to edit an entity using the "Modify" dialog box. You can also select Modify: from the MODIFY screen menu. You are first asked to select an object to modify:

Command: **DDMODIFY** ↵
Select object to modify: *(pick an object to modify)*

If you pick a line, you get the "Modify Line" dialog box, or if you pick a circle you get the "Modify Circle" dialog box shown in Figure 14-12. The following discussion details features that are commonly found in the "Modify" dialog box.

Figure 14-12.   The "Modify" dialog boxes, such as the "Modify Circle" dialog box, can be used to edit entities.

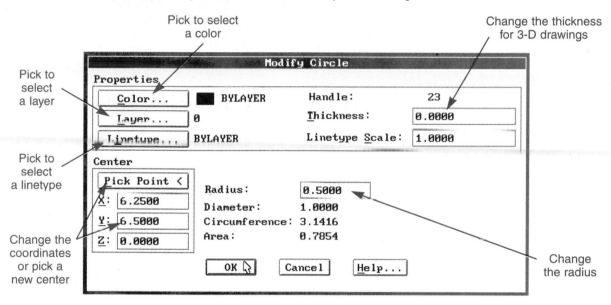

Properties

The Properties section of the "Modify" dialog box contains several common elements. These are:
* **Color....** Pick this button to get the "Select Color" subdialog box. This subdialog box displays the available colors. Simply pick a desired color for this entity, or enter a color name or number in the Color: edit box.
* **Layer....** Picking the Layer... button displays the "Select Layer" dialog box where you can set the selected entity to a desired layer. Layers are discussed in Chapter 19.
* **Linetype....** Pick this button to see the "Select Linetype" subdialog box. Here you can change the entity linetype by selecting one of the linetypes regardless of the LTSCALE system variable setting.
* **Thickness:.** This edit box lets you change the thickness of the entity. This is used in 3-D drawing, which is discussed in Chapter 29.

Changing the center point

When entities such as circles or arcs are selected using DDMODIFY, the following information is provided:
* **Pick Point ⟨.** Pick this button to establish a new center point location. The dialog box disappears, the graphics screen returns, and you see this prompt:

Center point: *(pick a new center point, or enter the coordinates for a new center location and press ENTER)*

• **X:, Y:, Z:.** Use these edit boxes to change the values of the X, Y, or Z coordinates, respectively. The Z coordinate is for 3-D drawings. The center location automatically changes when you enter new values and pick the OK button.

When modifying circular objects, related information for the Diameter, Circumference, and Area appear near the center of the "Modify" dialog box. The Radius is also given in an edit box. If you want to change the radius, double click on the Radius: edit box, enter a new value and the circle automatically changes to the new radius.

Each of the "Modify" dialog boxes is slightly different. For example, the "Modify Line" dialog box contains information about the line from the two endpoints, and edit boxes to change the endpoint coordinates. If you pick an entity such as a polygon you get the "Modify Polyline" dialog box. This dialog box contains items that allow you to automatically edit various aspects of a polyline. Remember from Chapter 8 that a polygon is a polyline.

The "Modify Text" dialog box is an excellent way to quickly and easily edit text. To get the "Modify Text" dialog box shown in Figure 14-13, enter the DDMODIFY command and pick the text to be modified.

Figure 14-13.   A simple means to edit text is through the use of the "Modify Text" dialog box.

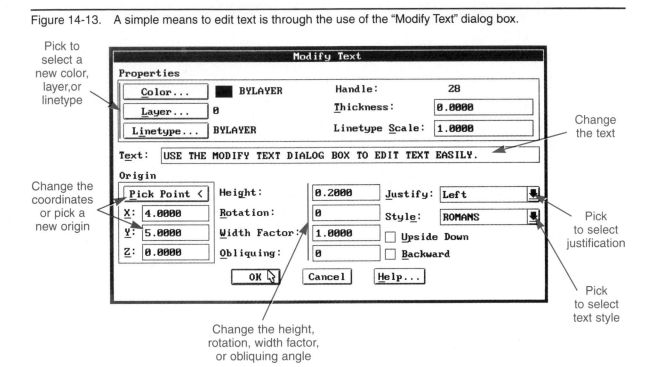

The Properties buttons allow you to change the color, layer, linetype, and thickness. You can edit the text wording by moving the cursor to the Text: edit box and remove, add, or change the text as needed. Change the text origin by selecting the Pick Point ⟨ button and picking a new point on the screen, or enter new X, Y coordinates. Automatically change the text height in the Height: edit box, or change the rotation angle, width factor, or obliquing angle by altering the values in these edit boxes. Pick the arrow at the right of the Justify: box to get the justification popup list. Pick the desired justification from this list. Select a text style that has been previously loaded by picking the desired style from the Style: popup list. Check either the Upside down or the Backward boxes if you want these conditions to be in effect.

EXERCISE 14-8

❏ Load AutoCAD and open TITLEA.
❏ Draw a line with endpoint coordinates X=2,Y=3 and X=2,Y=6.
❏ Draw a circle with a radius of 1.250 and a center location of X=6,Y=4.5.
❏ Use the DTEXT command with .25 in. text height and position the word "LINE" below the line and "CIRCLE" below the circle.
❏ Use the "Modify Line" dialog box to edit the line as follows:
  ❏ Change the "from point" to X=6.750,Y=3.770.
  ❏ Change the "to point" to X=6.750,Y=6.750.
❏ Use the "Modify Circle" dialog box to edit the circle as follows:
  ❏ Change the center location to X=7.125,Y=5.25.
  ❏ Change the radius to .375.
❏ Change the LINE label to .125 in. height and place it above the line.
❏ Change the CIRCLE label to read "Circle" and justify the middle of it with the center of the circle. Modify the text height to be .375 in.
❏ Save the drawing as A:EX14-8 and quit.

PROFESSIONAL TIP

If you are trying to pick an entity that is on top of another, AutoCAD may not pick the one you want. However, AutoCAD picks the last thing you drew if Object Selection is on in the "Object Sort Method" dialog box.

CHANGING THE PROPERTIES OF AN OBJECT   AUG 6, 11

In Chapter 13 you learned how to make changes to an object using the CHANGE command. This is a popular command because it is easy to use and allows you to change either the location of an object or properties related to the object. The CHANGE command prompts look like this:

Command: **CHANGE** ↵
Select objects: *(pick the object)*
Select objects: ↵

In Chapter 13 you used the default, Change point, to change the location of an object. You can also change properties of the feature by entering P:

Properties/〈Change point〉: **P** ↵
Change what property (Color/Elev/Layer/LType/ltScale/Thickness)?

The following properties can be changed with the CHANGE command:
* **Color.** Changes the color of the selected object.
* **Elev.** Used to change the elevation in 3-D drawing.
* **Layer.** Changes the layer designation. Layers are discussed in Chapter 19.
* **LType.** Changes the current linetype of a selected object to a linetype that has been loaded using the LINETYPE command.
* **ltScale.** Changes the linetype scale.
* **Thickness.** Used to change the thickness in 3-D drawing.

The CHPROP (CHange PROPerty) command lets you change only properties of an object. It does not allow for point change as in the CHANGE command. This is the command sequence if the FILE-DIA system variable is set to 0:

Command: **CHPROP** ↵
Select objects: *(pick the object)*
Select objects: ↵
Change what property (Color/Elev/Layer/LType/Thickness)?

The change property options are the same as those discussed in the CHANGE command.

If you like to use dialog boxes, you can change properties by entering DDCHPROP at the Command: prompt, or pick Ddchpro: from the MODIFY screen menu:

Command: **DDCHPROP** ↵
Select objects: *(pick the object)*
Select objects: ↵

Now the "Change Properties" dialog box, shown in Figure 14-14, is displayed.

As you look at this dialog box you can see some of the items discussed earlier. You can pick Color... to change the entity color, pick Layer... to change the layer, or pick Linetype... to change the linetype. The linetype scale representation can be changed using the Linetype Scale: edit box. The thickness of an object can be changed using the Thickness: edit box when performing 3-D functions.

Figure 14-14.   The "Change Properties" dialog box is accessed with the DDCHPROP command.

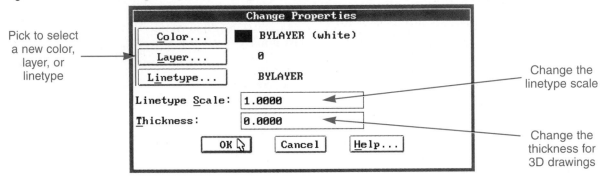

EXERCISE 14-9

❑ Load AutoCAD and open TITLEA.
❑ Draw a vertical line on the left side of the screen, a circle in the middle, and a hexagon on the right side.
❑ Load the CENTER, HIDDEN, and PHANTOM linetypes.
❑ Use the CHANGE command to change the linetype of the line to CENTER.
❑ Use the CHPROP command to change the circle's linetype to HIDDEN and the color to red.
❑ Enter the "Change Properties" dialog box and change the linetype of the hexagon to PHANTOM and the color to yellow.
❑ Save the drawing as A:EX14-9 and quit.

USING FILTERS TO CREATE A SELECTION SET   AUG 5

Even though the edit commands and selection methods that you have been using provide you with maximum flexibility, there are situations, especially on complex drawings, that limit your productivity. It would be nice, in these situations, if you could develop a selection set based on only specific characteristics of the drawing, such as all circles less than ∅1.00 or all text of a designated style. This is possible using filters. Filters allow you to create a selection set of only those items on the drawing that you designate.

Creating entity filters

You can create a filter list of items based on specific properties which restrict a selection set. These filter list selection sets may be used in the current drawing or in a future drawing, if needed. This is done using the FILTER command, which may be accessed by picking Selection Filters... from the Assist pull-down menu or by typing FILTER at the Command: prompt. This command may also be accessed transparently while inside another command at a Select objects: prompt by typing 'FILTER. These options access the "Object Selection Filters" dialog box shown in Figure 14-15. You can use this dialog box to identify filters for a variety of properties including type of entity such as line or circle, linetype, color, text style, or layer.

Figure 14-15. The "Object Selection Filters" dialog box. The list box, Select Filter area, and Named Filters area are highlighted here.

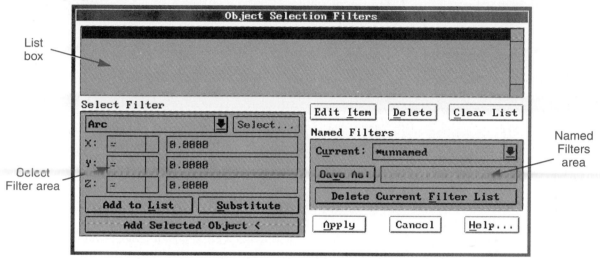

There are three major areas of the "Object Selection Filters" dialog box including the list box at the top of the dialog box, the Select Filter area, and the Named Filters area. There is nothing displayed in the list box until you add something to it. This is done by picking an item from the popup list just below Select Filter. Use the scroll bar to access the desired item. For example, pick Circle as shown in Figure 14-16. Follow this by picking the Add to List button.

Figure 14-16. Items picked from the popup list appear in the list box.

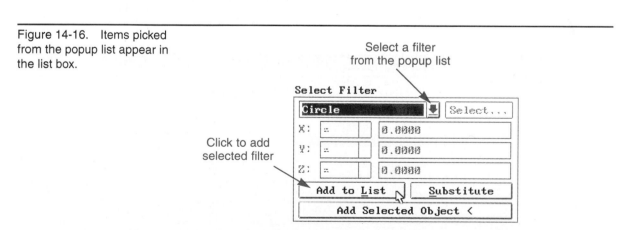

Now, Circle is placed in the list box. If you pick an item from the Select Filter list that has X, Y, and Z values such as Circle Center or Line Start, then the X:, Y:, and Z: coordinate popup lists and edit boxes are highlighted. Picking a coordinate popup arrow accesses the expanded popup shown in Figure 14-17. You can change the X, Y, and Z values in the edit boxes, and you can establish

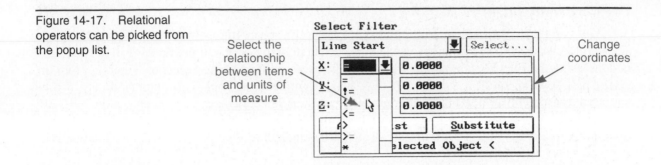

Figure 14-17.   Relational operators can be picked from the popup list.

relationships between the filtered items and designated units of measure. This is done by picking one of the symbols in the popup list. A description of these symbols follows:

= *Equals*
!= *Not equal to*
< *Less than*
<= *Less than or equal to*
> *Greater than*
>= *Greater than or equal to*
* *Multiply*

AutoCAD refers to these symbols as *relational operators.*

The Select… button is only highlighted if you pick an item from the Select Filter popup list that accesses a dialog box. For example, picking Text Style Name and then the Select button accesses the "Select Text Style Name(s)" dialog box. This dialog box shows you all of the currently defined text styles.

You can also add an entity from a drawing by picking the Add Selected Object 〈 button. This button returns you to the drawing editor and prompts with Select object:. If you pick an item such as text, the properties of this entity are displayed in the list box. Figure 14-18 shows part of the list now present in the list box. Move the scroll bar to see all of the items listed. You can have as many items in the filter list box as you wish.

Figure 14-18.   The filters list is displayed in the list box. You can edit, delete, apply, and substitute these items.

Items currently in the list

Edit highlighted item

Scroll thru the list

Object Selection Filters

Text Height   = 0.2000
Text Value   = USE THE MODIFY TEXT DIALOG BOX TO EDIT
Text Rotation   = 0
Text Style Name   = ROMANS
Normal Vector   X = 0.0000   Y = 0.0000   Z = 1.0000

Select Filter

Arc   [Select...]

X: =   0.0000
Y: =   0.0000
Z: =   0.0000

[Add to List] [Substitute]

[Add Selected Object 〈]

[Edit Item] [Delete] [Clear List]

Named Filters

Current: *unnamed

[Save As:]

[Delete Current Filter List]

[Apply] [Cancel] [Help...]

Clears entire list

Delete highlighted item

Substitute with highlighted item

Apply current list to drawing

Save the current filter list

Now that you have a filters list you can use some of the other items in the dialog box. For example, pick the Clear List button to get rid of everything you just put in the list. You can highlight any item in the list by moving the pointer to the item and picking it. When an item is highlighted, you can remove it from the list by selecting the Delete button. You can substitute an item in the Select Filter list with a highlighted item in the filters list by picking the Substitute button. For example, if the filter list displays "Text Style Name = ROMANS," you can change it to another existing text style (ROMANC). First, pick Text Style Name from the Select Filter popup list. Then, scroll down the list box and highlight the Text Style Name entry, followed by picking the Select... button. This accesses the "Select Text Style Name(s)" dialog box. Pick ROMANC followed by OK to close the dialog box. Finally, pick the Substitute button to execute the change.

If you want to edit an item in the filters list, first highlight it and then pick the Edit Item button. This places the current X, Y, and Z values of the item in the Select Filter: edit boxes for you to change as needed. Make the changes and pick the Substitute button for the alterations to take place.

The Named Filters area in Figure 14-15 shows the Current: filter as unnamed, which is what you can expect when you start a drawing. Use the Save As: edit box to save your current filter list. Enter the desired name in the edit box followed by picking the Save As: button. This name becomes the current named filter. If there were several filter names, you could access these through the Current: popup list. You can delete the current named filter list by picking the Delete Current Filter List button.

Finally, pick the Apply button to exit the dialog box and have the selection set filters ready for use. If AutoCAD finds a problem with your filter list, you will get a message at the bottom of the dialog box. Pick the Cancel button if you decide not to continue with the filter list.

Using filters on a drawing

Now, try using the filtering process on the drawing shown in Figure 14-19. Your supervisor likes the flowchart that you just finished, except you are asked to change all of the ROMANS text inside the flowchart and note to a new layer and color for special plotting or printing considerations. You could use the CHPROP command and individually select each word on the chart, but you decide to use the

Figure 14-19. Original flowchart requiring modification.

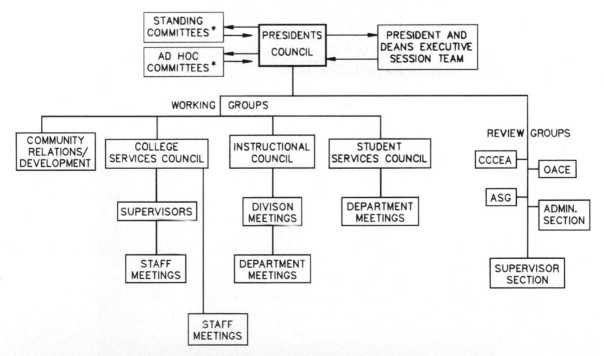

FILTER command to make the job easier. Access the "Object Selection Filters" dialog box and follow these steps:

1. Pick the Add Selected Object 〈 button.

> Command: FILTER
> Select object: *(pick one of the words in the chart such as PRESIDENTS)*

2. The dialog box returns and displays the characteristics of the text you picked. Highlight items such as Text Position and Text Value, and pick the <u>D</u>elete button for each. These filters are not needed because they limit the filter list to specific aspects of the text. See Figure 14-20.

Figure 14-20. Deleting selection filters.

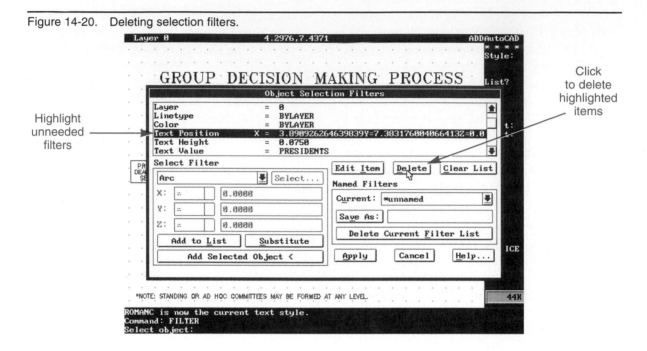

3. Enter a filter name such as TEXT in the Sa<u>v</u>e As: edit box and then pick the Sa<u>v</u>e As: button. The C<u>u</u>rrent: filter name is TEXT, as shown in Figure 14-21.

Figure 14-21. Setting the filter name.

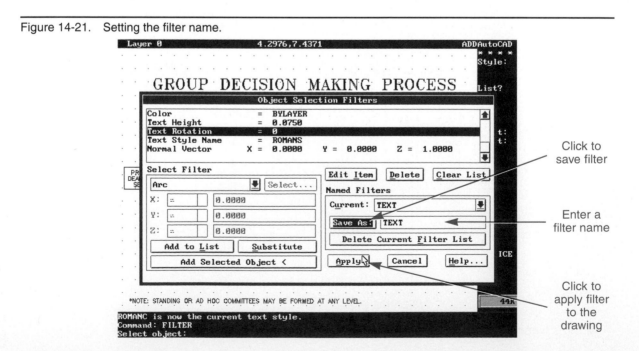

4. Pick the <u>A</u>pply button. The drawing returns and this prompt is given:

> Select object:
> Applying filter to selection.
> Select objects: *(window all of the drawing text to be included in the selection set)*

All of the text within the flowchart is now highlighted, and you see this prompt:

> 106 were filtered out.
> Select objects: ↵
> Existing filtered selection.

5. The highlighted text returns and the items that were previously highlighted become part of the selection set.
6. Now that the desired items are part of a selection set, the next step is to access the set and change the Layer.
7. At the Command: prompt, enter the CHPROP command so you can change the layer and color of the text that you placed in the filtered selection set. Enter P when you get Select objects: prompt. This retrieves the selection set that was previously established with the FILTER command:

> Command: **CHPROP** ↵
> Select objects: **P** ↵
> 106 found
> Select objects: ↵
> Change what property (Color/LAyer/LType/ltScale/Thickness)? **LA** ↵
> New Layer ⟨0⟩: **COLOR** ↵
> Change what property (Color/LAyer/LType/ltScale/Thickness)? ↵
> Command:

The COLOR layer was previously created with a color of red. You must create the layer before you can change to it. Now all of the text within the flow chart is on the COLOR layer in red.

The revised flowchart is shown in Figure 14-22.

Figure 14-22.   Revised flowchart.

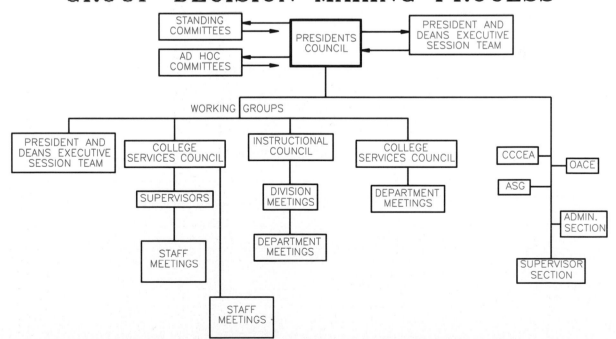

GROUP DECISION MAKING PROCESS

*NOTE: STANDING OR AD HOC COMMITTEES MAY BE FORMED AT ANY LEVEL.

CHAPTER TEST

Write your answers in the spaces provided.

1. Give the command and entries required to turn on grips:

   Command:_____

   New value for GRIPS ⟨⟩: _____

2. Give the prompts needed to rotate an object from an existing 60° angle to a new 25° angle:

   ⟨Rotation angle⟩/Base point/Copy/Undo/Reference/eXit: _____

   Reference angle⟨⟩: _____

   ⟨New angle⟩/Base point/Copy/Undo/Reference/eXit: _____

3. Give the prompts required to scale an object to become three-quarters of its original size:

   ⟨Scale factor⟩/Base point/Copy/Undo/Reference/eXit: _____

4. Name the two system variables that control the color of grips.

   _____

   _____

5. Name the six editing commands that can be accessed automatically. _____

   _____

   _____

6. Explain the difference between Noun/Verb selection and Verb/Noun selection. _____

   _____

   _____

7. Name the system variable that allows you to set the Noun/Verb selection. _____

8. What does "Use Shift to Add" mean? _____

   _____

   _____

9. Describe how "Press and Drag" works. _____

   _____

   _____

   _____

10. Name the system variable that is used to turn on "Press and Drag." _____

11. Name the system variable that turns on Implied Windowing. _____

12. Identify two ways to access the "Object Selection Settings" dialog box. _____

   _____

13. Explain two ways to change the pick box size. _____

   _____

   _____

14. Give the command sequence and explain how you would change the radius of a circle from 1.375 to 1.875 using a dialog box. _____

_____

_____

_____

_____

15. Identify the pull-down menu and the item you pick from this menu to access the dialog box described in question 14. _____

_____

16. How would you change the linetype of an entity using the dialog box described in question 14?

_____

_____

_____

17. Name three commands that allow you to change the properties of an object. _____

_____

_____

18. Which of the commands in question 17 accesses the "Change Properties" dialog box? _____

_____

19. How do you access the "Change Properties" dialog box through a screen menu? _____

_____

20. How do you change the color of an entity using the "Change Properties" dialog box? _____

_____

_____

DRAWING PROBLEMS

Use prototypes TITLEA or TITLEB as appropriate for each of the following problems. Use grips and the associated editing commands or other editing techniques discussed in this chapter.

1. Draw the objects shown at A below and then use the STRETCH command to make them look like the objects at B. Do not include dimensions. Save the drawing as A:P14-1.

P14-1

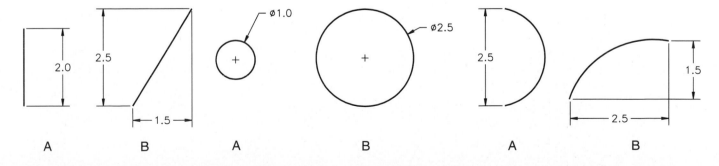

P14-2

2. Draw the object shown at A below. Then using the MOVE command's Copy option, copy the object to the position shown at B. Edit object A so that it resembles example C. Edit object B so that it looks like D. Do not include dimensions. Save the drawing as A:P14-2.

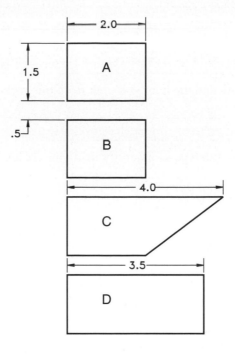

P14-3

3. Draw the object shown at A below. Then copy the object, without rotating it, to a position below as indicated by the dashed lines. Then, rotate the object 45°. Copy the rotated object at B to a position below as indicated by the dashed lines. Use the Reference option to rotate the object at C to 25° as shown. Do not include dimensions. Save the drawing as A:P14-3.

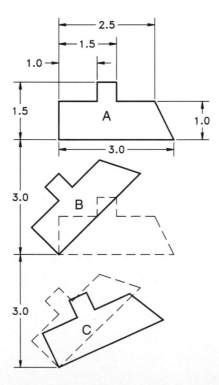

P14-4

4. Draw the individual entities (vertical line, horizontal line, circle, arc, and "C" shape) at A below using the dimensions given. Then, use grips and the editing commands to create the object shown at B. Do not include dimensions. Save the drawing as A:P14-4.

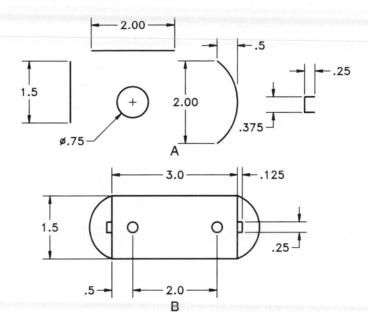

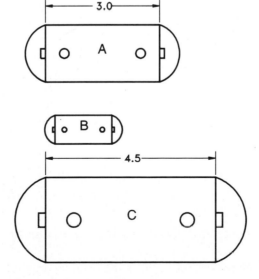

P14-5

5. Use the completed drawing from Problem 14-4. Erase everything except the completed object and move it to a position similar to A below. Copy the object two times to positions B and C. Use the SCALE command to scale the object at B to fifty percent of its original size. Use the SCALE command's Reference option to enlarge the object at C from the existing 3.0 length to a 4.5 length as shown in C. Do not include dimensions. Save as A:P14-5.

P14-6

6. Draw the dimensioned partial object shown at A. Do not include dimensions. Mirror the drawing to complete the four quadrants as shown at B. Change the color of the horizontal and vertical parting lines to red and Linetype to center. Save the drawing as A:P14-6.

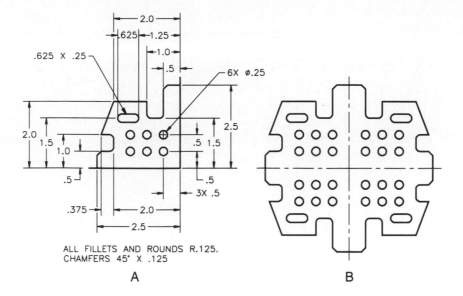

ALL FILLETS AND ROUNDS R.125.
CHAMFERS 45° X .125

A   B

P14-7

7. Load the final drawing you created in Problem 14-6. Use the "Modify Circle" dialog box to change the circles from ∅.25 to ∅.125. Use the "Change Properties" dialog box to change the linetype of the slots to PHANTOM. Be sure the linetype scale allows the linetypes to be displayed. Save the drawing as A:P14-7.

P14-8

8. Use the editing commands discussed in this chapter to assist you in drawing the following object. Draw the object within the boundaries of the given dimensions. All other dimensions are flexible. Do not include dimensions in the drawing. Save the drawing as A:P14-8.

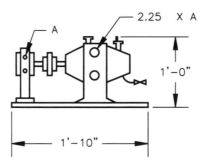

P14-9

9. Draw the following object within the boundaries of the given dimensions. All other dimensions are flexible. Do not include dimensions. After drawing the object, create a catalog page as follows:

   • All labels should be ROMAND text centered directly below the view. Use a text height of .125.
   • Keep the valve the same scale as the original drawing in each additional drawing.
   • Label the existing drawing: ONE-GALLON TANK WITH HORIZONTAL VALVE.
   • Copy the original tank to a new location and scale it so that it is two times its original size. Rotate the valve 45°. Label this tank: TWO-GALLON TANK WITH 45° VALVE.

- Copy the original tank to another location and scale it so that it is 2.5 times the size of the original. Rotate the valve 90°. Label this tank: TWO- AND ONE-HALF GALLON TANK WITH 90° VALVE.
- Copy the two-gallon tank to a new position and scale it so that it is two times this size. Rotate the valve to 22°30′. Label this tank: FOUR-GALLON TANK WITH 22°30′ VALVE.
- Left-justify this note at the bottom of the page:

  Combinations of tank size and valve orientation are available upon request.

- Use the "Modify Text" dialog box to make the following changes:
- Change all tank labels to ROMANC, .25 in. high.
- Change the note at the bottom of the sheet to ROMANS, centered on the sheet using uppercase letters.

Save the drawing as A:P14-9.

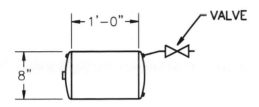

P14-10

10. Open Problem 13-14 if you have already drawn it. If you have not yet drawn this object, refer to this problem in Chapter 13 and draw it now. Do not include dimensions. Use the DDMODIFY command and other editing commands to change the drawing as follows:

    - Change the ∅2.125 circle to ∅1.50.
    - Change the R.50 dimension to R.375.
    - Change the 3.70 length to 4.80.

    Save the drawing as A:P14-10.

P14-11

11. Open Problem 11-7 and use the FILTER command as discussed in this chapter. Change all the text to a new Layer named COLOR and to color red. Save as A:P14-11.

Foundation Plan.   (Steve D. Bloedel)

Chapter 15

CREATING MULTIPLE OBJECTS WITH ARRAY

Learning objectives

After completing this chapter, you will be able to:
- ❍ Create an arrangement of objects in a rectangular pattern.
- ❍ Create an arrangement of any objects in a circular pattern.

Some designs require a rectangular or circular pattern of the same object. For example, office desks are often arranged in rows. Suppose your design calls for five rows, each having four desks. You could create this design by drawing one desk and copying it 19 times. You might also save the desk as a block and insert it 20 times. However, both of these options are time-consuming. A quicker method is to use AutoCAD's ARRAY command. Using ARRAY, you first select the object(s) to be copied. Then enter the type of arrangement (rectangular or polar).

A *rectangular array* creates rows and columns of the selected items, and you must provide the spacing. A *polar array* constructs a circular arrangement; you must specify the number of items to array, the angle between items, and the center point of the array. Some examples are shown in Figure 15-1.

Figure 15-1. Example arrays created with the ARRAY command.

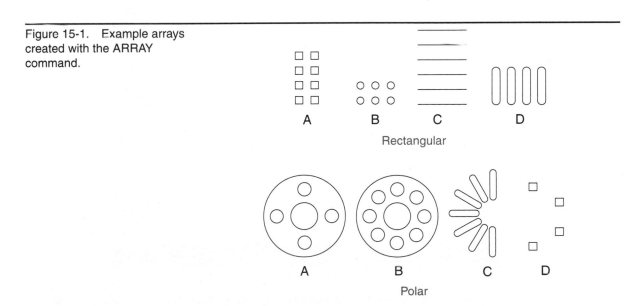

In this chapter, you will experiment with the ARRAY command on a .5 unit square. You may want to draw this object now to use as you study the chapter.

The ARRAY command may be typed at the Command: prompt, selected from the Construct pull-down menu, or picked from the CONSTRCT screen menu. After you enter the ARRAY command,

AutoCAD asks you to select objects to array. Use any selection method, such as a window. Then you must specify whether you want a rectangular or polar array. The command sequence is as follows:

> Command: **ARRAY** ↵
> Select objects: *(window the objects)*
> 1 found
> Select objects: ↵
> Rectangular or Polar array (R/P): *(type* **R** *or* **P**, *and press* ENTER*)*

RECTANGULAR PLACEMENT OF OBJECTS

AUG 5

A rectangular array places objects in line along the X and Y axes. You can request a single row, a single column, or multiple rows and columns. *Rows* are horizontal and *columns* are vertical. AutoCAD reminds you of this by indicating the direction in parentheses: (---) for rows and (ııı) for columns. The following process creates a pattern having 3 rows, 3 columns, and .5 spacing between objects.

> Rectangular or Polar array (R/P)⟨*current*⟩: **R** ↵
> Number of rows (---) ⟨1⟩: **3** ↵
> Number of columns (ııı) ⟨1⟩: **3** ↵
> Unit cell or distance between rows (---): **1** ↵
> Distance between columns (ııı): **1** ↵

The original object and resulting array are shown in Figure 15-2. When giving the distance between rows and columns, be sure to include the width and height of the object. Figure 15-2 shows how to calculate the distance between objects in a rectangular array.

Figure 15-2. The original object (dashed) and the created rectangular array. Note how the distance between rows and columns is determined.

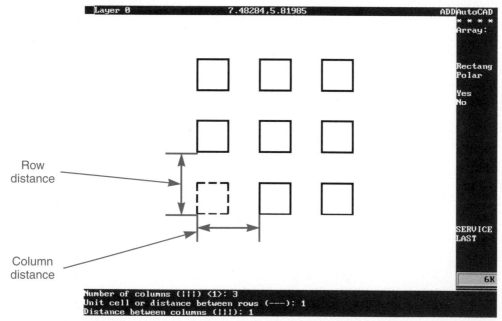

AutoCAD allows you to point to the distance separating objects. It calls this measurement the *unit cell*. The unit cell distance is the same as the distance between rows and columns. However, it is entered with the pointing device, just like selecting a window. See Figure 15-3.

> Unit cell or distance between rows (---): *(pick corner)* Other corner: *(pick second corner)*

Figure 15-3.   The unit cell spacing box is the same as the distance between rows and columns.

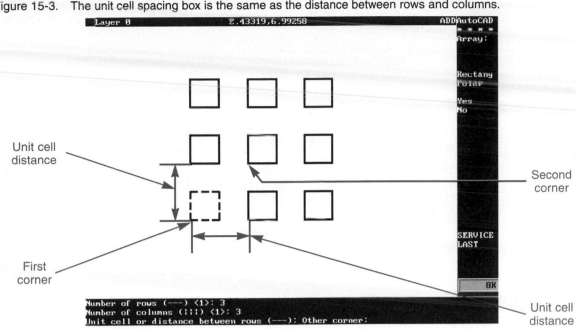

The command is then executed. The second point's distance and direction from the first point determines the X and Y spacing for the array.

Figure 15-4 shows how you can place arrays in four directions by entering either positive or negative row and column distance values. The dashed box is the original object. The row and column distance is one unit and the box is a .5 unit square.

Figure 15-4.   Placing arrays in one of four directions by giving positive or negative row and column distance values. The original object is shown highlighted here.

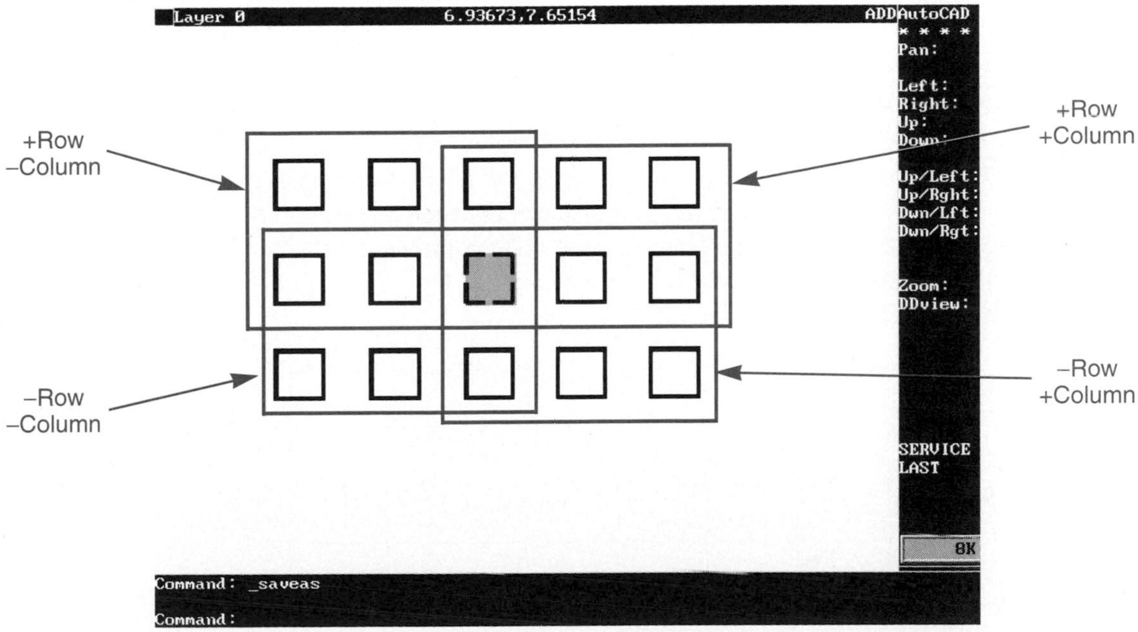

Specifying the unit cell distance can create a quick row and column arrangement in any direction. For example, in Figure 15-5, the second unit cell corner is picked to the left and below the first corner.

Figure 15-5. Creating a rectangular array by picking a negative unit cell distance.

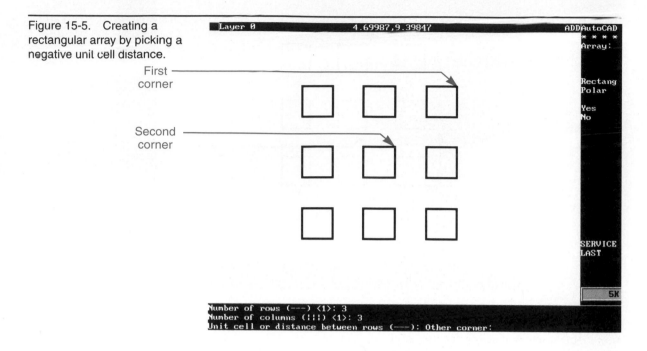

PROFESSIONAL TIP

Plan your drawing so you can array blocks. Blocks are symbols and shapes that are treated as a single entity. They are discussed in Chapter 25. Blocks save time when selecting the object. They also save drawing storage space. By setting the snap rotation to a specific angle before performing an array, a rotated rectangular array can be created.

EXERCISE 15-1

❑ Load AutoCAD and open TITLEA, or start a new drawing and set up your own variables.
❑ Construct the Bill of Materials form shown using the LINE and ARRAY commands. Line A is arrayed in nine rows and one column. The distance between rows is given. Line B is arrayed in one row and three columns. The distance between the columns is provided.
❑ Complete the headings using the DTEXT command.
❑ Save the drawing as A:EX15-1 and quit.

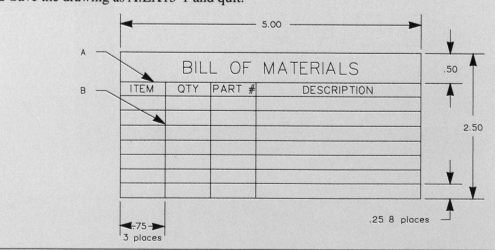

ARRANGING OBJECTS AROUND A CENTER POINT

AUC 5

To place objects in a circular pattern, use the Polar option of the ARRAY command. At this time, erase everything on your screen except for one .5 unit square. Enter the following command sequence:

Command: **ARRAY** ↵
Select objects: *(select the object using a window or other selection method)*
1 found
Select objects: ↵
Rectangular or Polar array (R/P)⟨*current*⟩: **P** ↵
Center point of array: *(pick the center point)*

Next, AutoCAD requests the number of objects you want in the array. If you know the exact number needed, enter that value. If you would rather specify an angle between items, just press ENTER. In the example below, no value is given. The next prompt you see is "Angle to fill."

Number of items: ↵
Angle to fill (+=ccw, −=cw) ⟨360⟩:

Notice the letters in parentheses (+=ccw, −=cw). You can array the object in a counterclockwise direction by entering a positive angle value. (Numbers entered without the plus sign are positive.) Objects can be arrayed clockwise by entering the minus sign before the angle value. Pressing ENTER at this prompt without entering a value copies the object through 360°. This is the default value.

The final value needed is the angular spacing between the arrayed objects.

Angle between items: **45** ↵

A number entered at this prompt is assumed to be the angle. This prompt is only displayed if you pressed ENTER at the Number of items: prompt. If you specify the number of items, you are not asked for the angle between them since AutoCAD calculates it for you. The last prompt is:

Rotate objects as they are copied? ⟨Y⟩: **N** ↵

You can have the objects rotated as they are copied around the pivot point. This keeps the same face of the object always pointing toward the pivot point. If objects are not rotated as they are copied, they remain in the same orientation as the original object, Figure 15-6.

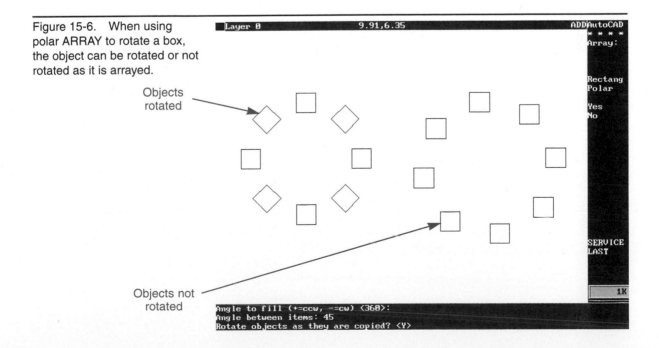

Figure 15-6.   When using polar ARRAY to rotate a box, the object can be rotated or not rotated as it is arrayed.

EXERCISE 15-2

❑ Load AutoCAD and open the TITLEA drawing, or start a new drawing and set up your own variables.

❑ Draw a .5 radius circle near the top of the screen.

❑ Create a 360° polar array of five circles.

❑ Copy one of the circles to the side of the polar array.

❑ Create an array with the copied circle. Each circle should be 30° apart through 270°.

❑ Save the drawing as A:EX15-2 and quit.

CHAPTER TEST

Write your answers in the spaces provided.

1. What is the difference between polar and rectangular arrays?_____

   _____

   _____

2. What four values should you know before you create a rectangular array?_____

   _____

   _____

3. Define "unit cell."_____

   _____

4. Suppose an object is 1.5 in. (38.1 mm) wide and you want a rectangular array with .75 in. (19.05 mm) spacing between objects. What should you specify for the distance between columns?_____

   _____

5. How do you create a rectangular array that is rotated? _____

6. What values should you know before you execute a polar array? _____

   _____

   _____

7. Suppose you enter a value for the Number of items: prompt in a polar array. Which of the following values are you not required to give? Circle one.

   A. Angle to fill.

   B. Angle between items.

   C. Center point.

   D. Rotate objects as they are copied.

8. What happens to an object drawn when it is not rotated as it is arrayed? _____

   _____

   _____

9. How do you request a clockwise array rotation? _____

   _____

DRAWING PROBLEMS

P15-1

1. Draw the following object views using the dimensions given. Use ARRAY to construct the bolt hole arrangement. Place the drawing on your prototype drawing TITLEB. Do not add dimensions. Save the drawing as A:P15-1.

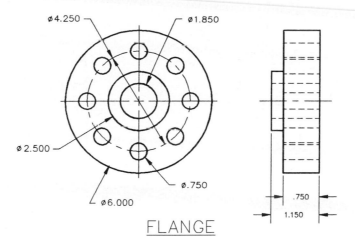

FLANGE

P15-2

2. Draw the object views shown below using the dimensions given. Use ARRAY to construct the hole arrangement. Place the drawing on your prototype drawing TITLEB. Do not add dimensions. Save the drawing as A:P15-2.

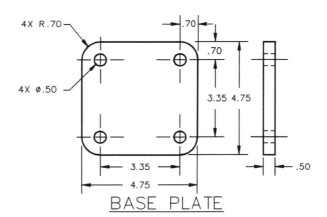

BASE PLATE

P15-3

3. You have been given an engineer's sketches and notes, and asked to construct a drawing of a sprocket. Create a front and side view of the sprocket using the ARRAY command. Place the drawing on your prototype drawing TITLEB. Do not add dimensions. Save the drawing as A:P15-3 and quit.

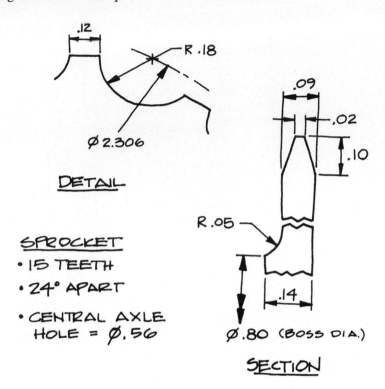

P15-4

4. The following engineering sketch shows a steel column arrangement on a concrete floor slab for a new building. The steel columns are represented by I-shaped symbols. The columns are arranged in "bay lines" and "column lines." The column lines are numbered 1, 2, and 3. The bay lines are labeled A through G. The width of a bay is 20'-0". Line balloons, or tags, identify bay and column lines. Draw the arrangement using ARRAY for the steel column symbols and for the tags. The following guidelines will help you.

A. Begin a new drawing and name it P15-4.

B. Select architectural units and 36 x 24 sheet size. Determine the scale required for this floor plan to fit on this sheet size, and determine your limits accordingly.

C. Set the grid spacing at 2'-0" (24").

D. Set the snap spacing at 12".

E. Use the PLINE command to draw the steel column symbol.

F. Do not dimension the drawing.

G. Draw all objects to dimensions given.

H. Place text inside the tag balloons. Set OSNAP to Center, use DTEXT, Middle, text height 6".

I. Place a title block on the drawing.

J. Save the drawing as A:P15-4.

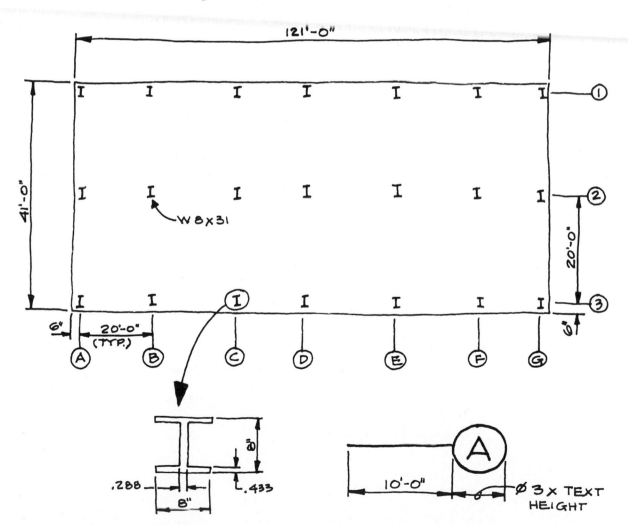

P15-5

5. The engineering sketch given is a proposed office layout of desks and chairs. One desk has been shown with the layout of chair, keyboard, monitor, and tower-mounted computer (dotted lines). All of the desk workstations should have the same configuration. Exact size and locations of doors and windows is not important for this problem. Set the SAVETIME variable to save your drawing every ten minutes. Use the following guidelines to complete this problem.

    A. Begin a new drawing called P15-5.

    B. Choose architectural units.

    C. Select an appropriate paper size. If you want to use the paper space prototype drawing for the final layout, be sure to create this drawing in model space without a border and title block.

    D. Use the appropriate drawing and editing commands to complete this problem quickly and efficiently.

    E. Draw the desk and computer hardware to the dimensions given.

    F. Do not dimension the drawing.

    G. Save the drawing as A:P15-5.

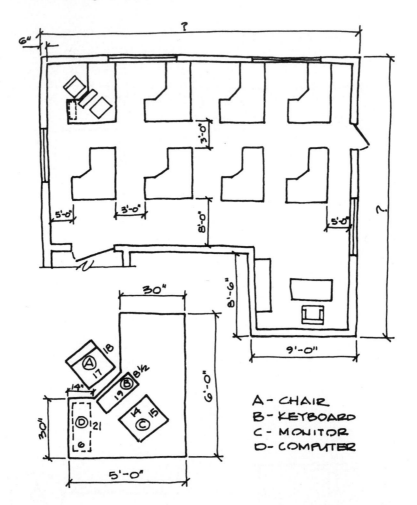

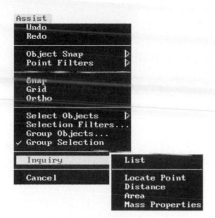

Chapter 16

OBTAINING INFORMATION ABOUT THE DRAWING

Learning objectives

After completing this chapter, you will be able to:

- ❍ Determine the area of an object by adding and subtracting entities.
- ❍ List data related to a single point, entity, group of entities, or an entire drawing.
- ❍ Discover the amount of time spent in a drawing session.

When working on a drawing, you may need to ask AutoCAD for information about the drawing, such as distances and areas. You can also ask AutoCAD how much time you have spent on a drawing. The commands that enable you to do this are located in the INQUIRY selection of the ASSIST screen menu, the Inquiry selection of the Assist pull-down menu, or can be typed at the Command: prompt. They include AREA, DBLIST (DataBase LIST), DIST (DISTance), ID (IDentification), LIST, STATUS, and TIME. The STATUS command was discussed in Chapter 5. The DBLIST, STATUS, and TIME commands are not listed in either the pull-down or screen menus. The last item in both menus is Mass Properties. This command provides data related to the properties of a region or 3-D object created with solids. These topics are discussed in *AutoCAD and its Applications–Advanced, R13 for DOS*.

FINDING THE AREA OF SHAPES AND ENTITIES

AUG 6

The most basic function of the AREA command is to find the area of any object, circle, polyline, or spline. To select an object for area calculation, use the Object option as follows:

Command: **AREA** ↵
⟨First point⟩/Object/Add/Subtract: **O** ↵
Select objects: *(pick object)*
Area = *(n.nn)*, Circumference = *(n.nn)*

The "n" given above represents the numerical values of the area and circumference of the object. The second value that is returned by the AREA command varies depending on the type of object selected.

Object	Value returned
Line	Perimeter
Pline	Perimeter
Circle	Circumference
Spline	Length

PROFESSIONAL TIP

   AutoCAD gives you the area between two or more points picked on the screen, even if these two points are not connected by lines. Although there is no area between two points, the distance between them is given.

Shapes drawn with lines or polylines do not have to be closed for AutoCAD to calculate their area. AutoCAD calculates the area as if a line connected the first and last points.

To find the area of a shape created with the LINE command, pick all the vertices of that shape. See Figure 16-1. This is the default mode of the AREA command. Set a running OSNAP such as ENDpoint or INTersection to help you pick the vertices.

Command: **AREA** ⏎
⟨First point⟩/Object/Add/Subtract: *(pick point 1)*
Next point: *(pick point 2)*
Next point: *(continue picking points until all corners of the object have been selected; then press* ENTER*)*
Next point: ⏎
Area = *(n.nn)*, Perimeter = *(n.nn)*

Figure 16-1.   Pick all corners to find the area of an object drawn with the LINE command.

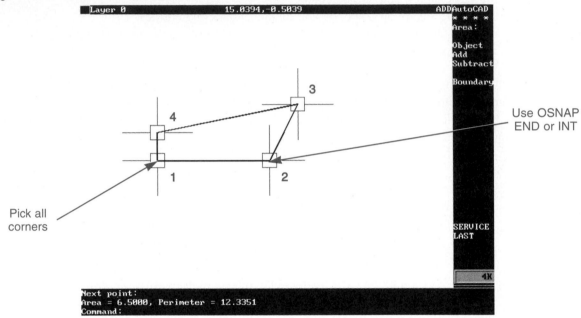

PROFESSIONAL TIP

Calculating area, circumference, and perimeter of shapes made with the LINE command can be time-consuming. You must pick each vertex on the object. If you know you will have to calculate areas, it is best to create lines and arcs with the PLINE or SPLINE command. Then choose the Object option when adding or subtracting entities.

Adding and subtracting areas

If you select the Add option, you can pick circles and entities drawn with PLINE. They are then automatically added to calculate the total area. After entities have been added, the Subtract option allows you to remove selected areas.

Once the Add option is chosen, the AREA command remains in effect until you cancel the command. You can continue to add or subtract entities and shapes using the Add and Subtract options.

The next example demonstrates using both Add and Subtract options. It also shows how entities drawn with the PLINE command are easier to pick. The object is shown in Figure 16-2. The command sequence is as follows:

```
Command: AREA ↵
⟨First point⟩/Object/Add/Subtract: A ↵
⟨First point⟩/Object/Subtract: O ↵
(ADD mode) Select objects: (pick polyline)
Area = 5.51, Perimeter = 13.61
Total area = 5.51
(ADD mode) Select objects: ↵
⟨First point⟩/Object/Subtract: S ↵
⟨First point⟩/Object/Add: O ↵
(SUBTRACT mode) Select objects: (pick first circle)
Area = 0.11, Circumference = 1.18
Total area = 5.40
(SUBTRACT mode) Select objects: (pick second circle)
Area = 0.11, Circumference = 1.18
Total area = 5.29
(SUBTRACT mode) Select objects: ↵
⟨First point⟩/Object/Add: ↵
```

Figure 16-2.   Example of object on which AREA Add and Subtract options can be used.

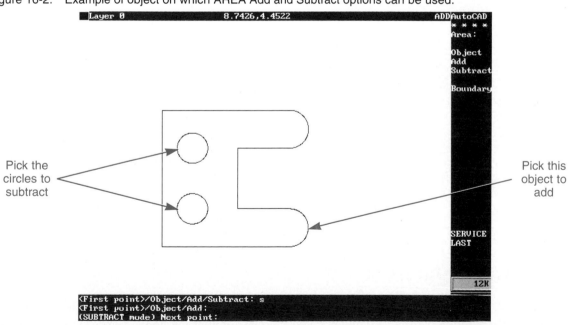

The total area of the object in Figure 16-2, subtracting the area of the two holes, is 5.29. Circumferences and perimeters are given for each object that is selected. These are not affected by the adding or subtracting functions.

Notice in the previous command sequence that if you are finished adding and wish to subtract, you must press ENTER at the (ADD mode) Select objects: prompt. The same is true if you have completed subtracting and wish to add.

EXERCISE 16-1

❑ Load AutoCAD, and begin a new drawing using the default AutoCAD prototype drawing. Set up your own variables.
❑ Draw the objects shown. Use the size dimensions given. The exact locations of the cutout and holes are not important.
❑ Use the AREA command to calculate the area of the entire object.
❑ Use the AREA command to subtract the areas of the rectangle and two circles.
❑ List the following information:

    Area of large rectangle _____

    Perimeter of large rectangle _____

    Perimeter of small rectangle_____

    Circumference of one circle_____

    Area of large rectangle minus the areas of the three shapes _____
❑ Save the drawing as A:EX16-1. This drawing is used for the next exercise.

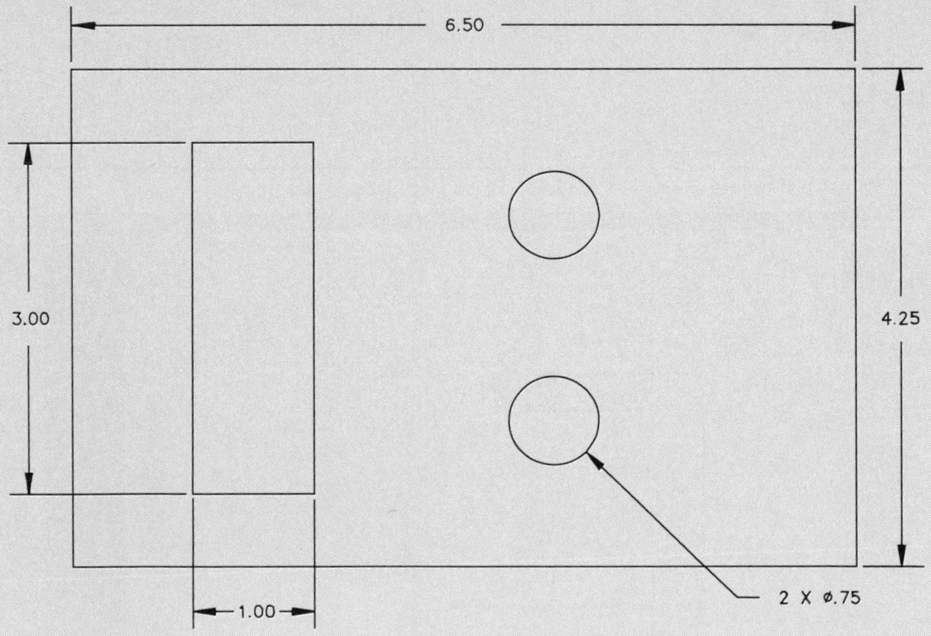

LISTING DRAWING DATA

AUG 6

The LIST command displays data about any AutoCAD object. Line length, circle and arc locations and radii, polyline widths, and object layers are just a few of the items AutoCAD gives you with the LIST command. You can select several objects to list.

```
Command: LIST ↵
Select objects: (pick object(s) using any selection option)
Select objects: ↵
```

When you press ENTER, the data for each of the objects picked is displayed. The information given for a line is:

```
LINE                 Layer: (layer name)
                     Space: Model space
                     Handle = (nn)
        from point, X  = (nn.nn)   Y  = (nn.nn)   Z = (nn.nn)
          to point, X  = (nn.nn)   Y  = (nn.nn)   Z = (nn.nn)
     Length = (nn.nn)   Angle in X-Y plane = (nn.nn)/
           Delta X  = (nn.nn)   Delta Y = (nn.nn)   Delta Z = (nn.nnn)
```

The Delta X and Y numbers show the horizontal and vertical distance between the *from point* and the *to point* of the line. These two numbers, the length, and angle provide you with four measurements for a single line. An example of the data provided for two-dimensional lines is shown in Figure 16-3. If a line is three-dimensional, an additional line of information is provided by the LIST command.

3D Length = *(nn.nn)*,   Angle from XY Plane = *(nn.nn)*

Figure 16-3.   Measurements of a line provided by the LIST command.

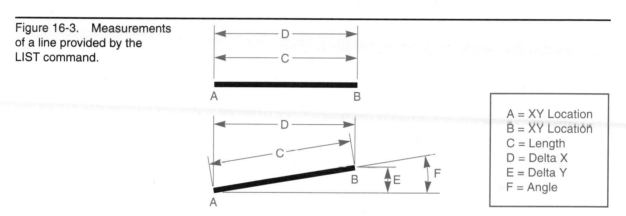

```
A = XY Location
B = XY Location
C = Length
D = Delta X
E = Delta Y
F = Angle
```

The data given by the LIST command for text, mtext, circles, and splines are as follows:

```
TEXT                 Layer:  (layer name)
                     Space: Model space
        Handle  = (nn)
          Style  = (name) Font file = (name)
        start  point, X = (n.nn) Y = (n.nn) Z =  (n.nn)
       height  (n.nn)
         text  (text label)
     rotation  angle (nn)
        width  scale factor (n.nn)
     obliquing  angle (nn)
    generation  normal


MTEXT                Layer:  (layer name)
                     Space: Model space
        Handle  = (nn)
      Location  X = (n.nn) Y = (n.nn) Z = (n.nn)
         Width  (n.nn)
        Normal  X = (n.nn) Y = (n.nn) Z = (n.nn)
      Rotation  (n.nn)
    Text style  (style name)
   Text height  (n.nn)
    Attachment  (corner of mtext insertion point)
Flow direction  (direction text is read based on language)
      Contents  (mtext contents)
```

```
CIRCLE          Layer:   (layer name)
                Space:  Model space
      Handle  = (nn)
center point  X = (n.nn) Y = (n.nn) Z = (n.nn)
      radius  (n.nn)
circumference  (n.nn), Area = (n.nn)
        area  (n.nn)


SPLINE          Layer:   (layer name)
                Space:  Model space
        Handle  = (nn)
        Length  (n.nn)
         Order  (n.nn)
     Properties  Planar, Non-Rational, Non-Periodic
Parametric Range  Start (n.nn)
                 End (n.nn)
 Control Points  X = (n.nn) , Y = (n.nn) , Z = (n.nn)
                 (All XYZ control points listed)
     User Data  Fit Points
                 X = (n.nn) , Y = (n.nn) , Z = (n.nn)
                 (All XYZ fit points listed)
```

PROFESSIONAL TIP

   The LIST command is probably the most powerful inquiry command in AutoCAD. It provides all of the information you need to know about the selected object. Practice listing as many different objects as possible in your drawings. This exercise will help you to gain a greater understanding of the different kinds of data stored with each AutoCAD object.

LISTING ALL THE DRAWING DATA   AUG 6

   The DBLIST (DataBase LIST) command lists all of the data about every object in the current drawing. Information provided is in the same format as the LIST command. As soon as you enter DBLIST, the data begins to quickly scroll up the screen. The scrolling stops when a complete page has been filled with database information. Press ENTER to scroll to the end of the next page. If you find the data you need, press CTRL+C to exit the DBLIST command.

FINDING THE DISTANCE BETWEEN TWO POINTS   AUG 6

   The DIST command finds the distance between two points. Use OSNAP modes to accurately pick location, or make sure the two points lie on snap points. See Figure 16-4. The DIST command provides distance and angle of the line. It also gives delta X, Y, and Z dimensions.

Command: **DIST** ↵
First point: *(select point)* Second point: *(select point)*
Distance = 2.85,   Angle in XY Plane = 353,   Angle from XY Plane = 0
Delta X = 2.83,   Delta Y = -0.37,   Delta Z = 0.000

Figure 16-4.   Use OSNAP ENDpoint and DIST to find the distance between two endpoints of a line

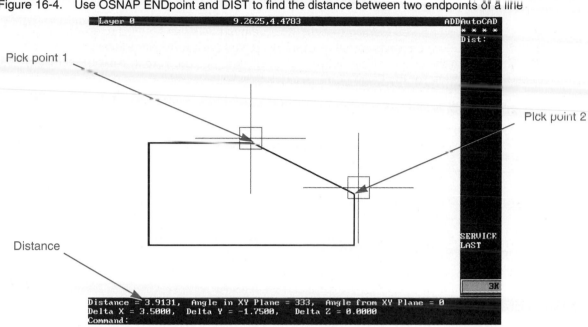

Delta Z refers to the third coordinate axis used in three-dimensional drawing. This value is zero unless the object was drawn with a thickness, or with 3-D drawing commands. An introduction to 3-D techniques and commands is provided in Chapter 29.

If you pick the Assist pull-down menu, then Inquiry and Distance, notice the syntax that is displayed at the Command: prompt.

Command: `__dist First point:

The apostrophe entered before "dist" indicates that this is a transparent command, and can be used while you are working inside of another command. The ID command, which is discussed in the next section, is also transparent if selected from the pull-down or screen menus. Be careful if you want to use a transparent DIST command by selecting it from the screen menu. If you pick AutoCAD at the top of the screen menu in order to locate the inquiry command, you will be cancelled out of the command you are in. It is best to use the pull-down menu if you need to use a transparent DIST or ID command.

IDENTIFYING A POINT LOCATION

AUG 6

The ID command gives the coordinate location of a single point on the screen. You might use it to find the endpoint of a line or the center of a circle. Simply pick the point to be identified. Use the OSNAP modes for accuracy.

Command: **ID** ⏎
Point: *(select the point)*
X = *(nn.nn)*   Y = *(nn.nn)*   Z = *(nn.nn)*

The ID command can also help you identify a coordinate location on the screen. Enter the exact coordinate values you wish to find. Suppose you want to see where the point X = 8.75, Y = 6.44 is located. Enter these numbers at the Point: prompt. AutoCAD responds by placing a blip (marker) at that exact location.

Command: **ID** ⏎
Point: **8.75,6.44** ⏎
X = 8.75 Y = 6.44 Z = 0.00

PROFESSIONAL TIP

From Chapter 8 you learned that the ID command can also be used to specify a point as the origin for relative coordinates. For example, if you wish to begin drawing a line 10'-6" on the X axis from the corner of a building, select ID and pick the corner. Next, select LINE and enter the following for the From point: prompt:

From point: **@10'6",0** ⏎

When you use the ID command, it automatically resets the system variable called LAST-POINT to the value of the ID point. When you include the *at sign* (@), this tells AutoCAD to work from the LASTPOINT value.

EXERCISE 16-2

Load AutoCAD and open EX16-1 if it is not currently on the screen.
❑ Use the LIST command to display information about one circle and one line on the drawing.
❑ Select the DBLIST command to display information about your drawing.
❑ Select DBLIST again and press CTRL+C to end the listing.
❑ Use OSNAP options to find the following information:
   A. Distance between the two circle center points.
   B. Between the lower circle center point and the left edge of the large rectangle.
   C. Distance between the lower-left and upper-right corners of the large rectangle.
   D. ID of the center point of the upper circle.
   E. ID of the lower-left corner of the small rectangle.
   F. ID of the midpoint of the large rectangle's right side.
   G. ID of point 6,4 on your screen.
❑ Save the drawing as A:EX16-2 and quit.

CHECKING THE TIME

AUG 4

The TIME command displays the current time and time related to your drawing and drawing session. The display for the TIME command is as follows:

Current time:	15 Sep 1995 at 13:39:22.210
Times for this drawing:	
Created:	15 Aug 1995 at 10:24:48.130
Last updated:	15 Aug 1995 at 14:36:23.46
Total editing time:	0 days 01:23:57.930
Elapsed timer *(on)*:	0 days 00:35:28.650
Next automatic save in:	0 days 01:35:26.680
Display/ON/OFF/Reset:	

There are a few things to keep in mind when checking the TIME display. First, the drawing creation time starts when you "OK" a new drawing with the NEW command, or by using the BLOCK command. (See Chapter 25.) Second, the END and SAVE commands affect the "Last updated" time. However, when QUIT is used to end a drawing session and you do not save the drawing, all time in that session is discarded. Finally, you can time a specific drawing task by using the Reset option to reset the elapsed timer.

While the TIME display is on the screen, it is static. That is, none of the times are being updated. You can request an update by choosing the Display option as follows:

Display/ON/OFF/Reset: **D** ⏎

When you enter the drawing editor, the timer is on by default. If you want to stop the timer, just enter OFF at the prompt. If the timer is off, enter ON to start it again.

If the date and time are incorrect, they can be reset with the DOS commands DATE and TIME. These must be set when you are at the DOS prompt. The SHELL command can help you reset the date and time quickly.

> Command: **SHELL** ↵↵
> C:\\⟩ **DATE** ↵
> Current date is Fri 08-18-1995
> Enter new date (mm-dd-yy): *(type the date; for example,* **09-15-95***)* ↵
> C:\\⟩ **TIME** ↵
> Current time is 6:49:57.00a
> Enter new time: *(type the time; for example,* **6:52p***)* ↵
> C:\\⟩ **EXIT** ↵

PROFESSIONAL TIP

The SHELL command executes a DOS shell, which means that you can work with DOS commands while in AutoCAD, without having to quit AutoCAD. It is like entering an enclosed shell while floating in the sea of AutoCAD. When you are finished working in the shell, just exit it back to AutoCAD. The SHELL command can also be selected by picking External Commands in the Tools pull-down menu.

EXERCISE 16-3

❑ Recall any one of your previous drawings.
❑ Select the TIME command and study the information that is displayed.
❑ If the current time and date are incorrect, inform your instructor or supervisor. Then use the DOS commands to set the correct date and time.
❑ Update the TIME display.
❑ Reset the elapsed timer.
❑ Use QUIT to exit the drawing editor without saving.

CHAPTER TEST

Write your answers in the spaces provided.

1. To add entity areas, when do you select the Add option? _____
   _____

2. When using the AREA command, explain how picking a polyline is different than picking an object drawn with the LINE command. _____
   _____

3. What information is provided by the AREA command? _____
   _____

4. What is the LIST command used for? _____
   _____

5. Describe the meaning of Delta X and Delta Y. _____
   _____
   _____

6. What is the function of the DBLIST command? _____

_____

7. How do you cancel the DBLIST command? _____

8. What are the two purposes of the ID command? _____

_____

9. What information is provided by the TIME command?_____

_____

10. When does the drawing time start? _____

_____

_____

DRAWING PROBLEMS

Load AutoCAD and start a new drawing for each of the following problems. Insert your floppy disk and name the drawing as P16-(problem number).

P16-1

1. Draw the object shown below using the dimensions given. Draw all of the features using PLINE and CIRCLE commands. Follow these instructions as you proceed:

   A. Check the time when you enter the drawing editor.

   B. Use the default units and limits.

   C. Set the grid spacing to .5 and snap spacing to .25.

   D. Measure the area of object A and subtract the areas of the other three features.

   E. Write your answers for the areas and perimeters in the chart provided.

   F. Use the Add, Subtract, and Object options of AREA to find the measurements. Do not exit the AREA command. Complete all of the following calculations in one selection of AREA.

   G. Select TIME and note your time in the drawing editor. _____

   H. Save the drawing as A:P16-1.

	OBJECT A	OBJECT B	OBJECT C	OBJECT A–OBJECT B	OBJECT A–CUTOUTS AND HOLES
AREA					
PERIMETER					

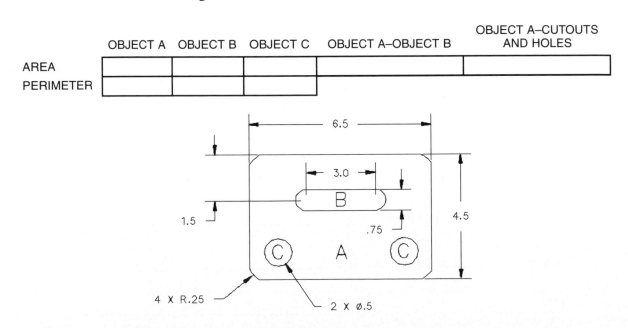

P16-2

2. Draw the object shown below using the LINE command. Draw the hexagon using the POLYGON command. Use the following settings and provide all measurements listed.

   A. Set architectural units. Use 1/2 in. fractions and decimal degrees. Leave remaining units settings at default values.

   B. Set the limits to 100',80'.

   C. Set the grid spacing to 2' and snap spacing to 1'.

   D. Calculate the measurements requested in the charts below.

   E. Select the DBLIST command.

   F. Select TIME and note the time in drawing editor. _____

   G. Save the drawing as A:P16-2.

	OBJECT A	OBJECT B	OBJECT A–OBJECT B
AREA			
PERIMETER			

	LINE CD	EC
DISTANCE		

	POINT C	POINT D	POINT F
ID			

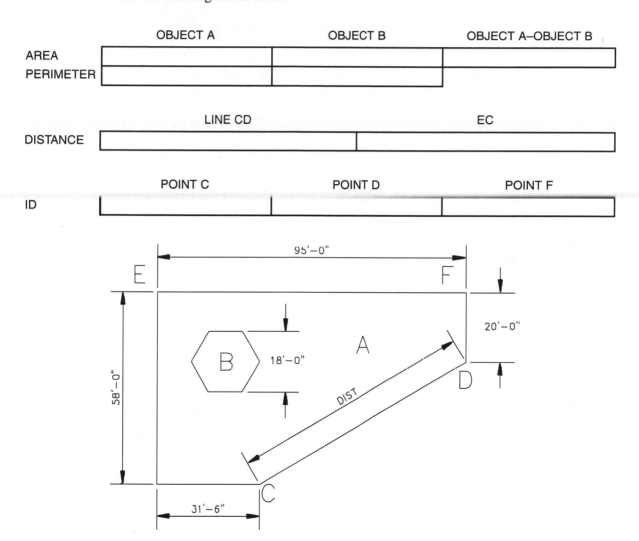

P16-3

3. In this problem you will draw a piece of property in the form of a plat. A *plat* is a map of a piece of land. The lengths of the sides are measured, as well as the bearing. A *bearing* is a direction measured from the north or south to the east or west. A bearing is never greater than 90°. Refer to the drawing as you do this problem.

    A. Set units to engineering. Select four digits to right of decimal.

    B. Select surveyor's units, and four fractional places for angle display.

    C. Select East (E) for angle direction.

    D. Set the limits at 440′,340′ and Zoom All.

    E. Draw the property lines using the LINE command. Enter the distance and bearing at the "To point" prompt as follows:

    From point: *(pick a point)*
    To point: @**130′**⟨**N45dE** ⏎
    To point: @**245′**⟨**S76d30′E** ⏎

    F. Continue in this manner for the next two sides. When entering tenths of a foot, they must be entered as feet and inches; for example, 264.5′ should be entered as 264′6″. Convert tenths of a foot to inches by multiplying by 12. Use the Close option to draw the fifth line.

    G. Select LIST and get the bearing of the last line.

    H. Use the PLINE, SPLINE, or LINE command to draw the road. It can be straight or curved. (See Chapter 18 for more information on the PLINE and SPLINE command.) The road should be 16 ft. wide.

    I. Use TRIM and EXTEND to clean up the ends of the road.

    J. Provide the following information:

	AREAS	PERIMETERS
PROPERTY		
LAKE		
ROAD		
PROPERTY–LAKE		
LAKE + ROAD		
PROPERTY–LAKE + ROAD		

    K. Label the drawing as shown.

    L. Select TIME and note the time in drawing editor. _____

    M. Save the drawing as A:P16-3.

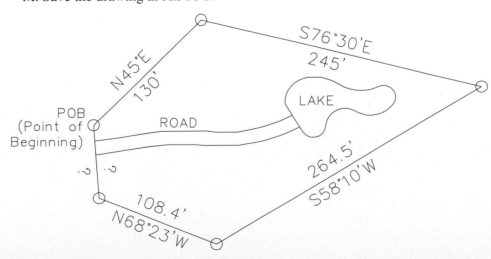

P16-4

4. This problem requires that you create a drawing of the proposed parking lot shown below. Do not dimension the drawing.

A. Set units to architectural.

B. Set the limits to 400',300'.

C. Use the PLINE command to draw the parking lot outline.

D. Calculate the following and record your answers:

   Area of asphalt (without landscape dividers). _____

   Area of landscape dividers (all trees and flowers). _____

   Area of landscape dividers (trees only). _____

E. Select TIME and note the time in the drawing editor. _____

F. Save the drawing as A:P16-4.

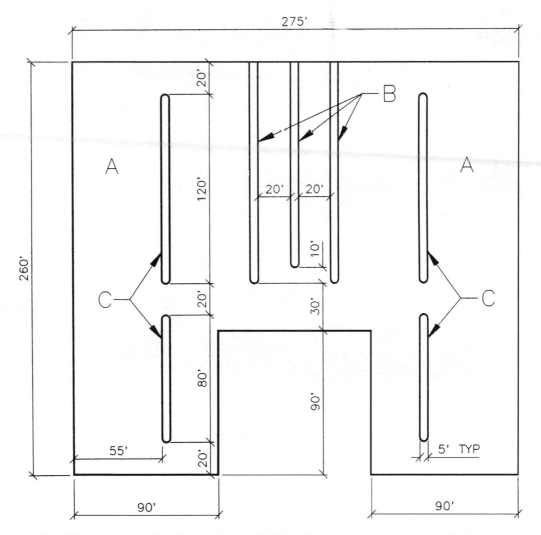

A–Parking Lot (asphalt)   B–Landscape Dividers (flowers)   C–Landscape Dividers (trees)

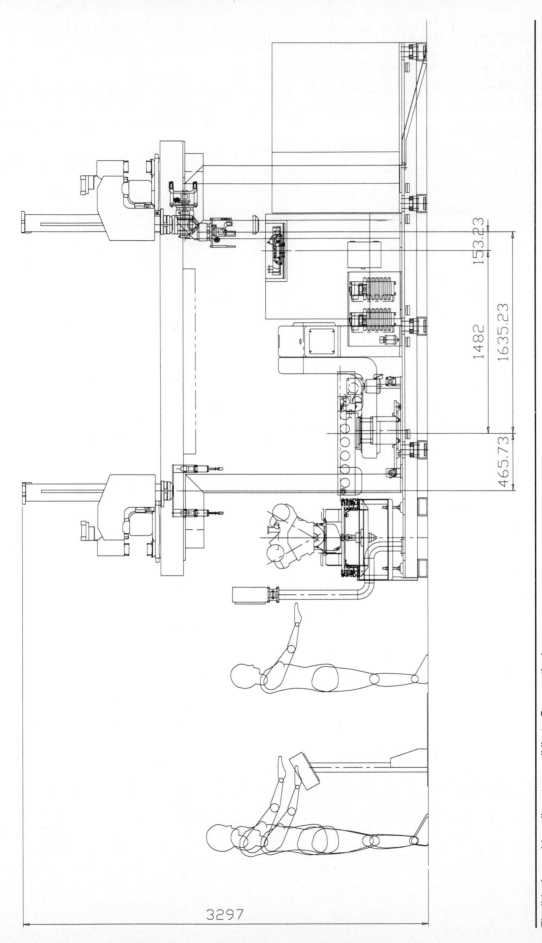

Flexible Assembly cell system.   (Hirata Corporation)

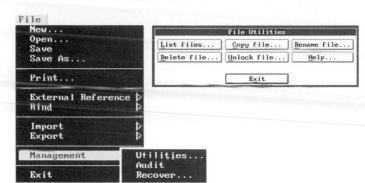

Learning objectives

After completing this chapter, you will be able to:
- ❍ Explain the meaning and use of DOS file extensions.
- ❍ List any type of file using the "File Utilities" dialog box.
- ❍ Copy, rename, and delete files using the "File Utilities" dialog box.
- ❍ Explain the use of file locking and unlocking.
- ❍ Import and export a variety of file types in AutoCAD.
- ❍ Define DOS file extensions.
- ❍ List any type of file using DOS commands.
- ❍ Copy, rename, delete, and undelete files using DOS commands.
- ❍ Copy disks using the DISKCOPY command.
- ❍ Create, delete, and manage DOS directories.

AutoCAD works with several types of computer files. These can be identified by a three-letter file type extension on the end of the file name. The "File Utilities" dialog box in AutoCAD allows the user to list, copy, erase, rename, and unlock files.

Working with files in this manner is easier than using DOS commands, which are also discussed later in this chapter. The "File Utilities" dialog box is accessible from the File pull-down menu by picking Management, then the Utilities… selection. From the FILE screen menu pick MANAGE, then Files:.

The AutoCAD drawing file format is potentially compatible with a variety of other software applications. You can export the industry standard DXF file for use with other CAD packages, or specific applications. Files can also be exported for use in the design and animation software 3D Studio, or for use in the stereolithography process. In addition, you can import several different file types into AutoCAD.

FILE NAME TYPES

AUG 14

Drawing file names can be up to eight characters long. They can contain letters, numbers, the dollar sign ($), hyphens (-), and underscores (_). When you begin a new drawing, AutoCAD adds a file extension to the end of the file name. This extension is .DWG. If you began a drawing called BLDG-34, AutoCAD creates the file as BLDG-34.DWG. When you open the drawing to edit, you only have to type BLDG-34. AutoCAD knows to look for that file, plus the .DWG extension.

After you edit the BLDG-34.DWG file and save it again, the original is converted to a backup file. Its file extension is automatically changed to .BAK (backup). AutoCAD maintains a current .DWG file and one .BAK file. If you revise the BLDG-34 drawing again, the .BAK file is erased and the previous .DWG copy becomes the backup. Only a newly revised drawing is given the .DWG file extension.

There are other extensions given to files by AutoCAD and MS-DOS. Some common file extensions are listed below. For a complete list, see Appendix C.

AutoCAD

- **.BAK.** Backup copy of a drawing file.
- **.DCL.** dialog Control Language description file.
- **.DWG.** Drawing file.
- **.LIN.** File containing the linetypes used by AutoCAD.
- **.MNU.** Menu source file.
- **.PAT.** Hatch patterns file.
- **.PLT.** Plot file.

MS-DOS

- **.BAT.** Batch file.
- **.COM.** Command file.
- **.EXE.** Executable file.

"FILE UTILITIES" DIALOG BOX   AUG 14

The "File Utilities" dialog box contains options that allow you to perform file management functions other than creating and editing drawings. This dialog box can be accessed three ways. Enter FILES at the Command: prompt, pick Management/Utilities from the Files pull-down menu, or pick MANAGE/Files: from the FILE screen menu. All three methods display the dialog box shown in Figure 17-1.

Figure 17-1.   The "File Utilities" dialog box can be used to manipulate files in a number of ways.

List your drawings

It is easy to find out which drawings are stored on a particular disk. The "File Utilities" dialog box allows you to list the drawings on any disk or directory. AutoCAD only needs to know which disk drive or directory you wish to list. Remember, your first floppy drive is usually a 3.5″, and it is usually designated the A: drive, and the second floppy drive is usually designated the B: drive. If you have a CD-ROM drive it is usually designated the D: drive. The first hard disk drive is always labeled C:. If there is more than one hard disk drive in your computer, the second is E:, the third is designated F:, and so on. To list the drawing files on a disk in the A: drive, first insert the diskette. Then pick List files... from the "File Utilities" box.

This displays the "File List" dialog box that is similar to the "Open Drawing" dialog box. Notice in Figure 17-2 that two list boxes are displayed. The box on the left contains a list of directories and disk drives, while the one on the right contains a list of files of the current pattern (file type). The current pattern is always given in the Edit box at the top of the dialog box.

Figure 17-2.   The "File List" dialog box shows directories and files.

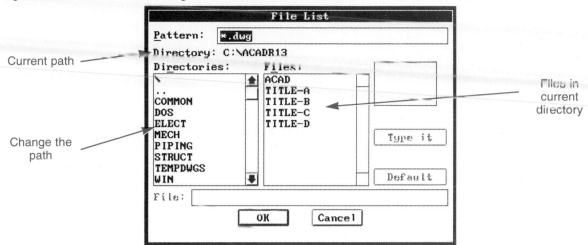

Current path

Change the
path

Files in
current
directory

Scroll down in the Directories: list box until you see ⟨A:⟩. Insert a disk that contains drawing files into the A: drive. Double click on the ⟨A:⟩ and a list of all drawing files is shown in the Files: list box. See Figure 17-3. If necessary, use the scroll arrows to move up and down in the list. If you pick OK, the next time you use the "File Utilities" dialog box, the A: drive will be current. If you pick Cancel, the default drive will be current.

Figure 17-3.   Files on a disk or in a directory are shown in the Files: list box.

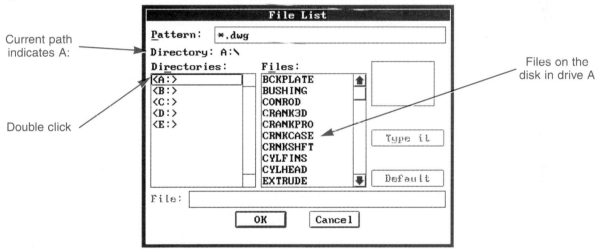

Current path
indicates A:

Double click

Files on the
disk in drive A

PROFESSIONAL TIP

Since all of the file management functions in the "File Utilities" dialog box use the same basic file dialog box, you can work easily with your files by performing the following basic steps for all file management operations.

1. Pick the file command to be used.
2. Scroll (if necessary) in the Directories box to find the drive or directory you wish to work in.
3. Enter the pattern (specific file group or file type) you wish to work with in the Pattern: box.
4. Select the file(s) you wish to work with.
5. Provide any final information required, such as a new name or location.

List any file type

You are not limited to listing just .DWG file types (drawing files). You can list any type of file by picking List files... in the "File List" dialog box. Notice that the default entry in the Pattern: text box is *.dwg. Therefore all of the files currently shown in the Files: list box are drawings. But suppose you need a list of all backup (.BAK) files in the C:\ACADR13\PROJ 01 subdirectory. They can be listed using the following steps:

1. Pick the List files... button in the "File List" dialog box.
2. If the current file type in the Pattern: text box is highlighted, you can begin typing the new file type to list, and it replaces the existing text. If the file type is not highlighted, click inside the text box and use Backspace, arrow keys, and the Delete key to edit the text. You can also double-click inside the text box to highlight the current entry. Now type the new text and it replaces everything in the box.
3. Using one of the techniques just described, enter *.BAK in the Pattern: text box and press ENTER.
4. Double-click on the directory or drive letter in which you wish to list files.

All of the files that have a .BAK file extension are listed in the Files: box. The asterisk (*) used in the above entry is a DOS wild-card character. It represents any number of characters. Used in this manner, it instructs AutoCAD to list all files with a .BAK extension.

If you are searching for one particular file, enter that name. If the file is not on the specified drive or directory, it will not be listed.

EXERCISE 17-1

❑ Load AutoCAD, and insert a floppy disk that contains drawing files.
❑ Use the "File Utilities" dialog box to do the following:
   A. List all .DWG files on the hard disk drive in the \ACADR13\COMMON\SAMPLE subdirectory.
   B. List all .DWG files on the floppy disk.
   C. List all files with an .EXP extension on the hard disk drive in the \ACADR13\DOS directory.
   D. List all file types beginning with ACAD.
   E. List all file types beginning with ACAD and ending with any extension that begins with an "E".
❑ Exit the "File Utilities" dialog box.

Deleting files

File deletion is a drastic measure to take with any type of file. *Before deleting a file, be sure that the file name you enter is the one you want to delete.* Select Delete file... in the "File Utilities" dialog box. The "File(s) to Delete" dialog box then appears.

Suppose you want to delete the drawing entitled JUNK.DWG on the disk in the A: drive. Be sure the A: drive is current. Scroll to find the file and pick it so the file name is highlighted. The selected name is displayed in the File: edit box. See Figure 17-4. If the file name displayed is correct, pick OK. Before AutoCAD deletes the file, it prompts you with an "AutoCAD Message" alert box as shown in Figure 17-5. Pick the Yes button to delete the file.

PROFESSIONAL TIP

 You may have noticed that many of the Edit boxes and buttons contain an uppercase, underlined letter. The options represented by these characters may be activated by pressing the character key and ALT key simultaneously. These are known as accelerator keys. Pressing one of these key combinations highlights the selected option. Press ENTER to execute it. You can also move around in a dialog box by pressing the Tab key. To cancel or exit a dialog box quickly, press the ESC key.

Figure 17-4.   The selected file to delete is placed in the File: text box.

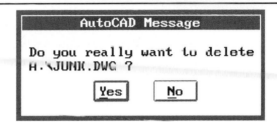

Select file
type

Current path

Select file
to delete

Selected
file

Click to select
all files in
the current
directory

Click to
deselect all
highlighted
files

Figure 17-5.   AutoCAD alerts
you before deleting a file.

You can delete more than one file at a time just by picking them. After you pick the second file, no name is displayed in the File: edit box. If you wish to "clean house" and delete all files on a disk or directory, simply pick the Select all button and all files are highlighted. If you do this by mistake, pick the Clear all button and all files are unselected.

If you want to delete a specific group of files, such as all drawing files that begin with "PIPE" and end with any three characters, you must first list them by typing the following in the Pattern edit box:

PIPE???.DWG

This displays only the specific files you requested. The question mark (?) is a DOS wild-card character that represents any single character. To delete the specified files, pick the Select all button, then pick OK. AutoCAD displays an "AutoCAD Message" alert box before deleting each file.

PROFESSIONAL TIP

Users who keep their drawing files on one or more backup disks or tapes occasionally erase all .BAK files on working disks in order to make room for additional files. Do not do this unless you are sure that you have backup copies of your files elsewhere.

Remember, a question mark represents any single character. The files PIPE123.DWG and PIPEABC.DWG are selected for deletion by the previous entry. However, the file PIPE1234.DWG is not because four characters follow PIPE.

PROFESSIONAL TIP

Deleting files is dangerous. Be careful when entering the file name. Always look at the file name you typed before pressing the ENTER key, or picking the OK button.

In order to manage your files properly, a working knowledge of directories and subdirectories is important. AutoCAD displays the name of the current directory in the Directory label of many dialog boxes. A label such as: C:\ACADR13\COMMON\SAMPLE indicates that the SAMPLE subdirectory located off the ACADR13\COMMON subdirectory on the C: drive is current. This is referred to as a *path.* An in-depth study of directories and DOS commands is given later in this chapter.

Changing file names

You can rename files by selecting <u>R</u>ename file... from the "File Utilities" dialog box. The standard file dialog box used for all file utility commands is displayed. This one is titled "Old File Name." Use the same method discussed previously to first select the disk drive or directory you wish to work in. Remember, you can specify the pattern of file to look for so that only specific file names are displayed. Then select the file name you wish to change from the <u>F</u>iles Name: list box and pick OK, or double click on the file name.

The "New File Name" dialog box appears. You can type the new name in the <u>F</u>ile: edit box and pick OK. Be sure to include the three-letter extension. A message indicates if the renaming operation was successful. If you want to put the file in another directory on the current disk drive, first pick the directory, then type the new name. This accomplishes the tasks of renaming and copying. You cannot copy from one drive to another using the Rename function.

Copying files

Copying files is similar to the functions previously discussed. When you pick <u>C</u>opy file... from the "File Utilities" dialog box, the "Source File" dialog box is displayed. Using the same procedure for all file manipulation functions, first select the disk drive and directory you wish to copy from, then select the file you wish to copy, such as P16-8.DWG, and pick OK. (You can also double click on the file name.) The "Destination File" dialog box is then displayed. Now select the disk drive and directory in which you want the copy placed. Finally, type the full name of the file, in this case P16-8.DWG and press ENTER or pick OK. If you wish to change the name of the file in addition to copying it, simply type the new name in the "Destination File" dialog box. A message (Copied 240107 bytes.) is displayed indicating the file was successfully copied. See Figure 17-6.

Figure 17-6.   The size of the copied file is indicated with a message.

Indicates the file was copied and gives the size of the file

PROFESSIONAL TIP

   AutoCAD can use a .BAK file if it is renamed to a .DWG file. This may be necessary when a drawing file is accidentally erased or is unreadable because of a disk failure. It is best to copy the backup file to another disk. Then rename the backup as a drawing file. This is easily done using the <u>C</u>opy file... selection and ensures that you still have a backup copy.

Unlocking a file

File locking can be set when AutoCAD is installed, or by using the CONFIG command. When AutoCAD is used in a network environment, and several people have access to the same drawings, it is good practice to lock files. A locked file can be used by only one person at a time. This prevents two or more people from revising the same drawing at the same time.

If you choose to configure AutoCAD to use file locking, be sure to first save your current drawing before using the CONFIG command. When you enable file locking, AutoCAD must exit, and you are not given a chance to save your work.

- First, save your current drawing.
- Type CONFIG at the Command: prompt, or pick Configure from the Options pull-down menu.
- The graphics screen flips to the text screen and the current configuration is displayed. Press ENTER.
- Select #7, Configure operating parameters.
- Select #12, File locking.
- Answer Yes (Y) to Do you wish to enable file-locking? prompt.
- Select #0, Exit to configuration menu.
- Select #0, Exit to drawing editor.
- Answer Yes (Y) to the Keep configuration changes? prompt. The following message and prompt is displayed:

  This configuration change requires AutoCAD to exit.
  Press RETURN to continue:

- Press ENTER at this prompt, and the program is terminated. The next time AutoCAD is loaded, file locking is enabled.

This procedure should be used to permanently enable or disable file locking. However, to unlock one file, you should use the option in the "File Utilities" dialog box.

NOTE   File locking should not be changed and files should not be unlocked unless you have proper authorization. File locking is enabled for a reason, and should you unlock and revise a file at the wrong time, it may cause problems in your classroom or company. Be sure you have permission before enabling file locking or unlocking files.

When AutoCAD is run on a single-user workstation, file locking is not needed. But should you wish to safeguard a file and protect it from being overwritten during an editing session, you can open it and assign read-only status to it. Execute the OPEN command and pick the Read Only Mode check box in the "Open Drawing" dialog box. See Figure 17-7.

Figure 17-7. Pick the Read Only Mode check box in the Open Drawing dialog box to safeguard a file from being overwritten.

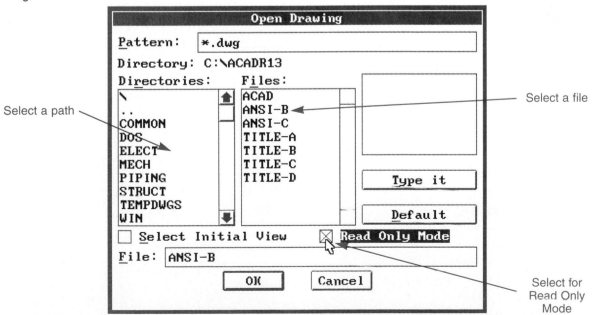

You can edit the drawing as you wish, but when you try to save it, an "AutoCAD Alert" box is displayed. See Figure 17-8.

Figure 17-8.   AutoCAD alerts
you if you try to save a file that
has read-only status.

> **NOTE**   One common function that creates a locked file is by an *ungraceful* exit from AutoCAD as a result of a power failure or system crash. These drawings may require unlocking before they can be edited again.

A file (or group of files) can be unlocked by using the Unlock file... selection in the "File Utilities" dialog box. The standard file dialog box entitled "File(s) to Unlock" is displayed. You can list only the lock files by entering *.DWK in the Pattern: edit box. Pick the file you need to unlock, then pick OK and the "AutoCAD Message" alert box shown in Figure 17-9 is displayed. Pick the Yes button if you wish to proceed with the unlocking.

Figure 17-9.   Information
about the locked file and who
locked it is provided in an
"AutoCAD Message" alert box.

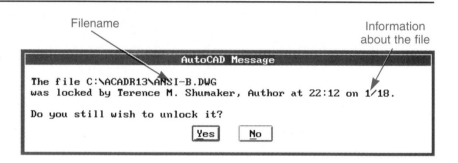

When file locking is enabled, AutoCAD automatically creates a small lock file with a .DWK extension. Therefore, when the ANSI-B.DWG file was loaded, a file named ANSI-B.DWK was also created. When this file was unlocked, the ANSI-B.DWK file was deleted.

PROFESSIONAL TIP

If your class or company works with drawings that must be accessed by more than one student or employee, it is good practice to enable file locking. Drawings such as basic site plans, floor plans, or templates or outlines that must have additional information added to them are examples of drawings that must be accessed by more than one person.

If file locking is enabled, AutoCAD creates locked versions of several file types. Keep this in mind when working with files other than drawings. The following activities create locked versions of the associated file:

Activity	File Type	Lock File
Auditing a drawing for errors.	.ADT	.ADK
Working with a drawing file.	.DWG	.DWK
Working with drawing interchange files.	.DXF, .DXB	.DFK, .DBK
Working with attribute extraction.	.DXX, .TXT	.DXK, .TXK
Altering line types.	.LIN	.LIK
Creating multiline styles.	.MLN	.MNK

Activity	File Type	Lock File
Compiling an AutoCAD menu file.	.MNX	.MNK
Writing mass properties to a text file.	.MPR	.MPK
Converting an older AutoCAD drawing.	.OLD	.OLK
Working with a plot configuration parameters file.	.PCP	.PCK
Creating plot files.	.PLT	.PLK
Working with an ASCIS (3-D solids) file.	.SAT	.SAK
Altering shape or font files.	.SHX	.SXK
Creating and displaying slides.	.SLD	.SDK
Creating a stereolithography file.	.STL	.STK
Using reference drawings.	.XLG	.XLK

It is not important that you understand the meaning of all of the file types previously mentioned. As you work through this text and gain experience with AutoCAD, you will become more familiar with these activities, and the file types that are used in each.

RECOVERING A DAMAGED DRAWING

AUG 14

A damaged drawing file is one that has been corrupted, and cannot be loaded into the AutoCAD drawing editor. Drawing files can be damaged in a number of ways. When they are damaged, it can be a frustrating experience, especially if you do not have a backup. Drawings are most often corrupted by the following actions:

• Removing a floppy disk before properly exiting AutoCAD.
• Changing floppy disks during a drawing session.
• Running out of disk space during a drawing session.
• Power failures.
• Hardware or software problems.

NOTE

Never start a new drawing on the floppy disk using the following naming convention:

A:FILENAME

This can lead to "disk full" errors and damaged drawings. Always start a new drawing on the hard disk. Use a directory other than the one that holds the AutoCAD program files. Create subdirectories in the ACADR13 directory for your drawing and data files. For example, use the DOS commands Make Directory (MD) and Change Directory (CD) to create work space on your hard disk. If your AutoCAD directory is named ACADR13, use the following commands to create a subdirectory called DWGS:

C:\〉 **CD ACADR13** ↵
C:\ACADR13〉 **MD DWGS** ↵

Now, you can load AutoCAD and start a new drawing called FRAMUS as follows:

New Drawing Name: **\ACADR13\DWGS\FRAMUS** ↵

You have given AutoCAD a "path" to follow in order to create and store a new drawing file. You should not run out of disk space as long as there are a few megabytes of open storage space on the hard disk that contains your directory. You can add a measure of security by specifying the name of a directory that AutoCAD can use for storage of temporary drawing files. This is an operating parameter option in the Configuration menu, which is accessed with the CONFIG command. This is discussed in the section titled *Understanding Disk Drives and Directories* in Chapter 2. Always get permission from your instructor or supervisor before altering any of the settings in the Configuration menu.

AutoCAD provides a method for recovering most damaged files. You can type RECOVER at the Command: prompt, or select Recover... from the Management section in the File pull-down menu.

Simply select the proper path and file and AutoCAD attempts to recover the damaged drawing. If the bad file is named \ACADR13\STRUCT\SLAB for example, pick the STRUCT subdirectory, and then pick the SLAB drawing name. AutoCAD then tries to recover the damaged file. If it is successful, the file is loaded into the drawing editor, and it can be worked on in the normal fashion. If you do not save the file before exiting AutoCAD, the recovered drawing is lost.

USING THE AUDIT COMMAND   AUG 14

You can perform a diagnostic check on your drawing files with the AUDIT command to check for, and correct errors. You can instruct AutoCAD to fix, or not to fix errors. A short report is generated as in the following example:

Command: **AUDIT** ↵
Fix any errors detected? ⟨N⟩ ↵
1   Blocks audited
Pass 1   145   objects audited
Pass 2   145   objects audited
Total errors found 0   fixed 0

Any errors are listed for your reference, but they are not fixed. To fix errors in the transferred drawing, answer Y as follows:

Command: **AUDIT** ↵
Fix any errors detected? ⟨N⟩: **Y** ↵

AutoCAD displays the errors and notifies you that they are fixed like this:

3 Blocks audited
Pass 29   objects audited
Pass 14   objects audited
Total errors found 2 fixed 2

If the system variable AUDITCTL is set to 1 (ON), AutoCAD automatically creates an audit report file that lists the corrections made. The report is given the same name as the drawing, but has an .ADT file extension. This file is placed in the same directory as the drawing. This is a text, or ASCII file (American Standard Code for Information Interchange), and can be listed by using the DOS command, TYPE, as follows:

Command: **TYPE** ↵
File to list: **\ACADR13\DWGS\FRAMUS.ADT** ↵

The contents of the FRAMUS.ADT file are then displayed on the screen.

NOTE   The use of dialog boxes is controlled by the FILEDIA system variable. If you do not want to work with the dialog boxes, simply set the FILEDIA variable to 0. All of the file utilities discussed in this chapter are still available, but they are accessed through the File Utility Menu on a text screen. All of your entries must be typed, including all paths, file names, and file extensions.

EXERCISE 17-2

❏ Insert one of your floppy disks with drawings into the A: drive.
❏ Use the "File Utilities" dialog box for this exercise.
❏ Copy one of your files and rename it using an .OLD file extension.
❏ Change the name of the file in the previous step to TEST.OLD.
❏ Copy and rename TEST.OLD to TEST-2.OLD.
❏ List all files with the .OLD extension.
❏ Delete all files with an .OLD extension.
❏ List the files on the floppy disk in the A: drive. Check to see whether there are any files with the .OLD extension.
❏ Exit the "File Utilities" dialog menu.

UNDERSTANDING AUTOCAD'S TEMPORARY FILES

AutoCAD maintains several temporary files while you are working on a drawing. You might consider these as "worksheets" that AutoCAD opens, much like the notes, references, sketches, and calculations you may have scattered around your desk. These files are created automatically to store portions of the AutoCAD program that is not currently in use, and for information related to the current drawing file. These files are critical to AutoCAD's operation, and must be maintained and safeguarded properly.

Program swap files

The main program file for AutoCAD is named ACAD.EXE. It is a very large file, over 5.5MB. If there is not enough room in your computer's physical memory (RAM) to store the program, AutoCAD creates *pages* of the program in free space on your hard disk drive. This total available RAM and hard disk space is called *virtual memory*. Therefore, AutoCAD employs a virtual memory system. This system maintains only that part of the program in physical memory that is needed. If additional portions of the program are needed, AutoCAD creates a *page* on the hard disk and writes the least-used portion of the program to that page. The new portion of the program that is requested is written to physical memory. Thus AutoCAD creates a *paging system* using virtual memory. The least-used pages are written to a page called a *swap file*, and are held there until needed again.

The important point to note regarding AutoCAD's paging system, is that when required, it creates a swap file in the root directory of the current disk drive, and gives it a .SWR extension. These files are critical to AutoCAD, and must never be deleted while you are in a drawing session. Should you experience an improper termination of AutoCAD, and the drawing file is not saved properly, these swap files may be left open. In that case the files are no longer of use and may be deleted. But only after you have exited AutoCAD.

CAUTION

If you feel that swap files have been left behind after an abnormal exit from AutoCAD, you may delete all files that have an .SWR extension, or that have names such as AOBCGFFE and have no extension. Never delete any of these temporary files while you are working in AutoCAD. Doing so may damage the current drawing and cause AutoCAD to terminate improperly.

Temporary files

The second piece of AutoCAD's virtual memory system is called the *pager*. This works similar to the swap file system, but creates temporary storage space for drawing file information. The entire contents of a small drawing may fit into your computer's physical memory, but as the drawing grows larger, portions of it must be temporarily removed. AutoCAD creates a *page file* for the least-used portion of your drawing, and opens the physical memory for new drawing data. When the drawing data contained in the page file is needed, it is *paged back* into memory. These temporary files are given the file extension of .AC$. These are vital files and must never be deleted while working in AutoCAD.

If AutoCAD should terminate improperly, these page files are left open in the current drawing directory. The .AC$ files that are left behind are no longer of any use, and may be deleted. Always delete these files at the DOS prompt using the DELETE command, and never while you are working in AutoCAD.

You can specify a directory on the hard disk drive for the storage of page files. Use the ACAD-PAGEDIR environment variable in the batch file that runs AutoCAD. A normal installation of AutoCAD creates a batch file titled ACADR13.BAT. The line in that file that specifies a directory for page files may look like this:

SET ACADPAGEDIR=C:\ACADR13\TEMP

Never alter the contents of a batch file unless you have the permission of your instructor or supervisor.

Create a workspace for temporary files

The procedure for creating a permanent storage location for temporary files was discussed in Chapter 2, but is important enough to warrant describing it again here.

The default workspace for AutoCAD's temporary files is the current disk drive and directory, or the drive and directory specified by the SAVE or SAVEAS commands. You can instruct AutoCAD to always use the same location for storage of temporary files. Use the following procedure to allocate space for these files.

1. Use the CONFIG command and press ENTER until the Configuration menu is displayed.
2. Select # 7; Configure operating parameters.
3. Select # 5; Placement of temporary files.
4. Enter a hard disk drive and directory reserved especially for temporary files.

The default setting is DRAWING, which causes temporary files to be stored in the same drive and directory as the drawing being edited. By setting this to a path that contains plenty of free space (e.g. C:\ACADR13\TEMP, or C:\ACADTEMP, etc.) you can be reasonably protected from "disk full" situations. Previous versions of AutoCAD placed tempory files on the floppy disk if it was specified as the path with SAVE or SAVEAS. This is no longer a problem in Release 13, because temporary files are always stored on the default hard drive, unless you use OPEN to retrieve a drawing from a floppy disk.

Automatically saved drawing files

You may remember from a previous discussion that the SAVETIME system variable allows you to specify the time interval at which AutoCAD automatically saves the current drawing file. This becomes your first line of backup, and is also considered a temporary file. Should you encounter a problem in AutoCAD and find your drawing file is corrupted as a result of an improper termination or system crash, this file may be a valuable backup. As a default setting, AutoCAD names the automatically saved file AUTO.SV$. If you ever need to use this drawing because the original was corrupted, you must rename it as a .DWG file. For example, use the RENAME command in DOS as follows:

C:\ACADR13⟩ **REN AUTO.SV$ FRAMUS.DWG**

This renaming action enables AutoCAD to load the file as a drawing.

The default name of the autosave file is established by AutoCAD, but can be changed by using the CONFIG command. If you want to have this file saved under a name other than AUTO.SV$, use the CONFIG command as follows:

1. Execute the CONFIG command.
2. Select #7 in the Configuration menu.
3. Select #7 in the Configure operating parameters menu.

roadblock:

4. Type the time between saves at the following prompt and press ENTER.

Interval between automatic saves, in minutes (1-600), or 0 for no automatic saves ⟨120⟩:10 ↵
Enter filename for automatic saves
⟨AUTO.SV$⟩ : **AUTOSAVE** ↵

5. Select #0 to Exit to configuration menu.
6. Select #0 to Exit to drawing editor.
7. Answer Yes (Y) to the Keep configuration changes? prompt.

Remember that any time you wish to change the interval between automatic saves, just use the SAVETIME system variable at the AutoCAD Command: prompt.

AUTOCAD'S DXF FILE FORMAT   ACG 16

AutoCAD users may need to exchange files to be used with other programs, or import other software files to be used in AutoCAD. For this purpose, Autodesk, Inc. created the DXF (Drawing interchange File) file format. This format has become the accepted standard for microcomputer CAD programs.

Files prepared using the DXF format are standard ASCII code. (ASCII stands for American National Standard Code for Information Interchange.) This means that the information contained in the file can be read by any computer.

Unfortunately computer translations, as with spoken languages, often lose something in the translation. The problem is not the ASCII code, but rather the way in which CAD systems create entities, layers, and other drawing characteristics. For example, AutoCAD allows layer names; some other programs use numbers. Even if layer numbers are used in AutoCAD, they may not translate to be the same number in another program. AutoCAD has polylines and some other programs do not. AutoCAD's blocks may become individual entities in other programs.

This may seem like a roadblock to drawing file translation, but often creates only minor problems, depending on the drawings and the systems involved. These problems may soon be eliminated. The field of microcomputer CAD (microCAD) is still young. Companies are beginning to realize the importance of standardization. The ability to translate files will become an even more valuable tool in the near future.

Creating a DXFOUT file

The DXFOUT command creates a .DXF file extension ASCII drawing file from an AutoCAD drawing. To test the use of the DXFOUT command, begin a new drawing and name it DXFTEST. Draw a single line on your screen using the LINE command. The DXF commands are located in the FILE screen menu by picking EXPORT, or by picking Export then DXF... in the File pull-down menu. You can also enter the DXFOUT command at the Command: prompt as follows:

Command: **DXFOUT** ↵

The "Create DXF File" dialog appears on the screen if the FILEDIA system variable is set at 1. Notice the file name default is the same as the drawing name. Look at the Pattern: text box and notice that the file has a .DXF extension. Pick the OK button to accept the file name.

AutoCAD then asks you to indicate the degree of accuracy you want for numeric values. The choices range between 0 and 16 decimal places. In this example, the default accuracy of six decimal places is accepted by pressing ENTER. The DXF file is created and stored on disk.

Enter decimal places of accuracy (0 to 16)/Objects/Binary ⟨6⟩: ↵
Command:

The Objects option allows you to select specific shapes or objects for inclusion in the DXF file. If you use this option, only the objects that you pick are placed in the file. When you pick the specific objects, AutoCAD asks for the desired accuracy as before:

Enter decimal places of accuracy (0 to 16)/Binary ⟨6⟩: ↵

Check to be sure that it was created by listing files as follows:

> Command: **DIR** ↵
> File specification: ***.DXF** ↵

This entry indicates that you want to see a list of all files with a .DXF extension. You can also use the "File Utilities" dialog box, to list .DXF files. To do so pick Management then Utilities… in the File pull-down menu. Pick the List files… selection to display the "File List" subdialog box. The default files that are listed are .DWG. Type *.DXF in the Pattern: text box and press ENTER. Only .DXF files will be listed. See Figure 17-10.

Figure 17-10   The "File List" subdialog box can be used to list .DXF files.

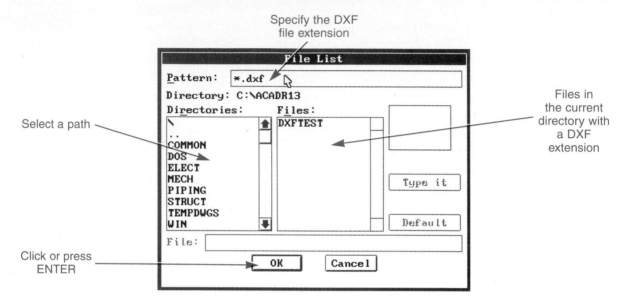

When using the DXFOUT command, you can specify a file name other than the default. Do not enter a file extension. AutoCAD automatically adds this to the file name you provide. If the file name you enter already exists, AutoCAD warns you by displaying the "AutoCAD Message" alert box shown in Figure 17-11. Pick the Yes button to replace the file, or the No button to cancel.

Figure 17-11   The "AutoCAD Message" alert box warns you that a file of the same name already exists.

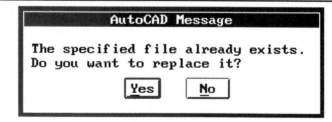

CAUTION

If FILEDIA is set to 0 (Off), a dialog box is not displayed when you create a .DXF file. In this case, you are prompted for a file name on the Command: line. If you enter a file name that already exists, AutoCAD does not warn you and the existing file is overwritten.

After using the DXFOUT command to create the DXF file, use the SAVEAS command to save your drawing file. The "Save Drawing As" dialog box appears. Accept the file name DXFTEST by picking the OK button. Notice the pattern extension is .DWG. Now exit AutoCAD.

comprise [kamprász]: comprender, abarcar, incluir, abrazar; constar de

Binary DXF file

The standard DXF file is in ASCII format, but you also have the option of creating a binary form of the DXF file. A *binary code* is one composed of data in the form of bits having a value of either 1 or 0. This type of file can be up to 25% smaller than an ASCII file, and it is just as accurate. The binary file is given the same extension of .DXF. It can be read quicker than an ASCII file, and AutoCAD can create it and load it using the DXFOUT and DXFIN command. Since DXF files are so much smaller than drawing files, and binary files are even smaller, using the DXFOUT command's Binary option may be a good practice if you must provide interchange files to a coworker or client who works with Release 10 or more recent versions of AutoCAD.

Contents of an ASCII DXF file

You do not need to understand the contents of a DXF file to successfully translate drawings. Yet, when customizing or programming AutoCAD and using AutoLISP, you will use information like that found in a DXF file. The contents of a DXF file is arranged into four sections.
- **Header.** Every drawing variable and its value is listed in this section.
- **Tables.** Named items, such as layers, linetypes, styles, and views, are found in this section.
- **Blocks.** All entities and their values that comprise blocks are listed in this section.
- **Entities.** Entities used in the drawing are located here.

The best method of displaying and examining a .DXF file is to open it with the DOS text editor named EDIT, or to use your favorite text editor or word processing program. The file is long, and contains a list of all the variables and settings used by AutoCAD. If you plan to study menu customization or programming, you should become familiar with the components of the .DXF file, and the syntax used in them. Refer to the *AutoCAD Customization Guide* for detailed information on this type of file.

Creating a DXFIN file

the information on the header, tables, and blocks sections are not considered.

The DXFIN command allows you to create an AutoCAD drawing file (.DWG extension) from a DXF file. It is important that you begin a new drawing in AutoCAD first. Do not add entities or make setup steps. If you use an old drawing, only the entities of the DXF file are inserted. The layers, blocks, and other drawing definitions of the old drawing will override those of the DXF file.

Begin a new drawing and name it DXFTEST1. Enter DXFIN at the Command: prompt, or select Import then DXF... from the File pull-down menu. When the "Select DXF File" subdialog box appears, pick DXFTEST from the Files: list box, Figure 17-12, or enter DXFTEST in the File: text box.

Figure 17-12   The "Select DXF File" subdialog box can also be used to list .DXF files.

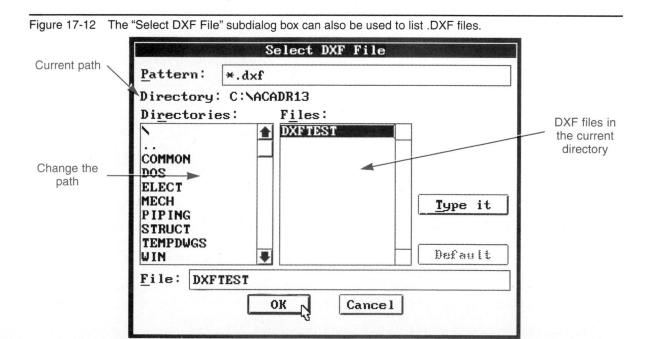

The line should appear on the screen as it was in the original DXFTEST drawing. The new drawing, DXFTEST1, with the inserted DXF file, is not listed as a .DWG file until you save it.

DXF applications

There are several applications where you will want to convert an AutoCAD file to DXF format. The most common application is translating drawings between CAD systems. Numerical control (NC) programs such as SmartCAM® and NCProgrammer® use DXF files. The file is used to translate the shape and features of a machine part to code that can be used for lathes, milling machines, and drill presses. Desktop publishing programs like QuarkXPress® and PageMaker® can use DXF files to translate drawings into images that are then inserted into a page layout. Programs that perform stress analysis and calculations often rely on DXF drawings.

Importing a scanned file

Scanning programs create a DXB (Drawing interchange Binary) file after scanning an existing paper drawing with a camera or plotter-mounted scanner. A plotter-mounted scanner is shown in Figure 17-13. The created file consists of binary code–a computer code composed of combinations of the numbers 1 and 0. The DXBIN command converts this code to drawing data to become an AutoCAD drawing file with a .DWG extension. The command is used as follows:

Command: **DXBIN** ↵

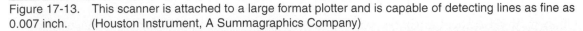

Figure 17-13.   This scanner is attached to a large format plotter and is capable of detecting lines as fine as 0.007 inch.   (Houston Instrument, A Summagraphics Company)

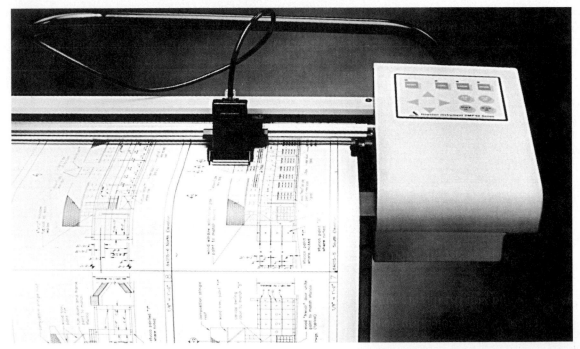

The FILEDIA system variable determines what you see on the screen. If FILEDIA is 1, the file dialog box automatically appears. If FILEDIA is 0, the file dialog box is replaced with a file name prompt. When the "Select DXB File" dialog box appears, accept the default file name, or enter the file name of a specific scanned drawing and pick the OK button or press ENTER. The following prompt then appears if the file dialog box is inactive:

DXB file: *(type the file name and press* ENTER*)*

The drawing file created can then be edited using typical AutoCAD commands.

variety [variáiati]: variedad

LOCATING ERRORS IN A TRANSFERRED FILE

AutoCAD generally does not check a DXF file for errors, but this function can be performed if you desire. In order for this to happen, instruct AutoCAD to automatically list errors in the file before you transfer a DXF file. Use the following steps:

1. At the Command: prompt type CONFIG.

   Command: **CONFIG** ↵

2. Press ENTER until the Configuration menu is displayed.
3. "7. Configure operating parameters" from the Configuration menu.
4. Select "10. Automatic Audit after DXFIN or DXBIN" from the Configure operating parameters menu.
5. Type Y, for yes, to this question:

   Do you want an automatic audit after DXFIN or DXBIN? ⟨N⟩: **Y** ↵

6. The automatic audit is ready to be performed. Press ENTER until you get back to the Configuration menu.
7. Be sure to press ENTER to update the configuration.

The automatic auditing process does not correct errors in the file. Errors must be corrected by editing the DXF file or by using the AUDIT command while working on the drawing. See the section earlier in this chapter titled *Using The AUDIT Command* for a discussion on the use of this command.

EXPORTING AND IMPORTING FILES

AutoCAD provides you with the ability to work with files other than DXF. You can export the current drawing file to files that can be used in other programs for rendering, animation, desktop publishing, presentations, stereolithography, and solids modeling. This section provides a brief overview of AutoCAD's capabilities in exporting and importing a variety of different files. All of these options can be selected from the FILE screen menu by picking either IMPORT or EXPORT, or from the File pull-down menu by picking either Import or Export. Figures 17-14A and B illustrate the File pull-down menu selections for importing and exporting files.

All of the following file export commands display the standard "Files" dialog box. The only difference between the functions is the title bar of the dialog box.

Figure 17-14.   A—File pull-down menu selections for importing files. B—File pull-down menu selections for exporting files.

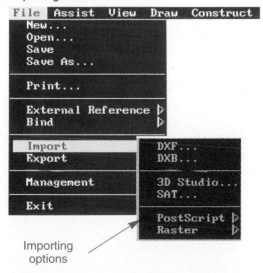

Importing options

A

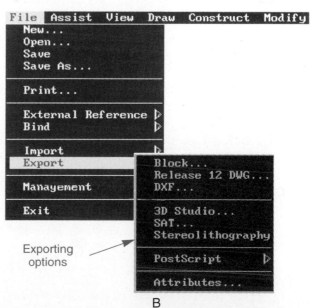

Exporting options

B

AutoCAD Release 12 files

This selection enables you to export an AutoCAD Release 13 drawing file out to Release 12 format. If FILEDIA is set to 1 (On), the "Save release 12 drawing as" dialog box is displayed. You can select any .DWG file from the files listing, or enter the file name in the File: text box. Press ENTER or pick OK when you are finished. This function can also be entered at the Command: prompt as SAVEASR12.

3D Studio files

The program 3D Studio is an Autodesk product that enables you to design, render, and animate 3-D models. AutoCAD Release 13 allows you to display 3D Studio files, but AutoCAD must first be given instructions for the type of rendering and hardcopy devices to use for this purpose. Therefore you must create a configuration file for the devices that you will be using to display and print rendered models. If you have not done so, you will be prompted to select a rendering display device when you select to either import or export a 3D Studio file. You are prompted as follows:

```
Select rendering display device:
    1. AutoCAD's configured P386 ADI combined display/rendering driver
    2. P386 Autodesk Device Interface rendering driver
    3. None (Null rendering device)
Rendering selection ⟨1⟩:
```

Check with your instructor or supervisor if you are unsure if a 3D Studio display driver has been installed for AutoCAD. The device can be changed at any time, so if you are uncertain, select #1, AutoCAD's configured P386 ADI combined display/rendering driver, and press ENTER. You will then be presented with a series of displays prompting you to select a variety of display options. For now just press ENTER to select all of the default settings.

Next you will be prompted to select a printing device with the following display:

```
Select rendering hard copy device:
    1. None (Null rendering device)
    2. P386 Autodesk Device Interface rendering driver
Rendering hard copy selection ⟨1⟩:
```

Select #1 (None) and press ENTER.

Now when you make the menu selection to export 3D Studio you are prompted to select objects. Select all of the 3-D objects you wish to export and press ENTER. The "3D Studio Output File" dialog box is displayed. Enter the new file name in the File: text box. Press ENTER or pick OK when you are finished. Exporting a 3D Studio file can also be executed by entering 3DSOUT at the Command: prompt.

You can also import an existing 3D Studio file into AutoCAD by selecting Import, then 3D Studio... from the File pull-down menu. The "3D Studio File Import" dialog box is displayed. Select the .3DS file from the listing and press ENTER or pick OK. Importing a 3D Studio file can also be executed by entering 3DSIN at the Command: prompt.

Solid model files

A *solid* is a three-dimensional object that is composed of a specific material, and possesses unique characteristics related to its shape and composition. These characteristics are called *mass properties*. Solids are created in AutoCAD with one of several commands found in the Solids cascading menu of the Draw pull-down menu. See Figure 17-15.

vat [væt] : tina, tanque

Figure 17-15.   File pull-down
menu selections for creating
solids.

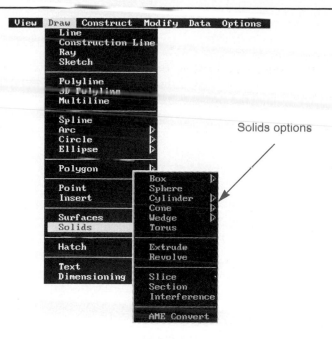

Solids options

The term *solid modeling* refers to the process of constructing a part from one or more 3-D solid shapes called *primitives,* and performing any necessary editing functions to create the final product. This procedure is discussed in detail in ***AutoCAD and Its Applications—Advanced, R13 for DOS;*** and in ***AutoCAD AME– Solid Modeling for Mechanical Design*** by Ted Saufley.

A solid model has many uses in software used for analysis and testing, or in the manufacturing of the part. AutoCAD drawings can be converted into a file that can be used for these purposes. The command that enables you to do this is ACISOUT. It can be entered at the Command: prompt, or choose Export from the File pull-down menu, then pick SAT…. You are first prompted to select objects. Use any of the standard selection methods to choose solid objects, then press ENTER. The "Create ACIS File" dialog box is displayed. Notice that the file type that is created is .SAT. Do not change this. Type the file name in the File: text box and press ENTER or pick OK. The .SAT file is stored in ASCII format.

Solid model data that is stored in the .SAT file can be read back into AutoCAD using the ACISIN command. From the File pull-down menu select Import then SAT…. This displays the "Select ACIS File" dialog box. Pick the file from the list and pick OK or press ENTER.

PROFESSIONAL TIP

The ASCII file created by the ACISOUT command may be three to four times smaller than the drawing file. For this reason, it may be efficient to store 3-D solid models as .SAT files instead of drawings. When you need to work with the model for any purpose in AutoCAD, simply use the ACISIN command. This command creates solid objects from the model data stored in the ASCII file.

Stereolithography files

Stereolithography is a technology in which a plastic prototype 3-D model is created using a computer-generated solid model, a laser, and a vat of liquid polymers. This technology is also referred to as *rapid prototyping* because a prototype 3-D model can be designed and formed in a short amount of time, without using standard manufacturing processes. Software that is used to facilitate the creation of a stereolithograph can read the .STL file. AutoCAD can only export a drawing file to the .STL format.

Choose Export from the File pull-down menu, then pick Stereolithography…. You are prompted to select a single object as follows:

    Select a single solid for STL output:
    Select objects:

If you select more than one object AutoCAD prompts you:

Only one solid per file permitted.

Select one object and press ENTER. You are then asked if you want to create a binary STL file. If you answer No to this prompt, an ASCII file is created. Keep in mind that a binary STL file may be at least five times smaller than the ASCII STL file. After you choose the type of file to create, the "Create STL File" dialog box is displayed. Type the file name in the File: text box and pick OK or press ENTER. An STL file can also be created by entering STLOUT at the Command: prompt.

PostScript files

PostScript is a copyrighted page description language which was developed by Adobe Systems, and is used in the desktop publishing industry. AutoCAD drawing files can be exported to the .EPS PostScript file format by typing PSOUT at the Command: prompt. You can also pick Export from the File pull-down menu, then pick PostScript, then Export…. The "Create PostScript File" dialog box is displayed. Type the file name in the File: text box and pick OK or press ENTER.

PostScript files can be imported into AutoCAD by picking Import from the File pull-down menu, then pick PostScript, then Import…. The "Select PostScript File" dialog box is displayed. Type the file name in the File: text box and pick OK or press ENTER.

USING DOS COMMANDS TO WORK WITH FILES

As you have read previously in this chapter, many of the typical file management functions can be handled from within AutoCAD using the "File Utilities" dialog box. But as you continue to create and store files, you will need to use DOS commands quickly and efficiently to help you create, manage, and maintain your files. Regardless of how well you can type, it is important that you learn to use the basic DOS commands at the DOS prompt. This will enable you to manage your files even when you are not running AutoCAD.

The quickest way to get to the DOS prompt from AutoCAD is to type SHELL at the Command: prompt and press ENTER twice. You can also pick External Commands from the Tools pull-down menu, then pick Shell. Press ENTER again to temporarily exit AutoCAD into DOS. When you use the SHELL command in this manner, notice that the DOS prompt is followed by two carets:

Command: **SHELL** ↵↵
C:\\〉〉

You can remain in DOS as long as you wish, but when you want to return to AutoCAD, type EXIT at the DOS prompt.

C:\\〉〉 **EXIT** ↵

The most-used DOS commands are DIR (Directory), DELETE, RENAME, and COPY. When using these commands with individual files, always give the path (if necessary) and include the file extension. Omitting the file extension at the end of the file name may cause an error to occur later.

File types

When using DOS to perform manipulations, remember file types, or extensions. A *file extension* is a three-letter combination that represents a specific type of file. AutoCAD recognizes several different file extensions. The most common ones are listed here.

File Extension	Description
.DWG	Latest version of a drawing file.
.BAK	Backup file–Previous version of a DWG file.
.MNU	Menu file–Contains AutoCAD screen and tablet menu commands.
.HLP	Help file–Contains help for AutoCAD commands.
.SCR	Script file–A file that automatically executes several AutoCAD commands.
.SLD	Slide file–A screen display of an AutoCAD drawing file.
.DXF	Drawing interchange file–Used to convert from one CAD system to another.

Some common DOS file extensions are:

File Extension	Description
.COM	Command file–A DOS external command.
.BAT	Batch file–An external DOS program that accomplishes specific tasks.
.TXT	Text file–A file composed of text.
.EXE	Executable file–An external command that is executed when its name is entered at the DOS prompt.
.SYS	System file–Contains information about your hardware.

Listing your files

The DIR command provides a view inside your diskette or any directory on the hard disk. It can give you several kinds of information, such as:

- Drawing names
- Number of files
- File size
- Space left on the disk

If your computer is on, be sure the DOS prompt is on the screen. If you used the SHELL command to exit AutoCAD, your DOS prompt may look like this:

C:\ACADR13⟩⟩

NOTE   Remember that you can change the current disk drive by typing the drive name at the DOS prompt.

C:\ACADR13⟩⟩ **A:** ⏎
A:\⟩⟩

You can also quickly list files in any directories by using the proper directory path with the DIR command.

C:\ACADR13⟩⟩ **DIR C:\PROJECTS\CIVIL** ⏎

Insert a diskette in drive A: and list its contents as follows:

C:\ACADR13⟩⟩ **A:** ⏎⏎
A:\⟩⟩ **DIR** ⏎

A listing of the disk's contents should be on the screen. The information you see is the volume label (name of the diskette), directory name, file name, file type (indicated by a three-letter extension), size of file in bytes, and the date and time it was last revised. A sample directory listing is shown in Figure 17-16.

If your disk contains many files, they may begin to scroll off the screen. Stop the scrolling by pressing the CTRL and S keys at the same time (CTRL+S). To begin scrolling again, press any key. Press CTRL+C to cancel the scrolling.

To prevent scrolling of large directories, specify a pause that shows a screen or "page" at a time.

C:\ACADR13⟩⟩ **DIR /P** ⏎ *(uppercase or lowercase letters are acceptable)*

Press any key to continue the scroll to the next page.

It is often not necessary to see all the information about the files. A "wide" display gives you only the file name and extension. It packs five columns of files on the screen.

C:\ACADR13⟩⟩ **DIR /W** ⏎

Figure 17-16.   An example of
the information provided by the
DIR command.

```
Volume in drive A is R13-SAMPLES
Volume Serial Number is 1003-055B
Directory of A:\

DIMDRAGR CLP       215,531 05-19    8:58a
CRANK3D  DWG       255,946 05-08    7:32p
CRANKPRO DWG        15,107 05-08    7:29p
EXTRUDE  DWG         5,334 05-19    1:51a
REGION   DWG         4,223 05-18   11:59p
REVOLVE  DWG         4,430 05-19    1:54a
SWRENCH  DWG         4,911 05-18   12:17a
BCKPLATE DWG        15,299 05-18    6:04a
BUSHING  DWG        12,536 05-18    6:05a
CRNKCASE DWG        34,231 05-18    6:15a
CRNKSHFT DWG        41,173 05-18    6:11a
CYLFINS  DWG        18,815 05-18    6:16a
CYLHEAD  DWG        56,955 05-18    6:13a
PINS     DWG        46,571 05-17    8:23a
PISTON   DWG         9,428 05-18    6:09a
SLEEVE   DWG        20,981 05-18    6:14a
ASSERT   CLP       240,107 05-20   10:16a
         17 file(s)       1,001,578 bytes
                           453,120 bytes free
```

If the disk or directory contains numerous files, even a wide display may scroll off the screen. If that happens, combine the "page" and "wide" formats like this:

C:\ACADR13⟩⟩ **DIR /P/W** ↵

A page at a time is displayed in the wide format.

NOTE   The DIR command has a variety of switches that are activated with the forward slash (/). These allow you to display and sort files and directory information in a variety of ways. Check your DOS manual for detailed instructions.

Special characters

When working with files, you may want to limit your commands and requests to specific files and file types. A couple of DOS characters come in handy for this.

*   Wild-card–Can be used as a substitute for any number of characters.
?   A substitute for any single character.

Try getting a listing of specific file types. For example, to list all files with a .DWG extension on drive C: in the ACADR13\COMMON\SAMPLE directory, enter:

C:\ACADR13⟩⟩ **DIR COMMON\SAMPLE*.DWG** ↵

You should have a listing of just drawing files (.DWG extension). If the list scrolled off the screen, how do you stop the scroll to display one screen at a time?

Try the same thing, only this time obtain a listing of all DWG files on the disk in the A: drive. (You can request a directory listing of any drive no matter which drive is current.) For example, try this:

C:\ACADR13⟩⟩ **DIR A:*.DWG** ↵

Even though drive C: is current, a listing of all .DWG files on the disk in drive A: appears. That is because you provided DOS with a "path" to the files you need to see. The "A:" pointed DOS to the disk on which the files were located.

The wild-card character (?) enables you to pick out files that may have similar characters. For example, suppose you have created several electrical drawings. The file names all begin with ELEC- and then have three additional numbers, such as ELEC-100, ELEC-101, etc. The files are located on the disk in the B: drive. To obtain a listing, enter:

    C:\ACADR13⟩⟩ **DIR B:ELEC-???.DWG** ↵

This lists only the drawing files that begin with ELEC- and have any three additional characters.

    Finally, list all files that begin with ELEC-, have three additional characters, and have any extension.

    C:\ACADR13⟩⟩ **DIR B:ELEC-???.* ** ↵

Suppose you knew there were over 70 possible files with that combination. How would you prevent them from scrolling off the screen? Try using the "P" switch to pause scrolling.

    C:\ACADR13⟩⟩ **DIR B:ELEC-???.* /P** ↵

PROFESSIONAL TIP

    Always enter a space after a DOS command. Omitting the space can result in a "Bad command" message.

EXERCISE 17-3

❑ Insert one of your disks in the A: drive.
❑ Make the C: drive current (show on the DOS prompt).
❑ Make the A: drive current.
❑ Obtain a directory of all files on the A: drive.
❑ Obtain a directory listing of just the .DWG files on the A: drive.
❑ Make the C: drive current.
❑ List all the files on drive C: in a wide format.
❑ List all the files on drive C: in a page format.

Erasing files

When it comes time to clean out your file drawers, you will want to use the DELETE (DEL) command. This command eliminates files, no questions asked. Always double-check the file name you enter before pressing ENTER. To delete a drawing file named JUNK on the C: drive, enter:

    C:\ACADR13⟩⟩ **DEL JUNK.DWG** ↵

PROFESSIONAL TIP

    When deleting files, it is a good practice to first change the DOS prompt to reflect the drive or directory in which you are doing the erasing. For example, suppose you plan to delete a drawing file named TEST on drive A:. The current prompt reflects the C: drive. Enter the following:
        C:\ **A:** ↵
        A:\ **DEL TEST.DWG** ↵

This prevents erasing files on the wrong drive.

You can erase entire groups of files by including wild-card characters. The asterisk (*) and question mark (?) can be used with several DOS commands. To delete all .DWG files on the A: drive, enter:

A:\ **DEL *.DWG** ↵

You can even erase all files within a directory or on a disk. This is a highly destructive procedure, but one you eventually might want to do. Enter the following:

A:\ **DEL *.*** ↵

At first, nothing happens. A prompt is displayed and asks you:

All files in directory will be deleted!
Are you sure (Y/N)?

If there is any doubt in your mind, type N and press ENTER. If you are sure, type Y and press ENTER. If you answer Y, all the files in the current directory of that disk are gone.

Retrieving deleted files

DOS 5.0+

Files that have been deleted can be retrieved using the UNDELETE command. Use this command as soon after deleting as possible because new files that are saved to this disk may take residence in the space that the deleted file occupied. If you can't remember what the deleted file name(s) was, DOS gives you a good idea if you type the following:

C:\\) **UNDELETE A: /LIST** ↵

A display similar to that in Figure 17-17 appears.

Figure 17-17.   Naming scheme for files that are to be undeleted (highlighted).

```
Directory: A:\
File Specifications: *.*

     Deletion-tracking file not found.

     MS-DOS directory contains     5 deleted files.
     Of those,     5 files may be recovered.

Using the MS-DOS directory method.

     ?13-10   PCX     25794  1-20     10:36a  ...A  Undelete (Y/N)?n
     ?13-11   PCX     25679  1-21      4:43p  ...A  Undelete (Y/N)?
```

If you don't care about the name of the file(s), but simply want it back, enter the following:

C:\\) **UNDELETE A:*.* /ALL** ↵

DOS finds all undeleted files, as best it can, and puts a number symbol (#) in place of the first character of each file. For example, the two deleted files in Figure 17-17 are given the following names after undeleting them:

?13-10.PCX
?13-11.PCX

You can return each file name to its original name (or any other desired name) by using the RENAME command, which is discussed next.

Renaming files

When you wish to change the name of a file, use the RENAME (REN) command. For example, to rename a file called FLOTSAM.DWG to JETSAM.DWG, enter the following:

A:\ REN FLOTSAM.DWG JETSAM.DWG ⏎

Note that the current name is given first, then a space, then the new name. Do not forget the file extensions. To see if the change has been made, list the directory.

Copying files

To copy files for backup purposes, use the COPY command. Give the source file first, the destination second, and remember the file extensions. Copy the ACAD.DWG file from the C: drive to a diskette in the A: drive.

C:\\> COPY ACAD.DWG A: ⏎

    1 File(s) copied

DOS lets you know that the file has been copied. Notice that a file name was not used for the destination. If the name is to remain the same, it does not need to be typed. You can copy and rename at the same time with the COPY command. To do this, type a new name after the destination drive. For example, to copy the ACAD.DWG file from the C: drive to a disk in the A: drive and rename it TEST.DWG, do the following:

C:\\> COPY ACAD.DWG A:TEST.DWG ⏎
    1 File(s) copied

Now the drawing has been both copied and renamed using just the COPY command.

Copying entire disks

You can copy the entire contents of one disk to another using the DISKCOPY command. Keep in mind that the *source* disk is the original you want copied. The *target* disk is the destination of the copied files. Type the following, regardless of the number of floppy drives included in your computer's configuration:

C:\DOS> DISKCOPY A: B: ⏎

A single-disk drive computer prompts for the source disk to be inserted into drive A:. It reads the disk and then asks for the target disk to be inserted into drive B:. Since DOS is using the one drive as both drive A: and B:, remove the source disk and insert the target disk. A computer with two flexible disk drives of the same size prompts for the source and target disks to be inserted into drives A: and B: respectively. Once the copy is made, a prompt asks if you wish to make additional duplicates.

    Do you wish to write another duplicate of this disk (Y/N)?

If you enter No (N), you are asked the following:

    Copy another disk (Y/N)?.

Type Y for Yes, or N for No and press ENTER.

CAUTION

There is no need to spend time formatting a disk before making a disk copy, since the DISKCOPY command not only copies, it erases. The target disk is formatted before any copying is done. Therefore, be certain your target disk is not one that already has files on it; unless, of course, you want to delete all the files on that disk.

The DISKCOPY command, as discussed previously, when used on a dual-disk drive machine only works if both disk drives are the same size. If you have an A: drive for 5.25″, 1.2MB floppy disks, and a B: drive for 3.5″, 1.44MB disks, then the two formats are incompatible. There are a couple of ways to copy disks in this situation. The first method allows you to copy disks in only one of the two disk drives. To do this, instruct DOS to copy disks in the A: drive only like this:

C:\DOS⟩ **DISKCOPY A: A:** ↵

You can copy disks in the B: drive only like this:

C:\DOS⟩ **DISKCOPY B: B:** ↵

The other method that allows you to copy from the 5.25″ disk format to the 3.5″ disk without formatting the target disk is this DOS command:

C:\DOS⟩ **COPY A:*.* B:** ↵

PROFESSIONAL TIP

 It is good practice to have backup copies of all of your flexible disks. These copies should be labeled as "backups" and stored separate from your work disks. Set up a routine in which you regularly back up the disks or individual files as you revise and add to them.

EXERCISE 17-4

❑ Choose a drawing file on your diskette to copy.
❑ Copy the file to the C: drive.
❑ List only DWG files on the C: drive to be sure it is there.
❑ Change the name of the drawing file on the C: drive to TRIAL.BAK.
❑ List only BAK files on the C: drive to see that the file was renamed.
❑ Erase TRIAL.BAK from the C: drive.
❑ Use DISKCOPY to copy one of your floppy disks.

USING DOS COMMANDS TO WORK WITH DIRECTORIES

A consistent method of file storage is one of the most important aspects of computer system management. Directories and subdirectories should reflect the nature of your work, whether it be in school or industry. Everyone who uses the files should know the system and method of creating and naming directories.

The filing cabinet of the hard disk is called the *root directory* and is indicated with a backslash by DOS. All other programs and subdirectories are accessed by first going through the root directory. A prompt set to reflect the current drive and directory should now look like that shown below when the root directory is current.

C:\⟩

If your DOS prompt does not look like this, use the PROMPT command to change it.

C⟩ **PROMPT PG** ↵
C:\⟩

The prompt indicates the C: drive is active and the root directory is current. This is a handy prompt to use because the current directory is always displayed.

Making a directory

Creating your own directories on the hard drive or on a flexible disk is easy. Just use the MD (Make Directory) command. Before making directories on the hard disk, obtain permission from your instructor or supervisor. Otherwise, use a floppy diskette and change the current drive to A:. Keep in mind that directory names are governed by the same restrictions that apply to file names.

Using the MD command, create a directory called PROJ-001 as follows:

    C:\\> **MD \PROJ-001** ↵

That is it. The new directory is made. You can now create subdirectories under PROJ-001 if they are required. To do so, you must specify the *path* of the new subdirectory. Make two subdirectories and call them ELEC and STRUCT.

    C:\\> **MD \PROJ-001\ELEC** ↵
    C:\\> **MD \PROJ-001\STRUCT** ↵

Now you have two new subdirectories under the PROJ-001 directory. Obtain a directory listing to be sure they are there.

    C:\\> **DIR** ↵

How many of your new directories do you see? Why are the ELEC and STRUCT directories not listed? Because they are subdirectories of PROJ-001, and it is not the current directory. You will not be able to see them listed until the PROJ-001 directory is current. This requires that you change from one directory to make another directory current.

Changing the current directory

You can be in one directory and manipulate files in another just by specifying the proper path. However, it is much safer to change over to the directory in which you plan to work. Move to another existing directory with the CD (Change Directory) command. To change from the root directory to the PROJ-001 directory, enter:

    C:\\> **CD \PROJ-001** ↵
    C:\PROJ-001>

Now the DOS prompt has changed to reflect the new current directory. Now list the files.

    C:\PROJ-001> **DIR** ↵

You should see the two directories ELEC and STRUCT, indicated by the 〈DIR〉 that follows. There are no files listed unless you have added some.

You can change to the ELEC or STRUCT directories using the same command.

    C:\PROJ-001> **CD ELEC** ↵
    C:\PROJ-001\ELEC>

The prompt reflects the new current directory. Notice the path. In order to have the prompt display the root directory again, type:

    C:\PROJ-001\ELEC> **CD ** ↵
    C:\>

510 AutoCAD and its Applications–Basics

Remove a directory

A directory can be removed from the disk with the RD (Remove Directory) command. There are two restrictions: you cannot remove a directory that contains files or subdirectories, and you cannot remove a directory that is current. First, delete the files from the directory you want to remove. To delete all files from the ELEC subdirectory, first use the CD command to make ELEC current:

C:\\> **CD \PROJ-001\ELEC** ⏎
C:\PROJ-001\ELEC> **DEL *.*** ⏎
All files in directory will be deleted!
Are you sure (Y/N)? **Y** ⏎

All files are deleted. Now you must get out of the ELEC subdirectory in order to remove it.

C:\PROJ-001\ELEC> **CD \PROJ-001** ⏎
C:\PROJ-001> **RD ELEC** ⏎
C:\PROJ-001>

You can check to be sure the ELEC directory is gone by getting a directory listing with the DIR command.

Any subdirectory can be removed from the root directory as long as the proper path is specified, and the subdirectory is empty.

C:\\> **RD \PROJ-001\STRUCT** ⏎

The STRUCT directory is now deleted. List the PROJ-001 directory to check.

EXERCISE 17-5

❏ Insert one of your disks in the A: drive.
❏ Make the A: drive current.
❏ Make a directory called CLASSES, and another called PROJECTS.
❏ Make two subdirectories in the CLASSES directory called CAD-I and CAD-II.
❏ Make two subdirectories in the PROJECTS directory called P-100 and P-200.
❏ List the directories to see that all new directories were properly created.
❏ Copy a group of drawing files from the hard disk to one of the subdirectories under either CLASSES or PROJECTS.
❏ List this directory to view the contents.
❏ Make the subdirectory that contains the copied files current.
❏ Delete all files from the current subdirectory.
❏ Remove the current subdirectory.
❏ Remove all the directories created in this exercise.

CHAPTER TEST

Write your answers in the spaces provided.

1. What is a file type extension?_____

_____

2. What do the following file extension types mean?
   A. .BAK_____
   B. .LIN_____
   C. .MNU _____
   D. .PLT_____
   E. .BAT _____
   F. .EXE _____

3. Which pull-down selection leads to the "File Utilities" dialog box? _____

4. How would you list the drawing files on the floppy disk in the A: drive?_____

_____

5. How would you list all .MNU files on the floppy disk in the B: drive? _____

_____

6. How would you delete all .BAK files from the current C:\ACADR13 directory? The files begin with PROJ2 and have three additional letters in their names. _____

_____

_____

7. What is the procedure for changing a file name?_____

_____

_____

8. What two functions can the Rename file option perform?_____

9. How is the Copy file option similar to the Rename file option? _____

_____

10. Which AutoCAD screen menu command gives you access to the "File Utilities" dialog box? ___

_____

11. Why are files locked? _____

_____

12. What type of file is created when file locking is enabled?_____

_____

13. How can a file be unlocked? _____

_____

14. How can a damaged file be recovered? _____

_____

15. Which command allows you to run a diagnostic check of a drawing file? _____

_____

16. What type of memory system does AutoCAD use to create pages of the program on the hard disk?
_____

17. What file type is created by the system in Question 16, and what is its three-letter file extension?
_____

18. What is AutoCAD's pager system, and what is the three-letter file extension that it creates?_____
_____
_____

19. What is the name of the backup drawing file that AutoCAD creates automatically based on the
value of the SAVETIME variable?_____

20. Explain why drawing file translations are needed._____
_____

21. Define the following abbreviations.
DXF– _____
DXB– _____

22. What is the purpose of the DXFOUT command? _____
_____
_____

23. When would you use the DXFIN command?_____
_____

24. Provide the input required to get a listing of all DXF files, assuming you are at the Command:
prompt.
Command:_____
File specification:_____

25. List the four sections contained in a DXF file.
_____

26. Suppose you plan to import a DXF file. What setup steps must you perform to the new drawing
before importing the DXF file? _____
_____

27. List programs that can use DXF files. _____
_____
_____

28. When would you use the DXBIN command? _____
_____

29. Name five types of files, other than DXF, that can be imported into AutoCAD._____
_____

30. Which type of exported file requires a configured rendering device? _____
_____

31. Why might it be more efficient to store solid models in the form of .SAT files rather than as drawing files? _____

_____

32. What is an .STL file and what is it used for? _____

_____

33. Provide the correct DOS command to list the directory of drive A: in a wide format displayed one page at a time.

    C:\) _____

34. Explain what the following command would accomplish.

    C:\) DIR B:ARCH-???.DWG

    _____

35. Given the following DOS prompt, provide the command that would erase the file named STRUCT05.BAK from the disk in the B: drive.

    C:\) _____

36. Explain how the COPY and RENAME commands are similar._____

    _____

37. What two commands enable you to remove files and then recover them again?_____

    _____

38. The DISKCOPY command can be used with single-disk drive computer. True or false?_____

39. Why should you exercise caution when using the DISKCOPY command? _____

    _____

40. Given the prompt below, provide the command to make a directory called DRAWINGS on the disk in the A: drive.

    C:\) _____

41. Name two restrictions when using the RD command. ____ _____

    _____

    _____

PROBLEMS

1. Write a short report on the importance of file maintenance. Present some uses of the "File Utilities" dialog box in file maintenance. Suggest a procedure to save drawing files and other types of files. Cover the following points in your report:

    A. Where drawing files are to be stored now: on hard disk or floppy disks.

    B. When files should be backed up.

    C. How many backups of each file should exist?

    D. Where should the original and backup disks be located?

    E. How often should .BAK files be deleted or should they be deleted at all?

    F. What file naming system should be used?

2. Make backup copies of all your diskettes. Use the "Copy File" option in the "File Utilities" dialog box. Copy the files in two different ways.

   A. Copy all files with the .DWG extension to the new disk. Then copy all .BAK files to the new disk.

   B. Copy a second disk, or recopy the first disk.

   C. List the files on your backup disk. Be sure that files with both .DWG and .BAK extensions have been copied. Then rename all files with the .BAK extension to have an .OLD extension.

3. Get a printed listing of the files contained on one disk. Ask your instructor or supervisor for assistance if you are not familiar with the printer.

4. Get a printed list of all drawing files contained on your floppy disk.

5. Load one of your simple drawings into AutoCAD. Create a DXF file of the drawing. Generate a printed copy of the contents of the DXF file.

P17-6

6. The purpose of this drawing is to create entities and generate a DXF file. Then, edit the DXF file with a text editor and use the DXFIN command to view the revised drawing. You must refer to Chapter 16 of the *AutoCAD Customization Guide* to complete this problem. Use the following steps:

   A. Begin a new drawing and name it P17-6.

   B. Draw circle A at 4,4 with a 1 in. radius.

   C. Draw circle B at a distance of 3,0 from circle A with radius of .5.

   D. Save the drawing.

   E. Make a DXF file of the drawing using the name of the drawing.

   F. Load the DXF file into your text editor and make the following changes to circles. They are listed in the ENTITIES section of the DXF file. Use a Search function of your text editor to find this section.
   Change the radius of circle B to 2.
   Change the location of the circle A to 4,2.

   G. Save the DXF file.

   H. Begin a new drawing named P17-6A. Use the DXFIN command to load the P17-6.DWG file. Do you notice any changes? Save the drawing.

Problems 7 and 8 require that you have access to another microCAD program or a program that is designed to work with AutoCAD output. Another school or company in your area may have one such program with which you can exchange files.

7. Load one of your drawings that contains layers, blocks, and a variety of entities into AutoCAD. Create a DXF file of the drawing. Import the file into another program that can accept DXF file translations. Compare the new drawings with the AutoCAD version. Look especially at layers, block definitions, and entities such as polylines.

8. Obtain a DXF file from another microCAD or CAD/CAM program. Use the DXFIN command to convert it to an AutoCAD drawing file. Compare the new AutoCAD drawing with the original version.

9. If you have access to a scanner, create a DXB file from an old, hand-drawn print. Import the DXB file using the DXBIN command. Compare the new AutoCAD drawing with the original.

10. Use one of the previous problems to fix errors that may exist in the transferred file using the AUDIT command.

NOTE   Have the permission of your instructor or supervisor before making or removing directories, formatting disks, deleting files, writing batch files, or using any DOS command that may alter the structure of the hard disk files and directories.

---

11. This problem involves making new subdirectories and copying drawing files to them. In addition, you will list the contents of the subdirectories.

 A. Make your own subdirectory of the ACADR13 directory. Name it using your initials.

 B. Make the subdirectory current.

 C. Copy all of your drawing files from one floppy disk to the subdirectory.

 D. Make a subdirectory within your new directory and name it BAK.

 E. Make the BAK subdirectory current.

 F. Copy all of your BAK files into the BAK subdirectory.

 G. List the files in each new subdirectory.

 H. Generate a printed copy of each directory listing.

12. Make a new subdirectory of the directory you created for Problem 1. Name the new subdirectory TEST.

 A. Copy the contents of the BAK subdirectory into TEST.

 B. List the contents of the TEST subdirectory.

 C. Rename one of the files in the TEST subdirectory HEY.YOU.

 D. List the contents of the TEST subdirectory.

 E. Copy the HEY.YOU file to the BAK subdirectory and rename it WHO.ME.

 F. List the contents of the BAK subdirectory.

 G. Copy WHO.ME to one of your floppy disks and name it YES.YOU.

 H. Delete the three files you just created.

 I. Make the BAK subdirectory current. Delete the entire contents of the BAK subdirectory.

 J. Remove the BAK subdirectory.

13. Format four disks in a row without exiting the FORMAT command. Provide names for the disks as they are formatted by using the proper FORMAT option.

Piping isometric drawing. (Harris Group Inc.)

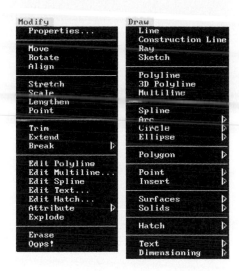

Chapter 18

DRAWING AND EDITING POLYLINES

Learning objectives

After completing this chapter, you will be able to:

- ❍ Use the PLINE command to draw given polylines.
- ❍ Preset the polyline width.
- ❍ Use the PEDIT command to make changes to existing polylines.
- ❍ Identify the PEDIT options.
- ❍ Use the EXPLODE command to remove all polyline width characteristics.
- ❍ Make a polyline boundary.

The PLINE command was introduced in Chapter 6 as a method to draw wide lines. As you will find, the PLINE command also draws a variety of special shapes, limited only by your imagination. The section on PLINE in Chapter 6 focused on line-related options, such as Width, Halfwidth, and Length. The editing functions were limited to ERASE and UNDO commands. This chapter covers using PLINE to make polyline arcs and advanced editing commands for polylines. The PLINE command is accessed through the DRAW 1 screen menu as PLine:, Draw pull-down menu as PolyLine, or by typing at the Command: prompt.

DRAWING PLINE ARCS   AUG 5

The PLINE command's Arc option functions like the ARC command except that PLINE options include Width and Halfwidth. The arc width may range from 0 up to the radius of the arc. A polyline arc with different end widths is drawn by changing the Width. The arc shown in Figure 18-1 was drawn with the following command sequence:

Command: **PLINE** ↵
From point: *(pick the first point)*
Current line-width is *(status specified)*
Arc/Close/Halfwidth/Length/Undo/Width/⟨Endpoint of line⟩: **W** ↵
Starting width ⟨*current*⟩: *(specify a starting width, such as* **.1***, and press* ENTER*)*
Ending width ⟨*current*⟩: *(specify an ending width, such as* **.4***, and press* ENTER*)*
Arc/Close/Halfwidth/Length/Undo/Width/⟨Endpoint of line⟩: **A** ↵
Angle/CEnter/CLose/Direction/Halfwidth/Line/Radius/Second pt/Undo/Width/⟨Endpoint of arc⟩: *(pick the arc endpoint)*
Angle/CEnter/CLose/Direction/Halfwidth/Line/Radius/Second pt/Undo/Width/⟨Endpoint of arc⟩: ↵

Figure 18-1. A polyline arc
with different starting and
ending widths.

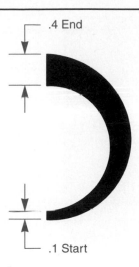

.4 End

.1 Start

Drawing a continuous polyline arc

A polyline arc drawn to continue from a previous line or polyline is tangent at the last point entered. The arc's center is determined automatically unless you pick a new center. If a polyline arc is drawn before a straight polyline, the arc's direction is the same as the previous line, arc, or polyline. This may not be what you want. In this event, it may be necessary to set one of the PLINE Arc options. These include Angle, CEnter, Direction, Radius, or Second point. They work much like the ARC command options.

Specifying the included angle

The following command sequence, shown in Figure 18-2, is used to enter the Angle option for a polyline arc:

Command: **PLINE** ↵
From point: *(pick the first point)*
Current line-width is *(status specified)*
Arc/Close/Halfwidth/Length/Undo/Width/⟨Endpoint of line⟩: **A** ↵
Angle/CEnter/CLose/Direction/Halfwidth/Line/Radius/Second pt/Undo/Width/⟨Endpoint
   of arc⟩: **A** ↵
Included angle: *(specify the included angle, such as **60**, and press ENTER)*
Center/Radius/⟨End point⟩: *(select the arc endpoint)*
Angle/CEnter/CLose/Direction/Halfwidth/Line/Radius/Second pt/Undo/Width/⟨Endpoint
   of arc⟩: ↵

Figure 18-2. Drawing a
polyline arc with a
specified angle.

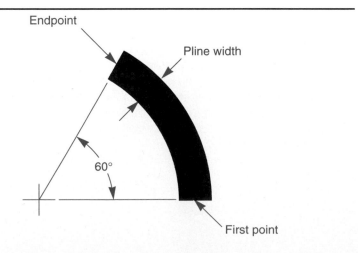

Endpoint

Pline width

60°

First point

Selecting the CEnter option

When a polyline arc continues from a drawn item, the center point is calculated automatically. You might want to pick a center point when the polyline arc does not continue from another item. Also pick a center point if the one calculated is not suitable. The CEnter option is chosen in this manner.

```
Command: PLINE ↵
From point: (select the first point)
Current line-width is (status specified)
Arc/Close/Halfwidth/Length/Undo/Width/⟨Endpoint of line⟩: A ↵
Angle/CEnter/CLose/Direction/Halfwidth/Line/Radius/Second pt/Undo/Width/⟨Endpoint
    of arc⟩: CE ↵ (notice that two letters, CE, are required for this option)
Center point: (select the arc center point)
Angle/Length/⟨End point⟩: (select the arc endpoint, or type A or L and press ENTER)
```

If A was entered at the last prompt, the next request is:

```
Included angle: (enter an included angle and press ENTER)
```

If L was entered, the next prompt would have been:

```
Length of chord: (select a chord length and press ENTER)
```

Using the Direction option

The Direction option alters the bearing of the arc. It changes the default option of placing the polyline arc tangent to the last polyline, arc, or line. This option may also be entered when you are drawing an unconnected polyline arc. The Direction option functions much like the ARC command's Direction option. It requests the following input after D is typed:

```
Direction from start point: (enter a direction in positive or negative degrees, or specify a
    point on either side of the start point)
End point: (select the endpoint of the arc)
```

Drawing a polyline arc by radius

Polyline arcs may be drawn by giving the arc's radius. This is done by typing R. Then respond to these prompts:

```
Angle/CEnter/CLose/Direction/Halfwidth/Line/Radius/Second pt/Undo/Width/⟨Endpoint
    of arc⟩: R ↵
Radius: (enter the arc radius and press ENTER)
Angle/⟨Endpoint⟩: (pick the arc endpoint)
```

or

```
Angle/⟨Endpoint⟩: A ↵
Included angle: (enter the included angle of the arc and press ENTER)
Direction of chord ⟨current⟩: (enter chord direction and press ENTER)
```

Specifying a three-point polyline arc

A three-point arc may be drawn by typing S for Second point. The prompts are as follows:

```
Angle/CEnter/CLose/Direction/Halfwidth/Line/Radius/Second pt/Undo/Width/⟨Endpoint
    of arc⟩: S ↵
Second point: (pick the second point on the arc)
End point: (pick the endpoint to complete the arc)
```

Using the CLose option

The CLose option adds the last segment to enclose a shape. It saves drafting time when you are drawing a polygon. This PLINE Arc option will CLose the shape with an arc, rather than a straight line. Notice that CL is typed at the prompt line; two letters are needed to separate this option from the CEnter option. Figure 18-3 shows how the command sequence below encloses a shape.

Angle/CEnter/CLose/Direction/Halfwidth/Line/Radius/Second pt/Undo/Width/⟨Endpoint of arc⟩: **CL** ↵

Figure 18-3.   Using the PLINE command's CLose option.

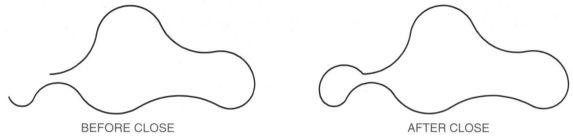

BEFORE CLOSE   AFTER CLOSE

EXERCISE 18-1

❑ Open TITLEA from Problem 11-1.
❑ Draw a continuous polyline arc with at least four segments. Select the CLose option to close the polyline.
❑ Draw a polyline arc by its endpoints and a 90° included angle. Then continue from the first arc with another 90° polyline arc.
❑ Draw a polyline arc using end and center points.
❑ Choose the endpoint, center, and included angle to draw a polyline arc.
❑ Select endpoints and a positive direction to draw a polyline arc. Then see how using a negative direction affects the arc.
❑ Specify the endpoints of a 1.5 unit radius arc.
❑ Draw a polyline arc using three points.
❑ Save the drawing as A:EX18-1 and quit.

PROFESSIONAL TIP

   The best way to learn and use AutoCAD's drafting tools is to practice. It is difficult for you to acquire skills unless you spend time on the computer. A successful CAD operator knows the commands and selects the best options.

REVISING POLYLINES USING THE PEDIT COMMAND | AUG 5 |

Polylines are drawn as single segments. A polyline joined to another polyline might then be joined to a polyline arc. Even though you draw connecting segments, AutoCAD puts them all together. The result is one polyline. When editing a polyline, you must edit it as one entity or divide it into its single segments. These changes are made with the PEDIT and EXPLODE commands.

INTRODUCTION TO PEDIT | AUG 5 |

The PEDIT command is found in the MODIFY screen menu as Pedit: and in the Modify pull-down menu as Edit PolyLine. When either is picked, AutoCAD then allows you to pick the polylines using any of the selection options.

Command. **PEDIT** ⏎
Select polyline: *(use one of the selection options and press* ENTER *when completed)*

When the Select polyline: or Select objects: prompt is issued, the screen cursor becomes a pick box. Move the cursor and pick the polyline to be changed. If the polyline is wide, place the cursor on an edge rather than in the center. You may also use the Window, Crossing, or Fence options if you need to select a group of polyline entities.

If the polyline is the last entity drawn, type L for Last. If the entity you pick is not a polyline, this message is displayed:

Entity selected is not a polyline
Do you want it to turn into one? ⟨Y⟩

A Y response or ENTER turns the entities into a polyline. Type N to leave them as is.

PROFESSIONAL TIP

 Place a window around a group of connected lines and arcs and turn them into a continuous polyline using the Join option discussed later in this chapter.

REVISING A POLYLINE AS ONE UNIT ⟨AUG 5⟩

A polyline may be edited as a single entity or it may be divided to revise each individual segment. This section shows you the options for changing the entire polyline. Note the number of options given in the prompt:

Command: **PEDIT** ⏎
Select polyline: *(pick a polyline)*
Close/Join/Width/Edit vertex/Fit/Spline/Decurve/Ltype gen/Undo/eXit ⟨X⟩:

The default option in brackets is X for eXit. Pressing ENTER returns you to the Command: prompt.

Closing an open polyline or opening a closed polyline

As mentioned before, polylines may be closed with the CLose option. You might later decide to close an open polyline, or you might want to reopen a closed polyline. Both of these functions are done with the Close option of PEDIT. Type C at the prompt line.

If you select Close for a polyline that is already closed, AutoCAD converts the request to Open. Also, typing O for Open will open a closed polyline. Picking an open polyline and the Close option yields the Close prompt. Keep in mind that the Open option will not work on a polyline that was closed by drawing the closing segment. You must have entered the Close option when you closed the polyline. Figure 18-4 shows open and closed polylines.

Figure 18-4.   Open and closed polylines.

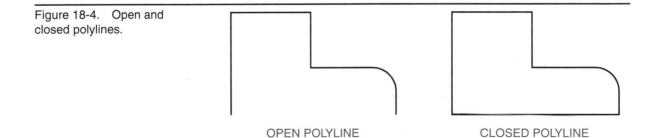

OPEN POLYLINE   CLOSED POLYLINE

Joining polylines to other polylines, lines, and arcs

Polylines, lines, and arcs may be joined together as one polyline. The Join option works only if the polyline and other entities meet exactly. They cannot cross, nor can there be spaces or breaks within the entities. These conditions are shown in Figure 18-5. The command sequence is as follows:

Command: **PEDIT** ↵
Select polyline: *(select the original polyline)*
Close/Join/Width/Edit vertex/Fit/Spline/Decurve/Ltype gen/Undo/eXit ⟨X⟩: **J** ↵
Select objects: *(select all of the objects to be joined)*
Select objects: ↵

Figure 18-5.   Enlarged views of features that are joined and not joined.

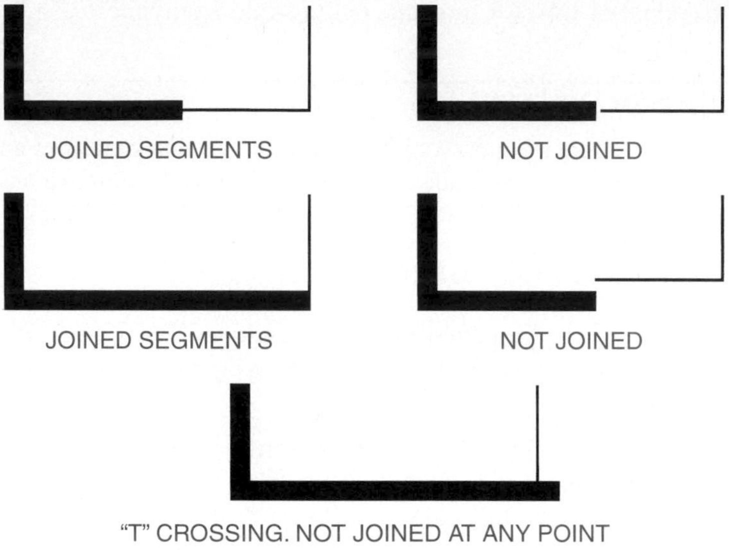

JOINED SEGMENTS   NOT JOINED

JOINED SEGMENTS   NOT JOINED

"T" CROSSING. NOT JOINED AT ANY POINT

Select each object to be joined, or group them with one of the selection options. The original polyline may be included in the group or left out; it does not matter. See Figure 18-6. The new additions will automatically assume the same width as the original polyline.

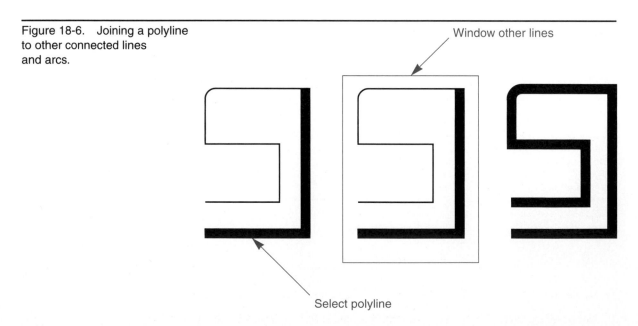

Figure 18-6.   Joining a polyline to other connected lines and arcs.

Window other lines

Select polyline

PROFESSIONAL TIP

Once items have been joined into a continuous polyline, the polyline may be closed using the Close option.

Changing the width of a polyline

The PEDIT command's Width option changes a polyline having a constant or varying width to a new width. To change a polyline from a .06 to .1 width, follow these steps:

Command: **PEDIT** ↵
Select polyline: *(pick the polyline)*
Close/Join/Width/Edit vertex/Fit/Spline/Decurve/Ltype gen/Undo/eXit ⟨X⟩: **W** ↵
Enter new width for all segments: **.1** ↵

Circles drawn with the CIRCLE command cannot be changed to polylines. Polycircles can be produced using the PLINE Arc option and drawing two 180° arcs, or by using the DONUT command. Change the width of doughnuts by individually picking each using the PEDIT command and Width option previously discussed. The Window, Crossing, or Fence selection will not change all doughnut widths at the same time. Figure 18-7 shows an existing polyline and a new polyline created using the PEDIT Width option.

Figure 18-7.   Changing the width of a polyline.

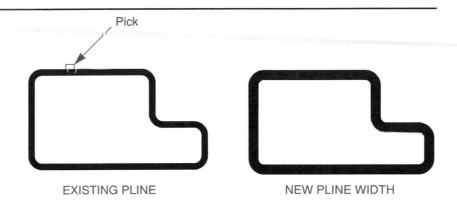

EXISTING PLINE   NEW PLINE WIDTH

EXERCISE 18-2

❑ Open TITLEB from Problem 11-1.
❑ Draw a series of connected lines and arcs. Then use the PEDIT command to change these items to a single polyline. Finally, change the width of the polyline.
❑ Draw a closed polyline. Use the Close option when drawing the final segment.
❑ Use the PEDIT command's Open option to open the previous polyline, and use Close to close it.
❑ Connect a series of lines and arcs to a polyline. Then join all items as one polyline.
❑ Draw two doughnuts, each with a .5 unit inside diameter and 1.0 unit outside diameter. Change the width of the doughnuts to .1 using the PEDIT command.
❑ Save the drawing as A:EX18-2 and quit.

Changing a polyline corner or point of tangency

Another PEDIT option is Edit vertex. When you enter E, an X appears on screen at the first vertex or point of tangency. This complex PEDIT option has nine suboptions:

Close/Join/Width/Edit vertex/Fit/Spline/Decurve/Ltype gen/Undo/eXit ⟨X⟩: **E** ↵
Next/Previous/Break/Insert/Move/Regen/Straighten/Tangent/Width/eXit ⟨N or P⟩:

The suboptions of the Edit vertex option are defined as follows:
- **Next (N).** Moves the screen X to the next vertex or point of tangency on the polyline.
- **Previous (P).** Moves the X to the previous vertex or tangency on the polyline.
- **Break (B).** Breaks a portion out of the polyline.
- **Insert (I).** Adds a new polyline vertex.
- **Move (M).** Moves a polyline vertex to a new location.
- **Regen (R).** Generates the revised version of the polyline.
- **Straighten (S).** Straightens polyline segments.
- **Tangent (T).** Specifies tangent direction for curve fitting.
- **Width (W).** Changes a polyline width.
- **eXit (X).** Returns you to the PEDIT menu and command prompt.

The Next and Previous options move the X between the vertices or points of tangency. The current point is affected by editing functions, Figure 18-8. If you edit the vertices of a polyline and nothing appears to happen, use the Regen option to regenerate the revised edition of the polyline.

Figure 18-8.   Using the Edit vertex, Next, and Previous suboptions. Note the position of the X.

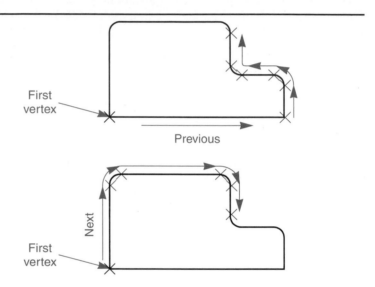

Making breaks in a polyline

The Edit vertex option breaks out a portion of a polyline. Select the N or P options to move the X to the correct vertex. Then follow this command sequence:

> Close/Join/Width/Edit vertex/Fit/Spline/Decurve/Ltype gen/Undo/eXit ⟨X⟩: **E** ↵
> Next/Previous/Break/Insert/Move/Regen/Straighten/Tangent/Width/eXit ⟨N⟩: *(move the screen X to the desired position where you want the break to begin)*
> Next/Previous/Break/Insert/Move/Regen/Straighten/Tangent/Width/eXit ⟨N⟩: **B** ↵

AutoCAD enters the point shown with an X as the first point to break.

> Next/Previous/Go/eXit ⟨N⟩: *(move the screen X to the next or previous position)*

Press ENTER to move the screen X to the Next or Previous vertex or point. The direction depends on which option is the default shown in brackets. Typing X exits the option. After moving the screen X to the desired location, enter G for Go. This instructs AutoCAD to remove the portion of the polyline between the two selected points. The steps below are illustrated in Figure 18-9.

> Next/Previous/Break/Insert/Move/Regen/Straighten/Tangent/Width/eXit ⟨N or P⟩: **B** ↵
> Next/Previous/Go/eXit ⟨N⟩: **P** ↵
> Next/Previous/Go/eXit ⟨P⟩: ↵
> Next/Previous/Go/eXit ⟨P⟩: ↵
> Next/Previous/Go/eXit ⟨P⟩: **G** ↵

Figure 18-9. Using Edit vertex to break out a portion of a polyline.

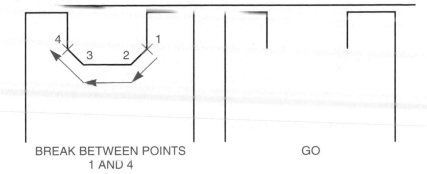

BREAK BETWEEN POINTS
1 AND 4

GO

Insert a new vertex in a polyline

A new vertex may be added to a polyline by typing I for Insert. Use the Insert option only after selecting the adjacent vertex.

Close/Join/Width/Edit vertex/Fit/Spline/Decurve/Ltype gen/Undo/eXit ⟨X⟩: **E** ↵
Next/Previous/Break/Insert/Move/Regen/Straighten/Tangent/Width/eXit ⟨N⟩: *(move the X cursor to the desired location using N or P)*
Next/Previous/Break/Insert/Move/Regen/Straighten/Tangent/Width/eXit ⟨N⟩: **I** ↵
Enter location of new vertex: *(move the screen crosshairs to the new vertex location and pick)*

The new vertex is drawn, as shown in Figure 18-10.

Figure 18-10. Using the Edit vertex Insert option to add a new vertex.

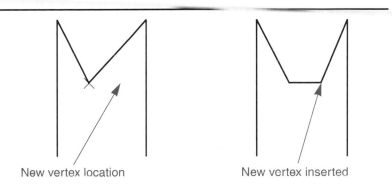

New vertex location   New vertex inserted

Moving a polyline vertex

The Move option of Edit vertex moves a vertex. The screen X cursor must be placed on the point to move before you enter M. The sequence shown in Figure 18-11 is as follows:

Close/Join/Width/Edit vertex/Fit/Spline/Decurve/Ltype gen/Undo/eXit ⟨X⟩: **E** ↵
Next/Previous/Break/Insert/Move/Regen/Straighten/Tangent/Width/eXit ⟨N⟩: *(move the X cursor to the vertex to be moved, using N or P)*
Next/Previous/Break/Insert/Move/Regen/Straighten/Tangent/Width/eXit ⟨N⟩: **M** ↵
Enter new location: *(pick the new point)*

Figure 18-11. Using the Edit vertex Move option to place a vertex in a new location.

Existing vertex location

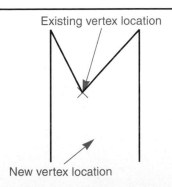
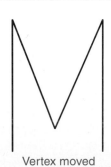

New vertex location   Vertex moved

Straightening polyline segments or arcs

You can straighten polyline segments or arcs between two points. Use the Edit vertex Straighten option as follows:

Close/Join/Width/Edit vertex/Fit/Spline/Decurve/Ltype gen/Undo/eXit ⟨X⟩: **E** ↵
Next/Previous/Break/Insert/Move/Regen/Straighten/Tangent/Width/eXit ⟨N⟩: *(move the*
X cursor to the first point of the segments to be straightened)
Next/Previous/Break/Insert/Move/Regen/Straighten/Tangent/Width/eXit ⟨N⟩: **S** ↵
Next/Previous/Go/eXit/ ⟨N⟩: *(move the X to the last point)*
Next/Previous/Go/eXit ⟨N⟩: **G** ↵

If the X is not moved before G is entered, AutoCAD straightens the segment to the next vertex. This option provides a quick way to straighten an arc, Figure 18-12.

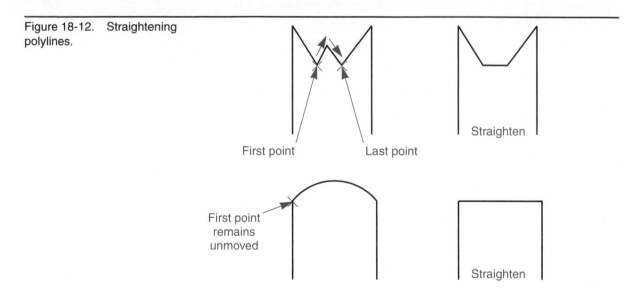

Figure 18-12.   Straightening polylines.

First point   Last point

First point remains unmoved

Straighten

Straighten

Changing polyline segment widths

The Edit vertex Width option is the only command that changes the starting and ending widths of an existing polyline. Move the screen X to the segment before the one to be altered. The command structure looks like this:

Close/Join/Width/Edit vertex/Fit/Spline/Decurve/Ltype gen/Undo/eXit ⟨X⟩: **E** ↵
Next/Previous/Break/Insert/Move/Regen/Straighten/Tangent/Width/eXit ⟨N⟩: **N** ↵
(move the X cursor to the segment prior to the one to be changed)
Next/Previous/Break/Insert/Move/Regen/Straighten/Tangent/Width/eXit ⟨N⟩: **W** ↵
Enter starting width ⟨*current*⟩: *(enter the revised starting width and press ENTER)*
Enter ending width ⟨revised start width⟩: *(enter the revised ending width and press ENTER,*
or press ENTER to keep the width the same as the starting width)
Next/Previous/Break/Insert/Move/Regen/Straighten/Tangent/Width/eXit ⟨N⟩: **R** ↵

Notice that the starting width default is the current setting. The ending width default is the same as the entered starting width. When you press ENTER to complete this command, nothing happens. You must select the Regen option to have AutoCAD draw the revised polyline. See Figure 18-13.

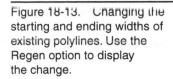

Figure 18-13.   Changing the starting and ending widths of existing polylines. Use the Regen option to display the change.

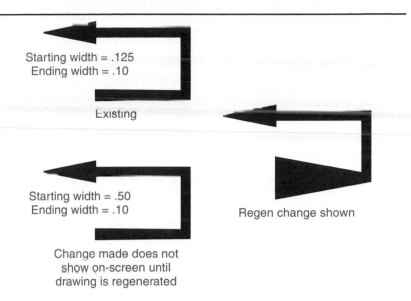

Starting width = .125
Ending width = .10

Existing

Starting width = .50
Ending width = .10

Regen change shown

Change made does not show on-screen until drawing is regenerated

---

EXERCISE 18-3

❑ Open TITLEB from Problem 11-1.
❑ Draw a polyline with a series of segments. Have at least eight corners and three arcs.
❑ Enter the Edit vertex option and move the screen X cursor around using the Next and Previous suboptions.
❑ Break the polyline between any three points. Then Undo the breaks.
❑ Insert a new vertex in the polyline.
❑ Move one vertex of the polyline.
❑ Straighten one arc segment or at least three line segments.
❑ Change the starting and ending widths of one segment.
❑ Save the drawing as A:EX18-3 and quit.

Making a smooth curve out of polyline corners

In some situations, you may need to convert a polyline into a series of smooth curves. One example is a graph. A graph may show a series of plotted points as a smooth curve rather than straight segments. This process is called *curve fitting* and is done with the Fit suboption. The Fit suboption constructs pairs of arcs passing through control points. You can specify control points or they may be the vertices of the polyline's corners. Many closely spaced control points produce a smooth curve. Prior to curve fitting, each vertex may be given a tangent direction. AutoCAD then fits the curve based on the tangent directions that you set. However, you do not have to enter tangent directions. Mainly, the option is used to edit vertices when Fit curve did not produce the best results.

To edit tangent directions, enter the Edit vertex option of the PEDIT command. Move the screen X to each vertex to be changed. Request the Tangent option and issue a tangent direction in degrees or pick a point in the expected direction. The direction you choose is indicated by an arrow placed at the vertex.

Close/Join/Width/Edit vertex/Fit/Spline/Decurve/Ltype gen/Undo/eXit/ ⟨X⟩: **E** ↵
Next/Previous/Break/Insert/Move/Regen/Straighten/Tangent/Width/eXit/ ⟨N⟩: *(move the screen X to the desired vertex)*
Next/Previous/Break/Insert/Move/Regen/Straighten/Tangent/Width/eXit ⟨N⟩: **T** ↵
Direction of tangent: *(specify a direction in positive or negative degrees and press* ENTER, *or pick a point in the desired direction)*

Once the tangent directions are given for vertices to be changed, select the Fit option. The polyline shown in Figure 18-14 was made into a smooth curve with these steps:

Command: **PEDIT** ↵
Select polyline: *(pick the polyline to be edited)*
Close/Join/Width/Edit vertex/Fit/Spline/Decurve/Ltype gen/Undo/eXit/ ⟨X⟩: **F** ↵

Figure 18-14.   Using the PEDIT command's Fit option.

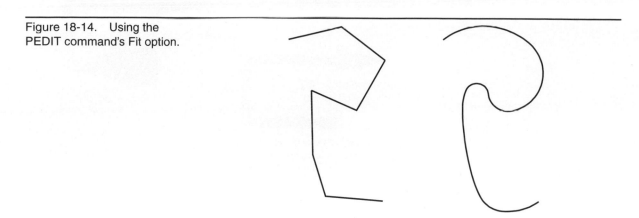

If the result does not look like the curve you anticipated, return to the Edit vertex suboption. Make changes using PEDIT options.

Using the Spline option

With the Fit option, the curve passes through polyline vertices. The Spline option also smoothes the corners of a straight segment polyline. This option produces a different result. The curve passes through the first and last control points or vertices. However, the curve "pulls" toward the other vertices but does not pass through them. The Spline curve option is used as follows:

Command: **PEDIT** ↵
Select polyline: *(pick the polyline to be edited)*
Close/Join/Width/Edit vertex/Fit/Spline/Decurve/Ltype gen/Undo/eXit/ ⟨X⟩: **S** ↵

A comparison of the Fit and Spline options is shown in Figure 18-15.

Figure 18-15.   A comparison between Fit and Spline options.

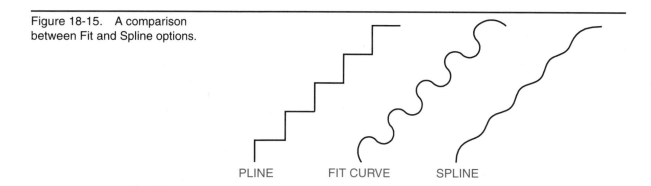

PLINE   FIT CURVE   SPLINE

Straightening all segments of a polyline

The Decurve option returns a polyline edited with Fit or Spline options to its original form. Information entered for tangent direction is kept for future reference. The Decurve option steps below are shown in Figure 18-16.

Command: **PEDIT** ↵
Select polyline: *(pick the polyline to be edited)*
Close/Join/Width/Edit vertex/Fit/Spline/Decurve/Ltype gen/Undo/eXit/ ⟨X⟩: **D** ↵

Figure 18-16.   Using the
Decurve option.

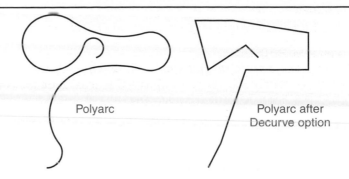

Polyarc

Polyarc after
Decurve option

PROFESSIONAL TIP

If you make a mistake, remember that the Undo option is always available. It removes the last polyline segment drawn. Entering Undo more than once removes each polyline segment in reverse order in which they were drawn. Use the eXit option to return to the previous prompt. Undo also cancels the last PEDIT function you used.

EXERCISE 18-4

❑ Open TITLEB from Problem 11-1.
❑ Draw a polyline with at least five vertices. Smooth the polyline using the PEDIT command's Fit option.
❑ Decurve the curved polyline.
❑ Practice with Undo by first drawing a series of polyline segments. After using PEDIT to make some changes, select Undo to return to the original polyline. Finally, select Redo to work on the edited polyline again.
❑ Save the drawing as A:EX18-4 and quit.

Changing the appearance of polyline linetypes

The Ltype gen option refers to "linetype generation." This option determines how linetypes, other than continuous lines, look in relation to the vertices of a polyline. For example, when a centerline is used and Ltype gen is off, then the line has a dash at each vertex. When Ltype gen is on, the line is generated with a constant pattern in relation to the vertices. Look at the difference between Ltype gen on and off in Figure 18-17, and also notice the effect these settings have on spline curves.

Figure 18-17.   Comparison
of Ltype gen On and Off.

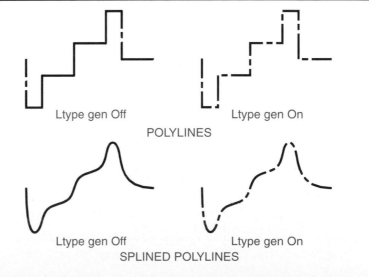

Ltype gen Off   Ltype gen On

POLYLINES

Ltype gen Off   Ltype gen On

SPLINED POLYLINES

Ltype gen is accessed by typing L at the prompt line, or by picking LT Updt from the screen menu. The Ltype gen option is either on or off. To turn on this option, follow these steps:

Command: **PEDIT** ↵
Select polyline: *(pick the polyline)*
Close/Join/Width/Edit vertex/Fit/Spline/Decurve/Ltype gen/Undo/eXit/ ⟨X⟩: **L** ↵
Full PLINE linetype ON/OFF ⟨Off⟩: **ON** ↵

You can also change the Ltype gen value using the PLINEGEN system variable as follows:

Command: **PLINEGEN** ↵
New value for PLINEGEN ⟨0⟩: **1** ↵

Ltype gen or PLINEGEN does not affect tapered polylines.

CONVERTING A POLYLINE INTO INDIVIDUAL LINE AND ARC SEGMENTS

AUG 5

Remember that a polyline is a single entity composed of polyline and polyline arc segments. The EXPLODE command changes the polyline to a series of lines and arcs. The EXPLODE command can be accessed from the MODIFY: screen menu, Modify pull-down menu, or typed at the Command: prompt.

When a wide polyline or polyarc is exploded, the resulting line or arc is redrawn along the centerline of the original polyline or polyarc, Figure 18-18. When the EXPLODE command is entered at the Command: prompt, AutoCAD makes the following request:

Command: **EXPLODE** ↵
Select objects: *(pick the polyline to be exploded)*
Select objects: ↵

Figure 18-18.   Exploding a wide polyarc.

POLYARC BEFORE   POLYARC AFTER

The EXPLODE command removes all width characteristics and tangent information. However, AutoCAD gives you a chance to change your mind by offering this message:

Exploding this polyline has lost (width/tangent) information.
The UNDO command will restore it.

EXERCISE 18-5

❑ Load AutoCAD and open TITLEB.
❑ Draw a polyline of your own design. Include some width changes. Then explode it and observe what happens.
❑ Restore the exploded polyline using the UNDO command.
❑ Save the drawing as A:EX18-5 and quit.

ADDITIONAL METHODS FOR SMOOTHING POLYLINE CORNERS

AUG 5

Earlier in this chapter, the Fit and Spline options of the PEDIT command were discussed. With the Fit option, the resulting curve passes through the polyline vertices. The Spline option creates a curve that passes through the first and last control points, or vertices. The curve then "pulls" toward the other vertices but does not pass through them. There are two spline curve options–Quadratic and Cubic. These options create B-spline curves. The *cubic curve* is extremely smooth because the elements of the curve pass through the first and last control points, and close to intermediate control points. The *quadratic curve* is not as smooth as the cubic curve. However, it is smoother than a curve made with the Fit option. Like a cubic curve, a quadratic curve passes through the first and last control points. The remainder of the curve is tangent to the polyline segments between intermediate control points, Figure 18-19.

Figure 18-19. A comparison of the Fit, Quadratic spline curve, and Cubic spline curve options.

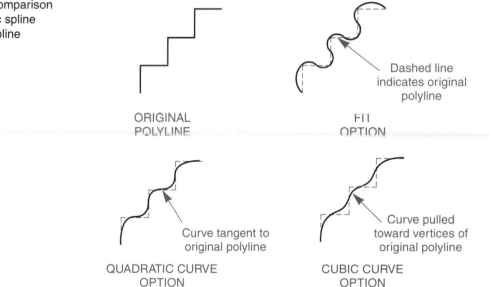

ORIGINAL POLYLINE

FIT OPTION

Dashed line indicates original polyline

QUADRATIC CURVE OPTION

Curve tangent to original polyline

CUBIC CURVE OPTION

Curve pulled toward vertices of original polyline

Editing a polyline into a B-spline curve requires that you first set the SPLINETYPE system variable. If you set SPLINETYPE to 5, AutoCAD draws a quadratic curve. If you set the value to 6, AutoCAD draws a cubic curve. Set the SPLINETYPE to draw a quadratic curve as follows:

Command: **SPLINETYPE** ↵
New value for SPLINETYPE ⟨6⟩: **5** ↵

If you want to draw a cubic curve, reset SPLINETYPE to 6.

EXERCISE 18-6

❏ Draw a polyline similar to the "ORIGINAL POLYLINE" shown in Figure 18-19.
❏ Use the COPY command to make three copies of the original polyline.
❏ Use PEDIT's Fit option to smooth the first copy.
❏ Set SPLINETYPE to 5 for a quadratic curve.
❏ Use PEDIT's Spline option to smooth the second copy.
❏ Set SPLINETYPE to 6 for a cubic curve.
❏ Use the Spline option again to smooth the third copy.
❏ Compare the original polyline with the three new curves.
❏ Save the drawing as A:EX18-6 and quit.

Another system variable, called SPLINESEGS, controls the number of line segments used to construct spline curves. The SPLINESEGS default value is 8. It allows you to create a fairly smooth spline curve with moderate regeneration time. If you decrease the value, the spline curve is less smooth. If you increase the value, the spline curve is more smooth. Although increasing the value above 8 creates a more precise spline curve, it also increases regeneration time and drawing file size. Change the SPLINESEGS variable as follows:

Command: **SPLINESEGS** ↵
New value for SPLINESEGS ⟨8⟩: **20** ↵

Figure 18-20 shows the relationship between several SPLINESEGS values.

Figure 18-20.   A comparison of SPLINESEGS values.

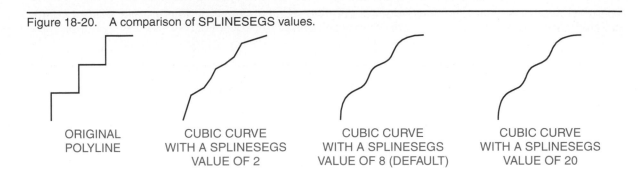

ORIGINAL
POLYLINE

CUBIC CURVE
WITH A SPLINESEGS
VALUE OF 2

CUBIC CURVE
WITH A SPLINESEGS
VALUE OF 8 (DEFAULT)

CUBIC CURVE
WITH A SPLINESEGS
VALUE OF 20

When you pick Edit PolyLine from the Modify pull-down menu and select the object to edit, the first PEDIT screen menu changes to display some of the PEDIT options. Also displayed at the end of this screen menu is PolyVars (Polyline Variables). Selecting PolyVars accesses a dialog box displaying five options, including Quadratic, Cubic, and Bezier.

EXERCISE 18-7

❑ Draw a polyline similar to the "ORIGINAL POLYLINE" shown in Figure 18-20.
❑ Use the COPY command to make three copies of the original polyline.
❑ Set SPLINETYPE to 6 for a cubic curve.
❑ Set the SPLINESEGS system variable to 2.
❑ Use PEDIT's Spline option to smooth the first copy.
❑ Set SPLINESEGS to 8.
❑ Use the Spline option to smooth the second copy.
❑ Set SPLINESEGS to 20.
❑ Use the Spline option to smooth the third copy.
❑ Compare the original polyline and the smoothness of the three new curves.
❑ Save the drawing as A:EX18-7 and quit.

MAKING CURVES USING THE SPLINE COMMAND   AUG 2

The SPLINE command provides the capability to create NURBS curves. A *NURBS* curve (Non-Uniform Rational B-Spline) is considered to be a true spline. The spline created by fitting a spline curve to a polyline is merely a linear approximation of a true spline and is not as accurate. An additional advantage of Spline objects over smoothed polylines is that Splines use less memory and disk space. You can access the SPLINE command by picking Spline in the Draw pull-down menu, Spline: in the DRAW 1 screen menu, or type at the Command: prompt A Spline is created by specifying the control points along the curve by any standard coordinate entry method:

```
Command: SPLINE ↵
Object/⟨Enter first point⟩: 2,2 ↵
Enter point: 4,4 ↵
Close/Fit Tolerance/⟨Enter point⟩: 6,2 ↵
Close/Fit Tolerance/⟨Enter point⟩: ↵
Enter start tangent: ↵
Enter end tangent: ↵
Command:
```

When you have given all of the necessary points along the Spline, pressing ENTER ends the point specification process and allows start and end tangencies to be issued. Specifying the tangencies allows the direction in which the spline curve begins and ends to be changed. Pressing ENTER at these prompts accepts the default direction as calculated by AutoCAD for the specified curve. The results of the previous command sequence is shown in Figure 18-21.

Figure 18-21.   Using the SPLINE command with the AutoCAD defaults for start and end tangents.

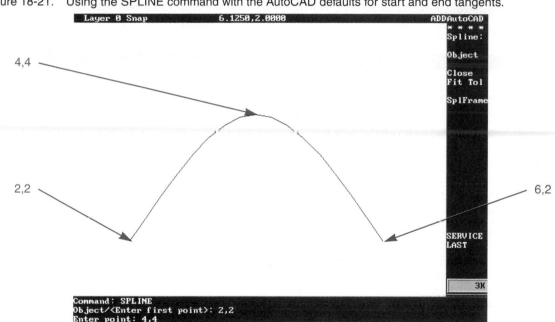

NOTE   If only two points are specified along the spline curve, an object that looks like a line is created, but the actual object is still a Spline.

Drawing closed splines

The Close option may be used to draw closed splines, as shown in Figure 18-22, using this command sequence:

```
Command: SPLINE ↵
Object/⟨Enter first point⟩: 2,2 ↵
Enter point: 4,4 ↵
Close/Fit Tolerance/⟨Enter point⟩: 6,2 ↵
Close/Fit Tolerance/⟨Enter point⟩: C ↵
Enter tangent: ↵
Command:
```

After closing a Spline, you are prompted to specify a tangent direction for the start/end point of the spline. Pressing ENTER accepts the AutoCAD default as shown in Figure 18-22.

Figure 18-22.   Using the SPLINE command Close option with AutoCAD default tangents. Compare this to the object in Figure 18-21.

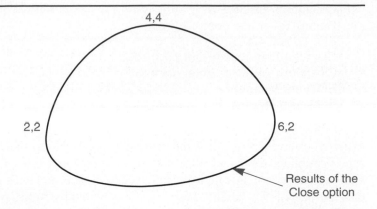

Results of the Close option

Altering the Fit Tolerance specifications

Different results can be achieved by altering the Fit Tolerance specifications. This setting has varied results depending on the configuration of the individual spline object. The way this works is that the spline curve passes through the fit points within the given tolerance. Figure 18-23 displays the Fit Tolerance for three test cases. The following is the command sequence for the example shown in color:

```
Command: SPLINE ↵
Object/⟨Enter first point⟩: 0,0 ↵
Enter point: 2,2 ↵
Close/Fit Tolerance/⟨Enter point⟩: 4,0 ↵
Close/Fit Tolerance/⟨Enter point⟩: 5,5.5 ↵
Close/Fit Tolerance/⟨Enter point⟩: 6,0 ↵
Close/Fit Tolerance/⟨Enter point⟩: F ↵
Enter Fit Tolerance ⟨0.0000⟩: 3 ↵
Enter start tangent: ↵
Enter end tangent: ↵
Command:
```

Figure 18-23.   The effect of different Fit tolerance values on a Spline. The line in color correlates to the command sequence given in the text.

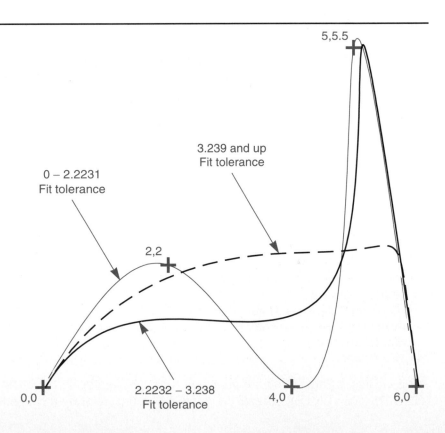

3.239 and up
Fit tolerance

0 – 2.2231
Fit tolerance

2.2232 – 3.238
Fit tolerance

Specifying the start and end tangencies

The previous examples used AutoCAD's default start and end tangencies. You can also issue a start and end tangency using the Tan or Perp object snap modes. Selecting a point causes the tangency direction to be in the direction of the selected point. An illustration showing the results of the Tan and Perp object snaps on two splines with the same point entries is displayed in Figure 18-24. This is the command sequence for the Perp selection:

Command: **SPLINE** ↵
Object/⟨Enter first point⟩: **2,2** ↵
Enter point: **4,4** ↵
Close/Fit Tolerance/⟨Enter point⟩: **6,2** ↵
Close/Fit Tolerance/⟨Enter point⟩: ↵
Enter start tangent: _per to *(pick the line)*
Enter end tangent: _per to *(pick the line)*
Command:

Figure 18-24.   Examples of start and end tangents perpendicular to a line and tangent to a line.

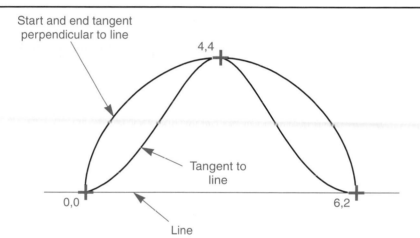

Start and end tangent perpendicular to line

Tangent to line

Line

Convert a spline fitted polyline to a spline

A spline fitted polyline object, either 2-D or 3-D, can be converted to a spline object using the Object option of the SPLINE command. This is the command sequence:

Command: **SPLINE** ↵
Object/⟨Enter first point⟩: **O** ↵
Select object to convert to splines.
Select objects: *(pick the polyline edited spline)*
Select objects: ↵
Command:

EXERCISE 18-8

❑ Load AutoCAD and open TITLEB.
❑ Draw a Spline with control points similar to Figure 18-21 and use the AutoCAD default tangencies.
❑ Draw a similar Spline to the right of the first one using the Close option and default tangencies.
❑ Draw three Splines each with the same control points similar to Figure 18-23. Set the Fit Tolerance for the Splines at 0, 3, and 4 respectively.
❑ Draw a line and two splines similar to Figure 18-24. Use the Perpendicular object snap mode for the start and end tangencies on one Spline and the Tangent object snap mode on the other.
❑ Save as A:EX18-8.

EDITING SPLINES

The SPLINEDIT command allows editing of Spline objects. Fit points can be added or moved to alter the shape of a curve. The spline can be opened, closed or joined, and start and endpoint tangencies can be changed. Pick Edit Spline in the Modify pull-down menu, SplinEd: in the MODIFY screen menu or type to get this:

Command: **SPLINEDIT** ↵
Select spline: *(pick a spline)*

When you pick a spline, the control points and fit tolerance data are displayed in the grip color, as demonstrated in Figure 18-25. The command continues with the following prompt:

Fit Data/Close/Move Vertex/Refine/rEverse/Undo/eXit ⟨X⟩:

Figure 18-25.   The control points on a Spline when using the SPLINEDIT command.

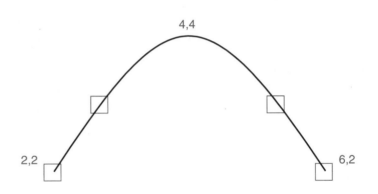

The SPLINEDIT command options are described in the following discussions.

Editing Fit Data

The Fit Data option of the SPLINEDIT command allows spline control points, called Fit Points, to be edited. Entering this option gives you the following suboptions:

Command: **SPLINEDIT** ↵
Select spline: *(pick a spline)*
Fit Data/Close/Move Vertex/Refine/rEverse/Undo/eXit ⟨X⟩: **F** ↵
Add/Close/Delete/Move/Purge/Tangents/toLerance/eXit ⟨X⟩:

The purpose of these suboptions is described in the following:
- **Add.** This allows new fit points to be added into the Spline definition. When adding, a fit point must be pointed to with the cursor, or you can type the X,Y location of the fit point to select. Fit points appear as unhighlighted grip boxes. When one is selected, it becomes highlighted along with the next fit point in the Spline toward the final point specified in the SPLINE definition. The added fit point occurs between the two highlighted fit points. If the start or end of the spline is selected, a prompt is issued asking whether to insert the new fit point Before or After the existing one. You respond with B or F accordingly. When a fit point is added, the spline curve is refit through the added point. See Figure 18-26.

Figure 18-26.   Demonstrations of using the SPLINEDIT command Fit Data suboptions. Compare the original Spline to edits that include adding a control point, closing an open Spline, deleting a control point, moving a control point, and changing the tangents.

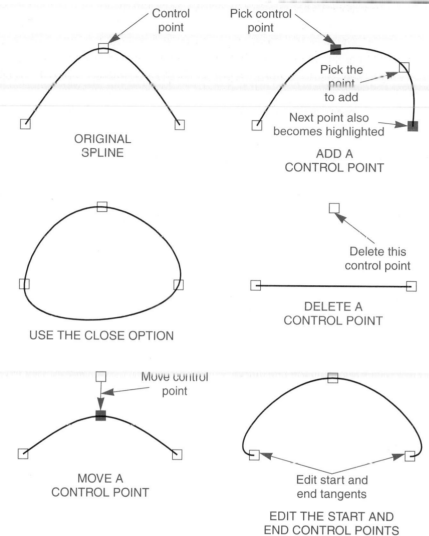

ORIGINAL SPLINE

ADD A CONTROL POINT

USE THE CLOSE OPTION

DELETE A CONTROL POINT

MOVE A CONTROL POINT

EDIT THE START AND END CONTROL POINTS

The Add option functions in a running mode. Running mode means that you can continue to add points as needed. Pressing ENTER at an Enter new point: prompt allows continued selection of another existing fit point so that points can be added anywhere on the spline until finished. The command sequence looks like this:

```
Command: SPLINEDIT ↵
Select spline: (pick a spline)
Fit Data/Close/Move Vertex/Refine/rEverse/Undo/eXit ⟨X⟩: F ↵
Add/Close/Delete/Move/Purge/Tangents/toLerance/eXit⟨X⟩: A ↵
Select point: (pick a fit point)
Enter new point: (pick a location to add a point)
Enter new point: (pick a location to add a point)
Enter new point: ↵
Select point: ↵
Add/Close/Delete/Move/Purge/Tangents/toLerance/eXit ⟨X⟩: ↵
Fit Data/Close/Move Vertex/Refine/rEverse/Undo/eXit ⟨X⟩: ↵
Command:
```

• **Close/Open.** This option appears as the opposite of the status of the spline object currently being edited. If the SPLINE is open, the option is Close. If the spline is closed, the option is Open. Using these options lets you open a closed spline or close an open spline, as shown in Figure 18-26.

- **Delete.** The Delete option allows fit points to be deleted as needed. However, at least two fit points must remain, and these last two cannot be deleted. Even when only two points remain, the object is still listed as a Spline and not a Line. See Figure 18-26. The delete option also operates in the running mode, allowing as many deletions as needed. The Spline curve is refit through the remaining fit points when fit points are deleted. The prompts work like this:

  Command: **SPLINEDIT** ↵
  Select spline: *(pick a spline)*
  Fit Data/Close/Move Vertex/Refine/rEverse/Undo/eXit ⟨X⟩: **F** ↵
  Add/Close/Delete/Move/Purge/Tangents/toLerance/eXit ⟨X⟩: **D** ↵
  Select point: *(pick a fit point)*
  Select point: *(pick a fit point)*
  Select point: ↵
  Add/Close/Delete/Move/Purge/Tangents/toLerance/eXit ⟨X⟩: ↵
  Fit Data/Close/Move Vertex/Refine/rEverse/Undo/eXit ⟨X⟩: ↵
  Command:

- **Move.** This option allows fit points to be moved as necessary. See Figure 18-26. The command sequence is as follows:

  Command: **SPLINEDIT** ↵
  Select spline: *(pick a spline)*
  Fit Data/Close/Move Vertex/Refine/rEverse/Undo/eXit ⟨X⟩: **F** ↵
  Add/Close/Delete/Move/Purge/Tangents/toLerance/eXit ⟨X⟩: **M** ↵
  Next/Previous/Select Point/eXit/⟨Enter new location⟩ ⟨N⟩: **S** ↵
  Next/Previous/Select Point/eXit/⟨Enter new location⟩ ⟨N⟩: ↵
  Add/Close/Delete/Move/Purge/Tangents/toLerance/eXit ⟨X⟩: ↵
  Fit Data/Close/Move Vertex/Refine/rEverse/Undo/eXit ⟨X⟩: ↵
  Command:

When Move is specified, the following options are available:
- **Next–**Highlights the next fit point.
- **Previous–**Highlights the previous fit point.
- **Select Point–**Allows you to pick a different point to move rather than using the Next or Previous options.
- **eXit–**Returns you to the Fit Data option prompt.
- **⟨Enter new location⟩.** Moves the currently highlighted point to the specified location.
- **Purge.** This option removes fit point data from a Spline, leaving it less easily edited. In very complex drawings such as Geographical Information Systems (GIS) where many very complex Splines are created, purging them reduces the file size by simplifying the definition. Once purged, the Fit Data option is no longer presented by the SPLINE command for the purged Spline.
- **Tangents.** This option allows editing of the start and end tangents for an open Spline and editing of the tangent for a closed Spline. Selecting a point causes the tangency direction to be in the direction of the selected point. See Figure 18-26. The System Default option sets the tangency values to the AutoCAD defaults. This is how you use the Tangents option to set the System Defaults:

  Command: **SPLINEDIT** ↵
  Select spline: *(pick a spline)*
  Fit Data/Close/Move Vertex/Refine/rEverse/Undo/eXit ⟨X⟩: **F** ↵
  Add/Close/Delete/Move/Purge/Tangents/toLerance/eXit ⟨X⟩: **T** ↵
  System Default/⟨Enter start tangent⟩: **S** ↵
  System Default/⟨Enter end tangent⟩: **S** ↵
  Add/Close/Delete/Move/Purge/Tangents/toLerance/eXit ⟨X⟩: ↵
  Fit Data/Close/Move Vertex/Refine/rEverse/Undo/eXit ⟨X⟩: ↵
  Command:

- **Tolerance.** The Fit Tolerance values can be adjusted using this option. The results are immediate, so the fit tolerance can be adjusted as necessary to produce different results.
- **eXit.** Returns you to the SPLINEDIT option line.

Opening or closing a Spline

This option appears as the opposite of the status of the Spline object currently being edited. If the Spline is open, the option is Close:

Fit Data/Close/Move Vertex/Refine/rEverse/Undo/eXit ⟨X⟩:

If the spline is closed, the option is Open:

Fit Data/Open/Move Vertex/Refine/rEverse/Undo/eXit ⟨X⟩:

Using these options lets you open a closed Spline or close an open spline.

Moving a Vertex

This SPLINEDIT option allows movement of the control points for the Spline. When you access this option you get a series of these suboptions:

Command: **SPLINEDIT** ⏎
Select spline: *(pick a spline)*
Fit Data/Close/Move Vertex/Refine/rEverse/Undo/eXit ⟨X⟩: **M** ⏎
Next/Previous/Select Point/eXit/⟨Enter new location⟩ ⟨N⟩: ⏎

The following outlines the purpose of the Move Vertex options:
- **Next.** Highlights the next fit point.
- **Previous.** Highlights the previous fit point.
- **Select Point.** Allows you a chance to pick a different point to move rather than using the Next or Previous options.
- **eXit.** Returns you to the Fit Data option prompt.
- ⟨**Enter new location**⟩. Moves the currently highlighted point to the specified location.

EXERCISE 18-9

❑ Load AutoCAD and open TITLEB.
❑ Draw a Spline with control points similar to the ORIGINAL SPLINE in Figure 18-26 and use the AutoCAD default tangencies.
❑ Copy the ORIGINAL Spline to five locations similar to the layout of Figure 18-26.
❑ Use the SPLINEDIT command on the upper right Spline to Add a control point similar to Figure18-26.
❑ Use the SPLINEDIT command to Close the middle left Spline similar to Figure 18-26.
❑ Use the SPLINEDIT command on the middle right Spline to Delete the top control point similar to Figure 18-26.
❑ Use the SPLINEDIT command on the lower left Spline to Move the top control point similar to Figure 18-26.
❑ Use the SPLINEDIT command on the lower right Spline to edit the start and end tangencies with the TAN object snap similar to Figure 18-26.
❑ Save as A:EX18-9.

Smoothing or reshaping a section of the Spline

The Refine option allows fine tuning of the Spline shape. Control points can be added to help smooth or reshape a section of the Spline.

Using Refine has the same effect as the Purge option with regards to removing the Fit Data option of the SPLINEDIT command. The command sequence for entering the Refine option is as follows:

Command: **SPLINEDIT** ↵
Select spline: *(pick a spline)*
Fit Data/Close/Move Vertex/Refine/rEverse/Undo/eXit ⟨X⟩: **R** ↵
Add control point/Elevate Order/Weight/eXit ⟨X⟩:

The following gives a description of each Refine suboption:

- **Add control point.** This allows new control points to be specified on a spline as needed. See Figure 18-26.
- **Elevate Order.** The order of a Spline is the degree of the Spline polynomial +1. For example, a cubic spline has order 4. Elevating the order of a Spline causes more control points to appear on the Spline for greater control. One of the Spline examples in Figure 18-27 has the control point order elevated from 5 to 9. The setting can be between 4 and 26, but cannot be adjusted downward. For example, once set to 24, the only remaining settings are 25 and 26. Integers less than 24 are rejected.

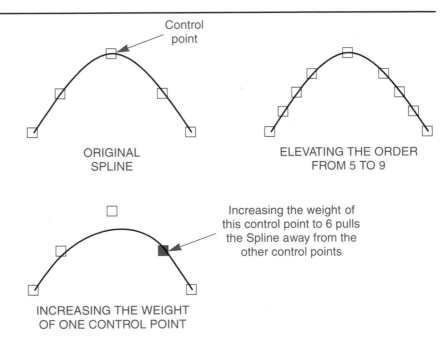

Figure 18-27.   Shows how elevating the order of control points and increasing the weight of a control point effect the curve.

- **Weight.** The default value is 1.0 and can be adjusted up or down from there. This controls the weight of individual control points. When all of the control points have the same weight factor, they all exert the same amount of pull on the resulting Spline. When a weight value is lessened, that control point is not able to pull the spline as close to it as before. Likewise, when the weight is increased, the control point puns harder and brings the Spline closer to it, as shown in Figure 18-27. The only valid settings for this are positive, non-zero real numbers. The control point selection options of this subcommand are the same as those discussed with Move Vertex except the request to change weight is ⟨New weight data⟩:

  Add control point/Elevate Order/Weight/eXit ⟨X⟩: **W** ↵
  Next/Previous/Select Point/eXit/⟨New weight data⟩ ⟨N⟩: *(enter a positive number up to 26)*

Reversing the order of Spline control points

The rEverse option of the SPLINEDIT command reverses the listed order of the Spline control points. This makes the previous start point the new end point and the previous end point the new start point. This has an effect on various selection options of the SPLINEDIT subcommand. For example, the control points are reversed, and the Tangent option changes the start first and end order.

Undoing SPLINEDIT changes

The Undo option undoes the previous change. This option can undo to the beginning of the current SPLINEDIT command.

Exiting the SPLINEDIT command

Using the eXit option in the SPLINEDIT command returns you to the Command: prompt. You can type X or press ENTER, because ⟨X⟩ (exit) is the default.

EXERCISE 18-10

❑ Load AutoCAD and open TITLEB.
❑ Draw a Spline with control points similar to the ORIGINAL SPLINE in Figure 18-27 and use the AutoCAD default tangencies.
❑ Copy the ORIGINAL Spline to two locations similar to the layout of Figure 18-27.
❑ Use the SPLINEDIT command on the upper right Spline to Elevate the order of control points similar to Figure 18-27.
❑ Use the SPLINEDIT command on the lower Spline to increase the Weight of a control point similar to Figure 18-27.
❑ Save as A:EX18-10.

MAKING A POLYLINE BOUNDARY

When you draw an object with the LINE command, each line segment is a single entity. You can create a polyline boundary of an area made up of closed line segments. To do this, pick Boundary from the Construct pull-down menu, Boundar: from the CONSTRCT screen menu, or enter the BOUNDARY command as follows:

Command: **BOUNDARY** ⏎

Now, the "Boundary Creation" dialog box shown in Figure 18-28 is displayed. The BPOLY command is still recognized from Release 12 and may also be used to access the "Boundary Creation" dialog box. Some of the items in this dialog box (related to hatching) are discussed in detail in Chapter 24.

Figure 18-28. The "Boundary Creation" dialog box.

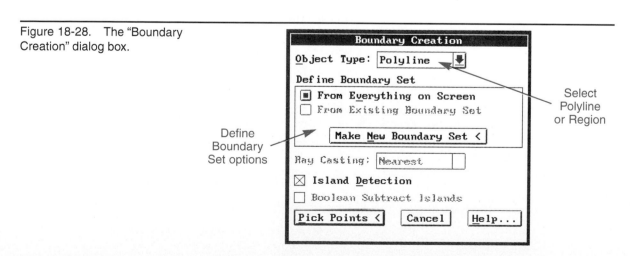

The first option in the "Boundary Creation" dialog box is the <u>O</u>bject Type: This can be set to either Polyline or Region. If set to Polyline, AutoCAD creates a polyline around the area. If set to Region, AutoCAD creates a closed 2-D area. A Region may be used for area analysis, shading or other purposes. The Define Boundary Set features are discussed in Chapter 24 of this text.

The Island <u>D</u>etection check box causes all objects within the outermost boundary to be used as boundary objects. Objects inside of a boundary are called islands, as shown in Figure 18-29.

Figure 18-29.   An example showing a boundary and islands.

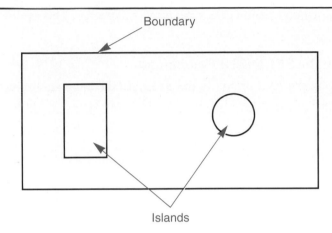

The Ray Casting options are disabled when Island <u>D</u>etection is checked. The Boolean Subtract Islands check box causes islands to be included in the outer boundary. Both Ray Casting and Boolean Subtract Islands are explained in Chapter 24 of this text.

Pick the <u>P</u>ick Points 〈 button to get these prompts:

Select internal point: *(pick a point inside a closed polygon)*
Selecting everything…
Selecting everything visible…
Analyzing selected data…
Select internal point: *(pick a point inside another closed polygon)*
Select internal point: ↵

If the point you pick is inside a closed polygon, then the boundary becomes highlighted, as shown in Figure 18-30. If the area you want is not closed, then you get the "Boundary Definition Error" alert box. Pick OK, close the area, and try again.

Figure 18-30.   When you select an internal point, the boundary becomes highligted. Boundaries must be closed objects.

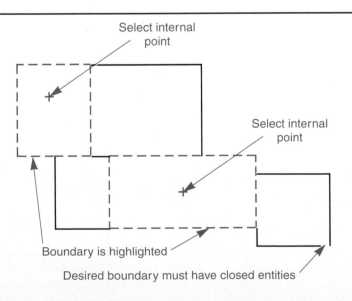

CHAPTER TEST

Write your answers in the spaces provided.

1. Give the command and entries required to make a polyline arc. It should have a starting width of 0 and ending width of .25. Draw it from a known center to an endpoint.

   Command:_____

   From point: _____

   Current line width is (status) _____

   Arc/Close/Halfwidth/Length/Undo/Width/⟨Endpoint of line⟩: _____

   Starting width ⟨*current*⟩: _____

   Ending width:_____

   Arc/Close/Halfwidth/Length/Undo/Width/⟨Endpoint of line⟩: _____

   Angle/CEnter/CLose/Directions/Halfwidth/Line/Radius/Second pt/Undo/Width/⟨Endpoint of arc⟩:

   _____

   Angle/Length/⟨⟩ _____

2. Give the command and entries required to turn three connected lines into a polyline:

   Command:_____

   Select polyline: _____

   Entity selected is not a polyline_____

   Do you want to turn it into one? ⟨Y⟩: __ _____

   Close/Join/Width/Edit vertex/Fit/Spline/Decurve/Ltype gen/Undo/eXit ⟨X⟩:

   Select objects:_____

   Select objects:_____

   2 segments added to polyline _____

   Close/Join/Width/Edit vertex/Fit/Spline/Decurve/Ltype gen/Undo/eXit ⟨X⟩: _____

3. Give the command and entries needed to change the width of a polyline from .1 to .25:

   Command:_____

   Select polyline: _____

   Close/Join/Width/Edit vertex/Fit/Spline/Decurve/Ltype gen/Undo/eXit ⟨X⟩: _____

   Enter new width for all segments: _____

   Close/Join/Width/Edit vertex/Fit/Spline/Decurve/Ltype gen/Undo/eXit ⟨X⟩: _____

For Questions 4 through 10, give the PEDIT Edit vertex option which relates to the definition given.

4. Moves the screen X to the next position. _____

5. Moves a polyline vertex to a new location. _____

6. Breaks a portion out of a polyline. _____

7. Required for AutoCAD to redraw the revised edition of a polyline. _____

8. Specifies tangent direction. _____

9. Adds a new polyline vertex._____

10. Returns you to the PEDIT menu. _____

11. Which PEDIT option and suboption allows you to change the starting and ending widths of a polyline?_____

12. Why does nothing appear to happen after you change the starting and ending widths of a polyline?_____

_____

13. How do you change the width of a doughnut?_____

14. Which command removes all width characteristics and tangency information from a polyline?

_____

15. What happens to the screen cursor after you select the PEDIT command?_____

_____

16. What occurs if you select Close for a polyline that is already closed? _____

_____

17. When you select the PEDIT command's Edit vertex option, where is the screen cursor X placed by AutoCAD?_____

18. How do you move the screen X to edit a different vertex? _____

_____

19. Can you use the PEDIT command's Fit option without using the Tangent option first?_____

_____

20. Explain the difference between a fit curve and spline curve._____

_____

_____

_____

21. Explain the relationship between the Quadratic curve, Cubic curve, and Fit options. _____

_____

_____

22. Discuss the construction of a quadratic curve._____

_____

_____

_____

23. What SPLINETYPE setting allows you to draw a quadratic curve?_____

24. What SPLINETYPE setting allows you to draw a cubic curve? _____

25. Name the system variable that adjusts the smoothness of a spline curve. _____

26. Name the pull-down menu where the Edit PolyLine options are found. _____

27. Explain how you can adjust the way polyline linetypes are generated in the PLINE command.

_____

_____

28. Name the system variable that also allows you to alter the way polyline linetypes are generated.

_____

29. Name the command used to create a polyline boundary._____

30. Name the command that may be used to create a true spline. _____

_____

31. How do you accept the AutoCAD defaults for the start and end tangencies of a Spline? _____

_____

32. Name the option that allows you to turn a spline fitted polyline into a true spline. _____

_____

33. Name the command that allows you to edit Splines. _____

_____

34. What is the purpose of the Add suboption in the Fit Data option? _____

_____

_____

35. What happens to the Spline if you use the Delete option and only two control points remain?

_____

36. Name the options that lets you move fit points in a Spline._____

37. What is the purpose of the Redefine option in the SPLINEDIT command? _____

_____

_____

_____

38. Identify the SPLINEDIT option that lets you increase the number of control points that appear
on a spline for greater control. _____

_____

39. Which option in the SPLINEDIT command controls the pull that a control point exerts on the
Spline? _____

_____

40. How many changes can you undo in the SPLINEDIT command when using the undo option?

_____

_____

DRAWING PROBLEMS

Start a new drawing for each of the following problems. Set up your own units, limits, and other variables to suit each problem.

1. Draw the polyline shown below. Use the Line, Arc, and Close options to complete the shape. The polyline width is 0, except where indicated. Save the drawing as A:P18-1.

P18-1

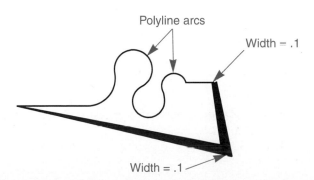

Polyline arcs

Width = .1

Width = .1

2. Draw the two curved arrows using the PLINE Arc and Width options. The arrowhead should have a starting width of 1.4 and ending width of 0. The arrow body should have a beginning width of .8 and ending width of .4. To draw the clockwise arrow, select the tanDir option of the PLINE Arc menu. Save the drawing as A:P18-2.

P18-2

3. The object of this problem is to change the object from Problem 18-1 into a rectangle. You will be using the PEDIT options Decurve, Straighten, Width, Insert, and Move. First, open P18-1, then make a copy of the object and edit them. Save the completed drawing as A:P18-3.

P18-3

4. Open P18-2 and make the following changes. Combine the two polylines using the Join option. Change the beginning width of the left arrow to 1.0 and the ending width to .2. Draw a polyline .062 wide similar to the one labeled as Line A. Save the drawing as A:P18-4.

P18-4

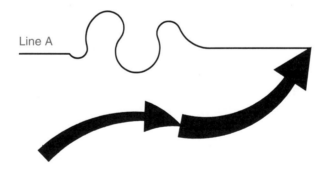

Line A

P18-5

5. Draw the object shown below, without dimensions, using the LINE command. Then change the object to a polyline, making the polyline .032 wide. Save the drawing as A:P18-5.

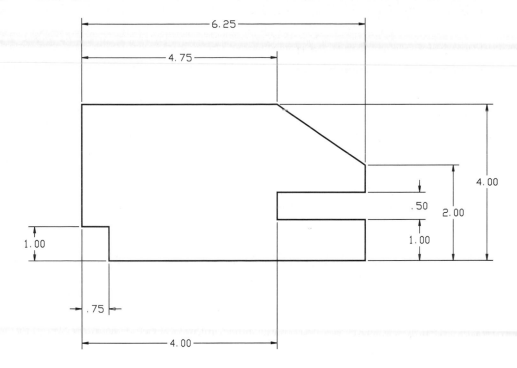

P18-6

6. Use the PLINE command to draw object A below. Then copy object A to a position directly below itself. Use the PEDIT command to edit the copy as shown at B. Save the drawing as A:P18-6.

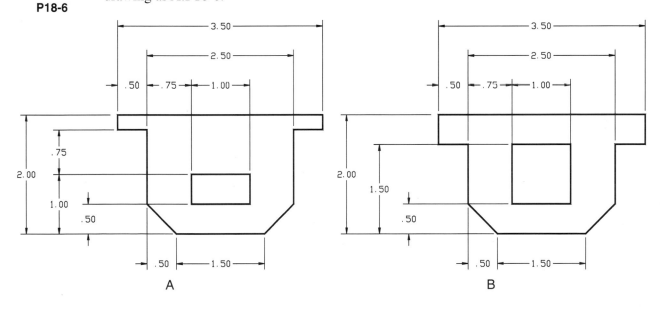

P18-7

7. Load AutoCAD and open drawing P18-1. Explode the polyline and observe the results. Restore the original polyline using the UNDO command. Save the drawing as A:P18-7 and quit.

P18-8

8. Draw a polyline .032 wide using the following absolute coordinates (bold text):

Point 1–**1,1**	Point 7–**4,4**
Point 2–**2,1**	Point 8–**5,4**
Point 3–**2,2**	Point 9–**5,5**
Point 4–**3,2**	Point 10–**6,5**
Point 5–**3,3**	Point 11–**6,6**
Point 6–**4,3**	Point 12–**7,6**

Copy the polyline three times. Use the PEDIT Fit option to smooth the first copy. Use the PEDIT Spline option to smooth the second copy. Use the PEDIT Quadratic curve option to smooth the third copy. Use the PEDIT Decurve option to return one polyline to its original form. Save the drawing as A:P18-8.

P18-9

9. Open drawing P13-14 for further editing. Change all of the object lines to .032 wide polylines. Then add centerlines. Save the revised version as A:P18-9.

P18-10

10. Draw a patio plan similar to the example shown at A below. Use the MLINE command to draw the house walls 6 in. wide. Copy the A drawing to the positions shown at B, C, D. Your client wants to see at least four different designs. Use the Fit option at B, Spline at C, and change SPLINETYPE to create a cubic curve at D. Save the drawing as A:P18-11.

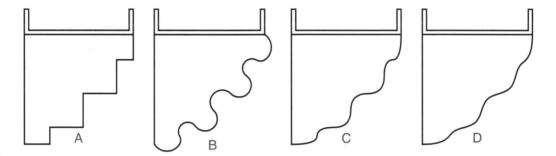

11. Open drawing P18-10 and make some new designs since your client is not satisfied with the first four proposals. This time, use the grips to edit the patio designs similar to the examples shown at A, B, C, and D below. Save the drawing as A:P18-11 and quit.

P18-11

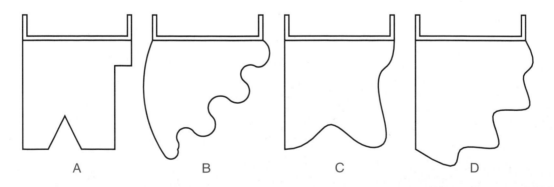

12. Use the SPLINE command to draw the curve for the cam displacement diagram below. Following the specifications given below the drawing.

P18-12

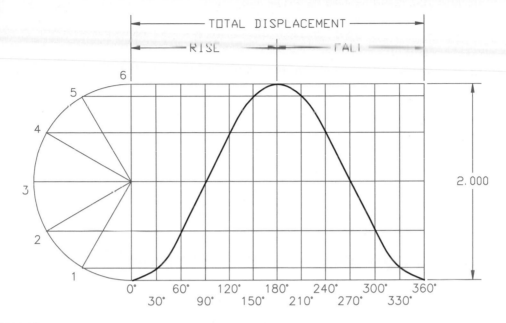

A. Total Rise = 2.000

B. Total Displacement may be any length.

C. Divide the Total Displacement into 30° increments.

D. Draw a half circle on one end divided into 6 equal parts.

E. Draw a horizontal line from each part of the half circle into the cam displacement diagram.

F. Draw the displacement curve with the SPLINE command by picking points where horizontal and vertical lines cross as shown in the given problem.

G. Label the degree increments along the horizontal scale as shown.

Save as A:P18-12.

13. Use the SPLINE command and other commands such as ELLIPSE, MIRROR, OFFSET, and PLINE to design an architectural door knocker similar to the one shown below. Use the Gothice text font to place your initials in the center. Save as A:P18-13.

P18-13

P18-14

14. Draw a spline similar to the original spline shown below. Copy the original spline to seven locations, similar to the layout shown below. Perform the SPLINEDIT operations as identified under each of the seven edited splines shown below. Save as A:P18-14.

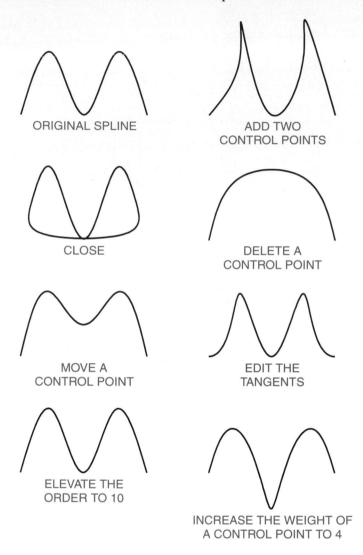

ORIGINAL SPLINE

ADD TWO
CONTROL POINTS

CLOSE

DELETE A
CONTROL POINT

MOVE A
CONTROL POINT

EDIT THE
TANGENTS

ELEVATE THE
ORDER TO 10

INCREASE THE WEIGHT OF
A CONTROL POINT TO 4

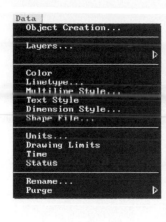
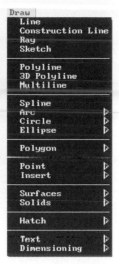

Chapter 19

MULTIVIEW DRAWINGS AND LAYERS

Learning objectives

After completing this chapter, you will be able to:
- ❍ Draw multiviews from given sketches.
- ❍ Properly draw object lines, hidden lines, and centerlines.
- ❍ Use the LINETYPE command to change linetypes.
- ❍ Change line color using the COLOR command.
- ❍ Use the LAYER command to draw items on separate layers.
- ❍ Identify guidelines for selecting the front view.
- ❍ Draw multiviews and associated auxiliary views from a given sketch.
- ❍ Use the dialog box to edit layers.
- ❍ Use standard borders and title block formats provided by AutoCAD.
- ❍ Customize the standard title block for your company or school.

Each field of drafting has its own method to present views of a product. Architectural drafting uses floor plans (and other plan views), exterior elevations, and sections. In electronics drafting, symbols are placed in a schematic diagram to show the circuit layout. In civil drafting, contour lines are used to show the topography of the land. This chapter describes views used in mechanical drafting, called *multiviews,* based on the standard ANSI Y14.3, *Multi and Sectional View Drawings.*

DRAWING MULTIVIEWS

Multiviews are made using orthographic projection. *Orthographic projection* is the projection of object features onto an imaginary plane, called a *projection plane.* The imaginary projection plane is placed parallel to the object. Thus, the line of sight is perpendicular to the object. This results in views that appear two dimensional, Figure 19-1.

Figure 19-1. How the front view is obtained by orthographic projection.

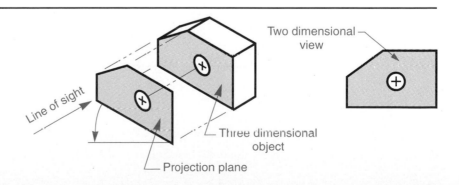

The term *multiview* refers to "many views." Six two-dimensional views completely show all sides of an object. The six views are the front, right side, left side, top, bottom, and rear. The views are placed in a standard arrangement so others can read the drawing. The front view is the central, or most important view. Other views are placed around it, Figure 19-2.

Views are aligned, rather than scattered about the drawing. It is easy to visualize the shape by looking from one view to the next. Chapters 20, 21, and 22 cover how this layout helps you read dimensions.

Figure 19-2.   Arrangement of the six orthographic views.

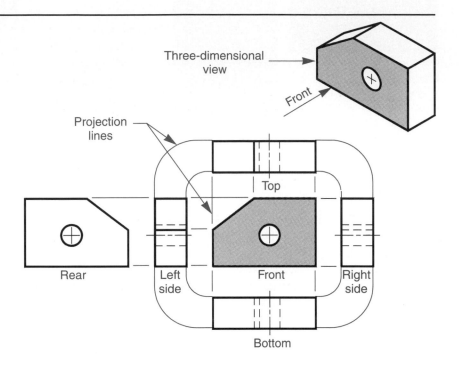

Six views are not always necessary. Actually, there are few products that require all six views. The number of views needed depends on the complexity of the object. Use only enough views to completely describe the object. Drawing too many views is time-consuming, and can clutter the drawing. In some cases, a single view may be enough to describe the object. The object shown in Figure 19-3 needs only two views. These two views completely describe the width, height, depth, and features of the object.

Figure 19-3.   The views you choose to describe the object should show all height, width, and depth dimensions.

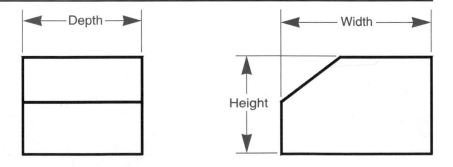

Selecting the front view

The front view is usually the most important view. The following guidelines should be considered when selecting the front view:

- Look for the best shape or most contours.
- Show the most natural position of use.
- Display the most stable position.
- Provide the longest dimension.
- Contain the least hidden features.

Look at Figure 19-4 and review the above guidelines. Do you agree with the front view chosen?

Additional views are selected relative to the front view. Choose only the number of views needed to completely describe the object's features.

Figure 19-4.   The front view should contain the most details whenever possible.

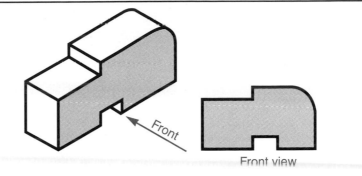

Showing hidden features in multiview drawings

Hidden features are those parts of the object not visible in the view you see. A visible edge appears as a solid line when the view is drawn. A hidden edge is shown by a hidden line. Hidden lines were discussed in Chapter 6. Notice in Figure 19-5 how hidden features are shown as hidden lines.

Figure 19-5.   Drawing hidden features.

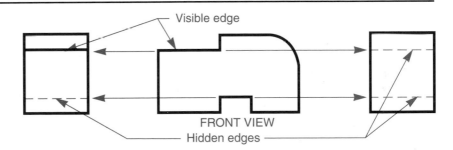

One-view drawings

In some instances, an object can be fully described using one view. A thin part, such as a gasket, is drawn with one view, Figure 19-6. The thickness is given as a note in the drawing or in the title block. A cylindrical object also may be drawn with one view. The diameter dimension is given to tell that the object is round.

Figure 19-6.   A one-view
drawing of a gasket. The
thickness is given in a note.

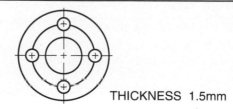

THICKNESS 1.5mm

Showing symmetry and circle centers

The centerlines of symmetrical objects and the centers of circles are shown using centerlines. For example, in one view of a cylinder, the axis is drawn as a centerline. In the other view, centerlines cross to show the center in the circular view. See Figure 19-7. The only place that the small centerline dashes should cross is at the center of a circle.

Figure 19-7.   Drawing
centerlines. A–For a cylinder.
B–For a round hole.

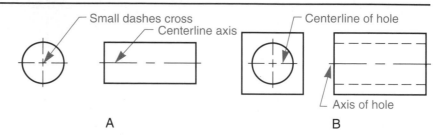

A   B

DRAWING AUXILIARY VIEWS

In most cases, an object is completely described using a combination of one or more of the six standard views. However, sometimes the multiview layout is not enough to properly identify some object surfaces. It may then be necessary to draw auxiliary views.

Auxiliary views are typically needed when a surface on the object is at an angle to the line of sight. These slanted surfaces are *foreshortened,* meaning they are shorter than the true size and shape of the surface. To show this surface in true size, an auxiliary view is needed. The reason that auxiliary views are needed is that dimensions should be placed in views showing a feature's true size and shape. Foreshortened dimensions are not recommended.

Auxiliary views are drawn by projecting perpendicular (90°) to a slanted surface. Usually, one projection line remains on the drawing. It connects the auxiliary view to the view where the slanted surface appears as a line. The resulting auxiliary view shows the surface in true size and shape. For most applications, the auxiliary view need only show the slanted surface, not the entire object. This is called a partial auxiliary view and is shown in Figure 19-8.

In many situations, there may not be enough room on the drawing to project directly from the slanted surface. Then, the auxiliary view is placed elsewhere, Figure 19-9. A viewing-plane line is drawn next to the view where the slanted surface appears as a line. The viewing-plane line is capped on the ends with arrowheads. The arrowheads point toward the slanted surface. Each end is labeled with a letter such as A. The letters relate the viewing-plane line with the proper auxiliary view. A title such as "VIEW A-A" is placed under the auxiliary view. When more than one auxiliary view is drawn, labels continue with B-B through Z-Z (if necessary). The letters I, O, and Q are not used because they may be confused with numbers. An auxiliary view drawn away from the multiview retains the same angle as if it were projected directly.

Figure 19-8.   Auxiliary views show the true size and shape of an inclined surface.

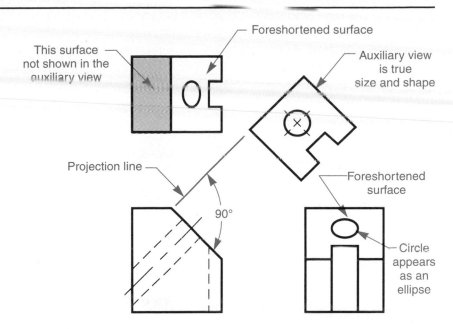

Figure 10 0.   Identifying an auxiliary view with a viewing-plane line. If there is not enough room, the view can be moved to a different location.

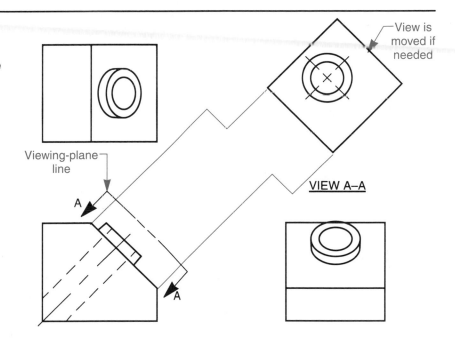

Changing the snap grid rotation angle

Changing the rotation angle of your snap grid, discussed in Chapter 4, is especially useful for drawing auxiliary views. After the views have been drawn, enter the SNAP command. Then pick the base point for rotation on the line which represents the slanted surface. Then enter the snap rotation angle equal to the angle of the slanted surface. If you do not know the angle, pick points on the slanted surface to graphically show the angle. The steps are as follows:

Command: **SNAP** ↵
Snap spacing or ON/OFF/Aspect/Rotate/Style ⟨*current*⟩: **R** ↵
Base point ⟨0,0⟩: *(pick an endpoint on the line which represents the slanted surface)*
Rotation angle ⟨0⟩: *(enter the angle of the slanted surface or pick two points on the surface)*
Command:

Once you have placed and rotated the snap grid, you may want to place grid points on the snap grid. Select the GRID command's Snap option. Then complete the auxiliary view, as shown in Figure 19-10A. When you finish drawing the auxiliary view, return the snap grid rotation value to 0°.

Figure 19-10.   A–Using the rotated snap grid and grid points to help draw the auxiliary view. B–Rotating the Z axis of the UCS system. Notice how the position of the UCS icon has been aligned with the auxiliary view angle. C–Moving the UCS icon display to the current UCS origin at the corner of the auxiliary view.

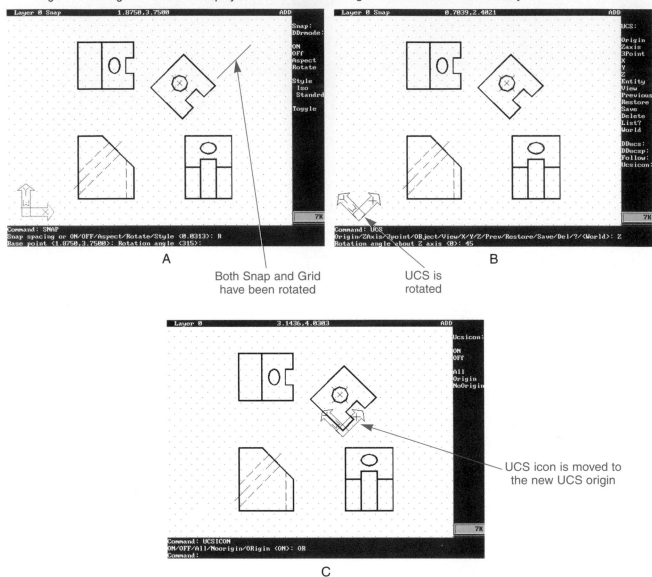

Using the User Coordinate System for auxiliary views

All of the features on your drawing originate from the *World Coordinate System (WCS)*, which is the X, Y, and Z coordinate values measured from the origin 0,0,0. The WCS is fixed. The *User Coordinate System (UCS)*, on the other hand, can be moved to any desired orientation. The UCS is discussed in detail in ***AutoCAD and its Applications–Advanced, R13 for DOS.*** In general, UCS allows you to set your own coordinate origin. The WCS 0,0,0 origin has been in the lower-left corner of the screen for the drawings you have done so far. In many cases this is fine, but when drawing an auxiliary view it is best to have the measurements originate from a corner of the view. This in turn makes all auxiliary view features and the coordinate display true as measured from the corner of the view. This method makes it easier to locate and later dimension the auxiliary view features as compared with the rotated snap grid previously discussed.

First, draw the principal views such as the front, top, and right side. Then, move the UCS origin to a location that coincides with a corner of the auxiliary view using this command sequence:

Command: **UCS** ↵
Origin/ZAxis/3point/Object/View/X/Y/Z/Prev/Restore/Save/Del/?/⟨World⟩: **0** ↵
Origin point ⟨0,0,0⟩: *(pick the origin point at the desired corner of the auxiliary view)*

Next, realign the UCS grid with the angle of the auxiliary view by adjusting the Z axis to the same angle, Figure 19-10B. For example, if the auxiliary view is projected at 45° from the slanted surface in the front view, then rotate the Z axis as follows:

Command: **UCS** ↵
Origin/ZAxis/3point/Object/View/X/Y/Z/Prev/Restore/Save/Del/?/⟨World⟩: **Z** ↵
Rotation angle about Z axis ⟨0⟩: **45** ↵

If you want the UCS icon displayed at the current UCS origin, use the UCSICON command as follows:

Command: **UCSICON** ↵
ON/OFF/ALL/Noorigin/ORigin/ ⟨ON⟩: **OR** ↵

This automatically moves the UCS icon to the revised UCS origin at the corner of the auxiliary view, as shown in Figure 19-10C. Although this is not required, it is convenient to see the location of the UCS origin. Before you begin drawing the auxiliary view, use the UCS command's Save option to name the new UCS and save it:

Command: **UCS** ↵
Origin/ZAxis/3point/Object/View/X/Y/Z/Prev/Restore/Save/Del/?/⟨World⟩: **S** ↵
?/Desired UCS name: **AUX** ↵

Now, proceed by drawing the auxiliary view. When you have finished drawing the auxiliary view, use the UCS command's Previous option to move the UCS icon to its previous position:

Command: **UCS** ↵
Origin/ZAxis/3point/Object/View/X/Y/Z/Prev/Restore/Save/Del/?/⟨World⟩: **P** ↵

You could also press ENTER to accept the World default and send the UCS icon display back to the WCS origin:

Command: **UCS** ↵
Origin/ZAxis/3point/Object/View/X/Y/Z/Prev/Restore/Save/Del/?/⟨World⟩: ↵

PROFESSIONAL TIP

Use the orthogonal mode (ORTHO command) to help align the projected auxiliary view with the slanted surface. Also consider using the object snap modes to assist you in connecting projection lines to the exact corners or features on the slanted surface.

DRAWING CONSTRUCTION LINES AND PROJECTING BETWEEN VIEWS

AUG 3

Construction lines in drafting terminology are lines that are used for layout purposes. They are not part of the drawing, and in manual drafting, they are either drawn very lightly or they are removed so they do not reproduce. AutoCAD has lines that may be used for such purposes. These are called *construction lines* and *rays*. These lines may be used in AutoCAD for the same purposes as in manual drafting. For example, you can use them to project features between views for accurate placement, for geometric constructions, or to coordinate imaginary places for object snap selections. The AutoCAD command that lets you draw construction lines is XLINE while rays are drawn with the RAY command. While both commands can be used for similar purposes, the XLINE command has more options and flexibility than the RAY command.

The XLINE command may be accessed by picking Construction line in the Draw pull-down menu, Xline: in the DRAW 1 screen menu, or by typing. The RAY command is found in the same menus.

Using the XLINE command

The XLINE command creates XLINE objects. The XLINE object is an infinite length line designed for use as a construction line. Although these lines are infinite, they do not change the total drawing area. They have no effect on zooming operations. They can be modified by moving, copying, trimming, and other editing operations. Editing changes such as TRIM or FILLET change the object type. For example, if one end of a construction line is trimmed off, the XLINE becomes a RAY object. A RAY is considered semi-infinite since it is infinite in one direction only as you will see later. If the infinite part of a ray is trimmed off, it becomes a LINE object.

Construction lines and rays print and plot the same as any other objects. Construction lines and rays are drawn on the current layer. This may cause conflict with the other lines on that layer. A good way to handle this problem is to set up a layer just for construction lines. Perhaps call it CONST and use a color such as blue. This is discussed in detail later in this chapter with the LAYER command. The XLINE command sequence is as follows:

Command: **XLINE** ⏎
Hor/Ver/Ang/Bisect/Offset/⟨From point⟩:

The XLINE command has several options that are described as follows:
- **⟨From point⟩.** The XLINE default option is ⟨From point⟩. This allows you to specify two points that the construction line passes through. After you pick the first point, you get a Through point: prompt. You can pick two points through which the first construction line is drawn, then draw another construction line by picking another second point. The first point of an Xline is called the *Root point.* Use the object snap options to help you accurately pick points:

    Command: **XLINE** ⏎
    Hor/Ver/Ang/Bisect/Offset/⟨From point⟩: *(pick a point)*
    Through point: *(pick a second point)*
    Through point: *(pick another second point)*
    Through point: *(draw more construction lines or press* ENTER*)*
    Command:

Figure 19-11 shows how construction lines can be used to help project features between views.
- **Hor.** This option draws a horizontal construction line through a specified point. It serves the same purpose as the default option, but it is automatically drawn horizontally and you only have to pick one point through which the construction line is drawn:

    Command: **XLINE** ⏎
    Hor/Ver/Ang/Bisect/Offset/⟨From point⟩: **H** ⏎
    Through point: *(pick a point)*
    Through point: ⏎
    Command:

- **Ver.** This option draws a vertical construction line through a specified point:

    Command: **XLINE** ⏎
    Hor/Ver/Ang/Bisect/Offset/⟨From point⟩: **V** ⏎
    Through point: *(pick a point)*
    Through point: ⏎
    Command:

Figure 19-11. Using the XLINE command default option.

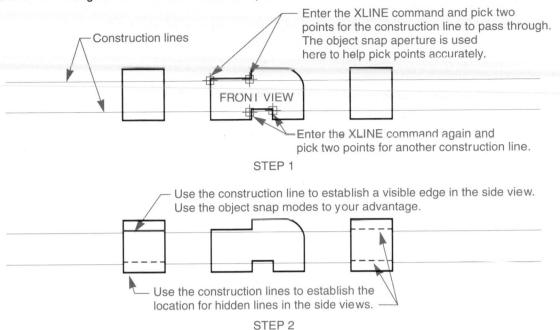

Construction lines

Enter the XLINE command and pick two
points for the construction line to pass through.
The object snap aperture is used
here to help pick points accurately.

FRONT VIEW

Enter the XLINE command again and
pick two points for another construction line.

STEP 1

Use the construction line to establish a visible edge in the side view.
Use the object snap modes to your advantage.

Use the construction lines to establish the
location for hidden lines in the side views.

STEP 2

EXERCISE 19-1

❑ Load AutoCAD and open TITLEB from Problem 11-1.
❑ Draw four views of the object shown below. Do not draw dimensions.

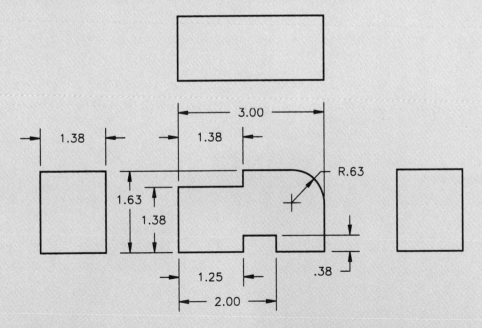

3.00

1.38

1.38

R.63

1.63

1.38

1.25

.38

2.00

❑ The top and side views are currently incomplete. Use construction lines to help you complete all
views by adding the missing lines. You were introduced to the LINETYPE command in Chapter
6. You may need to review before drawing the hidden lines.
❑ Save the drawing as A:EX19-1 and quit.

• **Ang.** This option draws a construction line at a specified angle through a specified point. The default lets you specify an angle and then pick a point for a construction line to be drawn at that angle. This works well if you know the angle that you want the construction line to be drawn:

Command: **XLINE** ⏎
Hor/Vor/Ang/Bisect/Offset/⟨From point⟩: **A** ⏎
Reference/⟨Enter angle (0.00)⟩: *(enter an angle such as* **45***)*
Through point: *(pick a point)*
Through point: ⏎
Command:

A specific reference angle from the angle of an existing line object may also be specified by using the Reference suboption. This may be used when you do not know the angle of the construction line, but you do know the desired angle between an existing object and the construction line:

Command: **XLINE** ⏎
Hor/Ver/Ang/Bisect/Offset/⟨From point⟩: **A** ⏎
Reference/⟨Enter angle (0.00)⟩: **R** ⏎
Select a line object: *(pick the line you want the construction line drawn from)*
Enter angle ⟨0.00⟩: **90** ⏎
Through point: *(pick a point)*
Through point: ⏎
Command:

Figure 19-12 shows the Ang option being used to draw construction lines to establish the location of an auxiliary view.

Figure 19-12.   Using the
XLINE command Ang option.

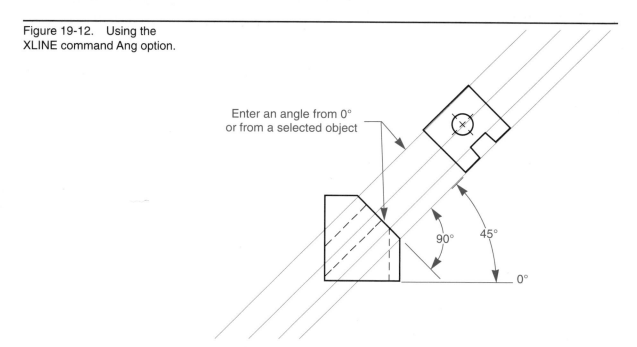

Enter an angle from 0°
or from a selected object

90°

45°

0°

EXERCISE 19-2

❏ Load AutoCAD and open TITLEB from Problem 11-1.
❏ Draw the front and auxiliary view of the object shown below. Do not draw dimensions or the top view. The top view is given to help you visualize the object.

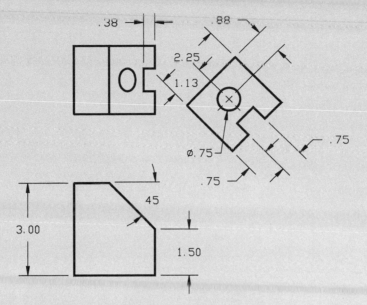

❏ The front view is currently incomplete. Use construction lines to help you complete the views by adding the missing lines.
❏ Save the drawing as A:EX19-2 and quit.

- **Bisect.** This option draws a construction line that bisects a specified angle. This is a convenient tool for use in some geometric constructions, as shown in Figure 19-13:

  ```
  Command: XLINE ↵
  Hor/Ver/Ang/Bisect/Offset/⟨From point⟩: B ↵
  Angle vertex point: (pick the vertex)
  Angle start point: (pick a point on a side of the angle)
  Angle end point: (pick a point on the other side of the angle)
  Angle end point: ↵
  Command:
  ```

Figure 19-13.   Using the XLINE command Bisect option.

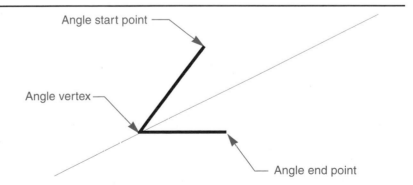

- **Offset.** This XLINE option draws a construction line a specified distance (offset) from a selected line object. It works just like the OFFSET command that you learned about in Chapter 9.

You have the option of specifying an offset distance or use the Through suboption to pick a point for the construction line to be drawn through:

Command: **XLINE** ↵
Hor/Ver/Ang/Bisect/Offset/⟨From point⟩: **O** ↵
Offset distance or Through ⟨0⟩: *(enter a distance such as* **.75**)
Select a line object: *(pick the object that you want to offset from)*
Side to offset? *(pick any point on the side you want the construction line drawn)*
Select a line object: ↵
Command:

The Through suboption works like this:

Command: **XLINE** ↵
Hor/Ver/Ang/Bisect/Offset/⟨From point⟩: **O** ↵
Offset distance or Through ⟨0⟩: **T** ↵
Select a line object: *(pick the object that you want to offset from)*
Through point: *(pick the specific point on the side you want the construction line drawn)*
Select a line object: ↵
Command:

EXERCISE 19-3

❑ Load AutoCAD and set the limits at 0,0 and 8.5,11.
❑ Draw the angle shown below using the given absolute coordinates.
❑ Use the XLINE command to bisect the angle. Also, draw a construction line parallel to the outer side of each leg of the angle at a distance of .525.

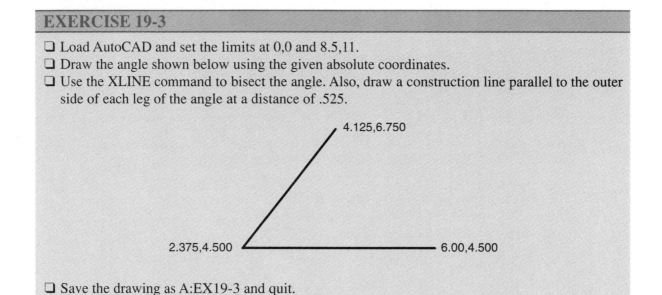

❑ Save the drawing as A:EX19-3 and quit.

Using the RAY command

The RAY command is limited when compared to the XLINE command. The RAY command allows you to specify the point of origin and a point the ray passes through. In this manner, the RAY command works much like the default option of the XLINE command, except that the ray only extends out beyond the second pick point. The XLINE command results in a construction line that extends both ways from the pick points. The RAY command works like this:

Command: **RAY** ↵
From point: *(pick a point)*
Through point: *(pick a second point)*
Through point: *(pick another second point)*
Through point: *(draw more construction lines or press* ENTER*)*
Command:

Both the RAY command and the XLINE command allow the creation of multiple objects, until you press ENTER to end the command. They do not allow you to undo a construction line that you previously drew while inside of the command.

MODIFYING THE XLINE   AUG 6

Earlier you used the DDMODIFY command to edit the properties of existing objects such as lines, circles, and text. You can also use this command to modify Xlines and Rays. When you enter the DDMODIFY command and select an Xline, you get the "Modify Xline" dialog box shown in Figure 19-14. You can use the dialog box to edit the color, layer, and linetype. You can also change the Root Point, the Second Point, and the Direction Vector. The Direction Vector is the coordinate values from the start point to the end point. If you pick a Ray while in the DDMODIFY command, you get the "Modify Ray" dialog box that has the same options as the "Modify Xline" dialog box.

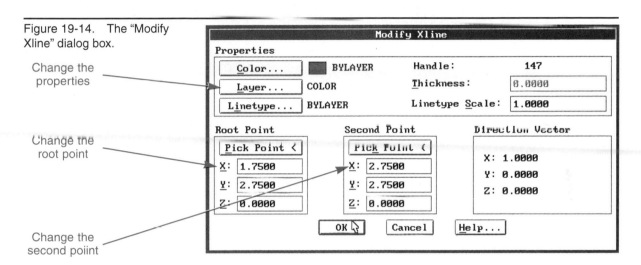

Figure 19-14.   The "Modify Xline" dialog box.

Change the properties

Change the root point

Change the second poiint

EDITING CONSTRUCTION LINES AND RAYS   AUG 5

The construction lines that you create using the XLINE and RAY commands may be edited using the TRIM command. XLINES and RAYS are infinite length lines. In many cases, their layer is turned off or frozen when they are no longer needed. However, you may prefer to trim them to specific lengths in some applications.

USING THE LINETYPE COMMAND   AUG 6

The lines that you have drawn so far have been solid. AutoCAD calls these lines "continuous." Continuous lines may be drawn thin using the LINE, ARC, and CIRCLE commands, or drawn thick with the TRACE or PLINE commands. Any entity is drawn with continuous lines unless you change the linetype. The LINETYPE command is found in the DATA screen menu and the Data pull-down menu. When you enter LINETYPE at the Command: prompt, a group of options appears. One option is a question mark (?). Typing ? accesses the "Select Linetype File" dialog box. ACAD should be the filename. Press ENTER for the list of AutoCAD's (ACAD) standard library of lines shown in Figure 19-15.

Command: **LINETYPE** ↵
?/Create/Load/Set: **?** ↵

Figure 19-15.   AutoCAD's
standard linetype library.

Name	Description
BORDER	
BORDER2	
BORDERX2	
CENTER	
CENTER2	
CENTERX2	
DASHDOT	
DASHDOT2	
DASHDOTX2	
DASHED	
DASHED2	
DASHEDX2	
DIVIDE	
DIVIDE2	
DIVIDEX2	
DOT	
DOT2	
DOTX2	
HIDDEN	
HIDDEN2	
HIDDENX2	
PHANTOM	
PHANTOM2	
PHANTOMX2	
ACAD_ISO02W100	
ACAD_ISO03W100	
ACAD_ISO04W100	
ACAD_ISO05W100	
ACAD_ISO06W100	
ACAD_ISO07W100	
ACAD_ISO08W100	
ACAD_ISO09W100	
ACAD_ISO10W100	
ACAD_ISO11W100	
ACAD_ISO12W100	
ACAD_ISO13W100	
ACAD_ISO14W100	
ACAD_ISO15W100	

Enter the LINETYPE command again and type ?. This time notice the LTYPESHP file name in the "Select Linetype File" dialog box. This is a group of symbol linetypes. Pick LTYPESHP to highlight it and then press ENTER to see the text screen displaying the symbol linetypes shown in Figure 19-16. If the FILEDIA system variable is off (0), the following prompt is displayed:

File to list ⟨ACAD⟩: ↵

If a custom linetype library such as MAPLINES has been designed, you may specify it by typing MAPLINES in the File: edit box, or pick it from the Files: list. The only linetypes available for your use at this point is the ACAD and LTYPESHP libraries. After listing the linetypes, AutoCAD returns the "?/Create/Load/Set:" prompt. Press F1 to return to the graphics screen.

Figure 19-16   LTYPESHP examples from \acadr13\common\support\ltypeshp.lin.

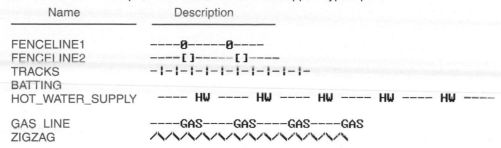

Setting the linetype

When drawing views of an object, you may need to draw hidden lines and centerlines. Select the linetype using the LINETYPE command's Set option. Type S at the prompt. You are then asked to name the linetype:

Command: **LINETYPE** ↵
?/Create/Load/Set: **S** ↵
New object linetype (or ?) ⟨BYLAYER⟩: **HIDDEN** ↵
?/Create/Load/Set:

The ?/Create/Load/Set: prompt returns; press ENTER to get the Command: prompt. Now, any lines you add are drawn with the linetype you just set. You must again use the Set option to draw continuous lines or set another linetype.

Loading custom linetypes

Many companies have custom linetypes. For example, cartographers may need special styles of lines to draw maps. These linetypes are usually stored in library files other than the ACAD library. To use one of these linetypes, type a question mark (?) to obtain a list of linetypes. Then, return to the prompt and type L for Load and press ENTER. Follow these steps:

Command: **LINETYPE** ↵
?/Create/Load/Set: ↵
?/Create/Load/Set: **L** ↵
Linetype(s) to load: *(enter the linetype name)*

If FILEDIA is set to one (1), the "Select Linetype File" dialog box is displayed. For example, if your company or school had previously installed a custom linetype library named MAPLINES, then this file name would be listed for your use. Pick MAPLINES from the F<u>i</u>les: list, or type it in the <u>F</u>ile: edit box. If the FILEDIA variable is 0, the following prompt appears:

Linetype(s) to load: **?** ↵
File to search: ↵

Now, suppose you want to use the PROPERTY linetype found in the MAPLINES linetype library. Enter PROPERTY as the name of the linetype to load and MAPLINES as the file to search.

If you try to load a linetype that is already loaded, such as the standard AutoCAD HIDDEN line-type, you get this message:

Linetype HIDDEN is already loaded. Reload it? ⟨Y⟩ ↵

Press ENTER to reload the linetype, or type N and press ENTER if you decide not to reload it.

Creating linetypes

To create custom linetypes or modify AutoCAD standard linetypes, use the Create option.

Command: **LINETYPE** ⏎
?/Create/Load/Set: **C** ⏎

After selecting C, AutoCAD requests the name of the linetype to create. It also must know the file for storing the linetype. Select a linetype name which represents the line's features. For example, suppose you are designing a line having long lines which alternate between three short dashes. This linetype might be for drawing property boundaries in mapping. Call the line D3D. You can store the linetype in the ACAD default file by pressing ENTER as follows:

Name of linetype to create: **D3D** ⏎

The "Create or Append Linetype File" dialog box appears. Pick and highlight ACAD and press ENTER.

Wait, checking if linetype already defined…
Descriptive text:

If the FILEDIA system variable is set to 0, the "Select Linetype File" dialog box does not appear and you get this prompt:

Name of linetype to create: **D3D** ⏎
File for storage of linetype ⟨C:\ACADR13\COMMON\SUPPORT\ACAD.LIN⟩: ⏎

AutoCAD first checks to see if the linetype already exists. Then you are asked for "Descriptive text." As the name implies, *descriptive text* describes the new linetype. The text should be in the format *LINETYPE-NAME ,DESCRIPTION and should be no longer than 47 characters long. The D3D linetype being created here might be described as follows:

Descriptive text: ***D3D ,LONG AND 3 SHORT DASHES** ⏎

The Enter pattern: prompt then appears. Describe the line based on the following code:

<u>**CODE**</u>

A,	=	alignment. This instructs AutoCAD to balance out the line ends with equal beginning length segments. The "A," always begins the set of pattern code.
–numeral	=	length of a space.
+numeral	=	length of a dash.
0	=	dot.

Suppose the D3D linetype is designed to be drawn as:

<u>LINE SEGMENT</u>	<u>LENGTH</u>	<u>CODE</u>
Long dash	= 1.5 units	= 1.5
Space	= .062 units	= –.062
Short dash	= .125 units	= .125
Space	= .062 units	= –.062
Short dash	= .125 units	= .125
Space	= .062 units	= –.062
Short dash	= .125 units	= .125
Space	= .062 units	= –.062

The linetype pattern is given as follows:

Enter pattern (on text line):
A,1.5,–.062,.125,–.062,.125,–.062,.125,–.062 ⏎

AutoCAD then responds with:

New definition written to file.
?/Create/Load/Set: **S** ⏎

You can begin using the new linetype by responding S to the previous prompt. When asked for the name of the new linetype, enter D3D. The new linetype, D3D is set to be used, as shown in Figure 19-17.

Figure 19-17.   The new D3D linetype.

Creating Complex Linetypes

You can create your own custom complex linetypes that use dashes, dots and spaces like simple linetypes, but you can also add shapes or text. The complex linetypes are used and managed the same as simple linetypes in every aspect except creation. Even in creation, the dash/dot definition is the same. However, additional options are available for defining symbols and parameters to be used in the complex linetype. Creating a complex linetype can be done either at the command line or using a text editor; the same as simple linetypes. Pen down and pen up lengths are defined as usual, with positive and negative numeric values. The symbols to use can be drawn from either SHX shape files or .SHX font files.

Introduction to creating custom shape linetypes

Shape files are similar to fonts in the means of description, and they have the same SHX file extension. The actual creation of SHX files is beyond the scope of this discussion, but AutoCAD Release 13 comes with the following sample shape files:

Common Linetype symbol shapes
File:C:\ACADR13\COMMON\SUPPORT\LTYPESHP.SHX

TRACK1	ZIG
BOX	CIRC1
BAT	

Electronics symbol shapes
File:C:\ACADR13\COMMON\SAMPLE\ES.SHX

CON1	ZENER	RES	OR
CAP	NOR	DIODE	XOR
PNP	AND	NPN	NAND
MARK	BUFFER	ARROW	INVERTER
JUMP	BOX	CON2	NBG

Other shape files include:

Printed circuit symbol shapes
File:C:\ACADR13\COMMON\SAMPLE\PC.SHX
Surface finish symbol shapes
File:C:\ACADR13\COMMON\SAMPLE\ST.SHX

To access shapes within a shape file, the shape file must first be loaded using the LOAD command. The LOAD command activates the "Select Shape File" dialog box if FILEDIA is set to 1. Otherwise the following command line sequence is used when the file is on the ACAD path:

```
Command: LOAD ↵
Name of shape file to load (or ?): LTYPESHP ↵
Command:
```

Do this in the "Select Shape File" dialog box by accessing the Directory: C:\ACADR13\COMMON\SUPPORT and then pick the LTYPESHP file or enter the file name in the File: edit box and pick OK. Any valid shape file may be specified. However, a font file also has the SHX file extension, but cannot be loaded. An error message is issued if you try to load a font file.

Now, the SHAPE command can be used to list the available shapes or to insert a shape. The listings shown previously for LTYPESHP.SHX and ES.SHX are displayed when the ? option, of the SHAPE command, is used after these files have been loaded.

After loading shape files, you are ready to proceed with creating a complex linetype using a shape definition. Only simple linetypes can be created at the AutoCAD command line, complex shapes must be created by entering them directly into the LIN file using a text editor.

Syntax for a Shape

Syntax means, the way words are put together. The syntax for a shape file is as follows:
[shapename,shxfilename]
or
[shapename,shxfilename, transform]

The *shapename* field should correspond to the name of a shape existing in the specified SHX file. The *transform* field refers to a series of optional modifiers for the shape where *n* = any number as follows:

R = *n*   Relative rotation angle (Angles default to degrees)
or
A = *n*   Absolute rotation angle use degrees, radians, or grads
S = *n*   Scale factor
X = *n*   X axis offset
Y = *n*   Y axis offset

The X and Y axis offsets are adjustments from the default insertion points. Angle specifications are numerical values as specified; however, S, X, and Y are in linetype scaled drawing units and are calculated with this formula n X LTSCALE = value.

These transform parameters can be used in any series with the n above indicating a signed (+ or –) decimal number such as 1, 0.125, or –3. The values are based on any desired size, rotation, and offset of shape or text. Some or all may be used in any order. An example of a shape and a transform specification is as follows:

[CAP,es.shx,S=2,R=10,X=0.5]

The elements of the shape transform specification mean this:
- **CAP.** shape name
- **es.shx.** shape file name
- **S = 2.** scale factor of 2
- **R = 10.** rotation angle of 10°
- **X = 0.5.** X axis offset is 0.5

To use this in a linetype definition, place the specification as you would a dash or dot description:

A,.25,–.125,[CAP,es.shx,S=2,R=10,X=0.5],–.125

A shape or text may not be the first specification in the linetype description, but square brackets, [ ], must enclose the shape specification. You need to use a text editor to enter the new linetype file. For example, enter a new file named MYLTYPE.LIN. The complete sequence used to create, load, and set the complex linetype shown in Figure 19-18 is as follows:

*CIR-SQ, Dashed line with alternating circles and squares
A,1.25,–.5,[CIRC1,ltypeshp.shx,S=.1,X=–.125]"–.5,1.25,–
    5,[BOX,ltypeshp.shx,S=.I,X=–.125],–.5

Figure 19-18.   A new linetype created with the command sequence in the text.

The following gives a brief description of each element in the above statement:
- ***.** All linetype names must be preceded with an asterisk.
- **CIR-SQ.** Linetype name followed by short descriptive text.
- **A.** Linetype is aligned, meaning that start and end dashes are equalized.
- **.125, .5.** Pen down and pen up are the same as simple linetype.
- **CIRC1.** Name of shape.
- **BOX.** Name of shape.
- **ltypeshp.shx.** Name of SHX file where shape is defined.
- **S.** Scale factor to modify size of shape.
- **X.** Offset value to help center or orient shape between dashes. X axis is considered to be the direction of the line, Y axis is the direction plus 90°.

Finally, save the file and exit the text editor, and return to AutoCAD. The linetype definition is now contained in the file named MYLTYPE.LIN. To load and set the new linetype, use the LINETYPE command:

```
Command: LINETYPE ↵
?/Create/Load/Set: L ↵
Linetype(s) to load: CIR-SQ ↵
?/Create/Load/Set: S ↵
New object linetype (or ?) ⟨BYLAYER⟩: CIR-SQ ↵
?/Create/Load/Set: ↵
Command:
```

Now, use any of the AutoCAD commands, such as LINE, PLINE, CIRCLE or ARC, to draw objects with the new linetype. See Figure 19-18.

Introduction to creating a custom text linetype

Creating a linetype that uses text is much the same as creating a shape linetype. The primary difference is that the specification is for text and font files, instead of shapes and shape files. The font linetype is still complex and must be entered directly into the .LIN file with a text editor. All other steps in the process are the same, except for the actual linetype specification entered into the .LIN file.

The syntax for a text linetype is as follows:

```
["string",stylename]
or
["string",stylename,transform]
```

The "string" field refers to any text to appear in the linetype placed within quote marks. The stylename can be specified or left out. If the stylename is left out, the default text style in the current drawing is used. The effects of the transform parameters are the same as for shapes. A sample font linetype specification is as follows, and the result is shown in Figure 19-19:

```
*TEXT, Sample linetype with text
A,1.25,−.25,["TEXT",romans,S=.1,X=−.18],−.25
```

Figure 19-19.   A sample linetype with text.

The following gives a brief description of each element in the above statement:
- ***.** All linetype names must be preceded with an asterisk.
- **TEXT.** Linetype name followed by short descriptive text.
- **A.** Linetype is aligned, meaning that start and end dashes are equalized.
- **.125,−.25.** Pen down and pen up are the same as simple linetype.
- **TEXT.** Text characters in quotation marks.

- **romans.** Text style name.
- **S.** Scale factor to modify size of shape.
- **X.** Offset value to help center or orient shape between dashes. X axis is considered to be the direction of the line, Y axis is the direction plus 90°.

Finally, save the file and exit the text editor, and return to AutoCAD. The linetype definition is now contained in the file named TEXT.LIN. To load and set the new linetype, use the LINETYPE command as previously explained.

SETTING LINETYPE USING THE PULL-DOWN MENU

The Object Creation Modes… selection in the Data pull-down menu accesses the "Object Creation Modes" dialog box shown in Figure 19-20. Pick the Linetype… button to access the "Select Linetype" subdialog box.

Figure 19-20. The "Object Creation Modes" dialog box.

Select for the "Select Linetype" subdialog box

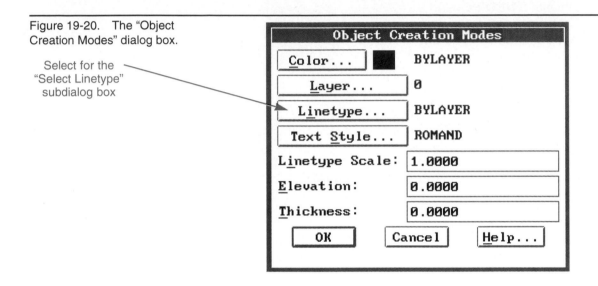

The AutoCAD linetypes that have been loaded are shown in the "Select Linetype" subdialog box, Figure 19-21. Use the scroll bar if you want to see more linetypes. If you want to set the HIDDEN linetype as current, pick it from the list and then pick the OK button. If HIDDEN is not showing, then it will need to be loaded.

Figure 19-21. The "Select Linetype" subdialog box displays linetypes that have been loaded.

Select a linetype to make current

Select for the "Load or Reload Linetypes" subdialog box

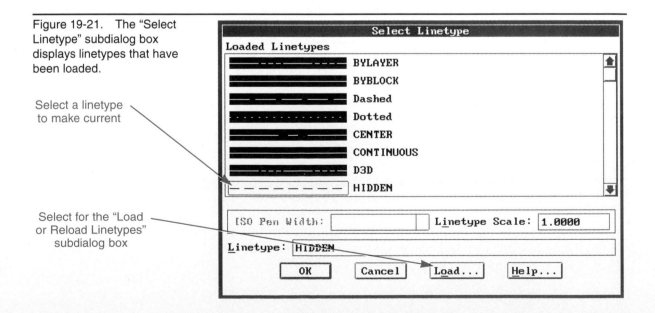

The "Select Linetypes" dialog box also offers an option to load linetypes. It is not necessary to use the LINETYPE command if you load linetypes here. To load linetypes, pick the Load... button to get the "Load or Reload Linetypes" subdialog box shown in Figure 19-22.

Figure 19-22.   The "Load or Reload Linetypes" subdialog box.

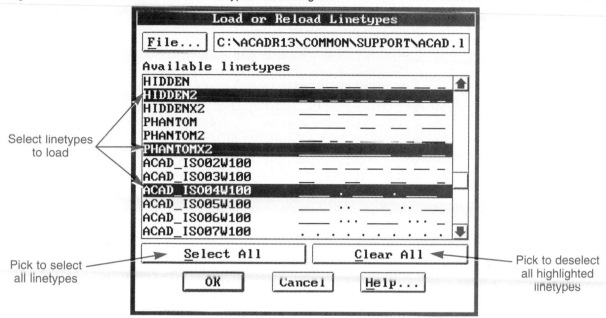

Scroll through the available linetypes and pick the one or more linetypes you want to load. Picking a desired linetype highlights it. You can continue to pick and highlight as many linetypes as you want to load. If you pick a linetype and decide that you do not want it, just pick it again and the highlight is removed. Pick the OK button to have the selected linetypes loaded and listed in the "Select Linetype" subdialog box. You can also pick the Select All button which automatically highlights all of the available linetypes. Pick the OK button and they are all loaded, or pick the Clear All button to have the selections cleared. The Clear All button is inactive until you pick one or more linetypes to load.

Pick the File... button in the "Load or Reload Linetypes" subdialog box to access the "Select Linetype File" dialog box. Here you can pick other linetype files that are listed such as LTYPESHP or other custom files that may be available. Pick a linetype file and then pick OK to have these linetypes listed and displayed in the "Load or Reload Linetypes" subdialog box. Then load them as needed.

When you pick one of the ACAD-ISO linetypes in the "Select Linetype" subdialog box, it activates the ISO Pen Width: list shown in Figure 19-23. Pick the down arrow to access the pop up list box. This list displays several line width options that are given in millimeters. The ISO Pen Width that you select also has an equal control of the Linetype Scale: value. Changing the ISO Pen Width: does not alter the appearance of these lines on the screen, but may be used when plotting. *ISO* stands for International Organization for Standardization.

Look at the "Select Linetype" subdialog box in Figure 19-21 or Figure 19-23 again. Notice the Linetype Scale: text box. You can use this to quickly adjust the linetype scale before returning to the drawing editor. If you forget to change the linetype scale before you leave the "Select Linetype" subdialog box, you can also do it in the "Object Creation Modes" dialog box. Look at Figure 19-20. You can also change the linetype scale at the Command: prompt using the LTSCALE command that is discussed later.

Figure 19-23.   Picking one of the AutoCAD ISO linetypes makes the ISO options available. Make any changes necessary and then pick OK.

Select ISO options

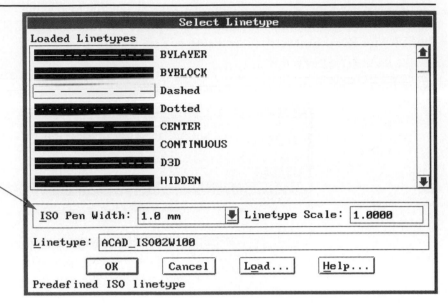

CHANGING THE LINETYPE SCALE

AUG 6

The linetype scale sets the length of dashes in linetypes having them. The default linetype scale factor is one. Any line with dashes initially assumes this factor. Figure 19-24 shows the effects of changing the scale factor for a centerline.

Figure 19-24.   A comparison of linetype scale factors.

Scale factor	Line
0.5	
1.0	
1.50	

You can change the scale factor to 1.5 as follows:

Command: **LTSCALE** ↲
New scale factor ⟨*current*⟩: **1.5** ↲

A "regenerating drawing" message appears as the linetype scale is changed for all lines on the drawing.

Changing the linetype of individual objects

The LTSCALE command may be used to make a global change to the linetype scale. Global means that the change affects everything on the drawing. Sometimes you may want to change the linetype of an individual or a select group of objects. You can do this with the CHPROP command. You can use this command to change many properties, each of which is identified by name in the list of options. The CHPROP command is a handy tool that works like this:

Command: **CHPROP** ↲
Select objects: *(select the objects to change)*
Select objects: ↲
Change what property (Color/LAyer/LType/ltScale/Thickness)? **S** ↲
New linetype scale ⟨1.0⟩: **.5** ↲
Change what property (Color/LAyer/LType/ltScale/Thickness)? ↲
Command:

The scale factors are the same as those displayed in Figure 19-24, but only the selected objects are affected.

You can also change the linetype scale of specific objects by using the DDMODIFY command:

Command: **DDMODIFY** ↵
Select object to modify: *(select the object or objects to modify)*

The "Modify Line" dialog box is displayed for your use. While this dialog box has several options for the modification of line properties, Linetype Scale: edit box allows you to enter the desired linetype scale. Pick the OK button when ready.

Using the CELTSCALE system variable

The CELTSCALE system variable stands for Current Entity LTSCALE. An LTSCALE setting is global, but a CELTSCALE setting is a system variable that is assigned to individual objects using a multiplier value of the LTSCALE setting. For example, if the CELTSCALE value is 0.5, all new objects created would reference this value. This indicates that the LTSCALE variable is multiplied by 0.5 for displaying these objects. A created object's linetype scale remains the same regardless of any CELTSCALE setting changes. A hidden line is drawn with a variety of CELTSCALE settings in Figure 19-25 for your reference.

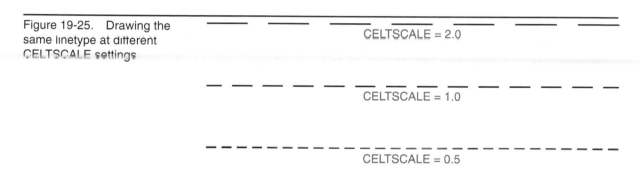

Figure 19-25.   Drawing the same linetype at different CELTSCALE settings.

CELTSCALE = 2.0

CELTSCALE = 1.0

CELTSCALE = 0.5

CELTSCALE may be set at the Linetype Scale: edit box using the "Select Linetype" subdialog box, or the DDMODIFY and DDCHPROP commands. CELTSCALE may also be changed using the ltScale option of the CHPROP command, or CELTSCALE can be entered at the Command: prompt as follows:

Command: **CELTSCALE** ↵
New value for CELTSCALE ⟨1.0⟩: **.5** ↵
Command:

EXERCISE 19-4

❑ Open TITLEB from Problem 10-1.
❑ Draw the two objects shown to approximate size.
❑ Change the linetype scale to .5, to 1.5, and then back to 1. Observe the effect each time it is changed.
❑ Save the drawing as A:EX19-4 and quit.

Object 1   Object 2

PROFESSIONAL TIP

 Changing the linetype scale affects all of the lines on the drawing. There is no standard way to change the scale of specific lines. Reset the linetype scale to obtain lines that come close to or meet your standards.

LAYERS

AUG 6

In manual drafting, details of a design might be separated by placing them on different sheets of media. This is called *overlay* or *pin register* drafting. Each overlay is perfectly aligned with the others. All of the layers may be reproduced together to reflect the entire design. Individual layers might also be reproduced to show specific details.

Drawing on different overlays, or *layers* as they are called with AutoCAD, has certain benefits:

* Specific information may be grouped on separate layers. For example, the floor plan could be drawn on one layer, the electrical plan on another, and the plumbing plan on a third layer.
* Drawings may be reproduced by individual layers or combined in any desired format. For example, the floor and electrical plan are reproduced together and sent to an electrical contractor for a bid. The floor and plumbing plan are reproduced together and sent to the plumbing contractor.
* Several drafters may work on a project at the same time for a marked increase in productivity.
* Each layer may be assigned a different color to help improve clarity.
* Each layer may be plotted in a different color or pen width.
* Selected layers may be turned off, or "frozen," to decrease the clutter of information displayed on the screen, and to speed up drawing regeneration.

AutoCAD allows drafters to turn on or off any individual layer and assign colors or linetypes to layers. Changes can be made to a layer promptly, often while the client watches. These capabilities increase productivity.

Layers used in different drafting fields

In mechanical drafting, views, hidden features, dimensions, sections, notes, and symbols might be placed on separate layers. In architectural drafting, there could be over a hundred layers. These could have plans for floor, foundation, partition layout, plumbing, electrical, structural, roof drainage, reflected ceiling, heating, ventilating, and air conditioning systems. Interior designers may have floor plan, interior partition, and furniture layers. In electronics drafting, each level of a multilevel circuit board is drawn on a separate layer.

Layer colors

The number of layer colors available depends on your graphics card and monitor. A monochrome monitor displays only one color, usually white, amber, or green. Color systems usually support 256 colors. Some graphics cards offer more. Layer colors are coded by name and number. The first seven standard color numbers are as follows:

Number	Color
1	Red
2	Yellow
3	Green
4	Cyan
5	Blue
6	Magenta
7	White

Assigning colors to layers is described later in the chapter.

Setting linetype by layer

AutoCAD allows you to select a linetype for individual entities. You can also assign linetypes to layers. Any item added to a layer assumes the linetype assigned to that layer.

You may have noticed that "Layer 0" has been shown in the upper-left corner of the AutoCAD screen. Layer 0 is the AutoCAD default layer. It has a continuous linetype and white color. You can assign linetype and color to other layers as discussed later in this chapter. However, to have entities take on the layer linetype, follow this procedure:

Command: **LINETYPE** ↵
?/Create/Load/Set: **S** ↵
New object linetype (or ?) ⟨*current*⟩: **BYLAYER** ↵
?/Create/Load/Set: ↵
Command:

Naming layers

Layers may be given names to reflect what is drawn on them. Layer names may have up to 31 characters and include letters, numbers, and special characters. Typical mechanical, architectural, and civil drafting layer names may be as follows:

Mechanical	Architectural		Civil
OBJ	OBJECTIVE	WALLS	PROPERTYLN
HID	HIDDEN	WINDOWS	STRUCTURES
CEN	CENTER	DOORS	ROADS
DIM	DIMENSION	ELECT	WATER
CONS	CONSTR	PLUMB	CONTOURS
HAT	HATCH		
BOR	BORDER		

For simple drawings, layers may be named by linetype and color. For example, the layer name OBJECT-WHITE would have white continuous lines. The linetype and layer color number, such as OBJECT-7, may also be used. Another option is to assign the linetype a numerical value. For example, object lines could be 0, hidden lines 1, and centerlines 2. If you use this method, keep a written record of the numbering system for reference.

Lastly, layers may be given more complex names. The name might include the drawing number, color code, and layer content. The name DWG100-2-DIMEN refers to drawing DWG100, color 2, and DIMENSIONS layer.

INTRODUCTION TO THE LAYER COMMAND   AUG 6

When a layer is *current*, it is the layer that newly created objects are placed on. The LAYER command is used to select a variety of options dealing with layer use. When you type LAYER at the Command: prompt, the response is as follows:

Command: **LAYER** ↵
?/Make/Set/New/ON/OFF/Color/Ltype/Freeze/Thaw/LOck/Unlock:

A list of LAYER command options and a brief description of each is given in Figure 19-26.

Figure 19-26.   LAYER command options and descriptions.

?	Typing a ? prompts:
	Layer name(s) for listing ⟨*⟩:
	Type a specific layer name(s) or press ENTER to get a list of all available layers. (The default means to list all layers.) The list might appear as:
	Layer name State Color Linetype -------------- ------ --------- ------------------ 0 On 7(white) CONTINUOUS Current layer: 0
Make	Used to create a new layer and make it current.
Set	This option sets a new current layer if the named layer exists.
New	This option creates new layers without affecting the status of the current layer.
ON	Layers turned ON are displayed and plotted.
OFF	Layers turned OFF are not displayed and are not plotted.
Color	Changes the color of specific layers, asking you for the color number of name.
Ltype	Used to change the linetype of specific layer or layers.
Freeze	Freeze is similar to OFF in that frozen layers are invisible and are not plotted. The difference is that frozen layers are not calculated by the computer when the drawing is regenerated. Freeze layers not in use to save regeneration time on complex drawings.
Thaw	Makes frozen layers visible again.
LOck	Lock layers that you do not want edited. However, they are visible.
Unlock	Unlock locked layers. These layers are then available for drawing and editing purposes.

USING THE LAYER COMMAND   ⎹ ARM 8 ⎸

Most prototype drawings have layers based on linetypes. Write down the specifications for each layer color and linetype. Use one of the systems described earlier. The linetype number followed by a color number is noted as follows:

Layer Name	Linetype	Color
0-7	CONTINUOUS	WHITE
1-1	HIDDEN	RED
2-2	CENTER	YELLOW
3-3	DIMENSION	GREEN

Making new layers

The LAYER command's MAKE option is used to create a new layer, and at the same time, make the new layer current. For example, if you want to establish a new layer named JUDY and make it current, enter the following:

```
Command: LAYER ↵
?/Make/Set/New/ON/OFF/Color/Ltype/Freeze/Thaw/LOck/Unlock: M ↵
New current layer ⟨0⟩: JUDY ↵
?/Make/Set/New/ON/OFF/Color/Ltype/Freeze/Thaw/LOck/Unlock: ↵
```

This procedure works fine if you want to create a new layer and make it current at the same time. However, new layers are usually created prior to beginning drawing, and then made current using the Set option. To create a new layer without making it current, follow this command sequence:

```
Command: LAYER ⏎
?/Make/Set/New/ON/OFF/Color/Ltype/Freeze/Thaw/LOck/Unlock: N ⏎
New layer name(s): ELECTRICAL ⏎
?/Make/Set/New/ON/OFF/Color/Ltype/Freeze/Thaw/LOck/Unlock: ⏎
```

The new layer named ELECTRICAL is created and ready to use when you need it. Notice the New layer name(s): prompt is either singular or plural. This means you can enter one or more layer names at the same time. Separate each name by a comma if you are specifying more than one layer. For example:

```
New layer name(s): ELECTRICAL,PLUMBING,WALLS ⏎
```

Setting the current layer

Layers must be created using the Make or New options before they can be set. However, once layers have been created, they can be set at any time. Layer 0 is the current layer which is set in the AutoCAD prototype drawing. If you want to make the ELECTRICAL layer (which you created earlier) current, follow this command sequence:

```
Command: LAYER ⏎
?/Make/Set/New/ON/OFF/Color/Ltype/Freeze/Thaw/LOck/Unlock: S ⏎
New current layer ⟨0⟩: ELECTRICAL ⏎
?/Make/Set/New/ON/OFF/Color/Ltype/Freeze/Thaw/LOck/Unlock: ⏎
```

Layer color and linetype

You can set a new layer's color and linetype, or change the color and linetype of an existing layer at any time. Use the Color and Ltype options as follows:

```
Command: LAYER ⏎
?/Make/Set/New/ON/OFF/Color/Ltype/Freeze/Thaw/LOck/Unlock: C ⏎
Color: BLUE or 5 ⏎
Layer name(s) for color 5 (blue) ⟨0⟩: ELECTRICAL ⏎
?/Make/Set/New/ON/OFF/Color/Ltype/Freeze/Thaw/LOck/Unlock: L ⏎
Linetype (or ?) ⟨CONTINUOUS⟩: PHANTOM ⏎
Layer name(s) for linetype PHANTOM ⟨0⟩: ELECTRICAL ⏎
?/Make/Set/New/ON/OFF/Color/Ltype/Freeze/Thaw/LOck/Unlock: ⏎
```

Putting it all together

Now, proceed by establishing the new layers 1, 2, and 3 with colors red, yellow, and green, respectively. Assign these layers the linetypes hidden, center, and continuous, respectively. Remember, you can name layers individually or enter several layer names separated by commas like this:

```
Command: LAYER ⏎
?/Make/Set/New/ON/OFF/Color/Ltype/Freeze/Thaw/LOck/Unlock: N ⏎
New layers name(s): 1,2,3 ⏎
?/Make/Set/New/ON/OFF/Color/Ltype/Freeze/Thaw/LOck/Unlock: C ⏎
Color: 1 ⏎
Layer name(s) for color 1 (red) ⟨0⟩: 1 ⏎
?/Make/Set/New/ON/OFF/Color/Ltype/Freeze/Thaw/LOck/Unlock: C ⏎
Color: 2 ⏎
Layer name(s) for color 2 (yellow) ⟨0⟩: 2 ⏎
?/Make/Set/New/ON/OFF/Color/Ltype/Freeze/Thaw/LOck/Unlock: C ⏎
Color: 3 ⏎
```

Layer name(s) for color 3 (green) ⟨0⟩: **3** ↵
?/Make/Set/New/ON/OFF/Color/Ltype/Freeze/Thaw/LOck/Unlock: **L** ↵
Linetype (or ?) ⟨CONTINUOUS⟩: **HIDDEN** ↵
Layer name(s) for linetype HIDDEN ⟨0⟩: **1** ↵
?/Make/Set/New/ON/OFF/Color/Ltype/Freeze/Thaw/LOck/Unlock: **L** ↵
Linetype (or ?) ⟨CONTINUOUS⟩: **CENTER** ↵
Layer name(s) for linetype CENTER ⟨0⟩: **2** ↵

Layer 3 contains dimensions. Dimension lines are solid lines so it is not necessary to assign a linetype. New layers are automatically given the default linetype, continuous. After entering layer values, type "?" to request a revised layer listing:

?/Make/Set/New/ON/OFF/Color/Ltype/Freeze/Thaw/LOck/Unlock: **?** ↵
Layer name(s) for listing⟨*⟩: ↵

Layer name	State	Color	Linetype
0	On	7 (white)	CONTINUOUS
1	On	1 (red)	HIDDEN
2	On	2 (yellow)	CENTER
3	On	3 (green)	CONTINUOUS
ELECTRICAL	On	5 (blue)	PHANTOM
JUDY	On	7 (white)	CONTINUOUS

Current layer: 0
?/Make/Set/New/ON/OFF/Color/Ltype/Freeze/Thaw/LOck/Unlock: ↵
Command:

Now, items added to layer 0 have white object lines. Items added to layer 1 have red hidden lines. Objects added to layer 2 have yellow centerlines. Dimensions added to layer 3 have solid green lines.

Once new layers and parameters are established, you can begin making the drawing. These steps outline the sequence for completing a mechanical drawing:
- Make a sketch and prepare a plan sheet.
- Draw all object lines.
- Use the LAYER command's Set option to select a new current layer on which to draw. At this point, select layer 1 which has the hidden linetype.
- Draw all hidden lines.
- Reset the current layer to layer 2, which has centerlines.
- Draw all centerlines.
- Use the LAYER command's Set option once again to select layer 3.
- Add dimensions. (Dimensioning is discussed in Chapters 20 through 23.)
- Set the current layer as necessary when editing the drawing.

Keep records listing how you set up drawing prototypes. If your notes are not handy, list the layers, colors, and linetypes by typing a ?.

EXERCISE 19-5

❑ Load AutoCAD and open PRODR1.
❑ Set up six layers, each having a different color and linetype as follows:

Layer name	Linetype	Color
0-7	Continuous	White
1-1	Hidden	Red
2-2	Center	Yellow
3-3	Continuous	Green
4-4	Phantom	Cyan
5-5	Dot	Blue

❑ Save as A:PRODR2, thus establishing a new prototype with the specified layers.
❑ Draw the objects shown below. Place objects on the layer that has their linetype. The dimension layer will not be used at this time.
❑ Save the drawing as A:EX19-5 and quit.

Object 1

Hidden

Phantom

Object 2

Object 3

Turning layers ON and OFF

Layers that are turned on may be displayed and plotted, but layers that are turned off may not be displayed or plotted. Even though a layer is turned off, it is still regenerated with the rest of the drawing. To turn off a layer, follow this procedure:

Command: **LAYER** ↵
?/Make/Set/New/ON/OFF/Color/Ltype/Freeze/Thaw/LOck/Unlock: **OFF** ↵
Layer name(s) to turn Off: **ELECTRICAL** ↵

This message then appears:

Really want layer ELECTRICAL (the CURRENT layer) off? ⟨N⟩ ↵

Press ENTER if you do not want the current layer turned off, or enter Y and press ENTER if you do want it turned off. You can draw with the current layer off, but you will not see the results until you turn it back on. Do not try to draw with the current layer off. Either turn it on or set another layer current. Simply use the ON option to turn layers back on.

Freezing and thawing layers

A frozen layer is similar to a layer that has been turned off, except that frozen layers are not calculated by the computer when a regeneration occurs, thus saving time. Freeze layers like this:

Command: **LAYER** ↵
?/Make/Set/New/ON/OFF/Color/Ltype/Freeze/Thaw/LOck/Unlock: **F** ↵
Layer name(s) to Freeze: **ELECTRICAL** ↵

If you try to freeze the current layer, AutoCAD responds with this message:

Cannot freeze layer ELECTRICAL. It is the CURRENT layer.

If you really want to freeze the ELECTRICAL layer, first make another layer current, and then freeze the ELECTRICAL layer. Use the Thaw option to unfreeze a frozen layer.

Locking and unlocking layers

Unlocked layers are available for you to use for drawing and editing purposes. Locked layers are visible, but they cannot be edited. Current layers can even be locked. For example, lock a layer (or several layers) if you want to be sure that no one tampers with the entities drawn on it. Lock a layer as follows. Note the use of the two-character response–LO.

Command: **LAYER** ↵
?/Make/Set/New/ON/OFF/Color/Ltype/Freeze/Thaw/LOck/Unlock: **LO** ↵
Layer name(s) to Lock: **ELECTRICAL** ↵

PROFESSIONAL TIP

Layers are meant to simplify the drafting process. They separate different details of the drawing and reduce the complexity of a displayed drawing. If you set color and linetype by layer, do not reset and mix entity linetypes and color on the same layer. Doing so can mislead you and your colleagues when trying to find certain details. Maintain accurate records of your prototype setup for future reference.

USING THE "LAYER CONTROL" DIALOG BOX   AUG 6

The LAYER command and all of its options may be used by accessing the "Layer Control" dialog box. Type DDLMODES at the Command: prompt, pick Layers… from the Data pull-down menu, or pick Ddlmode: from the DATA screen menu to display the dialog box. Only layers that have been previously created are displayed. Many of the dialog box items are grayed out until you move the arrow and pick one of the listed layers. You can pick as many layers as you want. When individual layers are picked, they become highlighted and are displayed in the edit box, as shown in Figure 19-27.

Figure 19-27.   The "Layer Control" dialog box.

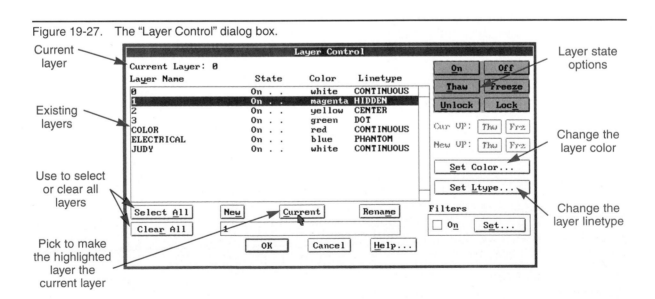

The Layer Name list

The current layer is displayed in the upper-left corner, followed by the Layer Name list box. Here you see the existing layer names, state, color, and linetype. (*State* means the layer status such as on, off, frozen, or locked.)

The Select and Clear buttons

Below the layer list is the Select All button, Figure 19-28. Pick this button if you want to select all of the layers in the list. Pick the Clear All button if you want to clear the list and remove the highlighting on all items picked. You can clear individual selections by repicking highlighted layers.

Figure 19-28.   All layers can be selected or deselected using the Select All or Clear All buttons. To create a new layer, enter a name in the edit box and pick the New button.

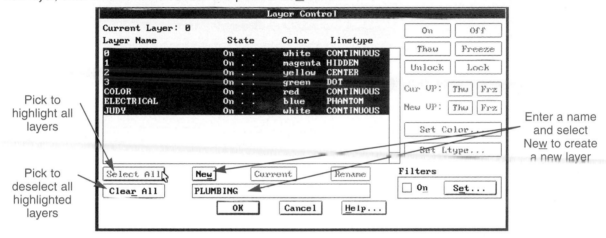

Pick to highlight all layers

Pick to deselect all highlighted layers

Enter a name and select New to create a new layer

The New, Current, and Rename buttons

To add a new layer to the list, first pick the edit box to activate the text cursor. Then type the new layer name, and pick the New button, Figure 19-28. The new layer name, in this case PLUMBING, is added to the list, with the color white and linetype continuous.

To make another layer current, pick a layer from the Layer Name list to highlight it, and then pick the Current button. Refer back to Figure 19-27. You can also use the CLAYER system variable to make a layer current. Type CLAYER at the Command: prompt, then type the name of the existing layer you want to make current.

When you pick a layer from the Layer Name list, its name is displayed in the edit box. To change the layer name, type the new name in the edit box and pick the Rename button. Notice in Figure 19-29 that the PLUMBING layer is being renamed as PLUMB.

Setting color and linetype

Note the Set Color… and Set Ltype… (linetype) buttons to the right of the Layer Name list box. You can change the color of a selected layer by picking the Set Color… button, which displays the "Select Color" subdialog box. In this case, the new PLUMB layer color is changed to magenta.

In order for a linetype to be changed, the desired linetype must first be loaded. Pick the Set Ltype… button to access the "Select Linetype" subdialog box. Pick the DASHED line from the line list to change the PLUMB layer linetype to dashed. Notice that Figure 19-30 displays the PLUMB layer with its color magenta and linetype dashed. Be sure to pick OK when you have completed making changes.

Figure 19-29.   To rename a layer, highlight the name in the Layer Name list box, change the name in the edit box, and then pick the Rename button.

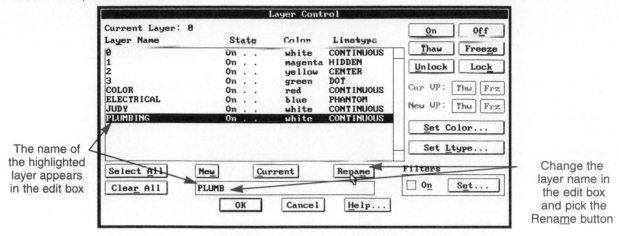

The name of the highlighted layer appears in the edit box

Change the layer name in the edit box and pick the Rename button

Figure 19-30.   Layer color and linetype can be changed in the "Layer Control" dialog box.

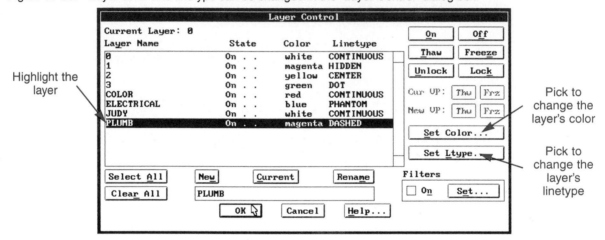

Highlight the layer

Pick to change the layer's color

Pick to change the layer's linetype

Using the On, Off, Thaw, Freeze, Unlock, and Lock buttons

The State column in the layer list provides the status of each layer. The first column in this list is for On/Off. The second column indicates Freeze/Thaw, and the third column is for Unlock/Lock. When a layer is off, thawed, or unlocked, a period (.) appears in the corresponding column.

Pick and highlight the desired layer in order to change the layer status. Then, pick the appropriate button–On, Off, Thaw, Freeze, Unlock, or Lock–as needed. Figure 19-31 shows the layers with their current style adjusted as desired. Remember, the current layer cannot be frozen.

Filtering layers

Layer filters are used to screen or "filter out" any layers that have features which you do not want displayed in the "Layer Control" dialog box. The Filters area of the "Layer Control" dialog box has an On check box and a Set... button. Filters may include layer features such as name, color, or linetype. Filters may also involve the status of layers, such as frozen/thawed, on/off, or locked/unlocked.

For example, assume you are working on an electrical drawing, and want layers 0, 1, 3, and ELECTRICAL displayed. You can freeze the other layers and filter them out. Layers can be filtered by any desired variable, such as name, state, color, or linetype. To do this, pick the Set... button to get the

Figure 19-31. When you highlight a layer in the Layer list box, the state of the layer can be changed. The state option buttons are shown here highlighted.

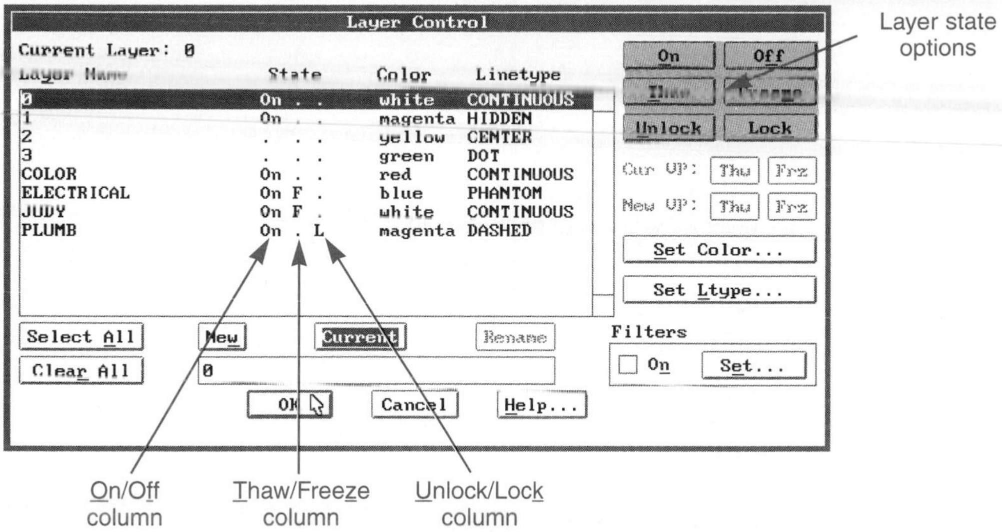

"Set Layer Filters" subdialog box, Figure 19-32. Filter the layer name, color, or linetype by entering the desired item in the related edit box. If you want to display only the ELECTRICAL layer, then filter it by listing its name.

Figure 19-32. Layers can be filtered by any desired variable using the "Set Layer Filters" dialog box.

You can use the wild card (*) to list a group of similar layers if desired. For example, if you want to filter all of the WALL layers, enter W*. This filters every layer name that starts with W.

Pick one of the pop-up arrows in the upper right to filter either On/Off:, Freeze/Thaw:, Lock/Unlock:, Current Vport: (Viewport), or New Vports:. For example, filter all of the thawed layers by setting Thawed, as shown in Figure 19-33A. Notice in Figure 19-33B that only the thawed layers are listed, and the filters On check box is checked. The On box is automatically checked when you pick the OK button in the "Set Layer Filters" subdialog box. However, you can turn filters on or off at any time by picking this check box.

Figure 19-33.   A–Layer filters being set. B–The result of filtering layers.

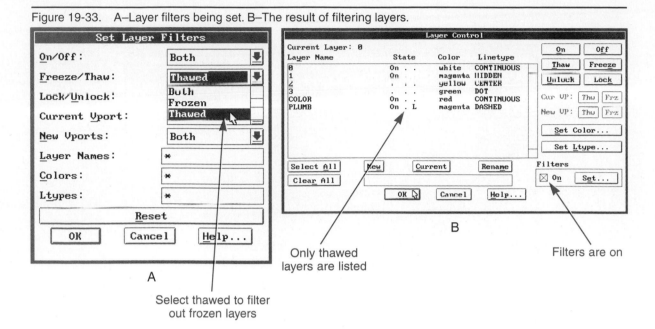

Select thawed to filter
out frozen layers

Only thawed
layers are listed

Filters are on

A

B

CONTROLLING LAYERS IN VIEWPORTS

The preceding discussion explained that the LAYER command's Freeze/Thaw and On/Off options set the visibility of layers in all viewports (known as *global control*). For example, if you freeze a layer globally, it is invisible in all viewports. If you want to set the visibility or invisibility of layers in one viewport or a specific set of viewports, use the VPLAYER command. This flexibility allows you to create a specific layer that is visible in a designated viewport. Refer to Chapters 10 and 26 for complete discussions of viewports, and Chapter 26 for the VPLAYER command.

USING ENTITY CREATION MODES

You can see the properties of the current layer, or set the color, linetype, text style, or layer using the "Object Creation Modes" dialog box. It is accessed by picking Object Creation… from the Data pull-down menu, or entered by typing DDEMODES at the Command: prompt.

A typical "Object Creation Modes" dialog box is shown in Figure 19-34. Notice that the color is currently set as BYLAYER, which is a common practice. Select a new color by picking the Color… button to access the "Select Color" subdialog box. Pick the Layer… button to make changes to the layer through the "Layer Control" subdialog box.

Figure 19-34.   The "Object Creation Modes" dialog box is used to view properties of the current layer. These properties can be changed, as well as a different layer made current (by accessing the "Layer Control" dialog box).

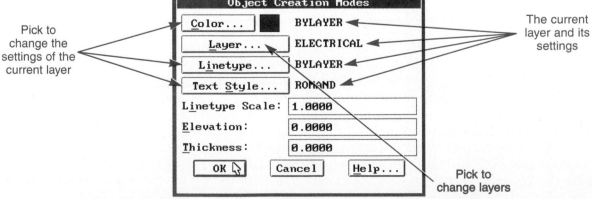

Pick to
change the
settings of the
current layer

The current
layer and its
settings

Pick to
change layers

The Text Style… button in the "Object Creation Modes" dialog box accesses the "Select Text Style" subdialog box shown in Figure 19-35. This is a convenient way to quickly change the text style. Simply pick one of the available styles in the list box, or type the name of a loaded text style in the Style Name: edit box. When you pick a new style, the image tile changes, displaying a sample of the selected style. You can change the sample by entering your desired text in the Sample Text: edit box. Pick the Show All… button to display the "Text Style Symbol Set" subdialog box, which shows all of the current text fonts. The current Height, Width, Obliquing angle, and Generation format are specified from your reference. The elevation and thickness items in this dialog box refer to 3-D values, which are discussed in Chapter 29.

Figure 19-35.   The "Select Text Style" subdialog box is a convenient way to view and change the text style.

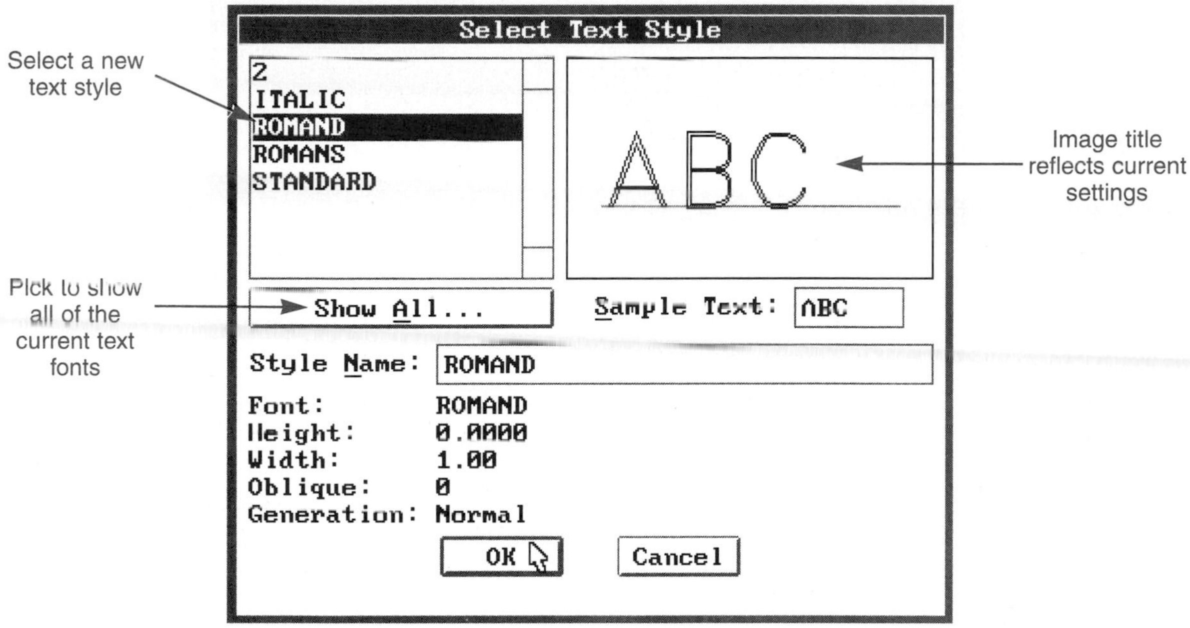

CHANGING LAYERS

AUG 6

In Chapters 11, 13, and 14, you were introduced to the CHANGE, CHPROP, and DDCHPROP commands. These commands are convenient for editing a drawing or changing a variety of properties. The CHPROP and DDCHPROP commands are the most convenient for changing layer, linetype, or color since they directly access the property options. For example, the CHPROP command's LA option moves an object or objects from one layer to another. This option only works if the intended layer has been created. When you enter LA and press ENTER, AutoCAD asks for the new layer. Suppose the current layer, shown in brackets, is FLPLAN. If the object should be on the ELECTRIC layer, proceed as follows:

```
Command: CHPROP ↵
Select objects: (pick or window the object to be changed)
Select objects: ↵
Change what property (Color/LAyer/LType/ltScale/Thickness)? LA ↵
New layer ⟨FLPLAN⟩: ELECTRIC ↵
Change what property (Color/LAyer/LType/ltScale/Thickness)? ↵
```

RENAMING LAYERS

Using the DDRENAME command, you can rename many items, including layer, linetype, and text style. This command accesses the "Rename" dialog box shown in Figure 19-36. Pick any of the named objects, such as Layer, to get a list of items related to the object. Notice the items in Figure 19-36 are the layers that were previously created. To change the name of a layer, pick that layer from the Items list. Picking ELECTRICAL, for example, places it in the <u>O</u>ld Name: edit box. Next, type the new name in the <u>R</u>ename To: edit box, followed by picking the <u>R</u>ename To: button. Finally, pick the OK button to exit the dialog box.

Figure 19-36.   The "Rename" dialog box is used to rename objects such as layers, viewports, and views.

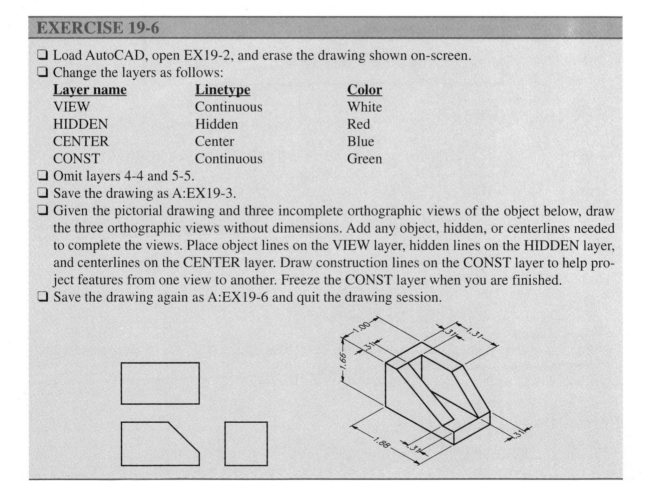

EXERCISE 19-6

❑ Load AutoCAD, open EX19-2, and erase the drawing shown on-screen.
❑ Change the layers as follows:

Layer name	Linetype	Color
VIEW	Continuous	White
HIDDEN	Hidden	Red
CENTER	Center	Blue
CONST	Continuous	Green

❑ Omit layers 4-4 and 5-5.
❑ Save the drawing as A:EX19-3.
❑ Given the pictorial drawing and three incomplete orthographic views of the object below, draw the three orthographic views without dimensions. Add any object, hidden, or centerlines needed to complete the views. Place object lines on the VIEW layer, hidden lines on the HIDDEN layer, and centerlines on the CENTER layer. Draw construction lines on the CONST layer to help project features from one view to another. Freeze the CONST layer when you are finished.
❑ Save the drawing again as A:EX19-6 and quit the drawing session.

SETTING UP YOUR SHEET FOR MULTIVIEW LAYOUT

AUG 10

AutoCAD provides you with the MVSETUP command that allows you to insert one of several different predrawn standard border and title block formats based on ANSI, ISO, architectural, or generic layouts. The border and title block can be set up before plotting where they can be scaled, and then plotted at FULL (1:1) scale. Refer to Chapter 12 for information regarding the use of paper space viewports, and scaling a viewport.

MVSETUP is an AutoLISP routine that can be customized to insert any type of border and title block. (AutoLISP is covered in *AutoCAD and its Applications–Advanced, R13 for DOS.*) To use MVSETUP, first open a drawing that you want to display. Enter the MVSETUP command by first picking Paper Space, then Floating Viewports followed by MV Setup in the View pull-down menu, or type MVSETUP. Then, enter paper space by answering Yes to the Enable paper space? prompt. The following command sequence is used to change the TILEMODE variable:

        Command: **MVSETUP**↵
        Initializing…
        Enable paper space? (No/⟨Yes⟩): ↵

Notice the paper space UCS icon is displayed and your drawing has disappeared. After the first use of MVSETUP, you can enter MVS as the command name. The Title block option is discussed first because it lets you establish a drawing border and title block:

        Align/Create/Scale viewports/Options/Title block/Undo: **T** ↵
        Delete objects/Origin/Undo/⟨Insert title block⟩: ↵

The default allows you to insert a title block. The options are summarized as follows:
   • **Delete objects.** Allows you to select objects to delete from paper space.
   • **Origin.** Permits you to relocate the sheet origin.
   • **Undo.** Undoes the previous operation.
   • **Insert title block.** Pressing ENTER to accept the default displays the following:

        Available title block options:
        0:      None
        1:      ISO A4 Size(mm)
        2:      ISO A3 Size(mm)
        3:      ISO A2 Size(mm)
        4:      ISO A1 Size(mm)
        5:      ISO A0 Size(mm)
        6:      ANSI-V Size(in) *(this is the vertical A-size format)*
        7:      ANSI-A Size(in) *(this is the horizontal A-size format)*
        8:      ANSI-B Size(in)
        9:      ANSI-C Size(in)
        10:     ANSI-D Size(in)
        11:     ANSI-E Size(in)
        12:     Arch/Engineering (24 x 36in)
        13:     Generic D-size Sheet (24 x 36in)
        Add/Delete/Redisplay/⟨Number of entry to load⟩: *(type the desired sheet size format,*
            *such as **7**, and press* ENTER*)*

Next, you get a message that asks if you want to create a drawing with the sheet size specifications you selected. This prompt is shown only if a file named ANSI-A.DWG is not in your AutoCAD directory. For example, the previous choice was number 7, which is the ANSI-A Size (in). The following prompt is displayed:

        Create a drawing named ansi-a.dwg? ⟨Y⟩: ↵

Pressing ENTER at this prompt creates a drawing file with the name shown. ANSI-A.DWG is now available to be used as a prototype for the future. When using this prototype, AutoCAD automatically draws the border and title block shown in Figure 19-37.

Figure 19-37.   One of the border and title block arrangements available with the MVSETUP command.

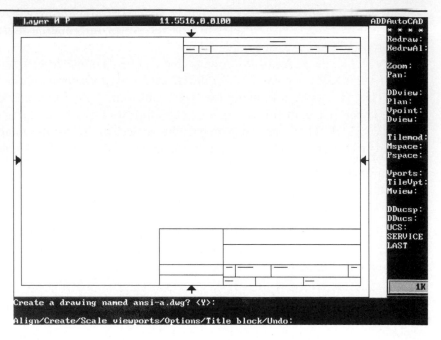

Now, the Create option is used to establish the viewports:

Align/Create/Scale viewports/Options/Title block/Undo: **C** ↵

Press ENTER at the following prompt to obtain a list of the viewport layout options:

Delete objects/Undo/⟨Create viewports⟩: ↵
Available Mview viewport layout options:
0:      None
1:      Single
2:      Std. Engineering
3:      Array of Viewports
Redisplay/⟨Number of entry to load⟩: **1** ↵

A single viewport works best for this application.

The next prompt asks you to identify the boundary for the viewport by picking the opposite corners (similar to forming a window).

Bounding area for viewports. First Point: *(pick a point)*
Other point: *(move the cursor and pick the second point)*

Look at Figure 19-38. The drawing you started with is now displayed inside the viewport.

Figure 19-38.   Opening a viewport.

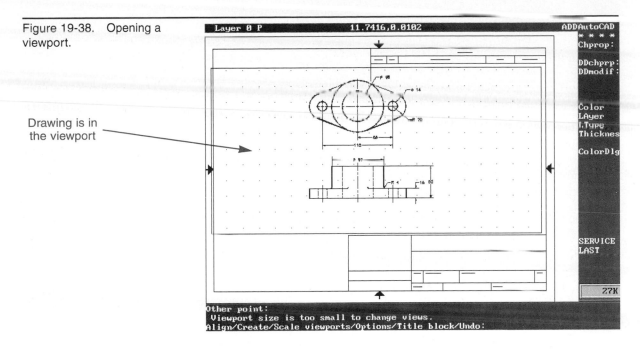

Drawing is in the viewport

The Scale option is used next to scale the drawing by using a ratio of paper space to model space units. For example, 1:2 is one paper space unit for two model space units, or a one-half scale, as shown in Figure 19-39.

Figure 19-39.   Viewports are scaled with the MVSETUP command's Scale viewport option.

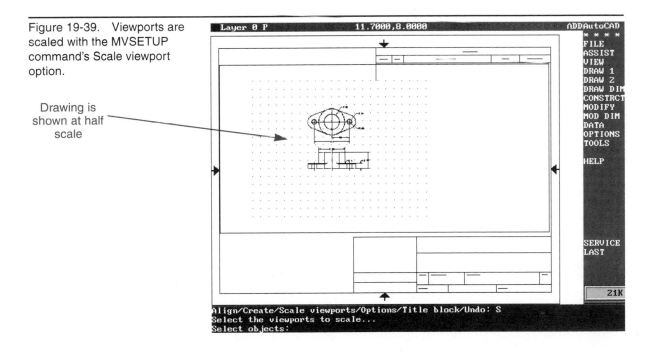

Drawing is shown at half scale

The defaults, used in the following example, are FULL scale, or 1:1. The drawing may not change much in size, depending on the size of the viewport, as demonstrated by the results in Figure 19-38. Note the following prompts:

Align/Create/Scale viewports/Options/Title block/Undo: **S** ↵
Select the viewports to scale...
Select objects: *(pick the viewport outline, not the drawing)*
Select objects: ↵
Enter the ratio of paper space units to model space units...
Number of paper space units. ⟨1.0⟩: ↵
Number of model space units. ⟨1.0⟩: **2** ↵
Align/Create/Scale viewports/Options/Title block/Undo: ↵

The viewport is an entity that may be altered in paper space using the MOVE or STRETCH commands, or with grips as needed. Part of your drawing may extend past the edge of the viewport after using the Scale option. Simply use the STRETCH command to compensate for the miscalculation. The MOVE command is used to position the drawing shown in Figure 19-38. Note the results in Figure 19-40A. You can also use grips to scale the viewport so the viewport borders do not overlap the title block and sheet border. To do this, pick the viewport, activate a hot grip, and press ENTER to access the SCALE command. Then enter a new scale factor like this:

** SCALE **
⟨Scale factor⟩/Base point/Copy/Undo/Reference/eXit: **.8** ↵
Notice that this only scales the viewport, not the drawing. The results are shown in Figure 19-40B.

Figure 19-40.   You can Move, Stretch, or Scale a viewport using grips or by first entering the desired command.

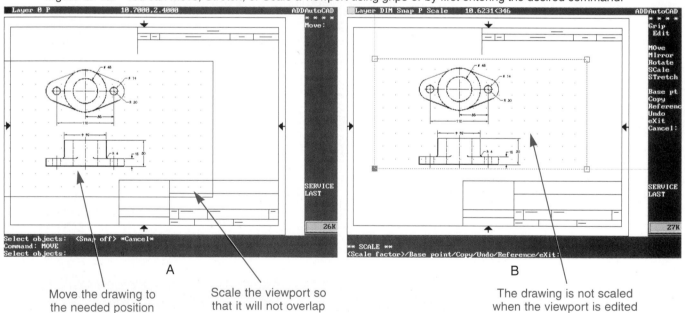

A

Move the drawing to
the needed position

Scale the viewport so
that it will not overlap

B

The drawing is not scaled
when the viewport is edited

Creating your own title block format

In the previous discussion, you saw how making a selection from the list of "Available title block options:" and responding with a Y (or pressing ENTER) to the following prompt created a drawing file with the name shown:

Create a drawing named ansi-a.dwg? ⟨Y⟩: ↵

The ANSI-A.DWG is now available to be edited and customized for your own applications. Figure 19-41A shows the ANSI-A title block and resulting customization. Figure 19-41B shows the entire new border and title block. Now that the title block is customized for your school or company, you can use the SAVEAS command to save the ANSI-A.DWG to any name you wish, such as MECH-A.

Figure 19-41. Customizing the ANSI-A title block.

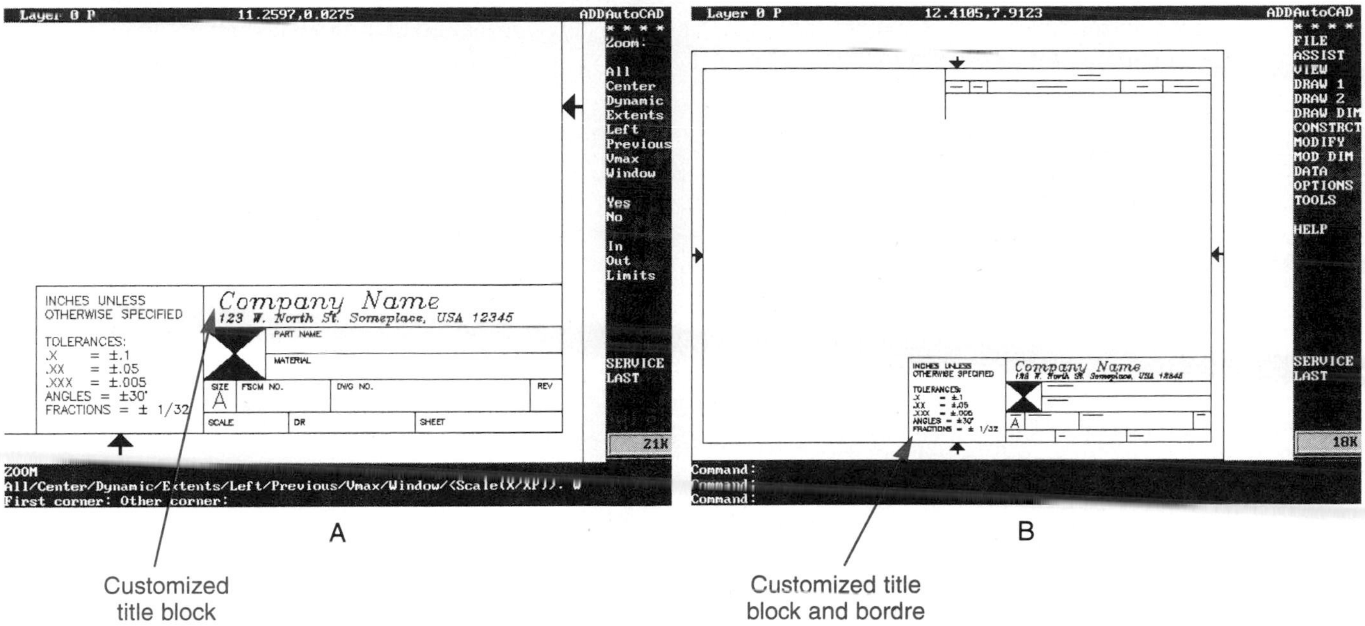

A

Customized
title block

B

Customized title
block and bordre

When you begin a new drawing, use MECH-A as the prototype and provide a new drawing name, such as PART001, as shown in Figure 19-42. The MECH-A format is loaded and ready for you to create the PART001 drawing, or use the MECH-A format and insert a drawing that was previously drawn. Using the MVSETUP command in this manner is very valuable because it can be used to create several prototypes for different sheet size and title block formats, and then not used again except for special needs, or used often to customize the list of drawings as explained in the next section.

Figure 19-42. Using the MECH-A prototype for the PART001 drawing.

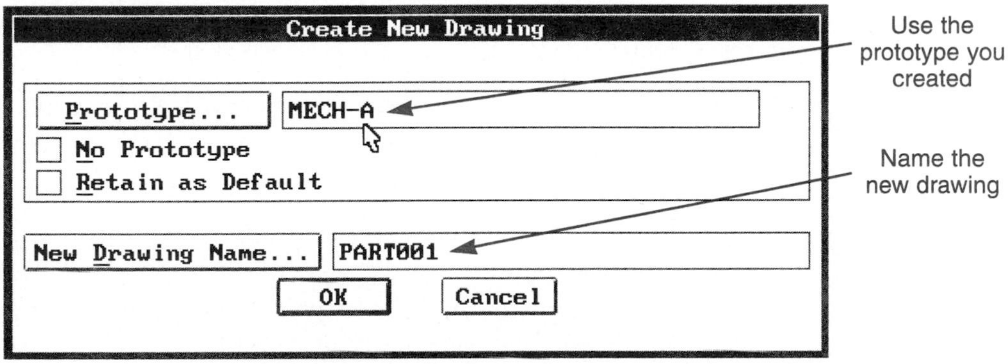

Adding title blocks to the MVSETUP list

Following the list of "Available title block options" is the Add/Delete/Redisplay/⟨Number of entry to load⟩: prompt. The Add option allows you to customize the list of prototype drawings by letting you name the drawing type, size, and insert a specific drawing. The following sequence gives you an idea of how this works:

> ALign/Create/Scale viewports/Options/Title block/Undo: **T** ↵
> Add/Delete/Redisplay/⟨Number of entry to load⟩: **A** ↵
> Title block description: **MECH (11 X 8.5 IN)** ↵
> Drawing to insert (without extension): **SAMPLE** ↵
> Specify default usable area? ⟨Y⟩: **N** ↵

The screen goes blank for a second and AutoCAD adds the new border and title block design to the list. A new "Available title block options:" list is displayed with your custom format listed as one of the options:

> 14. MECH (11 X 8.5 IN)
> Add/Delete/Redisplay/⟨number of entry to load⟩: *(enter a desired sheet format, such as* **14**,
>   *and press* ENTER*)*

If you only press ENTER to this prompt, the following is displayed:

> Specify default usable area? ⟨Y⟩: ↵

Pressing only ENTER accepts the Yes default. AutoCAD then asks you to either pick diagonal corners, or you can enter the lower-left and upper-right corner block coordinates. However, the N response described earlier is more convenient and works well in most situations.

Additional MVSETUP options

The following descriptions outline the purpose of the MVSETUP options that were not previously discussed:

- **Align.** This option is used to align views in multiple viewports. You get this prompt when you use the Align option:

    > Angled/Horizontal/Vertical alignment/Rotate view/Undo:

    - **Angled**–Used to pan a drawing in a viewport at a desired angle. The following prompts are displayed:

        > Base point: *(pick a point as an origin)*
        > Other point: *(pick a point in the viewport to be panned)*
        > Distance from base point: *(enter a distance and press* ENTER, *or pick two*
        >   *points to establish a distance from the base point)*
        > Angle from base point: *(enter an angular value and press* ENTER, *or pick two*
        >   *points representing an angle where the second point is to be positioned from*
        >   *the base point)*

    - **Horizontal**–This option allows you to align views in horizontal viewports:

        > Base point: *(pick a point as an origin)*
        > Other point: *(pick a point in the viewport to be aligned)*

    - **Vertical alignment**–This option allows you to align entities in vertical viewports in a manner similar to the Horizontal option.
    - **Rotate view**–You can rotate a drawing in a viewport around a selected base point:

        > Specify in which viewport the view is to be rotated.
        > Base point: *(pick a point as the pivot point for the rotation)*
        > Angle from base point: *(enter an angle and press* ENTER, *or pick two points*
        >   representing the angle)

- **Options.** This option lets you establish several different functions that are associated with your layout. The prompt issued with Options is:

    Set Layer/LImits/Units/Xref:

    - **Set Layer**–Allows you to specify an existing layer or create a new layer for your border and title block. It is a good idea to put your border and title block on a separate layer, perhaps BORDER. This gives you the flexibility to freeze, thaw, or otherwise manipulate the layer as needed. Enter L for layer to get this prompt:

        Layer name for title block or . for current layer: **BORDER** ↵

    - **Limits**–This suboption instructs AutoCAD to reset the drawing limits so it is equal to the extents when the border is inserted. The prompt has a No default:

        Set drawing limits? ⟨N⟩: ↵

    - **Units**–Allows you to specify if drawing information is to be presented in inch or millimeter values. Inch (in) units are the default. You can also enter F for feet, ME for meters, or M for millimeters:

        Paper space units are in Feet/Inches/MEters/Millimeters? ⟨in⟩:

    - **Xref**–This option determines if the border and title block is to be inserted in the drawing or referenced to a master drawing. A referenced drawing is not added to the current drawing file, but is displayed (also referred to as *attached*). This helps to keep the file smaller. Referencing drawings is discussed in detail in Chapter 26. The default is Insert, or you can type A and press ENTER for Attach as follows:

        Xref Attach or Insert title block? ⟨Insert⟩: ↵

Working with the TILEMODE system variable

The TILEMODE system variable is on when it is set to 1. TILEMODE must be turned off with a setting of 0, or you can answer Yes to the Enable paper space? (No/⟨Yes⟩): prompt to automatically have AutoCAD provide you with the standard border and title block formats that were previously discussed. The TILEMODE may be set to on (1) or off (0) like this:

Command: **TILEMODE** ↵
New value for TILEMODE ⟨0⟩: **1** ↵
Regenerating drawing.
Command:

You get the Enable paper space? (No/⟨Yes⟩): prompt with TILEMODE on when you enter the MVSETUP command:

Command: **MVSETUP**↵
Enable paper space? (No/⟨Yes⟩): **N** ↵

Answering No to the above prompt gives you the opportunity to establish your own drawing units, scale, and paper size. The prompts continue like this:

Units type (Scientific/Decimal/Engineering/Architectural/Metric): *(enter the desired units, for example* **D** *for decimal)*

The text screen is displayed with several scale options to choose from. Each of the Units type options give you a different list. This is the Decimal scale list:

```
Decimal Scales
(4.0)      4 TIMES
(2.0)      2 TIMES
(1.0)      FULL
(0.5)      HALF
(0.25)     QUARTER
Enter the scale factor: (enter the desired scale such as 1)
Enter the paper width: (enter the paper width such as 11)
Enter the paper height:(enter the paper height such as 8.5)
Command:
```

AutoCAD now uses the settings that you established to draw a polyline border at the drawing limits.

EXERCISE 19-7

❑ Use the MVSETUP command to insert the drawing from Exercise 19-6 (EX19-6) into a standard ANSI-A border and title block format.
❑ Adjust the scale and orientation as needed.
❑ Save the drawing as A:EX19-7 and quit the drawing session.

CHAPTER TEST

Write your answers in the spaces provided.

1. Give the command and entries required to display AutoCAD's standard linetypes:

   Command:_____

   ?/Create/Load/Set: _____

   File to list ⟨ACAD⟩:_____

   ?/Create/Load/Set: _____

2. Supply the command and entries needed to make CENTER the new linetype:

   Command:_____

   ?/Create/Load/Set: _____

   New entity linetype (or ?) ⟨*current*⟩: _____

   ?/Create/Load/Set: _____

3. Provide the command and entries that change the linetype scale to .5:

   Command:_____

   New scale factor ⟨1⟩: _____

4. Give the command and entries to create three layers named HIDDEN, CENTER, and DIMEN-
    SION. The names and associated linetypes and colors are given in the chart below.

Layer name	Linetype	Color
HIDDEN	HIDDEN	RED
CENTER	CENTER	YELLOW
DIMENSION	CONTINUOUS	GREEN

Command:_____

?/Make/Set/New/ON/OFF/Color/Ltype/Freeze/Thaw/LOck/Unlock: _____

New layer name(s): _____

?/Make/Set/New/ON/OFF/Color/Ltype/Freeze/Thaw/LOck/Unlock: _____

Color: _____

Layer name(s) for color red ⟨0⟩:_____

?/Make/Set/New/ON/OFF/Color/Ltype/Freeze/Thaw/LOck/Unlock: _____

Color: _____

Layer name(s) for color yellow ⟨0⟩: _____

?/Make/Set/New/ON/OFF/Color/Ltype/Freeze/Thaw/LOck/Unlock: _____

Color: _____

Layer name(s) for color green ⟨0⟩:_____

?/Make/Set/New/ON/OFF/Color/Ltype/Freeze/Thaw/LOck/Unlock: _____

Linetype (or ?) ⟨CONTINUOUS⟩: _____

Layer name(s) for linetype HIDDEN ⟨0⟩: _____

?/Make/Set/New/ON/OFF/Color/Ltype/Freeze/Thaw/LOck/Unlock: _____

Linetype (or ?) ⟨CONTINUOUS⟩: _____

Layer name(s) for linetype CENTER ⟨0⟩: _____

?/Make/Set/New/ON/OFF/Color/Ltype/Freeze/Thaw/LOck/Unlock: _____

5. Supply the command and entries that change the color from yellow to magenta. Assume that you
    are working on a single layer.
    Command:_____
    New entity color ⟨yellow⟩: _____

6. Identify five guidelines to consider when selecting the front view: _____

    _____

    _____

    _____

    _____

    _____

7. Suppose the axis of a hole is perpendicular to a slanted surface. The auxiliary view shows the
    hole as _____.

8. The default linetype of the LINE command is _____.

9. Name at least ten of AutoCAD's standard linetypes.

    _____   _____
    _____   _____
    _____   _____
    _____   _____
    _____   _____

10. In the chart provided, list the seven standard color names and their number.

Color Name	Color Number

11. When you enter the LAYER command and select the "?" option, the prompt Layer name(s) for listing ⟨*⟩: appears. What does the asterisk ⟨*⟩ in default brackets mean? _____

    _____

12. Describe the LAYER command's Make option. _____

    _____

    _____

13. Describe the LAYER command's Set option. _____

    _____

14. Describe the LAYER command's New option. _____

    _____

    _____

15. How are the new layer names entered when creating several layers at the same time? _____

    _____

16. Which pull-down menu contains the Layer option? _____

17. Name the command that is typed to access the "Layer Control" dialog box. _____

18. What condition must exist before a linetype can be chosen from the "Layer Control" dialog box?

    _____

19. How do you make another layer current in the "Layer Control" dialog box?_____

    _____

20. How do you change a layer's linetype in the "Layer Control" dialog box? _____

    _____

21. When is the "Select Color" subdialog box displayed?_____

    _____

22. How do you load several linetypes at the same time? _____

_____

23. When is a linetype displayed in the "Select Linetype" subdialog box?_____

_____

24. What is the state of a layer that is not displayed on the screen and is not calculated by the computer when the drawing is regenerated?_____

25. Describe the purpose of locking a layer. _____

_____

_____

26. Are locked layers visible? _____

27. What should you do if you want to freeze a layer, but you get this message: "Cannot freeze layer PROD002. It is the CURRENT layer"?_____

_____

28. How do you select all of the layers in the "Layer Control" dialog box list at the same time?

_____

29. When looking at the State column in the "Layer Control" dialog box, how do you know if a layer is either Off, Thawed, or Unlocked? _____

30. Describe the purpose of layer filters. _____

_____

31. Identify two ways to access the "Object Creation Modes" dialog box._____

_____

32. List at least four items that can be set using the "Object Creation Modes" dialog box. _____

_____

33. Name two commands that allow you to directly access property options for changing layer, linetype, or color. _____

34. Name the command that lets you rename layers, linetypes, and text styles. _____

35. The command that allows you to insert one of several different pre-drawn standard border and title block formats is _____.

36. Name the system variable that must be off (0) in order to enter paper space. _____

37. Explain the "Insert title block" default obtained after entering the Title block option in the MVS command. _____

_____

38. What happens when you press ENTER at this prompt:_____
Create a drawing named ansi-a.dwg?⟨Y⟩: _____

_____

39. Describe the purpose of the MVS command's Create option._____

_____

40. How is a drawing displayed when you set the MVS command's Scale option to 1 paper space unit and 2 model space units? _____

41. What should you do if the drawing is initially displayed too far to the upper right of the sheet format when inserted in the viewport using the MVS command?_____

_____

_____

42. Describe how you can customize a standard title block available in the MVS command and save it as a prototype called MECH-A. _____

_____

_____

43. How do you begin a new drawing named WALLEYE using the prototype described in Question 42?

_____

_____

44. How do you add the custom title block name ARCH-C to the Available title block options list?

_____

_____

45. Describe the function and importance of the Set Layer suboption in the MVS command's Options selection._____

_____

46. Explain the difference between the results obtained from the XLINE command and the RAY command._____

_____

_____

_____

_____

47. Describe how the XLINE default option works. _____

_____

_____

48. Name the XLINE option that lets you draw a construction line at a specified angle through a specified point. _____

_____

49. Identify the pull-down menu and the selection used to access the "Object Creation Modes" dialog box and then the pick needed to get the "Select Linetype" subdialog box? _____

_____

_____

_____

50. How is it possible to load all of the available linetypes when using the "Load or Reload Linetypes" subdialog box? _____

_____

_____

_____

DRAWING PROBLEMS

P19-1

1. Draw the views necessary to describe the object completely. Draw on one layer and use the LINETYPE command to change linetypes. Do not dimension. Use construction lines to your advantage on a CONST layer. Save your drawing as A:P19-1.

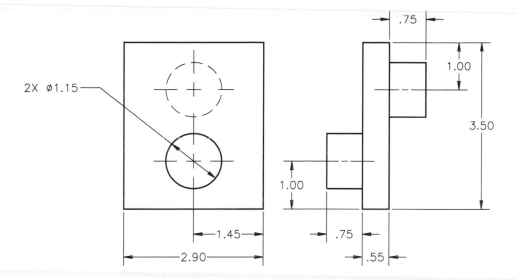

P19-2

2. Draw the views necessary to describe the object completely. Draw on one layer and use the LINETYPE command to change linetypes and the COLOR command to change colors. Draw object lines white, hidden lines red, and centerlines yellow. Do not dimension. Use construction lines to your advantage on a CONST layer. Save as A:P19-2.

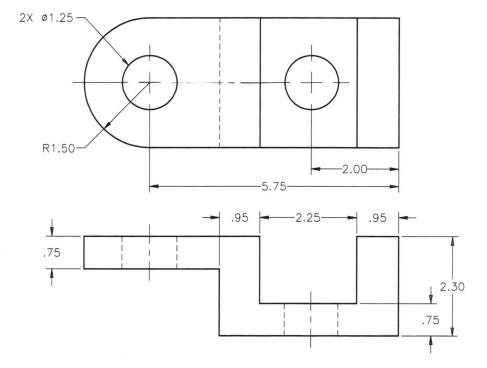

3-15. Draw the views necessary to describe each object completely. Set up the following layers, colors, and linetypes:

LAYER	COLOR	LINETYPE
OBJECT	WHITE	CONTINUOUS
HIDDEN	RED	HIDDEN
CENTER	YELLOW	CENTER
CONST	BLUE	CONTINUOUS

Do not dimension. Save each drawing on your floppy disk.

3.

P19-3

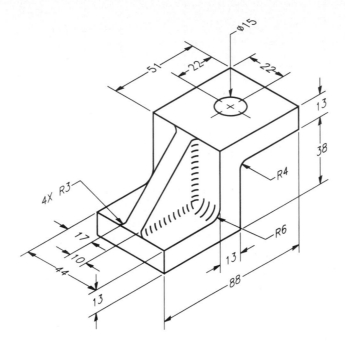

4.

P19-4

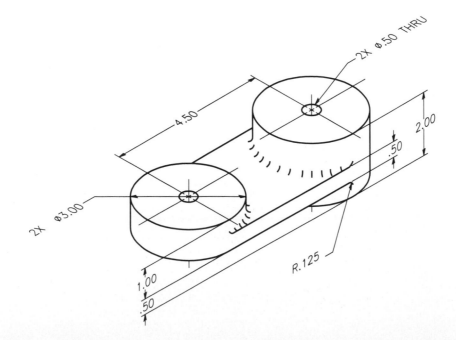

5.

P19-5

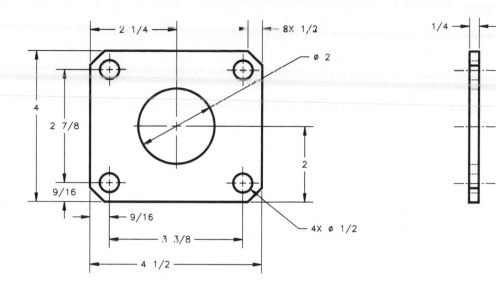

6.

P19-6

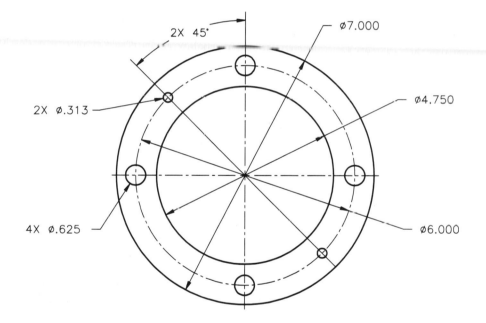

7.

P19-7

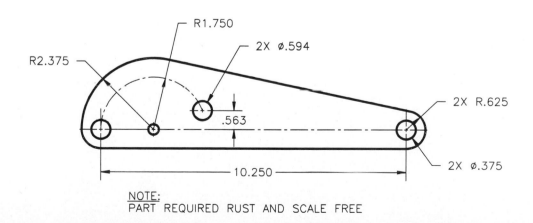

NOTE:
PART REQUIRED RUST AND SCALE FREE

8.

P19-8

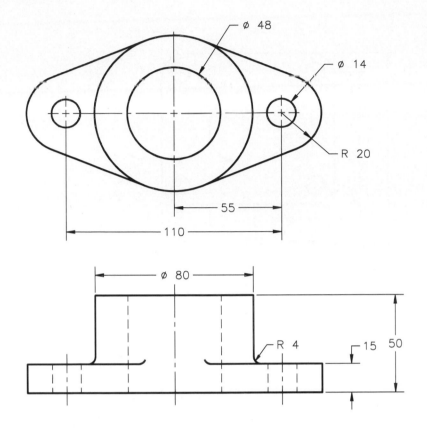

ø 48

ø 14

R 20

55

110

ø 80

R 4

15

50

 9.

P19-9

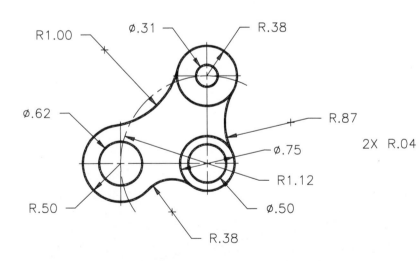

R1.00

ø.31

R.38

ø.62

R.87

ø.75

R1.12

R.50

ø.50

R.38

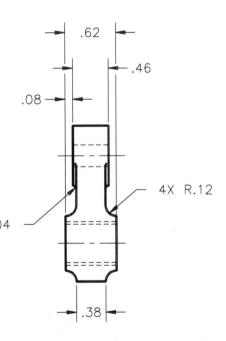

.62

.46

.08

4X R.12

2X R.04

.38

10.

P19-10

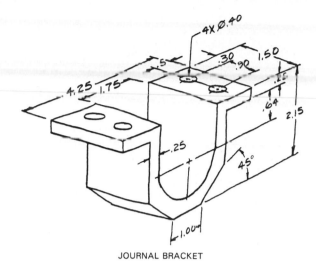

JOURNAL BRACKET

11.

P19-11

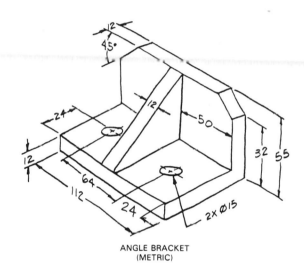

ANGLE BRACKET
(METRIC)

12.

P19-12

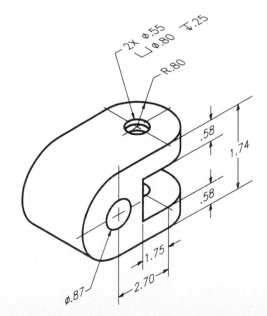

13.

P19-13

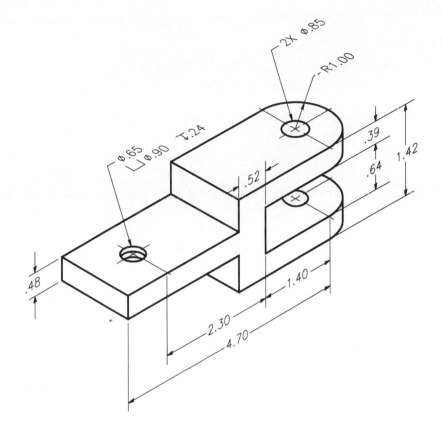

14.

P19-14

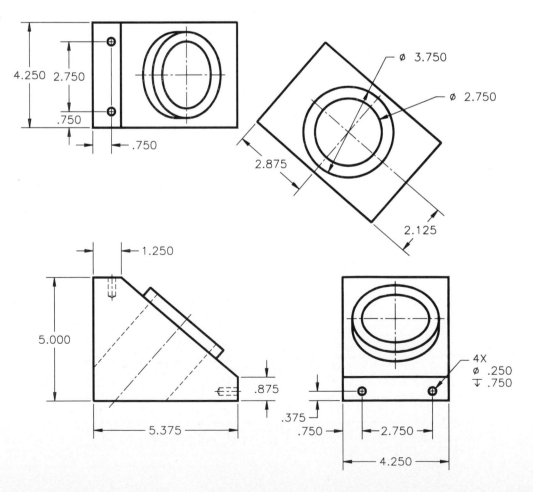

15.

P19-15

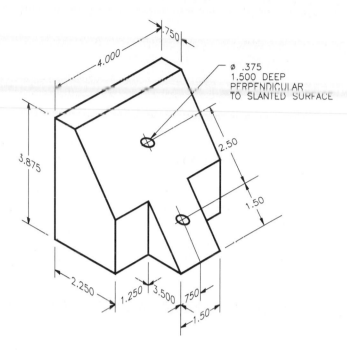

ø .375
1.500 DEEP
PERPENDICULAR
TO SLANTED SURFACE

.750
4.000
3.875
2.50
1.50
2.250
1.250
3.500
.750
1.50

16. Use the MVSETUP command to customize the ANSI-A, ANSI-B, and ANSI-C title blocks for your company or school. An example is provided in Figure 19-41, or refer to the border and title block arrangements of local industries. Be sure to include the following elements in your customized title block:

   - Company or school name, address, and telephone number.
   - Corporate logo or school mascot (if applicable).
   - Drafter's name.
   - Tolerance block for inch drawings (similar to Figure 19-41.)
   - Sheet size.
   - Part name.
   - Material.

17. Use the MVSETUP command to customize the ISO A4, ISO A3, and ISO A2 title blocks for your company or school. Include the following items in addition to the ones listed for Problem 16.

   - Tolerance block for metric drawings. For example:
   MILLIMETERS UNLESS OTHERWISE SPECIFIED.
   TOLERANCES:
   .X   = ±.1
   .XX   = ±.05
   .XXX = ±.010

18. Use the MVSETUP command to customize architectural title blocks for your company or school. Format the design for A-size, B-size, and C-size sheets as needed. Refer to title blocks of local architectural firms for examples of elements in them, or use the sample below as a guide.

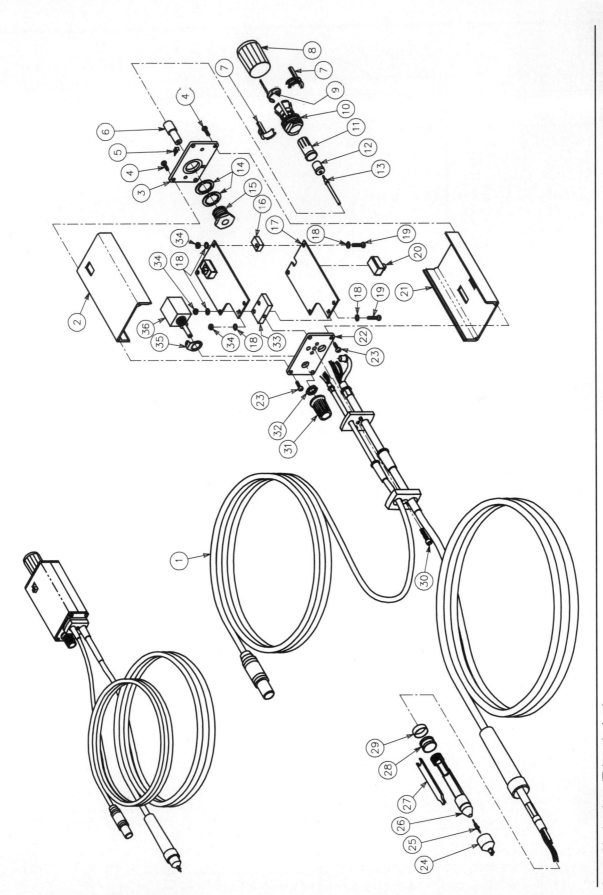

Assembly drawing. (Tektronix, Inc.)

Chapter 20

BASIC DIMENSIONING PRACTICES

Learning objectives

After completing this chapter, you will be able to:

- ○ Use the dimensioning commands to dimension given objects to ASME or other drafting standards.
- ○ Identify and set variables that affect the appearance of dimensions.
- ○ Add linear, angular, diameter, and radius dimensions to a drawing.
- ○ Set the appropriate units and decimal places for dimension numerals.
- ○ Use text size and style consistent with ASME or other professional standards.
- ○ Use the proper character codes to display symbols with dimension text.
- ○ Add dimensions to a separate layer.
- ○ Place general notes on drawings.

Dimensions are given on product designs for manufacturing and construction to describe the size, shape, and location of features on an object or structure. The dimension may consist of numerical values, lines, symbols, and/or notes, Figure 20-1. Each drafting field (mechanical, architectural, civil, electronics, etc.) uses a different type of dimensioning technique. Therefore, it is important for a drafter to place dimensions in accordance with company and industry standards. The standard emphasized in this text is ASME Y14.5M-1994, *Dimensioning and Tolerancing*. The "M" in ASME Y14.5M means the standard is written with metric numeric values. ASME Y14.5M, *Dimensioning and Tolerancing* is published by the American Society of Mechanical Engineers (ASME). The standard can be ordered directly from ASME, 345 47th Street, New York, NY 10017. It also can be obtained from The American National Standards Institute (ANSI), 1430 Broadway, New York, NY 10018. This text uses and discusses the correct application of both inch and metric dimensioning.

AutoCAD's dimensioning functions provide you with unlimited flexibility. Available commands allow you to dimension linear distances (DIMLINEAR and DIMALIGNED), circles (DIMDIAMETER), and arcs (DIMRADIUS). The LEADER command allows you to place a note with an arrow and leader line pointing to the feature. In addition to these commands, AutoCAD includes a number of variables that allow you to modify the appearance of dimensions. These affect the height, width, style, and spacing of individual components of a dimension.

This text covers the comprehensive elements of AutoCAD dimensioning in four chapters: this chapter, **Basic Dimensioning Practices** covers fundamental standards and practices; Chapter 21, **Intermediate Dimensioning** covers special applications and coordinate dimensioning; Chapter 22, **Advanced Dimensioning and Tolerancing** covers dimension styles and editing dimensions; and Chapter 23, **Geometric Dimensioning and Tolerancing (GD&T)** covers geometric dimensioning and tolerancing practices.

Figure 20-1.   Dimensions describe size and location. Follow accepted conventions when dimensioning drawings.

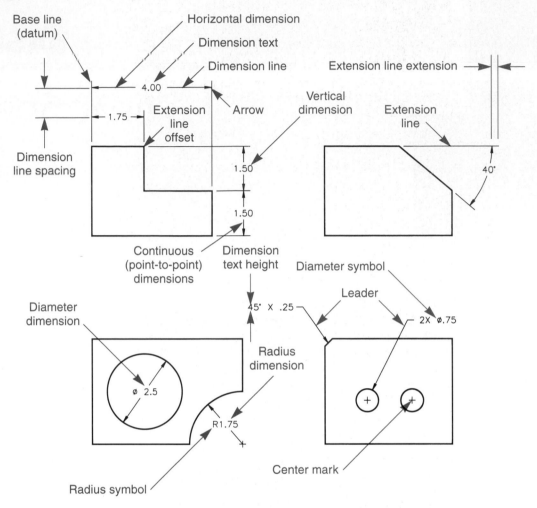

THE AUTOCAD DIMENSIONING COMMAND

AUG 9

Dimensioning is performed using DRAW DIM and MOD DIM screen menus, and Dimensioning in the Draw pull-down menu. When you select DRAW DIM from the screen menu or type DIM at the Command: prompt, the following options appear:

AutoCAD

* * * *

Linear:	*For drawing horizontal and vertical linear dimensions.*
Aligned:	*Used to draw dimensions that are aligned with an object.*
Diametr:	*For dimensioning circles, but can be used to dimension arcs.*
Radius:	*For dimensioning arcs, but can be used to dimension circles.*
Angular:	*Used to dimension angles.*
Ordinat:	*Used for arrowless coordinate dimensioning–Chapter 21.*
Baselin:	*This is for automatic datum dimensioning.*
Continu:	*Used for automatic chain dimensioning.*
Center:	*For drawing center marks in circles and arcs.*
Leader:	*Draws leader lines for notes.*
Toleran:	*Accesses geometric dimensioning and tolerancing GD&T–Chapter 23.*
DDim:	*Opens the Dimensioning Styles dialog box–Chapter 22.*
DimStyl:	*Used to access the Dimension Styles Edit options–Chapter 22.*

PROFESSIONAL TIP

It is the intent of AutoCAD Release 13 to provide the DIM command for compatibility with previous releases. You are encouraged to enter the dimensioning commands at the Command: prompt rather than using the DIM command. However, entering the Dim: mode shortens the typing requirements and can be faster for drafters who primarily use the keyboard for command entry, as opposed to menu picks. For example, one of the dimensioning commands is DIMDIA. This may be entered either of the following ways:

Command: **DIMDIA** ↵

or

Command: **DIM** ↵
Dim: **DIA** ↵

Typing at the Dim: prompt may be faster if you are doing several different dimensioning commands. This text presents both methods. You should experiment with all of the techniques and do what works best for the situation.

When you pick MOD DIM from the AutoCAD screen menu, the following dimension editing commands are displayed:

DimEDIT: *Used to edit dimension text and extension lines–Chapter 22.*
DimTedt: *This is used to move and rotate dimension text–Chapter 22.*
DDIM: *For creating and modifying dimension styles–Chapter 22.*
DimStyl: *Used to create, set, and apply dimensioning styles–Chapter 22.*
Overrid: *Used to override dimension system variables–Chapter 22.*

When you enter the DIM command, the only way to return to the Command: prompt is by typing EXIT at the Dim: prompt, CTRL+C, or puck button 3. If you plan to perform only one dimensioning operation, type DIM1 at the Command: prompt. After performing the one dimensioning task, AutoCAD returns to the Command: prompt.

PROFESSIONAL TIP

The dimensioning commands can also be accessed through the Draw pull-down menu. Pick the Dimensioning selection, and a cascading menu appears containing these options: Linear, Aligned, Radial, Angular, Ordinate, Baseline, Continue, Center Mark, Leader, Tolerance…, Oblique, and Align Text. Three of these options, Radial, Ordinate, and Align Text, also have cascading menus for additional selections. As you work with dimensions, try using the pull-down cascading menus to your advantage.

INTRODUCTION TO AUTOCAD'S DIMENSIONING VARIABLES

AUG 9

AutoCAD provides options that change the appearance of dimensions. These are called *dimensioning system variables,* or *dim vars* for short. All default values for dimensioning variables are set in the AutoCAD prototype drawing. To change a variable, type the variable name at the Command: or Dim: prompt, or select the variable from the "Dimension Styles" dialog box.

You can enter the entire dimension variable name at the Command: prompt. The following appears when you change the extension line offset:

Command: **DIMEXO** ↵
New value for DIMEXO ⟨0.12⟩:

You can also change a dimension variable if you are already in the DIM command without preceding it with the DIM prefix, like this:

Command: **DIM** ↵
Dim: **EXO** ↵
New value ⟨0.12⟩ New Value:

The default, or current value, is shown in brackets. Keep this value by pressing ENTER, or type a new value and then press ENTER.

In this chapter, dimensioning variables are introduced following the sequence in which you might use them. Notice the first three letters of each variable is "DIM." The remaining letters are a code giving the purpose of each variable. These codes make it easier for you to remember the content of each variable. Figure 20-2 displays the variables in a chart with a brief description of each. Page numbers are also included in the chart indicating the page number in this text to refer to for additional information.

Figure 20-2.   This chart gives AutoCAD dimensioning variables and their abbreviated meanings. The page numbers given refer to this text.

Dimensioning Variables								
Variable	Meaning	Pg	Variable	Meaning	Pg	Variable	Meaning	Pg
DIMALI	ALIgned dimensioning	626	DIMDEC	dimensioning DECimal places	613	DIMSOXD	Suppress Outside eXtension-Dimension lines	673
DIMALT	ALTernate units	730	DIMDIA	DIAmeter dimensioning	645	DIMSTYLE	gives current dimension STYLE and accesses the dimension style edit options	711
DIMALTD	ALTernate units Decimal places	730	DIMDLE	Dimension Line Extension	623	DIMTAD	Text Above Dimension line	622
DIMALTF	ALTernate units scale Factor	730	DIMDLI	Dimension Line Increment	642	DIMTDEC	Tolerance DECimal places	723
DIMALTTD	ALTernate Tolerance Decimal places	730	DIMEXE	EXtension line Extension	620	DIMTFAC	Tolerance text scale FACtor	726
DIMALTTZ	ALTernate Tolerance Zero suppression	730	DIMEXO	EXtension line Offset	620	DIMTIH	Text Inside extension lines, Horizontal	621
DIMALTU	ALTernate Units format	730	DIMGAP	dimension line GAP	675	DIMTIX	Text Inside eXtension lines	672
DIMALTZ	ALTernate units Zero suppression	730	DIMLFAC	Length FACtor	726	DIMTM	dimension with Minus Tolerance	723
DIMANG	dimensioning ANGles	629	DIMFIT	FIT text	647	DIMTOFL	Text Outside, Force Line inside	646
DIMAPOST	Alternate units Text Suffix	730	DIMJUST	JUSTification of text on dimension line	674	DIMTOH	Text Outside extension line, Horizontal	621
DIMASO	ASsOciative dimensioning	738	DIMLIM	LIMits tolerancing	726	DIMTOL	dimension with TOLerance	722
DIMASZ	Arrow SiZe	620	DIMLIN	LINear dimensions	616	DIMTOLJ	vertical TOLerance Justification	724
DIMAUNIT	dimensioning Angular UNITs format	632	DIMPOST	dimension Text suffix	728	DIMTP	dimension with Plus Tolerance	723
DIMBASE	BASEline dimensioning	639	DIMRAD	RADius dimension	653	DIMTSZ	Tick SiZe	622
DIMBLK	arrow BLocK display	623	DIMRND	RouND dimension units to specified value	731	DIMTVP	Text Vertical Placement	674
DIMBLK1	custom BLocK 1st extension line	676	DIMSAH	Separate custom ArrowHeads	676	DIMTXSTY	TeXt STYle	611
DIMBLK2	custom BLocK 2nd extension line	676	DIMSCALE	overall dimension SCALE factor	680	DIMTXT	dimension TeXT size	612
DIMCEN	CENter mark size	644	DIMSD1	Suppress Dimension line 1	621	DIMTZIN	Toggles Zero suppression in feet and INch values	613
DIMCLRD	CoLoR of Dimension line	681	DIMSD2	Suppress Dimension line 2	621	DIMZIN	Zero supression in feet and INch values	613
DIMCLRE	CoLoR of Extension line	681	DIMSE1	Suppress Extension line 1	621	DIMUNIT	dimensioning UNITs format	648
DIMCLRT	CoLoR of Text	681	DIMSE2	Suppress Extension line 2	621	DIMUPT	User Positioned Text	693
DIMCONT	CONTinuing dimensioning	641	DIMSHO	SHOw dragged dimensions	738			

DIMENSIONING UNITS

AUG 9

The standard units of measurement on engineering drawings are decimal inches and metric units (millimeters). When all dimensions are given in inches or millimeters, a general note should appear: UNLESS OTHERWISE SPECIFIED, ALL DIMENSIONS ARE IN INCHES (or MILLIMETERS). When using metric dimensions, a zero precedes the decimal point for measurements less than one millimeter. A metric measurement requires one less digit behind the decimal than inch measurements to maintain the same degree of accuracy, Figure 20-3.

Figure 20-3.   Examples of decimal-inch and metric dimensions. Note the zero preceding the decimal point for metric dimensions less than 1.

INCHES	MILLIMETERS
1.250	31.75
.500	12.70
.12	0.3
2.505	63.63

When dimensioning architectural or structural drawings, it is common to use feet and inches. For dimensions greater than one foot, the units are shown as FEET(′)-INCHES(″), such as 12′-6″. Distances less than one foot are noted in inches and fractions of an inch, Figure 20-4.

Figure 20-4.   Dimension formats for the construction trades.

DIMENSIONS GREATER THAN ONE FOOT			DIMENSIONS LESS THAN ONE FOOT		
8′–10 1/2″	4′–0″	24′–6″	0′–8″	8″	6 1/4″

The recommended ASME height for dimension numerals and notes on a drawing is .125 inch (3 mm). Some companies prefer .156 inch (4 mm) height. The larger text is recommended if the drawing is to be reduced. Titles and subtitles are usually .188 inch to .25 inch (5 mm to 6 mm) in height so they stand out from the rest of the drawing.

DIMENSIONING TEXT OPTIONS

AUG 9

AutoCAD gives you the flexibility to control the way the dimension text looks on your drawing. The way you set the text-related dimensioning variables may depend on your school or company standards, and on the type of drawing you are doing, such as mechanical or architectural.

Text style

When you begin a drawing, dimension text is drawn using the STANDARD text style. The text style on mechanical drawings is commonly ROMANS, while AutoCAD provides the CIBT PostScript font called City Blueprint that looks good for architectural applications. Use the STYLE command for the drawing text style and the DIMTXSTY (TeXt STYle) variable for dimension text style to make the text styles match. A text style must have been loaded using the STYLE command for it to be accessed. Use the DIMTXSTY variable like this to change the dimension text style to ROMANS:

```
Command: DIMTXSTY ↵
New value for DIMTXSTY ⟨"STANDARD" ⟩: ROMANS ↵
Command:
```

This can also be entered at the Dim: prompt as TXSTY.

Text size

If the text height is set to 0 in the STYLE command, then the dimension text height is controlled by the DIMTXT (TeXT) variable. AutoCAD's DIMTXT default (.1800) is in effect until a new value is entered. To change text to the standard .125 height used by most companies, type as follows:

> Command: **DIMTXT** ↵
> New value for DIMTXT ⟨0.1800⟩: **.125** ↵
> Command:

If the text height is set in the STYLE command, then the dimension text has the same height. If you want to have all of the text the same height, including the dimension text, then set the text height with the STYLE command. If you want to control the dimension text and the text on the rest of the drawing separately, then set the height to 0 in the STYLE command. Other dimension text can also be set. The following gives some advice on this:

> Command: **STYLE** ↵

While ROMANS font is desirable on mechanical drawings, setting the text style here does not affect the dimension text style.

> Text style name (or?) ⟨ROMANS⟩: ↵

Set the text height to 0 if you want to control dimension text height with the dimension variable:

> Height ⟨0.25⟩: **0** ↵
> Width factor ⟨1.0⟩: ↵

Most drawing text has a 0 obliquing angle, but some drafting applications or company standards prefer a 15° slant. Enter 15 here or keep the defaults (0):

> Oblique angle ⟨0⟩: ↵
> Backwards? ⟨N⟩: ↵
> Upside-down? ⟨N⟩: ↵

Be sure the text is horizontal by answering No to this prompt:

> Vertical? ⟨N⟩: ↵
> Command:

Determining drawing scale factors for dimension text height

Before plotting a drawing, you should determine the scale factor of the drawing. You can do this at the time of plotting, but at that time more work is required to update text heights. Scale factors are important since the number is used to ensure that the text is plotted at the proper height. The scale factor is multiplied by the desired plotted text height to get the AutoCAD text height that should be used while you are drawing. After the scale factor has been determined, you should then calculate the height of the text in AutoCAD. To do this, multiply the desired text height by the scale factor to get text that appears in correct proportion on the screen.

Scale factors and dimension text heights should be determined before beginning a drawing, and are best incorporated as values within your prototype drawing files.

PROFESSIONAL TIP

 If your text height was set to 0 when you used the STYLE command, then be sure the DIMTXT value is the same as the text height you specify when using the TEXT, DTEXT, or MTEXT commands. You will get different text heights for notes and dimensions if these values are not the same, giving the drawing an "amateur" appearance.

Dimension units

The DIMUNIT (UNITs) variable is used to set the units format for dimension text. The options are the same as you use in the UNITS command. Enter a value 1 through 5 for the following applications:

Value	Units	Example
1	Scientific	1.55E+01
2 (dofault)	Decimal	12.50
3	Engineering	1'-3.50"
4	Architectural	1'-3 1/2"
5	Fractional	12 1/2

The command works as follows:

Command: **DIMUNIT** ↵
New value for DIMUNIT⟨2⟩: **4** ↵
Command:

Decimal places

The DIMDEC (DECimal places) variable is used to set the number of decimal places for the value of the dimension numeral. The default is 4, but you can enter any value from 0 to 8.

Command: **DIMDEC** ↵
New value for DIMDEC⟨4⟩: **3** ↵
Command:

PROFESSIONAL TIP

Any settings that you make in the UNITS command are not altered by changes made with the DIMUNIT or DIMDEC variables.

Zero inch dimension

The DIMZIN (Zero INch) variable allows you to control the -0" part of feet-inch dimensions. When architectural or fractional units are used, the DIMZIN variable controls whether the dimension includes a "0" feet or "0" inches measurement. Valid responses to this variable for architectural dimensioning are 0, 1, 2, or 3. The following chart shows the results of selecting one of the DIMZIN variables.

Value	Results	Inches		Feet and Inches	
0 (default)	Removes 0 ft. or 0 in.	1/2"	4"	2'	1'-0 1/2"
1	Includes 0 ft. and 0 in.	0'-0 1/2"	0'-4"	2'-0"	1'-0 1/2"
2	Includes 0 ft. omits 0 in.	0'-0 1/2"	0'-4"	2'	1'-0 1/2"
3	Includes 0 in. omits 0 ft.	1/2"	4"	2'-0"	1'-0 1/2"

The DIMZIN variable is convenient when doing architectural drafting. However, other settings are preferred for mechanical drafting. For example, AutoCAD places a zero in front of all decimal dimensions when DIMZIN is set to the default (0). According to ASME standards, this is preferred for metric dimensions, but not for inch dimensions.

	Metric	Inch
	0.50	.50

In order to have AutoCAD automatically remove the 0 in front of the decimal point, set DIMZIN to 4 or 7. This is what you then get:

DIMZIN = 0	DIMZIN = 7
0.50	.50

It is more common to control the number of places after the decimal point with the UNITS command. However, you can have AutoCAD remove zeros after the decimal point by setting DIMZIN to 8. The results are:

DIMZIN = 0	DIMZIN = 8
0.50	0.5

You can even keep the zeros off the dimension before and after the decimal point with a DIMZIN setting of 15 (DIMZIN=7 + DIMZIN=8 = 15). You then will get the following results:

DIMZIN = 0	DIMZIN = 15
0.50	.5

PROFESSIONAL TIP

Autodesk documentation supports settings of 0, 1, 2, 3 as shown in the previous chart. However, DIMZIN settings above 3 do currently provide results that may be of value to the professional user. The settings have a variety of effects that may or may not be obvious. These settings also may not have any effect, depending on the type of dimensioning being used. For example, the settings 4 and 7 produce no noticeable difference when applied to decimal dimensions. The following chart displays DIMZIN settings of 0 through 15. These are the results of testing with a variety of dimensioning units. It is recommended that you can experiment with results that best suit your applications.

DIMZIN	Leading	Trailing	0 Feet	0 Inches
0			x	x
1				
2				x
3			x	
4	x		x	x
5	x			
6	x			x
7	x		x	
8		x	x	x
9		x		
10		x		x
11		x	x	
12	x	x	x	x
13	x	x		
14	x	x		x
15	x	x	x	

DIMENSION ARRANGEMENT

Dimensions are meant to communicate information about the drawing. Different industries and companies apply similar techniques for presenting dimensions. The two most-accepted arrangements of text are unidirectional and aligned.

Unidirectional dimensioning

Unidirectional dimensioning is typically used in the mechanical drafting field. The term *unidirectional* means "one direction." This system has all dimension numerals and notes placed horizontally on the drawing. They are read from the bottom of the sheet.

Unidirectional dimensions normally have arrowheads on the ends of dimension lines. The dimension numeral is usually centered in a break near the center of the dimension line, Figure 20-5.

Figure 20-5.   When applying unidirectional dimensions, all dimension numerals and notes are placed horizontally on the drawing.

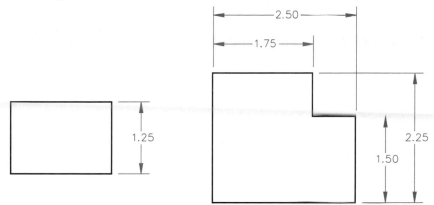

Aligned dimensioning

Aligned dimensions are typically placed on architectural or structural drawings. The term *aligned* means the dimension numerals are lined up with the dimension lines. The dimension numerals for horizontal dimensions read horizontally. Dimension numerals for vertical dimensions are placed so they read vertically from the right side of the sheet, Figure 20-6. Numerals for dimensions placed at an angle read at the same angle as the dimension line. Notes are usually placed so they read horizontally.

Figure 20-6.   In the aligned dimensioning system, dimension numerals for horizontal dimensions read horizontally. Dimension numerals for vertical dimensions are placed so they read from the right side of the sheet.

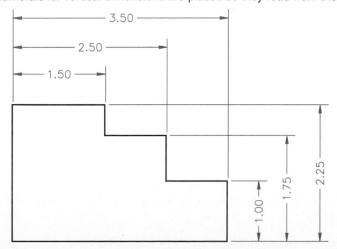

When using the aligned system, terminate dimension lines with tick marks, dots, or arrowheads. In architectural drafting, the dimension numeral is generally placed above the dimension line and the tick marks are used, Figure 20-7.

Figure 20-7. An example of aligned dimensioning in architectural drafting. Notice the tick marks used in place of the arrowheads and the placement of the dimensions above the dimension line.

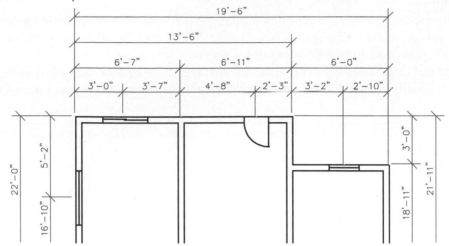

DRAWING LINEAR DIMENSIONS

AUG 9

Linear means straight. In most cases, dimensions measure straight distances, whether it be horizontal, vertical, or aligned with a slanted surface. The DIMLINEAR command allows you to measure the length of an object and place extension lines, dimension lines, dimension text, and arrowheads automatically. To do this, pick Linear: from the DRAW DIM screen menu, pick Linear in the Dimensioning cascading menu of the Draw pull-down menu, or type DIMLINEAR or DIMLIN at the Command: prompt as follows:

> Command: (type **DIMLINEAR** or **DIMLIN** and then press ENTER)
> First extension line origin or RETURN to select: (pick the origin of the first extension line)
> Second extension line origin: (pick the origin of the second extension line)

Your picks are the extension line origins. Place the crosshairs directly on the corners of the object where the extension lines begin; it may be helpful to use one of the object snap modes for accuracy. Dimensioning standards recommend that a small space or gap be left between the object and the start of the extension line. AutoCAD does this automatically with the DIMEXO setting, as shown in Figure 20-8. Do not be concerned if at first the extension lines appear to touch the object. The small spaces may not be displayed until you use REDRAW.

Figure 20-8.   Establishing the extension line origins. The object snap INTersection or ENDpoint options are useful in accurately locating the origins.

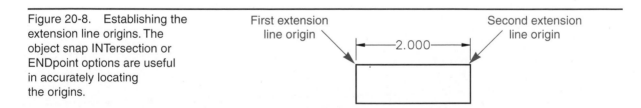

The DIMLINEAR command has many features, allowing you to generate horizontal, vertical, aligned, or rotated dimensions. After selecting the object or points of origin for dimensioning, the following options are available:

> Dimension line location (Text/Angle/Horizontal/Vertical/Rotated):

These options are outlined as follows:

- **Dimension line location.** This is the default. All you have to do is drag the dimension line to a desired location and pick, as shown in Figure 20-9. This is where preliminary plan sheets and sketches help you determine proper distances to avoid crowding. The extension lines, dimension line, dimension text, and arrowheads are automatically drawn without anymore prompting, and the Command: prompt returns:

  > Dimension line location (Text/Angle/Horizontal/Vertical/Rotated): *(pick the dimension line location)*
  > Command:

Figure 20-9.   Establishing the dimension line's location.

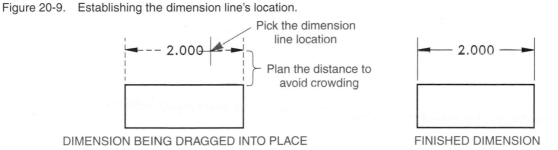

DIMENSION BEING DRAGGED INTO PLACE   FINISHED DIMENSION

- **Text.** If you type T and press ENTER, AutoCAD gives you the opportunity to provide a specified measurement or text format that you want displayed with the dimension. The value shown in brackets is the current dimension numeral. Press ENTER to accept this value, or type a new value. For example, you can type a numeral with parenthesis, called a reference dimension, like the one shown in Figure 20-10A by following this command sequence:

  > Dimension line location (Text/Angle/Horizontal/Vertical/Rotated): **T** ↵
  > Dimension text ⟨2.750⟩: **(2.750)** ↵
  > Dimension line location (Text/Angle/Horizontal/Vertical/Rotated): *(pick the dimension line location)*
  > Command:

Figure 20-10.   Using the Text and Angle options. A–A reference dimension. B–Press the space bar at the Dimension text: prompt to obtain a dimension line without text. C–The dimension text angle changed using the Angle option.

As shown in Figure 20-10B, you can have the dimension line drawn without text by pressing the space bar followed by pressing the ENTER key:

> Dimension line location (Text/Angle/Horizontal/Vertical/Rotated): **T** ↵
> Dimension text ⟨2.750⟩: *(press the space bar once and press ENTER)*
> Dimension line location (Text/Angle/Horizontal/Vertical/Rotated): *(pick the dimension line location)*
> Command:

- **Angle.** The Angle option allows you to change the dimension text angle, Figure 20-10C. While there are not many practical applications, the Angle option works like this:

  > Dimension line location (Text/Angle/Horizontal/Vertical/Rotated): **A** ↵
  > Enter text angle: **90** ↵
  > Dimension line location (Text/Angle/Horizontal/Vertical/Rotated): *(pick the dimension line location)*
  > Command:

- **Horizontal.** This option sets the dimension being created to a horizontal dimension only. The results are the same as shown in Figure 20-9. The Text/Angle options are available again in case you want to change the dimension text numeral or angle as explained before. The command sequence looks like this:

  > Dimension line location (Text/Angle/Horizontal/Vertical/Rotated): **H** ↵
  > Dimension line location (Text/Angle): *(use the T or A option, or pick the dimension line location)*
  > Command:

- **Vertical.** This option sets the dimension being created to a vertical dimension only. The command sequence looks like the following. Refer to Figure 20-11.

  > Dimension line location (Text/Angle/Horizontal/Vertical/Rotated): **V** ↵
  > Dimension line location (Text/Angle): *(use the T or A option, or pick the dimension line location)*
  > Command:

Figure 20-11.   Drawing a vertical dimension.

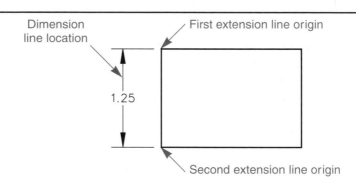

- **Rotated.** Using the Rotated option allows an angle to be specified for the dimension line. This results in a dimension line that is at an angle. A practical application is dimensioning to angled surfaces and auxiliary views. This is discussed and demonstrated later in this chapter.

  This option sets the dimension being created to a horizontal dimension only. The command sequence looks like this:

  > Dimension line location (Text/Angle/Horizontal/Vertical/Rotated): **R** ↵
  > Dimension line angle ⟨0⟩: **45** ↵
  > Dimension line location (Text/Angle/Horizontal/Vertical/Rotated): *(pick the dimension line location)*
  > Command:

PLACING HORIZONTAL AND VERTICAL DIMENSIONS INSIDE THE DIM COMMAND

AUG 9

The DIMLINEAR command, previously discussed, gives you the flexibility to place any straight dimension just by picking the extension line origins, or you can use the Horizontal option to specifically draw horizontal dimensions and the Vertical option for vertical dimensions. While the DIMLINEAR command offers much flexibility, you can also draw horizontal and vertical dimensions inside the DIM command. After entering the DIM command, enter either HOR or VERT at the Dim: prompt. When you are inside the DIM command, the HOR and VERT options work just like the Horizontal and Vertical options of the DIMLINEAR command.

This displays the following series of prompts:

> Command: **DIM** ↵
> Dim: **HOR** ↵
> First extension line origin or RETURN to select: *(pick one end of the feature to dimension)*
> Second extension line origin: *(pick the other point of the feature to dimension)*
> Dimension line location (Text/Angle): *(pick the dimension line location)*

When the dimension line location is picked, AutoCAD displays the measurement on the prompt line and allows you to change it.

> Dimension text ⟨2.0000⟩: ↵

If the numeral in brackets is what you expected, press ENTER. The extension lines, dimension lines, arrowheads, and numeral are drawn. If your drawing is accurate, the dimension numeral given is the proper measurement. However, if the number shown in brackets is not correct, type a new value, or start over again and correct your drawing.

You can also alter dimension text by entering T for the Text option, or A for the Angle option when you see this prompt:

> Dimension line location (Text/Angle):

If you type T and press ENTER, AutoCAD gives you the opportunity to provide a specified measurement or text format that you want displayed with the dimension. The value shown in brackets is the current dimension numeral. Press ENTER to accept this value, or enter a new value.

> Dimension line location (Text/Angle): **T** ↵
> Dimension text ⟨2.750⟩: **(2.750)** ↵
> Dimension line location (Text/Angle): ↵

You can have the dimension line drawn without text by pressing the space bar followed by pressing ENTER:

> Dimension line location (Text/Angle): **T** ↵
> Dimension text ⟨2.750⟩: *(press the space bar once and then press* ENTER*)*

The Angle option allows you to change the text angle as follows:

> Dimension line location (Text/Angle): **A** ↵
> Enter text angle: **90** ↵
> Dimension line location (Text/Angle): *(pick a point)*
> Dimension text ⟨2.750⟩: ↵

The Dim: prompt is issued after each dimension is complete. If the next dimension is vertical, the following command sequence is used:

> Dim: **VERT** ↵
> First extension line origin or RETURN to select: *(pick the origin of the first extension line)*
> Second extension line origin: *(pick the origin of the second extension line)*
> Dimension line location (Text/Angle): *(pick the dimension line location)*
> Dimension text ⟨2.500⟩: ↵
> Dim: *(Press* CTRL+C *or pick Exit from the screen menu)* *CANCEL*
> Command:

PROFESSIONAL TIP

Use object snap modes to your advantage when dimensioning. For example, to place exact extension line origins, use the INTersect option. This helps you find the exact corner of an object.

Setting the extension line offset

A small gap exists between the object and the start of the extension line. You can control the size of this space with DIMEXO (EXtension line Offset) variable. The default gap of 0.0625 units is the ASME standard. Suppose you needed to change the gap to .1 units. Then use the following command sequence:

Command: **DIMEXO** ↵
New value for DIMEXO ⟨0.0625⟩: **.1** ↵
Command:

Setting the extension line extension

Normally, extension lines extend beyond the last dimension line a short distance. In AutoCAD this is called the EXtension line Extension and is controlled by the DIMEXE variable. The default distance, 0.18, is an accepted standard. Figure 20-12 shows the extension line extension and offset. To change the extension line extension, enter DIMEXE at the Dim: or Command: prompts and enter a new value.

Command: **DIMEXE** ↵
New value for DIMEXE⟨0.18⟩: **.1** ↵
Command:

Figure 20-12.   The DIMEXE
and DIMEXO variables.

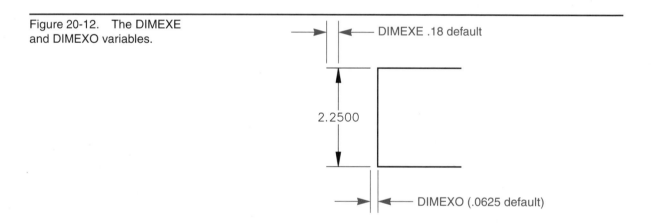

Suppressing the first extension line

Normally, extension lines are placed on both ends of the dimension line. The extension lines mark those edges of the feature you are dimensioning. However, a situation where you do not want the first extension line may occur. For example, suppose the extension line coincides with another line on the object. It is then best to omit the extension line, Figure 20-13.

Figure 20-13.   The DIMSE1
and DIMSE2 variables are used
to suppress extension lines.

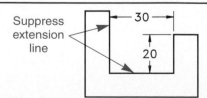

The DIMSE1 dimensioning variable is used to suppress the first extension line. The variable is either On (1) or Off (0). Off (default) places the extension line on the drawing.

Suppressing the second extension line

The DIMSE2 variable allows you to suppress the second extension line. This works the same as DIMSE1 except that the second extension line is left off the drawing. This is not a typical application and should be avoided unless absolutely necessary. Be sure to turn DIMSE1 and DIMSE2 back off before resuming normal dimensioning.

Suppressing the first dimension line

Use the DIMSD1 variable to suppress the dimension line and arrowhead referencing the first extension line. The options are On (1) and Off (2). The default is Off.

Suppressing the second dimension line

Use the DIMSD2 variable to suppress the dimension line and arrowhead referencing the second extension line. The options are On (1) and Off (2). The default is Off. Figure 20-14 compares the DIMSD1 and DIMSD2 variables.

Figure 20-14.   Using the DIMSD1 and DIMSD2 dimensioning variables.

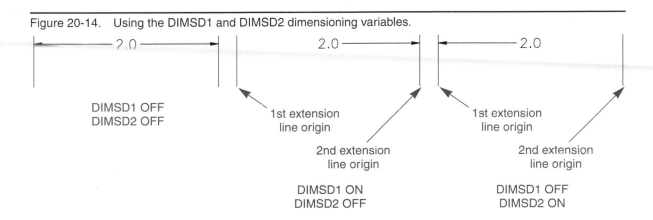

Alignment of dimension text between extension lines

When there is room, the dimension line, arrowheads, and text is placed between the extension lines. The numerals are normally placed horizontally when the DIMTIH (Text Inside Horizontal) variable is on. The DIMTIH variable is on for unidirectional dimensioning (Figure 20-5), but off for aligned dimensioning. DIMTIH off allows the text inside extension lines to align with the dimension line angle, and the dimension numerals are placed as shown in Figure 20-6.

Alignment of dimension text outside of extension lines

When there is not enough room between extension lines, AutoCAD automatically places the dimension lines, arrowheads, and numerals outside. In this instance, the DIMTOH (Text Outside Horizontal) variable works the same as DIMTIH. When this variable is on, text is drawn horizontally for unidirectional dimensioning. When it is off, text is drawn at the dimension line angle for aligned dimensioning, Figure 20-15.

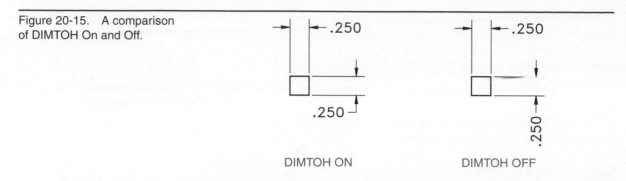

Figure 20-15.   A comparison
of DIMTOH On and Off.

DIMTOH ON   DIMTOH OFF

Placing the dimension text above the dimension line

In architectural drafting, the dimension numeral often appears above the dimension line. To do this, the DIMTAD (Text Above Dimension line) variable must be set to On (1). If it is Off (0), the default, dimension numerals are placed in a break in the dimension line. Figure 20-16 shows the effects of DIMTAD when turned On (1) and Off (0).

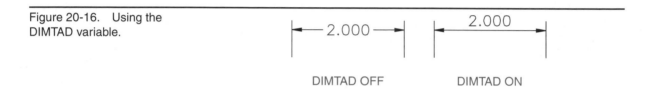

Figure 20-16.   Using the
DIMTAD variable.

DIMTAD OFF   DIMTAD ON

Controlling the size of arrowheads

In mechanical drafting, dimension lines are terminated with arrowheads where they meet the extension lines. The size of arrowheads is controlled by the DIMASZ (DIMension Arrowhead SiZe) variable. The default size, 0.18 units, is used for most drawings, Figure 20-17. To change the arrowhead size, enter the DIMASZ variable and the revised size value.

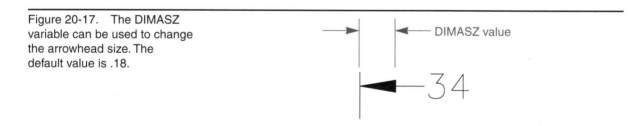

Figure 20-17.   The DIMASZ
variable can be used to change
the arrowhead size. The
default value is .18.

Drawing dimension line tick marks

The DIMTSZ (DIMension Tick SiZe) variable controls tick size. In architectural drafting, tick marks are often drawn at the ends of dimension lines. When DIMTSZ is set to 0 (default), arrowheads are drawn. If you want ticks, enter a value other than 0, such as .05. See Figure 20-18. If a value is set for DIMTSZ, the DIMASZ value is ignored.

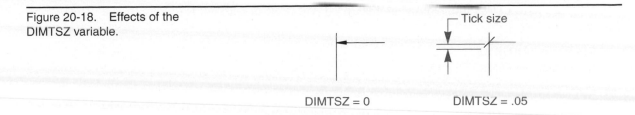

Figure 20-18.   Effects of the
DIMTSZ variable.

DIMTSZ = 0   DIMTSZ = .05

Extending the dimension line past the extension line

Normally, dimension lines meet, but do not cross extension lines. In architectural drafting, when tick marks are used, the dimension line may extend slightly beyond the extension line depending on your school or company standard. This procedure is controlled with the DIMDLE (Dimension Line Extension) variable. When DIMDLE is set to 0 (default), there is no dimension line extension. To extend the dimension line, enter a value such as .0625. See Figure 20-19.

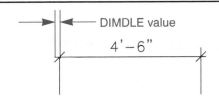

Figure 20-19.   Using the
DIMDLE variable to allow the
dimension line to extend past
the extension line. With the
default value of 0, the
dimension line will
not extend.

PROFESSIONAL TIP

It is easy to locate extension and dimension lines when grid and snap units align with the object. However, do not forget to use object snap options when it is difficult to find the extension line origins. For example, when you see the First extension line origin: prompt, type END and press ENTER. This issues the ENDpoint object snap option. Then pick the location where the dimension should begin. Object snap helps you save time and ensures accuracy.

Changing an arrowhead to a block

Another dimensioning variable, DIMBLK (BLocK), replaces arrowheads with a specific block. A block is an object, such as a symbol, that may be called up for use on the drawing. Blocks are discussed in Chapter 25. A block that might be used instead of an arrowhead is a custom-designed arrow or symbol. The DIMBLK default allows the standard arrowhead to be drawn.

AutoCAD has a standard block called DOT, which may be used at the ends of your dimension lines. Some architectural drafters like to use dots to terminate dimensions. The command sequence to use for dots is as follows:

Command: **DIM** ↵
Dim: **DIMBLK** ↵
Current value ⟨ ⟩ New value: **DOT** ↵

Figure 20-20 shows an example of the architectural dot. If the default dot is too big, make it smaller as follows:

Command: **DIMASZ** ↵
New value for DIMASZ ⟨0.18⟩: **.1** ↵

Figure 20-20.   Assigning a custom block to the DIMBLK variable. A–The DIMBLK variable is set to DOT. B–Assigning the DIMBLK variable to a custom block.

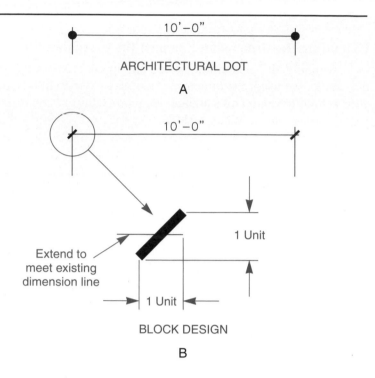

A common architectural arrowhead block is a bold tick mark, Figure 20-20. To define a customized tick mark as a block, first draw the block and give it a name such as TICK1. The block should be one unit square, and you must also draw a tail to connect with the dimension line. Then set the DIMBLK variable with the block name:

Command: **DIM** ↵
Dim: **DIMBLK** ↵
Current value ⟨ ⟩ New value: **TICK1** ↵
Dim:

Now place a horizontal dimension using this value. The DIMASZ and DIMTSZ variables should be set to their defaults. The DIMASZ variable affects the block size.

To disable the established DIMBLK, enter a period (.) at the New value: prompt:

Dim: **DIMBLK** ↵
Current value ⟨ ⟩ New value: **.** ↵

Additional block dimensioning variables are discussed later in this chapter. Detailed information regarding the creation and insertion of blocks is found in Chapter 25.

EXERCISE 20-1

❑ Load AutoCAD and open PRODR2.
❑ Draw the object lines of the following views on layer 0-7, and place all dimensions on layer 3-3.
❑ Use the proper dimensioning techniques and commands to dimension the objects exactly as shown.
❑ Save the drawing as A:EX20-1.

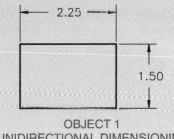

OBJECT 1
UNIDIRECTIONAL DIMENSIONING

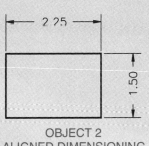

OBJECT 2
ALIGNED DIMENSIONING

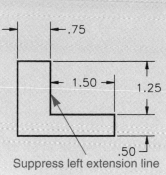

Suppress left extension line

OBJECT 3
SUPPRESS EXTENSION LINE,
UNIDIRECTIONAL DIMENSIONS,
TEXT OUTSIDE OF EXTENSION LINES

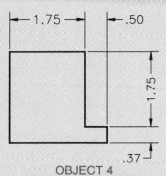

OBJECT 4
ALIGNED DIMENSION TEXT,
OUTSIDE OF EXTENSION LINES

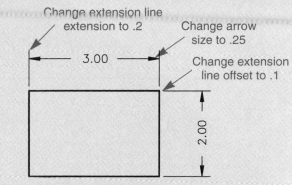

Change extension line
extension to .2

Change arrow
size to .25

Change extension
line offset to .1

OBJECT 5
CHANGING ARROWHEAD SIZE,
EXTENSION LINE OFFSET,
EXTENSION LINE EXTENSION

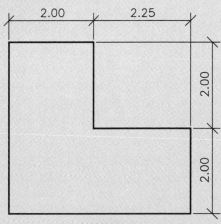

OBJECT 6
DIMENSION TEXT ABOVE DIMENSION LINE,
TICK MARKS .12

DIMENSIONING ANGLED SURFACES AND AUXILIARY VIEWS

AUG 9

When dimensioning a surface drawn at an angle, it may be necessary to align the dimension line with the surface. For example, auxiliary views are normally placed at an angle. In order to properly dimension these features, the DIMALIGNED or the DIMLINEAR Rotated option may be used.

Using the DIMALIGNED command

The DIMALIGNED command may be accessed by picking Aligned: from the DRAW DIM screen menu or by picking Dimensioning and then Aligned in the Draw pull-down menu. You can also type DIMALIGNED or DIMALI at the Command: prompt or if you are inside of the DIM command, you can type ALIGNED or ALI at the Dim: prompt. The results of the DIMALIGNED command are displayed in Figure 20-21. The following shows the command sequence if you are using the DIMALIGNED or the DIM command:

Command: *(type* **DIMALIGNED** *or* **DIMALI** *and press* ENTER*)*

or

Command: **DIM** ↵
Dim: *(type* **ALI** *or* **ALIGNED** *and press* ENTER*)*
First extension line origin or RETURN to select: *(pick first extension line origin)*
Second extension line origin: *(pick second extension line origin)*
Dimension line location (Text/Angle): *(pick the dimension line location)*
Dimension text ⟨2.250⟩: ↵
Dim:

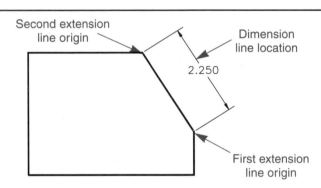

Figure 20-21. The DIMALIGNED dimensioning command allows you to place dimension lines parallel to angled features.

Using the DIMLINEAR command's Rotate option and Dim: ROTATE

Earlier, you were introduced to the DIMLINEAR command's Rotate option. This discussion continues with an explanation and example of how this option and the DIM command may be used to provide rotated dimensions to angled surfaces. This technique is different from other dimensioning commands because you are asked to provide a dimension line angle as shown in Figure 20-22. The command sequence works like this when you use either the DIMLINEAR command or the DIM command:

Command: *(type* **DIMLINEAR** *or* **DIMLIN** *and press* ENTER*)*
First extension line origin or RETURN to select: *(pick the first extension line origin)*
Second extension line origin: *(pick the second extension line origin)*
Dimension line location (Text/Angle/Horizontal/Vertical/Rotated): **R** ↵
Dimension line angle ⟨0⟩: *(type a dimension line angle such as* **45** *and press* ENTER, *or pick two points on the line to be dimensioned)*
Dimension line location (Text/Angle/Horizontal/Vertical/Rotated): *(pick the dimension line location)*
Command:

or

Command: **DIM** ↵
Dim: *(type* **ROT, ROTATED,** *or* **ROTATED** *and press* ENTER)
Dimension line angle ⟨0⟩: *(type the dimension line angle and press* ENTER, *or pick two
    points on the line to be dimensioned)*
First extension line origin or RETURN to select: *(pick the origin of the first extension line)*
Second extension line origin: *(pick the origin of the second extension line)*
Dimension line location (Text/Angle): *(pick the dimension line location)*
Dimension text ⟨2.0000⟩: ↵
Dim:

Figure 20-22.   Using the
DIMROTATED command allows
you to dimension an
angled view.

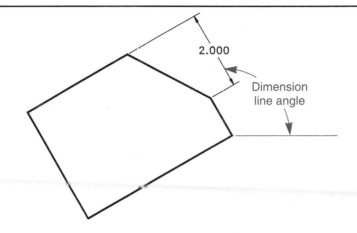

EXERCISE 20-2

❏ Open PRODR2.
❏ Draw the object lines of the following views on layer 0-7, and place all dimensions on layer 3-3.
❏ Use the proper dimensioning techniques and commands to dimension the objects exactly as
    shown.
Save the drawing as A:EX20-2.

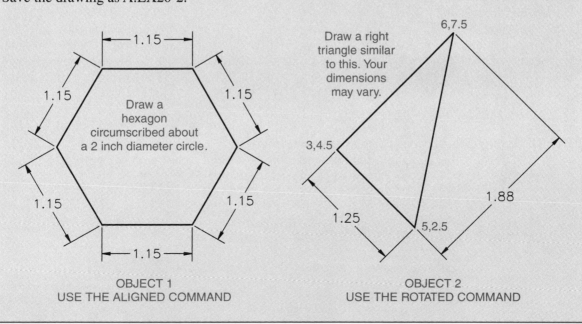

SELECTING AN OBJECT TO DIMENSION

AUG 9

In the previous discussion, the extension line origins were picked in order to establish the extents of the dimension. Another powerful AutoCAD option allows you to pick an object to dimension.

This works when you are using DIMLINEAR and DIMALIGNED commands, and the DIM subcommands HOR, VERT, ALI, and ROT. You can use this AutoCAD feature any time you see the First extension line origin or RETURN to select: prompt. At this prompt, just press the ENTER key or the SPACE bar to be asked to Select an object to dimension:. When you do this, AutoCAD automatically selects the endpoints of a line object. The endpoints of an arc are used to originate the extension lines, but if you pick a circle, the extension lines are drawn from the closest quadrant and its opposite quadrant. If the Rotate option is used, the extension lines are drawn tangent to the circle from the dimension line location. Figure 20-23 gives an example, and the DIMLINEAR command is used to demonstrate the command sequence as follows:

Command: **DIMLINEAR** ↵
First extension line origin or RETURN to select: ↵
Select object to dimension: *(pick an object on the drawing)*
Dimension line location (Text/Angle/Horizontal/Vertical/Rotated): *(pick the dimension line location)*
Dimension text ⟨1.250⟩: ↵
Command:

Figure 20-23.   Pressing ENTER at the First extension line origin: prompt allows you to pick the line, arc, or circle to be dimensioned. The cursor will change to the pick box.

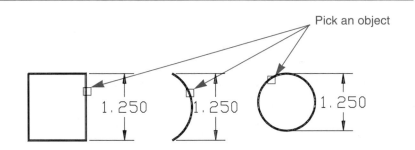

PROFESSIONAL TIP

AutoCAD does not place a diameter symbol in front of the dimension numeral when dimensioning a circle using any of the previously discussed options. For example, you may want to add a diameter symbol to the circle dimension in Figure 20-23 in compliance with ASME standards. Use the Text option by entering \U+2205 at the Dimension text: prompt like this:

Dimension text ⟨1.250⟩**: %%\U+22051.250** ↵

The resulting dimension is displayed as ⌀1.250.

Dimension text is multiline text, therefore, you need to use Unicode entries to provide special symbols. Unicode entries are discussed in Chapter 11.

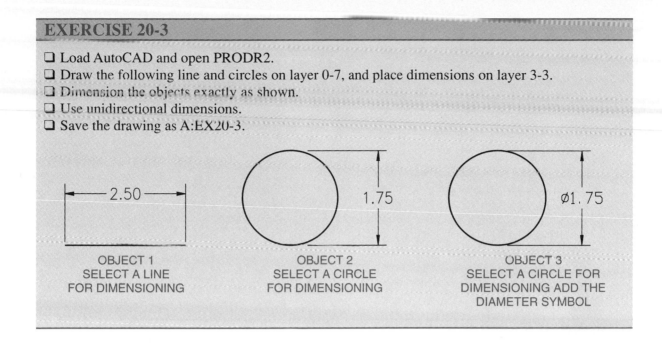

EXERCISE 20-3

❑ Load AutoCAD and open PRODR2.
❑ Draw the following line and circles on layer 0-7, and place dimensions on layer 3-3.
❑ Dimension the objects exactly as shown.
❑ Use unidirectional dimensions.
❑ Save the drawing as A:EX20-3.

OBJECT 1
SELECT A LINE
FOR DIMENSIONING

OBJECT 2
SELECT A CIRCLE
FOR DIMENSIONING

OBJECT 3
SELECT A CIRCLE FOR
DIMENSIONING ADD THE
DIAMETER SYMBOL

DIMENSIONING ANGLES IN DEGREES

AUG 9

Recommended standards for dimensioning angles are coordinate and angular dimensioning. *Coordinate* dimensioning of angles uses the DIMLINEAR command. These dimensions locate the corners of the angle, Figure 20-24.

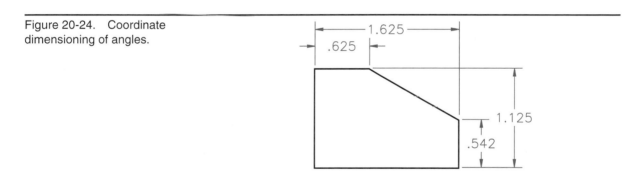

Figure 20-24.   Coordinate
dimensioning of angles.

The *angular* method gives a dimension to one corner and the angle in degrees, Figure 20-25. The angular method is established using the Angular: command found in the DRAW DIM screen menu, the Angular command in the Dimensioning cascading menu of the Draw pull-down menu, by typing DIMANG at the Command: line, or ANG at the Dim: prompt.

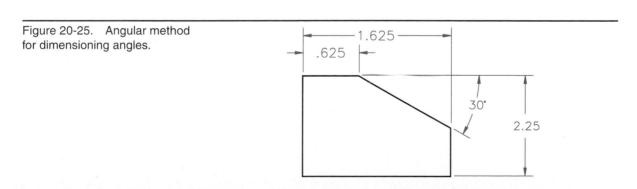

Figure 20-25.   Angular method
for dimensioning angles.

Dimensioning the angle between two nonparallel lines–the angular method

You can dimension the angle between two nonparallel lines. The intersection of the lines is the angle's vertex. AutoCAD automatically draws extension lines if they are needed, as shown in Figure 20-25 and detailed in Figure 20-26. The command sequence is as follows:

Command: *(type* **DIMANG** *or* **DIM** *and press* ENTER*)*

or

Command: **DIM** ↵
Dim: *(type* **ANG** *or* **ANGULAR** *and press* ENTER*)*
Select arc, circle, line, or RETURN: *(pick one of the lines of the angle to be dimensioned)*
Second line: *(pick the second line of the angle to be dimensioned)*
Dimension arc line location (Text/Angle): *(pick the desired location of the arc-shaped dimension line)*
Dimension text ⟨45⟩: *(press* ENTER *to accept the text, or type in a new value and press* ENTER*)*
Enter text location (or RETURN): ↵

Figure 20-26. Dimensioning angles with the text centered within the dimension line.

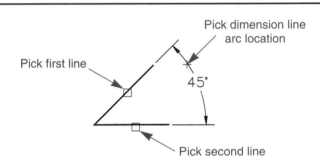

The last prompt asks you to enter the text location. Press ENTER to have AutoCAD draw the dimension line and center the numeral in the dimension line, as shown in Figure 20-26.

Suppose you want the text placed outside the extension lines, or you may not want the text centered. Then pick the text location yourself at the Enter text location (or RETURN): prompt. The position you pick is important. A leader is not connected to the numeral. Do not place the numeral where it could be confused with another part of the drawing. See Figure 20-27.

Figure 20-27. Manually locating the angle numeral.

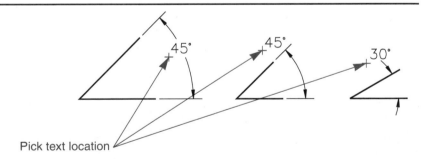

Placing angular dimensions on arcs

The ANGULAR command can also be used to dimension the angular relationship of an arc. When this is done, the arc's center point becomes the angle vertex and the two arc endpoints are the origin points for the extension lines, as shown in Figure 20-28. The command sequence is as follows:

Command: **DIMANG** ↵
Select arc, circle, line or RETURN: *(pick the arc)*
Dimension arc line location (Text/Angle): *(pick the desired dimension line location)*
Dimension text ⟨128⟩: ↵
Enter text location (or RETURN): *(press ENTER to accept the AutoCAD text location, or pick a desired location for the text)*

Figure 20-28.   Placing angular
dimensions on arcs.

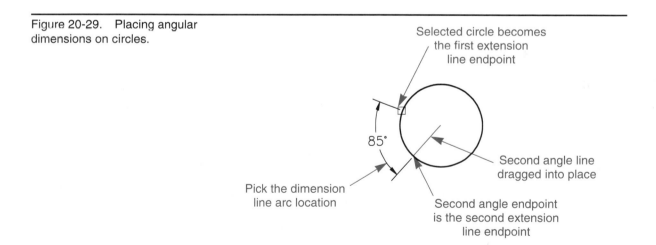

Arc center point
is automatically
determined

Pick the arc

128°

Pick the dimension
line arc location

Placing angular dimensions on circles

The ANGULAR command can also be used to dimension an angular feature related to a circle. When this is done, the circle's center point becomes the angle vertex and two picked points are the origin points for the extension lines, as shown in Figure 20-29. The command sequence is as follows:

Command: **DIMANG** ↵
Select arc, circle, line, or RETURN: *(pick the circle)*

Figure 20-29.   Placing angular
dimensions on circles.

Selected circle becomes
the first extension
line endpoint

85°

Second angle line
dragged into place

Pick the dimension
line arc location

Second angle endpoint
is the second extension
line endpoint

The point you pick on the circle becomes the endpoint of the first extension line. You are then asked for the second angle endpoint which becomes the endpoint of the second extension line. The command sequence is as follows:

Second angle endpoint: *(pick the second point)*
Dimension arc line location (Text/Angle): *(pick the desired dimension line location)*
Dimension text ⟨85⟩: ↵
Enter text location (or RETURN): *(press ENTER to accept the AutoCAD text location, or pick a desired location for the text)*

PROFESSIONAL TIP

The use of angular dimensioning for circles increases the number of possible solutions for a given dimensioning requirement, but the actual uses are limited. The first angle point is indicated by the point specified with the circle pick. Therefore, if this is to be an accurate point, it must coincide with a known point on the circle such as the intersection of a line and the circle using the OSNAP INTersection mode, or the quadrant of a circle using the OSNAP QUAdrant mode. One professional application may be dimensioning an angle from a quadrant point to a particular feature without having to first draw a line to dimension. This represents added convenience for specifying the angle. An additional positive aspect of this option is the ability to specify angles that exceed 180°.

Angular dimensioning through three points

You also have the flexibility to establish an angular dimension through three points. The points are the angle vertex and the two angle line endpoints. See Figure 20-30. To do this, press ENTER after the first prompt:

Command: **DIMANG** ↵
Select arc, circle, line or RETURN: ↵
Angle vertex: *(pick a vertex point)*

Figure 20-30. Angular dimensioning using three points.

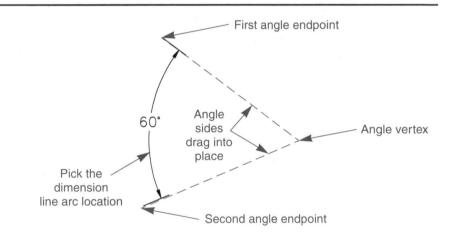

The side of the angle is dragged into place to assist in locating the first angle endpoint:

First angle endpoint: *(pick the first endpoint)*
Second angle endpoint: *(pick the second endpoint)*
Dimension arc line location (Text/Angle): *(pick the desired dimension line location)*
Dimension text ⟨60⟩: ↵
Enter text location (or RETURN): *(press* ENTER *to accept the AutoCAD text location, or pick a desired location for the text)*

Setting the angular units

The DIMAUNIT command allows you to set the dimension value format for angular units. The numerical options provide settings that are the same as the settings found in the UNITS command. The 0 setting for decimal degrees is the default value. The values are as follows:

Value	Format	Example
0	Decimal degrees	45.00
1	Degrees/minutes/seconds	45d30'15"
2	Gradians	50.00g
3	Radians	0.7549r
4	Surveyor's units	N45d30'15"E

Do this if you want to change from the decimal degrees format to the surveyor's units:

    Command: **DIMAUNIT** ⏎
    New value for DIMAUNIT ⟨0⟩: **4** ⏎
    Command:

PROFESSIONAL TIP

The DIMUNIT and DIMAUNIT variables affects dimensions only. The UNITS command, and the LUNITS and AUNITS variables still apply to coordinate displays and inquiry commands.

EXERCISE 20-4

❏ Open PRODR2.
❏ Draw the object lines of the views on layer 0-7 and dimensions on layer 3-3.
❏ Use the ANGULAR command to dimension the object exactly as shown.
❏ Save the drawing as A:EX20-4.

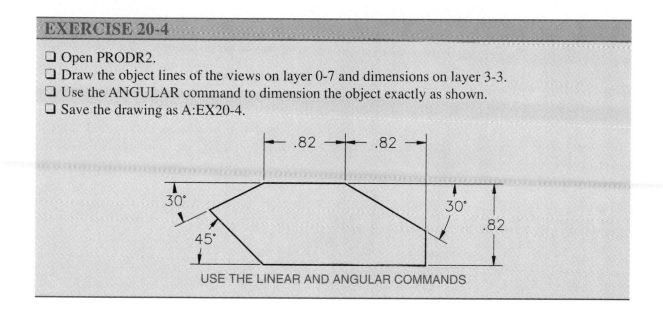

USE THE LINEAR AND ANGULAR COMMANDS

DIMENSIONING PRACTICES

Dimensioning practices often depend on product requirements, the manufacturing accuracy, standards, and tradition. Dimensional information includes size dimensions, location dimensions, and notes. Two techniques that identify size and location are chain and datum dimensioning. The method used depends on the accuracy of the product and the drafting field, such as mechanical or architectural drafting.

SIZE DIMENSIONS AND NOTES

Size dimensions provide the size of physical features, Figure 20-31. They include lines, dimension lines and numerals, or notes. Size dimensioning practices depend on the techniques used to dimension different geometric features. A *feature* is considered any physical portion of a part or object, such as a surface, slot, hole, window, or door. Dimensioning standards are used so an object designed in one area of the country may be manufactured or built somewhere else. This discussion provides short descriptions of common features and shows recommended dimensioning techniques.

There are two types of notes on a drawing: specific notes and general notes. *Specific notes* relate to individual or specific features on the drawing. They are attached to the feature being dimensioned using a leader line. *General notes* apply to the entire drawing and are placed in the lower-left corner, upper-left corner, or above or next to the title block depending on the company practices.

Figure 20-31. Size
dimensions and specific notes.

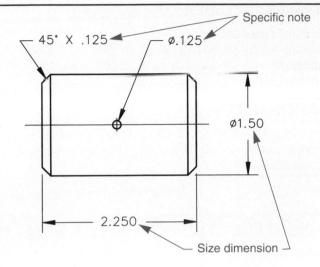

Dimensioning flat surfaces and architectural features

In mechanical drafting, flat surfaces are dimensioned by giving measurements for each feature. If there is an overall dimension provided, you can omit one of the dimensions because the overall dimension controls the dimension of the last feature. In architectural drafting, it is common to place all dimensions without omitting any of them. The idea is that all dimensions should be shown to help make construction easier. See Figure 20-32.

Figure 20-32. Dimensioning flat surfaces and architectural features.

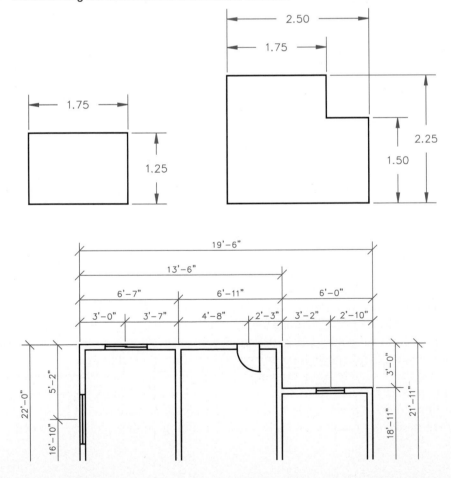

Dimensioning cylindrical shapes

The diameter and length of a cylindrical shape may be dimensioned in the view where the cylinder appears rectangular, Figure 20-33. Using this method, both the length of the cylindrical shape and the diameter can be dimensioned in the same view. Place dimension lines far enough apart so the dimension numerals are not crowded.

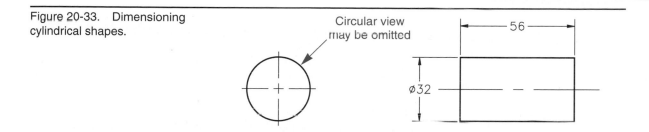

Figure 20-33.   Dimensioning cylindrical shapes.

Dimensioning square and rectangular features

Square and rectangular features are usually dimensioned in the views where the length and height are shown. The square symbol may be used preceding the dimension for the square feature, Figure 20-34. The square symbol must be developed as a block. Blocks are discussed in Chapter 25.

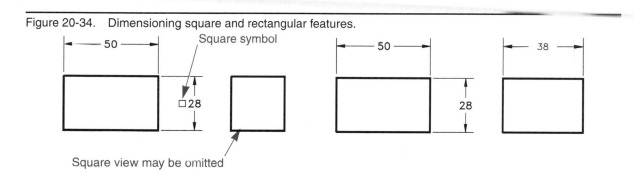

Figure 20-34.   Dimensioning square and rectangular features.

Dimensioning conical shapes

One method to dimension a conical shape is by giving the diameters at both ends and the length. See Figure 20-35. Another method is to give the taper angle and length.

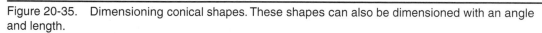

Figure 20-35.   Dimensioning conical shapes. These shapes can also be dimensioned with an angle and length.

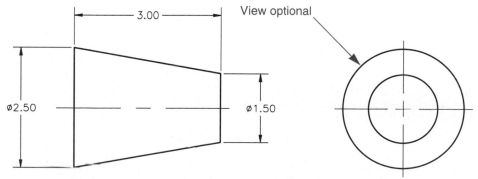

Dimensioning hexagons

Hexagonal shapes are dimensioned by giving the distance across the flats and the length. See Figure 20-36.

Figure 20-36.   Hexagons are dimensioned across their flats with a length given.

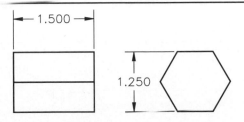

EXERCISE 20-5

❑ Open PRODR2.
❑ Draw the object lines of the following views on layer 0-7, and place all dimensions on layer 3-3.
❑ Use the proper dimensioning techniques and commands to dimension the objects exactly as shown.
❑ Save the drawing as A:EX20-5.

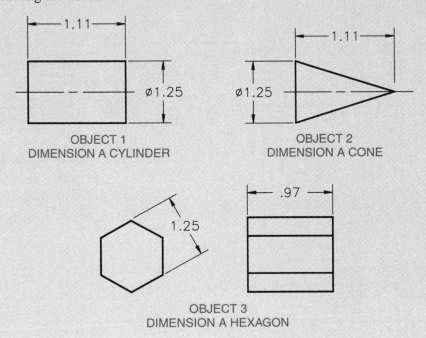

LOCATION DIMENSIONS

Location dimensions are used to locate features on an object. They do not provide the size. Holes and arcs are dimensioned to their centers in the view where they appear circular. Rectangular features are dimensioned to their edges, Figure 20-37. In architectural drafting, windows and doors are dimensioned to their centers on the floor plan.

Figure 20-37.   Locating circular and rectangular features.

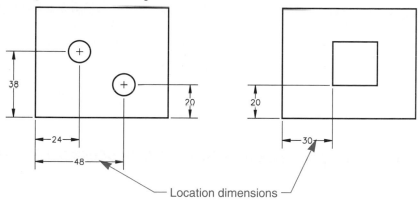

There are two basic location dimensioning systems: rectangular and polar coordinate dimensioning. *Rectangular coordinates* are linear dimensions used to locate features from surfaces, centerlines, or center planes. AutoCAD performs this type of dimensioning using a variety of dimensioning commands. The most frequently used command is DIMLINEAR and its options. See Figure 20-38.

Figure 20-38.   Rectangular coordinate location dimensions.

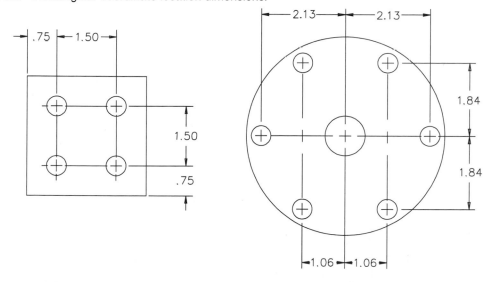

The *polar coordinate system* uses angular dimensions to locate features from surfaces, center-lines, or center planes. The angular dimensions in the polar coordinate system are drawn using AutoCAD's DIMANGULAR command. Results of the DIMANGULAR command are shown in Figure 20-39.

Figure 20-39. Polar coordinate location dimensions.

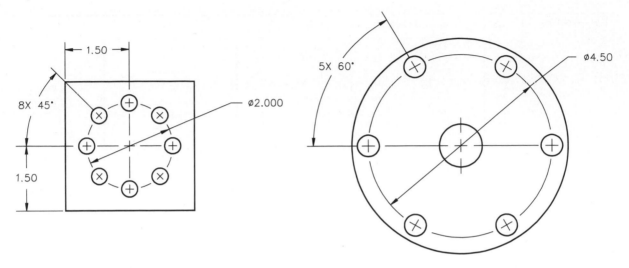

CHAIN DIMENSIONING

Chain dimensioning, also called *point-to-point dimensioning*, places dimensions in a line from one feature to the next. Chain dimensioning is sometimes used in mechanical drafting. However, there is less accuracy since each dimension is dependent on other dimensions in the chain. Architectural drafting uses chain dimensioning in most applications. Figure 20-40 shows examples of chain dimensioning. In mechanical drafting, it is common to leave one dimension blank and provide an overall dimension. Architectural drafting usually shows dimensions all the way across, plus an overall dimension.

Figure 20-40. Chain dimensioning.

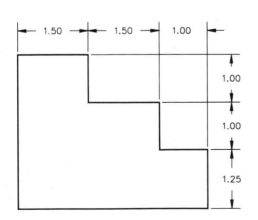
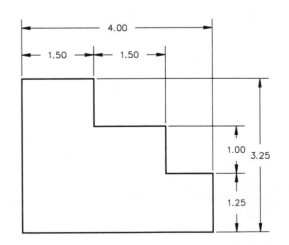

DATUM DIMENSIONING

With *datum*, or *baseline dimensioning*, dimensions on an object originate from common surfaces, centerlines, or center planes, Figure 20-41. Datum dimensioning is commonly used in mechanical drafting because each dimension is independent of the others. This achieves more accuracy in manufacturing.

Figure 20-41.   Datum dimensioning.

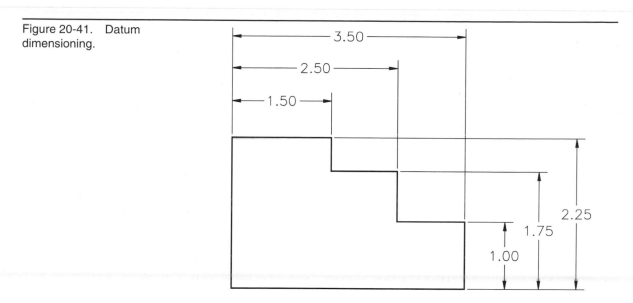

MAKING DATUM AND CHAIN DIMENSIONING EASY   AUG 9

AutoCAD refers to datum dimensioning as "baseline" and chain dimensioning as "continue." You can access these commands by picking Baselin: or Continu: in the DRAW DIM screen menu, or pick Baseline or Continue from the Dimensioning cascading menu of the Draw pull-down menu, or type either DIMBASE or DIMCONT at the command prompt. If you are using the DIM command, you can type BA (BAseline) or CO (COntinue) at the Dim: prompt. Baseline dimensions can be created with linear, ordinate, and angular dimensions. Ordinate dimensions are discussed in Chapter 21. You can draw baseline dimensions from an existing dimension or you can draw a linear or angular dimension and then proceed with baseline dimensioning. AutoCAD automatically spaces and places the extension lines, dimension lines, arrowheads, and numerals. When you begin a new drawing and enter the DIM-BASE command, AutoCAD asks you to Select base dimension:. You need to draw a dimension before using Baseline. Baseline then allows you to add additional datum dimensions to the previous dimension. For example, to dimension a series of horizontal baseline dimensions, Figure 20-42, use the following procedure:

Command: *(type* **DIMLIN** *or* **DIMLINEAR** *and press* ENTER*)*
First extension line origin or RETURN to select: *(pick the first extension line origin)*
Second extension line origin: *(pick the second extension line origin)*
Dimension line location (Text/Angle/Horizontal/Vertical/Rotated): *(pick the dimension line location)*
Command: *(type* **DIMBASE** *or* **DIMBASELINE** *and press* ENTER*)*
Second extension line origin or RETURN to select: *(pick the second extension line origin or the next baseline dimension)*
Second extension line origin or RETURN to select: *(pick the second extension line origin for the next baseline dimension)*
Second extension line origin or RETURN to select: ↵
Select base dimension: ↵
Command:

Figure 20-42.   Using the DIMBASELINE command. AutoCAD automatically spaces and places the extension lines, dimension lines, arrowheads, and numerals.

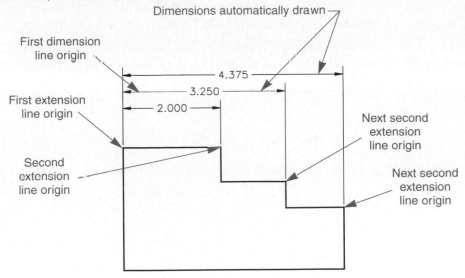

Baseline dimensions are automatically drawn until you press ENTER twice to return to the Command: prompt. This only occurs when DIMBASE is used. Only one dimension is drawn when the DIM subcommand BASE or BA is used, then the Dim: prompt returns. However, you can get immediately back to using the BAseline subcommand by pressing ENTER at the next Dim: prompt:

Command: **DIM** ⏎
Dim: *(type* **BASE** *or* **BA** *and press* ENTER*)*
Second extension line or RETURN to select: *(pick the second extension line origin for the next baseline dimension)*
Dimension text ⟨3.250⟩: ⏎
Dim: ⏎
BASE
Second extension line or RETURN to select: *(pick another second extension line origin for the next baseline dimension)*
Dimension text ⟨4.375⟩: ⏎
Dim:

In some cases, you may want to draw datum dimensions to existing dimensions other than the previously drawn dimension. Use this method:

Command: *(type* **DIMBASE** *or* **DIMBASELINE** *and press* ENTER*)*
Second extension line origin or RETURN to select: ⏎
Select base dimension: *(pick the existing linear dimension)*
Second extension line origin or RETURN to select: *(pick the second extension line origin for the next baseline dimension)*
Second extension line origin or RETURN to select: ⏎
Select base dimension: ⏎
Command:

You can also draw Baseline dimensions to angular features. To do this, draw an Angular dimension followed by entering the DIMBASE command or pick an existing Angular dimension. The result of this command sequence is shown in Figure 20-43:

Command: *(type* **DIMBASE** *or* **DIMBASELINE** *and press* ENTER*)*
Select next feature or RETURN to select: *(pick the next extension line origin for the next baseline dimension)*
Select next feature or RETURN to select: *(pick the next extension line origin for the next baseline dimension)*
Second extension line origin or RETURN to select: ↵
Select base dimension: ↵
Command:

Figure 20-43. Using the DIMBASELINE command to datum dimension angular features.

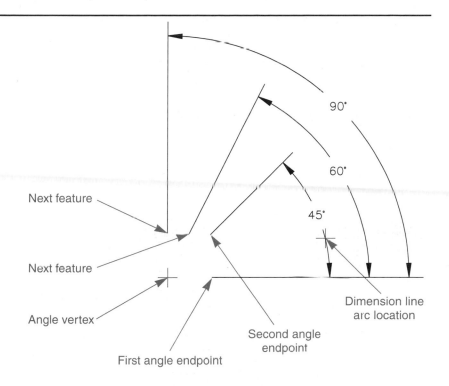

The DIMCONTINUE command is used in the same manner as the DIMBASELINE command. The prompts and options are the same. The result is the chain dimensioning shown in Figure 20-44.

Figure 20-44. Using the DIMCONTINUE command.

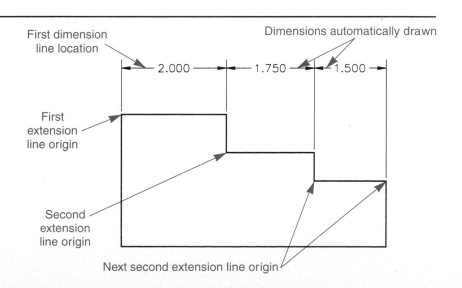

PROFESSIONAL TIP

The preceding discussion about the DIMBASE and DIMCONT commands illustrate how you can implement either datum or chain dimensioning immediately after placing your first horizontal or vertical dimension. However, you do not have to use DIMBASE or DIMCONT immediately after a dimension that is to be used as a base or chained with other dimensions. You can come back later and do it by pressing ENTER at the Select extension line origin or RETURN to select: option. For example, you can place the first dimension for reference, and then return to work on other drawing features before you proceed with the datum or chain dimensioning. When you want to finish the datum or chain dimensioning, enter the DIMBASE or DIMCONT command and use the Select base dimension: option. You can also type BASE or CONT at the Dim: prompt, or pick either as needed from the screen menu. AutoCAD automatically uses the last dimension you drew as reference for the next dimensions. This is the command sequence when you use the Dim: prompt:

Command: **DIM** ↵
Dim: *(type* **BASE** *or* **CONT** *and press ENTER)*
Second extension line origin or RETURN to select: *(pick the origin of the second extension line)*

SPACING DIMENSIONS ON A DRAWING | AUG 9 |

The primary concern when spacing dimensions on a drawing is to avoid crowding. Begin with the smallest dimension next to the object followed by increasingly larger dimensions. Place the overall dimension last. The minimum standard for dimension line spacing recommended by ASME is .4 inch (10 mm) away from the object. Place additional dimension lines .25 inch (6 mm) apart. However, these minimum distances are generally too close for most dimensioning. Use your own judgment. Dimension line spacing depends on:

- The size and complexity of the drawing. Complex drawings require careful consideration before dimensions are placed to avoid crowding.
- The amount of open area is important. If there is space available, use it to your best advantage to avoid crowding.
- The length of dimension numerals is important. Long numerals, such as 24.8750, require much space.

No matter what standard you use, dimension line spacing should be consistent. The drawing should look uniform. You can change dimension line spacing on different views, but keep the spacing of groups of dimension lines the same.

Setting dimension line spacing

The DIMDLI (Dimension Line Increment) variable controls the spacing between datum (baseline) dimension lines. The default spacing set in AutoCAD's prototype drawing is 0.38 units, Figure 20-45. The 0.38 default is too close for many applications. Additional spacing, such as .50, may be specified as follows:

Command: **DIMDLI** ↵
New value for DIMDLI: **.50** ↵
Command:

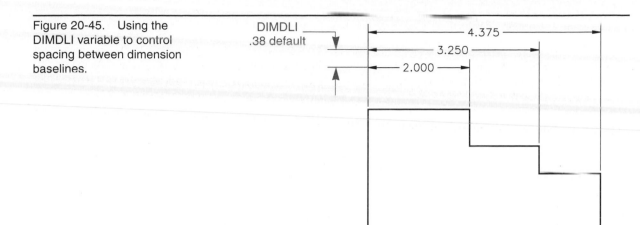

Figure 20-45.   Using the DIMDLI variable to control spacing between dimension baselines.

INCLUDING SYMBOLS WITH DIMENSION TEXT

AUG 8

After you select a feature to dimension, AutoCAD responds with the measurement, or dimensioning numeral. In some cases such as dimensioning radii and diameters, AutoCAD automatically places the radius (R) or diameter (Ø) symbol before the dimension numeral when dimensioning arcs and circles. However, in other cases related to linear dimensioning this practice is not automatic. The recommended ASME standard for a diameter dimension is to place the diameter symbol (Ø) before the numeral. Dimension numeral text is the same as multiline text discussed in Chapter 11. When adding special symbols to multiline text, you need to use the Unicode special characters. For example, to add the diameter symbol, you must type the Unicode followed by "⟨ ⟩." The "⟨ ⟩" tells AutoCAD to use the measurement it calculated. (See Chapter 11 for symbol codes.) You can also type the symbol code and the numeral to achieve the same result. This can be done using the Text option, or by entering the value as follows. Either of the following responses display the dimension text as (Ø)1.750.

Dimension text ⟨1.750⟩: **\U+2205⟨ ⟩** ↵

or

Dimension text ⟨1.750⟩:**\U+22051.750** ↵

Additional symbols are used in dimensions to point out certain features on the drawing. The diameter symbol (Ø) for circles and the radius symbol (R) for arcs are easily drawn. However, additional symbols, such as □ for a square feature, can be drawn individually, but this is time-consuming. Instead, save the symbol as a block and insert it in the drawing before the dimension text. Storing and inserting blocks is discussed in Chapter 25. Symbols used often are shown in Figure 20-46.

Figure 20-46.   Common dimensioning symbols and how to draw them.

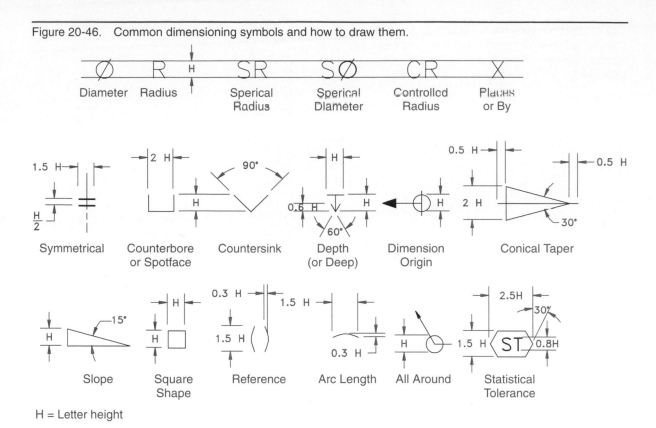

H = Letter height

DRAWING CENTER DASHES OR CENTERLINES IN A CIRCLE OR ARC

AUG 9

You may have noticed that circles and arcs are drawn without center dashes or centerlines. When small circles or arcs are dimensioned, the DIMDIAMETER and DIMRADIUS commands leave center dashes. If the dimension of a large circle crosses through the center, the dashes are left out. When you want to draw center dashes or centerlines, pick Center: from the DRAW DIM screen menu, pick Dimensioning followed by Center Mark in the Draw pull-down menu, or type DIMCENTER at the Command: prompt:

    Command: **DIMCENTER** ↵
    Select arc or circle: *(pick the arc or circle)*
    Command:

You can also enter CEN or CENTER at the Dim: prompt of the DIM command as follows:

    Command: **DIM** ↵
    Command: *(type* **CEN** *or* **CENTER** *and press* ENTER*)*
    Select arc or circle: *(pick the arc or circle)*
    Dim:

When the circle or arc is picked, center dashes are automatically drawn. The size of the center dashes or the amount that the centerlines extend outside the circle or arc is controlled by the DIMCEN (CENterline) variable. The default provides center dashes 0.09 units long. If DIMCEN is set to 0, center dashes or centerlines are not drawn. A positive value gives center dashes. For example, the value .125 displays center dashes that are .125 units long. When decimal inch units are used, .125 is the recommended length. A negative DIMCEN value draws complete centerlines in addition to center dashes. With a negative value, centerlines extend beyond the circle or arc by the amount entered. For example, a −.125 value extends centerlines .125 unit beyond the circle or arc. A zero (0) DIMCEN setting will not draw any center marks. The DIMCEN variable works like this, and is demonstrated in Figure 20-47:

Command: **DIMCEN** ↵
New value for DIMCEN ⟨0.09⟩: **–.125** ↵
Command:

Figure 20-47.   Using the DIMCEN variable. A positive value draws center dashes. A negative value draws complete centerlines. A value of 0 will not draw any center marks.

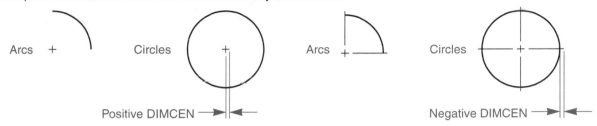

PROFESSIONAL TIP

The use of a negative DIMCEN value for small circles may result in placement of center dashes only. This is because AutoCAD needs room for the center dash and a space before the rest of the centerline symbol is placed. Don't be alarmed if this happens. Either try a smaller negative DIMCEN value or accept the results with the value you have set.

EXERCISE 20-6

❑ Load AutoCAD and open PRODR2.
❑ Draw circles and arcs similar to those shown in Figure 20-47.
❑ Set the DIMCEN value to add center dashes as shown. Use positive and negative values of .125.
❑ Place center dashes on layer 3-3.
❑ Save the drawing as A:EX20-6.

DIMENSIONING CIRCLES   AUG 9

Circles are normally dimensioned by giving the diameter. The ASME standard for dimensioning arcs is to give the radius. However, AutoCAD allows you to dimension either a circle or arc with a diameter dimension. The Diametr: command located in the DRAW DIM screen menu prompts you to select the arc or circle. You can use the Draw pull-down menu by picking Dimensioning followed by picking Radial and then Diameter. You can also type either DIMDIA or DIMDIAMETER at the Command: prompt.

When the AutoCAD dimension variables are set to their default values, the DIMDIA command automatically places the dimension line, arrowheads, and diameter dimension inside of a circle, when the circle is large enough. For medium size circles, the dimension line and arrowheads may be placed inside or outside depending on how you drag these items into place. The diameter dimension is placed with a short leader when the circle is small. Examples of these applications are shown in Figure 20-48. The DIMDIA command sequence is easy to operate, because all you have to do is pick a circle or arc to dimension. Once the circle or arc is selected, AutoCAD lets you drag the dimension line or leader to a desired position. The dimension line automatically passes through the center or the leader points to the center as preferred by ASME Y14.5M. This is the command sequence:

Command: (type **DIMDIA** or **DIMDIAMETER** and press ENTER)
Dimension line location (Text/Angle): (pick the dimension line location)
Command:

Figure 20-48.   Using the DIMDIA command with the AutoCAD dimension variable defaults.

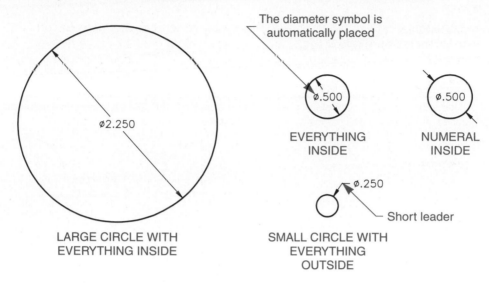

You also have the Text and Angle options that were introduced earlier. Use the Text option if you want to change the text numeral or the Angle option if you want to change the angle of the text. The Text option might be used if you are dimensioning an arc, because an R should precede the dimension numeral rather than a diameter symbol:

> Command: **DIMDIA** ⏎
> Dimension line location (Text/Angle): **T** ⏎
> Dimension text ⟨2.250⟩: **R2.250** ⏎
> Dimension line location (Text/Angle): *(pick the dimension line location)*
> Command:

Adjusting dimension variables to dimension circles with more flexibility

When you select an arc or circle to dimension as previously discussed, AutoCAD lets you drag the dimension line or leader to any desired angle, but the dimension line and numeral is either placed inside the circle or a short leader and the dimension numeral is automatically placed. You have little flexibility in this application. This practice is generally not the best solution when trying to place dimensions on a real drawing. There are dimension variables that may be set to help gain more flexibility when dimensioning circles using the DIMDIA command. These dimension variables include DIMTOFL, DIMFIT, and DIMUPT.

Using the DIMTOFL variable

The DIMTOFL (Text Outside, Force Line inside) variable allows you to cause a dimension line to be drawn between the arrowheads even when the text and arrowheads are placed outside as shown in Figure 20-49. The settings are Off (0) by default or On (1) as needed:

> Command: **DIMTOFL** ⏎
> New value for DIMTOFL ⟨Off⟩: **ON** ⏎
> Command:

Figure 20-49.   Diameter dimensions placed with DIMTOFL Off and DIMTOFL On.

DIMTOFL Off

DIMTOFL On

Using the DIMFIT variable

The DIMFIT (FIT text) variable controls the placement of arrowheads and text inside or outside of extension lines based on the space available. There are five settings available, but all of the settings will fit text and arrows inside if there is room, or outside in some cases based on how you drag the dimension. The DIMFIT settings are the options 0 through 4 and are used as follows:

0–If there is not enough room for both text and arrows, all are placed outside.

1–If there is room for text only, the text is placed inside and the arrowheads are placed outside. Otherwise, all are placed outside.

2–If there is room for arrows only, they are placed inside and the text is placed outside. Otherwise, all are placed outside.

3–This option is the default. If there is room for arrows only, arrows are placed inside. If there is room for text only, text is placed inside. Otherwise all are placed outside.

4–If there is room for text only, text is placed inside. Otherwise, a leader line is created.

Figure 20-50 shows how the DIMFIT variable can be used to alter the results of the DIMDIA command with DIMTOFL Off. Figure 20-51 shows how the DIMFIT variable can be used to alter the results of the DIMDIA command with DIMTOFL On. Change the DIMFIT setting like this:

Command: **DIMFIT** ↵
New value for DIMFIT ⟨3⟩: **4** ↵
Command:

Figure 20-50.   Diameter dimensions placed with DIMTOFL Off and DIMFIT options. Drag the dimensions if there is room inside, otherwise everything is placed outside. All examples are with DIMTOFL Off.

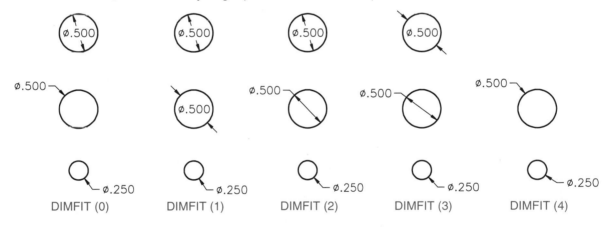

Figure 20-51.   Diameter dimensions placed with DIMTOFL On and DIMFIT options.

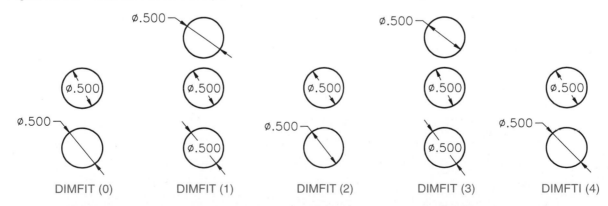

Using the DIMUPT variable

While the previous examples gave you some additional flexibility, the DIMUPT (User Positioned Text) variable gives you even more control. Part of the problem with the DIMTOFL and DIMFIT applications is the leader length may not be adjusted. In practical use, this may not provide the clearance you need to place the dimension correctly on a drawing. Also, the dimension text is placed at the center of the circle when the dimension line and text are placed inside. This text placement is not normally a recommended practice. The text should be offset from the center of the circle to allow a place for center marks. The DIMUPT variable allows you to adjust the leader length and control the dimension text location as shown in Figure 20-52. The DIMUPT variable is either Off (0) by default or On (1):

Command: **DIMUPT**↵
New value for DIMUPT ⟨Off⟩: *(type* **ON** *or* **1** *and press* ENTER*)*
Command:

Figure 20-52.   Using the DIMUPT variable provides more flexibility with the DIMDIA command.

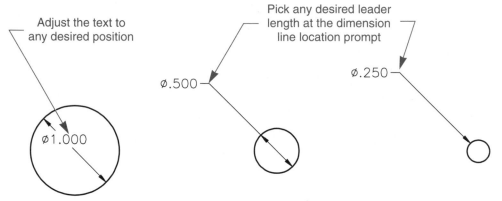

These examples are with DIMTOFL (Off) and DIMFIT (3)

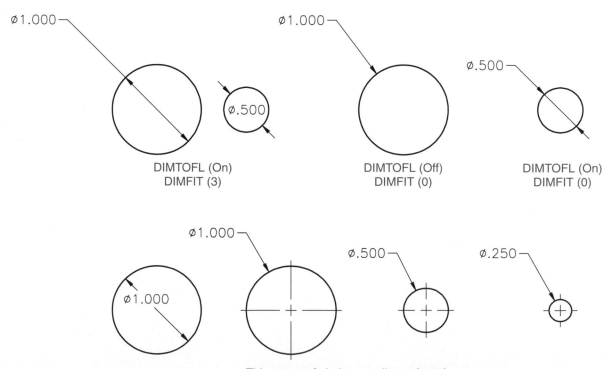

This group of circles are dimensioned
with the DIMDIA command and a DIMCEN setting of −.125

Draw the center marks automatically

When you use the DIMDIA or DIMRAD (discussed later) commands, center dashes are automatically drawn if the DIMCEN variable is set to a positive value or centerlines are drawn if DIMCEN is a negative value. The automatic centers are drawn if the dimension is placed outside of the circle or arc, otherwise no centers are drawn. See Figure 20-52.

Adjusting the DIMZIN variable

When the DIMZIN variable is set to its default (0), AutoCAD places a 0 in front of all decimal dimensions less than one, for example, 0.375. If the decimal dimension is in inches, this practice is not recommended. If the decimal dimension is metric (millimeters), then the practice is an accepted standard. Therefore, if you are using inch dimensioning, you should set the DIMZIN variable to have AutoCAD automatically remove the zero in front of decimal dimension numerals. To remove the zero in front of decimals, set the DIMZIN to 4 or 7 as follows:

Dim: **DIMZIN** ⏎
New value for DIMZIN ⟨0⟩: *(type* **4** *or* **7** *and press* ENTER*)*

NOTE   Remember, if the dimension placement is incorrect, just type a U at the Command:
      prompt after the incorrect application, and try again.

The DIAMETER command may also be used in the same manner to apply a diameter dimension to arcs. However, it is not standard to dimension arcs by diameter.

PROFESSIONAL TIP

When a dimensioning variable value is an on/off toggle, you can type YES or NO, or to save time, enter 0 for Off or 1 for On.

Command: **DIMTIX** ⏎
New value for DIMTIX ⟨0⟩: **1** ⏎

In addition, dimensioning variables can be entered transparently while in another command. For example:

Command: **DIMDIA** ⏎
Select arc or circle: **'DIMCEN** ⏎

When the dimension variables are set transparently, they are only active during the duration of the command you are working with.

EXERCISE 20-7

❑ Open PRODR2.
❑ Draw the object lines on layer 0-7, and place all center marks and dimensions on layer 3-3.
❑ Use the proper dimensioning techniques and commands to dimension the objects.
❑ Set the DIMCEN variable to −.125.
❑ With all other dimension variables at their default settings, draw and dimension four circles similar to the drawing in Figure 20-48.
❑ Draw and dimension a .500 diameter circle with DIMTOFL Off and another .500 diameter circle with DIMTOFL On, just like Figure 20-49. Label each dimensioned circle with its related DIMTOFL setting.
❑ With DIMTOFL Off experiment with the DIMFIT settings by drawing and dimensioning the same circles shown in Figure 20-50. Label each group of dimensioned circles with their correlated DIMFIT application.
❑ With DIMTOFL On experiment with the DIMFIT settings by drawing and dimensioning the same circles shown in Figure 20-51. Label each group of dimensioned circles with their correlated DIMFIT application.
❑ Turn the DIMUPT variable On. Use Figure. 20-52 as reference as you draw and dimension the following:
    ❑ Three circles (1.000, .500, and .250 diameters) with DIMTOFL Off and DIMFIT set to 3.
    ❑ Two circles (1.000 and .500 diameter) with DIMTOFL On and DIMFIT (3).
    ❑ A 1.000 diameter circle with DIMTOFL Off and DIMFIT (0).
    ❑ A .500 diameter circle with DIMTOFL On and DIMFIT (0).
❑ Save the drawing as A:EX20-7.

Dimensioning holes

    Holes are dimensioned in the view where they appear as circles. You should provide location dimensions to the center and a leader showing the diameter. As previously discussed, leader lines can be drawn with the DIMDIA command. The DIMUPT (On) variables gives you the most flexibility. Set the DIMCEN variable to get center marks. Same size holes may be noted with one hole dimension, such as 2X ⌀.50, as shown in Figure 20-53. However this must be typed using the Text option at the Dimension Line location (Text/Angle): prompt.

Figure 20-53.   Dimensioning holes.

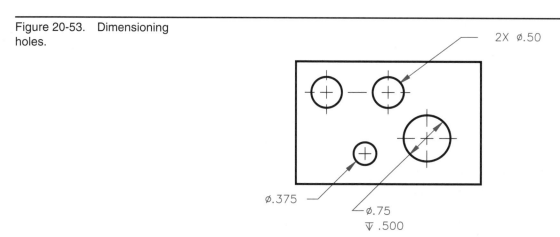

Dimensioning for manufacturing processes

    Manufacturing processes, such as counterbores, spotface, and countersink are dimensioned with two items. Locate the centers in the circular view. Place a leader providing machining information in a note, Figure 20-54. A *counterbore* is a larger diameter hole machined at one end of a smaller hole. It provides a recessed place for the head of a bolt. A *spotface* is similar to a counterbore except it is not as deep. The spotface provides a smooth recessed surface for a washer. A *countersink* is a cone-shaped recess at one end of a hole. It provides a mating surface for a screw head of the same shape. A note for these features is provided using symbols. Symbols for this type of application must be customized as blocks and are discussed in Chapter 25. These symbols are illustrated in Figure 20-46. Turn DIMUPT on to give you maximum flexibility using the DIMDIA command. DIMDIA gives you one line of text with the dimension. You need to use the DDEDIT command to place additional lines of dimension text. The LEADER command is discussed in Chapter 21 of this text.

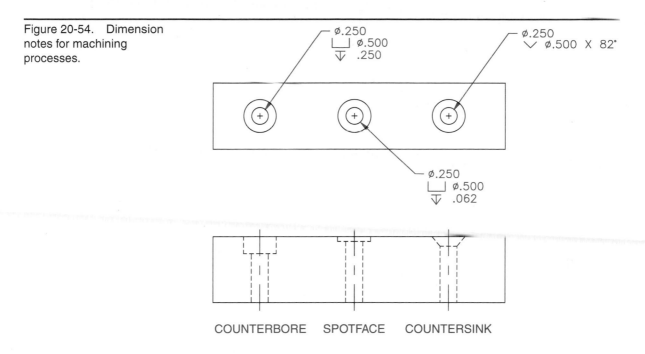

Figure 20-54.   Dimension notes for machining processes.

PROFESSIONAL TIP

After creating any dimension, the dimension text can be directly edited using the DDEDIT command. This allows entering multiline text and special notations.

Dimensioning repetitive features

Repetitive features refer to many features having the same shape and size. When this occurs, the number of repetitions is followed by an "X", a space, and the size dimension. The dimension is then connected to the feature with a leader as shown in Figure 20-55.

Figure 20-55.   Dimensioning repetitive features (shown in color).

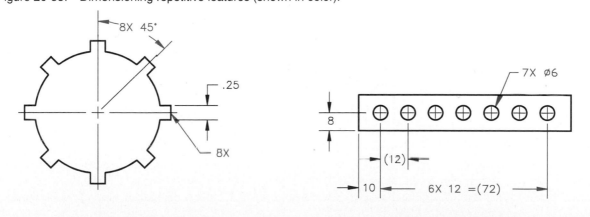

PROFESSIONAL TIP

      The ASME standard recommends a small space between the object and the extension line as shown in Figure 20-1. This happens when the DIMEXO variable is set to its default or some other desired positive value. This is very useful except when providing dimensions to center lines for the location of holes. A positive DIMEXO value leaves a space between the centerline and the beginning of the extension line, when the end of the centerline is picked, as shown at A below. This is not a preferred practice. It is recommended that you change DIMEXO to 0 for these applications. See Part B in the following figure.

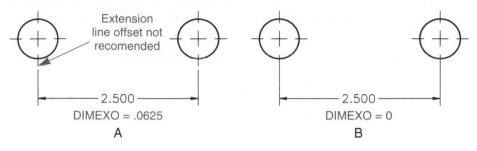

EXERCISE 20-8

❑ Load AutoCAD and open PRODR2.
❑ Draw the object lines of the following views on layer 0-7, and place all dimensions on layer 3-3.
❑ Use the proper dimensioning techniques and commands to dimension the objects exactly as they are shown.
❑ Save the drawing as A:EX20-8.

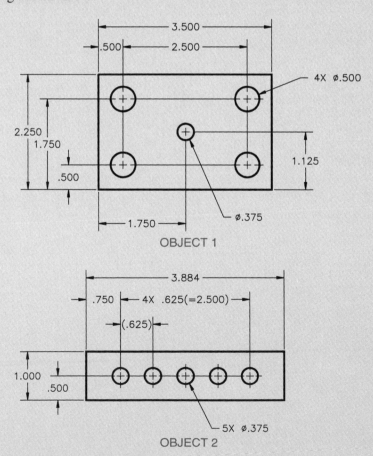

DIMENSIONING ARCS   AUG 9

The standard for dimensioning arcs is a radius dimension. A radius dimension is placed with the DIMRADIUS command. You can type either DIMRADIUS or DIMRAD at the Command: prompt, or type either RADIUS or RAD while in the DIM command at the Dim: prompt. This command may also be accessed by picking Radius: in the DRAW DIM screen menu. In the Draw pull-down menu, pick Dimensioning followed by Radial, and then pick Radius. The DIMRADIUS command allows you to dimension either an arc or circle in this manner. Using this command, AutoCAD places a leader line with an arrowhead pointing at the arc. The leader line either extends away from the arc, or from the arc through the center point depending on the size of the arc.

When the dimension variables are set to their default values, the leader length is automatically determined by AutoCAD. This leader length is often too short for practical applications. Examples using the DIMRAD command with default variables are shown in Figure 20-56 and the command sequence is like this:

    Command: *(type* **DIMRADIUS** *or* **DIMRAD** *and press* ENTER*)*
    Select arc or circle: *(pick an arc)*
    Dimension line location (Text/Angle): *(drag the leader to a desired location and pick)*
    Command:

Figure 20-56   Using the DIMRAD command to dimension arcs with AutoCAD dimension variable defaults.

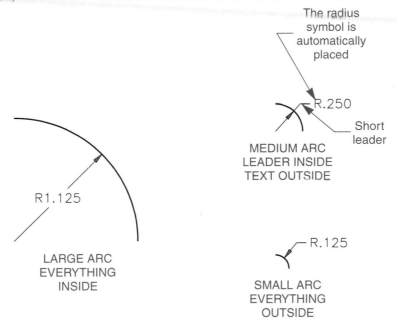

As with the previous dimensioning commands, you may use the text option to change the dimension text or use the Angle option to change the angle of the text numerals.

Adjusting the dimension variables with the DIMRAD command

Changing the dimension variables when using the DIMRAD command alters the way dimensions are presented in similar ways that you have seen before. While the effect of using the DIMTOFL variable is minor, it does force the leader inside when the arc is small as shown in Figure 20-57.

Figure 20-57.   Using the DIMRAD command with DIMTOFL Off and DIMTOFL On.

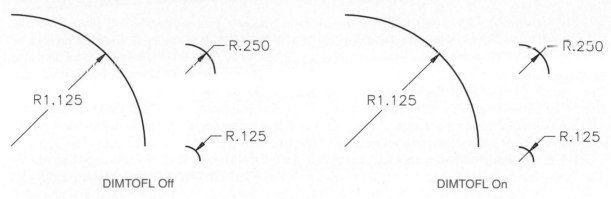

The DIMUPT variable gives you the flexibility to place the radius dimension for a large arc either inside or outside of the arc. DIMUPT also lets you adjust the text location when the leader is inside, and allows you to control the leader length when the leader is outside. See Figure 20-58.

Figure 20-58.   Using the DIMUPT variable provides more flexibility with the DIMRAD command.

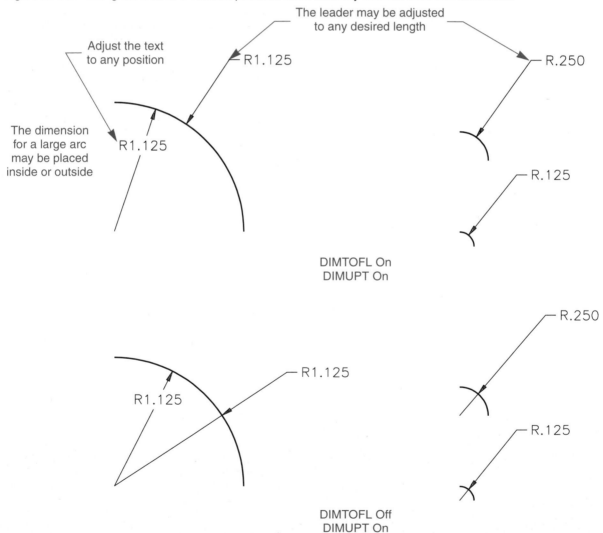

AutoCAD automatically adds the center dashes when the DIMCEN variable is nonzero, and when the leader is placed outside the arc.

If decimal inch units are used and the value is less than 1, AutoCAD places a 0 in front of the decimal, ASME Y14.5M recommends that a decimal inch be displayed without a 0 in front of the decimal point. Metric decimals, however, should have a 0 placed in front of the decimal point. To automatically delete the 0 in front of the decimal point, set the DIMZIN variable to 4.

Dimensioning fillets and rounds

Small arcs on the outside corners of a part are called *rounds*. Small inside arcs are called *fillets*. Rounds are used to relieve sharp corners. Fillets are designed to strengthen inside corners. Fillets and rounds may be dimensioned individually as arcs or in a general note if there are many of them on the part. When used, the general note for .125″ fillets and rounds is: ALL FILLETS AND ROUNDS R.125 UNLESS OTHERWISE SPECIFIED. See Figure 20-59.

Figure 20-59. Dimensioning fillets and rounds.

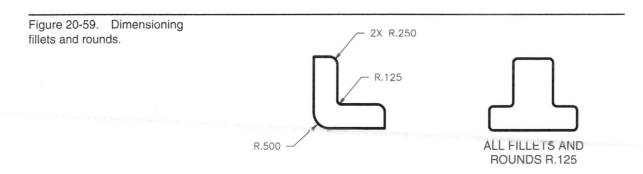

2X R.250

R.125

R.500

ALL FILLETS AND
ROUNDS R.125

EXERCISE 20-9

❑ Open PRODR2.
❑ Draw object lines on layer 0-7, and place all center dashes and dimensions on layer 3-3.
❑ Use the proper dimensioning techniques, variables, and commands to dimension the objects.
❑ Set the DIMCEN variable to .125.
❑ With all other dimension variables at their default settings, draw and dimension three arcs similar to the drawing in Figure. 20-56.
❑ Draw and dimension three arcs with DIMTOFL Off and three arcs with DIMTOFL On similar to Figure 20-57.
❑ Turn DIMUPT On and then draw and dimension three arcs with DIMTOFL Off and three arcs with DIMTOFL On similar to Figure 20-58.
❑ Save the drawing as A:EX20-9.

CHAPTER TEST

Write your answers in the spaces provided.

1. Give the command and entries required to change the dimensioning text style from STANDARD to ROMANS:

   Command:_____

   New value for_____ ⟨"STANDARD"⟩:_____ __

2. If the dimension reads 2.875 and you want it to read ∅2.875, what should you enter?

   Dimension text ⟨2.875⟩: _____

3. Give the command and entries needed to change the dimensioning text from the default size of 0.18 to .25:

   Command:_____

   New value for_____ ⟨0.1800⟩: _____ _____

4. Give the command and entries required to dimension a 30° angle between two existing intersecting lines. Let AutoCAD center the text in the dimension line.

   Command:_____

   Select arc, circle, line, or RETURN: _____

   Second line: _____ _____

   Dimension arc line location (Text/Angle): _____

   Dimension text ⟨30⟩: _____

   Enter text location (or RETURN): _____

5. Give the command and related responses used to dimension four holes, all having .250 inch diameter:

   Command:_____

   Select arc or circle: _____

   Dimension line location (Text/Angle): _____

   Dimension text ⟨0.250⟩: _____

   Dimension line location (Text/Angle): _____

6. Give the command and entries required to dimension an arc.

   Command:_____

   Select arc or circle: _____

   Dimension line location (Text/Angle): _____

7. Give the command and entries needed to set and draw centerlines that extend .25 unit beyond a circle's circumference:

   Command:_____

   New value for _____ ⟨0⟩: _____

   Command:_____

   Select arc or circle: _____

8. Describe the function of dimension variables._____

   _____

   _____

   _____

9. What is the Root Menu selection used to access the dimensioning screen menu? _____

   _____

10. Identify three ways to return to the Command: prompt when in the DIM command._____

    _____

    _____

    _____

11. What are the recommended standard units of measure on engineering drawings and related documents?_____

_____

12. Name the units of measure commonly used in architectural and structural drafting, and show an example. _____

13. What is the recommended height for dimension numerals and notes on drawings? _____

14. Name the screen menu where the Horizontal, Aligned, and Rotated dimensioning commands are found. _____

15. Name a dimensioning command that may be used to place a linear dimension on an angled surface. _____

16. Name the command used to dimension angles in degrees. _____

17. What are the two types of notes found on a drawing?_____

18. AutoCAD refers to chain dimensioning as _____.

19. AutoCAD refers to datum dimensioning as _____.

20. The command used to provide diameter dimensions for circles is_____.

21. The command used to provide radius dimensions for arcs is _____.

For Questions 22-38, identify the dimensioning variable that:

22. Controls the dimension text height. _____

23. Controls the -0″ part of a feet-inches dimension._____

24. Controls the size of the gap between the object and extension line. _____

25. Controls the distance the extension line projects past the last dimension line. _____

26. Suppresses the second extension line. _____

27. Provides for aligned dimensioning of dimensions inside of extension lines. _____

28. Places dimension text above the dimension line for architectural drafting. _____

29. Changes the arrowhead size. _____

30. Controls the display and size of dimension line ticks for architectural drafting._____

31. Controls dimension line spacing. _____

32. Establishes center marks for circles and arcs. _____

33. Used to set the dimension text style. _____

34. Sets the units format for dimension numerals._____

35. Establishes the number of decimal places for the value of the dimension numerals. _____

36. Sets the dimension value format for angular dimensions. _____

37. Controls the placement of arrowheads and text inside or outside of extension lines based on the space available. _____

38. Allows you to control the dimension text placement and leader length. _____

39. Name the dimensioning variable that, when turned on, forces dimension text inside the extension lines only when the dimension lines and arrowheads are placed outside. _____

_____

40. Give an example of a proper inch and metric (millimeters) decimal numeral less than one.

_____

41. Name the dimensioning variable and its value which is used to draw architectural dots at the end of the dimension lines. _____

_____

42. Name the dimensioning variable and its setting for suppressing the lead zero on decimal inch dimensions._____

_____

43. It is recommended that no gap exist between an extension line and a centerline when providing location dimensions to holes. Give the dimension variable and its value to use to achieve this task. _____

_____

44. What does the M mean in the title of the standard ASME Y14.5M?_____

_____

45. Does a text style have to be loaded using the STYLE command before it can be accessed for use in dimension text? _____

_____

46. If the text height is set to 0 in the STYLE command, then the dimension text height is controlled by this dimension variable. _____

_____

47. How do you access the DIMRADIUS and DIMDIAMETER in a pull-down menu?_____

_____

_____

48. How do you place a datum dimension from the origin of the previously drawn dimension?

_____

_____

_____

49. How do you place a datum dimension from the origin of a dimension that was drawn during a previous drawing session?

_____

_____

_____

_____

DRAWING PROBLEMS

1-15. Open each of the completed drawings in Chapter 19 (P19-1 through P19-15), or start a new drawing for those drawings which were not completed. Set limits, units, dimensioning variables, and other parameters as needed. Follow these guidelines:

A. Draw the views to exact size.

B. Use grid, snap, object snap modes, and the OSNAP command to your best advantage.

C. Apply dimensions accurately using ASME standards.

D. Set dimensioning variables to suit the drawing.

E. Use the LAYER command to set separate layers for views and dimensions.

F. Draw object lines using .032 in. wide polylines, or use LINE and plot object lines with pen.

G. Place general notes 1/2 in. from lower-left corner.

    2. REMOVE ALL BURRS AND SHARP EDGES.

    1. INTERPRET PER ASME Y14.5M–1994.

    NOTES:

H. Save the drawings to your floppy disk with names such as A:P20-X, where the X represents the problem number.

16-19. Draw and completely dimension the following manufacturing problems:

16.

P20-16

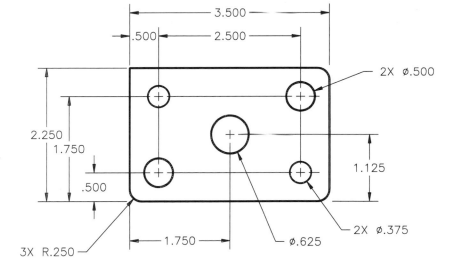

17.

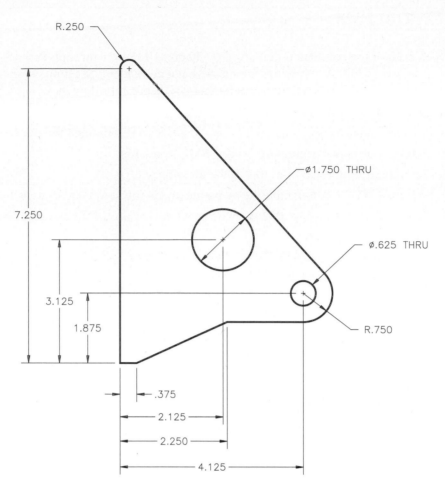

18.

P20-18

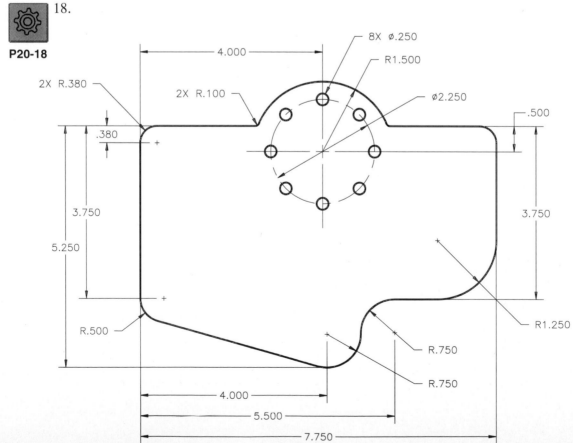

19.

P20-19

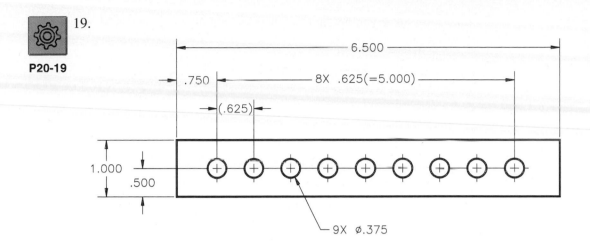

20-21. *Draw and completely dimension the following partial architectural floor plans:*

20.

P20-20

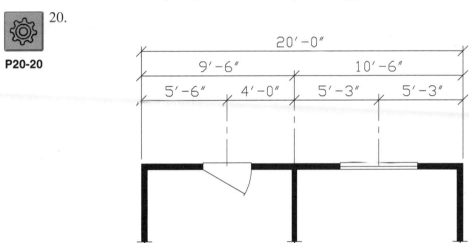

21.

P20-21

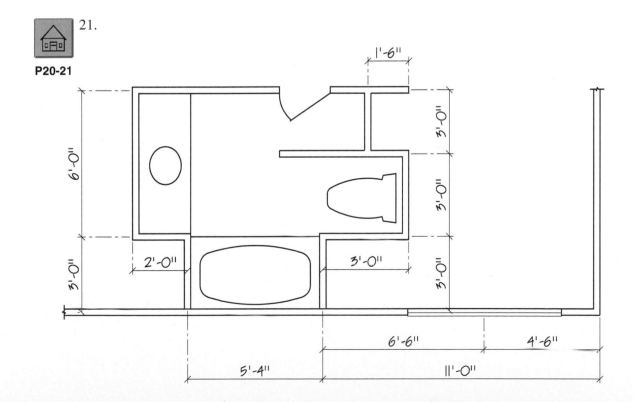

P20-22

22. The overall dimensions are given on the following kitchen drawing. Establish the rest of the dimensions using your own design.

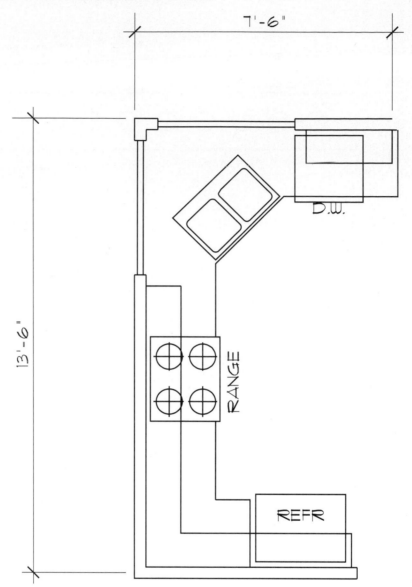

Chapter 21

INTERMEDIATE DIMENSIONING

Learning objectives

After completing this chapter, you will be able to:

- ○ Dimension curves that are not a specified radius.
- ○ Draw oblique dimensions.
- ○ Use the LEADER command to draw specific notes.
- ○ Use dimension variables to modify dimension text placement.
- ○ Alter dimension scales.
- ○ Change the color of dimension elements.
- ○ Edit dimensions.
- ○ Draw ordinate dimensions.
- ○ Place thread notes on a drawing.
- ○ Use dialog and subdialog boxes to control dimension variables.

The previous chapter introduced you to the basic dimensioning commands and how dimension variables may be used to provide you with flexibility in the way dimensions are presented. This chapter continues with additional dimensioning techniques that are used in a variety of situations where the applications require special consideration. The practices include dimensioning curves and drawing leaders to place specific notes. You will learn to use *ordinate dimensioning*. This is referred to as *arrowless dimensioning* because it replaces the traditional dimension lines and arrowheads. This chapter concludes with the use of the "Dimension Styles" dialog box to help you set dimension variables.

DIMENSIONING CURVES

AUG 9

When possible, curves are dimensioned as arcs. When they are not in the shape of a constant-radius arc, they should be dimensioned to points along the curve using the HORIZ or VERT commands. See Figure 21-1.

Figure 21-1. Dimensioning curves that are not a specified radius.

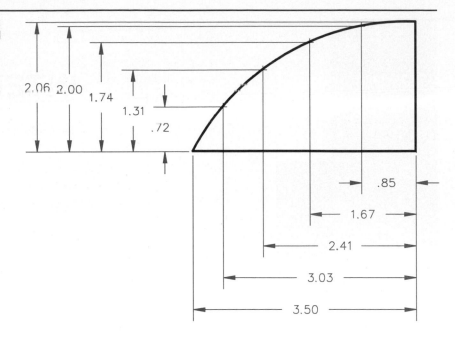

Dimensioning curves with oblique extension lines

The method of dimensioning a curve shown in Figure 21-1 is the normal practice, but in some cases, spaces may be limited and oblique extension lines are used. First, dimension the object using the LINEAR command, even if dimensions are crowded or overlap as shown in Figure 21-2A.

Figure 21-2. Drawing dimensions with oblique extension lines.

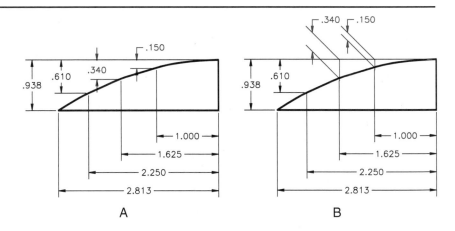

A   B

In this case, the drafter anticipated that the .150 and .340 dimensions are to be placed at an oblique angle above the view. Oblique extension lines are drawn using the DIM command and typing OBL or OBLIQUE at the Dim: prompt. The OBLIQUE command can also be accessed through the Oblique option of the Dim Edit: command in the MOD DIM screen menu. You can also pick Oblique from the Dimensioning cascading menu of the Draw pull-down menu. After entering OBL, you are asked to select the objects. At this time, you select the dimensions to be drawn at the oblique angle. The .150 and .340 dimensions are selected in this case:

Command: **DIM** ↵
Dim: *(type **OBL** or **OBLIQUE** and press* ENTER*)*
Select objects: *(pick the .150 and .340 dimensions)*
Select objects: ↵

Next, you are asked for the obliquing angle. Careful planning is need to ensure the dimensions oblique where you want them. Obliquing angles originate from 0° East and revolve counterclockwise:

Enter obliquing angle (RETURN for none): **135** ↵
Dim:

The result is shown in Figure 21-2B.

DRAWING LEADER LINES

AUG 9

The DIMDIAMETER and DIMRADIUS commands can automatically place leaders on the drawing depending on how dimensions are placed. The LEADER command allows you to begin and end a leader line where you desire. You can also place single or multiple lines of text with the leader. This command is ideal for the following situations:
- When you are working on a drawing and need more control of dimension placement than is available by adjusting dimension variables and using the DIMDIA and DIMRAD commands.
- Adding specific notes to the drawing.
- When a leader line must be staggered to go around other drawing features. Keep in mind that staggering leader lines is not a recommended ASME standard.
- Where a double leader is required. Drawing two leaders from one note is not normally recommended.
- When making custom leader lines.

AutoCAD's LEADER command creates leader lines and related notes. The leader segments and arrow are a single object and the text is an MTEXT object. This command provides you with the flexibility to place tolerances and multiple lines of text with the leader. The leader line characteristics, such as arrowhead size and text positioning are controlled by the current dimension variable settings. Other features, such as the leader format and annotation style are controlled by options in the LEADER command. *Annotation* means the addition of notes or text. This term is commonly used in computer-aided drafting. The LEADER command is accessed by picking Leader: in the DRAW DIM screen menu or in the Dimensioning cascading menu of the Draw pull-down menu. LEADER can also be typed at the command prompt: The initial prompts look like the LINE command with the From point: and To point: prompts. This allows you to pick where the leader starts and ends. Properly drawn leaders, for mechanical drafting, have one straight segment extending from the feature to a shoulder, and a horizontal shoulder about 1/4 inch (6mm). While architectural and other fields also use straight leaders, AutoCAD provides the option of drawing curved leaders. Examples are shown in Figure 21-3. The command sequence begins like this:

Command: **LEADER** ↵
From point: *(pick the leader start point)*
To point: *(pick the second leader point, which is the start of the leader shoulder)*
To point (Format/Annotation/Undo) ⟨Annotation⟩:

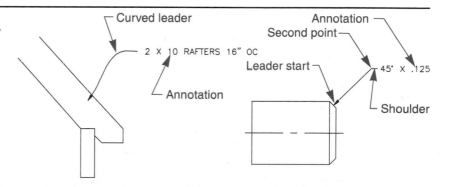

Figure 21-3.   The LEADER command can be used to draw a curved leader and a straight leader, and identification of the leader elements.

AutoCAD automatically draws a leader shoulder unless the leader line is 15° or less off of horizontal. While the ASME standard does not recommend a leader line that is less than 15° or greater than 75° from horizontal, it may sometimes be necessary. If you need to create a shoulder, pick the endpoint of the leader shoulder like this:

Command: **LEADER** ↵
From point: *(pick the leader start point)*
To point: *(pick the second leader point, which is the start of the leader shoulder)*
To point (Format/Annotation/Undo) ⟨Annotation⟩: *(pick the end of the leader shoulder)*
To point (Format/Annotation/Undo) ⟨Annotation⟩:

Annotation is the default, which means that you can press ENTER to access the Annotation option. Type the desired note at the next prompt and then press ENTER to get the MText: prompt. Press ENTER to get back to the Command: prompt, or type as many lines of text as you want and press the ENTER key after each line of text. The prompts continue like this for placing one line of text:

Annotation (or RETURN for options): **2 X 6 STUDS 16″ OC** ↵
MText: ↵
Command:

If you wanted to place more than one line of text, the prompts would have continued like this:

Annotation (or RETURN for options): **2 X 6 STUDS 16″ OC** ↵
MText: **W/ 5 1/2″ BATTS R-19 MIN** ↵
MText: **FOIL FACE 1 SIDE** ↵
MText: ↵
Command:

The results of using the previous leader commands are shown in Figure 21-4. Text placed using the LEADER command is a multiline text object where all of the lines of text are one object. You may want to review the MTEXT command in Chapter 11. When there is more than one line of text, the lines are justified on the left side if the leader is on the left or justified on the right if the leader is on the right. The leader shoulder is centered on the multiple lines of text as shown in Figure 21-4.

The DIMGAP variable controls the distance from the end of the leader shoulder to the text as shown in Figure 21-4

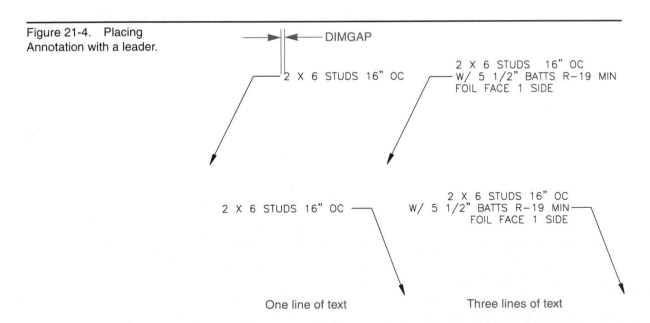

Figure 21-4.   Placing
Annotation with a leader.

PROFESSIONAL TIP

ASME Y14.5M recommends that the leader shoulder be centered at the start of the first line of text or at the end of the last line of text. After using the LEADER command and placing the desired text, use grips and cycle to the MOVE command and quickly move the text to the preferred position, or just use the MOVE command and do the same thing. Look at the difference between the multiline text position in Figure 21-4 and the recommended format shown below.

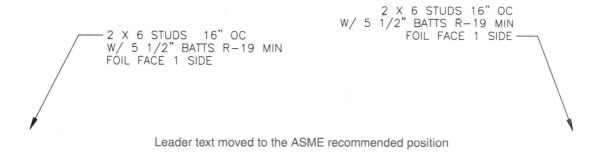

Leader text moved to the ASME recommended position

Using the Annotation sub options

The Annotation option any be accessed by pressing the ENTER key as previously described or type A and press the ENTER key. If you press ENTER again, you get the Annotation sub options:

> To point (Format/Annotation/Undo) ⟨Annotation⟩:
> Annotation (or RETURN for options): **A** ⏎
> Tolerance/Copy/Block/None/⟨Mtext⟩:

Now, you can press ENTER to access the MS DOS text editor where you can type paragraph text, or use one of the other options described as follows:

- **Tolerance.** Type T to use the Tolerance option. This displays the "Geometric Tolerance" dialog boxes for creation of a feature control frame. An example of a feature control frame is shown in Figure 21-5A; however, this is explained in detail in Chapter 23.

Figure 21-5. Examples of using the LEADER command's Annotation options.

Object picked to copy is copied here ➤ 2 X 6 STUDS 16" OC

.005   Tolerance A

2 X 6 STUDS 16" OC   Copy B

Block C

None D

- **Copy.** This option copies text, mtext, feature control frame, or a block and connects the new object to the leader being created. The option continues with the Select object: prompt. All you have to do is pick a single object feature and it is automatically copied to a position at the leader shoulder as shown in Figure 21-5B:

> Annotation (or RETURN for options): **A** ⏎
> Tolerance/Copy/Block/None/⟨Mtext⟩: **C** ⏎
> Select object: *(pick the object)*
> Command:

- **Block.** This option inserts a specified block at the end of the leader. A block is a symbol that was previously created and saved, and can be inserted in your drawing. These multiple use symbols are explained in detail in Chapter 25. Blocks may be scaled during the insertion process. A special symbol block called TARGET is inserted in Figure 21-5C. The command continues like this to insert the block at the default scale of 1:1 and 0° rotation angle:

```
Annotation (or RETURN for options): A ⏎
Tolerance/Copy/Block/None/⟨Mtext⟩: B ⏎
Block name (or ?): TARGET ⏎
Insertion point: X scale factor ⟨1⟩/Corner/XYZ: ⏎
Y scale factor (default=X): ⏎
Rotation angle ⟨0⟩: ⏎
Command:
```

- **None.** This option ends the leader with no annotation of any kind. See (Figure 21-5D):

```
Annotation (or RETURN for options): A ⏎
Tolerance/Copy/Block/None/⟨Mtext⟩: N ⏎
Command:
```

Using the LEADER command Format options

The LEADER command also allows you to modify the way a leader line is presented. This is done by accessing the Format option:

```
Command: LEADER ⏎
From point: (pick the leader start point)
To point: (pick the second leader point, which is the start of the leader shoulder)
To point (Format/Annotation/Undo) ⟨Annotation⟩: F ⏎
Spline/STraight/Arrow/None/⟨Exit⟩:
```

The Format options are shown in Figure 21-6 and are explained as follows:
- **Spline.** Enter S for the Spline option. This lets you draw leader lines using a spline object rather than straight segments. This practice is commonly used in architectural drafting and may meet other company standards.
- **STraight.** If you are inside the LEADER command and previously set Format to draw Spline leaders, then type ST to change back to the use of straight segments. AutoCAD automatically defaults back to drawing straight segment leaders when you leave the LEADER command.
- **Arrow.** Use the Arrow option if you selected the None (no arrow) option and then decided to change back to using an arrow while in the LEADER command. AutoCAD automatically defaults back to using an arrow when you leave the LEADER command.
- **None.** This allows you to draw a leader without an arrow.
- **Exit.** Exit is the default here. Press the ENTER key or type E and then ENTER to exit the Format options and return to To point: prompt.

Using the Undo option

The Undo option removes the last leader segment that you drew. This is handy if you accidentally draw an extra leader shoulder and want to remove it. You can use the Undo option by typing U during the following prompt:

```
To point (Format/Annotation/Undo) ⟨Annotation⟩: U ⏎
```

Figure 21-6. Examples of using the LEADER command's Format options.

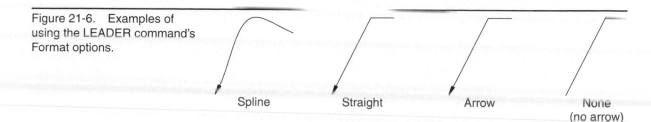

Spline   Straight   Arrow   None (no arrow)

The LEADER command may be used to connect notes to various features on a drawing. While single leader lines are the preferred ASME standard, some companies and industry practices, such as the placement of welding symbols, allow multiple leaders. See Figure 21-7. In order to draw multiple leader lines to the same note, you need to use the LEADER command to place the first leader and the note. Then enter the LEADER command again and pick a new start point followed by picking the beginning of the previous leader shoulder as the second point and then use the None Annotation option to terminate the command. The welding symbol shown in Figure 21-7B was created as a block and then inserted using the Annotation Block option.

Figure 21-7. Alternate applications of the LEADER command.

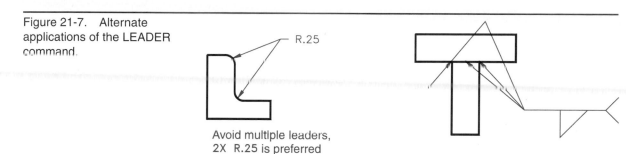

R.25

Avoid multiple leaders, 2X R.25 is preferred

A   B

Using the LEADER command inside the DIM command

You may also use the LEADER command inside of the DIM command by typing LEADER at the Dim: prompt. When you draw a leader in this manner, each element of the leader including the arrow, the straight segments, and the text are individual objects. The only option you have is to draw leaders with straight segments and you can not place multiline text. The DIM command's LEADER subcommand acts like the LINE command. AutoCAD asks you for the endpoints of the line segments. The second point determines the start of the leader shoulder. You must press enter to stop drawing other leader segments, and the leader shoulder is automatically drawn unless the leader line is 15° or less from horizontal. You may then type the desired dimension text. You have to cancel to get out of the DIM command:

Command: **DIM** ↵
Dim: **LEADER** ↵
Leader start: *(pick a point on the feature to be dimensioned)*
To point: *(pick the second leader point, which is usually the start of the shoulder)*
To point: *(pick the end of the leader shoulder)*
To point: ↵
Dimension text ⟨1.5000⟩: *(type the desired text)*
Dim: **^C**
Command:

PROFESSIONAL TIP

This is a version of the leader from previous AutoCAD releases. This type of leader generates a leader line that allows only one line of text to be entered, with no further options.

When using the DIM command's LEADER subcommand, the text in brackets at the Dimension text ⟨*current*⟩: prompt is the default text for the last drawn dimension in the current drawing. This includes any special symbology. For example, if the last drawn dimension was a 2.500 diameter, the default leader text is ⟨Ø2.500⟩. Sometimes when the DIMRADIUS or DIMDIAMETER commands do not give you enough flexibility to meet specialized dimensioning requirements, you can use the DIM command's LEADER subcommand to provide more flexibility of being able to manually place the leader.

EXERCISE 21-1

❑ Load AutoCAD and open PRODR2 or begin a new drawing with your own variables.
❑ Use the LEADER command to draw the following:
   ❑ Place one line of text with a straight leader and three lines of text with another leader just like Figure 21-4.
   ❑ Use the Copy and None Annotation options to place leaders similar to Figure 21-5. The Tolerance and Block options are not suggested at this time because these topics have not yet been introduced.
   ❑ Use the Spline, STraight, Arrow, and None Format options to draw leaders similar to Figure 21-6. Annotation may be placed, if you wish.
❑ Use the LEADER command inside of the DIM command to draw a leader line with a 1/4 inch shoulder and place the note: R.250. Notice the difference between using the LEADER command at the Command: prompt and at the Dim: prompt.
❑ Save the drawing as A:EX21-1.

DIMENSIONING CHAMFERS

A *chamfer* is an angled surface used to relieve sharp corners. The ends of bolts are commonly chamfered to allow them to engage the threaded hole better. Chamfers of 45° are dimensioned with a leader giving the angle and linear dimension, or with two linear dimensions. The LEADER command works well for this application as shown in Figure 21-8.

Figure 21-8. Dimensioning
45° chamfers.

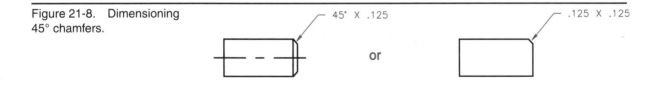

The leader placed in the first example of Figure 21-8 uses a note with the degree symbol. When you place a note with a special symbol, you need to use the Unicode for special characters. For example, the degree symbol is placed by using the Unicode \U+00B0. Unicodes are discussed in detail in Chapter 11 of this text.

Chamfers other than 45° must have the angle and linear dimension, or two linear dimensions placed on the view, Figure 21-9. The LINEAR and ANGULAR commands are used for this purpose.

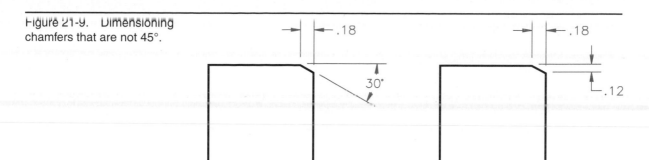

Figure 21-9.   Dimensioning chamfers that are not 45°.

PROFESSIONAL TIP

 Use the object snap modes to your best advantage when dimensioning. This helps save time and increase accuracy.

EXERCISE 21-2

❑ Open PRODR2.
❑ Draw the object lines of the views on layer 0-7 and place dimensions on layer 3-3.
❑ Use the proper dimensioning techniques and commands to dimension the objects exactly as shown.
❑ Save the drawing as A:EX21-2.

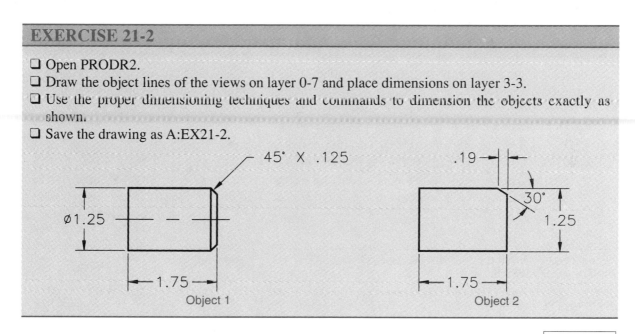

DIMENSIONING IN LIMITED SPACES   AUG 9

When space between extension lines is limited, AutoCAD places the dimension line, arrowheads, and numerals outside the extension lines, depending on the current DIMFIT setting. You need to plan ahead because the numeral is placed outside of the last extension line selected. See Figure 21-10. Remember, if you do not like where the dimension is placed, enter UNDO and try again.

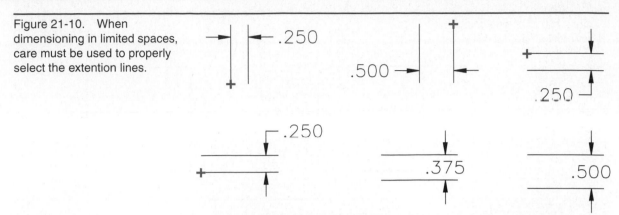

Figure 21-10. When dimensioning in limited spaces, care must be used to properly select the extention lines.

+ This symbol is used to represent the first extension line origin point when the text does not fit between the extension lines

ADJUSTING AUTOCAD FOR DIMENSION TEXT PLACEMENT, AND USING OTHER DIMENSIONING VARIABLES

AUG 9

AutoCAD provides you with maximum flexibility to make your dimensioning reflect proper drafting standards. For example, if you are dimensioning in a limited space and you want the numeral inside the extension lines with the arrowheads and dimension lines outside the extension lines, it is no problem with the dimensioning variables set appropriately.

Placing dimension text inside the extension lines

The DIMTIX (Text Inside eXtension lines) variable, when set ON, forces the dimension text inside the extension lines. This occurs only when the dimension lines and arrowheads are placed outside. The DIMTIX default value is OFF. See Figure 21-11.

Figure 21-11. How the DIMTIX variable affects the placement of dimension text between extension lines.

.500   .625   625

DIMTX = OFF   DIMTX = ON

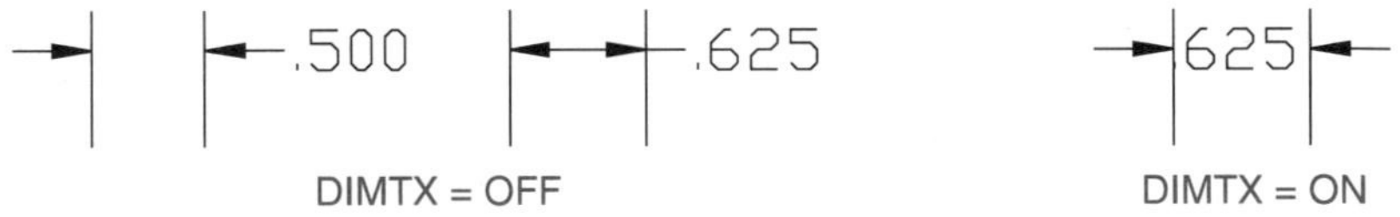

Drawing the dimension line between the extension lines when the text and arrowheads are outside

Some drafters prefer to place a dimension line between extension lines when the dimension text is outside. To do so, set DIMTOFL to ON and DIMTIX to OFF as shown in Figure 21-12. The default for DIMTOFL is OFF.

Figure 21-12. How the DIMTOFL variable affects dimensions.

.500   .500

DIMTOFL = OFF   DIMTOFL = ON

A review of the DIMFIT variable

The DIMFIT (FIT text) variable was introduced in Chapter 20. This variable controls the placement of arrowheads and text inside or outside of extension lines based on the space available. There are five settings available, but all of the settings will fit text and arrows inside if there is room, or outside

side in some cases based on how you drag the dimension. The DIMFIT settings are the options 0 through 4 and are used as follows:

- **0.** If there is not enough room for both text and arrows, all are placed outside.
- **1.** If there is room for text only, the text is placed inside and the arrowheads are placed outside. Otherwise, all are placed outside.
- **2.** If space is available, text and arrows are placed inside. If space is available for arrows only, they are placed inside and text is placed outside. Otherwise, all are placed outside.
- **3.** If space is available, place text and arrowheads between extension lines. If space is available for text, it is placed inside and arrowheads outside. If space is available for arrowheads, they are placed inside and text is placed outside. Otherwise all are placed outside.
- **4.** If there is room for text only, text is placed inside. Otherwise, a leader line is created.

Figure 21-13 shows how the DIMFIT variable can be used to alter the results of placing limited space dimensions. Some applications display no difference based on the space available.

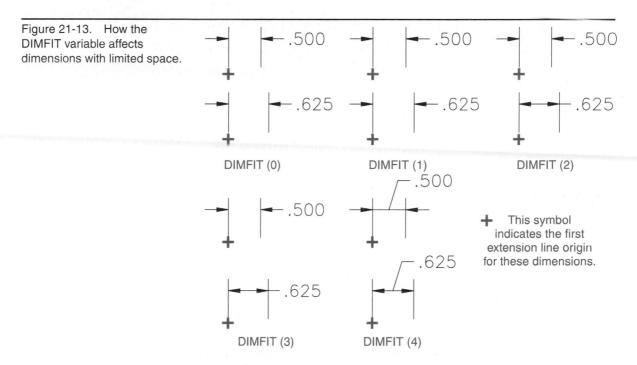

Figure 21-13. How the DIMFIT variable affects dimensions with limited space.

Placing the dimension text inside the extension lines and suppressing the dimension line

When several dimensions are adjacent, you may want to place one numeral inside the extension lines and suppress the dimension lines and arrowheads. To do this, set DIMTIX to ON and DIMSOXD to ON. The default value for each is OFF. The results are shown in Figure 21-14.

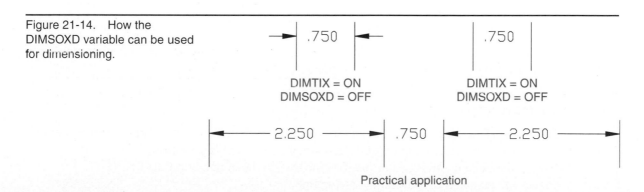

Figure 21-14. How the DIMSOXD variable can be used for dimensioning.

A review of the DIMUPT variable

The DIMUPT variable allows you to adjust the dimension line length and control the dimension text location by dragging the text to the right or left side of the extension lines as shown in Figure 21-15. Turn the DIMUPT variable On to have this flexibility.

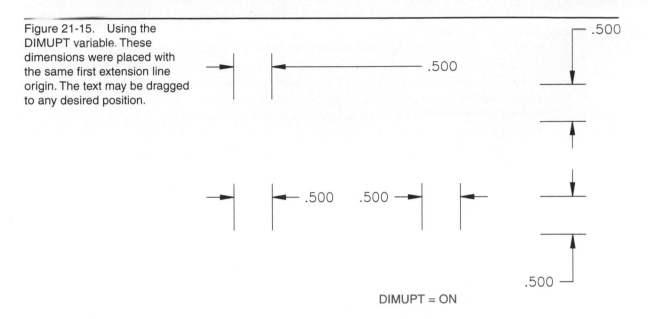

Figure 21-15. Using the DIMUPT variable. These dimensions were placed with the same first extension line origin. The text may be dragged to any desired position.

DIMUPT = ON

Adjusting dimension text placement in relation to the dimension line

AutoCAD allows you to place the dimension text above, below, or centered within a break in the dimension line. This is called "Text Vertical Position" and is controlled by the DIMTVP variable. As shown in Figure 21-16, DIMTVP has three settings:

- **DIMTVP = 0 (default).** Dimension text is centered within a break in dimension line. This is the normal practice for mechanical drafting.
- **DIMTVP = 1.** Dimension text is placed above the dimension line. This is common practice for architectural drafting and the construction trades.
- **DIMTVP = -1.** Dimension text is placed below the dimension line. This is an uncommon practice.

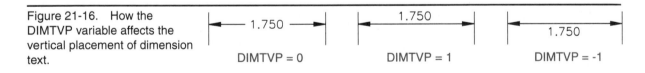

Figure 21-16. How the DIMTVP variable affects the vertical placement of dimension text.

DIMTVP = 0   DIMTVP = 1   DIMTVP = -1

PROFESSIONAL TIP

DIMTVP can be set to any value between 1 and –1 to achieve a text location that is off-center of the dimension line, but not completely above or below it.

Using the DIMJUST variable

DIMJUST (JUSTification) is used to justify text on the dimension line. There are five settings ranging from 0 to 4, with 0 being the default. Here are the results of these settings:

- **0.** This is the default and it center justifies the text on the dimension line.
- **1.** Places the text next to the first extension line.

- **2.** Places the text next to the second extension line.
- **3.** This option places the text aligned with and at the end of the first extension line.
- **4.** Places the text aligned with and at the end of the second extension line.

Results of the DIMJUST variable settings are displayed in Figure 21-17. Turn DIMTAD On if you want similar results with the text placed above the dimension line.

Figure 21-17.   How the DIMJUST variable affects dimension text.

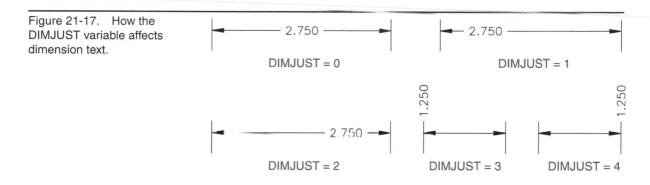

EXERCISE 21-3

- ❑ Open PRODR2 or begin a new drawing using your own variables.
- ❑ Adjust the dimension variables to their default values after each of the following exercises.
- ❑ Draw a .750 dimension with DIMTIX Off and draw the same dimension with DIMTIX On similar to Figure 21-11.
- ❑ Draw a .750 dimension with DIMTOFL Off and draw the same dimension with DIMTOFL On similar to Figure 21-12.
- ❑ Draw dimensions similar to the examples in Figure 21-13 by using the five DIMFIT settings.
- ❑ Set the dimension variables so you can draw the PRACTICAL APPLICATION shown in Figure 21-14.
- ❑ Use the DIMUPT variable to draw dimensions similar to the examples in Figure 21-15
- ❑ Draw three dimensions, similar to Figure 21-16, with a DIMTVP setting of 0, 1, and -1.
- ❑ Draw dimensions similar to the examples in Figure 21-17 by using the five DIMJUST settings.
- ❑ Save the drawing as A:EX21-3.

Controlling the gap between the dimension line and dimension text

When the dimension line is broken for placement of the dimension text, the space between the dimension line and text is controlled by the DIMGAP variable. The default distance for DIMGAP is .09. The default gap works well in most cases. However, in some instances the dimension text may be forced outside the extension line. Closing the dimension line gap allows more text to remain between the extension lines. Figure 21-18 shows the dimension line gap.

Figure 21-18.   The dimension line gap established with the DIMGAP dimensioning variable.

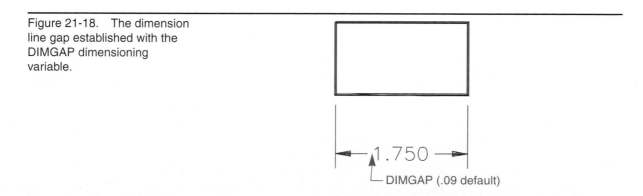

Drawing custom shapes at the ends of dimension lines

Creating shapes and symbols for multiple use is discussed in Chapter 25. You can place user-defined blocks rather than arrows at the ends of extension lines. The DIMBLK1 variable places a custom block at the first end of the dimension line. DIMBLK2 places a custom block at the second end of the dimension line. In order to place a block at both ends of the dimension line, set DIMBLK to the block name and have DIMSAH (Seperate custom Arrow Heads) OFF. To place a block at one end and use the default arrowhead type at the other end, DIMSAH must be ON, and either DIMBLK1 or DIMBLK2 set to the appropriate block name. DIMSAH must be ON for either DIMBLK1 or DIMBLK2 to be used, and DIMBLK must be set to none. Setting DIMBLK1 to one value and DIMBLK2 to another allows different blocks to be placed at each end of the dimension line. Figure 21-19 shows the dimension origin symbol used as a custom block at the first extension line. With DIMSAH set to ON, you can specify a custom block at both extension lines. Refer to Chapter 20 for a discussion regarding the use of the DIMBLK variable.

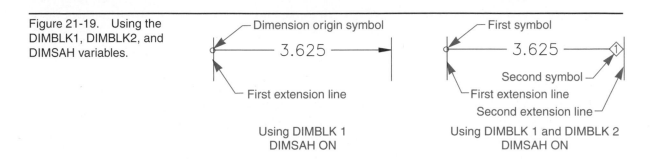

Figure 21-19.   Using the DIMBLK1, DIMBLK2, and DIMSAH variables.

USING DIMTEDIT TO EDIT DIMENSION TEXT POSITION AUG 9

In addition to the dimensioning variables that control the dimension text placement, the DIMTEDIT command lets you control the placement and orientation of an existing associative dimension. Remember, an associative dimension is a dimension drawn with DIMASO On, and all elements of the dimension act as one entity. Good dimensioning practice requires that adjacent dimension numerals be staggered rather than stacked up as shown in Figure 21-20A. The DIMJUST variable supports this practice if you set it before placing the dimension that needs to be staggered. Use the DIMTEDIT command to stagger the text after a dimension has been placed. Access this command by picking DimTedit: in the MOD DIM screen menu. The DIMTEDIT options are also found by picking Align Text in the Dimensioning cascading menu of the Draw pull-down menu. You can also type at the Command: prompt or in the DIM command:

Command: **DIMTEDIT** ↵
Select dimension: *(pick the dimension to be altered)*

or

Command: **DIM** ↵
Dim: **TEDIT** ↵
Select dimension: *(pick the dimension to be altered)*

If DIMASO was On when the dimension was created, the text of the selected dimension automatically drags with the screen cursor. This allows you to visually see where to place the text at the next prompt:

Enter text location (Left/Right/Home/Angle): *(pick the desired text location)*

AutoCAD automatically moves the text and re-establishes the break in the dimension line as shown in Figure 21-20B.

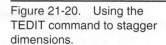
Figure 21-20.   Using the
TEDIT command to stagger
dimensions.

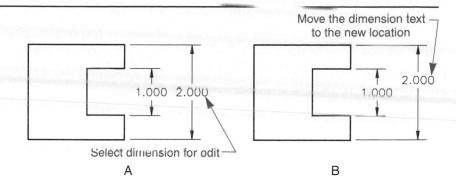

Move the dimension text
to the new location

Select dimension for edit

A   B

The DIMTEDIT command also allows you to automatically move the dimension text to the left or right, place it at an angle, or move it back to the original position. This is how the text location options work:

- **Left (L).** Moves horizontal text to the left or vertical text down. If you want to move text to the left, enter L as follows:

      Enter text location (Left/Right/Home/Angle): **L** ↵

- **Right (R).** Moves horizontal text to the right or vertical text up.
- **Home (H).** Moves text that had been changed previously back to its original position.
- **Angle.** Allows you to place dimension text at an angle. This works similar to the TROTATE command to be discussed later in this chapter. The text rotates around its middle point when you respond with a text angle or pick two points at the desired angle:

      Enter text location (Left/Right/Home/Angle): **A** ↵
      Text angle: **45** ↵

Figure 21-21 shows the affects of the TEDIT options.

Figure 21-21.   A comparison
of the TEDIT options.

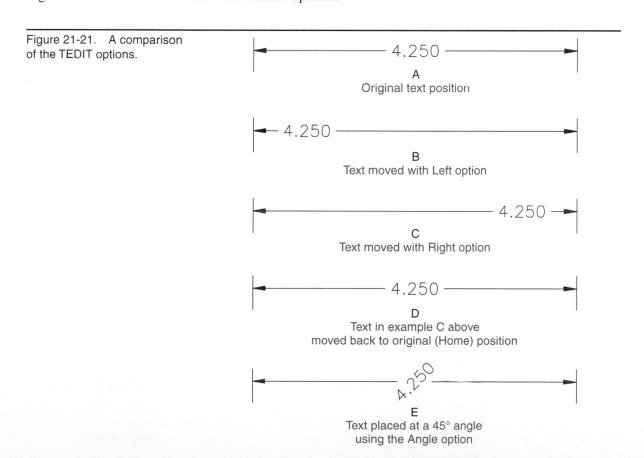

A
Original text position

B
Text moved with Left option

C
Text moved with Right option

D
Text in example C above
moved back to original (Home) position

E
Text placed at a 45° angle
using the Angle option

Using the DIMEDIT command

The DIMEDIT command may be used to change the text or extension lines of existing text. Type DIMEDIT or DIMED at the Command: prompt to use this command:

Command: *(type* **DIMEDIT** *or* **DIMED** *and press ENTER)*
Dimension Edit (Home/New/Rotate/Oblique) 〈Home〉:

This command has four options that may be used to edit individual dimensions, or multiple dimensions can be edited at the same time. The options are described as follows:

- **Home.** Home is the default option. You can press the ENTER key or type H and then press ENTER. This option restores the position and rotation of the dimension text to the original default position as shown in Figure 21-22. Use the Home option like this:

      Command: **DIMED** ⏎
      Dimension Edit (Home/New/Rotate/Oblique) 〈Home〉: ⏎
      Select objects: *(select the dimension or dimensions)*
      Select objects: ⏎
      Command:

- **New.** Type N for the New option which allows specification of new dimension text like this:

      Dimension Edit (Home/New/Rotate/Oblique) 〈Home〉: **N** ⏎
      Dimension text 〈0〉: **NEW TEXT** ⏎
      Select objects: *(select the dimension or dimensions)*

  See the example in Figure 21-22.

- **Rotate.** This option rotates the dimension text to an angle that you specify: See Figure 21-22.

      Dimension Edit (Home/New/Rotate/Oblique) 〈Home〉: **R** ⏎
      Enter text angle: **45** ⏎
      Select objects: *(select the dimension or dimensions)*

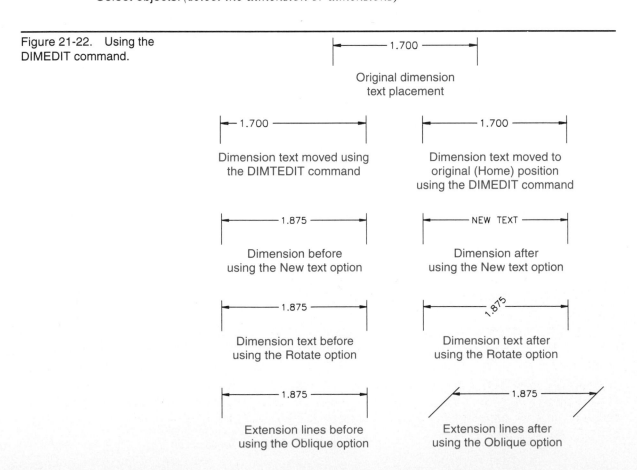

Figure 21-22. Using the DIMEDIT command.

|1.700|
Original dimension text placement

|1.700| Dimension text moved using the DIMTEDIT command

|1.700| Dimension text moved to original (Home) position using the DIMEDIT command

|1.875| Dimension before using the New text option

|NEW TEXT| Dimension after using the New text option

|1.875| Dimension text before using the Rotate option

|1.875| Dimension text after using the Rotate option

|1.875| Extension lines before using the Oblique option

|1.875| Extension lines after using the Oblique option

• **Oblique.** Changes the extension line angle to your specifications. This has the same effect as using the OBLIQUE command inside of the DIM command that was discussed previously in this chapter. See Figure 21-2 and 21-22.

> Dimension Edit (Home/New/Rotate/Oblique) ⟨Home⟩: **O** ⏎
> Select objects: *(select the dimension or dimensions)*
> Select objects: ⏎
> Enter obliquing angle (RETURN for none): *(press ENTER for no obliquing angle or type an angle such as* **45***)*

EXERCISE 21-4

❏ Open PRODR2 or start a new drawing with your own variables.
❏ Using Figure 21-21 as an example, draw an original dimension similar to A. Copy the original dimension to four places represented by B, C, D, and E.
  ❏ Use the Left option to edit the dimension at B.
  ❏ Use the Right option to edit the dimension at C.
  ❏ Use the Left option to edit the dimension at D. Then use the Home option to move the text back to the original position.
  ❏ Use the Angle option to edit the dimension at E by placing the text at a 45° angle.
❏ Using Figure 21-22 as an example, draw the original dimensions that are located on the left.
  ❏ Copy the original dimensions to the positions at the right.
  ❏ Perform the DIMTEDIT function on the middle top dimension.
  ❏ Use the DIMEDIT options on the rest of the dimensions as indicated in the caption for each example.
❏ Save the drawing as A:EX21-4.

USING THE UPDATE SUBCOMMAND   AUG 9

The UPDATE subcommand changes existing dimensions to reflect the current settings for dimension variables. The only dimension options not affected by UPDATE are those drawn using the DIMBASELINE or DIMCONTINUE commands. For example, suppose you change the DIMDLI variable, which changes the dimension line spacing. All new dimensions drawn with the BASELINE or CONTINUE commands reflect the revised dimension line spacing. However, the UPDATE command would not alter the existing dimension line spacing. Although, if you use the DIMASZ variable to change the arrowhead size, then any dimensions picked with the UPDATE command are automatically changed to reflect the new arrowhead size. The UPDATE command works like this:

> Command: **DIM** ⏎
> Dim: **UPDATE** ⏎
> Select objects: *(select dimension entities to be updated)*
> Select objects: ⏎
> Dim:

USING THE DIMOVERRIDE COMMAND   AUG 9

The DIMOVERRIDE command overrides dimension variables associated with an individual dimension or a specific selected group of dimensions. You can use this command by picking Overrid: in the MOD DIM screen menu, or type either DIMOVERRIDE or DIMOVER at the Command: prompt. This variable does not affect the current dimension variable settings on the rest of the drawing. For example, you are dimensioning features with a DIMEXO setting of .0625 and find that several extension lines have an undesirable .0625 space where they meet centerlines, similar to Figure 21-23A.

Use the DIMOVERRIDE command to change the DIMEXO setting and get the desired results shown in Figure 21-23B:

Command: *(type* **DIMOVERRIDE** *or* **DIMOVER** *and press* ENTER*)*
Dimension variable to override (or Clear to remove overrides): **DIMEXO** ↵
Current value ⟨0.0625⟩ New value: **0.**↵
Dimension variable to override: *(enter another dimvar to override or press* ENTER*)*
Select objects: *(select the dimension or dimensions to override)*
Select objects: ↵
Command:

Figure 21-23.   Using the DIMOVERRIDE command. Notice that the offset is removed in B.

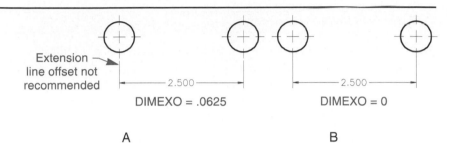

Extension line offset not recommended

2.500   DIMEXO = .0625

2.500   DIMEXO = 0

A   B

EXERCISE 21-5

❏ With DIMTIX set to OFF, draw a .750 in. dimension as shown in Figure 21-11.
❏ Set DIMTIX ON.
❏ Use the UPDATE command and pick the dimension again.
❏ With DIMTOFL set to OFF, draw a .750 dimension as shown in Figure 21-12.
❏ Turn on the DIMTOFL variable.
❏ Use the UPDATE command and pick the dimension again.
❏ With DIMEXO set to .0625, draw and dimension the objects in Figure 21-23A.
❏ Use the DIMOVERRIDE command to change DIMEXO to 0.
❏ Save the drawing as A:EX21-5.

DIM VARS THAT AFFECT DIMENSION SCALES | AUG 9 |

There are two dimensioning variables that alter the dimension scales. The DIMSCALE variable is an overall scale factor that applies to all dimensioning variables that specify size, distance, or offset. When DIMSCALE is set to the default factor of 1, all dimensioning variables are displayed as set. If it is changed to 2, all variable values are doubled. See Figure 21-24. Changing the DIMSCALE affects only future dimensions. If you are creating a drawing to be plotted at full (1:1) scale, then the DIMSCALE should equal 1. However, if the drawing is to be plotted at any other scale, the DIMSCALE should be set to the scale factor. The scale factor is the reciprocal of the drawing scale. For example, the scale factor for half scale (1:2) is 2, 1:2 is .5=1, and 1/.5=2. For the architect using a 1/4″ = 1′-0″ scale, the calculation is: .25″ = 12″, 12/.25 = 48 scale factor.

Figure 21-24.   Effects of the DIMSCALE variable.

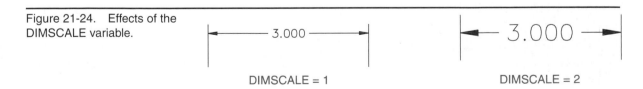

3.000   DIMSCALE = 1

3.000   DIMSCALE = 2

Another dimensioning variable, DIMLFAC (Length FACtor), sets a scale factor for all linear dimensions, except angles. The default value of 1 represents a 1:1, or full scale factor. A factor of 2 multiplies dimension numerals by two as shown in Figure 21-25.

Figure 21-25.   Using the
DIMLFAC variable.

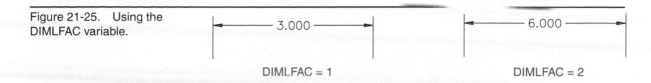

DIMLFAC = 1   DIMLFAC = 2

EXERCISE 21-6

❑ Draw the dimension shown on the left side of Figure 21-24 with a DIMSCALE value of 1. Copy it to a position at the right.
❑ Use the UPDATE command to change the DIMSCALE of the right dimension to a value of 2.
❑ Draw the dimension shown on the left side of Figure 21-25 with a DIMLFAC value of 1. Copy it to a position at the right.
❑ Use the DIMOVERRIDE command to change the DIMLFAC of the right dimension to a value of 2.
❑ Save as A:EX21-6.

VARIABLES THAT ASSIGN COLOR
TO DIMENSION COMPONENTS

AUG 9

There are three dimensioning variables that let you assign any valid color to dimension components. These variables are DIMCLRD, DIMCLRE, and DIMCLRT. You can set color values by number as follows:

1 = Red	5 = Blue
2 = Yellow	6 = Magenta
3 = Green	7 = White
4 = Cyan	

The DIMCLRD variable is used to set the CoLoR of all Dimension lines, arrowheads, and leaders. Use the DIMCLRD variable as follows:

Command: **DIMCLRD** ↵
New value for DIMCLRD: *(enter desired color, such as **1** for red)*

Now all new dimension lines, arrowheads, and leaders are drawn with red. Use the UPDATE command to change existing dimension colors.

The DIMCLRE variable changes the CoLoR of the Extension lines. The DIMCLRT variable is used to alter the CoLoR of the dimension Text. All three of these dimensioning variables are used in the same manner as previously described for the DIMCLRD variable.

PROFESSIONAL TIP

DIMCLRD, DIMCLRE, and DIMCLRT variables override any layer color settings. For example, even though a layer color may be yellow, the dimensions can still be different colors. You may want to avoid this practice, as it can cause confusion.

ROTATING THE DIMENSION TEXT

AUG 9

The unidirectional and aligned dimensioning systems are the standard placement of dimension text. However, AutoCAD does allow you to rotate the dimension text. First, draw the dimension in the usual way, as shown in Figure 21-26A, and then rotate the dimension text with the TROTATE command as follows:

Command: **DIM** ↵
Dim: **TROTATE** ↵
Enter text angle: *(set a text angle, **45** for example)*↵
Select objects: *(pick the dimension text to rotate)*

The selected dimension numeral is automatically rotated as shown in Figure 21-26B.

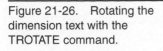

Figure 21-26. Rotating the dimension text with the TROTATE command.

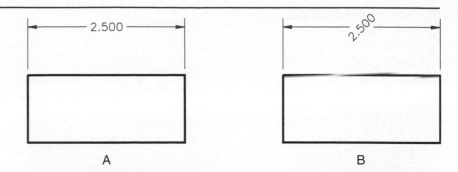

A   B

EXERCISE 21-7

❏ Draw a 1.750 dimension with the current DIMGAP setting. Then change DIMGAP and draw the dimension again to notice the difference.
❏ Set DIMCLRD to red, DIMCLRE to blue, and DIMCLRT to green. Draw the object shown in Figure 21-26A and see what happens.
❏ Use the TROTATE command to rotate some of the dimension text on your drawing. Rotate it back if you wish.
❏ Save the drawing as A:EX21-7.

ERASING DIMENSIONS USING VARIOUS SELECTION OPTIONS

AUG 9

In Chapter 6 you were introduced to the ERASE command. There are different ways to select objects for erasure. They include Last, Previous, Window, Crossing, WPolygon, CPolygon, and Fence.

Erasing features, such as large groups of dimensions, often becomes difficult. They are very close to other parts of the drawing. It is time-consuming to erase them individually. When this situation occurs, the Crossing, CPolygon, and Fence selection options are handy. Figure 21-27 shows a comparison between using ERASE Window and ERASE Crossing on a group of dimensions. For a review of these techniques, and the Modify pull-down menu, refer to Chapter 6.

Figure 21-27. Using the ERASE Window and Crossing options.

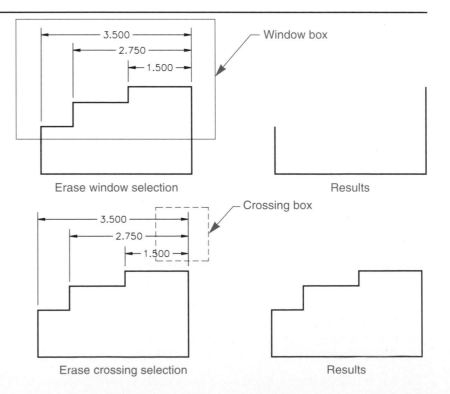

ALTERNATE DIMENSIONING PRACTICES

In industries where computer numerical control machining processes are used, it is becoming common to omit dimension lines. This type of dimensioning is called *arrowless*, or *tabular dimensioning*. Where changing values of a product are involved, dimensions are shown in a chart. This is referred to as *chart dimensioning*.

Arrowless dimensioning

Arrowless dimensioning is becoming popular in mechanical drafting. It is also used in electronics drafting, especially for chassis layout. This type of dimensioning has only extension lines and numerals. All dimension lines and arrowheads are omitted. Dimension numerals are aligned with the extension lines. Each dimension numeral represents a dimension originating from a common point. This starting, or "0" dimension is typically known as a *datum*, or *baseline*. Holes or other features are labeled with identification letters. Sizes are given in a table placed on the drawing as shown in Figure 21-28.

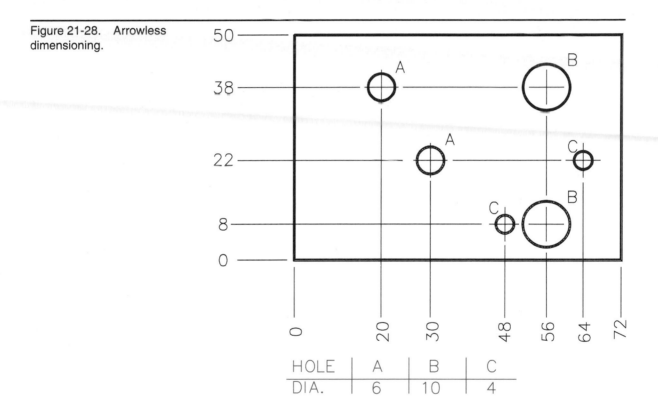

Figure 21-28.   Arrowless dimensioning.

HOLE	A	B	C
DIA.	6	10	4

Tabular dimensioning

Tabular dimensioning is a form of arrowless dimensioning where dimensions to features are shown in a table. The table gives the location of features from an X and Y axis. It also provides the depth of features from a Z axis when appropriate. Each feature is labeled with a letter or number that correlates to the table, Figure 21-29.

Figure 21-29.   Tabular dimensioning. (Doug Major)

HOLE	QTY.	DESCRIP.	X	Y	Z
A1	1	ø7	64	38	10
B1	1	ø5	5	38	THRU
B2	1	ø5	72	38	THRU
B3	1	ø5	64	11	THRU
B4	1	ø5	79	11	THRU
C1	1	ø4	19	38	THRU
C2	1	ø4	48	38	THRU
C3	1	ø4	5	21	THRU
C4	1	ø4	30	21	THRU
C5	1	ø4	72	21	THRU
C6	1	ø4	19	11	THRU
D1	1	ø2.5	48	6	THRU

UNLESS OTHERWISE SPECIFIED
■■■■■ – MILLIMETERS AND TOLERANCES FOR:
1 PLACE DIMS: ± .1
2 PLACE DIMS: ± .01
3 PLACE DIMS: ± .005
ANGULAR: ± 30'
FRACTIONAL: ± 1/32
FINISH: 3.2 ?m

❋ MAJOR DESIGN ❋

| DR: D. MAJOR | SCALE: 1.5:1 | DATE: 27FEB | APPD: |
MTRL: STAINLESS STEEL
NAME: MOUNTING BASE
B | PART NO: 10099 | REV: 0

2. REMOVE ALL BURRS AND SHARP EDGES.
1. INTERPRET DIMENSIONS AND TOLERANCES PER ASME Y14.5M–1994.
NOTES:

Chart dimensioning

Chart dimensioning may take the form of unidirectional, aligned, arrowless, or tabular dimensioning. It provides flexibility in situations where dimensions change depending on the requirements of the product. The views of the product are drawn and variable dimensions are shown with letters. The letters correlate to a chart in which the different options are shown, Figure 21-30.

Figure 21-30.   Chart dimensioning.

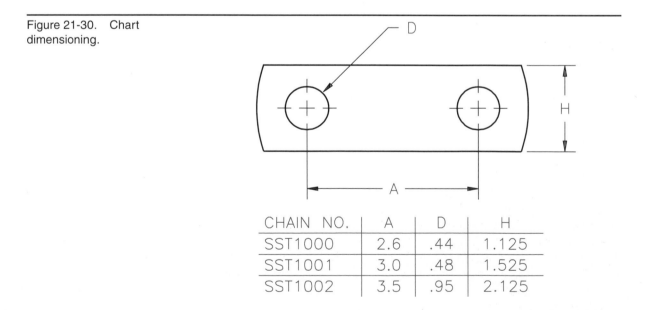

CHAIN NO.	A	D	H
SST1000	2.6	.44	1.125
SST1001	3.0	.48	1.525
SST1002	3.5	.95	2.125

Ordinate dimensioning

AutoCAD refers to arrowless dimensioning as *ordinate dimensioning*. This type of dimensioning is done using the Ordinat: command found in the DRAW DIM screen menu. You can also pick Ordinate from the Dimensioning cascading menu of the Draw pull-down menu. When typing the commands, enter DIMORDINATE or DIMORD at the Command: prompt, or type ORDINATE or ORD at the Dim: prompt in the DIM command. When using this command, AutoCAD automatically places an extension line and numeral along X and Y coordinates. Since you are working in X-Y axes it is best to have ORTHO on.

The World Coordinate System (WCS) 0,0 coordinate has been in the lower-left corner of the screen for the drawings you have already completed. In most cases, this is fine. However, when doing ordinate dimensioning it is best to have the dimensions originate from a corner of the object. The WCS is fixed; the User Coordinate System (UCS), on the other hand, can be moved to any orientation desired.

All of the ordinate dimensions originate from the current UCS origin. The UCS is discussed in detail in Chapter 3 of *AutoCAD and its Applications–Advanced, R13 for DOS*. In general, UCS allows you to set your own coordinate system. If you do this, then all of the Dimension text: prompts display the actual dimensions from the X-Y coordinates on the object. Move the UCS origin to the corner of the object using the following command sequence:

Command: **UCS** ↵
Origin/ZAxis/3point/Entity/View/X/Y/Z/Prev/Restore/Save/Del/?/⟨World⟩: **0** ↵
Origin point ⟨0,0,0⟩: *(pick the origin point at the corner of the object to be dimensioned as shown in Figure 21-31A)*

Next, if there are circles on your drawing, use the CENTER command to place center marks in the circles as shown in Figure 21-31B. This makes your drawing conform to ASME standards and provides something to pick when dimensioning the circle locations. Now, you are ready to start placing the ordinate dimensions. Enter the DIMORDINATE command as follows:

Command: *(type* **DIMORDINATE** *or* **DIMORD** *and press* ENTER*)*
Select Feature: *(pick the feature to be dimensioned)*

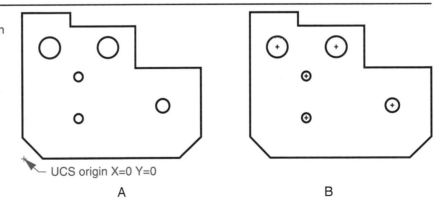

Figure 21-31. A–Draw the object and move the UCS origin to the X-Y corner. B–Add the center marks to the circular features using the CENTER command.

UCS origin X=0 Y=0

A   B

When the Select Feature: prompt appears, move the screen cursor to the feature to be dimensioned. If the feature is the corner of the object, pick the corner. Use the object snaps ENDpoint or INTersection to help if needed. If the feature is a circle, pick the end of the center mark. This leaves the required space between the center mark and the extension line if the DIMEXO variable is set appropriately. Zoom in if needed and use the object snaps to help. The next prompt asks for the leader endpoint, which really refers to the extension line endpoint:

Leader endpoint (Xdatum/Ydatum): *(pick the endpoint of the extension line)*
Dimension text: ⟨X.XXX⟩: ↵

If the X-axis or Y-axis distance between the feature and the leader endpoint is greater, then the default axis may not be the desired axis for the dimension. When this happens, use the Xdatum or Ydatum option to tell AutoCAD which axis originates the dimension:

Leader endpoint (Xdatum/Ydatum): **X** ↵
Leader endpoint: *(pick the endpoint of the extension line)*

Figure 21-32 shows the ordinate dimensions placed on the object. Notice the dimension text is aligned with the extension lines. Aligned dimensioning is standard with ordinate dimensioning, and is not altered by any change in the DIMTIH or DIMTOH variables. DIMTAD is off for the dimensions placed in Figure 21-32. You can have the dimension text placed above the extension line if you turn DIMTAD on.

Figure 21-32.   Placing the ordinate dimensions.

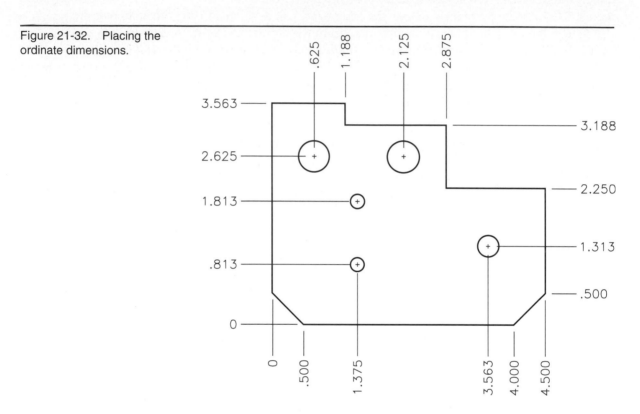

Finally, complete the drawing by adding any missing lines such as centerlines or fold lines. Identify the holes with letters A, B, C (as needed), and correlate a dimensioning table as shown in Figure 21-33.

You can leave the UCS origin at the corner of the object, or move it back to the corner of the screen (WCS) by pressing ENTER at the ⟨World⟩ default:

Command: **UCS** ↵
Origin/ZAxis/3point/Entity/View/X/Y/Z/Prev/Restore/Save/Del/?/⟨World⟩: ↵

Figure 21-33. Completing the drawing.

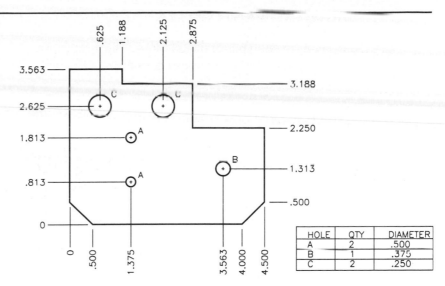

PROFESSIONAL TIP

Most ordinate dimensioning tasks work best with ORTHO on. However, when you have a situation where the extension line is too close to an adjacent dimension numeral, it is best to stagger the extension line as shown in the following illustration. With ORTHO off, the extension line is automatically staggered when you pick the offset second extension line point as demonstrated.

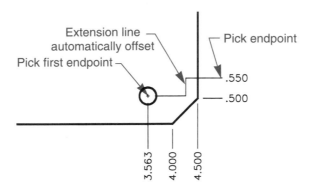

PROFESSIONAL TIP

AutoCAD's powerful DIMORDINATE dimensioning command allows you to quickly and accurately prepare arrowless dimensioning if you follow these steps:

- Draw the object carefully making sure that all features are accurate.
- Set the UCS origin to the X=0, Y=0 coordinates of the object.
- Place center marks in any circles or arcs requiring location dimensions.
- Set the units to the appropriate number of decimal places.
- Dimension the object.

EXERCISE 21-8

❑ Open PRODR2.
❑ Use ordinate dimensioning to draw and completely dimension the object shown in Figure 21-28.
❑ Save the drawing as A:EX21-8.

THREAD DRAWINGS AND NOTES

There are many different types of thread forms. The most common forms are the Unified and metric screw threads. The parts of a screw thread are shown in Figure 21-34.

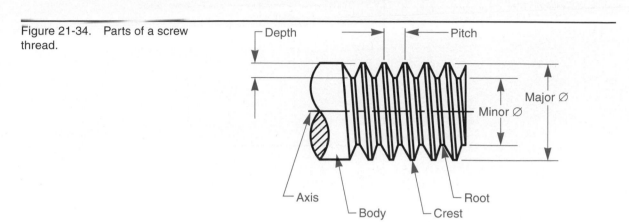

Figure 21-34. Parts of a screw thread.

Threads are commonly shown on a drawing with a simplified representation. Thread depth is shown with a hidden line. This method is used for both external and internal threads, Figure 21-35.

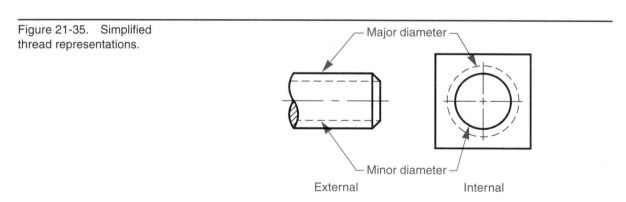

Figure 21-35. Simplified thread representations.

Showing the thread note

The view shows the reader that a thread exists, but the thread note gives exact specifications. The thread note for Unified screw threads must be given in the following order:

3/4 –   10UNC –   2A
(1)   (2) (3)   (4)(5)

- **1.** Major diameter of thread, given as fraction or decimal inch.
- **2.** Number of threads per inch.
- **3.** Thread series. UNC = Unified National Course. UNF = Unified National Fine.
- **4.** Class of fit. 1 = large tolerance. 2 = general purpose tolerance. 3 = tight tolerance.
- **5.** A = external thread. B = internal thread.

The thread note for metric threads is displayed in the following order:

M   14 X 2
(1) (2)   (3)

- **1.** M = metric thread.
- **2.** Major diameter in millimeters.
- **3.** Pitch in millimeters.

There are too many Unified and metric screw threads to discuss here. Refer to the *Machinery's Handbook* or a comprehensive drafting text for more information.

The thread note is typically connected to the thread view with a leader, Figure 21-36. Notice in Figures 21-35 and 21-36 that a chamfer is often placed on the external thread. This makes it easier to enter the mating thread.

Figure 21-36. Displaying the thread note with a leader.

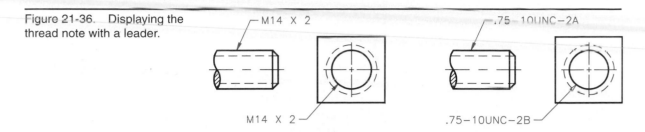

EXERCISE 21-9

❑ Open drawing PRODR2.
❑ Draw a simplified representation of an external and internal Unified screw thread. Do the same for a metric screw thread.
❑ Use the LEADER command to label each view. Label the Unified screw thread as 7/8-14UNF-2 and the metric screw thread as M25X1.5.
❑ Your drawing should look similar to Figure 21-36.
❑ Save the drawing as A:EX21-9.

USING DIALOG BOXES TO CONTROL DIMENSION VARIABLES

AUG 9

Entering the dimension variables at the Command: prompt, as you have done so far, has given you an opportunity to see exactly how each variable controls the way a dimension is drawn. Now that you have used many of the dimensioning variables at the Command: prompt, take a look at how the same variables may be accessed through the "Dimension Styles" dialog box shown in Figure 21-37. You can access this dialog box by entering DDIM at the Command: prompt, by picking "Dimension Style..." from the Data pull-down menu, or by picking DDim: from the DATA screen menu. As you review each dimension variable in the following discussion, it may be helpful to refer back to explanations and examples earlier in this chapter and in Chapter 20 of this text. When you become familiar with using the "Dimension Styles" dialog boxes, you will probably find that command-line adjustment of the dimension variables is slow by comparison. The dimension variables are changed in the dialog boxes by simply picking buttons or providing new settings in edit boxes. Some of the features are represented by image tiles. You can click on these image tiles with the cursor to cycle through the values while you see a display of the results. This can greatly speed up the dimension definition process.

An introduction to dimension styles

A *dimension style* in AutoCAD is a standard or customized set of dimension variables that conform to a particular drafting standard or office practice. How to create and use dimension styles is explained in detail in Chapter 22 of this text, *Advanced Dimensioning*. The Dimension Style area of the dialog box displays dimension style names, makes existing styles current, and may be used to Save and Rename dimension styles. The dimension style with all of the AutoCAD defaults is called STANDARD. If you change any of the standard dimension variables, AutoCAD stores the changes in another style named +STANDARD. Look at Figure 21-37 and notice the +STANDARD style listed as Current. This is a slightly modified version of the STANDARD dimension style. Pick the down arrow in the Current box to access any available dimension styles. When you place dimensions on a drawing, they are displayed in the current style. The only dimension styles that are available in this example are STANDARD and +STANDARD. The Name edit box is where you display a dimension style name to Save or Rename. The STANDARD dimension style is AutoCAD's default and may not be renamed.

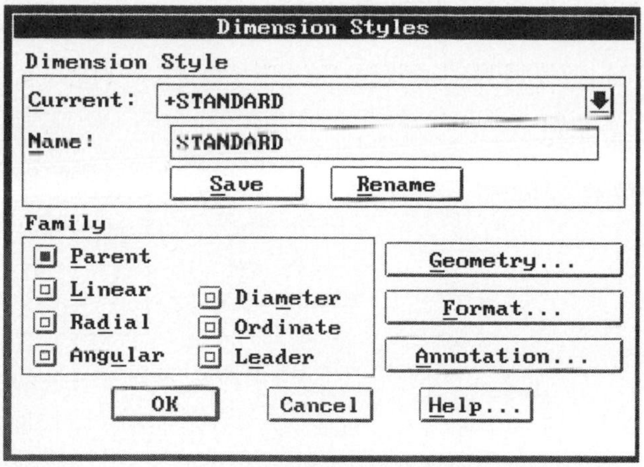

Figure 21-37. The "Dimension Styles" dialog box.

```
┌──────────────────────────────────────────┐
│            Dimension Styles                │
│  Dimension Style                           │
│  Current:  +STANDARD                    ▼ │
│                                            │
│  Name:     STANDARD                        │
│            ┌────────┐  ┌────────┐          │
│            │  Save  │  │ Rename │          │
│            └────────┘  └────────┘          │
│  Family                                    │
│   ■ Parent          ┌──────────────────┐  │
│   □ Linear   □ Diameter  │ Geometry... │  │
│   □ Radial   □ Ordinate  │ Format...   │  │
│   □ Angular  □ Leader    │ Annotation..│  │
│       ┌──────┐ ┌────────┐ ┌────────┐      │
│       │  OK  │ │ Cancel │ │ Help...│      │
│       └──────┘ └────────┘ └────────┘      │
└──────────────────────────────────────────┘
```

The dimension style family members

The Family area of the "Dimension Styles" dialog box contains AutoCAD's dimension style family members. A family member is turned on by picking the radio button next to the name. The family member that is turned on is the one that is displayed in the "Dimension Style" subdialog boxes that are discussed later. The Parent is default and contains all of the dimension style settings for the current style. The other family members contain only the specific dimension variables that are associated with their applications.

EXERCISE 21-10

❏ Begin a new drawing using the standard AutoCAD prototype.
❏ Access the "Dimension Styles" dialog box and notice the selections in the Current: list. Pick Cancel.
❏ Change any dimension variable. For example, enter DIMTXT and change the text height to .125.
❏ Access the "Dimension Styles" dialog box and notice the selections in the Current: list. +STANDARD should be an additional option. Pick Cancel.
❏ Save as A:EX21-10 or quit without saving.

Using the "Geometry" subdialog box

If you pick the Geometry... button in the "Dimension Styles" dialog box, you get the "Geometry" subdialog box shown in Figure 21-38 with the default values displayed. This subdialog box controls the appearance of dimension lines, extension lines, arrowheads, center marks, and dimension scale. The dimension variable name and related figure number from Chapter 20 and 21 are placed in parenthesis with each part of the following discussion. The elements of the "Geometry" subdialog box are described as follows:

• **Dimension Line.** This part of the subdialog box controls dimension variables that relate to the dimension line. The specific controls are as follows:
  • **Suppress:**–Pick the 1st check box if you want to suppress the first dimension line (DIMSD1, Figure 20-14). Pick the 2nd check box if you want to suppress the second dimension line (DIMSD2, Figure 20-14).
  • **Extension:**–This option is not available for use unless the dimension is set to draw tick marks (DIMTSZ, Figure 20-18). If DIMTSZ is set then this option allows you to enter a setting for dimension line extension beyond the extension line (DIMDLE, Figure 20-19).
  • **Spacing:**–This text box lets you change the spacing between dimension lines (DIMDLI, Figure 20-45) when the DIMBASELINE command is used.
  • **Color...**–Pick the Color... button to get the "Select Color" subdialog box. Here you can pick a desired color for the dimension line (DIMCLRD).

Figure 21-38.   The "Geometry" subdialog box is accessed by picking the Geometry... button in the "Dimension Styles" subdialog box.

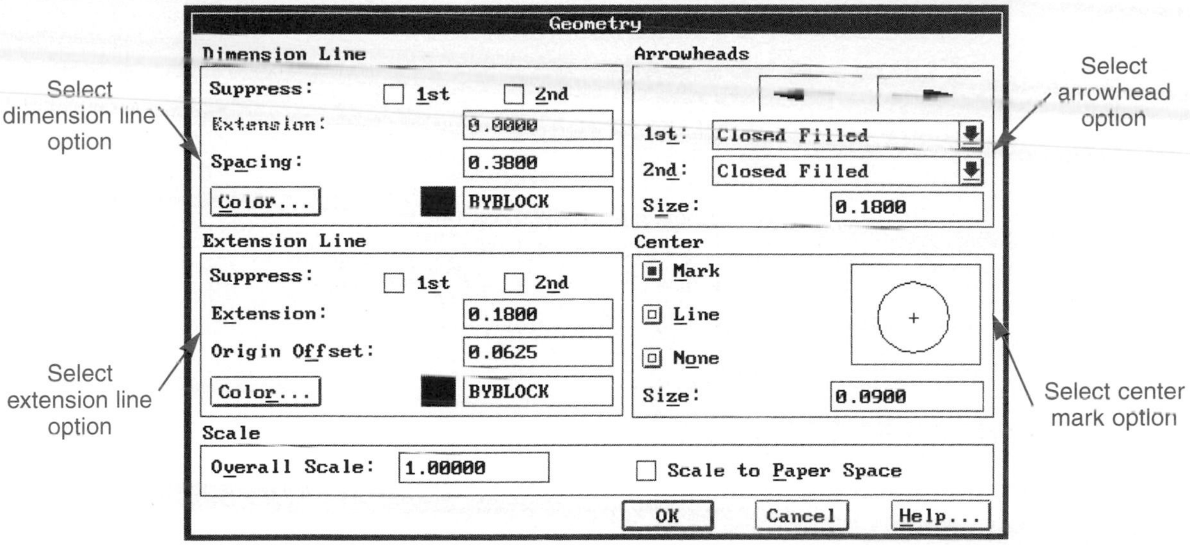

Select dimension line option

Select extension line option

Select arrowhead option

Select center mark option

- **Extension Line.** This part of the subdialog box controls dimension variables that relate to the extension line. The specific controls are as follows:
    - **Suppress:**–Pick the 1st check box if you want to suppress the first extension line (DIMSE1, Figure 20-13). Pick the 2nd check box if you want to suppress the second extension line (DIMSE2, Figure 20-13).
    - **Extension:**–Enter the amount that you want the extension line to extend beyond the last dimension line (DIMEXE, Figure 20-12).
    - **Origin Offset:**–Enter the distance of the space that you want between the extension line origin and the object being dimensioned (DIMEXO, Figure 20-12). Enter a value of 0 if you do not want a space between the extension line and the object (Figure 21-23).
    - **Color...**–Pick the Color... button to get the Select Color subdialog box. Here you can pick a desired color for the extension line (DIMCLRE).
- **Arrowheads.** This part of the subdialog box controls dimension variables that relate to arrowheads. You can change 1st, 2nd, or both arrowheads. To change arrowheads, pick the down arrow next to the 1st list box. The list contains the arrowhead options shown in Figure 21-39. When you pick an arrowhead option from the 1st: list, the 2nd arrowhead is automatically changed to match. You need to pick an arrowhead from the 2nd: list if you want the arrowheads to be different. Notice that the arrowhead image tile changes to display a representation of your selection. Representations of the arrowhead options are shown in Figure 21-40. The None option draws a dimension line or leader without an arrowhead. The Origin Indication option gives you the origin symbol that is used to display where a specific dimension is intended to originate on the drawing. Picking the User Arrow... option gets you the "User arrow" subdialog box where you enter the name of a previously customized arrowhead block (Figure 20-20). The Size: text box lets you change the arrowhead size as needed (DIMASZ, Figure 20-17).

Figure 21-39. Setting desired arrowheads inside of the "Geometry" subdialog box.

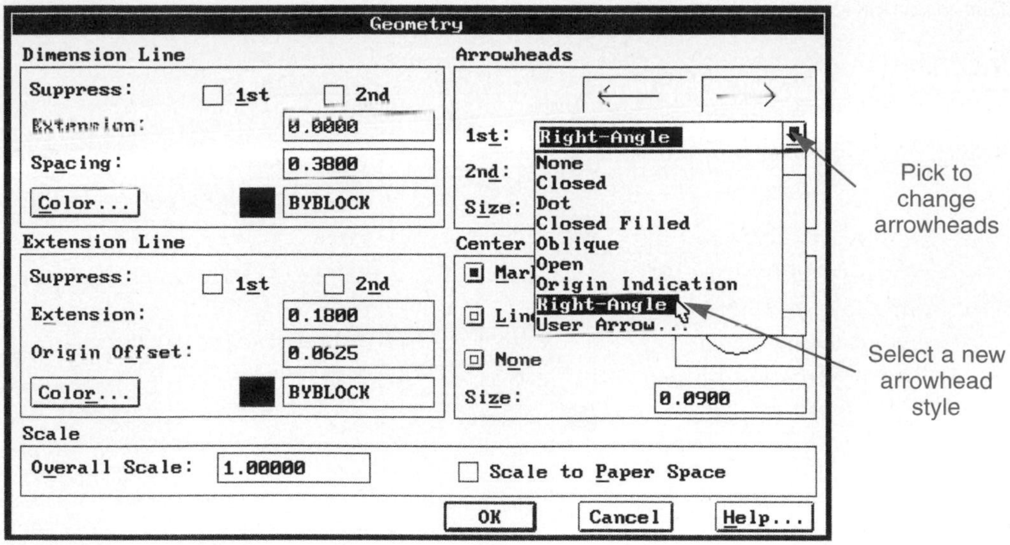

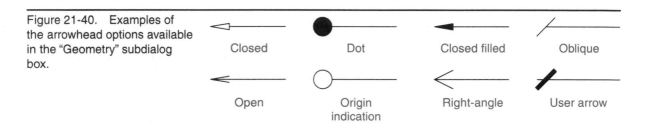

Figure 21-40. Examples of the arrowhead options available in the "Geometry" subdialog box.

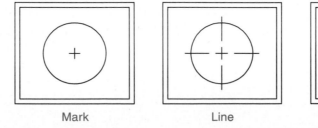

- **Center.** The Center options include radio buttons that allow you to quickly set desired center marks when using the DIMCENTER, DIMDIAMETER, and DIMRADIUS commands (DIMCEN, Figure 20-47). The circle image tile at the right automatically displays the results of the button you pick. Figure 21-41 shows the appearance of the image tile when the different options are selected. The options include:
  - **Mark–**Pick this button to get the center marks that would be drawn with a positive DIMCEN value.
  - **Line–**This option allows you to draw the center mark and centerlines that project beyond the circle as with a negative DIMCEN value.
  - **None–**Pick this if you want circles and arcs dimensioned without any center marks.
  - **Size:–**Enter a value in the text box that you want used for the center mark length.
- **Scale.** The Scale options allow you to change the overall scale factor by entering a value in the Overall Scale: text box (DIMSCALE, Figure 21-24). Pick the Scale to Paper Space check box if you want the dimension scaling to be a factor based on settings between model space and paper space. The Overall Scale: text box is disabled when the Scale to Paper Space check box is picked.

Figure 21-41. Examples of the Center options found in the "Geometry" subdialog box. Pick the desired Center button or pick on the image to cycle through the available options.

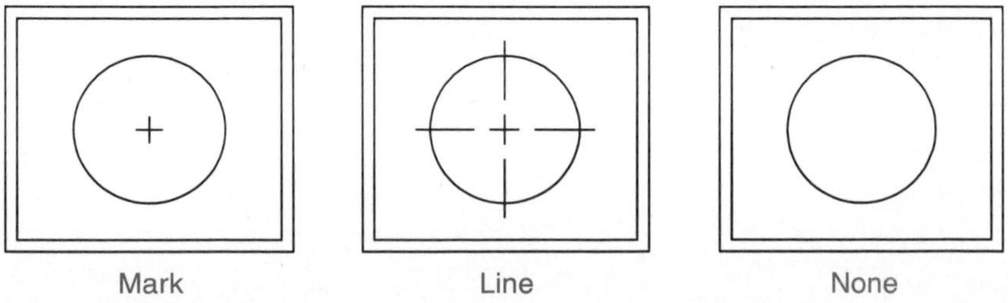

Mark   Line   None

EXERCISE 21-11

❏ Begin a new drawing using the standard AutoCAD prototype.
❏ Access the "Dimension Styles" subdialog box and pick the Geometry button.
❏ Experiment with the options in the "Geometry" subdialog box by doing the following:
   ❏ Change the dimension line spacing to .5.
   ❏ Change the extension line extension to .125.
   ❏ Access the Arrowhead list and pick each of the options while you observe the results. Now, pick inside the left image tile as you watch the image and the option in the text box change. Pick the right image tile and see the results. Pick the left image tile until you get the Closed Filled arrowhead option.
   ❏ Pick each of the Center radio buttons and observe the changing image tile at the right. Now, pick inside the image tile and see the results.
   ❏ Pick either the OK or Cancel button.
❏ Save as A: EX21-11 or quit without saving.

Using the "Format" subdialog box

If you pick the Format... button in the "Dimension Styles" dialog box, you get the "Format" subdialog box shown in Figure 21-42. This subdialog box is used to control the dimension variables that are used to adjust the location of dimension lines, dimension text, arrowheads, and leader lines. The elements of the "Format" subdialog box are described in the following:

- **User Defined.** Picking the User Defined check box turns on the DIMUPT variable. In previously discussed applications, you learned that DIMUPT provides you with the flexibility to place dimension text at any desired position. This variable also allows you to drag the dimension line and leader length as needed. (Figures 20-52, 20-58, and 21-15).
- **Force Line Inside.** Pick this check box if you want the dimension lines to be forced inside of the extension lines even when the arrowheads are placed outside of the extension lines (DIMTOFL, Figures 20-49, 20-51, 20-57, and 21-12).
- **Fit:.** Pick the down arrow to get the list of fit options. Best Fit is the default, but the list also includes Text and arrows, Text Only, Arrows Only, and Leader. These options are the various settings of the DIMFIT variable (Figures 20-50, 20-51, and 21-13). The options are described as follows:
  - **Best Fit–**If there is room for arrowheads only, arrowheads are placed inside of the extension lines. If there is room for text only, then text is placed inside of the extension lines. Otherwise all are placed outside. (DIMFIT =3).

Figure 21-42. The "Format" subdialog box is accessed by picking the Format... button in the "Dimension Styles" dialog box.

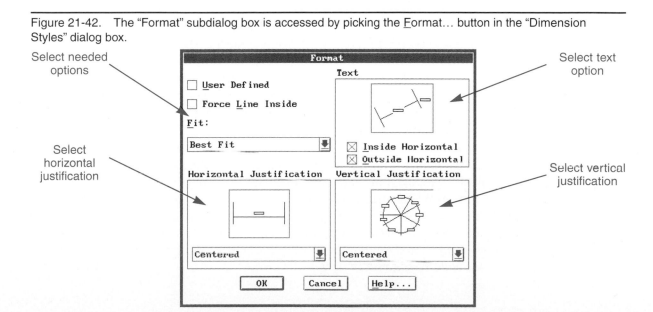

- **Text and Arrows–** If there is not enough room for both text and arrows, all are placed outside of the extension lines. (DIMFIT = 0).
- **Text Only–** If there is room for text only, it is placed inside of the extension lines and the arrowheads are placed outside. Otherwise all are placed outside. (DIMFIT = 1).
- **Arrows Only–** If there is room for arrowheads only, they are placed inside of the extension lines and the text is placed outside. Otherwise all are placed outside. (DIMFIT = 2).
- **Leader–** If there is room for text only, it is placed inside of the extension lines. Otherwise a leader line is created that connects the text to the dimension line. (DIMFIT = 3).

- **Horizontal Justification.** Pick the down arrow to access a list of Horizontal justification options. These options are the settings of the DIMJUST variable (Figure 21-17). Notice the image tile just above the Horizontal Justification list in Figure 21-42. The rectangle in the image tile represents the dimension text position. You can also pick on the image tile to cycle through the options as with any image tile. The following describes the options and the representative image is displayed in Figure 21-43:
  - **Centered –**This is the default and it center justifies the text on the dimension line. (DIMJUST =0)
  - **1st Extension Line–**Places the text next to the first extension line. (DIMJUST =1)
  - **2nd Extension Line–**Places the text next to the second extension line. (DIMJUST =2)
  - **Over 1st Extension –**This option places the text aligned with and at the end of the first extension line. (DIMJUST =3)
  - **Over 2nd Extension–**Places the text aligned with and at the end of the second extension line. (DIMJUST =4)

Figure 21-43. Examples of the Horizontal Justification options found in the "Format" subdialog box. Pick the desired option from the Horizontal Justification list or pick on the image to cycle through the available options.

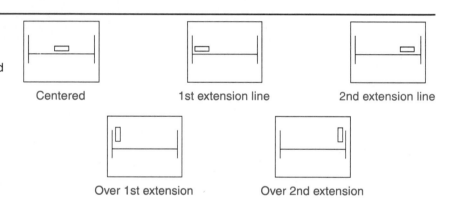

Centered   1st extension line   2nd extension line

Over 1st extension   Over 2nd extension

- **Text.** The Text options in the "Format" subdialog box allow you to control the alignment of dimension text inside (DIMTIH, Figure 20-5, 20-6) and outside (DIMTOH, Figure 20-15) of the extension lines. The options are available by using two check boxes. The default is for these boxes to be checked. Any change to the settings is represented by a change in the image tile displaying the effects of the change. The image tile represented when both boxes are checked is shown in Figure 21-42. Examples of the other image tile displays are shown in Figure 21-44. The options are explained in the following:
  - **Inside Horizontal–**When there is room, the dimension line, arrowheads, and text is placed between the extension lines. The numerals are normally placed horizontally when this box is checked, or aligned with the dimension line when this box is not checked.
  - **Outside Horizontal–**When there is not enough room between extension lines, AutoCAD automatically places the dimension lines, arrowheads, and numerals outside, depending on the status of the DIMFIT variable. When this box is checked, text placed outside of the extension lines is drawn horizontally. When not checked, the dimension text placed outside is drawn aligned with the dimension lines.

Figure 21-44.   The Text options found in the "Format" subdialog box. Look at Figure 21-42 to see the defaults with the Inside Horizontal On and Outside Horizontal On. Notice how the image changes as the check boxes are adjusted. A–Inside Horizontal Off and Outside horizontal On. B–Inside Horizontal On and Outside horizontal Off. C–Inside Horizontal Off and Outside horizontal Off.

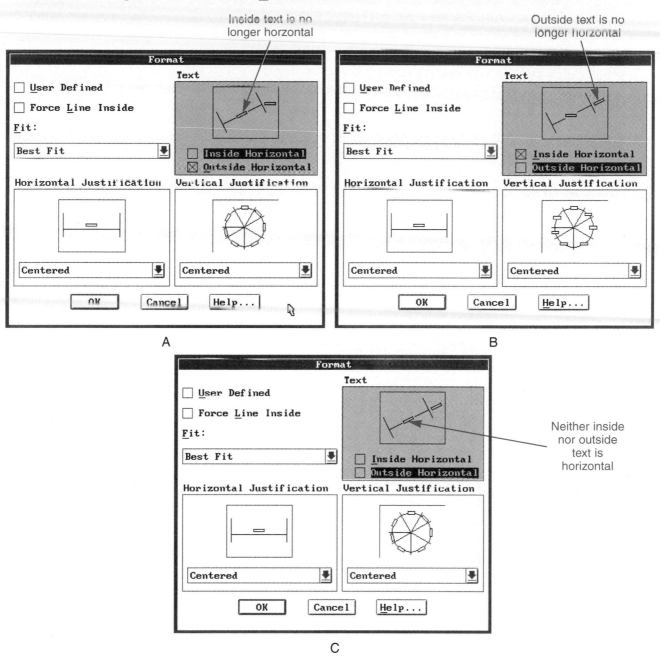

A

B

C

- **Vertical Justification.** Pick the down arrow to access a list of Vertical Justification options. These options are the settings of the DIMTAD variable (Figure 20-16). Notice the image just above the Vertical Justification list in Figure 21-42. The rectangle in the image represents the dimension text position. The following describes the options:
  - **Centered**–This is the default and it center justifies the text on the dimension line. The image in Figure 21-42 represents the Centered option.
  - **Above**–This option places the dimension text centered above the dimension line (DIMTAD ON). This is a common practice in architectural drafting. The distance that the text is placed above the dimension line is equal to the DIMGAP (Figure 21-18) setting. The subdialog box image is shown in Figure 21-45A.

- **Outside**–Using this option places the dimension text on the side of the dimension line that is farthest away from the first extension line origin. This may be an uncommon practice for most applications. The subdialog box image that displays this is shown in Figure 21-45B.
- **JIS**–This option allows you to place dimension text as related to the Japanese Industrial Standard (JIS). See the image in Figure 21-45C.

Figure 21-45.   The Vertical Justification options found in the "Format" subdialog box. Notice the Centered default shown in Figure 21-42. Pick the desired option from the Vertical Justification list, or pick on the image to cycle through the available options. A–Vertical Justification Above the dimension line. B–The Outside option. C–The JIS option.

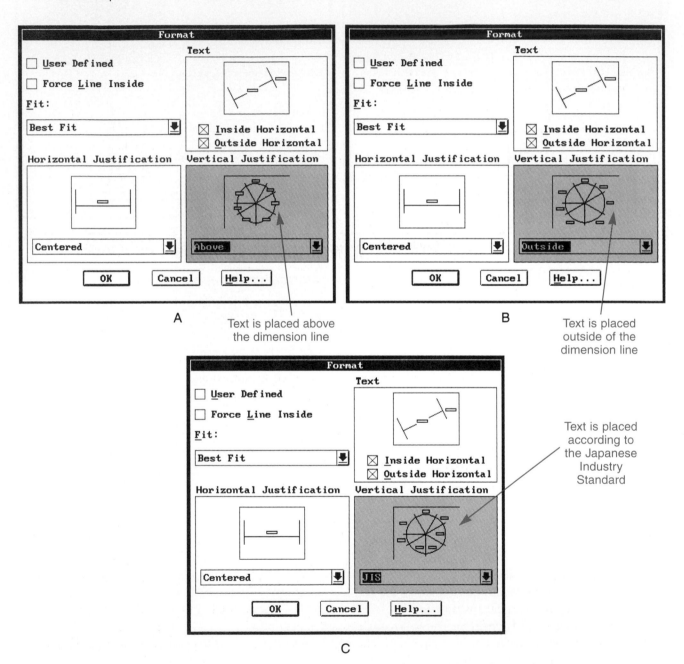

EXERCISE 21-12

❑ Begin a new drawing using the standard AutoCAD prototype.
❑ Access the "Dimension Styles" subdialog box and pick the Format... button.
❑ Experiment with the options in the "Format" subdialog box by doing the following:
  ❑ Pick the User Defined check box.
  ❑ Access the Fit: list and see the options.
  ❑ Pick each of the options in the Horizontal Justification list and see what happens to the image tile. Now, pick the image tile several times and observe the results.
  ❑ Watch the results when you pick the Text check boxes, also pick the image tile and see what happens.
  ❑ Pick each of the options in the Vertical Justification list and see what happens to the image tile. Now, pick the image tile several times and observe the results.
❑ Save as A:EX21-12 or quit without saving.

Using the "Annotation" subdialog box

If you pick the Annotation... button in the "Dimension Styles" dialog box, you get the "Annotation" subdialog box shown in Figure 21-46. This subdialog box is used to control the dimension variables that display the dimension text. Some of the features found in this subdialog box relate to topics that are discussed in Chapter 22, *Advanced Dimensioning and Tolerancing*. These advanced topics are introduced here and explained in detail in Chapter 22. The elements of the "Annotation" subdialog box are described in the following:

Figure 21-46. The "Annotation" subdialog box is accessed by picking the Annotation... button in the "Dimension Styles" dialog box. The Primary Units area is shown here highlighted.

Primary Units area

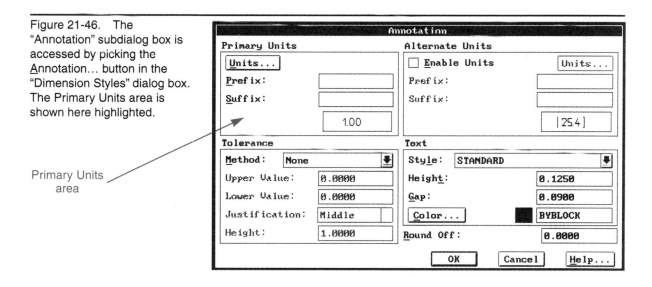

• **Primary Units.** *Primary units* are considered the main part of the dimension text. For example, if you have the dimension 2.875±.005, the primary units is 2.875. This is also referred to as the *specified dimension* in mechanical drafting. In some applications, there may be items added to the primary units, such as prefixes, suffixes, tolerances, or symbols. The following items are found in the Primary Units compartment of the "Annotation" subdialog box:
  • **Units....** Pick the Units... button to access the "Primary Units" subdialog box shown in Figure 21-47. This is where you find items such as Units, Dimension–Precision: and Zero Suppression that may sound familiar. Each of the items in the "Primary Units" subdialog box are described in the following:

- **Units.** Pick the down arrow to access the traditional list of dimension unit options (DIMUNIT). These include:

Scientific	Decimal (default)
Engineering	Architectural
Fractional	

  Pick the desired units format from the list to make it active.

- **Dimension.** The Dimension area has a pop-up list box with selections that are used to control the number of decimal places (DIMDEC) for the primary units. Pick the down arrow to access the choices from 0 to 8 decimal places. Four decimal places (0.0000) is the default.

  The Zero Suppression area gives you four check boxes. These options are used to suppress or keep leading and trailing zeros for the primary units (DIMZIN). Refer to Chapter 20 for a complete review of the DIMZIN variable and its options. The options are explained as follows:

  - **Leading**–Check this box to remove the zeros that are placed before the decimal point in units less than one. Omit the check in this box to keep the zeros that are placed before the decimal point in units less than one. The ASME dimensioning standard recommends that inch values less than one have the zero removed, while metric values less than one keep the zero. (DIMZIN = 4)
  - **Trailing**–This box is not checked by default. This leaves the zeros after the decimal point up to the number of zeros specified in the Dimension Precision (DIMDEC) option. Put a check in this box to remove zeros after the decimal point. (DIMZIN = 8)
  - **0 Feet**–A check in this box is the default which removes the zero in feet measurements like this: 2′. Remove the check to keep 0 feet like this: 2′-0″. (DIMZIN = 0)
  - **0 Inches**–A check in this box is the default which removes the zero in inch measurements like this: 1/2″. Remove the check to keep 0 inches like this: 0′-0 1/2″. (DIMZIN = 3)

- **Angles.** Pick the down arrow to access the traditional list of angular unit options (DIMAUNIT). These include:

Decimal Degrees (default)	Deg/Min/Sec
Grads	Radians
Surveyor	

  Pick the selection that you want to make active.

- **Tolerance.** The Tolerance area has the same options as the Dimension area. The difference is they control the Precision (DIMTDEC) and Zero Suppression (DIMTZIN) for dimension tolerances. This is explained fully in Chapter 22 of this text.

- **Scale.** This area of the subdialog box controls the scale factor of linear dimension numerals on the entire drawing (DIMLFAC, Figure 21-25). This does not effect angles, text height, or tolerance values. The options are:

  - **Linear:**–The default is 1 which represents a 1:1 or FULL scale factor. Enter 2 in the text box to get a factor of 2 which multiplies dimension numerals by 2. For example, if a dimension numeral reads 3.000 with a Linear setting of 1, it would read 6.000 with a setting of 2.
  - **Paper Space Only**–Pick the Paper Space Only check box if you want the dimension scaling to be a factor based on settings between model space and paper space. The Linear: text box is disabled when the Paper Space Only check box is picked.

Figure 21-47   The "Primary Units" subdialog box is accessed by picking the Units... button in the Primary Units area of the "Annotation" subdialog box.

Select units

Select dimension options

Select angles units

Select tolerance options

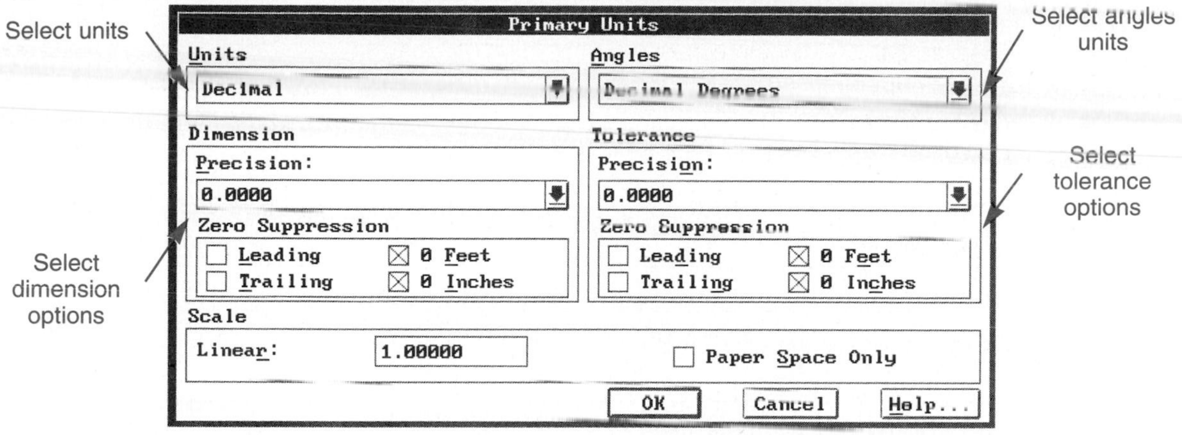

EXERCISE 21-13

❏ Begin a new drawing using the standard AutoCAD prototype.
❏ Access the "Dimension Styles" dialog box and pick the Annotation... button.
❏ Experiment with the options in the "Annotation" subdialog box by doing the following:
   ❏ Pick the Units... button.
      ❏ Experiment with the options in the "Primary Units" subdialog box by doing the following:
         ❏ Look at the options in the Units list.
         ❏ Set the Dimension Precision: to three places (0.000).
         ❏ Suppress the leading zeros for inch dimensioning.
         ❏ Look at the options in the Angles list.
      ❏ Pick OK.
   ❏ Pick each of the options in the Tolerance Method: list and see what happens to the Primary Units image tile. Pick the image tile several times and see the results.
   ❏ Pick the Text Style: list and see the options.
   ❏ Pick OK.
❏ Use the STYLE command to set the ROMANS and ROMAND text fonts.
❏ Access the "Dimension Styles" dialog box again and pick the Annotation... button. Do the following:
   ❏ Pick the Text Style: list and see the options now.
   ❏ Change the text height to .125.
   ❏ Pick OK.
❏ Pick OK.
❏ Save as A:EX21-13 or quit without saving.

CHAPTER TEST

Write your answers in the spaces provided.

1. Oblique extension lines are drawn using the _____ command and by typing _____

   or _____ at the Dim: prompt.

2. Define annotation. _____

   _____

3. Identify how to access the leader command using the following methods:

   Screen menu–_____

   Pull-down menu–_____

   Typing at the Command: prompt– _____   _____

4. Text placed using the LEADER command is a _____ text object where all of the lines of

   text are _____ object.

5. Describe the purpose of the LEADER command's Annotation Copy option. _____

   _____

   _____

6. Name and briefly describe the LEADER command's five Format options. _____

   _____

   _____

   _____

   _____

   _____

7. This LEADER command option removes the last leader segment that you drew. _____

   _____

8. Name the command that may be used to easily move the text in the dimension line after the

   dimension has been placed. _____

   _____

9. Identify the option from the following brief DIMEDIT command option descriptions:

   Restores position and rotation of dimension text to the original default position– _____

   Allows specification of new dimension text– _____

   Rotates the dimension text to an angle that you specify– _____

   Changes the extension line angle to your specifications– _____

10. This command may be used to override dimension variables associated with an individual

    dimension or selected group of dimensions. _____

11. Define arrowless dimensioning. _____

    _____

12. AutoCAD refers to arrowless dimensioning as _____ dimensioning.

13. Name the screen menu and pull-down menu selections that allow you to draw arrowless dimen-

    sions with AutoCAD. _____

    _____

    _____

    _____

14. What is the importance of the User Coordinate System (UCS) when doing arrowless dimensioning?

    _____

    _____

    _____

15. Identify the elements of this Unified screw thread note. 1/2-13 UNC 2B

    1/2 _____

    13 _____

    UNC _____

    2 _____

    B _____

16. Identify the elements of this metric screw thread: M 14 X 2

    M _____

    14 _____

    2 _____

17. Name the dialog box that may be used to control dimension variables. _____

18. Identify at least three ways to access the dialog box identified in question number 17. _____

19. Define an AutoCAD dimension style. _____

20. If you change any of the standard dimension variables, AutoCAD stores the changes in another style named _____.

21. Provide a general description of dimension style family members._____

    _____

    _____

    _____

22. Identify the parent family member. _____

    _____

    _____

23. Name the subdialog box that may be used to control the appearance of dimension lines, extension lines, arrowheads, center marks, and dimension scale._____

    _____

24. Name the subdialog box that may be used to control dimension variables that are used to adjust the location of dimension lines, dimension text, arrowheads, and leader lines._____

    _____

25. Name the subdialog box that is used to control the dimension variables that display the dimension text. _____

26. This DIM command's subcommand is used to change existing dimensions to reflect the current settings for dimension variables. _____

27. This command may be used to change the text or extension lines of existing dimensions._____

    _____

28. You can use this command to move dimension text within the dimension line of an existing dimension. _____

For 29 through 40, identify the dimension variables associated with each of the following short definitions:

29. Forces dimension text inside of extension lines. _____

30. Places a dimension line between extension lines when the dimension text is outside. _____

702   AutoCAD and its Applications–Basics

31. Used to suppress the dimension lines and arrowheads. _____

32. Allows you to place the dimension text above, below, or centered in a break in the dimension line. _____

33. Controls the space between the dimension line and the dimension text. _____

34. Lets you insert a block in place of the first arrowhead. _____

35. Allows you to adjust the dimension line or leader length and control the dimension text location by dragging the text to the right or left side of the extension line. _____

36. This variable is an overall scale factor that applies to all dimension variables that specify size, distance, or offset. _____

37. Sets a scale factor for all linear dimensions, except angles. _____

38. Sets the color of all dimension lines, arrowheads, and leaders. _____

39. This variable controls the placement of arrowheads and text inside or outside of extension lines based on the space available. _____

40. Used to adjust the placement of the dimension text within the dimension line relative to the extension line or aligned with and at the end of an extension line. _____

_____

DRAWING PROBLEMS

Set limits, units, dimensioning variables, and other parameters as needed. Follow the following guidelines.

A. Draw the needed Multiviews to exact size. Problems presented in 3-D require you to select the proper multiviews.

B. Use grids, object snap options, and the OSNAP command to your best advantage.

C. Apply dimensions accurately using ASME standards. Dimensions are in inches unless otherwise specified.

D. Set dimensioning variables to suit the drawing.

E. Use the LAYER command to set separate layers for views and dimensions.

F. Draw object lines using .032 in. wide polylines, or use the LINE command and plot with a wide pen.

G. Place general notes 1/2 in. from lower-left corner:
   3. UNLESS OTHERWISE SPECIFIED, ALL DIMENSIONS ARE IN MILLIMETERS *(or* INCHES *as applicable).*
   2. REMOVE ALL BURRS AND SHARP EDGES.
   1. INTERPRET PER ASME Y14.5M-1994.
   NOTES:

H. Save the drawing to a floppy disk as **P21** *(problem number.)*

P21-1

1. **Dimensioning Undefined Curve**

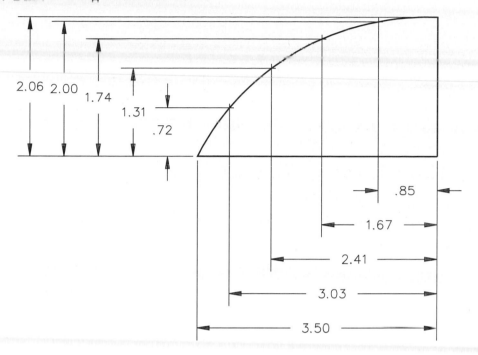

P21-2

2. **Placing Oblique Dimensions**

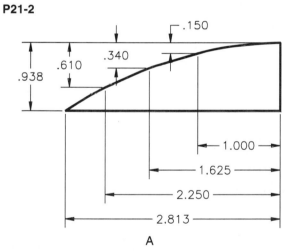

A

Draw the object as shown at A.

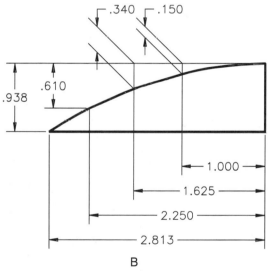

B

Use the OBLIQUE command to modify
the dimension as shown at B.

3. **Shaft SAE 1030**

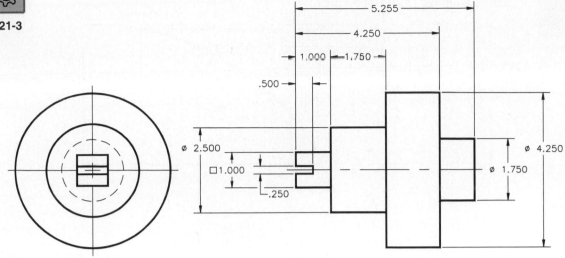

4. **Step Block**

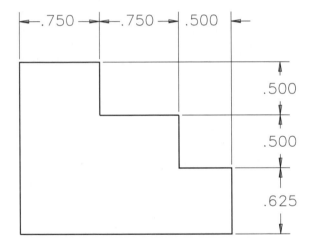

5. **Step Block 2**

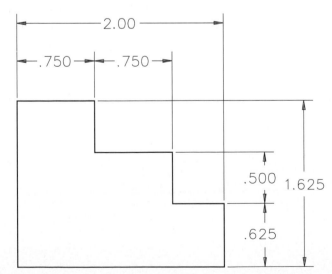

P21-3

P21-4

P21-5

P21-6

6. **Pin SAE 4320**

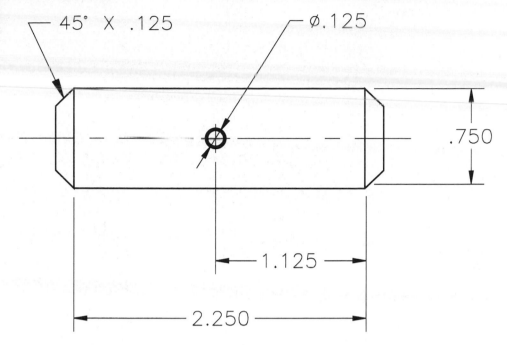

P21-7

7. **Spline–MS .125 THK**

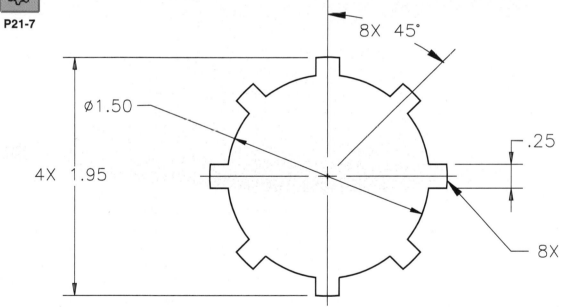

P21-8

8. Bracket–Aluminum

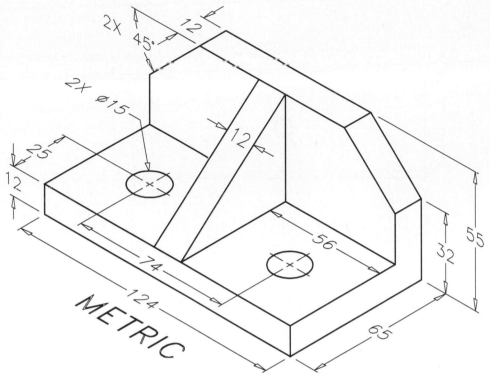

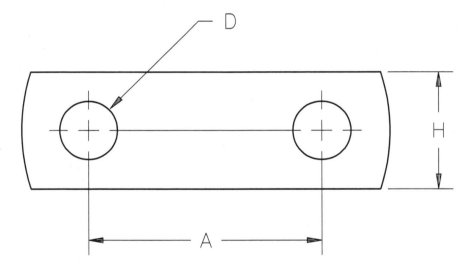

P21-9

9. Chain Link–Tool Steel

CHAIN NO.	A	D	H
SST1000	2.6	.44	1.125
SST1001	3.0	.48	1.525
SST1002	3.5	.95	2.125

P21-10

10. **Base–Bronze** Convert the given drawing to a drawing with the holes located using arrowless dimensioning based on the X and Y coordinate dimensions given in the table. Place a table above your title block with Hole (identification), Quantity, Description, and Depth (Z axis).

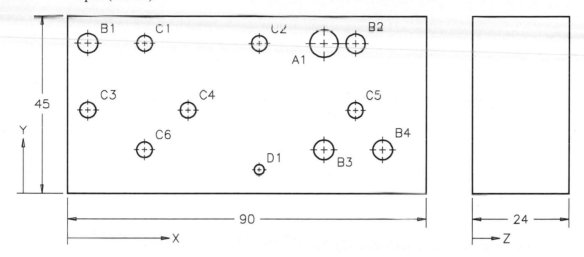

HOLE	QTY.	DESCRIP.	X	Y	Z
A1	1	⌀7	64	38	18
B1	1	⌀5	5	38	THRU
B2	1	⌀5	72	38	THRU
B3	1	⌀5	64	11	THRU
B4	1	⌀5	79	11	THRU
C1	1	⌀4	19	38	THRU
C2	1	⌀4	48	38	THRU
C3	1	⌀4	5	21	THRU
C4	1	⌀4	30	21	THRU
C5	1	⌀4	72	21	THRU
C6	1	⌀4	19	11	THRU
D1	1	⌀2.5	48	6	THRU

11. **Chassis–Aluminum .100 THK**

P21-11

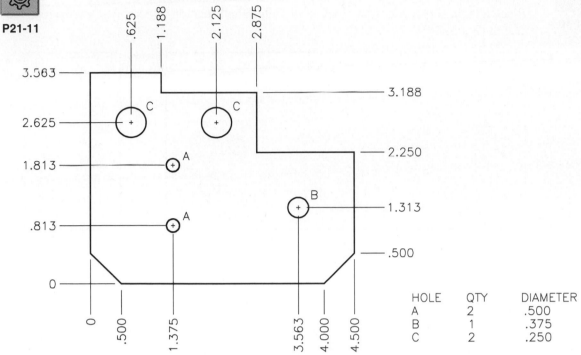

HOLE	QTY	DIAMETER
A	2	.500
B	1	.375
C	2	.250

12. **Shim MS**

P21-12

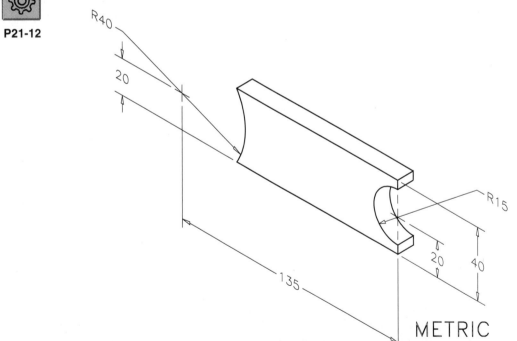

METRIC

P21-13

13. **Shaft Support–Cast Iron (CI)** Half of the object is removed for clarity. The entire object should be drawn.

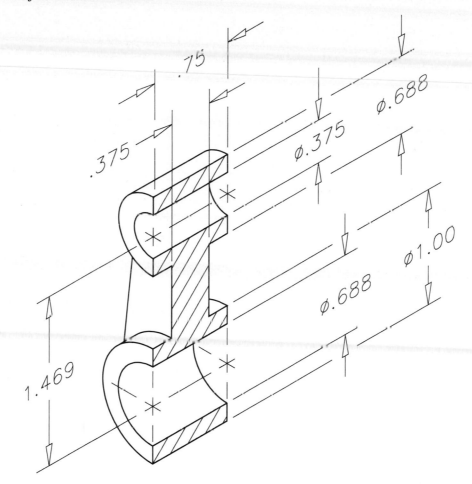

14. **Transmission Cover–Cast Iron (CI)** Half of the object is removed for clarity. The entire object should be drawn.

P21-14

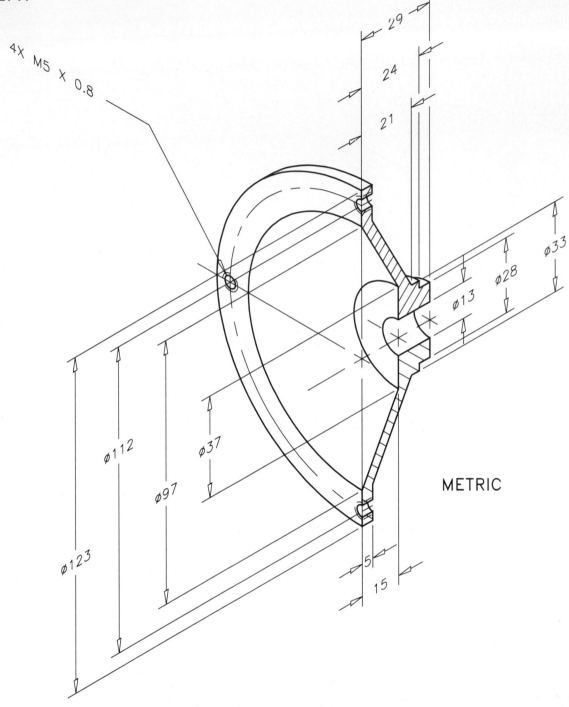

METRIC

Chapter 22

ADVANCED DIMENSIONING AND TOLERANCING

Learning objectives

After completing this chapter, you will be able to:
- ○ Establish AutoCAD dimensioning styles to conform with drafting standards.
- ○ Override existing dimensioning variables.
- ○ Prepare drawings with dimensions and tolerances from engineering sketches.
- ○ Modify dimensioning variables to perform specific dimensioning and tolerancing operations.
- ○ Identify and use dual dimensioning techniques.
- ○ Use dimension variable dialog boxes.
- ○ Apply associative dimensioning.
- ○ Use the STRETCH, TRIM, and EXTEND commands to revise existing dimensioned objects.
- ○ Make changes to existing dimension entities using the UPDATE, HOMETEXT, and NEWTEXT commands.

This chapter shows you how to establish AutoCAD dimensioning styles to conform with drafting standards. It explains tolerancing and dual dimensioning, along with the AutoCAD techniques used to edit dimensions. Also introduced is *associative dimensioning,* a technique that allows you to revise drawings using the STRETCH, TRIM, and EXTEND commands. Changes made to an object automatically affect associated dimensions.

The number of decimal places usually reflects the accuracy of a dimension. For example, a three-place decimal dimension is more precise than a two-place decimal. You can control the number of places behind the decimal point using dimension variables that control the dimension and tolerance format. These are setups that you should enter on the drawing plan sheet.

CREATING AND CONTROLLING DIMENSIONING STYLE `AUG 9`

AutoCAD refers to dimensioning standards as *style.* You can customize your dimensioning style to correspond to drafting standards such as ASME/ANSI, ISO (International Organization for Standardization), MIL (military), architectural, structural, civil, or for your own corporate or school standards. With a basic knowledge of AutoCAD dimensioning techniques and how to control the dimensioning variables, you can now decide how to establish your own dimensioning styles. If you do more than one type of drafting such as mechanical and architectural, or if you create drawings for clients who require different standards such as ASME/ANSI, ISO, or MIL, then you can set up AutoCAD to assist you in preparing the type of dimensioning needed. The AutoCAD dimensioning command that helps you identify and create dimensioning styles is DIMSTYLE. The DIMSTYLE command is found in the DRAWDIM screen menu as DimStyl:, or can be typed as DIMSTYLE at the Command: prompt:

Command: **DIMSTYLE** ⏎
  dimension style: STANDARD
Dimension Style Edit (Save/Restore/STatus/Variables/Apply/?) ⟨Restore⟩:

After you enter the DIMSTYLE command, AutoCAD gives you a message identifying the current dimension style. The dimension style identified on previous page is STANDARD. This is the AutoCAD default dimension style that is set up in the AutoCAD prototype.

Creating dimension styles

Dimension styles can be created in a prototype drawing. When using this practice, you can begin a new drawing and set the dimensioning style(s) that you want used in the drawing. For example, you may typically do drawings that are either drawn to ARCHFL (architectural floor plans) or ASME/ANSI standards (inch or metric). If this is the case, then you should make a complete list of the dimensioning variables that you commonly use for each type of drafting and create dimensioning styles accordingly. Lists for architectural or mechanical styles may look like this:

ARCHFL (1/4″ = 1′-0″)	**ASME/ANSI (in)**	**ASME (mm)**
DIMTSZ = 4	DIMASZ = .125	DIMASZ = 3
DIMCEN = 6	DIMCEN = -.1	DIMCEN = -3
DIMDLE = 2	DIMDLI = .5	DIMDLI = 15
DIMDLI = 12	DIMTXT = .125	DIMTXT = 3
DIMEXO =	DIMZIN = 4 or 7	DIMZIN = 8
DIMEXE = 3	DIMDEC = 3	DIMDEC = 0
DIMTAD = ON	DIMUPT = 1	DIMUPT = 1
DIMTIX = ON	STYLE = ROMANS	STYLE = ROMANS
DIMTXT = 6	DIMTXSTY = ROMANS	DIMTXSTY = ROMANS
DIMZIN = 1		

(the following dimension variables are for tolerance control and are explained later in this chapter)

DIMTIH = OFF	DIMTDEC = 3	DIMTDEC = 0
DIMTOH = OFF	DIMTZIN = 1	
DIMUNIT = 4		
DIMAUNIT = 1		
DIMTOFL = 1		
DIMFIT = 4		
DIMUPT = 1		
STYLE = CIBT		
DIMTXSTY = CIBT		

Any of the dimensioning variables that remain unchanged continue as AutoCAD default values. If you find that a particular dimensioning variable is not set the way you want it, then you can change it and modify the dimensioning style at any time.

Saving dimension styles

Now, you are ready to create each of the dimensioning styles listed. Use AutoCAD to change all of the dimensioning variables that you have listed for your ARCHFL standard. After all of the dimensioning variables are set to your satisfaction, use the Save option of the DIMSTYLE command to enter the desired dimension style name. To do this, access the DimStyle: screen menu and pick Save or type S, as shown in the following example:

Command: **DIMSTYLE** ↵
 dimension style: STANDARD
Dimension Style Edit (Save/Restore/STatus/Variables/Apply/?) ⟨Restore⟩: **S** ↵
?/Name for new dimension style: **ARCHFL** ↵
Command:

When used at the Dim. prompt, the SAVE subcommand saves the current dimensioning variable settings to a dimension style and makes the new dimension style current. Type the desired dimension style:

Command: **DIM** ↵
Dim: **SAVE** ↵
?/Name for new dimension style: **ARCHFL** ↵

Now, proceed in the same manner to change the dimensioning variables reflecting your proposed ASME/ANSI styles, and again use the Save option for the created styles. Do this for any dimensioning style that you want created in your prototype drawing.

Listing the dimension styles

If you want to list the dimension styles created for the current drawing, enter a question mark (?). List the name or names of styles you want listed to help you remember if they have been created, or press ENTER to accept the wild card ⟨*⟩ for all dimension styles:

Command: **DIMSTYLE** ↵
 dimension style: STANDARD
Dimension Style Edit (Save/Restore/STatus/Variables/Apply/?) ⟨Restore⟩: **?**↵
Dimension style(s) to list ⟨*⟩: ↵

The AutoCAD Text Screen is displayed. This gives a list of available dimension styles:

Named dimension styles:
  ARCHFL
  ASMEIN
  ASMEMM
  STANDARD
Command:

Press the F1 key to return to the Command: prompt.
This is how you list the dimension styles in the DIM command:

Command: **DIM** ↵
Dim: **SAVE** ↵
?/Name for new dimension style: **?** ↵
Dimension style(s) to list ⟨*⟩: ↵
Named dimension styles:
ARCHFL
ASMEIN
ASMEMM
STANDARD
?/Name for new dimension style:

Using the Restore option

The Restore option lets you change dimensioning variable settings by reading new settings from an existing dimension style. You can access Restore at the keyboard, or pick Restore from the DimStyl: screen menu. The current dimension style is listed. Change to a different dimension style by entering a dimension style name as follows:

Command: **DIMSTYLE** ↵
 dimension style: STANDARD
Dimension Style Edit (Save/Restore/STatus/Variables/Apply/?) ⟨Restore⟩: ↵
?/Enter dimension style name or RETURN to select dimension: **ARCHFL** ↵
Command:

Using the DIM command, the sequence is as follows:

> Command: **DIM** ↵
> Dim: **RES** ↵
> ?/Enter dimension style name or RETURN to select dimension: **ARCHFL** ↵
> Dim:

You can also press ENTER to determine the dimensioning style of any existing dimension by picking that dimension. Restore is the default in the DIMSTYLE command, so you can type R and press ENTER or just press the ENTER key:

> Command: **DIMSTYLE** ↵
>   dimension style: ARCHFL
> Dimension Style Edit (Save/Restore/STatus/Variables/Apply/?) ⟨Restore⟩: ↵
> ?/Enter dimension style name or RETURN to select dimension: ↵
> Select dimension: *(pick a dimension on the drawing)*
>   dimension style: ARCHFL
> Command:

Using the DIM command, the sequence is as follows:

> Command: **DIM** ↵
> Dim: *(Type* **RES** *or* **RESTORE** *and press* ENTER*)*
> Current dimension style: ARCHFL
> ?/Enter dimension style name or RETURN to select dimension: ↵
> Select dimension: *(pick a dimension on the drawing)*
> Current dimension style: ARCHFL
> Dim:

Now you know that the dimension you picked was drawn using the ARCHFL style, which is the current style. The Restore option lets you list the dimension styles in the current drawing by entering a ? in the same manner as described with the Save option.

If you want to display the difference between one of your dimension styles and the current style enter the tilde character (~) followed by the style to compare and ENTER:

> ?/Enter dimension style name or RETURN to select dimension: **~ASMEIN** ↵

AutoCAD shows you the difference between styles on the Text Screen:

> Difference between ASMEIN and current settings:
>
> | ASMEIN | | Current Setting |
> |---|---|---|
> | DIMASZ | 0.125 | 0.180 |
> | DIMCEN | -0.100 | 6.000 |
> | DIMDEC | 3 | 4 |
> | DIMDLI | 0.500 | 12.000 |
> | DIMTDEC | 3 | 4 |
> | DIMTXSTY | ROMANS | CIBT |
> | DIMTZIN | 1 | 0 |
> | DIMZIN | 4 | 1 |

Keep in mind that the Text Screen only displays the dimension variable settings that are *different* between the current style and the style name that you entered. You can do the same thing using the Save option, at the ?/Name for new dimension style: prompt.

Using the STatus option

The STatus option of the DIMSTYLE command is used to display the settings of all dimension variables for the current dimension style. Pick the Status option in the DimStyle screen menu, or type ST, as follows:

Command: **DIMSTYLE** ↵
  dimension style: ARCHFL
Dimension Style Edit (Save/Restore/STatus/Variables/Apply/?) ⟨Restore⟩: **ST** ↵

The Text Screen displays all of the dimension variable names, the settings, and a descriptive statement about each variable. There are three pages, so press ENTER to read each of the additional pages and press F1 to get back to the Command: prompt when done. This works the same as the STATUS subcommand:

Command: **DIM** ↵
Dim: **STATUS** ↵

Using the Variables option

Another way to list the current dimension style and variable settings of a dimension style without changing the current settings is with the Variables option. You can name a dimension style to list the variables, or pick a dimension on the screen just as you did with the Restore option:

Command: **DIMSTYLE** ↵
  dimension style: ARCHFL
Dimension Style Edit (Save/Restore/STatus/Variables/Apply/?) ⟨Restore⟩: **V** ↵
?/Enter dimension style name or RETURN to select dimension: ↵
Select dimension: *(pick a dimension on the drawing)*

In the DIM command, the sequence is as follows:

Command: **DIM** ↵
Dim: **VAR** ↵
Current dimension style: ARCHFL
?/Enter dimension style name or RETURN to select dimension: ↵
Select dimension: (pick a dimension on the screen)

The screen changes to the Text Screen, with a listing of the current dimensioning variable settings for the dimension you picked. Press ENTER to see more pages of the list, or press the F1 key to return to the graphics screen.

Use the ? option if you want to look at the dimensioning variables used in the current drawing. You can compare the current dimension style with another style by entering a ~ and the style name to compare. The following is an example:

Command: **DIMSTYLE** ↵
Dimension Style Edit (Save/Restore/STatus/Variables/Apply/?) **?** ↵
Dimension style(s) to List ⟨*⟩: **~ASMEIN** ↵

The Text Screen then displays only the dimension variables that are different between the current style and the ASMEIN style.

Using the Apply option

Use the Apply option in the DIMSTYLE command if you want to select a dimension and have it applied to the current dimension style settings. Pick the Apply option in the DimStyle screen menu, or type A, as follows:

Command: **DIMSTYLE** ↵
Dimension Style Edit (Save/Restore/STatus/Variables/Apply/?) ⟨Restore⟩: **A** ↵
Select objects: *(select the dimension or dimensions that you want to have applied to the current dimension style)*
Select objects: ↵
Command:

EXERCISE 22-1

❑ Open one of your previous mechanical drawings or exercises containing dimensions.
❑ Design dimensioning variables that may be used for two different dimension styles. One is named ARCHFL for use when drawing architectural floor plans at a scale of 1/4″ =1′–0″, and the other is named ASMEIN for decimal-inch, ASME standard drawings. Use the following dimension variable settings:

ARCHFL	ASMEIN
DIMTSZ = 4	DIMTSZ = .125
DIMCEN = 6	DIMCEN = -.1
DIMDLE = 2	DIMDLI = .5
DIMEXO = 2	DIMEXE = .125
DIMEXE = 3	DIMTXT = .125
DIMTAD = ON	DIMZIN = 4
DIMTIX = ON	DIMDEC = 3
DIMTXT = 6	DIMUPT = 1
DIMZIN = 1	STYLE = ROMANS
DIMTIH = OFF	DIMTXSTY = ROMANS
DIMTOH = OFF	DIMTDEC = 3
DIMUNIT = 4	DIMTZIN = 4
DIMAUNIT = 1	
DIMFIT = 4	
DIMTOFL = 1	
DIMUPT = 1	
STYLE = CIBT	
DIMTXSTY = CIBT	

❑ Save these dimension styles under the name identified with each.
❑ Use the Restore option to restore the dimension style that is not currently set.
❑ Use the tilde (~) to have AutoCAD show you the difference between the styles.
❑ Use the ? option to list the available dimension styles.
❑ Use the STatus option to display the dimension variable names of the current dimension style.
❑ Access the dimension variable status screen with the Variable option.
❑ Restore the ASMEIN dimension style if it is not current. Use the Apply option and select the dimensions on the drawing to have converted to the current dimension style.
❑ Save as A:EX22-1.

OVERRIDING EXISTING DIMENSIONING VARIABLES AUG 9

Generally, it is appropriate to have one or more dimensioning variables set to perform specific tasks that relate to your dimensioning practices. However, situations may arise where it is necessary to alter dimensioning variables to modify one or more specific dimensions on the final drawing. For example, assume you have the DIMEXO (EXtension line Offset) variable set at .062, which conforms to ASME standards. However, in your final drawing there are three specific dimensions that require a 0 extension line offset. You can pick these three dimensions and alter the DIMEXO variable exclusively by using the DIMOVERRIDE command that was introduced in Chapter 21. As a review, the command works like this:

Command: *(type* **DIMOVERRIDE** or **DIMOVER** *and press* ENTER*)*
Dimension variable to override (or Clear to remove overrides): **DIMEXO** ↵
Current value ⟨.06200⟩ New value: **0** ↵
Dimension variable to override: *(type another variable name to override or press* ENTER*)*
Select objects: *(select the dimension or dimensions to override)*
Select objects: ↵
Command:

You can also override a dimension variable in the DIM command:

Command: **DIM** ↵
Dim: **OVER** ↵
Dimension variable to override: **DIMEXO** ↵
Current value ⟨.0625⟩: New value: **0** ↵
  Dimension variable to override: ↵
Select objects: *(pick the specific dimensions for change)*

The DIMEXO variable automatically changes from .062 to 0 on the three selected dimensions. You can also clear any previous overrides by using the Clear option like this:

Command: **DIMOVER** ↵
Dimension variable to override (or Clear to remove overrides): **C** ↵
Select objects: *(select the dimension or dimensions to clear an override)*
Select objects: ↵
Command:

PROFESSIONAL TIP

It may be better to use the DDIM command rather than the DIMOVERRIDE command, depending on the nature of the change. In the dialog box, you can pick an existing style, change the variable, then make a new style.

It is also sometimes better to generate a new style, since certain situations require specific dimension styles in order to prevent conflicts with drawing geometry or dimension crowding. For example, if a number of the dimensions in the current drawing all require the same overrides, then generating a new dimension style is a good idea. If only one or two dimensions need the same overrides, then just using the DIMOVERRIDE command may be more productive.

EXERCISE 22-2

❑ Load AutoCAD and open PRODR2.
❑ Make a drawing similar to Figure 21-1 with dimensioning variables set as follows:
  ❑ DIMASZ = .1
  ❑ DIMGAP = .05
  ❑ DIMDLE = .12
  ❑ DIMDLI = .5
  ❑ DIMEXO = .06
❑ Use datum (baseline) dimensioning to make your job easier.
❑ After completing the entire drawing, with the dimensioning variables set as required, use the DIMOVERRIDE command to change only the DIMEXO variable to 0 on all dimensions except the overall dimensions.
❑ Save the drawing as A:EX22-2.

USING THE DIALOG BOX TO CONTROL DIMENSION STYLES

The "Dimension Styles" dialog box was introduced in Chapter 21 as an easy way to work with dimension variables. This dialog box is also used to list, save, and restore dimension styles. The dialog box is accessed by picking Dimension Style... from the Data pull down menu, picking Ddim: in the DRAW DIM screen menu, or by typing DDIM at the Command: or Dim: prompt.

The Dimension Style area of the dialog box is where you can access dimension styles that were previously created, or name and save additional dimension styles. See Figure 22-1. The current active dimension style is identified in the Current: list box. Figure 22-1 shows STANDARD as the current dimension style. STANDARD is the AutoCAD default dimension style. Pick the down arrow to see additional dimension styles that are available as shown in Figure 22-2. These are dimension styles that were saved earlier using the DIMSTYLE command. Each of the dimension styles saved using the DIMSTYLE command or in the "Dimension Styles" dialog box are referred to as a *dimension style family* by AutoCAD.

Figure 22-1.   The "Dimensions Styles" dialog box can be used to list, save, and restore dimension styles.

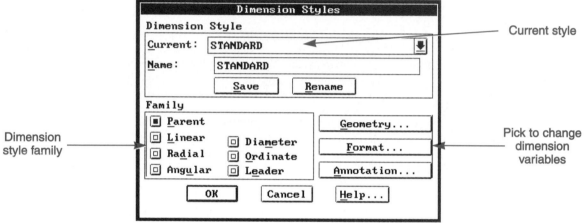

Figure 22-2.   Pick the down arrow next to the Current: edit box to see additional dimension styles that are available

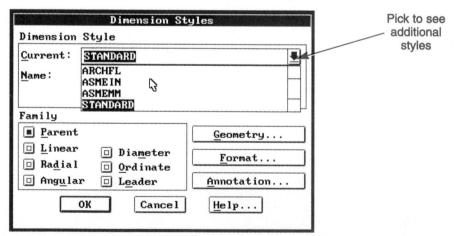

You can return to AutoCAD and make changes to the dimension variables or change dimension variables using the "Geometry" subdialog box, "Format" subdialog box, and "Annotation" subdialog box inside the "Dimension Styles" dialog box. When you have made the dimension variable changes, use the "Dimension Styles" dialog box to type the name of a new dimension style in the Name: text box. A dimension style name may have up to 31 characters. For example, you can modify the ARCH-FL dimension style for use on roof plan drawings by changing the variables to a 1/8″ = 1′-0″ scale. Then type ARCHRP (ARCHitectural Roof Plans) in the Name: text box and pick the Save button, as shown in Figure 22-3. AutoCAD gives you the following message at the bottom of the "Dimension Styles" dialog box: Created ARCHRP from ARCHFL. Creating a new dimension style from an existing style is an easy way to establish new dimension styles.

Figure 22-3.   To create a new dimension style, type the name in the Name: edit box and pick the Save button. Note the message in the lower-left corner of the dialog box (shown highlighted here).

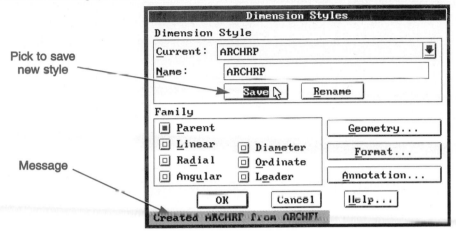

PROFESSIONAL TIP

Although AutoCAD allows a dimension style name to be up to 31 characters, care should be taken in applying long names. Dimension style names and drawing names are linked together for certain applications. The combination of characters in these linked names may not exceed 31 characters. If a drawing name has up to 8 characters, then the dimension style name should have no more than 23 characters.

The Rename button is used to rename a current dimension style. To rename a dimension style, type the style name in the Name: text box and then pick the Rename button. You cannot rename the AutoCAD STANDARD dimension style.

Using dimension style family members

Dimension style family members are very useful in AutoCAD. Just as with people, members of dimension families have different needs. This feature makes it possible to have various types of dimensions use alternate dimension variable settings. For example, in a drawing, you may want to show linear dimensions with the text placed above the dimension line, but maintain centered placement on radial dimensions. Rather than create and maintain an additional dimension style, you can specify that the Parent of this style uses DIMTAD = 1 (Text Above Dimension line), then select the Radial member of this dimension family and specify centered text placement with DIMTAD = 0. Now the DIMTAD variable is On for linear dimensions and not for radial dimensions.

A second example of dimension family use might be if you want all diameter dimensions to place text outside the feature and force a dimension line (DIMTOFL) inside, without affecting any other types of dimensions. Again, using DDIM, select the Parent of the current style and specify all settings that are used globally. Then select the Diameter members of the family and turn DIMTOFL On.

A third example of dimension family use is for center marks placed by diameter dimensions (DIMCEN = .09 or -.09) but not by radius dimensions (DIMCEN = 0). This is a common practice in mechanical drafting, especially when the radii are small. To do this, use the "Geometry" subdialog box and set the Center to None for the Parent, and then set the Center to either Mark or Line as desired for the Diameter family member.

There are many possible uses of the dimension style families. Using the dimension style families allows maximum flexibility with a minimal number of dimension styles.

NOTE   The descriptive nature of the term "family" may be used to explain the dimension style family. For example, in a family, many family members may share specific qualities or features, yet each member is unique—having certain qualities or features all their own. My son and daughter share my name (DIMSTYLE name) and some of my general tendencies and features (Parent setting), yet each of them look and act different than I do (individual family member settings).

EXERCISE 22-3

❑ Open EX22-2.
❑ Access the "Dimension Styles" dialog box.
❑ Look at the list of current dimension styles.
❑ Make the ASMEIN variable current.
❑ Note that the Parent Family member radio button is active.
❑ Use the "Dimension Styles" dialog box to change the following dimension variables to the values indicated, and pick the OK button when done. Answer Yes when AutoCAD asks if you want to Save changes to current style?:
　❑ Use the "Geometry" subdialog box:
　❑ Center = None (DIMCEN = 0)
❑ Pick the Diameter family button to make it active and then set these dimension variables:
　❑ Use the "Geometry" subdialog box:
　❑ Center = Line, Size = .125 (DIMCEN = –.125)
　❑ Use the "Format" subdialog box:
　❑ Force Line Inside (DIMTOFL = ON)
❑ The changes are for a new dimension style that is slightly different from the ASMEIN style. This may be used for drawing standards that require the centerlines to be placed with diameter dimensions, but not with radius dimensions. This also forces the dimension line inside when using the DIMDIAMETER command. Name this dimension style ASMEIN2 and save it.
❑ You should keep a manual that lists the dimension style names and their family member dimension variable settings for reference.
❑ Save as A:EX22-3.

USING EXTERNALLY REFERENCED DIMENSION STYLES

An externally referenced drawing (XREF) is one that is not added to the current drawing, but rather *referenced* to it. This is explained in detail in Chapter 26. The Dimension Styles list box may contain externally referenced styles. These referenced styles cannot be made current, changed, or renamed. You can easily identify these names, since the Xref name is given first, followed by a vertical bar, and then the dimension style name. Refer to the following example: FOUNDATIONıARCH.

If you want to use an externally referenced style, simply pick the style from the list box and then change the name and pick the Save button. Now, the new dimension style contains all the characteristics of the referenced style.

TOLERANCING

A *tolerance* is the total amount that a specific dimension is allowed to vary. It is the difference between the maximum and minimum limits. A tolerance is not given to values that are identified as reference, maximum, minimum, or stock sizes. The tolerance may be applied to the dimension, Figure 22-4, indicated by a general note, or identified in the drawing title block.

The dimension in Figure 22-4 is 2.750±.005. This is referred to as *plus/minus tolerancing*. The maximum and minimum limits of the feature are then 2.755 (2.750 +.005) and 2.745 (2.750 –.005). By subtracting the lower limit from the upper limit, you find the tolerance is .010. The *specified dimension*, 2.750, is the value that the limits are calculated from. AutoCAD refers to the specified dimension as the *primary units*.

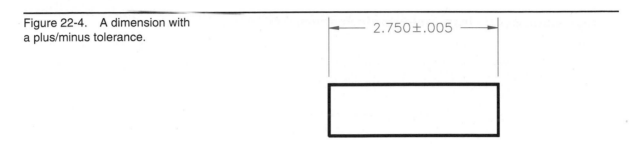

Figure 22-4. A dimension with a plus/minus tolerance.

2.750±.005

The dimension on the drawing may show only the limits, without the specified dimension, as shown in Figure 22-5. This is referred to as *limits dimensioning*. Many companies prefer limits dimensioning over plus/minus tolerancing. Since the limits are shown, calculating them is not required.

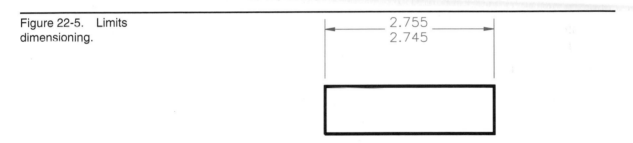

Figure 22-5. Limits dimensioning.

2.755
2.745

A *bilateral tolerance* is permitted to vary in both directions from the specified dimension. The dimension 2.750±.005 is an equal bilateral tolerance. The variation from the specified dimension, 2.750, is the same in both directions.

An unequal bilateral tolerance occurs when the variation is not equal. The dimension $2.750 \, ^{+.005}_{-.003}$ is an unequal bilateral tolerance. A *unilateral tolerance* allows the dimension to vary in only one direction. The dimensions $2.750 \, ^{+.000}_{-.005}$ and $2.750 \, ^{+.005}_{-.000}$ are unilateral tolerances.

The tolerancing for inch and metric dimensions are shown differently on a drawing. Refer to the following examples

INCH	METRIC
1.500±.005	25± 0.5
$1.500 \, ^{+.000}_{-.005}$	$25 \, ^{+ \; 0}_{- \; .5}$
$1.500 \, ^{+.005}_{-.000}$	$25 \, ^{+ \; .5}_{- \; 0}$

Notice the 0 preceding the decimal point for metric values less than one, while the 0 is not shown for inch dimensions less than one. Also, compare the difference between inch and metric unilateral tolerances in the above examples.

Drawing tolerance dimensions with AutoCAD

The DIMTOL (TOLerance) variable is used to draw dimension numerals with or without tolerances. The default value is Off. This draws dimensions without specified tolerances. Turn DIMTOL On to have tolerances drawn with the specified dimension:

Command: **DIMTOL** ↵
New value for DIMTOL ⟨Off⟩: **ON** ↵
Command:

Setting AutoCAD to draw metric or inch dimension numerals

In Chapter 20, you learned that you can control whether or not a zero is placed in front of a decimal unit less than one. When the values are in millimeters, a zero should precede a value less than one millimeter, such as 0.5mm. However, when the dimensions are in inches, a zero is not placed in front of a decimal inch less than 1, such as .5″. The DIMZIN variable controls this for the specified dimension. DIMZIN is set to the default value of 0 for metric dimensioning. This automatically enters the zero when the decimal is less than one, as in 0.8. DIMZIN is set to 4 or 7 for inch dimensioning. This automatically removes the zero when the decimal is less than one, as in .75.

The DIMTZIN (Tolerance Zero INch) variable allows you to suppress the zero for the tolerance values. The default value is 0. This places the zero in front of tolerance values. A DIMTZIN setting of 4 removes the zeros in front of any decimal tolerance numeral. If your drawing is in inches with tolerance dimensions, set DIMTZIN like this:

Command: **DIMTZIN** ↵
New value for DIMTZIN ⟨0⟩: **4** ↵
Command:

DIMENSION AND TOLERANCE DECIMAL PLACES

The ASME Y14.5M-1994 *Dimensioning and Tolerancing* standard has separate recommendations for the way the number of decimal places are displayed for inch and metric dimensions. The following are some general rules:

Inch

- A specified inch dimension is expressed to the same number of decimal places as its tolerance. Zeros are added to the right of the decimal point if needed. For example, the inch dimension .250±.005 has an additional zero added to the .25 to match the three decimal tolerance. The following two examples also have zeros added to match the tolerance: 2.000±.005 and 2.500±.005.

- Both plus and minus values of an inch tolerance have the same number of decimal places, and zeros are added to fill in where needed. For example, $^{+.005}_{-.010}$ *not* $^{+.005}_{-.01}$.

Metric

- The decimal point and zeros are omitted when the metric dimension is a whole number. For example, the metric dimension 12 has no decimal point followed by a zero. This rule is true unless tolerance values are displayed.
- When a metric dimension is greater than a whole number, the last digit to the right of the decimal point is not followed by a zero. For example, the metric dimension 12.5 has no zero to the right of the five. This rule is true unless tolerance values are displayed.
- Both plus and minus values of a metric tolerance have the same number of decimal places, and zeros are added to fill in where needed.
- Examples in ASME Y14.5M-1994 show no zeros after the specified dimension to match the tolerance. For example, 24±0.25 or 24.5±0.25 are correct. However, some companies prefer to add zeros after the specified dimension to match the tolerance, as in 24.00±0.25 or 24.50±0.25.

Examples of inch and metric decimal dimension numerals are shown in Figure 22-6.

Figure 22-6.   Examples of inch and metric decimal dimension numerals.

$$28 \qquad 24.5$$
$$0.5$$
$$24^{+0.08}_{-0.20}$$
$$24 \pm 0.1$$
$$24^{\;\;\;0}_{-0.2} \quad 24^{+0.2}_{\;\;\;0}$$
$$24.25$$
$$24.30$$
METRIC

$$2.375 \qquad .625$$
$$.750^{+.002}_{-.003}$$
$$.750 \pm .005$$
$$.625^{+.000}_{-.004}$$
$$.625^{+.004}_{-.000}$$
INCH

$$24.5° \quad 30°15'35" \quad 30° \pm 0°5'$$
ANGLE

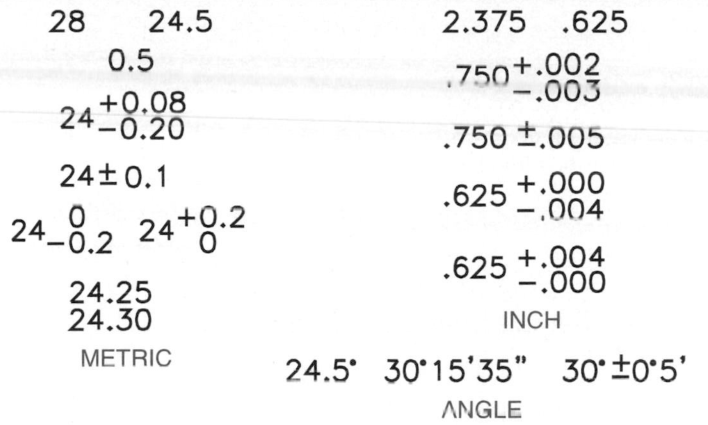

Controlling the decimal places with AutoCAD

The DIMDEC (DECimal) variable was introduced in Chapter 20. This variable is used to set the number of decimal places for the value of the primary units. The default is 4, but you can set between 0 and 8. Inch dimensions for manufacturing drawings are often set to three place decimals:

Command: **DIMDEC** ↵
New value for DIMDEC ⟨4⟩: **3** ↵
Command:

With metric dimensions, the last digit to the right of the decimal point is not followed by a zero. This is true unless the dimension needs to have places added after the decimal point to match tolerances given in a general note or in the title block.

When DIMTOL is On and dimensions are drawn with plus minus tolerances displayed, it is important to match the number of decimal places in the tolerance with the number of decimal places in the specified dimension. This is done with the DIMTDEC (Tolerance DECimal) variable. DIMTDEC also has a default of 4 and options between 0 and 8. If the specified dimension is set to three decimal places, then the tolerance decimal places should be three places:

Command: **DIMTDEC** ↵
New value for DIMTDEC ⟨4⟩: **3** ↵
Command:

DRAWING BILATERAL AND UNILATERAL TOLERANCES WITH AUTOCAD

AUG 9

Three dimension variables control how bilateral and unilateral tolerances are set up in AutoCAD. These are DIMTOL, DIMTP (Tolerance Plus), and DIMTM (Tolerance Minus). DIMTOL was introduced earlier and must be turned On before tolerance dimensions can be drawn. DIMTP sets the plus part of the tolerance, while DIMTM is used for the minus part of the tolerance.

Setting an equal bilateral tolerance

Use this procedure to set an equal bilateral tolerance of .001:

Command: **DIMTP** ↵
New value for DIMTP ⟨0.0000⟩: **.001** ↵
Command: **DIMTM** ↵
New value for DIMTM ⟨0.0000⟩: **.001** ↵
Command:

Before you set DIMTP and DIMTM, be sure that DIMZIN, DIMTZIN, DIMDEC, and DIMTDEC are in the desired settings and values. Any dimensions drawn from now on are given the plus and minus tolerance, as shown in Figure 22-7.

Figure 22-7. Once an equal bilateral tolerance of .001 is set-up, all dimensions drawn will have a tolerance that looks like this.

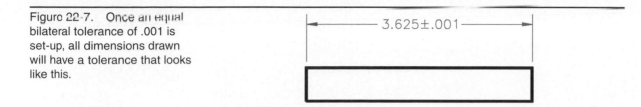

Setting an unequal bilateral tolerance

Use this procedure to set an unequal bilateral tolerance:

Command: **DIMTP** ↵
New value for DIMTP ⟨0.0000⟩: **.002** ↵
Command: **DIMTM** ↵
New value for DIMTM ⟨0.0000⟩: **.005** ↵
Command:

Now you can use a desired dimensioning command, such as DIMLIN, to draw the dimension shown in Figure 22-8.

Figure 22-8.   A dimension with an unequal bilateral tolerance.

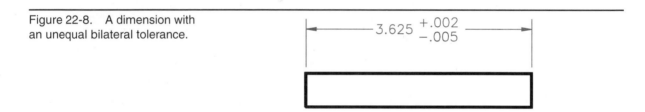

Controlling the tolerance position of a bilateral tolerance

AutoCAD provides the DIMTOLJ (TOLerance Justification) variable. This may be used to control vertical justification of the bilateral tolerance in relation to the specified dimension. Using an option other than the default may not be practical, since the default places the bilateral tolerance centered on the specified dimension. This is shown in examples throughout this chapter. If you find an application, the options are as follows:

Option	Results
0	*The specified dimension text is aligned with the lower tolerance text.*
1 (*default*)	*The specified dimension text is centered vertically between the tolerance text.*
2	*The specified dimension text is aligned with the upper tolerance text.*

Setting a unilateral tolerance

To set a unilateral tolerance, enter 0 for either the DIMTP or DIMTM variables as needed. Remember, DIMTP is tolerance plus and DIMTM is tolerance minus. Setting the following dimension variables allows you to draw the dimension shown in Figure 22-9:

Command: **DIMTP** ↵
New value for DIMTP ⟨0.0000⟩: **0** ↵
Command: **DIMTM** ↵
New value for DIMTM ⟨0.0000⟩: **.005** ↵
Command:

Figure 22-9.   Notice that AutoCAD automatically omits the plus (+) symbol in front of the zero part of a unilateral tolerance.

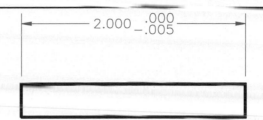

Notice in Figure 22-9 that AutoCAD automatically omits the plus (+) symbol in front of the zero part of the unilateral tolerance. The minus (–) symbol is removed if the unilateral tolerance is –.000. The plus (+) symbol is removed if the unilateral tolerance is +000. This is in violation of the ASME standard for inch dimensioning. However, it is in accordance with the ASME and ISO format for metric dimensions, where the plus and minus symbol should be removed for the zero part of the unilateral tolerance.

When DIMTZIN is 0 for metric dimensions, AutoCAD leaves the zero in front of the decimal point. This is the preferred practice. When DIMTDEC is 1, for placement of one unit past the decimal point, AutoCAD places a decimal point and a zero as shown in Figure 22-10A. This is not a preferred way to display a metric unilateral tolerance. If you set DIMTDEC to 0, then you will only be able to place a tolerance equal to or greater than 1, because the tolerance is rounded up to the nearest whole number. This makes the metric format correct, as shown in Figure 22-10B, but it may not be an acceptable tolerance. See Figure 22-6 for examples of the recommended dimension text formats.

Figure 22-10.   A–For metric tolerances, a zero should not be followed by a decimal and another zero. B–The proper way to show a metric tolerance of zero is with no decimal.

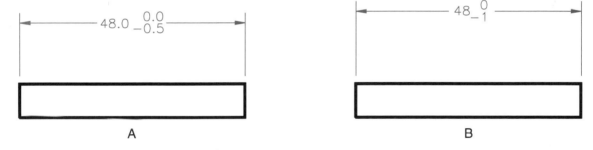

A

B

PROFESSIONAL TIP

As previously discussed, ASME Y14.5M-1994 recommends a plus and minus symbol be displayed for inch tolerances, even for a unilateral tolerance. AutoCAD does not do this automatically. There is a way to have the plus or minus symbol placed with the zero part of a unilateral tolerance, but caution should be used. If the specified dimension and the tolerance values are three place decimals, then set DIMDEC = 3 and DIMTDEC = 3. Now, turn DIMTOL On. If you want the plus tolerance to be .005, then set DIMTP to .005. If you want the minus tolerance to be .000, then set the DIMTM to .0001. Notice that this is a four place decimal. The DIMTDEC value of 3 automatically sets the tolerance value to a three place decimal, regardless of the DIMTM setting. Therefore, if you set DIMTM to .0001, the last digit (1) is automatically removed. This results in a display of –.000 for the minus tolerance. This is because AutoCAD thought that the tolerance had a value other than zero, but it was not displayed because DIMTDEC only allowed a three place decimal.

Caution should be taken when using this method if the drawing is transmitted in electronic format or is run through a translator. In this application, the four place value that you set may be transferred to the destination drawing. This may result in incorrect information. If this is the case, but you want to continue with this technique, then set the tolerance out to 8 places (.00000001). Hopefully it will be recognized as a ridiculous value and questioned, rather than simply integrated into the manufacturing plan. If you are in doubt, stick with the normal AutoCAD application.

PROFESSIONAL TIP

The dimension text often becomes very long for dimensions having a plus/minus tolerance. Horizontal dimension text will take up more space between extension lines. Vertical dimension text will require more space between dimension lines. Allow for this space during the planning and sketching process. If you make an error when dimensioning, simply try again or move the dimension text. Remember to keep dimension lines equally spaced for a uniform appearance. The DIMDLI variable controls the dimension line spacing for baseline dimensions.

DRAWING DIMENSIONS USING LIMITS TOLERANCING   AUG 9

Limits tolerances can be drawn with AutoCAD by setting one extra variable in addition to DIMTP and DIMTM. Enter the DIMLIM variable and respond with "On." This automatically turns DIMTOL Off (if it is On). Enter the DIMTP and DIMTM values, if you have not already done so. AutoCAD calculates the upper and lower limits, and places this as the dimension text. The following sequence was used before drawing the dimension shown in Figure 22-11:

```
Command: DIMLIM ↵
New value for DIMLIM 〈Off〉: ON ↵
Command: DIMTP ↵
New value for DIMTP 〈Off〉: .005 ↵
Command: DIMTM ↵
New value for DIMTM 〈Off〉: .005 ↵
Command:
```

Figure 22-11.   Limits tolerancing.

If the specified dimension in Figure 22-11 is 3.625, then AutoCAD automatically adds .005 and subtracts .005 (3.625 + .005 = 3.630 and 3.625 − .005 = 3.620)

Setting the tolerance text height

You can control the text height for tolerance dimensions when DIMTOL is On and DIMTP is different than DIMTM, or DIMLIM is on and DIMTP and DIMTM are at any setting. When these conditions occur you can alter the tolerance text height with the DIMTFAC (DIMension Tolerance scale FACtor) variable. With DIMTFAC set at the default of 1, the tolerance text height is equal to the specified dimension text height. This practice is consistent with the ASME standard. However, if you want to change the text height of the tolerance to 3/4 (.75) of the normal text height, for example, then alter the DIMTFAC variable as follows:

```
Command: DIMTFAC ↵
New value for DIMTFAC 〈1〉: .75 ↵
Command:
```

Figure 22-12 shows how changing the DIMTFAC variable affects the dimension text.

Figure 22-12. The affect of different DIMTFAC settings on plus/minus tolerances and limits tolerances.

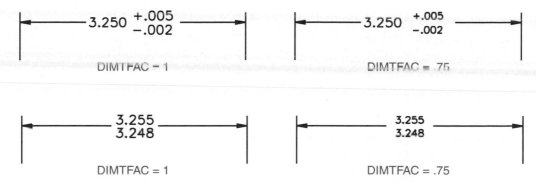

EXERCISE 22-4

❑ Open PRODR2 or begin a new drawing with your own variables.
❑ Draw object lines of the views on layer 0-7. Add dimensions to layer 3-3.
❑ Set the dimensioning variables as required to obtain the tolerances shown. Objects 1, 2, 3, and 4 are in inches. Objects 5, 6, and 7 are metric.

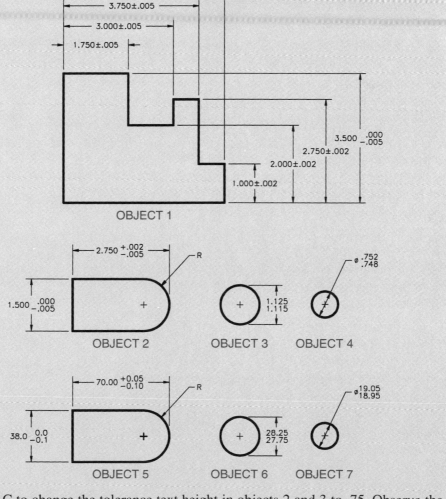

❑ Use DIMTFAC to change the tolerance text height in objects 2 and 3 to .75. Observe the difference and then change back to 1.
❑ Save the drawing as A:EX22-4.

DIMENSIONING UNITS AND DUAL DIMENSIONING

Dimensions in the ASME standard Y14.5M-1994, *Dimensioning and Tolerancing,* are given in SI (International System of Units) units. The accepted SI linear unit for engineering drawings and related documents is the millimeter. The accepted US linear unit for engineering drawings is the decimal-inch. The unit of measurement chosen should be in accordance with the policy of your company or school, or the product design. When all dimensions on a drawing are given in either millimeters or inches, place this general note on the drawing: UNLESS OTHERWISE SPECIFIED, ALL DIMENSIONS ARE IN MILLIMETERS (or INCHES).

The abbreviation "IN." follows all inch dimensions on a drawing dimensioned in millimeters. The abbreviation "mm" follows all millimeter dimensions on a drawing dimensioned in inches.

Placing a dimension suffix or prefix

AutoCAD allows you to place "IN." or "mm" after any or all dimension numerals using the DIM-POST (POST, meaning "after") variable. Common suffixes might be IN. for inch on mechanical drawings or " for inch on architectural drawings, mm for millimeters, MAX for maximum, or MIN for minimum in mechanical drafting. Architectural drafting may have suffixes such as TYP for typical or OC for on center. However, it is not likely that a specific suffix would be used on all dimensions. Use the suffix IN. like this:

> Command: **DIMPOST** ↵
> New value for DIMPOST, or . for none ⟨""⟩: **IN.** ↵
> Command:

Now, any new dimensions carry the IN. suffix. The DIMPOST default is no suffix. You can remove a suffix by typing a period (.) like this:

> Command: **DIMPOST** ↵
> New value for DIMPOST, or . for none ⟨"IN."⟩: **.** ↵
> Command:

It is not common to place a suffix after every dimension. However, you might have an inch dimension on a metric drawing. Rather than using DIMPOST, it may be easier to enter a desired suffix by using the Text option during the dimensioning process. This is done by placing the desired suffix after the closed brackets ⟨⟩. The ⟨⟩ symbol tells AutoCAD to automatically place the measured dimension text in the place of the symbol. This keeps the default text:

> Dimension line location (Text/Angle/Horizontal/Vertical/Rotated): **T** ↵
> Dimension text ⟨2.750⟩: ⟨⟩ **IN.** ↵
> Dimension line location (Text/Angle/Horizontal/Vertical/Rotated): *(pick the dimension line location)*
> Command:

You can also use the DIMPOST to place a prefix, or a prefix and a suffix, at the same time with dimension text. This is done by placing the desired prefix in front of open and closed brackets ⟨⟩. This keeps the default text as previously discussed. For example, enter the prefix SR (spherical radius) followed by ⟨⟩ if you need to dimension a group of spherical radii.

> Command: **DIMPOST** ↵
> New value for DIMPOST, or . for none ⟨""⟩: **SR⟨⟩** ↵
> Command:

You may enter a prefix and a suffix like this:

> Command: **DIMPOST** ↵
> New value for DIMPOST, or . for none ⟨""⟩: **SR⟨⟩IN.** ↵
> Command:

PROFESSIONAL TIP

Using the brackets ⟨⟩ as previously discussed to keep the default text also maintains the associative dimension. An *associative dimension* allows the dimension to automatically change as the dimension is edited. Associative dimensions are explained in detail later in this chapter. If the text is typed without using the default text ⟨⟩, then the text is not changed when the dimension is edited. This is the normal application, but there may be some specific applications when you need to type a value that is different from the default text.

PROFESSIONAL TIP

It is not a common practice to have a prefix or suffix on every dimension on the drawing. A general note usually takes care of these applications effectively. Additionally, you need to be careful when using the DIMPOST variable to set a prefix, since this prefix takes the place of any standard AutoCAD prefixes, such as the R symbol for radius and the ∅ symbol for diameter.

Dual dimensioning

Dual dimensioning means to place both inches and millimeters on each dimension. The current ASME standard ***does not*** recognize dual dimensioning. Yet, a few companies prefer to use it. One technique is to show inch dimensions followed by millimeter equivalents in brackets. This is referred to as the *bracket method*. The opposite is millimeters followed by inch equivalents in brackets. When this is done, the general note DIMENSIONS IN [ ] ARE MILLIMETERS, or DIMENSIONS IN [ ] ARE INCHES, should be placed on the drawing. Another method of dual dimensioning has inch and millimeter dimensions separated by a slash. This is referred to as the *position method*. When this is done, the general note MILLIMETER/INCH or INCH/MILLIMETER should be placed on the drawing.

Military (MIL) standards recommend the bracket method when dual dimensioning is used, or to display dual dimensioning by giving a decimal equivalent table in the upper left corner of the drawing. This table lists the inch and metric equivalent values of every dimension on the drawing. The table begins with the smallest dimension and continues to the largest. This eliminates the need for dual dimensioning at each dimension and cleans up the drawing. Examples of the bracket and position methods of dual dimensioning are shown in Figure 22-13.

Figure 22-13. Two different ways of showing dual dimensions.

1.250 [31.75]	1.250 31.75
IN [MM]	IN/MM
31.75 [1.250]	31.75 1.250
MM [IN]	MM/IN
BRACKET METHOD	POSITION METHOD

To convert inches to millimeters, use the formula: $25.4 \times INCH = MILLIMETER$. To convert millimeters to inches, use the formula: $MILLIMETER \div 25.4 = INCH$.

The same degree of accuracy is achieved by giving one less digit to the right of the decimal point for millimeter dimensions. The following are considered equivalent conversions:

INCH	MILLIMETER
.1	2.5
.01	0.3
.001	0.03
.0001	0.003

USING AUTOCAD FOR DUAL DIMENSIONING

AutoCAD refers to dual dimensions as *alternate* dimensions. The DIMALT, DIMALTF, and DIMALTD variables set a dual dimensioning system for the specified dimension. The variables are as follows:

DIMALTU = *ALTernate Units.*
DIMALTZ = *ALTernate unit Zero suppression.*
DIMALT = *ALTernate units.*
DIMALTF = *ALTernate units scale Factor.*
DIMALTD = *ALTernate units Decimal places.*

The DIMALTU variable sets the unit format for alternate unit dimensions. The options are the normal unit formats:

Options	Format
1	Scientific
2 *(default)*	Decimal
3	Engineering
4	Architectural
5	Fractional

DIMALTZ is the variable that controls alternate unit zero suppression. The options are the same as the DIMZIN variable, where the default 0 places a zero before decimals less than one for metric dimensioning. A value of 4 automatically removes the zero in front of decimals less than one. Review the DIMZIN variable in Chapter 20 for additional options and their applications.

DIMALTF allows you to set the multiplication factor. The DIMALTF default value for metric conversion is 25.4. Next, use the DIMALTD variable. This allows you to set the number of decimal places for the conversion value. If one-place millimeters are desired, set the DIMALTD value to 1. (The default is 2.) After setting the DIMALTF and DIMALTD variables, set the DIMALT variable to On. This places the millimeter dual dimensions in brackets after each dimension numeral, such as 2.500 [63.50].

The DIMAPOST variable places information after the alternate dimension. The normal dual dimension appears as 2.50 [63.5]. With DIMAPOST set as "mm," the same dimension reads 2.50 [63.5mm]. You can remove the suffix by typing "" at the New value: prompt. The general note discussed earlier is better for dual dimensioning. Do not confuse DIMAPOST with DIMPOST. DIMPOST sets up a dimension suffix for the non-dual dimensioning system.

Displaying alternate units with tolerance dimensions

When tolerance dimensions are placed on a drawing and dual dimensioning is used, the alternate units need to be applied to the specified dimension and the tolerance. AutoCAD gives you these variables to help control the alternate unit tolerance values:

DIMALTTD = *ALTernate Tolerance Decimal places.*
DIMALTTZ = *ALTernate Tolerance Zero suppression.*

The DIMALTTD variable is used to set the number of decimal places for the tolerance values of an alternate dimension. The options are integers between 0 and 8, with 2 being the default. These options are the same as any variable controlling decimal places. DIMALTTZ controls zero suppression of alternate unit tolerances. The options are the same as the DIMZIN variable.

Rounding dimensions

Dimension numerals may be rounded using the DIMRND variable. The DIMRND default value of 0 means no rounding takes place. Dimension numerals are given exactly as measured. If DIMRND is set at .5, then all numerals are rounded to the nearest .5 unit. For example, 2.875 is rounded to 3.000. Rounding is seldom needed.

EXERCISE 22-5

❏ Open PRODR2 or begin a new drawing with your own variables.
❏ Draw the object lines on layer 0-7 and place dimensions on layer 3-3.
❏ Undimensioned features may be drawn to your own specifications.
❏ Set the following dimension variables:
  ❏ DIMTXSTY = ROMANS
  ❏ DIMTXT = .125
  ❏ DIMUPT = ON
  ❏ DIMZIN = 4
  ❏ DIMCEN = .1
❏ In addition to the previous settings, use the appropriate dimension variables to draw the dimensions shown below.

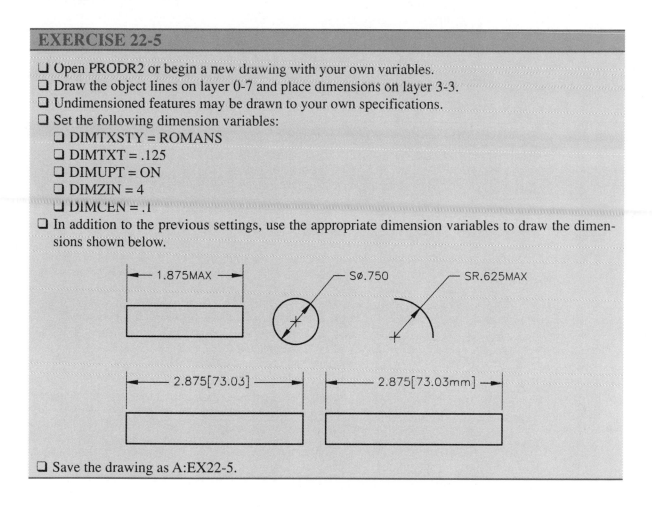

❏ Save the drawing as A:EX22-5.

USING THE DIALOG BOX TO CONTROL TOLERANCING AND DUAL DIMENSIONING

AUG 9

The "Dimension Style" dialog box is a convenient way to work with dimension variables since the selections indicate the function performed. The "Dimension Styles" dialog box was introduced in Chapter 21, but as a review, you can access this dialog box by picking DDim: from the DATA screen menu, picking Dimension Style... from the Data pull-down menu, or typing DDIM at the Command: prompt. Pick the Annotation... button, as shown in Figure 22-14, to access the "Annotation" subdialog box shown in Figure 22-15.

Figure 22-14. Pick the Annotation... button in the "Dimension Styles" dialog box to open the "Annotation" subdialog box.

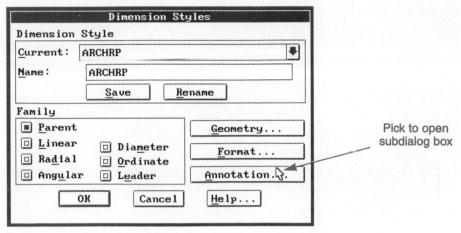

Figure 22-15. The different areas of the "Annotation" subdialog box.

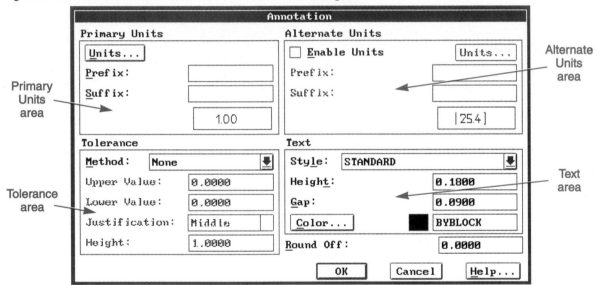

Review Chapter 21 for an overview of the "Dimension Styles" and the "Annotation" subdialog boxes. The following discussion explains the elements of the "Annotation" subdialog box that control dimension tolerance, prefix, suffix, and alternate units.

Primary Units

Pick the Units... button to access the "Primary Units" subdialog box shown in Figure 22-16. The features that control the specified dimension were explained in Chapter 21. For this discussion, look at the Tolerance portion. Adjust the DIMDEC variable by picking one of the options in the Precision: list box. Access this list box by picking the down arrow. The default is 0.0000 (four digits past the decimal place). If you want three-place tolerance units, pick 0.000, as shown in Figure 22-17.

Figure 22-16. Select the units, dimension precision, zero suppression, and tolerance precision in the "Primary Units" subdialog box. Note that the zero suppression has 0 Feet and 0 Inches checked by default.

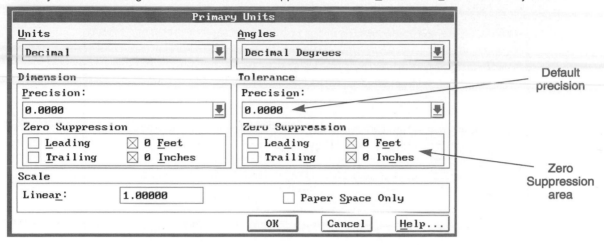

Figure 22-17. Pick the drop-down arrow next to Precision: and select a new precision. Here, a three-place precision is being selected.

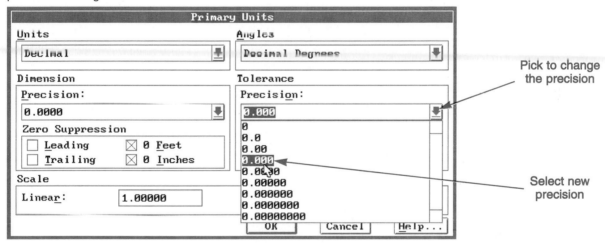

The Zero Suppression (DIMZIN) area has 0 Feet and 0 Inches suppressed by default. This is indicated by the checks in the check boxes. See Figure 22-16. The Leading and Trailing boxes are not checked by default. The Leading box remains unchecked for metric dimensioning. Pick the Leading check box if you want zeros omitted before decimal units less than one (for inch dimensioning). The Trailing check box is normally left unchecked, because Precision: sets the number of units past the decimal point, including zeros. In most cases, the number of decimal places is the same between the tolerance of a plus/minus or a limits tolerance. However, you may pick the Trailing check box if you want any zeros removed from the end of a tolerance value.

The Prefix: and Suffix: (DIMPOST) text boxes, in the "Annotation" subdialog box, are where you can type a desired prefix or suffix, or both. Figure 22-18 shows SR entered in the Prefix: box and IN. in the Suffix: box. When a suffix is used, it is added to the specified dimension and the tolerance. Keep in mind that a prefix entered here with the DIMPOST variable takes the place of a diameter or radius symbol when using the DIMDIA and DIMRAD commands. You can have AutoCAD draw special symbols by typing the text control characters in the Prefix: and Suffix: text boxes. For example, type %%C to have a diameter symbol drawn, or %%d for a degree symbol.

Look at Figure 22-18 and notice the box with 1.00 inside. This is an image box. Moving the cursor to this box and picking changes the image and also changes display in the Tolerance area of the "Annotation" subdialog box. The images change to represent the various tolerance options that are available. These are explained in the following discussion covering the Tolerance area.

Figure 22-18. In the "Annotation" subdialog box, you can enter a prefix and/or a suffix for all dimensions. Here, SR (spherical radius) is entered as a prefix and IN (inches) is entered as a suffix. The image box will change to reflect the settings you choose in this subdialog box.

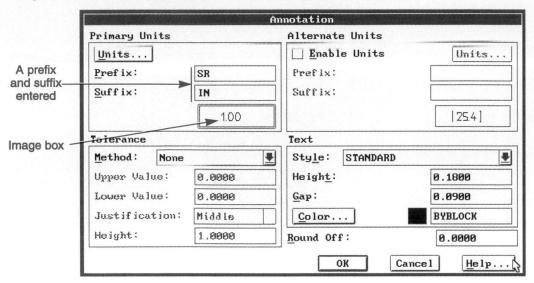

Tolerance

This is the area of the "Annotation" subdialog box where you set the dimension variables that control tolerance dimensioning for the specified dimension (primary units) and the alternate units.

The Method: list box displays the tolerance options. None is the default, which is no tolerance. Pick the down arrow to get the list of options shown in Figure 22-19. The options may be picked from the list, or accessed automatically by picking the tolerance image in the Primary Units area or in the Alternate Units area (if alternate units are enabled). Alternate units tolerance is discussed later. Keep picking the image until it cycles to the option you want, or access the desired option in the Method: list.

The Symmetrical option (DIMTOL = On and DIMLIM = Off) lets you draw equal bilateral tolerances. Picking the Symmetrical option changes the image in the primary Units area. The image is similar to what you can expect the tolerance dimension to look like, but keep in mind that it is only a representation. The image representing each of the Tolerance Method: options is shown in Figure 22-20. The Upper Value: text box is activated when you select the Symmetrical option. Type the

Figure 22-19. Pick the drop-down arrow next to Method: in the Tolerance area to select the tolerancing option that you want.

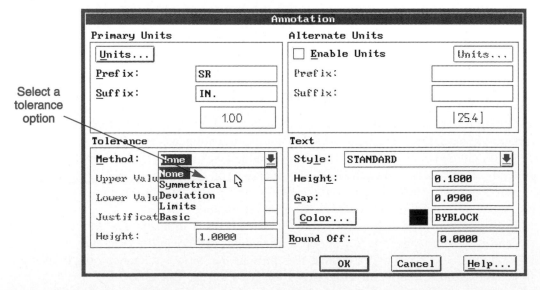

Figure 22-20. Examples of the different tolerancing options available in the Method: drop-down list of the "Annotation" subdialog box (See Figure 22-19).

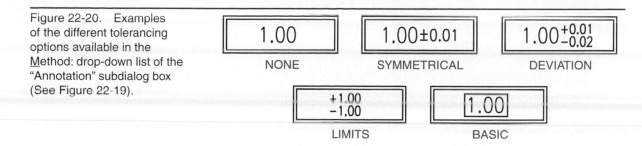

desired tolerance, such as .001 (DIMTP and DIMTM = .001). Then when you draw a dimension, such as 2.750, it reads 2.750±.001. The Lower Value: text box is deactivated because it is not needed for an equal bilateral tolerance.

The Deviation option (DIMTOL = On and DIMLIM = Off) lets you draw unequal bilateral tolerances. The representative tolerance image is shown in Figure 22-20. The Upper Value: and Lower Value: text boxes are now both active so you can enter the desired plus and minus tolerance values. If you type .001 (DIMTP = .001) in the Upper Value: box and .002 (DIMTM = .002) in the Lower Value: box, a 2.750 dimension looks like this: $2.750^{+.001}_{-.002}$. AutoCAD places a + symbol for positive values and a – symbol for negative values. The plus or minus symbol is omitted for zero tolerance values in a unilateral tolerance.

The Limits option (DIMTOL = Off and DIMLIM = On) allows you to draw limit dimensions. The tolerance image shown in Figure 22-20 is a rather strange representation of limits dimensioning. However, it does show one value above another. The image is meant to indicate that AutoCAD adds the tolerance you specify in the Upper Value: box, and subtracts the value you enter in the Lower Value: box. If you type .002 (DIMTP = .002) in the Upper Value: box and .002 (DIMTM = .002) in the Lower Value: box, a 2.750 dimension looks like this: $\frac{2.752}{2.748}$.

The Basic option allows you to draw a basic dimension. A basic dimension is one with a box drawn around it. This type of dimension is used in geometric dimensioning and tolerancing (GD&T) and is discussed in detail in Chapter 23. The representative tolerance image is shown in Figure 22-20. The Upper Value: and Lower Value: text boxes are both inactive, because a basic dimension has no tolerance values displayed with it.

The Justification: (DIMTOLJ) list box contains the tolerance justification options in name form. These may be used to control vertical justification of the bilateral tolerance in relation to the specified dimension. Using an option other than the Middle default may not be practical. The options provide the following results:

Option	Results
Top	*The specified dimension text is aligned with the upper tolerance text.*
Middle	*The specified dimension text is centered vertically between the tolerance text. This is the default and is the common practice.*
Bottom	*The specified dimension text is aligned with the lower tolerance text.*

The Height: (DIMTFAC) text box allows you to change the tolerance text height relative to the specified dimension text height. The default is 1.0. This draws the tolerances text equal to the specified dimension text height. The default setting is the preferred practice. Examples of different DIMTFAC settings are shown in Figure 22-12.

Alternate Units

This is the area of the "Annotation" subdialog box where you set dual dimensioning with inches followed by millimeters in brackets, or millimeters followed by inches in brackets. Look at the Alternate Units part of Figure 22-15. While this practice is not recommended by ASME, it is recognized by the MIL standard. Other applications displaying equivalents in brackets might be used for specific purposes.

The <u>E</u>nable Units (DIMALT) check box is used to activate the dual dimensioning feature. DIMALT is On when this box is checked.

- **U<u>n</u>its... button.** The U<u>n</u>its... button is used to access the "Alternate Units" subdialog box shown in Figure 22-21. The features found in this subdialog box work just like those found in the "Primary Units" subdialog box, except that the controls are for alternate units. The following provides a brief overview of the items found in this subdialog box:

Figure 22-21.   Select the various options you need in the "Alternate Units" subdialog box. This subdialog box functions like the "Primary Units" subdialog box. Note that the <u>A</u>ngles option in not available.

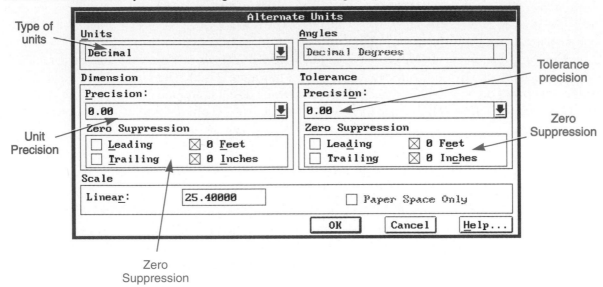

- **U<u>n</u>its–(DIMALTU)** Pick the down arrow to access the units options that include Scientific, Decimal (default), Engineering, Architectural, and Fractional. The selection you make establishes the units for the alternate dimension numerals.
- **Dimension–**The <u>P</u>recision: (DIMALTD) lists allows you to select the number of digits past the decimal point for the alternate units associated with the primary dimension. Zero Suppression (DIMALTZ) provides check boxes for you to control the display of zeros before and after the alternate primary units decimal point.
- **Scale–(DIMALTF)** The Li<u>n</u>ear: text box allows you to set the multiplication factor for the conversion units. The default factor for inch to metric conversion is 25.4. Pick the Paper Space Only check box to apply the scale factor to dimensions created in paper space.
- **<u>A</u>ngles–**You cannot access the Angles options for alternate units applications.
- **Tolerance–**The Precisi<u>o</u>n: (DIMALTTD) list allows you to select the number of digits past the decimal point for the alternate units associated with the tolerance dimension. Zero Suppression (DIMALTTZ) provides check boxes for you to control the display of zeros before and after the tolerance alternate units decimal point.

The Prefix: and Suffix: (DIMAPOST) text boxes allow you to enter a desired prefix or suffix to go along with the alternate units.

The features found in the Tolerance area of the "Annotation" subdialog box were discussed earlier. Any changes made to the tolerance options for primary units also affect the alternate units, if alternate units are enabled. As a review, the <u>M</u>ethod: list box displays the options None, Symmetrical, Deviation, Limits, and Basic. These options mean the same thing to alternate units as they do to primary units. You may change the tolerance method for primary and alternate units by picking one of the options from the <u>M</u>ethod: list, or by picking the image box in the Alternate Units area if alternate units are enabled. Every time you pick the image box, a different tolerance method option is displayed and the items in the Tolerance area automatically change to match. The image representing each of the alternate tolerance <u>M</u>ethod: options is shown in Figure 22-22.

Figure 22-22. Examples of the tolerancing options available in the "Alternate Units" subdialog box.

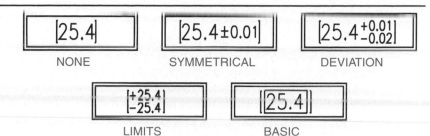

[25.4]	[25.4±0.01]	[25.4$^{+0.01}_{-0.02}$]
NONE	SYMMETRICAL	DEVIATION

[+25.4] [−25.4]	[25.4]
LIMITS	BASIC

EXERCISE 22-6

❑ Open PRODR2 or begin a new drawing with your own variables.
❑ Draw the object lines on layer 0-7 and place dimensions on layer 3-3.
❑ Undimensioned features may be drawn to your own specifications.
❑ Set these dimension variables:
  ❑ DIMTXSTY = ROMANS
  ❑ DIMTXT = .125
  ❑ DIMUPT = ON
  ❑ DIMZIN = 4
  ❑ DIMCEN = .1
❑ In addition to the previous settings, use the appropriate dimension variables by using the DDIM command to draw the dimensions shown below:

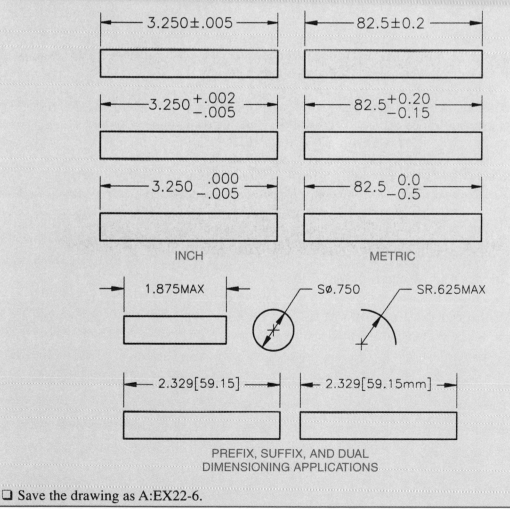

❑ Save the drawing as A:EX22-6.

PROFESSIONAL TIP

Note that the techniques used by AutoCAD to handle tolerance numerals is not exactly as preferred in the ASME standard. For example, AutoCAD omits the + (or –) in the unilateral tolerance. This is fine for metric dimensions, but it is recommended that the + (or –) be displayed for an inch tolerance. In addition, only one zero is recommended for a metric unilateral tolerance, while AutoCAD places a number of zeros after the decimal place (equal to the number specified in the DIMDEC and DIMTDEC variables). The following illustration shows the preferred method.

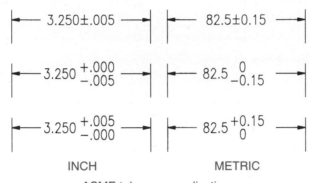

INCH   METRIC

ASME tolerance applications

USING AUTOCAD'S ASSOCIATIVE DIMENSIONING   AUG 9

Associative dimensioning permits dimensions to change as an object is edited. With the DIMASO (ASsOciative) variable turned On, stretching, trimming, or extending an object also changes the dimensions associated with that object. DIMASO is On by default. With the DIMASO variable turned Off, elements of the dimension are considered separate. Thus, you could edit the dimension line, arrowheads, extension lines, and dimension numerals as individual items. With DIMASO turned On, these items act together as one entity. You could then erase the entire dimension by picking any part of the dimension. The DIMLINEAR, DIMALIGNED, DIMANGULAR, DIMDIAMETER, DIMRADIUS, and DIMORDINATE commands are influenced by associative dimensioning. The DIMCENTER and DIMLEADER commands remain as unique items and are not affected.

Another variable that works with associative dimensioning is DIMSHO (SHOw dragged dimensions). If DIMASO and DIMSHO are both on, the dimension for an object being stretched (for example) is visually recalculated as the object is dragged into position. The DIMSHO default is Off since this function slows down the computer on complex drawings.

Revising drawings and associated dimensions

When a drawing is changed using the GRIPS, MIRROR, ROTATE, or SCALE commands, the dimensions are also changed when DIMASO is On. Linear and Angular dimensioning options are altered by the STRETCH command. Only linear dimensions are affected by the EXTEND and TRIM commands.

Stretching an object and its dimensions

When stretching an object, select the object and dimension using the Crossing or polygon option. The command sequence, illustrated in Figure 22-23, is as follows:

Command: **STRETCH** ↵
Select objects to be stretched by crossing-window or polygon...
Select objects: **C** ↵
First corner: *(pick the first corner of the crossing box)*
Other corner: *(pick the second crossing box corner)*
Select objects: ↵
Base point or displacement: *(pick the base point on the object to be stretched)*
Second point of displacement: *(pick the new point where the object is to be stretched to, and observe the object being dragged into position)*
Command:

Figure 22-23.   When you stretch an object and dimension when the dimension is associative, the dimension text is automatically changed to reflect the new values.

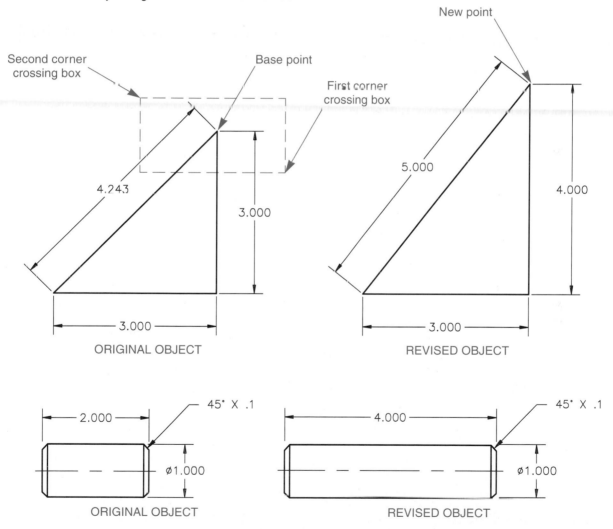

PROFESSIONAL TIP

The examples of editing associative dimensions that are discussed throughout this section demonstrate the power and efficiency that may be achieved when the DIMASO variable is On. When the two objects in Figure 22-23 were stretched, the dimensions automatically assumed the actual size of the object after the editing process was complete. You may not fully understand the power of this feature until you try to edit an object without associative dimensions. For example, if the original objects in Figure 22-23 had been drawn with DIMASO turned Off, then the dimension values remain the same even when the objects are stretched, as shown below. If you compare this example with Figure 22-23, you quickly see the advantage of associative dimensions. In order to make the dimensions in the example below read to the correct size of the objects, you would first need to calculate the correct values followed by using the DIMEDIT command to change the dimension text.

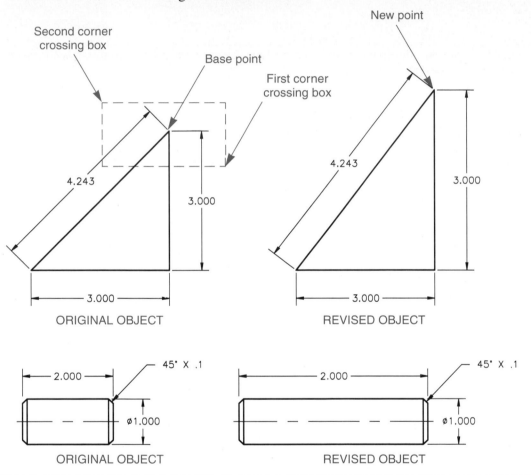

Moving a dimension numeral

The ASME standards advise that adjacent dimensions be staggered. However, AutoCAD centers all dimension text, unless the DIMUPT variable is On. The STRETCH command moves dimension text within the dimension line, Figure 22-24, as follows:

Command: **STRETCH** ↵
Select objects to be stretched by crossing-window or polygon...
Select objects: **C** ↵
First corner: Other corner: *(place the crossing box around the text to be moved)*
Select objects: ↵
Base point or displacement: *(pick the base point at the center of the existing text)*
Second point of displacement: *(pick the new point at the desired text location)*
Command:

Figure 22-24. You can stretch text to a different location when needed.

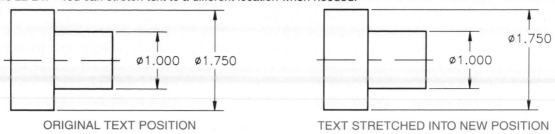

ORIGINAL TEXT POSITION   TEXT STRETCHED INTO NEW POSITION

The TEDIT command also works well for this application. Try this:

Command: **DIM** ↵
Dim: **TEDIT** ↵
Select dimension: (pick the dimension numeral to be moved)
Enter text location (Left/Right/Home/Angle): *(move the text to a new location and pick, or
    use one of the available options)*
Dim:

Refer to Chapter 21, Figure 21-21 for a detailed discussion of all TEDIT options.

You can also add or subtract size from an object to be stretched using relative coordinates. For example, at the Second point of displacement: prompt, typing @2,0 adds 2 units horizontally. Typing @–1.25,0 deletes 1.25 units horizontally. Typing @0,–.5 deletes .5 units vertically.

PROFESSIONAL TIP

The DIMUPT variable allows you to position the text as desired during the dimensioning process. The default for this variable is Off, but you can turn it on if you want this flexibility. DIMUPT was explained in Chapter 20 as related to Figure 20-52 and reviewed again in Chapter 21 with Figure 21-15.

Trimming and extending

It is possible to extend or trim an object and related dimensions to meet another object. The TRIM and EXTEND commands were introduced in Chapter 13 to trim or extend lines of an object. The EXTEND command format is as follows:

Command: **EXTEND** ↵
Select boundary edges: (Projmode = UCS, Edgemode = No extend)
Select objects: *(pick the boundary edge)*
Select objects: ↵

The boundary edge is the line that the desired object will extend to, Figure 22-25. Then pick the dimension and lines to extend.

⟨Select object to extend⟩/Project/Edge/Undo: *(pick the dimension to be extended)*
⟨Select object to extend⟩/Project/Edge/Undo /Undo: *(pick a line to extend)*
⟨Select object to extend⟩/Project/Edge/Undo /Undo: *(pick a line to extend)*
⟨Select object to extend⟩/Project/Edge/Undo /Undo: ↵
Command:

Notice in Figure 22-25 that one line of the original object remains. This line may be removed using the ERASE command.

Figure 22-25. When you extend an associative dimension, the dimension text is automatically updated to reflect the new value.

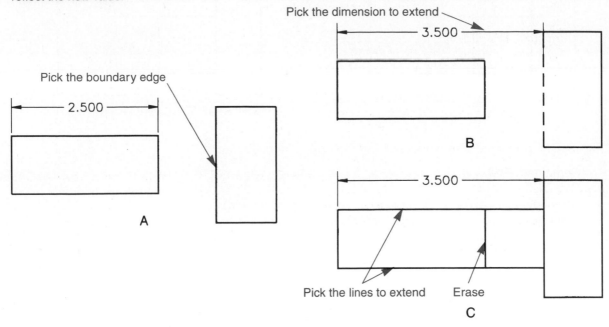

The TRIM command is the opposite of the EXTEND command. Look at Figure 22-26. First, draw a line on the Original Object to trim to. Then, follow this TRIM command sequence:

Command: **TRIM** ⏎
Select cutting edges: (Projmode = UCS, Edgemode = NO extend)
Select objects: *(pick cutting edges that lines and dimensions will be shortened to)*
Select objects: ⏎

Figure 22-26. When you trim an associative dimension, the dimension text is automatically updated to reflect the new value.

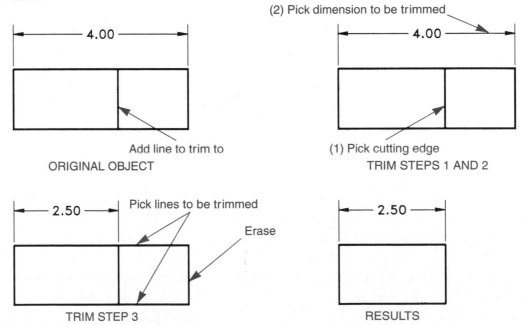

The location where you pick the dimension establishes the trim position the dimension takes. Pick as shown in Figure 22-26 for the results shown.

⟨Select object to trim⟩/Project/Edge/Undo: *(pick the dimension to be trimmed)*
⟨Select object to trim⟩/Project/Edge/Undo: *(pick the line to be trimmed)*
⟨Select object to trim⟩/Project/Edge/Undo: *(pick the line to be trimmed)*
⟨Select object to trim⟩/Undo: ↵
Command : **ERASE** ↵
Select objects: *(select the line on the right)*
Select objects: ↵
Command:

MAKING CHANGES TO DIMENSIONS

AUG 9

The component parts of a dimension may be edited after using the EXPLODE command. Dimensions also may be changed individually or in groups using the UPDATE, HOMETEXT, or NEWTEXT commands.

Exploding an associative dimension

An associative dimension is treated as one entity even though it consists of extension lines, a dimension line, arrowheads, and numerals. At times it is necessary to work with the individual parts. You can then select objects to edit. For example, you can erase the text without erasing the dimension line, arrowheads, or extension lines. To do this, you must break the dimension into its individual parts with the EXPLODE command as follows:

Command: **EXPLODE** ↵
Select objects: *(pick the dimension to be exploded)*
Select objects: ↵
Command:

PROFESSIONAL TIP

Caution should be exercised when using the EXPLODE command on dimensions, because the dimension loses its layer and color definition. Once exploded, the dimension is placed on layer 0. This is not normally acceptable. You may want to use the CHPROP command to set the exploded dimension elements back to the dimensioning layer and color and set them to BYLAYER. An easier way to remove the associative dimension feature from a dimension is to use the DIMOVERRIDE command or the UPDATE option, which is discussed next. If you know in advance that you need to work with the individual elements of the dimensions, then turn the DIMASO variable Off before starting the drawing.

Changing variables or text of existing dimensions

You can change the text or variables of individual dimensions or all dimensions on the drawing. The UPDATE, HOMETEXT, and NEWTEXT subcommands may be used to perform these tasks when you are inside the DIM command. The HOMETEXT and NEWTEXT subcommands work just like the DIMEDIT command that was discussed in Chapter 21 and shown in Figure 21-22.

The UPDATE subcommand updates existing dimensions with the current dimensioning variables, units, or text style. For example, the DIMASZ (arrowhead size) default value is .18. Suppose that after completing a drawing you learn the company standard requires .25 arrowheads. This is easy to fix. Select DIMASZ and enter the new value as .25. At the Dim: prompt, type UPDATE and press ENTER. Then select the items to be changed by picking them individually or windowing. It is common to change the entire drawing using the window selection process. The steps are as follows:

Command: **DIM** ↵
Dim: *(type* **UPDATE** *or* **UPD** *and press* ENTER*)*
Select objects: *(pick individual dimensions, a group of dimensions, or window the entire drawing for change)*

The entire drawing is now automatically updated with the new current variables, Figure 22-27.

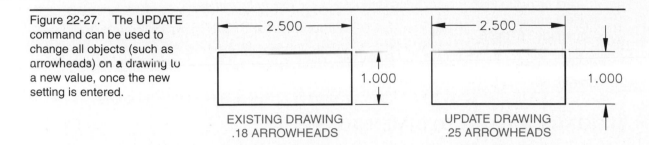

Figure 22-27.   The UPDATE command can be used to change all objects (such as arrowheads) on a drawing to a new value, once the new setting is entered.

The HOMETEXT subcommand changes the position of dimension text to its original location. For example, suppose the STRETCH or TEDIT command was used to move a dimension numeral to a new location. The HOMETEXT command moves the numeral back to the center, Figure 22-28.

Command: **DIM** ↵
Dim: *(type* **HOMETEXT** *or* **HOM** *and press* ENTER*)*
Select objects: *(pick the dimension(s) to be changed)*
Select objects:
Dim:

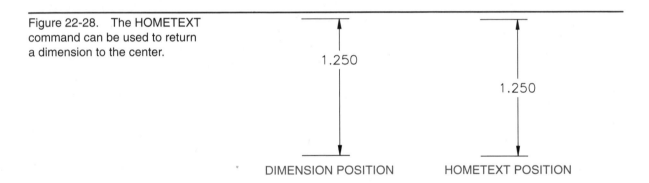

Figure 22-28.   The HOMETEXT command can be used to return a dimension to the center.

The NEWTEXT subcommand is used to edit dimension text. Suppose you find that a diameter symbol was left off of a dimension. Enter the NEWTEXT command, Figure 22-29, to select and change the numeral as follows:

Command: **DIM** ↵
Dim: *(type* **NEWTEXT** *or* **NEW** *and press* ENTER*)*
Enter new dimension text: **%%C2.500** ↵
Select objects: *(pick the dimension to be changed)*
Select objects:
Dim:

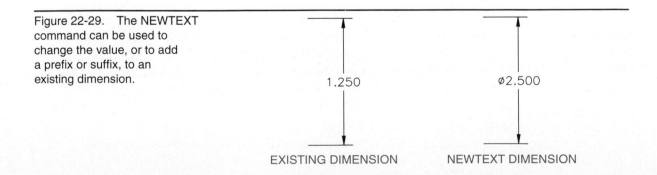

Figure 22-29.   The NEWTEXT command can be used to change the value, or to add a prefix or suffix, to an existing dimension.

DIMENSION DEFINITION POINTS

AUG 9

When you draw an associative dimension, the points used to specify the dimension and the middle point of the dimension text are called *definition points*, or DEFPOINTS. When a dimension is redefined, the revised position is based on the definition points. The definition points are located on the DEFPOINTS layer. This layer is automatically created by AutoCAD. The definition points are displayed with the dimension. The DEFPOINTS layer will not plot. The definition points are plotted only if the DEFPOINTS layer is renamed. The definition points are displayed when the dimensioning layer is on, even if the DEFPOINTS layer is off.

If you select an object for editing and wish to include the dimensions in the edit, then you must include the definition points of the dimension in the selection set. If you need to snap to a definition point only, use the Node object snap.

PAPER SPACE DIMENSIONING

Be cautious when placing associative dimensions on a drawing created in model space when you are currently in the paper space mode. These dimensions remain unchanged when you use editing commands like STRETCH, TRIM, or EXTEND, or display commands such as ZOOM or PAN in a model space viewport. To ensure that AutoCAD calculates a scale factor that is compatible between model and paper space, check the Paper Space Only check box in any of the subdialog boxes accessed through the "Dimension Styles" dialog box.

When you draw dimensions in paper space that describe something from your model space drawing, first set the Viewport option in the DIMLFAC variable while in paper space like this:

Command: **DIMLFAC** ↵
New value for DIMLFAC ⟨1.000⟩: **V** ↵
Select viewport to set scale: *(pick the desired viewport)*

AutoCAD automatically makes the DIMLFAC variable adjust to the zoom scale factor of the model space viewport. This does not work when dimensioning with the ORDINATE command.

PROFESSIONAL TIP

Dimensions should normally be created in model space. Use caution when dimensioning in paper space, because linear dimensions of model space objects can be created in paper space, but radius and diameter dimensions of model space objects cannot be created in paper space. This means that some of your dimensions are in model space and others in paper space. This situation would require a lot of dimension variable juggling and space swapping. However, there are valid reasons to place notes in paper space when they are part of the drawing format.

EXERCISE 22-7

❑ Open EX22-6.
❑ Select the following dimensioning variable values:
   ❑ DIMEXE = 125
   ❑ DIMEXO − .08
   ❑ DIMCEN = −.25
   ❑ DIMASZ = .25
   ❑ DIMDLI = .75
   ❑ DIMTXT = .125
❑ Use the STRETCH or TEDIT command to stagger the last vertical dimension.
❑ For object 2, use the STRETCH command to make it .25 in. longer and .5 in. higher.
❑ Enter the UPDATE command to change the entire drawing to the current variables.
❑ Use the HOMETEXT command to move the staggered vertical dimension in object 1 back to its original position.
❑ Use the NEWTEXT command to remove the plus/minus tolerances from the horizontal dimensions on object 1.
❑ Save the drawing as A:EX22-7.

CHAPTER TEST

Write your answers in the spaces provided.

1. The _____ command and the _____ option save dimensioning variable settings to a dimension style and make the new dimension style current.

2. The _____ command and the _____ option let you change dimensioning variable settings by reading new settings from an existing dimension style.

3. Give the command and responses needed to list all of the available dimension styles through the DIMSTYLE command:

   Command:_____

     dimension style: ASME

   Dimension Style Edit (Save/Restore/STatus/Variable/Apply/?)⟨Restore⟩: _____

   Dimension style(s) to list ⟨*⟩: _____

4. Give the command and responses used to have AutoCAD display the difference between an existing MIL dimension style and the current dimension style:

   Command:_____

     dimension style: ASME _____

   Dimension Style Edit (Save/Restore/STatus/Variable/Apply/?)⟨Restore⟩: _____

   Dimension style(s) to list ⟨*⟩: _____

5. Give the command and responses used to override the DIMEXO variable on an existing dimension from the existing setting of .06 to 0, without changing the current dimension style:

Command:_____

Dimension variable to override (or clear to remove overrides):_____

Current value (.062): New value:_____

Dimension variable to override:_____

Select objects:_____

Select objects:_____

Command:_____

6. Give the command and entries required to create all dimensions with a tolerance of ±.005:

Command:_____

New value for 〈〉 〈Off〉: _____

Command:_____

New value for 〈〉 〈0.000〉: _____

Command:_____

New value for 〈〉 〈0.000〉: _____

Command:_____

7. Give the command and entries needed to create all dimensions as limits tolerancing of ±.002:

Command:_____

New value for 〈〉 〈Off〉: _____

Command:_____

New value for 〈〉 〈0.0000〉: _____

Command:_____

New value for 〈〉 〈0.0000〉: _____

Command:_____

8. Define "tolerance."_____

_____

9. Give an example of a bilateral tolerance._____

10. Give an example of a unilateral tolerance._____

11. What are the limits of the dimension 1.875±.002? _____

12. Give the general note that would accompany a drawing dimensioned in millimeters. _____

_____

_____

13. Give the general note used when millimeter dimensions are provided in brackets next to inch dimensions._____

14. Name the dialog box that allows you to work with dimension styles._____

_____

15. Identify at least two ways to access the dialog box discussed in question number 14.

_____

_____

16. How do you save a new dimension style using the dialog box that was accessed in question number 15? _____

_____

17. Describe the procedure to use if you want dimensions displayed with plus/minus equal bilateral tolerances of ±.002 using the dialog box. _____

_____

_____

_____

18. Describe the procedure to use if you want dimensions displayed with limits dimensioning ±.005 from the specified dimension using the dialog box. _____

_____

_____

_____

19. Define "definition points." _____

_____

20. What is the importance of selecting definition points when editing an object that includes dimensions in the edit? _____

_____

_____

21. Name the object snap mode used to snap to a definition point. _____

22-35. Identify the dimensioning variable associated with each of the definitions.

22. The dimension variable used when in paper space to make the dimension scale factor adjust to the zoom scale factor of the model space viewport. _____

23. Identifies the current dimension style. _____

24. Used to change the text height for tolerance dimensions without affecting the primary dimension text height. _____

25. When on, it shows a dimension numeral with tolerance. _____

26. Controls plus part of tolerance. _____

27. Controls minus part of tolerance. _____

28. When on, automatically calculates and displays tolerance limits. _____

29. Allows you to place a specified suffix after dimension numerals. _____

30. Automatically places millimeter dual dimensions in brackets. _____

31. Allows you to set a multiplication factor for alternate units. _____

32. Sets the number of decimal places for alternate units. _____

33. Used to turn on or off associative dimensioning. _____

34. Allows dimensions to be shown as they are edited. _____

35. Allows dimension numerals to be rounded as specified. _____

36-40. Name the commands that do the following.

36. Moves dimension text within a dimension line. _____

37. Breaks an existing associative dimension into its individual parts. _____

38. Changes existing dimensions to take on current dimensioning variable values. _____

39. Changes the position of dimension text to its original location. _____

40. Used to edit existing dimension text. _____

41. When would it be better to create a new dimension style rather than using the DIMOVERRIDE command? _____

_____

_____

_____

42. Define dimension "style family" and "dimension style family members." _____

_____

_____

_____

_____

_____

43. Give a practical example of how dimension style family members might have different settings for a useful application in AutoCAD. _____

_____

_____

_____

44. Give the following dimension variable settings needed before you can draw an equal bilateral tolerance of .750±.001 in inches:

DIMDEC _____

DIMTDEC _____

DIMZIN _____

DIMTZIN _____

DIMTOL _____

DIMTP _____

DIMTM _____

45. Give the following dimension variable settings if you plan to draw this limits dimension: 2.752 / 2.748

DIMLIM _____

DIMTP _____

DIMTM _____

46. What is the purpose of typing 〈〉IN. at the Dimension text prompt as follows:

Dimension text 〈2.750〉: 〈〉IN. _____

_____

_____

_____

DRAWING PROBLEMS

Set limits, units, dimensioning variables, and other parameters as needed. Follow these guidelines.

    A. Draw the needed multiviews to exact size. Problems presented in 3-D require that you select the proper multiviews.

    B. Use grids, object snap options, and the OSNAP command to your best advantage.

    C. Apply dimensions accurately using ASME standards. Dimensions are in inches unless otherwise specified.

    D. Set dimensioning variables to suit the drawing.

    E. Use the LAYER command to set separate layers for views and dimensions.

    F. Draw object lines using .032″ wide polylines, or use the LINE command and plot with a wide pen.

    G. Place general notes 1/2≈ from lower-left corner:

        3. UNLESS OTHERWISE SPECIFIED, ALL DIMENSIONS ARE IN MILLIMETERS (or INCHES as applicable).

        2. REMOVE ALL BURRS AND SHARP EDGES.

        1. INTERPRET PER ASME Y14.5M-1994.

        NOTES:

    H. Create dimension styles with family members that suit the specific needs of each drawing. For example, save dimension styles for metric, inch, or architectural drawings as appropriate.

    J. Save the drawings to floppy disk as P22-(problem number).

P22-1

1.

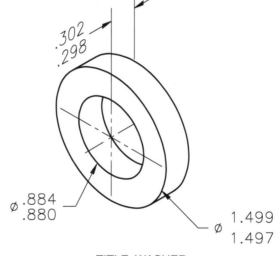

.302
.298

⌀ .884
.880

⌀ 1.499
1.497

TITLE: WASHER
MATERIAL: SAE 1020

P22-2

2.

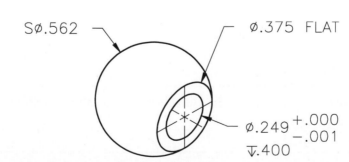

S⌀.562

⌀.375 FLAT

⌀.249 +.000 −.001

∇.400

TITLE: HANDLE

3.

P22-3

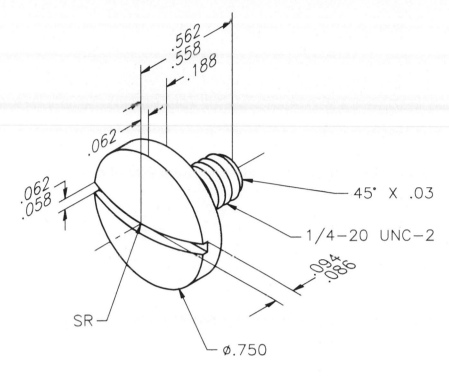

.562
.558
.188
.062
.062
.058
45° X .03
1/4−20 UNC−2
.094
.086
SR
ø.750

TITLE: SCREW
MATERIAL: SAE 4320

4.

P22-4

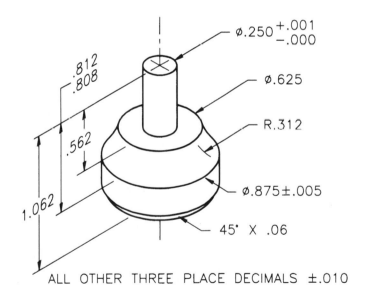

ø.250 $^{+.001}_{-.000}$
.812
.808
ø.625
.562
R.312
1.062
ø.875±.005
45° X .06

ALL OTHER THREE PLACE DECIMALS ±.010

TITLE: PIN
MATERIAL: MILD STEEL

5.

P22-5

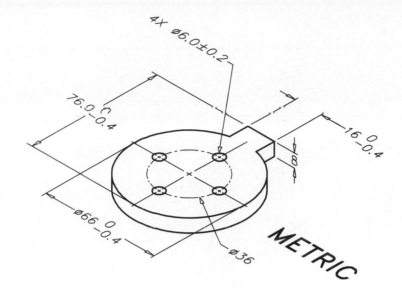

TITLE: SPACER
MATERIAL: COLD ROLLED STEEL

6.

P22-6

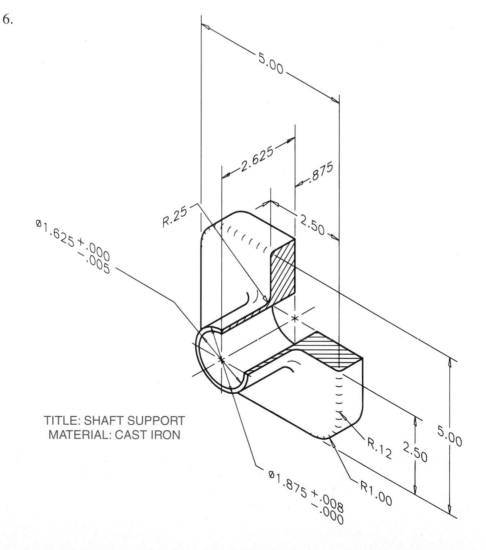

TITLE: SHAFT SUPPORT
MATERIAL: CAST IRON

P22-7

1.

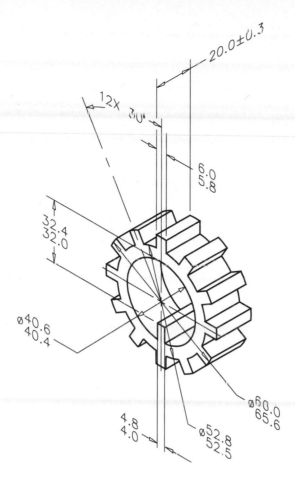

TITLE: SPLINE
MATERIAL: BRONZE

P22-8

8.

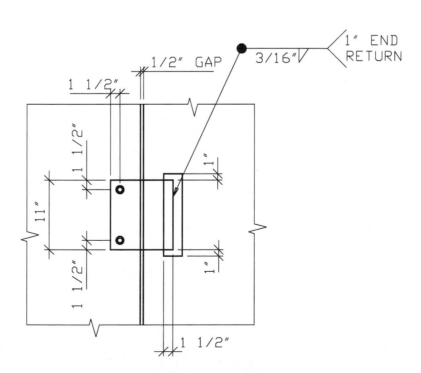

TITLE: COLUMN BASE

9.

P22-9

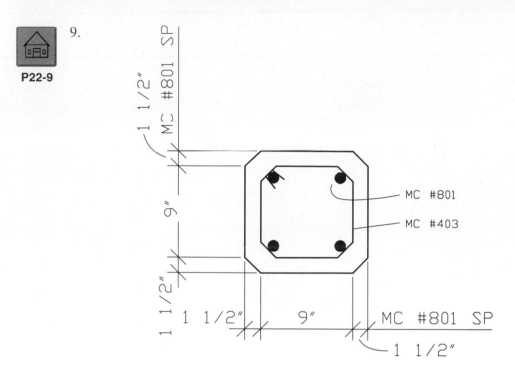

TITLE: COLUMN REINFORCING

10. Complete the partial floor plan by adding the needed dimensions.

P22-10

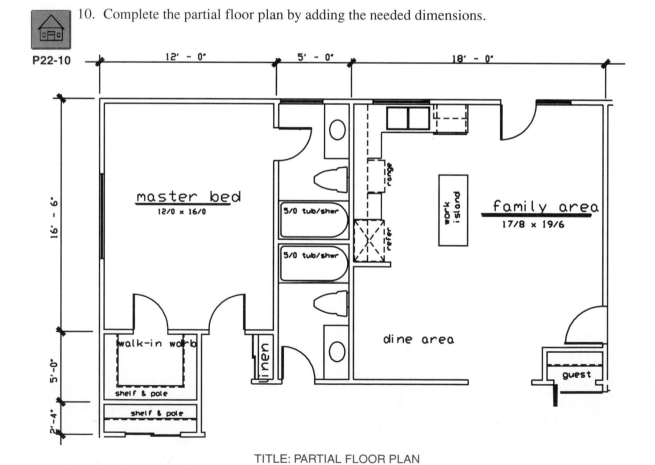

TITLE: PARTIAL FLOOR PLAN

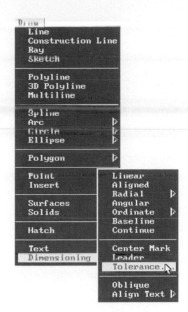

Chapter 23

Geometric Dimensioning and Tolerancing

Learning objectives:

After completing this chapter, you will be able to:

○ Identify geometric tolerancing symbols.
○ Use the TOLERANCE and LEADER commands.
○ Draw feature control frames.
○ Edit feature control frames.
○ Place basic dimensions on a drawing.
○ Draw datum feature symbols.
○ Identify how to draw projected tolerance zone symbols.

This chapter is an introduction to geometric dimensioning and tolerancing (GD&T) as adopted by the American National Standards Institute (ANSI) and published by the American Society of Mechanical Engineers (ASME) for engineering and related document practices. The standard is titled ASME Y14.5M-1994 *Dimensioning and Tolerancing*. *Geometric tolerancing* is a general term that refers to tolerances used to control form, profile, orientation, runout, and location of features on an object. The drafting applications identified in this chapter use the AutoCAD geometric tolerancing capabilities and additional recommendations to comply with the ASME Y14.5M-1994 standard. This chapter is only an introduction to geometric dimensioning and tolerancing (GD&T). For complete coverage of GD&T refer to *Geometric Dimensioning and Tolerancing* published by The Goodheart-Willcox Company, Inc. Before beginning this chapter, it is also recommended that you have a solid understanding of dimensioning and tolerancing standards and AutoCAD applications, which is covered in Chapters 20 through 22 of this text.

The discussion in this chapter divides the dimensioning and geometric tolerancing symbols into the following five basic types:

1. Dimensioning symbols.
2. Geometric characteristic symbols.
3. Material condition symbols.
4. Feature control frame.
5. Datum feature and datum target symbols.

When you draw GD&T symbols, it is recommended that you use a dimensioning layer so the symbols and text may be printed or plotted as thin lines that are the same thickness as extension and dimension lines (.01 inch or .3 mm). The suggested text font is ROMANS. These practices correspond with ASME Y14.2M-1992 *Line Conventions and Lettering*.

DIMENSIONING SYMBOLS

Symbols represent specific information that would otherwise be difficult and time consuming to duplicate in note form. Symbols must be clearly drawn to the required size and shape so they communicate the desired information uniformly. Symbols are recommended by ASME Y14.5M because symbols are an international language and are read the same way in any country. It is important in an international economy to have effective communication on engineering drawings. Symbols make this communication process uniform. ASME Y14.5M also states that the adoption of dimensioning symbols does not prevent the use of equivalent terms or abbreviations in situations where symbols are considered inappropriate.

Symbols aid in clarity, ease of drawing presentation, and save time. Creating and using AutoCAD symbols is covered later in this chapter and in Chapter 25 of this text. Figure 23-1 shows recommended dimensioning symbols.

Figure 23-1.   Dimensioning symbols recommended by ASME Y14.5M-1994.

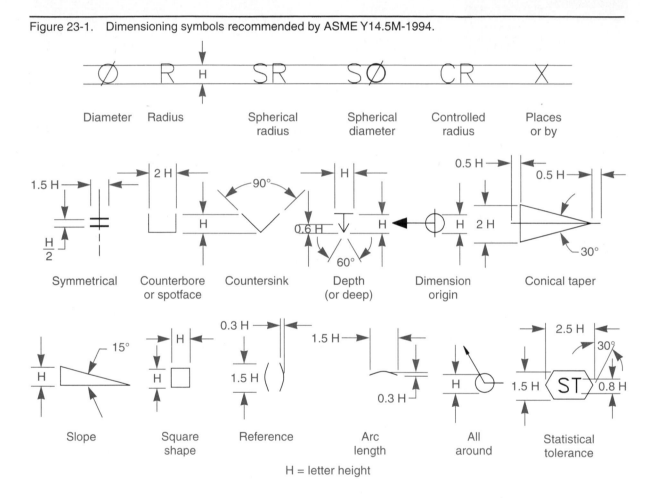

GEOMETRIC CHARACTERISTIC SYMBOLS

Symbols used in geometric dimensioning and tolerancing to provide specific controls related to the form of an object, the orientation of features, the outlines of features, the relationship of features to an axis, or the location of features are known as geometric characteristic symbols. *Geometric characteristic symbols* are separated into five types: form, profile, orientation, location, and runout, as shown in Figure 23-2.

The symbols in Figure 23-2 are drawn to the actual size and shape recommended by ASME Y14.5M based on .125 in. (3 mm) high lettering.

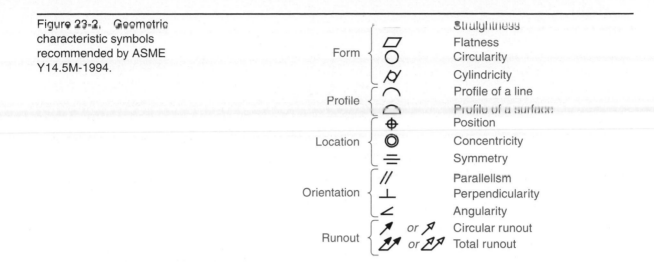

Figure 23-2. Geometric characteristic symbols recommended by ASME Y14.5M-1994.

MATERIAL CONDITION SYMBOLS

Material condition symbols are often referred to as "modifying symbols" because they modify or change the geometric tolerance in relation to the produced size or location of the feature. Material condition symbols are only used in geometric dimensioning applications. The symbols used in the feature control frame to indicate maximum material condition (MMC) or least material condition (LMC) are shown in Figure 23-3A. Regardless of feature size (RFS) is also a material condition. However, there is no symbol for RFS because it is assumed for all geometric tolerances and datum references unless MMC or LMC is specified.

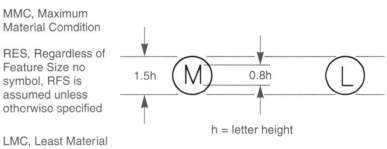

Figure 23-3A. Material condition symbols. In ASME Y14.5M-1994, there is no symbol for RFS since it is assumed.

Surface control regardless of feature size

Regardless of feature size is assumed when there is no material condition symbol following the geometric tolerance in the feature control frame. *Regardless of feature size* means that the geometric tolerances remains the same regardless of what the actual produced size happens to be. The term *produced size,* when used here, means the actual size of the feature when measured after manufacture. When the feature control frame is connected to a feature surface with a leader or an extension line, it is referred to as *surface control,* as shown in the drawing of Figure 23-3B. Even though the geometric characteristic symbol is straightness, the applications are the same for any geometric characteristic.

Look at the chart in Figure 23-3B and notice the possible produced sizes range from 6.20 (MMC) to 5.80 (LMC). With surface control, perfect form is required at MMC. *Perfect form* means that the object may not exceed a true geometric form boundary established at maximum material condition. This means that the geometric tolerance at MMC is zero, as shown in the chart in Figure 23-3B. Then, as the produced size goes away from MMC, the geometric tolerance increases until it equals the amount specified in the feature control frame, at which time the geometric tolerance remains the same, as shown in the chart in Figure 23-3B.

Figure 23-3B.   The drawing specifies surface control regardless of feature size. The related meaning is shown at the bottom.

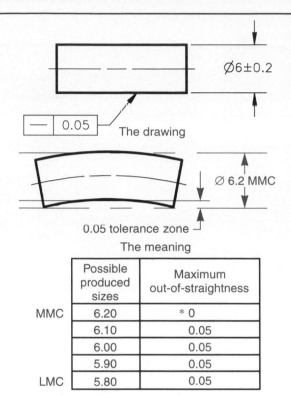

The drawing

The meaning

	Possible produced sizes	Maximum out-of-straightness
MMC	6.20	* 0
	6.10	0.05
	6.00	0.05
	5.90	0.05
LMC	5.80	0.05

* Perfect form required

Axis control regardless of feature size

Axis control is used when the feature control frame is with the diameter dimension, as shown in Figure 23-3C. Regardless of feature size is assumed. With axis control, perfect form is not required at MMC. Therefore, the specified geometric tolerance stays the same at every produced size, as shown in the chart in Figure 23-3C.

Figure 23-3C.   The drawing specifies axis control regardless of feature size. The related meaning is shown at the bottom.

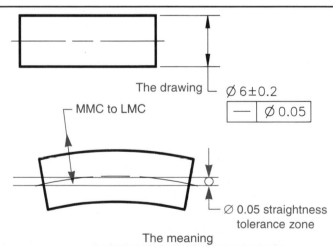

The drawing

The meaning

	Possible produced sizes	Maximum out-of-straightness
MMC	6.20	0.05
	6.10	0.05
	6.00	0.05
	5.90	0.05
LMC	5.80	0.05

Maximum material condition control

If the material condition control is maximum material condition, then the symbol for MMC must be placed in the feature control frame, as shown in Figure 23-3D. When this application is used, the specified geometric tolerance is held at the maximum material condition produced size, as in the Figure 23-3D chart. Then as the produced size goes away from MMC, the geometric tolerance increases equal to the change. The maximum geometric tolerance is at the LMC produced size.

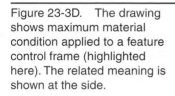

Figure 23-3D. The drawing shows maximum material condition applied to a feature control frame (highlighted here). The related meaning is shown at the side.

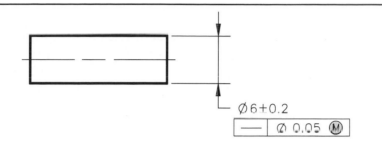

The meaning

	Possible produced sizes	Maximum out-of-straightness
MMC	6.20	0.05
	6.10	0.15
	6.00	0.25
	5.90	0.35
LMC	5.80	0.45

Least material condition control

If the material condition control is least material condition, then the symbol for LMC must be placed in the feature control frame. When this application is used, the specified geometric tolerance is held at the least material condition produced size. Then, as the produced size goes away from LMC, the geometric tolerance increases equal to the change. The maximum geometric tolerance is at the MMC produced size.

FEATURE CONTROL FRAME

A geometric characteristic, geometric tolerance, material condition, and datum reference (if any) for an individual feature is specified by means of a feature control frame. The *feature control frame* is divided into compartments containing the geometric characteristic symbol in the first compartment followed by the geometric tolerance. Where applicable, the geometric tolerance is preceded by the diameter symbol to describe the shape of the tolerance zone, and followed by a material condition symbol if other than RFS. See Figure 23-4.

Figure 23-4. Feature control
frames with geometric
characteristic symbol,
geometric tolerance, diameter
symbol (when used), and
material condition symbol
(when used). The material
condition symbol is left off for
RFS, since it is assumed. Note
that the geometric tolerance is
total, not plus/minus.

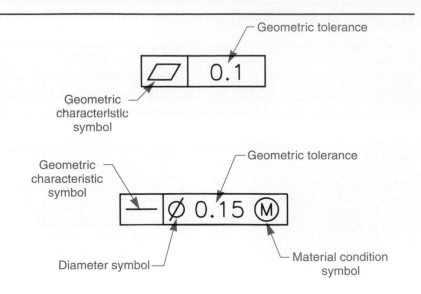

Where a geometric tolerance is related to one or more datums, the datum reference letters are placed in compartments following the geometric tolerance. Where a datum reference is multiple (that is, established by two datum features such as an axis established by two datum diameters) both datum reference letters, separated by a dash, are placed in a single compartment after the geometric tolerance. This is known as a *multiple datum reference*. Figure 23-5 shows several feature control frames with datum references.

Figure 23-5. Feature control
frames with datum references.

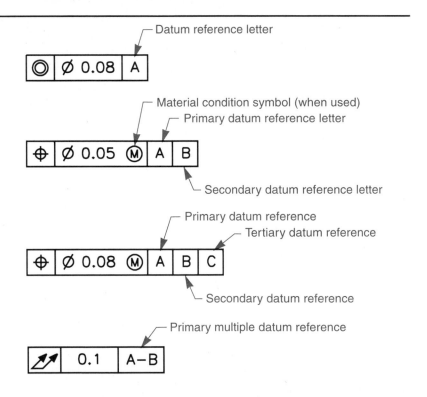

The order of elements in a feature control frame is shown in Figure 23-6. Notice in Figure 23-6 that the datum reference letters may be followed by a material condition symbol where applicable.

Figure 23-6.   Order of elements in a feature control frame.

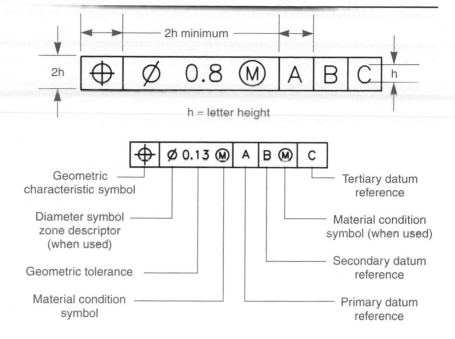

Geometric characteristic symbol

Diameter symbol zone descriptor (when used)

Geometric tolerance

Material condition symbol

Tertiary datum reference

Material condition symbol (when used)

Secondary datum reference

Primary datum reference

BASIC DIMENSIONS

A *basic dimension* is considered a theoretically perfect dimension. Basic dimensions are used to describe the theoretically exact size, profile, orientation, or location of a feature or datum target. These dimensions provide the basis where permissible variations are established by tolerances on other dimensions, in notes, or in feature control frames. In simple terms, all a basic dimension does is tell you where the geometric tolerance zone or datum target is located. Basic dimensions are shown on a drawing by placing a rectangle around the dimension, as shown in Figure 23-7. A general note may also be used to identify basic dimensions in some applications. For example, the note "UNTOLER-ANCED DIMENSIONS LOCATING TRUE POSITION ARE BASIC" indicates the dimensions that are basic.

Figure 23-7.   Basic dimensions.

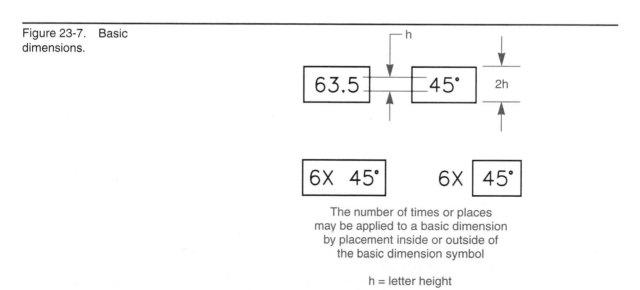

The number of times or places may be applied to a basic dimension by placement inside or outside of the basic dimension symbol

h = letter height

The basic dimension symbol around a dimension is a signal to the reader to look for a geometric tolerance in a feature control frame related to the features being dimensioned.

ADDITIONAL SYMBOLS

A few other symbols used in geometric dimensioning and tolerancing are shown in Figure 23-8. These symbols are used for specific applications and are identified as follows:

Figure 23-8. Additional dimensioning symbols.

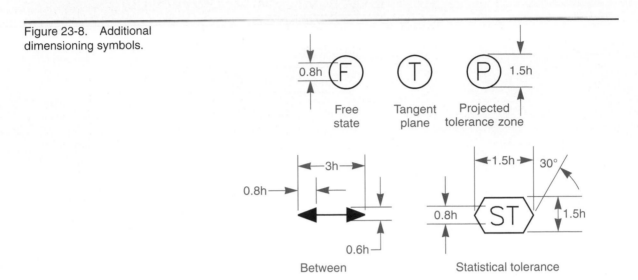

- **Free state.** Free state describes distortion of a part after the removal of forces applied during manufacture. The free state symbol is placed in the feature control frame after the geometric tolerance and the material condition (if any) if the feature must meet the tolerance specified while in free state.
- **Tangent plane.** A tangent plane symbol is placed after the geometric tolerance in the feature control frame when it is necessary to control a feature surface by contacting points of tangency.
- **Projected tolerance zone.** A projected tolerance zone symbol is placed in the feature control frame to inform the reader that the geometric tolerance zone is projected away from the primary datum.
- **Between.** The between symbol is used with profile geometric tolerances to identify where the profile tolerance is applied.
- **Statistical tolerance.** The *statistical tolerance* symbol is used to indicate that a tolerance is based on statistical tolerancing. *Statistical tolerancing* is the assigning of tolerances to related dimensions in an assembly based on the requirements of statistical process control (SPC). *Statistical process control* is a method of monitoring a manufacturing process by using statistical signals to either leave the process alone or change it as needed to maintain the quality intended in the dimensional tolerancing. The statistical tolerancing symbol is placed after the dimension or geometric tolerance that requires SPC, Figure 23-9. When the feature may be manufactured either by using SPC or by using conventional means, both the statistical tolerance with the statistical tolerance symbol and the conventional tolerance must be shown. An appropriate general note should accompany the drawing. Either of the two notes shown below are acceptable:
  - FEATURES IDENTIFIED AS STATISTICAL TOLERANCED SHALL BE PRODUCED WITH STATISTICAL PROCESS CONTROL.
  - FEATURES IDENTIFIED AS STATISTICAL TOLERANCED SHALL BE PRODUCED WITH STATISTICAL PROCESS CONTROL, OR THE MORE RESTRICTIVE ARITHMETIC LIMITS.

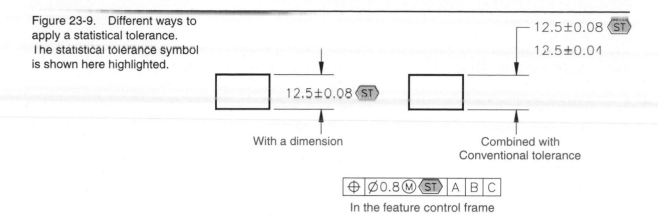

Figure 23-9.   Different ways to apply a statistical tolerance. The statistical tolerance symbol is shown here highlighted.

With a dimension

Combined with Conventional tolerance

In the feature control frame

DATUM FEATURE SYMBOL

Datums are considered theoretically perfect surfaces, planes, points, or axes. This is only an introduction to the appearance of datum-related symbols. In these applications, the datum is assumed. In geometric dimensioning and tolerancing, the datums are identified with a *datum feature symbol*.

Any letter of the alphabet may be used to identify a datum except for I, O, or Q. These letters may be confused with the numbers 1 or 0. Each datum feature requiring identification must have its own identification letter. On drawings where the number of datums exceed the letters in the alphabet, then double letters are used starting with AA through AZ, and then BA through BZ. Datum feature symbols may be repeated only as necessary for clarity. Figure 23-10 shows the datum feature symbol that is recommended by ASME 14.5M-1994.

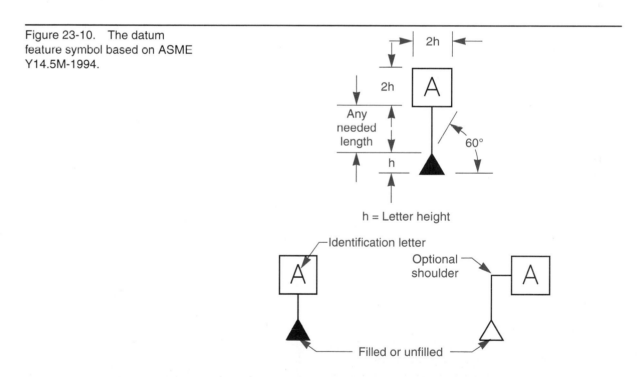

Figure 23-10.   The datum feature symbol based on ASME Y14.5M-1994.

The datum feature used in drawings prior to the release of ASME 14.5M-1994 is distinctively different. Figure 23-11 shows the datum feature recommended by ANSI Y14.5M-1982.

Figure 23-11.   The datum feature symbol based on ANSI Y14.5M-1982. (Note: This standard has been revised to ASME Y14.5M-1994.)

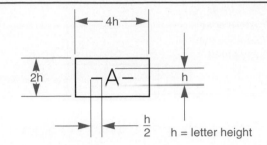

APPLICATIONS OF THE ASME Y14.5M-1994 DATUM FEATURE SYMBOL

When a surface is used to establish a datum plane on a part, the datum feature symbol is placed on the edge view of the surface, or on an extension line in the view where the surface appears as a line. Refer to Figure 23-12. A leader line may also be used to connect the datum feature symbol to the view in some applications.

Figure 23-12.   The datum feature symbol is placed on the edge view or on an extension line in the view where the surface appears as a line.

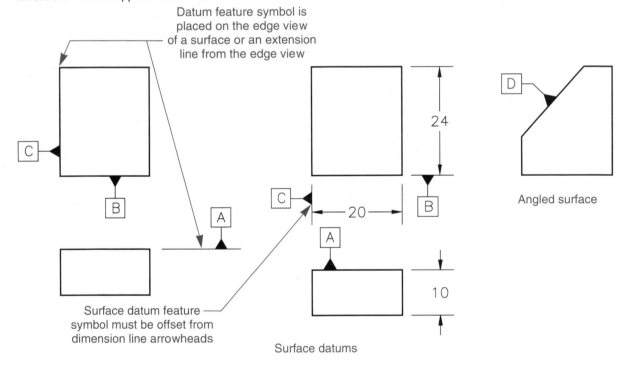

When the datum is an axis, the datum feature symbol may be placed on the drawing using one of the following methods (also shown in Figure 23-13):
- The symbol can be placed on the outside surface of a cylindrical feature.
- The symbol can be centered on the opposite side of the dimension line arrowhead.
- The symbol can replace the dimension line and arrowhead when the dimension line is placed outside of the extension lines.
- The symbol can be placed on a leader line shoulder.
- The symbol can be placed below, and attached to, the center of a feature control frame.

Elements on a rectangular shaped symmetrical part or feature may be located and dimensioned in relationship to a datum center plane. The representation of datum center plane symbols are shown in Figure 23-14.

Figure 23-13.   Methods of representing the datum axis.

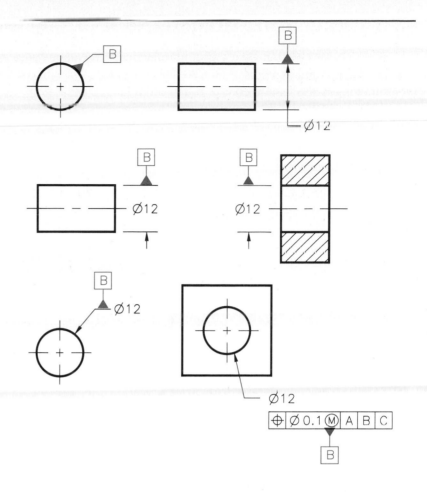

Figure 23-14.   Placement of center plane datum feature symbols. Axis and center plane datum feature symbols must align wlth, or replace, the dimension line arrowhead. Or, the datum must be placed on the feature, leader shoulder, or feature control frame.

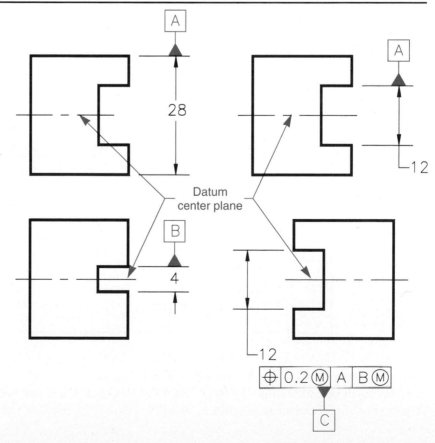

GEOMETRIC DIMENSIONING AND TOLERANCING WITH AUTOCAD

The previous section gave a brief introduction to the appearance and use of geometric dimensioning and tolerancing symbols. AutoCAD has provided you with the ability to add GD&T symbols to your drawings. The feature control frame and related GD&T symbols may be created using the TOLERANCE and LEADER commands.

Using the TOLERANCE command

The TOLERANCE command provides tools for creating GD&T symbols. Access this command by picking Toleran: from the DRAW DIM screen menu, pick Dimensioning followed by Tolerance… in the Draw pull-down menu, or type either TOL or TOLERANCE at the Command: prompt. When you enter this command, you get the "Symbol" dialog box shown in Figure 23-15.

Figure 23-15. The "Symbol" dialog box. Pick the desired geometric characteristic symbol.

Select the symbol you need

Pick OK and the "Geometric Tolerance" subdialog box appears

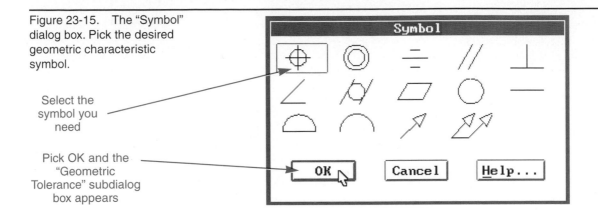

The "Symbol" dialog box contains the geometric characteristic symbols. The last option is blank. When you pick a symbol, it becomes highlighted. Next, pick the OK button and you get the "Geometric Tolerance" subdialog box shown in Figure 23-16.

Figure 23-16. The "Geometric Tolerance" subdialog box is used to build a feature control frame to desired specifications.

Tolerance compartments

The symbol selected in the "Symbol" dialog box. Pick here to access that dialog box

Enter a datum identifier

Datum reference compartments

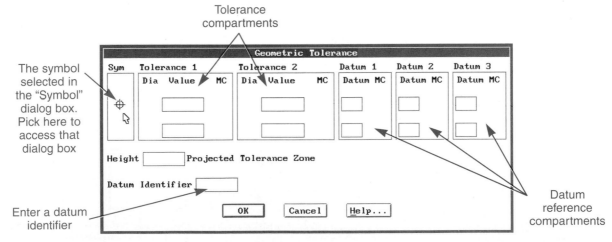

The symbol that you picked in the "Symbol" dialog box is displayed in the Sym text box. You can pick the Sym box to get the "Symbol" dialog box back again if you want to pick a different symbol. The rest of the "Geometric Tolerance" subdialog box is divided into compartments that relate to the

compartments found in the feature control frame. The elements of the "Geometric Tolerance" dialog box are described as follows:

- **Tolerance 1.** This compartment allows you to enter the first geometric tolerance value found in the feature control frame. You can also add a diameter symbol by picking below the Dia and a material condition symbol by picking below MC if needed. When you pick below MC, the "Material Condition" subdialog box shown in Figure 23-17 appears. Highlight the desired material condition symbol by picking it, and then pick the OK button. The desired material condition symbol is now displayed under MC. Notice the ⑤ symbol in Figure 23-17. This is the regardless of feature size (RFS) symbol used in ANSI Y14.5M-1982. In the current standard, ASME Y14.5M-1994, RFS is assumed unless otherwise specified.

Figure 23-17. The "Material Condition" subdialog box. Pick the desired material condition symbol for the geometric tolerance and datum reference as needed. Notice the symbol for RFS appears here. This symbol is not used in ASME Y14.5M-1994, but may be needed when editing older drawings.

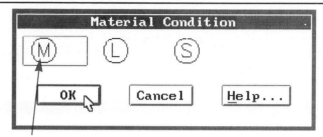

Pick the material condition symbol you need

There are two text edit boxes in each compartment. The text edit boxes are located below Value. The top text edit box is for the information found in a single feature control frame, while the bottom text edit box is for information needed for a double feature control frame. Double feature control frames are used for applications such as unit straightness, unit flatness, composite profile tolerance, composite positional tolerance, or coaxial positional tolerance. Refer to *Geometric Dimensioning and Tolerancing* published by The Goodheart-Willcox Company, Inc., or ASME Y14.5M-1994 for a complete discussion and examples. Figure 23-18 shows 0.5 entered in the Tolerance 1 first text box, preceded by a diameter symbol and followed by an MMC symbol.

Figure 23-18. The "Geometric Tolerance" subdialog box with a diameter symbol, geometric tolerance, and MMC material condition symbol added to the Tolerance 1 area (shown highlighted here).

The value, diameter symbol, and material condition symbol are entered

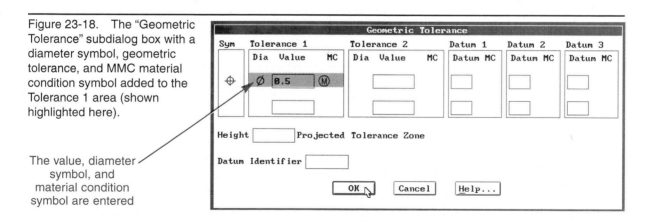

- **Tolerance 2.** This compartment is used for the addition of a second geometric tolerance to the feature control frame. This is not a common application, but it may be used in some cases where there are restrictions placed on the geometric tolerance specified in the first compartment. For example, ⌀0.8 MAX, which means that the specification given in the first compartment is maintained but may not exceed 0.8 maximum (MAX) as given in the second compartment. The Tolerance 2 text box is left blank in Figure 23-18 for this example.

- **Datum 1.** This is used to establish the information needed in the primary datum reference compartment. You can also enter a material condition symbol by picking MC if needed.
- **Datum 2 and Datum 3.** These work the same as Datum 1, but are for setting the secondary and tertiary datum reference information. Look back at Figure 23-6 to see how the datum reference and related material condition symbols are placed in the feature control frame.
- **Height.** Enter the height of a projected tolerance zone and pick to the right of Projected Tolerance Zone to access the symbol. This topic is discussed later in this chapter.
- **Datum Identifier.** You can specify a datum feature symbol here for the ANSI Y14.5M-1982 standard. However, you need to design a datum feature symbol and save it as a block if you want to comply with ASME Y14.5M-1994. Creating your own dimensioning symbols is discussed later in this chapter and in Chapter 25 of this text.

Figure 23-19.   The "Geometric Tolerance" subdialog box with a diameter symbol, geometric tolerance, and MMC material condition symbol added to the Tolerance 1 area. Identifiers A at Datum 1, B and MMC symbol at Datum 2, and C at Datum 3 are also added. (These items are shown highlighted here.)

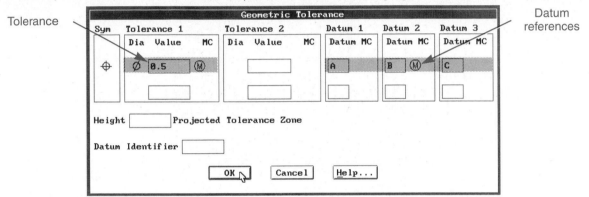

When you have entered all of the desired information in the "Geometric Tolerance" subdialog box, as shown in Figure 23-19, pick the OK button. Now the following prompt is issued:

Enter tolerance location: *(pick the place for the feature control frame to be drawn)*
Command:

The feature control frame shown in Figure 23-20 is placed on the drawing at the point you picked.

Figure 23-20.   The feature control frame created by the information displayed in Figure 23-19.

Using the LEADER command to place GD&T symbols

You can also use the LEADER command to access the same dialog boxes and draw a feature control frame connected to a leader line using the following command sequence:

Command: **LEADER** ↵
From point: *(pick the leader starting point)*
To point (Format/Annotation/Undo) ⟨Annotation⟩: *(pick the end of the shoulder)*
To point (Format/Annotation/Undo) ⟨Annotation⟩: *(press ENTER for the default)*

Annotation means notes. The Annotation option allows you to enter a single line of text, or press the ENTER key to get a list of Annotation options:

Annotation (or RETURN for options): ↵
Tolerance/Copy/Block/None/⟨Mtext⟩: **T** ↵

Enter T to access the Tolerance option. This activates the "Symbol" and "Geometric Tolerance" dialog boxes that were previously discussed. Establish the feature control frame information that you want and pick OK. The feature control frame is automatically connected to the leader shoulder, as shown in Figure 23-21.

Figure 23-21.   Using the LEADER command to draw a feature control frame.

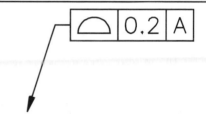

EXERCISE 23-2

❑ Load AutoCAD and open EX23-1.
❑ Draw the same feature control frame with a leader that is displayed in Figure 23-21.
❑ Save the drawing as A:EX23-2.

PROJECTION TOLERANCE ZONE INTRODUCTION   AUG 9

In some situations where positional tolerance is used entirely in out-of-squareness, it may be necessary to control perpendicularity and position next to the part. The use of a *projected tolerance zone* is recommended when variations in perpendicularity of threaded or press-fit holes could cause the fastener to interfere with the mating part. A projected tolerance zone is usually specified for fixed fastener situations, such as the threaded hole for a bolt or the press-fit hole of a pin application. The length of a projected tolerance zone may be specified as the distance the fastener extends into the mating part, the thickness of the part, or the height of a press fit stud. The normal positional tolerance extends through the thickness of the part. However, this application may cause an interference between the location of a thread or press-fit object and its mating part. This is because the attitude of a fixed fastener is controlled by the actual angle of the threaded hole. There is no clearance available to provide flexibility. For this reason, the projected tolerance zone is established at true position and extends away from the primary datum at the threaded feature.

The projected tolerance zone provides a bigger tolerance because it is projected away from the primary datum, rather than within the thread. The projected tolerance is also easier to inspect than the tolerance applied to the pitch diameter of the thread, because a thread gauge with a post projecting above the threaded hole may be used to easily verify the projected tolerance zone with a coordinate measuring machine (CMM).

One method for displaying the projected tolerance zone is where the projected tolerance zone symbol and height is placed in the feature control frame after the geometric tolerance and related material condition symbol. The related thread specification is then connected to the sectional view of the thread symbol. With this method, the projected tolerance zone is assumed to extend away from the threaded hole at the primary datum. Refer to Figure 23-22A.

Figure 23-22A.   Projected tolerance zone representation with the length of the projected tolerance zone given in the feature control frame. The projected tolerance zone symbol is shown here highlighted.

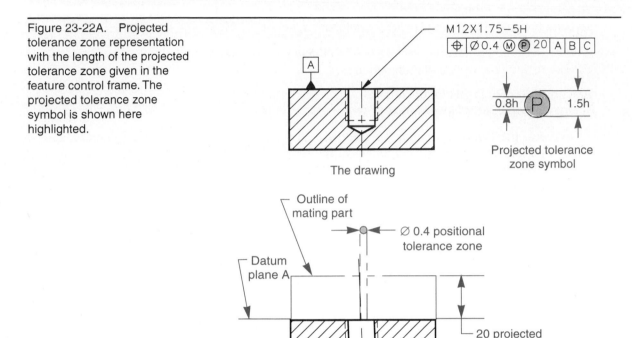

To provide additional clarification, the projected tolerance zone may be shown using a chain line in the view where the related datum appears as an edge and the minimum height of the projection is dimensioned. Refer to Figure 23-22B. When this is done, the projected tolerance zone symbol is shown alone in the feature control frame after the geometric tolerance and material condition symbol (if any). The meaning is the same as previously discussed.

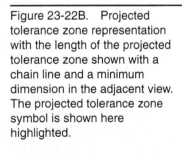

Figure 23-22B.   Projected tolerance zone representation with the length of the projected tolerance zone shown with a chain line and a minimum dimension in the adjacent view. The projected tolerance zone symbol is shown here highlighted.

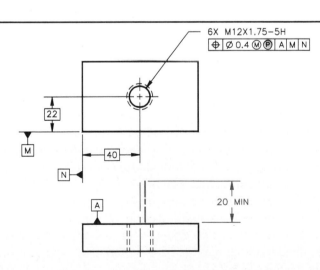

Drawing the projected tolerance zone with AutoCAD

AUG 9

You can add projected tolerance zone specifications to the feature control frame by using the "Geometric Tolerance" subdialog box. To do this, use either the TOLERANCE or LEADER command to access the "Symbol" dialog box. Select the desired geometric characteristic symbol and press the OK button to access the "Geometric Tolerance" subdialog box. Type the desired geometric tolerance, diameter symbol, material condition symbol, and datum reference as previously discussed. Type the projected tolerance zone height in the Height text box. Notice that 24 is entered in the Height text box in Figure 23-23. Pick to the right of Projected Tolerance Zone to insert the projected tolerance zone symbol. Pick the OK button when ready.

Figure 23-23. Entering the projected tolerance zone height and symbol in the "Geometric Tolerance" subdialog box.

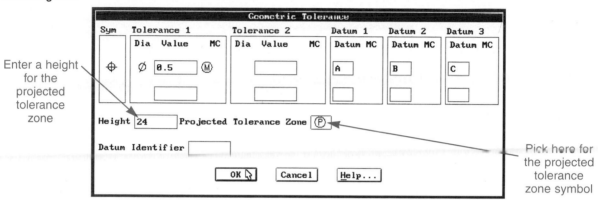

Now follow the screen prompts and place the feature control frame in the desired location. Notice in Figure 23-24 that AutoCAD displays the projected tolerance zone height in a separate compartment below the feature control frame. This representation is in accordance with ANSI Y14.5M-1982, but does not match the ASME Y14.5M-1994 examples that are displayed in Figures 23-22A and 23-22B. If you want to dimension the projected tolerance zone height with a chain line as in Figure 23-22B, then omit the Height in the "Geometric Tolerance" subdialog box and only pick the Projected tolerance Zone symbol. This adds a compartment below the feature control frame with only the projected tolerance zone symbol.

Figure 23-24. The AutoCAD feature control frame and projected tolerance zone compartment conforms to ANSI Y14.5M-1982 standards.

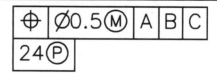

EXERCISE 23-3

❑ Load AutoCAD and open EX23-1.
❑ Draw the feature control frame and projected tolerance zone compartment shown in Figure 23-24.
❑ Save the drawing as A:EX23-3

DRAWING A DOUBLE FEATURE CONTROL FRAME WITH AUTOCAD

AUG 9

Several GD&T applications require that the feature control frame be doubled in height with two sets of geometric tolerancing information provided. These applications include unit straightness and flatness, composite positional tolerance, and coaxial positional tolerance. Use the TOLERANCE or LEADER command as previously discussed and pick the desired geometric characteristic symbol from the "Symbol" dialog box. When the "Geometric Tolerance" subdialog box is displayed, pick below the current geometric characteristic symbol in the Sym box. The "Symbol" dialog box is displayed again. Pick another geometric characteristic symbol. This results in two symbols displayed in the Sym box, as shown in Figure 23-25. Continue picking and typing the needed information in both sets of tolerance and datum compartments.

Figure 23-25.   Double feature control frame information displayed in the "Geometric Tolerance" subdialog box.

Pick here to select a second symbol

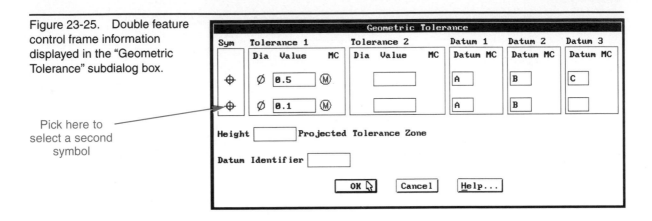

If the two symbols in the Sym box are the same, then the double feature control frame is drawn with one geometric characteristic symbol displayed in the first compartment as shown in Figure 23-26A. If you are drawing a double feature control frame with different geometric characteristic symbols for a combination control, then the feature control frame is drawn, as shown in Figure 23-26B.

Figure 23-26.   A–If the same symbol is entered in the Sym box of the "Geometric Tolerance" subdialog box, it will be displayed once in the first compartment of the feature control frame. B–Enter two different symbols in the Sym box of the "Geometric Tolerance" subdialog box to have them displayed in two separate compartments of the feature control frame.

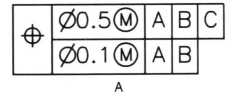

A

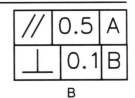

B

EXERCISE 23-4

❑ Load AutoCAD and open EX23-1.
❑ Draw the feature control frames shown in Figure 23-26.
❑ Save the drawing as A:EX23-4

DRAWING THE DATUM FEATURE
SYMBOL WITH AUTOCAD

AUG 9

To draw the datum feature symbol with AutoCAD, use the TOLERANCE command or the LEADER command if you want the symbol connected to a leader line. When you get the "Symbol" dialog box, pick the blank option and then pick OK. This accesses the "Geometric Tolerance" subdialog box without any geometric characteristic symbol displayed. Type the desired datum identification (- A -) in the Datum Identifier text box, as shown in Figure 23-27.

Figure 23-27.   Enter a datum identifier in the text box found in the "Geometric Tolerance" subdialog box.

Picking the blank area in the "Symbol" dialog box leaves this area blank

	Geometric Tolerance				
Sym	Tolerance 1	Tolerance 2	Datum 1	Datum 2	Datum 3
	Dia Value MC	Dia Value MC	Datum MC	Datum MC	Datum MC

Height [   ] Projected Tolerance Zone

Datum Identifier [- A -]

Enter a datum identifier

[OK]   [Cancel]   [Help...]

Pick the OK button and then place the datum feature symbol in the desired position on the drawing. The resulting datum feature symbol correlates with ANSI Y14.5M-1982, Figure 23-28A. You can also draw an ANSI Y14.5M-1982 datum feature symbol connected to a feature control frame, as shown in Figure 23-28B, by selecting the desired geometric characteristic symbol and entering the needed information in the "Geometric Tolerance" subdialog box.

Figure 23-28.   A–A datum feature symbol drawn without a feature control frame. B–A datum feature symbol drawn with a feature control frame. Note: These datum feature symbols are drawn to the ANSI Y14.5M-1982 standards.

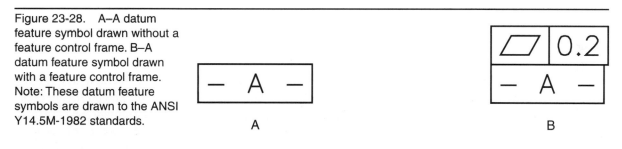

A

B

EXERCISE 23-5

❑ Load AutoCAD and open EX23-1.
❑ Draw the datum feature symbol shown in Figure 23-28A.
❑ Draw the feature control frame and datum feature symbol shown in Figure 23-24.
❑ Save the drawing as A:EX23-5

PROFESSIONAL TIP

Chapter 25 of this text gives you a detailed discussion on how to create your own custom symbol libraries. It is recommended that you design a group of dimensioning symbols that are not available in AutoCAD. Dimensioning symbols might include the counterbore, countersink, depth, and other symbols displayed in Figure 23-1. Geometric tolerancing symbols may include the datum feature symbol that is currently recognized by ASME Y14.5M-1994 as shown in Figure 23-10.

CONTROLLING THE HEIGHT OF THE FEATURE CONTROL FRAME | AUG 9 |

Figure 23-6 showed the height of the feature control frame as being twice the height of the text. Text on engineering drawings is generally .125 in. (3 mm). This makes the feature control frame height equal to .25 in. (6 mm). The distance from the text to the feature control frame is controlled by the DIMGAP dimension variable. The DIMGAP default is .09 in. If the drawing text is .125 in., then the space between the text and the feature control frame should be .0625 in. to get a .25 in. high frame. Change the DIMGAP like this:

Command: **DIMGAP** ↵
New value for DIMGAP ⟨0.09⟩: **.0625** ↵
Command:

The results of this setting is shown in the feature control frame in Figure 23-29.

Figure 23-29.   The DIMGAP dimension variable controls the distance from the text to the box in the feature control frame and the basic dimension. Note: This value applies to both sides of the text.

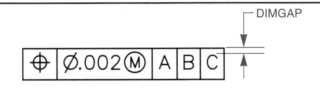

DRAWING BASIC DIMENSIONS WITH AUTOCAD | AUG 9 |

You can have AutoCAD automatically draw basic dimensions by using the "Dimension Styles" dialog box. Remember, access this dialog box by picking DDim: in the MOD DIM screen menu, picking Dimension Style... in the Data pull-down menu, or by typing DDIM at the command prompt.

When inside the "Dimension Styles" dialog box, pick the Annotation button to get the "Annotation" subdialog box. To access the basic dimension feature, go to the Tolerance Method: list and pick BASIC, as shown in Figure 23-30. Notice that the image tile in the Primary and Alternate Units areas display basic dimension examples.

You can also activate the basic dimension feature by picking the image tile and cycling through the options until you get the basic dimension example. Pick the OK button in the "Annotation" subdialog box and the "Dimension Styles" dialog box to return to the drawing editor and begin drawing basic dimensions, as shown in Figure 23-31.

The DIMGAP variable also controls the space between the basic dimension text and the box around the dimension.

Figure 23-30.   Use the DDIM command to access the "Dimension Styles" dialog box. Then, pick Basic in the "Annotation" subdialog box to draw basic dimensions. You can also click on the image tile to cycle through the options.

The image title adjusts to basic dimensions

Select Basic from the list

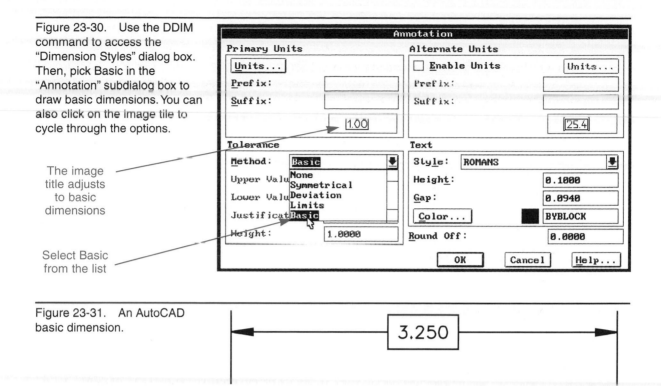

Figure 23-31.   An AutoCAD basic dimension.

3.250

EXERCISE 23-6

❑ Load AutoCAD and open EX23-1.
❑ The dimension text height was set to .125 in. in EX23-1. Set the DIMGAP dimension variable so the feature control frame height is two times the text height.
❑ Draw the feature control frame shown in Figure 23-29.
❑ Draw the basic dimension shown in Figure 23-31.
❑ Save the drawing as A:EX23-6.

EDITING THE FEATURE CONTROL FRAME

AUG 9

A feature control frame acts as one object. So, when you pick anywhere on the frame, the entire object is selected. You can edit feature control frames using ERASE, COPY, MOVE, ROTATE, and SCALE. The STRETCH command and GRIPS have the affect of only moving the feature control frame, similar to when they are used with text objects.

You can edit the information inside of a feature control frame by using the DDEDIT command. When you enter DDEDIT and select the desired feature control frame, the familiar "Geometric Tolerance" subdialog box is displayed with all of the current feature control frame values shown. Make any desired changes and pick the OK button. The feature control frame is now revised as needed. You can also use the DDEDIT command to edit basic dimensions. This displays the "Edit MText" dialog box where you can edit the basic dimension as any other dimension.

SAMPLE GD&T APPLICATIONS

This chapter is intended to give you a general overview of GD&T applications and how to draw GD&T symbols using AutoCAD. If you are in the manufacturing industry, you may have considerable use for geometric dimensioning and tolerancing. The support information may be reviewed or it may inspire you to learn more about this topic. The drawings in Figure 23-32 are intended to show you some common GD&T applications using the available geometric characteristics.

Figure 23-32. Examples of typical geometric dimensioning and tolerancing applications using the various geometric characteristics.

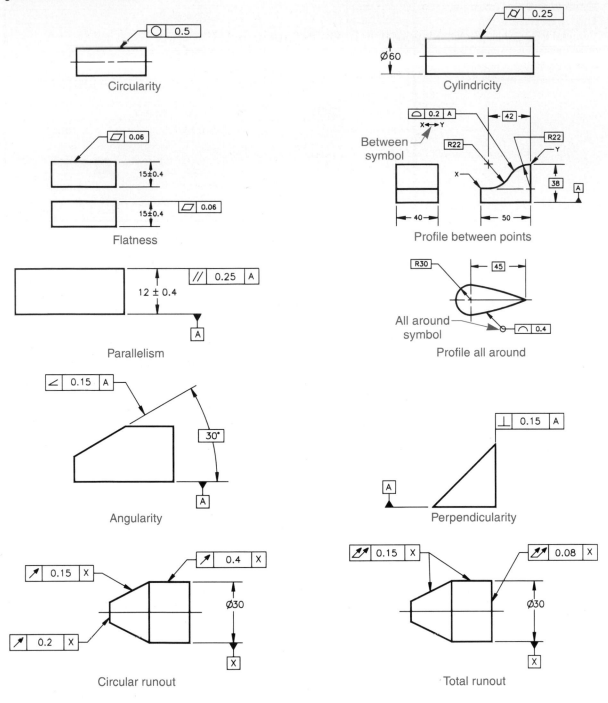

CHAPTER TEST

Write your answers in the spaces provided:

1. Name each of the following geometric characteristic symbols:

A. _____   H. _____

B. _____   I. _____

C. _____   J. _____

D. _____   K. _____

E. _____   L. _____

F. _____   M. _____

G. _____   N. _____

2. Label the parts of the following feature control frame:

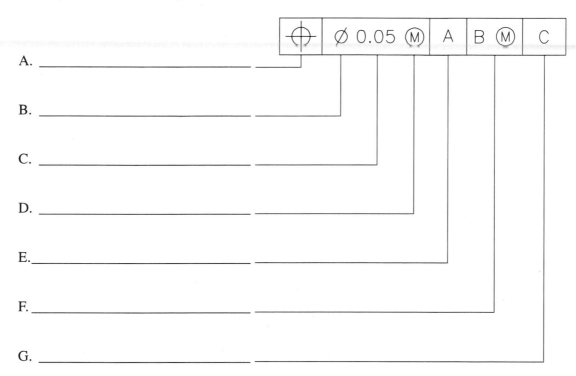

A. _____

B. _____

C. _____

D. _____

E. _____

F. _____

G. _____

3. Name two commands that can be used to draw a feature control frame._____

_____

4. Identify the dialog box that contains the geometric characteristic symbols. _____

_____

5. What do you get after you pick a geometric characteristic symbol followed by picking OK in the dialog box identified in Question 4? _____

_____

6. Identify the procedure used if you want to draw a feature control frame connected to a leader.

_____
_____
_____
_____
_____

7. Describe how to place a projected tolerance zone height and symbol compartment with the feature control frame. _____

_____
_____
_____
_____

8. How do you get one symbol in the first compartment of a double height feature control frame?

_____
_____
_____
_____

9. How do you get two different geometric characteristic symbols in the first compartment of a double height feature control frame? _____

_____
_____
_____
_____

10. Describe how to draw a basic dimension with AutoCAD. _____

_____
_____
_____

11. Identify the dimension variable that controls the space between the text in a feature control frame and basic dimension and the box surrounding these items. _____

_____

12. Describe how to draw a datum feature symbol with AutoCAD, without drawing an attached feature control frame. _____

_____
_____
_____

13. Name the command that may be used to change the information in an existing feature control frame.

_____

14. How do you get a "Geometric Tolerance" subdialog box without any symbol shown in the Sym box?

_____
_____

15. Name the current standard for dimensioning and tolerancing that is adopted by the American National Standards Institute. _____

_____

DRAWING PROBLEMS

Create dimension styles that will assist you in the solution of these problems. Draw fully-dimensioned multiview drawings. The required number of views depends upon the problem and is to be determined by you. Apply geometric tolerancing as discussed in this chapter. Use ANSI Y14.5M-1982 standards as applied by AutoCAD, or modify the available applications to use ASME Y14.5M-1994 standards. The problems are presented with ASME Y14.5M-1994 standards.

P23-1

1. Open P22-5 and edit by adding the geometric tolerancing shown below. If you did not draw P22-5, then open a new drawing or a prototype and draw the problem. Untoleranced dimensions are ±0.5. Save as A:P23-1.

   METRIC

   Name: SPRING CLIP

   Material: SAE 1085

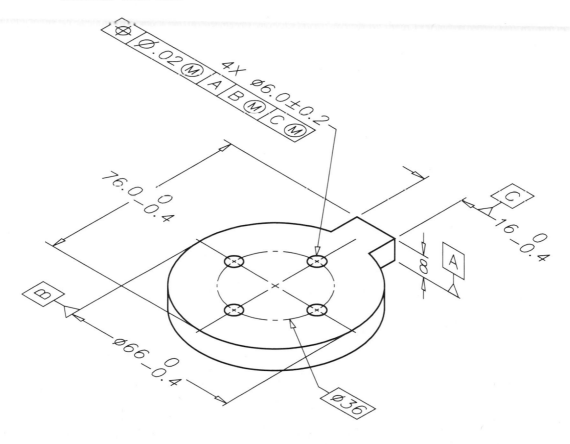

P23-2

2. Open P22-6 and edit by adding the geometric tolerancing shown below. If you did not draw P22-6, then open a new drawing or a prototype and draw the problem. Note: the problem is shown with a cut-away for clarity. You do not need to draw a section. Untoleranced dimensions are ±.02. Save as A:P23-2.

INCII

Name: THRUST WASHER

Material: SAE 5150

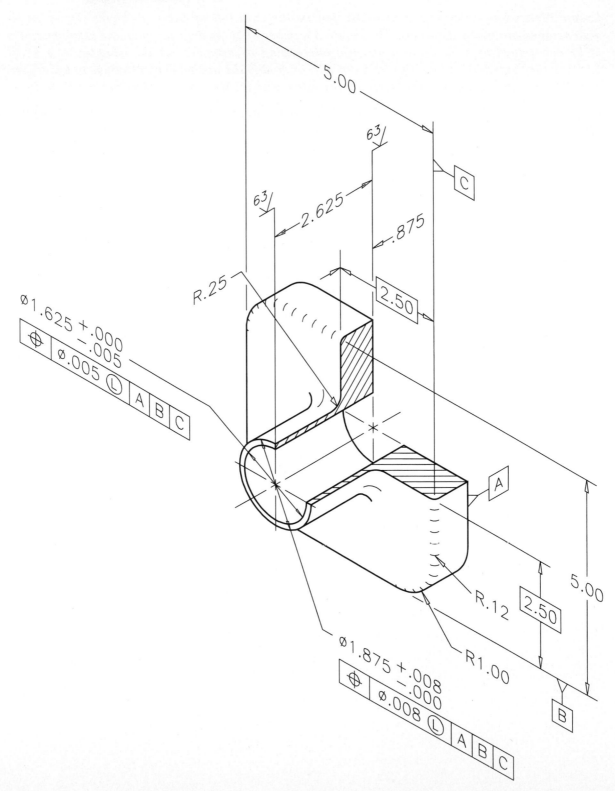

3. Open P22-7 and edit by adding the geometric tolerancing shown below. If you did not
draw P22-7, then open a new drawing or a prototype and draw the problem. Save as
A:P23-3.

P23-3

METRIC

Name: LOCKING COLLAR

Material: SAE 1080

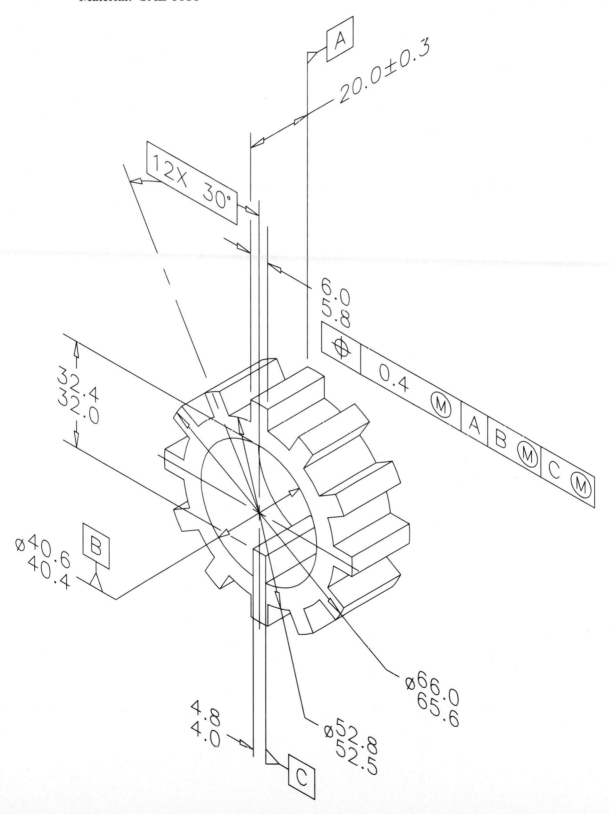

P23-4

4. Draw the following object as previously instructed. Untoleranced dimensions are ±0.3. Save as A:P23-4.

METRIC

Name: SHAFT GUIDE

Material: CAST IRON

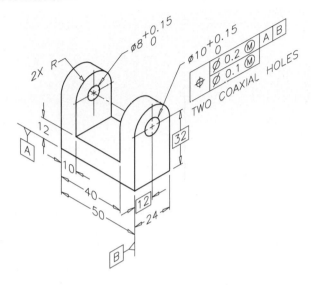

P23-5

5. Draw the following object as previously instructed. Note: the problem is shown with a cut-away for clarity. You do not need to draw a section. Untoleranced dimensions are ±.010. Save as A:P23-5.

INCH

Name: VALVE PIN

Material: PHOSPHOR BRONZE

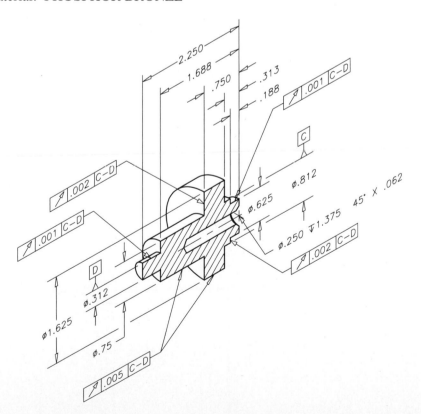

P23-6

6. Draw the following object as previously instructed. Note: the problem is shown with a cut-away for clarity. You do not need to draw a section. Untoleranced dimensions are ±.010. Save as A:P23-6.

INCH

Name: HUB

Material: CAST IRON

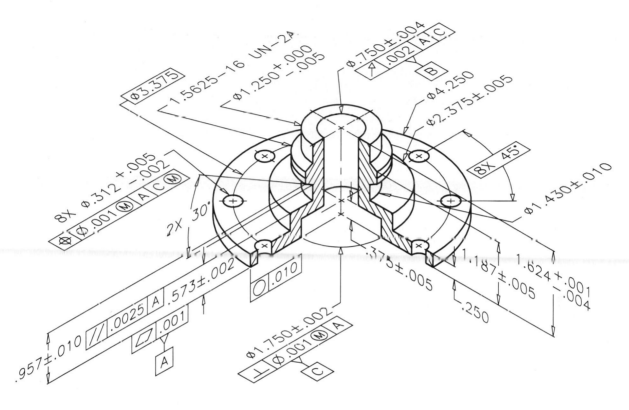

Assembly drawing. (Tektronix, Inc.)

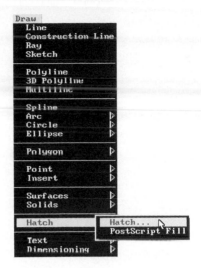

Chapter 24

DRAWING SECTION VIEWS AND GRAPHIC PATTERNS

Learning objectives

After completing this chapter, you will be able to:

○ Identify sectioning techniques.

○ Use sections and dimensioning practices to draw objects given on engineering sketches.

○ Draw sectioned material using the HATCH, BHATCH, and SOLID commands.

○ Prepare graphic displays, such as graphs and logos, using the HATCH and SOLID commands.

In mechanical drafting, internal features in regular multiviews appear as hidden lines. These features must be dimensioned. However, it is poor practice to dimension to hidden lines. Therefore, section views are used to clarify the hidden features. They show internal features as if a portion of the object is cut away. Section views are used in conjunction with multiviews to completely describe the exterior and interior features of an object.

When sections are drawn, a cutting-plane line placed in one of the views shows where the cut was made. The cutting-plane line is the "saw" that cuts through the object to expose internal features. The arrows on the cutting-plane line indicate the line of sight when looking at the section view. The cutting-plane lines are often labeled with letters which relate to the proper section view. This practice is necessary for drawings with multiple sections. It is optional when only one section view is present and its location is obvious. Section lines are used in the section view to show where material has been cut away, Figure 24-1.

Figure 24-1. A three-view multiview drawing with a section view.

REGULAR MULTIVIEWS

SECTION A—A

SECTION VIEW

Sectioning is also used in other drafting fields such as architectural and structural drafting. Cross sections through buildings show the construction methods and materials, Figure 24-2. The cutting-plane lines used in these fields are often composed of letter and number symbols. This helps coordinate the large number of sections found in a set of architectural drawings.

Figure 24-2. An architectural section view. (Drawing courtesy of Alan Mascord, Design Associates.)

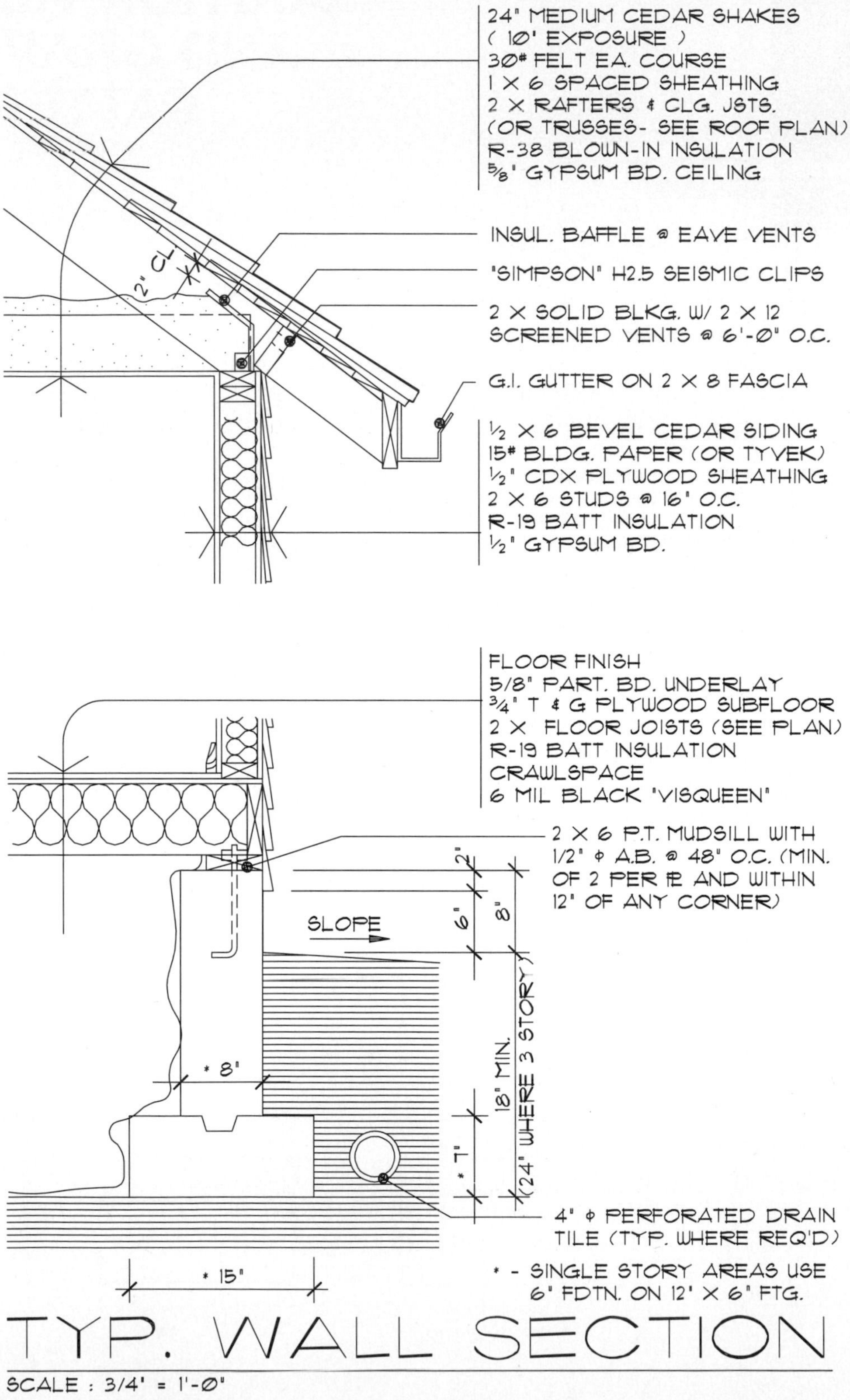
24" MEDIUM CEDAR SHAKES
(10' EXPOSURE)
30# FELT EA. COURSE
1 X 6 SPACED SHEATHING
2 X RAFTERS & CLG. JSTS.
(OR TRUSSES- SEE ROOF PLAN)
R-38 BLOWN-IN INSULATION
5/8' GYPSUM BD. CEILING
INSUL. BAFFLE @ EAVE VENTS
"SIMPSON" H2.5 SEISMIC CLIPS
2 X SOLID BLKG. W/ 2 X 12
SCREENED VENTS @ 6'-0" O.C.
G.I. GUTTER ON 2 X 8 FASCIA
2' CL
1/2 X 6 BEVEL CEDAR SIDING
15# BLDG. PAPER (OR TYVEK)
1/2" CDX PLYWOOD SHEATHING
2 X 6 STUDS @ 16' O.C.
R-19 BATT INSULATION
1/2" GYPSUM BD.
FLOOR FINISH
5/8" PART. BD. UNDERLAY
3/4" T & G PLYWOOD SUBFLOOR
2 X FLOOR JOISTS (SEE PLAN)
R-19 BATT INSULATION
CRAWLSPACE
6 MIL BLACK 'VISQUEEN"
2 X 6 P.T. MUDSILL WITH
1/2" ϕ A.B. @ 48" O.C. (MIN.
OF 2 PER PL AND WITHIN
12" OF ANY CORNER)
2"
6"
8"
SLOPE
18" MIN.
(24" WHERE 3 STORY)
* 8"
* 7"
* 15"
4" ϕ PERFORATED DRAIN
TILE (TYP. WHERE REQ'D)
* - SINGLE STORY AREAS USE
6" FDTN. ON 12" X 6" FTG.
TYP. WALL SECTION
SCALE : 3/4" = 1'-0"

TYPES OF SECTIONS

There are many types of sections available for the drafter to use in specific situations. The section used depends on the detail to be sectioned. For example, one object may require the section be taken completely through the object. Another may only need to remove a small portion to expose the interior features.

Full sections

Full sections, such as the one shown in Figure 24-1, are used when it is necessary to remove half of the object. In this type of section, the cutting-plane line passes completely through the object along a center plane.

Offset sections

Offset sections are the same as full sections, except that the cutting-plane line is staggered. This allows you to cut through features that do not lie in a straight line, Figure 24-3.

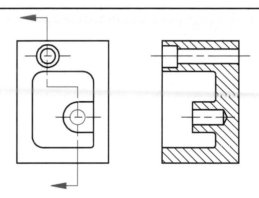

Figure 24-3.   An offset section.

Half sections

Half sections show one-quarter of the object removed. The term *half* is used because half of the view appears in section and the other half is shown as an exterior view. Half sections are commonly used on symmetrical objects. A centerline is used to separate the sectioned part of the view from the unsectioned portion. Hidden lines are normally omitted from the unsectioned side, Figure 24-4.

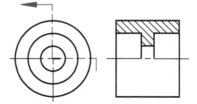

Figure 24-4.   A half section.

Aligned sections

Aligned sections are used when a feature is out of alignment with the center plane. In this case, an offset section would distort the image. The cutting-plane line cuts through the feature to be sectioned. It is then rotated to align with the center plane before projecting into the section view. See Figure 24-5.

Figure 24-5.   An aligned
section.

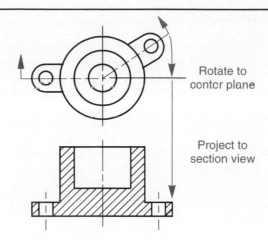

Rotate to
center plane

Project to
section view

Revolved sections

Revolved sections clarify the contour of objects that have the same shape throughout their length. The section is revolved in place within the object or part of the view may be broken away. Refer to Figure 24-6. The advantage of breaking away part of the view is to make dimensioning easier.

Figure 24-6.   A revolved
section.

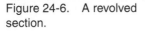
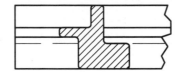

Removed sections

Removed sections serve much the same function as revolved sections. The section view is removed from the regular view. A cutting-plane line shows where the section was taken. When multiple removed sections are taken, the cutting planes and related views are labeled. The section views are placed in alphabetical order. The letters I, O, and Q are not used because they may be mistaken for numbers. Drawing only the ends of the cutting-plane lines simplifies the views. See Figure 24-7.

Figure 24-7.   Removed
sections.

SECTION A–A

SECTION C–C

SECTION B–B

Broken-out sections

Broken-out sections show only a small portion of the view removed to clarify a hidden feature. See Figure 24-8.

Figure 24-8.   A broken-out section.

SECTION LINE SYMBOLS

AUG C

Section lines are placed in the section view to show where material has been cut away. Some rules that govern section line usage are:

- Section lines are placed at 45° unless another angle is required to satisfy the following rules.
- Section lines should not be drawn parallel or perpendicular to any other adjacent lines on the drawing.
- Section lines should not cross object lines.

Section lines may be drawn using different patterns to represent the specific type of material. The equally spaced section lines shown in the preceding examples represent a general application. This is adequate in most situations. Additional patterns are not necessary if the type of material is clearly indicated in the title block. Different section line material symbols are needed when several connected parts of different materials are sectioned. AutoCAD has standard section line symbols available. These are referred to as *hatch patterns*. These symbols may be seen in the "acad.pat" file. The AutoCAD pattern labeled ANSI31 is the general section line symbol and is the default pattern in a new drawing. When you change to a different hatch pattern, the new pattern becomes the default until it is changed. It is also used for cast iron. The ANSI32 symbol is used for sectioning steel. Other standard AutoCAD hatch patterns are shown in Figure 24-9. When very thin objects are sectioned, the material may be completely blackened or filled in. AutoCAD refers to this as "solid."

Figure 24-9.   Standard AutoCAD hatch patterns. (Autodesk, Inc.)

ANGLE	ANSI31	ANSI32	AR-BRELM	AR-BRSTD	AR-CONC
ANSI33	ANSI34	ANSI35	AR-HBONE	AR-PARQ1	AR-RROOF
ANSI36	ANSI37	ANSI38	AR-RSHKE	AR-SAND	BOX
AR-B816	AR-B816C	AR-B88	BRASS	BRICK	BRSTONE

Figure 24-9.   Standard AutoCAD hatch patterns. (Autodesk, Inc.)

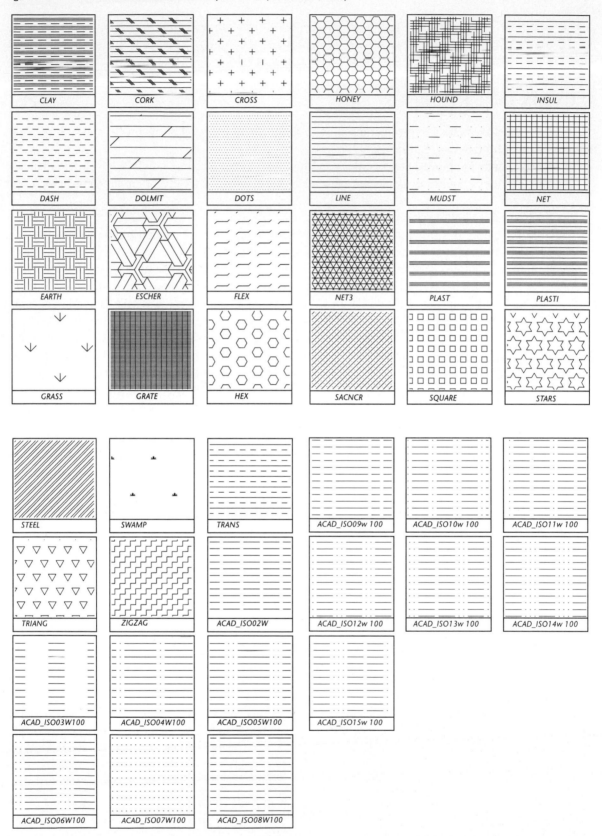

DRAWING SECTION LINES AND HATCH PATTERNS

AUG 2

The previous discussion explained the different sectioning techniques and introduced section line hatch patterns. AutoCAD hatch patterns are not limited to sectioning. They may be used as artistic patterns in a graphic layout for an advertisement or promotion. They might also be added as shading on an architectural elevation or technical illustration.

Introduction to the HATCH command

AutoCAD allows you to draw section lines or other patterns using the HATCH command, by typing HATCH at the Command: prompt as follows:

    Command: **HATCH** ↵
    Pattern (? or name/U,style) ⟨ANSI31⟩:

Typing ? gives you this prompt:

    Pattern(s) to ⟨*⟩:

You can type the name or names of specific hatch patterns, or press ENTER to accept the wild card ⟨*⟩ and list all the hatch patterns. AutoCAD displays the names of all standard hatch patterns each followed by a brief description. The list is three pages long so press ENTER, the space bar, or function key F1 after each page. Press flip screen, F1, when finished.

To draw a hatch pattern, press ENTER to accept the default pattern name, ANSI31, or type a different pattern name and press ENTER. You are then asked to define the pattern scale and angle.

    Pattern (? or name/U,style) ⟨ANSI31⟩: ↵
    Scale for pattern ⟨1.0000⟩: ↵
    Angle for pattern ⟨0⟩: ↵

Press ENTER after each prompt to use the default value shown in brackets. The pattern scale default is 1, or full scale. If the drawn pattern is too tight or too wide, type a new scale. Figure 24-10 shows different scale factors.

Figure 24-10.   Hatch pattern scale factors.

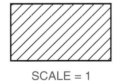

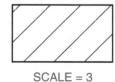

SCALE = 1   SCALE = 2   SCALE = 3

The default scale factor of 1 specifies one drawing unit. A relationship exists between the hatch scale in model space and paper space. This relationship is controlled by the scale factor. Respond to the scale prompt with the desired size of the pattern in model space or paper space. The hatch scale can still be specified referencing model space if desired, but it is much simpler to reference the scale to paper space. This allows the scale factor to be based on the plotted scale of the drawing. To do this, enter XP after the scale. The XP indicates relative to paper space units. Therefore, entering 1XP as the scale factor causes AutoCAD to automatically calculate the actual scale required within model space to match the specified value of 1 in paper space:

    Scale for pattern ⟨1.0000⟩: **1XP** ↵

When you do this, notice that the next use of the HATCH command offers the actual pattern scale which was calculated by AutoCAD as a default. It is not necessary to reenter 1XP, since the default value shown is the model space equivalent of this already. Model space and paper space are discussed in detail in Chapter 12.

An alternate method of entering values for this prompt is by picking two points in the drawing. AutoCAD then measures the distance and uses the number of units as the scale factor. This method does not allow the XP option to be used.

PROFESSIONAL TIP

 It is recommended that you enter a large scale factor when hatching big areas. This makes your section lines look neater and saves regeneration and plot time.

The pattern default angle is 0. This gives you the same pattern angle shown in Figure 24-9. To alter the pattern angle, type a new value.

Selecting objects to be hatched

It is important to consider the boundary of the area you plan to hatch. It is easy to hatch within a circle or square. All you do is pick the circle, or window the square, when you see the Select objects: prompt. If the square was drawn as one closed polyline, then pick it as one entity. The circumference of the circle and the perimeter of the square automatically become the hatch boundary. See Figure 24-11.

```
Command: HATCH ↵
Pattern (? or name/U,style) ⟨ANSI31⟩:↵
Scale for pattern ⟨1.0000⟩: ↵
Angle for pattern ⟨0⟩: ↵
Select hatch boundaries or RETURN for direct hatch option,
Select objects: (pick the circle)
1 found
```

Now select a square that was drawn as four lines.

```
Select objects: W ↵
First corner: (pick the first window corner)
Other corner: (pick the second window corner)
4 found
```

Now select a square that was drawn as one closed polyline.

```
Select objects: (pick the closed polyline)
1 found
Select objects: ↵
Command:
```

Figure 24-11.   Selecting objects to be hatched.

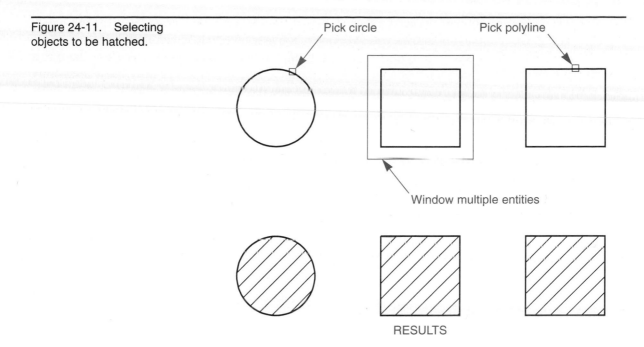

Hatching without selecting objects

A problem may arise when you try to hatch an object that is composed of more than one enclosed area. If adjacent areas are drawn with interconnecting lines, the hatching may not be what you expect. The plan in Figure 24-12 is to hatch only the right side of each pair of blocks. Notice the possible results using Window selection and picking the lines of the right side.

Figure 24-12.   When selecting an area made up of interconnecting lines, the results may be undesirable. A–AutoCAD would not hatch the area and issued the error message "Hatching did not intersect the figure." B–The hatch extends into the adjacent area.

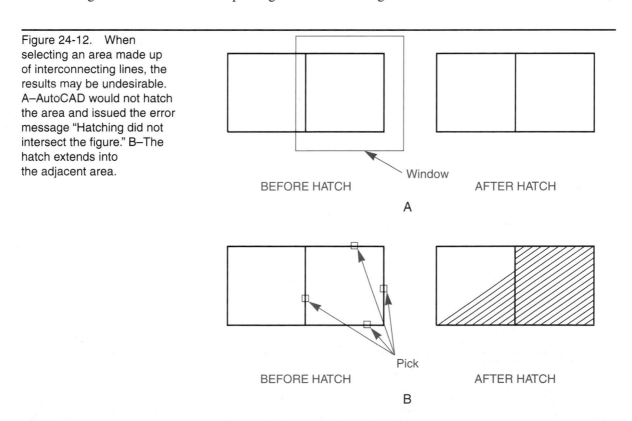

To overcome the problem that can occur in Figure 24-12, AutoCAD provides a feature called direct hatching. *Direct hatching* allows you to define a boundary without selecting any objects. So, if you want to successfully hatch an object such as the right side of Figure 24-12, you use the direct hatching option to place a polyline boundary around the area to be hatched. The polyline is temporary if you want to discard it or you can keep it. When you see the Retain polyline? ⟨N⟩: prompt, press ENTER to accept the default to have the polyline boundary removed after the hatch is drawn, or type Y and press ENTER to keep the polyline boundary. If you type Y to keep the polyline boundary, then the ⟨Y⟩ option becomes the default for the next HATCH operation until changed again. When you draw the polyline boundary, you get options that are just like the PLINE command:

    Command: **HATCH** ↵
    Pattern (? or name/U, style) ⟨ANSI31⟩: ↵
    Scale for pattern ⟨1.0000⟩: ↵
    Angle for pattern ⟨0⟩: ↵
    Select hatch boundaries or RETURN for direct hatch option,
    Select objects: ↵
    Retain polyline? ⟨N⟩ ↵
    From point: *(pick the first point at a corner of the right square in Figure 24-13)*
    Arc/Close/Length/Undo/⟨Next point⟩: *(pick point 2)*
    Arc/Close/Length/Undo/⟨Next point⟩: *(pick point 3)*
    Arc/Close/Length/Undo/⟨Next point⟩: *(pick point 4)*
    Arc/Close/Length/Undo/⟨Next point⟩: **C** ↵

Figure 24-13. Using the direct hatching option.

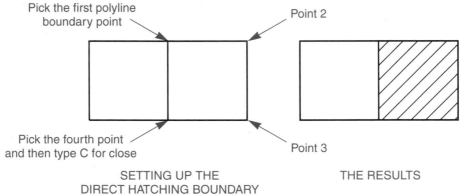

SETTING UP THE
DIRECT HATCHING BOUNDARY   THE RESULTS

You can draw another polyline boundary or you can press ENTER to have the hatch drawn in the boundary that you just finished:

    From point or RETURN to apply hatch: ↵
    Command:

You do not have to draw a hatch pattern in a predefined area. You can draw a hatch pattern anyplace using the direct hatching method. The hatch pattern can be drawn with or without the polyline boundary, as shown in Figure 24-14.

Figure 24-14. You can draw a
hatch pattern with or without
the polyline boundary
displayed.

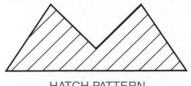

HATCH PATTERN   HATCH PATTERN
WITHOUT THE BOUNDARY   WITH THE BOUNDARY

The hatch pattern is nonassociative

If you remember, in dimensioning an associative dimension automatically changes to match the object when the object is edited. Patterns drawn with the HATCH command are nonassociative. This means that if you pick only the hatch boundary to edit, the hatch pattern does not change with it. For example, if you pick a hatch boundary to scale, only the boundary is scaled while the pattern remains the same. You need to select both the boundary and the pattern before editing.

Making individual line hatch patterns

When you use the HATCH command and draw a hatch pattern using any of the designated hatch names, the pattern is drawn as a block. This means that the entire hatch pattern acts as one object. So, if you pick one line of the pattern to erase, for example, the entire hatch pattern is erased. You can make each line of the hatch pattern act as an individual object by typing an asterisk (*) before the hatch pattern name:

```
Command: HATCH ↵
Pattern (? or name/U, style) ⟨ANSI31⟩: *ANSI31 ↵
```

The rest of the command sequence works as previously discussed. Now, each line in the hatch pattern is a single object. This allows you to edit the lines individually. You must use a selection method that includes all of the lines in the pattern if you want to edit them together. The individual line hatch pattern remains as default until changed, so be sure to change back to a pattern name without the asterisk if you want to draw the next hatch pattern as a block. After a hatch pattern has been drawn, the EXPLODE command may be used to make individual objects out of the hatch pattern element.

EXERCISE 24-1

❑ Load AutoCAD and open PRODR2.
❑ Draw all object lines on layer 0-7.
❑ Create a new layer for hatch lines with color magenta. Name the layer HATCH.
❑ Practice using the HATCH command by drawing the objects from the following figures with the specified patterns:
   ❑ Figure 24-10. Set the scale as shown, use ANSI31, and angle 0.
   ❑ Figure 24-11. The first object is a circle. The second object is a square drawn using the LINE command and Close the last line. The third object is a square drawn using the PLINE command and Close the last polyline segment. Use ANSI31, scale 1, and angle 0.
   ❑ Figure 24-13. Draw the figure shown on the left using any combination of interconnecting lines. Hatch only the right side using the direct hatching option. Use ANSI31, scale 1, and angle 0.
   ❑ Figure 24-14. Use the direct hatching option to draw shapes that are similar to the examples. Draw one with the polyline boundary omitted and the other with the polyline boundary shown. Use ANSI31, scale 1, and angle 0.
❑ Save the drawing as A:EX24-1 and quit.

Hatching around text

AutoCAD automatically places an imaginary box around the text in a hatch boundary. The text must also be selected as an element of the hatch boundary for this to work properly. Hatch patterns are not allowed to enter. An example is the bar graph shown in Figure 24-15. Always place the text before hatching the area. For this to work, be sure you pick the object and the text:

```
Command: HATCH ⏎
Pattern (? or name/U,style) ⟨current⟩: ⏎
Scale for pattern ⟨1.0000⟩: ⏎
Angle for pattern ⟨0⟩: ⏎
Select hatch boundaries or RETURN for diroot hatch option,
Select objects: (pick the object to be hatched)
n found
Select objects: (pick the text to be hatched around)
Select objects: ⏎
```

Figure 24-15.   Hatching around text.

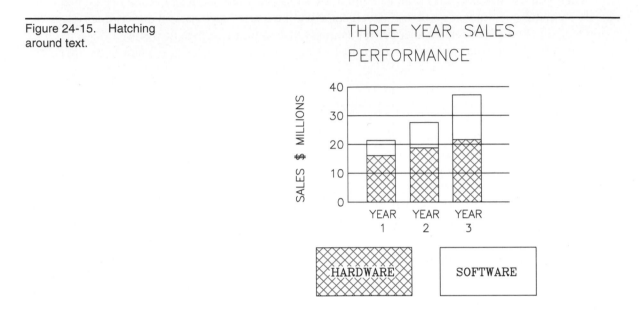

The previous example allowed you to pick the object and the text. You can also window both for this to work.

Drawing your own simple hatch patterns

When you enter HATCH at the Command: prompt, one of the options is U. This allows you to provide angle, spacing, and single or double specifications for a very simple hatch pattern, Figure 24-16. The commands are as follows:

```
Command: HATCH ⏎
Pattern (? or name/U,style) ⟨current⟩: U ⏎
Angle of crosshatch lines ⟨0⟩: (specify an angle or pick two points on the screen; press
    ENTER to accept the default angle)
Spacing between lines ⟨1.000⟩: (type the spacing desired or pick two points on the screen to
    define the spacing; press ENTER to accept the default spacing)
Double hatch area? ⟨N⟩ (type Y and press ENTER for double hatch lines, or press ENTER
    for the single hatch default)
Select hatch boundaries or RETURN for direct hatch option,
Select objects: (pick the object to be hatched)
n found
Select objects: ⏎
Command:
```

Figure 24-16.   Using the HATCH command's U option.

0 ANGLE
.125 SINGLE HATCH

45° .125 SPACE
SINGLE HATCH

45° .125 SPACE
DOUBLE HATCH

45° .25 SPACE
DOUBLE HATCH

A relationship exists between the hatch line spacing in model space and paper space. This relationship is controlled by the scale factor. If you are planning to plot a drawing at a 1/2″ = 1″ (HALF) scale then the scale factor is 2. This means that one model space unit is equal to 2 paper space units. AutoCAD automatically controls this line spacing when you enter a line spacing of 1XP:

Spacing between lines ⟨1.0000⟩: **1XP** ↵

This was discussed earlier in this chapter. Model space and paper space are explained in Chapter 26.

PROFESSIONAL TIP

Sometimes the HATCH spacing is too wide or too close. Select ERASE Last or Undo to remove the pattern. Try a smaller or larger value.

Using the HATCH Style option

An object may have several areas enclosed within each other, Figure 24-17. The HATCH command's Style option allows you to decide which features are to be hatched and which are not. The three style options are:
- **N.** Normal style; hatches every other feature.
- **O.** Hatches outermost feature area only.
- **I.** Ignores all interior features and hatches the entire object.

Figure 24-17.   This object has three enclosed features.

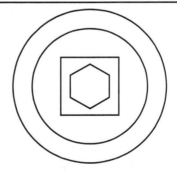

Any one of the options may be chosen. Type the desired pattern followed by the option, and separated by a comma. For example:

Command: **HATCH** ↵
Pattern (? or name/U,style): **NET3,N** ↵
Scale for pattern ⟨1.000⟩: **2** *(for example)* ↵
Angle for pattern ⟨0⟩: ↵
Select hatch boundaries or RETURN for direct hatch option,
Select objects: **W** ↵
First corner: *(pick first corner)*
Other corner: *(pick second corner)*
n found
Select objects: ↵
Command:

Figure 24-18 shows the results of using each HATCH style option on the object in Figure 24-17.

Figure 24-18.   The HATCH command's Style option allows you to hatch enclosed features differently. Shown here is the object from Figure 24-17.

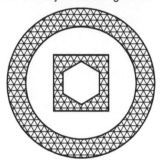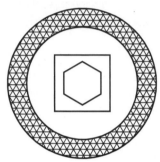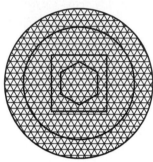

PROFESSIONAL TIP

You can fill an area solid by specifying a dense pattern scale or close line spacing. Set the scale or line spacing equal to the width of the plotter pen. This ensures a solid fill without excessive use of plot or regeneration time. However, keep this type of application to a minimum because it slows down regeneration and plot time.

EXERCISE 24-2

❏ Load AutoCAD and open PRODR2.
❏ Draw all object lines on layer 0-7.
❏ Create a new layer for hatch lines. Set a magenta color. Name this layer HATCH.
❏ Practice using the HATCH command by drawing the objects from the following figures with the patterns as shown.
  ❏ Figure 24-15. Draw the "HARDWARE" and "SOFTWARE" legend boxes to practice hatching around text.
  ❏ Figure 24-16.
  ❏ Figure 24-18.
❏ Save the drawing as A:EX24-2 and quit.

AUTOMATIC BOUNDARY HATCHING   AUG 2

So far you have seen how the HATCH command is used to place hatch patterns inside defined areas. In addition, you were cautioned about hatching adjacent areas, as demonstrated in Figure 24-12. It is important that the hatch boundary be clearly defined, otherwise strange things could happen. The BHATCH command simplifies the hatching process by automatically hatching any enclosed area. All you have to do with the BHATCH command is pick inside an enclosed area rather than picking the entities to be hatched or drawing a polyline boundary as you did with the HATCH command. The BHATCH command creates associative hatch patterns by default, but can be set to create nonassociative patterns. *Associative hatch patterns* can be edited with ease, since they update automatically when the boundary is edited. This means that if the boundary is stretched, scaled or otherwise edited, the hatch pattern automatically updates to fill the new area with the original hatch pattern scale, angle and other settings. Also associative hatch patterns can be edited using the HATCHEDIT command to be discussed later. The BHATCH command may be typed at the Command: prompt, or by picking Hatch... in the Hatch option of the Draw pull-down menu. Entering the BHATCH command displays the "Boundary Hatch" dialog box shown in Figure 24-19.

Figure 24-19. The "Boundary Hatch" dialog box.

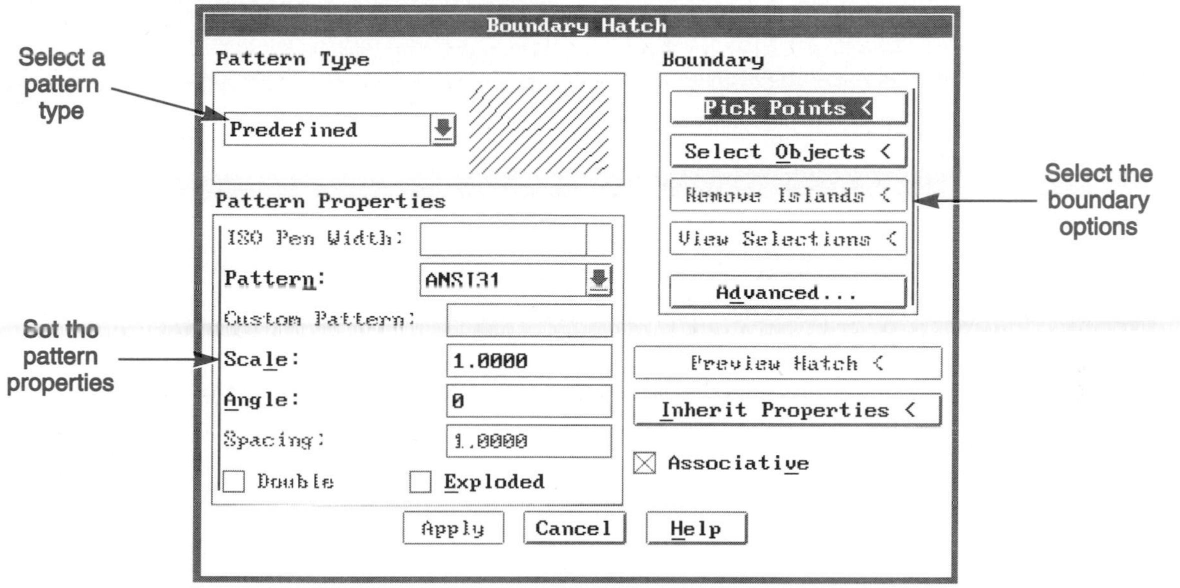

The "Boundary Hatch" dialog box contains the following elements:
- **Pattern Type.** The Pattern Type area has the Pattern Type list and an image tile at the right. The Pattern Type list has three options described as follows:
  - **Predefined–**This is AutoCAD's standard hatch patterns that are available in the ACAD.PAT file. A Predefined pattern is displayed in the image tile.

    When the Predefined patterns are active, picking on the image tile at the right allows you to scroll through the available AutoCAD hatch patterns until you find the one you want. This is a convenient way to see and select a desired hatch pattern. The patterns that display in the image tile are the same ones that are shown in Figure 24-9.
  - **User-defined–**When you pick the User-defined option, the image tile goes away. This selection allows you to draw a U style pattern using the current linetype just as described earlier and displayed in Figure 24-16.
  - **Custom–**This is used for you to access a custom pattern defined in a pattern file other than the ACAD.PAT file.
- **Pattern Properties.** This is the area of the "Boundary Hatch" dialog box where you set the properties that are related to the selected hatch pattern. These are the features:
  - **ISO Pen Width:–**This is a list that is available when a predefined ISO pattern is selected. The list shown in Figure 24-20 allows you to pick a desired pen width for ISO pattern scaling.

Figure 24-20. Pick the desired pen width for ISO pattern scaling from the list (shown here highlighted).

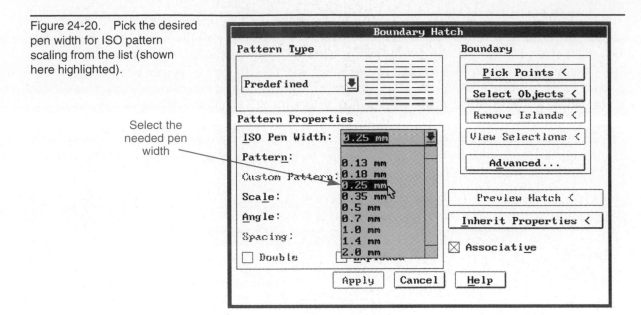

Select the needed pen width

• **Pattern:**–This list provides an easy way to access the predefined patterns. When you pick a pattern name from this list, the Pattern Type image tile automatically displays a representation of the pattern for you to see as shown in Figure 24-21.

Figure 24-21. The Pattern Type image tile automatically displays a representation of the pattern selected from the list. (The list and the image tile are shown here highlighted.)

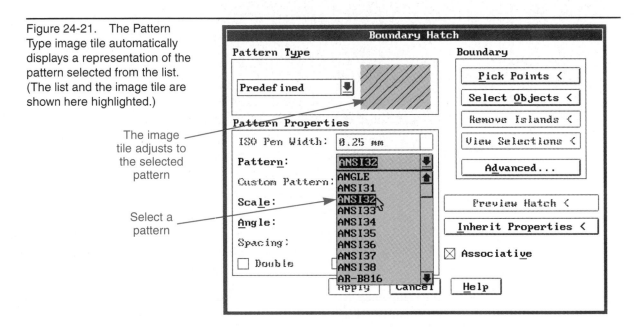

The image tile adjusts to the selected pattern

Select a pattern

• **Custom Pattern:**–This is available only if Custom is selected in the Pattern Type. This allows you to enter a custom pattern name in the text box.
• **Scale:**–This text box allows you to set the pattern scale as discussed earlier and displayed in Figure 24-10. AutoCAD stores the hatch pattern scale in the HPSCALE system variable.
• **Angle:**–This text box allows you to set the pattern angle as discussed earlier in this chapter. AutoCAD stores the hatch pattern angle in the HPANG system variable.
• **Spacing:**–This is the text box available if User-defined is selected in the Pattern Type area and it allows you to set user-defined hatch spacing as explained earlier and shown in Figure 24-16. AutoCAD stores the hatch pattern spacing in the HSPACE system variable.

- **Double**—Pick this check box to activate double hatch lines for a user-defined hatch pattern as shown in Figure 24-16. AutoCAD stores this setting in the HPDOUBLE system variable.
- **Explode**—Pick this check box if you want the hatch pattern to be drawn with individual line objects rather that as a block pattern. When this box is checked, an asterisk is placed in front of the pattern name in the HPNAME system variable.
- **Boundary.** This area of the "Boundary Hatch" dialog box controls the way you hatch objects. The features are described as follows:
    - **Pick Points** ⟨—Everything you have done so far with the "Boundary Hatch" dialog box has prepared you to draw a hatch pattern. Refer back to Figure 24-13 and the discussion about using the HATCH command's polyline boundary that was used to hatch the right side of the object. You can hatch the same feature using BHATCH just by picking inside the area to be hatched. The Pick Points ⟨ button is highlighted as default. Press ENTER or use the cursor and pick this button. The drawing now returns and the following prompts are displayed:

        Select internal point: *(pick a point inside the area to be hatched)*
        Analyzing the selected data…
        Analyzing internal islands…
        Select internal point: *(pick an internal point of another object or* ENTER*)*
        Command:

        When you press ENTER, the "Boundary Hatch" dialog box returns. You can make adjustments to the hatch pattern, such as change the pattern, scale, or angle. You can also preview the pattern. The Preview Hatch ⟨ button is explained later. Pick the Apply button or press ENTER. Apply is highlighted by default. The feature is automatically hatched, as shown in Figure 24-22. When you are at the Select internal point: prompt, you can type U or UNDO to undo the last selection just in case you picked the wrong area. You can also undo the hatch pattern by typing U at the Command: prompt after the pattern is drawn. However, the preview hatch allows you to look at the hatch while inside the BHATCH command to help save time.

Figure 24-22.   Applying a hatch to a feature.

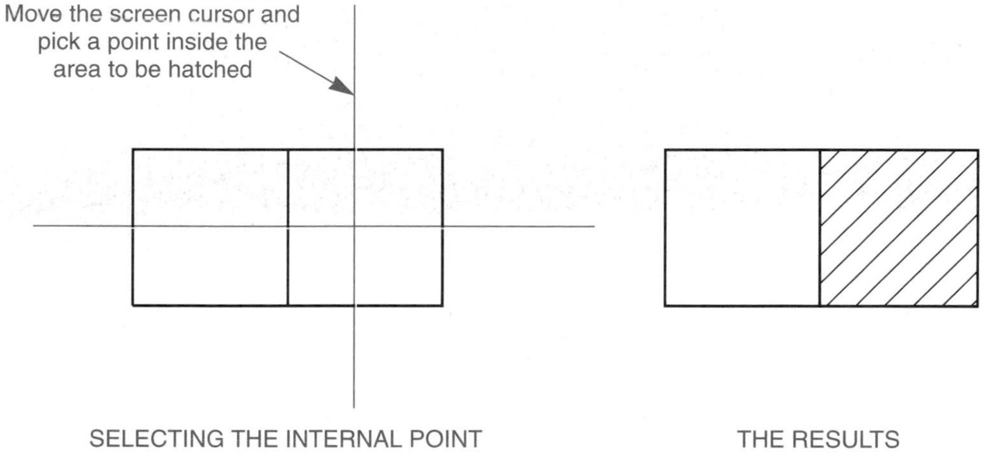

Move the screen cursor and pick a point inside the area to be hatched

SELECTING THE INTERNAL POINT   THE RESULTS

- **Select Objects** ⟨–This button is used if you have items such as circles, polygons, or closed polylines that you want to hatch by picking the object rather than picking inside the object. This works especially well if the object to be hatched is crossed by other objects such as the graph lines that cross the bars in the bar graph shown in Figure 24-23. Picking a point inside the bar results in the hatch displayed in Figure 24-23A. You could pick inside each individual area of each bar, but this might be time consuming. If the bars were drawn using a closed polyline, all you would have to do is use the Select Objects ⟨ button to pick each bar for hatching as shown in Figure 24-23B.

Figure 24-23.   A–Applying a hatch pattern to objects that cross each other using the Pick Points ⟨ button. B–Applying a hatch pattern to a closed polygon using the Select Objects ⟨ button.

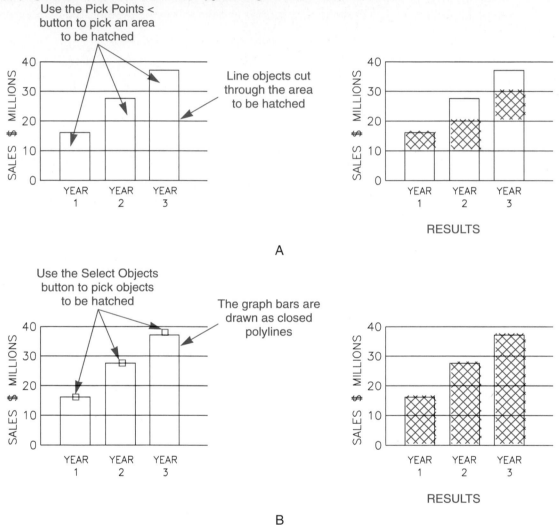

The Select Objects ⟨ button may also be used to pick an object inside an area to be hatched if you want it excluded from the hatch pattern. An example of this is the text shown inside the hatch area of Figure 24-24. When you pick the Select Objects ⟨ button, the following prompts are issued:

Select objects: *(pick or select an object or objects)*
Select objects: *(pick the object or objects to be removed from the hatch)*
Select objects: ↵

The "Boundary Hatch" dialog box returns. Preview the hatch, make any desired changes, or press ENTER to apply the hatch.

Figure 24-24.   Using the Select Objects ⟨ button to exclude an object from the hatch pattern.

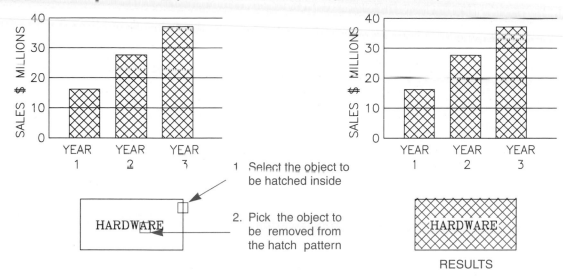

- **Remove Islands** ⟨–An *island* is defined as a closed area inside of a hatch area. When you use the Pick Points ⟨ button to hatch an internal area, islands are automatically left unhatched, as shown in Figure 24-25A. This may be the results you desire. However, if you want the island to be hatched, follow these steps:
  1. Use the Pick Points ⟨ button and select an internal point, as shown in Figure 24-25.
  2. When the "Boundary Hatch" dialog box returns, pick the Remove Islands ⟨ button which is now active. The following prompts are now issued:

     Select island to remove: *(pick an island or islands to remove)*
     ⟨Select island to remove⟩/Undo: ↵

The "Boundary Hatch" dialog box returns. You can preview the hatch pattern, modify the hatch pattern, or pick the Apply button. The results of removing an island is shown in Figure 24-25B.

Figure 24-25.   A–Using the <u>P</u>ick Points ⟨ button to hatch an internal area leaves islands unhatched. B–After picking an internal point, use the Remove Island ⟨ button and pick an island. This allows the island to be hatched.

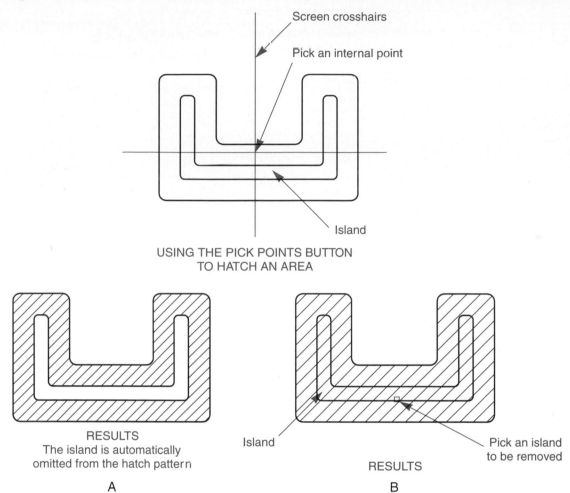

USING THE PICK POINTS BUTTON
TO HATCH AN AREA

RESULTS
The island is automatically
omitted from the hatch pattern

A

RESULTS

B

- **Vie<u>w</u> Selection** ⟨–You can instruct AutoCAD to let you see the boundaries of selected objects. The Vie<u>w</u> Selections ⟨ button is available after picking objects to be hatched. Pick this button to have the drawing displayed with the hatch boundaries highlighted. Look at the highlighted boundary and then pick the Continue button to return to the "Boundary Hatch" dialog box.
- **A<u>d</u>vanced…**–Picking the A<u>d</u>vanced… button accesses the "Advanced Options" subdialog box which is explained later in this chapter.
- **Preview Ha<u>t</u>ch** ⟨–Pick the Preview Ha<u>t</u>ch ⟨ button if you want to look at the hatch pattern before you apply it to the drawing. This feature allows you to make changes to the hatch pattern before it is drawn. AutoCAD temporarily places the hatch pattern on your drawing and displays the "Boundary Hatch Continue" dialog box. Press ENTER or pick Continue. The "Boundary Hatch" dialog box is displayed again. Use it to change the hatch pattern as needed, preview the hatch again, or pick the Apply button to have the hatch pattern drawn.
- **<u>I</u>nherit Properties** ⟨–If you pick this button, AutoCAD allows you to select a previously drawn hatch pattern and use it as the current hatch pattern settings. For example, you may be working with a particular hatch pattern and then want to draw a different one with the same hatch pattern settings as the one you drew previously. Pick the <u>I</u>nherit Properties ⟨ button to choose the desired previously drawn pattern and have AutoCAD automatically make all current hatch settings the same. The prompts are as follows:

Select hatch object: *(pick the desired hatch pattern)*

The "Boundary Hatch" dialog box is displayed with the selected hatch pattern settings.

*   **Associative**–This is a check box. The default is to have associative ON with a check in the box. As discussed earlier, an associative hatch pattern is automatically updated to match any changes to the boundary area, such as scaling, rotating, moving, or copying. Pick this box to remove the associative hatching feature.

EXERCISE 24-3

❑ Open PRODR2.

❑ Use the LINE command to draw the object to be hatched similar to the following example. The exact dimensions are up to you. Be sure each area of the object is closed, but the line sequence is up to you.

❑ Use the BHATCH command to make a full section of the object as displayed at the right. Use the ANSI31 hatch pattern.

❑ Draw the bar graph shown in Figure 24-24 without text (except for HARDWARE inside the legend box). Use a closed polyline to draw the graph bars and the box around the HARDWARE legend. Use the BHATCH Select Objects option to select the bars for hatching. Use the same option to hatch the area inside the HARDWARE legend box without hatching through the text.

❑ Use closed polylines to draw the object at the left in Figure 24-25A. Copy the drawing to a position directly below. Use the Pick Points ⟨ option to hatch the top object as shown in Figure 24-25A. Use the Pick Points ⟨ button again and the Remove Islands ⟨ button to hatch the bottom object as shown in Figure 24-25B.

❑ Preview each hatch pattern before you apply to be sure the results are what you expected.

❑ Enter the BHATCH command and pick the Inherit Properties ⟨ button. Pick a hatch pattern on your drawing that is different from the current hatch pattern settings. Notice that the name and settings of the selected pattern becomes current.

❑ Save the drawing as A:EX24-3.

OBJECT TO BE HATCHED   APPLIED HATCH

Correcting errors in the boundary

The BHATCH command works well unless you have an error in the hatch boundary. The most common error is a gap in the boundary. This may be very small and difficult to detect. However, AutoCAD is quick to let you know by displaying the "Boundary Definition Error" alert box shown in Figure 24-26. Pick the OK button then return to the drawing to find and correct the problem.

Figure 24-27 shows an object where the corner does not close. The error is too small to see on the screen, but using the ZOOM command reveals the problem.

Another error message occurs when you pick a point outside the boundary area. When this happens, you also get the "Boundary Definition Error" alert box. All you have to do is pick OK and select a new point that is inside the boundary you want hatched.

Figure 24-26.   A "Boundary Definition Error" alert box is displayed if problems occur in your hatching operation.

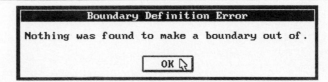

Figure 24-27.   Using the Look at it button to find the source of a hatching error.

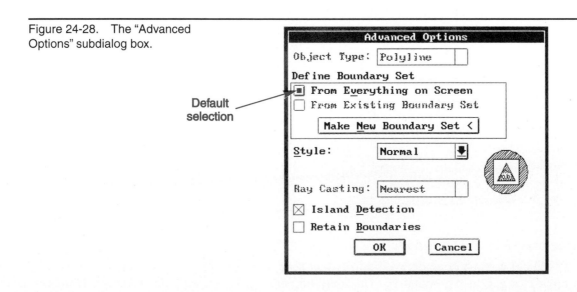

LOOK AT THE BOUNDARY ERROR   HATCH AFTER THE ERROR IS FIXED

Improving boundary hatching speed using Advanced Options...

In most situations, boundary hatching works well, and with satisfactory speed. Normally the BHATCH command evaluates the entire drawing that is visible on the screen when establishing a boundary around the internal point that you pick. This process can take some time on a large drawing. You can improve the hatching speed, or resolve other problems by picking Advanced Options... in the "Boundary Hatch" dialog box. This displays the "Advanced Options" subdialog box shown in Figure 24-28. Notice in the Define Boundary Set area that the From Everything on Screen radio button is active. This is the default which evaluates everything on the screen for hatching.

Figure 24-28.   The "Advanced Options" subdialog box.

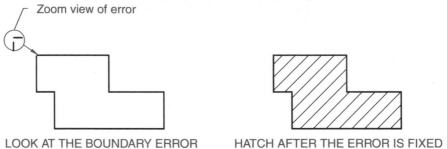

If you want to limit what AutoCAD evaluates when hatching you can define the boundary area so the BHATCH command only considers a specified portion of the drawing. To do this, pick the Make New Boundary Set ⟨ button in the "Advanced Options" subdialog box and then use a window to select the features of the object to be hatched, as demonstrated in Figure 24-29:

Select objects: *(pick the first window corner)*

Notice that the window is automatic if you move the box to the right of the first pick point.

Other corner: *(pick the second corner of the window)*
Select objects: ↵
Analyzing the selected data…

Figure 24-29.   The boundary set limits what AutoCAD evaluates during a boundary hatching operation.

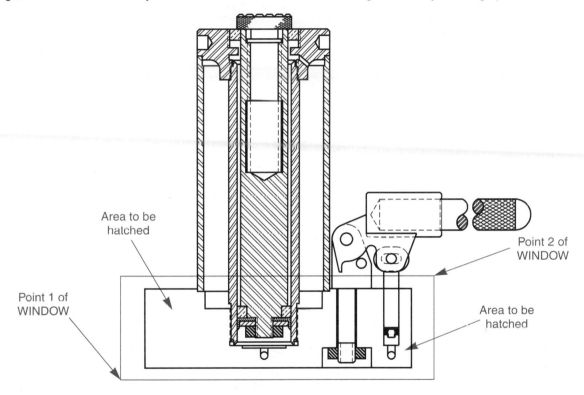

Now the "Advanced Options" subdialog box returns and the From Existing Boundary Set ⟨ radio button is active, as shown in Figure 24-30. Pick the OK button and the "Boundary Hatch" dialog box appears. Use the Pick Points ⟨ button to pick the areas to be hatched. The results are shown in Figure 24-31.

You can make as many boundary sets as you wish; however, the last one made remains current until another is created. The Retain Boundaries check box becomes selectable as soon as a boundary set is made. Checking this box allows you to keep the boundary of a hatched area as a polyline, and continues to save these as polylines every time you create a boundary area. The default is no check in this box so the hatched boundaries are not saved as polylines.

Figure 24-30.   When the From Existing Boundary Set option is selected, AutoCAD only evaluates objects in the boundary for the hatch.

Now the current selection

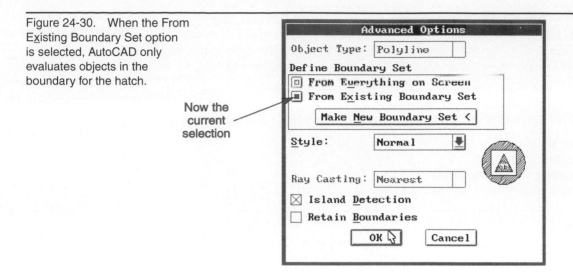

Figure 24-31.   Results of hatching the drawing in Figure 24-29 after selecting a boundary set.

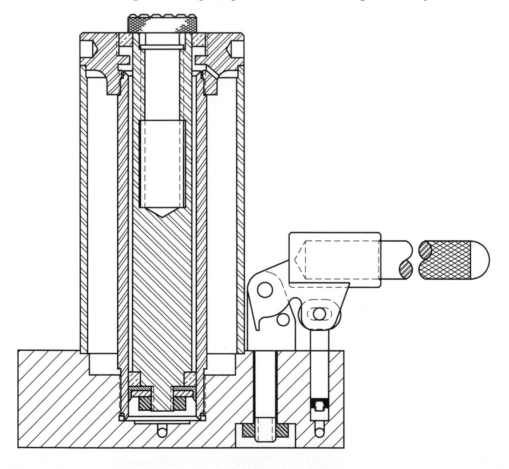

Directing the way AutoCAD selects a boundary for hatching

When you pick an internal point for hatching an area, AutoCAD sends an imaginary line, by default, to the nearest object and then turns left in an effort to make a boundary around the object. This is known as *ray casting*. If the first ray hits an internal area or internal text, a boundary definition error is given. For example, look at the internal cavity in Figure 24-32.

Figure 24-32.   Ray casting affects the objects selected for boundary hatching. If the first ray hits an internal area or internal text, a boundary definition error is given.

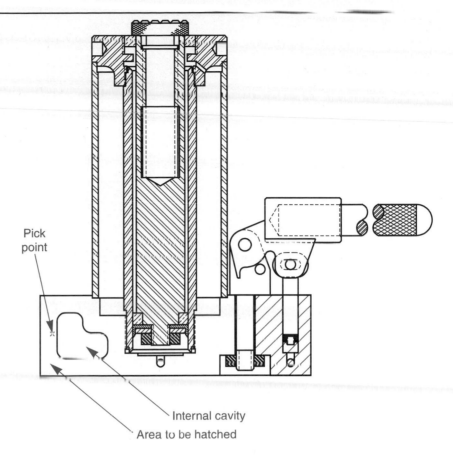

Pick point

Internal cavity

Area to be hatched

A Boundary Definition Error occurred because AutoCAD made a boundary around the cavity and could not continue with the desired hatch if the Island Detection box is not checked. You can control the way AutoCAD does ray casting. Notice in Figure 24-28 the Ray Casting: edit box specifies "Nearest." This is the default, but you can change it by picking the down arrow to access the ray casting list. Figure 24-33 shows the ray casting options: +X, –X, +Y, and –Y. Selecting one of these determines which way the first ray is cast. For example, selecting a –X value for ray casting causes the same pick point in Figure 24-32 to make the correct boundary definition. Picking this point followed by picking inside the cavity area results in the desired hatching shown in Figure 24-34.

Figure 24-33.   A–The Ray Casting: list box. B–Ray casting directions.

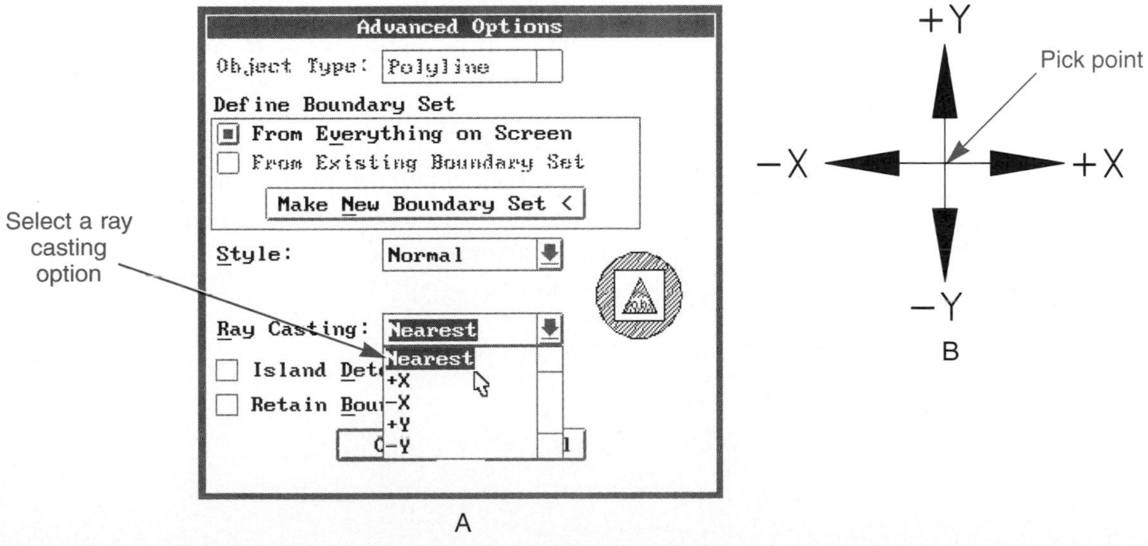

Advanced Options

Object Type: Polyline

Define Boundary Set

☑ From Everything on Screen
☐ From Existing Boundary Set

Make New Boundary Set <

Style: Normal ▼

Ray Casting: Nearest ▼
              Nearest
☐ Island Det +X
☐ Retain Bou –X
              +Y
              –Y

Select a ray casting option

+Y

Pick point

–X ◄———————► +X

–Y

B

A

Figure 24-34. The results of
using the appropriate ray
casting selection on the
drawing in Figure 24-29.

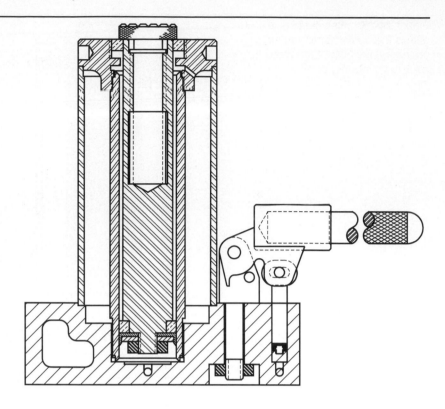

PROFESSIONAL TIP

There are a number of techniques that can help save you time when hatching, especially with large and complex drawings. These include the following:

✓ Zoom in on the area to be hatched to make it easier for you to define the boundary. When you zoom into an area to be hatched, the hatch process is much faster because AutoCAD doesn't have to search the entire drawing to find the hatch boundaries.

✓ Preview the hatch before you apply it. This allows you to easily make last minute adjustments.

✓ Turn off layers where there are lines or text that might interfere with your ability to accurately define hatch boundaries.

✓ Create boundary sets of small areas within a complex drawing to help save time.

Accessing Hatch Style options through the "Boundary Hatch" dialog box

Earlier in this chapter, you learned about using the Style option in the HATCH command. This feature allows you to decide which features are to be hatched and which are not. Refer back to Figures 24-17 and 24-18 for examples. You can create the same hatch styles through the "Boundary Hatch" dialog box. To do this, pick the A*d*vanced... button to display the "Advanced Options" subdialog box. Now, pick the down arrow in the *S*tyle: list to get the options. When you pick one of the options, the image tile to the right displays the expected results. The selection and representative image tile for each option is shown in Figure 24-35. The options are reviewed as follows:

• **Normal.** Hatches every other feature.
• **Outer.** Hatches the outermost feature only.
• **Ignore.** Ignores all interior features and hatches the entire object.

Figure 24-35.   Shown are the three options for hatch style. Notice how the image tile (shown here highlighted) changes to reflect how the hatch will appear on the drawing.

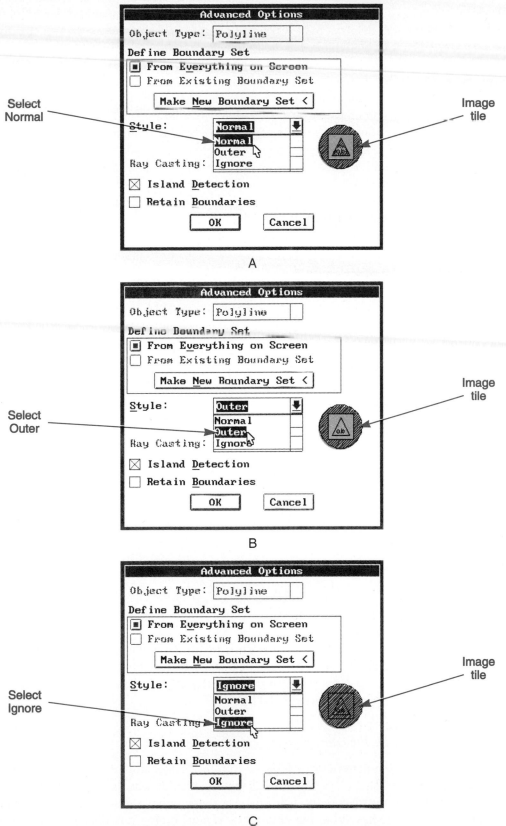

Island Detection and Retaining Boundaries

Earlier in this chapter, you were introduced to hatching around or through islands as shown in Figure 24-25 as associated with the Remove Islands ⟨ button in the "Boundary Hatch" dialog box. Look at Figure 24-30 which displays the "Advanced Options" subdialog box. Notice that the Island Detection check box is active by default. This setting leaves internal objects (islands) unhatched. Pick the check box and remove the check if you want to hatch through islands.

Notice also in Figure 24-30 that the Retain Boundaries check box is not checked by default. When you use the BHATCH command and pick an internal area to be hatched, AutoCAD automatically creates a temporary boundary around the area. If the Retain Boundaries check box is unchecked then the temporary boundaries are automatically removed when the hatch is complete. However, if you check the Retain Boundaries check box then the hatch boundaries are kept when the hatch is completed. Additionally, when the Retain Boundaries check box is checked, the Object Type: edit list, at the top of the "Advanced Options" subdialog box is activated, as shown in Figure 24-36. Notice that the Object Type: list has two options: Polyline and Region. Polyline is the default. This means that the boundary is a polyline object around the hatch area. If you select the Region option, then the hatch boundary is the hatched region. A region is a closed two-dimensional area.

Figure 24-36.   There are two object type options for the boundary.

Select the boundary object type

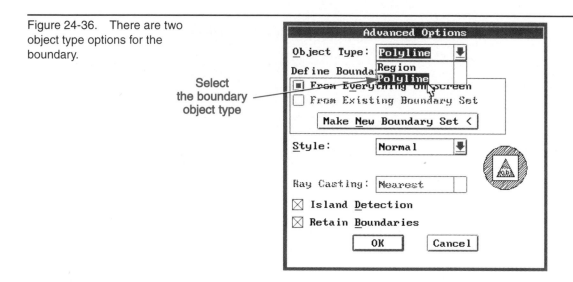

EDITING HATCH PATTERNS

AUG 5

You can edit hatch boundaries and hatch patterns with GRIPS and editing commands such as ERASE, COPY, MOVE, ROTATE, and SCALE. If a hatch pattern is associative, then what ever you do to the hatch boundary is automatically done to the associated hatch pattern. As explained earlier, a hatch pattern is associative if the Associative check box in the "Boundary Hatch" dialog box is active. A convenient way to edit the characteristics of a hatch pattern is by using the HATCHEDIT command. You can access this command by picking HatchEd: in the MODIFY screen menu, pick Edit Hatch… in the Modify pull-down menu, or type HATCHEDIT as follows:

Command: **HATCHEDIT** ↵
Select hatch object: *(pick the hatch pattern to edit)*

When you select a hatch pattern or patterns to edit, the "Hatchedit" dialog box shown in Figure 24-37 is displayed. The "Hatchedit" dialog box has the same features as the "Boundary Hatch" dialog box, except that only the items that control hatch pattern characteristics are available. The features that are available work just like they do in the "Boundary Hatch" dialog box discussed earlier. You can change the pattern type, scale, angle, explode the pattern, remove the associative qualities, inherit properties of an existing hatch pattern, or use the "Advanced Options" dialog box to edit the hatch pattern.

Figure 24-37. The "Hatchedit" dialog box is used to edit hatch patterns. Notice that only the options related to the hatch are available.

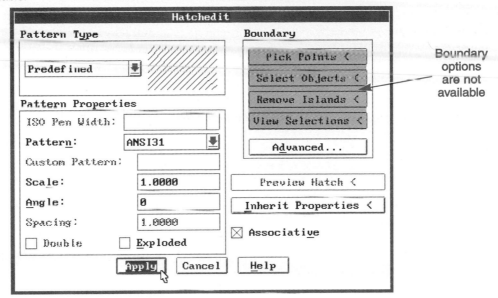

EXERCISE 24-4

❑ Open PRODR2.
❑ Draw each of the objects displayed at each of the A positions shown below.
❑ Be sure the hatch pattern is associative.
❑ Copy the objects at the A positions to B and C positions.
❑ Use the HATCHEDIT command to change the hatch pattern of the A objects to the representation found at B and C positions.
❑ Adjust the hatch pattern, scale, angle, and style to get the results shown below.
❑ Save as A:EX24-4.

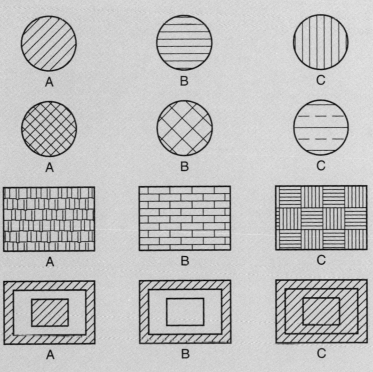

DRAWING OBJECTS THAT ARE FILLED IN SOLID $\boxed{\text{AUG 2}}$

Chapter 7 introduced how polyline and trace segments may be filled solid when the Fill mode is On. They are drawn as an outline with Fill turned Off. The SOLID command works in much the same manner except that it fills objects or shapes that are already drawn, or fills areas that are simply defined by points you pick. Fill in the sectioned area rather than use a hatch pattern. It may also be used to accent certain features or objects on a drawing. The SOLID command is found in the DRAW 1 screen menu, or SOLID can be typed at the Command: prompt. It prompts you to pick a point. If the object is rectangular, pick the corners in the sequence numbered in Figure 24-38. The command format is as follows:

Command: **SOLID** ↵
First point: *(pick point 1)*
Second point: *(pick point 2)*
Third point: *(pick point 3)*
Fourth point: *(pick point 4)*
Third point:

Figure 24-38.   Using the SOLID command. Select the points in the order shown.

Notice that AutoCAD prompts you for another third point after the first four. This prompt allows you to fill in additional parts of the same object, if needed. Press ENTER when you want to stop, or continue, as shown in Figure 24-39.

Figure 24-39.   The SOLID command allows you to enter a second "third" point (point 5 here) after entering the fourth point.

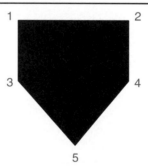

Different types of SOLID arrangements can be drawn by altering the numbering sequence. See Figure 24-40. Also, the SOLID command can be used to draw shapes without prior use of the LINE or PLINE commands; simply pick the points.

Figure 24-40.   Using a different numbering sequence for the SOLID command will give you different results.

PROFESSIONAL TIP

It is very difficult and time-consuming to fill a circle using the SOLID command. The best solution to this problem is to use the DOUGHNUT command and set a 0 inside diameter. You could also use the HATCH command with a dense pattern. An irregular shape such as a lake on a map may be filled in solid to denote water. This is done by drawing the outline of the lake using lines, arcs, or polylines. Then select a dense pattern. If lines and arcs are used, a window selection is best. If polylines and polyline arcs are used, pick any point on the polyline. The lake must be a full enclosure. Keep in mind that many solids and dense hatches require extensive regeneration and plot time. Make check plots with the Fill mode off.

EXERCISE 24-5

❑ Open PRODR2.
❑ Draw all object lines on layer 0-7.
❑ Create a new layer named SOLID-MAGENTA and draw all solids on this layer.
❑ Practice using the SOLID command by drawing the objects shown in Figures 24-38, 24-39, and 24-40.
❑ Save the drawing as A:EX24-5.

CHAPTER TEST

Write your answers in the spaces provided.

1. Give the command and entries required to use the ANSI37 hatch pattern with double scale to hatch the inside of a given circle:

   Command:_____

   Pattern (? or name/U,style): _____

   Scale for pattern ⟨1.0000⟩: _____

   Angle for pattern ⟨0⟩: _____

   Select hatch boundaries or RETURN for direct hatch option,_____

   Select objects:_____

   Select objects:_____

   Command:_____

2. Give the command and entries needed to draw your own hatch pattern. Set a 30° hatch angle, 1.5 spacing, and single hatch lines pattern to hatch the inside of a rectangle drawn with polylines:

   Command:_____

   Pattern (? or name/U,style): _____

   Angle of crosshatch lines ⟨0⟩: _____

   Spacing between lines ⟨1.0000⟩:_____

   Double hatch area? ⟨N⟩: _____

   Select hatch boundaries or RETURN for direct hatch option,_____

   Select objects:_____

   Select objects:_____

   Command:_____

3. Given a square within a square, provide the command and entries used to hatch between the two squares (the outermost area). Use the default values of the ANSI31 hatch pattern:

   Command:_____

   Pattern (? or name/U,style):_____

   Scale for pattern ⟨1.0000⟩:_____

   Angle for pattern ⟨0⟩:_____

   Select hatch boundaries or RETURN for direct hatch option,_____

   Select objects:_____

   First corner:_____

   Other corner:_____

   Select objects:_____

   Command:_____

4. Give the command and entries needed to fill in a rectangular area. Identify specific corners on the rectangle as you give the prompts. For example, specify "upper-right corner."

   Command:_____

   First point:_____

   Second point:_____

   Third point:_____

   Fourth point:_____

   Third point:_____

5. Give the command and responses to show a list and description of all the hatch patterns:

   Command:_____

   Pattern (? or name/U,style):_____

   Pattern(s) to list ⟨*⟩:_____

6. Give the command and responses used to hatch an object while providing an imaginary box around text located inside the hatch area.

   Command:_____

   Pattern (? or name/U,style) ⟨*current*⟩:_____

   Scale for pattern ⟨1.0000⟩:_____

   Angle for pattern ⟨0⟩:_____

   Select hatch boundaries or RETURN for direct hatch option,_____

   Select objects:_____

   Select objects:_____

   Select objects:_____

For Questions 7-12, name the type of section identified in each of the following statements:

7. Half of the object is removed; the cutting-plane line generally cuts completely through along the center plane._____

   _____

8. Used primarily on symmetrical objects; the cutting-plane line cuts through one-quarter of the object._____

   _____

9. The cutting-plane line is staggered through features that do not lie in a straight line. _____
_____

10. The section is rotated in place to clarify the contour of the object. _____

11. This section is revolved and removed from the object. The location of the section is normally
identified with a cutting-plane line. _____

12. Remove a small portion of the view to clarify an internal feature. _____

13. AutoCAD's standard section line symbols are called _____ _____.

14. To use the same hatch pattern again, you must _____.

15. Give the code and results of using the three HATCH Style options: _____
_____
_____
_____

16. In which pull-down menu is Hatch located? _____

17. Name the command that lets you automatically hatch an enclosed area just by picking a point
inside the area. _____

18. Identify at least two ways to select a predefined hatch pattern in the "Boundary Hatch" dialog
box. _____
_____
_____
_____
_____

19. Explain how you set a hatch scale in the "Boundary Hatch" dialog box. _____
_____

20. Identify two ways to change a hatch pattern (where all elements of the hatch are one unit) so that
each element is an individual entity. _____
_____

21. Explain how to use an existing hatch pattern on a drawing as the current pattern for your next
hatch. _____
_____
_____

22. Describe the purpose of the Preview Hatch ⟨ button found in the "Boundary Hatch" dialog box.
_____
_____

23. What happens if you try to hatch an area where there is a gap in the boundary? _____
_____
_____

24. How do you limit AutoCAD hatch evaluation to a specific area of the drawing? _____
_____
_____
_____

25. Define "ray casting." _____

    _____

    _____

26. Define associative hatch pattern. _____   _____

    _____

    _____

    _____

27. How do you change the hatch scale and angle in the "Boundary Hatch" dialog box? _____

    _____

    _____

28. Describe the fundamental difference between using the Pick Points ⟨ and the Select Objects ⟨
    buttons in the "Boundary Hatch" dialog box. _____

    _____

    _____

    _____

    _____

29. If you use the Pick Points ⟨ button inside the "Boundary Hatch" dialog box to hatch an area, how
    do you remove an island, inside the area, from the hatch pattern? _____

    _____

    _____

    _____

    _____

30. How do you use the BHATCH command to hatch an object with text inside, without hatching
    the text? _____

    _____

    _____

    _____

31. How do you access the hatch style options through the "Boundary Hatch" dialog box? _____

    _____

    _____

    _____

32. Name the command that may be used to edit existing associative hatch patterns. _____

    _____

33. What do you get when you enter the command identified in Question 32? _____

    _____

34. How does the item identified in Question 33 compare and differ from what you get when you
    enter the BHATCH command? _____

    _____

    _____

35. What would you do if you want an existing hatch pattern on a drawing to take on the same characteristics as another different hatch pattern on the same drawing? _____

_____

_____

_____

_____

DRAWING PROBLEMS

Name each of the drawings P24-(problem number). Follow these guidelines for all of the problems.

    A. Draw the views to full size.
    B. Set grids, snap, limits, and units values as needed. Use object snap to your best advantage.
    C. Apply dimensions accurately following ANSI standards.
    D. Set dimensioning variables to suit the drawing.
    E. Use the LAYER command to set separate layers for views, dimensions, and section lines.
    F. Place these general notes 1/2 in. from the lower-left corner.
    2. REMOVE ALL BURRS AND SHARP EDGES
    1. INTERPRET PER ASME Y14.5M-1994.
    NOTES:

1-2. Draw the full sections as indicated. For Problem 2, add the additional general note:
    UNLESS OTHERWISE SPECIFIED, ALL DIMENSIONS ARE IN MILLIMETERS.

1.

P24-1

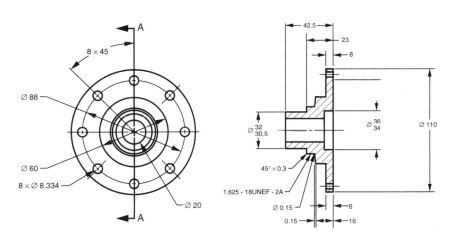

2.

P24-2

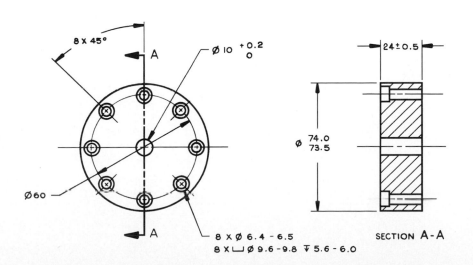

P24-3

3. Draw the half section. Add the additional notes: OIL QUENCH 40-45C, CASE HARDEN .020 DEEP, 59-60 ROCKWELL C SCALE, and MATERIAL: AISI 1018.

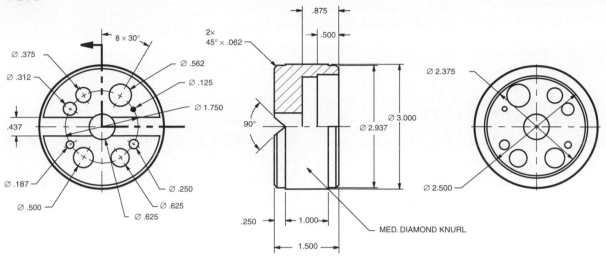

4-5. Draw the aligned sections as indicated. Add the additional notes:

FINISH ALL OVER 1.6μM UNLESS OTHERWISE SPECIFIED and ALL DIMENSIONS ARE IN MILLIMETERS

4.

P24-4

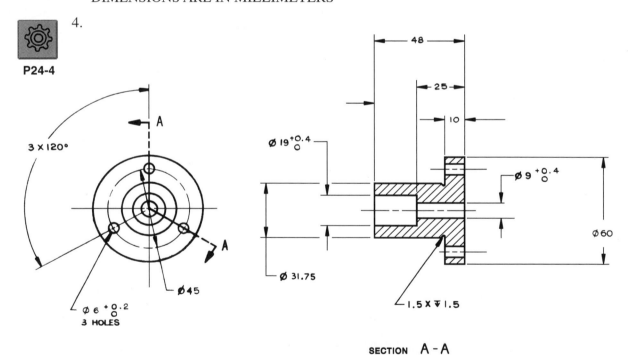

SECTION A-A

5.

P24-5

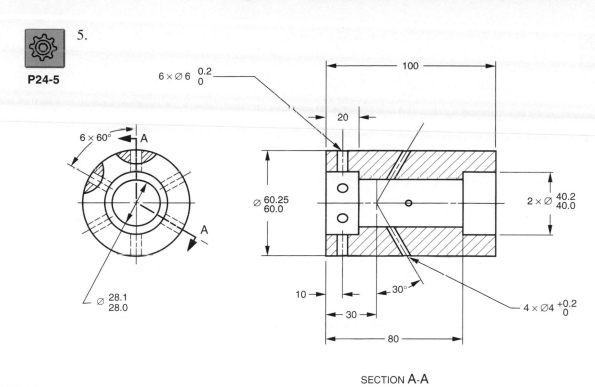

SECTION A-A

6. Draw the offset sections.

P24-6

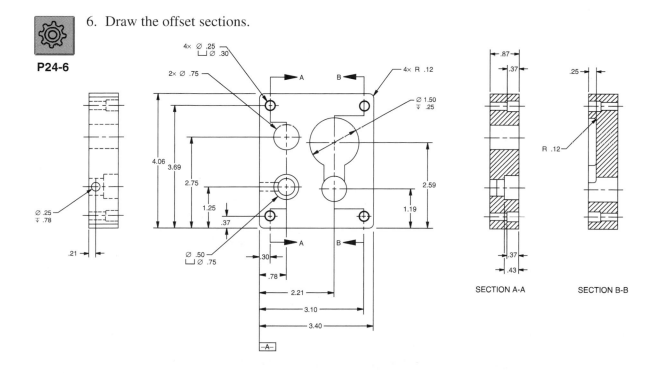

SECTION A-A   SECTION B-B

7. Draw the removed section and enlarged view.

P24-7

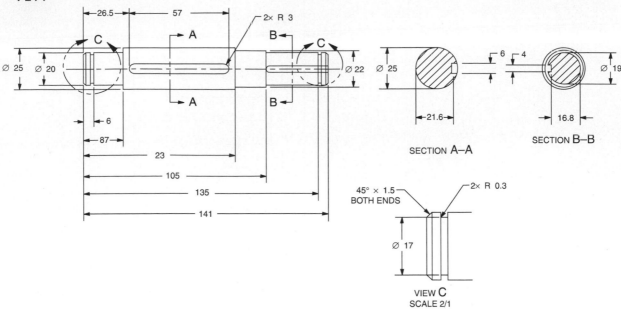

SECTION A–A

SECTION B–B

VIEW C
SCALE 2/1

8. Draw the revolved section. Use the SOLID command to fill in the thin section.

P24-8

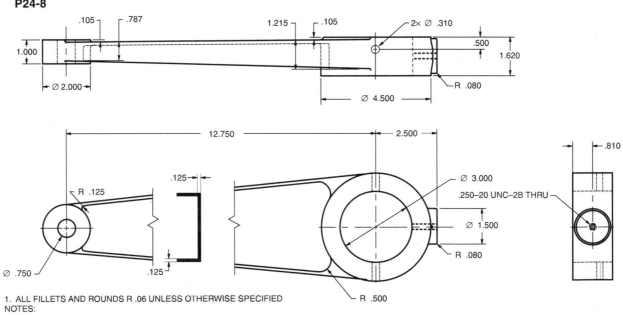

NOTES:
1. ALL FILLETS AND ROUNDS R .06 UNLESS OTHERWISE SPECIFIED

For Problems 9-16, use the HATCH, BHATCH, and SOLID commands as necessary. Establish appropriate grid, snap, limits, and units values.

9.

P24-9

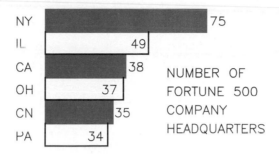

STATES WITH TOP COMPANIES

NY — 75
IL — 49
CA — 38
OH — 37
CN — 35
PA — 34

NUMBER OF FORTUNE 500 COMPANY HEADQUARTERS

10.

P24-10

COMPONENT LAYOUT

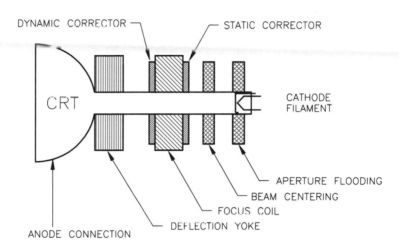

DYNAMIC CORRECTOR
STATIC CORRECTOR
CRT
CATHODE FILAMENT
APERTURE FLOODING
BEAM CENTERING
FOCUS COIL
DEFLECTION YOKE
ANODE CONNECTION

11.

P24-11

SOLOMAN SHOE COMPANY

PERCENT OF TOTAL SALES EACH DIVISION

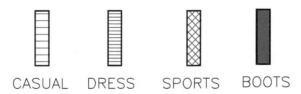

CASUAL   DRESS   SPORTS   BOOTS

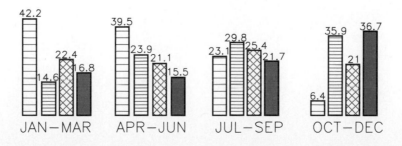

JAN–MAR   APR–JUN   JUL–SEP   OCT–DEC

42.2 14.6 22.4 16.8
39.5 23.9 21.1 15.5
23.1 29.8 25.4 21.7
6.4 35.9 21 36.7

12.

P24-12

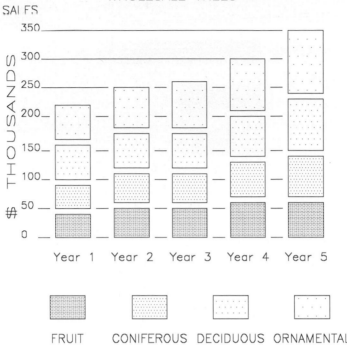

13.

P24-13

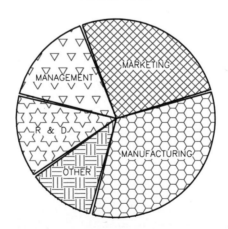

14.

P24-14

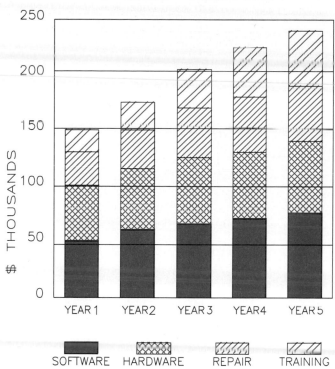

SALES HISTORY

SOFTWARE   HARDWARE   REPAIR   TRAINING

15.

P24-15

X-RAY

16.

P24-16

Architectural
Design
Consultants

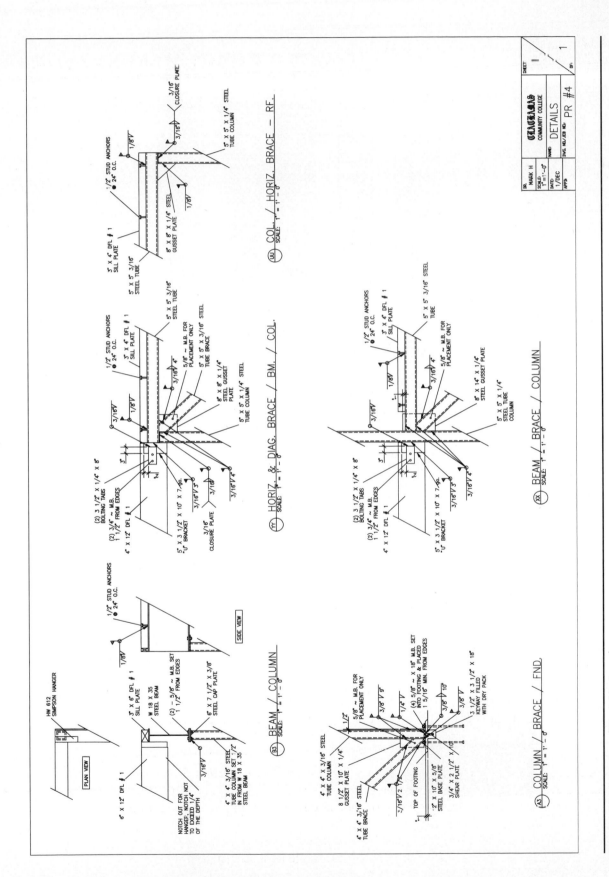

Roof framing details.　(Mark Hartman)

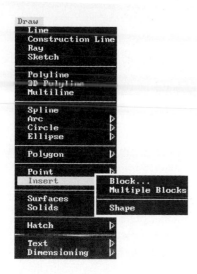

Chapter 25

CREATING SYMBOLS FOR MULTIPLE USE

Learning objectives

After completing this chapter, you will be able to:

- ○ Create and save blocks.
- ○ Insert blocks into a drawing.
- ○ Edit a block and update it in a drawing.
- ○ Create, or write blocks that are saved independent of the drawing.
- ○ Construct and use a symbol library of blocks.

One of the greatest benefits of AutoCAD is in its ability to store often-used geometry as symbols for future use. These symbols, or *blocks,* can be inserted into a drawing full size, or scaled and rotated. If a block is edited, drawings having the block can be updated to include the new version. The term *wblock* refers to the command WBLOCK, which is used to write a *block* description as a separate drawing file. Since any AutoCAD drawing can be inserted into another drawing, this provides *global* access (any drawing), as opposed to *local* access (current drawing). Therefore, a *block* can be used only in the drawing in which it was created. Both types can be used to create a symbol library, which is a related group of symbols.

AutoCAD also allows you to "reference" drawings instead of inserting them into a drawing. When a drawing is referenced, it becomes part of the drawing on the screen, but its content is not added to the current drawing file. Referenced drawings and any named entities, such as blocks and layers, are referred to as *dependent symbols.* When a dependent symbol is revised, the drawing(s) it is referenced to are automatically updated the next time it is loaded into AutoCAD.

CREATING SYMBOLS AS BLOCKS

AUG 7

The ability to draw and store a symbol once, and then insert it when needed, has been the greatest time-saving feature of CAD. AutoCAD provides the BLOCK command to create a symbol and keep it with a specific drawing file. You can insert a predrawn block as many times as needed into any drawing. Upon insertion, the block can be scaled and rotated to meet the drawing requirements.

Constructing blocks

A block can be any shape, symbol, view, or drawing that you use more than once. Before constructing a block, review the type of drawing you are working on. (This is where a sketch of your drawing is convenient.) Look for shapes, components, notes, and assemblies that are used more than once. These can be drawn once and then saved as blocks.

Existing drawings can also be used as blocks. This can be done two different ways:

- • Use the BASE command on the drawing to assign an insertion point.
- • Insert the existing drawing into the drawing you are working on.

These two methods are discussed later in this chapter.

PROFESSIONAL TIP

Blocks that vary in size from one drawing to the next should be drawn to fit inside a one unit square. It does not matter if the object is measured in feet, inches, or millimeters. This makes it easy to scale the symbol when you later insert it in a drawing.

Drawing the block components

Draw a block as you would any other drawing geometry. Use any AutoCAD commands you need. If you want the block to have the color and linetype of the layer it will be inserted on, be sure that you set layer 0 as current before you begin drawing the block. If you forget to do this, and draw the objects on another layer, simply use the CHPROP command to place all the objects on layer 0 before using the BLOCK command. When you finish drawing the object, decide what is the best place on the symbol to use as an insertion point. When you insert the block into a drawing, the symbol is placed with its insertion point on the screen cursor. Figure 25-1 illustrates some common blocks and their insertion points, shown as dots.

Figure 25-1.   Common symbols are inserted on drawings using their insertion points for placement. The insertion points are shown here as color dots.

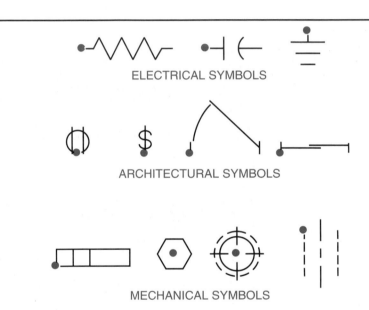

ELECTRICAL SYMBOLS

ARCHITECTURAL SYMBOLS

MECHANICAL SYMBOLS

If it is important that the block maintains a specific color and linetype, regardless of the layer it is to be used on, be sure to set the color and linetype before drawing the objects. On the other hand, if it is okay for the block to assume the current color and linetype when the block is inserted into the drawing, use the BYBLOCK options of the COLOR and LINETYPE commands. This is easily achieved by picking Object Creation… in the Data pull-down menu. The "Object Creation Modes" dialog box displays the current settings of color, layer, linetype, text style, linetype scale, elevation, and thickness. See Figure 25-2.

The block will have color and linetype of the layer it will be inserted on

① • Layer 0

• use BYBLOCK option of the COLOR and LINETYPE commands   • set the color and linetype before drawing the object }   block maintains its color and linetype.

② • draw the object

③ • enter the BLOCK command

④ •   "   the block name

⑤ •   "   insertion point

⑥ • select the object

Figure 25-2. The "Object Creation Modes" dialog box displays the current settings of object characteristics. You can change these settings by clicking on one of the four buttons or entering new values in the text boxes.

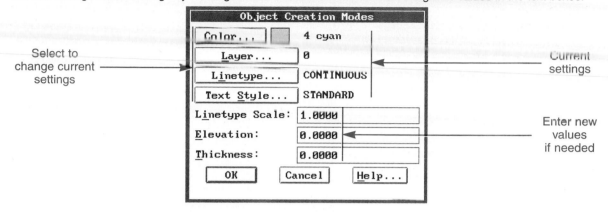

Select the Color... button and then pick the BYBLOCK button in the "Select Color" subdialog box, as shown in Figure 25-3, then pick OK.

Figure 25-3. The "Select Color" subdialog box is used to change the color of an object. Select a new color or enter a logical color.

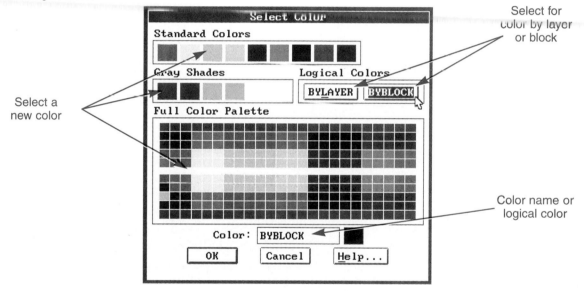

Next pick the Linetype... button in the "Object Creation Modes" dialog box to display the "Select Linetype" subdialog box. Scroll to the top of the linetype list and pick the BYBLOCK entry, then pick OK. See Figure 25-4.

Figure 25-4.   The "Select Linetype" subdialog box is used to change an object's linetype.

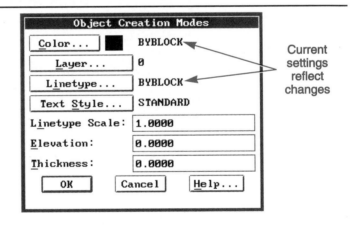

The "Object Creation Modes" dialog box should now display the settings of BYBLOCK for color and linetype. See Figure 25-5. Now you can use any AutoCAD commands to create your block shapes. Whenever a block that was created with these BYBLOCK settings is inserted into a drawing, it will assume the current color and linetype, regardless of the current layer values.

Figure 25-5.   The color and linetype have been set to BYBLOCK in the "Object Creation Modes" dialog box.

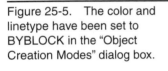

Creating blocks

Although you may have drawn a shape, you have not created a block yet. To save your object as a block, select the BLOCK command. The BLOCK command can be typed in at the Command: prompt, or picked from the Construct pull-down menu. Then enter the block's name and insertion point. Finally, you must select those objects on the screen that will become the block. The following procedure saves the symbol under the name PUMP.

Command: **BLOCK** ↵
Block name (or ?): **PUMP** ↵
Insertion base point: *(pick an insertion point)*
Select objects: *(select the object)*
Select objects: ↵

The block name can be no longer than 31 characters. The insertion point should be accurate. You can type exact coordinate values of a point on the object, or use OSNAP options. Select the object with any of the standard object selection options. Type W and press ENTER at the Select objects: prompt to use a window, or F to use a fence.

AutoCAD informs you that a block was made by removing it from the screen. It is stored as a part of the drawing file. Remember, a block can be used only in the drawing in which it was created. If you want the block geometry to return to the screen, type OOPS, or pick Oops from the screen menu. The geometry reappears in the same position.

Check to see that the block was saved properly by selecting the BLOCK command again. At the prompt, type a question mark as follows:

Command: **BLOCK** ↵
Block name (or ?): **?** ↵
Block(s) to list ⟨*⟩:

Press ENTER to list all of the blocks in the current directory. The following information is then displayed.

Defined blocks.
PUMP

User Blocks	External Reference	Dependent Blocks	Unnamed Blocks
1	0	0	0

This display indicates the name and number of blocks. When you create a block, you have actually created a *block definition*. Therefore, the first entry in the block listing is that of *defined* blocks. *User blocks* are those created by you, the user. *External references* are drawings referenced with the XREF command, which is discussed later in this chapter, and in greater detail in Chapter 26. Blocks that reside in a referenced drawing are called *dependent blocks*. *Unnamed blocks* are entities such as associative dimensions and hatch patterns.

Step through the process of drawing a block again. Draw a one unit square and name it PLATE. See Figure 25-6. Draw the object using the LINE command. Select the BLOCK command. Name the block PLATE. Pick the insertion point at the lower-left corner. Select the object using the Window option. Select BLOCK again and use the ? option to see that it was saved.

Figure 25-6.   The procedure for drawing a one unit square block. A–Draw the block. B–Pick the insertion point. C–Select the box using a window or other selection option.

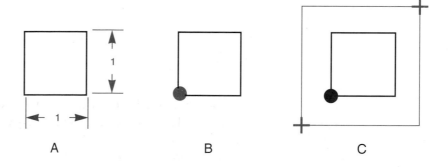

A   B   C

EXERCISE 25-1

❏ Load AutoCAD and open one of your prototype drawings with decimal units to use for this exercise.
❏ Draw the circle with a one unit diameter and add centerlines on layer 0.
❏ Make a block of the circle and centerlines and name it CIRCLE.
❏ Pick the center of the circle as the insertion point.

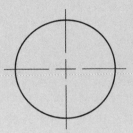

❏ Save the drawing as A:EX25-1 and quit.

PROFESSIONAL TIP

Blocks can be used when creating other blocks. Suppose you design a complex part or view that will be used repeatedly. You can insert existing blocks into the view and then save the entire object as a block. This is called *nesting;* larger blocks contain smaller blocks. The larger block must be given a different name. Proper planning and knowledge of all existing blocks can speed the drawing process and creation of complex parts.

USING BLOCKS IN A DRAWING   AUG 7

Once a block has been created, it is easy to insert it on a drawing. Before inserting a block, give some thought to the size the block should be and the rotation angle needed. Blocks are normally inserted on specific layers. Set the proper layer *before* inserting the block. Once a block has been inserted into a drawing, it is referred to as a *block reference.*

Inserting blocks

Blocks are placed on your drawing with the INSERT command, found in the Draw pull-down menu, or the Draw 2 screen menu. Know beforehand where the insertion point of the block will be located in the drawing. Insert the PLATE block into your drawing as follows:

Command: **INSERT** ↵
Block name (or ?): **PLATE** ↵ ← *If there is not block definition for "PLATE" in the current drawing, AutoCAD searches the drives and directories on the PATH for a drawing of name "PLATE" and inserts it instead.*
    Insertion point: *(pick the point)*
    X scale factor ⟨1⟩ / Corner / XYZ: *(pick a point, type a number and press* ENTER, *or press* ENTER *to accept the default)*
    Y scale factor (default=X): *(type a number and press* ENTER, *or press* ENTER *to accept the default)*
    Rotation angle ⟨0⟩: *(pick a point, or type a number and press* ENTER)

The X and Y scale factors allow you to stretch or compress the block to suit your needs. This is why it is a good idea to draw blocks to fit inside a one unit square. It makes the block easy to scale because you can type the exact number of units for the X and Y dimensions. If you want the block to be three units long and two units high, respond:

    X scale factor ⟨1⟩ / Corner / XYZ: **3** ↵
    Y scale factor (default=X): **2** ↵

Notice that the Y prompt allows you to accept the X value for Y by just pressing ENTER. The object shown in Figure 25-7 was given several different X and Y scale factors during the INSERT command.

Figure 25-7. Shown is a comparison of the PLATE block inserted using different X and Y scale factors.

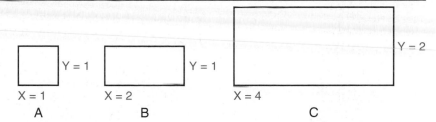

Block insertion options

It is possible to obtain a mirror image of a block just by typing a negative value for the scale factor. For example, a -1,-1 scale factor mirrors the block to the opposite quadrant of the coordinate system, but retains the original size. Figure 25-8 illustrates mirroring techniques; the insertion point is indicated with a dot.

An approximate dynamic scaling technique is achieved using the Corner option. You can see the block change size as you move the cursor if DRAGMODE is set to Auto. Select the Corner option at the X scale factor prompt as follows:

X scale factor ⟨1⟩ / Corner / XYZ: **C** ↵
Other corner: *(move cursor to change size and pick a point)*

A coordinate value can be typed or a point can be picked. Be sure to pick a point above and to the right of the insertion point to insert the block as drawn. Picking corner points to the left or below the insertion points will generate mirror images such as those in Figure 25-8.

Figure 25-8. Negative and positive scale factors have different effects when inserting a block.

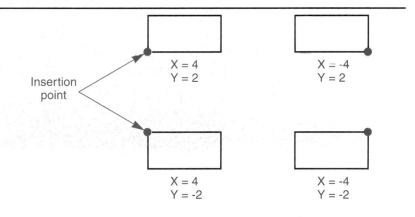

NOTE Before a block can be edited, it must be returned to its original objects with the EXPLODE command. Block editing and redefinition are covered later in this chapter.

EXERCISE 25-2

❑ Open EX25-1 if it is not currently on your screen.
❑ Draw a 1 x 1 square on layer 0 and make it a block named PLATE.
❑ Insert the PLATE block into the drawing. Enter an X scale factor of 6 and a Y scale factor of 4.
❑ Insert the CIRCLE block twice into the PLATE block as shown. The small circle is one unit in diameter and the large circle is 1.5 units in diameter.

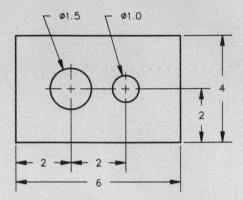

❑ Make a block of the entire drawing and name it PLATE-1. Pick the lower-left corner as the insertion point.
❑ Insert the PLATE-1 block on your drawing and enter a scale of –1, –1. Also rotate the object 45°.
❑ Save the drawing as A:EX25-2.

The effects of layers on blocks

Blocks retain the characteristics of the layer on which they are drawn. All objects in AutoCAD are created in BYLAYER mode by default. This means that an object's color and linetype are governed by the layer on which they are created.

For example, suppose the CIRCLE block is drawn on layer 1 having the color red and a dashed linetype. When inserted, the block appears red and dashed, no matter what layer it is inserted on. If different colors, linetypes, or even layers are used in a block, they also remain the same when the block is inserted on a different layer. Therefore, a block defined in BYLAYER mode retains its properties when inserted into another drawing. If the layers which comprise the inserted block do not exist in the current drawing, AutoCAD automatically creates them.

For a block to assume the property characteristics of the layer it is inserted on, it must be created on layer 0. Suppose you create the CIRCLE block on layer 0 and insert it on layer 1. The block becomes part of layer 1 and thus assumes the color and linetype of that layer. Exploding the CIRCLE block returns the entities back to layer 0 and to the original color and linetype assigned to layer 0.

Changing the layer and color of a block

If you insert a block on the wrong layer, select CHPROP to move it to the proper layer. Then enter the LAyer option of the CHPROP command:

Command: **CHPROP** ⏎
Select objects: *(pick the block to change)*
Select objects: ⏎
Change what property (Color/LAyer/LType/LtScale/Thickness)?: **LA** ⏎
New layer ⟨0⟩: *(enter new layer name and press* ENTER*)*
Change what property (Color/Elev/LAyer/LType/LtScale/Thickness)?: ⏎

The block is now changed to the proper layer. If the block was originally created on layer 0, it will assume the color of the new layer. If it was created on another layer, it will keep its original color.

To prevent a block from assuming a different color than the assigned layer color, set the COLOR command to BYLAYER before creating blocks:

Command: **COLOR** ↵
New object color ⟨1 (red)⟩: **BYLAYER** ↵

Now any entities or blocks that are drawn assume the color of the current layer.

The same is true of the linetype of an entity. In order to avoid problems, the linetype should be set as a function of the layer rather than using the LINETYPE command. Check to be sure the LINETYPE command is set to BYLAYER.

Command: **LINETYPE** ↵
?/Create/Load/Set: **S** ↵
New object linetype (or ?) ⟨HIDDEN⟩: **BYLAYER** ↵

All entities and blocks are drawn with the linetype of the current layer.

INSERTING MULTIPLE COPIES OF A BLOCK

The INSERT and ARRAY features are combined in the MINSERT (Multiple INSERT) command. This method of inserting and arraying not only saves time, but also disk space.

An example of an application using MINSERT is to place an arrangement of desks on a drawing. Suppose you want to draw the layout shown in Figure 25-9. Change to architectural units and set the limits to 30',22'. Draw a rectangle 4 ft. by 3 ft. and save it as a block called DESK. The arrangement is to be three rows and four columns. Spacing between desks should be two feet horizontally and four feet vertically. Follow this sequence.

Command: **MINSERT** ↵
Block name (or ?): **DESK** ↵
  Insertion point: *(pick a point)*
  X scale factor ⟨1⟩ / Corner / XYZ: ↵
  Y scale factor ⟨default=X⟩: ↵
  Rotation angle ⟨0⟩: ↵
Number of rows (---) ⟨1⟩: **3** ↵
Number of columns (⎪⎪⎪) ⟨1⟩: **4** ↵
Unit of cell or distance between rows (---): **7'** ↵
Distance between columns (⎪⎪⎪): **6'** ↵

The resulting arrangement is shown in Figure 25-9. The total pattern takes on the characteristics of a block, except that a MINSERT array cannot be exploded. If the initial block is rotated, all arrayed objects are also rotated about their insertion points.

Figure 25-9. To create an arrangement of desks using MINSERT, first create a block called "desk".

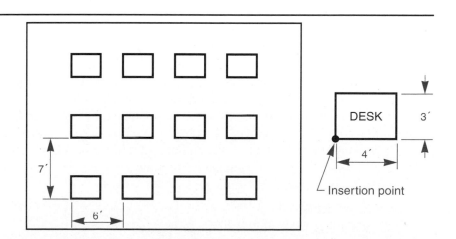

PROFESSIONAL TIP

In the previous example, if you were working with a lot of different desk sizes, a one unit square may serve your purposes better than an exact size block. To create a 5′ x 3′-6″ (60″ x 42″) desk, insert a one unit square block using INSERT or MINSERT, and enter the following for the X and Y values:

X scale factor⟨1⟩/Corner/XYZ: **60** ↵
Y scale factor⟨default = X⟩: **42** ↵

A one unit square block can be used in this manner for a variety of objects.

EXERCISE 25-3

❑ Load AutoCAD and start a new drawing named EX25-3. Set architectural units and 80′,60′ limits.
❑ Draw the chair shown below and save it as a block named CHAIR.
❑ Use the MINSERT command twice to create the theater arrangement. The sides of the chairs should touch. Each row on either side of the aisle should have 10 chairs. The spacing between rows is 4 feet. The width of the center aisle is 5 feet.
❑ Consider where you should insert the first chair to obtain the pattern.

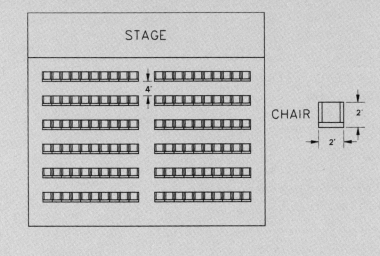

❑ Save the drawing as A:EX25-3.

Inserting entire drawings

The INSERT command can be used to insert an entire drawing into the current drawing. When one drawing is inserted into another, the inserted drawing becomes a block reference. Since it is a block, it is a single object. If you pick it, one grip appears at the insertion point. This makes it easy to move the inserted drawing if it is placed incorrectly. A drawing that is inserted does not inherit the color, linetype, and thickness values of the current layer, even though it is placed on the current layer. If you explode the inserted drawing, its objects revert back to their original layers.

All drawings have a default insertion point of 0,0,0. You can specify a different insertion point on a drawing by using the BASE command. The nature of the view or drawing should determine the best location for the base point.

Command: **BASE** ↵
Base point ⟨0.0000,0.0000,0.0000⟩: *(pick a point)*

The base point now becomes the insertion point.

EXERCISE 25-4

❑ Open drawing EX25-2 if it is not already on your screen.

❑ If your drawing does not have a RED layer, make one and be sure it is current.

❑ Draw a 6 × 4 unit rectangle. Insert two CIRCLE blocks into the rectangle, both one unit in diameter. Make a new block of this drawing and name it PLATE-2.

❑ Erase the screen. Set the current layer to 0. Insert both the PLATE-1 and PLATE-2 blocks.

❑ The PLATE-2 block should appear red because it was created on the red layer. PLATE-1 should be black.

❑ Make sure RED is the current layer. Insert the PLATE-1 block into your drawing. It should appear red because it was created on layer 0 and will assume the color of the layer on which it is inserted.

❑ Enter the BASE command. Choose an insertion point below and to the left of the objects on the screen.

❑ Save the drawing as A:EX25-4.

❑ Start a new drawing named PLATES.

❑ Insert drawing EX25-4 into your new drawing. The insertion point you pick is the one established using the BASE command.

❑ Pick any editing command and select a line of one of the plates. The entire drawing should highlight since the drawing is actually one large block.

❑ Save the drawing as A:EX25-4.

Presetting block insertion variables

You can dramatically speed the insertion of blocks by presetting the scale or rotation angle. These preset options are available by typing them at the Insertion point: prompt of the INSERT command, or when using the "Insert" dialog box, which is discussed in the next section. The preset options not only save time, but also allow you to see the scaled size and rotation angle before you pick the insertion point. This helps you determine if the scale and rotation angle are correct.

Preset options can be used two ways. If the S option is entered at the Insertion point: prompt, you are asked for the scale factor, then the insertion point and rotation angle. If you enter P and S, a prompt requests the scale factor for insertion display purposes only. After you pick the insertion point, the normal INSERT prompts are displayed. This second method is a "temporary" preset. That difference is illustrated in the following examples. The first example inserts the block PLATE at a preset scale factor of 2.

```
Command: INSERT ↵
Block name (or ?) ⟨current⟩: PLATE ↵
    Insertion point: S ↵
    Scale factor: 2 ↵
    Insertion point: (pick an insertion point)
    Rotation angle ⟨0⟩: ↵
```

The next example illustrates a temporary preset of the scale factor.

```
Command: INSERT ↵
Block name (or ?) ⟨current⟩: PLATE ↵
    Insertion point: PS ↵
    Scale factor: 2 ↵
    Insertion point: (pick an insertion point)
    X scale factor ⟨1⟩ / Corner / XYZ: ↵
    Y scale factor (default=X): ↵
    Rotation angle ⟨0⟩: ↵
```

The temporary preset allows you to see the preset scale or rotation angle as you drag the block. You can also change the scale and rotation angle by entering a value at the normal prompts. Remember to use temporary preset type P, then the option you wish to preset at the Insertion point: prompt. For example, to temporarily set the rotation angle, enter PR at the Insertion point: prompt. The following list describes the functions of the preset options:

- **S.** Affects the overall scale of X, Y, and Z axes. Rotation angle is also requested.
- **X.** Affects only the X scale. Rotation angle is also requested.
- **Y.** Affects only the Y scale. Rotation angle is also requested.
- **Z.** Affects only the Z scale. Rotation angle is also requested.
- **R.** Sets the rotation angle. Prompts for X and Y scale factors.

The AutoCAD system variable INSNAME (Insert NAME) may be used to preset the name of a block you wish to insert. For example, if you will be inserting several copies of the DESK block, use INSNAME as follows:

Command: **INSNAME** ⏎
New value for INSNAME, or . for none ⟨""⟩: **DESK** ⏎

Now when you use the INSERT command, the name "DESK" appears as the default for the block name.

Command: **INSERT** ⏎
Block name (or ?) ⟨DESK⟩: *(press ENTER to accept this block name, or provide another block name and press ENTER)*

As shown above, you may provide another block name at the INSERT prompt, such as CHAIR, regardless of the current INSNAME setting. The name CHAIR is then stored as the INSNAME value.

USING THE INSERT DIALOG BOX   AUG 7

All of the functions of the INSERT command previously discussed can be accessed using the DDINSERT command. DDINSERT can be typed at the Command: prompt, or Insert then Block … can be picked from the Draw pull-down menu. This displays the "Insert" dialog box shown in Figure 25-10.

Figure 25-10.   Shown is the "Insert" dialog box that is activated by the DDINSERT command.

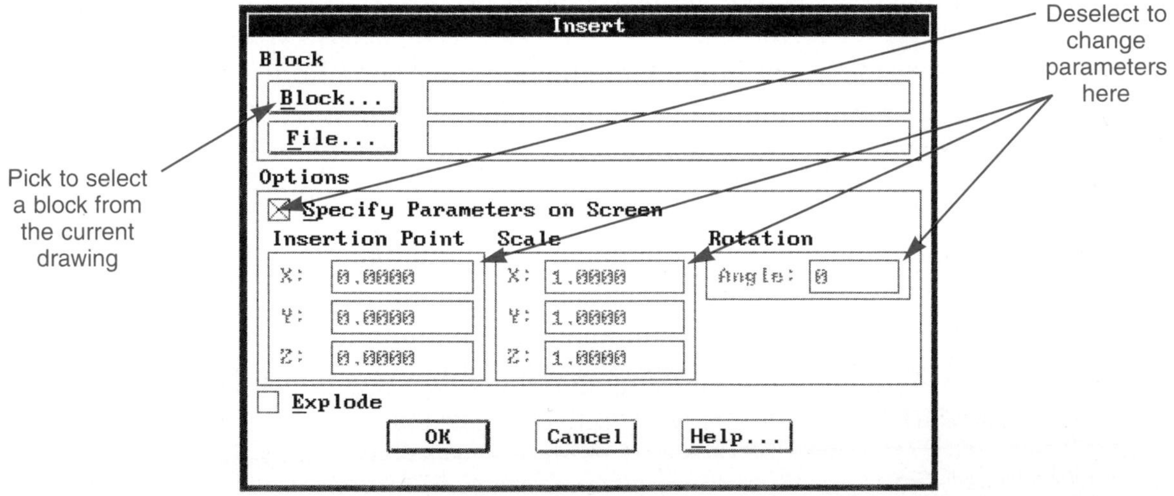

You can choose the block to insert by picking the Block… button. When you pick this box, a file list of all blocks defined in the current drawing is displayed. See Figure 25-11. Pick the block name you wish to use and it is displayed in the Selection: text box. If the list of block names is long, and the name you need is not displayed, you can enter the name in the Selection: box, and then pick OK.

Figure 25-11. Picking the Block... button in the "Insert" dialog box shows the blocks defined in the current drawing. If the list is long, you can scroll through it or enter the block name in the Selection: text box.

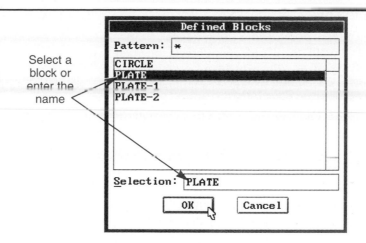

Notice that the presets of Insertion point, Scale, and Rotation in the "Insert" dialog box are initially grayed out. (Refer back to Figure 25-10.) If you wish to preset the insertion point, scale, and rotation angle values, pick the Specify Parameters on Screen check box. Now the preset values are no longer grayed out, and can be changed in the dialog box.

If you wish to have the block exploded upon insertion, simply pick the Explode check box to turn it on. (Editing blocks is discussed in the next section.) When you are finished, pick OK. If presets were used, look quickly because the block is immediately inserted. If presets were not used, the specified block appears on the crosshairs and the standard INSERT command prompts are issued.

PROFESSIONAL TIP

A block's rotation angle can also be based on the current UCS. Should you wish to insert a block at a specific angle based on the current, or an existing UCS, first be sure the proper UCS is restored. Then insert the block and use a zero rotation angle. If you subsequently change the UCS, the inserted objects retain their original angle.

EDITING BLOCKS

AUG 7

Blocks must first be broken into their original components before they can be edited. This is especially important when an entire view or drawing has been inserted. Two methods can be used to break blocks apart. The first method–asterisk insertion–is done at the time of insertion. The second–the EXPLODE command–can be done at any time.

Breaking a block apart with asterisk insertions

A block is a single object. Individual objects that make up the block, such as lines, arcs, and circles, cannot be edited. The MOVE, COPY, ROTATE, and SCALE commands affect the block as a single item.

If you plan to edit the individual items upon insertion, you can insert a block exploded into its original components. To do this, type an asterisk before the block name as follows:

Command: **INSERT** ↵
Block name (or ?): ***PLATE-1** ↵
   Insertion point: *(pick a point)*
   Scale factor ⟨1⟩: ↵
   Rotation angle ⟨0⟩: ↵

The inserted geometry is not part of a block. It consists of individual objects that can be edited.

Exploding the block

The EXPLODE command is used to break apart any existing block, polyline, or dimension. When the block is exploded, the component objects are quickly redrawn.

Command: **EXPLODE** ↵
Select objects: *(pick the block)*
Select objects: ↵

The exploded block is now composed of objects that may be edited individually. To see if EXPLODE worked properly, select any object formerly part of the block. Only that entity should highlight. If so, the block was exploded properly.

NOTE   You can explode a block that was scaled using different X, Y, and Z values when it was inserted in the drawing. This is technically called a non-uniformly scaled block. Previous versions of AutoCAD did not allow exploding non-uniformly scaled Blocks.

Redefining existing blocks

A situation may arise where you discover that a block definition must be changed. This is an easy process, even if you have placed the block on a drawing many times. To redefine an existing block, follow this procedure:

1. Insert the block to be redefined anywhere on screen.
2. Explode the block you just inserted using the EXPLODE command.
3. Edit the block as needed.
4. Recreate the block using the BLOCK command.
5. Give the block the same name it had before. Answer Yes to redefine the block.
6. Give the block the same insertion point as the original.
7. All insertions of the block are updated when the BLOCK command is complete.

A common mistake is to forget to use the EXPLODE command. When you try to create the block again with the same name, the following error message is displayed and the command is aborted:

Block ⟨name⟩ references itself
Invalid

This means that you are trying to recreate a block that already exists. Enter the EXPLODE command and try again.

This concept of a block "referencing itself" may be a little difficult to understand at first, so let's take a closer look at how AutoCAD works with blocks.

A block can be composed of any AutoCAD objects, including other blocks. When using the BLOCK command to incorporate an existing block into the new block, AutoCAD must make a list of all the objects the new block is composed of. This means that AutoCAD must refer to any existing block definitions that are selected to be part of the new block. But if you select an instance (reference) of the block being redefined as a component object for the new definition, a problem occurs. You are trying to redefine a block name using a previous version of the block with the same name. In other words, the new block refers to a block of the same name, or "references itself."

For example, use a block called BOX that is composed of four line objects. The block should be changed so that it contains a small circle in the lower left corner. If the block is exploded, all that is left is the four line objects. After drawing the required circle, the block command is activated and the block named BOX can be redefined by selecting the four lines and the circle as the component objects. Redefining a block destroys the old definition and creates a new one. See Figure 25-12A.

Alternately, if you do not explode the block, but still draw the circle and try to redefine the block, the objects selected to define the block BOX would now be a block reference of the block BOX, and a circle. The old definition of BOX has not been destroyed, but a new definition has been attempted, which is a circle and the old block named BOX. Thus AutoCAD is trying to define the block BOX by using an instance of the block BOX. This is referred to as a circular reference, meaning a block references itself. See Figure 25-12B.

Figure 25-12. A—The correct procedure for redefining a block. B—Redefining a block that has not first been exploded creates an invalid circular reference where the block references itself.

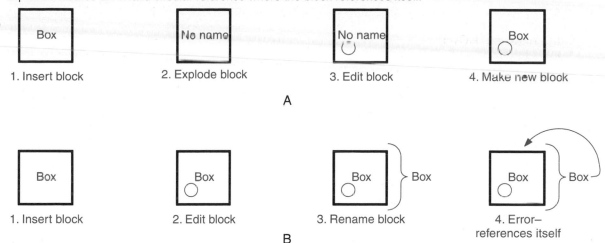

1. Insert block   2. Explode block   3. Edit block   4. Make new block

A

1. Insert block   2. Edit block   3. Rename block   4. Error—
references itself

B

Creating a block from a drawing file

You can create a block from any existing drawing. This allows you to avoid redrawing the object as a block, thus saving time. Remember, if something has already been drawn, try to use it as a block rather than redrawing it. In this case, use the INSERT command in the following manner to define a block named BOLT from an existing drawing file named FASTENER.

Command: **INSERT** ↵   *or* PATH_NAME
Block name (or ?): **BOLT=FASTENER** ↵
   Insertion point: *(press* CTRL+C*)*

The drawing is not inserted on screen because the command is canceled. However, a block named BOLT is added to the drawing file and can be used like any other block.

EXERCISE 25-5

❑ Open EX25-3.
❑ Insert a block named CHAIR anywhere on the drawing.
❑ Explode the chair you just inserted.
❑ Add a feature to the chair, such as a headrest. Keep it simple.
❑ Make a block named CHAIR of the revised chair.
❑ Answer Yes to redefine the block, and pick the same insertion point as the original chair.
❑ When the BLOCK command is completed, all chairs should be updated to reflect the changes.
❑ Save the drawing as A:EX25-5 and quit.

MAKING PERMANENT BLOCKS

AUG 7

Symbols created with the BLOCK command can only be used in the drawing on which they were made. However, you may want to use blocks on many different drawings without having to redraw them. The WBLOCK command allows you to create a drawing file (.DWG extension) out of a block or any other shape. This drawing can then be inserted as a block in any other drawing.

There are several ways to use the WBLOCK command. For the first method, open drawing EX25-1. Convert your CIRCLE block to a permanent symbol by making it a separate drawing file using the following procedure:

Command: **WBLOCK** ↵

The "Create Drawing File" dialog box appears, displaying a listing of all drawing files in the current directory. Move the pointer to the <u>F</u>ile: text box and type the name of the wblock, HOLE, and press ENTER. Each time you select the WBLOCK command, the "Create Drawing File" dialog box appears, unless the FILEDIA system variable is set to the value of zero (0).

File name: HOLE⏎

      Block name: **CIRCLE** ⏎

unhappy sentence (confusing)

The above sequence wrote a new block, HOLE, to a drawing file on disk. The prompt asked for the name of an existing block, CIRCLE, to convert into a separate drawing file. Select Management and then Utilities… from the File pull-down menu, or type FILES at the Command: prompt. The "File Utilities" dialog box appears; pick <u>L</u>ist Files… to see if HOLE.DWG is now on your disk. When another drawing is inserted into the current drawing, though, it acts like a block. It is a single object and cannot be edited unless broken into its original components.

To assign the new drawing name to the same name as the block, type an equal symbol (=) for the block name as follows:

      Command: **WBLOCK** ⏎
      File name: **CIRCLE** ⏎
      Block name: **=** ⏎

If you want to name the new drawing "CIRCLE", the same as the block you had just created (the block already exists)

First of all…

When you enter WBLOCK, the "Create Drawing File" dialog box appears if FILEDIA is set to 1. Pick the <u>T</u>ype it button to obtain the previous prompts.

Making a new wblock

Suppose you want to create a separate drawing file from a shape you just drew, but have not made a block yet. Enter the WBLOCK command, but do not supply a block name. Press ENTER instead. Then select the insertion point and the objects to be included in the new drawing.

      Command: **WBLOCK** ⏎
      File name: **DESK** ⏎
      Block Name: ⏎
        Insertion base point: *(pick a point)*
      Select objects: *(select objects to be in the new drawing)*
      Select objects: ⏎

This sequence is exactly like that of the BLOCK command. Remember that this drawing is saved to disk not to the current drawing file. Be sure to specify a path before the file name, if needed. The previous drawing file would be saved in the current hard disk directory because no path was given. If you want to save the WBLOCKed drawing file on a floppy disk in the A: drive, enter the file name as A:DESK. A drawing file that is to be saved into the BLOCKS directory on the C: hard drive would be named C:\BLOCKS\DESK.

Preparing a drawing for use as a symbol

An entire drawing can also be stored as a wblock. Type an asterisk (*) for the block name.

      Command: **WBLOCK** ⏎
      File name: *(type a file name and press ENTER)*
      Block name: * ⏎

In this case, the whole drawing is saved to disk as if you used the SAVE command. The difference is that all unused blocks are deleted from the drawing. If the drawing contains any unused blocks, this method reduces the size of a drawing considerably.

PROFESSIONAL TIP

    The WBLOCK-asterisk method is a good technique to clean your drawing of unused named objects to reduce the file size. Use this routine when you have completed a drawing and know that the unused blocks, layers, styles, and objects are no longer needed.

Inserting a separate drawing file with the "Select Drawing File" dialog box

When you pick Insert, then Block... from the Draw pull-down menu, you have the choice of inserting a block or file using the "Insert" dialog box shown in Figure 25-10. If you want to look through a listing of your drawing files, pick the File... button in the screen menu. This displays the "Select Drawing File" dialog box. You can now scroll through listings in any directory and pick the file name you need.

If you type INSERT at the Command: prompt, you can access the "Select Drawing File" dialog box by entering a tilde (~) at the Block name (or '?): prompt as follows:

Command: **INSERT** ↵
Block name (or ?): **~** ↵

You can type this character whenever any AutoCAD command prompt requests a file name. One of several dialog boxes is then displayed regardless of the FILEDIA system variable setting.

EXERCISE 25-6

❑ Open drawing EX25-2.
❑ Create a drawing file called PLATE-1 using the existing block of the same name.
❑ Select Management, then Utilities... from the File pull-down menu to get a listing of your .DWG files. Be sure PLATE-1.DWG is listed.
❑ Quit the drawing editor.
❑ Start a new drawing called EX25-6.
❑ Insert the PLATE-1 drawing into the current drawing. Remember, drawings can be inserted into the current drawing.
❑ Save the drawing as A:EX25-6 and quit.

Revising an inserted drawing

One of the basic principles of drawing, design, and engineering is that things will inevitably change. You may find that you have to revise a drawing file that has previously been inserted in other drawings. If this happens, you can quickly update any drawing in which the revised drawing is used. For example, if the drawing file named PUMP is revised, but its previous version was inserted several times in a drawing, simply use the INSERT command, and place an equal sign (=) after the block name in the following manner to update all the old PUMP symbols:

Command: **INSERT** ↵
Block name (or ?): **PUMP=** ↵
Block PUMP redefined
Regenerating drawing.
  Insertion point: *(press* CTRL+C*)*

All of the old PUMP symbols are automatically updated to reflect the revised version, and by canceling the command, no new symbols are added to the drawing.

Suppose you had inserted a drawing file named FASTENER into your current drawing, but gave it the block name of SCREW. Now you have decided to revise the FASTENER drawing. The SCREW block can be updated using the INSERT command as follows:

Command: **INSERT** ↵
Block name (or ?): **SCREW=FASTENER** ↵
Block SCREW redefined
Regenerating drawing.
  Insertion point: *(press* CTRL+C*)*

PROFESSIONAL TIP

     If you work on projects in which inserted drawings may be revised, it is more productive to use reference drawings instead of inserted drawing files. Reference drawings are used with the XREF command, which is introduced later in this chapter, and discussed in detail in Chapter 26. All referenced drawings are automatically updated when a drawing file that contains the Xrefed material is loaded into AutoCAD.

CREATING A SYMBOL LIBRARY

     As you become proficient with AutoCAD, begin to construct symbol libraries. A *symbol library* is a collection of related shapes, views, and symbols that are used repeatedly. You may eventually want to incorporate symbols into your screen and tablet menus. This is discussed in detail in ***AutoCAD and its Applications–Advanced, R13 for DOS.*** First, you need to know where symbols (blocks and drawing files) are stored and how they can be inserted into different drawings.

Blocks vs. separate drawing files

     As discussed earlier, the principal difference between the BLOCK command and the WBLOCK command is that a *block* is saved with the drawing in which it is created. The WBLOCK command saves a separate individual drawing file. This means that a block can only be used in the current drawing. See Figure 25-13. A complete drawing file occupies considerably more disk space than a block.

     If you decide to use blocks, each person in the office or class must have a copy of the drawing that contains the blocks. This is often done by creating the blocks in a prototype drawing. If drawing files are used, each student or employee must have access to the files via hard disks, optical disks, or a network server.

Figure 25-13.   Blocks can only be used in the drawing where they were created. Drawing files can be inserted into any drawing.

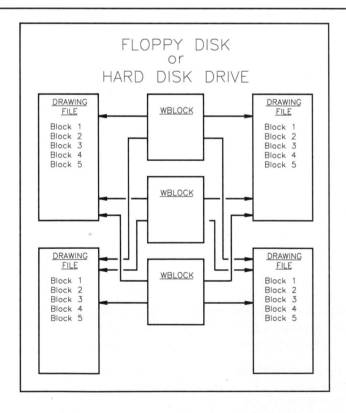

Using floppy diskettes

Floppy diskettes are good for temporarily storing backup copies of drawing and data files. They also allow you to transport files from one workstation to another in the absence of a network or modem. However, avoid making floppies the primary means for storage of symbols, especially if you have sufficient room on the hard disk drive, optical drive, or network server drives. Inserting and removing floppy diskettes from a disk drive is tedious and time-consuming because it takes more time for the computer to access the floppy disks. If you must adopt this method, follow these guidelines.

• Create all symbols as separate drawing files.
• Assign one person to initially create the symbols for each specialty.
• Follow class or company symbol standards.
• Create a symbol library listing using a printer or plotter. Include a picture of the symbol, its insertion point, necessary information, and the disk on which it is located. See Figure 25-14. Provide all persons who use the symbols with a copy of the listing.

Figure 25-14.   Piping flow diagram blocks used for prototype drawings are illustrated in this Symbol library listing. The colored dot indicates the insertion point, and is not part of the block.

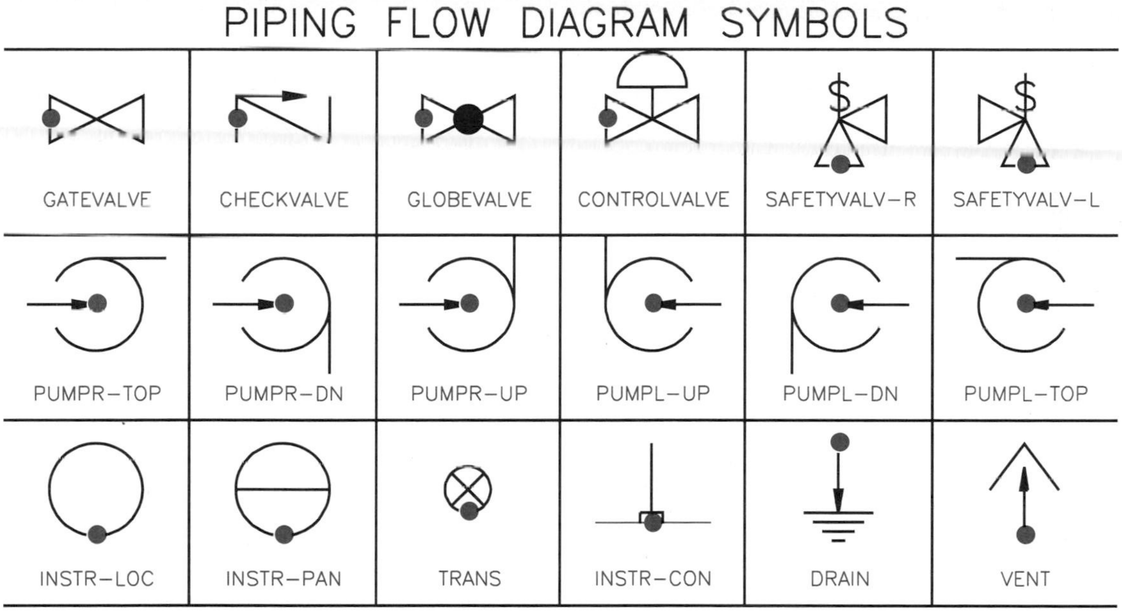

PIPING FLOW DIAGRAM SYMBOLS

GATEVALVE	CHECKVALVE	GLOBEVALVE	CONTROLVALVE	SAFETYVALV–R	SAFETYVALV–L
PUMPR–TOP	PUMPR–DN	PUMPR–UP	PUMPL–UP	PUMPL–DN	PUMPL–TOP
INSTR–LOC	INSTR–PAN	TRANS	INSTR–CON	DRAIN	VENT

• Save one group of symbols per diskette. For example, individual disks may contain the following types of symbols:
  ✓ Electronic   ✓ Structural
  ✓ Electrical   ✓ Architectural
  ✓ Piping   ✓ Landscaping
  ✓ Mechanical   ✓ Mapping
• Label floppy disks two ways:
  ✓ Use the DOS LABEL command to assign a name to each floppy disk in the following manner:

C:\\)**LABEL A:STRUCTURAL** ↵

This gives the disk in the A: drive the name of STRUCTURAL. Eleven characters can be used for a label. Use the DOS VOL command to find out the label of a disk.

C:\\)**VOL A:** ↵

DOS responds:

> Volume in drive A is STRUCTURAL
> Volume Serial Number is 2309-OCFA

A label can also be given to a disk when it is formatted.

> C:\)**FORMAT A:/V** ⏎

The /V (Volume) switch activates the DOS LABEL command.

✓ Use stick-on floppy disk labels on all disks. Write on the label before attaching it to the disk. Use the same name as the volume label.
- Copy symbols disks and provide a copy for each workstation in the class or office.
- Keep backup copies of all symbol library disks in a secure place.
- When symbols are revised, update all copies of diskettes containing the edited symbols.
- Inform all users of any changes to symbols.

Using the hard disk drive

The hard disk drive is the best place to store symbol libraries. It is easily accessible, quicker, and more convenient to use than floppy disks. Symbols should be created with the WBLOCK command, as they were with floppy disks. The drawing files can be saved in the current directory (usually ACADR13) or a subdirectory. If drawing files are stored in the ACADR13 directory, they are easier to enter the first time. There is less typing at the INSERT command. However, storing symbols in separate subdirectories keeps the ACADR13 directory uncluttered and easy to manage.

A symbol named PUMP is retrieved from the ACADR13 directory with the INSERT command as follows:

> Command: **INSERT** ⏎
> Block name (or ?) ⟨*current*⟩: **PUMP** ⏎

If the same symbol is stored in a subdirectory of ACADR13 called BLK, it is retrieved the first time as follows:

> Command: **INSERT** ⏎
> Block name (or ?) ⟨*current*⟩: **\ACADR13\BLK\PUMP** ⏎

After its initial insertion, a drawing file is saved as a block definition in the current drawing, and can be accessed by just entering its file name.

Drawing files are saved on the hard disk drive using the same systematic approach as with floppy disks. These additional guidelines also apply:
- All workstations in the class or office should have directories and subdirectories with the same names.
- One person should be assigned to update and copy symbol libraries to all workstation hard drives.
- Drawing files should be copied onto each workstation's hard drive from a master disk or network server.
- The master disks and backup disks of the symbol libraries should be kept in separate locations.

Creating prototype symbol drawings

In addition to obtaining a printed copy, you can display all the symbols on the screen. This technique requires that you create symbols in a prototype drawing. The symbols (blocks) are then inserted into a special area of the drawing outside the drawing limits, then labeled. They can be copied from this library and placed in the drawing. An example of this arrangement was shown in Figure 25-14. The following steps should be used to create this type of symbol library.
- Draw each symbol on layer 0 and save as a block.
- Increase the limits beyond the needed drawing area to provide space for the symbols. The amount of space required is determined by the number of symbols stored in the library.

- Draw a grid in which to place the symbols (if desired). Insert symbols inside the grid boxes.
- Make a layer named INSERT. Assign a unique color to the layer.
- Use the DONUT or POINT commands to place a dot or an "X" at the insertion point of each symbol.
- Label each symbol on the INSERT layer.
- To use a block, copy it from the library to the drawing rather than using the INSERT command.

Using prototype symbol libraries

The symbol library can be used in several different ways. Symbols can be copied directly from the library to the drawing as they are needed. You might also insert one copy of each symbol into the drawing limits when you begin. Then zoom the drawing to display only the limits. This hides the symbol library and also enlarges the view of your work. Use COPY to place symbols in your drawing. This method has limitations because you cannot scale or rotate with COPY as you can with INSERT.

Turn Quick Text mode on so that symbol labels are not recalculated when a regeneration takes place. This saves much time. Descriptive symbol names, like those in Figure 25-14, can be replaced with numbers or letters.

The on-screen library also serves as a reference. You can check the shape, block name, or insertion point of a symbol. When using the on-screen library for this method only, create the library on layers not used in the drawing. The symbol library layers are normally frozen to speed regeneration time. To check a symbol, thaw the library layers.

PROFESSIONAL TIP

Create one or more views of your symbol library using the VIEW command, especially if you use them for reference purposes. It is faster to display a view than it is to use the ZOOM or PAN commands.

Copying a symbol library into a new drawing

A symbol library of blocks that are part of a prototype drawing can be copied into a new drawing file. This technique is an invisible function that transfers blocks from an existing drawing to a new drawing. The incoming blocks are not displayed, only included in the drawing file. It enables you to use blocks created on one drawing without also having to use the drawing. The process is simple. If the drawing PIPEFLOW on the disk in the A: drive contains the needed blocks, enter the following:

Command: **INSERT** ↵
Block name (or ?) ⟨*current*⟩: **A:PIPEFLOW** ↵
  Insertion point: (*press* CTRL+C *to cancel*)

The blocks are now included with your drawing. Check this by selecting BLOCK and the ? option.

These methods of placing symbol libraries on prototype drawings are just several possibilities. As you learn more about AutoCAD, other avenues will open. After reading the menu customizing chapters in ***AutoCAD and its Applications–Advanced, R13 for DOS,*** you will see additional possibilities. Regardless of the method chosen, it is important that you maintain consistency and adhere to standards.

Create a symbol library listing

After deciding which method of using symbols is best for you, create a symbol library listing. Distribute it to all persons who will be using the symbols. The list can be a pen or printer plot of the symbol libraries on each prototype drawing. These lists should be updated when revisions are made to symbols. A copy on 8.5 by 11 in. paper should be given to all AutoCAD users. A larger copy should be placed on a wall or bulletin board. Examples of symbol library lists used in engineering offices are shown in Figures 25-15 and 25-16.

Figure 25-15.   Shown are instrumentation loop diagram symbols.   (Willamette Industries, Inc.)

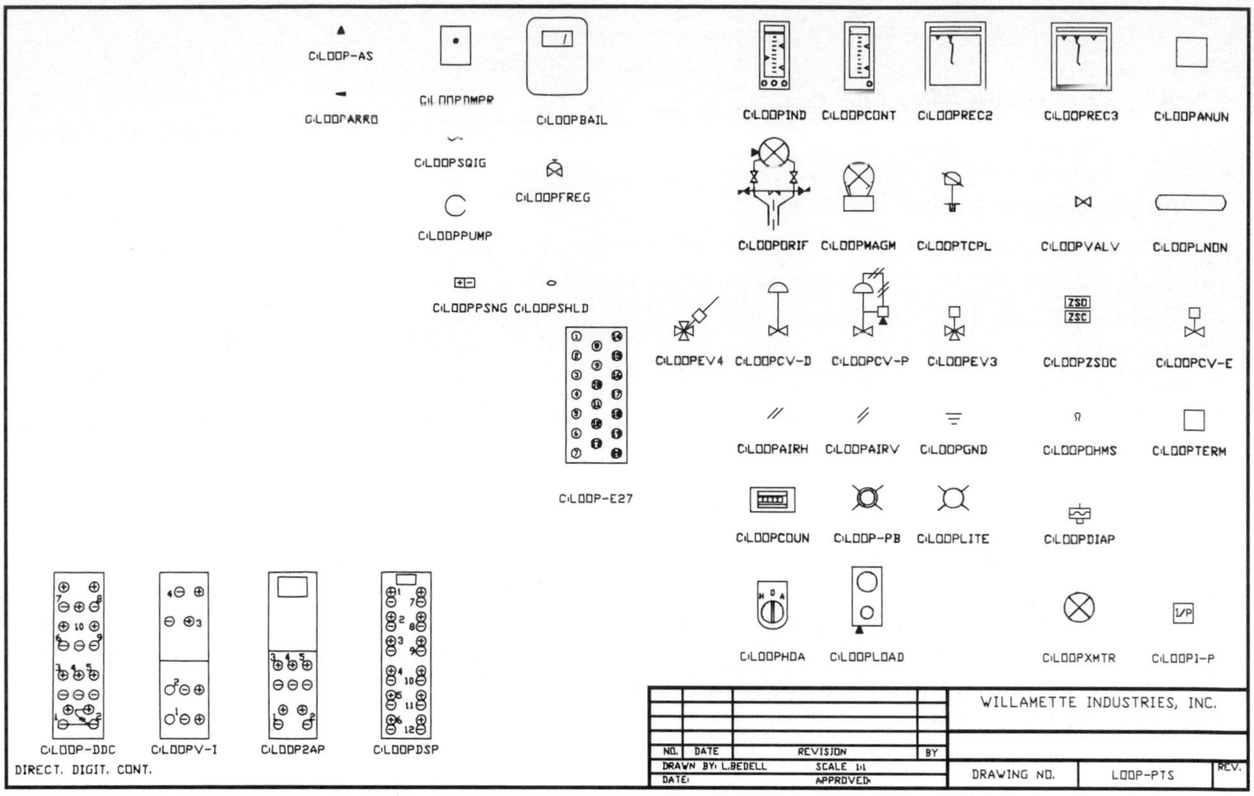

Figure 25-16.   Shown are isometric piping symbols.   (Willamette Industries, Inc.)

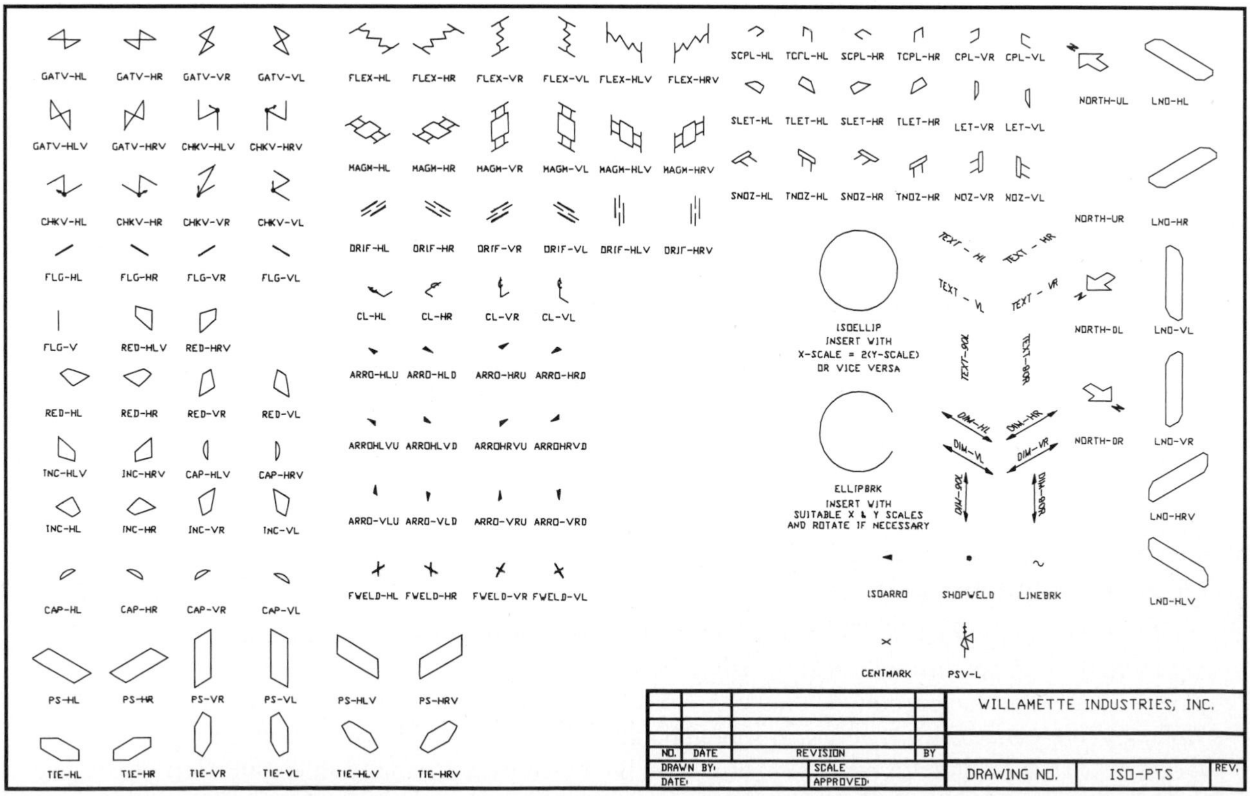

RENAMING BLOCKS

Block names can be changed with the RENAME command. It is found by picking Management, then Utilities... in the File pull-down menu. To change the name of the CIRCLE block to HOLE, enter the RENAME command as follows:

```
Command: RENAME ↵
Block/Dimstyle/LAyer/LType/Style/Ucs/VIew/VPort: B ↵
Old block name: CIRCLE ↵
New block name: HOLE ↵
```

The block name is changed. To check that the name was changed, select the BLOCK or INSERT command. Use the ? option to get a listing. The list will appear similar to this:

```
Defined blocks.
PLATE
HOLE
PLATE-1
User            External        Dependent       Unnamed
Blocks          References      Blocks          Blocks
  3                0               0               0
```

The RENAME command in AutoCAD only works for blocks, not wblocks. To change the name of a wblock, use either the File Utilities Menu's Rename option or the DOS RENAME command. See Chapter 17 for a discussion of the "File Utilities" dialog box and for use of the DOS RENAME command.

Renaming blocks using a dialog box

Blocks can also be renamed using a dialog box. In addition, the "Rename" dialog box can be used to change the names of dimension styles, layers, linetypes, text styles, UCSs, named views, and saved viewports. Enter DDRENAME at the Command: prompt, and the "Rename" dialog box is displayed. Pick Block from the Named Objects list on the left and a list of the block definitions is displayed in the Items list on the right. To change the name of CIRCLE to HOLE, pick the CIRCLE item and notice that this name is then displayed in the Old Name: text box. See Figure 25-17. Now enter the name HOLE in the Rename To: text box, then pick the Rename To: button. The new name HOLE appears in the Items list. Pick OK to close the "Rename" dialog box.

Figure 25-17.   The "Rename" dialog box allows you to change the name of items in a block.

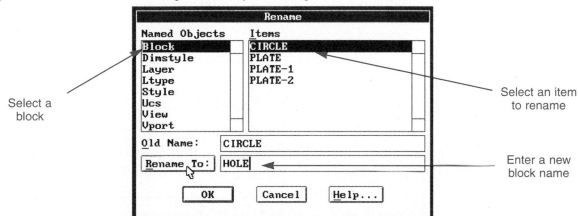

DELETING NAMED ENTITIES

Blocks are a "named entity," or object. Other such named objects are dimension styles (dimstyles), layers, linetypes, shapes, text styles, applications registered for ADS or AutoLISP, and multiline styles. In many drawing sessions, not all of the named entities in a drawing are used. For example, your prototype drawing may contain several layers, text styles, and blocks that are not used. Since these entities occupy drawing file space, it is good practice to delete, or "purge" the unused objects using the PURGE command. You can use PURGE in the following manner to delete a block named LINESPEC:

>Command: **PURGE** ↵
>Purge unused Blocks/Dimstyles/LAyers/LTypes/SHapes/STyles/APpids/Mlinestyles/ALL: **B** ↵
>Purge block LINESPEC? ⟨N⟩ **Y** ↵

The PURGE command individually lists all unused blocks and gives you the option to answer YES or NO. Use the PURGE command in the same manner to delete any of the unused entities listed above. The All option can be used to delete all unused named objects.

A part of your efforts in file maintenance should be to remove any unused named objects from drawings that you have completed. This reduces the file size, thus creating more space on your storage media for additional files. The WBLOCK-asterisk method mentioned earlier accomplishes the same thing as the PURGE command, but does so automatically.

CHAPTER TEST

Write your answers in the spaces provided.

1. Define "symbol library." _____
   _____

2. Which option of the COLOR and LINETYPE commands should be set, and what dialog box should they be set in, if you want the block to assume the current color and linetype when it is inserted into a drawing? _____
   _____

3. When should blocks be drawn to fit inside a one unit square? _____
   _____

4. A block name can be _____ characters long.

5. To obtain a listing of all blocks in the current drawing, you must _____

6. Describe block nesting. _____
   _____

7. How do you preset block insertion variables using a dialog box? _____
   _____
   _____

8. Describe the effect of entering negative scale factors when inserting a block. _____
   _____

9. Why would the Corner option be used when scaling a block during insertion? _____
   _____
   _____

10. What properties do blocks drawn on a layer other than 0 assume when inserted? _____

_____

11. Why would you draw blocks on layer 0? _____

_____

12. What are the limitations of the MINSERT command?_____

_____

13. What is the purpose of the BASE command? _____   _____

_____

14. What is the purpose of the INSNAME system variable?_____

_____

15. Explain why a drafter would choose to use preset options when inserting a block. _____

_____

16. Explain the difference between "PS" or "S" as preset options. _____

_____

_____

17. Name the two methods that break a block into its individual entities for editing._____

_____

18. Suppose you have found that a block was incorrectly drawn. Unfortunately, you have already
    inserted the block 30 times. How can you edit all of the blocks quickly? _____

_____

19. What is the primary difference between a block and a wblock? _____

_____

_____

_____

20. The WBLOCK command asks for block name. What would you enter at the Block name: prompt
    to make a wblock out of an existing block? _____

21. What would you enter at the Block name: prompt to remove all unused blocks from a drawing?

_____

22. Suppose you revise a drawing named DESK. However, the DESK drawing had been inserted
    several times into another drawing as wblocks named DESK2. How would you update the
    DESK2 insertions? _____

_____

_____

23. Why is it best to put symbol libraries on the hard disk drive rather than floppy disks? _____

_____

_____

24. What would you enter at the DOS C:⟩ prompt to name a diskette located in the B: drive
    CADCLASS? _____

25. How do you request the disk-naming procedure at the DOS prompt when formatting a disk in the
    A: drive?_____

26. What advantage is offered by having a symbol library of blocks in a prototype drawing, rather than using wblocks? _____

    _____

27. Give the command and entries needed to insert all of the blocks from a drawing named A:STRUCT-1 into the current drawing.

    Command: _____

    Block name (or ?) ⟨*current*⟩:_____

    Insertion point: _____

28. What is the purpose of the PURGE command, and what conditions govern its use? _____

    _____

DRAWING PROBLEMS

P25-1

1. Choose one of the diagrams shown and draw it using blocks. Use the following guidelines:

    A. Start a new drawing using an A-size or B-size prototype.

    B. Create a block for each different shape in the drawing.

    C. Arrows should be drawn as a block.

    D. Use a thick polyline for the flow lines.

    E. Label the drawing as shown.

    F. Place a border and title block on the drawing.

    G. Save the drawing as A:P25-1.

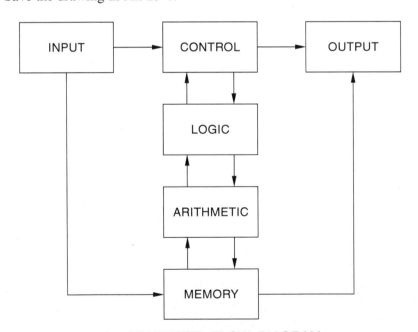

A. COMPUTER FLOW DIAGRAM

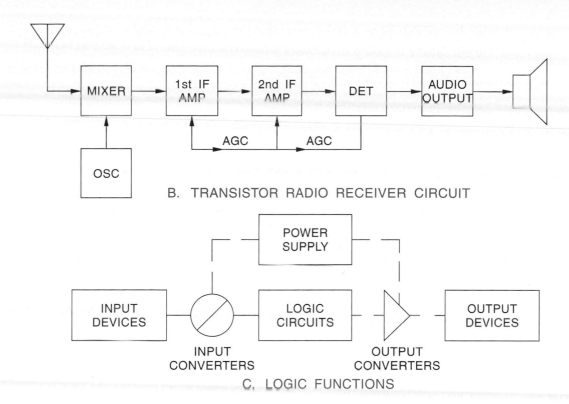

B. TRANSISTOR RADIO RECEIVER CIRCUIT

C. LOGIC FUNCTIONS

P25-2

2. Create a symbol library for one of the drafting disciplines listed below on a prototype drawing. Then, after checking with your instructor, draw one problem using the library. You can use the prototype drawings in two ways:

• Start a new drawing using a standard prototype drawing named PROTO. Name the new drawing NEWDWG.
• Insert the prototype into the current drawing (perhaps a different size drawing) and cancel at the Insertion point: prompt.

Specialty areas you might create symbols for include:

• Mechanical (machine features, fasteners, tolerance symbols).
• Architectural (doors, windows, fixtures).
• Structural (steel shapes, bolts, standard footings).
• Industrial piping (fittings, valves).
• Piping Flow Diagrams (tanks, valves, pumps).
• Electrical Schematic (resistors, capacitors, switches).
• Electrical One-Line (transformers, switches).
• Electronics (IC chips, test points, components).
• Logic Diagrams (and gates, nand gates, buffers).
• Mapping, Civil (survey markers, piping).
• Geometric Tolerancing (feature control frames).

Save the drawing as A:P25-2, or choose an appropriate name for the prototype, such as ARCH-PRO or ELEC-PRO.

P25-3

3. Display the prototype drawing symbol library on the screen and make a print with your dot matrix or laser printer. If you are not familiar with your printer, read Chapter 12 and consult your printer's reference manuals for specific information on its operation. Put the printed copy of symbol library in your notebook as a reference.

P25-4

4. Open Problem 4 from Chapter 15 (P15-4). Erase all copies of the symbols that were made, leaving the original intact. This includes steel column symbols and the bay and column line tags. Then follow these steps:

A. Make a block of each of the remaining steel column and tag symbols.

B. Use the MINSERT or ARRAY commands to place the symbols in the drawing.

C. Dimension the drawing as shown in the problem drawing of Chapter 15. Set the proper dimension variables for this type of drawing. Dimensions should be given in feet and inches. Show zero inches as follows: 20'-0".

D. Save the drawing as A:P25-4.

P25-5

5. Open Problem 5 from Chapter 15 (P15-5). Erase all of the desk workstations except one. Then follow these directions:

A. Create a block of the remaining workstation.

B. Insert the block in the drawing using the MINSERT command.

C. Dimension one of the workstations as shown in the original problem.

D. Save the drawing as A:P25-5.

6-10. The following problems are presented as real-world engineering sketches, and may contain layout errors. They are non-scale, schematic-type drawings made using symbols. The symbols should first be drawn as blocks and then saved in a symbol library. Use one of the methods discussed in this chapter. Place a border and title block on each of the drawings.

P25-6

6. This is a one-line diagram of an electrical substation. Set limits for an A-size or B-size sheet. Save the drawing as A:P25-6.

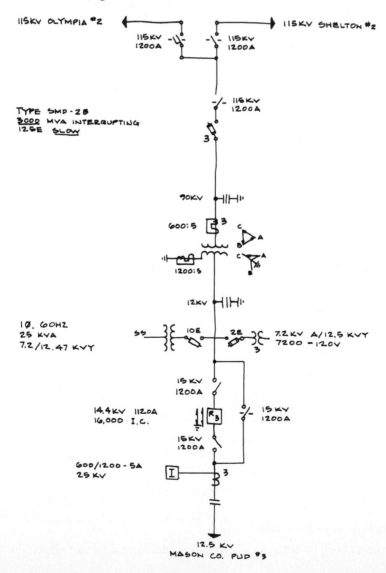

P25-7

7. This is an electrical schematic of a light flasher circuit. Set limits for a B-size sheet. Align components when possible. Eliminate as many bends in the circuit lines as possible. See Appendix H for standard electronic symbols. Save the drawing as A:P25-7.

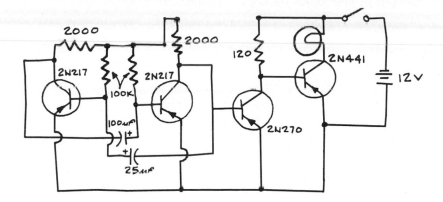

P25-8

8. This is a logic diagram of a portion of a computer's internal components. Create the drawing on a C-size sheet. Save the drawing as A:P25-8.

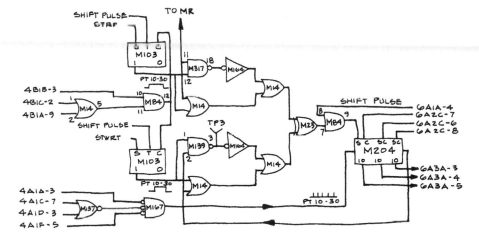

P25-9

9. Draw the piping flow diagram of a cooling water system on a B-size sheet. Look closely at this drawing. Using editing commands, it may be easier than you think. Draw thick flow lines with polylines. Save the drawing as A:P25-9.

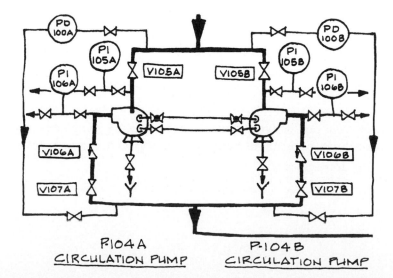

P25-10

10. This piping flow diagram is part of an industrial effluent treatment system. Draw it on a C-size sheet. Eliminate as many bends in the flow lines as possible. Place arrowheads at all flow line intersections and bends. Flow lines should not run through valves or equipment. Use polylines for thick flow lines. Save the drawing as A:P25-10.

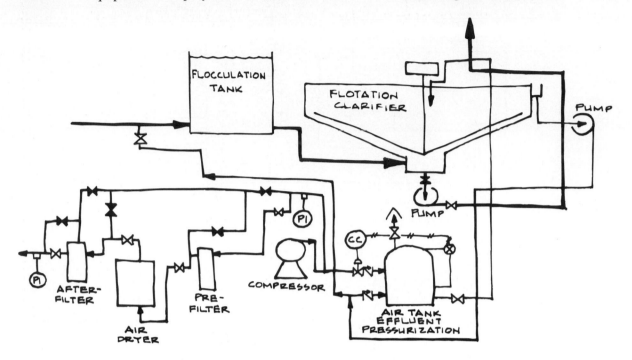

P25-11

11. The general arrangement of a basement floor plan for a new building is shown at the top of the next page. The engineer has shown one example of each type of equipment. Use the following instructions to complete the drawing:

A. Drawing should fit on C-size sheet.

B. All text should appear 1/8″ high, except bay and column line tags, which are 3/16″ high. The text balloons for bay and column lines should be twice the diameter of the text height.

C. The column and bay line steel symbols represent wide-flange structural shapes, and should be 8″ x 12″.

D. The PUMP and CHILLER installations (except PUMP #5) should be located per the dimensions given for PUMP #1 and CHILLER #1. Use the dimensions shown on the sketch for other PUMP and CHILLER units.

E. TANK #2 and PUMP #5 (P-5) should be located exactly as TANK #1 and P-4, and should be the same respective sizes.

F. Tanks T-3, T-4, T-5, and T-6 are all the same size, and are aligned 12′ from column line A.

G. Plan this drawing carefully and create as many blocks or wblocks as possible to increase your productivity. Dimension the drawing completely as shown, and provide location dimensions for all equipment not shown in the engineer's sketch.

H. Save the drawing as A:P25-11.

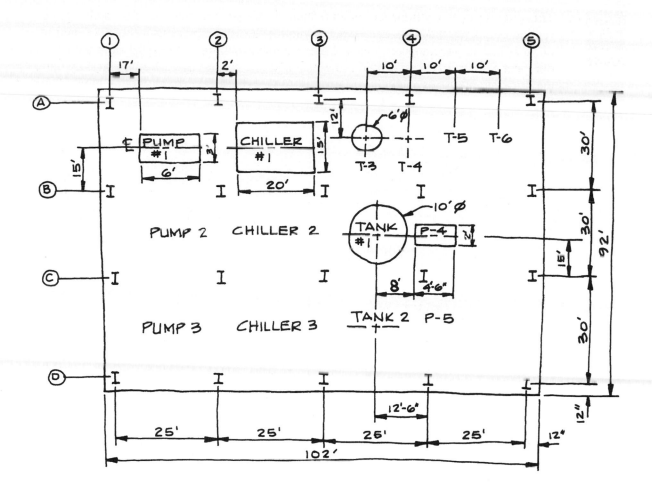

 12. The drawing in Problem 25-11 (P25-11) must be revised. The engineer has provided you
with a sketch of the necessary revisions. It is up to you to alter the drawing as quickly
and efficiently as possible. The dimensions shown on the sketch *do not* need to be added
to the drawing; they are provided for construction purposes only. Revise P25-11 so that
all CHILLERS, and TANKS #3, #4, #5, and #6 reflect the changes. Save your drawing as
A:P25-12.

P25-12

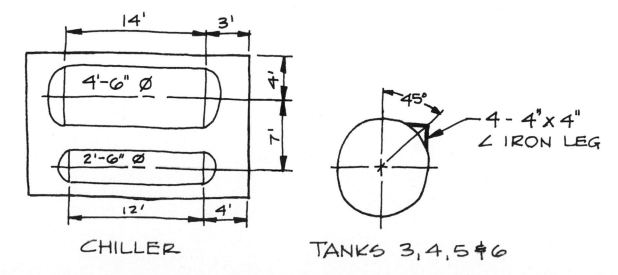

CHILLER   TANKS 3, 4, 5 & 6

P25-13

13. This drawing is an instrumentation loop diagram of software functions for the drying section of a paper machine. Each large box in the drawing represents a specific function or algorithm in the computer program. The smaller blocks on the left and right indicate different signals that are received and sent (input and output) by each function. Lay out the drawing exactly as shown on a B size or C-size sheet. Use your own title block. Save the drawing as A:P25-13.

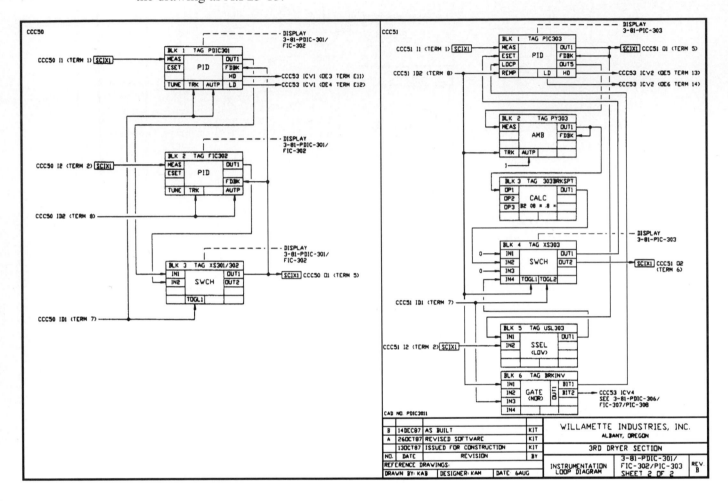

14-15. Make multiview drawings from the following engineer drawings. Add any sectioning necessary to completely describe the object. Completely dimension the drawing and apply geometric dimensioning and tolerancing symbols as shown on the sketch. Refer to Appendix section for the proper size and format of geometric dimensioning and tolerancing symbols. Be sure to include the following general notes:

INTERPRET DIMENSIONS AND TOLERANCES PER ASME Y14.5M-1994.
REMOVE ALL BURRS AND SHARP EDGES.

Save the drawings as A:P25-14 and A:P25-15, respectively.

14.

P25-14

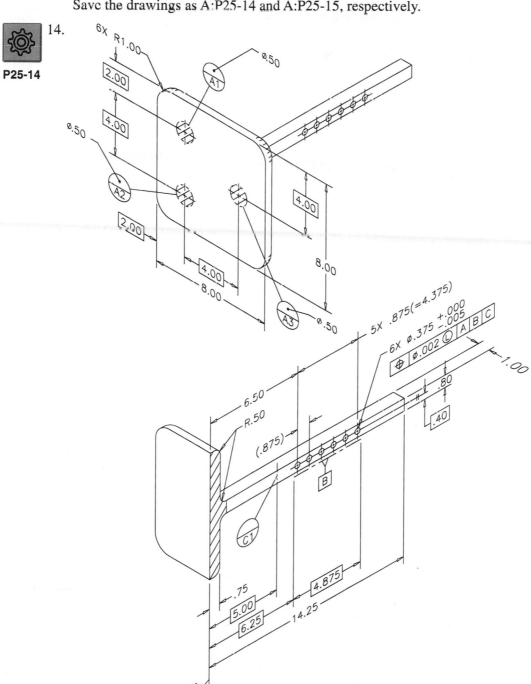

15.

P25-15

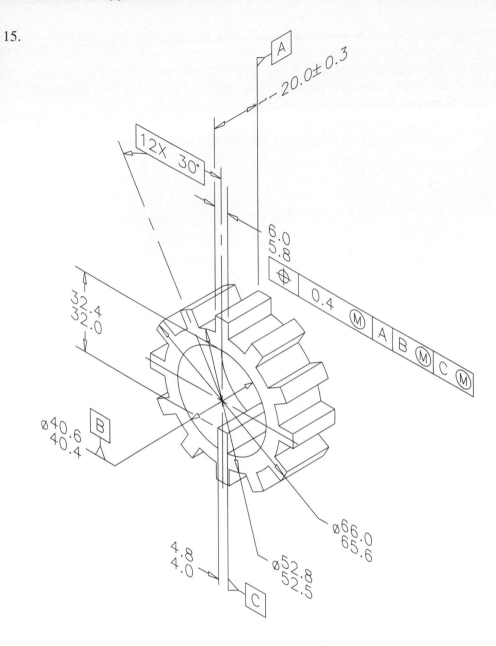

CHAPTER 26

EXTERNAL REFERENCES AND MULTIVIEW LAYOUTS

Learning objectives

- ○ Define the function of external references.
- ○ Reference an existing drawing into the current drawing using the XREF command.
- ○ Overlay an existing drawing onto the current drawing.
- ○ Change the path of external references.
- ○ Bind dependent symbols to a drawing.
- ○ Construct multiple viewports in a paper space drawing.
- ○ Construct a multiview drawing using external references of different scales.
- ○ Control the display of layers using the VPLAYER command.

As you create multiple objects in a drawing by copying, the drawing file grows quickly in size. That is because AutoCAD must maintain a complete description of the geometry of each one of the copied objects. On the other hand, when you use a block to represent repetitive objects, AutoCAD must maintain only one description of the block's geometry. All of the other instances of the block are recorded as X, Y, Z coordinates, and AutoCAD refers to the original *block definition* to obtain the block's data. This decreases the size of a drawing considerably if many blocks are used.

AutoCAD enables you to go even further in your efforts to control the size of drawing files, with the use of the XREF command. This command allows you to incorporate one or more existing drawings into the current drawing without adding them to the contents of the current file. This procedure is excellent for applications in which existing base drawings, or complex symbols and details must be shared by several users, or used often. This chapter explores the use of the XREF command, and steps you through a typical application of its capabilities when used to create a multiview architectural layout with a variety of scales.

USING REFERENCE DRAWINGS

AUG 7

Any machine or electrical appliance contains a variety of subassemblies and components. These components are assembled to create the final product. The final product occupies a greater amount of space and weighs more than any of the individual parts. In the same way, a drawing composed of a variety of blocks and wblocks grows much larger and occupies more disk space than the individual symbols and components. Imagine creating a design model of an automobile by projecting numerous holograms (laser-generated 3-D pictures) onto a viewing area. The design occupies perceived space, yet weighs nothing. When the lasers are turned off, the image of the car vanishes. Yet, the individual components that were projected still exist in computer storage and can be displayed again if needed. That is the principle behind the AutoCAD reference drawing concept.

AutoCAD allows you to "reference" existing drawings to the master drawing you are currently working on. When you reference (Xref) a drawing, its geometry is not added to the current drawing (as are inserted drawing files), but it is displayed on the screen. This makes for much smaller files. It also allows several people in a class or office to reference the same drawing file, and always be assured that any revisions to the reference drawing will be included in the master. Reference drawings are used with the XREF command, which is found in the FILE screen menu, File pull-down menu, or typed as XREF at the Command: prompt.

Reference drawings can be used in two basic forms:
- Constructing a drawing using predrawn symbols or details (similar to the use of blocks).
- Laying out a drawing to be plotted, which is composed of multiple views or details, using existing drawings. This technique is discussed in detail later in this chapter.

Benefits of external references

An important benefit of using Xrefs is that whenever the master drawing is loaded into AutoCAD, the latest version of the Xrefs are displayed. If the Xrefs are modified between the time you revise the master and the time you plot it, all of the revisions are automatically reflected. This is because AutoCAD reloads each Xref whenever the master drawing is loaded.

Other significant aspects of Xrefs is that they can be nested, and you can use as many Xrefs as needed for the drawing. This means that a detail referenced to the master drawing can be composed of smaller details that are themselves Xrefs. You can also use OSNAP options to attach entities or other Xrefs to the referenced drawing.

Attaching an external reference to the current drawing

Using the XREF command is similar to the BLOCK or WBLOCK commands. Suppose, for example, that you want to add a standard arrangement of a pump and valves to a piping flow diagram. The pump and valve arrangement is named PUMP-VLV, and is located in the \ACADR13\PIPE subdirectory. Use the Attach option of the XREF command as follows:

Command: **XREF** ↵
?/Bind/Detach/Path/Reload/Overlay/⟨Attach⟩: ↵

The "Select File to Attach" dialog box is displayed, which is the standard files list. Choose the file to attach and pick OK.

Attach Xref PUMP-VLV: \ACADR13\PIPE\PUMP-VLV.DWG
PUMP-VLV loaded.
Insertion point: *(pick an insertion point)*
\X scale factor ⟨1⟩/Corner/XYZ: ↵
\Y scale factor (default = X): ↵
 Rotation angle ⟨0⟩: ↵

As you can see, the only outward differences between the XREF command and the BLOCK or WBLOCK commands are the options of the command. All of the commands function in a similar manner, yet it is the internal workings of the commands that are different. Remember that Xrefs are not added to the drawing file, thereby reducing the size of the master drawings.

Overlaying the current drawing with an external reference

As you have learned in the previous discussion, you can attach an Xref to the current, or master drawing. Then, each time you open the master drawing in AutoCAD, the xref is also loaded, and appears on the screen. This attachment remains permanent until you remove it by using the Detach option of the XREF command.

There are many situations in which you may just want to see what your drawing looks like with another drawing overlaid on it. In manual drafting terms, this was called *overlay drafting,* and involved the use of a pin bar, and registered holes punched along the top of all the drawings used in the overlay. The Overlay option of the XREF command temporarily lays an existing drawing over the one currently on your screen. Because this is a temporary operation, the overlay Xref does not appear on your screen the next time you open the master drawing. This is an important distinction between the Attach and Overlay options of XREF. Use the following to remember the functions of each option.
- **Attach.** The Xref drawing is loaded each time the master drawing is opened.
- **Overlay.** The Xref drawing is loaded only when this command option is used.

Clipping an external reference

The XREFCLIP command combines several functions into one powerful procedure. It enables you to construct a paper space viewport, attach an external reference, and zoom to a specific portion of the drawing. This command can be picked from the File pull-down menu by picking External Reference, and then Clip. The following Command: prompt entry illustrates the use of the XREFCLIP command.

```
Command: XREFCLIP ↵
Initializing...
Enable paper space? ⟨Y⟩: ↵
```

If you are currently in paper space, this prompt does not appear. If you are in model space and answer Yes to this prompt, the TILEMODE variable is set to 0 (Off), and all layers and viewports are turned off temporarily.

```
Entering Paper space. Use MVIEW to insert Model space viewports.
Regenerating drawing.
Xref name: \ACADR13\ARCH\FOOTING ↵
Clip onto what layer? (enter a layer name that does not exist)
First corner of clip box: (pick a corner of the clip box)
Other corner: (pick the opposite corner of the clip box)
```

The next prompts establish a scale for the drawing inside the new paper space viewport. As you will see in the upcoming tutorial in this chapter, it is important that you plan the drawing and layout early. For example, if the plotted scale of this footing detail is to be 3/4" = 1'-0", the scale factor is 16. The plotted drawing is 16 times smaller than the footing. Use that information as follows:

```
Enter the ratio of paper space units to model space units...
Number of paper space units ⟨1.0⟩ 16 ↵
Number of model space units ⟨1.0⟩ ↵
```

The existing layers and viewports are redisplayed and you can accurately position the new viewport containing the clipped reference drawing.

```
Insertion point for clip: (pick an insertion point)
```

Figure 26-1 now shows the original viewport created with XREFCLIP and the new one constructed with XREF Attach.

Figure 26-1.   The XREFCLIP command allows you to construct a viewport with a clipped drawing.

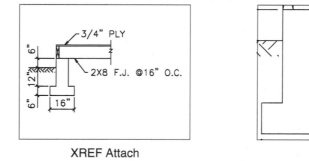

XREF Attach   XREFCLIP

XREF command options

A complete discussion of the use of Xrefs and the creation of multiview drawings for plotting is discussed later in this chapter. This discussion covers many of the options of the XREF command, and the manner in which they can be used to create any type of drawing that is composed of several views, details, or components of varying scales.

A brief description of each of the XREF command options is given here to provide a better understanding of their capabilities.

- **?.** Lists the Xrefs used in the current drawing.
- **Bind.** Allows you to permanently join an Xref to the master drawing. This is similar to using the WBLOCK command. Whereas the WBLOCK command takes a portion of the current drawing and writes it to a file on disk, the Bind option of XREF imports all data from an external drawing file into the current drawing. The Bind option is useful if you must send a drawing file on disk to a plotting service, or give a copy of the drawing file to a client.
- **Detach.** Removes an Xref from the master drawing. It is used if you must delete a detail, view, or portion of a drawing, and wish to remove all its dependent symbols.
- **Path.** Allows you to change the location (path) of the Xref. It is convenient if you must locate the Xrefs in a different hard drive directory or disk drive.
- **Reload.** Enables you to reload any Xrefs without reloading the master drawing. It is useful if you know that an Xref has been updated while you were working on your drawing.
- **Overlay.** An Xref that has been inserted into the drawing, but does not remain attached when the drawing is saved. Unlike the Attach option, AutoCAD does not create a block definition of an overlaid drawing.
- **Attach.** An Xref drawing that has been attached becomes a part of the master drawing in the form of a block definition. Therefore, whenever the master drawing is opened in AutoCAD, the attached Xref is automatically loaded.

BINDING DEPENDENT SYMBOLS TO A DRAWING ◻ AUG 7

AutoCAD refers to *dependent symbols* as named items such as blocks, dimension styles, layers, linetypes, and text styles. If you reference a drawing, you cannot directly use any of its dependent symbols. For example, a layer that exists only on a referenced drawing cannot be made current in the master drawing in order to draw on it. It is the same for text styles. If one of the dependent symbols, such as a dimension style, or linetype, is one that you would like to use on the master drawing, you can permanently "bind," or affix any of these symbols to the master drawing. After a permanent bind is created, the dependent symbol, such as the text style, can be used on the master drawing.

When a drawing is referenced to the master, the layer names of the Xref are given the name of the referenced drawing, followed by the ı symbol, and then the name of the layer. This enables you to quickly identify which layers belong to the specific referenced drawing. See Figure 26-2.

Figure 26-2. Layer names on a reference drawing are preceded by the Xref drawing name and the ı symbol.

Name of referenced drawing

Layer name

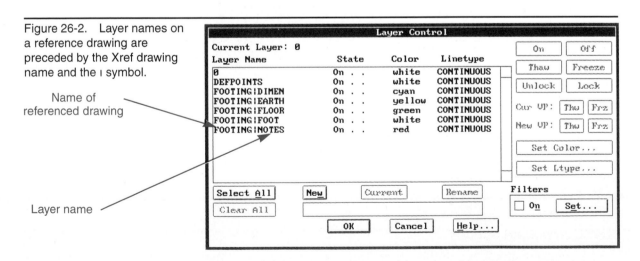

Remember, you are not allowed to draw on any layer that belongs to an Xref. If you wish to use one of these layers or any other dependent symbol in an Xref drawing, use the XBIND command. The

XBIND command and its options are also located in the File pull-down menu as Bind, Figure 26-3. The command sequence is as follows:

Command: **XBIND** ⏎
Block/Dimstyle/LAyer/LType/Style: **LA** ⏎
Dependent layer name(s): **FOOTING:DIMEN,FOOTING:NOTES** ⏎
  Scanning...
2 Layer(s) bound.
Command:

Figure 26-3.   The XBIND command options in the File pull-down menu (shown here highlighted).

XBIND command

Options

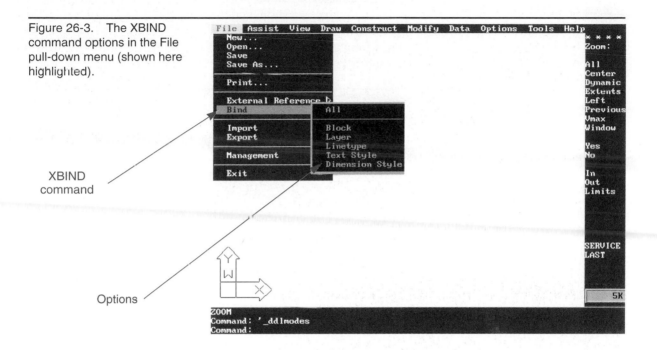

When a layer has been bound to the master drawing, it is renamed. The FOOTING:DIMEN layer becomes FOOTING0DIMEN. Another view of the "Layer Control" dialog box (DDLMODES), shown in Figure 26-4, illustrates this concept.

Keep in mind that when a dependent symbol is bound to the master drawing using XBIND, it becomes a permanent part of the drawing, thus increasing the drawing file size.

Figure 26-4.   Layers that are bound using the XBIND command are renamed. Note the use of the 0.

Layer is bound to the master drawing

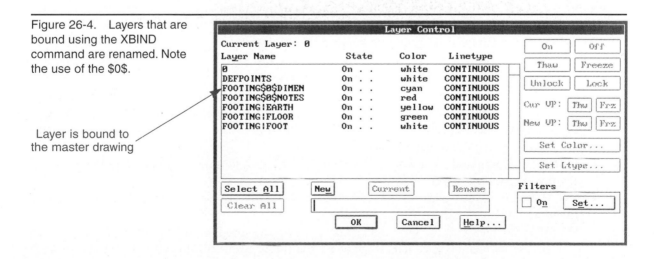

NOTE You can instruct AutoCAD to create and maintain a log file of the Attach, Detach, and Reload functions used on any drawing containing Xrefs. Simply set the XREFCTL system variable to 1. AutoCAD creates an .xlg file having the same name as the current drawing, and locates it in the same directory. Each time you load a drawing that contains Xrefs, or use the Attach, Detach, and Reload options of the XREF command, AutoCAD appends information to the log file. A new heading, or title block, is added to the log file each time the related drawing file is opened. The log file provides the following information:

* Drawing name, date, time, and type of Xref operation.
* Nesting level of all Xrefs affected by the operation.
* A list of the symbol tables affected by the operation, and the names of the symbols added to the drawing. A few examples of symbol tables are blocks, styles, linetypes, and layers.

You can also select Log Files from the Options pull-down menu. This displays a cascading menu that enables you to control the creation of standard drawing editor log files, audit logs, or Xref logs.

CREATING MULTIPLE VIEWPORTS IN PAPER SPACE AUG 10

Multiview mechanical drawings and architectural construction drawings often contain sections or details drawn at different scales. AutoCAD allows you to lay out a multiview drawing with views of different scales, and plot at full scale.

Imagine that you have manually developed three separate drawings of a house floor plan and construction details. Now, assume that you lay a C-size piece of vellum (with preprinted border and title block) on a table. Take the three drawings, each at a different scale, and arrange them on the sheet of vellum. Now, take a full-size photograph of the entire drawing. The photo contains all drawings at the proper scale, including the border and title block. Finally, remove the views from the original sheet of vellum and return them to storage. That's the concept behind creating multiple viewports in paper space.

One of the productive reasons for creating multiple viewport layouts in paper space using drawings and details of different scales, is the ability to plot the layout at the scale of 1:1. This means that scales do not have to be calculated prior to plotting, but they must be considered during the planning stages of your drawing.

Understanding model space and paper space

Creating a multiple viewport layout requires a basic understanding of two concepts–model space and paper space. Model space is the "space" that you draw and design in. It is the default space you enter when AutoCAD is loaded. All of your drawings and models should be created here. Paper space is the mode that you select when you wish to create a layout of your drawing prior to plotting. The powerful aspect of using paper space is that you can create a layout of several different drawings and views, each with different scales. You can even mix 2-D and 3-D views in the same paper space multiview layout.

As mentioned in Chapter 10, four commands govern how you work with model space and paper space. The discussion provided in this chapter will step you through the use of these commands, but a short preview here will help you understand their functions.

* **TILEMODE = 1.** Represents model space, and the VPORTS command is used to establish multiple "tiled" viewports. This is the default setting when you enter AutoCAD.
* **TILEMODE = 0.** Represents paper space, and the MVIEW command is used to create multiple floating viewports in paper space.
* **MSPACE.** Command used when TILEMODE is set to 0, to move from paper space to one of the model space viewports.
* **PSPACE.** Command used when TILEMODE is set to 0, to move from one of the model space viewports to paper space.
* **MVIEW.** Enables you to "cut" model space viewports into the "paper" of paper space. Can only be used when TILEMODE is set to 0. You might even call this command the X-acto™ knife of AutoCAD. Using it, you can cut any number and size of rectangular viewports, at any location on your paper. A viewport created with MVIEW is an AutoCAD object, and can be moved, copied, or resized.

NOTE   The creat option of the MVSETUP command can also be used to construct an arrangement of viewports in paperspace.

If this seems a bit confusing to you, try using the following to help you understand the relationship between model and paper space.

ACTIVITY	SPACE	TILEMODE	COMMAND
Drawing and design	Model	1	VPORTS (tiled)
Plotting and printing layout	Paper	0	MVIEW (objects)

After you use these commands and procedures a few times, you will begin to see how easy they are to understand. Everything you draw is constructed in model space. When preparing a drawing or model for plotting, the necessary views are created in paper space.

Drawing in model space

When you begin a new drawing in AutoCAD, you are automatically in model space. This is the default setting in the ACAD.DWG file. The standard UCS icon is displayed in the lower-left corner of the screen when you are in model space. In addition, a system variable called TILEMODE controls the setting of model space and paper space. The model space default setting of TILEMODE is 1, and the paper space setting is 0. Enter the following to change the paper space:

Command: **TILEMODE** ↵
New value for TILEMODE ⟨1⟩: **0** ↵
Entering Paper space. Use MVIEW to insert Model space viewports.
Regenerating drawing.

Note the special paper space UCS icon resembling a triangle is displayed. See Figure 26-5.

Figure 26-5.   The paper space
UCS icon resembles a triangle.

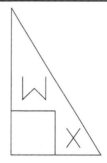

The TILEMODE variable can also be set using the View pull-down menu. Take note of the function of the following three selections in the View pull-down menu:
- **Tiled Model Space.** Sets TILEMODE to 1 (model space). Use the VPORTS command to created tiled viewports.
- **Floating Model Space.** Executes the MSPACE command and activates the crosshairs in the current viewport. If there are no viewports in paper space, the MVIEW command is executed.
- **Paper Space.** Sets TILEMODE to 0 (paper space). Use the MVIEW command to create viewports in paper space.

The TILEMODE, MSPACE, and PSPACE commands can also be selected in the VIEW screen menu.

PROFESSIONAL TIP

All system variable names can be entered at the Command: prompt.

MULTIPLE VIEWPORT CREATION OVERVIEW

AUG 10

An overview of creating multiple viewports for plotting will first be discussed to introduce the commands and options, before detailing the creation of a multiview plot. The most important visualization aspect involved in creating a multiview layout is to imagine that the sheet of paper you are creating will contain several cutouts *(viewports)*, through which you can see other drawings *(models)*. See Figure 26-6.

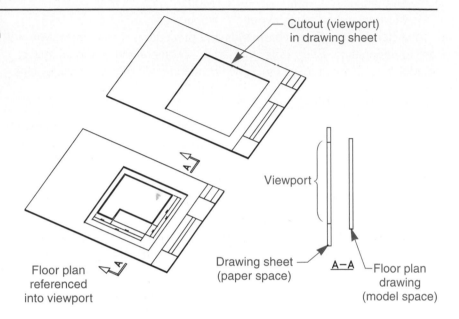

Figure 26-6.   Views of other drawings can be seen through viewports "cut into" paper space.

Imagine holding a sheet of paper with a border and title block in front of you. Now, use a knife to cut a rectangle out of the paper. This is a viewport. Place a scaled print (model) of a house floor plan behind the opening. Use your knife to cut another smaller rectangular opening in the paper to the left of the first. Cut a third viewport above the second one. Find scaled prints of a stair detail and a footing detail drawing. Place each of these behind the two new viewports. Now, take a photograph of the completed drawing. That's a simplified version of the process used to create viewports in paper space.

As you know, objects and designs should be created at full size in model space. If you are designing a machine part, you are probably using decimal units. If you are designing a house, you are using architectural units. When constructing each of these, you likely used the full dimensions of the part or house.

Now, imagine the C-size paper is hanging up in front of you, and the first viewport is cut to be 12″ wide and 10″ high. You want to display the floor plan of a house inside the opening. If you then place the full-size model of the floor plan directly behind the C-size paper, the house will extend many feet beyond the edges of the paper. How can you place the drawing within the viewport? You know that the floor plan should be displayed inside the viewport at a scale of 1/4″ = 1′-0″. The scale factor of 1/4″ = 1′-0″ is 48. Therefore, you need to move the floor plan model away from the C-size paper until it is 1/48 (reciprocal of 48) the size it is now. This is accomplished with ZOOM command's XP (Times Paper space) option discussed later. When you do that, the entire floor plan fits inside the viewport you cut. See Figure 26-7.

Remember to zoom to the appropriate scale after referencing *(inserting)* a drawing into a viewport so that your multiview plots work properly. Review the brief step-by-step procedure for constructing multiview plots. The first six steps can be omitted if your prototype drawing contains these settings and entities.

- Set TILEMODE to 0 to enter paper space.
- Set UNITS to match the type of drawing you are creating.
- Set LIMITS to match paper size and plotter limits.
- Make a layer for referenced drawings.

Figure 26-7.   The floor plan is placed inside a viewport.

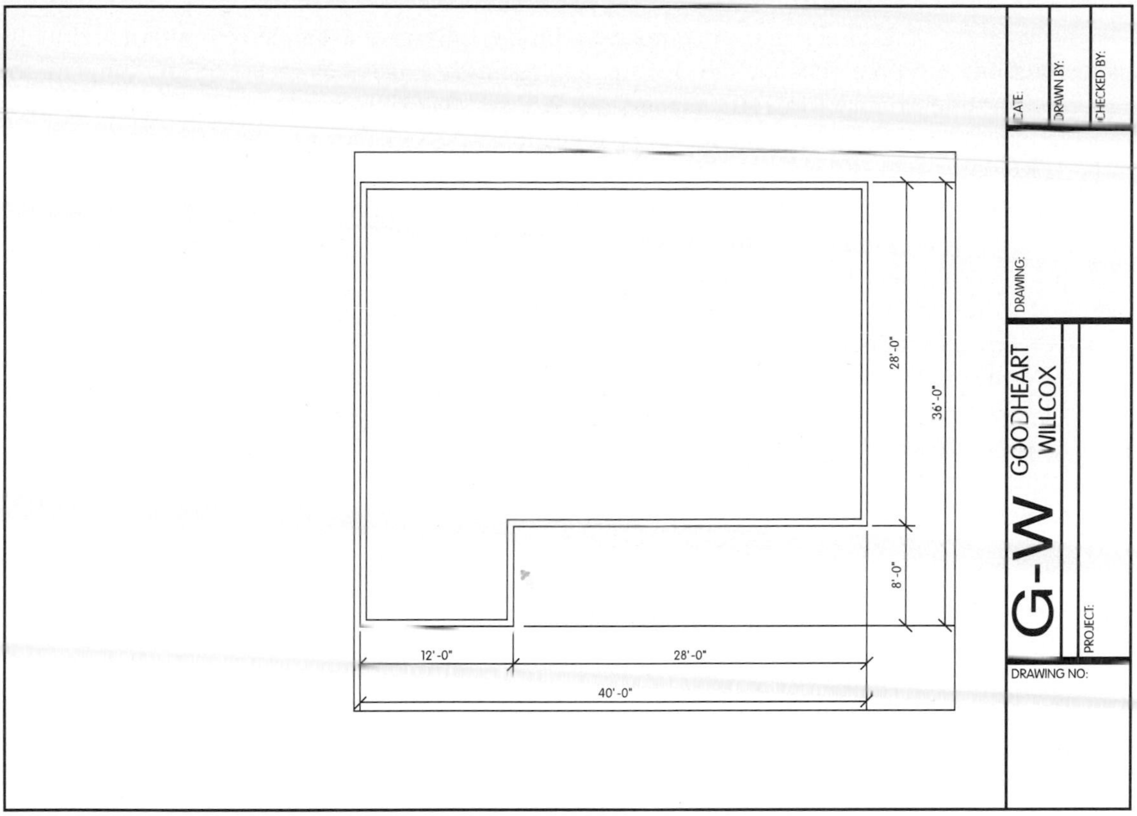

- Create a border layer or reference a drawing that has a border and title block. You may want to use MVSETUP (discussed in Chapter 19).
- Make a layer for viewport entities, and set this as the current layer.
- Enter MVIEW and make the size viewport needed.
- Change to model space.
- Use the XREF command to reference an existing drawing. Insert the drawing at 0,0 and use the remaining defaults.
- Zoom to the extents of the drawing.
- Set the scale to the appropriate value using the ZOOM command's XP option.
- Use VPLAYER (Viewpoint Layer) and either the Vpvisdflt (ViewPort VISibility DeFauLTs) or Freeze options to freeze layers of this referenced drawing in all new viewports or selected viewports.
- Return to paper space.
- Repeat the process using the MVIEW command.

CONSTRUCTING A MULTIVIEW DRAWING FOR PLOTTING | AUG 7 |

Now that you have a good idea of the multiview plotting process, the following example leads you through the details of the procedure. This example uses a house floor plan, a stair detail, and a footing detail. This drawing is not among the sample drawings furnished with the AutoCAD. Instead, the drawing is based on Exercise 26-1. Complete Exercise 26-1 before working through the example. It is composed of three simple architectural drawings.

EXERCISE 26-1

❑ If you wish to work along at your computer with the following example of multiview drawing construction, complete this exercise before reading further. It is not necessary to complete this exercise in order to understand the process discussed in the following example, but it may assist you in quickly grasping the concepts of the procedure.

❑ The three drawings shown at the bottom of this page–the floor plan, stair detail, and footing detail–should be created for this exercise. They are highly simplified for the purpose of this exercise and explanation, and should not be regarded as complete representations of actual designs. Exact dimensions are not necessary, because the purpose of this exercise is to illustrate the creation of a multiview drawing. You may simplify the drawings further to speed up the exercise.

❑ Each drawing should be created, named, and stored separately with different names. Do not put a border or title block on the drawings. The names are shown in the following table.

FLOOR.DWG		STAIR.DWG		FOOTING.DWG	
Layer	**Color**	**Layer**	**Color**	**Layer**	**Color**
Wall	White	Wall	Yellow	Floor	Green
Dimen	Cyan	Floor	White	Foot	White
Notes	Red	Stair	Green	Dimen	Cyan
		Foot	White	Notes	Red
		Dimen	Cyan	Earth	Yellow
		Notes	Red		

❑ Use the following scales and scale factors when constructing each of the drawings.
  FLOOR.DWG: 1/4″ = 1′-0″ (Scale factor = 48)
  STAIR.DWG: 3/8″ = 1′-0″ (Scale factor = 32)
  FOOTING.DWG: 3/4″ = 1′-0″ (Scale factor = 16)
The scale factors are important when setting the DIMSCALE dimensioning variable, and when establishing text height. Remember to multiply the plotted text height, such as .125, by the scale factor, such as 48, to get the text height to use in AutoCAD (.125 x 48 = 6). The scale factor is also used with the ZOOM XP command discussed later in the text.

❑ Save the drawings to a hard disk subdirectory, preferably not in the AutoCAD directory. Check with your instructor or supervisor before creating or using hard disk space. Save backup copies on a floppy disk.

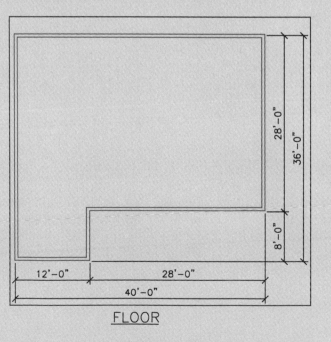

FLOOR

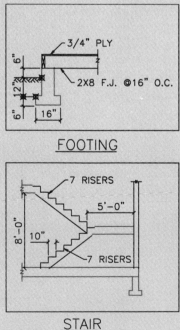

FOOTING

STAIR

Initial drawing setup

The first aspect of drawing setup is to place a border and title block on the screen. It should be the proper size for the plot you wish to make. This can be accomplished in one of several ways, depending on the depth of your preparation. First, set TILEMODE to 0, then:

- Draw a border on a separate layer, then draw a title block.
- Draw a border and insert a predrawn title block.

or

- Insert a predrawn standard border and title block prototype containing all constant text and attributes for variable information.

The method you use is not of primary importance for this example, but it is always best to use existing borders and title blocks for reasons that are discussed later.

PROFESSIONAL TIP

    This initial setup phase is unnecessary if your school or company uses preprinted border and title block sheets. You might use a "phantom" border and title block sheet on the screen for layout purposes, and to add additional information to the title block. This phantom information can be frozen before plotting.

When setting up a drawing, first enter paper space, then set the units and limits to match the type of drawing you are creating. Be sure that the extents of your border and title block match the maximum active plotting area, or "clip limits" of your plotter. This example uses a standard architectural C-size sheet (18 × 24), and assumes that the plotter's active area is .75″ less on all sides, for a total plotting area of 16.5″ × 22.5″.

```
Command: TILEMODE ↵
New value for TILEMODE ⟨1⟩: 0 ↵
Entering Paper space. Use MVIEW to insert Model space viewports.
Regenerating drawing.
Command: UNITS ↵
```

Use the following UNITS settings and then reply to the Command: prompts.

- Architectural units.
- Units precision = 1/2″.
- Systems of angle measure = Decimal degrees.
- Angle precision = 0.
- Direction for angle 0 = East (0).
- Angles measured counterclockwise.

```
Command: LIMITS ↵
Reset Paper space limits:
ON/OFF/⟨Lower left corner⟩ ⟨0′-0″,0′-0″⟩: ↵
Upper right corner ⟨1′-0″,0′-9″⟩: 26,20 ↵
```

The upper-right corner limits of 26,20 provides additional space on the screen outside the paper limits.

```
Command: ZOOM ↵
All/Center/Dynamic/Extents/Left/Previous/Vmax/Window/⟨Scale(X/XP)⟩: A ↵
Regenerating drawing.
```

Creating new layers

The border and title block should be on a separate layer, so you may want to create a new layer, called BORDER or TITLE, and assign it a separate color. Be sure to make this new layer current before you draw the border, insert a prototype, or use MVSETUP.

At this point you can set an appropriate snap grid and visible grid values. If you wish to use an existing border and title block, insert it now, and those values should already be set in the prototype drawing.

One of the principle functions of this example is to use existing drawings of the house floor plan, stairs, and footing. These drawings will not become a part of our new drawing, but they will be "referenced" with the XREF command in order to save drawing file space. Therefore, you should also create a new layer for these drawings and name it XREF. Assign the XREF layer the color of 0.

The referenced drawings will fit inside viewports that are made with the MVIEW command. These viewports are rectangles and are given the entity name of Viewport. Therefore, they can be edited like any other AutoCAD entity. Create a layer called VIEWPORTS or VPORT for these entities and assign it a color.

The layers of any existing drawings that you reference (Xref) into your new drawing remain intact. Therefore, you do not have to create additional layers unless you want to add information to your drawing.

If you do not have an existing C-size architectural border and title block, you can draw a border at this time. Make the BORDER layer current and draw a polyline border using the dimensions of 16.5″ × 22.5″. Draw a title block if you wish. Your screen should look similar to Figure 26-8.

Figure 26-8.   The border and title block in paper space.

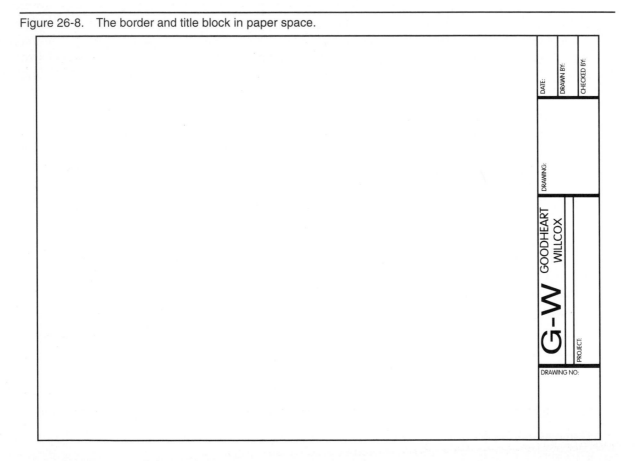

Creating a viewport in paper space

The process of creating viewports is completed in paper space because viewports are "cut" out of the paper. When creating a drawing in paper space, your screen represents a sheet of paper. You must now create an opening, called a viewport, through which you can view a model, design, or drawing. In this case, the model is a floor plan. First, cut an opening in the paper so you can see the floor plan that is behind it. Keep in mind that the sheet of paper measures 18″ × 24″ and the first viewport to be cut measures 11.5″ × 12″.

The MVIEW command is used to create the viewports. Since viewports are entities, make the VIEWPORTS layer current, so they reside on their own layer. This allows them to be frozen later to avoid being plotted. The first viewport can be located from the lower-left corner of the border by using the From object snap mode to locate the corner. Enter the following:

Command: **MVIEW** ⏎
ON/OFF/Hideplot/Fit/2/3/4/Restore/⟨First Point⟩: **FROM** ⏎
Base point: **INT** ⏎
of *(pick lower-left corner of border)*
⟨Offset⟩: **@7,3** ⏎
Other corner: **@12,11.5** ⏎
Regenerating drawing.

Your screen should now look like Figure 26-9.

At this point, you can continue creating as many viewports as required. However, this example continues the process, and references a drawing into the new viewport. The other options of the MVIEW command are discussed in detail later in this chapter.

Figure 26-9.   A viewport added to the border and title block in paper space.

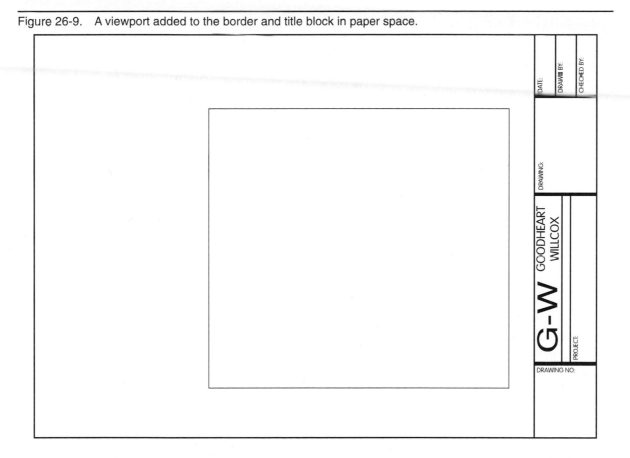

Placing views in the drawing

A viewport has now been created into which you can insert a view of the 2-D or 3-D model (drawing) that has been previously created. In this case, we will reference the drawing of the floor plan named FLOOR. Instead of using the INSERT command, which combines an existing drawing with the new one, use the XREF command so that AutoCAD creates a "reference" to the FLOOR drawing. This allows the size of the new drawing to remain small because the FLOOR drawing has not been combined with it.

The following procedure allows you to enter model space, reference an existing drawing to the new one, and ZOOM to see the referenced drawing.

    Command: **MSPACE** ↵
    Command: **LAYER** ↵
    ?/Make/Set/New/ON/OFF/Color/Ltype/Freeze/Thaw/LOck/Unlock: **S** ↵
    New current layer ⟨VIEWPORTS⟩: **XREF** ↵
    ?/Make/Set/New/ON/OFF/Color/Ltype/Freeze/Thaw/LOck/Unlock:↵
    Command: **XREF** ↵
    ?/Bind/Detach/Path/Reload/Overlay/⟨Attach⟩: ↵

The "Select File to Attach" dialog box is displayed. See Figure 26-10.

Figure 26-10.   The "Select Files to Attach" dialog box.

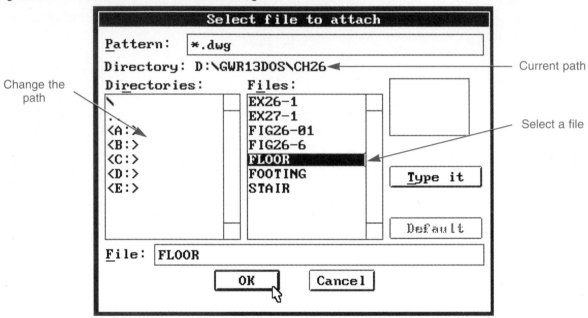

PROFESSIONAL TIP

If you have disabled the display of dialog boxes by setting the FILEDIA system variable to 0, you can still force the dialog box to appear by entering the tilde (~) at the Xref to Attach: prompt.

Select the FLOOR drawing in the dialog box, or the filename can be typed at the Xref to Attach: prompt. The following prompt then appears:

    Insertion point: **0,0** ↵
      X scale factor ⟨1⟩/Corner/XYZ: ↵
        scale factor (default = X): ↵
      Rotation angle ⟨0⟩: ↵
    Command: **ZOOM** ↵
    All/Center/Dynamic/Extents/Left/Previous/Vmax/Window/⟨Scale(X/XP)⟩: **E** ↵

Your drawing should now resemble the one shown in Figure 26-11.

Figure 26-11.   The floor plan is referenced into the first viewport.

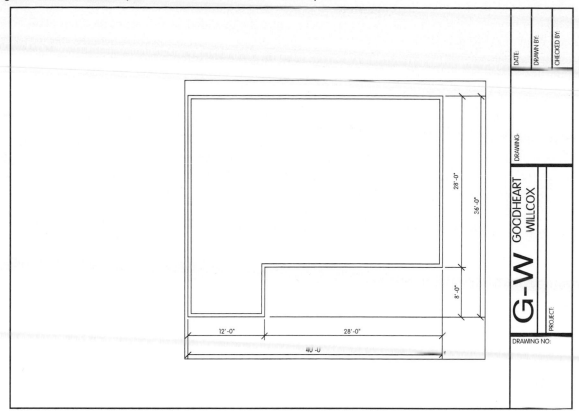

All of the layers on the referenced drawing are added to the new drawing. These layers can be distinguished from existing layers because the drawing name is automatically placed in front of the layer name and separated by the ı symbol. Pick Layers… in the Data pull-down menu to see this layer-naming technique. See Figure 26-12.

Figure 26-12.   The "Layer Control" dialog box shows the technique used for naming layers on referenced drawings. The name of the referenced drawing appears first, followed by the ı symbol and the name of the layer.

Layers on a referenced drawing

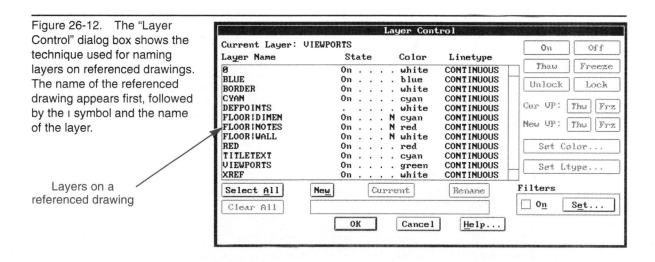

Scaling a drawing in a viewport

When a drawing has been referenced and placed in a viewport, it is ready to be scaled. After using the ZOOM command's Extents option, the referenced drawing fills the viewport. However, this does not imply that the drawing is displayed at the correct scale.

The scale factor of each view of the multiview drawing is an important number to remember; it is the number you use to size your drawing in the viewport. The scale factor is used in conjunction with the ZOOM command's XP option (Times Paper space). Since the intended final scale of the floor plan on the plotted drawing is to be 1/4″ = 1′-0″, the scale factor is 48, or 1/48 of full size. A detailed discussion of determining scale factors is given in this Chapter 12 of this text. Be sure you are still in model space, and that the crosshairs are present in the viewport where you are working. Enter the following:

Command: **ZOOM** ↵
All/Center/Dynamic/Extents/Left/Previous/Vmax/Window/⟨Scale(X/XP)⟩: **1/48XP** ↵

The drawing may not change much in size depending on the size of the viewport. Also, keep in mind that the viewport itself is an entity that can be moved or stretched if needed. Remember to change to paper space when editing the size of the viewport. If part of your drawing extends beyond the edge of the viewport after using the ZOOM command's XP option, simply use the STRETCH command to change the size of the viewport.

Controlling viewport layer visibility

If you now create another viewport using MVIEW, the floor plan will immediately fill it. This is because a viewport is just a window through which you can view a drawing or 3-D model that has been referenced to the current drawing. One way to control what is visible in subsequent viewports is to freeze all layers of the FLOOR drawing in any new viewports that are created. The VPLAYER (ViewPort LAYER) command controls the display of layers in specific viewports, whereas the LAYER command controls layers in all viewports.

The following example uses the VPLAYER command and the Vpvisdflt option to control the display of layers in new viewports.

Command: **VPLAYER** ↵
?/Freeze/Thaw/Reset/Newfrz/Vpvisdflt: **V** ↵
Layer name(s) to change default viewport visibility: **FLOOR*** ↵
Change default viewport visibility to Frozen/⟨Thawed⟩: **F** ↵
?/Freeze/Thaw/Reset/Newfrz/Vpvisdflt: ↵

The asterisk (*) after the name FLOOR instructs AutoCAD to freeze all of the layers on the FLOOR drawing in subsequent viewports. Look at the "Layer Control" dialog box in Figure 26-13 and note the "N" after the layer name, directly to the left of the color. This indicates the layer is frozen in a new viewport.

Figure 26-13.   The "N" to the left of the color indicates the layer is frozen in new viewports. Layers can be frozen in selected viewports using the Cur VP and New VP buttons (shown here highlighted).

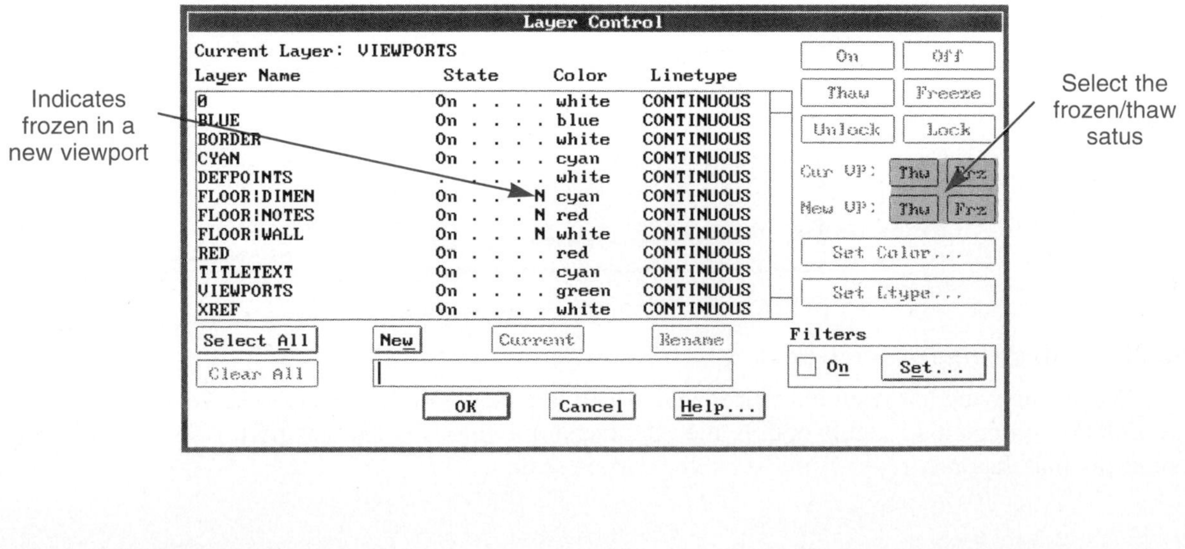

Any layer's frozen or thawed status in a viewport can also be controlled by using the Cur VP: and the New VP: buttons on the right side of the "Layer Control" dialog box. See Figure 26-13. Select one of the FLOOR layers, then pick the Thw button of the New VP: option. Notice that the "N" is removed. These buttons are the same as using the VPLAYER command. The remaining options of the VPLAYER command are discussed later in the chapter.

Using menus to control viewport layer visibility

The VPLAYER command options are found in the Data pull-down menu by selecting Viewport Layer Controls, and by picking VPlayer: in the DATA screen menu. Both selections display all of the options of the VPLAYER command. See Figure 26-14.

Figure 26-14.   The VPLAYER command options are found in the Data pull-down menu by selecting Viewport Layer Controls, or by picking VPlayer: in the DATA screen menu.

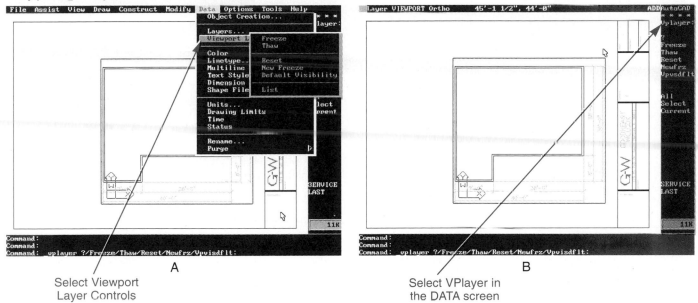

A

B

Select Viewport
Layer Controls

Select VPlayer in
the DATA screen

Creating additional viewports

The previous example of creating a viewport and referencing a drawing to it is the same process that is used to create the additional two viewports in our example. In this case, two viewports are created before using the XREF command. If you know the number, size, and location of all viewports needed on a multiview drawing, it may save time to create them all at once.

PROFESSIONAL TIP

If your class or company uses standard sheet layouts containing several views, create prototype drawings that contain viewports. Viewports can always be added, deleted, or resized on a drawing. Custom prototype drawings with viewports can be added to the list in the MVSETUP command.

The following command sequence resets paper space, changes the current layer to VIEWPORT, and uses the MVIEW command and GRIPS to create new viewports. It then returns to model space to reference new drawings, and uses the ZOOM command to size the drawing in the viewport. The VPLAYER command is also used to control layer visibility in new viewports.

Command: **PSPACE** ↵
Command: **LAYER** ↵
?/Make/Set/New/ON/OFF/Color/Ltype/Freeze/Thaw/LOck/Unlock: **S** ↵
New current layer ⟨current⟩: **VIEWPORTS** ↵
?/Make/Set/New/ON/OFF/Color/Ltype/Freeze/Thaw/LOck/Unlock: ↵
Command: **MVIEW** ↵
ON/OFF/Hideplot/Fit/2/3/4/Restore/⟨First Point⟩: **.5,3** ↵ *(this is the location relative to the lower-left corner of the border)*
Other corner: **6.5,9** ↵

Be sure grips are on and pick the viewport you just drew. Copy the viewport to a position directly above the first. Next, use the grips and STRETCH command to change the height of the top viewport

Figure 26-15.   Two additional viewports are placed and sized on the drawing.

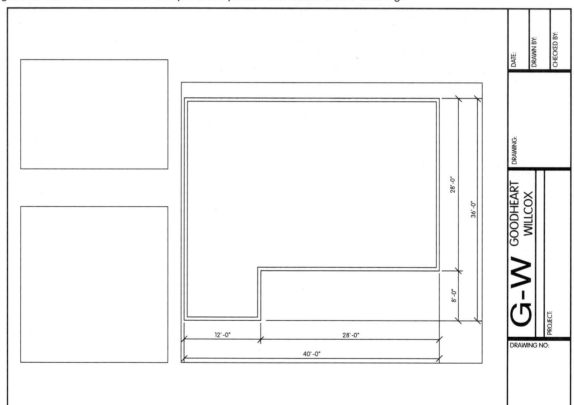

to 5″ while keeping the width the same. The final arrangement of the three viewports is shown in Figure 26-15.

Now that the viewports are complete, you can begin referencing the remaining two drawings. Change to model space, set the current layer to XREF, and pick the lower-left viewport to make it active. The STAIR drawing can now be referenced.

Command: **XREF** ↵
?/Bind/Detach/Path/Reload/Overlay/⟨Attach⟩: ↵
Xref to Attach ⟨FLOOR⟩: **STAIR** ↵

Insert the drawing at 0,0 or pick an insertion point, and accept the defaults for the remaining prompts. Notice in Figure 26-16 that the stair drawing is shown in all three viewports. The VPLAYER command must be used to freeze the stair layers in selected viewports.

```
Command: VPLAYER ⏎
?/Freeze/Thaw/Reset/Newfrz/Vpvisdflt: F ⏎
Layer(s) to freeze: STAIR* ⏎
Select/〈Current〉: S ⏎
Switching to Paper space.
Select objects: (pick the outlines of both the large and upper-left viewports)
Select objects: ⏎
Switching to Model space.
?/Freeze/Thaw/Reset/Newfrz/Vpvisdflt: ⏎
```

Use the ZOOM command's Extents option to display the drawing completely in the lower-left viewport, then scale the drawing with ZOOM XP.

Figure 26-16.   The reference drawing, STAIR, is displayed in all viewports. VPLAYER must be used to restrict its visibility.

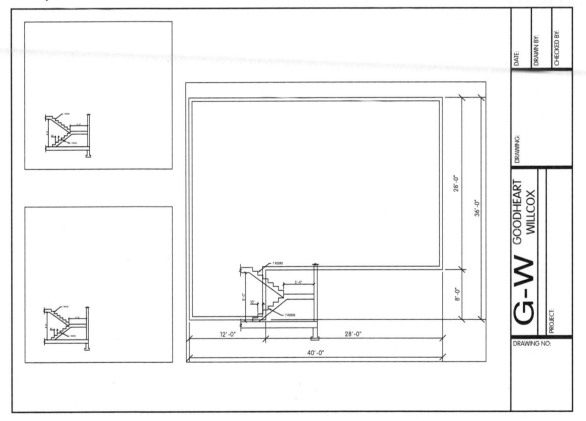

NOTE   If you do not use ZOOM Extents first, your drawing may disappear after using ZOOM XP. This may occur if you pick the insertion point when using the XREF command, rather than entering 0,0 for the insertion point.

The plotted scale of the stair detail should be 3/8″ = 1′-0″. The scale factor is calculated as follows:

$$3/8'' = 1'\text{-}0''$$
$$.375'' = 12''$$
$$12/.375 = \mathbf{32}$$

The scale factor is 32, but you must use the reciprocal (1/32) for the ZOOM XP command.

    Command: **ZOOM** ↵
    All/Center/Dynamic/Extents/Left/Previous/Vmax/Window/⟨Scale⟩(X/XP)⟩: **1/32XP** ↵

Your drawing should now resemble the one shown in Figure 26-17.

Figure 26-17.   The scaled STAIR drawing in the second viewport.

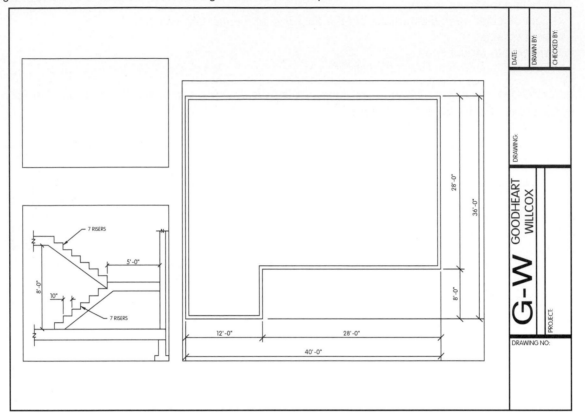

PROFESSIONAL TIP

    You can use any display command inside a viewport. If a drawing is not centered after using ZOOM XP, simply use PAN to move it around. If lines of a drawing touch a viewport edge, those lines will not be visible if the viewport layer is frozen or turned off.

    The final drawing can now be inserted into the last viewport. Pick the top viewport with your pointing device to make it active. Notice that the current viewport is surrounded by a line. Crosshairs should now be displayed in the active viewport. Try to prepare the third view by following these steps.
- Model space should be active.
- The XREF layer should be current.
- XREF Attach the FOOTING drawing.
- Freeze the FOOTING layers in the other two viewports with VPLAYER.
- Zoom Extents, then ZOOM XP for proper scale. Plotted scale is to be 3/4″ = 1′-0″.
- Use the PAN command if necessary to center the drawing.

NOTE   Be sure to set the current layer to XREF when referencing a drawing so that the inserted drawing is not placed on another layer, such as VIEWPORTS.

When the final drawing has been referenced and scaled, your screen should look like Figure 26-18.

Figure 26-18. The new drawing is completed with the referencing of the footing.

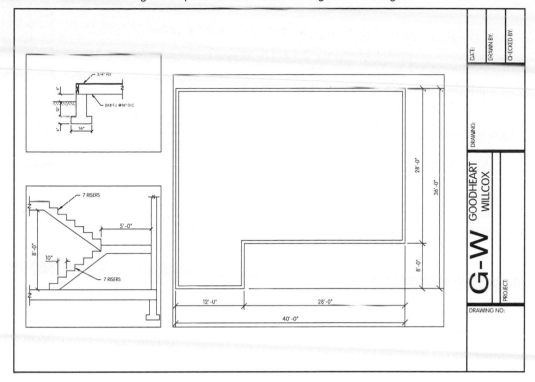

Adjusting viewport display, size, and location

If you need to adjust a drawing within a viewport, first be sure that you are in model space. Then, pick the desired viewport to make it active, and use an appropriate display command such as ZOOM or PAN.

The entire viewport can be moved to another location, but you must first be in paper space. Pick the viewport box and its grips appear. An object inside the viewport is not selected when picked because those objects are in model space. After selection, adjust the location of the viewports. Remember the following when adjusting viewports:

• **Model space.** Adjust the display of a drawing or model inside a specific viewport.
• **Paper space.** Adjust the size or location of a viewport.

Adding notes and titles

There are two ways in which titles and notes can be added to a multiview drawing. The first method is to add the notations to the original drawing. In this manner, all titles and notes are referenced to the new drawing. This is the best system to use if the titles, scale label, and notes will not change.

However, titles may change. You may want to be sure that all titles of views are the same text style, or you might want to add a special symbol. This is easily completed after the drawings are referenced. The most important thing to remember is that you must be in paper space to add text. You can use new or existing text styles to add titles and notes to a drawing using DTEXT.

Removing viewport outlines

The viewport outlines can be turned off for plotting purposes, as shown in Figure 26-19. Turn off or freeze the VIEWPORTS layer as follows:

```
Command: LAYER ↵
?/Make/Set/New/ON/OFF/Color/Ltype/Freeze/Thaw/LOck/Unlock: F ↵
Layer name(s) to Freeze: VIEWPORTS ↵
?/Make/Set/New/ON/OFF/Color/Ltype/Freeze/Thaw/LOck/Unlock: ↵
```

Figure 26-19.   The completed drawing with titles added and viewport outlines turned off.

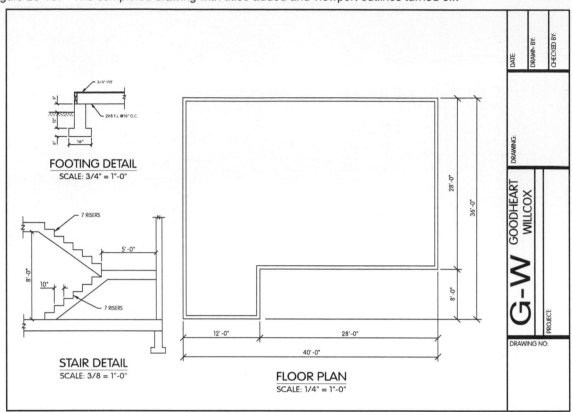

PROFESSIONAL TIP

Paperspace viewport can also be placed on the DEFPOINTS layer, which is automatically created when you draw a dimension. Objects on this layer are seen but never plotted. You can also creat a DEFPOINTS layer if it does not exist.

NOTE   If you turn off the VIEWPORTS layer, and a box still surrounds one of the views, you are probably still in model space. Remember that a box outlines the current viewport in model space. Type PS to enter paper space and the outline disappears.

PLOTTING A MULTIVIEW DRAWING

You have already taken care of scaling the views when you referenced them and used the ZOOM XP command. The drawing that now appears on your screen in paper space can be plotted at full scale, 1=1, with the PLOT command.

Using the PLOT command in this manner is a simple procedure, but only if you planned your drawing(s) at the start of the project. The process of creating a properly scaled multiview layout will go smoothly if you have planned the project. Review the following items, and keep them in mind when starting any drawing or design project–especially one which involves the creation of a multiview paper space layout.

- Determine the size of paper to be used.
- Determine the type of title block, notes, revision blocks, parts lists, etc. that will appear on the drawing.
- Prepare a quick sketch of the view layouts and their plotted scales.
- Determine the scales to be used for each viewport.
- Establish proper text styles and heights based on the drawing scale factors.
- Set the DIMSCALE variable using the proper scale factor when creating drawings in model space.

There is no substitute for planning a project before you begin. It may seem like an unnecessary expense of time, but it will save time later in the project, and may help you become more productive in all your work.

PROFESSIONAL TIP

 You may never have to specify a scale other than full (1=1) when plotting. Any object or design, whether 2-D or 3-D, can be referenced into a border and title block drawing, scaled with ZOOM XP, and then plotted. Try using the paper space layout procedure for all your drawings, even if they are just a single view. You will find that you need fewer border and title block prototype drawings, and the process will become quicker.

MVIEW COMMAND OPTIONS   AUG 10

The primary purpose of the MVIEW command is to create viewports in paper space. If you use the MVIEW command in model space when TILEMODE is set to 0, AutoCAD changes to paper space for the rest of the command, then returns you to model space. The MVIEW command also allows you to change the size of viewports, fit them in the displayed screen area, or default to a specific value. Brief descriptions of each follow:

- **ON/OFF.** The contents of a viewport (the drawing or design in model space) can be turned on or off. If viewports are turned off, less time is required to regenerate the drawing.
- **Hideplot.** Allows you to select the viewports you wish to have hidden lines removed from when plotting in paper space. Hidden lines are removed by selecting ON, and are shown by selecting OFF.
- **Fit.** Creates a viewport to fit the current screen display. You can zoom into an area first, then use the MVIEW command's Fit option to create a viewport in the windowed area.
- **2/3/4.** AutoCAD automatically creates a configuration of 2, 3, or 4 viewports. The prompt is similar to the same option for the VPORTS command. When 2 or 3 is selected, you are prompted for specific locations and arrangements.

    2–Horizontal/⟨Vertical⟩:
    3–Horizontal/Vertical/Above/Below/Left/⟨Right⟩:

When 4 is selected, four equal size viewports are created within a specified area.
- **Restore.** This option works if you have used the VPORTS command to create and save viewport configurations. AutoCAD asks for the configuration name, then allows you to either specify the locations and size of the viewports, or fit it into the current display.

    ?/Name of window configuration to insert ⟨*ACTIVE⟩: *(enter the name and press*
       ENTER)
    Fit/⟨First Point⟩:

If you accept the default, you can position and size the new viewports by selecting two points to window an area in paper space. If you select Fit, the restored viewports are scaled to fit the graphics area.
- **⟨First Point⟩.** The default option allows you to select or enter the coordinates of the first corner of the viewport. Then, you are prompted for the other corner and a window is attached to the crosshairs. Pick the opposite corner and the viewport is drawn.

EXERCISE 26-2

❑ Use the prototype method to recall the border and title block drawing you used in Exercise 26-1. Name the drawing EX26-2.
❑ Create layers for referenced drawings (XREF) and viewports (VIEWPORT).
❑ Use the MVIEW 2/3/4 option to create an arrangement of three viewports on the VIEWPORT layer. Leave space in the upper-right corner for an additional viewport.
❑ Use the ZOOM command's Window option to display the open area in the upper-right corner of the drawing.
❑ Select the MVIEW command's Fit option to create a viewport in the current screen display.
❑ Reference the FLOOR drawing used in Exercise 26-1 into one of the viewports in the group of three viewports. Be sure the XREF layer is current.
❑ Turn off the contents of that viewport with the MVIEW command's OFF option.
❑ Save the drawing as A:EX26-2, then quit the drawing session.

VPLAYER COMMAND OPTIONS

AUG 10

The VPLAYER (ViewPort LAYER) command controls the visibility of layers within selected viewports. This function differs from the LAYER command that controls the visibility of all layers in the drawing. The following list describes the function of each of the VPLAYER command option.

- **?.** After entering a question mark, AutoCAD prompts you to select a viewport. If you select the upper-left viewport in Figure 26-18, the following display appears on your screen:

```
Layers currently frozen in viewport 4:
FLOORiWALL
FLOORiDIMEN
FLOORiNOTES
STAIRiDIMEN
STAIRiFLOOR
STAIRiNOTES
STAIRiSTAIR
STAIRiWALL
?/Freeze/Thaw/Reset/Newfrz/Vpvisdflt:
```

- **Freeze.** Enables you to selectively freeze one or more layers in any selected viewport(s).
- **Thaw.** This option allows you to thaw layers that were frozen with the Freeze option. As with the Freeze option, you can selectively thaw one or more layers in any viewport(s).
- **Reset.** Removes any viewport visibility default settings that were established with the Vpvisdflt option, and resets it to the default setting for a layer in a given viewport. This means that if you reset layers in a selected viewport, they become visible.
- **Newfrz.** Enables you to create a new frozen layer in all viewports, then you can thaw it in the viewport you wish it to be displayed in. The prompt for this option is:

```
?/Freeze/Thaw/Reset/Newfrz/Vpvisdflt: N ↵
New Viewport frozen layer name(s): WALLS ↵
?/Freeze/Thaw/Reset/Newfrz/Vpvisdflt: T ↵
```

After entering the Thaw option, you can select the viewport(s) in which you want the new layer named WALLS to be visible.

- **Vpvisdflt (ViewPort VISibility DeFauLT).** This option enables you to control the visibility of layers in new viewports. Use this option if you do not want existing layers to be visible in new viewports.

```
?/Freeze/Thaw/Reset/Newfrz/Vpvisdflt: V ↵
Layer name(s) to change default viewport visibility: (enter layer name)
```

EXERCISE 26-3

❑ Recall the drawing that you constructed in this chapter. It should contain three viewports, each containing an architectural detail.
❑ Be sure that the VIEWPORTS layer is on so that the viewport outlines are visible.
❑ List the layers currently frozen in the large viewport.
❑ Freeze the DIMEN layers in all viewports. Remember that in each viewport, the DIMEN layer name has been altered. For example, in the STAIR drawing, the layer is STAIRıDIMEN.
❑ Thaw the DIMEN layers in all viewports. Use a wild-card character (*) to thaw them all at once.
❑ Use the VPLAYER command's Reset option to remove all Vpvisdflt settings. The viewports should become crowded with multiple views. Use UNDO to remove the effects of the last command.
❑ Create a new frozen layer with the VPLAYER command's Newfrz option, and name it BOM. List the frozen layers in any of the viewports to see if BOM is frozen.
❑ Thaw BOM in the FOOTING viewport, then list the frozen layers in that viewport.
❑ Do not save your drawing.

XREF COMMAND OPTIONS

AUG 7

The XREF (eXternal REFerence) command enables you to add existing models or drawings to the current drawing without actually combining the files. AutoCAD creates a reference to an existing drawing. This allows you to keep the size of drawing files to a minimum. The following options are included when the XREF command is used.

- **?.** All Xrefs in your drawing are displayed.

      Command: **XREF** ↵
      ?/Bind/Detach/Path/Reload/⟨Attach⟩: **?** ↵
      Xref(s) to list ⟨*⟩: ↵

Xref Name	Path
FLOOR	\gwr13dos\ch26\floor
FOOTING	\gwr13dos\ch26\footing
STAIR	\gwr13dos\ch26\stair
Total Xref(s): 3	

- **Bind.** This option permanently attaches an external reference to your drawing. It is a good idea to bind Xrefs on drawings that are completed and are to be stored (archived), or drawings that are to be sent to a client, instructor, or service bureau for plotting.
- **Detach.** Referenced drawings that have been erased from your drawing, or that are no longer needed, can then be detached. AutoCAD deletes the specified Xref(s) from the drawing file.
- **Path.** AutoCAD remembers the location, or "path" of a referenced drawing. If, for any reason, you must move the referenced drawings to another directory or disk drive, use the Path option to tell AutoCAD the new location. For example, if you were to relocate the FOOTING drawing to the \ACADR13\STRUCT subdirectory, use the following sequence:

      Command: **XREF** ↵
      ?/Bind/Detach/Path/Reload/Overlay/⟨Attach⟩: **P** ↵
      Edit path for which xref(s): **FOOTING** ↵
        Scanning…
      Xref name: FOOTING
      Old path: \gwr13dos\ch26\footing
      New path: **\ACADR13\STRUCT** ↵

- **Reload.** You can update any of the referenced drawings at any time by using the Reload option. This may be appropriate if someone in the class or office made revisions to a drawing that you referenced.

  Reload Xref FOOTING: \acadr13\struct\footing

- **Overlay.** Using the Overlay option of the XREF command you can temporarily lay an existing drawing over the top of the one currently on your screen. This is a temporary operation, and the overlay xref does not appear on your screen the next time you open the master drawing because the overlay has not been attached.
- **Attach.** This option enables you to attach an Xref to the drawing currently displayed on the screen. This is the default option and can be selected by pressing ENTER after the initial prompt is displayed.

CHAPTER TEST

Write your answer in the space provided.

1. How does the XREF Overlay option differ from the Attach option?_____

2. What command enables you to construct a paper space viewport, attach an external reference, and zoom to a specific portion of the drawing? _____

3. What effect does the use of referenced drawings have on drawing file size? _____
   _____

4. When are Xrefs updated in the master drawing? _____
   _____

5. Why would you want to bind a dependent symbol to a master drawing? _____
   _____

6. What does the layer name WALL0NOTES mean? _____
   _____

7. Name the system variable that controls the creation of the Xref log file. _____

8. Your drawings should be created in what "space?" _____

9. Which system variable allows you to switch from model space to paper space? _____

10. What value should the variable mentioned in Question 9 be set to in order to draw in the space mentioned in Question 8?_____

11. What value should the variable mentioned in Question 9 be set to in order to use the MVIEW command? _____

12. What is the function of the MVIEW command? _____

13. Why would you want to reference one drawing to another rather than insert it? _____
    _____

14. Indicate the command, option, and value you would use to specify a scale of 1/2″ = 1′-0″ inside a viewport. _____

15. Name the command and option you would use to freeze all layers of drawings inside any new viewports._____

16. Do you need to be in paper space or model space in order to resize a viewport? _____
    _____

17. Why would you plot a multiview drawing at full scale (1=1) if it was created with MVIEW, and contained several views at different scales?_____

_____

18. Explain why you should plan your plots._____

_____

_____

DRAWING PROBLEMS

P26-1

1. Open one of your dimensioned drawings from Chapter 20. Construct a multiview layout and generate a final plot on C-size paper.
   A. Set TILEMODE to 0 and create four viewports of equal size, but separated by 1 in. of empty space.
   B. Select each viewport and display a different view of the drawing.
   C. Plot the drawing and be sure to use the scale of 1=1.
   D. Save the drawing as A:P26-1.

P26-2

2. Open one of your dimensioned drawings from Chapter 21. Construct a multiview layout and generate a plot on C-size or B-size paper. Create a single viewport and plot at the scale of 1:1. Save the drawing as A:P26-2.

P26-3

3. Open one of your dimensioned drawings from Chapter 22. Construct a multiview layout and generate a plot on C-size or B-size paper. Create a single viewport and plot at the scale of 1:1. Save the drawing as A:P26-3.

P26-4

4. Open one of your dimensioned drawings from Chapter 23. Construct a multiview layout and generate a plot on C-size or B-size paper. Create a single viewport and plot at the scale of 1:1. Save the drawing as A:P26-4.

P26-5

5. Open one of your dimensioned drawings from Chapter 24. Construct a multiview layout and generate a plot on C-size or B-size paper. Create a single viewport and plot at the scale of 1:1. Save the drawing as A:P26-5.

P26-6

6. Open one of your dimensioned drawings from Chapter 25. Construct a multiview layout and generate a plot on C-size or B-size paper. Create a single viewport and plot at the scale of 1:1. Save the drawing as A:P26-6.

Joist hangers. (Mark Hartman)

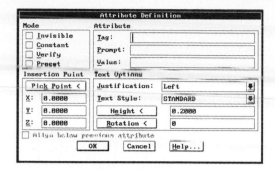

Chapter 27

ASSIGNING ATTRIBUTES AND GENERATING A BILL OF MATERIALS

Learning objectives

After completing this chapter, you will be able to:

❍ Assign visible or hidden values (attributes) to blocks.
❍ Edit attributes in existing blocks.
❍ Create a template file for the collection of block attributes.
❍ Collect attribute values in a bill of materials.

Blocks become more useful when written information is given with them. It is even more helpful to assign information that is visible (displayed) and information that is hidden. From these data, a list, much like a bill of materials, can be requested and printed.

Written or numerical values assigned to blocks are called *attributes* by AutoCAD. Attribute information can be extracted from the drawing rather than used only as text labels. Examples of blocks with attributes are shown in Figure 27-1. The ATTDEF (ATTribute DEFined) command allows you to specify attribute text and determine how it is displayed. The ATTDISP (ATTribute DISPlay) command governs which attributes are displayed. You can selectively or collectively edit attributes using the ATTEDIT (ATTribute EDIT) command. Using the ATTEXT (ATTribute EXTract) command, you can extract any or all attributes from a drawing in a list or report form.

Figure 27-1. Examples of blocks with attributes.

```
DESK
JONES CO.
$985.00
WOOD
```

```
TABLE
ACME, INC.
$340.00
6' X 4'
```

```
CHAIR
JONES CO.
SECRETARY'S
$260.00
BLUE
```

FURNITURE

```
GLOBE VALVE
JAMESBURY
6" ø
$325.00
95 LBS.
```

```
WELD NECK FLANGE
GRINNELL
8" ø
150# PSI
$170.00
37 LBS.
```

```
90' ELBOW
TAYLOR FORGE
8" ø
300# PSI
$146.00
48 LBS
```

PIPING

The creation, editing, and extraction of attributes can also be handled with dialog boxes that are displayed with the DDATTDEF, DDATTE, DDMODIFY, and DDATTEXT commands.

ASSIGNING ATTRIBUTES TO BLOCKS | AUG 7 |

The first step in defining block attributes is to decide what information about the block is needed. Then decide how the computer should ask you for the attribute. This might be a prompt, such as "What is the size?" The name of the object should be your first attribute. This is followed by items such as manufacturer, type, size, price, and weight. Suppose you are drawing a valve symbol for a piping flow diagram. You might want to list all product-related data. The number of attributes needed are limited only by the project requirements.

Once the symbol is completed and shown on the screen, select the ATTDEF command.

Command: **ATTDEF** ↵
Attribute modes – Invisible:N Constant:N Verify:N Preset:N
Enter (ICVP) to change, RETURN when done:

At this prompt, there are four decisions you must make. All of the options affect the attributes, and all are toggle switches. The default option is N for no, or normal.
- **Invisible.** Should the attribute be visible? Type I to make the attribute invisible. It will not be displayed when the block is inserted.
- **Constant.** Should the attribute always be the same? Typing C to turn on the Constant option means that all future uses of the block display the same value for the attribute. You will not be prompted for a new value.
- **Verify.** Do you want a prompt to remind you about the value you entered? When creating an attribute, you enter the attribute value at the prompt. To check that the value you entered is correct, turn Verify on.
- **Preset.** Should all attributes assume preset values and not display prompts? The Preset option creates variable attributes, but disables all attribute prompts during the insertion of a block. Default values are used instead. This works only with normal attributes. The setting does not affect dialog box entry discussed later.

If you do not turn on any of these options, the display shows Normal. A normal display means that you will be prompted for all attributes and they will be visible. Request the Normal option by pressing ENTER. The next three prompts let you assign a value to the attribute.

Attribute tag: **TYPE** ↵
Attribute prompt: **Enter valve type:** ↵
Default attribute value: **GATE** ↵

The information needed by the ATTDEF prompts is as follows:
- **Attribute tag.** Enter the name of the attribute here. You must give a name or number. There can be any character in the tag, but blanks are not allowed.
- **Attribute prompt.** Enter the statement you want the computer to ask when this block is inserted. For example, "What is the valve size?" or "Enter valve size:" are good prompts if the attribute tag is "size." If Constant or Preset mode is set, this prompt is not displayed.
- **Default attribute value.** The entry you type here is placed in the drawing as a default when the block is inserted unless you change it at the prompt. You do not have to enter anything here. You might type a message regarding the type of information needed. The default is displayed in brackets (⟨ ⟩). You might have a message, such as "10 spaces max" or "numbers only." Only the prompt "Attribute value" is displayed if the Constant mode is set.

The remainder of the ATTDEF command is the same series of prompts found with the TEXT command. Since attributes are text, they need to be positioned and sized. The current text style is assigned unless a new one is selected. When you complete the ATTDEF command, press ENTER. A label appears on screen. This is the attribute tag. Do not be dismayed; this is the only time the tag name appears. When the block is inserted, you are asked for information that takes the place of the tag.

Click inside the appropriate text box to edit the current value. The Origin area in the lower left of the dialog box displays the current X, Y, and Z values of the attribute. These can be edited by clicking in the appropriate text box. You can also select the Pick Point ⟨ button and the dialog is temporarily dismissed while you pick a new origin for the attribute. The dialog box returns immediately after the point is picked.

Figure 27-4.   The "Modify Attribute Definition" dialog box allows all aspects of the attribute's text to be changed.

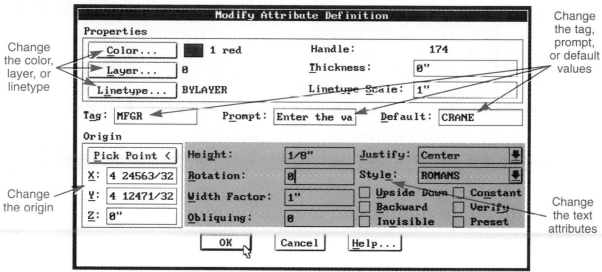

All of the aspects of the attribute's text can be changed. Use the Height, Rotation, Width Factor, Obliquing, and Justify buttons, for this purpose. Or select the Upside Down and Backward check boxes. Changing any of these items overrides settings in the current text style–which is shown in the Style: drop-down list. Pick this drop-down list to select another existing text style.

The four attribute modes of invisible, constant, verify, and preset can also be changed in the "Modify Attribute Definition" dialog box. Notice in Figure 27-4 that the Constant: check box mode is checked. This means that no prompt is issued when a block with this attribute is inserted into the drawing. If you wish to turn off the constant mode and provide a prompt, pick the Constant check box to remove the X. Next pick the Prompt: text box and enter the prompt.

INSERTING BLOCKS WITH ATTRIBUTES ⟨ AUG 7 ⟩

When you use the INSERT command to place a block in your drawing, you are prompted for additional information after the insertion point, scale factors, and rotation angle. The prompt that you entered in the ATTDEF command appears, and the default attribute value appears in brackets. Accept the default by pressing ENTER, or provide a new value. Then the attribute is displayed.

Attributes can be entered using a dialog box if the ATTDIA system variable is set to a value other than 0. After entering the rotation angle at the INSERT command, the "Enter Attributes" dialog box appears. See Figure 27-5. It can list up to eight attributes. If a block has more than eight attributes, you can display the next "page" of attributes by picking the Next button. Move forward through the attributes by pressing the Tab key, or move in reverse by pressing the Shift+Tab key combination. When you are finished editing, pick OK and the block with attributes is inserted in your drawing.

Figure 27-5. The "Enter Attribute" dialog box allows you to enter or change attributes when a block is inserted. If the block has more than eight attributes, pick the Next button to see the next "page." (The button is shown here "grayed-out" since there are only three attributes.)

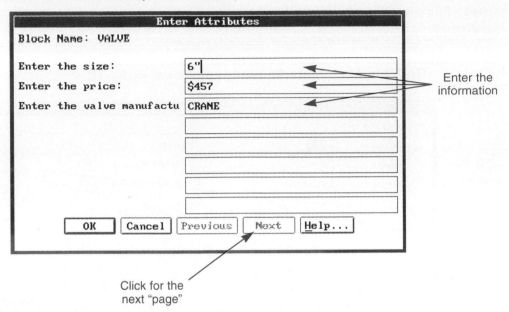

Enter the information

Click for the next "page"

Attribute prompt suppression

Some drawings may use blocks with attributes that always retain their default values. In this case, there is no need to be prompted for the attribute values. You can turn off the attribute prompts by entering a 0 for the ATTREQ system variable.

Command: **ATTREQ** ↵
New value for ATTREQ ⟨1⟩: **0** ↵

Try inserting the VALVE block. Notice that none of the attribute prompts appear. The ATTREQ value is saved with the drawing. To display attribute prompts again, change the value of ATTREQ back to 1.

PROFESSIONAL TIP

Part of your project and drawing planning should involve system variable settings such as ATTREQ. Setting ATTREQ to 0 before using blocks can save time in the drawing process.

EXERCISE 27-1

❑ Load AutoCAD and start a new drawing. Name the drawing EX27-1, and use an A-size or B-size architectural prototype drawing.
❑ Draw the valve symbol shown below.

```
GATE
CRANE
6"
$457
```

❑ Select the ATTDEF command and assign the following attributes:

TAG	PROMPT	VALVE	MODE
Type	(None)	Gate	Constant
Mfgr	Enter the valve manufacturer:	Crane	Invisible
Size	Enter the size	6"	Normal and Preset
Price	Enter the price	$365	Invisible and Verify

❑ Select the BLOCK command. Include the valve and all of the attributes in the block and name it VALVE.
❑ Select the INSERT command to place a copy of the VALVE block on your screen. Enter new values for the attributes if you wish. You should be prompted twice for the price if the Verify option was set properly.
❑ Save the drawing as A:EX27-1

CONTROLLING THE ATTRIBUTE DISPLAY

Attributes are meant to contain valuable information about the blocks in your drawings. This information is normally not displayed on the screen or during plotting. Its principal function is to generate materials lists and to speed accounting. Use the DTEXT and MTEXT commands for specific labels. You can control the display of attributes on the screen using the ATTDISP command.

Command: **ATTDISP** ⌐
Normal/ON/OFF ⟨Normal⟩

The Normal mode displays attributes exactly as you created them. This is the default mode for ATTDISP. The ON option displays *all* attributes. The OFF position suppresses *all* attributes.

PROFESSIONAL TIP

After attributes have been drawn, added to blocks, and checked for correctness, hide them by turning off ATTDISP. If left on, they clutter the screen and lengthen regeneration time.

CHANGING ATTRIBUTE VALUES

Attributes can be edited with normal editing commands before they are included in a block. Once the block is created, the attributes are part of it and must be changed using the ATTEDIT command. This discussion covers the use of ATTEDIT when entered at the Command: prompt. The next section covers editing attributes using a dialog box. Type ATTEDIT as follows:

Command: **ATTEDIT** ⌐
Edit attributes one at a time? ⟨Y⟩

This prompt asks if you want to edit attributes individually. It is possible to change the same attribute on several insertions of the same block. Pressing ENTER at this prompt allows you to select any number of different attributes. AutoCAD lets you edit them all, one at a time, without leaving the ATTEDIT command. If you respond with N (NO), you may change specific letters, words, and values of a single attribute. This can affect all insertions of the same block. For example, suppose a block named RESISTOR was inserted on a drawing in 12 places. However, you misspelled the attribute as RESISTER. Answer N to the Edit attributes one at a time? prompt. This is a "global" attribute editing method.

Each ATTEDIT technique allows you to determine the exact block and attribute specifications to edit. These prompts appear:

Block name specification ⟨*⟩:
Attribute tag specification ⟨*⟩:
Attribute value specification ⟨*⟩:

To selectively edit attribute values, respond to the prompt with a name or value. Suppose you enter an attribute and receive the following message:

0 attributes selected. *Invalid*

You have picked an attribute that was not specified. It is often quicker to press ENTER for the three specification prompts and then *pick* the attribute you need to edit.

Editing several insertions of the same attribute

A situation may occur when a block having a wrong or misspelled attribute is inserted several times. For example, in Figure 27-6 the VALVE block was inserted three times with the manufacturer's name as CRANE. Unfortunately, the name was supposed to be POWELL. Use ATTEDIT and respond in the following manner:

Command: **ATTEDIT** ↵
Edit attributes one at a time? ⟨Y⟩ **N** ↵
Global edit of attribute values.
Edit only attributes visible on screen? ⟨Y⟩: ↵
Block name specification ⟨*⟩: ↵
Attribute tag specification ⟨*⟩: ↵
Attribute value specification ⟨*⟩: ↵
Select attributes: *(pick CRANE on all VALVE blocks and press* ENTER *when completed)*
(N) attributes selected. *(N equals the number of attributes picked)*
String to change: **CRANE** ↵ *(words or characters to change)*
New string: **POWELL** ↵

Figure 27-6.   Global editing changes the same attribute on several block insertions.

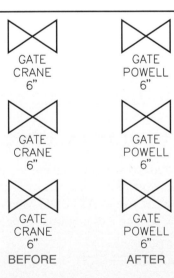

GATE
CRANE
6"

GATE
POWELL
6"

GATE
CRANE
6"

GATE
POWELL
6"

GATE
CRANE
6"

GATE
POWELL
6"

BEFORE   AFTER

After pressing ENTER, CRANE attributes on the blocks selected are changed to read POWELL.

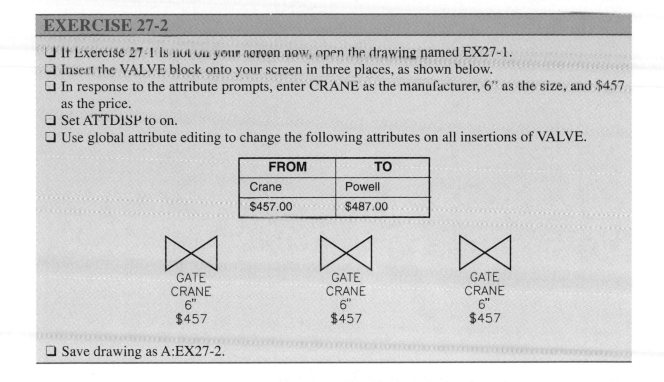

EXERCISE 27-2

❏ If Exercise 27-1 is not on your screen now, open the drawing named EX27-1.
❏ Insert the VALVE block onto your screen in three places, as shown below.
❏ In response to the attribute prompts, enter CRANE as the manufacturer, 6" as the size, and $457 as the price.
❏ Set ATTDISP to on.
❏ Use global attribute editing to change the following attributes on all insertions of VALVE.

FROM	TO
Crane	Powell
$457.00	$487.00

❏ Save drawing as A:EX27-2.

PROFESSIONAL TIP

Use care when assigning the Constant mode option to attribute definitions. An attribute with the Constant setting cannot be changed using ATTEDIT. If you try to edit an inserted block attribute with the Constant mode setting, the following error message is displayed:

0 attributes selected. *Invalid*

The inserted block must be exploded and redefined. Assign Constant to only those attributes you know will not change.

Editing different attributes one at a time

Global editing is a more precise method of changing specific attributes and text strings. On the other hand, individual editing allows you to change any value on any attribute. Several attributes and text strings can be done without leaving the ATTEDIT command. The ATTEDIT command can also be selected from the Modify pull-down menu. Pick Attribute, then Edit Globally. After you answer Y to the Edit attributes one at a time prompt, and press ENTER for the three "specification" options, select the attributes. Press ENTER when you are finished; then this prompt appears:

(N) attributes selected.
Value/Position/Height/Angle/Style/Layer/Color/Next ⟨N⟩:

With this prompt, a small "X" appears at the lower-left corner of the first attribute in the last block selected. The "X" indicates the attribute that is being edited. The Next option is the default. Pressing ENTER causes the "X" to jump to the next attribute in sequence. The "X" does not jump to the next attribute automatically after you make a change. It remains in case you want to make more than one change to the attribute. Figure 27-7A shows the order in which attributes were picked. The order in which AutoCAD selects them for editing is shown in Figure 27-7B.

Figure 27-7.   A–The order
attributes were selected. B–The
order in which AutoCAD
edits them.

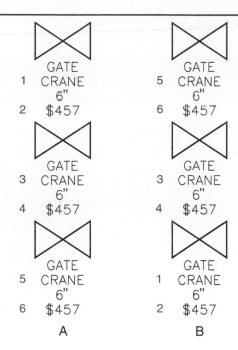

The prompts for all attribute editing options are as follows:
- **Value.** "Change or Replace? ⟨R⟩:" Pressing ENTER here indicates you want to replace the attribute. AutoCAD requests a new attribute value. You can change any part of the attribute by typing C for Change. AutoCAD responds with String to change and New string prompts. A string is any sequence of consecutive characters.
- **Position.** "Enter text insertion point:"
- **Height.** "New height ⟨*current*⟩:"
- **Angle.** "New rotation angle ⟨0⟩:"
- **Style.** "Text style: (current)
        New style or RETURN for no change:"
- **Layer.** "New layer ⟨current⟩:"
- **Color.** "New color ⟨BYLAYER⟩:"

Individual editing of attributes can be used to correct misspelled words, replace a word, or change the attribute information. Look at the attributes attached to the block in Figure 27-8. The manufacturer was changed from POWELL to CRANE. The price was changed from $565.00 to $556.00. Suppose these are the only two attributes to be edited. The entire command sequence looks like this:

    Command: **ATTEDIT** ↵
    Edit attributes one at a time? ⟨N⟩ **Y** ↵
    Select Attributes: *(select the two attributes)*
    2 attributes selected. *(the "X" appears at POWELL, the first attribute selected)*
    Value/Position/Height/Angle/Style/Layer/Color/Next ⟨N⟩: **V** ↵
    Change or Replace? ⟨R⟩: **R** ↵
    New attribute value: **CRANE**
    Value/Position/Height/Angle/Style/Layer/Color/Next ⟨N⟩: ↵ *(pressing ENTER moves the "X"*
        to the next attribute, $565.00)
    Value/Position/Height/Angle/Style/Layer/Color/Next ⟨N⟩: **V** ↵
    Change or Replace? ⟨R⟩: **C** ↵
    String to change: **65** ↵
    New string: **56** ↵
    Value/Position/Height/Angle/Style/Layer/Color/Next ⟨N⟩: ↵ *(press ENTER at this prompt to*
        get out of the ATTEDIT command and see the final change take place)

The completed attribute edit is shown in Figure 27-8C.

Figure 27-8.   The attributes
to be changed are indicated
with an "X."

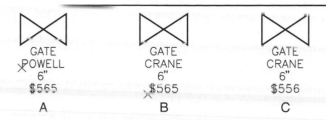

PROFESSIONAL TIP

When making blocks that contain attributes, add as many attributes you think will be needed. If you do not have values for some of them, just enter TO COME as the value, or enter something to remind you that information is needed. Adding an attribute to a block is much more time-consuming than changing an attribute using the ATTEDIT command.

EXERCISE 27-3

❑ Load AutoCAD and open drawing EX27-2 if it is not already on screen.
❑ Be sure there are three insertions of the VALVE block. Align them as shown below.
❑ Set ATTDISP to on to display all attributes.
❑ Select the ATTEDIT command and choose the individual edit option.
❑ Assuming the blocks are numbered 1 to 3, top to bottom, change the individual attributes to the following values:

	1	2	3
Type	Gate	Gate	Gate
Mfrg.	Crane	Powell	Jenkins
Size	4″	8″	10″
Price	$376.00	$563.00	$837.00

❑ Connect the valves with straight lines as shown.
❑ Save the drawing as A:EX27-3.

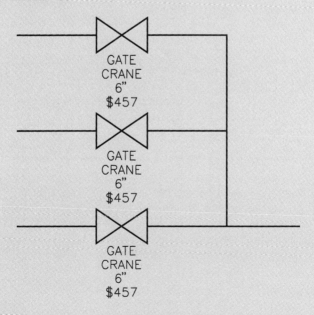

EDITING ATTRIBUTES USING A DIALOG BOX   AUG 10

The DDATTE (Dynamic Dialog ATTribute Editing) command allows you to edit attributes in a dialog box. You can edit single blocks or use the MULTIPLE command to edit as many block attributes as needed. The DDATTE command can be typed at the Command. prompt, or selected from a pull-down or screen menu. Pick the Modify pull-down menu, then select Attribute. Next pick Edit... from the cascading menu. If you use the screen menu pick MODIFY, then AttEd:.

Editing attributes in a single block

If attributes in one block need editing, enter DDATTE and select the block as follows:

Command: **DDATTE** ↵
Select block: *(select block)*

The "Edit Attributes" dialog box appears on screen, Figure 27-9. The attributes of the selected block are listed on the left. Their current values are shown in the edit boxes on the right. Move the cursor to the value to be edited and double click so the box is highlighted, and enter the new value. Remember, that if you pick the box, you can move the cursor to the incorrect letter, then use the delete key to remove a letter, type to insert characters, or use Backspace to delete. You can then pick CANCEL or OK, or you can press ENTER to move to the next attribute. If CANCEL is picked, the attribute value is left unchanged. When finished, pick OK at the bottom of the dialog box. The attribute associated with the block is changed. If CANCEL is picked, no changes are made and the drawing is redisplayed.

Figure 27-9.   The "Edit Attributes" dialog box displays all of the attributes assigned to the selected block. You can change any of these attributes.

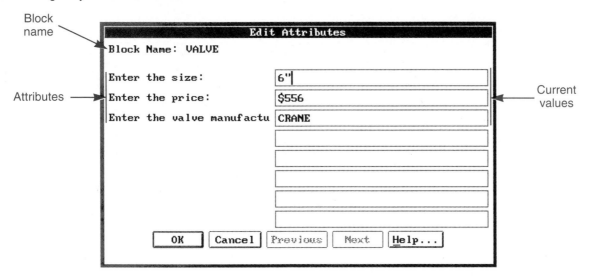

NOTE   When editing attributes using the dialog box, keep in mind that the attribute value can have up to 256 characters. The maximum number of characters that will be displayed in the edit box is 32. The attribute prompt is limited to 23 characters in the dialog box for display purposes only. Longer attribute prompts entered remain intact in the drawing file.

USING ATTRIBUTES FOR DRAWING ANNOTATIONS

An important aspect of any drawing documentation is the written information it contains. The annotations on a drawing are the title block information, parts list data, and revision list notes. Adding these to a drawing can require a considerable investment of time if standard text entry methods are used. But these functions can be automated with the use of blocks that contain attribute definitions

Using attributes in title blocks

It is time-consuming to add written information to title blocks each time a drawing is completed. Using a command such as DTEXT requires that each line of text be located, sized and typed. This process can be automated by creating a block that contains an attribute definition for each part of the title block that is different from one drawing to the next. These items include drawing name, part number, date, scale, material, drawn by, drawing size, revision number, and approved by. The following steps illustrate the procedure for creating a block with attribute definitions for use in a drawing title block.

1. Construct an appropriate title block and border that can be used as a prototype for future drawings. The MVSETUP command provides this capability, and is discussed in Chapter 19. Any prototype drawing that you create for this purpose should adhere to school or company standards. An existing drawing from your school or company can also be used. An example of an A-size sheet that adheres to ANSI Y14.1, *Drawing Sheet Size and Format* is shown in Figure 27-10. Note the two "FSCM NO." blocks. This is the Federal Supply Code for Manufacturers. This code is used by manufacturers, suppliers, and designers of materials used by the federal government.

Figure 27-10. A title block sheet must adhere to applicable standards. This title block is for an A-size sheet and adheres to ANSI Y14.1, *Drawing Sheet Size and Format.*

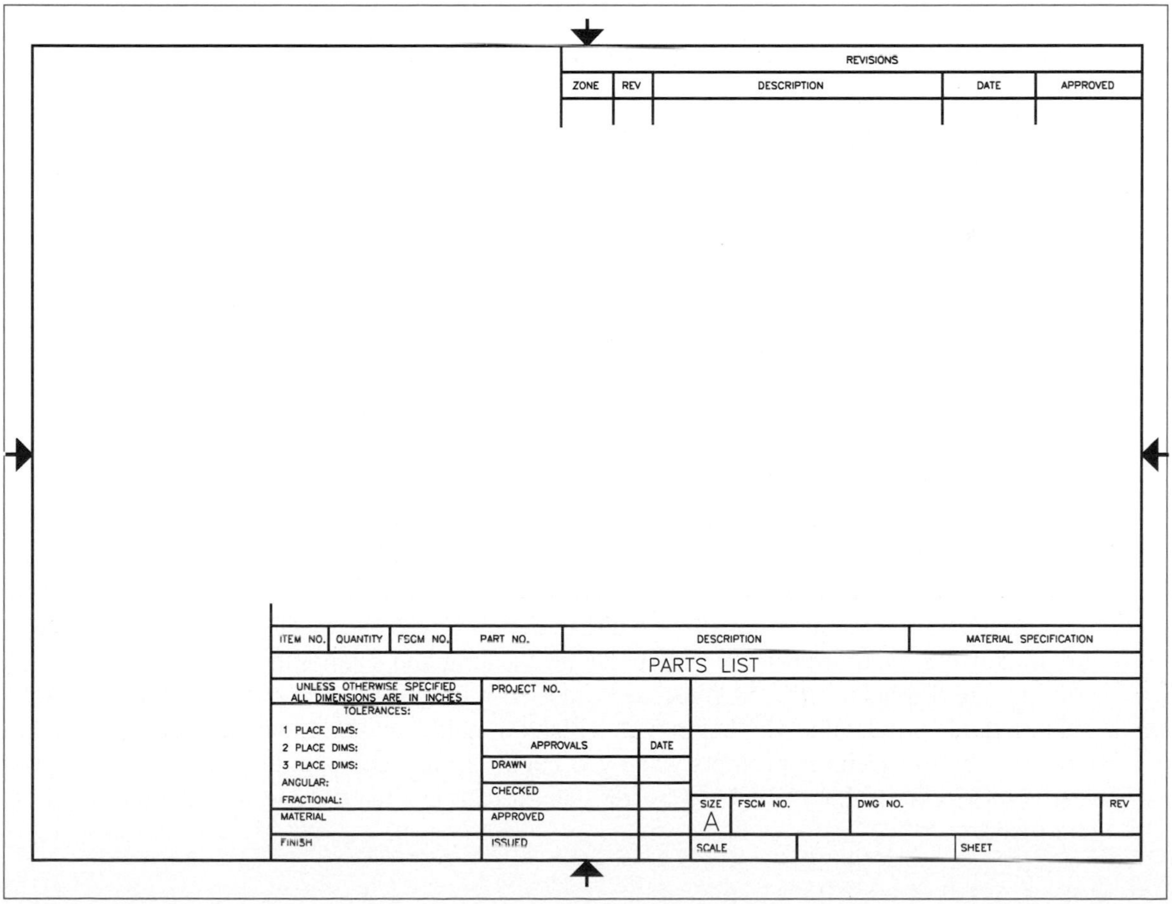

2. Create a layer for defined attributes that will be used in the title block.

3. Determine the text fonts and heights that will be used in the attributes, and create any text styles that are needed. Determine the text locations within each box in the title block. Base the locations on middle justified text. If your applications regularly call for multiline drawing titles or names, take this into account when planning text heights and locations.

4. Create defined attributes for all areas of the title block. Remember to use the appropriate text style for each area. If certain areas of the title block use the same value most of the time, enter this value at the Default attribute value: prompt. This saves time during the creation of each new drawing. Figure 27-11 shows attributes that have been defined for a title block.

Figure 27-11.   This shows attributes that have been defined for a title block.

ITEM NO.	QUANTITY	FSCM NO.	PART NO.	DESCRIPTION	MATERIAL SPECIFICATION

PARTS LIST

UNLESS OTHERWISE SPECIFIED ALL DIMENSIONS ARE IN INCHES TOLERANCES:	PROJECT NO. PROJECT			
1 PLACE DIMS: TOL1				
2 PLACE DIMS: TOL2	APPROVALS	DATE		TITLE
3 PLACE DIMS: TOL3	DRAWN DRAWN	DATE		
ANGULAR: ANGL	CHECKED CHECKED	DATE	SIZE FSCM NO.	DWG NO.
FRACTIONAL: FRAC			A	NUMBER REV
MATERIAL MATERIAL	APPROVED APPROVED	DATE		REV
FINISH FINISH	ISSUED ISSUED	DATE	SCALE SCALE	SHEET SHEET

Insertion point

PROFESSIONAL TIP

The size of each title block area imposes limits on the number of characters you can have in a line of text. You can provide a handy cue to yourself or anyone who uses the prototype drawing with attributes, by including a reminder in the attribute. When defining an attribute in which you wish to place a reminder, use something like the following when entering text for the attribute prompt:

Attribute prompt: **Enter drawing name 〈15 characters max〉:**

Each time the block or prototype drawing is used that contains this attribute, the prompt will display the reminder shown above.

After all of the attributes have been defined, the WBLOCK command can be used to create a prototype drawing that can be inserted into a new drawing, or the BLOCK command can be used to create a block of defined attributes within the current prototype drawing file. Either method is acceptable, and the uses of both are explained in the following descriptions.

• **WBLOCK method.** The WBLOCK command saves a drawing file to disk which can be inserted into any other drawing. Prototype drawings used in this manner should be given descriptive names such as TITLE-A, PROTO-A, or TITLBLKA. The name should provide some indication of the drawing size. To utilize the prototype file created in this manner, begin a new drawing, then insert the prototype. After locating and scaling the drawing, the attribute prompts are displayed. As you enter the requested information, it is placed in the title block. This method requires that you begin with a blank drawing, and that you know the information requested by the attribute prompts when you begin. Remember, should you enter information that is incorrect, or that changes at a later date, it can be altered using the ATTE (DDATTE) command.

- **BLOCK method.** The BLOCK command prompts you to select objects. Be sure to select *only* the defined attributes you just created. Do not select the headings of title block areas, or any of the geometry in the title block. When prompted to pick the Insertion base point, select a corner of the title block that will be convenient to use each time this block is inserted into a drawing. The bold X in Figure 27-11 shows an appropriate location for the insertion base point. The current prototype drawing now contains a block of defined attributes for use in the title block. To begin a new drawing you must open this prototype and give it a new name to protect the integrity of the prototype. The title block data can be entered at any time during the creation of the new drawing. To do so, just use the INSERT command, and pick the proper insertion base point. The attribute prompts are then either displayed on the command line, or in a dialog box, depending on the value of the ATTDIA variable. If ATTDIA is set to 1, all of the attributes can be entered in a dialog box like the one shown in Figure 27-12. The WBLOCK command can be used to save the defined attributes to disk as a file should you wish to have the ability to use the attributes on any drawing.

Figure 27-12.   Attributes can be entered in a dialog box when ATTDIA is set to 1. If there are more than eight attributes defined, pick the Next button to see the next "page." Pick OK when the final page of attributes is completed.

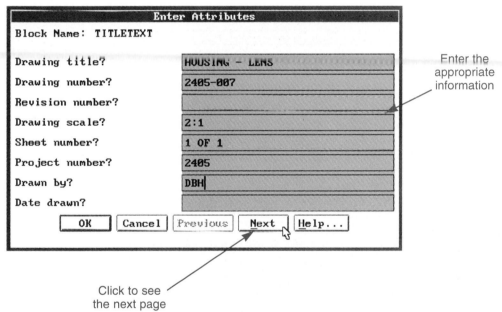

Regardless of the method used, title block data can be entered quickly and accurately without the use of text commands. If the attributes are entered in a dialog box, all of the information can be seen at one time, and mistakes can be corrected quickly. Attributes can be easily edited at a later date if necessary. Attribute text height or position can be changed with the ATTEDIT command, and the content of the attribute is changed with the DDATTE command. The completed title block after insertion of the attribute block is shown in Figure 27-13.

Figure 27-13.   The title block after insertion of the attributes. When the drawing is complete, dates and approvals can be added with the DDATTE command.

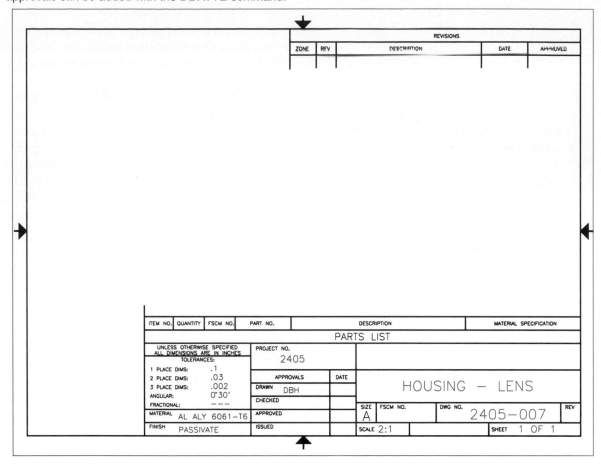

Using attributes in a parts list or revision block

Any text on a drawing that is confined to a constant position or relationship can be a candidate for attributes. Parts lists and revision blocks are two prime candidates. Most schools and companies have standards regarding the placement and layout of parts lists and revisions. In fact, prototype title block drawings may already have the headings for these two items. They are always printed whether they are used or not. Some organizations may maintain a drawing file of the parts list or revision block that can be inserted into the current drawing when needed. Familiarize yourself with the appropriate method used in your organization.

Creating attributes for either of these purposes is similar to the process used for title blocks. Before you begin, plan the number of attributes needed, the text height, justification, and location. Some items, such as the revision or part Description areas may require that you use middle justified text, while other items require left justified text. Plan these before you begin. The following items may assist you in your task:

• Draw the lines for the revision block or parts list. Use proper drawing layers and colors.
• Define the attributes for each area, paying close attention to the text style, height and location. Be sure to set the appropriate layer before beginning.
• WBLOCK the lines and attributes to disk, or BLOCK them into the current prototype drawing. Use descriptive names such as PARTLIST, REVBLOCK, PL, or REV. Keep in mind that each line of the parts list or revision block needs its own border lines. Therefore, the borders must be saved with the attributes. See Figure 27-14.

Figure 27-14.   The revision block is comprised of lines, attributes, and an insertion point. The border lines must be drawn as part of the block.

When a drawing requires a parts list or revision block, just insert the appropriate block, and enter the proper text at the ensuing attribute prompts. Again, if ATTDIA is set to 1, the attributes can be entered in a dialog box. See Figure 27-15.

Figure 27-15.   Drawing revisions are entered in the "Enter Attributes" dialog box when ATTDIA is set to 1.

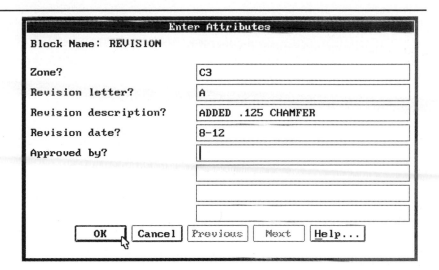

These are a few of the situations in which attributes can be used to automate drawing annotations. A little time invested in developing these features can save accumulated hours of tedious labor in the future. Figure 27-16 shows the revision block that is the result of the information entered in the dialog box in Figure 27-15.

Figure 27-16.   The revision block after it is inserted into the drawing.

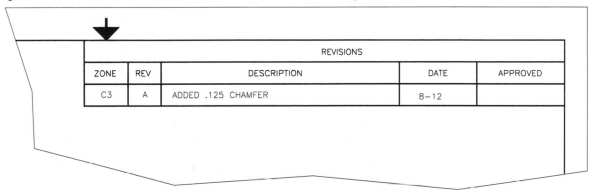

COLLECTING ATTRIBUTE INFORMATION $\boxed{\text{AUG 7}}$

AutoCAD provides a method for listing attributes associated with any specified blocks. It is helpful for tabulating block information. This method involves creating a special *template file*. This file is a list of attributes that can be used in a bill of materials by third-party packages, or in databases. It is used with drawings that contain specific blocks and attributes you wish to list. The ATTEXT command creates an *extract file* that allows AutoCAD to find and list the attributes specified in the template file. This extract file can display the attributes on the screen or send them to a printer.

Creating a template file

You often need to be selective in the blocks and attributes that are listed. This requires guidelines for AutoCAD to use when sorting through a drawing. To pick out specific block attributes, these guidelines are in the form of a *template file*. The AutoCAD template file allows you to pick out specific items from blocks and list them. First, you have to make the template file.

The template file, a simple text file, can be made using database, word processing, or text editor programs. The text editor that resides in DOS, is discussed in Chapter 32.

In addition to listing attributes, the template file can be designed to extract block properties. Those include:

- **Level.** This refers to the nesting level of the block. If the block was nested inside another block, this number would be "2" in the extracted list.
- **Name.** Block name.
- **X.** The X coordinate location of the block insertion point.
- **Y.** The Y coordinate location of the block insertion point.
- **Layer.** Layer name.
- **Orient.** Rotation angle of the block.
- **XScale.** The X coordinate scale factor of the block.
- **YScale.** The Y coordinate scale factor of the block.

PROFESSIONAL TIP

Your application determines which properties need to be included in the template file. Template files can be created for different groups or departments of a company. The following chart lists possible attributes for a desk in the left column. Across the top are several different departments in a company. An "X" indicates which item is to be included in that department's template file.

ATTRIBUTE	SHIPPING	PURCHASING	ACCOUNTING	ENGINEERING
Manufacturer		X	X	
Size	X	X		X
Price		X	X	
Weight	X			X
Color		X		X
Material	X	X		X

The example template file shown below could be used to extract information from the piping flow diagram in Exercise 27-3.

BL:NAME	C010000
BL:LAYER	C005000
BL:X	N008002
BL:Y	N008002
BLANK	C004000
MFGR	C010000
SIZE	C008000
PRICE	C010000

You would write this file using database or text editing programs such as EDLIN or the DOS text editor. Notice that the items that are block characteristics begin with BL:. The items that are block attributes are given the name used at the Attribute tag: prompt of the ATTDEF command. The item BLANK is placed in the file to provide spacing between the Y coordinates and MFGR. Had this been omitted there would be no line space between those two items.

The numbers in the right column all begin with either C or N. The C indicates that character information is to be extracted and N represents numerical information. If a character other than a number is included in an attribute, use C instead of N. Notice that the PRICE attribute uses C. That is because the dollar sign ($) is used in front of the price in the attribute.

The first three numbers after the C or N character indicate the number of spaces allotted for the attribute. There are ten spaces allotted for MFGR. The following three digits specify the number of decimal places in the attribute. The X and Y locations have been assigned two decimal places. This is detailed in Figure 27-17.

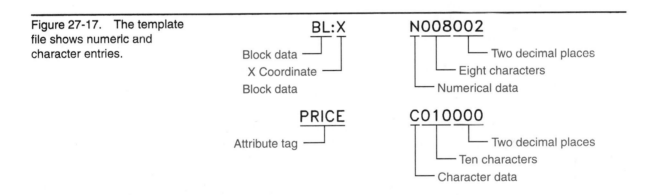

Figure 27-17.   The template file shows numeric and character entries.

EXERCISE 27-4

❑ This exercise steps you through the construction of a template file for drawing EX27-3. The DOS text editor program named EDIT can be used to create the file.
❑ Open drawing EX27-3 if it is not already on your screen.
❑ At the Command: prompt, type the following:

      Command: **EDIT** ↵
      File to edit: **EX22-4.TXT**

❑ You are now in the DOS text editor. A flashing cursor should appear at the upper left of the screen. Enter the following text at the cursor:

BL:NAME	C010000
BL:LAYER	C005000
BL:X	N008002
BL:Y	N008002
BLANK	C004000
MFGR	C010000
SIZE	C008000
PRICE	C010000

When you are finished the text editor screen should appear as shown below.

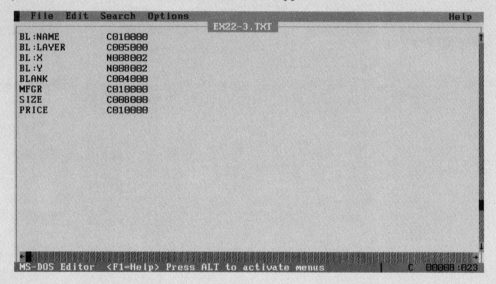

❑ Check the title bar to be sure the filename is EX22-3.TXT. If the name is correct select Save from the File pull-down menu. If the name is incorrect, select Save As...from the File pull-down menu.
❑ Select Exit from the File pull-down menu to return to AutoCAD.

Listing block attributes

AutoCAD provides three different formats for listing extracted information. The *DXF format* is related to programming and is the most complex. See the *AutoCAD Customization Guide*, Chapter 16 for information on the DXF format. The other two–SDF and CDF–are formats that can be used with a variety of other programs. The *SDF (Space Delimited Format)* is the easiest for the average user to interpret. It means that the different *fields*, or groups of data are separated by spaces. The *CDF (Comma Delimited Format)* uses commas instead of spaces to separate fields.

Execute the ATTEXT command by entering ATTEXT at the Command: prompt. Specify the format you want or type O to list the attributes of specific objects. At this point, select the SDF format. The response here needs to be only the first letter.

Command: **ATTEXT** ↵
CDF, SDF, or DXF Attribute extract (or Objects)? ⟨C⟩: **S** ↵

The "Select Template File" dialog box is then displayed. Select the file you wish to use from the Files: list box. Note in Figure 27-18 that the file named EX22-3.TXT is selected. Pick OK and the "Create extract file" dialog box appears.

Figure 27-18.   The "Select Template File" dialog box allows you to choose a file.

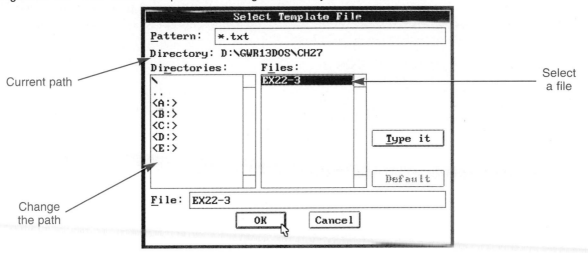

Current path

Change
the path

Select
a file

If you wish to have the extracted attributes saved in a file, enter a name in the File: edit box. The current drawing name is the default. Be sure the extract filename you enter is slightly different than the template filename, for example, EX27-4A.TXT. See Figure 27-19. If you use the same name, your original template file will be deleted. Pick OK after entering the filename. If all goes well, AutoCAD prompts that you have "n records in extract file." The number of records listed in the file is based on the number of blocks that contain the attributes you were searching for.

Figure 27-19.   An extract
filename selected from the
"Create extract file"
dialog box.

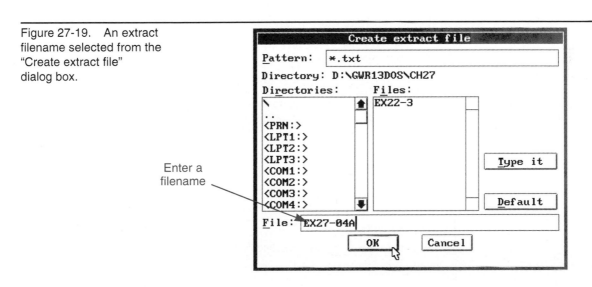

Enter a
filename

PROFESSIONAL TIP

The extract file can be displayed on the text screen by using the DOS TYPE command, or can be sent to a printer with the DOS PRINT command as follows:

C:\ACADR13⟩ **TYPE EX27-04A.TXT** ↵
C:\ACADR13⟩ **PRINT EX27-04A.TXT** ↵

When the "Create extract file" dialog box is on screen, you can have an immediate screen display of the extracted attributes by entering CON in the File: edit box. You can also pick the Type it button and enter CON (console) or PRN (printer) at the Extract file name: prompt to send the contents of the extract file to the console or to the printer as follows:

Extract file name ⟨drawing name⟩: **CON** ↵

The list should be displayed as:

VALVE 0	14.50	16.00	CRANE	4″	$376.00
VALVE 0	14.50	17.50	POWELL	8″	$563.95
VALVE 0	14.50	14.40	JENKINS	10″	$873.00

If you select the CDF format at the initial ATTEXT prompt, the extract listing will look like this:

'VALVE','0',14.50,16.00,",'CRANE','4"','376.00'
'VALVE','0',14.50,17.50,",'POWELL','8"','$563.95'
'VALVE','0',14.50,14.40,",'JENKINS','10"','$837.00'

The CDF format, of the three discussed, appears the most cumbersome. Yet, it as well as SDF can be used with specific database programs such as dBASE. Decide which format is most suitable for your application.

Listing block attributes with the DDATTEXT command

The DDATTEXT command enables you to use dialog boxes for all steps in the attribute extraction process. The "Attribute Extraction" dialog box appears after entering the DDATTEXT command. This command is found in the screen menu by first picking FILE, then EXPORT, then DDattEx:. In the File pull-down menu it is found by picking Export, then Attributes.... See Figure 27-20. Pick the file format, such as SDF, by selecting the appropriate radio button. If you want specific blocks in the extract file, pick the Select Objects ⟨ button, and use any selection method to pick the blocks. If you do not select objects, all blocks in the drawing (specified by the template file) will be used.

Figure 27-20.   The DDATTEXT command displays the "Attribute Extraction" dialog box.

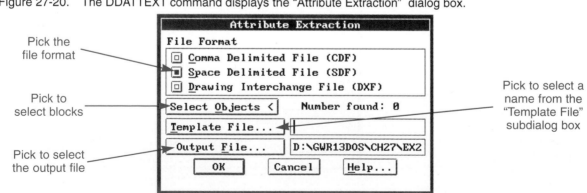

Pick the Template File... button to select a filename from the "Template File" subdialog box. This subdialog box is exactly the same as the one in Figure 27-9. The output file, or extract file, can be selected by picking the Output File... button. This displays the "Output File" subdialog box, which is exactly the same as the "Create extract file" dialog box shown in Figure 27-19.

If you want the contents of the output file displayed on the screen, type CON in the Output file edit box, or if you want the file sent to the printer, type PRN.

The bill of materials listing discussed in this chapter is a basic list of each block's selected attributes. As you become familiar with AutoCAD, customize it to meet your needs. Study magazines devoted to AutoCAD and read the *AutoCAD Resource Guide*. You will find numerous software packages that generate specialized bills of materials containing quantities and totals, rather than just a list of blocks.

EXERCISE 27-5

❑ Open EX27-4 if it is not already on your screen.
❑ Select the ATTEXT command and enter SDF format.
❑ Enter the template filename as EX27-4. Enter EX27-4A for the extract filename.
❑ Select ATTEXT again and display the bill of materials on the screen.

CHAPTER TEST

Write your answers in the spaces provided.

1. Define an "attribute." _____

   _____

2. Explain the purpose of the ATTDEF command. _____

   _____

3. Define the function of the following four ATTDEF modes:

   A. Invisible– _____

   B. Constant– _____

   _____

   C. Verify– _____

   _____

   D. Preset–_____

4. What attribute information does the ATTDEF command request?

   _____

   _____

5. List the three options for the ATTDISP command. _____

   _____

6. What is meant by "global" attribute editing?_____

   _____

7. How does individual attribute editing differ from global editing?_____

   _____

   _____

   _____

8. Identify the purpose of the following two prompts in the global attribute editing routine.

   String to change: _____

   New string: _____

9. List the different aspects of the attribute that you can change when you edit attributes one at a time. _____

10. Which command allows you to use a dialog box to create attributes? _____

11. Explain the function of the DDATTE command. _____

    _____

12. How does editing an attribute with DDEDIT differ from using DDMODIFY? _____

    _____

    _____

    _____

13. What purpose does the ATTREQ system variable serve? _____

    _____

14. To enter attributes using the dialog box, you must set the ATTDIA system variable to _____

    _____.

15. When created, a drawing extract file is given the file extension. _____

16. The command that allows you to create the file type mentioned in Question 15 is _____

    _____.

17. How is character and numerical data specified in a template file? _____

    _____

18. What would you type at the Extract file name: prompt to display the extracted attributes on the screen? _____

19. How many characters are allowed for an attribute name in the template file? _____

    _____

20. How do you create a template file? _____

    _____

21. Define all of the aspects of each of the following template file entries.

    BL:X _____

    N006002 _____

    PRICE _____

    C010003 _____

22. Describe the difference between CDF and SDF attribute extract formats. _____

    _____

23. The first time you create a file using the ATTEXT command, it is given a _____ extension.

24. Suppose you have used the ATTEXT command a second time. To display on screen the bill of materials, what do you enter at the following prompt?

    Extract file name ⟨drawing name⟩: _____

DRAWING PROBLEMS

P27-1

1. Load AutoCAD and start a new drawing named P27-1. Draw the structural steel wide flange shape shown below using the dimensions given. Do not dimension the drawing. Create attributes for the drawing using the information given. Make a block of the drawing and name it W12X40. Insert the block once to test the attributes.

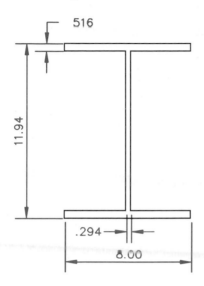

Attributes			
	Steel	W12 x 40	Visible
	Mfgr	Ryerson	Invisible
	Price	$.30/lb	Invisible
	Weight	40 lbs/ft	Invisible
	Length	10 ft	Invisible
	Code	03116Wf	Invisible

P27-2

2. Load the drawing in Problem 1 (P27-1) and construct the floor plan shown using the dimensions given at a scale of 1/4″ = 1′-0″. Dimension the drawing. Insert the block W12X40 six times as shown. Required attribute data is given in the chart below the drawing. Enter the appropriate information for the attributes as you are prompted for it. Note that the steel columns labeled 3 and 6 require slightly different attribute data. You can speed the drawing process by using MINSERT, ARRAY, or COPY. Save the drawing as A:P27-2.

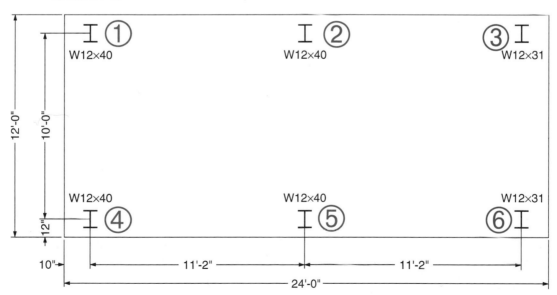

	Steel	Mfgr	Price	Weight	Length	Code
Blocks ❶, ❷, ❹, & ❺	W12×40	RYERSON	$.30/LB	40LB/FT	10′	03116WF
Blocks ❸ & ❻	W12×31	RYERSON	$.29/LB	31LB/FT	8.5′	03125WF

P27-3

3. Load Problem 2 (P27-2) into the drawing editor. Create a template file for use in extracting the data from structural steel blocks inserted in Problem 2. Use the following information in your template file:

ITEM	CHARACTERS	DECIMAL PLACES
Block name	8	0
Tag	8	0
Mfgr	20	0
Price	12	0
Weight	8	0
Length	6	1
Code	8	0

Use the ATTEXT command to create a listing of the attribute information. When using ATTEXT, give the extract file a slightly different name than the template file. If not, your template file will be converted into the extract file. Using a different name enables you to easily revise the template file to extract different information.

The extract file that is created from Problem 2 should appear as follows:

```
W12X40    RYERSON    $.30/LB    40LB/FT    10FT     03116WF
W12X40    RYERSON    $.30/LB    40LB/FT    10FT     03116WF
W12X40    RYERSON    $.30/LB    40LB/FT    10FT     03116WF
W12X40    RYERSON    $.30/LB    40LB/FT    10FT     03116WF
W12X31    RYERSON    $.29/LB    31LB/FT    8.5FT    03125WF
W12X31    RYERSON    $.29/LB    31LB/FT    8.5FT    03125WF
```

P27-4

4. Select one of your drawings from Chapter 25 and create a bill of materials for it using the template file method and the ATTEXT command. Follow these guidelines.

A. The template file should list all of the attributes of each block in the drawing.

B. Use the SDF format to display the file.

C. Display the file on the screen.

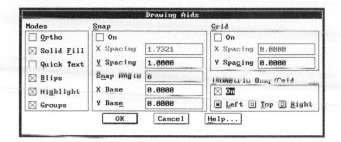

Chapter 28

ISOMETRIC DRAWING

Learning objectives

After completing this chapter, you will be able to:

○ Understand the nature of isometric and oblique views.
○ Set an isometric grid and construct isometric objects.
○ Create isometric text styles.
○ Demonstrate isometric and oblique dimensioning techniques.

Three-dimensional visualization and drawing are skills that every drafter, designer, and engineer should possess. This is especially important now that most CAD systems support 3-D modeling. However, be aware that there is a distinct difference between drawing a three-dimensional looking view and a true 3-D model. Once a 3-D model is made, it can be rotated on the display screen to view from any angle. The computer actually calculates the points, lines, and surfaces of the object in space. The topic of 3-D is presented in Chapter 29. This chapter focuses on creating three-dimensional *look-ing* views using two-dimensional objects and some special AutoCAD functions.

PICTORIAL DRAWING OVERVIEW

The word *pictorial* means "like a picture." It refers to any realistic form of drawing. Pictorial drawings show height, width, and depth. Several forms of pictorial drawings are used in industry today. The simplest and least realistic is *oblique*. The most realistic is *perspective*. *Isometric* drawing falls midway between the two in terms of realism.

Oblique drawings

An oblique drawing shows objects with one or more parallel faces having true shape and size. A scale is selected for the orthographic, or front faces. Then, an angle for the depth or receding axis is chosen. Three types of oblique drawings are used: *cavalier, cabinet*, and *general*, Figure 28-1. They vary in the angle and scale of the receding axis. Both cavalier and cabinet drawings use an angle of 45°. The cabinet view receding axis is drawn at half scale and a cavalier's is at full scale. The general oblique is normally drawn at an angle other than 45° and at 3/4 scale.

Figure 28-1. The three types of oblique drawings differ in the scale, and angle, of the receding axis.

Cavalier   Cabinet   General

Isometric drawings

Isometric drawings are more realistic than obliques. The entire object appears to have been tilted toward or away from the viewer. The word "isometric" means equal measure. This equal measure refers to the angle between the three axes, 120°, after the object has been tilted. The tilt angle is 35°16'. This is shown in Figure 28-2. The angle of 120° is cumbersome to measure, so an angle of 30° from horizontal is used when laying out the drawing.

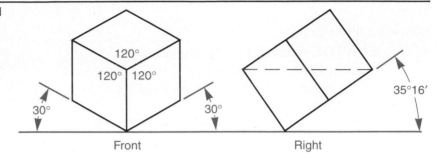

Figure 28-2. An object is tilted 35°16' to achieve an isometric view having 120° between the three axes.

NOTE When constructing isometric drawings, remember that lines parallel in the orthogonal views must be parallel in the isometric view.

The most appealing aspect of isometric drawing is that all three axis lines can be measured using the same scale. This saves time, while still producing a pleasing pictorial representation of the object. This type of drawing is produced when you use the Isometric option of the SNAP command, which is detailed later.

Closely related to isometric drawing is *dimetric* and *trimetric*. These forms of pictorial drawing differ from isometric in the scales used to measure the three axes. Dimetric drawing uses two different scales, whereas trimetric uses three scales. The use of different scales is an effort to create *foreshortening*, in which the length of the sides appear to recede. The relationship between isometric, dimetric, and trimetric drawings is illustrated in Figure 28-3.

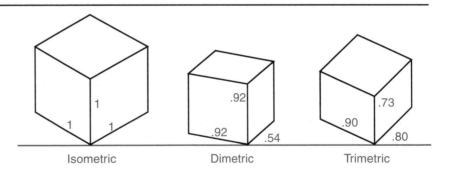

Figure 28-3. Isometric, dimetric, and trimetric differ in the scales used to draw the three axes. The isometric shown here has the scales represented as one. You can see how the dimetric and trimetric scales vary from that.

Perspective drawing

The most realistic form of pictorial drawing is perspective. This is done with the aid of *vanishing points*. The eye naturally sees objects in perspective. Look down a long hall and note that the wall and floor lines seem to converge in the distance at an imaginary point, or the *vanishing point*. The most common types of perspective drawings are *one-point* and *two-point*. These forms of pictorial drawing are often used in architecture, and somewhat in the automotive and aircraft industries. Examples of one-point and two-point perspectives are shown in Figure 28-4. A perspective view of a 3-D model can be produced in AutoCAD using the DVIEW command. See *AutoCAD and Its Applications–Advanced, R13 for DOS* for a complete discussion of the DVIEW command.

Figure 28-4.   Example of a one-point and a two-point perspective.

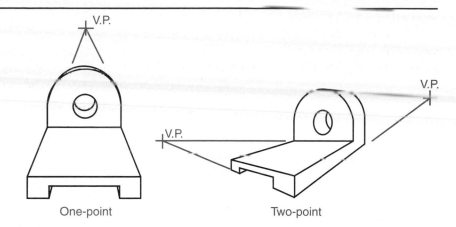

One-point

Two-point

ISOMETRIC DRAWING

AUG 3

The most common method of pictorial drawing used in industry is isometric. The drawing provides a single view showing three sides that can be measured using the same scale. An isometric view has no perspective and may appear somewhat distorted. Isometric axes are drawn at 30° to horizontal, as shown in Figure 28-5.

Figure 28-5.   Isometric axis layout. Lines not parallel to any of the three axes are called nonisometric.

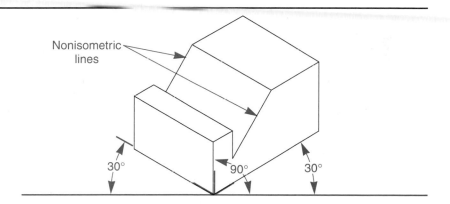

Nonisometric lines

30°   90°   30°

The three axes shown in Figure 28-5 represent the width, height, and depth of the object. Lines which would appear horizontal in an orthographic view are placed at a 30° angle. Lines vertical in an orthographic view are placed vertically. These are parallel to the axes. Any line parallel to the three axes can be measured and is called an *isometric line*. Lines not parallel to the axes cannot be measured and are called *nonisometric lines*. Note the two nonisometric lines in Figure 28-5.

Circular features shown on isometric objects must be oriented properly or they will appear distorted. Figure 28-6 shows the correct orientation of isometric circles on the three principal planes. These circles appear as ellipses on the isometric object. The small diameter of the ellipse must always align on the axis of the hole or circular feature. Notice that the centerline axes of the holes in Figure 28-6 are parallel to one of the isometric planes.

A good basic rule to remember about isometric drawing is that lines parallel in an orthogonal view must be parallel in the isometric view. AutoCAD's feature makes that task, and the positioning of ellipses easy.

Figure 28-6.   Proper ellipse
orientation on isometric planes.
The minor axis always aligns
with the axis centerline.

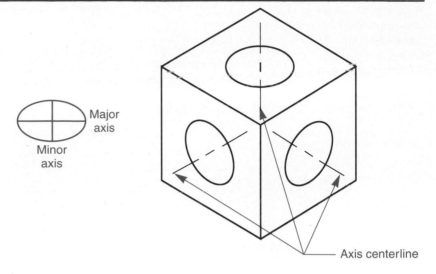

PROFESSIONAL TIP

If you are ever in doubt about the proper orientation of an ellipse in an isometric drawing, remember that the minor axis of the ellipse must always be aligned on the centerline axis of the circular feature. This shows clearly in Figure 28-6.

Setting the isometric snap

When the grid is turned on, horizontal and vertical lines of dots are displayed. To begin drawing an isometric object it is helpful to have the grid dots at an angle. The angle represents the three axis lines of the isometric layout. This is easy using the SNAP command. Enter the Style (S) option, then the Isometric (I) option. Finally, enter the vertical spacing.

Command: **SNAP** ↵
Snap spacing or ON/OFF/Aspect/Rotate/Style ⟨current⟩: **S** ↵
Standard/Isometric ⟨S⟩: **I** ↵
Vertical spacing ⟨current⟩: **.25** ↵

The grid dots on the screen change to the isometric orientation, as shown in Figure 28-7. If your grid dots are not visible, turn the grid on. Notice the crosshairs have also changed and appear angled. This aids you in drawing lines at the proper angles.

Try drawing a four-sided surface using the LINE command. Draw it so that it appears to be the left side of a box in an isometric layout. See Figure 28-8. To draw nonparallel surfaces, change the angle of the crosshairs to make your task easy.

Changing the crosshairs orientation

Drawing an isometric shape is possible without ever changing the crosshairs' angle. Yet, the drawing process is easier and quicker if the angles of the crosshairs align with the axes. This is a simple task with a multibutton digitizer puck. Button 8 is a toggle for the crosshairs when the isometric snap is active. Press the button and the crosshairs immediately change to the next position. The positions are displayed on the prompt line as a reference.

Command: ⟨Isoplane Left⟩ ⟨Isoplane Top⟩ ⟨Isoplane Right⟩

The three crosshairs positions are shown in Figure 28-9.

Figure 28-7.   An example of
an isometric grid setup in
AutoCAD.

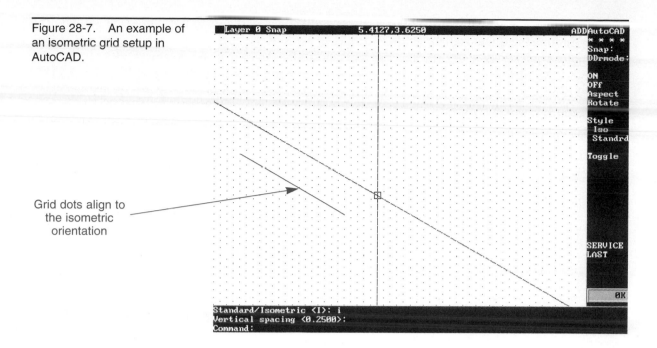

Grid dots align to
the isometric
orientation

Figure 28-8.   A four-sided
object drawn with the LINE
command can be used as the
left side of an isometric box.

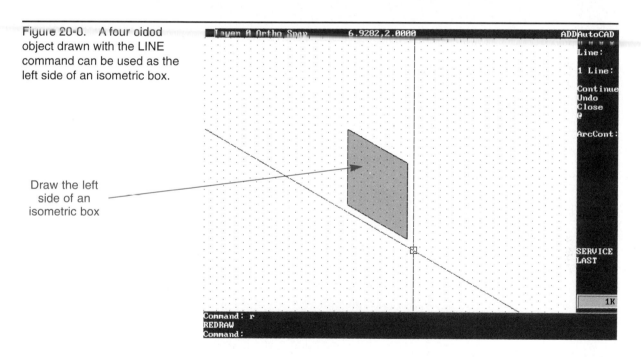

Draw the left
side of an
isometric box

Figure 28-9.   The three
isometric crosshairs positions
are set with the ISOPLANE
command.

Left   Top   Right

A second method that is just as fast as pressing the puck button is to press function key F5. This toggles through the three isoplane settings with each press of the key.

Another quick way to change the crosshairs' position is to use the toggle keys CTRL+E. Pressing these two keys performs the same function as the puck button. The fourth method is to use the ISO-PLANE command.

Command: **ISOPLANE** ↵
Left/Top/Right/⟨Toggle⟩:

Press ENTER to toggle the crosshairs to the next position. The command line displays the following message:

Current Isometric plane is: Right

You can toggle immediately to the next position by pressing ENTER at the Command: prompt and ENTER again. The prompt should now read:

Current Isometric plane is: Left

To specify the plane of orientation, type the first letter of that position:

Left/Top/Right/⟨Toggle⟩: **R** ↵
Current Isometric plane is: Right

The crosshairs are always in one of the isoplane positions when the isometric snap option is in effect. The one exception occurs when the Window or Crossing selection options are used for display and editing commands. At this time the crosshairs change to the normal vertical and horizontal positions.

Setting isometric variables with a dialog box

You can quickly pick your isometric variables from a dialog box. Pick the Options pull-down menu, then pick the Drawing Aids... option. The "Drawing Aids" dialog box displayed was discussed earlier in this text. It contains the options for isometric drawing. The isometric buttons are located at the lower right of the dialog box. See Figure 28-10.

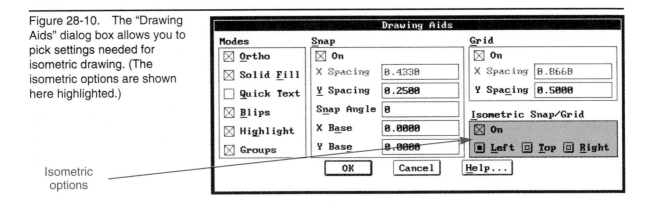

Figure 28-10. The "Drawing Aids" dialog box allows you to pick settings needed for isometric drawing. (The isometric options are shown here highlighted.)

Isometric options

To activate the isometric snap grid, pick the On check box. Notice that the X spacing for Grid and Snap are grayed out. You can only set the Y spacing for grid and snap in isometric. Since X spacing relates to horizontal measurements, it is not used in the isometric mode. What would normally be horizontal lines on an isometric object, are drawn at a 30° angle from horizontal. Three radio buttons at the lower right of the dialog box allow you to select the isoplane orientation. Be sure to pick the On buttons for Snap and Grid if you want to turn them on. Pick OK when you have completed all of your settings.

To turn off the Isometric mode, simply select DDRMODES to display the "Drawing Aids" dialog box, and pick the On check box in the isometric area. The X disappears, and the Isometric mode is turned off when you pick OK.

EXERCISE 28-1

❏ Start a new drawing and name it EX28-1.
❏ Set the grid spacing at .5.
❏ Set the snap style to the Isometric option. Specify .25 vertical spacing.
❏ Use the LINE command to draw the objects shown. Dimensions are given.
❏ Change the ISOPLANE orientation as needed.
❏ Save the drawing as A:EX28-1.

The isometric ellipse

Placing an isometric ellipse on an object is made easy by AutoCAD. An ellipse is positioned automatically to the current ISOPLANE setting. All you must do is pick the center point and the diameter after selecting Isocircle from the ELLIPSE command options.

Command. **ELLIPSE** ↵
Arc/Center/Isocircle/⟨Axis endpoint 1⟩: **I** ↵
Center of circle: *(pick a point)*
⟨Circle radius⟩/Diameter:

Three options are available for determining the size of the ellipse at this last prompt.
- When DRAGMODE is on, the ellipse changes size as the cursor moves. Set the radius by picking a point.
- Enter a numeric value and press ENTER to have AutoCAD draw the ellipse to a specific radius.
- Type D and you are asked for the circle diameter. Enter a number, press ENTER, and the ellipse appears.

Always check the ISOPLANE position before locating an ellipse on your drawing. You can dynamically view the three positions that an ellipse can take. Select ELLIPSE, pick the Isocircle option, and then toggle the ISOPLANE option. See Figure 28-11. The ellipse rotates each time you toggle the crosshairs.

Figure 28-11.   The orientation of the isometric ellipse is determined by the ISOPLANE position.

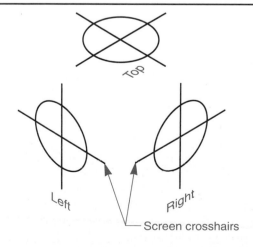

EXERCISE 28-2

❏ Open EX28-1 if this drawing is not already on your screen.
❏ Select the ELLIPSE command to place an ellipse on the three sides of the object.
❏ Draw the ellipses in the following manner:
   1. Pick a radius of .5 using the cursor.
   2. Enter a radius of .75 at the keyboard.
   3. Type D and enter a diameter of .6 at the keyboard.
❏ The finished drawing should look like the example given here.
❏ Save the drawing as A:EX28-2.

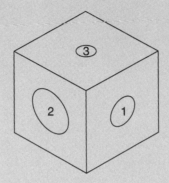

Creating isometric text styles

Isometric text should look like part of the drawing, because it appears to lie in one of the isometric planes. It should not look like it was added at the last minute. Drafters and artists occasionally neglect this aspect of pictorial drawing and it shows on the final product. Text should align with the plane it applies to. This involves creating several new text styles.

Figure 28-12 illustrates possible orientation of text on an isometric drawing. Text could be located on the object or positioned away from it as a note. These examples were done using only two text styles.

Figure 28-12.   Isometric text applications. The text shown here indicates the ISO style used and the angle used.

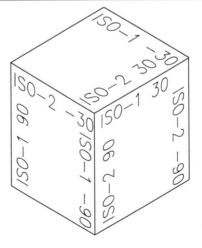

The text styles in Figure 28-12 are based on styles that use either a 30° or –30° obliquing angle. The labels refer to the style numbers given below. The angles shown in Figure 28-12 indicate the rotation angle entered when using the TEXT command. The two isometric styles used are:

NAME	FONT	OBLIQUING ANGLE
ISO-1	Romans	30°
ISO-2	Romans	–30°

Find the text sample in Figure 28-12 that says ISO-2 90. This means that the ISO-2 style was used and the text was rotated 90°. This technique can be applied to any font.

EXERCISE 28-3

❑ Load AutoCAD and open drawing EX28-1.
❑ Create one text style to label the angled (nonisometric) surface of the wedge. See the illustration.
❑ Create a second style to label the front of the wedge.
❑ Save the drawing as A:EX28-3.

Drawing solid isometric shapes

Isometric drawing can be used to produce both *wireframe* constructions and objects that appear to be solid. Wireframes are objects that you can see through, as if they are made of wire. The objects you drew in Exercise 28-1 appeared solid even though the surfaces were not colored or filled in.

Using the SOLID command, you can construct simple colored shapes that appear to be solid. Keep in mind the following points as you draw an isometric object using the SOLID command.
• The sequence of points needed to draw a rectangular shape must be correct.
• A solid fill cannot be drawn with a curved edge.
• An ellipse or circle placed on a solid surface will not open a hole in the solid shading.

The sequence you choose to pick the points is important. Figure 28-13 shows the proper order to construct solid planes.

Figure 28-13.   The correct sequence of points to create solid isometric planes.

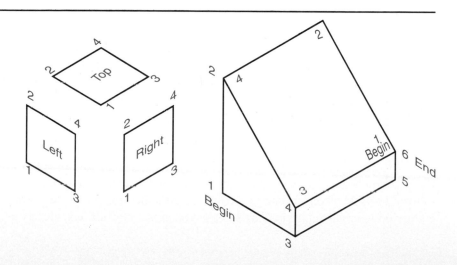

PROFESSIONAL TIP

Solids are drawn without the benefit of a rubberband line. Isometric snap and grids are especially helpful when creating solid surfaces.

EXERCISE 28-4

❏ Start a new drawing and name it EX28-4.
❏ Set the visible grid to .5 and isometric snap to .25.
❏ Set the colors as indicated for each side of the object. Enter the COLOR command before drawing each side with the SOLID command.
❏ Use the SOLID command to construct the object shown.
❏ Save the drawing as A:EX28-4.

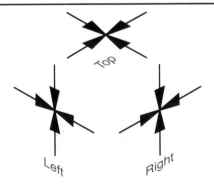

ISOMETRIC DIMENSIONING

AutoCAD does not automatically dimension isometric objects. You must create isometric arrowheads and text styles. Then, manually draw the dimension lines and text as they should appear in each of the three isometric planes. This is a laborious task when compared to dimensioning two-dimensional drawings. Yet, it is much faster than manual drafting.

There are only two drawing entities you must develop in an isometric format: the arrowheads and the text styles. You have already learned how to create isometric text styles. These can be set up in an isometric prototype drawing if you draw isometrics often. The arrowheads must be drawn individually. Examples of arrows for the three isometric planes are shown in Figure 28-14.

Figure 28-14.   Examples of arrowheads in each of the three isometric planes.

Arrowheads can be drawn open with the LINE command or filled in with the SOLID command. Every arrowhead does not have to be drawn individually. First, draw two isometric axes as shown in Figure 28-15A. Then draw one arrowhead like the one shown in Figure 28-15B. Use the MIRROR command to create additional arrows. As you create new arrows, move them to their proper plane. Save each arrowhead as a block in your isometric prototype drawing. Use block names that are easy to remember and type.

Figure 28-15.   A–Draw the two isometric axes for arrowhead placement. B–Draw the first arrowhead on one of the axis lines. Then, mirror the arrowhead to create others.

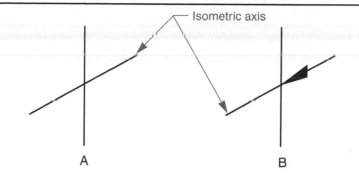

Isometric axis

A

B

An important aspect of isometric dimensioning is to place dimension lines, text, and arrowheads in the proper plane. Remember these guidelines:
- The extension lines should always extend the plane being dimensioned.
- The heel of the arrowhead should always be parallel to the extension line.
- The strokes of the text that would normally be vertical should always be parallel with the extension lines or dimension lines.

These techniques are shown on a dimensioned isometric part in Figure 28-16.

Figure 28-16.   A dimensioned isometric part. Note the text and arrowhead orientation in relation to the extension lines.

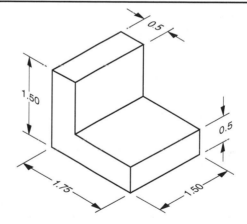

OBLIQUE DIMENSIONING

AutoCAD provides a method for semiautomatic dimensioning of oblique lines. The dimensions must already be drawn using any of the linear dimensioning commands. Figure 28-17A illustrates an object that has been dimensioned using the DIMALIGNED and VERTICAL commands. The next step is to select the Oblique option of the DIMEDIT command. Oblique is a dimension editing function. It is found in the Draw pull-down menu by picking Dimensioning. In the screen menu pick MOD DIM, then DimEdit: to locate the Oblique option.

The Oblique option requires that you select the dimension and enter the obliquing angle desired. It is used as follows:

Command: **DIMEDIT** ↵
Dimension Edit (Home/New/Rotate/Oblique) ⟨Home⟩: **O** ↵
Select objects: *(pick dimension number 1)*
Enter obliquing angle (RETURN for none): **30** ↵

Figure 28-17A shows numbers by each dimension. The following list gives the obliquing angle required for each numbered dimension in order to achieve the finished drawing shown in Figure 28-17B.

Dimension	Obliquing angle
①	30°
②	–30°
③	30°
④	–30°

Figure 28-17. The OBLIQUE dimensioning command requires that you select an existing dimension (shown in A) and enter the desired obliquing angle (shown in B). Refer to the text for the angles represented by the circled numbers.

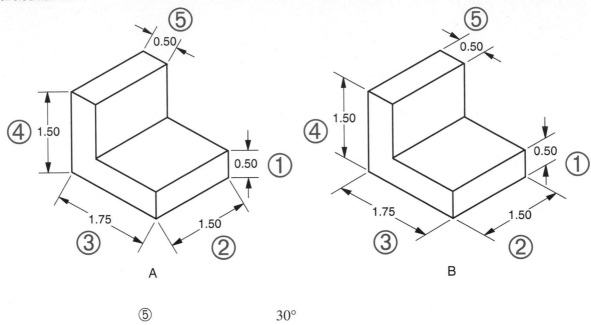

A   B

⑤	30°

This technique creates suitable dimensions for an isometric drawing, and is quicker than the previous method discussed. Bear in mind that the oblique method does not rotate the arrows so that the arrowhead heels are aligned with the extension lines, nor does it draw the dimension text aligned in the plane of the dimension.

CHAPTER TEST

Write your answers in the spaces provided.

1. The simplest form of pictorial drawing is _____.

2. How does isometric drawing differ from oblique drawing? _____
   _____
   _____

3. How do dimetric and trimetric drawings differ from isometric drawings? _____
   _____
   _____

4. The most realistic form of pictorial drawing is _____.

5. Provide the correct entries at the following prompts to set an isometric snap with a spacing of .2.

   Command:_____

   Snap spacing or ON/OFF/Aspect/Rotate/Style ⟨current⟩: _____

   Standard/Isometric ⟨S⟩: _____

   Vertical spacing ⟨current⟩: _____

6. What function does the ISOPLANE command perform? _____

   _____

   _____

7. The pull-down menu that contains the "Drawing Aids" dialog box is _____.

8. What factor determines the orientation of an isometric ellipse? _____

   _____

9. List the three methods to define the size of an isometric ellipse. _____

   _____

   _____

10. Which aspect of the TEXT Style option allows you to create text that can be used on an isometric

    drawing?_____

11. You can create angled surfaces in an isometric drawing using the SOLID command. (True/False)

12. What technique does AutoCAD provide for dimensioning isometric objects? _____

    _____

13. What value must you enter to achieve the kind of dimensioning referred to in Question 12? ____

    _____

DRAWING PROBLEMS

1-13. Before drawing any of the objects, create an isometric prototype drawing. Then use the prototype to construct each isometric drawing. Items that should be set in the prototype include: grid spacing, snap spacing, ortho setting, and text size. Save the prototype as ISOPROTO. Use ISOPROTO as the prototype drawing for the following isometric drawings. Save the drawings as A:P28-(problem number).

 1.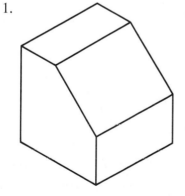

P28-1

 2.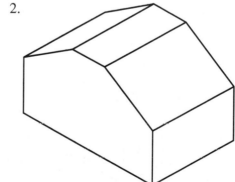

P28-2

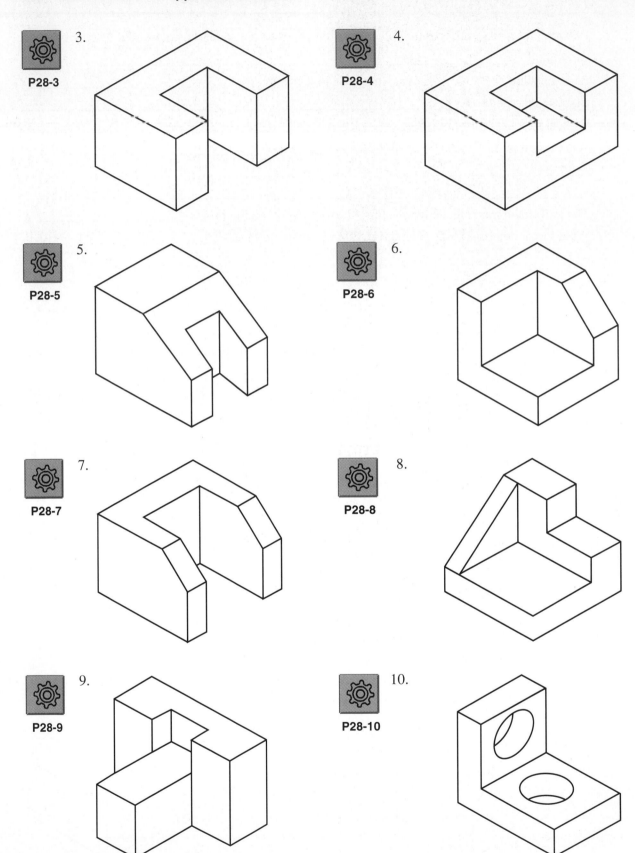

3.
P28-3

4.
P28-4

5.
P28-5

6.
P28-6

7.
P28-7

8.
P28-8

9.
P28-9

10.
P28-10

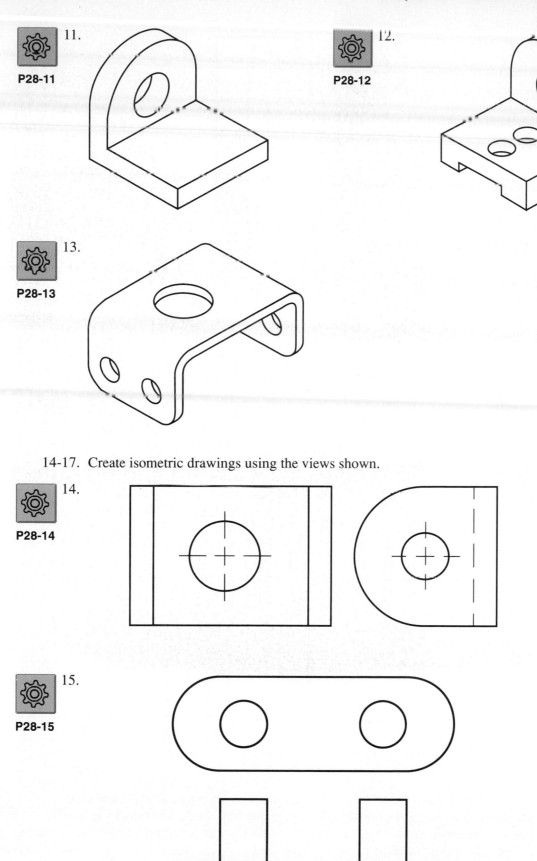

11.

P28-11

12.

P28-12

13.

P28-13

14-17.   Create isometric drawings using the views shown.

14.

P28-14

15.

P28-15

16.

P28-16

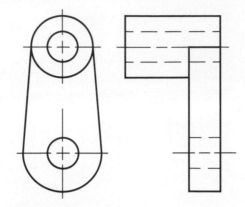

17.

P28-17

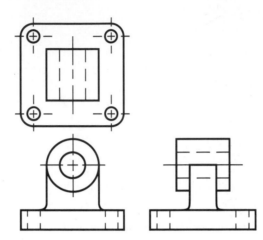

18. Construct a set of isometric arrowheads to use when dimensioning isometric drawings. Load your isometric prototype (ISOPROTO). Create arrowheads for each of the three isometric planes. Save each arrowhead as a block. Name them with the first letter indicating the plane: T for top, L for left, and R for right. Also number them clockwise from the top. See the example for the right isometric plane. Save the prototype again when finished.

P28-18

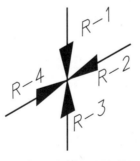

19. Create a set of isometric text styles like those shown in Figure 28-12. Load your prototype drawing; make one complete set in one font. Make additional sets in other fonts if you wish. Enter a text height of 0 so that you can specify the height when placing the text. Save the prototype again when finished.

P28-19

20. Begin a new drawing named P28-20 using your prototype. Select one of the following problems to dimension fully: 2, 6, 10, 11, or 12. When adding dimensions, be sure to use the proper arrowhead and text style for the plane in which you are working. Save the drawing when completed.

P28-20

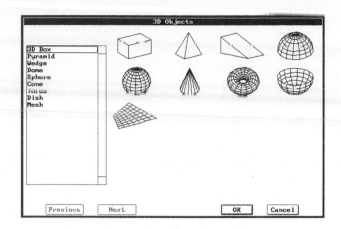

Chapter 29

INTRODUCTION TO THREE-DIMENSIONAL DRAWING

Learning objectives

After completing this chapter, you will be able to:

○ Understand the nature and function of rectangular 3-D coordinate systems.
○ Understand the "right-hand rule" of 3-D visualization.
○ Construct extruded and wireframe 3-D objects.
○ Display 3-D objects at any desired viewpoint.

Computers are especially suited to handle information about points in space. However, in order for computer software to accept and use this information, the drafter or designer must first have good 3-D visualization skills. These skills include the ability to see an object in three dimensions and to visualize it rotating in space. These skills can be obtained by using 3-D techniques to construct objects, and by trying to see two-dimensional sketches and drawings as 3-D models. This chapter provides an introduction to several aspects of 3-D drawing and visualization. A thorough discussion of 3-D drawing, visualization, and display techniques is provided in *AutoCAD and its Applications–Advanced, R13 for DOS.*

RECTANGULAR 3-D COORDINATES

AUG 11

A computer can draw lines because it knows the X and Y values of the endpoints. The line does not really exist in the computer, only the points do. You see one plane and two dimensions in 2-D drawing. However, when drawing in 3-D you add another plane and coordinate axis. You define the third dimension with a third coordinate measured along the Z axis. A computer can only draw lines in 3-D if it knows the X, Y, and Z coordinate values of each point on the object.

Compare the 2-D coordinate system to the 3-D system in Figure 29-1. Note that the positive values of Z in the 3-D system come up from the XY plane of a 2-D drawing. Consider the surface of your screen as the new Z plane. Anything behind the screen is negative Z and anything in front of the screen is positive Z.

Figure 29-1.   A comparison of 2-D and 3-D coordinate systems.

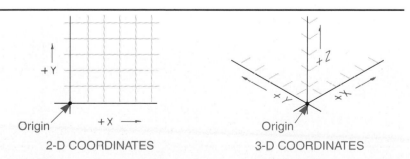

2-D COORDINATES

3-D COORDINATES

The object in Figure 29-2A is a 2-D drawing showing the top view of an object. The XY coordinate values of each point are shown, given the lower-left corner as the origin (0,0). To convert this object to its three-dimensional form, Z values are given to each vertex, or corner. Figure 29-2B shows the object pictorially with the XYZ values of each point listed.

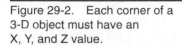

Figure 29-2.　Each corner of a 3-D object must have an X, Y, and Z value.

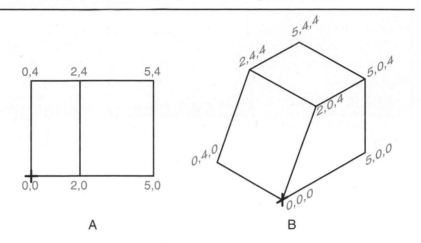

A   B

This same object could have been drawn using negative Z coordinates. It would extend behind the screen. Although the sign of the Z value makes no difference to AutoCAD, it is time-consuming for you to deal with negative values.

Study the nature of the 3-D coordinate system. Be sure you understand Z values before you begin constructing 3-D objects. It is especially important that you carefully visualize and plan your design when working with 3-D constructions.

Three-dimensional objects can be drawn in AutoCAD using two additional coordinate systems–spherical and cylindrical. These two systems enable you to work with point locations using distances and angles in order to draw a variety of shapes. For a complete discussion of spherical and cylindrical coordinate systems please refer to *AutoCAD and its Applications–Advanced, R13 for DOS.*

EXERCISE 29-1

❑ Study the multiview sketch.
❑ Given the 3-D coordinate axes, freehand sketch the object pictorially.
❑ Each tick mark is one unit. Use correct dimensions as given in the multiview drawing.
❑ When you complete the freehand sketch, draw the object in AutoCAD with the LINE command by entering XYZ coordinates for each point.
❑ Save the drawing as A:EX29-1 and quit.

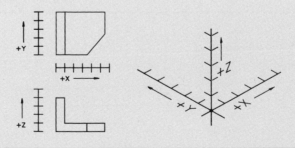

CREATING EXTRUDED 3-D SHAPES

AUG 11

Most shapes drawn with AutoCAD are extruded shapes. *Extruded* means that a 2-D shape is given a base elevation and a thickness. The object then rises up, or "extrudes" to its given thickness. The ELEV command controls the base elevation and thickness. ELEV does not draw, it merely sets the base elevation and thickness for the next objects drawn. ELEV can be typed at the Command: prompt, or set in a dialog box by picking Object Creation... from the Data pull-down menu, or DDemode from the DATA screen menu. The DDEMODES command displays the "Object Creation Modes" dialog box in which the current elevation and thickness can be set. See Figure 29-3.

Figure 29-3.   The "Object Creation Modes" dialog box enables you to set the current elevation and thickness.

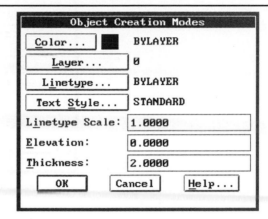

NOTE   Keep in mind that the current elevation established by the value set using the ELEV command, or entered in the "Object Creation Modes" dialog box, is the level on which the next objects will be drawn. Therefore, if you set the elevation at 2.0, then draw the bottom of a machine part, the bottom of that part is now sitting at an elevation of 2.0 units above the zero elevation.

On the other hand, the setting of the *thickness* is the value that determines the height of the next object you draw. Therefore, if you want to draw a part 2.0 units high, with the bottom of the part resting on the zero elevation plane, set elevation to 0.0 and thickness to 2.0.

The process of drawing a rectangular box four units long by three units wide by two units high begins with the ELEV command:

Command: **ELEV** ↵
New current elevation ⟨0.0000⟩: ↵
New current thickness ⟨0.0000⟩: **2** ↵

Nothing happens on screen. Now use the LINE command to draw the top view of the rectangular box. Although it appears that you are drawing lines, you are actually drawing XY planes. Each plane has a height (the thickness) that you cannot see yet.

Before you display the 3-D construction, use the following instructions to add a hexagon and a circle as shown in Figure 29-4. The hexagon should sit on top of the rectangle and extend three units above. The circle should appear to be a hole through the rectangle. Since the circle and rectangle have the same elevation, there is no need to use the ELEV command.

Figure 29-4.   A hexagon and a circle added to rectangle for the command sequence given in the text.

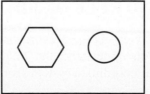

Before drawing the hexagon, set the base elevation to the top surface of the rectangle and thickness (height) of the hexagon feature using the ELEV command as follows:

Command: **ELEV** ↵
New current elevation ⟨0.0000⟩: **2** ↵
New current thickness ⟨2.0000⟩: **3** ↵

These values can also be set in the "Object Creation Modes" dialog box as shown in Figure 29-5.

Figure 29-5.   The elevation and thickness values can be set in the "Object Creation Modes" dialog box.

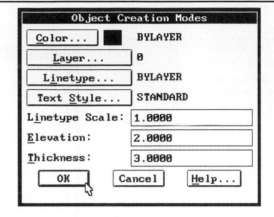

Now, draw the hexagon. The bracketed numbers after each prompt reflect the current values. A 2 was entered for the elevation because the hexagon sits on top of the rectangle, which is two units thick. This is where the hexagon starts. The 3 is the thickness, or height of the hexagon above its starting point.

Next the elevation and thickness for the circle is set:

Command: **ELEV** ↵
New current elevation ⟨2.0000⟩: **0** ↵
New current thickness ⟨3.0000⟩: **2** ↵

Now draw the circle to the right of the hexagon as shown in Figure 29-4. The object is now ready to be viewed in 3-D.

PROFESSIONAL TIP

   Keep in mind that a "hole" drawn using ELEV and CIRCLE is not really a hole to AutoCAD. It is a cylinder with solid ends. This becomes clear when you display the objects in a 3-D view with hidden lines removed.

Some 3-D drawing hints

- Erasing a line drawn with the ELEV thickness value set other than zero erases an entire plane.
- Shapes drawn using the LINE and ELEV commands are open at the top and bottom. Circles drawn with ELEV are closed at the ends.
- The PLINE and TRACE commands give thickness to lines and make them appear as walls in the 3-D view.

THE RIGHT-HAND RULE OF 3-D   AUG 11

Before we discuss viewing the 3-D drawing, it is worthwhile to review a good technique for 3-D visualization. Once you understand the following procedure, viewing a 3-D object oriented in AutoCAD's rectangular coordinate system should be simplified.

The right-hand rule is a graphic representation of positive coordinate values in the three axis directions of a coordinate system. The *UCS* (User Coordinate System) is based on a concept of visualization called the *right-hand rule*. This requires that you use the thumb, index finger, and middle finger of your right hand and hold them open in front of you, as shown in Figure 29-6.

Figure 29-6.   Try positioning your hand like this to understand the relationship of the X, Y, and Z axes.

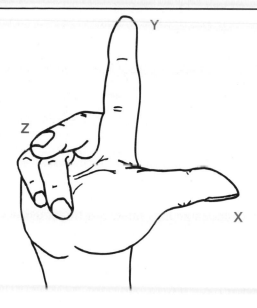

Although this may seem a bit unusual to do (especially if you are sitting in the middle of a school library or computer lab), it can do wonders for your understanding of the nature of the three axes. It can also help in understanding how the UCS can be rotated about each of the axis lines, or fingers.

Imagine that your thumb represents the X axis, your index finger is the Y axis, and your middle finger is the Z axis. Hold your hand directly in front of you and bend your middle finger so it is pointing directly at you. Now you see the plan view. The positive X axis is pointing to the right and the positive Y axis is pointing up. The positive Z axis comes toward you, and the origin of this system is the palm of your hand.

This concept can be visualized even better if you are sitting at a computer and the AutoCAD graphics screen is displayed. If the UCS icon is not displayed in the lower-left corner of the screen, turn it on as follows:

Command: **UCSICON** ⏎
ON/OFF/All/Noorigin/ORigin ⟨ON⟩: **ON** ⏎

Now orient your right hand as shown in Figure 29-6 and position it next to the UCS icon on the screen. Your index finger and thumb should point in the same directions as Y and X respectively on the UCS icon. Your middle finger will be pointing out of the screen directly at you. This technique can also be used to eliminate confusion when the UCS is rotated to odd angles.

When you use the VPOINT command (discussed later in this chapter), a tripod appears on the screen. It is composed of three axis lines–X, Y, and Z. When you see the tripod, you should be able to make the comparison with the right-hand rule. See Figure 29-7.

Figure 29-7. Compare the use of three fingers on the right hand and the tripod used by AutoCAD for 3-D viewing.

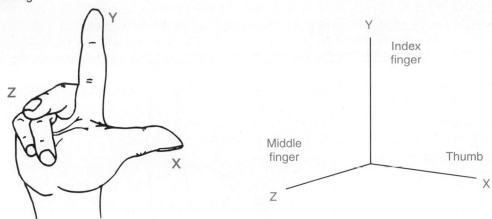

The User Coordinate System (UCS) can be rotated to any position desired. The coordinate system rotates on one of the three axis lines, just like a wheel rotates on an axle. Therefore, if you want to rotate the X plane, keep your thumb stationary, and turn your hand toward or away from you. If you wish to rotate the Y plane, keep your index finger stationary and turn your hand to the left or right. When rotating the Z plane, you must keep your middle finger stationary and rotate your entire arm to the right or left.

If you discover that your 3-D visualization skills are weak, or that you are having trouble with the UCS method, don't be afraid to use the right-hand rule. It is a useful technique for improving your 3-D visualization skills. The ability to rotate the UCS around one or more of the three axes can become confusing if proper techniques are not used to visualize the rotation angles. A complete discussion of these techniques is provided in *AutoCAD and its Applications–Advanced, R13 for DOS.*

DISPLAYING 3-D DRAWINGS   AUG 11

Once you draw a 3-D object in the plan view, you should change your point of view so that the object can be seen in three dimensions. The VPOINT command allows you to display the current drawing at any angle. It may be easier to understand the function of this command as establishing your position relative to the object. Imagine that you can position yourself at a coordinate location in 3-D space, in relation to the object. The VPOINT command basically provides AutoCAD with the XYZ coordinates of your eyes, so the object can be positioned properly. VPOINT can be selected from the View pull-down menu by picking 3D Viewpoint, then Tripod, or by picking Vpoint: from the VIEW screen menu. It can also be typed at the Command: prompt as follows:

Command: **VPOINT** ↵
Rotate/⟨View point⟩ ⟨0.0000,0.0000,1.0000⟩:

The three numbers reflect the XYZ coordinates of the current viewpoint. You change these coordinates to select different viewpoints. The VPOINT values shown above represent the coordinates for the plan view. This means that you see the XY plane. Since it is difficult to visualize a numerical viewpoint, you can display a graphic representation of the XYZ axes, and pick the desired viewpoint with your pointing device. Press ENTER at the Rotate: prompt or select the Axes option from the screen menu. The screen display changes to one similar to Figure 29-8.

Figure 29-8.   The VPOINT
axes display enables you to
position yourself in relation
to the object.

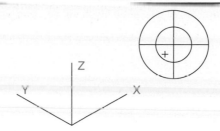

    As you move the pointing device, notice what happens on screen. The XYZ coordinate tripod moves and the small crosshairs near the concentric circles also move. The concentric circles divided into quarters represent a compass. When the small crosshairs are inside the small circle, you are viewing the object from above. When the crosshairs are located between the two circles, you are viewing the object from below.

    The easiest way to locate the viewpoint is to move the cursor while observing the XYZ axes tripod movement. Pick the location where you are satisfied with the appearance of the axes. It may take some practice. Remember that in the top or plan view, the X axis is horizontal, Y axis is vertical, and Z axis comes out of the screen. As you move the tripod, keep track of where the crosshairs are located inside the compass. Compare their position to that of the tripod. Move the tripod until it is positioned like the one given in Figure 29-9. Press the pick button. The display should then resemble that shown in the figure.

Figure 29-9.   The three axes
and a 3-D view.

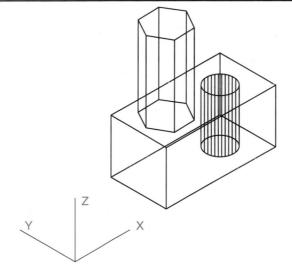

    The number of viewpoints you can select is endless. To get an idea of how the axes tripod and compass relate to the viewpoint, see the examples in Figure 29-10. It can be hard to distinguish top from bottom in wireframe views. Therefore, the viewpoints shown in Figure 29-10 are all from above the object and the HIDE command has been used to clarify the views. Use the VPOINT command to try each of these 3-D positions on your computer.

Figure 29-10. Examples of viewpoint locations and their related axes positions.

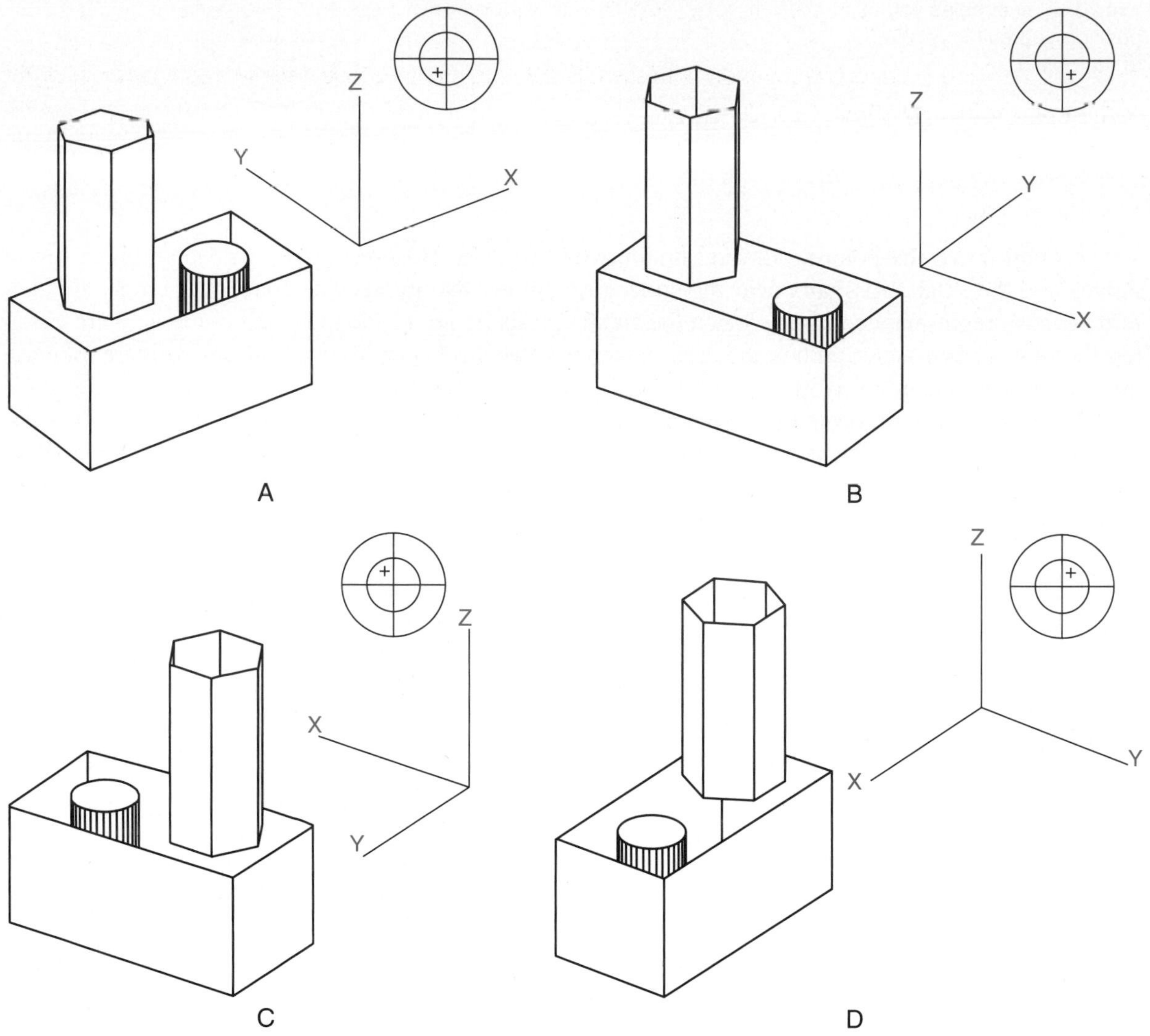

A

B

C

D

When you are ready to return to the plan view, type PLAN at the Command: prompt, or type the XYZ coordinates for the plan view.

Command: **VPOINT** ↵
Rotate/⟨View point⟩ ⟨*current*⟩: **0,0,1** ↵

This returns your original top view which fills the screen. You can use the ZOOM command's All option to display the drawing limits.

EXERCISE 29-2

❑ Set the grid spacing to .5 and snap spacing to .25.
❑ Set the elevation at 0 and the thickness at 2.
❑ Using the LINE command, draw a rectangle 2 x 3 units.
❑ Add a 180° arc to each end of the rectangle.
❑ Set the elevation at 2 and the thickness at 3.
❑ Draw a 1 unit diameter circle in the center of the rectangle.
❑ Use the VPOINT command to display the 3-D view of your drawing. Display it from three viewpoints using the axes tripod.
❑ Save the drawing as A:EX29-2.

Creating extruded 3-D text

Text added on the plan view is displayed in 3-D when you use the VPOINT command. However, the displayed text does not have thickness, and it always rests on the zero elevation plane. You can give text thickness and change the elevation with the CHPROP command. Select the text to change, pick the Thickness option, and enter a value.

Command: **CHPROP** ↵
Select objects: *(select the text)*
Select objects: ↵
Change what property (Color/LAyer/Ltype/ltScale/Thickness)? **T** ↵
New thickness ⟨*current*⟩: **1.5** ↵
Change what property (Color/LAyer/Ltype/ltScale/Thickness)? ↵

The selected text now has a thickness of 1.5. It is that simple. The CHPROP command does not leave the properties prompt until you press ENTER. Figure 29-11 shows examples of 3-D text with thickness added, before and after using the HIDE command.

Figure 29-11. Thickness applied to 3-D text with and without the HIDE option.

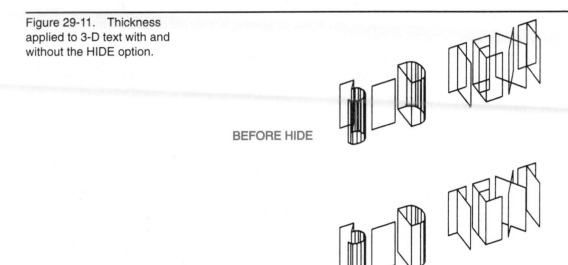

BEFORE HIDE

AFTER HIDE

Removing hidden lines in 3-D displays

The previous displays have been wireframe; every edge can be seen. This view can be confusing, especially if there are several circular features in your drawing. The best way to mask all lines that would normally be hidden is to use the HIDE command. Use HIDE only after you have selected a viewpoint to display a 3-D view.

Command: **HIDE** ↵
Regenerating drawing
Hiding lines 100% done

The size and complexity of the drawing, and the speed of your computer, determines how long you must wait for the lines to be hidden. The final display of the object in Figure 29-9 is shown in Figure 29-12 with hidden lines removed.

Figure 29-12.   Hidden lines
removed using the HIDE
command.

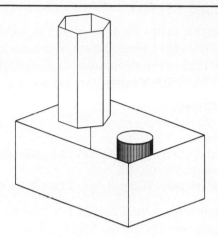

The view in Figure 29-12 may not look quite right. You probably expected the rectangle to appear solid with a circle in the top representing a hole. Think back to the initial construction of the rectangle. When drawn in the plan view, it consisted of four lines, or planes. It was not drawn with a top or bottom, just four sides. Then you placed a hexagon on top of the box and a cylinder inside. That is what appears in the "hidden line removed" display.

The individual features that compose the object in Figure 29-12 are shown in Figure 29-13. Both wireframe and hidden line views are given. To redisplay the wireframe view, just select another viewpoint or enter REGEN and press ENTER. A regeneration displays all lines of the objects.

Figure 29-13.   Individual features of the object in Figure 29-12 shown in wireframe and with hidden lines removed.

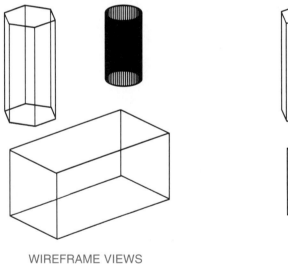
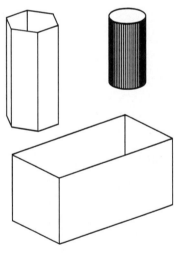

WIREFRAME VIEWS   HIDDEN LINES REMOVED

3-D CONSTRUCTION TECHNIQUES

Three-dimensional objects can be drawn in three basic forms–wireframe, surface models, and solid models. The following section discusses the construction of wireframes, and the use of 3-D faces to apply a surface to the wireframe. A *wireframe construction* is just that; an object that looks like it was made of wire. You can see through it. There are not a lot of practical applications for wireframe models unless you are an artist designing a new object using coat hangers. Wireframe models can be hard to visualize because it is difficult to determine the angle of view and the nature of the surfaces. Compare the two objects in Figure 29-14.

Figure 29-14.   A wireframe
object may be harder to visualize
than a surface model.
(Autodesk, Inc.)

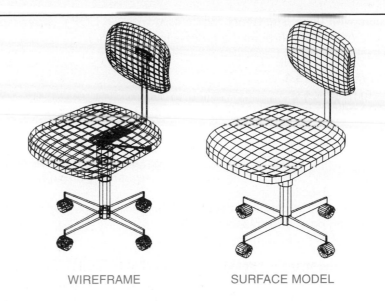

WIREFRAME   SURFACE MODEL

Surface modeling, on the other hand, is much more easily visualized. It looks more like the real object. Surface models can be used to imitate solid models, and most importantly, can be used for shading and rendering models. These shaded and rendered models can then be used in any number of presentation formats including slide shows, black and white or color prints, walk-arounds or walk-through animations, or animations that are recorded to videotape. A surface model can also be exported from AutoCAD for use in animation and rendering software such as Autodesk's 3D Studio. In addition, surface models are the basis for the construction of composite 3-D models, often called *virtual worlds,* which are used in the field of virtual reality. The possibilities are endless. However, remember that their usefulness is defined by the word "presentation." This means "seeing" what the model looks like while viewing it from different angles, with different lighting, shading, and surface textures.

On the other hand, *solids modeling* more closely represents designing an object using the materials from which it is to be made. This type of 3-D design involves using primitive solid shapes such as boxes, cylinders, spheres, and cones to construct an object. These shapes are added together and subtracted from each other to create a finished product. The solid model can then be shaded, rendered, and more importantly, analyzed and tested for mass, volume, moments of inertia, and centroids. Some third-party programs allow you to perform finite stress analysis on the model.

Before constructing a 3-D model, you should determine the purpose of your design. What will the model be used for–presentation, or analysis and manufacturing? This helps you determine which tools you should use to construct the model. The discussions and examples in this chapter provide an introductory view of the uses of wireframe, 3-D faces, and basic surfaced objects in order to create 3-D constructions. Further details of surface and solids modeling techniques are covered in ***AutoCAD and its Applications–Advanced, R13 for DOS.***

CONSTRUCTING WIREFRAMES AND 3-D FACES | AUG 11 |

Wireframes can be constructed using the LINE, PLINE, SPLINE, and 3DPOLY commands. AutoCAD provides a number of methods to use, but one particularly useful method is called filters. A *filter* is an existing point, or vector in your drawing file. When using a filter, you instruct AutoCAD to find the coordinate values of a selected point, then you supply the missing value–X, Y, or Z, or a combination. Filters can be used when working in two-dimensional space or when using a pictorial projection resulting from the VPOINT command.

Using filters to create 3-D wireframe objects

When using LINE, you must know the XYZ coordinate values of each corner on the object. To draw an object, first decide the easiest and quickest method using the LINE command. One technique is to draw the bottom surface. Then, make a copy at the height of the object. Finally, connect the corners with lines. The filters can be used with the COPY command, or by using grips to copy. From the plan view, step through the process in this manner:

> Command: **LINE** ↵
> From point: **3,3** ↵
> To point: **@1,0** ↵
> To point: *(continue picking points to construct the box)*

Next, copy the shape up to the height of 3 units.

> Command: **COPY** ↵
> Select objects: *(select the box using a window or crossing box)*
> Select objects: ↵
> ⟨Base point or displacement⟩/Multiple: *(pick a corner of the box)*
> Second point of displacement: **.XY** ↵
> of *(pick the same corner) (need Z):* **3** ↵

Since the shape is copied straight up, the top surface of the cube has the same XY values as the bottom surface. That is why .XY was entered as the second point of displacement. This filter picks up the XY values of the previous point specified and applies them to the location of the new copy. Now, all AutoCAD needs is the Z value, which it requests.

Check your progress by looking at the object using the VPOINT command. Enter the coordinates given below. Your display should look like that in Figure 29-15.

Figure 29-15.   A partially constructed 3-D box using Line and XYZ filters.

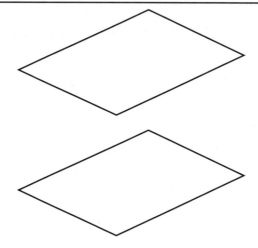

> Command: **VPOINT** ↵
> Enter view point ⟨*current*⟩: **–1,–2,0.5** ↵

Return the drawing to the plan view and finish the object using LINE command and point filters. The four remaining lines are vertical and three units long.

> Command: **LINE** ↵
> From point: *(pick the lower-left corner)*
> To point: **.XY** ↵
> of *(pick the lower-left corner again) (need Z):* **3** ↵
> To point: ↵

In this example, you instructed the computer to draw a line from the lower-left corner of the object to the same XY position 3 units above. The new line connects the top and bottom planes of the object. The same process can be used to draw the other three vertical lines. If you forget to enter the XY filter at the To point: prompt, AutoCAD will not ask for the Z distance. If this happens, cancel the command and start again. Use the VPOINT command again, and your drawing should look like Figure 29-16.

Figure 29-16.   A completed
3-D box using the LINE
command.

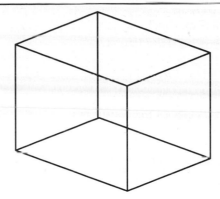

PROFESSIONAL TIP

If the process of drawing Z axis lines in the plan view is difficult to visualize, there is an easier option; draw them in the pictorial view. After drawing the top and bottom faces of the box, select a viewpoint and zoom in on the object. Now use the LINE command to construct the vertical lines using OSNAP modes ENDpoint, MIDpoint, and INTersection. This method allows you to see the lines in 3-D as you draw them.

EXERCISE 29-3

❑ Set the grid spacing at .5, snap spacing at .25, and elevation at 0.
❑ Draw the object below to the dimensions indicated.
❑ Use the LINE and COPY commands to construct the object.
❑ Construct the top and bottom planes in the plan view. Connect the vertical lines in a 3-D view.
❑ Save the drawing as A:EX29-3.

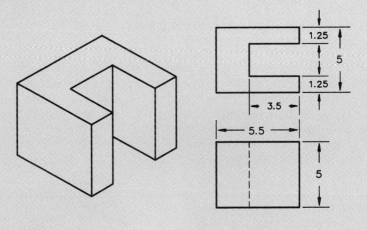

Constructing 3-D faces

Surfaces that appear solid and not wireframe are called *3-D faces*. They can be made with the 3DFACE command. Its prompt structure is similar to that of the SOLID command, but you can specify points in a clockwise or counterclockwise manner. A 3-D face must have at least three corners, but cannot have any more than four corners. The 3DFACE command is accessed in the DRAW 2 screen menu by picking SURFACES, and in the Draw pull-down menu by selecting Surfaces.

Draw the familiar box again, beginning with the bottom face, with the elevation set at 0. Then draw the top face. Draw the bottom face using the following command sequence.

Command: **3DFACE** ↵
First point: *(pick a point)*
Second point: *(pick a point)*
Third point: *(pick a point)*
Fourth point: *(pick a point)*
Third point: ↵

Notice that after you placed the fourth point, a line automatically connected the first point. A prompt then asks for the third point again if you want to continue to draw additional faces. Press ENTER to end the command.

The 3-D face can be copied using the same steps taken to copy the line surface. Remember to use XY filters for copying.

Command: **COPY** ↵
Select objects: *(pick the 3-D face)*
Select objects: ↵

Finally, the four sides of the box are drawn. First, set a viewpoint and then connect corners of each 3-D face using a running OSNAP mode of ENDpoint or INTersection.

Command: **VPOINT** ↵
⟨view point⟩ ⟨*current*⟩: **–1,–1,.75** ↵

PROFESSIONAL TIP

When moving or copying objects in 3-D space, it can simplify matters to use the displacement option to specify positioning data. This allows you to specify the X,Y, and Z movement simultaneously. For example, to copy the 3-D face to a position 3 units above the original on the Z axis, use the following command sequence:

Command: **COPY** ↵
Select objects: *(pick the 3-D face)*
Select objects: ↵
⟨*Base point or displacement*⟩*/Multiple:* **0,0,3** ↵
⟨Second point of displacement⟩: ↵

Because ENTER was pressed at the ⟨Second point of displacement⟩: prompt, the X,Y, Z values entered are used as a relative displacement instead of a base point. In this example, the object is copied to a position that differs from the original by 0 on the X axis, 0 on the Y axis and +3 on the Z axis. To move an object +1 on the X, –4 on the Y, and +2 on the Z axis, the displacement value would be 1,–4,2.

The drawing should look like that shown in Figure 29-17. Zoom in at this time if the view is too small.

Figure 29-17. Top and bottom faces of a 3-D box. The numbers indicate the points to pick when using the 3DFACE command.

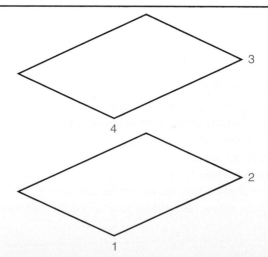

Complete the box using the 3DFACE command and pick the points as numbered in Figure 29-17.

Command: **OSNAP** ⏎
Object snap modes: **INT** ⏎
Command: **3DFACE** ⏎
First point: *(pick point 1)*
Second point: *(pick point 2)*
Third point: *(pick point 3)*
Fourth point: *(pick point 4)*
Third point: ⏎
Command:

The first face is complete. Now draw the remaining faces in the same manner. The finished box should appear similar to that in Figure 29-18.

Figure 29-18.   A completed 3DFACE appears to be a wireframe construction before using HIDE.

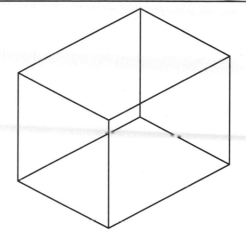

How does a 3-D face object differ from ones drawn using the ELEV and LINE commands? For comparison, Figure 29-19 shows boxes drawn using the ELEV, LINE, and 3DFACE commands with hidden lines removed by HIDE.

Figure 29-19.   A comparison of boxes drawn with ELEV, LINE, and 3DFACE after the HIDE command was selected.

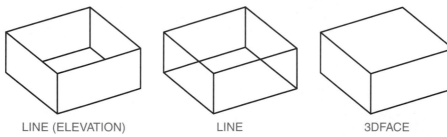

LINE (ELEVATION)   LINE   3DFACE

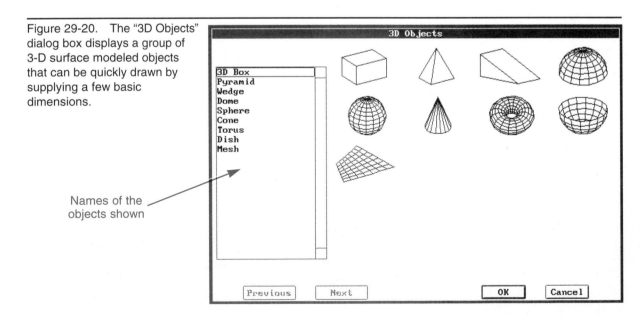

EXERCISE 29-4

❑ Set the grid spacing at .5, snap spacing at .25, and elevation at 0.
❑ Use the 3DFACE command to construct the object to the dimensions given.
❑ Draw the bottom, two end faces, and the two top angled surfaces in the plan view. Draw the front and rear V-shaped surfaces in a 3-D view. Hint: Each V-shaped end surface must be made of two 3-D faces.
❑ Use the HIDE command when you complete the object.
❑ Save the drawing as A:EX29-4.

CONSTRUCTING 3-D SURFACE MODELED OBJECTS

Several predrawn 3-D objects can be quickly drawn by providing AutoCAD with a location and basic dimensions of the object. A list of these objects is accessed by picking DRAW 2 in the screen menu, then SURFACES. A graphic dialog box display of the objects is available by picking Surfaces from the Draw pull-down menu, then 3D Objects… in the cascading menu. The "3D Objects" dialog box appears. See Figure 29-20.

Figure 29-20.   The "3D Objects" dialog box displays a group of 3-D surface modeled objects that can be quickly drawn by supplying a few basic dimensions.

Names of the objects shown

Notice the list box to the left of the dialog box. These are the names of all the objects shown. An object can be selected for drawing by picking either the name or the image. When an image or its name is selected, the image is highlighted with a box, and the name in the list box is also highlighted. See Figure 29-21. Pick OK after the object you wish to draw is highlighted.

Figure 29-21.   When an image or its name is selected, the image is highlighted with a box and the name is highlighted in the list box.

Select the object or the name

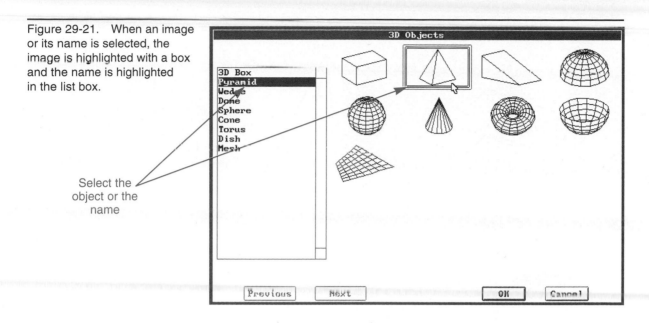

Regardless of the object that is selected, the first prompt requests a location point for the object. The remaining prompts request sizes in the form of length, width, height, diameter, radius, or number of longitudinal and latitudinal segments. For example, select Dome in the "3D Objects" dialog box. The prompt sequence is as follows:

Center of dome: *(pick a point)*
Diameter/⟨radius⟩: *(enter a radius or pick on the screen)*
Number of longitudinal segments ⟨16⟩: ↵
Number of latitudinal segments ⟨16⟩: ↵

The object is drawn in the plan view as shown in Figure 29-22A. Use the VPOINT command to produce a 3-D view of the object, and use HIDE to remove hidden lines. The illustration in Figure 29-22B provides an explanation of longitudinal and latitudinal segments. Longitudinal refers to an east-west measurement, and latitudinal means north-south. Note that the default of 16 latitudinal segments creates only eight segments in the dome or dish, since these shapes are half of a sphere.

Figure 29-22.   A–The plan view of a dome. B–Longitudinal segments are measured east-west, and latitudinal segments are measured north-south.

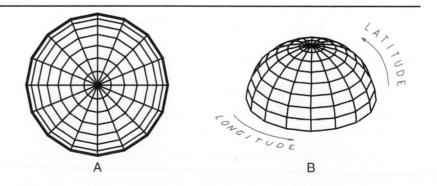

A   B

The group of objects provided in the "3D Objects" dialog box are not difficult to draw, and are fun to work with. Remember that if the current display is a plan view, and you draw 3-D objects, you must use the VPOINT command in order to see a 3-D view. The illustrations in Figure 29-23 show all of the dimensions required to construct the predrawn 3-D objects provided by AutoCAD.

Figure 29-23.   These dimensions are required to draw AutoCAD's various 3-D surface objects.

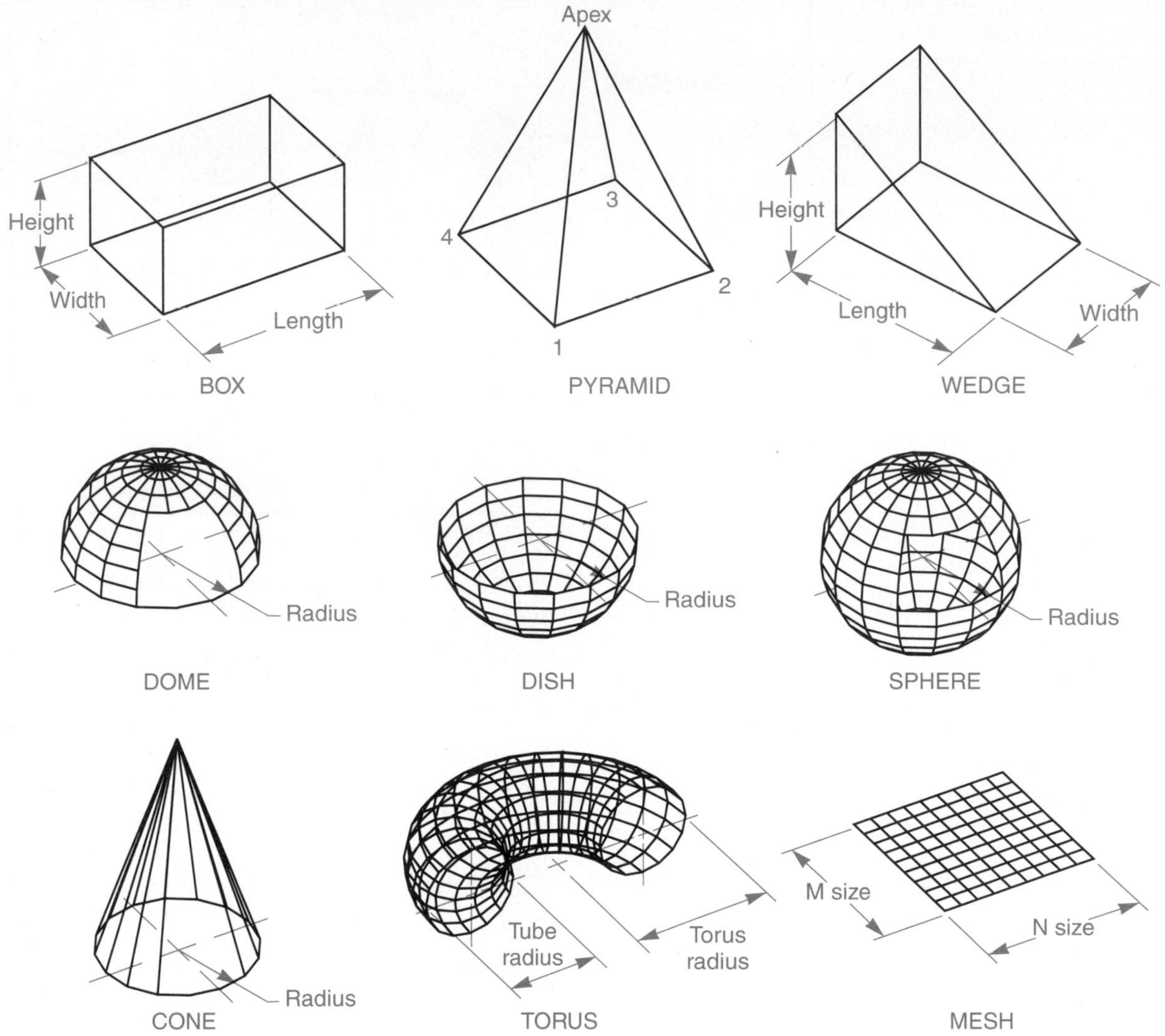

CHAPTER TEST

Write your answers in the spaces provided.

1. When looking at the screen, in which direction does the Z coordinate project? _____
    _____

2. Which command displays the "Object Creation Modes" dialog box?_____

3. Which two aspects of 3-D can be set in the "Object Creation Modes" dialog box? _____

4. Which command allows you to give objects thickness? _____

5. If you draw a line after setting a thickness, what have you actually drawn?_____
    _____

6. What is the purpose of the right-hand rule? _____

_____

_____

7. According to the right-hand rule, name the coordinate axes represented by the following fingers:

Thumb– _____

Middle finger– _____   _____

Index finger– _____

8. What is the purpose of the VPOINT command? _____

_____

9. When the VPOINT command's tripod is displayed, what are the concentric circles in the upper

right called? _____

10. How are you viewing an object when the little crosshairs are inside the small circle in the

VPOINT command display? _____

11. How are you viewing an object when the little crosshairs are between the small circle and the

large circle in the VPOINT command display? _____

12. How do you create 3-D extruded text? _____

_____

13. What is the function of the HIDE command? _____

_____

14. Define "point filters." _____

_____

_____

_____

_____

15. Compare the 3DFACE and SOLID commands. _____

_____

_____

_____

_____

16. How do you select one of AutoCAD's predrawn 3-D shapes? _____

_____

_____

DRAWING PROBLEMS

P29-1

1. Draw Problem 12 from Chapter 28 using the ELEV command. Display the object in two different views. Use HIDE on one view. Save the drawing as A:P29-1.

P29-2

2. Draw the object shown below using the ELEV command. Display the object in two different views. Use HIDE on one view. Save the drawing as A:P29-2.

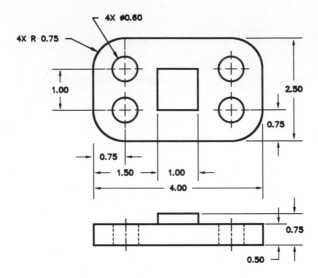

P29-3

3. Choose Problem 5, 6, 7, 8, or 9 from Chapter 28 and draw it in wireframe using the LINE command. Display the drawing with VPOINT in four different views. Save the drawing as A:P29-3.

P29-4

4. Load AutoCAD and open P29-3. Use the 3DFACE command to create faces on the entire part. Display the part in four different views. Save the revised drawing as A:P29-4.

5-7. Draw the objects shown below in 3-D form. Use the LINE and 3DFACE commands with the dimensions given to create the drawings. Can you create 3-D blocks for use in these drawings? Display the drawings from three different viewpoints. Select the HIDE command for one of the views. Save the drawings as A:P29-5, A:P29-6, and A:P29-7.

P29-5

5.

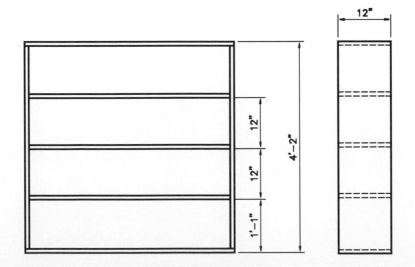

6.

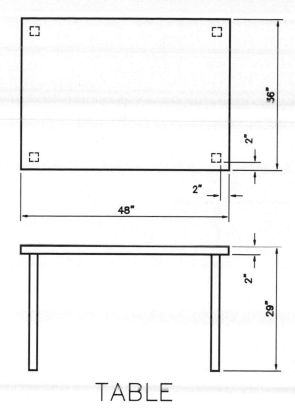

TABLE

7.

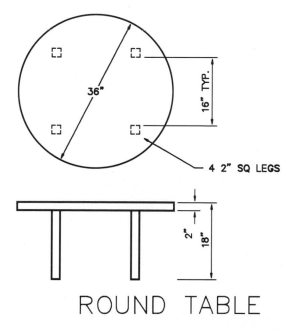

ROUND TABLE

P29-8

8. Construct a 3-D model of the table shown.
   A. Use any 3-D construction techniques required.
   B. Use the dimensions given.
   C. Alter the design of the table to include rounded tabletop corners or rounded feet. Try replacing the rectangular feet shown with spheres.
   D. Use the DVIEW command to display the model.
   E. Use the HIDE command to remove hidden lines.
   F. Plot the table both in wireframe and with hidden lines removed.

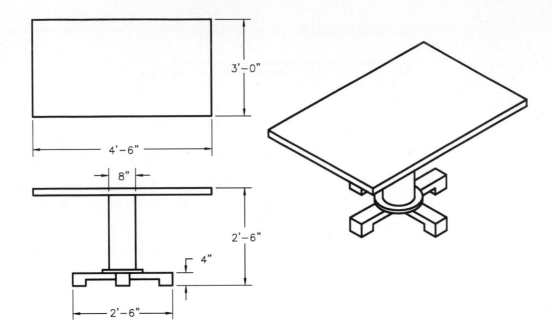

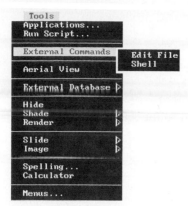

Chapter 30

EXTERNAL COMMANDS, SCRIPT FILES, AND SLIDE SHOWS

Learning objectives

After completing this chapter, you will be able to:

- ❍ Edit the ACAD.PGP file.
- ❍ Use a text editor to create script files.
- ❍ Create a continuous slide show of existing drawings.
- ❍ Use the SLIDELIB command to create a slide library.

This chapter introduces you to the use of scripts. A *script* is a series of commands and variables listed in a text file. When the script file is activated by AutoCAD, the entire list of commands is performed without additional input from the user. One useful script is a continuous slide show. It is excellent for client presentations, demonstrations, and for grading drawings.

Word processing or text editor programs can be used to write scripts. There are three tools available under the MS-DOS operating system for writing ASCII text files–the COPY command with the CONsole input source, the EDLIN line editor, and the MS-DOS EDIT text editor. Check for the presence of the last two files on your hard disk drive by typing the following at the DOS prompt:

C:) DIR\DOS\ED*.* ↵

If EDLIN.COM or EDIT.COM are not listed, consult your instructor or supervisor.

NOTE The EDIT text editor is a feature of DOS Version 5.x or later. If you have an earlier version of DOS, this program is not available. Type VER at the DOS prompt to determine your DOS version. The EDLIN line editor is not available if you are using MS-DOS version 6.x.

USING TEXT EDITORS

The more experienced you become with AutoCAD, the more you will want to alter the program to suit specific needs. Most of these alterations are done with a text editor program. The EDLIN program that comes with DOS is not really powerful or flexible enough for production work. However, it is satisfactory for creating simple files. The MS-DOS EDIT text editor is sufficient for most text file creation tasks.

Word processors

Many AutoCAD users rely on full-fledged word processing programs to create their text files. The files are saved in ASCII format so that they can be read by AutoCAD. There are a number of word processing programs commercially available. Two of which you might recognize are WordPerfect and Microsoft Word. These are excellent programs when used for writing documents, but exceed what is needed to create text files for AutoCAD. If you choose to use a word processor, save the text file as

"MS-DOS" text. This prevents the inclusion of special formatting codes, and produces an ASCII format file.

PROFESSIONAL TIP

If you have used EDLIN before, you noticed that EDLIN numbers each line of the file. This is unique to EDLIN, and the numbers are not included when AutoCAD reads the file. Do not include line numbers when using a word processor or other text editor. The EDIT text editor is a full-screen editor and does not number the lines in a file. EDLIN is actually a "line editor," and therefore its lines are numbered.

Programmer's text editors

The best type of text editor to use is a programmer's editor. There are a wide variety of inexpensive but powerful text editors commercially available. They all are designed for creating the type of files needed to customize AutoCAD. Programmer's editors are recommended over word processors because of their design, size, function, ease of use, and price. The Norton Editor is an example of an excellent text editor. If you are using DOS Version 5.x or later, the EDIT text editor is excellent for many of the custom files you will write for AutoCAD.

Introduction to the MS-DOS Editor

The MS-DOS text editor named EDIT is included with the DOS software, and was introduced with Version 5.0. It is easy to run and to use, and contains only four pull-down menus. In order to load EDIT you must first have the DOS prompt displayed. Text editors can also be loaded while AutoCAD is running, and that is discussed in the next section. Load EDIT from the DOS prompt as follows:

C:\\> **EDIT** ↵

The initial screen display of EDIT is shown in Figure 30-1. Press the ESC key to clear the dialog box.

Figure 30-1. The "MS-DOS Editor" dialog box is displayed when EDIT is loaded without specifying a filename.

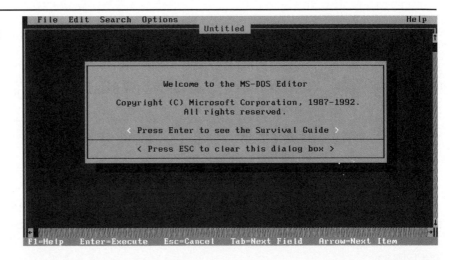

PROFESSIONAL TIP

The initial display of the "MS-DOS Editor" dialog box can be bypassed by entering a filename after the EDIT command. For example, to create a new text file named PLOT-1.SCR, enter the following at the DOS prompt:

C:\\> **EDIT PLOT-1.SCR \H** ↵

The editor is loaded, and the filename PLOT-1.SCR is displayed in the title bar of the top of the editor. The \H forces EDIT into high-resolution mode if supported by your system.

Use of the MS-DOS Editor is made easier by the availability of instant, on-screen help. Pick the Help pull-down menu, then select Getting Started. This displays a help screen that provides several selections for additional help. See Figure 30-2. These items are bracketed by green triangles. When you select one of these items, you "jump" to a new help screen. In addition, three jump text items are located at the top of any help screen that provide access to the Getting Started help, Keyboard help, or the previous help screen (Back). You can get help on any item enclosed in brackets by double-clicking on that item, or by clicking once on the item, then pressing ENTER. If you are new to the EDIT program, take a few minutes to familiarize yourself with the function of the on-screen help. Any help screen can be cleared by pressing the ESC key.

Figure 30-2.   The Getting Started help screen lists five selections for additional help.

Help screen

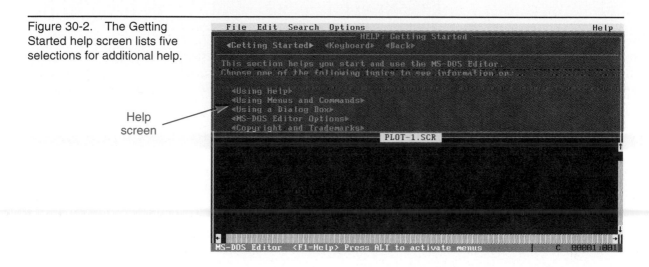

Pointer control in the editor is either by mouse or cursor keys. See the Keyboard help screen for detailed information on using cursor keys. Locate the blinking cursor in the upper-left corner of the screen and begin typing your file. A short, blinking, underline cursor indicates the "insert" mode in which you can move the pointer to a location and insert new text just by typing. Existing text is moved as new text is entered. Press the INSERT key on the keyboard to toggle the "overstrike" move. The cursor changes to a solid blinking rectangle. When the overstrike mode is active, and the cursor is positioned on existing text, any new characters that are typed, replace existing text.

The MS-DOS Editor allows you to cut, copy, paste, and delete selected text. Text is selected by pressing down on the pointer's pick button and dragging across the characters, words, or lines. Once the text is selected it is highlighted. All of the editing capabilities mentioned are found in the Edit pull-down menu.

The Search pull-down menu provides the ability to find any text string, or to replace existing text with new text. Use the Find... selection to just find existing text. The item is highlighted when it is found. Use the Change... selection to find existing text and replace it with new text.

When you are finished writing the file, use the Save or Save As... selections in the File pull-down menu. Use the Print... command to print either the entire file, or only the selected (highlighted) items. Pick Exit to close the Editor. Some of these file manipulation commands are discussed and illustrated later in the chapter.

EXTERNAL COMMANDS–THE ACAD.PGP FILE

ACG 1

You will often encounter situations, while working in AutoCAD, in which you need to access the text editor, or use one or more of the operating system commands. It is time-consuming to exit AutoCAD to execute these *external* commands. They are called external because they are not a part of AutoCAD.

All of these external commands are defined in the ACAD.PGP (ProGram Parameters) file. The default location of this file is in the \ACADR13\COMMON\SUPPORT subdirectory. The first portion of this file is shown in Figure 30-3 as it appears in the MS-DOS Editor.

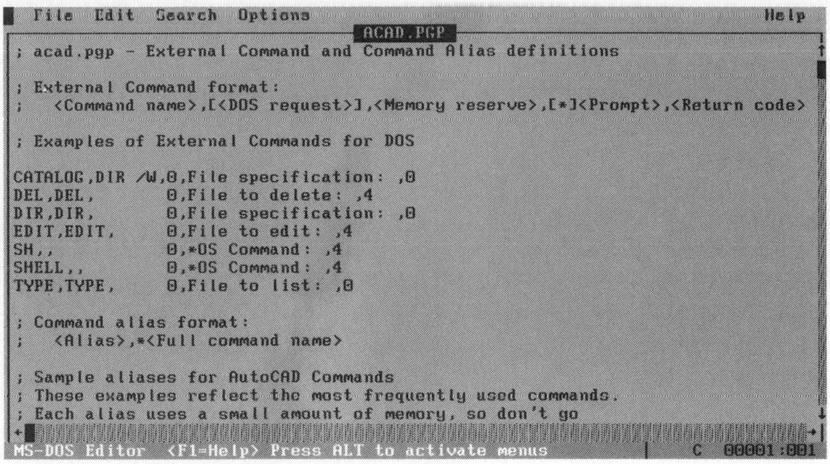

Figure 30-3.   The first part of the ACAD.PGP file is shown as it appears in the MS-DOS Editor.

To view this file without executing the MS-DOS Editor, enter the DOS TYPE command at the Command: prompt as follows:

Command: **TYPE** ⏎
File to list: **\ACADR13\COMMON\SUPPORT\ACAD.PGPⁱMORE** ⏎

The screen display is the same as that shown in Figure 30-3. Press any key to view additional pages of the file.

Find the seven lines in Figure 30-3 that begin with CATALOG, and end with TYPE. The first word on each line is the command name that should be typed at AutoCAD's Command: prompt to execute the command. The second word represents the DOS command or program to be executed. Notice that typing EDIT at the Command: prompt runs the EDIT text editor. Each part of the ACAD.PGP file is separated by a comma. These parts are called *fields*. The fields of the EDIT entry are defined as follows:

- **EDIT.** The command to be typed at the AutoCAD command prompt.
- **EDIT.** The command or program name executed after the external command name is typed. This is the file name normally entered at the DOS prompt to run the text editor. Instructions on how to edit the ACAD.PGP file to run your own text editor are provided later in this chapter.
- **0.** Previous versions of AutoCAD require a specified memory reserve for the command to function. Release 13 handles this automatically. The 0 is used only as a placeholder for compatability with previous releases.
- **File to edit.** The prompt that you want to appear after a command is typed.
- **4.** To return to the graphics screen, a number 4 is placed in this location. Entering a 0 here instructs AutoCAD to remain in the text mode. These are two of the more commonly used *return code* placed at this location.

The SH and SHELL commands

The SH and SHELL commands allow you to enter multiple DOS commands while AutoCAD is still active. You are allowed to type only one external command at the AutoCAD Command: prompt. When the command is completed the AutoCAD Command: prompt is redisplayed. But if you use SH or SHELL, the following prompt appears:

Command: **SH** ⏎
OS Command: *(type an external command or press* ENTER*)*

You can enter a single external command at the OS Command: prompt, but the screen will automatically return to the AutoCAD graphics display. It is best to press ENTER in order to have access to as many external commands as you need to use. The DOS system prompt will be displayed until you exit the DOS shell. After pressing ENTER at the OS Command: prompt, the following display appears:

```
Type EXIT to return to AutoCAD.
Microsoft (R) MS-DOS (R)  Version 6.xx
     (C) Copyright Microsoft Corp. 1981-1994.
C:\ACADR13⟩⟩
```

Notice that two carets (⟩⟩) are displayed after the DOS system prompt. This indicates that DOS is running as a "shell" in AutoCAD. Therefore, in order to return to AutoCAD you must type EXIT.

```
C:\ACADR13⟩⟩ EXIT ⏎
```

The graphics screen returns and the AutoCAD Command: prompt is displayed.

PROFESSIONAL TIP

The SH and SHELL commands are convenient for performing basic file manipulation functions such as deleting, copying, renaming, and listing. But avoid using hard disk utilities, or the CHKDSK command while shelled out of AutoCAD. In addition, never delete temporary and locked files with extensions such as .ac$, .$a, .swr, or .??k. These files are needed by AutoCAD while it is running.

Command aliases

AutoCAD allows you to abbreviate command names. This feature is called *command aliasing*. A list of predefined aliases furnished with AutoCAD can be displayed by viewing the contents of the ACAD.PGP file. You can do this by using the TYPE command as explained earlier in this chapter, or by loading the MS-DOS Editor or another text editor of your choice. Scroll down to the second screen, and you will see the list of command aliases:

```
A,        *ARC
C,        *CIRCLE
CP,       *COPY
DV,       *DVIEW
E,        *ERASE
L,        *LINE
LA,       *LAYER
M,        *MOVE
MS,       *MSPACE
P,        *PAN
PS,       *PSPACE
PL,       *PLINE
R,        *REDRAW
T,        *MTEXT
Z,        *ZOOM
```

If you continue to scroll down into the file you will find a long list of aliases for dimensioning commands. You can easily create your own aliases, by editing the ACAD.PGP file. If you do so, keep the number to a minimum if your computer does not have a lot of extra memory. Each command alias uses a small amount of memory, which reduces the amount available for drawing purposes.

If you want to add an alias for the SPLINE command, for example, enter the following below the REDRAW command in the ACAD.PGP file:

```
S,        *SPLINE
```

Be sure to include the asterisk since it indicates to AutoCAD that this is an alias. The revised .PGP file will not work until you exit AutoCAD and re-enter the drawing editor, which reloads the ACAD.PGP file. You can also reload the ACAD.PGP file by entering the REINIT command. This displays the "Re-initialization" dialog box. See Figure 30-4. Pick the PGP File check box, then pick OK to re-initialize the ACAD.PGP. Now your new command alias will work.

Figure 30-4.   The
"Re-initialization" dialog box.
Select the item and then OK
to re-initialize AutoCAD.

Pick to
re-initalize the
ACAD.PGP

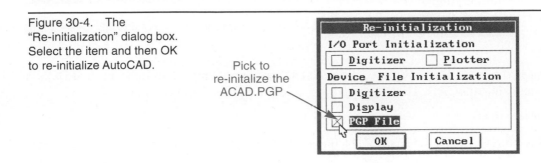

NOTE   The "Re-initialization" dialog box can be used if you have one of your communications ports such as COM1 configured for both a plotter and digitizer. If you physically change the cable from plotter to digitizer, pick the Digitizer box in both areas of the dialog box, then pick OK. The digitizer will be re-initialized.

Editing the ACAD.PGP file

The ACAD.PGP file can easily be altered to contain new external commands, or to contain a command that executes any text editor of your choosing. New commands can be added to the ACAD.PGP file as long as they do not have the same name as an AutoCAD command. They can be inserted anywhere within the group of predefined external commands in the ACAD.PGP file. Should you wish to substitute your personal text editor (TE), for the DOS editor EDIT, simply alter the entry shown in Figure 30-5. Enter the following at the Command: prompt.

Command: **EDIT** ↵
File to edit: **\ACADR13\COMMON\SUPPORT\ACAD.PGP** ↵

Figure 30-5.   The ACAD.PGP
file can be altered using the
DOS Editor. The text editor
used from within AutoCAD
has been edited here.

The text editor
is changed here

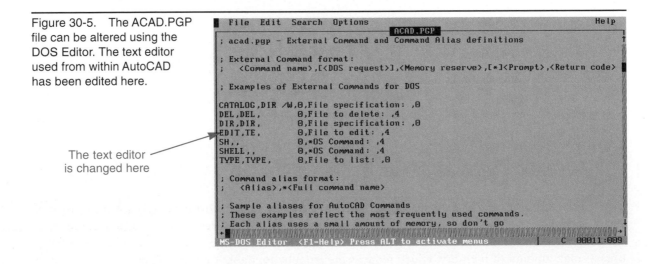

The DOS Editor is loaded and the screen displays the file shown in Figure 30-3. The flashing cursor can be moved by using the up, down, left, and right arrow keys, or by using your pointing device. In addition, the HOME, END, DELETE, PAGE UP, PAGE DOWN, and INSERT keys can be used for editing purposes. Move the blinking cursor to the following line:

EDIT,EDIT,   0,File to edit: ,4

Change the second EDIT to the appropriate name of your text editor using the BACKSPACE or DELETE keys. In this example, TE is used as the command to run the text editor. After the ACAD.PGP file is altered it should appear as shown in Figure 30-5.

The edited file can be saved by selecting Save from the File pull-down menu. Use your pointing device, or press ALT+F, to activate the File pull-down menu, then type S to save the file. See Figure 30-6.

Figure 30-6. Select Save from the File pull-down menu (shown here highlighted) to save the edited ACAD.PGP file.

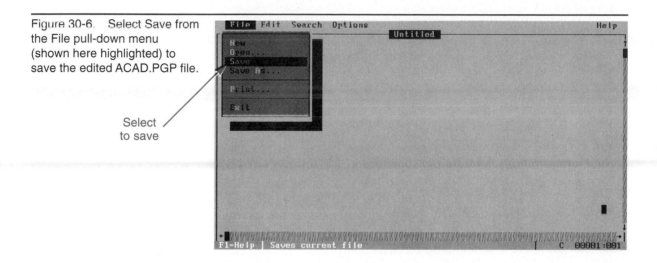

Select to save

The file will be saved quickly because it is small. To exit the DOS Editor, activate the File pull-down menu again, and select the Exit command with the pointing device, or type X, Figure 30-7.

Figure 30-7. Selecting Exit from the File pull-down menu (shown here highlighted) exits the DOS Editor and returns to the AutoCAD Command: prompt.

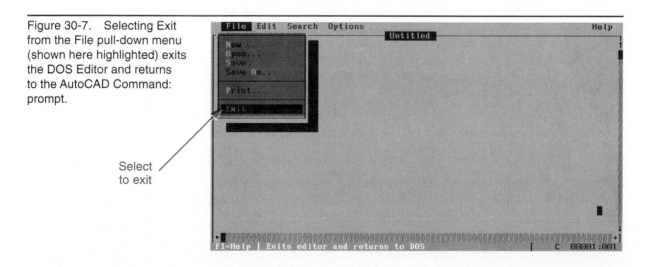

Select to exit

You are returned to the Command: prompt if the file was saved properly. If there was a problem saving the file, or you made even a single small change after saving it, a dialog box shown in Figure 30-8 appears. You are asked if you want to save the file. Pressing ENTER saves the file, since Yes is highlighted and is the default answer

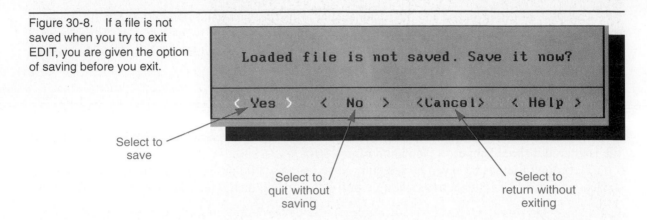

Figure 30-8.   If a file is not saved when you try to exit EDIT, you are given the option of saving before you exit.

Loaded file is not saved. Save it now?

< Yes >   <   No   >   <Cancel>   < Help >

Select to save

Select to quit without saving

Select to return without exiting

If you try using the new commands now, they will not work. This is because AutoCAD is still using the original version of the ACAD.PGP file. You must reinitialize the .PGP file with the REINIT command before the TE command can function properly.

EXERCISE 30-1

❏ Enter the AutoCAD drawing editor.
❏ Use the EDIT external command to edit the ACAD.PGP file.
❏ Create a new command named DIRDWG that lists only DWG files on the A: drive. The DOS command to use (if you haven't already devised it) is DIR A:*.DWG.
❏ The new command does not need a prompt. Therefore, place two commas after the 0 memory value.
❏ The line should end with 0 so that the screen remains in text mode.
❏ Save the file and use the REINIT command.
❏ Test the new command.

CREATING SCRIPT FILES TO AUTOMATE AUTOCAD   ACG 6

A *script file* is a list of commands that AutoCAD performs in sequence without input from the user. Scripts enable non-programmers to automate AutoCAD functions. They can be used for specific functions such as plotting a drawing with the correct PLOT command values and settings, or to create a slide show. A good working knowledge of AutoCAD commands and options is needed before you can confidently create a script file.

When writing a script file, put just one command or option per line in the text file. This makes the file easier to fix if the script does not work properly. A RETURN is specified by pressing ENTER after typing a command. If the next option of a command is a default value to be accepted, press ENTER again. This leaves a blank line in the script file, which represents pressing ENTER.

The following example shows how a script file can be used to plot a drawing. At your computer, enter these files with EDIT or your favorite text editor. The file extension of the script name must be .SCR. Also, place the file in the ACADR13 directory of the hard disk. This occurs automatically if you enter EDIT at the Command: prompt to run the text editor. If the file is written outside AutoCAD, enter the filename as C:\ACADR13\filename.SCR.

A drawing plotting script

In Chapter 12, you learned that you can save plotter settings for a specific drawing in the form of a .PCP file. This eliminates setting all of the plot values each time you plot the same drawing. You can automate this process by including all of the plot values in a script file. If you have drawings that will always be plotted with the same settings, use script files to plot them.

The following script plots a C-size drawing. The contents of the script file are shown in the left column, and a description of each line is given to the right. This script file is named ARCH24-C.SCR. The "ARCH" indicates an architectural drawing, the "24" is the scale factor, and "C" is the paper size.

NOTE   When writing a script file, it is important to include every keystroke that is required to accomplish the task at the keyboard. It is also important to know how many plotters and printers are configured in AutoCAD, and how they are listed when using the PLOT command at the Command: line.

---

cmddia	*(executes CMDDIA system variable)*
0	*(disables the "Plot Configuration" dialog box)*
plot	*(executes PLOT command)*
E	*(what to plot–extents)*
Y	*("Y" to change plot settings)*
Y	*("Y" to change plotters)*
3	*(description #3 for HP DraftPro)*
E	*(what to plot–extents)*
Y	*("Y" to change plot settings)*
N	*("N"–not to change plotters)*
60	*(number of seconds to wait for plotter port)*
Y	*("Y" to request hard clip limits)*
Y	*("Y" to change plot parameters)*
C1	*(specify color number 1)*
1	*(pen 1 for color 1)*
0	*(linetype 0 for color 1)*
10	*(pen speed for color 1)*
0.010	*(pen width for color 1)*
C2	*(specify color 2)*
2	*(pen 2 for color 2)*
0	*(linetype 0 for color 2)*
10	*(pen speed for color 2)*
0.010	*(pen width for color 2)*
C3	*(specify color 3)*
3	*(pen 3 for color 3)*
0	*(linetype 0 for color 3)*
10	*(pen speed for color 3)*
0.010	*(pen width for color 3)*
C4	*(specify color 4)*
4	*(pen 4 for color 4)*
0	*(linetype 0 for color 4)*
10	*(pen speed for color 4)*
0.010	*(pen width for color 4)*
X	*(exit parameter settings)*
N	*(do not write plot file)*
I	*(size units in inches)*
0,0	*(plot origin)*
C	*(paper size)*
0	*(plot rotation angle)*
N	*(do not adjust for pen width)*
N	*(do not remove hidden lines)*
1 = 24	*(drawing scale)*

CAUTION

A single incorrect entry in a script file can cause it to malfunction. Test the keystrokes at the keyboard before you write the script file, and record them for future reference. When writing a script for plotting purposes, this is an important step. Plotters and printers have different settings, and thus have different prompts in the PLOT command. Always step through the PLOT command and specify the plotter or printer you wish to use before writing the script file.

PROFESSIONAL TIP

Avoid pressing the space bar at the end of a line in the script file. This adds a space, and can cause the script to crash. Plus, finding spaces in a script file can be tedious work.

At the Command: prompt, type SCRIPT and then select the filename ARCH24-C from the "Select Script File" dialog box. See Figure 30-9. Then sit back and watch the script run.

Command: **SCRIPT** ↵

Figure 30-9.   The "Select Script File" dialog box.

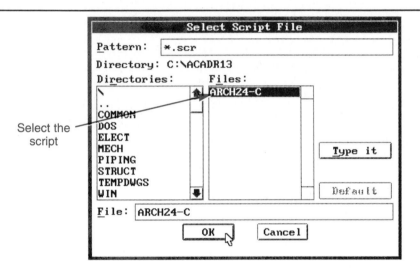

Select the script

All of the commands, options, and text screens associated with the commands in the script are displayed in rapid succession on the screen. If the script stops before completing, a problem has occurred. Flip the screen to text mode (F1) to determine the last command executed. Return to your text editor and correct the problem. Most often, there are too many or too few RETURNs. Another problem is spaces at the end of a line. If you suspect these errors, retype the line.

Running a script from the DOS prompt

A script file can be run from the DOS prompt by entering a drawing name and script name after typing ACADR13. The default batch file that was initially created to run AutoCAD is named ACADR13.BAT. This file is automatically created when AutoCAD is first installed on the hard disk. Check with your instructor or supervisor for the correct name of this batch file, if you suspect its name has been changed. Otherwise enter the following at the DOS prompt:

C:\\ **ACADR13 FLRPLAN2 ARCH24-C** ↵

In this case, AutoCAD is executed by the ACADR13 batch file, and the FLRPLAN2 drawing file is opened. Then, the ARCH24-C script is run. This is enabled by a line in the batch file that runs AutoCAD. A *batch file* executes a group of DOS commands automatically. You can examine the contents of this batch file to see the commands that are used. Find the batch file that runs AutoCAD in your computer and use the TYPE command to list it. Locate the following line:

ACAD %1 %2

In DOS terminology, the two percent symbols are called replaceable parameters. A *replaceable parameter* is a symbol that holds a place for a command or filename that is entered at the DOS prompt. The first percent symbol holds a place for the first command or name that is entered after the batch filename is entered at the DOS prompt. The second percent symbol holds a place for the second command or name entered after the batch filename. Therefore, if your batch file that runs AutoCAD is named ACADR13.BAT, you can type the following at the DOS prompt:

C:\) **ACADR13 FLRPLAN2 ARCH24-C** ⏎

DOS finds the batch file named ACADR13 and runs it. When the ACAD %1 %2 line is encountered, DOS looks back at the initial command to find a substitute for %1. In this case, it finds FLRPLAN2, which for AutoCAD is a drawing name to open. Then DOS substitutes ARCH24-C for the %2, which AutoCAD interprets as a script filename and runs it.

EXERCISE 30-2

❑ Begin a new drawing named SCRPTEST.
❑ Use the DTEXT command to write your name in the lower-right corner.
❑ Save the drawing.
❑ Use your text editor and write a script file named TEST.SCR. The script file should do the following:
  ❑ Draw a circle at coordinates 4,4 with a radius of 1.
  ❑ Change the color to green.
  ❑ Draw a donut centered on the circle with an inside diameter of 2.5 and an outside diameter of 2.8.
❑ Save the script file and exit AutoCAD if you are not currently at a DOS prompt.
❑ Use your batch file to load AutoCAD, open the SCRPTEST drawing, and run the TEST.SCR file.
❑ If the script file does not run to completion, use your text editor to correct it. Exit AutoCAD and run the script file again until it works.

SLIDES AND SLIDE SHOWS   ACG 6

A *slide* in AutoCAD, similar to a slide in photography, is a snapshot of the screen display. Because of its nature, it cannot be edited or plotted. Slides can be viewed one at a time or as a continuous show. This is why slides are excellent for demonstrations, presentations, displays, and grading procedures.

Students and prospective employees can create an impressive portfolio using a slide show. A *slide show* is a group of slides that are displayed at preset intervals. The slide show is controlled by a script file–a list of commands similar to the previous script examples. Each slide is displayed for a specific length of time. The show can be continuous or a single pass.

Making and viewing slides

Creating slides is easy. First display the drawing for which you need a slide. You might display the entire drawing or zoom to a specific area or feature. AutoCAD creates a slide of the current screen display, no questions asked. Make as many slides of one drawing as you want. For each, select the MSLIDE command and provide a filename for the slide. Do not enter a file type, as AutoCAD automatically attaches an .SLD file extension. If FILEDIA is set to 1, a dialog box appears after entering MSLIDE. From the screen menu pick TOOLS, then Mslide:, or pick Slide, then View... from the Tools pull-down menu. Use MSLIDE at the Command: prompt as follows:

Command: **MSLIDE** ⏎

The "Create Slide File" dialog box is displayed. This is the standard file dialog box. Pick the drive and directory in which the file is to be stored, then enter the name in the File: text box, and pick the OK button.

Slide names should follow a pattern. Suppose you are making slides for a class called CAD1. Filenames such as CAD1SLD1 and CAD1SLD2 are appropriate. If working on project #4305 for the Weyerhauser Company, you might name the slide to reflect the client name or project number, such as WEYERSL1 or 4305SLD1. Slide names can use the full eight characters allowed by DOS.

Viewing a slide is as simple as making one. The VSLIDE command asks for the slide filename. Do not enter the .SLD file extension because AutoCAD knows it is looking for a slide. From the screen menu pick TOOLS, then Vslide:, or pick Slide, then Save… from the Tools pull-down menu.

Command: **VSLIDE** ↵

The "Select Slide File" dialog box appears. Pick the slide you want to display and pick OK.

Keep the \ACADR13 directory free of drawing, slide, and AutoLISP files. This speeds the computer's access to AutoCAD files. Create a separate hard disk directory for slides or save slides on a floppy disk. See Chapter 32. If using floppy disks, be sure to give the appropriate filename when creating slides. A filename of CAD1SLD1 is entered to place a slide on a floppy disk in the A: disk drive.

Command: **MSLIDE** ↵
Slide file: **A:CAD1SLD1** ↵

PROFESSIONAL TIP

The screen display should be set to its highest resolution before making a slide. To do this, set the VIEWRES circle zoom percent to the maximum value of 20000. After the slide is created, reset VIEWRES to its previous value.

EXERCISE 30-3

❑ Load any one of your drawings into the drawing editor.
❑ Create a slide of the entire drawing, using an appropriate filename.
❑ Make slides of two more drawings. Use similar naming techniques.
❑ View each of the slides as they are created.
❑ These slides are required to complete the next exercise.

Writing a slide show script file

A slide show script file contains only two or three commands. This depends on whether it is a single pass or continuous show. The RSCRIPT (Repeat SCRIPT) command is used at the end of a continuous script file. Any slide file can be displayed for up to 33 seconds using the DELAY command. Delays are given in milliseconds. A delay of four seconds is written as DELAY 4000. The next slide is "preloaded" into computer memory for quick display by placing an asterisk before the slide name. A slide is displayed with the VSLIDE command.

A slide show begins with the creation of a script file using a text editor. The following script uses four slides. Each appears for three seconds and the script repeats. Notice that the next slide is preloaded while the previous one is viewed. The file, SHOW.SCR, is created using a text editor as follows:

Command: **EDIT** ↵
File to edit: **SHOW.SCR** ↵
   VSLIDE CAD1.SLD1 ↵
   VSLIDE *CAD1SLD2 ↵
   DELAY 3000 ↵
   VSLIDE ↵
   VSLIDE *CAD1SLD3 ↵
   DELAY 3000 ↵
   VSLIDE ↵
   VSLIDE *CAD1SLD4 ↵
   DELAY 3000 ↵
   VSLIDE ↵
   DELAY 3000 ↵
   RSCRIPT ↵

The SHOW.SCR file is shown in Figure 30-10 as it would appear in the DOS Editor. Also, keep in mind that when using slide files on diskettes, include the disk drive path in front of the filename, such as A:CAD1SLD2. Use this method with each VSLIDE command.

Figure 30-10. A slide show script file is shown as it would appear in the DOS Editor.

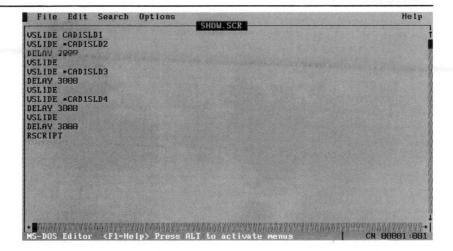

Viewing the slide show

A slide show is started with the SCRIPT command, which is found in the TOOLS screen menu, or by picking Run Script... from the Tools pull-down menu. Enter SCRIPT at the Command: prompt as follows:

Command: **SCRIPT** ↵

Select the script filename SHOW.SCR from the "Select Script File" dialog box, and pick OK. The show begins and the commands in the script file are displayed at the Command: prompt as the slides appear. To stop the show, press the BACKSPACE key. You can then work on a drawing, use DOS commands, or work with a text editor on another script file. When finished, resume the slide show where it left off by typing RESUME. Any script file can be interrupted and restarted in this manner.

Your slide show may run into a bug and not finish the first time through. This is not unusual, so do not panic. Take the following steps to "debug," or correct, problems in your script file.
- Run the script to see where it crashes (quits working).
- Check the command line for the last command that was executed.
- Look for error messages, such as:
  - ✓ "Can't open slide file *xxxxx*" (incorrect slide filename).
  - ✓ "*xxxxx* Unknown command" (command spelled incorrectly or a space left at the end of the line).

✓ "Requires an integer value" (delay value not all numerical characters. Possibly a space at the end of the line).
- Correct the problem in the script file, and save the file.
- Test the script.

The most common errors are misspelled commands and spaces at the end of lines. If you suspect there is a space at the end of a line, it is best to retype the line.

If you use a text editor, it is easy to see if a space exists. The flashing cursor, when placed at the end of a line, does not rest on the last character. This feature is not possible with EDLIN.

EXERCISE 30-4

❑ Create a script file named EX30-4. Use the MS-DOS Editor or your own text editor. It is not necessary to be in the AutoCAD drawing editor to create the script file.
❑ Include the three slides created in Exercise 30-3. If these slides have not been created, make slides of any three of your drawings.
❑ Delay each slide for two seconds.
❑ Make the show run continuously.
❑ Run the slide show. Correct any errors and run it again until it recycles without failing.

CREATING AND USING SLIDE LIBRARIES | AUG 14 |

A *slide library* is a list of slide files that can be used not only for slide shows, but also for constructing image tile menus. Image tile menus are groups of slides or vector images displayed in a dialog box. Examples are the Geometric Dimensioning and Tolerancing symbols displayed after selecting Dimensioning, then Tolerance… in the Draw pull-down menu. Image tile menus were known as *icon menus* in previous releases of AutoCAD. Constructing image tile menus is discussed in *AutoCAD and its Applications–Advanced, R13 for DOS.*

Creating the slide library

To create the slide library, you must use a utility program, called SLIDELIB.EXE, that operates from the DOS prompt. By default, the SLIDELIB.EXE utility is installed in the ACADR13\COMMON\SUPPORT subdirectory. Be sure to include this path when using the utility. SLIDE.EXE can be used to create slide libraries one of two ways. The first method involves listing the slides and their directory location after entering the SLIDELIB command. For example, suppose you have four slides of pipe fittings in the PIPE subdirectory of \ACADR13. List these in a slide library called PIPE in the following manner:

```
Command: SH ↵
OS Command: \ACADR13\COMMON\SUPPORT\SLIDELIB PIPE ↵
SLIDELIB 1.2 (3/8/89)
(C) Copyright 1987-89 Autodesk, Inc.
 All Rights Reserved
\ACAD\PIPE\90ELBOW ↵
\ACAD\PIPE\45ELBOW ↵
\ACAD\PIPE\TEE ↵
\ACAD\PIPE\CAP ↵
 ↵
 ↵
Command:
```

After entering the last slide, press ENTER three times to end the SLIDELIB command. The new slide library file is saved as PIPE.SLB.

The second way to use SLIDELIB is to first create a list of the slides you will eventually want in the library. Do this with an ASCII text editor, such as MS-DOS EDIT. This method allows you to accumulate slides over a period of time. Then, when you are finally ready to create the slide library, the list is prepared. A list of those same pipe fittings slides would be entered in a file named PIPE.TXT, for example. That file would appear as follows in the MS-DOS Editor:

90ELBOW
45ELBOW
TEE
CAP

After completing the list of slides to include, use the SLIDELIB command. The SLIDELIB command needs to find the PIPE.TXT file and use it to create a slide library file called PIPE.SLB. This can all be handled with one entry at the DOS prompt.

Command: **SH** ⏎
OS Command: **COMMON\SUPPORT\SLIDELIB PIPE PIPE.TXT** ⏎
SLIDELIB 1.0 (7/29/87)
(C) Copyright 1987 Autodesk, Inc.
 All Rights Reserved
Command:

The SLIDELIB command automatically creates a file called PIPE.SLB using the information it found in the PIPE.TXT file. The reverse caret (⟨) instructs the SLIDELIB program to use the contents of PIPE.TXT to create the PIPE.SLB file. To see the results, obtain a directory listing of all SLB files and look for PIPE.SLB.

Viewing slide library slides

The VSLIDE command also is used to view slides contained in a slide library. Provide the library name plus the slide name in parentheses as follows:

Command: **VSLIDE** ⏎
Slide file: *(pick* T*ype it* in the dialog box, and enter **PIPE(90ELBOW)** *in the edit box)*

To remove the slide from the screen to display the previous drawing, enter REDRAW.

Making a slide show using the slide library

The advantage of using a slide library for a slide show is that you do not need to preload slides. A slide show of the four slides in the PIPE.SLB file would appear as follows:

```
VSLIDE PIPE(90ELBOW)
DELAY 1000
VSLIDE PIPE(45ELBOW)
DELAY 1000
VSLIDE PIPE(TEE)
DELAY 1000
VSLIDE PIPE(CAP)
DELAY 1000
REDRAW
```

The REDRAW command at the end of the slide show clears the screen and replaces the previous display. An RSCRIPT command instead of REDRAW repeats the show continuously.

CHAPTER TEST

Write your answers in the spaces provided.

1. What is the name of the MS-DOS text editor? _____

2. What precautions should you take when using word processor software to create text files for AutoCAD? _____

    _____

3. What is the best type of text editor to use with AutoCAD? _____

    _____

4. What would you type at the DOS prompt, to use the DOS text editor and enter the filename of PLOT-B.SCR at the same time? C:_____

5. How do you know that additional help is available for items in the DOS text editor help screens?

    _____

6. How do you know if the DOS text editor is in insert, or overstrike mode?_____

    _____

    _____

7. Describe external commands. _____

    _____

8. Commands located in the ACAD.PGP file are executed by _____.

9. Name the parts of a command listing found in the ACAD.PGP file._____

    _____

    _____

10. What is a command alias, and how would you write one for the POLYGON command? _____

    _____

11. Define "script file." _____

    _____

12. Why is it a good idea to put one command on each line of a script file? _____

    _____

13. List two common reasons why a script file might not work._____

    _____

14. The commands that allow you to make and view slides are _____ and _____.

15. The file extension that AutoCAD assigns slides is _____.

16. Explain why it is a good idea to keep slide files in a separate directory and not in the ACAD directory._____

    _____

17. List the three commands that are included when writing a slide show._____

    _____

18. To stop a slide show press the _____ key.

19. To begin a slide show that has been stopped _____.

20. Briefly explain the two methods used to create a SLIDELIB file. _____

_____

_____

_____

21. Suppose you want to view a slide named VIEW1 that is in a slide library file called VIEWS. How must you enter its name at the Slide file: prompt?

Slide file: _____

22. What is the principal difference between a slide show script file written for a slide library and one simply written for a group of slides?

_____

DRAWING PROBLEMS

1. If you use a text editor or word processor other than MS-DOS EDIT, create a new command in the ACAD.PGP file that loads the text editor. Set the screen mode to return to the graphics display.

2. Create a new command for the ACAD.PGP file that generates a directory listing of all your slide files. Be sure to specify the directory path that contains the slides. For example, if your slides are kept on a floppy disk, the DOS command to execute is: DIR A:*.SLD. Set the screen mode to remain in the text display.

3. Write a script file called NOTES.SCR that does the following:

   A. Executes the TEXT command.

   B. Selects the Style option.

   C. Enters a style name.

   D. Selects the lastpoint using the @ symbol.

   E. Enters a text height of .25.

   F. Enters a rotation angle of 0.

   G. Inserts the text: "NOTES:".

   H. Selects the TEXT command again.

   I. Enters location coordinates for first note.

   J. Enters a text height of .125.

   K. Enters a rotation angle of 0.

   L. Inserts the text: "1. Interpret dimensions and tolerances per ASME Y14.5."

   M. Enters an ENTER keystroke.

   N. Inserts the text: "2. Remove all burrs and sharp edges."

   O. Enters ENTER twice to exit the command.

   Immediately before this script file is used, select the ID command and pick the point where you want the notes to begin. That point will be the "lastpoint" used in the script file for the location of the word "NOTES:". The script file when executed should draw the following:

   NOTES:

   1. Interpret dimensions and tolerances per ASME Y14.5.

   2. Remove all burrs and sharp edges.

4. Create a slide show of your best AutoCAD drawings. This slide show should be considered as part of your portfolio for potential employers. Place all of the slides and the script file on a floppy disk. Make two copies of the portfolio disk: a 5.25″ high-density floppy disk, and a 3.5″ high-density floppy disk. Since employers may have different machines, be prepared. Keep the following guidelines in mind:

A. Do not delay slides longer than 5 seconds. You can always press the BACKSPACE key to view a slide longer.

B. One view of a drawing is sufficient unless the drawing is complex. If so, make additional slides of the drawing's details.

C. Create a cover slide, or title page slide that gives your name.

D. Create an ending slide that says "THE END."

5. Create a slide show that illustrates specific types of drawings. For example, you might make a slide show for dimensioned mechanical drawings or for electrical drawings. These specialized slide shows in your portfolio are useful if you apply for a job in a specific discipline. Store all slide shows on the same disk. Identify slide shows by their content as follows:

MECH.SCR–Mechanical

ARCH.SCR–Architectural

PIPE.SCR–Piping

STRUCT.SCR–Structural

ELECT.SCR–Electrical or Electronics

MAP.SCR–Mapping

CIVIL.SCR–Civil

6. Create a script file to plot your most frequently used drawing. Use the following guidelines to write the script:

A. Run a trial plot of the drawing first. Record all of the keystrokes required to plot the drawing correctly.

B. Check the results of the trial plot to be sure that the use of pens and the location of the drawing on the paper is correct.

C. Write the script file using the exact keystrokes you recorded.

D. Test the script and note where problems occur.

E. Fix the problems in the script file and test the script until it runs properly.

F. Run the script file from the DOS prompt so the drawing is loaded and plotted from one entry.

Chapter 31

DIGITIZING EXISTING DRAWINGS

Learning objectives

After completing this chapter, you will be able to:
- ○ Describe the digitizer and the digitizing process.
- ○ Digitize existing drawings into AutoCAD.
- ○ Define scanning and discuss the advantages and disadvantages of scanning over manually digitizing a drawing.

Digitizing is the process of transferring information from a digitizing tablet into the computer. You might send commands to the computer by digitizing a command cell on the menu overlay. A *digitizing tablet,* or *digitizer,* also is used to convert existing paper drawings into AutoCAD drawing files. Digitizers range in size from 6 in. square to 44 × 60 in. Many schools and industries use 12 in. square digitizers to input commands from standard and custom tablet menus. Most companies do not have the time to convert existing drawings to CAD because they rely on the CAD system for new product drawings. Therefore, an increasing number of businesses digitize existing drawings for other companies. These commercial operations use larger digitizers so that D-size and E-size drawings can be digitized.

Another way to convert existing drawings to CAD files is with a scanner. It sends a light or camera over the drawing to transfer the image to the computer. This technique is called *scanning.*

THE DIGITIZER

A digitizer consists of a plastic surface, called a *tablet,* and a pointing device for picking locations on the tablet. The digitizer provides extremely accurate location in the form of XY coordinates. Figure 31-1 shows a pointing device and a 12 in. × 12 in. digitizer with an AutoCAD menu overlay.

Figure 31-1.   A 12″ × 12″ digitizer with pointing device.

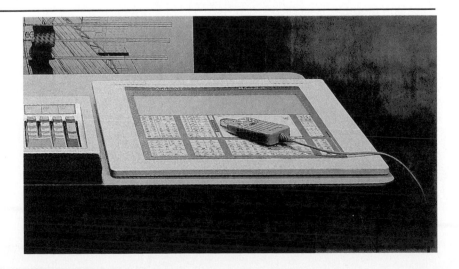

DIGITIZING AN EXISTING DRAWING

When a company begins converting to CAD, the normal procedure is to have a manual drafting group and a CAD group. Selected new drawings are done on the computer. This situation may continue until the full capabilities of CAD are realized. Manual drafters remain important because older drawings are often revised in the original format. There comes a time when a company must make a decision to convert existing paper drawings to CAD drawing files. This problem is not confined to paper drawings. Sometimes it is necessary to convert one type of computer-generated drawing to another CAD system. This might be done with a translation program.

However, in some situations the only solution is to redraw the existing drawings with AutoCAD. However, time is usually saved by digitizing the existing drawing, depending on the type of drawing. A digitizer large enough to accommodate the largest drawings is best, yet large drawings can be digitized on small digitizers. The process consists of a combination of digitized points and AutoCAD drawing and editing commands. Also plan to use SNAP, ORTHO, and OSNAP modes to your best advantage.

Configuring the tablet

Before digitizing a drawing, you must configure the tablet even if it was previously configured for another application. This is done to utilize the maximum area on the tablet. To configure the tablet, select Tablet: from the OPTIONS screen menu and then pick Config:, or type TABLET at the Command: prompt, followed by CFG at the Option: prompt as follows:

Command: **TABLET** ↵
Option (ON/OFF/CAL/CFG): **CFG** ↵

Next, AutoCAD asks for the number of tablet menus. Since the entire tablet is used when digitizing an existing drawing, there are no menu areas. Type 0 and press ENTER. When asked if you want to respecify the screen pointing area, answer Y. Then pick the lower-left corner followed by the upper-right corner. If your digitizer has proximity lights, watch them as you do this. One of the lights is on when the puck is in the screen pointing area, and off when the puck leaves the area. Move the pointing device slowly to the extreme corners until you find the location where the light comes on. This will help you gain use of the entire screen pointing areas when digitizing. See Figure 31-2. The prompt sequence is as follows:

Enter number of tablet menus desired (0-4) ⟨ ⟩: **0** ↵
Do you want to respecify the screen pointing area? ⟨N⟩: **Y** ↵
Digitize lower-left corner of screen pointing area: *(pick the lower-left corner of the pointing area)*
Digitize the upper-right corner of screen pointing area: *(pick the upper-right corner of the pointing area)*
Command:

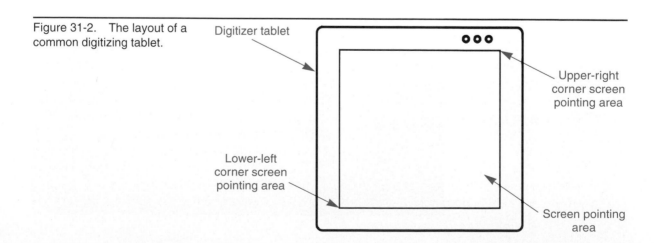

Figure 31-2.   The layout of a common digitizing tablet.

Preparing the drawing and calibrating the tablet

The next step, calibrating the tablet, aligns the drawing to be digitized with the tablet. Attach the drawing to the tablet using drafting tape. The drawing does not have to be exactly square on the screen pointing area, but it should be flat. Figure 31-3 shows a plot plan attached to the digitizer tablet.

Figure 31-3.   A drawing to be digitized is placed on the tablet.

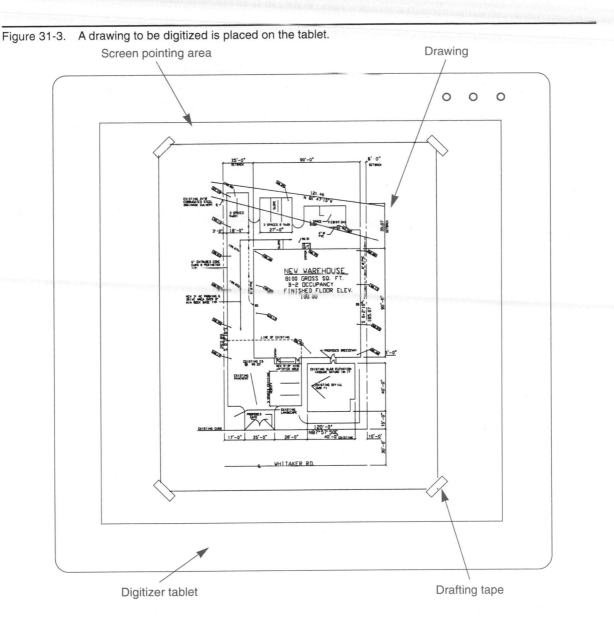

The number of points that you digitize when calibrating the drawing to the tablet determines how accurately the existing drawing coordinates are transferred to the computer. This is called *transformation*. The following are the AutoCAD transformation options:

- **Orthogonal transformation.** AutoCAD allows you to enter two coordinates. Two points work well if the existing drawing is dimensionally accurate. A dimensionally accurate drawing normally has stable length and width measurements, and angles are not distorted.
- **Affine.** This is digitizing three points for calibration. It is necessary when lines are generally parallel, but the horizontal dimensions are stretched in relationship to the vertical dimensions. The calibration of three points provides accuracy by triangulation of three points.
- **Projective calibration.** This is the calibration of four points. When the existing drawing has stretched or has been distorted to the point where parallel lines tend to converge, then the calibration of four points may be necessary.

- **Multiple-point transformation.** This is the digitizing of more than four points. AutoCAD mathematically calculates the relationship between the points with increased accuracy, which is proportional to the number of points digitized. However, nine points are usually the maximum number of points needed since additional points tend to slow down the transformation process without improving the accuracy. Entering more than four points slows the process.

PROFESSIONAL TIP

When selecting points for calibration, choose locations that are as accurate as possible. For example, in mapping applications, pick property corners or bench marks. In mechanical drafting, use datums on the drawing. Select points that are distributed in a wide area around the drawing. In addition, the points should be in a triangular relationship rather than in a straight line.

When attaching a drawing to the digitizer, use the following guidelines:
- Set the limits to correlate with the drawing dimensions. The limits for the drawing in Figure 31-3 should relate to the overall dimensions of the plot, plus space for notes. The plot is approximately 120′ × 200′. Allowing an additional 40′ in the horizontal and vertical directions for dimensions and notes makes the limits 160′ × 240′, or 1920″ × 2880″.
- Set the drawing units to correspond with the type of drawing you are transferring. The drawing in Figure 31-3 is a surveyed plot plan where engineering units are used, angles are measured in degrees/minutes/seconds, the direction of angle 0 is North 90d, and angles are measured clockwise.
- Set the grid and snap to a convenient value. A 20′ (240″) value works well for the plot plan.
- The property lines on the plot plan are based on a survey and are probably accurate. With this in mind, use the UCS command to set the origin to one of the property corners:

```
Command: UCS ↵
Origin/ZAxis/3point/Entity/View/X/Y/Z/Prev/Restore/Del/?/⟨World⟩: O ↵
Origin point: ⟨0,0,0⟩: (pick the lower-left property line corner)
```

This establishes the property corner at a 0,0 origin for convenience in locating other property corner points.

PROFESSIONAL TIP

Be sure to look straight down on the target point if you are digitizing points using a puck with crosshairs. Looking at an angle through the puck viewing glass results in inaccuracies when picking points.

Now you are ready to calibrate the tablet. The orthogonal, or two-point calibration is used on the plot plan because the existing drawing was done with ink on polyester film and there is very good accuracy. To do this, enter the TABLET command and respond with CAL for calibrate. At this point, the tablet mode is turned on and the screen cursor no longer appears.

```
Command: TABLET ↵
Option (ON/OFF/CAL/CFG): CAL ↵
```

AutoCAD then requests that you digitize two points on the drawing and give the coordinates of each point. These two points may be anywhere, but usually are the endpoints of a vertical line. Drafters often pick two points on the left side of the object such as the west property line on a plot plan. This begins the orientation of the digitizer in relation to the object as you work from left to right. AutoCAD next asks for the exact coordinates of the two points. Look at the existing drawing to be digitized in Figure 31-4 as you follow these prompts:

Digitize first known point: *(pick the lower-left property corner where you set the UCS origin)*
Enter coordinates for first point: *(enter 0,0 to coincide with the UCS origin)*
Digitize second known point: *(pick the north end of the west property line)*

Figure 31-4.   To calibrate the tablet, carefully select two points and provide the coordinates of those points.

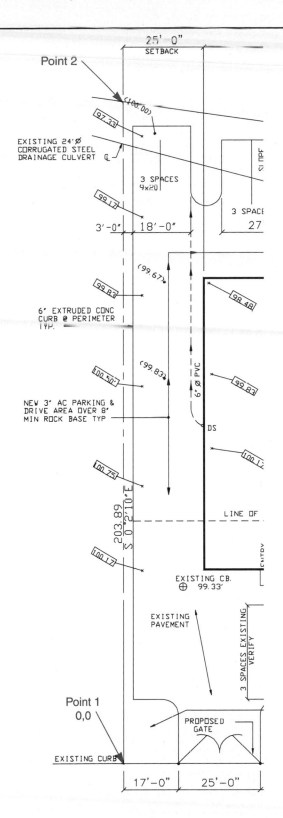

Enter the length of the property line relative to the first point (X = 0, Y = 203.89′ or 2446.68″) when entering the coordinates for the second point:

Enter coordinates for the second point: **0,2446.68** ↵

Pressing ENTER for the third point request automatically makes AutoCAD use the orthogonal transformation format:

Digitize third known point: ↵

Enter the TABLET command and turn the tablet on now that the existing drawing has been calibrated to the digitizer:

Command: **TABLET** ↵
Option (ON/OFF/CAL/CFG): **ON** ↵

The screen cursor returns for you to use AutoCAD commands to draw lines and other features. Use the LINE command to draw the property boundaries by picking each property corner when you see the From point: and To point: prompts. Use the Close option for the last line. The resulting property boundaries are shown in Figure 31-5.

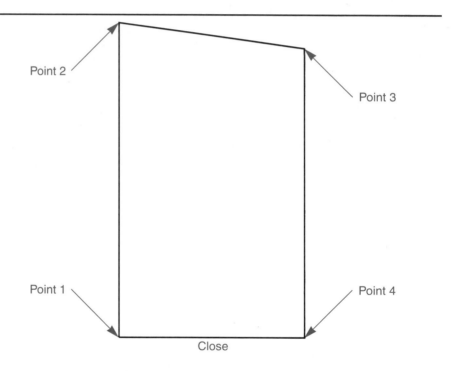

Figure 31-5.   Use the LINE command to construct the property boundaries.

Point 2

Point 3

Point 1

Point 4

Close

Proceed by digitizing the buildings, roads, walkways, utilities, and other features using AutoCAD commands such as LINE, PLINE, ARC, or CIRCLE. Use the dimensioning commands to dimension the plot plan, and use the MTEXT command to add notes. The finished drawing is shown in Figure 31-6.

When the tablet mode is on, the screen menu is disabled. Commands may only be input from the keyboard. To use the screen menu, turn the tablet mode off by entering OFF at the TABLET command's Option prompt. You can also press function key F10. Turning the tablet off allows you to use the screen cursor. The command sequence is as follows:

Command: **TABLET** ↵
Option (ON/OFF/CAL/CFG): **OFF** ↵

Figure 31-6. The completed digitized drawing.

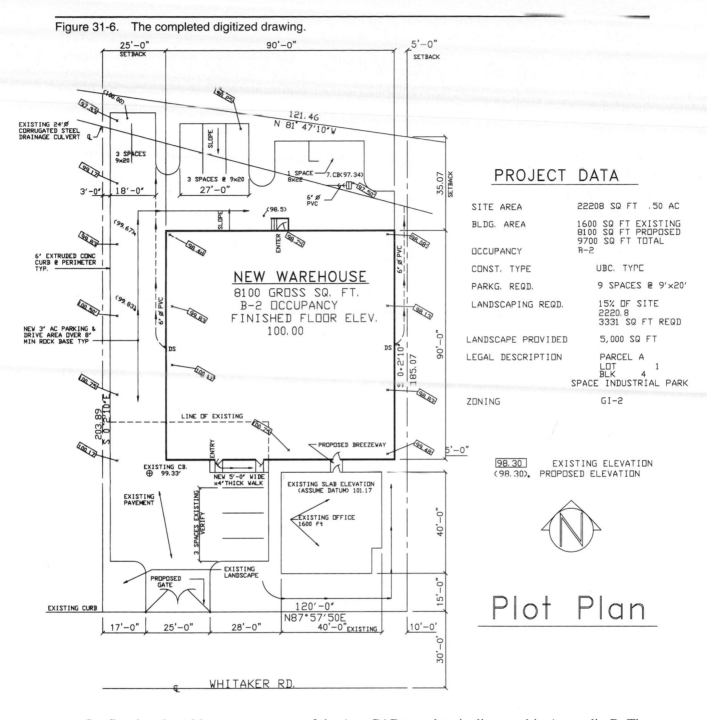

PROJECT DATA

SITE AREA	22208 SQ FT .50 AC
BLDG. AREA	1600 SQ FT EXISTING 8100 SQ FT PROPOSED 9700 SQ FT TOTAL
OCCUPANCY	B-2
CONST. TYPE	UBC. TYPE
PARKG. REQD.	9 SPACES @ 9'x20'
LANDSCAPING REQD.	15% OF SITE 2220.8 3331 SQ FT REQD
LANDSCAPE PROVIDED	5,000 SQ FT
LEGAL DESCRIPTION	PARCEL A LOT 1 BLK 4 SPACE INDUSTRIAL PARK
ZONING	GI-2

98.30   EXISTING ELEVATION
(98.30). PROPOSED ELEVATION

Plot Plan

Configuring the tablet to menu areas of the AutoCAD template is discussed in Appendix B. The tablet may also be turned On and Off using the TABMODE system variable, or by pressing CTRL+T. When using TABMODE, 0 is Off and 1 is On.

PROFESSIONAL TIP

Remember, when digitizing an existing drawing, use the SNAP and ORTHO commands to your advantage. Also be careful when you pick points on the existing drawing. Place the digitizing tablet at a convenient angle. Look directly into the crosshairs of the puck.

The plot plan example in the previous discussion used two calibration points. The existing drawing was very accurate, allowing for two-point calibration to be successfully used. If you successfully enter two points, AutoCAD automatically calculates an orthogonal transformation and ends the command. Three or more points may be digitized to help provide greater accuracy. The same example may have been used to continue calibrating a third point. The third point would be another property line corner, forming a triangular relationship between the points. Press ENTER when you have picked three calibration points. When three points are digitized, AutoCAD calculates the relationship between orthogonal, affine, and projective transformation types. When AutoCAD is finished making the calculations, a table is displayed on the text screen, providing you with this information:

3 calibration points

Transformation type:	Orthogonal	Affine	Projective
Outcome of fit:	success	exact	impossible
RMS error:	6.324		
Standard deviation:	2.941		
Largest residual:	9.726		
At point:	2		
Second largest residual:	8.975		
At point:	1		

These elements can be interpreted as follows:
- **Outcome of fit.**
  - **success**–AutoCAD was successful in calibrating the points, and this is the only category that gives the calculation results.
  - **exact**–There were exactly enough points for AutoCAD to complete the transformation.
  - **impossible**–AutoCAD was not given enough points to provide a projective transformation.
  - **failure**–If this message is displayed, there may have been enough points, but AutoCAD was unable to complete a transformation, because of co-linear or coincident points.
  - **canceled**–Can happen in a projective transformation.
- **RMS Error.** RMS means Root Mean Square, which is a calculation of the accuracy of your calibration points. The smaller this number is, the closer it is to a perfect fit.
- **Standard deviation.** This indicates how much difference there is between the accuracy of points. If this value is near zero, then the points have nearly the same degree of accuracy.
- **Largest residual** Estimates the worst error you might have in the digitized points, and tells you which point this occurs across from the At point: specification.
- **Second largest residual.** Gives the next least accurate calculation at the point specified.

When you pick more than three points, a successful calibration reports back to you in all three types of transformation with a table similar to this:

7 calibration points
Transformation type:OrthogonalAffineProjective

Outcome of fit:	success	success	success
RMS error:	6.324	5.852	2.602
Standard deviation:	2.941	2.469	0.508
Largest residual:	9.726	8.984	4.7634
At point:	3	3	3
Second largest residual:	8.975	8.233	4.012
At point:	5	5	5

Now, AutoCAD allows you to select the desired transformation type or repeat the table by pressing ENTER at the following prompt:

Select transformation type…
Orthogonal/Affine/Projective?⟨Repeat table⟩: *(press* ENTER *or type* **O**, **A**, *or* **P** *for the desired transformation type)*
Command:

Digitizing large drawings

Companies with many large drawings to digitize typically invest in a table-size digitizer. A variety of digitizers and pointing devices were discussed in Chapter 1.

The drawing you plan to digitize may be too large for your tablet. Then you must divide the drawing into sections that fit the tablet area. Establish the coordinates of the boundaries for each section. The over-size drawing in Figure 31-7 is divided into four sections. The coordinates of each section are labeled and shown with dots for reference.

Figure 31-7.   Dividing a large drawing into sections for digitizing. Label the sections and the coordinates of the points defining the sections.

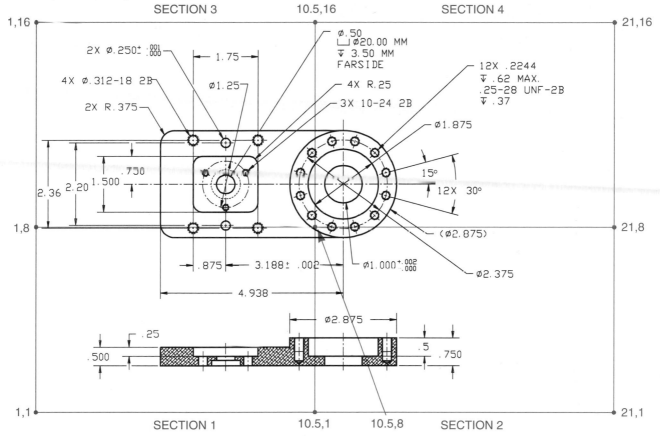

Next, tape the portion labeled as SECTION 1 to the tablet and calibrate the tablet to the coordinates 1,1 and 1,8. Digitize the portion of the object shown as SECTION 1, Figure 31-8.

Figure 31-8.   Place the first section to be digitized on the tablet and calibrate the tablet.

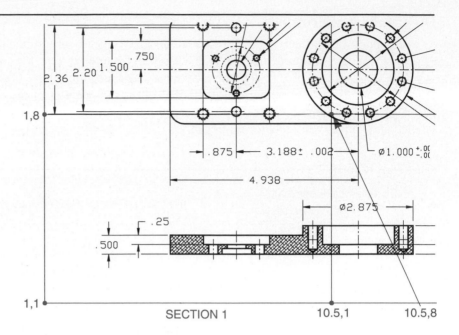

SECTION 1

Proceed by placing the portion of the drawing labeled as SECTION 2 on the digitizer. Calibrate the tablet to the coordinates 10.5,1 and 10.5,8. Digitize the portion of the object shown as SECTION 2. See Figure 31-9.

Figure 31-9.   Place the second section to be digitized on the tablet and calibrate the tablet.

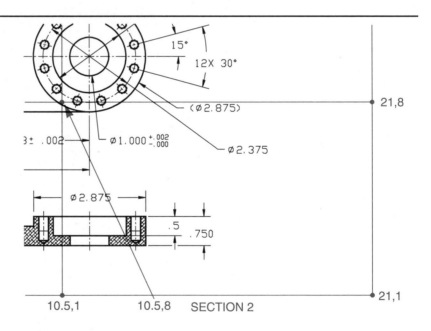

SECTION 2

Proceed by moving SECTION 3 of the drawing into place on the digitizer. Calibrate the tablet to the coordinates 1,8 and 1,16. Digitize the portion of the object shown as SECTION 3.

Proceed by moving SECTION 4 into place on the digitizer. Calibrate the tablet to the coordinates 10.5,8 and 10.5,16. Digitize the portion of the object shown as SECTION 4. The entire drawing has now been digitized.

OPTICAL SCANNING OF EXISTING DRAWINGS

Scanning is a method of automatically digitizing existing drawings to become computer draw
ings. Scanners work much the same way as taking a photograph of the drawing. One advantage of
scanning over manually digitizing drawings is that the entire drawing–including dimensions, symbols,
and text–is transferred to the computer. A disadvantage is that some drawings, when scanned, require
much editing to make them presentable. The scanning process picks up images from the drawing.
What appears to be a dimension, for example, is only a graphic representation of the dimension, it is
not an "entity." If you want the dimensional information to be technically accurate, the dimensions
must be edited and redrawn.

After the drawing is scanned, the image is sent to a raster converter that translates information to
digital or vector format. A *raster* is an electron beam that generates a matrix of pixels. As you learned
previously, pixels make up the drawing image on the display screen. A raster editor is then used to display the images for changes.

Companies using scanners can, in many cases, reproduce existing drawings more efficiently than
companies that manually digitize existing drawings. When an existing drawing has been transferred to
the computer, it becomes an AutoCAD drawing that may be edited as necessary.

Scanners transfer drawings from paper, vellum, film, or blueline prints and convert the hardcopy
image into a raster data file. An example of a scanner in operation is shown in Figure 31-10.

Figure 31-10. An optical scanner in operation. (Houston Instrument, A Summagraphics Corporation)

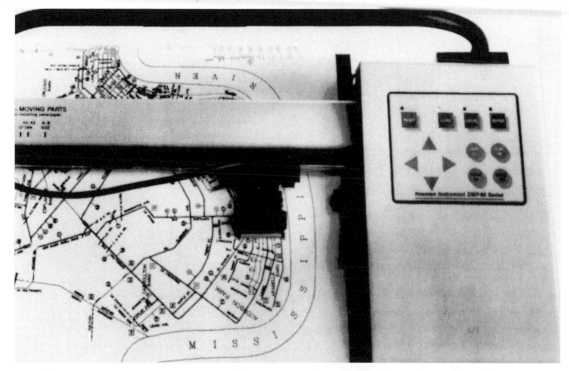

PROFESSIONAL TIP

Current technology limits the capability to scan old faded drawings, especially blueprints
or faded blueline prints. Raster to vector conversions are not very reliable and text recogni-
tion is weak or nonexistent. Text is usually converted to vectors. A common approach to scanning is referred to as overlay, where a raster image is displayed in AutoCAD for on-screen
digitizing.

CHAPTER TEST

Write your answers on a separate sheet of paper.

1. Give the command and related entries to configure the tablet so that the entire area is available as the screen pointing area:

   Command:_____

   Option (ON/OFF/CAL/CFG): _____

   Enter number of tablet menus desired (0-4) ⟨ ⟩: _____

   Do you want to respecify the screen pointing area? ⟨ N ⟩: _____

   Digitize lower-left corner of screen pointing area: _____

   _____

   Digitize upper-right corner of screen pointing area: _____

   _____

2. Give the command and related entries needed to calibrate an existing drawing for digitizing using orthogonal transformation:

   Command:_____

   Option (ON/OFF/CAL/CFG):_____

   Digitize first known point: _____

   Enter coordinates for first point: _____

   Digitize second known point:_____

   Enter coordinates for second point: _____

   Digitize third known point: _____

3. Explain why commands must be typed at the keyboard when the tablet mode is on.

   _____

   _____

4. List at least three methods to turn the tablet mode on and off. _____

   _____

5. Describe the function of a digitizer. _____

   _____

   _____

   _____

6. List the four types of transformation and give the number of points required to digitize each.

   _____

   _____

7. Why is it generally never necessary to digitize more than nine points? _____

   _____

8. List at least three things to consider when digitizing points for drawing transformation.

   _____

   _____

   _____

9. Explain the relationship of the limits, units, grid, and snap to digitizing an existing drawing.

    _____

    _____

10. Why is it important to look straight down into the puck crosshairs when digitizing points?

    _____

    _____

11. Define the following terms related to digitizing three or more points when transferring an existing drawing.

    Outcome of fit:

    A. success– _____

    B. exact– _____

    _____

    C. impossible–_____

    _____

    D. largest residual– _____

    _____

12. How are sections of a drawing coordinated when a large drawing is ditigized? _____

    _____

13. Define "scanning." _____

    _____

    _____

14. List an advantage and a disadvantage of scanning over digitizing drawings. _____

    _____

    _____

    _____

    _____

DRAWING PROBLEMS

1. Make a photocopy of the drawing in Figure 31-6 or 31-7. Use the process for digitizing an existing drawing to convert the drawing to AutoCAD.

2. Make a photocopy of one or more of your previous drawing problem solutions. Use the process for digitizing an existing drawing to convert the drawings to AutoCAD.

3. Obtain an existing industrial or class drawing which was created using manual techniques. Use the process for digitizing an existing drawing to convert it to AutoCAD.

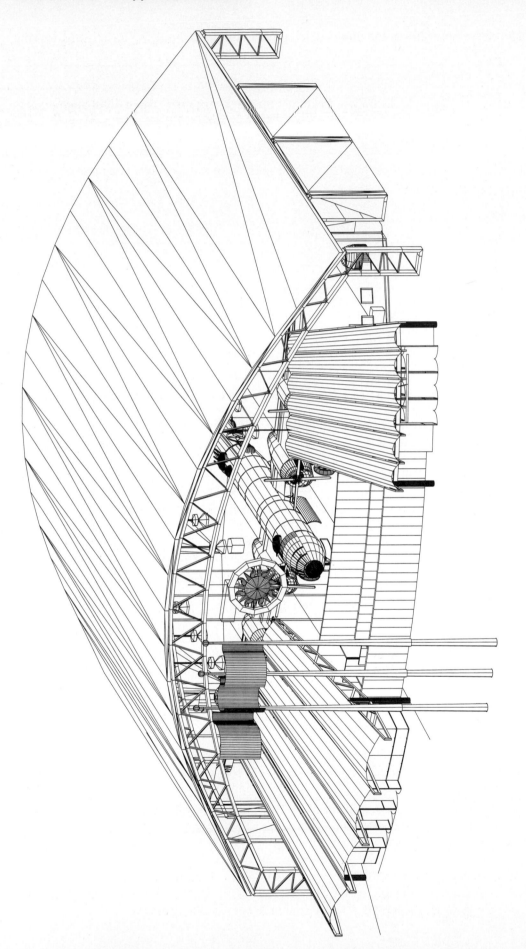

Drawing of an airplane hanger. (David Ward)

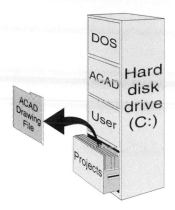

CHAPTER 32

USING MS-DOS COMMANDS

Learning objectives

After completing this chapter, you will be able to:

- ○ Format, label, and examine the contents of floppy disks.
- ○ Recover a formatted disk with the UNFORMAT command.
- ○ Repair disk problems with SCANDISK.
- ○ Assign read-only and hidden features to files using the ATTRIB command.
- ○ Relocate files with the MOVE command.
- ○ Copy directories with the XCOPY command.
- ○ Set the date and time in your computer.
- ○ Write quick files with the COPY command.
- ○ Examine the contents of files.

The Disk Operating System (DOS) is a program that handles the movement of files in your computer. It is basically the traffic cop, or system manager, that enables AutoCAD to work with your computer, and the computer to work with attached equipment. DOS is the first program installed onto your hard disk drive when you purchase a computer. It manages your disk drives and files much like you use a filing cabinet. You might even think of the hard disk drive as one large filing cabinet.

There are two types of DOS commands: internal and external. Internal commands reside in the computer's memory once DOS is loaded. (DOS is loaded when the computer is turned on, or booted.) *Internal commands* are the most used functions of DOS. They perform file manipulations, such as listing, deleting, renaming, and copying files on or between disks. *External commands* are DOS files that are actually individual programs. These must be run from the DOS prompt, just as you might run AutoCAD, because they do not reside in memory.

Some of the more common DOS commands were discussed in previous chapters, and are not repeated here. For a review of selected DOS commands, please refer to the appropriate chapter shown in the chart on the following page.

CAUTION

 The improper use of MS-DOS commands can cause severe problems, such as deleted and damaged files and directories. Therefore, it is critically important that you obtain permission from your instructor or supervisor before using DOS commands that you are unfamiliar with.

WORKING WITH DISKS

The basic function of the FORMAT command was discussed in Chapter 2 of this text. Here we look at techniques used to format a variety of disk sizes and capacities, and to create a disk that can be used to boot your computer should you lose critical files on your hard drive.

Command	Chapter
CD (Change Directory)	17
COPY	17
DIR (Directory)	2 and 17
FORMAT	2
DISKCOPY	17
MD (Make Directory)	17
Paths	2
PROMPT	17
RD (Remove Directory)	17
RENAME	17
UNDELETE	17

Formatting different sizes of disks

Most floppy disk drives are high-density drives. A *high-density disk* has smaller particles of magnetic material, and thus can have more tracks on it. When you format high-density disks, either 5.25″ or 3.5″, in a high-density drive, the only thing you have to type is:

C:\\> **FORMAT A:** ↵

or

C:\\> **FORMAT B:** ↵

The two standard sizes of floppy disks are 5.25″ and 3.5″. The following chart provides you with the most commonly used disk sizes and capacities. The third column in the chart indicates the FORMAT command syntax to use when formatting the disk in a high-density drive.

Disk	Capacity	Format Syntax (for A: or B:)
5.25″	360K	Format A: /F:360
5.25″	1.2MB	Format A:
3.5″	720K	Format B: /F:720
3.5″	1.44MB	Format B:

You may want to create a *system* disk in addition to formatting. This procedure puts two hidden files and the COMMAND.COM file on the disk, which can then be used to boot the computer. The COMMAND.COM file contains *internal* commands such as DIR, COPY, RENAME, and others discussed in the following sections. Create a system disk in drive B: as follows:

C:\\> **FORMAT B: /S** ↵

The system disk that you create with the FORMAT /S command should always be kept with you when you work at a computer. If you work at more than one computer, keep a system disk at each computer. Should you ever encounter a problem that prevents the computer from booting, turn the power off, insert the system disk into the A: drive and turn the power on again. The computer will boot from the A: drive and you will then have access to the hard drive in order to solve the problem.

PROFESSIONAL TIP

The FORMAT command, in addition to preparing a new disk, will erase any data on a previously formatted disk. It will also erase your entire hard disk. Therefore, take two precautions. First, make sure you are inserting a new, blank floppy. Then, read the command you type several times and make sure it reads FORMAT A:. Many hard disks have been accidentally erased because the C: drive was specified when the FORMAT command was issued. Newer versions of DOS provide the following warning if a hard disk is about to be formatted:

```
WARNING: ALL DATA ON NON-REMOVABLE DISK
DRIVE C: WILL BE LOST!
Proceed with Format (Y/N)?
```

By all means, answer NO to this prompt unless you are certain that you wish to delete all files from the hard drive.

Recovering a formatted disk   DOS 5.0

The FORMAT command doesn't really erase the data on your disk; it simply deletes the information in its file directory. This list is called the *File Allocation Table,* or *FAT,* for short. It's like throwing away your phone book. All the people and houses are still in town, but to find one, you have to drive all over town looking for the street and address. It's the same with DOS. If you format a disk safely, as previously described, the files are still on the disk! DOS can find all the files again, but it just has to drive all over the disk to locate them because it no longer has a phone book, or file directory (FAT).

Using the FORMAT command as previously described conducts a "safe" format. You can specifically instruct DOS to perform this type of format by using the "quick" switch. This option can only be used on disks that have been previously formatted. A "quick format" does not create sectors or check for bad spots, it simply deletes the File Allocation Table. Use the "quick" switch as follows:

C:\\⟩ **FORMAT A: /Q** ↵

If you format a disk that contains files you need, you can recover from that mistake by using the UNFORMAT command. This command attempts to rebuild the file directory on the floppy disk.

C:\\⟩ **UNFORMAT A:** ↵

Follow the instructions displayed on screen, and be prepared to wait awhile.

You can provide greater insurance for your disks, and the data on them, if you do the following:

1. Label your disks with the adhesive labels that come with them.
2. Label your disks using DOS as described later on this page.
3. Use the write-protect tabs on flexible disks to protect data. See page 990.

The format of no return

You can unconditionally format a disk from which you will not be able to recover information. This option erases everything on the disk, and the UNFORMAT command cannot recover the lost data. Use this option only if you wish to format disks for security purposes.

C:\\⟩ **FORMAT A: /U** ↵

Be sure you want to perform this type of formatting; DOS does not ask whether you are "really sure."

Giving your disk a name

You can assign a name to your disk by using the *volume* parameter as follows:

C:\\DOS⟩ **FORMAT A: /V** ↵

When the format is complete, you are prompted for a volume label. This label can be up to 11 characters long. Get in the habit of naming your disks. The label is the first item displayed in a directory listing of a disk. Also write the disk name on the adhesive label that comes with the disk before attaching it to the disk. Attempting to write on the label after attaching it to a 5.25″ disk may damage it.

If you forget to label a disk when formatting, use the LABEL command to name the disk. Enter LABEL in the following manner to name a backup disk of chapter problems·

    C:\\ **LABEL A:PROBLEM-BAK** ↲

EXERCISE 32-1

❏ Insert a blank floppy disk into the A: drive and use FORMAT to create a system disk. Be sure that you use the proper disk size for the A: drive, and also be sure that you use the A: drive rather than B:.

❏ Copy several files to a blank disk. Now format the disk that contains the copied files. Next use the UNFORMAT command on the disk you just formatted. You should be able to recover all of the files on the formatted disk.

❏ Change the label of the newly formatted disk to DOSTEST.

❏ Use the appropriate DOS command to display the name of any one of your disks.

What is the name of this disk?

You can easily determine the volume label of any disk using one of two quick methods. The first is to use the DIR command to get a list of the disk's files. The first line that is displayed after you press ENTER contains the disk label. For example:

    C:\ **DIR A:** ↲
    Volume in drive A is PROJECT-02

The second method is to use the VOL command. This command can be used to determine the label on any fixed, or floppy disk.

    C:\ **VOL A:** ↲
    Volume in drive A is PROJECT-02
    Volume Serial Number is *xxxx-xxxx*

Giving your disk a checkup

You can get a quick examination of a disk by using the CHKDSK (CHecK DiSK) command. Insert the disk in drive A: and type:

    C:\DOS)**CHKDSK A:** ↲

The computer then gives you a short report on the status of the disk. It looks similar to this:

    1,457,644 bytes total disk space
      7168 bytes in 7 directories
    651,264 bytes in 12 user files
    805,888 bytes available on disk
    512 bytes in each allocation unit
    2,847 total allocation units on disk
    1,574 available allocation units on disk
    655,360 total bytes memory
    571,840 bytes free

If you are using DOS 6.x, the following message is displayed:

    Instead of using CHKDSK, try using SCANDISK. SCANDISK can reliably detect
    and fix a much wider range of disk problems. For more information,
    type HELP SCANDISK from the command prompt.

Again, the information that appears on screen may differ slightly from what is shown here, depending on the version of DOS you are using.

Most computer programs create open files to use while they are working. AutoCAD is no exception. When you exit the program properly, the open files are closed and put away. Some files are just closed and tossed out. However, if you exit the program improperly, reset the computer while in a program, or the computer crashes, those open files are left "hanging" and can no longer be used. These files are referred to as "lost clusters" or "lost chains." They are disk units that cannot be used, but they are occupying space on the disk. You can use the CHKDSK command to find these lost clusters as follows:

C:\\> **CHKDSK /F**↵
 49 lost allocation units found in 1 chains
Convert lost chains to files (Y/N)?

If you answer N to this prompt, DOS fixes the disk and recovers the lost chains. If you answer Y, the files DOS creates are given names such as FILE0001.CHK, and are placed in the root directory. In most cases, these files cannot be viewed, so you might as well delete them as follows:

C:\\> **DEL *.CHK** ↵

NOTE   Floppy disks can collect lost clusters if you open AutoCAD drawings on the floppy, or if you remove or insert disks at the wrong time while AutoCAD is in session. Lost clusters can also accumulate on your disk as a result of program or system crashes. Therefore, use the CHKDSK command regularly on your floppy disks like this:

C:\\> **CHKDSK A: /F** ↵

Never use CHKDSK if you are shelled out of AutoCAD.

Giving your disk a thorough checkup

┌─────────┐
│ **DOS 6.2** │
└─────────┘

The SCANDISK command was introduced in MS-DOS version 6.2, and provides a much more complete checkup for your disk than the CHKDSK command. Simply log on to the drive you wish to check, then use SCANDISK:

C:\\> **SCANDISK** ↵

As SCANDISK goes to work, a screen is displayed that lists the items being checked. See Figure 32-1. The final item in the list is Surface Scan. You are asked if you want to proceed with the surface scan. See Figure 32-2. This function performs a detailed examination of the disk, and takes several minutes. It is recommended that you perform a surface scan approximately once a month.

Figure 32-1. The "ScanDisk" dialog box displays the items that are being checked.

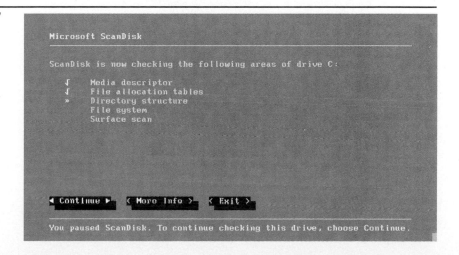

Figure 32-2. ScanDisk displays a dialog box that allows you to answer Yes or No to perform a surface scan.

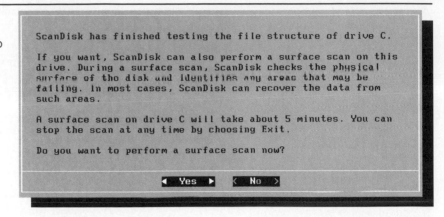

ScanDisk has finished testing the file structure of drive C.

If you want, ScanDisk can also perform a surface scan on this drive. During a surface scan, ScanDisk checks the physical surface of the disk and identifies any areas that may be failing. In most cases, ScanDisk can recover the data from such areas.

A surface scan on drive C will take about 5 minutes. You can stop the scan at any time by choosing Exit.

Do you want to perform a surface scan now?

◄ Yes ► ◄ No ►

Protecting your disks

Dust, heat, cold, magnets, cigarette smoke, and coffee do great damage to your disks. Placing your disk on or near the digitizer tablet or any other electrical or magnetic device can quickly ruin your files. A ringing telephone can even be a dangerous enemy of the disk because of its magnetic field. Beyond physical damage, you or someone else could write over the files on a disk or put files on the wrong disk, making them difficult or impossible to find.

The easiest way to protect the data on your floppy disk from accidental erasure by formatting, saving, or copying files, is to use the *write-protect tab*. For 5.25″ disks, the write-protect tab is a small, rectangular adhesive-backed piece that is placed over the write-protect notch. See Figure 32-3. A 3.5″ disk uses a small, sliding tab located on the bottom side of the disk. Notice in Figure 32-3 that the write-protect tab is in effect when it is moved toward the edge of the disk. Use the point of a pen or your fingernail to slide the tab.

When the tab is covering the notch, or moved to the write-protect position, you cannot format, save, or copy files to that disk, but the files can be read from it. Trying to format or save to the disk gives you a write-protect error in DOS. If you must use the disk for writing or formatting purposes, simply remove the tab or move it to the appropriate position.

Figure 32-3. A–Protect your 5.25″ disks by placing a write-protect tab over the notch on the disk. B–On a 3.5″ disk, move the write-protect tab to the "Read Only" position.

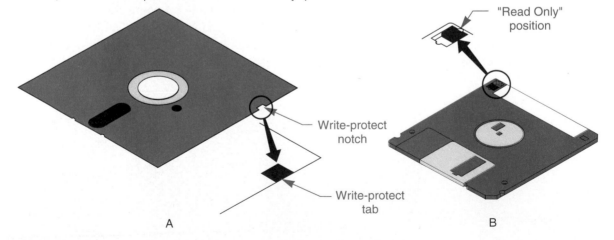

"Read Only" position

Write-protect notch

Write-protect tab

A

B

EXERCISE 32-2

❏ Insert one of your floppy disks into drive A:. Use the CHKDSK command to determine usage and capacities of the disk.

❏ Use the CHKDSK command on the disk in drive A: to check for, and fix, lost clusters or chains.

❏ Use the SCANDISK command (if you have DOS version 6.2) to give the hard disk a checkup. Do not conduct a surface scan.

❏ Use the SCANDISK command on one of your floppy disks. Perform a surface scan.

❏ Find the system disk that you created in Exercise 32-1 and use the appropriate write-protect tab to ensure that it is write-protected.

WORKING WITH FILES

The most commonly used commands for file manipulation are DIR, COPY, RENAME, and DELETE. These commands were discussed thoroughly in Chapter 17. In addition to these common commands, there are three others that are useful when working with file management. They are MOVE, XCOPY, and ATTRIB.

Relocating a file with MOVE
DOS 6.0

The MOVE command is actually a combination of the COPY and DELETE commands. The file is copied to the new location, and the original is deleted, just as you would expect if you physically move anything to a new location. Files can be moved between directories or disk drives as follows:

C:\ACADR13\PROJECT⟩ **MOVE FLRPLN26.DWG D:\ARCHIVE** ↵
c:\acadr13\project\flrpln26.dwg =⟩ d:\archive\flrpln26.dwg [ok]

If a file of the same name exists, DOS allows you to approve the move or change your mind with the following prompt:

Overwrite d:\archive\flrpln26.dwg (Yes/No/All)?

If you respond with YES, the file in the destination is overwritten by the file being moved. If a group of files is being moved, and files of the same names exist in the destination, respond to the above prompt with ALL to overwrite all of the files in the destination.

CAUTION

Always use caution when working with the MOVE command if duplicate files are involved. Be sure that you have permission to overwrite duplicate or archived files. Some companies keep records of previous drawing versions as a revision history. Familiarize yourself with school or company procedures before using MOVE for this purpose.

Renaming a directory with MOVE
DOS 6.0

The MOVE command can be used to quickly rename a directory. Use the following technique to rename the DATA directory to DRAWINGS.

C:\⟩ **MOVE DATA DRAWINGS** ↵

Be sure to put a space after the MOVE command, and between the two directory names. If the move (rename) is successful, DOS responds with:

c:\data =⟩ c:\drawings [ok]

Using the XCOPY command to copy directories

Situations may arise in which you need to copy an entire directory of files, or even entire directory trees. For these situations the XCOPY command picks up where COPY leaves off. What makes XCOPY so powerful is that it can duplicate directories and subdirectories as it copies files. The following example copies all files in the C:\ACADR13\PROJECT subdirectory to a new directory named C:\PROJECT. The new directory name does not have to exist for XCOPY to perform the function.

```
C:\ACADR13⟩ XCOPY PROJECT\*.* C:\PROJECT ↵
Does PROJECT specify a file name
or directory name on the target
(F = file, D = directory)? D
```

It is not necessary to press ENTER after typing a D or F. DOS automatically executes the command.

The above example of XCOPY showed how to create a new directory and copy a group of files to the new directory. But XCOPY can also be used to copy an entire directory tree. A directory tree structure refers to the current directory, plus all subdirectories that reside within it. Suppose for example, that the C:\ACADR13\PROJECT directory contained several subdirectories for a variety of projects. And, within each one of the subdirectories there were several additional sub-subdirectories. Your task is to copy this entire tree structure to another hard drive partition. Use the following switches to accomplish this:

```
C:\ACADR13⟩ XCOPY PROJECT\*.* D:\PROJECT /S /E ↵
Does PROJECT specify a file name
or directory name on the target
(F = file, D = directory)? D
```

In this example, the XCOPY command is copying all files in the C:\ACADR13\PROJECT directory to a new location on the D: hard drive named D:\PROJECT. In addition, the /S switch copies directories and subdirectories that contain files. The /E switch copies all subdirectories, even if they contain no files.

PROFESSIONAL TIP

The XCOPY command can be especially useful when working with a network server. When a directory tree must be copied between stations, XCOPY can be used to copy to the server, then down to the other station. If a computer experiences problems that leads to directory damage or loss, backup directories can be transferred from the server with **XCOPY.**

The XCOPY command has a variety of switches that enable you to be specific in your instructions. These are clearly listed in the DOS help screen. You can quickly view these by entering the following at any DOS prompt:

```
C:\⟩ HELP XCOPY ↵
```

File security with the ATTRIB command

Files have features called *attributes*. Two of these features are *read-only* and *hidden*. Using the ATTRIB command, a file can be marked as read-only, in which case you can only read from the file. An "Access denied" error message is displayed should you try to rename, alter, or delete the file. Although this command is rather useless as security against anyone purposely damaging or destroying your files, it is good protection against inadvertent damage or deletion. Use the proper notation to mark a file as read-only:

```
C:\PROTOS⟩ ATTRIB PROTO-B.DWG +R ↵
```

Be sure to put a space after the file extension, but do not put a space between the plus sign and R.

To remove the read-only marker so the file can be modified, renamed, or deleted, simply replace the plus sign with a minus:

```
C:\PROTOS⟩ ATTRIB PROTO-B.DWG –R ↵
```

Now the file is unprotected and can be deleted.

Files and directories can be hidden with a similar notation. When a file or directory is hidden, it will not be displayed when the DIR command is used. Hide a file as follows:

C:\PROTOS⟩ **ATTRIB PROTO-B.DWG +H** ↵

In order to hide an entire directory it must not be current. Change to the parent directory before trying to hide it.

C:\ ⟩ **ATTRIB PROTOS +H** ↵

The C:\PROTOS directory is now hidden, and will not show in a directory listing. But you can still use CD to change to that directory, and its name will show in the DOS prompt if the PROMPT command has been used to display directory names. See Chapter 17 for more details on the PROMPT command. In addition, all files within hidden directories are available for use with any software, and by any DOS command, depending of course on the attributes that have been assigned to the files.

MISCELLANEOUS COMMANDS

The DOS program contains more commands than can be discussed in this text. Most AutoCAD users will not use these additional commands. Consult your DOS manual for a detailed discussion of other commands if extensive DOS programming is required.

There are several commands that are useful when creating text or batch files. These commands let you set the date and time, create a text file, and display any file on the screen.

Setting the date and time

The DATE and TIME commands allow you to set the date and time and ask the computer for the date and time. Enter the following:

C:\⟩ **DATE** ↵
Current date is Tue 8-15-1995
Enter new date (mm-dd-yy):

If you just wanted to know the date, press ENTER now and the DOS prompt returns. If you need to reset the date for any reason, enter it in the following manner:

Enter new date (mm-dd-yy): **8-29-95** ↵
C:\⟩

If you enter the date incorrectly, the "Invalid date" error message appears and a prompt asks you to enter the new date again.

The TIME command is used in the same manner:

C:\⟩ **TIME** ↵
Current time is 8:37:12.82a
Enter new time:

Press ENTER if you are just checking the time. Notice that the time is given in hundredths of a second. When entering a new time, only the hour and minute is needed, and if it is A.M. or P.M.:

Enter new time: **7:37a** ↵
C:\⟩

Some users make the date and/or the time part of the DOS prompt. Enter the following to make the date part of the prompt:

C:\⟩ **PROMPT $P DG** ↵
C:\ Tue 8-29-1995⟩

Notice that a space was left after the "$P" in the prompt entry. This adds a space after the current directory in the new prompt. The time can be added to the prompt in the same manner:

    C:\ Tue 8-29-95⟩ **PROMPT $P TG** ↵
    C:\ 7:46:58.04⟩

The time displayed reflects the last time you pressed ENTER. To know the current time, press ENTER.

    C:\ 7:46:58.04⟩ ↵
    C:\ 7:47:05.89⟩

PROFESSIONAL TIP

Include DATE and TIME in the AUTOEXEC.BAT file if your computer does not have a clock, or if the battery in your computer is not functioning. It is important that the internal clock is working, especially if you customize the screen and tablet menus. AutoCAD uses the menu file with the latest date and time.

Writing quick files

The COPY command with the CONsole output source allows you to create small text or batch files without using a text editor program, such as EDIT. Files created using COPY CON cannot be edited; therefore, make them short. If you discover a mistake in a file, you must rewrite it using the COPY CON command, or edit it with a text editor. Create a short batch file to clear the screen and display the date and time:

    C:\⟩ **COPY CON TEST.BAT** ↵
    ECHO OFF ↵
    CLS ↵
    DATE ↵
    TIME ↵

Press function key F6 to end the file. This displays a "^Z," which terminates the file. Then press ENTER. A message appears indicating the file has been copied. You can test the file by entering TEST at the DOS prompt:

    C:\⟩ **TEST** ↵

The file runs and the screen clears. The date prompt appears, allowing you to change the date. After pressing ENTER, the time prompt appears. When you press ENTER a second time, the DOS prompt returns.

Try entering this short batch file from within AutoCAD using the COPY CON command.

    Command: **SHELL** ↵
    OS Command: ↵
    C:\ACADR13⟩⟩ **COPY CON TEST.BAT** ↵
    ECHO OFF ↵   *(do not display DOS commands)*
    CLS ↵   *(clear the screen)*
    DIR A:*.DWG ↵   *(list all .DWG files in drive A:)*
    PAUSE ↵   *(pause to read the list)*
    CD \ACADR13\COMMON\SAMPLE ↵   *(change directory to \ACADR13\COMMON\SAMPLE)*
    DIR *.DWG ↵   *(list all .DWG files in the\ ACADR13\ COMMON*
                                           SAMPLE subdirectory)
    PAUSE ↵   *(pause to read the list)*
    CLS ↵   *(clear the screen)*
    CD..   *(change to the previous or "parent" directory)*
    (Press key F6 and ENTER*)*

Execute this file by typing TEST at the DOS prompt. When this is completed, type EXIT to return to the drawing editor.

Displaying the contents of files

The TYPE command allows you to see the data a file contains. Enter the TYPE command at the DOS prompt, followed by the name and extension of the file to display. Display the contents of your AUTOEXEC.BAT file by entering:

C:\\> **TYPE AUTOEXEC.BAT** ↵

The contents of the entire file scroll up the screen. The DOS prompt then returns. If the file is long, the screen display does not automatically stop when the first page scrolls. Stop the file by entering CTRL+S, then press CTRL+S to start the scroll again. This requires quick fingers and a measured eye to stop the scroll exactly where you want to look at the file.

A more precise method of displaying only one screen at a time is the MORE command. It allows only one screen display at a time to scroll by. To see the next screen, press any key. You are using two commands in one entry, so you must use the *pipe* symbol (|) before the MORE command. This is a vertical bar (|), or two short vertical dashes (¦), usually located on the backslash key (\\). Use SHIFT to activate this symbol. The pipe symbol takes output from one command (file) and sends it to another. In this case, it takes the output of the TYPE command (a continuous list) and sends it to the MORE command (breaks the list into separate pages).

Try this with the ACAD.MNU file. First change directory to ACADR13\\DOS\\SUPPORT. Then use the TYPE and MORE commands:

C:\\> **CD \\ACADR13\\DOS\\SUPPORT**
C:\\ACADR13\\DOS\\SUPPORT> **TYPE ACAD.MNU¦MORE** ↵

When one page scrolls by, the following prompt appears at the bottom of the screen:

–More–

Press any key and the next page appears. The ACAD.MNU file is long. When you have seen enough, press CTRL+C to cancel the command.

NOTE   Most computer programs come with files such as README.DOC, README, or README.NOW. Anytime you see one of these files, especially if you have just installed new software or received files via a modem, you should read them first. These files are usually ASCII files, so they can be displayed without using special software. Use the TYPE command to view these files:

C:\\> **TYPE README.DOC¦MORE** ↵

In addition, many of the files that come with software or *shareware* (software that is free or available for a nominal fee), are registration forms or instruction manuals. These usually have a .DOC file extension. They can be printed like this:

C:\\> **PRINT REGISTER.DOC** ↵

Before initiating this command, be sure to have paper in your printer.

EXERCISE 32-3

❑ Using COPY CON, write a batch file named EX32-3.BAT that does the following:
  ❑ Turns the screen echo off.
  ❑ Clears the screen,
  ❑ Sets the prompt to display the current directory, the words "hi there," and the caret (〉).
  ❑ Sets the date.
  ❑ Sets the time.
  ❑ Changes the current directory to ACADR13.
❑ Use the TYPE command to list the file.
❑ Run the file by entering EX32-3 at the DOS prompt.

CHAPTER TEST

Write your answers in the spaces provided.

1. The name of the DOS command that lets you prepare a floppy disk for use is. _____

2. What command allows you to recover a disk that has been prepared with the command in Question 1?_____

3. What would you enter at the DOS prompt to prepare and assign a name to a floppy disk in the A: drive?
   C〉_____

4. Explain the function of the CHKDSK command. _____
   _____
   _____

5. What command provides a much more thorough checkup for disks than CHKDSK? _____

6. Describe how you can protect your floppy disks from having data written to them accidentally.
   _____

7. What command enables you to relocate a file to a new location? _____

8. What would you enter at the DOS prompt to quickly rename the C:\ARCH directory to C:\ARCH-01?
   C:\〉 _____

9. What command would you use to copy an entire directory tree to a different location?_____
   _____

10. What would you enter at the DOS prompt to copy the C:\ACADR13\ELEC directory and all of its files and subdirectories to a new directory named C:\ELEC?
    C:\〉 _____

11. What command would you use to mark a file as hidden? _____

12. What would you enter at the DOS prompt to hide the file AUTOEXEC.BAT? _____
    C:\〉 _____

13. Define a BAT file. _____

14. Explain why it is important that AutoCAD have the current date and time. _____
    _____

15. List the proper DOS entry to begin writing a small batch file called FIRST, without using a text editor such as EDIT.

    C:\\) _____

16. Explain how you would display a long file on the A: drive named MYFIRST.BAT, one page at a time. _____

    C:\\) _____

17. Provide complete, but brief explanations of the following DOS commands:

    A. FORMAT B: /F:720 /V– _____

    B. CHKDSK B: /F– _____

    C. FORMAT A: /U– _____

    D. MOVE EL024-01.DWG D:\ELEC– _____

    E. HELP ATTRIB– _____

    F. ATTRIB CONFIG.SYS +R +H– _____

PROBLEMS

NOTE   Have the permission of your instructor or supervisor before making or removing directories, formatting disks, deleting files, writing batch files, or using any DOS command that may alter the structure of the hard disk files and directories.

---

1. Format four disks in a row without exiting the FORMAT command. Provide names for the disks as they are formatted by using the proper FORMAT option.

2. If you have not done so already, use the FORMAT command to create a system disk. Be sure the disk is inserted into the A: hard drive. After the disk has been formatted, perform a "warm boot" by simultaneously pressing the CTRL+ALT+DELETE keys on the keyboard. The computer will boot itself from the system disk in the A: drive. When the DOS prompt is displayed, it will show as A:\\). You can change the drive and continue with your work. Remove the disk from drive A: and perform a warm boot again. If your computer has a RESET button, press it. The computer will boot up normally from the hard disk.

3. Use the SCANDISK command to perform disk checks of all of your floppy disks. Perform surface scans if you wish. Use SCANDISK to perform a check of your hard drive. Answer Yes to perform a surface scan. This may take several minutes, so do not conduct this scan if you are working under tight time constraints.

4. List the contents of one of your newly formatted diskettes. Use the CHKDSK command on your old diskettes. (If there are any lost clusters, do not convert them to files.)

5. Use a text editor or COPY CON to write a batch file called CHECK.BAT that does the following:

   A. Turns the display of DOS commands off.

   B. Clears the screen.

   C. Lists all files on the disk.

   D. Pauses to view the files.

   E. Checks the disk in drive A:.

   F. Pauses.

   G. Clears the screen.

6. Use a text editor or COPY CON to write a batch file called DELBAK.BAT that does the following:

   A. Turns the display of DOS commands off.

   B. Clears the screen.

   C. Changes the current drive to A:.

   D. Lists the contents of the disk.

   E. Pauses.

   F. Deletes all BAK files.

   G. Changes the current disk to C:.

   H. Clears the screen.

INSTALLING AND CONFIGURING AUTOCAD

Before you can use AutoCAD, it must be loaded onto the hard disk and then configured to work with your specific hardware. When AutoCAD is installed on the hard disk, you begin the continuous process of disk and system management. This involves creating storage space for files and maintaining them. The configuration procedure should have to be used only once, unless equipment is upgraded or new peripherals are added. To use two or more different menu systems, you can duplicate and alter AutoCAD's standard configuration file, ACAD.CFG.

LOADING AUTOCAD ONTO THE HARD DISK

Before loading AutoCAD, follow these preparation and setup steps:
- Determine the hard disk drive to install AutoCAD on.
- If installing from disks, make backup copies of the AutoCAD diskettes.
- Label the backup disks.

These steps require only a few minutes and can prevent problems later.

Making backup copies of the AutoCAD disks

Always make backup copies of original disks before loading the software onto the hard disk. Be sure you have the correct number of blank disks before starting to copy the AutoCAD disks. Attach labels to the blank disks that contain the disk name, number, and AutoCAD serial number. Enter the DISKCOPY command at the DOS prompt. This program prepares the blank disk (formats) and then copies onto it the contents of the original. DISKCOPY can be used with a single- or dual-disk drive computer if both drives are the same type. For a two-drive system, enter:

C) **DISKCOPY A: B:** ↵
Insert SOURCE disk in drive A:
Insert TARGET disk in drive B:
Press any key when ready…

Insert the AutoCAD Disk 1 into drive A: and the blank "target" disk into drive B:. Press a key and the copy begins. If you have only one disk drive, enter DISKCOPY A: A: and insert the source disk in drive A:. You are prompted to insert the target disk into drive A:. When the copy is complete, you are asked if you want to copy another diskette. Answer Y and continue the process above until all of the disks have been copied.

Copy another diskette (Y/N)? **Y** ↵

When you finish copying the disks, return the originals to the packaging and store them in a safe place. Use the backup copies for loading AutoCAD, and any other future needs.

Using the CD ROM

Release 13 is the first version of AutoCAD that is available on CD-ROM. This format is less expensive, and requires the use of only one flexible disk. In addition, the CD-ROM has greater integrity than disks, and many of the extra precautions required when handling and storing flexible disks, are not concerns with a CD. Advantages of a CD are the speed of the installation, and the need to handle only a single installation disk. Once the installation of files begins from the CD, the computer can be left unattended, since there are no disks to remove or insert.

The installation process discussed here is based on the use of a CD-ROM, but is similar if installing from disks. The only difference is that you are prompted to insert the next disk.

Installing AutoCAD onto the hard disk

Installing AutoCAD on a hard disk is a simple process, but it does require that you are somewhat prepared before beginning. First, be sure that you have enough physical hard disk space for the program files. Approximate storage areas required for some of the components are given below.

Files	Disk Space
Complete installation	40.6MB
Minimum installation	21.1MB
Typical installation	34.6MB
AutoCAD fonts: TrueType	1.7MB
AutoCAD fonts: PostScript	600K
AutoCAD English Spelling Dictionary	238K
AutoCAD External Database Access	10.6MB
AutoCAD Example & Sample files	4.1MB
AutoCAD Application Development	1.6MB
AutoCAD Learning tools	800K

In an effort to run smoothly through the installation process, know the following information before starting:

Disk drive on which to install AutoCAD. _____

Portion of the AutoCAD files to install. See previous list. _____

Dealer's name. _____

Dealer's telephone number. _____

NOTE   If you are installing AutoCAD from disks, use only your backup disks for installation, not the original disks. If you have not yet created backup disks as explained at the beginning of this chapter, do so before you continue. If you are installing from a CD, you should also make a backup copy of the installation disk before continuing.

After you have created backup disks of all of the AutoCAD program disks, you are ready to install the software. Insert the Installation Disk, into the disk drive and enter the following at the DOS prompt:

C:\ 〉 **A:INSTALL** ↵

The screen shown in Figure A-1 is displayed. If the installation disk is write-protected, AutoCAD will not be able to transfer your personal information to the disk, and you will get an error message to that effect. To remove write-protection from a 3.5″ disk, move the tab away from the edge of the disk. See Figure 32-3 if you are unfamiliar with the write-protect tab.

Figure A-1.   AutoCAD informs
you that write-protection must
be removed from the
installation disk.

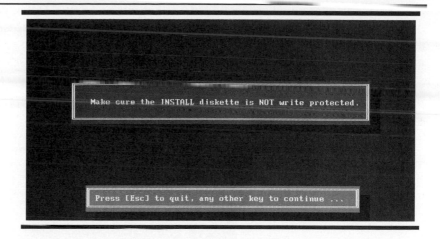

Next, you are asked for specific information that becomes a permanent part of the Installation disk. This is both a security measure, and enables AutoCAD to display the name and phone number of your dealer in the "About AutoCAD" dialog box. The screen shown in Figure A-2 (with your personalized information) appears whenever you re-install your copy of AutoCAD.

Figure A-2.   The personal data
you enter becomes a permanent
part of the Installation disk.

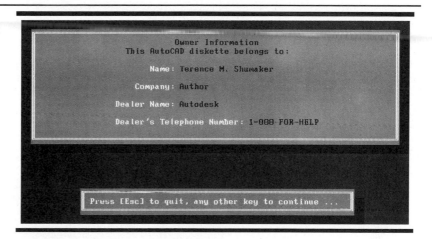

After entering the required information, you are given a chance to change your mind or correct anything you entered, and you are warned that the data entered becomes permanent. The next screen is information providing you with brief instructions for using the installation program. See Figure A-3.

Figure A-3.   Information on
using the installation program is
provided in this display.

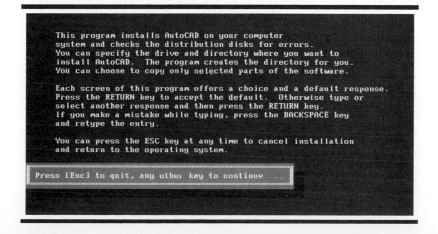

Next, you are required to select the components of AutoCAD that you wish to install. See Figure A-4. If you planned your installation as mentioned previously, refer to those notes now. If you are unsure about the applications that will be needed, install all files. Just remember, you'll need about 41 megabytes of storage space for all files.

Figure A-4.   Choose the components to install from this list.

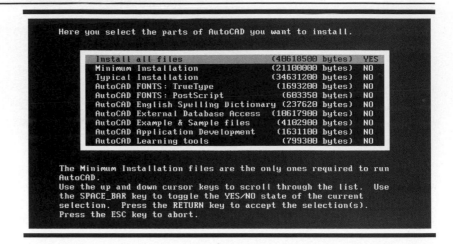

If you will be working with databases and SQL, install the AutoCAD External Database Access files. If you wish to have access to AutoCAD Development System (ADS) files (additional sample programs with an .EXP, .EXE, or .C extension), install the AutoCAD Application Development files. You will gain access to the AutoCAD tutorials by installing the AutoCAD Learning tools.

After you have selected the components you wish to install, a display indicates your selection(s). See Figure A-5.

Figure A-5.   The components selected for installation are displayed.

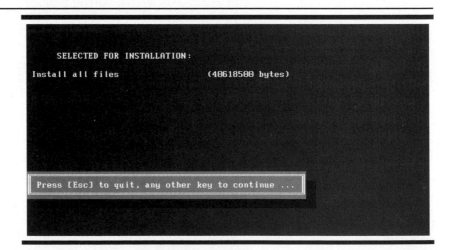

You next need to indicate which hard disk drive AutoCAD is to be installed on. A list of possible drives is displayed, and the current selected drive is flashing. See Figure A-6. Use the up and down cursor keys to highlight the appropriate drive, then press ENTER.

Figure A-6.   Select the hard
drive on which to install
AutoCAD .

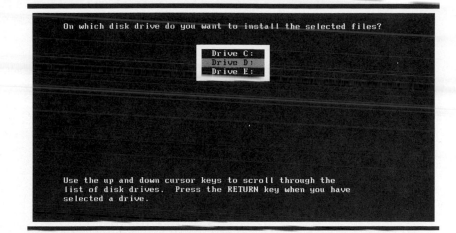

The next two screens prompt you for the name of the directory in which the AutoCAD files and
the shared files will be installed. Shared files are those used by both the DOS and Windows versions of
Release 13. Press ENTER to accept the default, unless you wish to change the names. See Figures A-7
and A-8.

Figure A-7.   Press ENTER to
accept the default name of the
AutoCAD for DOS directory,
or enter a new one.

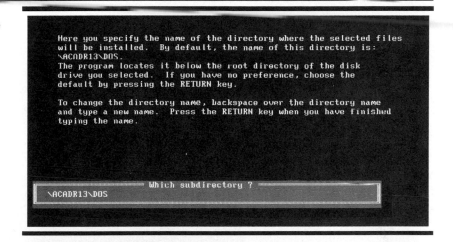

Figure A-8.   Press ENTER to
accept the default name of the
shared files directory, or
enter a new one.

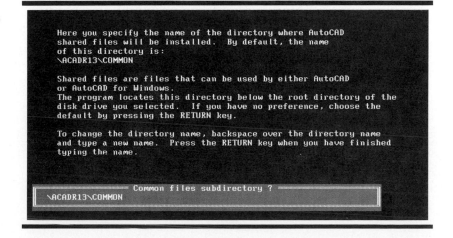

The next screen prompts you for the name of your CD-ROM drive. Use the up and down cursor keys to highlight it, then press ENTER. See Figure A-9.

Figure A-9. Select your CD-ROM drive from the list.

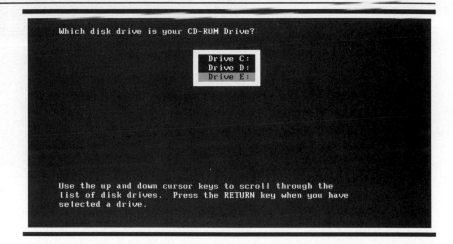

The last selection before installation begins is for choosing the Metric or English system of measurement. See Figure A-10. Highlight your selection, press ENTER, and the installation begins.

Figure A-10. Select the default unit of measurement.

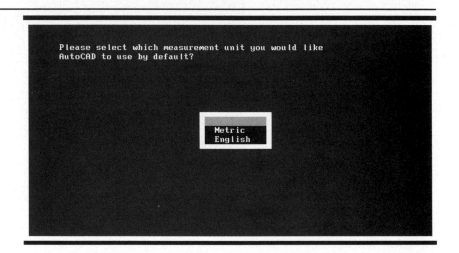

When the installation is complete, your CONFIG.SYS file is checked to see if two statements have appropriate values. These are the FILES= and BUFFERS= statements. The install program will suggest automatic changes to this file, or you can manually change the file if you wish. See Figure A-11. It is suggested that you agree to these changes by entering Yes.

Figure A-11.   After installation, changes to your CONFIG.SYS files are suggested (if required).

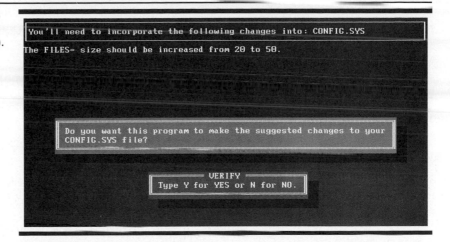

Lastly, the install program suggests creating a new file called ACADR13.BAT. If you answer Yes, this file is automatically created. See Figure A-12. Unless you plan to write your own file to load AutoCAD, it is suggested that you answer Yes. This file sets critical environment statements that enable AutoCAD to run efficiently. This file can be edited later, using any text editor, to suit your application. See Appendix C for examples of this and other batch files.

Figure A-12.   A batch file can be automatically created that sets the proper environment prior to loading AutoCAD.

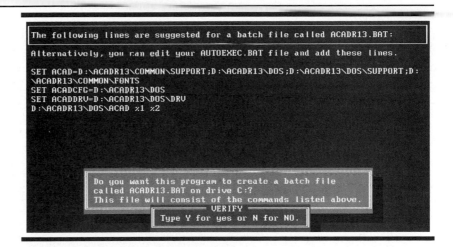

CONFIGURING AUTOCAD

The configuration process allows you to tell AutoCAD the specific brands and styles of equipment you are using. Before you begin, make a list of the following pieces of equipment that comprise your workstation:

Video Display_____

Input Device (Digitizer or Mouse)_____

Size_____

Number of buttons _____

Plotter _____

Printer_____

Once you have a list of your equipment, the configuring process should go quickly. At the DOS prompt, make the ACADR13 directory current with the Change Directory (CD) command.

C:\ ⟩ **CD ACADR13** ↵
C:\ACADR13 ⟩

Remember, if you did not change the prompt's appearance using the PROMPT command, the display will not show the current directory:

C ⟩ **CD ACADR13** ↵
C ⟩

Start AutoCAD by entering ACADR13 if you are using the suggested startup batch file.

C:\ACAD ⟩ **ACADR13** ↵

If AutoCAD has not yet been configured, it will proceed past the copyright notice and display a message saying "AutoCAD is not yet configured." You are then instructed:

You must specify the devices to which AutoCAD will interface.
Press ENTER to continue:

You are then presented with a list of the following video display selections.

Available video displays:
1. Null display
2. Accelerated Driver V1.0.1 ADI by Vibrant Graphics for Autodesk

There are a wide variety of video graphics adapters on the market. If drivers for one of these devices have been installed in your computer, the list that is displayed on your screen may contain additional selections. Make the appropriate selection and then be prepared to answer the following questions:

- What is the brand and model of your video card? _____
- What is the screen resolution? (number of horizontal pixels and number of vertical pixels)____
- Are you using single or dual screens? _____
- Do you want to create a custom configuration? (screen layout, menu colors, fonts, etc.) _____
- Do you want to correct the aspect ratio of the graphics screen? _____
- Do you want a status line? _____
- Do you want a command prompt area? _____
- Do you want a screen menu area? _____

Depending on the type of display devices that you may select, you may be asked different questions regarding detailed configurations or specific screen color settings. Consult your video card documentation for instructions.

After configuring your video display, you are asked to choose a digitizer. This is actually referring to the pointing device. You are given the following list:

Available digitizers:
1. None
2. ADI digitizer (Real Mode)
3. Calcomp 2500 (obsolete) and 3300 Series ADI 4.2 - by Autodesk, Inc
4. Hitachi HICOMSCAN HDG Series ADI 4.2 - by Autodesk, Inc
5. Kurta IS/ONE (obsolete) ADI 4.2 - by Autodesk, Inc
6. Kurta XLC, IS/THREE (obsolete) ADI 4.2 - by Autodesk, Inc
7. Kurta XLP, ADI 4.2 - by Autodesk, Inc
8. Microsoft Mouse Driver ADI 4.2 - by Autodesk
9. Summagraphics MicroGrid v1.1 (Series II/later) ADI 4.2 - by Autodesk, Inc
10. Summagraphics MM Series v2.0, ADI 4.2 - by Autodesk, Inc
Select device number or ? to repeat list ⟨1⟩: (*enter your selection and press* ENTER)

You are next asked a variety of questions regarding digitizer size, number of buttons, mouse scaling parameters, etc., depending on which pointing device you selected.

The configuration process continues, presenting available plotters and printers. Choose the appropriate hardware and answer the ensuing questions. After the printer or plotter is configured, you are required to provide the following information:

- Authorization number.
- Default login name–The default name is the one entered when AutoCAD was installed.
- Enable file locking? (Y/N)
- Available spelling dialects:
  - 1. American English
  - 2. British English (ise)
  - 3. British English (ize)
- Select dialect number or ? to repeat list ⟨1⟩:
- Run the executable from a read-only directory? (Y/N)

After answering these questions, the screen displays the current AutoCAD configuration. This is only a display; you cannot change anything here. If you wish to change something, you can do so at the Configuration menu after pressing ENTER, or you can use the CONFIG command when you are in AutoCAD.

Press ENTER to continue:

Pressing ENTER displays the Configuration menu. Correct any configuration errors or add a piece of equipment that you may have forgotten.

```
Configuration menu
      0.  Exit to drawing editor
      1.  Show current configuration
      2.  Allow detailed configuration

      3.  Configure video display
      4.  Configure digitizer
      5.  Configure plotter
      6.  Configure system console
      7.  Configure operating parameters
Enter selection ⟨ 0 ⟩: ↵
```

Press ENTER if you do not wish to configure any additional equipment or change the hardware you chose. Be sure to press ENTER at the following prompt, or enter Y, to save the configuration file:

```
If you answer N to the following question, all configuration
changes you have just made will be discarded.
Keep configuration changes? ⟨ Y ⟩ ↵
```

The AutoCAD drawing editor then appears, and you can begin a drawing session. Test the equipment you configured and reconfigure those which do not operate properly.

When you enter the AutoCAD drawing editor, if you have a digitizer, notice that the entire surface of the digitizer tablet represents the screen. The tablet menu will not work until you use the TABLET command to configure it. This is explained in detail in Appendix J. After the tablet is configured, this information is added to the ACAD.CFG file, which is saved in the \ACADR13\DOS subdirectory.

ALTERNATE CONFIGURATIONS

The ACAD.CFG file contains all of the information needed to allow AutoCAD to work with the equipment you specified during configuration. It also includes information about the screen and tablet menus, and additional system variable settings. As you gain experience with AutoCAD, you will use additional configurations of tablet and screen menus, and possibly different input devices. Creating and maintaining multiple configuration files is discussed in Appendix C, Hard Disk Management. If you plan to work with projects that require different menus, become familiar with multiple configuration techniques. These eliminate the need to reconfigure the tablet and load new menus each time you begin a new project or work on a different drawing.

SYSTEM REQUIREMENTS FOR AUTOCAD RELEASE 13

AutoCAD is the industry standard design and drafting software for desktop computers and workstations. One reson for AutoCAD's popularity over the years has been its consistent technical superiority.

This Appendix lists the system requirements for AutoCAD Release 13 and outlines the hardware, software, and data exchange options available for this latest AutoCAD release. It is intended to be used as a guide for configuring the AutoCAD system that best meets your needs. Your local authorized AutoCAD dealer will provide you with detailed information about system configuration options and assist you in selecting the platform, peripherals, and companion programs that are right for you. See the AutoCAD Release 13 *Installation Guide for DOS* for detailed information on peripheral configurations and settings.

SOFTWARE AND HARDWARE

The following software and hardware, unless noted as optional, is required to run AutoCAD Release 13.

- DOS 5.0 or later
- Intel 386, Intel 486, Pentium processor or compatible
- 80387 math coprocessor (or 80486 internal)
- 8 MB of RAM (minimum)
- 26 MB of hard disk space
- 20 MB of disk swap space (minimum)
- 1.44 MB, 3 1/2-inch, or 1.2 MB, 5 1/4-inch floppy drive
- A video display adapter
- IBM-compatible parallel port
- Hardware lock (for networks and single-user international version only)

The following hardware is optional:

- Mouse or supported digitizing tablet
- Printer/plotter
- Serial port (for digitizers and some plotters)
- CD-ROM drive for running AutoCAD in both DOS and Windows formats.

Video graphics boards and chip sets		
Manufacturer	**Graphics boards**	**Chip sets**
ATI Technologies	VGA Wonder XL, Graphics Ultra	ATI 28800
	Graphics Ultra	ATI38800
	Graphics Ultra & Ultra Plus/Pro	ATI 68800
Compaq	QVision	Compaq LTE
	Advanced VGA	Compaq QVision
Diamond Computer	Stealth	S3 911
	Stealth 24	S3 801/805
	Stealth VRAM	S3 924
	Stealth Pro	S3 928
	SpeedStar	Tseng ET 4000
	SpeedStar 24	Western Digital 90C31
	Viper VLB	Weitek P9000
Focus Information	2themax 6700	Oak Technology 0x7
Genoa	Windows VGA 24	Cirrus 542x
	Super VGA 6400 AV	Genoa GVGA
IBM	18514/a with expansion kit	IBM 8514/a
	IXGA, XGA with 512 KB memory	IBM XGA
	IVGA, Compaq VGA	IBM VGA, WDAVGA
Matrox	MG 1xx Series	Western Digital 95C00/01
	HiPER VGA	S3 911
Metheus	Premier	CnT 82C452
	Premier 1 meg	ET 4000
Nth Graphics	150	CnT 82C481, CnT 82C480
Number Nine	#9GXe	S3 928
Orchid Technology	Fahrenheit VA, VA-LB	S3 801,S3 805
	Fahrenheit 1280	S3 911, S3 924
	Pro Designer	Tseng ET 3000
	Pro Designer II	Tseng ET 4000
Paradise	VGA 1024	Western Digital 90C00
	Value Card	Oak 0x7
Trident	TVGA 8916	Trident 8900
Truevision	TARGA+	TARGA+
	SVGA & GUI-X Boards	VESA 1.1
Video 7	VRAM	Headland HT205
	1024i	Headland HT208
	VRAM II	Headland HT209
Null display		

Digitizers supported by AutoCAD	
Driver files	**Company**
(internal)	Real-mode ADI versions 4.0 and 4.1 or earlier
(internal)	Protected-mode ADI
dgcal.exp	CalComp® Drawing Board 25120 and 25180
	CalComp 2500 Series tablets
	CalComp Drawing Board II 3300 Series
dgphit.exp	Hitachi® HDG Series tablets
dgkur1.exp	Kurta® Tablet IS/ONE
dgkur23.exp	Kurta Tablet XLC
	Kurta Tablet IS/THREE
dgpsg.exp	Kurta Tablet XLP
dgpms.exp	Microsoft Mouse
	Mouse Systems Mouse PC Mouse II IBM PS/2 Mouse
dgpsg.exp	Summagraphics® MioroGrid Series II (or later)
	Summagraphics SummaSketch® MM Series
	Summagraphics SummaSketch II
	Summagraphics SummaSketch III
(internal)	Null pointing device

Plotters supported by AutoCAD		
Driver file	**Plotter**	**Model**
plexport.exp	Raster file format	BMP GIF Fax Image FITS IFF/ILBM PBM PCX PostScript Image Sun Rasterfile TGA TIFF XWD
plpadi.exp	Real-mode ADI	
plpcan.exp	Canon Laser Beam printer	LBP-4 LBP-8 mkII/III
plpcanbj.exp *rhpcanbj.exp*	Canon Bubble Jet printer	BJ-200 BJ-230 BJC-600 BJC-800
plpcc.exp	CalComp ColorMaster plotter	Plus 6613VRC Plus 6603VRC 5913* 5912* 5902A*
plpcc.exp	CalComp DrawingMaster plotter	Pro 52436 Pro 52424 Plus 52236
plpcc.exp	CalComp Electrostatic plotter	68444 Color EPP 68436 Color EPP 67436 Mono EPP 58444 Color EPP* 58436 Color EPP* 58424 Color EPP* 57444 Mono* 57436 Mono* 57424 Mono*
plpcc.exp	CalComp pen plotter	1043*, 1044* Artisan 1023* Artisan 1025* Artisan 1026* Designmate 3024 Designmate 3036 Pacesetter 2024 Pacesetter 2036 Classic 4036
ppep.exp	Epson printer	9 pin (parallel) 24 pin
plpfile.exp	AutoCAD file format	ASCII plot file Binary plot file Binary printer/plot

Plotters supported by AutoCAD (continued)		
Driver file	**Plotter**	**Model**
plphlp.exp	Houston Instument DMP plotter	DMP-51* DMP-51MP* DMP-52* DMP-52MP* DMP-56* DMP-56MP* DMP-61* DMP-61MP* DMP-62 DMP-62MP DMP-161 DMP-162 DMP-162R
plhpgl2.exp	Hewlett-Packard plotter (HP-GL/2)	7600 Color* 7600 Mono* DesignJet 200 DesignJet 600 DesignJet 650C DraftMaster Roll Feed DraftMaster SX/RX/MX DraftPro Plus Series LaserJet III, 4 Series PaintJet XL300
plphplj.exp	Hewlett-Packard LaserJet printer (PCL)	LaserJet II LaserJet II w/1.5 MB LaserJet III LaserJet III w/1+ MB LaserJet 4 Series
plphplp.exp	Hewlett-Packard plotters (HP-GL)	7475 7550 7580 7585 7586 7586B Roll Feed 7596A Roll Feed DraftMaster I* DraftPro DXL DraftPro EXL
plphppj.exp	Hewlett-Packard color printer (PCL)	DeskJet 500C DeskJet 550C PaintJet (parallel)
rhppj.exp	Hewlett-Packard PaintJet printer (PCL)	DeskJet 500C DeskJet 550C PaintJet (parallel)
rhprtl.exp	Hewlett-Packard plotter	7600 Color* 7600 Mono* DesignJet 200 DesignJet 600 DesignJet 650C
	Null plotter	
plppost.exp	PostScript laser printer	300 dpi 600 dpi 1270 dpi
plppro.exp	IBM ProPrinter	ProPrinter III ProPrinter III XL ProPrinter XL ProPrinter XL24 ProPrinter X24E

Appendix C

HARD DISK AND SYSTEM MANAGEMENT

Any business–be it a bakery or engineering firm–relies on structure, organization, and standard procedures. A business lacking in one of these areas does not operate efficiently. The widespread use of computers in business and industry has introduced another facet to business operations. Computer systems can be used within the company structure for organization and procedure; or computers can contain the structure and organize procedures. In either case, the method in which computer systems are managed greatly affects the operation of the entire company.

Effective management of an AutoCAD system in a school or business means paying careful attention to the following items:

- The structure and makeup of the hard disk.
- The location of all files and drawings.
- Storage procedures for student/employee drawing files.
- Drawing file backup procedures.
- The kind of prototype drawings used for specific projects.
- The location and use of symbol libraries and reference drawings.
- The location and use of special screen and tablet menus.
- Drawing naming procedures.
- Drawing file creation procedures.
- Creation and distribution of new symbols and menus.
- Timely updating of software and hardware.
- Hardware maintenance.

Effective procedures and management techniques must be practiced by all students or employees. In addition, look for ways that the standards can be improved and revised for greater efficiency. Read the section in Chapter 1 on system management and the section in Chapter 25 on creating and using symbol libraries.

DOS HARD DISK STRUCTURE

The hard disk drive is the heart of the AutoCAD computer system. It is the storage center for AutoCAD and other programs you use. In addition, it may hold hundreds of additional files, including drawings, menus, AutoLISP programs, slides, scripts, and text files. The manner in which you work with the hard disk and arrange its contents can affect your productivity and efficiency at the computer. Take some time to learn the nature of the hard disk drive.

The root directory and its contents

The root directory is the trunk of the hard disk tree from which every other directory, subdirectory, and file branches. After your computer is set up and DOS installed, the root directory contains only a DOS directory. See Figure C-1. No other programs are on the hard disk. In addition to the DOS directory, three files occupy the root directory–COMMAND.COM, CONFIG.SYS, and AUTOEXEC.BAT.

Figure C-1.   The root directory
contains only the DOS directory
when the computer is set up
and DOS is installed.

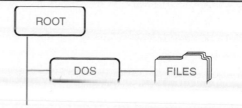

Before a program is installed on the hard disk, a directory should first be created. (Most programs create their own directory during installation.) The program files are copied into that directory. Program files should not be placed in the root directory. The default name for the AutoCAD directory is ACADR13, and all AutoCAD files reside in its subdirectories. After AutoCAD is installed, the structure of the hard disk resembles Figure C-2.

Figure C-2.   AutoCAD files are
stored in the ACADR13
directory.

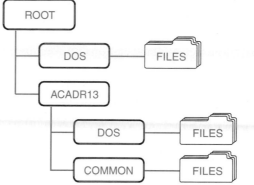

The AutoCAD installation program creates a directory tree that contains a location for files required by the DOS version. In addition, a shared subdirectory, named COMMON, is created in which files are stored that can be used by both the DOS and Windows versions of Release 13. Thus, after installation, the ACADR13 directory is completely free of files, and contains only the two subdirectories mentioned above. See Figure C-2.

The files that reside in the ACADR13 subdirectories after the software is installed are the only ones that need to be there. Any files that you create should be stored in either the appropriate subdirectory, or in new subdirectories. See Chapter 17 for information on creating and working with directories. Additional information is provided in this Appendix for creating and maintaining an efficient directory tree.

Designing and building a hard disk tree

When you install AutoCAD using the INSTALL program provided on the disks, several subdirectories are automatically created depending on which files you instruct AutoCAD to install. These subdirectories are created so that the ACADR13 directory is not filled with files it does not need. Take some time to look at the contents of these subdirectories and notice the files that are stored there.

PROFESSIONAL TIP

If you are responsible for hard disk organization and management in your school or company, it is a good idea to keep a printed copy of the contents of each subdirectory. Get a print of each directory and subdirectory immediately after installing the software. Periodically check the contents of each directory and look for unnecessary files. Compare the contents with your printed list. Then, delete all unnecessary files.

You can automate this process with a batch file. This file can delete all file types, such as .DWG, that are not supposed to be in the directory. See the next section for batch file examples and instructions.

After installing the software, you will be faced with other decisions about where to store new files that must go on the hard disk. Only you can decide which files should be saved on the hard disk and where they are to be saved. Regardless of the decisions you make, they should be based on careful consideration of the following:

Questions to ask

✓ Are the computers used for training or production?
✓ Will the computers be used for demonstrations?
✓ Will the system hardware be upgraded often?
✓ How often will drawings be saved to the hard disk?
✓ How many drawings, from how many users, are to be saved on the hard disk?
✓ Will custom menus, AutoLISP, and ADS programs be used?
✓ Will users have their own subdirectories?

Points to consider

✓ Load new software in its own directory.
✓ Store nonessential files in subdirectories of the parent software directory.
✓ Use short names or abbreviations for directory names.
✓ If you have multiple hard drives, leave an empty buffer of at least five megabytes per hard drive for workspace over and above the working space required by software such as AutoCAD.
✓ If users have their own subdirectory, encourage them to work in it, not in the program directory.

When you answer these questions, and keep these points in mind, you can better estimate what to store on the hard disk and how it should be structured.

Regardless of what you store on the hard disk, have a plan for it. Drawings should not be saved in the ACADR13 directory. Users should not be allowed to save files in the root directory. Decide on the nature of the hard disk structure and then stick to it. Make sure that all users are informed by documenting and distributing standard procedures to all who use the system. Place copies of procedures at each workstation.

Files to be used in conjunction with AutoCAD should be located in subdirectories of the ACADR13 directory. Possible subdirectories include drawings, AutoLISP files, drivers, slides, and user directories. Within each of these subdirectories reside the individual files. This is clearly illustrated in Figure C-3. The subdirectories of \ACADR13 in Figure C-3 are some of those that are automatically created when AutoCAD is installed. If you plan to store files within the AutoCAD directory tree, plan on creating new subdirectories with names such as DRAWINGS, LISP, and SCRIPTS. When specific types of files are kept in their own subdirectory, file maintenance is easier.

Your hard disk planning should take into account future software. New programs should be stored in their own directories on the hard disk, and managed in the same fashion as the AutoCAD files. The structure of a well-planned and closely managed hard disk should appear like that shown in Figure C-4.

USING BATCH FILES FOR AUTOCAD EFFICIENCY

After turning on your system, the computer checks itself, and the COMMAND.COM file (the DOS command interpreter) searches for a file named AUTOEXEC.BAT. If found, this file is executed. The AUTOEXEC.BAT file may simply set the date and time, or establish operating parameters for the entire drawing session. It can also automatically run other batch files.

A batch file (.BAT file extension) is a short DOS program that processes a group of commands. Batch files can be used to display menu selections, perform disk checking functions, and call other programs. Periodic use of special batch files can allow the user to accomplish tasks such as cleaning unwanted files from directories, formatting disks, displaying directory contents, and giving the disk a checkup.

PROFESSIONAL TIP

One of your goals should be to work toward automating as many of the routine functions as possible. Use batch files to help achieve this goal in preliminary set up functions.

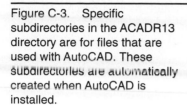

Figure C-3.   Specific subdirectories in the ACADR13 directory are for files that are used with AutoCAD. These subdirectories are automatically created when AutoCAD is installed.

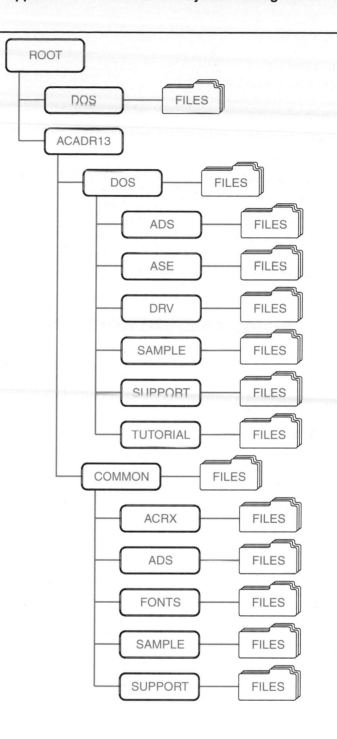

AUTOEXEC.BAT files

The AUTOEXEC.BAT file is one of several files needed in the root directory. After the computer is turned on, it reads the CONFIG.SYS file, then reads the AUTOEXEC.BAT file. If you want to display this file, list the contents of AUTOEXEC.BAT as follows:

C:\⟩ **TYPE AUTOEXEC.BAT** ↵

You may not understand the contents of the file now, but soon you will be writing your own. Several commands you may see in the file are:

- **CLS.** Clears the screen of everything except the DOS prompt.
- **ECHO OFF.** Turns off the display of DOS commands when the batch file is run.

- **PATH.** Indicates the different directories that DOS can search through to find batch files and commands.
- **SET.** Enables you to set specific values and functions.

These commands are discussed later with batch files. For now, take a look at sample AUTOEXEC.BAT files.

Figure C-4.   The directory structure of a well-managed hard disk appears clean and organized.

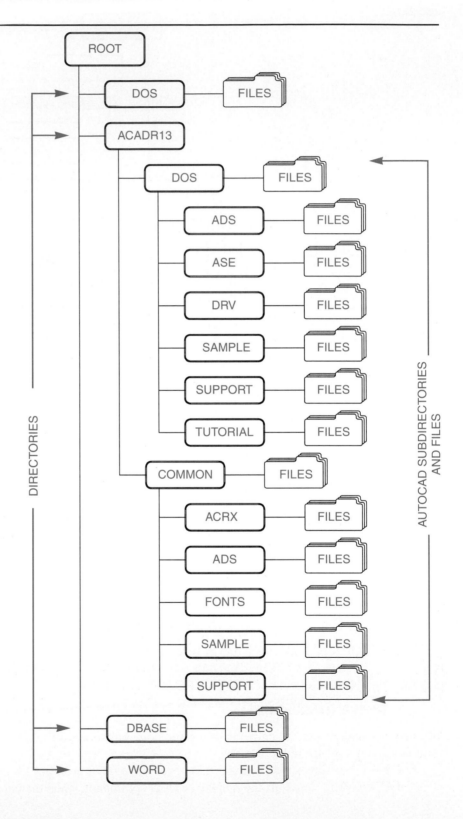

PROFESSIONAL TIP

When experimenting with new AUTOEXEC.BAT files, give them names other than AUTOEXEC.BAT. Names should indicate that the files are preliminary. Typical names might be AUTOTEST.BAT, BATTEST1.BAT, or BATTEST2.BAT. When you develop a file to replace the old AUTOEXEC.BAT file, rename the original AUTOEXEC.OLD, and rename the new one AUTOEXEC.BAT.

AutoCAD's default batch file

When you install AutoCAD, you are asked if you want a batch file automatically created that is named ACADR13.BAT. If you are not sure about constructing batch files, and the settings and commands that they should contain, it is a good idea to let AutoCAD create this batch file for you. Later, when you learn more about batch files, you can easily edit the default file, or even create a new one.

The file named ACADR13.BAT provides AutoCAD with locations for support files, video drivers, and its configuration file. Then, it changes to the directory containing AutoCAD, executes the program, and also allows you to enter a drawing name and script file to run.

```
SET ACAD=C:\ACADR13\COMMON\SUPPORT;C:\ACADR13\DOS;C:\ACADR13\DOS\
SUPPORT;C:\ACADR13\COMMON\FONTS
SET ACADCFG=C:\ACADR13\DOS
SET ACADDRV=C:\ACADR13\DOS\DRV
C:\ACADR13\DOS\ACAD %1 %2
```

The last line loads AutoCAD and allows you to enter a drawing name to begin or edit (%1), and executes a script file that has already been written (%2). The script file can perform any additional operations you desire. The following is an example of a simple setup script file.

SETUP.SCR

VIEW	(executes the VIEW command)
R	(selects the Restore option of VIEW)
TBLOCK	(restores the view named TBLOCK)

In order to run the ACADR13.BAT file to load an existing prototype drawing named PIPEPROT, enter the following at the DOS prompt.

C:\ ⟩ **ACADR13 PIPEPROT SETUP** ↵

This not only runs the ACADR13 batch file, but loads the PIPEPROT drawing and displays the view of the title block as specified in the file SETUP.SCR.

In the next three sample batch files, notice that the ACADR13.BAT file is called at the end of each file. This is a good example of how one batch file can run another.

Batch file 1

Batch files can be written using the COPY CON command in DOS, EDLIN, or a text editor such as the DOS EDIT text editor. A text editor gives you the greatest flexibility in creating and editing batch files. Enter the lines given here exactly as shown, pressing ENTER at the end of each line.

This first batch file allows the user to set the date and time. Then it clears the screen, changes to the ACADR13 directory, and executes AutoCAD. Give this file the name ACADBAT1.BAT.

```
DATE
TIME
CLS
CD \ACADR13
ACADR13
```

Run this program by entering the filename at the DOS prompt:

C:\ > **ACADBAT1** ⏎

Batch files can be executed by entering the name without the file .BAT extension.

As the batch file begins, the DATE and TIME prompts appear and ask for the date and time. The commands appear only because the DOS command ECHO is ON. All commands in the batch file are displayed on the screen. You can prevent displaying these commands by inserting ECHO OFF at the start of your batch file. Notice also that the batch file does not begin with a CLS (Clear screen) command. Any text left on the screen from previous computer self-checks, DOS commands, or batch files still shows. Finally, the last line in the ACADBAT1.BAT file runs the ACADR13.BAT file in order to properly load AutoCAD. This file and the ACADR13 file can easily be combined into one file and function exactly the same. When you exit AutoCAD, the DOS prompt does not reflect the current directory. Revise this batch file as shown below to incorporate the items just discussed. Comments are contained inside parentheses; do not type them.

```
ECHO OFF        (turns off the display of DOS commands)
CLS             (clears the screen)
PROMPT $P$G     (sets DOS prompt to reflect current directory)
DATE
TIME
CLS
CD \ACADR13
ACADR13
```

Run this file and compare it to the previous version. The DATE and TIME commands do not have to be included in the AUTOEXEC.BAT file if your computer has an internal clock and battery backup.

Batch file 2

This batch file is a bit more specific in its instructions. The function of the file is to set the operating *environment* for AutoCAD, and then execute the program. The environment is modified by the values given in the SET and PATH commands. The PATH provides a route for DOS to use when searching for files. Name this file ACADBAT2.BAT.

```
ECHO OFF
CLS
PROMPT $P$G
PATH = C:\;\DOS;\ACADR13
SET ACADALTMENU=C:\CADPIPE\PIPING
SET ACADPAGEDIR=C:\TEMP
ACADR13
CD \
```

This batch file is a little more involved than the previous one. It contains three new lines that should be examined closer.

- **PATH=C:\;\DOS\ACAD.** The PATH is the route DOS uses to search for programs, commands, and batch files. The path is most often different directories, which are separated by a semicolon (;). In this example, DOS first searches through the root directory, then the DOS directory, and finally the ACAD directory.
- **SET ACADALTMENU=C:\CADPIPE\PIPING.** This environment variable specifies the location of the alternate menu that is used when the CHANGE TEMPLATE command is picked on the tablet menu. See *AutoCAD and its Applications—Advanced, R13 for DOS* for a discussion of this process.
- **SET ACADPAGEDIR=C:\TEMP.** This environment variable provides a location for "pages" of a drawing file that is being worked on. AutoCAD divides drawings into pages and places these pages in memory. If the allotted memory space fills, the "pager" removes the least

recently accessed page and places it as a file in the current directory. If the ACADPAGEDIR variable has been set prior to entering AutoCAD, the page file is placed in the location specified by the variable, in this case, the C:\TEMP directory.

PROFESSIONAL TIP

AutoCAD contains several *environment variables* that enable you to fine-tune the operating environment in which AutoCAD is placed. An environment variable generally specifies an exact value for a specific aspect of AutoCAD's operation. Since AutoCAD requires considerable memory and can be tailored to suit any user, it is important that you become familiar with some of the settings that can make the program work efficiently for you. Read the Installation Guide for DOS and the *AutoCAD Customization Guide* for specific information on environment variables and memory management. Using some of these variables in your batch files can enhance the operation of the software and hardware.

The previous batch file is typical of AUTOEXEC.BAT files used on AutoCAD systems. You can add a variety of functions to the AUTOEXEC.BAT file, such as displaying a menu or maintaining the hard disk.

MENU SELECTIONS

New computer users should not be required to deal with the step-by-step functions of DOS and AutoCAD. Therefore, the goal of designing menus is to automate tasks as much as possible. The repetitive functions of commands should be transparent, so that the user can spend more productive time working with drawing and design. With batch files, you can automate execution of programs and DOS functions.

A good menu displays a list of program options. This allows the user to enter a number in response to a list of programs. An example of such a menu is shown below.

AutoCAD Training Center
MAIN MENU

1. AutoCAD
2. 3D Studio
3. Softdesk Civil
4. AutoCAD LT
5. Dbase
6. Text Editor
7. Utilities Menu

TYPE THE NUMBER OF YOUR CHOICE AND PRESS ENTER

The user merely decides which program to use, types a number, and presses ENTER. The program automatically loads. This removes many possible errors and frustrations from novice users trying to enter the exact directory and file names.

NOTE TO INSTRUCTORS AND TRAINERS

People learning AutoCAD, or any computer program for the first time, should be taught that specific program only. Do not request that they wade through the many details of entering DOS commands. That can come later. Make the entrance into AutoCAD as smooth as possible. Menus help avoid some of those problems.

The menu screen just shown is not a batch file. Its a text file (.TXT) that is called by the AUTOEXEC.BAT file. The menu, possibly named MENU.TXT, is written with a text editor exactly as you see it. Each of the selections in the menu execute their own batch file. An example of an AUTOEXEC.BAT file that calls the above menu is as follows:

```
ECHO OFF
CLS
PROMPT $P$G
PATH=C:\;\DOS;\BAT;\ACADR13;\3DS4\SDC;\ACADLT;\DBASE;\TE
CD \BAT
TYPE MENU.TXT
```

PROFESSIONAL TIP

Create a new directory called BAT if you will be using batch and text files in menus and other applications. This helps keep the root directory clean.

This AUTOEXEC.BAT file is brief because additional values that must be set for individual programs are specified in the batch files for those programs. Notice that the PATH command lists several new directories. Each program should have its own directory. The last line displays the MENU.TXT file using the TYPE command.

PROFESSIONAL TIP

You can eliminate the need to use several different batch files in a menu system like the one described here. Software utilities are available commercially that enable you to create menus that require only a single keystroke to activate a selection. In addition, you can custom design the menu appearance. One such utility, called Batch Enhancer, found in the Norton Utilities software, allows you to create a single batch file to run an entire menu.

The individual selections in the Main Menu must now be established as batch files. Since the user enters a number in response to the menu selections, the names of batch files must correspond to numbers. For example, the batch file to run AutoCAD must be 1.BAT. The batch file that calls the Utilities Menu must be 7.BAT. An example of 1.BAT is shown as follows:

```
ECHO OFF
CLS
SET ACAD=C:\ACADR13\COMMON\SUPPORT;C:\ACADR13\DOS;
   C:\ACADR13\DOS\SUPPORT;C:\ACADR13\COMMON\FONTS
SET ACADCFG=C:\ACADR13\DOS
SET ACADDRV=C:\ACADR13\DOS\DRV
SET ACADPAGEDIR=C:\TEMP
C: \ACADR13\DOS\ACAD %1 %2
CLS
CD \BAT
TYPE MENU.TXT
```

This batch file does not have to set the PATH because that was taken care of by the AUTOEXEC.BAT file. Notice also that when the user exits AutoCAD, the current directory is changed to BAT, and the Main Menu is redisplayed.

The Utilities Menu can contain disk functions that enable you to perform hard disk organizing, floppy disk formatting, and other tasks. The batch file 7.BAT calls the Utilities Menu and should appear like this:

```
ECHO OFF
CLS
TYPE UTIL.TXT
```

This short batch file displays the Utilities Menu, which is also a TXT file, the same as MENU.TXT. The UTIL.TXT file looks like this:

```
                    AutoCAD Training Center
                       UTILITIES MENU
M.  Return to Main Menu
A.  Format a diskette in drive A:
B.  Fomat a disk in drive B:
D.  Defragment the hard disk
S.  Scan a disk in A: for virus
TYPE THE LETTER OF YOUR CHOICE AND PRESS ENTER
```

The functions shown above are just a few possibilities that you might choose. Letters are used instead of numbers because batch files in the Main Menu use numbers. Keep in mind that menus should not contain an overwhelming number of selections.

The individual batch files that perform the functions listed in the menu above are given as follows:

A. Format a diskette in drive A:

It is wise to have this command in a menu, especially in a training environment. (The mere sound of the word FORMAT sends shivers down the spine of instructors and managers. Many users have accidentally erased the hard disk with FORMAT.) When this menu selection is made, the user can format a disk only in drive A:. This file can be made safer by renaming the FORMAT.COM command and using the new name in the batch file. The batch file is named F.BAT to correspond to the menu selection.

```
ECHO OFF
CLS
FORMAT A:
CLS
TYPE UTIL.TXT
```

Quick and easy. The user never sees the commands. After entering A, and pressing ENTER, insert a diskette in drive A: when the computer prompts, and press ENTER. The formatting is performed by line 3 in the batch file. Look at the line closely. The FORMAT command is applied to drive A: only. The batch file named B.BAT would be exactly the same as A.BAT, except the third line reads FORMAT B:.

D. Defragment the hard disk

Through normal use of a computer, the hard disk drive begins to fragment files because it does not put data back where it found them. Over several weeks, accessing data on the hard disk slows down as the drive must search far and wide to find all parts of a single file. This can be remedied by any number of commercially available disk organizing programs. Computers that are used every day should have their hard disks organized at least once a month, and preferably once a week. One such program, DEFRAG, is included in DOS 6.x, and is called by the following batch file, named D.BAT.

```
ECHO OFF
CLS
CD \DOS
DEFRAG C: /F
CD \BAT
TYPE UTIL.TXT
```

Even though the C:\DOS directory may be in the current path statement, it is always safe to first change to the appropriate directory before running a program. Notice the /F switch in the line that runs the DEFRAG program. This ensures that when the C: drive is reorganized, there are no spaces left between files on the hard disk. The last line displays the Utilities Menu again.

S. Scan a disk in drive A: for virus

An important safeguard for any computer system is a regular virus-scanning procedure. A wide variety of virus-scanning software is commercially available. Some offer regular updates to protect your system from newly created viruses, and others claim to be able to detect any abnormal alterations of data, thus requiring no updates. The MSAV command (Microsoft Anti-Virus), is available with DOS 6.x, and can be used as protection against most common viruses.

NOTE New viruses are being created all the time, and therefore new "antidotes" must be developed as well. You can keep your anti-virus software up-to-date by contacting the software vendor, or subscribing to an on-line service such as CompuServe. Most vendors post updated files on CompuServe that can be downloaded to your computer via modem in a matter of minutes.

Using DEFRAG to scan a disk for viruses is handled by the S.BAT file shown below.

```
ECHO OFF
CLS
CD \DOS
MSAV C: /C
CD \BAT
TYPE UTIL.TXT
```

The fourth line of this file instructs the MSAV command to scan the C: drive. In addition, the /C switch will clean any detected virus from the drive. See the DOS help file for more information on MSAV settings.

ENSURING EFFICIENT OPERATION

AutoCAD and DOS require a certain amount of reserve memory for efficient operation. AutoCAD opens several files at once, and DOS needs space for input/output operation. To have adequate memory, these parameters must be entered in the CONFIG.SYS file, which the computer looks for when turned on.

The CONFIG.SYS file is a text file that should reside in the root directory. When the computer is booted, DOS reads the CONFIG.SYS file, reserves the amount of memory specified, then runs the AUTOEXEC.BAT file. The CONFIG.SYS file can be written using any text editor. A CONFIG.SYS file should always contain the following two lines:

```
BUFFERS=20
FILES=50
```

The "BUFFERS=20" line states that 20 input/output buffers are reserved for DOS. Each buffer is approximately 520 bytes, or about one-half K of memory. If the CONFIG.SYS file does not exist, DOS sets the default number of two buffers. The more buffers available, the more efficiently the computer and your programs can run because disk access is reduced. Too many buffers can increase the time DOS spends searching the buffers for data. A value between 10 and 20 is recommended. DOS allows up to 99 buffers. AutoCAD contains a DOS extender to handle memory, so the setting for buffers is not important for its operation.

The "FILES=50" line sets the number of open files allowed. AutoCAD opens several files during operation. These include overlays, text fonts, slides, and AutoLISP programs. If too few files are specified by CONFIG.SYS, AutoCAD must temporarily close some open files in order to open others. This can detract from performance of the software. The default value for open files is eight, but should be set to at least 50 for AutoCAD to run efficiently.

SETTING A HEALTHY ENVIRONMENT

Several commands found in the AUTOEXEC.BAT file form what is called the *environment*. The environment is a source of information that programs refer to for specific instructions. The DOS commands that comprise the environment are PATH and SET. The form of these commands is an equation, such as:

    PATH=C:\;\DOS;\ACADR13

This instruction occupies "environment space." If you include too many environment instructions in your AUTOEXEC.BAT and CONFIG.SYS files, the error message "Out of environment space" may appear. This can be remedied by including the following command in the CONFIG.SYS file:

    SHELL=COMMAND.COM /P /E:512

This entry uses the DOS SHELL command, and instructs the COMMAND.COM program to operate as it normally does (/P), but increase the environment space to 512 bytes of memory (/E:512). See your DOS manual for further discussion of the SHELL command. The CONFIG.SYS file should now appear like this:

    BUFFERS=20
    FILES=20
    SHELL=COMMAND.COM /P /E:512

ESTABLISHING MULTIPLE CONFIGURATIONS

When configured, AutoCAD is set up to operate with certain pieces of equipment, using a specific tablet menu and screen menu. These parameters are all stored in the ACAD.CFG file. Some schools and companies may need to change from a digitizer to a mouse, or switch tablet menus for certain applications. It is time-consuming and frustrating to reconfigure AutoCAD each time hardware or menus are switched. This can be avoided by having multiple configurations.

Assessing the need

How do you know if you need multiple configurations? If you answer YES to any of the following questions, multiple configurations will help:
- Do you occasionally switch between different pieces of computer hardware?
- Do you use a mouse for certain applications and a digitizer tablet for others?
- Do you use more than one tablet menu?

Creating batch files for multiple configurations

Multiple configurations can be established through the use of batch files. Two methods can be used to execute the batch files.
1. At the DOS prompt, the user enters the name of a batch file and directory. The configuration specified in that batch file is loaded by AutoCAD. The current directory is set to the one entered after the batch file name. When the SAVE command is entered, the drawing is automatically placed in the current directory.
2. The user chooses a menu selection that executes a batch file. The batch file sets a current directory, searches for a specific configuration, and loads it with AutoCAD.

Method one

With the first method, the user enters the batch file name followed by the name of the directory that contains the desired configuration. The DOS variable "%1 " allows you to provide for user input. This variable is used in the following batch file named STRUCT-1.BAT to specify a directory:

```
ECHO OFF
CLS
CD\%1
SET ACAD=C:\ACADR13\COMMON\SUPPORT;C:\ACADR13\DOS;
  C:\ACADR13\DOS\SUPPORT;C:\ACADR13\COMMON\FONTS
SET ACADCFG=C:\STRUCT
SET ACADDRV=C:\ACADR13\DOS\DRV
SET ACADPAGEDIR=C:\TEMP
ACAD
CD \
```

Look closely at the following three lines in this batch file.
  • **CD\%1.** Changes the current directory to one specified by the user. The "%1" variable is assigned to the first group of characters entered after the batch file name. For example, this batch file is executed by entering STRUCT-1 at the DOS prompt. If a directory name is given after the batch file name, DOS uses the directory name as the "%1" variable. Then DOS sets the current directory to the one entered by the user.

     C:\) **STRUCT-1 PROJ-005** ⏎

     This sets the current directory to PROJ-005.
  • **SET ACAD=C:\ACADR13\COMMON\SUPPORT;C:\ACADR13\DOS;C:\ACADR13\ DOS\SUPPORT;C:\ACADR13\COMMON\FONTS.** This tells AutoCAD to look in the four specified directories for AutoCAD and related files such as hatch patterns, PGP files, shape files for text fonts, LISP routines, and prototype drawings.
  • **SET ACADCFG=C:\STRUCT.** This instructs AutoCAD to look in the STRUCT directory to find the configuration file, ACAD.CFG. This line is important because it allows you to use alternate configurations.

The batch file shown above, STRUCT-1.BAT, should be duplicated if additional configurations are required. Be sure to create separate directories for each project, or configuration. Specify each configuration location with the "SET ACADCFG=" statement.

NOTE The first time you run a batch file that specifies a new directory containing an alternate configuration, AutoCAD requires that you go through the configuration routine. After that, AutoCAD loads each time using the configuration found in the directory specified in the batch file.

Method two

Menus allow users to select exactly what they want to do, without entering DOS commands or specifying directories. It is an efficient method, and maintains consistency in the office or classroom while at the same time eliminating time-wasting errors. The menu system is appropriate where several classes or projects require different configurations. The configurations may be alternative default drawings or prototype drawings. Each prototype drawing might contain a different menu. Thus, with one pick, the user can access a specific project directory and use a prototype drawing that contains the proper screen and tablet menus. One such menu is shown below.

AutoCAD Training Center
PROJECTS MENU

1. AutoCAD Standard Menu
2. Mechanical
3. Structural
4. Piping
5. Electrical
6. Return to MAIN MENU
TYPE THE NUMBER OF YOUR CHOICE AND PRESS ENTER

This menu could be used with the Main Menu discussed earlier in this Appendix. The batch file for the selection 1 AutoCAD in the Main Menu shown on page 1023, AutoCAD should look like this:

```
ECHO OFF
CLS
TYPE PROJ.TXT
```

The PROJ.TXT file would be a text file that looks exactly like the Projects menu.

PROFESSIONAL TIP

When using more than one menu, you cannot use the same numbers for menu selections if the batch files reside in the same directory. If numbers are used in the Main Menu, continue with higher numbers in the Projects Menu, or use letters instead. A second solution is to create a new directory for batch and text files relating to the Projects Menu. Then, the numbers for the menu items can duplicate those in the Main Menu. For example, the batch file for the selection 1, AutoCAD, in the Main Menu might read:

```
ECHO OFF
CLS
CD \BAT2
TYPE PROJ.TXT
```

In this case, the directory must be changed to BAT2 where the files for the Project Menu are stored.

With method two, batch files in the Project Menu are the same as those in method one except for the directory names. The batch file must specify the name of the current directory. An example of the batch file for the selection 4, Piping, is given. It must be understood that each of the projects has its own directory on the hard disk.

```
ECHO OFF
CLS
CD\PIPE\DWG
SET ACAD=C:\ACADR13\COMMON\SUPPORT;C:\ACADR13\DOS;C:\ACADR13\DOS
    \SUPPORT;C:\ACADR13\COMMON\FONTS
SET ACADCFG=C:\PIPE
SET ACADPAGEDIR=C:\TEMP
ACAD
CD \BAT
TYPE MENU.TXT
```

With this batch file, the user does not need to specify a path when saving an AutoCAD drawing. The drawing is saved in the current directory specified in the batch file.

USEFUL BATCH FILES

With a little time and experimenting, you will find that batch files have a variety of applications. These functions can be executed by entering the name of the batch file or by accessing batch files from a menu. Set aside a few minutes each day to develop useful batch files for your applications. The reward is a smooth-functioning system that removes the routine nature of many tasks.

The following examples will help you get started. Enter them exactly as given with your text editor. Remember, batch files are executed by entering the name of the file at the DOS prompt. Adding the BAT extension is not required to run the file.

Looking through several directories

This file is useful in training situations when the instructor or trainer needs to check whether students have saved their required exercises, problems, or drawings. The batch file searches the selected directories and lists files. You can specify certain file types, or display the entire contents of a directory. Any number of directories can be included in this file. The batch file name might be LOOK.BAT. Alternative B allows you to enter specific directory names after typing LOOK.BAT.

```
A.  ECHO OFF              B.  ECHO OFF
    CLS                       CLS
    CD \DIR-1                 CD \%I
    DIR *.DWG/P               DIR *.DWG/P
    PAUSE                     PAUSE
    CD \DIR-2                 CD \%2
    DIR*.DWG/P                DIR *.DWG/P
    PAUSE                     PAUSE
    CD \                      CD \
```

Delete backup files from a drawing directory

As drawings are edited and resaved, a collection of BAK files begins to accumulate. If you regularly backup the drawing files on separate disks, these files are not needed. To reclaim valuable space on the hard disk, use this batch file, possibly named DELBAK.BAT.

```
ECHO OFF
CLS
CD\PROJ-002
DEL *.BAK
CD \
```

Delete drawings that do not belong

Try to keep the ACAD directory free of nonessential files. Create subdirectories for DWG, LSP, and SLD files. Nonessential files have a way of creeping into the most guarded directories, especially in an instructional environment. A handy batch file is one that can delete those wayward files and leave the essential ones intact. The following batch file deletes all DWG files in the \ACADR13 directory. (Make sure needed drawings are stored in the proper directory first.) The file name might be ACAD-PURG.BAT or DELDWG.BAT.

```
ECHO OFF
CLS
CD \ACADR13
DEL *.DWG
DIR/P
PAUSE
CD \
```

MANAGING THE AUTOCAD SYSTEM

One of your goals as an AutoCAD user should be to keep the computer system as efficient as possible. This means being organized and knowledgeable of school or company standards. Also know who has the authority to manage the system, and follow the system manager's guidelines.

If you are the system manager, develop standards and procedures, relay these to system users, and distribute up-to-date documentation, symbol libraries, menus, and standards. Revise standards as needed and distribute these to all users. In addition, handle software updates in a consistent and timely manner and make the maintenance of hardware a priority.

The system manager

One or two people, depending on the size of the department or company, should be assigned as system manager. The manager has control over all functions of the computer system, preventing inconsistencies in procedure, drawing format, and file storage caused by lack of organization and structure. The manager is responsible for the following:

- Scheduling computer use.
- Structure of the hard disk directories.
- Appearance and function of start-up menus.
- Drawing naming techniques.
- File storage procedures.
- File backup procedures.
- Drawing file access.
- Creation of symbol libraries.
- Development of written standards.
- Distribution of standards to users.
- Upgrading software and hardware.
- Hardware hygiene and maintenance.

When tasks are delegated, such as the creation of symbol library shapes, be sure to include accurate sketches or drawings. Check and approve final drawings before distributing them to users.

Developing operating standards and procedures

The crux of system management is that everyone performs their job using the same procedures, symbols, and drawing techniques. When this happens, the details of drawing and designing are transparent because they are established routines. A department that operates smoothly is probably using standards such as the following:

- File naming conventions.
- Methods of file storage: location and name.
- Drawing sheet sizes and title blocks to be used.
- Prototype drawings.
- Creation of blocks and symbols.
- Dimensioning techniques.
- Use of dimensioning variables.
- Use of layers and colors.
- Text styles.
- Line types.
- Color schemes for plotting.
- Creation of screen and tablet menus.
- File backup methods and times.

Take the time initially to study the needs of your school or company. Meet with other department managers and users to determine the nature of their drawings. Always gain input from people who use the system and avoid making blanket decisions on your own. When needs have been established, develop a plan for implementing the required standards and procedures. Assign specific tasks to students or employees. Assemble the materials as they are completed and distribute the documentation and procedures to all users.

When developing procedures, begin with start-up procedures and work through the drawing process. Develop prototype drawings for specific types of projects first. The final aspects of system development should be screen and tablet menus and AutoLISP programs.

File maintenance

The integrity of files must be protected by all who work with the system. Procedures for file maintenance must be documented. Files of every type, including DWG, SLD, BAT, LSP, .MNU, and BAK must have a secure storage area. This can be hard disk directories, floppy disks or magnetic tape storage areas, kept clean of nonessential files. File maintenance procedures should include the following:

- Location of essential AutoCAD files.
- Location of backup AutoCAD files.
- Print the contents of all hard disk directories for each workstation.
- Location and contents of all prototype drawings, supplemented with printed listings.
- Location and contents of all batch files and associated menus.
- Location of all user files including drawings, slides, and text files.
- Proper creation of drawings using prototypes, layers, dimensioning techniques, linetypes, text styles, and symbols.
- Storage and backup methods for drawing files.
- Storage of printed or plotted copies of all drawing files.

Symbol libraries and menus

The development of symbol libraries and menus is a primary concern of managing an AutoCAD system. Symbols must be consistent and up-to-date. Menus must also be consistent throughout the department or company. A vital aspect of maintaining standards and consistency is a facility for updating symbol libraries and menus. This task should be given to certain students or employees and the results distributed to all users. Maintaining symbol libraries and menus includes the following:

- Standards for drawing symbols.
- System for naming symbols (blocks).
- System for block storage.
- Post a printed or plotted copy of all symbol libraries, their names, and locations.
- Creation and maintenance of custom screen and tablet menus.
- Use of custom menus by specific departments.
- Revisions to custom menus.
- Upgrading of menus on all hard disks.

Maintaining the software

Software upgrades and releases are issued regularly. If you purchase upgrades, converting to the new version should be smooth and have little, if any, effect on production. Establish a procedure for upgrading all computers in the classroom or office. Inform all users of changes by providing a printed listing of new features. Offer training sessions on the new release if necessary. Make backup copies of the new software and store the originals in a safe place.

Maintain the management system

All systems require continuous maintenance to function efficiently. Enable users to contribute to the function of the system. Foster creativity by inviting suggestions from users. Meet with users and managers on a regular basis to learn what is functioning well and what is not. Remember, the system will function efficiently if a majority of those using it enjoy working with the system, and are encouraged to contribute to its growth and development.

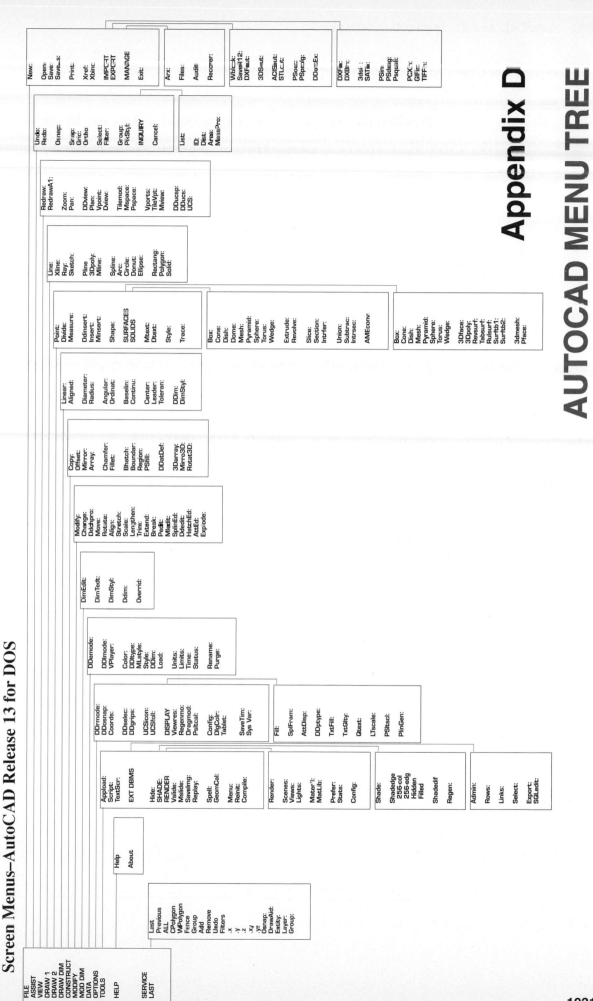

Screen Menus–AutoCAD Release 13 for DOS

Appendix D

AUTOCAD MENU TREE

Pull-Down and Cascading Menus–AutoCAD Release 13 for DOS

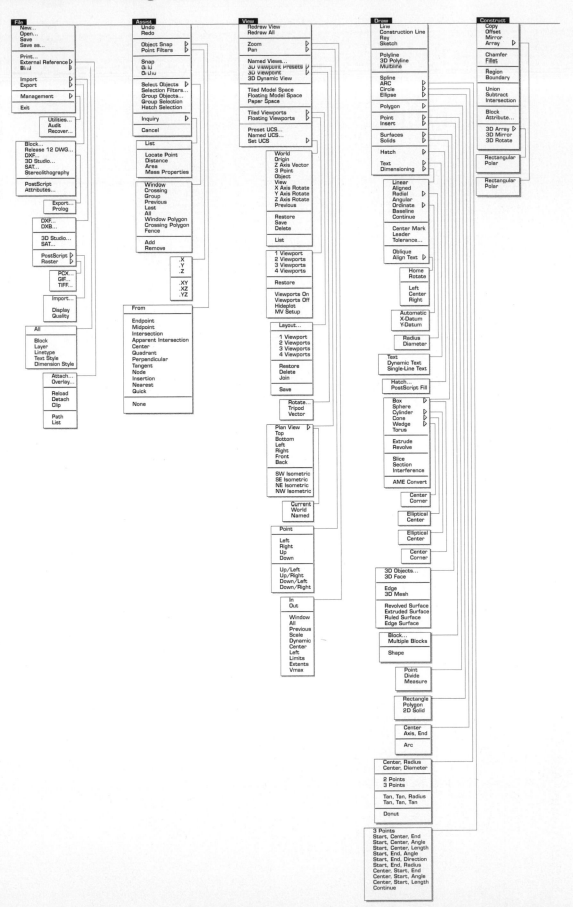

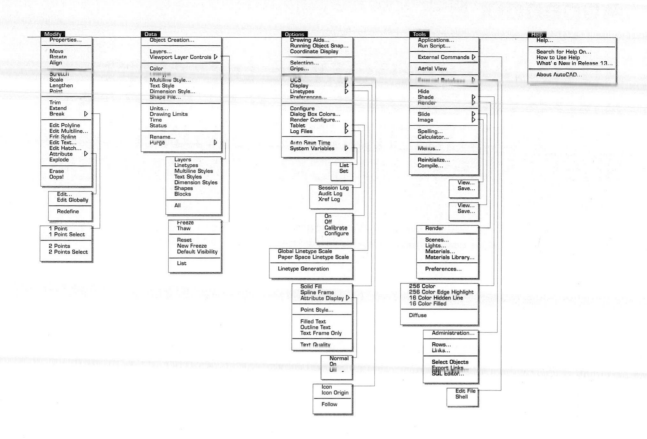

Modify
Properties...

Move
Rotate
Align

Stretch
Scale
Lengthen
Point

Trim
Extend
Break   ▷

Edit Polyline
Edit Multiline...
Edit Spline
Edit Text...
Edit Hatch...   ▷
Attribute
Explode

Erase
Oops!

Edit...
Edit Globally

Redefine

1 Point
1 Point Select

2 Points
2 Points Select

Data
Object Creation...

Layers...
Viewport Layer Controls ▷

Color
Linetype
Multiline Style...
Text Style
Dimension Style...
Shape File...

Units...
Drawing Limits
Time
Status

Rename...
Purge   ▷

Layers
Linetypes
Multiline Styles
Text Styles
Dimension Styles
Shapes
Blocks

All

Freeze
Thaw

Reset
New Freeze
Default Visibility

List

Options
Drawing Aids...
Running Object Snap...
Coordinate Display

Selection...
Grips...

UCS   ▷
Display   ▷
Linetypes   ▷
Preferences...

Configure
Dialog Box Colors...
Render Configure...
Tablet   ▷
Log Files   ▷

Auto Save Time
System Variables   ▷

List
Set

Session Log
Audit Log
Xref Log

On
Off
Calibrate
Configure

Global Linetype Scale
Paper Space Linetype Scale

Linetype Generation

Solid Fill
Spline Frame
Attribute Display ▷

Point Style...

Filled Text
Outline Text
Text Frame Only

Text Quality

Normal
On
Off

Icon
Icon Origin

Follow

Tools
Applications...
Run Script...

External Commands ▷

Aerial View

External Database ▷

Hide
Shade   ▷
Render   ▷

Slide   ▷
Image   ▷

Spelling...
Calculator...

Menus...

Reinitialize...
Compile...

View...
Save...

View...
Save...

Render

Scenes...
Lights...
Materials...
Materials Library...

Preferences...

256 Color
256 Color Edge Highlight
16 Color Hidden Line
16 Color Filled

Diffuse

Administration...

Rows...
Links...

Select Objects
Export Links...
SQL Editor...

Edit File
Shell

Help
Help...

Search for Help On...
How to Use Help
What's New in Release 13...

About AutoCAD...

Appendix E

AUTOCAD PROTOTYPE DRAWING AND SYSTEM VARIABLE DEFAULTS AND DESCRIPTIONS; DRAWING SHEET SIZES AND SCALE PARAMETERS

The following listing shows the AutoCAD system variables that can be stored within a prototype drawing file. The value of each of these variables is written into the drawing file when the drawing is saved, so that the next time the drawing is opened the values remain the same. Setting the values for most of these variables can be done by entering the associated command or by using the SETVAR command. Some variable values are derived by AutoCAD from the current condition of the drawing or the drawing environment, and cannot be directly set. The variables that cannot be directly set are referred to as "Read-only".

Each listing provides a brief description of the variable and the default setting when no prototype drawing is referenced. The symbol ᜂ (eyeglasses) indicates that the variable is "read-only."

Variable Name	Default Value	Description
ANGBASE	0.0000	Direction for base angle 0 relative to current UCS.
ANGDIR	0	Counter-clockwise or Clockwise angle measurement.
ATTDIA	0	Prompt on Command: line or use Dialog box.
ATTMODE	1	Display mode for block attributes.
ATTREQ	1	Use attribute defaults or request values from user.
AUNITS	0	Format for angular units.
AUPREC	0	Precision of angular units.
BACKZ	ᜂ	Back clipping plane offset from the target plane.
BLIPMODE	1	Controls display of marker blips.
CECOLOR	"BYLAYER"	Color of newly-created objects.
CELTSCALE	1.0000	Individual object linetype scaling for new objects.
CELTYPE	"BYLAYER"	Linetype for newly-created objects.
CHAMFERA	0.0000	First chamfer distance.
CHAMFERB	0.0000	Second chamfer distance.
CHAMFERC	0.0000	Chamfer length.
CHAMFERD	0.0000	Chamfer angle.
CLAYER	"0"	Currently active layer.
COORDS	1	Controls dynamic coordinate updating.
CVPORT	2	Identification number of current viewport.
DELOBJ	1	Controls deletion of objects used to create other objects.
DIMALT	Off	Enables or disables alternate units dimensioning.
DIMALTD	2	Decimal places for alternate units dimensions.
DIMALTF	25.4	Alternate units dimension scale factor.
DIMALTTD	2	Decimal places for alternate units tolerance values.
DIMALTTZ	0	Zero suppression for alternate units tolerance values.
DIMALTU	2	Units format for alternate units dimensions.

Variable Name	Default Value	Description
DIMALTZ	0	Zero suppression for alternate units dimension values.
DIMAPOST	""	Prefix/Suffix for alternate units dimensions.
DIMASO	On	Toggles associative dimensioning.
DIMASZ	0.1800	Dimension line and arrowhead size.
DIMAUNIT	0	Unit format for angular dimension values.
DIMBLK	""	Block name to use for both arrowheads.
DIMBLK1	""	Block name to use for first arrowhead.
DIMBLK2	""	Block name to use for second arrowhead.
DIMCEN	0.0900	Center mark size.
DIMCLRD	0	Dimension line, arrowhead and leader line color.
DIMCLRE	0	Dimension extension line color.
DIMCLRT	0	Dimension text color.
DIMDEC	4	Decimal places for dimension values.
DIMDLE	0.0000	Dimension line extension beyond extension lines.
DIMDLI	0.3800	Incremental spacing between baseline dimensions.
DIMEXE	0.1800	Extension line distance beyond dimension line.
DIMEXO	0.0625	Distance from origin to begin extension line.
DIMFIT	3	Controls placement of text and arrowheads.
DIMGAP	0.0900	Gap size between dimension line and dimension text.
DIMJUST	0	Horizontal justification of dimension text.
DIMLFAC	1.0000	Linear units scale factor for dimension values.
DIMLIM	Off	Toggles creation of limits style dimensions.
DIMPOST	""	Prefix/Suffix for primary units dimension values.
DIMRND	0.0000	Rounding value for dimensions.
DIMSAH	Off	Toggles use of separate arrowhead blocks.
DIMSCALE	1.0000	Global dimension feature scale factor.
DIMSD1	Off	Toggles suppression of first dimension line.
DIMSD2	Off	Toggles suppression of second dimension line.
DIMSE1	Off	Toggles suppression of first extension line.
DIMSE2	Off	Toggles suppression of second extension line.
DIMSHO	On	Controls dynamic update of dimensions while dragging.
DIMSOXD	Off	Suppress dimension lines outside of extension lines.
DIMSTYLE	~	Name of current dimension style.
DIMTAD	0	Toggles placement of text above dimension line.
DIMTDEC	4	Decimal places for primary units tolerance values.
DIMTFAC	1.0000	Scale factor for tolerance text size relative to dimensions.
DIMTIH	On	Orientation of text inside extension lines.
DIMTIX	Off	Toggles forced placement of text between extension lines.
DIMTM	0.0000	Lower tolerance value for limits or toleranced dimensions.
DIMTOFL	Off	Toggles forced dimension line creation.
DIMTOH	On	Orientation of text outside extension lines.
DIMTOL	Off	Toggles creation of tolerance style dimensions.
DIMTOLJ	1	Vertical justification for dimension tolerance text.
DIMTP	0.0000	Upper tolerance value for limits or toleranced dimensions.
DIMTSZ	0.0000	Size for dimension line tick marks instead of arrowheads.
DIMTVP	0.0000	Vertical position of text above/below dimension line.
DIMTXSTY	"STANDARD"	Text style used for dimension text.
DIMTXT	0.1800	Size of dimension text.

Variable Name	Default Value	Description
DIMTZIN	0	Zero suppression for primary units tolerance values.
DIMUNIT	2	Units format for primary dimension values.
DIMUPT	Off	Controls user placement of dimension line/text
DIMZIN	0	Zero suppression for primary units dimensions.
DISPSILH	0	Toggles display of wire frame curve silhouettes.
DRAGMODE	2	Controls object "dragging" feature.
DWGCODEPAGE	⌇	SYSCODEPAGE value when drawing was created.
ELEVATION	0.0000	Current 3D elevation relative to current UCS.
EXPLMODE	1	EXPLODE support for nonuniformly scaled blocks.
EXTMAX	⌇	Upper-right extents of drawing.
EXTMIN	⌇	Lower-left extents of drawing.
FACETRES	0.5	Smoothness of shaded and hidden line removed objects.
FILLETRAD	0.0000	Current fillet radius setting.
FILLMODE	1	Toggles fill for SOLID objects.
FRONTZ	⌇	Front clipping plane offset from the target plane.
GRIDMODE	0	Toggles display of grid.
GRIDUNIT	0.0000, 0.0000	Current grid spacing in drawing units.
HANDLES	⌇	Provides support for applications requiring handle access.
HPBOUND	1	Object type created by BHATCH and BOUNDARY
INSBASE	0.0000, 0.0000	Insertion point set by BASE command.
ISOLINES	4	Number of isolines per surface on 3D objects.
LASTPOINT	0.0000, 0.0000, 0.0000	Last entered UCS coordinates for current space.
LENSLENGTH	⌇	Length of lens in millimeters for perspective view.
LIMCHECK	0	Toggles active limit checking for object creation.
LIMMAX	12.0000, 9.0000	Upper-right limits.
LIMMIN	0.0000, 0.0000	Lower-left limits.
LTSCALE	1.0000	Current global linetype scale.
LUNITS	2	Current display format for linear units.
LUPREC	4	Current linear units precision value.
MIRRTEXT	1	Toggles mirroring technique for text objects.
ORTHOMODE	0	Toggles orthogonal drawing control.
OSMODE	0	Current Object Snap mode bit value.
PDMODE	0	Current POINT object display mode.
PDSIZE	0.0000	Current POINT object display size.
PELLIPSE	0	Controls the object type created with ELLIPSE.
PICKSTYLE	3	Controls group and associative hatch selection.
PLINEGEN	0	Toggles linetype generation along a polyline.
PLINEWID	0.0000	Current polyline width value.
PLOTROTMODE	1	Controls the orientation of plots.
PSLTSCALE	1	Paper space tintype scale factor.
PSQUALITY	75	Controls rendering quality and fill on postscript images.
QTEXTMODE	0	Toggles quick text display mode.
RASTERPREVIEW	0	Toggles drawing preview saving and sets format.
REGENMODE	1	Toggles automatic drawing regeneration.
SHADEDGE	3	Controls edge shading during rendering.
SHADEDIF	70	Sets ratio of diffuse reflective light to ambient light.
SKETCHINC	0.1000	Current SKETCH record increment value.
SKPOLY	0	Toggles creation of polyline objects by SKETCH.

Variable Name	Default Value	Description
SNAPANG	0	Snap/grid rotation angle in current viewport
SNAPBASE	0.0000, 0.0000	Snap/Grid origin point in current viewport.
SNAPISOPAIR	0	Isometric plane for current viewport.
SNAPMODE	0	Toggles snap mode.
SNAPSTYL	0	Current snap style.
SNAPUNIT	1.0000, 1.0000	Snap spacing for current viewport.
SPLFRAME	0	Toggles display of frames for spline-fit polylines.
SPLINESEGS	8	Current number of segments generated for each spline.
SPLINETYPE	6	Current type of spline generation by PEDIT.
SURFTAB1	6	Tabulations generated for RULESURF/ TABSURF, and M direction mesh density for REVSURF/ EDGESURF.
SURFTAB2	6	N direction mesh density for REVSURF and EDGESURF.
SURFTYPE	6	Surface fitting type performed by PEDIT Smooth.
SURFU	6	M direction surface density.
SURFV	6	N direction surface density.
SYSCODEPAGE	∽	System code page specified in *acad.xmf*.
TARGET	∽	Location of target point in current viewport.
TDCREATE	∽	Time and date when the current drawing was created.
TDINDWG	∽	Total editing time for the current drawing.
TDUPDATE	∽	Time and date of last update and save.
TDUSRTIMER	∽	User timer time elapsed.
TEXTFILL	1	Controls fill for Bitstream/True Type/Adobe Type 1 fonts.
TEXTQLTY	50	Resolution for Bitstream/True Type/Adobe Type 1 fonts.
TEXTSIZE	0.2000	Default height of text drawn in current style.
TEXTSTYLE	"STANDARD"	Current text style name.
THICKNESS	0.0000	Current 3D thickness.
TILEMODE	1	Controls access to paper space.
TRACEWID	0.0500	Current width for TRACE objects.
TREEDEPTH	3020	Maximum number of branches for tree-structured spatial index.
UCSFOLLOW	0	Toggles automatic change to plan view of current UCS.
UCSICON	1	Controls the display of the UCSICON.
UCSNAME	∽	Name of the current UCS for the current space.
UCSORG	∽	Origin point for the current UCS for the current space.
UCSXDIR	∽	X direction for the current UCS for the current space.
UCSYDIR	∽	Y direction for the current UCS for the current space.
UNITMODE	0	Current units display format.
VIEWCTR	∽	Center point location for current view in current viewport.
VIEWDIR	∽	Viewing direction of the current view in current viewport.
VIEWMODE	∽	Current viewing mode for the current viewport.
VIEWSIZE	∽	Height of the current view in the current viewport.
VIEWTWIST	∽	View twist angle for current viewport.
VISRETAIN	0	Controls visibility of layers in XREF files.
VSMAX	∽	Upper-right corner of the current viewport virtual screen.
VSMIN	∽	Lower-left corner of the current viewport virtual screen.
WORLDVIEW	1	Controls automatic change of UCS for DVIEW/VPOINT.

This listing shows the AutoCAD system variables that are saved with the AutoCAD configuration. These variables are not associated with or saved in the drawing file. The values will be the same in the next drawing session as they are when you leave the current drawing.

The default values shown here represent the values existing prior to AutoCAD's initial configuration.

Variable Name	Default Value	Description
APERTURE	10	Object snap target aperture height.
AUDITCTL	0	Toggles AutoCAD's creation of an audit file (.adt).
CMDDIA	1	Enables/disables dialog boxes for a variety of commands.
CMLJUST	0	Current multiline justification.
CMLSCALE	1.0000	Scale factor for multiline features.
CMLSTYLE	""	Current multiline style name.
DCTCUST	""	Current custom dictionary file name and path.
DCTMAIN	""	Main dictionary file name.
FFLIMIT	0	Maximum number of Post Script/True Type fonts that can be stored in memory.
FILEDIA	1	Enables/disables file dialog boxes.
FONTALT	""	Font file to be used when specified file is not found.
FONTMAP	""	Font mapping file to be used when specified file is not found.
GRIPBLOCK	0	Controls assignment of grips within block objects.
GRIPCOLOR	5	Color of nonselected grips.
GRIPHOT	1	Color of selected grips.
GRIPS	1	Toggles availability of grip editing modes.
GRIPSIZE	3	Size of grip box in pixels.
MAXSORT	200	Maximum number of symbols or file names sorted by listing commands.
MENUCTL	1	Toggles screen menu switching in response to commands.
MTEXTED	""	Name of text editor for editing MTEXT objects.
PICKADD	1	Toggles additive selection of objects.
PICKAUTO	1	Toggles automatic windowing during selection process.
PICKBOX	3	Object selection pickbox height in pixels.
PICKDRAG	0	Controls selection window drawing method.
PICKFIRST	1	Controls selection and editing sequence.
PLOTID	""	Current default plotter description.
PLOTTER	0	Current default plotter identification.
PROJMODE	1	Controls projection mode for TRIM/EXTEND.
PSPROLOG	""	Name for prologue section read from *acad.psf* for PSOUT.
SAVEFILE	ᴸ	Current autosave destination file name.
SAVETIME	120	Autosave interval, in minutes.
SCREENBOXES	ᴸ	Number of available boxes in screen menu area.
SCREENMODE	ᴸ	Current graphics/text state of the AutoCAD display.
SORTENTS	96	Controls object sort order operations.
TEMPPREFIX	ᴸ	Directory name for placement of temporary files.
TOOLTIPS	1	Toggles display of toolbar ToolTips.
TREEMAX	10000000	Limits maximum number of nodes in spatial index tree.
XREFCTL	0	Controls creation of *.xlg* files (XREF Log).

The next listing shows the AutoCAD system variables that are not saved at all. These variables revert to default values when opening an existing drawing or starting a new one. Many of these variables are read-only and reference drawing or operating system specific information. Other variables in this section are used to change standard features of AutoCAD, and are restored to default values in subsequent editing sessions to avoid unexpected results in common drafting procedures.

Many of the variables shown here are commonly referenced or set when customizing

Variable Name	Default Value	Description
ACADPREFIX	⌁	Current support directory search path.
ACADVER	⌁	Current AutoCAD version number, including patch level.
AFLAGS	0	Current attribute flags settings.
AREA	⌁	Stores the last area calculated by AREA/LIST/DBLIST.
CDATE	⌁	Current date and time presented as a real number.
CHAMMODE	0	Current chamfer method.
CIRCLERAD	0.0000	Radius of last circle drawn.
CMDACTIVE	⌁	Indicates what type of command is active.
CMDECHO	1	Controls echo of prompts and commands during the AutoLISP (command) function.
CMDNAMES	⌁	Name of the currently active command(s).
DATE	⌁	Current Julian date.
DBMOD	⌁	Drawing modification status.
DIASTAT	⌁	Exit method of last dialog session.
DISTANCE	⌁	Last distance calculated by DIST.
DONUTID	0.5000	Default ID for donuts.
DONUTOD	1.0000	Default OD for donuts.
DWGNAME	⌁	Name of current drawing.
DWGPREFIX	⌁	Directory path for current drawing.
DWGTITLED	⌁	Indicates if current drawing has been named.
DWGWRITE	1	Toggles initial state of "read-only" switch for OPEN.
EDGEMODE	0	Cutting and boundary edge determination method for TRIM/EXTEND.
EXPERT	0	Suppression level of warnings and double-checks.
HIGHLIGHT	1	Toggles highlighting of selected objects.
HPANG	0.0000	Current default hatch pattern angle.
HPDOUBLE	0	Toggles double hatching for "U" user-defined patterns.
HPNAME	""	Current default hatch pattern name.
HPSCALE	1.0000	Current default hatch pattern scale.
HPSPACE	1.0000	Current spacing for "U" user-defined patterns.
INSNAME	""	Name of last block inserted.
LASTANGLE	⌁	Last angle entered or drawn.
LOCALE	⌁	ISO language code for running AutoCAD version.
LOGINNAME	⌁	Currently configured user login name.
MAXACTVP	16	Maximum number of active model space viewports.
MENUECHO	0	Controls level of menu echo.
MENUNAME	⌁	Currently loaded menu file and path names.
MODEMACRO	""	Displays text on status line - used in DIESEL.
OFFSETDIST	-1.0000	Last entered offset distance.

Variable Name	Default Value	Description
PERIMETER	⟿	Last perimeter value calculated by AREA/LIST/DBLIST.
PFACEMAX	⟿	Maximum number of vertices per face.
PLATFORM	⟿	Current operating system.
POLYSIDES	4	Default number of POLYGON sides.
POPUPS	⟿	Support level of display driver for pull-down menus.
RE-INIT	0	Controls action of REINIT command.
RIASPECT	0.0000	Aspect ratio for imported raster images.
RIBACKG	0	Background color for imported raster images.
RIEDGE	0	Edge detection feature for imported raster images.
RIGAMUT	256	Number of colors used for imported raster images.
RIGREY	0	Gray-scale conversion for imported raster images.
RITHRESH	0	Controls importing an image based on luminance.
SAVENAME	⟿	Default drawing save name.
SCREENSIZE	⟿	Current viewport size in pixels.
SHPNAME	""	Default shape file name.
TABMODE	0	Enables/disables tablet mode.
TEXTEVAL	0	Controls evaluation method for text strings.
TRIMMODE	1	Controls object trimming for FILLET and CHAMFER.
UNDOCTL	⟿	Current status of UNDO feature.
UNDOMARKS	⟿	The number of UNDO Marks that have been placed.
WORLDUCS	⟿	Comparison of current UCS to WORLD UCS.

Prototype Drawing Sheet Size Parameters

Drawing Scale	"D" Size (34" × 22") Drawing Limits	"C" Size (22" × 17") Drawing Limits	"B" Size (17" × 11") Drawing Limits
1" = 1"	34,22	22,17	17,11
1/2" = 1"	68,44	44,34	34,22
1/4" = 1"	136,88	88,68	88,44
1/8" = 1"	272,176	176,136	136,88
1" = 1'-0"	408,264	264,204	204,132
3/4" = 1'-0"	544,352	352,272	272,176
1/2" = 1'-0"	816,528	528, 408	408,264
3/8" = 1'-0"	1088,704	704, 544	544,352
1/4" = 1'-0"	1632,1056	1056,816	816,528
3/16" = 1'-0"	2176,1408	1408,1088	1088,704
1/8" = 1'-0"	3264,2112	2112,1632	1632,1056
3/32" = 1'-0"	4352,2816	2816,2176	2176,1408
1/16" = 1'-0"	6528,4224	4224,3264	3264,2112

Prototype Drawing Scale Parameters

Drawing Scale	Dimension Scale (DIMSCALE)	Linetype Scale (LISCALE)	Inversion Scale of Border & Parts List Blocks
1" = 1"	1	.5	1=1
1/2" = 1"	2	1	1=2
1/4" = 1"	4	2	1=4
1/8" = 1"	8	4	1=8
1" = 1'-0"	12	6	1=12
3/4" = 1'-0"	16	8	1=16
1/2" = 1'-0"	24	12	1=24
3/8" = 1'-0"	32	16	1=32
1/4" = 1'-0"	48	24	1=48
3/16" = 1'-0"	64	32	1=64
1/8" = 1'-0"	96	48	1=96
3/32" = 1'-0"	128	64	1=128
1/16" = 1'-0"	192	96	1=192

Appendix F

SAMPLE TABLET MENUS

The tablet menu templates illustrated here show how the AutoCAD menu template can be altered to suit the needs of a company or individual. The menu shown in Figure F-1 is used creating electrical loop and wiring diagrams. Look closely at some of the special commands. Also note that different menus can be called from this template.

Figure F-1. Tablet menu for electrical loop and wiring diagrams. (Fitzgerald, Hagan & Hackathorn, Inc., Norwest Engineering)

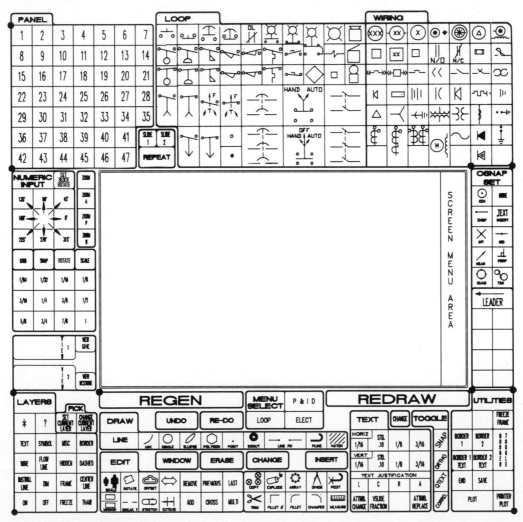

The tablet menu template shown in Figure F-2 was developed specifically for isometric piping drawings. All symbols are displayed in an orderly manner at the top of the menu. Note the section at the left of the screen area for isometric text.

Figure F-2. Tablet menu template for isometric piping symbols. (Fitzgerald, Hagan & Hackathorn, Inc., Norwest Engineering)

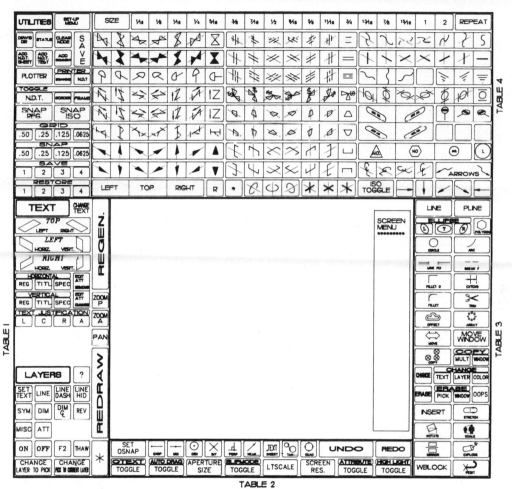

The tablet menu template shown in Figure F-3 was created for instrumentation loop diagrams. This menu does not have the detail as those shown earlier, but still reflects the needs of the individual using it. Notice the conversion chart on the right side of the template. Also note the cursor button references inside the screen area.

Figure F-3. Tablet menu template for instrumentation loop diagrams. (Courtesy R.L. Dunn, Harris Group, Inc.)

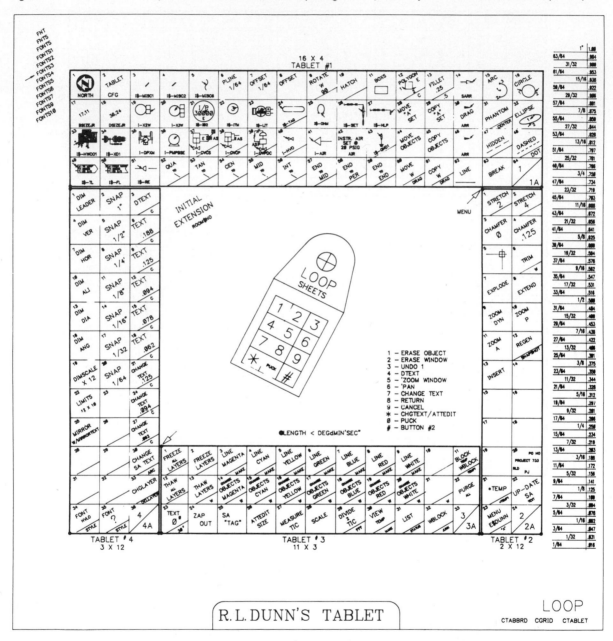

Appendix G

DRAFTING STANDARDS AND RELATED DOCUMENTS

The following is a list of ANSI/ASME drafting standards or related documents. They are ANSI/ASME adopted, unless another standard developing organization, such as ANSI/NFPA, is indicated.

ABBREVIATIONS

Y1.1-1989, *Abbreviations for Use on Drawings and in Text*

CHARTS AND GRAPHS (Y15)

Y15.1M-1979 (R1993), *Illustrations for Publication and Projection*

Y15.2M-1979 (R1986), *Time-Series Charts*

Y15.3M-1979 (R1986), *Process Charts*

DIMENSIONS

B4.1-1967 (R1987), *Preferred Limits and Fits for Cylindrical Parts*

B4.2-1978 (R1994), *Preferred Metric Limits and Fits*

B4.3-1978 (R1994), *General Tolerances for Metric Dimensioned Products*

B4.4M-1981 (R1987), *Inspection of Workpieces*

B32.1-1952 (R1994), *Preferred Thickness for Uncoated, Thin, Flat Metals (Under 0.250/in.)*

B32.2-1969 (R1994), *Preferred Diameters for Round Wire-0.500 Inches and Under*

B32.3M-1984 (R1994), *Preferred Metric Sizes for Flat Metal Products*

B32.4M-1980 (R1994), *Preferred Metric Sizes for Round, Square, Rectangle and Hexagon Metal Products*

B32.5-1977 (R1994), *Preferred Metric Sizes for Tubular Metal Products Other Than Pipe*

B32.6M-1984 (R1994), *Preferred Metric Equivalents of Inch Sizes for Tubular Metal Products Other Than Pipe*

B36.10M-1985, *Welded and Seamless Wrought Steel Pipe*

B36.19M-1985, *Stainless Steel Pipe*

DRAFTING STANDARDS

Y14.1-1980 (R1987), *Drawing Sheet Size and Format*

Y14.1M-1992, *Metric Drawing Sheet Size and Format*

Y14.2M-1992, *Line Conventions and Lettering*

Y14.3M-1992, *Multi- and Sectional-View Drawings*

Y14.4M-1989 (R1994), *Pictorial Drawings*

Y14.5M-1994, *Dimensioning and Tolerancing*

Y14.5.1-1994, *Mathematical Definition of Y14.5*

Y14.5.2, *Certification of GD&T Professionals*

Y14.6M-1978 (R1993), *Screw Thread Representation*

14.6aM-1981 (R1993), *Engineering Drawing and Related Documentation Practices (Screw Thread Representation) (Metric Supplement)*

Y14.7.1-1971 (R1993), *Gear Drawing Standards-Part 1-Spur, Helical, Double Helical, and Rack*

Y14.7.2-1978 (R1994), *Gear and Spline Drawing Standards-Part 2-Bevel and Hypoid Gears*

Y14.8M-1989 (R1993), *Castings and Forgings*

Y14.13M-1981 (R1992), *Engineering Drawing and Related Documentation Practices-Mechanical Spring Representation*

Y14.18M-1986 (R1993), *Engineering Drawings and Related Documentation Practices-Optical Parts*

Y14.24M-1989, *Types and Applications of Engineering Drawings*

14.34M-1989 (R1993), *Parts Lists, Data Lists, and Index Lists*

Y14.35M-1992, *Revision of Engineering Drawings and Associated Documents*

Y14.36-1978 (R1993), *Surface Texture Symbols*

Y14 Report 1, *Digital Representation of Physical Object Shapes*
Y14 Report 2, *Guidelines for Documenting of Computer Systems Used in Computer-Aided Preparation of Product Definition Data-User Instructions*
Y14 Report 3, *Guidelines for Documenting of Computer Systems Used in Computer-Aided Preparation of Product Definition Data-Design Requirements*
Y14 Report 4-1989, *A Structural Language Format for Basic Shape Description*
ANSI/US PRO/IPO-100-1993, *Digital Representation for Communication of Product Definition Data (Replaced ANSI Y14.26M-1981)*

GRAPHIC SYMBOLS

Y32.2-1975, *Electrical and Electronic Diagrams*
Y32.2.3-1949 (R1988), *Pipe Fittings, Valves, and Piping*
Y32.2.4-1949 (R1993), *Heating, Ventilating, and Air Conditioning*
Y32.2.6-1950 (R1993), *Heat/Power Apparatus*
Y32.4-1977 (R1987), *Plumbing Fixture Diagrams Used in Architectural and Building Construction*
Y32.7-1972 (R1987), *Railroad Maps and Profiles*
Y32.9-1972 (R1989), *Electrical Wiring and Layout Diagrams Used in Architecture and Building*
Y32.10-1967 (R1987), *Fluid Power Diagrams*
Y32.11-1961 (R1993), *Process Flow Diagrams in the Petroleum and Chemical Industries*
Y32.18-1972 (R1993), *Mechanical and Acoustical Elements as Used in Schematic Diagrams*
ANSI/AWS A2.4-91, *Symbols for Welding, Brazing, and Nondestructive Examination*
ANSI/IEEE 200-1975 (R1989), *Reference Designations for Electrical and Electronics Parts and Equipment*

ANSI/IEEE 315-1975 (R1989), *Electrical and Electronics Diagrams (Including Reference Designation Class Designation Letters)*
ANSI/IEEE 623-1976 (R1989), *Grid and Mapping Used in Cable Television Systems*
ANSI/ISA S5.1-1984 (R1992), *Instrumentation Symbols and Identification*
ANSI/NFPA 170-1991, *Public Fire Safety Symbols*

LETTER SYMBOLS

Y10.1-1972 (R1988), *Glossary of Terms Concerning Letter Symbols*
Y10.3M-1984, *Mechanics and Time-Related Phenomena*
Y10.4-1982 (R1988), *Heat and Thermodynamics*
Y10.11-1984, *Acoustics*
Y10.12-1955 (R1988), *Chemical Engineering*
Y10.17-1961 (R1988), *Greek Letters Used as Letter Symbols for Engineering Math*
Y10.18 1967 (R1977), *Illuminating Engineering*
ANSI/IEEE 260-1978 (R1992), *SI Units and Certain Other Units of Measurement*

METRIC SYSTEM

SI-1, *Orientation and Guide for use of SI (Metric) Units*
SI-2, *SI Units in Strength of Materials*
SI-3, *SI Units in Dynamics*
SI-4, *SI Units in Thermodynamics*
SI-5, *SI Units in Fluid Mechanics*
SI-6, *SI Units in Kinematics*
SI-7, *SI Units in Heat Transfer*
SI-8, *SI Units in Vibration*
SI-9, *Metrification of Codes and Standards SI (Metric) Units*
SI-10, *Steam Charts, SI (Metric) and U.S. Customary Units*

At the time of publication all information in this appendix is correct. Some of the standards are, and may in the future be, under review. Information in this appendix is subject to change.

DRAFTING SYMBOLS

STANDARD DIMENSIONING SYMBOLS

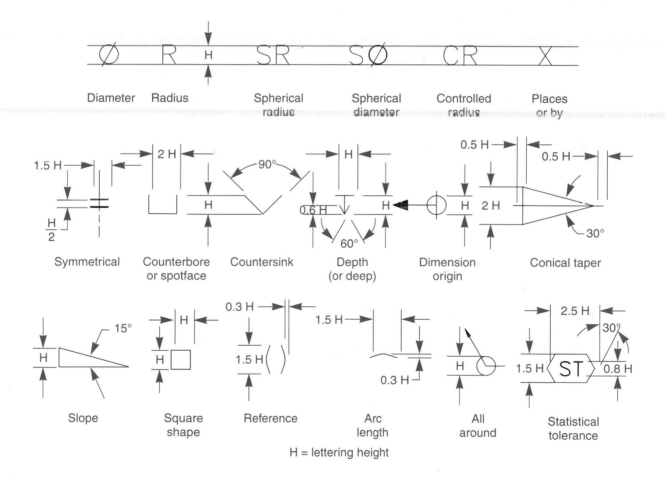

H = lettering height

GEOMETRIC DIMENSIONING AND TOLERANCING SYMBOLS

Additional GD&T information is found in *Geometric Dimensioning and Tolerancing* by David A. Madsen, and is available through Goodheart-Willcox.

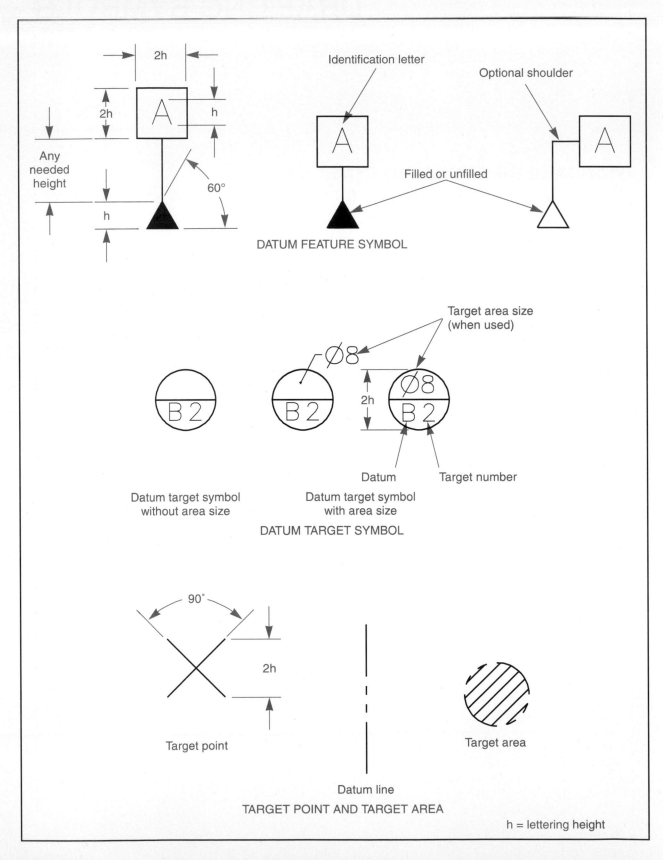

GEOMETRIC DIMENSIONING AND TOLERANCING SYMBOLS, Cont.

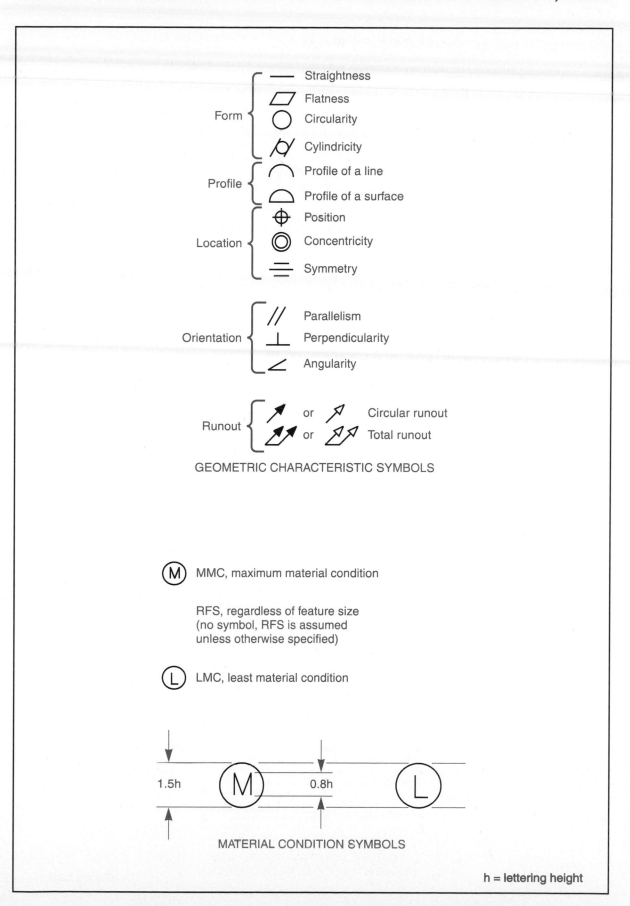

GEOMETRIC CHARACTERISTIC SYMBOLS

Ⓜ MMC, maximum material condition

RFS, regardless of feature size
(no symbol, RFS is assumed
unless otherwise specified)

Ⓛ LMC, least material condition

MATERIAL CONDITION SYMBOLS

h = lettering height

GEOMETRIC DIMENSIONING AND TOLERANCING SYMBOLS, Cont.

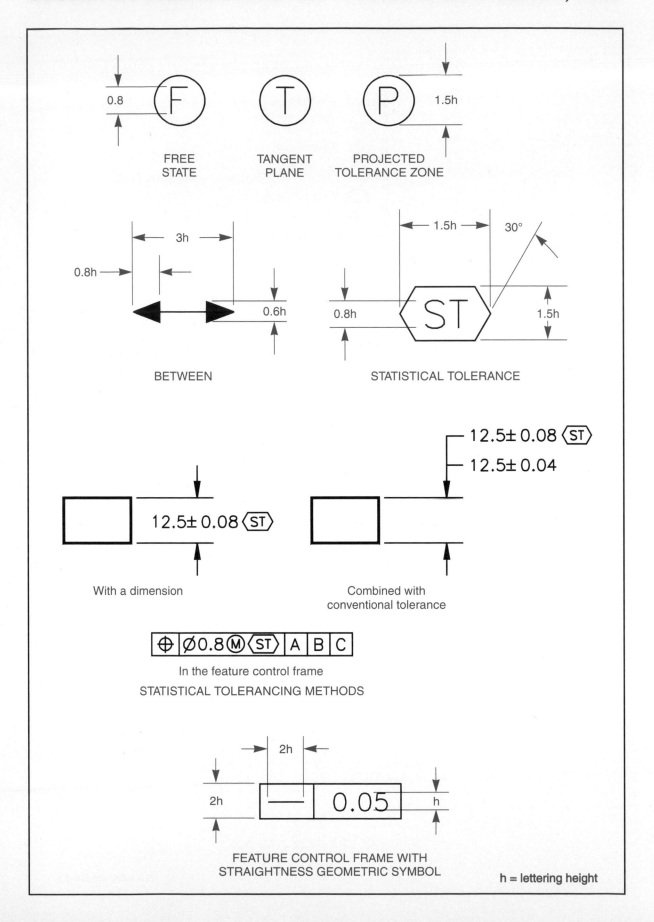

GEOMETRIC DIMENSIONING AND TOLERANCING SYMBOLS, Cont.

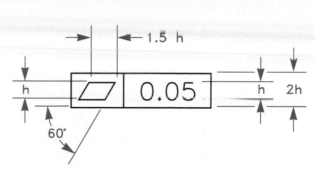

FEATURE CONTROL FRAME WITH THE FLATNESS
GEOMETRIC CHARACTERISTIC SYMBOL

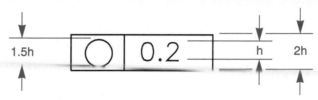

FEATURE CONTROL FRAME WITH CIRCULARITY
GEOMETRIC CHARACTERISTIC SYMBOL

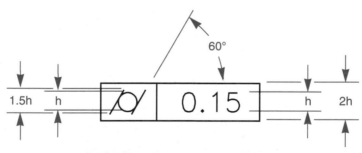

FEATURE CONTROL FRAME WITH CYLINDRICITY
GEOMETRIC CHARACTERISTIC SYMBOL

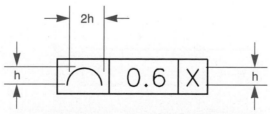

FEATURE CONTROL FRAME WITH PROFILE
OF A LINE GEOMETRIC CHARACTERISTIC
SYMBOL AND A DATUM REFERENCE

h = lettering height

GEOMETRIC DIMENSIONING AND TOLERANCING SYMBOLS, Cont.

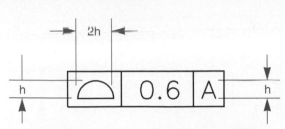

FEATURE CONTROL FRAME WITH PROFILE
OF A SURFACE GEOMETRIC CHARACTERISTIC
SYMBOL AND A DATUM REFERENCE

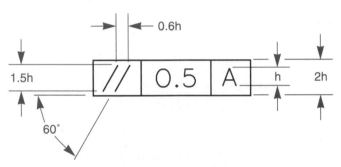

FEATURE CONTROL FRAME WITH
PARALLELISM GEOMETRIC CHARACTERISTIC
SYMBOL AND A DATUM REFERENCE

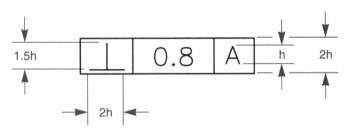

FEATURE CONTROL FRAME WITH
PERPENDICULARITY GEOMETRIC CHARACTERISTIC
SYMBOL AND A DATUM REFERENCE

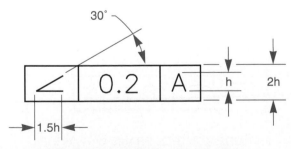

FEATURE CONTROL FRAME WITH
ANGULARITY GEOMETRIC CHARACTERISTIC
SYMBOL AND A DATUM REFERENCE

h = lettering height

GEOMETRIC DIMENSIONING AND TOLERANCING SYMBOLS, Cont.

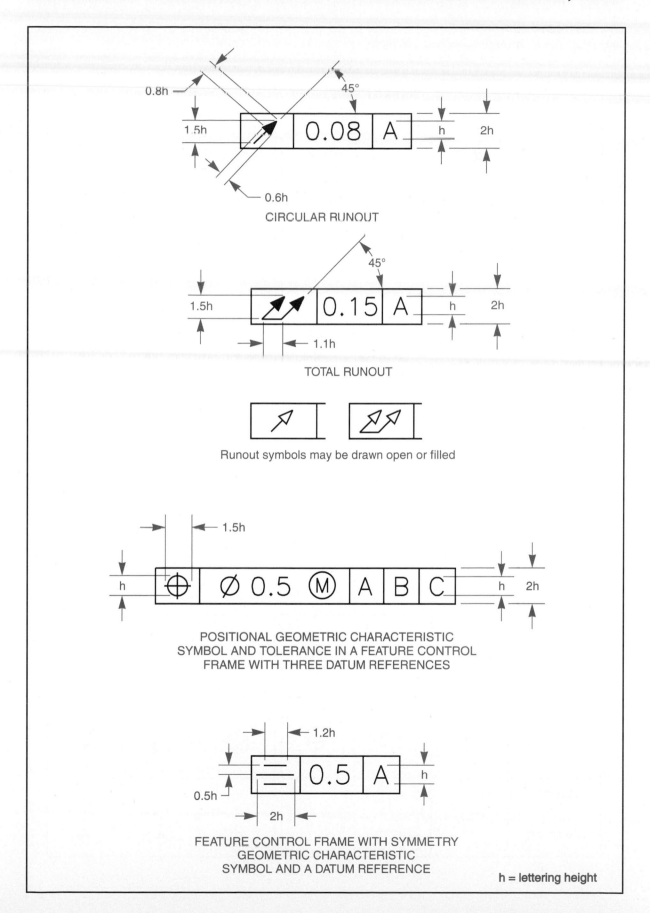

CIRCULAR RUNOUT

TOTAL RUNOUT

Runout symbols may be drawn open or filled

POSITIONAL GEOMETRIC CHARACTERISTIC
SYMBOL AND TOLERANCE IN A FEATURE CONTROL
FRAME WITH THREE DATUM REFERENCES

FEATURE CONTROL FRAME WITH SYMMETRY
GEOMETRIC CHARACTERISTIC
SYMBOL AND A DATUM REFERENCE

h = lettering height

COMMON SINGLE LINE PIPE FITTING SYMBOLS

Additional pipe drafting information is found in *Process Pipe Drafting* by Terence M. Shumaker, and is available through Goodheart-Willcox.

Name	Screwed			Buttwelded		
	Left side	Front	Right side	Left side	Front	Right side
90° Elbow						
45° Elbow						
Tee						
45° Lateral						
Cross						
Cap						
Concentric Reducer						
Eccentric Reducer						
Union						
Coupling						

COMMON SYMBOLS FOR ELECTRICAL DIAGRAMS

Amplifier		Triode with directly heated cathode and envelope connection to base terminal		Fluorescent, 2-terminal lamp	
Antenna, general				Incandescent lamp	
Antenna, dipole		Pentode using elongated envelope		Microphone	
Antenna, dipole				Receiver, earphone	
Antenna, counterpoise		Twin triode using elongated envelope		Resistor, general	
Battery, long line positive					
Multicell battery		Voltage regulator, also, glow lamp		Resistor, adjustable	
Capacitor, general				Resistor, variable	
Capacitor, variable		Phototube		Transformer, general	
Capacitor, polarized					
Circuit breaker		Inductor, winding, reactor, general		Transformer, magnetic core	
Ground		Magnetic core inductor		Shielded transformer, magnetic core	
Chassis ground					
Connectors, jack and plug		Adjustable inductor		Auto-transformer, adjustable	
Engaged connectors		Balast lamp			

COMMON ARCHITECTURAL SYMBOLS

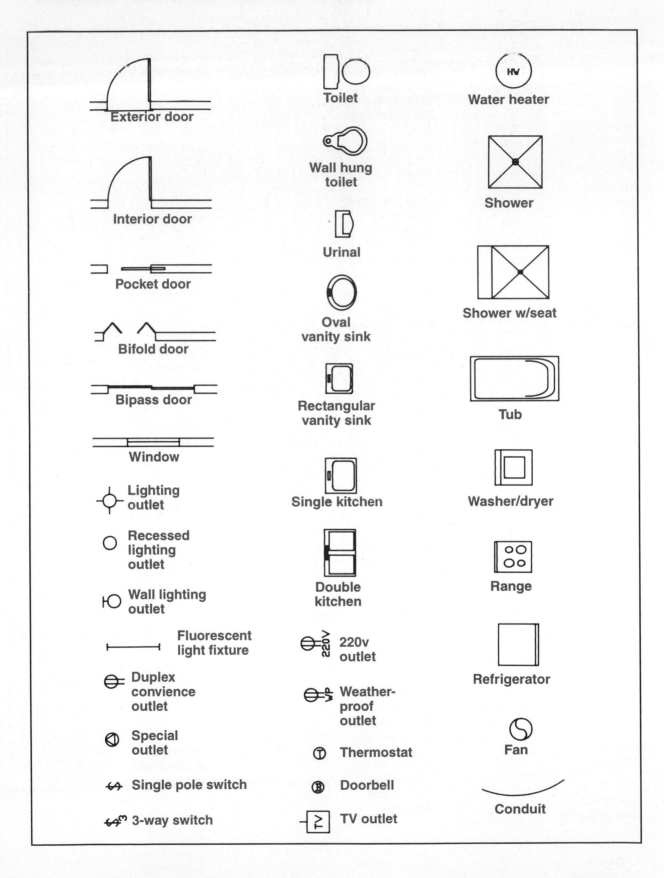

Exterior door

Interior door

Pocket door

Bifold door

Bipass door

Window

Lighting outlet

Recessed lighting outlet

Wall lighting outlet

Fluorescent light fixture

Duplex convience outlet

Special outlet

Single pole switch

3-way switch

Toilet

Wall hung toilet

Urinal

Oval vanity sink

Rectangular vanity sink

Single kitchen

Double kitchen

220v outlet

Weather-proof outlet

Thermostat

Doorbell

TV outlet

Water heater

Shower

Shower w/seat

Tub

Washer/dryer

Range

Refrigerator

Fan

Conduit

METRIC CONVERSION CHART

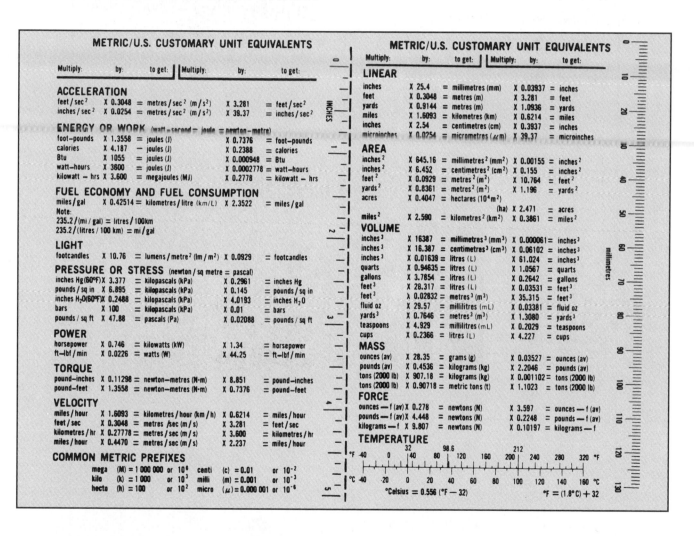

METRIC/U.S. CUSTOMARY UNIT EQUIVALENTS

ACCELERATION

Multiply:	by:	to get:	Multiply:	by:	to get:
feet/sec^2	X 0.3048	= metres/sec^2 (m/s^2)	X 3.281	= feet/sec^2
inches/sec^2	X 0.0254	= metres/sec^2 (m/s^2)	X 39.37	= inches/sec^2

ENERGY OR WORK (watt-second = joule = newton-metre)

foot-pounds	X 1.3558	= joules (J)	X 0.7376	= foot-pounds
calories	X 4.187	= joules (J)	X 0.2388	= calories
Btu	X 1055	= joules (J)	X 0.000948	= Btu
watt-hours	X 3600	= joules (J)	X 0.0002778	= watt-hours
kilowatt-hrs	X 3.600	= megajoules (MJ)	X 0.2778	= kilowatt-hrs

FUEL ECONOMY AND FUEL CONSUMPTION

miles/gal	X 0.42514	= kilometres/litre (km/L)	X 2.3522	= miles/gal

Note:
235.2/(mi/gal) = litres/100km
235.2/(litres/100 km) = mi/gal

LIGHT

footcandles	X 10.76	= lumens/metre^2 (lm/m^2)	X 0.0929	= footcandles

PRESSURE OR STRESS (newton/sq metre = pascal)

inches Hg(60°F)	X 3.377	= kilopascals (kPa)	X 0.2961	= inches Hg
pounds/sq in	X 6.895	= kilopascals (kPa)	X 0.145	= pounds/sq in
inches H$_2$O(60°F)	X 0.2488	= kilopascals (kPa)	X 4.0193	= inches H$_2$0
bars	X 100	= kilopascals (kPa)	X 0.01	= bars
pounds/sq ft	X 47.88	= pascals (Pa)	X 0.02088	= pounds/sq ft

POWER

horsepower	X 0.746	= kilowatts (kW)	X 1.34	= horsepower
ft-lbf/min	X 0.0226	= watts (W)	X 44.25	= ft-lbf/min

TORQUE

pound-inches	X 0.11298	= newton-metres (N·m)	X 8.851	= pound-inches
pound-feet	X 1.3558	= newton-metres (N·m)	X 0.7376	= pound-feet

VELOCITY

miles/hour	X 1.6093	= kilometres/hour (km/h)	X 0.6214	= miles/hour
feet/sec	X 0.3048	= metres/sec (m/s)	X 3.281	= feet/sec
kilometres/hr	X 0.27778	= metres/sec (m/s)	X 3.600	= kilometres/hr
miles/hour	X 0.4470	= metres/sec (m/s)	X 2.237	= miles/hour

COMMON METRIC PREFIXES

mega	(M) = 1 000 000	or 10^6	centi	(c) = 0.01	or 10^{-2}
kilo	(k) = 1 000	or 10^3	milli	(m) = 0.001	or 10^{-3}
hecto	(h) = 100	or 10^2	micro	(μ) = 0.000 001	or 10^{-6}

METRIC/U.S. CUSTOMARY UNIT EQUIVALENTS

Multiply:	by:	to get:	Multiply:	by:	to get:

LINEAR

inches	X 25.4	= millimetres (mm)	X 0.03937	= inches
feet	X 0.3048	= metres (m)	X 3.281	= feet
yards	X 0.9144	= metres (m)	X 1.0936	= yards
miles	X 1.6093	= kilometres (km)	X 0.6214	= miles
inches	X 2.54	= centimetres (cm)	X 0.3937	= inches
microinches	X 0.0254	= micrometres (μm)	X 39.37	= microinches

AREA

inches^2	X 645.16	= millimetres^2 (mm^2)	X 0.00155	= inches^2
inches^2	X 6.452	= centimetres^2 (cm^2)	X 0.155	= inches^2
feet^2	X 0.0929	= metres^2 (m^2)	X 10.764	= feet^2
yards^2	X 0.8361	= metres^2 (m^2)	X 1.196	= yards^2
acres	X 0.4047	= hectares (10^{4}m^2)		
		(ha)	X 2.471	= acres
miles^2	X 2.590	= kilometres^2 (km^2)	X 0.3861	= miles^2

VOLUME

inches^3	X 16387	= millimetres^3 (mm^3)	X 0.000061	= inches^3
inches^3	X 16.387	= centimetres^3 (cm^3)	X 0.06102	= inches^3
inches^3	X 0.01639	= litres (L)	X 61.024	= inches^3
quarts	X 0.94635	= litres (L)	X 1.0567	= quarts
gallons	X 3.7854	= litres (L)	X 0.2642	= gallons
feet^3	X 28.317	= litres (L)	X 0.03531	= feet^3
feet^3	λ 0.02832	= metres^3 (m^3)	X 35.315	= feet^3
fluid oz	X 29.57	= millilitres (mL)	X 0.03381	= fluid oz
yards^3	X 0.7646	= metres^3 (m^3)	X 1.3080	= yards^3
teaspoons	X 4.929	= millilitres (mL)	X 0.2029	= teaspoons
cups	X 0.2366	= litres (L)	X 4.227	= cups

MASS

ounces (av)	X 28.35	= grams (g)	X 0.03527	= ounces (av)
pounds (av)	X 0.4536	= kilograms (kg)	X 2.2046	= pounds (av)
tons (2000 lb)	X 907.18	= kilograms (kg)	X 0.001102	= tons (2000 lb)
tons (2000 lb)	X 0.90718	= metric tons (t)	X 1.1023	= tons (2000 lb)

FORCE

ounces-f (av)	X 0.278	= newtons (N)	X 3.597	= ounces-f (av)
pounds-f (av)	X 4.448	= newtons (N)	X 0.2248	= pounds-f (av)
kilograms-f	X 9.807	= newtons (N)	X 0.10197	= kilograms-f

TEMPERATURE

°Celsius = 0.556 (°F — 32)

°F = (1.8°C) + 32

FRACTION, DECIMAL, AND METRIC EQUIVALENTS

INCHES (FRACTIONS)	DECIMALS	MILLIMETERS
	.00394	.1
	.00787	.2
	.01181	.3
1/64	.015625	.3969
	.01575	.4
	.01969	.5
	.02362	.6
	.02756	.7
1/32	.03125	.7938
	.0315	.8
	.03543	.9
	.03937	1.00
3/64	.046875	1.1906
1/16	.0625	1.5875
5/64	.078125	1.9844
	.07874	2.00
3/32	.09375	2.3813
7/64	.109375	2.7781
	.11811	3.00
1/8	.125	3.175
9/64	.140625	3.5719
5/32	.15625	3.9688
	.15748	4.00
11/64	.171875	4.3656
3/16	.1875	4.7625
	.19685	5.00
13/64	.203125	5.1594
7/32	.21875	5.5563
15/64	.234375	5.9531
	.23622	6.00
1/4	.2500	6.35
17/64	.265625	6.7469
	.27559	7.00
9/32	.28125	7.1438
19/64	.296875	7.5406
5/16	.3125	7.9375
	.31496	8.00
21/64	.328125	8.3344
11/32	.34375	8.7313
	.35433	9.00
23/64	.359375	9.1281
3/8	.375	9.525
25/64	.390625	9.9219
	.3937	10.00
13/32	.40625	10.3188
27/64	.421875	10.7156
	.43307	11.00
7/16	.4375	11.1125
29/64	.453125	11.5094

INCHES (FRACTIONS)	DECIMALS	MILLIMETERS
15/32	.46875	11.9063
	.47244	12.00
31/64	.484375	12.3031
1/2	.5000	12.70
	.51181	13.00
33/64	.515625	13.0969
17/32	.53125	13.4938
35/64	.546875	13.8907
	.55118	14.00
9/16	.5625	14.2875
37/64	.578125	14.6844
	.59055	15.00
19/32	.59375	15.0813
39/64	.609375	15.4782
5/8	.625	15.875
	.62992	16.00
41/64	.640625	16.2719
21/32	.65625	16.6688
	.66929	17.00
43/64	.671875	17.0657
11/16	.6875	17.4625
45/64	.703125	17.8594
	.70866	18.00
23/32	.71875	18.2563
47/64	.734375	18.6532
	.74803	19.00
3/4	.7500	19.05
49/64	.765625	19.4469
25/32	.78125	19.8438
	.7874	20.00
51/64	.796875	20.2407
13/16	.8125	20.6375
	.82677	21.00
53/64	.828125	21.0344
27/32	.84375	21.4313
55/64	.859375	21.8282
	.86614	22.00
7/8	.875	22.225
57/64	.890625	22.6219
	.90551	23.00
29/32	.90625	23.0188
59/64	.921875	23.4157
15/16	.9375	23.8125
	.94488	24.00
61/64	.953125	24.2094
31/32	.96875	24.6063
	.98425	25.00
63/64	.984375	25.0032
1	1.0000	25.4001

CHORD LENGTH–SEGMENTS OF CIRCLES

Length of arc (l=radians), height of segment (h), length of chord (c), and area of segment (A) for angles from 1 to 180 degrees and radius = 1. For other radii, multiply the values given for distance by the radius, and the values given for the area by r^2, the square of the radius. The values in the table can be used for U.S. customary or metric units.

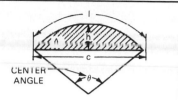

Center Angle θ, Degrees	l	h	c	Area of Segment A	Center Angle θ, Degrees	l	h	c	Area of Segment A	Center Angle θ, Degrees	l	h	c	Area of Segment A	Center Angle θ, Degrees	l	h	c	Area of Segment A
1	0.01745	0.00004	0.01745	0.00000	46	0.803	0.0795	0.781	0.04176	91	1.588	0.2991	1.427	0.2942	136	2.374	0.6254	1.854	0.8395
2	0.03491	0.00015	0.03490	0.00000	47	0.820	0.0829	0.797	0.04448	92	1.606	0.3053	1.439	0.3032	137	2.391	0.6335	1.861	0.8548
3	0.05236	0.00034	0.05235	0.00001	48	0.838	0.0865	0.813	0.04731	93	1.623	0.3116	1.451	0.3123	138	2.409	0.6416	1.867	0.8697
4	0.06981	0.00061	0.06980	0.00003	49	0.855	0.0900	0.829	0.05025	94	1.641	0.3180	1.463	0.3215	139	2.426	0.6498	1.873	0.8850
5	0.08727	0.00095	0.08724	0.00006	50	0.873	0.0937	0.845	0.05331	95	1.658	0.3244	1.475	0.3309	140	2.443	0.6580	1.879	0.9003
6	0.10472	0.00137	0.10467	0.00010	51	0.890	0.0974	0.861	0.05649	96	1.676	0.3309	1.486	0.3405	141	2.461	0.6662	1.885	0.9158
7	0.12217	0.00187	0.12210	0.00015	52	0.908	0.1012	0.877	0.05978	97	1.693	0.3374	1.498	0.3502	142	2.478	0.6744	1.891	0.9314
8	0.13963	0.00244	0.13951	0.00023	53	0.925	0.1051	0.892	0.06319	98	1.710	0.3439	1.509	0.3601	143	2.496	0.6827	1.897	0.9470
9	0.15708	0.00308	0.15692	0.00032	54	0.942	0.1090	0.908	0.06673	99	1.728	0.3506	1.521	0.3701	144	2.513	0.6910	1.902	0.9627
10	0.17453	0.00381	0.17431	0.00044	55	0.960	0.1130	0.923	0.07039	100	1.745	0.3572	1.532	0.3803	145	2.531	0.6993	1.907	0.9786
11	0.19199	0.00460	0.19169	0.00059	56	0.977	0.1171	0.939	0.07417	101	1.763	0.3639	1.543	0.3906	146	2.548	0.7076	1.913	0.9945
12	0.20944	0.00548	0.20906	0.00076	57	0.995	0.1212	0.954	0.07808	102	1.780	0.3707	1.554	0.4010	147	2.566	0.7160	1.918	1.0105
13	0.22689	0.00643	0.22641	0.00097	58	1.012	0.1254	0.970	0.08212	103	1.798	0.3775	1.565	0.4117	148	2.583	0.7244	1.923	1.0266
14	0.24435	0.00745	0.24374	0.00121	59	1.030	0.1296	0.985	0.08629	104	1.815	0.3843	1.576	0.4224	149	2.601	0.7328	1.927	1.0428
15	0.26180	0.00856	0.26105	0.00149	60	1.047	0.1340	1.000	0.09059	105	1.833	0.3912	1.587	0.4333	150	2.618	0.7412	1.932	1.0590
16	0.27925	0.00973	0.27835	0.00181	61	1.065	0.1384	1.015	0.09502	106	1.850	0.3982	1.597	0.4444	151	2.635	0.7496	1.936	1.0753
17	0.29671	0.01098	0.29562	0.00217	62	1.082	0.1428	1.030	0.09958	107	1.868	0.4052	1.608	0.4556	152	2.653	0.7581	1.941	1.0917
18	0.31416	0.01231	0.31287	0.00257	63	1.100	0.1474	1.045	0.10428	108	1.885	0.4122	1.618	0.4669	153	2.670	0.7666	1.945	1.1082
19	0.33161	0.01371	0.33010	0.00302	64	1.117	0.1520	1.060	0.10911	109	1.902	0.4193	1.628	0.4784	154	2.688	0.7750	1.949	1.1247
20	0.34907	0.01519	0.34730	0.00352	65	1.134	0.1566	1.075	0.11408	110	1.920	0.4264	1.638	0.4901	155	2.705	0.7836	1.953	1.1413
21	0.36652	0.01675	0.36447	0.00408	66	1.152	0.1613	1.089	0.11919	111	1.937	0.4336	1.648	0.5019	156	2.723	0.7921	1.956	1.1580
22	0.38397	0.01837	0.38162	0.00468	67	1.169	0.1661	1.104	0.12443	112	1.955	0.4408	1.658	0.5138	157	2.740	0.8006	1.960	1.1747
23	0.40143	0.02008	0.39874	0.00535	68	1.187	0.1710	1.118	0.12982	113	1.972	0.4481	1.668	0.5259	158	2.758	0.8092	1.963	1.1915
24	0.41888	0.02185	0.41582	0.00607	69	1.204	0.1759	1.133	0.13535	114	1.990	0.4554	1.677	0.5381	159	2.775	0.8178	1.967	1.2084
25	0.43633	0.02370	0.43288	0.00686	70	1.222	0.1808	1.147	0.14102	115	2.007	0.4627	1.687	0.5504	160	2.793	0.8264	1.970	1.2253
26	0.45379	0.02563	0.44990	0.00771	71	1.239	0.1859	1.161	0.14683	116	2.025	0.4701	1.696	0.5629	161	2.810	0.8350	1.973	1.2422
27	0.47124	0.02763	0.46689	0.00862	72	1.257	0.1910	1.176	0.15279	117	2.042	0.4775	1.705	0.5755	162	2.827	0.8436	1.975	1.2592
28	0.48869	0.02970	0.48384	0.00961	73	1.274	0.1961	1.190	0.15889	118	2.059	0.4850	1.714	0.5883	163	2.845	0.8522	1.978	1.2763
29	0.50615	0.03185	0.50076	0.01067	74	1.292	0.2014	1.204	0.16514	119	2.077	0.4925	1.723	0.6012	164	2.862	0.8608	1.981	1.2934
30	0.52360	0.03407	0.51764	0.01180	75	1.309	0.2066	1.218	0.17154	120	2.094	0.5000	1.732	0.6142	165	2.880	0.8695	1.983	1.3105
31	0.54105	0.03637	0.53448	0.01301	76	1.326	0.2120	1.231	0.17808	121	2.112	0.5076	1.741	0.6273	166	2.897	0.8781	1.985	1.3277
32	0.55851	0.03874	0.55127	0.01429	77	1.344	0.2174	1.245	0.18477	122	2.129	0.5152	1.749	0.6406	167	2.915	0.8868	1.987	1.3449
33	0.57596	0.04118	0.56803	0.01566	78	1.361	0.2229	1.259	0.19160	123	2.147	0.5228	1.758	0.6540	168	2.932	0.8955	1.989	1.3621
34	0.59341	0.04370	0.58474	0.01711	79	1.379	0.2284	1.272	0.19859	124	2.164	0.5305	1.766	0.6676	169	2.950	0.9042	1.991	1.3794
35	0.61087	0.04628	0.60141	0.01864	80	1.396	0.2340	1.286	0.20573	125	2.182	0.5383	1.774	0.6813	170	2.967	0.9128	1.992	1.3967
36	0.62832	0.04894	0.61803	0.02027	81	1.414	0.2396	1.299	0.21301	126	2.199	0.5460	1.782	0.6950	171	2.985	0.9215	1.994	1.4140
37	0.64577	0.05168	0.63461	0.02198	82	1.431	0.2453	1.312	0.22045	127	2.217	0.5538	1.790	0.7090	172	3.002	0.9302	1.995	1.4314
38	0.66323	0.05448	0.65114	0.02378	83	1.449	0.2510	1.325	0.22804	128	2.234	0.5616	1.798	0.7230	173	3.019	0.9390	1.996	1.4488
39	0.68068	0.05736	0.66761	0.02568	84	1.466	0.2569	1.338	0.23578	129	2.251	0.5695	1.805	0.7372	174	3.037	0.9477	1.997	1.4662
40	0.69813	0.06031	0.68404	0.02767	85	1.484	0.2627	1.351	0.24367	130	2.269	0.5774	1.813	0.7514	175	3.054	0.9564	1.998	1.4836
41	0.71558	0.06333	0.70041	0.02976	86	1.501	0.2686	1.364	0.25171	131	2.286	0.5853	1.820	0.7658	176	3.072	0.9651	1.999	1.5010
42	0.73304	0.06642	0.71674	0.03195	87	1.518	0.2746	1.377	0.25990	132	2.304	0.5933	1.827	0.7803	177	3.089	0.9738	1.999	1.5184
43	0.75049	0.06958	0.73300	0.03425	88	1.536	0.2807	1.389	0.26825	133	2.321	0.6013	1.834	0.7950	178	3.107	0.9825	2.000	1.5359
44	0.76794	0.07282	0.74921	0.03664	89	1.553	0.2867	1.402	0.27675	134	2.339	0.6093	1.841	0.8097	179	3.124	0.9913	2.000	1.5533
45	0.78540	0.07612	0.76537	0.03915	90	1.571	0.2929	1.414	0.28540	135	2.356	0.6173	1.848	0.8245	180	3.142	1.0000	2.000	1.5708

DECIMAL EQUIVALENTS AND TAP DRILL SIZES

Starrett® PRECISION TOOLS — DECIMAL EQUIVALENTS AND TAP DRILL SIZES

Left Chart

Fraction or Drill Size	Decimal Equivalent	Tap Size
NUMBER SIZE DRILLS 80	.0135	
79	.0145	
1/64	.0156	
78	.0160	
77	.0180	
76	.0200	
75	.0210	
74	.0225	
73	.0240	
72	.0250	
71	.0260	
70	.0280	
69	.0292	
68	.0310	
1/32	.0312	
67	.0320	
66	.0330	
65	.0350	
64	.0360	
63	.0370	
62	.0380	
61	.0390	
60	.0400	
59	.0410	
58	.0420	
57	.0430	
56	.0465	
3/64	.0469	0–80
55	.0520	
54	.0550	
53	.0595	1–64, 72
1/16	.0625	
52	.0635	
51	.0670	
50	.0700	2–56, 64
49	.0730	
48	.0760	
5/64	.0781	
47	.0785	3–48
46	.0810	
45	.0820	3–56
44	.0860	
43	.0890	4–40
42	.0935	4–48
3/32	.0938	
41	.0960	
40	.0980	
39	.0995	
38	.1015	5–40
37	.1040	5–44
36	.1065	6–32
7/64	.1094	
35	.1100	
34	.1110	
33	.1130	6–40
32	.1160	
31	.1200	
1/8	.1250	
30	.1285	
29	.1360	8–32, 36
28	.1405	
9/64	.1406	
27	.1440	
26	.1470	
25	.1495	10–24
24	.1520	
23	.1540	
5/32	.1562	
22	.1570	
21	.1590	10–32
20	.1610	
19	.1660	
18	.1695	
11/64	.1719	
17	.1730	
16	.1770	12–24
15	.1800	
14	.1820	12–28
13	.1850	
3/16	.1875	
12	.1890	
11	.1910	
10	.1935	
9	.1960	
8	.1990	
7	.2010	1/4–20
13/64	.2031	
6	.2040	
5	.2055	
4	.2090	
3	.2130	1/4–28
7/32	.2188	
2	.2210	
LETTER SIZE DRILLS 1	.2280	
A	.2340	

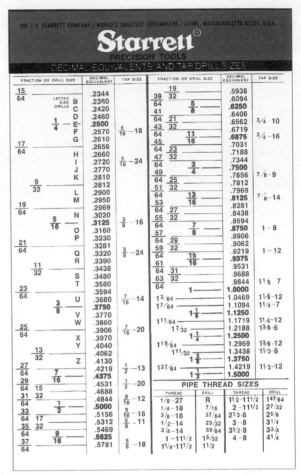

Right Chart

Fraction or Drill Size	Decimal Equivalent	Tap Size
15/64	.2344	
LETTER SIZE DRILLS B	.2380	
C	.2420	
D	.2460	
1/4 E	.2500	5/16–18
F	.2570	
G	.2610	
17/64	.2656	
H	.2660	
I	.2720	5/16–24
J	.2770	
K	.2810	
9/32	.2812	
L	.2900	
M	.2950	
19/64	.2969	
N	.3020	
5/16	.3125	3/8–16
O	.3160	
P	.3230	
21/64	.3281	
Q	.3320	3/8–24
R	.3390	
11/32	.3438	
S	.3480	
T	.3580	
23/64	.3594	
U	.3680	7/16–14
3/8	.3750	
V	.3770	
W	.3860	
25/64	.3906	7/16–20
X	.3970	
Y	.4040	
13/32	.4062	
Z	.4130	
27/64	.4219	
7/16	.4375	1/2–13
29/64	.4531	
15/32	.4688	
	.4844	9/16–12
1/2	.5000	
33/64	.5156	9/16–18
17/32	.5312	5/8–11
35/64	.5469	
9/16	.5625	
37/64	.5781	5/8–18
19/32	.5938	
39/64	.6094	
5/8	.6250	
41/64	.6406	
21/32	.6562	3/4–10
43/64	.6719	
11/16	.6875	3/4–16
45/64	.7031	
23/32	.7188	
47/64	.7344	
3/4	.7500	
49/64	.7656	7/8–9
25/32	.7812	
51/64	.7969	
13/16	.8125	7/8–14
53/64	.8281	
27/32	.8438	
55/64	.8594	
7/8	.8750	1–8
57/64	.8906	
29/32	.9062	
59/64	.9219	1–12
15/16	.9375	
61/64	.9531	
31/32	.9688	
63/64	.9844	
1	1.0000	1 1/8–7
1 3/64	1.0469	1 1/16–12
1 7/64	1.1094	1 1/4–7
1 1/8	1.1250	
1 11/64	1.1719	1 1/4–12
1 17/32	1.2188	1 3/8–6
1 1/4	1.2500	
1 19/64	1.2969	1 3/8–12
1 11/32	1.3438	1 1/2–6
1 3/8	1.3750	
1 27/64	1.4219	1 1/2–12
1 1/2	1.5000	

PIPE THREAD SIZES

Thread	Drill	Thread	Drill
1/8–27	R	1 1/2–11 1/2	1 47/64
1/4–18	7/16	2–11 1/2	2 7/32
3/8–18	37/64	2 1/2–8	2 5/8
1/2–14	23/32	3–8	3 1/4
3/4–14	59/64	3 1/2–8	3 3/4
1–11 1/2	1 5/32	4–8	4 1/4
1 1/4–11 1/2	1 1/2		

Courtesy of the L.S. Starrett Company

AREA, TEMPERATURE, WEIGHT, AND VOLUME EQUIVALENTS

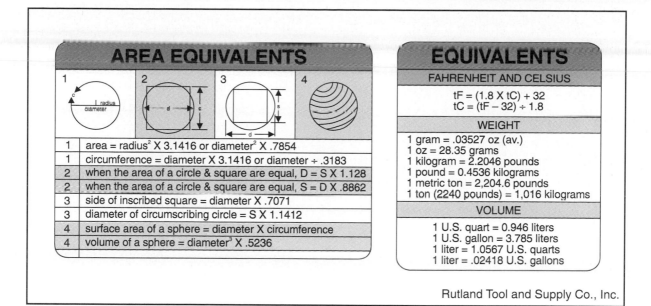

AREA EQUIVALENTS

1	area = radius^2 X 3.1416 or diameter^2 X .7854
1	circumference = diameter X 3.1416 or diameter ÷ .3183
2	when the area of a circle & square are equal, D = S X 1.128
2	when the area of a circle & square are equal, S = D X .8862
3	side of inscribed square = diameter X .7071
3	diameter of circumscribing circle = S X 1.1412
4	surface area of a sphere = diameter X circumference
4	volume of a sphere = diameter^3 X .5236

EQUIVALENTS

FAHRENHEIT AND CELSIUS

$$tF = (1.8 \times tC) + 32$$
$$tC = (tF - 32) \div 1.8$$

WEIGHT

1 gram = .03527 oz (av.)
1 oz = 28.35 grams
1 kilogram = 2.2046 pounds
1 pound = 0.4536 kilograms
1 metric ton = 2,204.6 pounds
1 ton (2240 pounds) = 1,016 kilograms

VOLUME

1 U.S. quart = 0.946 liters
1 U.S. gallon = 3.785 liters
1 liter = 1.0567 U.S. quarts
1 liter = .02418 U.S. gallons

Rutland Tool and Supply Co., Inc.

LENGTH AND SQUARE CONVERSIONS

LENGTH CONVERSIONS

multiply	by	to obtain
INCHES	25.4	MILLIMETERS
FEET	304.8	MILLIMETERS
INCHES	2.54	CENTIMETERS
FEET	30.48	CENTIMETERS
MILLIMETERS	.03937008	INCHES
CENTIMETERS	.3937008	INCHES
METERS	39.37008	INCHES
MILLIMETERS	.003280840	FEET
CENTIMETERS	.03280840	FEET
INCHES	.0254	METERS

SQUARE AREA CONVERSIONS

multiply	by	to obtain
MILLIMETERS	.00001076391	FEET
MILLIMETERS	.00155003	INCHES
CENTIMETERS	.1550003	INCHES
CENTIMETERS	.001076391	FEET
INCHES	645.16	MILLIMETERS
INCHES	6.4516	CENTIMETERS
INCHES	.00064516	METERS
FEET	.09290304	METERS
FEET	929.0304	CENTIMETERS
FEET	92,903.04	MILLIMETERS

Rutland Tool and Supply Co., Inc.

NATURAL TRIGOMETRIC FUNCTIONS

Degree	Sine	Cosine	Tangent	Cotangent
0	.00000	1.0000	.00000	∞
1	.01745	.9998	.01745	57.2900
2	.03490	.9994	.03492	28.6360
3	.05234	.9986	.05241	19.0810
4	.06976	.9976	.06993	14.3010
5	.08716	.9962	.08749	11.4300
6	.10453	.9945	.10510	9.5144
7	.12187	.9925	.12278	8.1443
8	.13920	.9903	.14050	7.1154
9	.15640	.9877	.15840	6.3138
10	.17360	.9848	.17630	5.6713
11	.19080	.9816	.19440	5.1446
12	.20790	.9781	.21260	4.7046
13	.22500	.9744	.23090	4.3315
14	.24190	.9703	.24930	4.0108
15	.25880	.9659	.26790	3.7321
16	.27560	.9613	.28670	3.4874
17	.29240	.9563	.30570	3.2709
18	.30900	.9511	.32490	3.0777
19	.32560	.9455	.34430	2.9042
20	.34200	.9397	.36400	2.7475
21	.35840	.9336	.38390	2.6051
22	.37460	.9272	.40400	2.4751
23	.39070	.9205	.42450	2.3559
24	.40670	.9135	.44520	2.2460
25	.42260	.9063	.46630	2.1445
26	.43840	.8988	.48770	2.0503
27	.45400	.8910	.50950	1.9626
28	.46950	.8829	.53170	1.8807
29	.48480	.8746	.55430	1.8040
30	.50000	.8660	.57740	1.7321
31	.51500	.8572	.60090	1.6643
32	.52990	.8480	.62490	1.6003
33	.54460	.8387	.64940	1.5399
34	.55920	.8290	.67450	1.4826
35	.57360	.8192	.70020	1.4281
36	.58780	.8090	.72650	1.3764
37	.60180	.7986	.75360	1.3270
38	.61570	.7880	.78130	1.2799
39	.62930	.7771	.80980	1.2349
40	.64280	.7660	.83910	1.1918
41	.65610	.7547	.86930	1.1504
42	.66910	.7431	.90040	1.1106
43	.68200	.7314	.93250	1.0724
44	.69470	.7193	.96570	1.0355
45	.70710	.7071	1.00000	1.0000
46	.71930	.6947	1.03550	.9657
47	.73140	.6820	1.07240	.9325
48	.74310	.6691	1.11060	.9004
49	.75470	.6561	1.15040	.8693

Degree	Sine	Cosine	Tangent	Cotangent
50	.7660	.64280	1.1918	.8391
51	.7771	.62930	1.2349	.8098
52	.7880	.61570	1.2799	.7813
53	.7986	.60180	1.3270	.7536
54	.8090	.58780	1.3764	.7265
55	.8192	.57360	1.4281	.7002
56	.8290	.55920	1.4826	.6745
57	.8387	.54460	1.5399	.6494
58	.8480	.52990	1.6003	.6249
59	.8572	.51500	1.6643	.6009
60	.8660	.50000	1.7321	.5774
61	.8746	.48480	1.8040	.5543
62	.8829	.46950	1.8807	.5317
63	.8910	.45400	1.9626	.5095
64	.8988	.43840	2.0503	.4877
65	.9063	.42260	2.1445	.4663
66	.9135	.40670	2.2460	.4452
67	.9205	.39070	2.3559	.4245
68	.9272	.37460	2.4751	.4040
69	.9336	.35840	2.6051	.3839
70	.9397	.34200	2.7475	.3640
71	.9455	.32560	2.9042	.3443
72	.9511	.30900	3.0777	.3249
73	.9563	.29240	3.2709	.3057
74	.9613	.27560	3.4874	.2868
75	.9659	.25880	3.7321	.2680
76	.9703	.24190	4.0108	.2493
77	.9744	.22500	4.3315	.2309
78	.9781	.20790	4.7046	.2126
79	.9816	.19080	5.1446	.1944
80	.9848	.17360	5.6713	.1763
81	.9877	.15640	6.3138	.1584
82	.9903	.13920	7.1154	.1405
83	.9925	.12187	8.1443	.1228
84	.9945	.10453	9.5144	.1051
85	.9962	.08716	11.4301	.0875
86	.9976	.06976	14.3007	.0699
87	.9986	.05234	19.0811	.0524
88	.9994	.03490	28.6363	.0349
89	.9998	.01745	57.2900	.0175
90	1.0000	.00000	∞	.0000

TRIANGLE SOLUTIONS

SOLUTIONS TO TRIANGLES

	$A + B + C = 180°$ $S = \dfrac{a+b+c}{2}$	RIGHT	OBLIQUE

HAVE	WANT	FORMULAS FOR RIGHT	FORMULAS FOR OBLIQUE
abc	A	$\tan A = a/b$	$1/2A = \sqrt{(s-b)(s-c)/bc}$
	B	$90° - A$ or $\cos B = a/c$	$\sin 1/2B = \sqrt{(s-a)(s-c)/a \times c}$
	C	$90°$	$\sin 1/2C = \sqrt{(s-a)(s-b)/a \times b}$
	AREA	$a \times b/2$	$\sqrt{s \times (s-a)(s-b)(s-c)}$
aAC	B	$90° - A$	$180° - (A + C)$
	b	$a \cot A$	$a \sin B/\sin A$
	c	$a/\sin A$	$a \sin C/\sin A$
	AREA	$(a^2 \cot A)/2$	$a^2 \sin B \sin C/2 \sin A$
acC	A	$\sin A = a - c$	$\sin A = a \sin C/c$
	B	$90° - A$ or $\cos B = a/c$	$180° - (A + C)$
	b	$\sqrt{c^2 - a^2}$	$c \sin B/\sin C$
	AREA	$1/2a\sqrt{c^2 - a^2}$	$1/2\, ac \sin B$
abC	A	$\tan A = a/b$	$\tan A = a \sin C/b - a \cos C$
	B	$90° - A$ or $\tan B = b/a$	$180° - (A + C)$
	c	$\sqrt{a^2 + b^2}$	$\sqrt{a^2 + b^2 - 2ab \cos C}$
	AREA	$a \times b/2$	$1/2ab \sin C$

Rutland Tool and Supply Co., Inc.

Appendix J

CONFIGURING THE DIGITIZER

If you have a digitizer, the AutoCAD standard tablet menu is an alternative to keyboard entry or using screen commands. The tablet menu template is a thick piece of plastic that measures 11 in. × 12 in. Printed on it are most of the commands available in AutoCAD. Some commands are accompanied by small symbols, or icons, that indicate the function of the command. The menu is helpful because it provides a clear display of various AutoCAD commands.

Like the screen menus, the tablet menu can be customized. Notice the empty spaces at the top of Figure J-1. This space is available for adding commands or symbols, to aid in the picking and inserting functions. You can have several overlays for this area.

You do not have to use the template supplied with AutoCAD. Most people discover that many of the AutoCAD commands are not used for specific types of drawings, so they construct their own tablet menus. This is similar to creating screen menus, but there are different techniques involved when making tablet menus. Customizing tablet menus is discussed in Chapter 17 of *AutoCAD and its Applications–Advanced, R13 for DOS.*

USING THE AUTOCAD TABLET MENU

To use a tablet menu, the digitizer must first be configured for the specific menu you have. When you initially configure AutoCAD to recognize a digitizer, the entire surface of the tablet represents the screen pointing area. The TABLET command allows you to configure the digitizer to recognize the menu. This includes telling AutoCAD the exact layout of the menu areas and the size and position of the screen pointing area.

Tablet menu layout

The AutoCAD tablet menu presents commands in related groups. See Figure J-1. Notice the headings below each menu area.

Item	Group
A	Monitor
B	User area
C	DRAW/ZOOM
D	DISPLAY/INQUIRY/LAYER
E	TEXT/DIMENSION
F	BLOCK/XREF/SETTINGS
G	SNAP/TOGGLE/EDIT
H	UTILITY
I	NUMERIC

Find the TEMPLATE command in the UTILITY section in the lower-right corner of the template. This command changes the meaning of the digitizer to recognize additional third-party software packages or your own custom menu. Each third-party package must work with AutoCAD, and must be installed on your hard disk drive for this command to work.

Figure J-1.   The AutoCAD tablet menu template. (Autodesk, Inc.)

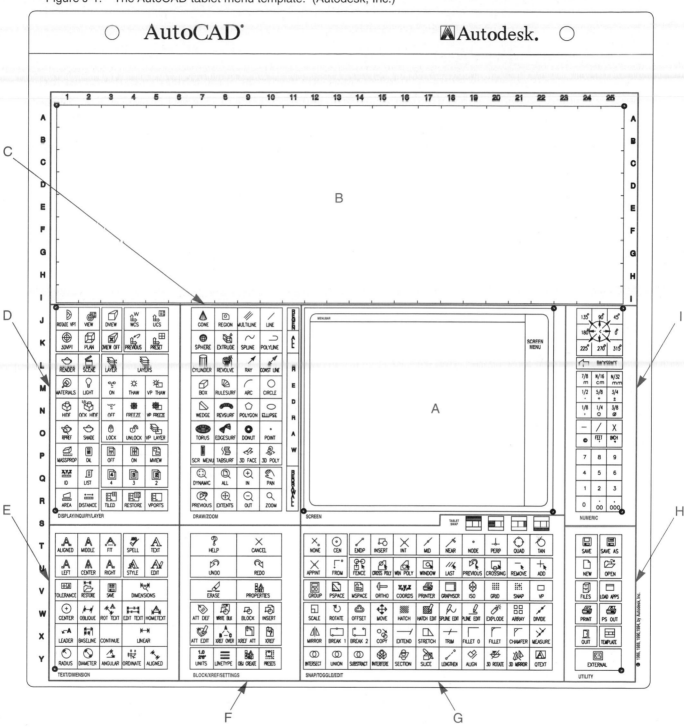

In order for the TEMPLATE command to work, you must set an environment variable called ACADALTMENU. This variable must be set in a batch file before loading AutoCAD. For example, if you have an alternate menu called PIPING.MNU located in the C:\CADPIPE subdirectory, add the following statement to a batch file before AutoCAD is loaded:

    SET ACADALTMENU = C:\CADPIPE\PIPING.MNU

Now, when you pick TEMPLATE it looks for a value in the ACADALTMENU environment variable and loads the menu. Keep in mind that the alternate menu can be an entirely new menu composed of button, screen, pull-downs, icons, and tablet menus.

Configuring the tablet menu

The TABLET command allows you to tell AutoCAD the layout of the tablet menu. It prompts for three corners of each menu area and the number of columns and rows in each area. The screen pointing area is defined by picking two opposite corners. Three corners of each menu area are marked with small doughnuts. As you read the following example, look at Figure J-2. It illustrates how the standard AutoCAD tablet menu is configured and shows the doughnuts marking menu area corners.

Figure J-2.   Small doughnuts mark the corners of the menu areas on the AutoCAD template. (Autodesk, Inc.)

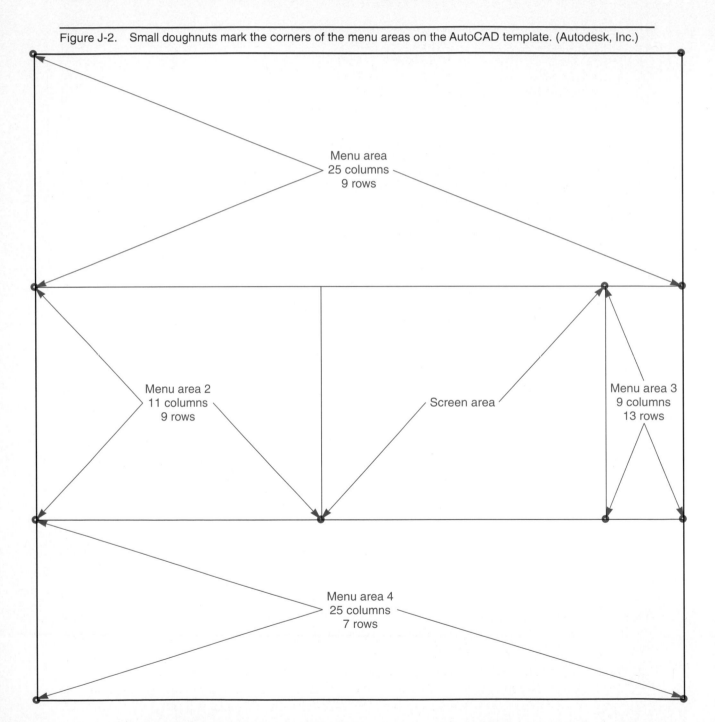

```
Command: TABLET ↵
Option (ON/OFF/CAL/CFG): CFG ↵
Enter number of tablet menus desired (0-4) ⟨4⟩: ↵
Do you want to realign tablet menu areas? ⟨N⟩ Y ↵
Digitize upper left corner of menu area 1: (pick the doughnut at the upper-left corner)
Digitize lower left corner of menu area 1: (pick the point)
Digitize lower right corner of menu area 1: (pick the point)
Enter the number of columns for menu area 1: 25 ↵
Enter the number of rows for menu area 1: 9 ↵
```

You have now given AutoCAD the location of menu area 1 and specified the number of boxes that are available. The command continues with menu area 2:

```
Digitize upper left corner of menu area 2: (pick the point)
Digitize lower left corner of menu area 2: (pick the point)
Digitize lower right corner of menu area 2: (pick the point)
Enter the number of columns for menu area 2: 11 ↵
Enter the number of rows for menu area 2: 9 ↵
Digitize upper left corner of menu area 3: (pick the point)
Digitize lower left corner of menu area 3: (pick the point)
Digitize lower right corner of menu area 3: (pick the point)
Enter the number of columns for menu area 3: 9 ↵
Enter the number of rows for menu area 3: 13 ↵
Digitize upper left corner of menu area 4: (pick the point)
Digitize lower left corner of menu area 4: (pick the point)
Digitize lower right corner of menu area 4: (pick the point)
Enter the number of columns for menu area 4: 25 ↵
Enter the number of rows for menu area 4: 7 ↵
```

Next, you must locate opposite corners of the screen pointing area:

```
Do you want to respecify the screen pointing area? ⟨N⟩ Y ↵
Digitize lower left corner of screen pointing area: (pick doughnut at lower-left corner of
  screen area)
Digitize upper right corner of screen pointing area: (pick upper-right corner)
Command:
```

The tablet configuration is saved in the ACAD.CFG file, which is in your ACADR13\DOS directory. The system reads this file when loading AutoCAD to determine what kind of equipment you are using. It also determines which menu is current. Use this same process when configuring the tablet for your custom menus.

Configuring the AutoCAD template is made quicker by selecting the TABLET command from the screen menu. Pick OPTIONS in the Root Menu, then pick Tablet:, or pick Tablet in the Options pull-down menu.

Select the Re-Cfg option from the Tablet: screen menu. The configuration prompts appear as shown earlier, but you do not have to enter the number of columns and rows. The Re-Cfg option assumes you are reconfiguring the AutoCAD template. Therefore, it only requires the locations of the menu areas and the screen pointing area. Use this option when you wish to return to the standard AutoCAD template after using a custom menu.

Swapping template areas

Look at the digitizer template below the monitor area and you can see the "Tablet swap" icons. These four picks allow you to swap each of the four tablet areas. The black area of each icon indicates the area that is swapped when the icon is picked. In addition, a prompt on the monitor indicates the type of swap. For example, if you pick area 1, the current custom menu picks are removed and the entire area is available for an alternate custom menu. Customizing this area is discussed in *AutoCAD and its Applications–Advanced, R13 for DOS*. In addition, the number 1 is placed below the word

AutoCAD in the screen menu, in the position of the first asterisk. The following list indicates the area swapped, the prompt, and the number placed in the line of asterisks in the screen menu.

- Area 1 prompt:
  Alternate tablet area 1 loaded.
  This area is for your personal applications and menu items.
  1 * * *
- Area 2 prompt:
  Alternate tablet area 2 loaded.
  Zoom and other commands issue CTRL+Cs: VPOINT and DVIEW in current UCS mode.
  *2 * *
- Area 3 prompt:
  Alternate tablet area 3 loaded.
  Select Metric units from the Numeric menu.
  * * 3 *
- Area 4 prompt:
  Alternate tablet area 4 loaded.
  Object snap modes issue running modes: commands repeat.
  * * * 4

Any of the areas can be swapped back to the default menu by just picking the icon again. You can have more than one swapped menu at a time. For example, if areas 2 and 4 are swapped, the asterisk line reads:

*2 * 4

You will always know if you are working with a swapped menu because one or more numbers are displayed on the asterisk line below AutoCAD in the screen menu.

The prompt that is issued after picking a swap icon can be shortened or eliminated if you decide that you do not need to see it. Use the EXPERT system variable to change the prompt. A value of 0 for EXPERT displays the entire prompt. A value of 1 to 3 displays only the first part of the prompt:

Alternate tablet area 3 loaded.

A value of 4 for the EXPERT variable displays no prompt when a swap icon is picked. A value of 3 displays an abbreviated prompt. Set the variable as follows:

Command: **EXPERT** ↵
New value for EXPERT ⟨0 ⟩: **3** ↵

INDEX

M